AFRO-AMERICAN ARTISTS

A Bio-bibliographical Directory

Compiled and edited by
Theresa Dickason Cederholm

Trustees of the Boston Public Library

1973

This project is supported by grants from the National Endowment for the Arts in Washington, D.C., a Federal agency, and the Massachusetts Council on the Arts and Humanities, a state agency.

The findings, conclusions, etc. do not necessarily represent the view of either agency.

Copyright © Boston Public Library 1973

Library of Congress Catalog Card Number: 73-84951

Preface

The need to bring together data on black artists exists today because of the past isolation of black artists from the mainstream of their profession. Relatively few of the Afro-American painters and sculptors who have contributed notably to the cultural richness of their country have received due recognition. Historically their works were rarely exhibited in major museums or included in art shows. National acclaim, widespread critical consideration, and imprint recognition were for the most part not accorded black artists. As a result, up to now, there has been a dearth of bibliographical tools which point definitively to black American artists.

In this publication the Boston Public Library attempts to fill this void. The scope of this work covers retrospective as well as contemporary artists, spanning the time period from the slave craftsman of the 18th century to the present. It brings together obscure, hard-to-locate data from exhibition catalogues, reviews, periodicals, books and questionnaires and serves as a nucleus of information which can be constantly and periodically updated and expanded. Furthermore, it demonstrates one more way in which a major research institution can make a creative interpretation of its resources and services.

In completing the research for this project the Library called upon many institutions across the country for aid and assistance. It also wishes to acknowledge the contributions of many individuals for their helpful suggestions and their generous permission to consult their private collections.

Especial indebtedness is owed to Mrs. Dorothy Porter of Howard University for her helpful early guidance and generosity; to Mrs. Evangeline J. Montgomery of the Oakland Museum who made available the considerable material in the museum's Archives of California Black Artists as well as material in her own collection; to Mrs. Roslyn Walker Randall of the Black Studies Program of Indiana University who generously contributed the results of her own research; and to Miss Joanne Abbott, Miss Ruth Wagner, and especially Mrs. Deborah Williams for their help in preparing and editing the manuscript.

Because of the strong bibliographic approach of this work, we are immensely indebted to the authors of many fine books, some of which like *Modern Negro Art* by James A. Porter, *The Negro in Art* by Alain Locke, *American Negro Art* by Cedric Dover, and *Black Artists on Art* by Samella Lewis and Ruth Waddy are used with such consistency they appear only in abbreviated form in each artist's entry, with full listing in the bibliography.

Art historian Edmund B. Gaither, Curator, Museum of the National Center of Afro-American Artists and two leading black artists in the area: Mrs. Harriet Kennedy, Assistant Registrar, Boston Museum of Fine Arts, and J. Marcus Mitchell, President, Boston Negro Artists Association, generously served on the Advisory Board. Their advice and assistance have been invaluable to the successful completion of the project.

This project was made possible with an initial grant from the Massachusetts Council on the Arts and Humanities and further supported with funding from the National Endowment for the Arts. The Library is grateful to Mr. Brian O'Doherty, Director for Visual Arts, National Endowment for the Arts, for his kind understanding and support, and above all, to Miss Louise Tate, Executive Director, Massachusetts Council on the Arts and Humanities, for her unfailing support and generous encouragement from the very inception of the project.

Under the general direction of William R. Lewis, Coordinator of Afro-American Programs at the Boston Public Library, and with the support of Miss Florence Connolly, Curator of Fine Arts, the entire project has been initiated and completed by Mrs. Theresa Cederholm, Reference Librarian in Fine Arts. The Library is truly pleased to be able to present the result of this project—more than two years in the making—in this published form, and it welcomes comments and suggestions from its users. It is hoped that the biobibliographic directory will be updated as more data are assembled and cumulated.

Philip J. McNiff
Director

The following list represents those institutions whose collections aided us in our research for the project.

New York Public Library & The Schomburg Collection of Negro Literature and History
Studio Museum in Harlem
Howard University
Martin Luther King Memorial Library, Washington, D.C.
Smith-Mason Gallery, Washington, D.C.
National Gallery of Art, Washington, D.C.
Library of Congress
Atlanta University
Montgomery Public Library
University of South Alabama
Mobile Public Library
Fisk University
Public Library of Nashville and Davidson County

Chicago Public Library
DuSable Museum of African-American History, Chicago
Art Institute of Chicago
Minneapolis Public Library
Minneapolis Institute of Arts
San Francisco Public Library
Oakland Museum
University of California Libraries
Portland State University
Indianapolis-Marion County Public Library
Indianapolis Museum of Art
Indiana University
Detroit Public Library
Detroit Institute of Arts

Introduction

The black American artist is no newcomer to American art, for even within the narrow arena of the "Fine Arts," he has been a regular although unheralded contributor since the eighteenth century. Some of the most interesting landscapists and religious painters of the nineteenth century were black, and without doubt, twentieth century American art has been enhanced by the work of Romare Bearden, Charles White, Richard Hunt, Benny Andrews and others. Moreover, some directions in contemporary American art have been influenced by largely black developments such as the wall-mural movement.

In spite of his long and varied arts participation, the black artist has not been integrated into the history of American art. Most books do not mention him at all and in others his citation is token and cursory. Even the popular interest in "black art" and the "black show" has done little to broaden the existing literature, and to stimulate art historical consideration of his work and plight.

The most substantial and penerating discussions of the art of the Afro-American are still the earlier one; consequently, they deserve a moments consideration.

The first major advocate, patron, critic and writer on Afro-American art was Alain LeRoy Locke. A believer in cultural democracy, Locke held that every people had a self-validating historical culture, and that in the global community, all cultures are co-equal. Thus he urged the Afro-American artist to study African art and to use its formal and spiritual ideas. Additionally, they were to portray sympathetically black life. The body of works created at Locke's urgings come to be called "New Negro Art" in contra-distinction to "Old Negro" or African art.

Locke's earliest formulations of the ideals of New Negro Art appeared in "The Legacy of the Ancestral Arts" (1924). A more amplified statement was published in *Negro Art, Past and Present* (1936), and *The Negro in Art* (1940).

James A. Porter, Locke's colleague at Howard University and author of *Modern Negro Art* (1943), was a more cautious art historian. His scientific approach plus the vast scope of his researches assures a high place in art historical scholarship for his book. More than anyone else, he laid the groundwork for the integration of the Afro-American artist into the mainstream of American art and history. His apologia is absolutely convincing and his analysis is thorough and persuasive.

Cedric Dover's *American Negro Art* (1960), although it is built on Porter's work, is important for its updated commentary and its generous illustrations. Along with Samella Lewis and Ruth Waddy's *Black Artists on Art*, it is among the more complete pictorial works on Afro-American art.

Recently, the number of publications focusing on Afro-American art has increased; nevertheless, much still needs to be done. There remains a great need for short, precise articles on manageable topics, for monographs and critical writings. Until such material exists in sufficient quantity, it will be difficult for the historian to find a firm foundation on which to base his concepts and generalizations. It is our hope that this directory will stimulate research in these directions. If the directory can be instrumental in widening and encouraging the examination of oeuvre of black America, it will have served its purpose.

Edmund B. Gaither
1973

ABDULRASHID, EILEEN
Craftsman. Studied at Chicago Art Institute, Chicago American Academy of Art; Institute of Design; Illinois Institute of Technology, Chicago.
Works: *Enamel on Copper on Plastic.*
Exhibitions: Art Inst., Chicago; Fie Gallery, Chicago; H. Horner Gallery, Chicago; Brockman Gallery, Los Angeles; Gallery 32, Los Angeles; South Side Art Center, Chicago; Arts Gallery, Chicago; East Gallery, Chicago; Mills College Art Gallery, Oakland, 1970.
Sources: Mills College Art Gallery. *California Black Craftsmen,* 1970.

ABELE, JULIAN F.
Painter.
Works: *Formal Garden.*
Exhibited: James A. Porter Gallery, 1970.
Sources: Howard Univ. *James A. Porter Gallery of African Amer. Art,* 1970.

ACHILLE, LOUIS
Painter.
Works: *Peinture Vecue.*
Exhibited: Atlanta Univ., 1942.
Sources: *Atlanta Univ. Annual Exhibition,* 1942.

ADAMS, JACK
Painter, graphic artist. Born in Atlanta. Studied at Clark College.
Works: *Melancholy; Country Homes; Bird Cage,* 1965 (mural); untitled print, 1970; untitled acrylic, 1963; PRIDE, illustrations, Aug./Sept. 1972; *Julian Bond,* 1971; *Georgia Artist,* 1971.
Exhibited: Atlanta Univ., 1940-65; Mead Painting of the Year Annual, 1963; Creative Arts Guild, Dalton, Ga., 1969-70; High Museum, Atlanta, 1971; Atlanta Center for Black Arts, 1970; Rowell Arts Festival, 1971-72; New Image Gallery, 1969-71; Creative Cancer, 1971; Emory Univ., 1969; Studio Gallery #1, Jacksonville, Fla., 1969; Blakesly's Gallery, Martha's Vineyard, Mass., 1965-71; Arts Festival, Atlanta.
Collections: Atlanta Univ.; Morris Brown College; Mr. Julian Bond; Mr. Maynard Jackson; Mr. Eliot Haas; Dr. S. Isenberg.
Awards: 1st award, painting, Atlanta Univ.; 2nd award, graphics, Atlanta Univ.; 1st award, mixed media, Roswell Annual.
Member: National Conference of Artists; Arts Festival of Atlanta; Creative Arts Guild.
Represented by: Creative Cancer, Atlanta; Blakesly's Gallery, Martha's Vineyard, Mass.
Sources: Siddons, A. R. "The Selling of Butterflies, Ants, and Dandylion Stems," *Pride,* Aug. 1972, pp. 41-45; Information from artist.

ADAMS, JOHN HENRY, JR.
Graphic artist, educator. Teacher in Atlanta.
Sources: Walker, Roslyn. *A Resource Guide to the Visual Arts of Afro-Americans,* South Bend, Ind., 1971; Harmon Foundation. *Exhibition of Productions by Negro Artists,* 1933; "Negro Artist Wins Praise," *Star of Zion,* Charlotte, N.C., Feb. 28, 1924; Porter, James. "Negro Artists Gain Recognition after Long Battle," *Pittsburgh Courier,* July 29, 1950; Roucek/Kiernan. *The Negro Impact on Western Civilization;* Dover. *American Negro Art;* Porter. *Modern Negro Art;* Indiana Univ. *Fine Arts and the Black American;* Harley, Ralph L., Jr. "A Checklist of Afro-American Art & Artists," *Serif,* Dec., 1970.

ADAMS, LEROY
Painter.
Works: *Sketch for a Painting.*
Exhibited: Market Place Gallery.
Collections: David Brown.
Sources: *Market Place Gallery Catalog.*

1

ADAMS, RON

Painter, graphic artist. Born in Detroit in 1934. Studied at Otis Art Institute (1965).
Sources: Lewis/Waddy. *Black Artists on Art*; Walker, Roslyn. *A Resource Guide to the Visual Arts of Afro-Americans,* South Bend, Ind., 1971.

ADEN, ALONZO J.

Painter, gallery director. Director of Barnet Aden Gallery, Washington, DC.
Sources: Walker, Roslyn. *A Resource Guide to the Visual Arts of Afro-Americans,* South Bend, Ind., 1971; Dover. *American Negro Art*; Indiana Univ. *Fine Arts and the Black American*; Boning, Richard A. *Profiles of Black Americans,* NYC, 1968, p. 50.

AKOIO, J. B.

Printmaker.
Works: *Plate Washing Hands & Feet* (etching).
Collections: Oakland Museum.
Sources: Oakland Museum Archives, gift of the Harmon Foundation.

AKUBUIRO, DOROTHY

Graphic artist. Artist in the Art Department of R.R. Bowker, NYC.
Sources: Jackson, Dorothy. "The Black Experience in Graphic Design," *Print,* Nov./Dec. 1968.

ALEXANDER, BILLIE

Painter.
Works: *Translucent Metropolis* (oil).
Collections: Johnson Pub. Co.
Sources: Johnson Pub. Co. *The JPC Art Collection.*

ALEXANDER, ERNEST

Sources: DuSable Museum of African-Amer. History. *Contemporary Black Artists,* 1970, calendar; Walker, Roslyn. *A Resource Guide to the Visual Arts of Afro-Americans,* South Bend, Ind., 1971.

ALEXANDER, IDA

Painter.
Works: *To Market.*
Exhibited: Atlanta Univ., 1944.
Sources: *Atlanta Univ. Catalog,* 1944.

ALEXANDER, L. H.

Source: Harley, Ralph, Jr. "Checklist of Afro-American Art & Artists," *The Serif,* Dec. 1970.

ALLEN, FREDERICK DOUGLASS

Painter. Born in Toledo, Ohio in 1886. Studied at Toledo Polytechnic School; Toledo Art Museum; Chicago Art Institute. Worked as portrait painter.
Works: *Louisa; W.T. Huntsman.*

Exhibited: 135th St. Branch of NY Library; Chicago Art Institute, 1916; Toledo Art Museum, 1927, 1931.
Sources: Harmon Foundation. *Non Jury Exhibit of Works of Negro Artists,* 1933.

ALLEN, JAMES LATIMER

Photographer. Born in New York City in 1907.
Works: *A Dancer of the East; Mara-Mara; Richard B. Harrison; Still Life.*
Exhibited: Carnegie Institute, Pittsburgh, 1928; Rotherham Salon, London, 1929, 1930; Harmon Exhibition, 1929, 1931, 1933; National Gallery of Art, 1933; PWAP Exhibit, 1934; Harmon Foundation-College Art Assn. Touring Exhibition, 1934-35; Texas Centennial Exposition, 1936.
Awards: Harmon Commission Prize, 1931; Commission on Race Relations Prize, 1933.
Sources: Harmon Foundation. *Exhibition of Productions by Negro Artists*; Harley, Ralph, Jr. "Checklist of Afro-American Art & Artists," *The Serif,* Dec. 1970; Indiana Univ. *Fine Arts & the Black American*; Dover. *American Negro Art*; Mallett. *Index of Artists*; DuSable Museum of African-Amer. History. *Contemporary Black Artists,* 1970, calendar; Texas Centennial Exposition. *Thumbnail Sketches of Exhibiting Artists,* 1936; Harmon Foundation. *Negro Artists,* 1935; *Art Digest,* March 1, 1933, p. 18; Walker, Roslyn. *A Resource Guide to the Visual Arts of Afro-Americans,* South Bend, Ind., 1971; *Opportunity,* Dec. 1926, p. 369.

ALLEN, RICHARD

Painter.
Works: *Crucifixion; De-Vision; Black Messiah; Sign of Protest; Flight into Egypt; Black Horsemen; Cry of the Ghetto; Black Model; Three Brothers; Man with Turban.*
Exhibited: Studio 1.
Sources: Afro-American Slide Depository, Catalog; Studio 1. *6 Black Artists.*

ALLEN, VANCE

Photographer.
Exhibited: Addison Gallery, 1971.
Sources: James Van DerZee Institute. *The Black Photographer (1908-1970): A Survey.*

A'LLERIO, MIGUEL

Sources: DuSable Museum of African-Amer. History. *Contemporary Black Artists,* 1970.

ALSTON, CHARLES H.

Painter, sculptor, graphic artist, illustrator, educator. Born in Charlotte, North Carolina, 1907. Studied at Columbia University (BA, MA); New York University. Teacher at Harlem Community Art Center and Harlem Art

Workshop (1934-36); Pennsylvania State University; Art Students League, New York.
Works: *Black Man and Woman—USA;* Illustrations in JUDGE, COLLIER'S, AMERICAN MAGAZINE, NEW YORKER; *Woman with Two Sons and a Baby on the Way; Farm Boy; Refugees;* Murals in Women's Pavilion, Harlem Hospital, NYC; *Mystery and Magic Contrasted with Modern Science and Medicine; Sons and Daughters; Red Hook, New York; Head of a Girl; Formal; Rockin' in Rhythm; Deserted Barn; Girl in Red Dress; Nude; Portrait of a Boy; Tobacco Farmer; Ruins; Torso; Walking; Girl with Necklace, Ritual of the Mask,* 1951; *African Theme: Nos. 1-4,* 1952-54; *Mneumonic,* 1954; *Across the River,* 1959; *Arrangement—Blue and Gray,* 1961; *Still Life with Eggplant,* 1961; *Hudson River,* 1966; *Astral #1,* 1960; *Astral #2,* 1960; *Ancient Place,* 1956; *Pompeian,* 1956; *Blastoff,* 1966; *Black and White: Nos. 1-8,* 1960-61; *Paintings of Protest* series—*Crucifixion,* 1953, *Statistics,* 1955, *Pieta,* 1957, *School Girl,* 1958, *Walking,* 1958, *Sons and Daughters,* 1966, *You really didn't mean it, did you, Mr. Charlie,* 1968, *March,* 1968; *The Family: Nos. 1-8,* 1955-68; *The Blues* series—*Blues Singer: Nos. 1-6,* 1950-57, *Blues with Guitar and Bass,* 1957, *Blues Song,* 1958; *Youth* series—*Boy: Nos. 1-3,* 1947, 1957, 1958, *Sisters,* 1950; *Mother and Child* (mahogany); *Head of a Virginian* (bronze); *Head of a Woman* (limestone); *Heroic Heads* series—*God's Angry Man,* 1964, *Nobody Knows,* 1966, *Frederick Douglass,* 1968.
Exhibited: High Museum, Atlanta; Univ. of Cal.; Oppenheimer Gallery, Chicago; Dunbarton Gallery, Boston; Gallery of Modern Art; Harmon Foundation, 1933-34; ACA Gallery, NY, 1936; Museum of Modern Art, 1936; Baltimore Museum, 1937, 1939; Amer. Negro Exhibition, 1940; Pyramid Club, Phila., 1952; Whitney Museum, 1952; Metropolitan Museum, 1950; Pa. Academy of Fine Arts; Downtown Gallery, NY; Univ. of Nebraska; Brussels World's Fair, 1958; Corcoran Gallery of Art; Art Students League, NY; Feingarten Gallery; City College of NY, 1967; La Jolla Museum of Art; Dillard Univ., 1941; James A. Porter Gallery, 1970; John Heller Gallery, NYC, 1956; Fairleigh Dickinson Gallery of Modern Art, NY, 1968-69 (1-man).
Collections: Metropolitan Museum of Art; Whitney Museum; Butler Art Institute; Detroit Institute of Arts; Ford College; IBM; Women's Pavilion, Harlem Hospital, NYC; Univ. of Nebraska; Atlanta Univ.; Howard Univ.; Art Students League; Johnson Pub. Co.; Dr. and Mrs. Lloyd Barnes, NY; Mr. & Mrs. William Anderson, NY; Frederick Douglass Institute, Washington, DC; Mrs. Miriam Snibbe,

NY; Mr. & Mrs. Lloyd Greenidge, White Plains, NY; Mr. & Mrs. John Hammond, NY; Mr. & Mrs. George Gregory, NY; Mr. & Mrs. Charles Gorham, Westport, Conn.; Dr. & Mrs. Thomas Day, NY; Jamestown (Va.) Museum; Mr. and Mrs. Robert Popper, White Plains, NY.
Awards: Dow Fellowship; Rosenwald Fellowship; Grant, National Institute of Arts & Letters; Atlanta Univ.; Dillard Univ.; Joe & Emily Lowe Award; DeWitt Clinton Alumni Award, 1961; Thomas B. Clarke Award, National Academy of Design, 1971; Golden State Insurance Co. Award.
Member: Dept. of Fine Arts, City College of NY; Board of Directors, National Society of Mural Painters, NY; Spiral.
Represented by: Kennedy Gallery, 20 E. 56th St., NYC.
Sources: DuSable Museum of African-Amer. History. *Contemporary Black Artists,* 1970, calendar; Cahill. *New Horizons in American Art;* Dover. *American Negro Art;* Mallett. *Index of Artists; Who's Who in American Art,* 1966, 1970; City College of NY. *Evolution of Afro-American Artists 1800-1950,* 1967; *Pictures on Exhibit,* May 1956, p. 18; "The Dead Conquers: A Drawing by Charles Alston," *Modern Quarterly,* Fall 1940, p. 24; Storm, John. *Malcolm MacBeth,* NY, Lothrop, Lee & Shepard Co., 1946; Harley, Ralph, Jr. "Checklist of Afro-Amer. Art & Artists," *Serif,* Dec. 1970; Porter. *Modern Negro Art;* La Jolla Museum of Art. *Dimensions of Black;* Baltimore Museum of Art. *Contemporary Negro,* 1939; Tanner Art Galleries. *Art of the American Negro,* 1940; Brown, Evelyn S. "The Harmon Award," *Opportunity,* Mar., 1933; Locke. *The Negro in Art,* 1940; Bardolph. *The Negro Vanguard,* 1959; Jefferson, Louise. *Contemporary Afro-American Art,* 1969; Brawley, Benjamin. *The Negro Genius;* Dillard Univ. *Arts Festival,* 1941; Roucek/Kiernan. *The Negro Impact on Western Civilization;* Harmon Foundation. *Negro Artists,* 1935; Howard Univ. *James A. Porter Gallery of African-Amer. Art,* 1970; *Daily News,* Greensboro, NC, May 6, 1951; L.I. Univ. *Spiral;* "Honoring Negro History," *Art Digest,* Feb. 15, 1949, p. 20; Drummond, Dorothy. "Coast-to-Coast," *Art Digest,* Mar. 1, 1952, p. 12; Greene, Carroll, Jr. "Perspective: The Black Artist in America," *Art Gallery,* Apr. 1970, p. 19; "Amer. Negro Art Given Full Length Review in NY Show," *Art Digest,* Dec. 15, 1941; "Negro Art Annual," *Art Digest,* May 1, 1942; "The Negro Comes of Age," *Art News,* Feb. 1, 1945; Pierre-Noel, Lois Jones. "American Negro Art in Progress," *Negro History Bulletin,* Oct. 1967; McCausland, Elizabeth. "Jacob Lawrence," *Amer. Magazine of Art,*

Nov. 1945; "Negro in Art," *Art News,* Dec. 19, 1941, p. 24; Siegel, Jeanne. "Why Spiral?," *Art News,* Sept. 1966, pp. 48-50; "American Negro Art," *Design,* Feb. 1942, p. 28; Johnson Pub. Co. *The JPC Art Collection;* Greene, Carroll, Jr. "Afro-Amer. Artists, Yesterday & Now," *The Humble Way,* Vol. 8, No. 3, 1968; "Leading Negro Artists," *Ebony,* Sept. 1963, pp. 131-2; Shorewood Reproductions. *The Art of Black America,* 1969; Alston, Charles. *Art Student League News,* Feb. 1956; Brown, Marion. "The Negro in the Fine Arts," *The Negro Heritage Library,* Vol. 2; Ploski, Harry, & Ernest Kaiser. "The Black Artist," *Afro USA,* 1971; The Negro Handbook, Composed by editors of *Ebony,* Chicago, 1966; Schatz, Walter. *Directory of Afro-American Resources,* 1970; Adams, Russell. *Great Negroes Past & Present,* Chicago, 1969; Fairleigh Dickinson Gallery of Modern Art. *Charles Alston,* catalogue of Dec. 1968-Jan. 1969 exhibition, NYC, 1971; Myers, Carol L. *Black Power in the Arts,* Flint, Mich., 1970; Glueck, Grace. "The Best Painter I Can Possibly Be," *New York Times,* Dec. 8, 1970; John Heller Gallery. *Exhibition of Paintings, Sculpture, Drawing & Watercolors,* NY, 1958; Walker, Roslyn. *A Resource Guide to the Visual Arts of Afro-Americans,* South Bend, Ind., 1971.

ALSTON, ERNEST G.
Painter. Born in Detroit on May 23, 1931. Studied at University of Hawaii; Society of Arts & Crafts, 1953-4.
Works: *Solitude; Butterfly; Fish & Fruit; Aquiescence; Still Life with Fish.*
Exhibited: Nat'l Gallery Competition, Denver; Detroit Institute of Arts, 1959-65.
Sources: Detroit Institute of Art, exhibition files.

ALSTON, FRANK H., JR.
Painter, educator, designer. Born in Providence, Rhode Island, 1913. Studied at Rhode Island School of Design (1933); Rhode Island College of Education (1933). Heraldic designer in US Army, Washington, DC in 1960.
Works: *Eastern Branch; Summer Storm.*
Exhibited: Atlanta Univ., 1951; National Gallery, Washington, DC, 1945; NY World's Fair; San Francisco Golden Gate Exposition; Corcoran Art Gallery; NY Historical Society.
Collections: Howard Univ.; Senate Office Building, Washington, DC.
Awards: 1st prize, oils, National Gallery, 1945; 14 major scholarships.

ADAMS, FRANK H., JR.
Sources: Mallett. *Index of Artists;* Dover. *American Negro Art;* Atlanta Univ. *10th Annual for Negro Artists,* 1951; "Oil by Local Artist Given 1st Prize at Exhibit of 500,"

Washington Afro-American, Nov. 17, 1945; Woodruff, Hale. "Negro Artists Hold 4th Annual in Atlanta," *Art Digest,* Apr. 15, 1945; Barnet Aden Gallery. *Exhibition of Paintings & Watercolors,* Washington, DC; Walker, Roslyn. *A Resource Guide to the Visual Arts of Afro-Americans,* 1971.

ALSTON, FREDERICK CORNELIUS
Painter, educator, illustrator. Born in Wilmington, North Carolina, 1895. Studied at the Philadelphia School of Industrial Arts; Shaw University. Studied under Thornton Oakley, George Harding.
Works: *Industrial Education* (mural); *Genesis; Exodus; The Good Book Says; Sunshine.*
Exhibited: Tanner Art League, 1922; Harmon Foundation, 1929-31, 1933; Exhibition of Negro Painters, St. Louis, 1930; Library of Congress, 1940; Barnet Aden Gallery, 1948 (1-man); Howard Univ., 1961; Smithsonian Institution, 1929.
Collections: Tuskegee Institute.
Awards: 1st prize, 1930-1, 2nd prize, 1932, Citizen's Art Commission; 1st prize, Exhibition of Negro Artists, St. Louis, 1930.
Member: St. Louis Independent Artists; Amer. Federation of Artists; St. Louis Citizen's Art Commission.
Sources: Mallett. *Index of Artists;* Harmon Foundation. *Exhibition of Productions by Negro Artists;* Indiana Univ. *Fine Arts and the Black American; Who's Who in American Art,* 1940-1; *American Art Annual,* 1929; Clermont, R. "Paintings by Frank Alston," *La Revue Moderne,* July 1948; *Catalogue of the Third Annual Exhibition of the Tanner Art League,* 1922; Library of Congress. *Catalog of the Exhibition of Oils, Watercolors and Drawings,* 1940; Harley, Ralph, Jr. "Checklist of Afro-Amer. Art & Artists," *Serif,* Dec. 1970; DuSable Museum of African-Amer. History. *Contemporary Black Artists,* 1970; Harmon Foundation. *Negro Artists,* 1935; Harmon Foundation. *Exhibit of Fine Arts,* 1930; Smithsonian Institution. *Painting & Sculpture by American Negro Artists,* 1929; Walker, Roslyn. *A Resource Guide to the Visual Arts of Afro-Americans,* South Bend, Ind., 1970.

ALSTON, TOUSSAINT
Painter.
Works: *Harvest Time; Roses & Vase.*
Exhibited: Atlanta Univ., 1944.
Sources: Atlanta Univ. Annual Exhibition Catalog, 1944; Harley, Ralph, Jr. "Checklist of Afro-American Art and Artists," *The Serif,* Dec. 1970.

AMERINO, VICTOR
Collections: NY Public Library, Schomberg Collection.

Sources: Schatz, Walter. *Directory of Afro-American Resources,* 1970.

AMÉVOR, CHARLOTTE

Born in Harlem, New York, on September 17, 1932. Studied at Brooklyn Museum School; Art Students League, New York City.
Works: *Village Drummers; Determination.*
Exhibited: Fulton Art Fair, Brooklyn, 1964.
Sources: Fax, Elton C. *Seventeen Black Artists.*

AMOS, EMMA

Painter, printmaker. Born in Atlanta, Georgia in 1938. Studied at Antioch College, Yellow Springs, Ohio (BA, 1958); London Central School of Art; New York University (MA, 1966); Slade School of Art, London.
Works: *Baby,* 1966 (oil); *The Ladies,* 1969 (etching & seriograph); *The Window,* 1965 (oil); *Harvest II; Flower Sniffer; Two Women; Three Ladies; Nature; Horizons; Bathers; Summer, 1968; Black Magic Mirror; Without Father Boa.*
Exhibited: Alexander Galleries, Atlanta; Minneapolis Inst. of Art, 1968; Boston Museum of Fine Arts, 1970; Young Contemporaries Annual, London, 1959; Intaglio Workshop, NY, 1961, 1963; Spiral Group, NY, 1964, 1965; Harlem Cultural Council, 1966; Society of Amer. Graphic Artists, NY, 1966; Long Island Univ., 1965-6; Arts Festival, Provincetown, Mass., 1958; Atlanta Univ. Annuals, 1953, 1958, 1959, 1960; St. Georges Gallery; Amer. Art Assn., NY; Ruder & Finn Fine Arts, NY, 1969.
Collections: US Embassy, London; Museum of African Art, Washington, DC; Spelman College, Atlanta; Oakland Museum; Mr. Edmund B. Gaither.
Sources: Myers, Carol L. *Black Power in the Arts,* Flint, Mich., 1970; Boston Museum of Fine Arts. *Afro-American Artists: New York & Boston,* 1970; Roelof-Lanner. *Prints by American Negro Artists;* Morrison, Allan. "New Surge in the Arts," *Ebony,* Aug. 1967; NY State Education Dept. *Fifteen Under Forty;* Harley, Ralph, Jr. "Checklist of Afro-American Art & Artists," *The Serif,* Dec. 1970; Bowling, Frank. "The Rupture," *Arts,* Summer 1970; Siegel, Jeanne. "Why Spiral?," *Art News,* Sept. 1966; "What is Black Art?," *Newsweek,* June 22, 1970; Minneapolis Inst. of Art. *30 Contemporary Black Artists,* 1968; Ruder & Finn Fine Arts. *Contemporary Black Artists,* 1969; Harlem Cultural Council. *Art of the American Negro,* 1966; Walker, Roslyn. *A Resource Guide to the Visual Arts of Afro-Americans,* South Bend, Ind., 1971; Gaither, Edmund B. "The Evolution of the Afro-American Artist," *Artists Proof,* 1971; Hollingsworth, Alvin. "Wealth of Expression in Black Artists' RISD Show," *Providence Sunday Journal,* June 29, 1969; LeBrun, Caron. "Black Art," *Herald Traveler,* Sunday Supplement, Boston, May 24, 1970; "Afro-American Issue," *Art Gallery,* April 1968; DuSable Museum of African-Amer. History. *Contemporary Black Artists,* 1970, calendar; "Afro-American Artists: NY & Boston," *Prudential Center News,* March 1, 1970, p. 4.

ANDERSON, CHARLES HENRY

Born in New York City in 1882.
Works: *Her Evening Prayer; A Quiet Moment; River Stay Away From My Door; Self Portrait.*
Exhibited: Harmon Foundation, 1933, 1935, 1944.
Sources: Harmon Foundation. *Negro Artists,* 1935; Harmon Foundation. *Non-Jury Exhibit of Works of Negro Artists,* 1933; Harmon Foundation. *Exhibition of Productions by Negro Artists;* Indiana Univ. *Fine Arts & the Black American;* Harley, Ralph, Jr. "Checklist of Afro-Amer. Art & Artists," *The Serif,* Dec. 1970; Walker, Roslyn. *A Resource Guide to the Visual Arts of Afro-Americans,* South Bend, Ind., 1971.

ANDERSON, EILEEN

Painter.
Works: *Airport; Love Structure.*
Collections: Johnson Pub. Co., Chicago.
Sources: Johnson Pub. Co. *The JPC Art Collection,* Chicago.

ANDERSON, ERIC

Painter.
Exhibited: Harmon Foundation, 1933.
Sources: Walker, Roslyn. *A Resource Guide to the Visual Arts of Afro-Americans,* South Bend, Ind., 1971; Myers, Carol L. *Black Power in the Arts,* Flint, Mich., 1970; "Afro-Amer. Issue," *Art Gallery,* April 1968; Indiana Univ. *Fine Arts & the Black American;* DuSable Museum of African-Amer. History. *Contemporary Black Americans,* 1970, calendar.

ANDERSON, FREDDIE

Painter, illustrator. Born in Denver, Colorado on August 24, 1932. Studied at Kansas University (BFA, 1956).
Works: *Rappin; Lil Brother; Victoria; Hossin' Roun'; Playtime; Market Woman; Boy Sitting on Steps; Why Me.*
Exhibited: Chicago outdoor art fairs; South Side Community Art Center; Old Town Ale House.
Collections: Byron Minor; Grace Leaming; Sylvia Guldager; Woodlawn Mental Health Center; Fern Gayden; Geraldine Mardis.
Member: South Side Community Art Center (Board Member); National Conference of Artists.

Sources: National Conference of Artists. *A Print Portfolio by Negro Artists*; King, Helen. *Soul of Christmas* (illustrator); "Everybody Loves Saturday Night," *Follett Song Book* (illustrator); Haydon, Harold. "Galleries— The Older Generation Strikes Back," *Chicago Sun Times*, April 1971; Information from the artist.

ANDERSON, HORACE G.

Painter. Born in Washington, DC. Studied at Howard University; Armour Institute.

Works: *Autumn Landscape; Road in the Rock Creek Park.*

Exhibited: Harmon Foundation, 1930, 1933, 1935.

Sources: Harmon Foundation. *Negro Artists,* 1935; Harmon Foundation. *Exhibit of Fine Arts,* 1930; Harmon Foundation. *Exhibition of Productions by Negro Artists*; Indiana Univ. *Fine Arts & the Black American*; Harley, Ralph, Jr. "Checklist of Afro-Amer. Art & Artists," *The Serif,* Dec. 1970; Walker, Roslyn. *A Resource Guide to the Visual Arts of Afro-Americans,* South Bend, Ind., 1971.

ANDREWS, BENNY

Painter, mixed media, illustrator, educator. Born in Madison, Georgia on November 13, 1930. Studied at Fort Valley (Georgia) State College; University of Chicago; Art Institute of Chicago (BFA, 1958). Teacher at New York School of Social Research, New York City; Queens College, New York City.

Works: *Man; Roz; Redhead; Bliss; Madam; Shadow on the Land; Witness; Streets; Interruption; Man with a Bow Tie; Dawn's Early Light; Louie; Seated Woman; Mary; Champion; Gypsy; Introspective; Man & His History; Yesterday; War Baby* (oil collage); *Meditation* (oil collage); *Every Man* (collage sculpture); *Mother & Baby; Red Hat; Gertrude; Primping Ladies; Black Cat; Young Rabbi; Artist's Wife; St. Francis Talking to the Birds; Christ & the Nude; Someone Somewhere; The Old Jew; Julie; Flora; Mom & Dad; Orator; Man at the Rail; Mourners; Head of a Woman; Running Wild; Charley; Placidity; The Milkers; The Survivors; Landscape; Sitter; Young Lady; Girl in the Garden; The Arrival; He-Man; Stars; Woman with Vase; Studio; Human's Love; Young Maiden at the Window; Ourselves; Poor Boy Drinking; Secrets; Hat; No More Games; Symbols; Trash; Mr. America; L.D.; Threshold; Sweet Charity; Bike Rider; No Title; Bread; Washer Woman; The Ascension; Worker's Table; City Bird; Black Man; Mother of the World; Lady; Odd Man In; Self Portrait; Cradle; Mary in Blue; Oedipus; Mrs. A.; Woman Washing; Ecstasy; Destiny; On Request; Nina; Exhibitors; Despair; Prickley Plant* (oil collage); *Artist's Hommage; Portrait of a Young Lady; Rebecca; Swing Low; A Soul; Watchers; The Answer is Si; But See; American Heritage; Girl; Cicara A; Cage Sculpture; Spokesman; Woman; Front Porch; Window; Isle of Woman; Praying Woman; Introspective; Smoker; Temptation of Chastity; The Virgin; Eve; Lady with Animal; Man in the Sun; Carressed Flowers; Turtle Logging; Gypsy Revisited; The New Hat; Landscape #5; Adam & Eve; Doctor; Raphael; Queen of the May; The Loser; The New Day; Windowless World; Showdown; Burden; End; Mouthful; Mode; Flower #3; Ah Bliss; Airling; Seeker; Woman with Shawl; Painter & His Sculpture; Piggyback; Visitor; Cop; Did the Bear Sit Under the Tree; The Invisible Man; Cotton Chopper; Farmer; There Must Be a Heaven; Mother Earth; The Family,* 1965 (oil); *Wounded SGT.; Georgian Funeral; Apple Pie,* 1969 (collage); *People.*

Exhibited: Forum Gallery, NYC, 1962-6; Henri Gallery, Alexandria, Va., 1963-6; Mari Gallery, Woodstock, NY, 1963; Bray-Hampton Gallery, Atlanta, Ga., 1966; New School for Social Research, NYC, 1968; Cal. State College, Hayward, 1969; Windy Glass Gallery, NYC, 1970; Univ. of Bridgeport, Conn., 1970; Point Gallery, Kittery Point, Me., 1970; Acts of Art Gallery, NYC, 1970; Spelman College, Atlanta, 1971; Wabash (Ind.) College, 1971; Talladega College, Atlanta, 1971; Studio Museum, NYC, 1971; Carlow College, Pittsburgh, 1971; Western Mich. Univ., 1972; ACA Gallery, NYC, 1972; Detroit Institute of Art, 1959; Phila. Academy of Art, 1960; Brooklyn Museum of Art, 1963; New York World's Fair, 1965; Eastern Mich. Univ., Ypsilanti, Mich.; Chrysler Museum, Provincetown, Mass.; Amer. Academy of Arts & Letters, NYC; Art Students League, NYC; Butler (Ohio) Inst. of American Art, 1967; Minneapolis Art Inst.; Museum of Modern Art, NYC; Riverside Museum, NYC, 1969; Brooklyn College; Martha Jackson's Gallery, NYC; Boston Museum of Fine Arts; Hudson River Museum, Yonkers, NY; The Currier Gallery, 1971; Univ. of New Hampshire; Nat'l Center of Afro-Amer. Artists, Boston; Illinois Bell Tel. Gallery, Chicago; Illinois State Museum, Springfield; Univ. of Wisconsin, Milwaukee; Sloan Galleries, Valpariso, Ind.; Peoria Art Guild, Ill.; Burpee Gallery, Rockford, Ill.; Davenport Municipal Gallery, Iowa; Univ. of Iowa; Carnegie Inst., Pittsburgh; Scripps College, Claremont, Cal.; High Art Museum, Atlanta, 1969; Everson Museum of Art, Syracuse, NY, 1969; IBM Gallery of Arts & Sciences, NYC, 1969; Rhode Island School of Design, 1969; Memorial Art Gallery, Rochester, NY, 1969; San Francisco Museum of Art, 1969; Contemporary Arts Museum, Houston, 1970; Flint (Mich.) Board of Education; Pan

Amer. Building, NYC; Rainbow Sign Gallery, 1972; Gallery 1199, NYC, 1972.

Collections: ACA Gallery, NYC; Museum of African Art, Washington, DC; Norfolk Museum, Va.; Chrysler Museum, Provincetown, Mass.; Joseph H. Hirshhorn Collection; Internat'l Harvester Co., Chicago; Butler (Ohio) Institute of Amer. Art; Russ Thompson Collection; Aarson Midtown Gallery, Atlanta; Wisconsin State Univ.; Stout State Univ., Wisc.; Slater Memorial Museum, Norwich, Conn.; Mr. & Mrs. William Paley, Manhasset, NY; Richard Brown Baker, NYC; Museum of Modern Art, NYC; La Jolla Museum, Cal.; Mr. George Axelrod; Mr. Chaim Gross; Mr. Raphael Soyer.

Awards: John Hay Whitney Fellowship, 1965-6; Dorne Professorship, Bridgeport Univ.; New York State Council Creative Arts Program Award, 1971; The Atlanta Univ. Negro Art Collection Award for "Educational Arts," 1971.

Sources: Who's Who in American Art, 1970; "Afro-American Issue," Art Gallery, April 1968, 1970; Afro-American Slide Depository, catalog; Minneapolis Institute of Arts. 30 Contemporary Black Artists; Boston Museum of Fine Arts. Afro-American Artists: New York & Boston, 1970; Andrews, Benny. "The Black Emergency Cultural Coalition," Arts, Summer 1970, pp. 18-20; Lewis/Waddy. Black Artists on Art, Vol. 2; Harley, Ralph, Jr. "A Checklist of Afro-American Art and Artists," The Serif, Dec. 1970; Illinois Bell Telephone. Black American Artists/71, 1971-2; Hudson River Museum. Contemporary American Black Artists; Ruder & Finn Fine Arts. Contemporary Black Artists, 1969; "Art," Newsweek, June 22, 1970; Flint (Mich.) Community Schools. Black Reflections; Miller, Earl. Rhode Island School of Design Bulletin, 1969; L.C. "Black is Political," Art News, Oct. 1970, p. 30; Bowling, Frank. "It's Not Enough to Say 'Black is Beautiful,'" Art News, April 1971; Bowling, Frank. "Silence: People Die Crying When They Should Love," Arts, Sept. 1970, p. 31; Fax, Elton C. Seventeen Black Artists; Kiah, Virginia. "Black Artists," Savannah Magazine, April 1972, p. 16; Berkman, Florence. "Some Black Artists Irate Over Whitney Exhibit," Times, Hartford, Conn., April 25, 1971; Glueck, Grace. "Black Show Under Fire At The Whitney," New York Times, Jan. 31, 1971; Hinchcliffe, Diane. "Black Art Exhibit: Future Looks A Little Brighter," Chronicle Citizen, Brookline, Mass., June 4, 1970; Bourne, Kay. "Black Artists Shown at Museum," Bay State Banner, May 28, 1970; "Museum of Fine Arts to Hold Black Art Show," Chronicle, Ipswich, Mass., April 30, 1970; "What is Black Art," Newsweek, June 22, 1970; Museum of Nat'l Center of Afro-Amer.

Artists. Taking Care of Business; Loercher, Diana. "Nat'l Center of Afro-Amer. Artists & Art Benefit Premier," Christian Science Monitor, May 4, 1971; Driscoll, Edgar. "Art Show Reflects Black Rage, Pride," Boston Globe, April 28, 1971; "Museum to Hold Black Art Show," Tri-Town Transcript & Pennysaver, April 29, 1970; "Now Showing: The Black Artist," Contact, Sept. 1970; Kramer, Hilton. "Is Politics Submerging Black Art?," Courier-Journal & Times, Louisville, Ky., June 7, 1970; Ploski, Harry, & Ernest Kaiser. "The Black Artist," Afro USA, 1971; Van Almelo, Frederick. "In The American Grain," Boston After Dark, May 26, 1970; Walsh, Rose. "Artist to Meet Public at Art Exhibit Preview," Record American, May 19, 1970; LC. "Black is Political," Art News, Oct. 1970, p. 30; Metropolitan Applied Research Center. Six Painters; Grillo, Jean B. "Black Art-White Museum," Phoenix, May 23, 1970; Schwartz, Therese. "The Political Scene," Arts, April 1971; Paris, Jean. "Black Art Experience in Art," Long Island Press, Jamaica, NY, June 14, 1970; Ploski, Harry, Ernest Kaiser, & Otto Lindenmeyer. "The Black Artist," Reference Library of Black America, Book 4, 1971; Atkinson, J. Edward. Black Dimensions in Contemporary American Art, NYC, 1971; DuSable Museum of African-Amer. History. Contemporary Black Artists, 1970, Calendar; Brooklyn College. Afro-American Artists: Since 1950, 1969; Myers, Carol L. Black Power in the Arts, Flint, Mich., 1970; Adoff, Arnold. I Am the Darker Brother, 1968 (Illustrator); Walker, Roslyn. A Resource Guide to the Visual Arts of Afro-Americans, South Bend, Ind., 1971; Bowling, Frank. "It's Not Enough To Say 'Black Is Beautiful,'" Art News, April 1971; Riverside Museum. Eight Plus Eight, 1969; A Collection of Negro Poems, MacMillan Co., March 1968 (Illustrator); Hollingsworth, Alvin. "Wealth of Expression in Black Artists' RISD Show," Providence Sunday Journal, June 29, 1969; Amer. Academy of Arts & Letters. Exhibition of Paintings Eligible for Purchase Under the Childe Hassam Fund, NYC, 1972; Rainbow Sign Gallery. Black Arts Day II, Press Release, 1972; Black Shades, Oct. 1972.

ANDREWS, OPHELIA G.

Educator, painter. Chairman, Department of Art, West Virginia State College.

Sources: Dover. American Negro Art, p. 38; Indiana Univ. Fine Arts & the Black American; Harley, Ralph, Jr. "A Checklist of Afro-Amer. Art & Artists," The Serif, Dec. 1970; Walker, Roslyn. A Resource Guide to the Visual Arts of Afro-Americans, South Bend, Ind., 1971.

ARCHER, EDMUND

Sources: Indiana Univ. *Fine Arts & the Black American*; Walker, Roslyn. *A Resource Guide to the Visual Arts of Afro-Americans*, South Bend, Ind., 1971.

ARCHIE, JAMES LEE

Painter. Born in Orlander, North Carolina in 1924. Self-taught.
Works: *The Horse; Destitute Meets Tranquility.*
Exhibited: Studio Museum, Harlem, 1969.
Sources: Studio Museum in Harlem. *Harlem Artists 69*, 1969.

ARCHIE, WILLIAM

Painter. Born in Portsmouth, Virginia in 1925. Self-taught.
Works: *Country Scene: Teens in Country; Beach Scene: Boy Running.*
Exhibited: Studio Museum, Harlem, 1969.
Sources: Studio Museum in Harlem. *Harlem Artists 69*, 1969.

ARGUDIN Y PEDROSO, PASTOR

Born in Havana, Cuba, 1889. Government scholar to Madrid and Paris.
Works: Murals, Church of Our Lady, Havana; *Sengalese Warrior; Dance of Salome; Girl Warrior.*
Exhibited: Harmon Foundation, NY, 1935 (1-man); Works, Havana (1-man); Pavilion de Cuba, Seville, Spain (1-man); Phila. Sesquicentennial Exposition; NJ State Museum, 1935; Berean Manual Training & Industrial School, Phila., 1935.
Collections: Church of Our Lady, Havana; NY Public Library, Schomburg Collection; Museum of Andalusia, Seville.
Awards: Madrid Academy Prize, 1915.
Sources: Locke. *The Negro in Art*; Schatz, Walter. *Directory of Afro-American Resources*, 1970; DuSable Museum of African-Amer. History. *Contemporary Black Artists*, Calendar, 1970; Harmon Foundation. *Negro Artists*, Catalog, 1935; "Negro Artists Reveal Genius in Trenton Show," *Art Digest*, April 15, 1935.

ARNOLD, RALPH

Painter, mixed media, graphic artist, educator. Born in Chicago in 1928. Studied at University of Illinois; School of Art Institute of Chicago; Hyde Park Art Center; Roosevelt University (BA).
Works: *Untitled* (color lithograph); *Coastal; Rain & Rainbow; Some of My Favorite Things*, 1969 (etching); *Confrontation Series—Drawings on the Chicago Convention*, 1968; *Celebration*, 1970 (crayon & pencil); *Arcade with Bridge*, 1970 (intaglio); *Soul Box; Open Bag; Drexel Square; Steel Painting; The Sum of Two Numbers* (collage based on the Kennedy-King assassinations); *Unfinished Collage.*
Exhibited: Whitney Museum, 1971; Univ. of Iowa Museum of Art, 1971-2; Festival of the Arts, Rockford College, Ill., 1965; Museum of Contemporary Art, Chicago, 1969; NY State Fair, 1969; Phila. Art Alliance, 1969; Illinois Bell Tel. Co., Chicago, 1970; Phila. Civic Center, 1970; Museum of Art, Utica, NY, 1970; Illinois State Museum, 1971; Ball State Univ., Muncie, Ind., 1971; Fisk Univ., Nashville, 1972; Sneed Gallery 35, Rockford, Ill.; Rockford (Ill.) College, 1968, 1970; College of the St. Benedict, St. Joseph, Minn.; Benjamin Galleries, 1966, 1968; Barat College, Lake Forest, Ill., 1969, 1971; Gilman Galleries, Chicago, 1969, 1971; Illinois Arts Council, 1970; Van Staaten Gallery, Chicago, 1972.
Collections: J. G. Powers; Theodore Zekman; Rockford College; Illinois Bell Telephone; Container Corporation of America; Museum of African Art, Washington, DC; Playboy Club International; Borg-Warner Corporation; Whitney Museum; Fisk Univ.; Luther College, Iowa; Johnson Pub., Chicago; Tuesday Foundation, Chicago; Oakland Museum.
Member: Arts Club of Chicago.
Sources: "Afro-American Issue," *Art Gallery*, April 1968; Indiana Univ. *Fine Arts and the Black American*; Museum of Contemporary Art. *Violence in American Art*, Chicago, 1969, Unpublished list; Doty. *Contemporary Black Artists in America*; NY State Fair. *Graphics 1969*, Unpublished list; Illinois Bell Telephone. *Black American Artists*, 1971; Rockford College. *Creativity and the Negro*; Johnson Pub. Co. *The JPC Art Collection*; DuSable Museum of African-Amer. History. *Contemporary Black Artists*, 1970; *Collage and Found Art*, Reinhold and Co., 1964; *Creating Art From Anything*, Reilly and Lee, 1968; Phila. Art Alliance. *New Approaches in Printmaking*, 1969, Unpublished list; Illinois Bell Tel. *American Drawings & Prints of the 60's*, 1970; Phila. Civic Center. *Afro-American Arts 1800-1969*, 1970; Museum of Art. *American Prints Today*, Utica, NY, 1970; Whitney Museum of Art. *Contemporary Black Artists in America*, 1971; Illinois State Museum. *24th Invitational Exhibition*, 1971; Ball State Univ. Gallery. *All Collage Exhibition*, 1971; Information from artist; Myers, Carol L. *Black Power in the Arts*, Flint, Mich., 1970; Oakland Museum Archives, Ruth Waddy Collection; Walker, Roslyn. *A Resource Guide to the Visual Arts of Afro-Americans*, South Bend, Ind., 1971; Preston, Malcolm. "Art: Black Exhibit," *Boston Herald Traveler*, April 19, 1971; Haas, Joseph. "A Big Brilliant & Exciting Exhibition of Black Art," *Chicago Daily News*, 1971; Cultural Exchange Center. *Prints by American Negro Artists.*

ARTIS, WILLIAM E.

Sculptor, printmaker, educator, ceramist, illustrator. Born in Washington, North Carolina on February 2, 1914. Studied at Chadron State College, Nebraska (BS); Syracuse University (BFA, MFA); New York State University, College of Ceramics; Long Beach State College, California; Pennsylvania State University; Art Students League (1933-5); New York State College of Ceramics; Greenwich House Ceramic Center. Teacher at Harlem YMCA; Nebraska State Teachers College.

Works: *Chinese Green Jar & Cover; Mauve Bowl; Turquoise Blue Bowl; White Cracker Jar with Cover; Yellow Brown Bowl; Yellow Dish; Planter; Two Vases; Pugilist; A Studio Exhibition; Six Heads; Bowl; Woman with Kerchief; Draped Head; Geomorphic Form; Jar with Cover; African Youth; Young Mother; Afro; Mississippi Swamps; Compote; Vita; Vase; Michael; Habiticle; Orbit; Boy with Cap; Girl with Turban; Head of Dottie; Caricature Head; Head of a Boy; Head of a Girl; Blue & White Bowl; Blue & White Vase; Mother Love; Mama Look at Bobo; Detail from Mama Look at Bobo; The Quiet One; Poet of Hope; Ash Trays Green; Two Yellow Vases, One Yellow & One Brown; Two Dishes, One Green, One Green Blue; Jar; Blue Vase; Two Highly Glazed Jars; Green Vase with Flowers; Two Glazed Bowls; One Deep Yellow Bowl; Black Bowl; Eddie; Antone; Dr. Lewis Wright; Two (Yellow, Green) Shallow Dishes; Three Vases; C.C. Spaulding; Vase & Jar; Four Shallow Dishes; Low & Tall Vases; Two Highly Glazed Yellow Bowls; Colored Youth; Girl with Long Bob; Two Highly Glazed Yellow Dishes; Two Shallow Gray Dishes; Two Highly Glazed Bottles; Bottle, with Three Small Cups; Two Coarse Terracotta Bowls; Three Shallow Glazed Dishes, Green; Group of Six Pieces; Medium Dish, Blue Crackle Finish; Two Glazed Buff Colored Jars; Head with Caps; Vernon Bisque Sculpture; A Decorative Head; Head-Terracotta; Nlysterier.*

Exhibited: Harmon Foundation, 1933; Grace Horne Galleries, Boston, 1942; Atlanta Univ., 1944, 1951; USO Exhibit, NYC, 1944; NJ State Museum, Trenton; Albany Inst. of History & Art; Nat'l Portrait Gallery; Walker Art Center; Joslyn Art Museum, Neb.; Chadron State College; Pennsylvania State College; City College of NY, 1967; IBM; Slater Memorial Museum, Norwich, Conn.; Howard Univ.; Goodall Art Gallery, Doane College, Crete, Neb.; Fisk Univ.; Johnson Pub. Co., Chicago; Nat'l Arts Club, NYC, 1940; Nat'l Sculpture Society, NYC; Whitney Museum of American Art; Syracuse Museum of Fine Arts, 1940, 1947-51; Hetzel Union Building, 1956-61; Lang Art Gallery, Scripps College, Claremont, Cal.; Amer. Negro Exposition, Chicago, 1940; Art Students League, 1933; Salons of America, 1934; Harlem Art Committee, 1935; Texas Centennial, 1936; James A. Porter Gallery, 1970; Xavier Univ., 1963; Art Center, NYC, 1933.

Collections: Walker Art Center, Minneapolis; IBM; Slater Memorial Art Museum, Norwich, Conn.; Howard Univ.; Joslyn Art Museum, Neb.; Goodall Art Gallery, Doane College, Crete, Neb.; Chadron State College; Johnson Pub. Co., Chicago; Smithsonian Institution; Atlanta Univ.

Awards: Outstanding Educator of America, 1970; Outstanding Afro-American Artist, 1970; John Hope Prize, sculpture, 1933, 1935; Sculpture Purchase Prize, Atlanta Univ., 1951; Rosenwald Fellowship, 1947; Atlanta Univ. Purchase Award, 1944, 1947, 1952, 1959, 1962, 1965; Smith-Mason Gallery Award, 1971.

Member: American Ceramic Society; Nat'l Sculpture Society; College Art Assn. of America; Nat'l Art Education Assn.; New York Society of Arts & Crafts.

Sources: Mallett. *Index of Artists*; Dover. *American Negro Art*, pp. 31, 42, 54, 142; Locke. *The Negro in Art; Art Digest*, April 15, 1935, 1951; Albany Inst. of History & Art. *The Negro Artist Comes of Age*, 1945; Afro-American Slide Depository, Catalog; Johnson Pub. Co. *The JPC Collection*, Chicago; Harmon Foundation. *Exhibition of Productions by Negro Artists*, 1933; Indiana Univ. *Fine Arts & the Black American; Who's Who in American Art*, 1970; City College of NY. *Evolution of Afro-American Artists 1800-1950*, 1967; Information from artist; Porter. *Modern Negro Art*; Lewis/Waddy. *Black Artists on Art*, Vol. 2; Butcher, Margaret J. *The Negro in American Culture; The National Sculpture Review*, Vol. 20, No. 3; Vol. 21, No. 4; Vol. 22, No. 4; *Artists/USA 1972-3*, Feasterville, Pa., Artists/USA Inc., 1972; Chase, Judith. *Afro-American Art & Craft*; Harmon Foundation. *Negro Artists; Mankato Citizens Telephone Co./1968*; Buck, Dr. Benjamin. *Mankato State College Today*, Vol. 3, No. 2, 1972, p. 7; *National Sculpture Review*, Vol. 22, No. 3; Smith-Mason Gallery of Art. *Nat'l. Exhibition: Black Artists 1971*; Smithsonian Institution. *National Portrait Gallery*; Fisk Univ. *Carl Van Vechten Gallery of Fine Arts*, 1971; *Time*, April 9, 1951; Harley, Ralph, Jr. "A Checklist of Afro-Amer. Art & Artists," *The Serif*, Dec. 1970; DuSable Museum of African-Amer. History. *Contemporary Black Artists*, 1970, Calendar; Tanner Art Galleries. *Art of the American Negro*, 1940; Texas Centennial Exposition. *Thumbnail Sketches of Exhibiting Artists*, 1936; Howard Univ. *James A. Porter Gallery of African American Art*, 1970; Harmon Foundation. *Select Picture List*; *New York Times*, April 4, 1948; April 1, 1951; *Art Digest*, March 1, 1933, p. 18; "Negro Artists Reveal Genius in Trenton Show," *Art Digest*, April 15, 1935; Greene, Carroll, Jr. "Perspective: The Black Artist in America," *The Art Gallery*, April 1970, p. 19; Woodruff, Hale. "Negro Artists Hold Fourth Annual in Atlanta," *Art Digest*, April 15, 1945; Pierre-Noel, Lois Jones. "American Negro Art in Progress," *Negro History Bulletin*, Oct. 1967; "Atlanta's Annual," *Time*, April 9, 1945; *Art News*, April 15, 1945, pp. 8-9. "Negro Art Prizes," *Art News*, May 1, 1944. "The Negro Artist Comes of Age," *Art News*, Feb. 1, 1945; Xavier Univ. *Emancipation Proclamation Centennial National Art Exhibition*; Ploski, Harry, & Ernest Kaiser. "The Black Artist," *Afro USA*, 1971; Ploski, Harry, Ernest Kaiser, & Otto Lindenmeyer. "The Black Artist," *Reference Library of Black America*, Book 4, 1971; *The Negro Handbook*, Composed by Editors of *Ebony*, Chicago, 1966; "Exhibition of Work by Negro Artists," *Afro-American Presbyterian*, Feb. 23, 1933; Schatz, Walter. *Directory of Afro-American Resources*, 1970; Myers, Carol L. *Black Power in the Arts*, Flint, Mich., 1970; Walker, Roslyn. *A Resource Guide to the Visual Arts of Afro-Americans*, South Bend, Ind., 1971.

ATKINS, DOROTHY

Painter, sculptor, jeweler. Born in Brooklyn in 1936. Studied at University of California at Berkeley.
Works: Untitled metal design; Untitled fused silver ring; Untitled cast silver necklace with rare wood.
Exhibitions: Wurster Hall; Cal. State Exposition; Space Art Show; Scranton Museum; Oakland Museum, 1971.
Collections: Space Art Show.
Sources: Lewis/Waddy. *Black Artists on Art*, Vol. 2; Oakland Museum. *The Metal Experience*, 1971.

ATKINSON, JOHN I.

Painter.
Works: *After '29.*
Exhibited: Amer. Negro Exposition, Chicago, 1940.
Sources: Tanner Art Galleries. *Art of the American Negro*, 1940.

AUDUBON, JOHN JAMES

Painter, naturalist. Born in Les Cayes, Haiti, 1785; died 1851. Studied drawing under Louis David.
Works: *A Covey of Blackcock* (oil); *Canada Otter* (oil).
Exhibited: Centennial Exhibition, 1876.

Member: Honorary Member, Professional, National Academy, 1833.
Sources: Audubon, John J. *Birds of America*; Boning, Richard A. *Profiles of Black Americans*, NYC, 1968; Audubon, Maria R. *Audubon & His Journals*, Dover, 1960; Peattie, Donald C. *Audubon's America: The Narratives & Experiences of John J. Audubon*, Boston, Houghton-Mifflin, 1940; Ford, Alice. *Audubon's Animals: The Quadrupeds of North America*, NY, Studio Pub., 1951. Dock, George, Jr. *The Audubon Folio*, NY, H.N. Abrams, 1964; Ford, Alice. *Audubon, By Himself*, NY, National Historical Press, 1969; McDermott, John Francis. *Audubon in the West*, Univ. of Okla. Press, 1965; Teale, Edwin Way, ed. *Audubon's Wildlife*, NY, Viking Press, 1964; Herrick, Francis Hobart. *Audubon the Naturalist*, NY & London, D. Appleton, 1917; Ford, Alice. *Bird Biographies*, NY, MacMillan, 1957; Payne, Raphael Semmes. *The Baltimore Oriole & A Biographical Sketch of Audubon*, Norman, Remington Co., 1923; Hanaburgh, Emory F. *Audubon's Birds of America*, Buchanan, NY, Enterprise Press, 1941; Audubon, John J. *Delineations of American Scenery & Character*, NY, G.A. Baker, 1926, Edited by Francis Hobart Herrick; Anon. *The Story of Audubon, The Naturalist*, London, Nelson, 1895; Adams, Alexander B. *John H. Audubon: A Biography*, NY, Putnam, 1966; Audubon, John J., & John Bachman. *The Vivparous Quadrupeds of North America*, NY; Bradford, Mary Fluker. *Audubon*, L. Graham & Son, Ltd., 1897; John, Burroughs. *John J. Audubon*, Boston, Small, Maynard & Co., 4th edition; Fisher, George Clyde. *The Life of Audubon*, NY, Harper, 1949; Ford, Alice. *Audubon's Butterflies, Moths & Other Studies*, NY, Studio Pub., 1952; Godwin, Parke. *Commemorative Addresses*, NY, Harper, 1895; Harris, Edward. *Up the Missouri with Audubon*, Norman, Univ. of Okla. Press, 1951; Hogeboom, Amy. *Audubon and His Sons*, NY, Lothrop, Lee & Shepard, 1956; Kieran, Margaret & John. *John J. Audubon*, NY, Random House, 1954; Lauder, Sir Thomas Dick, & Capt. Thomas Brown. "Biological Sketch of Natural History," *The Miscellany of Natural History*, Vol. 1; Muschamp, Edward A. *Audacious Audubon, the Story of a Great Pioneer, Artist, Naturalist, & Man*, NY, Brentano's, 1929; Peare, Catherine O. *John J. Audubon, His Life*, NY, Holt, 1953; Peattie, Donald Culross. *Singing in the Wilderness: A Salute to John J. Audubon*, NY, Putnam, 1935; Rourke, Constance M. *Audubon*, NY, Harcourt, Brace, 1936; St. John, Mrs. Horace S. R. *Audubon, the Naturalist of the New World: His Adventures & Discoveries*, Boston, Crosby & Nichols, 1864; Towles, Susan

S. *John J. Audubon in Henderson, Kentucky: A Sketch*, John P. Morton, 1925; Townsend, Charles W. *In Audubon's Labrador*, Boston, Houghton-Mifflin, 1918; Benezit, E. *Dictionnaire Critique et Documentaire Des Peintres*, Paris, 1913; Champlin, J.D., & C.C. Perkins. *Cyclopedia of Painters & Paintings*, NY; *Dictionary of American Biography*, NY; *Encyclopedia Britannica*, 14th edition; Thieme, U., & F. Becker. *Allgemeines Lexikon Der Bildenden Kunstler Von Der Antike Bis Zur Gegenwart*, Leipzig, 1934; Tuckerman, H. T. *Book of the Artists*, NY, 1867; Clement, C.E., & L. Hutton. *Artists of the 19th Century*, 3rd edition, Boston, 1907; Bolton, T. *Early American Portrait Draughtsmen in Crayons*, NY, 1923; Audubon, John J. *Life of John James Audubon*, NY, 1869; Mallett. *Index of Artists*; Audubon, John J. *Ornithological Biography*, Phila., Carey & Hart, 1832-39; Graves, Algernon. *A Dictionary of Artists Who Have Exhibited Works in the Principal London Exhibitions of Oil Paintings from 1760-1880*, London, 1884; Cowdrey, Mary B. *National Academy of Design Exhibition Record*, 1926-60, NY, 1943; Alabama Dept. of Archives & History. *New York City Directory*, 1843-49; McDermott, John F. "Likeness by Audubon," *Antiques*, June 1955, pp. 499-501; Flexner, James T. *The Light of Distant Skies, 1760-1835*, NY, 1954; Groce, George C., & David H. Wallace. *NY Historical Society's Dictionary of Artists in America*; Fielding. *Dictionary of American Painters, Sculptors & Engravers*, NY, 1965; "Audubon's Story of His Youth," preface by Maria R. Audubon, *Scribner's Magazine*, 1893.

AUGUSTE, T.

Collections: NY Public Library, Schomburg Art Collection.
Sources: Schatz, Walter. *Directory of Afro-American Resources*, 1971.

AUSBY, ELLSWORTH

Painter, illustrator. Born in Portsmouth, Virginia in 1942. Studied at American Art School; School of Visual Arts, New York City; Pratt Institute, New York City.
Works: *Ancestral Spirit* (acrylic); *Regeneration of the Spirit* (acrylic); *Time; Reptiles; Imperialism; Inside the Pyramid; Today, Yesterday, & Tomorrow; Spirits Revisited #1; Spirits Revisited #2*, Untitled, 1970 (painted wood); *Passing Through; In the Valley of the Kings; Afternoon; Totem; Spirits Regenerated*.
Exhibited: School of Visual Arts, NYC, 1970; Pratt Institute, NYC, 1960; Adelphi Univ., Garden City, NY, 1967; Princeton Univ., 1967; Pan-American Building, NYC, 1968; Bowdoin Univ., Brunswick, Me., 1969; Loeb Center, NY

Univ., NYC, 1969; Boston Museum of Fine Arts, 1970; Cinque Gallery, NYC, 1970 (1-man); Brooklyn Museum, 1969; Whitney Museum, 1971; Columbia Univ., NYC, 1969; Nat'l Center of Afro-Amer. Artists, Boston, 1970; Elma Lewis Art School, Boston, 1970; Rice Univ.; Pa. Academy of the Fine Arts, 1972; Finch College; Countee Cullen Library; St. Marks Church; Stout State Univ.; Univ. of Florida; Saratoga Springs Performing Arts Center; Reading Museum.
Collections: Jean de Menil; Mr. Leon Banks; Mr. James Haskins; Ms. Verta Grosvenor; Mr. Charles Lewis; Cinque Gallery.
Sources: Boston Museum of Fine Arts. *Afro-American Artists: New York & Boston*, 1970; Brooklyn Museum. *New Black Artists*, 1969; NY State Education Dept. *Fifteen Under Forty*; Doty. *Contemporary Black Artists in America*; Rose, Barbara. "Black Art in America," *Art in America*, Vol. 58; Walsh, Rose. "Artists to Meet Public in Art Exhibit Preview," *Record American* (Boston), May 19, 1970; *Black Creation*, Vol. 3, No. 3; Information from artist; Ausby, Ellsworth. *Slavery*, Silvermine; Lewis/Waddy. *Black Artists on Art*; Walker, Roslyn. *A Resource Guide to the Visual Arts of Afro-Americans*, South Bend, Ind., 1971; Loercher, Diana. "Art: Idioms of Blackness at the Elma Lewis School," *Christian Science Monitor*, July 10, 1970; Grospiner, Verta. *Tuesdays & Every Other Sundays Off*, Doubleday (cover); "Afro-American Artists: NY & Boston," *Prudential Center News*, March 1, 1970, p. 4.

AUSTIN, DOROTHY ELEASE

Medical illustrator, muralist, printmaker. Born in Columbus, Ohio, in 1926. Studied at Pleasant Hill School of Cartooning; Columbus Art School; Ohio State University; Academie De La Grande Chaumière, Paris.
Sources: Nat'l Conference of Artists. *A Print Portfolio by Negro Artists*.

AUSTIN, JO
See: Fundi, Ibibio.

AVERY, HENRY

Painter, sculptor, muralist. Born in Margatan, North Carolina in 1906. Studied at South Side Settlement House, Chicago.
Works: *Still Life;* Murals, Center Masonic Temple, Chicago; Murals, Regal Theater, Chicago; Murals, Civic Center, Alton, Ill.; *Feather; Big Apples; Man Sketching; The Revival; Still Life with Grapes.*
Exhibited: 48th Annual Art Institute of Chicago Show; Chicago Artists' Group, 1937, 1938; American Painters & Sculptors Annual, Chicago, 1939; Evanston Public Library, 1939; Institute of Modern Art, Boston, 1943; Howard

Univ., 1941; Library of Congress, 1940; Amer. Negro Exposition, 1940; James A. Porter Gallery, 1970; South Side Community Art Center, Chicago, 1941, 1945; Easel Division, Ill. Federal Arts Project, 1937-9; Tanner Art Galleries, 1940.
Member: United American Artists; South Side Community Art Center, Chicago.
Sources: Mallett. *Index of Artists; Who's Who in American Art*, 1940-1; Dover. *American Negro Art*, p. 48; Locke. *The Negro in Art*; Indiana Univ. *Fine Arts & the Black American*; Howard Univ. *Exhibit of Negro Artists of Chicago at Howard University Gallery of Art*, 1941; Porter. *Modern Negro Art*; Library of Congress. *Catalog of Exhibitions of Oils, Watercolors, Prints & Drawings*, 1940; Motley, Willard F. "Negro Art in Chicago," *Opportunity*, Jan. 1940; Harley, Ralph, Jr. "A Checklist of Afro-Amer. Art & Artists," *The Serif*, Dec. 1970; DuSable Museum of African-Amer. History. *Contemporary Black Artists*, 1970; Tanner Art Galleries. *Art of the American Negro*, 1940; Howard Univ. *James A. Porter Gallery of African Amer. Art*, 1970; "American Negro Art Given Full Length Review in N.Y. Show," *Art Digest*, Dec. 15, 1941; Locke, Alain. "Chicago's New South Side Art Center," *American Magazine of Art*, Aug. 1941, p. 373; South Side Community Art Center. *National Negro Art Exhibition*, Chicago, 1941; South Side Community Art Center. *Opening Exhibition of Paintings by Negro Artists*, Chicago, 1940-41; Walker, Roslyn. *A Resource Guide to the Visual Arts of Afro-Americans*, South Bend, Ind., 1971.

AXT, CHARLES

Sculptor, painter. Born in New York City in 1935. Studied at Alfred University, New York (BFA).
Works: *Bird Form*, 1969; *Female Form*, 1969; untitled form (mahogany); untiled form, 1972 (elm); untitled form, 1972 (cedar); *Sparticus*, 1970.
Exhibited: Newark Museum, 1971; Trenton State Museum, 1972; Riise Gallery, St. Thomas, Virgin Islands; Black Expressions, West Orange, NJ.
Represented by: Mid-Block Art Service, East Orange, NJ.
Sources: Newark Museum. *Black Artists: Two Generations*, 1971; Trenton State Museum. *Black Artist*, 1972; Information from artist.

AYERS, ROLAND

Born in Philadelphia in 1932.
Works: *House of the Seven Sons; Elements Returning; Atlantis Rising; The Creation*.
Exhibited: Whitney Museum, 1971.
Sources: Doty. *Contemporary Black Artists in*

America; Craig, Randall J. "Focus on Black Artists: A Project for Schools and Community," *School Arts*, Nov. 1970, pp. 30-3.

BABB'C

Painter, sculptor. Studied painting privately. Self-taught sculptor.
Exhibited: Boston City Hall, 1973 (1-man).
Sources: Information from artist.

BACON, FREDERICK

Works: *Confrontation*.

BACOT, ANNABELLE G.

Painter, educator. Studied at Howard University (BA); George Washington; Catholic University; District of Columbia Teachers College. Teacher in District of Columbia Public Schools.
Works: *Candles*.
Exhibited: Margaret Dickey Gallery; Oxon Hill Library; Zion Baptist Church; District of Columbia Art Assn.; Anacostia Neighborhood Museum—Smithsonian Institution, 1971.
Sources: District of Columbia Art Ass'n. *Exhibition '71*.

BAILEY, CALVIN

Painter, caricaturist. Born in 1915. Studied at New Jersey Vocational School; Newark School of Fine & Applied Arts.
Works: *The Old Man; Solo Session; Portrait of Dianne at the Age of Nine*.
Exhibited: YMCA, Phila.; South Side Community Art Center, Chicago, 1945.
Sources: Harley, Ralph, Jr. "A Checklist of Afro-American Art & Artists," *The Serif*, Dec. 1970; South Side Community Art Center. *Chicago Collectors Exhibit of Negro Art*, Chicago, 1945; Atkinson, J. Edward. *Black Dimensions in Contemporary American Art*, NY, 1971; "Youthful Artist Winning Notice of the Art World with his Work," *Journal & Defender*, April 2, 1932; *Ebony*, Oct. 1953, pp. 81-4; Spradling, Mary, ed. *In Black & White: Afro-Americans in Print*.

BAILEY, GEORGE EDWARD

Painter. Born in Philadelphia.
Works: *Cigarettes; Ships*.
Exhibited: Harmon Foundation, 1933.
Awards: 1st prize for city & county in WCTU contest, 1929.
Sources: Harmon Foundation. *Negro Artists*, 1935; Harmon Foundation. *Exhibition of Productions by Negro Artists*; Indiana Univ. *Fine Arts & the Black American*; DuSable Museum of African-Amer. History. *Contemporary Black Artists*, 1970, Calendar; Harley, Ralph, Jr. "A Checklist of Afro-Amer. Art & Artists," *The Serif*, Dec. 1970; Walker, Roslyn. *A Resource Guide to the Visual Arts of Afro-Americans*, South Bend, Ind., 1971.

BAILEY, H. KOFI

Painter, printmaker. Studied at Howard University; Alabama State College; University of Southern California (MFA).
Works: *Queen; W.E.B. DuBois; Kwame Nkrumah; New Blacks; Untitled.*
Exhibited: National Center of Afro-American Artists, Boston; Spelman College, Atlanta.
Sources: Museum of the Nat'l Center of Afro-Amer. Artists. *Taking Care of Business,* 1971; Loercher, Diana. "National Center of Afro-Amer. Artists Art & Benefit Premier," *Christian Science Monitor,* May 4, 1971; "Home Fold: Africa," *Christian Science Monitor,* April 8, 1971; Harley, Ralph, Jr. "A Checklist of Afro-American Art & Artists," *The Serif,* Dec. 1970; Contemporary Crafts, Inc. *H. Kofi Bailey: Portfolio of Prints,* Los Angeles, 1972?; Driscoll, Edgar. "Art Show Reflects Black Rage, Pride," *Boston Globe,* April 28, 1971.

BAILEY, HERMAN

See: Bailey, H. Kofi.

BAILEY, JOSEPH C.

Sculptor, painter, educator. Studied at Philadelphia College of Art; Pennsylvania Academy of Fine Arts. Art instructor at Antioch-Putney Graduate Program, Antioch College. Artist-in-residence, Intensive Learning Center, Philadelphia.
Works: *Death Takes a Bride; Dream; Stillness; Bronze Head; Blue; Spring.*
Exhibited: State Armory, Wilmington, Del., 1971 (1-man); Arts & Crafts Center, Pittsburgh, 1955; Provident Nat'l Bank; Buena Vista Country Club, NJ; Art Alliance of Phila.; Pa. Academy of Fine Arts; Phila. College of Art; American Exhibiting Artists; Atlantic City Boardwalk Shows; Greene Gallery, Westchester, N.Y; Jersey City Museum Annual Nat'l Exhibits; Glassboro State College, NJ; Phila. Civic Center, 1969; Textile Institute of Phila. (3-man); Delaware State Museum; 252 Gallery, Phila.
Collections: Theatre of the Living Arts; Yale Univ.; Dr. Anthony Shelfo & Assoc., Brooklyn; Wagner Jr. High School; Webster Elem. School, Phila.; Lee Cultural Center; Cassway & McGee; New Bryant School; Del. Valley Hospital Laundry Assn.; Sherwood Center, Dept. of Recreation; Amer. Negro Commemorative Society; Bright Hope Baptist Church.
Awards: 1st prize, drawing, Packard Award, Academy of Fine Arts, 1959; 2nd prize, painting, Greene Gallery, NY, 1961; 3rd prize, painting, Atlantic City, NJ, 1961; Sculpture Prize, Jersey City Museum, 1961; Finalist, Tiffany Foundation, Nat'l Fellowship competition, 1967-8.
Sources: Aesthetic Dynamics. *Afro-American*

Images, 1971; Phila. Division of Art. *Afro-American Artists 1800-1969.*

BAILEY, MALCOLM

Painter, educator. Born in New York in 1947. Studied at the High School of Art and Design (1965); Pratt Institute (BFA, 1969). Teacher at Cooper Union.
Works: *How to Beat a Pig; Hold (Separate but Equal); Untitled,* 1969 (acrylic/masonite).
Exhibited: Cinque Gallery (1-man); Brooklyn College, 1969; Whitney Museum Annual, 1969; Boston Museum of Fine Arts, 1970.
Awards: Yaddo Scholarship, 1969-70; Pratt Institute Scholarship.
Sources: Boston Museum of Fine Arts. *Afro-American Artists: NY & Boston,* 1970; *Time,* Apr. 6, 1970, pp. 80-6; Brooklyn College. *Afro American Artists: Since 1950,* 1969; "Black Art: What Is It?," *Art Gallery,* April 1970; NY State Education Dept. *Fifteen Under Forty;* Harley, Ralph, Jr. "A Checklist of Afro-Amer. Art & Artists," *The Serif,* Dec. 1970; Rose, Barbara. "Black Art in America," *Art in America,* July-Dec. 1970; Walker, Roslyn. *A Resource Guide to the Visual Arts of Afro-Americans,* South Bend, Ind., 1971; Fine, Elsa H. "Mainstream, Blackstream and the Black Art Movement," *Art Journal,* Spring 1971; Cinque Gallery. *Malcolm Bailey: Paintings & Drawings Untitled,* NYC, Dec. 22, 1966-Jan. 17, 1967.

BAILEY, RUBY HYACINTH

Graphic artist, fashion illustrator. Born in Bermuda in 1908. Studied at National Academy of Design.
Works: *Doris; Still Life.*
Exhibited: Harmon Foundation, 1933; Art Students Club, 1928; YWCA, 1928; Gumby's Book Studio, 1929; Boykins School of Art, 1932.
Sources: Harmon Foundation. *Non Jury Exhibit of Works of Negro Artists,* 1933.

BAIRD, FRANCIS B.

Painter.
Exhibited: Smith-Mason Gallery of Art, 1971.
Sources: Smith-Mason Gallery. *National Exhibition of Black Artists,* 1971.

BAIYERMAN, EUGENIE

Collections: NY Public Library-Schomburg Art Collection.
Sources: Schatz, Walter. *Directory of Afro-American Resources,* 1970.

BAKER, ANNABELLE

Works: *Laundry Woman.*
Exhibited: Atlanta Univ., 1944; Museum of Modern Art, 1943.
Sources: *Design 46,* Sept. 1944; Atlanta Univ.

Catalog, 1944; Harley, Ralph, Jr. "A Checklist of Afro-Amer. Art & Artists," *The Serif,* Dec. 1970; "Young Negro Art Impresses New York," *Art Digest,* Oct. 15 1943; Lowenfeld, Viktor. "New Negro Art in America," *Design,* Vol. 46.

BALDRIDGE, CYRUS LEROY

Painter. Born in 1889.
Collections: Fisk Univ. Library.
Sources: Schatz, Walter. *Directory of Afro-American Resources,* 1970.

BALLARD, E. LORETTA

Educator, painter. Studied at Indiana State University (BS); Howard University; District of Columbia Teachers College. Teacher at District of Columbia elementary schools; District of Columbia Adult Education Demonstration Center.
Works: *The Strike; Black; Trapped.*
Exhibited: State Armory, Wilmington, Del., 1971; Negro Artist Show, Chicago; DC Teachers College; Phyllis Wheatley YWCA; Margaret Dickey Gallery; Anacostia Neighborhood Museum; Import Gallery.
Sources: Aesthetic Dynamics. *Afro-American Images,* 1971; DC Art Assn. *Exhibition '71.*

BALLENTINE, JENE

Painter. Born in Memphis, Tennessee in 1942. Studied at University of California, Los Angeles (BA, 1964).
Works: *Had I Been Bold or Slightly Brave; Born Free.*
Sources: Lewis/Waddy. *Black Artists on Art,* Vol. 1; Walker, Roslyn. *A Resource Guide to the Visual Arts of Afro-Americans,* South Bend, Ind., 1971.

BANJO, CASPER

Sculptor, educator. Born in Memphis, Tennessee. Studied at University of California at Berkeley.
Exhibited: Raymond Howell Art Gallery, San Francisco; Black Odyssey Festival, Berkeley.
Sources: Lewis/Waddy. *Black Artists on Art,* Vol. 2.

BANKS, BILL

Painter.
Works: *Birthplace of the Stars.*
Exhibited: Smith-Mason Gallery, 1971.
Sources: Smith-Mason Gallery. *National Exhibition of Black Artists,* 1971.

BANKS, ELLEN

Painter. Born in Boston. Studied at Massachusetts College of Art (BA); School of the Museum of Fine Arts, Boston.
Works: *Black & White Plus #194,* 1970 (acrylics); *Black & White Plus #180,* 1970 (acrylics); *City Shape; Claudia.*

Exhibited: Dunbarton Galleries, Boston, 1962 (1-man); Boston Museum of Fine Arts, 1970; Smith-Mason Gallery, 1971 (1-man); Nat'l Center of Afro-Amer. Artists, Boston.
Awards: Prix de Paris, 1967.
Sources: Smith-Mason Gallery. *National Exhibition Black Artists,* 1971; Boston Museum of Fine Arts. *Afro-American Artists: NY & Boston,* 1970; *Newsweek,* June 22, 1970; Driscoll, Edgar. "Abstract is Beautiful, Too," *Boston Globe,* Jan. 11, 1972, p. 21; Goodman, Ellen, "What Black Artists Are Doing and Why," *Boston Globe,* June 18, 1970, p. 28; Giuliano, Charles. "Ellen Banks' Works Shown," *Boston Herald Traveler,* Jan. 27, 1972; Setlik, Robert. "Cultural Cross Currents 19th Century Style," *Patriot Ledger,* Jan. 20, 1972; Grillo, Jean B. "Black Artists: Three Views," *Phoenix,* Boston, n.d.

BANKS, JANETTE E.

Painter, educator, graphic artist, mixed media. Born in Philadelphia in 1934. Studied at Murrell Dobbins Technical School (BFA); Philadelphia College of Art; Tyler School of Art (MFA); Temple University.
Works: *Blacker Shade of Black; Gathered in His Name; His Grace; Higher Ground; An Etude in Knots,* 1970; *Behold All Flesh Is As the Grass,* 1965; *Fruit of the Earth,* 1966; *Linear Confrontation,* 1971; *Prelude in Green; Out-Group Barriers,* 1965; *No Way,* 1972; *Collective Bargaining,* 1972; *Considered Collectively,* 1971; *My Way,* 1971; *Be,* 1970; *We Are,* 1970; *Apathy,* 1967; *Committed to Non-Commitment,* 1966; *Cecil's People,* 1965; *Black Backlash,* 1965; *Let It Be,* 1970; *By and By,* 1968; *Peace Be Still,* 1964; *Be Still and Know,* 1970 (mixed media); *I Am,* 1970 (mixed media); *Restrain,* 1970 (pen & ink).
Exhibited: Univ. City Arts League, Phila., 1972 (1-man); Glassboro State College, NJ, 1972; West Chester State College, Pa., 1971 (1-man); Free Library of Phila., 1966 (1-man); Tyler School of Art, Temple Univ., 1964 (1-man); Phila. Art Teachers' Assn., 1960-72; Phila. Art Alliance, 1970-2; Museum of the Phila. Civic Center, 1969, 1971; Moore College of Art, 1966-8, 1970; Moravian College, Bethlehem, Pa.; William Penn Memorial Museum; Nat'l Guard Armory, Wilmington, Del., 1971; Temple Univ., 1965, 1970; Bucks County Links, New Hope, Pa.; Belmont YWCA; Lee Cultural Center, Phila., 1967; Designer's Gallery, 1966; Woodmere Art Gallery, 1970; Cheltenham Township Art Center, 1964; Women's Univ. Club; Barnegat Light Gallery.
Collections: Cheyney State College.
Awards: 1st Prize, painting, Jeanette W. Rosenbaum Exhibition; 1st Prize, drawing,

Jeanette W. Rosenbaum Exhibition; 1st Prize, drawing, 50th Anniversary Regional Craft & Watercolor Show, Phila. Art Alliance; 1st Award, painting, Phila. Art Teachers' Assn. Annual Exhibition; Dobbins Graduate Award, 1968.

Member: Phila. Art Alliance; Artists Equity Assn., Inc.; Woodmere Art Gallery; Phila. Art Teachers' Assn.; National Art Teachers' Assn.; American Assn. of Univ. Professors; American Assn. of Univ. Women; Phila. Art Education Assn.

Sources: Phila. Division of Art Education. *Afro-American Artists 1800-1969*; Aesthetic Dynamics. *Afro-American Images 1971*; Wasserman, Burt. "The Banks of the Tigers, You Fraidies," *Camden Courier Post,* Feb. 12, 1972; Univ. City Arts League. "News Release," Oct. 29, 1972; Phila. Art Alliance. *Hangings,* 1972, Unpublished list; Phila. Art Alliance. *Black and White,* 1971, Unpublished list; Lee Cultural Center. *American Exhibiting Artists,* 1967, Unpublished list; Woodmere Art Gallery. *Best of the Year,* 1970, Unpublished list; Cheltenham Township Art Centre. *Eighth Annual New Talent Show,* 1964, Unpublished list; Information from artist.

BANNARN, HENRY W.

Painter, sculptor, educator. Born in Wetunka, Oklahoma on July 17, 1910. Studied at Minnesota School of Art; Beaux Arts, New York City; Art Students League, New York City. Studied under B.J.C. Nordfelt; George Oberteuffer; S. Chatwood Burton; Carl Mose; Ahron Ben-Schumel. Teacher at Alston-Bannarn Workshop, 1934-5; Harlem Community Center; Federal Arts Projects, 1937-9.

Works: *Frederick Douglass; Daywork; City; Portrait; John Brown; Fantasy; Swampwater; Colt; Booby; The Crossing; The Showers; Winter Sports; The Head of Amy Fong.*

Exhibited: Minnesota State Fair, 1928; Carnegie Institute, 1929; YMCA, NYC; Harmon Foundation, 1933; Baltimore Museum, 1939; Amer. Negro Exhibition, 1940; Minn. State Artists Annual, 1940; Atlanta Univ., 1943-4; Hanley Gallery, St. Paul, Minn. (1-man); Arthur U. Newton Gallery; Western Art Assn.; Pa. Academy.

Collections: Nat'l Archives.

Awards: Purchase Award, Atlanta Univ., 1943; 2nd prize, Minn. State Fair, 1928; 1st prize, Minn. State Artists Annual, 1940; 1st prize, Minneapolis Institute of Arts, 1932.

Member: American Artists Congress; Artists Union; Harlem Art Guild.

Sources: Mallett. *Index of Artists*; Locke. *The Negro in Art*; Dover. *American Negro Art*; Albany Institute of History & Art. *The*

Negro Artist Comes of Age; Baltimore Museum of Art, records; Harmon Foundation. *Exhibition of Productions by Negro Artists*; Harmon Foundation. *Non-Jury Exhibit of Works of Negro Artists,* 1933; Harmon Foundation. *Negro Artists,* 1935; Porter. *Modern Negro Art*; Harley, Ralph L., Jr. "A Checklist of Afro-Amer. Art & Artists," *The Serif,* Dec. 1970; Baltimore Museum of Art. *Contemporary Negro,* 1939; Locke, Alain. "Advance on the Art Front," *Opportunity,* May 1939; Brawley, Benjamin. *The Negro Genius*; Afro-American Slide Depository, Catalog; *Who's Who in American Art,* 1940-1; DuSable Museum of African-Amer. History. *Contemporary Black Artists,* 1970 Calendar; "Negro Annual," *Art Digest,* April 15, 1943; Woodruff, Hale. "Negro Artists Host Fourth Annual in Atlanta," *Art Digest,* April 15, 1945; Pierre-Noel, Lois Jones. "American Negro Art in Progress," *Negro History Bulletin,* Oct. 1967; "Negro Annual," *Art News,* April 15, 1943; *Art News,* April 15, 1945, pp. 8-9; "The Negro Artist Comes of Age," *Art News,* Feb. 1, 1945; Xavier Univ. *Emancipation Proclamation Centennial National Art Exhibition,* 1963; Ploski, Harry, & Ernest Kaiser. "The Black Artist," *Afro USA,* 1971; Ploski, Harry, & Ernest Kaiser, & Otto Lindenmeyer. "The Black Artist," *Reference Library of Black America,* Book 4, 1971; Myers, Carol L. *Black Power in the Arts,* Flint, Mich., 1970; Walker, Roslyn. *A Resource Guide to the Visual Arts of Afro-Americans,* South Bend, Ind., 1971.

BANNISTER, EDWARD MITCHELL

Painter. Born in St. Andrews, New Brunswick in 1828. Died in 1901 in Providence, Rhode Island. Studied at Lowell Institute. Studied under Dr. Rimmir.

Works: *Under the Oaks; Sabin Point, Narragansett Bay; After the Storm; Sad Memories; Flower Study; Approaching Storm; Pleasant Pastures; Swale Land; Morning on the Shore; Sunset; Driving Home the Cows; Landscape; Sheep; Water Scene; The Old Ferry; Landscape with Sailboat; Autumn Landscape; Landscape with Trees; After the Shower; Lady with Bouquet; Portrait Sketch of Judith; Street Scene; Sunset; Two Men & Oxen; Hillside Pasture; Landscape; Pleasant Pastures; Repose; Sunrise; Morning of the Shore; Palmer River; Mill in Knightsville; At Pawtucket; Fort off Jamestown; Still Life.*

Exhibited: Boston Art Club; Providence Art Club; Centennial Exhibition, Phila., 1876; Atlanta Univ.; Rhode Island School of Design; Howard Univ.; Nat'l Center of Afro-Amer. Artists, Boston, 1972; Museum of Fine Arts, Boston; Barbizon School, Providence.

Collections: Frederick Douglass Inst. of Negro Arts & History, Washington, DC; Rhode Island School of Design Museum of Art; NY Public Library, Schomburg Art Collection.

Awards: Gold Medal, Centennial Exhibition, Phila., 1876.

Member: Providence Art Club (Founding Member).

Sources: Mallett. *Index of Artists*; Clement/ Hutton. *Artists of the 19th Century*; Fielding. *Dictionary of American Artists*; Appleton. *Cyclopedia of American Biography*; Dover. *American Negro Art*; *Art Annual*, Vol. IV (obit.); *Providence Journal*, Jan. 11, 1901 (obit.); *Negro Almanac*; *American Negro Reference Book*; *Art in America*, Jan. 1936, pp. 16-27; Indiana Univ. *Fine Arts & the Black American*; Rhode Island School of Design Museum of Art. *Edward Mitchell Bannister, 1828-1901*, 1966; City College of NY. *The Evolution of Afro-American Artists: 1800-1950*; Wellington, Muriel B. "Edward M. Bannister," *The Negro History Bulletin*, Oct. 1941; Phila. Division of Art Education. *Afro-American Artists 1800-1969*; Chicago Art Institute. *The Negro in Art Week*; Brown, John S. "Edward Mitchell Bannister," *Crisis*, Nov. 1933; Porter. *Modern Negro Art*; Harley, Ralph, Jr. "A Checklist of Afro-Amer. Art & Artists," *The Serif*, Dec. 1970; Brown, W. Alden. *Edward Mitchell Bannister*, Providence, RI, 1950; Benezit. *Dictionnaire Des Peintres, Sculpteurs, Dessinateurs et Gravenurs*, Librairie Grund, France, 1948, Vol. 1, p. 379; Thieme-Becker. *Allgemeines Lexikon Der Blindenden Künstler*; NY Historical Society. *Dictionary of Artists in America 1564-1860*; Boston Directories, 1858-60; Young, William. *Dictionary of American Artists, Sculptors & Engravers*; Simmons, W.J. *Men of Mark, Eminent, Progressive, & Rising*; Herring, James V. "The American Negro Craftsman," *Crisis*, April 1942; Howard Univ. *Ten Afro-American Artists of the 19th Century*; Arnold, John N. *Art & Artists of Rhode Island 1905*, p. 37-9; Howard Univ. *Art of the American Negro*, 1937; Brawley, Benjamin. *The Negro Genius*; Butcher, Margaret. *The Negro in American Culture*, p. 125; Roucek & Kiernan. *The Negro Impact on Western Civilization*; Rogers. *Africa's Gift to America: The Afro-American in the Making & Saving of the United States*; "American Negro Review in New York Show," *Art Digest*, Dec. 15, 1941; Greene, Carroll, Jr. "Perspective: The Black Artist in America," *The Art Gallery*, April 1970, p. 3; Pierre-Noel, Lois Jones. "American Negro Art in Progress," *The Negro History Bulletin*, Oct. 1967; *Apollo*, Feb. 1968, p. 141; Locke, Alain. "The American Negro as Artist," *American Magazine of Art*, Sept. 1931, Vol. 23; Craig, Randall J. "Focus on Black Artists: A Project For Schools & Community," *School Arts*, Nov. 1970, pp. 30-3; Kiah, Virginia. "Black Artist," *Savannah Magazine*, April 1972, p. 14; Greene, Carroll, Jr. "Afro-Amer. Artists: Yesterday & Now," *The Humble Way*, 1968, Vol. 8, No. 3; Greene, Carroll, Jr. *Afro-American Artists: 1800-1968*, 1968, slides; Boning, Richard A. *Profiles of Black Americans*, NYC, 1968; Brawley, Benjamin. *The Negro in Literature & Art in the United States*; Nat'l Center of Afro-Amer. Artists. *19th Century Afro-Amer. Artists: Duncanson & Bannister*, Jan. 13, 1972; Driscoll, Edgar. "Blacks Duncanson & Bannister Honored in Fine Arts Exhibit," *Boston Globe*, Jan. 16, 1972; Setlick, Robert. "Cultural Cross Currents 19th Century Style," *Patriot Ledger*, Jan. 20, 1972; "Afro-American Paintings at Boston Museum," *Fence Viewer*, Jan. 20, 1972; "Afro-Art," *Jewish Advocate*, Jan. 20, 1972; "Paintings of Afro-Amer. Artists Now at Museum," *Chronicle*, Needham, Mass., Jan. 27, 1972; Brown, Marion. "The Negro in Fine Arts," *The Negro Heritage Library*, Vol. 2; Museum of Art, Rhode Island School of Design. *Edward Mitchell Bannister, 1828-1901*, Providence, 1966; "Negro Has Given Much to Art, Survey Shows," *Boston Traveler*, Feb. 23, 1933; Adams, Russell. *Great Negroes Past & Present*, Chicago, 1969; DuSable Museum of African-Amer. History. *Contemporary Black Artists*, 1970, Calendar; Boston Museum of Fine Arts. *Afro-Amer. Artists: NY/Boston*; Myers, Carol L. *Black Power in the Arts*, Flint, Mich., 1970; Holbrook, Francis C. "A Group of Negro Artists," *Opportunity*, July 1923, pp. 211-3; Walker, Roslyn. *A Resource Guide to the Visual Arts of Afro-Americans*, South Bend, Ind., 1971; Robinson, Wilhelmina S. *Historical Negro Biographies*, p. 47; Spradling, Mary M., ed. *In Black & White; Afro-Americans in Print*; Patterson, Lindsay. *The Negro in Music & Art*, NYC, 1969; Danikian, Caron Le Brun. "Duncanson & Bannister," *Sunday Herald Traveler*, Jan. 23, 1972; *American Art Annual*, Vol. IV, 1903-4, p. 136; Locke, Alain. *Negro Art: Past and Present*, Washington, DC, Assoc. in Negro Folk Education, 1936; Locke, Alain. *The Negro in Art*.

BARBOUR, JOHN E.

Sources: Walker, Roslyn. *A Resource Guide to the Visual Arts of Afro-Americans*, South Bend, Ind., 1971; DuSable Museum of African-Amer. History. *Contemporary Black Artists*, 1970.

BARBOZA, ANTHONY

Photographer.

Exhibited: Addison Gallery, 1971.

Sources: James Van DerZee Institute. *The Black Photographer (1908-1970): A Survey*.

BARNES, ERNIE E., JR.
Painter. Born in Durham, North Carolina. Studied at North Carolina Central University.
Works: *Three Hustlers*, 1970; *Jake*, 1969; *Rock of Ages*, 1970; *High Aspirations*, 1971; *The Runner*, 1965; *Charlton Heston*, 1968; *O.J.*, 1969; *Pool Hall*, 1970; *The Fullback*, 1965; *Uppity*, 1971; *Practice Wall*, 1969; *Fourth & One*, 1969; *The Loose Ball*, 1966; *The Bench*, 1960; *The Plan*, 1971; *The Pulling Guards; The Hand-off; Two Linemen; The Bomb; To Know Defeat; From Here on Up*, 1970; *Closed Set*, 1970.
Exhibited: North Carolina Central Univ., Durham, 1960; Private Sponsorship, San Diego, 1963 (1-man); Denver Country Club, 1965 (1-man); Incurable Collectors Gallery, NYC, 1966 (1-man); Grand Central Art Gallery, NYC, 1966; McKenzie Gallery, Los Angeles, 1968 (1-man); 1969; Agra Gallery, Washington, DC, 1971 (1-man); Elizabeth City State Univ., NC, 1971 (1-man); Heritage Gallery, Los Angeles, 1972 (1-man).
Collections: Mr. & Mrs. Barron Hilton, Beverly Hills; Mr. & Mrs. Michael Wayne, Toluca Lake, Cal.; Mr. & Mrs. David Werblin, NYC; Mr. & Mrs. Herb Klein, Washington, DC; Mr. & Mrs. Mike Franovich, Beverly Hills; Mr. & Mrs. Sheldon Leonard, Beverly Hills; Mr. & Mrs. Charlton Heston, Beverly Hills; Mr. Jack Palance, Malibu; Mr. & Mrs. Danny Arnold, Beverly Hills; Mr. & Mrs. Ron Mix, San Diego; Mr. & Mrs. Howard Cosell, NYC; Mrs. Maria Cole, Los Angeles; Mr. & Mrs. Jack Murphy, San Diego; Mr. & Mrs. Joe O'Donnell, Buffalo, NY; Mr. & Mrs. Don Freeman, San Diego; Mr. & Mrs. Ernie Wright, San Diego; Mr. Barry Lowen, Los Angeles; Mr. William Nauls, Los Angeles; Mr. & Mrs. H.M. Michaux, Jr., Durham, NC; Mr. & Mrs. William Asher, Beverly Hills; Mr. & Mrs. John Mabee, San Diego; Mr. & Mrs. Elbert Keimbrough, San Diego; Mr. & Mrs. William Berger, Denver; Mr. Willie Mays, San Francisco; Mr. Carlton C. Gilcrist, Los Angeles; Mr. & Mrs. James Campbell, Wilkinsbury, Pa.; Mr. Norman Schide, Albuquerque, NMex.; Mr. & Mrs. Robert Swanhauser, San Diego; Mr. & Mrs. Ross Bowman, Beverly Hills; Mr. & Mrs. Dominic Frontiere, Beverly Hills; Mr. & Mrs. Paul Maguire, Buffalo, NY; Mr. & Mrs. Tom Harmon, Beverly Hills; Mr. & Mrs. Lionel Taylor, Las Vegas; Mr. & Mrs. Sam Jones, Washington, DC; Mr. Merrill Jacobsen, Los Angeles; Mr. & Mrs. Sherwin Samuels, Los Angeles; Mr. & Mrs. Joey Bishop, Beverly Hills; Mr. & Mrs. Ed Hookstraten, Beverly Hills; Mr. & Mrs. William Sullivan, Boston; Mr. & Mrs. Wayne Valley, Oakland, Cal.; Mr. & Mrs. Bernard Whitkin, Denver; Mr. & Mrs. Jerry Seifert, Denver; Mr. Ronald Rosen, Beverly Hills; Mr. Irving Zeiger, Beverly Hills; Mr. & Mrs. Jason Shrinsky, Washington, DC; Mr. Larry Shriver, Los Angeles; Mr. & Mrs. M.I. Golden, Beverly Hills; Mr. Tom Gries, Beverly Hills; Mrs. K. Mirman, NYC; Mr. & Mrs. Walter Seltzer, Sherman Oaks, Cal.; Mr. & Mrs. G.D. Spratlin, Beverly Hills; Mr. & Mrs. Ralph Andrews, Lake Arrowhead, Cal.; Miss Diana Muldaur, Los Angeles; Mr. & Mrs. Saul Turtletaub, Beverly Hills; Mr. & Mrs. Myron Slobodien, Tarzana, Cal.; Mr. & Mrs. Sam Denoff, Beverly Hills; Mr. Jack Haley, Jr., Beverly Hills; Mrs. Adela Rogers St. Johns, Beverly Hills; Mr. & Mrs. Charlie Jones, La Jolla, Cal.; Mr. & Mrs. W.B. Smedley, Oakland, Cal.; Mr. & Mrs. Gordon Ritz, Minneapolis; Mr. Steave Blauner, Westwood, Cal.; Mr. Sidney Poitier, Beverly Hills; Mrs. W.D. McElliot; Univ. of Cal. at La Jolla; Heritage Hall, Univ. of So. Cal.
Sources: Heritage Gallery. *Ernie Barnes: A 20th Century Genre Painter.*

BARNETT, EDWARD
Photographer. Born in 1933.
Sources: Dunbar, Ernest, ed. *Black Expatriates*, pp. 148-65. Spradling, Mary M., ed. *In Black & White: Afro-Americans in Print.*

BARNETT, RITA WOLPÉ
Painter.
Exhibited: Phila. Invitational Exhibition, Pyramid Club, 1952.
Sources: Drummond, Dorothy. "Coast-to-Coast," *Art Digest*, Mar. 1, 1952, p. 12.

BARTHÉ, RICHMOND
Sculptor, painter. Born in Bay St. Louis, Missouri in 1901. Studied at Art Institute of Chicago; Art Students League, New York City, 1931. Studied under Charles Schroeder; Albin Polasek.
Works: *Toussaint L'Ouverture; Henry Ossawa Tanner; Booker T. Washington; Paul Lawrence Dunbar; The Devil Crab Man; The Blackberry Woman; The Harmonica Player; The African Dancer; Portrait of Dr. J.E.K. Aggrey; John Gielgud; Green Pastures bas-reliefs; Fallen Aviator; Head; The Grocer Boy* (plaster); *George Washington Carver; Langston Hughes; Exodus; The Negro Looks Ahead; Dance; General Dessalines; Wetta; Mary; Shoeshine Boy; Ferran Benga; Ram Gopal; Lawrence Olivier; Singing Slave; Maurice Evans; Stevedore; West Indian Girl; Black Narcissus; Shilluk Warrior; The Mother; Bust of Rev. Austin; Comedian; Mary From a Family Portrait; Head of a Boy; Arthur Brisbane; Kenneth McPherson; Lot's Wife; Gypsy Rose Lee; Sermon On The Mount; Angry Christ; African Boy Dancing; The Seated Figure; Frank Durdy; Bernadette; Bust of Rose McClendon; Ram Gopal (Dance of Siva); Dawn Radin; Edgar Kaufman, Jr.; Dr. Weir; Julius;*

Dr. G.W. Carver; Katherine Cornell; The Boxer; John The Baptist; Jimmy; Harald Kreutzberg Dancer; Abraham Lincoln; The Acrobat; Feral Benza; Blanche; Barthe With His Figure of Christ; Cyrina; Kalambwan; Jimmie; Jesus Christ; Supplication; Rug Cutters; James Mitchell; Fania Marionoff As Ariel; Male Figure; Tortured Negro; West Indian Girl; African Man; African Woman; Torso; Mask of a Faun; Mask of a Boy; Prayer; Mother & Son; Sarah; Head of a Young Man; Male Torso; Detail of Dance; Christina; Singing Slave; The Breakaway; Fawn; Boxer; Head of Alain Locke.

Exhibited: Texas Centennial Exposition, 1936; James A. Porter Gallery, 1970; Women's City Club, Chicago, 1927; Harmon Foundation, 1929, 1931, 1933; Whitney Museum, 1933, 1935, 1939; Century of Progress Show, 1933-4; Howard Univ., 1934; Pa. Academy of Fine Arts, 1938, 1939; Worlds Fair, NYC, 1939; Pa. Museum Sculpture Show, 1940; Grand Central Gallery, NYC, 1947; Margaret Brown Gallery, Boston, 1947; Newark Museum, 1971; City College of NY; Baltimore Museum, 1939; Amer. Negro Expo; Caz-Delbos Gallery, NYC, 1933 (1-man); Delphic Studios, NYC, 1925 (1-man); Salons of America, NYC, 1934 (1-man); Arden Gallery, NYC, 1938 (1-man); NJ State Museum, 1935 (1-man); Rankin Gallery, Washington (1-man); Univ. of Wisconsin (1-man); Harmon College Traveling Exhibit.

Collections: Univ. of Wisconsin; Oberlin College; Pa. Academy of Fine Arts; Virginia Museum; Metropolitan Museum of Art, NYC; NY Public Library, Schomburg Collection; Atlanta Univ.; Countee Cullen Collection; Lake Country Children's Home, Gary, Ind.; Armstrong High School, Richmond, Va.; Whitney Museum of American Art; Anson Phelps Stokes Foundation; New Theater, London; Harlem River Houses, US Treasury Project.

Awards: Eames McVeagh Prize, 1928; Rosenwald Fellowship, 1928-9; Guggenheim Fellowship, 1940-1; Honorary MA from Xavier Univ., New Orleans, 1934; Edward B. Alford Award.

Member: Chicago Art League; Sculpture Guild.

Sources: Dover. *American Negro Art*, pp. 31, 35, 40, 54, 142; *Negro Almanac; American Art Annual*, 1940-1; Albany Institute of History & Art. *The Negro Artist Comes of Age;* Indiana Univ. *Fine Arts & the Black American;* Harmon Foundation. *Exhibition of Productions by Negro Artists;* Harmon Foundation. *Sculpture*, Portfolio; Harmon Foundation. *Negro Artists*, 1935; Harmon Foundation. *Select Picture List;* "Afro-American Issue," *Art Gallery*, April 1968; Newark Museum. *Black Artists: Two Generations;* City College of New York. *Evolution of Afro-American Artists 1800-1950;* Porter. *Modern Negro Art;* Har-

ley, Ralph L., Jr. "A Checklist of Afro-Amer. Art & Artists," *The Serif*, Dec. 1970; Moore, William H.A. "Richmond Barthé-Sculpture," *Opportunity VI*, Nov. 1928, p. 334; "Negro's Exhibit of Works in Arts Stirs Interest," *Chicago News*, June 17, 1930; "John Gielgud as Hamlet: A Bust by Barthé," *Theatre Arts*, XXI, May 1936-7; *Pictures on Exhibit*, March 1939, pp. 21-2; "Richmond Barthé," *Tarrytown News*, March 1940; Howard Univ. *James A. Porter Gallery of African American Art*, 1970; *New York Times*, April 4, 1948; Woodson, Carter G., & Charles H. Wesley. *The Story of the Negro Retold*, p. 403; Furr, Arthur. *History & Progress of Negroes in US;* "Negro Artists Reveal Genius in Trenton Show," *Art Digest*, April 15, 1935; "Harmon Foundation Spreads Public Appreciation of Negro Art," *Art Digest*, June 1, 1935; "Story of Barthé," *Art Digest*, March 1, 1939; Greene, Carroll, Jr. "Perspective: The Black Artist in America," *The Art Gallery*, April 1970, p. 19; "American Negro Art Given Full Length Review in NY Show," *Art Digest*, Dec. 15, 1941; "Fort Huachuca, Arizona Art Show," *Art Digest*, Aug. 1, 1943; "The Negro in Art," *Art Digest*, June 1, 1944; "Negro Art Scores Without Double Standards," *Art Digest*, Feb. 1, 1945; Woodruff, Hale. "Negro Artists Hold Fourth Annual in Atlanta," *Art Digest*, April 15, 1945; *Art Digest*, April 15, 1946, p. 3; Pierre-Noel, Lois Jones. "American Negro Art in Progress," *Negro History Bulletin*, Oct. 1967; Locke, Alain. "The American Negro as Artist," *American Magazine of Art*, Vol. 23; Locke, Alain. "Chicago's New South Side Art Center," *American Magazine of Art*, Aug. 1941; *Art News*, April 15, 1945; "Negro Art Show," *Art News*, July 1, 1944; Craig, Randall. "Focus on Black Artists: A Project for Schools & Community," *School Arts*, Nov. 1970, pp. 30-3; Kiah, Virginia. "Black Artists," *Savannah Magazine*, April 1972, p. 14; Greene, Carroll, Jr. "Afro-American Artists," *The Humble Way*, Vol. 8, No. 3; Xavier Univ. *Emancipation Proclamation Centennial National Art Exhibition*, 1963; Greene, Carroll, Jr. *Afro-American Artists: 1800-1968*, slides; Boning, Richard A. *Profiles of Black Americans;* Brown, Evelyn S. "The Harmon Awards," *Opportunity*, March 1933; Huggins, Nathan Irvin. *Harlem Renaissance;* Brown, Marion. "The Negro in Fine Arts," *The Negro Heritage Library*, Vol. 2; Morsbach, Mabel. *The Negro in American Life;* Winslow, Vernon. "Negro Art & the Depression," *The Negro in Music & Art*, 1969; Ploski, Harry, & Ernest Kaiser. "The Black Artist," *Afro USA*, 1970; Schatz, Walter. *Directory of Afro-American Resources*, 1970; Adams, Russell. *Great Negroes Past & Present*, Chicago, 1970; South Side Community Art

Center. *National Negro Art Exhibition*, Chicago, 1941; Myers, Carol L. *Black Power in the Arts*, Flint, Mich., 1970; Walker, Roslyn. *A Resource Guide to the Visual Arts of Afro-Americans*, South Bend, Ind., 1971; "Two Negro Artists Win Awards in Artists for Victory Exhibition," *Opportunity*, July 1943, p. 18; Spradling, Mary M., ed. *In Black & White: Afro-Americans in Print; Richardson, Ben. Great American Negroes*, pp. 92-100; Robinson, Wilhelmina S. *Historical Negro Biographies*, pp. 161-2; *Negro Digest*, June 1944, p. 27; *Negro History Bulletin*, March 1939, p. 52; "Leading Negro Artists," *Ebony*, Sept. 1963; Ames, Winslow. "Richmond Barthé," *Parnassus*, Vol. XII, 1940.

BASKERVILLE, MARY EFFIE

Sculptor, educator. Born in North Carolina in 1874. Teacher of kindergarten.
Works: *Edwin A. Harleston.*
Exhibited: Charlestown Museum, 1929-33; Harmon Foundation, 1933; NY Public Library, 135th St. Branch, 1933.
Sources: Harmon Foundation. *Non Jury Exhibit of Works of Negro Artists*, 1933; "Harlem Library Shows Negro Art," *Art News*, May 20, 1933, p. 14.

BASSETTE, BEATRICE

Illustrator, educator.
Sources: *Ebony*, Feb. 1961, pp. 48-50; Spradling, Mary M., ed. *In Black and White: Afro-Americans in Print.*

BATTEY, C. M.

Photographer. Worked in Tuskegee, Alabama.
Sources: "Battey," *Opportunity*, May 1927, p. 126.

BAYTON, HARRY W.

Painter.
Works: *Alexis; Steve.*
Exhibited: Phila. Civic Center.
Sources: Phila. Division of Art. *Afro-American Artists 1800-1969.*

BEAN, JOHN

Painter.
Exhibited: Museum of Modern Art, 1943.
Sources: "Young Negro Art Impresses New York," *Art Digest*, Oct. 15, 1943.

BEARD, DANIEL CARTER

Painter, graphic artist.
Sources: Harley, Ralph L., Jr. "A Checklist of Afro-American Art & Artists," *The Serif*, Dec. 1970; "Celebrating the Fourth in New York in 1834," *NY Times Magazine*, July 4, 1937; ". . . Original Drawings are being Exhibited . . .," *Pictures on Exhibit*, June 1940.

BEARDEN, ROMARE

Painter, mixed media. Born in Charlotte, North Carolina, 1912. Studied at New York University (BS); University of Pittsburgh; American Artists School; Art Students League, NYC, under George Grosz; Columbia University (1943); La Sorbonne, Paris (1950-1).

Works: *Adoration of the Wise Men; The Evening Meal of Prophet Peterson; Evening 9:30 461 Lenox Avenue; Mysteries; Interior; City Scene; Spring Planting; Factory Workers; He Is Arisen; Sharecroppers; Two Generations; After Church; Baptism; Circe Preparing a Banquet for Ulysses; Serenade; Tomorrow I May Be Far Away; Family; Palm Sunday Procession; Chicago Grand Terace; Jazz 1930's; The Walls of Jericho; Cotton; The Dove; She-ba; Burial; Train Whistle Blues #1; Fiddle Riff; Dream Dream; Early Morning; Guitar Executive; Watching the Trains Go By; 1930's Chicago Jazz; Blue Projection; The Woodshed; The Farmer; Mother & Child; Morning; Express to Memphis; Carolina Family; The Basket Woman; Urban Blues; The Street; Projections; Conjur Woman; Conjur Woman as an Angel; Pittsburgh Memory; The Passion of Christ; Expulsion from Paradise; Woman Picking Cotton; Visitation; Mama's Knee; Woman in a Blue Dress; Block II; Block I; Blue Maternity; Girl in a Garden; Tidings II; Sketch for Block II; Ancestral Legend; Carolina Blue; Two of Them; Rites of Spring; Golgotha; Blue Interior, Morning; Conjunction* (collage).
Exhibited: G Place Gallery, Washington, DC, 1945 (1-man); Corcoran Gallery, Washington, DC, 1965; Bundy Museum, Waitesfield, Vt., 1967; J. L. Hudson Gallery, Detroit; Spelman College, Atlanta, 1968; Williams College, Williamstown, Mass., 1969; Cordier & Ekstrom Gallery, NYC, 1970; Tricia Karliss Gallery, Provincetown, Mass., 1970; Dartmouth College, 1968; Rockford (Ill.) College, 1965; Carnegie Museum, Pittsburgh; Harlem Art Center, 1937, 1939; American Art Gallery, 1938; McMillen Gallery, 1941; Downtown Gallery, NYC, 1941; Institute of Modern Art, Boston, 1943; Smith College, 1943; Minneapolis Art Gallery; Columbus (Ohio) Museum of Art; Albany Institute of History; Newark Museum, 1971; James A. Porter Gallery, 1970; Oakland Art Museum, 1967; Fine Arts Gallery of San Diego, 1966; Amer. Academy of Arts & Letters, 1966, 1972; Atlanta Univ., 1944; Univ. of Iowa, 1971-2; Boston Museum of Fine Arts, 1970; Samuel M. Kootz Gallery, NY, 1945-7; Ekstrom Gallery, 1961, 1964, 1967; State Univ. of NY, Albany, 1968; Caresse Crosby Niveau Gallery, NY, 1948; Barone Gallery, NY, 1955; Michael Warren Gallery, 1960; National Center of Afro-Amer. Artists, Boston, 1970; Sidney Janis Gallery, 1972; Pace Gallery, NY, 1972; Rhode

Island School of Design, 1969; Memorial Art Gallery, Rochester, 1969; San Francisco Museum of Art, 1969; Contemporary Arts Museum, Houston, 1970; NJ State Museum, 1970; Roberson Center for the Arts & Sciences, Binghamton, NY, 1970; Univ. of Cal., Santa Barbara, 1970; Visual Arts Gallery, NY.

Collections: Whitney Museum; North Carolina Museum, Charlotte; Cordeir & Ekstrom Gallery, NYC; Johnson Pub. Co., Chicago; Schomburg Collection, NYC; Chase Manhattan Bank, NYC; Newark Public Library; Mr. Thomas Sills; Mr. Russ Thompson; Museum of Fine Arts, Boston.

Member: Charter member, Advisory Committee, Community Gallery of the Brooklyn Museum; Co-director/founder, Cinque Gallery, NYC; National Institute of Arts & Letters; Spiral.

Sources: Ghent, Henri. "A Powerful 'Spokesman' for the Negro—With His Brush," *Elegant,* March 1967; "Afro-American Art: 1800-1950," *Ebony,* Feb. 1968; Cover, *Time,* Nov. 1, 1968; McLean, Deckle. "What Blacks Say Is Missing in Met Show: 'Harlem on My Mind' Hit for Lack of Art, Dignity," *Boston Globe,* Mar 9, 1969; Ghent, Henri. "And So It Is . . .," *School Arts,* April 1969; Smith, Alvin. "Not Judicious," Art Mailbag, *New York Times,* April 19, 1970; Ghent, Henri. "Gide's Words," Art Mailbag, *New York Times,* April 19, 1970; "Object Diversity," Art Section, *Time,* April 6, 1970; Aldridge, Cathy. "Bearden's Collages Sold though Exhibit Goes On," *Amsterdam News* (NY), Nov. 4, 1967; p. 23; Ashton, Dore. "Romare Bearden: Projections," *Quadrum* (Brussels), 1968, pp. 99-110; "Bearden at Cordier & Elkstrom," *Arts,* March 1970, p. 57; "Bearden Painting in Presidential Suite," *Amsterdam News* (NY), Jan. 7, 1961, p. 7; "Brilliant Artist's Work Appears in European Art Magazine," *The African* (NY), April/May 1948, pp. 14, 19; Burrows, Carlyle. "Bearden's Return," *New York Herald Tribune,* Jan. 24, 1960, p. 6; Canaday, John. "Romare Bearden Focuses on the Negro," *New York Times,* Oct. 14, 1967; Childs, Charles. "Bearden: Identification and Identity," *Art News,* Oct. 1964; Doar, Harriet. "Charlotte Native Is in NY Art World Spotlight," *Charlotte Observer,* Nov. 12, 1967, p. G2; "Romare Bearden," *Arts,* Dec. 1967/Jan. 1968, p. 62; Glueck, Grace. "A Brueghel from Harlem," *New York Times,* Feb. 22, 1970, p. 29; "Minority Artists Find a Welcome in a New Showcase," *New York Times,* Dec. 23, 1969, p. 22; "Negro Art from 1800-1950 Is on Display at City College," *New York Times,* Oct. 16, 1967, pp. 47-8; "Negroes' Art Is What's in Just Now," *New York Times,* Feb. 27, 1969, p. 34; "New York Gallery Notes," *Art in America,* Sept./Oct. 1967, p. 111;

"1930's Show at Whitney Picketed by Negro Artists Who Call It Incomplete," *New York Times,* Nov. 18, 1968, p. 31; Greene, Carroll, Jr. "Afro-American Artists: Yesterday and Now," *The Humble Way,* Houston, Fall 1968, pp. 10-15; "Bearden, Gerard Display Paintings," *New York Times,* Nov. 12, 1948, p. 21; Kramer, Hilton. "Black Art and Expedient Politics," *New York Times,* June 7, 1970; "Black Experience and Modernist Art," *New York Times,* Feb. 14, 1970, p. 23; Lane, James W. "Afro-American Art on Both Continents," *Art News,* Oct. 15, 1941, p. 25; "Negro in Art," *Art News,* Dec. 15, 1941, p. 24; McCausland, Elizabeth. "American Negro Art of the 19th & 20th Centuries," *Springfield* (Mass.) *Union and Republican,* Dec. 21, 1941; "Romare Bearden," *Art Students League,* 93rd Regular Session Report, Sept. 16, 1968-May 28, 1969, p. 94; Sharp, Marynell. "Bearden Paints 'The Iliad,'" *Art Digest,* Nov. 15, 1948, pp. 32-3; "Romare Bearden Bull-Fight Inspirations," *Art News,* April 1946, pp. 53-4; Wolf, Ben. "Bearden Abstracts Drama of the Bull-Ring," *Art Digest,* April 1, 1946; "Bearden—He Wrestles with Angels," *Art Digest,* Oct. 1, 1945, p. 16; "Bearden Sings of the Cup that Cheers," *Art Digest,* March 1, 1947, p. 19; National Center of Afro-Amer. Artists. *Five Black Artists,* 1970; City College of NY. *The Evolution of Afro-American Artists: 1800-1950;* "Home Forum," *Christian Science Monitor,* May 24, 1972; Howard Univ. *James A. Porter Gallery of African-Amer. Art,* 1970; Boston Museum of Fine Arts. *Afro-American Artists: NY & Boston,* 1970; Museum of Modern Art. *Romare Bearden: The Prevalence of Ritual;* Henderson, Harry. *Six Black Masters of American Art,* Doubleday, 1972; "The Black Artist in America: A Symposium," *Metropolitan Museum of Art Bulletin,* Jan. 1969; "The Artist Responds," *Harvard Art Review,* Summer 1969; Porter. *Modern Negro Art;* "The Negro Artist and Modern Art," *Opportunity,* Dec. 1934, pp. 371-2; "Eighth Avenue Market, New York City, Sketches from an Art Student's Notebook," *Opportunity,* Jan. 1935; "Exhibition, Kootz Gallery," *Pictures on Exhibit,* Vol. 7, Oct. 1945; *Pictures on Exhibit,* Vol. 26, April 1946; "The Negro Artist's Dilemma," *Critique,* Nov. 1946, pp. 16-22; La Jolla Museum of Art. *Dimensions of Black;* Bearden, Romare. "The Negro Artist and Modern Art," *Opportunity,* Dec. 1934; DuSable Museum of African-Amer. History. *Contemporary Black Artists,* 1970; Tanner Art Galleries. *Art of the American Negro,* 1940; Illinois Bell Telephone. *Black American Artists/71,* 1972; Roucek/Kiernan. *The Negro Impact on Western Civilization;* Newark Museum. *Black Artists: Two Generations,* 1971; Afro-American Slide Depository,

Catalog; Harmon Foundation. *Select Picture List;* Glueck, Grace. "Works of Bearden and Hunt Are Displayed: Scenes of Negro Life Depicted by Painter," *New York Times,* March 24, 1971; Gratz, Roberta B. "Ten Black Artists Quit the Whitney in Protest," *New York Post,* March 27, 1971; Ghent, Henri. *Encyclopedia of World Biography,* Sept. 1972. Genauer, Emily. "Art and the Artist," *New York Post,* April 3, 1971; Musée Rath. *8 Artistes Afro-Americains;* Fax, Elton C. *17 Black Artists;* Dartmouth College. *Six Black Artists,* 1968; L.I. Univ. *Spiral,* catalog; Werner, Alfred. "Black Is Not a Colour," *Art and Artists,* May 1969, pp. 14-7; "Art by Negroes," *Art Digest,* Oct. 15, 1949; Amer. Academy of Arts & Letters and National Institute of Arts & Letters. *Exhibition of Work by Newly Elected Members and Recipients of Honors and Awards;* Greene, Carroll, Jr. "Perspective: The Black Artist in America," *Art Gallery,* April 1970, p. 19; "American Negro Art Given Full Length Review in NY Show," *Art Digest,* Dec. 15, 1941; Pierre-Noel, Lois Jones. "American Negro Art in Progress," *Negro History Bulletin,* Oct. 1967; Rockford (Ill.) College. *Creativity and the Negro;* "The Negro Artist Comes of Age," *Art News,* Feb. 1, 1945; Siegel, Jeanne. "Why Spiral?," *Art News,* Sept. 1966, pp. 48-50; "American Negro Art," *Design,* Feb. 1942, p. 28; Kiah, Virginia. "Black Artists," *Savannah,* April 1972, p. 14; Johnson Pub. Co. *The JPC Art Collection;* "Black Art: What Is It?," *Art Gallery,* April 1970; Jacobs, Jay. "The Cinque Gallery," *Art Gallery,* April 1970; Driscoll, Edgar, Jr. "Exhibit Features Black Artists," *Boston Globe,* Feb. 16, 1970, p. 17; Greene, Carroll, Jr. *Afro-American Artists: 1800-1968,* slides; "Leading Negro Artists," *Ebony,* Sept. 1963, pp. 131-2; Shorewood Reproductions. *The Art of Black America,* 1969; Mt. Holyoke College. *10 Afro-American Artists,* 1969; Giuliano, Charles. "Five Black Artists," *Boston After Dark,* March 4, 1970; "Winthrop Students Visit Arts Center," *Bay State Banner,* March 19, 1970; Loercher, Diana. "Black Artists Exhibition Reveals Visual Eloquence," *Christian Science Monitor,* March 2, 1970; Haydon, Harold. "Coming of Age of Black Art," *Chicago Sun Times,* July 26, 1970; Bourne, Kay. "Black Artists Shown at Museum," *Bay State Banner,* May 28, 1970; Museum of Fine Arts to Hold Black Art Show," *Chronicle,* Ipswich, Mass., April 30, 1970; "What Is Black Art?" *Newsweek,* June 22, 1970; Driscoll, Edgar. "Blacks Duncanson & Bannister Honored in Fine Arts Exhibit," *Boston Globe,* Jan. 16, 1972; Drysdale, Susan. "Black Arts: Alive & Struggling in America," *Christian Science Monitor;* "Museum of Fine Arts to Hold Black Art Show," *Tri Town Transcript & Pennysaver,* April 29, 1970; Kramer, Hilton. "Is Politics Submerging Black Art?," *Courier Journal & Times,* Louisville, Ky., June 7, 1970; Brown, Marion. "The Negro in Fine Arts," *Negro Heritage Library,* Vol. 2; Ploski, Harry A., & Ernest Kaiser. "The Black Artist," *Afro USA,* 1971; Berkman, Florence. "Afro-Amer. Exhibit Fosters Understanding of Black Artist," *Times,* Hartford, Conn., May 24, 1970; Walsh, Rose. "Artists to Meet Public at Art Exhibit Preview," *Record American,* May 19, 1970; Le Brun, Caron. "Blacks' Art on Display," *Herald Traveler,* Boston, May 26, 1970; Minneapolis Institute of Art. *30 Contemporary Black Artists,* 1968; Ploski, Harry, Otto J. Lindenmeyer, & Ernest Kaiser. "The Black Artist," *Reference Library of Black America,* Book 4, 1971; *The Negro Handbook,* Composed by Editors of *Ebony,* Chicago, 1966; Schatz, Walter. *Directory of Afro-American Resources,* 1970; Bessye J. Bearden Papers; Locke. *The Negro in Art;* Dover. *American Negro Art; Negro Almanac; Art News,* Feb. 1, 1945; *Who's Who in American Art,* 1970; Boston Museum of Fine Arts. *Afro-American Artists: NY & Boston,* 1970; "Afro-American Issue," *Art Gallery,* April 1968, April 1970; Indiana Univ. *Fine Arts & the Black American;* State Univ. of NY at Albany. *Romare Bearden: Paintings & Projections,* 1968; Myers, Carol L. *Black Power in the Arts,* Flint (Mich.), 1970; Walker, Roslyn. *A Resource Guide to the Visual Arts of Afro-Americans,* South Bend, Ind., 1971; Driscoll, E. J., Jr. "Showcase for Black Artists," *Boston Sunday Globe,* July 6, 1969, p. A73; Glueck, Grace. "America Has Black Art on Her Mind," *New York Times,* Feb. 27, 1969, p. C34; McMillen Inc. Galleries. *Contemporary Negro Art,* NY, 1941; Mashek, Joseph. "Morris Louis, Rubin Gallery; Michael Steiner, Marlbourough Gallery; Black Artists, Visual Arts Gallery," *Art Forum,* Sept. 1970, p. 80; School of Visual Arts. *Black Artists,* 1970; Fine, Elsa H. "Mainstream, Blackstream and the Black Art Movement," *Art Journal,* Spring 1971; Gaither, Edmund B. "The Evolution of the Afro-American Artists," *Artists Proof,* Vol. 2; *Crisis,* March 1970, pp. 81-6; Spradling, Mary M., ed. *In Black & White: Afro-Americans in Print;* Hollingsworth, Alvin. "Wealth of Expression in Black Artists' RISD Show," *Providence Sunday Journal,* June 29, 1969; Bearden, Romare, & Carl Holty. *The Painters Mind,* Crown Pub., 1969; Albany Institute of History and Art. *The Negro Artist Comes of Age;* Amer. Academy of Arts & Letters and National Institute of Arts & Letters. *Paintings by Members,* 1972; Bearden, Romare. *Prevalence of Ritual,* NY, Museum of Modern Art.

BEATTY, RICHARD

Sources: "Negro Art from Cleveland's Karamu House," *Art Digest*, Jan. 15, 1942.

BECK, SHERMAN

Painter, mixed media. Born in Chicago.
Works: *Untitled #1; Untitled #2.*
Exhibited: Nat'l Center of Afro-Amer. Artists, Boston, 1970, 1972; Howard Univ., 1970, 1972; Studio Museum in Harlem, 1970, 1972.
Collections: Johnson Pub. Co., Chicago.
Member: AFRICOBRA.
Sources: Myers, Carol L. *Black Power in the Arts,* Flint, Mich., 1970; "Afro-American Issue," *Art Gallery,* April 1968; Indiana Univ. *Fine Arts & the Black American;* DuSable Museum of African-Amer. History. *Contemporary Black Artists,* 1970, Calendar; Johnson Pub. Co. *The JPC Art Collection;* Grillo, Jean B. "Where Down Home Meets Back Home," *Boston After Dark,* Sept. 1970; *Black Shades,* Oct. 1970; Howard Univ. *AFRICOBRA I,* Catalog, 1970; Howard Univ. *AFRICOBRA II,* Catalog, 1972; Walker, Roslyn. *A Resource Guide to the Visual Arts of Afro-Americans,* South Bend, Ind., 1971.

BECKET, HUMPHREYS WILLIAM

Painter, interior decorator, muralist. Born in Providence, Rhode Island, 1894. Grade school education; three years of weekend study at Rhode Island School of Design.
Works: *Boys Head; Mid-Ocean; The New Hat.*
Exhibited: Harmon Foundation, 1933.
Sources: Harmon Foundation. *Negro Artists,* 1935; Harmon Foundation. *Non-Jury Exhibit of Works of Negro Artists,* 1933; DuSable Museum of African-Amer. History. *Contemporary Black Artists,* 1970, Calendar; Harmon Foundation. *Exhibition of Productions by Negro Artists;* Indiana Univ. *Fine Arts & the Black American;* Harley, Ralph, Jr. "A Checklist of Afro-Amer. Art & Artists," *Serif,* Dec. 1970; Walker, Roslyn. *A Resource Guide to the Visual Arts of Afro-Americans,* South Bend, Ind., 1971.

BEGAUD, WILSON

Painter.
Collections: Johnson Pub. Co.
Sources: Johnson Pub. Co. *The JPC Art Collection,* Pamphlet.

BELL, COLUMBUS

Painter.
Works: *Shinertown.*
Exhibited: Dillard Univ., 1941.
Sources: Dillard Univ. *Arts Festival,* 1941.

BELL, JOANNE

Studied at Fisk University.
Works: *Self-portrait at Term.*

Exhibited: Sun Times/Daily News Gallery, Chicago, 1970.
Sources: United Negro College Fund. *Art 1970,* Chicago, 1970.

BELL, RICHARD E.

Painter, graphic artist. Born 1953.
Works: *This World* (mixed media); *Still Life* (crayon); *Still Life* (pastel); *My Lady* (pencil & ink); *People; Inner City Blues.*
Exhibited: Mayor's Art on Human Rights Exhib., 1970, Boston.
Awards: 1st place, Mayor's Art on Human Rights Exhib., 1970.
Sources: Information from the artist.

BELL, ROBERT E.

Painter, sculptor.
Works: *Bust of Booker T. Washington* (commissioned for sunken gardens at 18th St. & Paeso, Kansas City, Mo.); *Paul Lawrence Dunbar.*
Exhibited: South Side Community Art Center, Chicago, 1945.
Collections: Mrs. Katie E. Bell.
Sources: South Side Community Art Center. *Chicago Collectors Exhibit of Negro Art,* Chicago, 1945; "Booker T. Washington—Plan Statue of," *Pittsburgh Courier,* May 19, 1923.

BELL, T. L.

Exhibited: NY Public Library, 1921.
Sources: NY Public Library. *Catalog of the Negro Arts Exhibit,* 135th St. Branch, NYC, 1921; Harley, Ralph, Jr. "A Checklist of Afro-Amer. Art & Artists," *Serif,* Dec. 1970.

BELLINGER, LOUIS A. S.

Architect, educator. Born in South Carolina, 1891. Studied at Howard University; Carnegie Institute of Technology.
Exhibited: Harmon Foundation, 1928, 1933.
Sources: DuSable Museum of African-Amer. History. *Contemporary Black Artists,* 1970, Calendar; Harmon Foundation. *Negro Artists,* 1935; Harmon Foundation. *Exhibition of Productions by Negro Artists;* Harley, Ralph, Jr. "A Checklist of Afro-Amer. Art & Artists," *Serif,* Dec. 1970; Indiana Univ. *Fine Arts & the Black American;* Downing, Lewis K. "Contributions of Negro Scientists," *Crisis,* June 1939; Walker, Roslyn. *A Resource Guide to the Visual Arts of Afro-Americans,* South Bend, Ind., 1971.

BELLOW, CLEVELAND

Painter, printmaker, photographer. Born in San Francisco in 1946. Studied at California College of Arts and Crafts (BFA, 1969; MA, 1971). Teacher at Alcorn College, Art Department, Lorman, Mississippi.
Works: *Don* (photoprint); *Untitled* (billboard

poster); *Emancipation of a Son*; *Untitled* (silk-screen); *Duke*; *Marin*; *Wash Woman*; *There Is No Need for a Title*, Series-Nos. 1-7, 1969-71.

Exhibited: Oakland Museum, Kaiser Center, 1968; Monterey Jazz Festival, 1969; San Francisco Arts Festival, 1969, 1970, 1972; College of Marin, 1969; Berkeley Art Center, 1970; La Jolla Museum of Art, 1970; Illinois Bell, Chicago, 1971; Oakland Museum, 1970-1; Society's Child Gallery, Seattle, 1972; Alcorn A & M College, 1972; Rainbow Sign, Berkeley, 1972; Southern Ill. Univ., 1972; Black Expo, San Francisco, 1972; Whitney Museum, 1971; San Francisco Museum of Art, 1971; Jackson, Miss. Municipal Art Gallery, 1971; Cal. State Fair, 1971; Pacific Grove Museum, 1970; Monte Vista, 1970; Cal. College of Arts & Crafts, 1970; Pleasant Hill City, Cal., 1969; Studios I & II, Oakland, 1968; Univ. of Cal., 1968; Billboard Exhibit, Oakland & Berkeley, 1970; Billboard Nat'l Exhibit, March & April, 1972; Oakland Recreation Dept.; Links Nat'l Convention.

Collections: Stanford Univ.; Oakland Museum; City of Pleasant Hill; City of San Francisco; Cal. College of Arts & Crafts; Illinois Bell Telephone Co.; Mrs. Thomas Berkeley; Mrs. Dorothy Weiss; Johnson Pub. Co.

Awards: Links Art Scholarship, 1969; Permanent Pigments Award, Spring 1971; Cal. College of Arts & Crafts, Bank of Amer. Achievement Award, 1965; Purchase Award, San Francisco Arts Festival, 1970; Merit Award, San Francisco Arts Festival, 1970; Honorable Mention, Jackson, Miss. Municipal Art Gallery, 1971; Purchase Award, City of Pleasant Hill, 1969.

Member: Contemporary Arts Council, Oakland Museum; Art West Associated North; Nat'l Conference of Artists; College Art Assn.; Board of Directors, Alpha Phi Alpha Educational Foundation; Museum Intercultural Exchange, San Francisco Museum of Art, Advisory Board.

Sources: Lewis/Waddy. *Black Artists on Art*, Vol. 2; Oakland Museum Archives; Oakland Art Museum. *New Perspectives in Black Art;* Indiana Univ. *Fine Arts & the Black American;* Harley, Ralph, Jr. "A Checklist of Afro-American Art & Artists," *The Serif,* Dec. 1970; La Jolla Museum of Art. *Dimensions of Black;* Oakland Museum. *Black Untitled II,* 1971; Illinois Bell Telephone. *Black American Artists/71,* Catalog, 1972; Information from the artist; Walker, Roslyn. *A Resource Guide to the Visual Arts of Afro-Americans,* South Bend, Ind., 1971.

BENNETT, FRED

Photographer, printmaker.

Works: *The Sign* (print); *Untitled* (photograph).

Exhibited: Lee Cultural Center, Phila.

Sources: Phila. Dept. of Recreation. *Love . . . and the Black Community.*

BENNETT, GWENDOLYN

Painter, educator, director. Born in Giddings, Texas in 1902. Studied at Pratt Institute, New York; Academie Julian, Paris. Teacher of Art at Howard University; Tennessee State College. Director of Harlem Community Art Center, 1937-40.

Sources: Locke. *The Negro in Art;* Indiana Univ. *Fine Arts & the Black American;* Porter. *Modern Negro Art;* Harley, Ralph L., Jr. "A Checklist of Afro-Amer. Art & Artists," *The Serif,* Dec. 1970; *Negro Yearbook;* Walker, Roslyn. *A Resource Guide to the Visual Arts of Afro-Americans,* South Bend, Ind., 1971.

BEREAL, EDWARD

Sculptor. Born in Los Angeles, California in 1937. Studied at the Chouinard Art Institute.

Exhibited: Pomona College, Claremont; Huysman Gallery, Los Angeles; Metropolitan College, Los Angeles (3-man); Dickson Art Center, Los Angeles, 1966.

Collections: Dr. & Mrs. Leonard Asher; Mr. & Mrs. Donald Factor.

Awards: William Copley Award, NY.

Sources: Myers, Carol L. *Black Power in the Arts,* Flint (Mich.), 1970; DuSable Museum of African-Amer. History. *Contemporary Black Artists,* 1970 calendar; "Afro-American Issue," *Art Gallery,* April 1968; UCLA Art Galleries. *The Negro in American Art,* 1966; Harley, Ralph L., Jr. "Checklist of Afro-American Art & Artists," *The Serif,* Dec. 1970; Walker, Roslyn. *A Resource Guide to the Visual Arts of Afro-Americans,* South Bend, Ind., 1971.

BERRY, ARTHUR

Sculptor, educator. Born in Tulsa, Oklahoma in 1923. Studied at Fisk University (BA, 1923); Columbia University (MA, 1952); School of Painting and Sculpture, Skowhegan, Maine. Teacher of art at Albany State College, Georgia.

Works: *Unfinished Figure; Still Life.*

Exhibited: Xavier Univ., 1963.

Sources: Lewis/Waddy. *Black Artists on Art,* Vol. 1; Xavier Univ. *Emancipation Proclamation Centennial National Art Exhibition,* 1963; Walker, Roslyn. *A Resource Guide to the Visual Arts of Afro-Americans,* South Bend, Ind., 1971.

BERRY, REUBEN

Painter, sculptor. Born in Montgomery, West Virginia in 1923. Studied at Famous Artists

School (1950-3); School of Visual Arts (1956-7).
Works: *The Bridge; The Warrior.*
Exhibited: Studio Museum in Harlem, 1969.
Sources: Studio Museum in Harlem. *Harlem Artists 69.*

BESCHOFF, E. H.
Collections: NY Public Library Schomburg Art Collection.
Sources: Schatz, Walter. *Directory of Afro-American Resources,* 1970.

BEVERLY, JUANITA MILLER
Painter, mixed media.
Works: *Target Practice* (acrylic & oil); *All* (acrylic).
Exhibited: Lee Cultural Center, Phila.
Sources: Phila. Dept. of Recreation. *Love . . . and the Black Community.*

BEY, MOHAMMED S.
Sculptor.
Works: *Abraham & The Ram.*
Exhibited: Smith-Mason Gallery, 1971.
Sources: Smith-Mason Gallery. *National Exhibition Black Artists,* 1971.

BIBLE, CHARLES
Painter, graphic artist. Born in Waco, Texas in 1937. Studied at Pratt Institute.
Works: *The Afro-American Hero Series* (posters).
Sources: Groom, Gladys. Black Means . . . , 1970.

BIGGERS, JOHN T.
Painter, sculptor, graphic artist, educator, muralist. Born in Gastonia, North Carolina, 1924. Studied at Hampton Institute; Pennsylvania State University. Chairman, Art Department, Texas Southern University, Houston (1970).
Works: *Mother and Children; Cradle, Mother and Child; The Contribution of the Negro Women; Slave; Dying Soldier; Coal Man; Coal Pickers; The Timi of Ede, Nigeria;* Murals for Pa. State Univ., Texas Old Folks Home, YWCA, Texas Southern Univ. Science Building; *The Market Women; Market Women, Ghana; Nigerian Festival; Jubilee (Harvest Festival); Houston.*
Exhibited: Atlanta Univ., 1944; City College of NY; La Jolla Museum, 1970; Texas Painting & Sculpture Exhibition, 1971-2; Black Art Gallery, Houston, 1972; National Center of Afro-Amer. Artists, 1971; Benin Sculpture Exhibit, 1968; Denver Museum of Art, 1966-8; Rockford (Ill.) College, 1965; Xavier Univ., 1963.
Collections: Houston Museum of Fine Arts;

Dallas Museum of Fine Arts; Lubbock Museum; Howard Univ.; Atlanta Univ.; Texas Southern Univ.; Pa. State Univ.; Golden State Mutual Life Insurance Co.; Ms. Nina Cullinan; Mrs. Susan Macashan; Mr. Frank Wardlow.
Awards: Purchase Prizes—Houston Museum, 1950, Dallas Museum, 1952, Atlanta Univ. Annuals, 1950-3; Honorable Mention, Architectural League; UNESCO Fellowship, 1957; Piper Professor Award, 1964; Dallas Museum Award; Excellence of Design Award, 1963; Citation of Merit, Society of Illustrators Annual National Exhibit, 1967; Harbison Award for Distinguished Teaching, 1968.
Member: Nat'l Society of Mural Painters; Amer. Federation of Art; Texas Commission of Arts & Humanities; Texas Institute of Letters.
Sources: *"Afro-American Issue,"* Art Gallery, April 1968; City College of NY. *Evolution of Afro-American Artists 1800-1950,* 1967; Biggers, John T. *Ananse, the Web of Life in West Africa; Negro Almanac,* p. 625; *American Negro Reference Book,* p. 771; Lowenfeld, Viktor. *Creative Mental Growth,* NY, McMillan, 1957; *Contribution of the Negro Woman to American Life and Education:* A Mural Presentation, Ann Arbor, Mich., Univ. Microfilms, 1955; Harley, Ralph, Jr. "Checklist of Afro-Amer. Art & Artists," *Serif,* Dec. 1970; Roelof-Lanner, T.V. *Prints by American Negro Artists;* "Working on Hampton Mural," *Chicago Defender,* Feb. 20, 1943; "Lone Star Artist," *Time,* June 30, 1952; "Contemporary Art from Texas in New York," *Christian Science Monitor,* July 12, 1952; Martinsen, Dick. "Folk Art of Texas," *Houston Chronicle Rotogravure,* March 6, 1955; Miller, Inez. "John Biggers," *Southern Artist,* March/April 1956; "American Artist Wins UNESCO Fellowship," *US Commission for UNESCO News,* Sept. 8, 1957; "The Art World. . . . ," *Philadelphia Sunday Bulletin,* July 17, 1960; "Texas Artists," *Texas Architect,* May 1964; "Africa Impressions," *Texas A&M Review,* Summer 1964; "Harlem's Artists," *Harlem USA,* 1965; DuSable Museum of African-Amer. History. *Contemporary Black Artists,* 1970 Calendar; Brown, Evelyn S. "The Harmon Awards," *Opportunity,* March 1933; Fax, Elton C. "Four Rebels in Art," *Freedomways,* Spring 1961; Roucek/Kiernan. *The Negro Impact on Western Civilization;* Dover. *American Negro Art;* Indiana Univ. *Fine Arts & the Black American;* La Jolla Museum of Art. *Dimensions of Black;* Information from artist; Brewer, J. Mason. *Aunt Dicy Tales;* Brewer, J. Mason. *Dog Ghost & Other Negro Folk Tales;* Buck, Pearl. *The Good Earth;* Bywaters, Jerry. *Texas Painting & Sculpture: 20th Century;* Walker, Roslyn. *A Resource*

Guide to the Visual Arts of Afro-Americans, South Bend, Ind., 1971; Dale, Edward E. *Cross Timbers,* 1966; International Library of Negro Life & History. *The Negro in Music & Art,* 1965; Shikes, Ralph E. *The Indignant Eye: The Artist as Social Critic in Prints & Drawings from the 15th Century to Picasso,* 1969; Chase, Judith W. *Afro-American Art,* 1972; Atkinson, J. Edward. *Black Dimensions in Contemporary American Art,* 1971; Clark, John H. *Harlem, USA,* 1971; Fax, Elton C. *17 Black Artists,* 1971. Anderson, A., & A. Wooster. *Texas & Texans Text Book,* 1971 (6 paintings by Bigger's students); Greene, Carroll, Jr. "Perspective: The Black Artist in America," *Art Gallery,* April 1970, p. 23; Holmes, Ann. "It Is Almost Genetic," *Art Gallery,* April 1970; "Young Negro Impresses New York," *Art Digest,* Oct. 15, 1943; Rockford (Ill.) College. *Creativity and the Negro; Art News,* Nov. 15, 1943, p. 22; Lowenfeld, Viktor. "The Negro Art in America," *Design,* Sept. 1944; "Young Negro Artists," *Design,* Nov. 1943, p. 7; Greene, Carroll, Jr. "Afro-American Artists: Yesterday & Now," *The Humble Way,* Vol. 8, No. 3, 1968; Xavier Univ. *Emancipation Proclamation Centennial National Art Exhibition,* 1963; "Home Folk: Africa," *Christian Science Monitor,* April 8, 1971; Brown, Marion. "The Negro in the Fine Arts," *The Negro Heritage Library,* Vol. 2; Morsbach, Mabel. *The Negro in American Life;* Ploski, Harry, & Ernest Kaiser. "The Black Artist," *Afro USA,* 1971; Ploski, Harry, Ernest Kaiser, & Otto J. Lindenmeyer. "The Black Artist," *Reference Library of Black America,* Book 4, 1971; *The Negro Handbook,* Composed by Editors of *Ebony,* Chicago, 1966; Myers, Carol L. *Black Power in the Arts,* Flint, Mich., 1970; Spradling, Mary, Ed. *In Black & White: Afro-Americans in Print;* "Leading Negro Artists," *Ebony,* Sept. 1963.

BIRCHER, JAMES
Painter, printmaker.
Sources: DuSable Museum of African-Amer. History. *Contemporary Black Artists,* 1970 calendar.

BISHOP, ELOISE
Sculptor, educator. Born in Pittsburgh, Pennsylvania in 1921. Studied at Bennington College (1938-42); and under Simon Molselsio; Columbia University.
Works: *Head of Boy.*
Exhibited: Independent Artists Show, NY; Atlanta Univ.; Columbia Univ.; King-Smith School, Washington, DC.
Sources: Albany Inst. of History & Art. *The Negro Artist Comes of Age;* Indiana Univ. *Fine Arts & the Black American;* Ploski,

Harry, Ernest Kaiser. "The Black Artist," *Afro USA,* 1971; Ploski, Harry, Ernest Kaiser, Otto Lindenmeyer. "The Black Artist," *Reference Library of Black America,* Book 4, 1971; Walker, Roslyn. *A Resource Guide to the Visual Arts of Afro-Americans,* South Bend, Ind., 1971.

BLACKBURN, ANTONIO M.
Sculptor, educator, ceramist. Born in Louisville, Kentucky in 1929. Studied at Indiana University (BS, MFA); Konstfactskolan, Sweden.
Works: *Black Star; Stoneware Bowl,* 1958; *See How They Run,* 1959.
Exhibited: Smith-Mason Gallery, DC, 1971; Butler Institute of Amer. Art, Youngstown, Ohio, 1958; Decorative Arts & Ceramics Exhibition, 1959, 1961; American House, NY, 1960; J. B. Speed Museum, Louisville, 1958.
Collections: Butler Institute of Amer. Art; Konstfactskolan, Stockholm, Sweden; Indiana Univ.
Sources: Smith-Mason Gallery. *National Exhibition of Black Artists,* 1971; *Form* Magazine, May 1960. Information from artist.

BLACKBURN, LEROY
Sources: Harley, Ralph, Jr. "A Checklist of Afro-American Art and Artists," *The Serif,* Dec. 1970.

BLACKBURN, MAUDE C.
Painter.
Works: *Ice House; Down Cellar.*
Exhibited: Atlanta Univ., 1943.
Sources: Atlanta Univ. Exhibition files.

BLACKBURN, ROBERT
Painter, graphic artist. Born in New York City, 1921. Studied at Art Students League; FAP (1938-40); Uptown and Harlem Community Art Centers (1935-9); Wallace Harrison School of Art (1950-2). Operated a graphic workshop in New York.
Works: *The Toiler; Upper New York; Boy with Green Head; Table for Two; Dream World; Blue Thing; Sun Burst; Space Ship; Windowed Shapes; Heavy Forms; House Tops; Horses in Moonlight; Cafe Composition; Cafe Scene; Coal Pile; Farm; Refugees; Upper New York #2; Man with Mule; Providence Houses; Still Life; Easter #1; Negro Mother; Ominous Black.*
Exhibited: Baltimore Museum, 1939; Amer. Negro Exposition, Chicago, 1940; Atlanta Univ., 1949; Boston Museum of Fine Arts, 1970; City College of NY, 1967; Hotel Diplomat, 1948; Albany Institute of History & Art, 1942; Contemporary Art of the Amer. Negro, 1966; James A. Porter Gallery, 1970; Xavier Univ., 1963.

Collections: Brooklyn Museum; Baltimore Museum of Art; Library of Congress; DeWitt Clinton High School, NY (murals); National Archives; Mr. Edmund B. Gaither, Boston.
Awards: 3rd prize, Amer. Negro Exposition, Chicago, 1940; John Hay Whitney Fellowship, 1953-4.
Sources: *New York Times,* April 4, 1968; City College of NY. *The Evolution of Afro-American Artists 1800-1950,* 1967; Dover. *American Negro Art;* Locke. *The Negro in Art;* Boston Museum of Fine Arts. *Afro-American Artists: NY & Boston,* 1970; Porter. *Modern Negro Art; Daily Worker,* NY, May 5, 1948; Howard Univ. *James A. Porter Gallery of African-American Art,* 1970; Afro-American Slide Depository, catalog; Tanner Art Galleries. *Art of the American Negro,* 1940; DuSable Museum of African-Amer. History. *Contemporary Black Artists,* 1970 Calendar; "American Negro Art Given Full Length Review in NY Show," *Art Digest,* Dec. 15, 1941; Xavier Univ. *Emancipation Proclamation Centennial National Art Exhibition,* 1963; Porter, James. "Negro Artists Gain Recognition after Long Battle," *Pittsburgh Courier,* July 29, 1950; "Six Paintings of City Life," *Arts Quarterly,* Dec. 1939, pp. 13-9; "Now Showing: The Black Artist," *Contact,* Sept. 1970; Baltimore Museum of Art. *Contemporary Negro,* 1939; Library of Congress. *Catalogue of the Exhibition of Oils, Watercolors, Prints, & Drawings;* Harley, Ralph, Jr. "Checklist of Afro-Amer. Art & Artists," *Serif,* Dec. 1970; Locke, Alain. "Advance on the Art Front," *Opportunity,* May 1939; Gaither, Edmund B. "The Evolution of the Afro-American Artists," *Artists Proof,* Vol. 2; Le Brun, Caron. "Black Art," *Boston Herald Traveler,* Sunday Supplement, May 24, 1970; *Affairs of Black Artists,* 1972; Albany Institute of History & Art. *The Negro Artist Comes of Age;* Walker, Roslyn. *A Resource Guide to the Visual Arts of Afro-Americans,* South Bend, Ind., 1971; Afro-American Artists: NY & Boston," *Prudential Center News,* March 1, 1970, p. 4.

BLACKWELL, CHARLES
Photographer.
Exhibited: Addison Gallery, 1971.
Sources: James Van DerZee Institute. *The Black Photographer (1908-1970): A Survey.*

BLAIR, SHEILA
Photographer. Studied at Fisk University.
Exhibited: Sun Times/Daily News Gallery, Chicago, 1970.
Sources: United Negro College Fund. *Art 1970,* Chicago, 1970.

BLAIRE, JERRY
Sources: NY NAACP. *Art Exhibition of Negro Expression Sponsored by Minars Furniture,* April 1964.

BLANCO, TEODORO RAMOS
Sculptor. Born 1901 in Havana, Cuba. Studied at the Art Academy, San Alejandro; and Rome (1927-30).
Works: *Memorial to the Maceos; Heroic Head of Ant. Maceo; The Invading Soldier; The Slave; Langston Hughes; Mother of the Maceos.*
Exhibited: Seville, 1929; Rome, 1930; Harmon Foundation, 1933 (1-man); Club Atenas, Havana, 1934; National Cuban Shows, 1935, 1938; Riverside Museum, NY, 1939; American Negro Exposition, Chicago, 1940.
Awards: Gold Medal, Seville, 1939; Prize Awards, National Cuban Shows, 1939, 1938.
Collections: Municipal and public collections, Havana; Harmon Foundation; Howard Univ.; Schomburg Collection, NY.
Sources: Harmon Foundation. *Exhibition of Productions by Negro Artists;* DuSable Museum of African-American History. *Contemporary Black Artists,* 1970 calendar; Tanner Art Galleries. *Art of the American Negro,* Catalog, 1940; Harmon Foundation. *Negro Artists,* Catalog, 1935; "Blanco, A. Colored Sculptor in Cuba," *Crisis,* Sept. 1931, p. 299.

BLAND, GARNETT W.
Sources: Harley, Ralph, Jr. "A Checklist of Afro-American Art and Artists," *The Serif,* Dec. 1970.

BLAND, JAMES
Designer, printmaker. Born in Providence, Rhode Island in 1909. Studied at Commercial School, Providence; Rhode Island School of Design.
Works: *Manning Hall* (lithograph); *On the Hill* (lithograph); *New England House.*
Exhibited: Harmon Foundation 1928, 1933, 1935.
Collections: National Archives.
Sources: Harmon Foundation. *Negro Artists,* 1935; Harmon Foundation. *Non-Jury Exhibit of Works of Negro Artists,* 1933; Harmon Foundation. *Exhibition of Productions by Negro Artists;* Indiana Univ. *Fine Arts & the Black American;* Harley, Ralph L., Jr. "A Checklist of Afro-American Art & Artists," *The Serif,* Dec. 1970; DuSable Museum of African-Amer. History. *Contemporary Black Artists,* 1970, calendar; Afro-American Slide Depository, catalog; Walker, Roslyn. *A Resource Guide to the Visual Arts of Afro-Americans,* South Bend, Ind., 1971.

BLANTON, DONALD R.
Painter. Born in Richmond, Indiana, 1941. Self-taught.

Exhibited: Mystic (Conn.) Art Festival; Groton (Conn.) Art Festival; Hartford Arts Festival; Sterns Square, Springfield, Mass.; Dunbar Afro-Amer. Outdoor Show; Springfield (Mass.) College; Amer. Internat'l College, Springfield; Black Bank, Hartford; Western Mass. Electric Co.
Member: Afro-Art Alliance.
Sources: Information from the artist.

BLANTON, PAUL L.

Painter. Born in Combs, Kentucky, 1936. Self-taught.
Exhibited: Springfield College; Amer. Internat'l College, Springfield, Mass.; Stage West, West Springfield, Mass.; Dunbar Community Center.
Member: Afro-Art Alliance, Springfield; Springfield Art League.
Sources: Information from the artist.

BLAYTON, BETTY

Painter, mixed media, educator. Born in Williamsburg, Virginia on July 10, 1937. Studied at Syracuse University, New York (BFA, 1959); Art Students League, New York City; Brooklyn Museum Art School, New York City. Executive director of the Children's Art Carnival.
Works: *Evolved; Steady State; Lower Octave; Consume; Souls Ascended; Uranus; Penetration; Signals; Energy; Magnetic Angles; Thoughts; Alive; Souls Descend; An Inner View; Mind's Rot; Dance if Water; Above & Below; Souls Interact; Opposition; Transcendence; State of Mind; Being & Becoming, I, II, III; Concentrated Energies; Reaching for Center; Childhood's End; Conductive Mind; I An Me,* 1968 (oil).
Exhibited: Metropolitan Applied Research Center, NY; Ruder & Finn, NY; Boston Museum of Fine Arts, 1970; Brooklyn Museum, 1969; Collectors Corner Gallery, Washington, DC, 1965; Counterpoint Exhibit, Lever House, NYC, 1965; Reder Store, NYC; American Greetings Gallery, NYC, 1968; MARC, NYC, 1969; Riverside Museum, NYC, 1969; traveling exhibit, 1969-70; St. Thomas Gallery, Virgin Islands, 1960 (1-woman); Adair Gallery, Atlanta, 1963 (1-woman); Capricorn Gallery, NYC, 1966, 1968 (1-woman); Collectors Corner, Washington, DC, 1959 (1-woman); Univ. of Iowa Museum of Art, 1971-2; Newark Museum, 1971; Hudson River Museum, Yonkers, NY; Rhode Island School of Design, 1969; Memorial Art Gallery, Rochester, NY, 1969; San Francisco Museum of Art, 1969; Contemporary Arts Museum, Houston, 1970; New Jersey State Museum, 1970; Roberson Center for the Arts & Sciences, Binghamton, NY, 1970; Art Galleries, Univ. of Cal. at Santa Barbara,

1970; Pan American Building, NYC; High Museum, Atlanta; Minneapolis Institute of Art; Everson Museum of Art, Syracuse; Milwaukee Art Center; San Diego Museum of Art; Staten Island Museum; Brooklyn College; Hunter College, NY; A & T College, NC; NY State Univ., Saratoga.
Collections: Dr. Kenneth Marshall; Ms. Evelyn Cunningham; Mr. Sidney Poitier; Ms. Caroline S. Lerner; Mr. Charles Hobson; Mr. & Mrs. David Rockefeller; Mr. Walter N. Thayer; Mr. & Mrs. Peter Haas; Miss Carolyn Lerner; Mr. & Mrs. J. Hart Lyon; Mr. & Mrs. William Kernan.
Member: Executive Director, The Children's Art Carnival, Harlem (Sponsored by the Museum of Modern Art); Secretary, Board of Trustees of the Studio Museum in Harlem.
Sources: DuSable Museum of African-American History. *Contemporary Black Artists,* Calendar, 1970; Boston Museum of Fine Arts. *Afro-American Artists: New York & Boston,* 1970; *Negro Year Book;* Indiana Univ. *Fine Arts and the Black American;* Afro-American Slide Depository, Catalog; Newark Museum. *Black Artists: Two Generations,* 1971; Illinois Bell Telephone. *Black American Artists/71,* 1972; Ruder & Finn Fine Arts. *Contemporary Black Artists,* 1969; Hudson River Museum. *Contemporary American Black Artists;* Brooklyn College. *Afro-American Artists: Since 1950,* 1969; Greene, Carroll, Jr. "Perspective: The Black Artist in America," *The Art Gallery,* 1970; NY State Education Department, *Fifteen Under Forty;* Minneapolis Institute of Arts. *30 Contemporary Black Artists;* Harley, Ralph, Jr. "A Checklist of Afro-American Art and Artists," *The Serif,* Dec. 1970; Blayton, Betty. "The Children's Art Carnival," *The Art Gallery,* April 1970. Metropolitan Applied Research Center (MARC), NY. *Six Painters,* 1969; Patterson, Lindsay. "Contemporary Artists," *The Negro in Music and Art,* 1969; Ploski, Harry, Ernest Kaiser. "The Black Artist," *Afro USA,* 1971; Grillo, Jean B. "Black Art-White Museum," *Phoenix,* May 23, 1970; Ploski, Harry, Ernest Kaiser, & Otto Lindenmeyer. "The Black Artist," *Reference Library of Black America,* 1971; "Women in the Arts," *Ebony,* Aug. 1966, pp. 90-4; Riverside Museum. *8+8,* NY, 1969; American Greetings Gallery. *New Voices: 15 New York Artists,* NY, 1968; Lever House. *Counterpoints,* NY, 1965; Myers, Carol L. *Black Power in the Arts,* Flint, Mich., 1970; Lee, Timothy. "Daily Closeup, A Carnival of Art," *New York Post,* Apr. 6, 1972; Information from artist. Hollingsworth, Alvin. "Wealth of Expression in Black Artists' RISD Show," *Providence Sunday Journal,* June 29, 1969; Walker, Roslyn. *A Resource to the Visual*

Arts of Afro-Americans, South Bend, Ind., 1971.

BLISH, ALAN

Painter.

Exhibited: World's Fair Tower of Light Pavillion.

BLOUNT, REGINALD

Painter, mixed media.

Works: *Expression* (papier mâché); *Reggie B* (oil).

Exhibited: Lee Cultual Center, Phila.

Sources: Phila. Dept. of Recreation. *Love . . . and the Black Community.*

BLOUNT, SAMUEL ELLIS

Free-lance cartoonist. Born in New Bern, North Carolina, 1896. Studied at City College of New York; Pratt Institute; National Academy of Design.

Works: *Fairmount Park, Philadelphia; The Model; Erie Basin, Brooklyn; Camilla; Savin Rock, Conn.; Ruins-Roper Saw Mill; Man with Red Cap; Bible Student,* 1970; *Bimsha,* 1970; *Janice,* 1932; *The Committee Reports,* 1939; *Summer Nights,* 1944; *Off Yankees,* 1940.

Exhibited: Harmon Foundation, 1928-31, 1933, 1936; National Gallery of Art, 1929, 1930; Smithsonian Institution, 1929.

Sources: Information from artist; Harmon Foundation. *Exhibition of Productions by Negro Artists;* Indiana Univ. *Fine Arts & the Black American;* Harley, Ralph, Jr. "Checklist of Afro-Amer. Art & Artists," *Serif,* Dec. 1970; DuSable Museum of African-Amer. History. *Contemporary Artists,* 1970 Calendar; Harmon Foundation. *Non-Jury Exhibit of Works of Negro Artists,* 1933; Harmon Foundation. *Negro Artists,* 1935; Harmon Foundation. *Exhibit of Fine Arts,* 1930; Smithsonian Institution. *Painting & Sculpture by American Negro Artists,* 1929; Walker, Roslyn. *A Resource Guide to the Visual Arts of Afro-Americans,* South Bend, Ind., 1971; "Our Young Negro Artists," *Opportunity,* Jan. 1923, pp. 16-8.

BOHANON, GLORIA

Painter, textile artist. Born in Atlanta. Studied at Wayne State University (BS, 1962; MA, 1968); Society of Arts and Crafts; Los Angeles City College; California State College, Los Angeles; Otis Art Institute (MFA).

Works: *Untitled painting; In the Park; Who Reflects Who.*

Exhibited: Wayne State Univ.; Brockman Gallery; Watts Summer Art Festival; Galeria del Sol, Santa Barbara, 1969; Ankrum Gallery, Los Angeles; Gallery 32, Los Angeles; Royal Oak Art Assn; Mills College; Temple Israel, Hollywood; Cal. State College, Los Angeles; Art Teachers Exhibits, Detroit, 1962-67; Scarab Club, Detroit, 1966-8; UAW-CIO Art Show, 1966; Dialogue through Art, Los Angeles, 1969; Art for Funds Sake, 1969-70; Inner City Art Exhibition, 1969; Pasadena City College, 1970; Los Angeles County Museum of Art, 1972; Otis Art Institute, 1972; Neighborhood Arts; Chaffey College; Pomona Public Library.

Collections: Detroit Edison; Detroit Public Schools; Johnson Pub. Co.; First National Bank of Phoenix; Scarab Club, Detroit; Detroit Institute of Arts.

Awards: 2 awards, Westwood Art Assn.; 1 award, Royal Oak Art Assn., 1965.

Member: Black Arts Council; Black Artists Assn., Los Angeles.

Represented by: Brockman Gallery, 4334 Degnan Blvd., Los Angeles.

Sources: Lewis/Waddy; *Black Artists on Art,* Vol. 2; Mills College. *California Black Craftsmen;* Johnson Pub Co. *The JPC Art Collection.*

BOLLING, LESLIE GARLAND

Sculptor. Born in Richmond, Virginia, 1898. Studied at Hampton Institute; Wayland Academy; Virginia Union University. Self-taught in pen-knife sculpture.

Works: *Salome I; Salome II; The Shopper; Rock of Ages;* portraits of Rev. Dr. W.T. Johnson & Bishop W. Sampson Brooks; *Aunt Monday (Washing); Sister Tuesday (Ironing); Washerwoman; The Market Woman; The Head of a Woman; Ice Man; Soap Making; The Janitor; The Boxer; The Shot Putter; Bust of a Friend; Study in Curves; Gossip on Thursday; Cooking on Saturday; Cousin on Friday; Mana on Wednesday; The Redcap; The Runner; Figure Reclining; The Fish Man; Parson on Sunday; Puff Sleeves; The Workmen; Head.*

Exhibited: William D. Cox Galleries, Richmond, Va.; Harmon Foundation, 1933, 1935; Richmond (Va.) Academy of Arts, 1935 (1-man); NJ State Museum, Trenton, 1935; College Art Assn., 1934; Amer. Negro Exposition, Chicago, 1940; Texas Centennial Exposition, 1936; Smithsonian Institution, 1933; Valentine Museum, Richmond, Va., 1935; Va. Artist Exhibition, 1934.

Awards: Harmon Foundation, 1933.

Sources: Mallett. *Index of Artists; American Art Annual,* 1940-1; Harmon Foundation. *Exhibtion of Productions by Negro Artists;* Indiana Univ. *Fine Arts & the Black American;* Texas Centennial Exposition. *Thumbnail Sketches of Exhibiting Artists,* 1936; Porter. *Modern Negro Art;* Dover. *American Negro Art;* "Exhibition of Works by Negro Artists," *Washington Star,* Nov. 5, 1933; DuSable Museum of African-Amer. History. *Contemporary Black Artists,* 1970 Calendar; Tanner Art Galleries. *Art of the American Negro,* 1940; Brawley, Benjamin. *The Negro Genius;* Afro-American Slide Depository, 1971-2 Catalog; Harmon Foundation. *Negro Artists,* 1935; Harmon Foundation. *Select Picture List;* "Negro Artists Reveal Genius in Trenton Show," *Art Digest,* Apr. 15, 1935; Porter, James A. "Negro Art on Review," *American Magazine of Art,* Jan. 1934; Harley, Ralph, Jr. "Checklist of Afro-Amer. Art & Artists," *Serif,* Dec. 1970; Walker, Roslyn. *A Resource Guide to the Visual Arts of Afro-Americans,* South Bend, Ind., 1971; "Woodcarvings," *Opportunity,* Aug. 1937.

BOLTEN, LORRAINE

Painter. Born in Hampton, Virginia. Studied at the Institute of Chicago (BFA); School of Design, Illinois Institute of Technology (MFA). Instructor of Art at Hampton Institute.
Works: *Dance Linda.*
Exhibited: Winston-Salem (NC) Public Library, 1960 (1-man); Hampton Institute, 1960 (1-man); Panoras Gallery, NY, 1959, 1960; Washington Water Color Assn. Nat'l Exhibit, Washington, DC, 1961; Brockton Art Assn., Brockton, Mass., 1960, 1961; Winston-Salem Gallery of Fine Arts 5-State Show, 1961; New Directions Gallery, NY, 1960; Hunter Gallery Annual 5-State Show, Chattanooga, Tenn., 1960; The Studio, Newport News, Va., 1959; American Water Color Society National, NY, 1958; Art Institute of Chicago, 1943; Macmillan Gallery, NY, 1943; Internat'l Water Color Show, Chicago, 1942.
Collections: Johnson Pub. Co., Chicago.
Sources: A & T Univ. 15 *Afro-American Women;* Johnson Pub. Co. *The JPC Art Collection,* pamphlet.

BOLTON, SHIRLEY L.

Painter, educator, illustrator. Born in Lexington, Georgia on January 9, 1945. Studied at University of Georgia (BFA, 1966; MFA, 1970; Ed D, 1970). Assistant professor of art at University of West Florida, Pensacola.
Works: *Help the People in Cathy's World,* 1970 (acrylic); *Tenement,* 1970 (acrylic); *Black Man,* 1969 (oil); *The New Democracy,* 1971 (acrylic); *The World Outside,* 1971 (pencil); *Relics,* 1972 (pencil); *Theme & Variations,* 1971 (acrylic); *The Jazz Quintet; The Ghosts of Man; Jazz Strings; Expo; Neon; Urban III; Symphysis; Illusion; Tenement Series-Asunder, City, Renovation,* 1970 (acrylic); *Horizon; Images; Opus 1; Peace.*
Exhibitions: Atlanta Univ., 1964-70; Univ. of Georgia, 1970 (1-woman); Nat'l Exhibition Black Artists, Washington, DC, 1971; High

Museum of Art, Atlanta 1971, 1973; Carnegie Inst., 1971-2; Nat'l Bank of Washington, 1971; Newark Museum, 1972; Warbeke Gallery, Mt. Holyoke College, So. Hadley, Mass., 1972; So. Illinois Univ., 1972; Museum of Arts & Sciences, Macon, Georgia, 1972; Black Exposé, San Francisco, 1972; Florida Faculties Traveling Show, 1973; Banks-Haley Gallery, Albany, Georgia, 1973; Univ. of West Florida Gallery, 1973; The Citizens & Trust Bank Building, Atlanta, 1971; Smith-Mason Gallery, 1971.
Collections: Atlanta Univ. Negro Collection; Carnation Milk Co., Los Angeles; Univ. of Georgia; Johnson Pub. Co., Chicago; Georgia Commission on the Arts-High Museum, Atlanta.
Awards: Popular Ballot Award, painting, Atlanta Univ. Annual Exhibition, 1969; 2nd Award, painting, Atlanta Univ. Annual Exhibition, 1970; The James V. Herring Award in Painting, Nat'l Exhibition Black Artists, Washington, DC, 1971.
Member: Nat'l Conference of Artists; College Arts Assn. of America.
Represented by: Aronson-Midtown Gallery, Atlanta; The Creative Cancer Art Gallery, Atlanta.
Sources: Smith-Mason Gallery. *Nat'l Exhibition Black Artists* 1971; Kiah, Virginia. "Black Artist," *Savannah Magazine,* April 1972, p. 16; Johnson Pub. Co. *The JPC Art Collection;* Lewis/Waddy. *Black Artist on Art,* Vol. 2, 1971; Bolton, Shirley L. "Art as Creative Learning for the Rural Disadvantaged," *Studies in Art Education,* Winter 1969; Bolton, Shirley L. *Museum of Fine Arts Bulletin for Summer Institute Studies,* Atlanta Univ., 1970; Bolton, Shirley L. *Georgia Artists Magazine,* High Museum, Atlanta, 1971 (cover design); *The Atlanta Magazine,* Dec. 1972. *The Washington Post,* Nov. 7, 1971; Afro-American Slide Depository, Catalog; So. Illinois Univ. *Existence/Black,* Edwardsville, 1972.

BOND, MAX

Architect. Studied at Harvard School of Design. Practices in Atlanta, Georgia.
Works: Library, Bolgatanga, Ghana.
Sources: Rose, Barbara. "Black Art in America," *Art in America,* July-Dec. 1970.

BONNER, CHARLES

Painter, physician.
Sources: *Ebony,* Sept. 1951, pp. 29-33; Spralding, Mary M., ed. *In Black & White: Afro-Americans in Print,* 1971.

BORICAN, JOHN

Painter. Studied at Columbia University (MA). Deceased.
Works: *Portrait of John M. Gandy; Tiger Lilies.*

Sources: Rose, Lester. "Artful Athlete," *Negro Digest,* n.d.; "Amer. Negro Art Given Full Length Review in NY," *Art Digest,* Dec. 15, 1941; J.W.L. "Negro in Art," *Art News,* Dec. 19, 1941.

BOSTELLE, TOM
Painter.
Works: *Inside the Cave.*
Exhibited: 12th Annual Invitational Exhibition, Pyramid Club, Phila. 1952.
Sources: Drummond, Dorothy. "Coast-to-Coast," *Art Digest,* March 1, 1952, p. 12.

BOUGH, MARTIN
Photographer.
Exhibited: Addison Gallery, 1971.
Sources: James Van DerZee Institute. *The Black Photographer (1908-1970): A Survey.*

BOULDIN, SUSIE VERA
Artist, educator. Born in Centreville, Mississippi, April 16, 1888. Studied at Harper College, Gloster, Mississippi; Howe Institute, Memphis, Tennessee (1914); Western University, Kansas City, Kansas (1924); under John Patrick (1922-6). Art teacher at Summer Night School, Kansas City (1924-32); conducted Susie V. Bouldin Art School, Kansas City (1927-30); art teacher at Kansas Vocational School, Topeka, Kansas.
Member: National Chairman, Arts & Crafts Dept., National Assn. of Colored Women (1933-); Chairman, Arts & Crafts Dept., Central Assn.; National Assn. of Colored Women, (1924-); Chairman, Art Dept., Kansas Assn. (1923-33); Chairman, National Jr. Arts & Crafts Dept., National Assn. of Colored Women; Organizer, Wyandotte Co. Assn. of Colored Women, Kansas City; General Chairman, Norene Davis Memorial Committee; SVB Lovers of Art Club; Inter-City Dames Club; Business & Professional Women's Club; Progressive Literary Club; Chicago Art League.
Sources: *Who's Who in Colored America,* 3rd edition.

BOUSER, LULA BISSANT
Painter.
Works: *Swirls; Landscape; Man & The Universe; The Sea.*
Exhibited: Xavier Univ., 1963.
Sources: Xavier Univ. *Emancipation Proclamation Centennial National Art Exhibition,* 1963.

BOUTTÉ, RONALD
Painter, graphic artist. Born in Boston. Studied at Suffolk University; School of the Museum of Fine Arts, Boston.
Works: *Interior with Figures* (charcoal); *Untitled.*

Exhibited: Boston Museum of Fine Arts, 1970.
Awards: Ford Foundation; Clough Fund Scholarship; Dana Pond Prizes.
Sources: Boston Museum of Fine Arts. *Afro-American Artists: New York & Boston,* 1970; Gerson, Sareen R. "Black Art New York-Hub Set For Museum of Fine Arts," *Minuteman,* March 19, 1970.

BOWE, JOHN
Sculptor.
Exhibited: NJ State Museum, Trenton, 1935.
Sources: "Negro Artists Reveal Genius in Trenton Show," *Art Digest,* April 15, 1935.

BOWEN, JOYCE
Painter.
Works: *The Pool Shark; Boy Wonder.*
Exhibited: Wilson City College, Chicago, 1970.
Sources: "Expressions in Black," *Chicago Sun Times,* March 25, 1970.

BOWERS, DAVID BUSTILL
Painter. Born in Philadelphia on January 16, 1820. Died 1900. Self-taught. Started as a sign painter in Philadelphia. His works were primarily landscapes, portraits, marines and banners. Early works were emblems and banners for local firemen and organizations. Among his portraits are several of Abraham Lincoln who is believed to have sat for one of the originals. Bowers' relatives claim to own an unredeemed check to him in Lincoln's own hand.
Sources: Young. *Dictionary of Amer. Artists, Sculptors, & Engravers;* Runes/Schrickel. *Encyclopedia of the Arts,* pp. 36-7; Porter. *Modern Negro Art;* Brown, Marion. "The Negro in the Fine Arts," *The Negro Heritage Library,* Vol. 2.

BOWERS, LYNN
Painter, mixed media. Born in Canada, 1933. Studied at Art Students League (1958-9); New School of Social Research (1959).
Works: *Barbara First* (acrylic); *Barbara in Three Parts,* 1969; *Many Thought in Barbara; Move, Barbara, Move; My Barbara is Beautiful; Shape in Barbara; My Thought in Barbara; Untitled* (1968); *Untitled 1970; Many Thoughts in Barbara; My Barbara in Three; Untitled 1967; Untitled 1969.*
Exhibited: Martha Jackson Gallery; Rose Fired Gallery; Boston Museum of Fine Arts, 1970; Illinois Bell Telephone Traveling Show, 1971-2.
Collections: Mr. Benny Andrews.
Awards: John Hay Whitney finalist, 1964.
Sources: Boston Museum of Fine Arts. *Afro-American Artists: NY & Boston,* 1970; Afro-American Slide Depository, Catalog; Bourne, Kay. "Black Artists Shown at Museum," *Bay State Banner,* May 28, 1970; Van Almelo,

Frederik. "In the American Grain," *Boston After Dark,* May 26, 1970, p. 24; Illinois Bell Telephone. *Black American Artists/71,* 1972; Le Brun, Caron. "Black Art," *Herald Traveler,* Sunday Supplement, Boston, May 24, 1970.

BOWLING, FRANK

Painter, educator. Born in Guyana, 1936. Studied at Chelsea School of Art; London University; The Slade School; Royal College of Art. Teacher of art history at Massachusetts College of Art.
Works: *Mel Edwards Decides,* 1969 (oil); *Where Is Lucienne?,* 1970 (synthetic polymer on canvas); *Stations of the Cross from St. John's Street, New Amsterdam: Nos. 1 & 2.*
Exhibited: Grabowski Gallery, London, 1962 (1-man); First World Festival of Negro Art, Dakar, Senegal, 1966; Whitney Museum of American Art, 1966, 1971; Boston Museum of Fine Arts, 1970.
Collections: Whitney Museum of American Art.
Awards: Guggenheim Fellowship, 1967; Grand prize, First World Festival of Negro Art, 1966.
Sources: Boston Museum of Fine Arts. *Afro-American Artists: NY & Boston,* 1970; Doty. *Contemporary Black Artists in America;* "Black Art III," *Arts,* Dec. 1969/Jan. 1970; "Discussion on Black Art II," *Arts,* May 1969; "The Rupture: Ancestor Worship, Revival, Confusion, or Disguise," *Arts,* Summer 1970; "Silence: People Die Crying When They Should Love," *Arts,* Sept./Oct. 1970; Bloom, Janet. "5+1," *Arts,* Dec. 1969/Jan. 1970, p. 56; Kramer, Hilton. "Is Politics Submerging Black Art," *Courier Journal & Times,* Louisville, Ky., June 7, 1970; Van Almelo, Frederik. "In the American Grain," *Boston After Dark,* May 26, 1970, p. 24; Bowling, Frank. "It's Not Enough to Say 'Black Is Beautiful'," *Art News,* April 1971.

BOYD, DAVID PATTERSON

Painter. Born in St. Louis, Missouri in 1913. Studied in public schools; no formal art training.
Works: *The St. Louis Blues; Landscape; Still Life; The Voodoo.*
Exhibited: St. Louis Public Library, 1929-32; Harmon Exhibits, 1928, 1933, 1935; St. Louis Urban League; Negro Exposition.
Awards: 2nd Prize, Negro Exhibit of the St. Louis Urban League.
Sources: Indiana Univ. *Fine Arts & The Black American;* Harmon Foundation. *Exhibition of Productions by Negro Artists;* Harmon Foundation. *Non-Jury Exhibit of Works of Negro Artists,* 1933; Harmon Foundation. *Negro Artists,* 1935; Harley, Ralph, Jr. "A Checklist of Afro-Amer. Art & Artists," *The Serif,* Dec.

1970; DuSable Museum of African-Amer. History. *Contemporary Black Artists,* calendar, 1970; Walker, Roslyn. *A Resource Guide to the Visual Arts of Afro-Americans,* South Bend, Ind., 1971.

BOYKIN, CLOYD LEE

Painter. Born 1877 in Hampton, Massachusetts.
Exhibited: Harmon Foundation, 1925, 1931; NY Public Library, 1921.
Sources: Harmon Foundation. *Negro Artists.* Catalog, 1925; Harmon Foundation. *Exhibit of Productions by Negro Artists;* Indiana Univ. *Fine Arts & the Black American;* NY Public Library. *Catalog of the Negro Arts Exhibit,* 1921; Harley, Ralph, Jr. "Checklist of Afro-American Artists," *The Serif,* Dec. 1970; DuSable Museum of African-American History. *Contemporary Black Artists,* "Cloyd L. Boykin," *Crisis,* July 1913, p. 119; "African Art—Harlem," *American Magazine of Art,* Oct. 1932, p. 244; Walker, Roslyn. *A Resource Guide to the Visual Arts of Afro-Americans,* South Bend, Ind., 1971.

BOYKIN, ETHEL L.

Painter. Worked in Atlanta.
Works: *View from the Window* (watercolor).
Exhibited: Atlanta Univ., 1944.
Sources: Atlanta Univ. Exhibition files.

BRACEY, HENRY

Painter. Studied at Shaw University.
Works: Untitled watercolor.
Exhibited: Sun Times/Daily News Gallery, Chicago, 1970.
Sources: United Negro College Fund. *Art 1970,* Chicago, 1970.

BRACKETT, M.

Ceramist.
Works: *Vase, California Peppers in Gold; Vase, Wysteria; Bon Bon Box, Hard Enamel; Compote; Pitcher; Cup, Saucer, enamel.*
Exhibited: Art Inst. of Chicago, 1927.
Sources: Art Inst. of Chicago. *The Negro in Art Week,* 1927.

BRADFORD, DAVID PHILIP

Painter, educator. Born in Chicago, 1937. Studied at Chicago Art Institute; Otis Art Institute, Los Angeles; Lincoln University (BS, 1963); University of California at Berkeley (MS). Teacher of art at Grove Street Community College; University of California at Berkeley.
Works: *Yes, Leroi; Untitled* (oil); *Pride; Portrait of Alvin Ayler* (dwg.); *Portrait of Emamu Baraka* (dwg.); *Self-Portrait* (dwg.); *Portrait of Angela Davis* (dwg.); *Portrait of Don L. Lee* (dwg.); *Portrait of Lela Wafer* (dwg.).

Exhibited: Missouri State Fair; Atlanta Univ.; National Conference of Artists, 1962; Oakland Museum; Virginia Museum; Quay Gallery, San Francisco; Worth Ryder Gallery of UC, Berkeley; Lakeside Gallery, Chicago; Brockman Gallery; Watts Community Art Center (one-man); Watts Festival, Chicago.
Awards: 1st place, Missouri State Fair, 1962; 1st place, Chicago, 1968; 2nd place, Atlanta Univ., 1962; 2nd place, National Conference of Artists, 1962; Watts Festival, 1970-1.
Represented by: Brockman Gallery, Los Angeles.
Sources: Oakland Museum. *Black Untitled II,* 1971; DuSable Museum of African-Amer. History. *Contemporary Black Artists,* 1970, calendar; Indiana Univ. *Fine Arts & the Black American;* Lewis/Waddy. *Black Artists on Art,* Vol. 1; Brockman Gallery. Press release, April 19, 1971; Harley, Ralph, Jr. "A Checklist of Afro-Amer. Art & Artists," *The Serif,* Dec. 1970; Bradford, David. *Portraits in Black: Portfolio of Recent Drawings,* Los Angles, Brockman Gallery; Walker, Roslyn. *A Resource Guide to the Visual Arts of Afro-Americans,* South Bend, Ind., 1971; Oakland Museum. *New Perspectives in Black Art.*

BRADLEY, OMAR
Photographer.
Exhibited: Addison Gallery, 1971.
Sources: James Van DerZee Institute. *The Black Photographer (1908-1970): Survey*

BRADLEY, PETER
Painter. Born September 15, 1940 in Connellsville, Pennsylvania. Studied Cranbrook Academy, Bloomfield, Michigan (BA, 1963); Society of Arts and Crafts, Detroit; Yale University.
Works: *M.F.R.,* 1968 (oil); *Mutourni Maki.*
Exhibited: Yale Univ., 1968; USIA Exhibit of American Print Makers, USSR, 1966; Museum of Modern Art, NY, 1966; Detroit Institute of Arts, 1962; Minneapolis Institute of Arts, 1968; High Museum of Art, Atlanta, 1969; Flint (Mich.) Institute of Arts, 1970; Everson Museum of Art, Syracuse, NY, 1970; IBM Gallery of Arts & Sciences, NY, 1970; Rhode Island School of Design, 1969; The Memorial Art Gallery, Rochester, NY, 1969; San Francisco Museum of Art, 1969; Contemporary Arts Museum, Houston, 1970; NJ State Museum, 1970; Roberson Center for the Arts & Sciences, Binghamton, NY, 1970; The Art Galleries, Univ. of Cal. at Santa Barbara, 1970.
Collections: Metropolitan Museum of Art, NY; Museum of Modern Art, NY; Joseph H. Hirshhorn Collection; Mr. & Mrs. Thomas H. Benenson; Mr. Daniel Robbins; Ms. Mary Frances Rand; Mrs. Caroline S. Lerner.

Sources: Yale University Art Gallery. *Painters of Yale,* 1968; USIA. *American Print Makers,* 1966; Museum of Modern Art. *Young Print Makers,* NY, 1966; Detroit Institute of Arts. *Michigan Annual,* 1962; Minneapolis Institute of Arts. *30 Contemporary Black Artists,* 1968; Ruder & Finn Fine Arts. *Contemporary Black Artists,* 1969; Harley, Ralph, Jr. "A Checklist of Afro-American Art and Artists," *The Serif,* Dec. 1970; Schatz, Walter, ed. *Directory of Afro-American Resources,* 1970; Myers, Carol L. *Black Power in the Arts,* Flint, Mich., 1970.

BRADLEY, WILLIAM
Works: *Mutsumi Maki.*
Collections: Metropolitan Museum.
Sources: Afro-American Slide Depository, Catalog, 1971-72.

BRAHMIN, J. I.
Collections: NY Public Library, Schomburg Art Collection.
Sources: Schatz, Walter. *Directory of Afro-American Resources,* 1970.

BRANCH, HARRISON
Photographer. Born in New York City, June 6, 1947. Studied at San Francisco Art Institute.
Works: *A-Brother; Two Old Cars; Rocks & Grass; Torn Posters; Fire Hydrant & Wall; Scribbling & a Pipe; Clubhouse; Soul Sister; Steam & Rocks; Broken Door; The Couch.*
Exhibited: Oakland Museum, Kaiser Center, 1968; Western Addition Library, San Francisco, 1967 (1-man); Merritt Campus, Peralta College, 1967.
Collections: Oakland Museum.
Sources: Oakland Museum. *New Perspectives in Black Art,* 1968; Harley, Ralph, Jr. "Checklist of Afro-Amer. Art & Artists," *The Serif,* Dec. 1970.

BRANDFORD, EDWARD JOSCELYN
Painter. Born in Jamaica, British West Indies, 1905. Studied at Barile School; Cooper Union.
Works: *Broken Toys.*
Exhibited: 135th St. Branch, NY Public Library (1-man); Harmon Foundation, 1931-1935.
Collections: National Archives.
Sources: Afro-American Slide Depository, catalog, 1971-2; Harmon Foundation. *Negro Artists,* 1935; Harmon Foundation. *Exhibition of Productions by Negro Artists;* Indiana Univ. *Fine Arts & the Black American;* DuSable Museum of African-Amer. History. *Contemporary Black Artists,* 1970 Calendar; Harmon Foundation Exhibit, *Art Digest,* Feb. 15, 1931; Harley, Ralph, Jr. "Checklist of Afro-Amer. Art & Artists," *Serif,* Dec. 1970; Walker, Roslyn.

A Resource to the Visual Arts of Afro-Americans, South Bend, Ind., 1971.

BRANDON, BRUMSIC, JR.
Graphic artist.
Works: *Sit In; The Non-Violent; The March; Picket; The Martyred; The Militant; Common Cold; Gossip; Understanding Man; Successful Man; Eligible Man; Man With Patience; Ambitious Man; Social Error; Growing Man; Adversary; Mourning the Martyred.*
Collections: Oakland (Cal.) Museum, Ruth Waddy Collection.
Sources: Roelof-Lanner, T.V. *Prints by American Negro Artists;* "Poison Pen Art: Washington GI Artist Develops Unique Oneline Drawings to Jibe Pointedly at Human Foibles," *Ebony,* July 1952, pp. 59-61; Oakland Museum Archives; Walker, Roslyn. *A Resource Guide to the Visual Arts of Afro-Americans,* South Bend, Ind., 1971.

BRANTLEY, JAMES
Painter. Born in Philadelphia in 1945.
Works: *Red, White, Green, and Black; Red, Black and Green; The Informer,* 1970 (oil); *Brother James; Dreams* (oil); *Peace, Peace* (oil); *War* (oil).
Exhibited: Whitney Museum, NY, 1971; Lee Cultural Center, Phila.
Collections: Pa. Academy of Fine Arts.
Sources: Phila. Division of Art. *Afro-American Artists 1800-1969;* Doty. *Contemporary Black Artists in America;* Afro-American Slide Depository, catalog, 1971-2; Phila. Dept. of Recreation. *Love . . . and the Black Community.*

BRAXTON, MILDRED A.
Painter. Born in Newport News, Virginia, 1930. Studied at Hampton Institute, Hampton, Virginia.
Sources: Dover. *American Negro Art,* p. 51; Harley, Ralph,, Jr. "Checklist of Afro-Amer. Art & Artists," *The Serif,* Dec. 1970.

BRAXTON, WILLIAM ERNEST
Painter, illustrator. Born in Washington, DC in 1878. Died in 1932. Studied at Adelphi University; and under John Barnard Whittaker. He was considered the first American Negro expressionist painter.
Works: *Figural Study; Seascape; Winter; The Good Book; Portraits of Aleksander Sergeevich Pushkin; D'Artagnan; Alexander Dumas; Placido; Ira Aldridge; Capitien Jacobus Eliza.*
Exhibited: Harmon Exhibits, 1928-9; Smithsonian Institution, 1929; NY Public Library, 1921; National Gallery of Art, 1929.
Collections: NY Public Library, Schomburg Collection.

Member: League of NY Artists; Society of Independent Artists.
Sources: Harmon Foundation. *Negro Artists,* 1935; Harmon Foundation. *Exhibit of Productions by Negro Artists;* Fielding. *Dictionary of Painters, Sculptors & Engravers; Mallett. Index of Artists;* Indiana Univ. *Fine Arts & the Black American;* City College of NY. *The Evolution of Afro-American Artists 1800-1950; American Art Annual,* 1933; DuSable Museum of African-Amer. History. *Contemporary Black Artists,* 1970 calendar; Smithsonian Institution. *Painting & Sculpture by American Negro Artists,* 1929; "Afro-American Artists 1800-1950," *Ebony,* Vol. 23, p. 116-22; Harley, Ralph, Jr. "A Checklist of Afro-Amer. Art & Artists," *The Serif,* Dec. 1970; *First Annual Exhibit of Books, Manuscripts, Paintings, Sculptures, etc. by The Negro Library Association.* Aug. 7-16, 1918; Schatz, Walter. *Directory of Afro-American Resources,* 1970; Myers, Carol. *Black Power in the Arts,* Flint, Mich., 1970; Walker, Roslyn. *A Resource Guide to the Visual Arts of Afro-Americans,* South Bend, Ind., 1971.

BREEDEN, LALOREE
Sculptor. Studied at Claflin College.
Exhibited: Sun Times/Daily News Gallery, Chicago, 1970.
Sources: United Negro College Fund. *Art 1970,* Chicago, 1970.

BRICE, CHARLES AUSTIN
Painter. Born in New York City, 1909. Studied at Cooper Union; Pratt Institute; Art Students League; National Academy of Design.
Works: *Houses, Trees and Clouds; Houses, Liberty Ave.; Seated Nude.*
Exhibited: Atlanta Univ., 1942, 1945; Dillard Univ., 1941; 135th St. YMCA, NY; 135th St. Public Library.
Awards: Honorable Mention, oil, Atlanta Univ., 1945.
Sources: Dillard Univ. *Arts Festival,* Catalog, 1941; Information from the artist; Woodruff, Hale. "Negro Artists Hold Fourth Annual in Atlanta," *Art Digest,* April 15, 1945.

BRIDGES, RUTH
Printmaker.
Works: *The Subway* (silk screen).
Exhibited: Lee Cultural Center, Phila.
Sources: Phila. Dept. of Recreation. *Love . . . and the Black Community.*

BRISCO, CLARENCE
Painter, mixed media.
Works: *Slave Auction; Black Smith Shop; Tina; Medium of Art.*
Exhibited: Xavier Univ., 1963.

Sources: Xavier Univ. *Emancipation Proclamation Centennial National Art Exhibition,* 1963.

BRITT, ARTHUR L., SR.

Painter, educator. Born in Cuthbert, Georgia, 1934. Studied at Winston-Salem College, under Hayward Oubre; University of Japan, under Dr. Tomosa; Art Academy, Los Angeles, under Walter Khulmann; University of New Mexico (MS, 1965); Alabama State College (BS, 1959). Teacher at Savannah State; served as Acting Chairman, Art Department, Southern University, New Orleans.

Works: *Swamp; The Dream; Gradually Dreams; At Last; Demonstration; Little & Big Black Image; Black Cat; The Dawn Is Breaking; Blacker Grass across the Fence; Our Social Jungle; Corrupt Political Brain; The Love Maker; The Dream—The Story of Dr. King's Life; Black Athlete Excellency; The Big House; In the Beginning #1; In the Beginning #2; Broken Fence; Our Social Web; The Black Remains; Swamp #1; Swamp #2; Burned, Baby It's Burned; Our Social Struggle; Swamp Five; Entanglement; It's Nation Time; Miss Duck; Looking Out; The Black Movement; The Family; Swamp Fire.*

Exhibited: Southern Univ., Baton Rouge & New Orleans; College Art Gallery, Baton Rouge; Ala. State College, Montgomery; Sumter County Training School, Livingston, Ala.; Calloway School, Birmingham, Ala.; Carver High School, Birmingham; Nenival Baptist Church, Birmingham; Univ. of N Mex.; Crystal Caves, Birmingham; Lincoln Univ., Jefferson City, Mo.; Dillard Univ., New Orleans; Stillman College, Tuscaloosa, Ala.; Mountain Brook Presbyterian Church; Miss. Valley State College, Itta Bena; Indiana Univ.; Capital City, Santa Fe, New Mexico; Ala. State College Library; Atlanta Univ.; Louisiana State Univ., New Orleans; Savannah State College; Maryland State College; Pittsburgh Talking Theater; Smith-Mason Gallery, Washington, DC; Voorhees College, Denmark, SC; Rainbow Sign Gallery, Berkeley, 1971; High Museum, Atlanta; Birmingham (Ala.) Festival; Glo Gallery, Accra, Ghana; Kiah Museum, Savannah; Citizen Trust Bank, Atlanta; Virginia State College.

Collections: Savannah State College; Atlanta Univ.; Lincoln Univ., Jefferson City, Mo.; Miss. Valley State College, Itta Bena; Univ. of N Mex., Alburquerque; Ala. State College; Mr. & Mrs. Thomas Noland, Birmingham, Ala.; Dean Emmett W. Bashful, Southern Univ., New Orleans; Mrs. Julian Johnson, Eurarla, Ala.; Mr. & Mrs. W. R. Lawson, Abbeville, Ala.; Stillman College, Tuscaloosa, Ala.; Dr. Anthony Donfor, Southern Univ., New Orleans; Pres. of Md. State College; Kiah Museum, Savannah; Glo Gallery, Accra, Ghana; Dr. Prince A. Jackson, Jr.

Awards: WVa. State College National Conference Artist Merit Award; 1st prize, sculpture, Atlanta Univ.; Savannah State College National Conference Artist Merit Award; Outstanding Service Award, Chicago, 1972; Man of the Year Award, Savannah State College; Outstanding Service Award, National Links; 1st prize, Crystal Caves.

Sources: Rainbow Sign Gallery. *Black Arts Day II,* Press Release, Berkeley, 1972; Lewis/Waddy. *Black Artists on Art,* Vol. 1; Afro-American Slide Depository, Catalog; Smith-Mason Gallery. *National Exhibition Black Artists,* 1971; Kiah, Virginia. "Black Artists," *Savannah,* April 1972; *National Conference of Artists,* Winter 1971; Atkinson, J. E. *Black Dimensions in Contemporary Art; Atlanta Journal,* 1966-7; Walker, Roslyn. *A Resource Guide to the Visual Arts of Afro-Americans,* South Bend, Ind., 1971.

BRITT, AVERY L.

Sources: Harley, Ralph, Jr. "Checklist of Afro-Amer. Art & Artists," *The Serif,* Dec. 1970.

BRITT, BENJAMIN

Painter, printmaker. Born in Philadelphia in 1923.

Works: *Taurus; Alpha; A House Divided; Yield Not; Adolescence* (oil); *Environment* (oil).

Exhibited: State Armory, Wilmington, Del., 1971; Smith-Mason Gallery, 1971; Xavier Univ., 1963; Lee Cultural Center, Phila.

Sources: Dover. *American Negro Art,* p. 51; Indiana Univ. *Fine Arts & The Black American;* Phila. Division of Art. *Afro-Amer. Artists 1800-1969;* Aesthetic Dynamics. *Afro-Amer. Images 1971;* Smith-Mason Gallery. *National Exhibition Black Artists,* 1971; Kiah, Virginia. "Black Artists," *Savannah Magazine,* April 1972; Xavier Univ. *Emancipation Proclamation Centennial National Art Exhibition,* 1963; Harley, Ralph, Jr. "Checklist of Afro-Amer. Art & Artists," *The Serif,* Dec. 1970; Phila. Dept. of Recreation. *Love . . . and the Black Community;* Walker, Roslyn. *A Resource Guide to the Visual Arts of Afro-Americans,* South Bend, Ind., 1971.

BRITTON, JOHN

Graphic artist.

Works: *Jesus Before Pontius Pilate.*

Represented by: Blackman's Art Gallery, San Francisco.

Sources: *Black Shades,* Vol. 3, #2.

BRITTON, SYLVESTER

Painter, printmaker. Born in Chicago, Illinois in 1926. Studied at the Art Institute of Chi-

cago; School of Painting & Sculpture, Mexico City; Academie de la Grande Chaumière, Paris.
Works: *Across the Land; Untitled woodcut.*
Exhibited: Oak Park Library, Ill.; Atlanta; Paris; Art Institute of Chicago; Stockholm.
Awards: Eisendrath Prize, Art Institute of Chicago, 1956.
Collections: Oakland Museum.
Sources: Oak Park Library. *Exhibition of Black Artists;* Dover. *American Negro Art,* p. 51; Roelof-Lanner, T.V., ed. *Prints by American Negro Artists;* "Afro-American Issue," *Art Gallery,* April 1968; Indiana Univ. *Fine Arts & the Black American;* DuSable Museum of African-Amer. History. *Contemporary Black Artists,* 1970 calendar; Nat'l Conference of Artists. *A Print Portfolio by Negro Artists;* Art Institute of Chicago. *Scrapbook of Art & Artists of Chicago,* 1956, p. 48; Harley, Ralph, Jr. "Checklist of Afro-Amer. Art & Artists," *The Serif,* Dec. 1970; Myers, Carol L. *Black Power in the Arts,* Flint, Mich., 1970; Oakland Museum Archives; Walker, Roslyn. *A Resource Guide to the Visual Arts of Afro-Americans,* South Bend, Ind., 1971.

BROCK, KING
Sources: Harley, Ralph, Jr. "Checklist of Afro-Amer. Art & Artists," *The Serif,* Dec. 1970.

BROOKE, RICHARD MORRIS
Sources: "A Pastoral Visit," *Washington Star,* July 18, 1936; Harley, Ralph, Jr. "Checklist of Afro-Amer. Art & Artists," *The Serif,* Dec. 1970.

BROOKINS, MARCIA J.
Painter, printmaker, educator. Born in St. Paul, Minnesota, 1947. Studied at Howard University (BFA); University of Hartford (MEd).
Works: *African Masks,* 1969 (silkscreen); *Mama Na Wototo (Mother and Children),* 1971 (scratchboard); *Hair,* 1970 (oil).
Exhibited: Community Gallery, Wadsworth Atheneum, Hartford, 1970, 1971; North Hartford Community Art Exhibit, 1970.
Awards: Blue ribbon & cash prize, graphics, Through Young Black Eyes, 1970; 2nd prize, drawing, Through Young Black Eyes, 1971.
Member: Artists' Studio Workshop, Hartford.
Sources: Information from the artist.

BROOKS, BERNARD W.
Studied at University of Maryland; Philadelphia Museum College of Art; Corcoran Gallery School of Art; Howard University. Illustrator, American Chemical Society.
Works: *Two Different Worlds.*
Exhibited: Exhibition '71, Washington, DC, 1971; National Hospital Week, Alexandria Hospital Art Show; National Capitol Dental Assistants Art Show; Cornell Univ. Women's Club Art Show; Howard Univ. Student Art Shows; Corcoran Gallery of Art 18th Area Exhibit; Woodridge Civic Assn. Art Show; Neighbors, Inc. Art Show; Capital Plaza Fine Arts Gallery; Group Showing by Attorneys Alan Mendelsohn, Herman Levy; Amer. Chemical Society Art Show; Alexandria Plaza Art Show; United Planning Organization Art Show; Montgomery Mall Art Show; Taylor Ray Fine Arts Galleries (1-man); Home Studio.
Awards: 1st place, DC Recreation Outdoor Art Show, Professional Division-Watercolors; 2nd place, Montgomery Mall Art Show; Honorable mention, Corcoran Gallery of Art 18th Area Exhibit; 2nd place, Amer. Cancer Society Poster Contest; 2nd place, Washington Post Christmas Painting Contest.
Collections: Secretary to Congressman Thomas Foley; NYC Mission Society; Mr. Murray Socolof, president of Grand Union Food Co.
Sources: DC Art Assn. *Exhibition '71,* Washington, DC, 1971.

BROOKS, DAISY CHAPMAN
Painter. Born in Virginia. Studied at Hampton Institute; Pratt Institute, New York.
Works: *The Country Home.*
Exhibited: Harmon Foundation, 1930-1935; National Gallery of Art, 1930.
Collections: National Archives.
Sources: Harmon Foundation. *Exhibition of Productions by Negro Artists;* Indiana Univ. *Fine Arts & the Black American;* DuSable Museum of African-American History. *Contemporary Black Artists,* Calendar, 1970; Harmon Foundation. *Negro Artists,* 1935; Harley, Ralph L., Jr. "A Checklist of Afro-Amer. Art & Artists," *The Serif,* Dec. 1970; Walker, Roslyn. *A Resource Guide to the Visual Arts of Afro-Americans,* South Bend, Ind., 1971.

BROOKS, HOWARD
Painter.
Works: *Two Young Men By the Sea.*
Exhibited: McMillen Inc. Galleries, NY, 1941.
Sources: McMillen Inc. Galleries. *Contemporary Negro Art,* NY, 1941.

BROOKS, MABEL RANDOLPH
Painter, designer of tapestries. Born 1899 in Maryland. Studied at Radcliffe College; studied mural painting at Yale School of Fine Arts.
Works: *The Dancers.*
Exhibited: Harmon Exhibit, 1930.
Sources: Harmon Foundation. *Exhibition of Productions by Negro Artists;* Harmon Foundation. *Exhibit of Fine Arts,* 1930; Indiana Univ. *Fine Arts & the Black American;* Harley, Ralph, Jr. "Checklist of Afro-American Art & Artists," *The Serif,* Dec. 1970; Brooks,

Mabel. "The Autobiography of an Artist," *Crisis,* Feb. 1932; Walker, Roslyn. *A Resource Guide to the Visual Arts of Afro-Americans,* South Bend, Ind., 1971.

BROOKS-EL, ORASTON
Painter, commercial artist, photographer, designer. Born in Brooklyn, New York on July 18, 1937.
Works: 12 murals, US Army Mess Hall, Hanau, Germany; murals, Post Theater, Hanau, Germany; *Miles Davis; Les Ballets Africans; Hands; Self Portrait; Voo Doo; The Rage; Cubano Chant; Indian Summer; Carolyn Ward; Diablo; Spartacus;* illustrations for Caedmon Records, 1966-1972.
Exhibitions: Churchill Restaurant, 1960; Fulton Art Fair, 1959-1972.
Sources: Information from artist.

BROWN, CHARLES E.
Works: *Determination.*
Sources: Phila. Division of Art. *Afro-American Artists 1800-1969.*

BROWN, CLEMSON
Sculptor. Born in Lancaster, South Carolina in 1939. Studied at City College (1966-8). Coordinator of Cultural Activities, Police Athletic League.
Works: *Cactus Flower; Man in Search.*
Exhibited: Bowery Savings Bank (1-man); Studio Museum in Harlem, 1969.
Sources: Studio Museum in Harlem. *Harlem Artists 69.*

BROWN, DAVID SCOTT
Painter. Born in Greenwich, Connecticut, 1931. Studied at Pratt Institute.
Works: *Three Jazz Musicians; Delat Cab; Gospel Singers.*
Exhibited: Market Place Gallery; Greenwich Library Gallery; Studio Museum, Harlem, 1969; NY Newspaper Guild, 1957; Greenwich Society of Artists; Brooklyn Museum.
Awards: Best in Show, NY Newspaper Guild; Best in Show, Greenwich Society of Artists, 1958.
Sources: *Market Place Gallery* Catalog; Studio Museum in Harlem. *Harlem Artists 69;* Brooklyn College. *Afro-American Artists: Since 1950,* 1969.

BROWN, DIANA L.
Painter. Born in New York, 1946. Studied at AAS Junior College; City College.
Works: *Mischievous Teenager; Freedom; Untitled; Yesterday & Today; Struggles.*
Exhibited: St. Mark's AME Church, 1968; 5th Annual Harlem Outdoor Art Festival, 1968; Nyumba Ya Sanaa, 1968; Research Committee of African Amer. Art.

BROWN, EDITH
Painter. Born in Akron, Ohio. Teacher at Akron Art Institute.
Exhibited: Akron Art Institute, 1965; Packard Gallery, 1968; Bennett College, Greensboro, NC; Group Shows at Akron Spring Show, Cleveland Museum, Butler Museum and Cuyahoga Falls Art Show.
Awards: Akron Spring Shows.
Collections: Akron Art Institute; Akron National Bank; Akron Public Library; Madison Architects, Cleveland.
Sources: A & T University Lyceum Program. *15 Afro-American Women.*

BROWN, ELMER W.
Painter, educator, decorator, cartoonist, illustrator, designer. Born in Pittsburgh, 1909. Studied at Cleveland School of Art under Paul Travis; John Huntington Polytechnic Institute. Teacher at the Playhouse Settlement, Cleveland.
Works: *Freedom of Expression; Candy Dancers; Cross Section* (batik); *Spotlight;* Costumes for Cleveland Summer Operas; Sets for Gilpin Players of Cleveland for PORGY and EMPEROR JONES.
Sources: Dover. *American Negro Art; Who's Who in American Art,* 1940-41; Mallett. *Index of Artists;* Indiana Univ. *Fine Arts & the Black American;* DuSable Museum of African-Amer. History. *Contemporary Black Artists,* 1970; Roucek/Kiernan. *The Negro Impact on Western Civilization;* "Negro Art from Cleveland's Karamu House," *Art Digest,* Jan. 15, 1942; Porter. *Modern Negro Art;* Harley, Ralph, Jr. "Checklist of Afro-Amer. Art & Artists," *Serif,* Dec. 1970; *The Negro Handbook,* Composed by Editors of *Ebony,* Chicago, 1966; "Zell Ingram, Painter of 'America's Most Tragic Figure,' Talks about Mothers," *New York Post,* Jan. 13, 1942; Walker, Roslyn. *A Resource Guide to the Visual Arts of Afro-Americans,* South Bend, Ind., 1971.

BROWN, EUGENE JESSE
Painter. Worked in Langston, Oklahoma.
Works: *Old Ice Plant; Bachelor's Shack; Town Hall.*
Exhibited: Atlanta University, 1943, 1944, 1951.
Sources: Harley, Ralph, Jr. "Checklist of Afro-Amer. Art & Artists," *The Serif,* Dec. 1970.

BROWN, FRED
Painter. Born in Conway, Arkansas, 1941. Studied at City College of San Francisco.
Exhibited: Blackman's Gallery; San Francisco Art Festival, 1968.
Sources: Lewis/Waddy. *Black Artists on Art,* Vol. 1.

BROWN, GENA MAY

Sources: Harley, Ralph, Jr. "Checklist of Afro-Amer. Artists," *The Serif,* Dec. 1970.

BROWN, GLORIA JEANNE

Filmmaker, ceramist, exhibit designer and specialist. Born in Easton, Pennsylvania, 1948. Studied at Fisk University (BA); Smithsonian Institution Summer Program.
Works: *Rain Drinkers; Under Water Jelly Forms.*
Exhibited: Vanderbilt Univ., 1970; Checkwood Fine Arts Center, 1969; Peabody College, 1971; Smithsonian Institution & Children's Museum, 1968-70; Utica College, NY; Fisk Univ.
Collections: Fisk Univ. Art Dept., Nashville; Sengstacke Collection, Chicago.
Awards: High School Sr. Award in Art; College Sr. Award in Art; Smithsonian Institution Summer Scholarship, 1968; Artist-in-residence, Children's Museum, Nashville, 1970.
Sources: Information from artist; Smithsonian Institution. *Color Me Mankind,* Washington, DC, 1968.

BROWN, GRAFTON TYLER

Painter, graphic artist. First Negro artist in California. Active between 1860's and 1880's in California, Nevada Territory and the Pacific Northwest. Worked for Kuchel and Dresel, San Francisco lithographers.
Works: *Grand Canyon of the Yellowstone from Hayden Point* (oil); *Mount Tacoma (Mt. Ranier, Washington),* 1885 (oil).
Exhibited: Oakland Museum, 1972.
Collections: Oakland Museum.
Sources: Oakland Museum Archives; Groce, George C., & David H. Wallace. *NY Historical Society's Dictionary of Artists in America;* Peters, Harry T. *California on Stone,* Garden City, 1935; Stokes, I. N. Phelps, & Daniel C. Haskell. *American Historical Prints,* NY Public Library, 1933.

BROWN, HILDA WILKINSON

Painter, educator. Born in Washington, DC. Studied at Howard University Miner Teachers' College; Columbia University; National Academy of Design; Cooper Union. Instructor of art at Miner Teachers' College.
Works: *Still Life with Tulips.*
Exhibited: Howard Univ., 1932, 1937; 1st Annual Metropolitan State Art Contest, US National Museum, 1936; 2nd Independent Art Exhibit, 1936; Texas Centennial Exposition, 1936.
Collections: Howard Univ.
Sources: Howard Univ. *Art of the American Negro,* 1937; Texas Centennial Exposition. *Thumbnail Sketches of Exhibiting Artists,* 1936; Harley, Ralph, Jr. "Checklist of Afro-Amer. Art & Artists," *Serif,* Dec. 1970.

BROWN, HUNTLEY

Painter, educator. Born in New York City, 1924. Studied at City College of New York (BA, Art Education, 1952); Columbia University (MA, Fine Arts & Art Education, 1958). Art teacher, New York City Board of Education.
Works: *Cane Field Workers.*
Exhibited: Nicholas Roerich Museum; Lynn Kottler Galleries, NY; Institute of Jamaica (WI); Studio Museum in Harlem, 1969.
Sources: Studio Museum in Harlem. *Harlem Artists 69.*

BROWN, KEN

Photographer.
Works: *Love Yesterday; Love Tomorrow.*
Exhibited: Lee Cultural Center, Phila.
Sources: Phila. Dept. of Recreation. *Love . . . and the Black Community.*

BROWN, MALCOLM M.

Painter.
Works: *Bayou Fishing Party.*
Exhibited: Smith-Mason Gallery, 1971.
Sources: Smith-Mason Gallery. *National Exhibition Black Artists,* 1971.

BROWN, MARJORIE WHEELER

Painter.
Works: *Dahlias; Red Gladiolas; Magnolia Blossoms; Night Flower; Pink Peonies; Flowering Primrose; The City Is a Pattern.*
Exhibited: Atlanta Univ., 1942-4.
Sources: Woodruff, Hale. "Negro Artists Hold Fourth Annual in Atlanta," *Art Digest,* Apr. 15, 1945; *Art News,* Apr. 15, 1945, pp. 8-9; Harley, Ralph, Jr. "Checklist of Afro-Amer. Art & Artists," *Serif,* Dec. 1970.

BROWN, MARVIN P.

Painter, educator. Born in New York City, 1943. Studied at Brooklyn Museum Art School (1961-2); Philadelphia Museum College of Art (BFA, 1965); Indiana University School of Fine Arts (1965-6). Teacher at Brooklyn Museum; Brooklyn Institute of Arts and Sciences.
Works: *Saratoga's Memory,* 1969 (liquetex); Untitled synthetic polymer & oil on canvas, 1970; *Location Piece; Undertow.*
Exhibited: Whitney Museum of Amer. Art, 1969-72; Boston Museum of Fine Arts, 1970; Silvermine Guild of Artists, 1962; Phila. Art Alliance, 1963; Cheltenham Gallery, 1964, 1965; Univ. of Ky., 1965; Western Mich. Univ., 1966; Butler Institute of Amer. Art, 1966; Purdue Univ., 1966; Dorsky Gallery, 1966; The Guild Hall, East Hampton, NY, 1967, 1969; NY State Fair; Eastern Mich. Univ., 1968, 1970; Univ. of Cincinnati, 1970; Thorne Art Gallery, Keene State College, NH, 1970; Van

Alstyne Gallery, Horace Mann School, NY, 1971; Museum of Modern Art, 1971; Finch College, 1971; Phila. College of Art, 1971; O.K. Harris Gallery, NY, 1971; Katonah (NY) Gallery, 1971; Univ. of Tenn., 1972; Newark Museum, 1972; Hudson River Museum, 1972; Univ. of Rhode Island, 1972; Richmond (Cal.) Art Center, 1972.

Awards: Purchase Grant-in-Aid, Warner-Lambert Pharmaceutical Co., Morris Plains, NJ; Yale-Norfolk Fellowship; Irma Rosenau Prize, 18th Annual Award Show, Cheltenham (Pa.) Gallery, 1965; Max Beckmann Scholarship, Brooklyn Museum Art School, 1965; Purchase Award, Second National Polymer Exhibition, Eastern Mich. Univ., 1968; Fellowship, Edward MacDowell Assn., 1970.

Sources: Boston Museum of Fine Arts. *Afro-American Artists: NY & Boston*, 1970; Doty. *Contemporary Black Artists in America*; Rose, Barbara. "Black Art in America," *Art in America*, July/Dec. 1970; Glueck, Grace. "Black Show under Fire at the Whitney," *New York Times*, Jan. 31, 1971; Kramer, Hilton. "Is Politics Submerging Black Art?," *Courier Journal & Times*, Louisville, Ky., June 7, 1970; Ratcliffe, Carter. "The Whitney Annual, Part I," *Art Forum*, Apr. 1972, pp. 28-32; Swan, Bradford F. "At the Fine Arts Center," *Providence Journal*, Aug. 6, 1972; Information from artist.

BROWN, RICHARD LONSDALE

Painter. Born 1886; died 1915.

Exhibited: NY Public Library, 1921; Tanner Art League, 1922; Harmon Exhibition, 1936.

Sources: *Encyclopedia of Art*; DuSable Museum of African-American History & Art. *Contemporary Black Artists*, 1970 Calendar; *Negro Yearbook*; Indiana Univ. *Fine Arts & the Black American*; Pierre-Noel, Lois Jones. "American Negro Art in Progress," *Negro History Bulletin*, Oct. 1967; "Rising Colored Painter Loyal to His Art," *Christian Science Monitor*, Clippings LXVIII-LXIX; Maclean, Mary D. "Richard Lonsdale Brown," *Crisis*, Apr. 1912; Porter. *Modern Negro Art*; Porter, James. "Negro Artists Gain Recognition after Long Battle," *Pittsburgh Courier*, July 29, 1950; Brawley, Benjamin. *The Negro in Literature & Art in the US*; *1st Annual Exhibit of Books, Manuscripts, Paintings, Sculptures, etc. by the Negro Library Assn. at Carlton Ave. YMCA*, Aug. 7-16, 1918; "Richard Lonsdale Brown," *Crisis*, Jan. 1918, p. 128; Holbrook, Francis C. "A Group of Negro Artists," *Opportunity*, July 1923, pp. 211-3; Walker, Roslyn. *A Resource Guide to the Visual Arts of Afro-Americans*, South Bend, Ind., 1971.

BROWN, SAMUEL JOSEPH

Painter, printmaker, educator, sculptor, mixed media. Born in Wilmington, North Carolina, 1907. Studied at Pennsylvania Museum School of Industrial Art; Teachers College of University of Pennsylvania. Teacher at Bok Vocational School, Philadelphia.

Works: *The Picnic; Mrs. Simmons; We Thank Thee Lord; Impressions of Mexico; Global War; Global Peace; Illustrations ' for Text; Unite Mankind; Food for Israel; Portrait of Fiske Kimball; Portrait of Robert Krewsen; Portrait of Elmer Briggs; Portrait of William Donavan; Portrait of Dr. George F. Ellison; Portrait of Councilman James H. Irvin; Universal Madonna; Devil May Care; Moon Women; Temperance; Prudence; Abstraction III; A Child's Prayer; The Scrubwoman; A Writing Lesson; Little Black Girl; Maryella; Le Passe* (mixed); *Male or Female* (oil).

Exhibited: Pa. College of Art, 1933 (1-man); Barnet Aden Galleries, Washington, DC, 1946; Art Alliance, 1946-7; Bryn Mawr Baptist Church, 1966; River Park Apt. Community Gallery, Phila., 1968; John Wanamaker Store Gallery, 1969; WPA Art Project, Howard Univ., 1935; Univ. of Pa., 1936; Temple Univ., 1936; Phila. Museum of Art, 1937; Baltimore Museum of Art, 1937; Museum of Modern Art, NYC, 1935, 1937; New Horizons in American Art, 1939; Nat'l Forum of Professional Artists, Phila., 1969, 1970; Phila. Board of Education, 1970; Nat'l Convention Negro Physicians, 1971; Nat'l Forum of Professional Artists, NYC, 1970-1; Pa. Museum of Art, 1928, 1930, 1934; NJ State Museum, 1935; Harmon Foundation, 1933; Corcoran Gallery, 1934; Phila. YWCA; YMCA; Newark Museum, 1971; James A. Porter Gallery of African Amer. Art, 1970; South Side Community Center, Chicago, 1941; Lee Cultural Center, Phila.

Collections: Phila. Museum of Art; Metropolitan Museum of Art; Hyde Park Elem. School; Huey Elem. School, Phila.; Hamilton Elem. School, Phila.; Temple Univ.; Hanna Elem. School, Phila.; Internat'l Ladies Garment Workers, Phila.; Howard Univ.; National Archives; Workers Progress Alliance.

Awards: 1st prize, Nat'l Competition Serigraph in Colors; 1st prize, Latham Foundation Nat'l Competition; 1st prize, sculpture, Willingboro (NJ) Art Show; One of the Best 100 Designs, *House Beautiful* cover competition, 1928, 1930, 1933.

Member: Phila. Water Color Club; Nat'l Forum of Professional Artists; Internat'l Graphic Arts Educational Assn.; Delaware Valley Artist Guild.

Sources: Dover. *American Negro Art*; Harmon Foundation. *Exhibition of Productions by Negro Artists*; Indiana Univ. *Fine Arts and the Black American*; Mallett. *Index of Artists*; *Who's Who in American Art*, 1940-41; Short,

Walker, & Elliot O'Hara. *Watercolor Portraiture*; Locke. *Negro in Art*; Locke, Alain. "Advance on the Art Front," *Opportunity*, May 1939; Locke, Alain. "Chicago's New Southside Art Center," *Amer. Mag. of Art*, Aug. 1941; Porter. *Negro in Art*; Roberts, George & Mary. *Triumph on Fairmount: Fiske Kimball and the Philadelphia Museum of Art*; *Liberty Magazine*, 1946; *Parnassus*, Oct. 1936, p. 4; Information from artist; "Howard Univ. Gallery: Paintings by 3 Artists Are Displayed," *Washington Star*, Feb. 18, 1940; Baltimore Museum of Art. *Contemporary Negro*, 1939; DuSable Museum of African Amer. History. *Contemporary Black Artists*, 1970 Calendar; "Samuel Brown Exhibits Mexican Watercolors," *Phila. Art Alliance Bulletin*, X, Dec. 1945; "Exhibition at the Art Alliance, Phila.," *Pictures on Exhibit*, VIII, Jan. 1946, p. 51; Harley, Ralph L., Jr. "A Checklist of Afro-Amer. Art & Artists," *The Serif*, Dec. 1970; Porter, James. *Modern Negro Art*; Harmon Foundation. *Non-Jury Exhibit of Works of Negro Artists*, 1933; Texas Centennial Exposition. *Thumbnail Sketches of Exhibiting Artists*, 1936; Newark Museum. *Black Artists: Two Generations*, 1971; Afro-Amer. Slide Depository, 1971-2; Harmon Foundation. *Negro Artists*, 1935; "Negro Artists Reveal Genius in Trenton Show," *Art Digest*, Apr. 15, 1935; "Amer. Negro Art Given Full Length Review in NY Show," *Art Digest*, Dec. 15, 1941; Craig, Randall J. "Focus on Black Artists: A Project for Schools and Community," *School Arts*, Nov. 1970, pp. 30-3; *The Negro Handbook*, Composed by Editors of *Ebony*, Chicago, 1966; South Side Community Art Center. *Nat'l Negro Art Exhibition*, Chicago, 1941; Phila. Dept. of Recreation. *Love . . . and the Black Community*; Walker, Roslyn. *A Resource Guide to the Visual Arts of Afro-Americans*, South Bend, Ind., 1971.

BROWNE, VIVIAN E.

Painter, graphic artist, educator. Born in Laural, Florida. Studied at Hunter College, NY (BFA, MFA); Teachers College, Columbia University; New School for Social Research; New York University; Art Students League; Pratt Institute. Teacher at Rutgers University. Co-director, organizer, Lever House Annual. Coordinator, "Black Artists of the 1930's," Studio Museum in Harlem.
Works: *Peopled Mountain; Seven Deadly Sins; Getting Out; View of the Window; Atavisms; Warning; The Dance; Two Men.*
Exhibited: Ahda Artz Gallery, 1954; Lenox, Mass., 1958; Sunken Meadow, Long Island, 1960; Pacific Palisades, Cal., 1965; Yonkers Annual, NY, 1966; Harlem Cultural Council, NY, 1966; Atlanta Univ., 1965-7; Grove Street Gallery, 1967; Museum of Modern Art, NYC, 1968; Wilson College, Pa., 1968; Brooklyn College, 1969; Lyrit Gallery, 1970; Soho Art Festival, 1970; Aesthetic Dynamics, Del., 1970; Illinois Bell Telephone, 1970-1; English in Action, 1971; Acts of Art Gallery, 1971; Carnegie Institute, 1971; Civil Liberties Exhibition Benefit, 1972; Mount Holyoke College, 1972; Rhode Island Univ., 1971; Seligmann Gallery, 1972; State Armory, Wilmington, Del., 1971; Brooklyn Public Library; NYC Community College.
Collections: Mr. James Baldwin; Ms. Jean Edwards; Mr. Henri Ghent; Ms. June Shagaloff; Mr. & Mrs. Milton Ehre, Ms. Carol Reigen.
Awards: Huntington Hartford Fellowship, 1964; Achievement Award, National Assn. of Business & Professional Negro Women, 1965.
Member: College Arts Assn.; Textbook Committee, Board of Education, NYC, 1963; National Conference of Artists; National Art Education Assn.
Sources: Lewis/Waddy. *Black Artists on Art*, Vol. 2; Aesthetic Dynamics. *Afro-American Images*, 1971; Illinois Bell Telephone. *Black American Artists/71*, 1972; Brooklyn College. *Afro-American Artists Since 1950*, 1969; Schwartz, Therese. "The Political Scene," *Arts*, April 1971.

BROWNLEE, HENRY

Painter. Born in Savannah, Georgia, 1940. Studied at Washington School of Art; Savannah State College. Writer and artist for Southern Christian Leadership Conference.
Works: *Three Black Sisters.*
Exhibited: Sears Roebuck Art Show; Savannah Art Assn., Drawing & Print Competition, 1968.
Sources: Lewis/Waddy. *Black Artists on Art*, Vol. 1; Walker, Roslyn. *A Resource Guide to the Visual Arts of Afro-Americans*, South Bend, Ind., 1971.

BRUCE, CHARLES AUSTIN

Exhibited: Atlanta Univ., 1942.
Sources: Harley, Ralph, Jr. "Checklist of Afro-Amer. Art & Artists," *The Serif*, Dec. 1970.

BRUCE, HERBERT

Painter.
Works: *We're Tired of Grinning.*
Collections: Johnson Pub. Co.
Sources: Johnson Pub. Co. *The JPC Art Collection*, Pamphlet.

BRUCE, JONATHAN

Painter, photographer, graphic artist, commercial artist, educator. Born in Hartford, 1948. Studied at Hartford School of Art, University of Hartford (BFA, 1973).
Works: *Abstract Woman; Miss Twentieth Century; Children of Time Waits; Reconstructing in an Alien Land; Alienated Idolessence.*

Exhibited: Union Carbide Exhibition Hall, NYC, 1969; Wadsworth Atheneum, Hartford, 1970-1; Conn. Savings and Loan Assn., Hartford, 1971 (1-man); Univ. of Hartford, 1971; Travelers Insurance Co., Hartford, 1970; Amer. Internat'l College, Springfield, Mass., 1971-2; G. Fox & Co., Hartford, 1972; Jewish Community Center Gallery, New Haven, 1972 (1-man).

Collections: Univ. of Hartford, Mortensen Library; Mr. & Mrs. Milton Lewis Howard, Bloomfield, Conn.; Mr. B. Piper, Bronx, NY; Mr. Michael Thomas, Manchester, Conn.; Mr. & Mrs. F. Gaddy, Hartford; Ms. A. Deparolis, Vernon, Conn.; Mr. & Mrs. Ellsworth Davis, Hartford; Ms. Marion Cutler, West Hartford; Mr. & Mrs. Edgar Coleman, Hartford; Mr. & Mrs. H. Campbell, Wethersfield, Conn.; Dr. & Mrs. James A. Smith, Springfield, Mass.; Mr. R. N. Parendes, Hartford; Mr. & Mrs. Tom Tinnins, Bronx, NY; Waverly Elem. School, Hartford; Freddie D. Wish Elem. School, Hartford; Mr. Edgar Honer, Phila.; Ms. Marybeth Harper, Los Angeles; Thomas S. Weaver Sr. High School, Hartford; Mr. & Mrs. Henry Allen.

Awards: Placement Awards, 1964-5, 1967-8, 1969, 4 Blue Ribbons, 2 Gold Keys, & Portfolio Award to Univ. of Hartford, 1969—National Scholastic Art Awards, NYC; Cicuso Club Scholarship Prize, 1969, Alpha Wives Cash Prize, 1970 & 1971—Through Young Black Eyes, Hartford; Univ. of Hartford Core City Scholarship, 1969-73; Greater Hartford Sunday School Fellowship Union Scholarship, 1969; Greater Hartford Inter-racial Scholarship, 1969-72; Hartford Arts Festival Student Book Prize, 1971; Wethersfield Congregational Church Scholarship, 1971-2.

Represented by: Mrs. Jorena Bruce, 24 Greenwich Street, Hartford.

Sources: Information from artist; Univ. of Hartford. *Black Week—Journey Through a Black Kaleidoscope*, 1972; Gaines, Regina. "What Is Black Art," *New Paper*, Univ. of Hartford, Oct. 25, 1972.

BRUCE, RICHARD

Sources: Thurman, Wallace. "Negro Artists and the Negro," *New Republic*, Aug. 31, 1927; Harley, Ralph, Jr. "Checklist of Afro-Amer. Art & Artists," *Serif*, Dec. 1970; Thurman, Wallace. *Fire:* A Quarterly Devoted to the Younger Negro Artists, NY, Vol. 1, No. 1; Johnson, Charles S. *Ebony & Topaz, A Collectanea*, 1927.

BRYANT, JOAN

Painter.
Works: *Evening Sundown; Street Scene in Paris.*

Collections: Johnson Pub. Co.
Sources: DuSable Museum of African-Amer. History. *Contemporary Black Artists*, 1970 Calendar; Johnson Pub. Co. *The JPC Art Collection*, Pamphlet; Walker, Roslyn. *A Resource Guide to the Visual Arts of Afro-Americans*, South Bend, Ind., 1971.

BRYANT, LAWRENCE, SR.

Painter.
Works: *In the Mohawk; Red Maple; Fruit.*
Exhibited: South Side Community Art Center, Chicago, 1945.
Collections: Mrs. William Melton; Mr. & Mrs. William H. Patterson.
Sources: South Side Community Center. *Chicago Collectors Exhibit of Negro Art*, Chicago, 1945.

BRYANT, REGINALD

Graphic artist, filmmaker, educator. Studied at Temple University (BFA & BSEd, 1963); University of Pennsylvania; Pratt Institute; Johns Hopkins University; American Film Institute; University of California at Santa Barbara. Assistant Professor and Director of the undergraduate program in Community Design at Philadelphia College of Art.
Works: *Castration; Assassination Totem; Dilemma-if she ain't part of the solution; Ode to Negative Space*, 1969 (ink); *Long Live the Albatross*, 1969 (ink); *Study for Puppet on Yellow Paper*, 1969 (ink with paint); *Ritual of Fugitive Images*, 1969 (mixed media); *Pope Phallus the Fifth*, 1969 (ink); *Untitled*, 1970 (ink); *You Are What You See*, 1970 (ink).
Exhibited: State Armory, Wilmington, 1971; Temple Univ., 1970; Pa. Academy of the Fine Arts; Phila. Art Alliance; Phila. Civic Center; Lee Cultural Center (1-man).
Sources: Phila. Division of Art. *Afro-American Artists Abroad 1800-1969*; Aesthetic Dynamics. *Afro-American Images*, 1971; Tyler School of Art. *Seven by Seven*, Temple Univ., 1970.

BUCHANAN, BEVERLY

Painter, health educator. Born in Fuquay, North Carolina, 1940. Studied at Bennett College (BS); Columbia University (MS, MPH).
Works: *Today & Tomorrow; Passage; Untitled; Surface.*
Exhibited: Carroll Condit Galleries; Hudson River Museum, 1971; Annex Gallery, 1971; 4th Annual Panorama of African-Amer. Culture; Art in the Park, 1971; Staten Island Museum, 1963; Riverdale Neighborhood House, 1968; Paperback Forum, 1968; Northside Savings Bank, 1969; Vassar College, 1972.
Collections: Cinque Gallery; Ms. Elizabeth Sewell; Ann & Martin Scheiner; Miss Joan Lasky; Mr. & Mrs. Burne Hogarth; Mr. & Mrs. Dan Wallace Clark; Miss Ruth Healy;

Mr. & Mrs. George A. Woods; Dr. Jane Spragg; Chris Shelton; Mr. & Mrs. Barry Abrams; Ms. Anna Mitch.
Awards: 3rd prize, Art in the Park.
Represented by: Carroll Condit Galleries.
Sources: *Reporter Dispatch*, Mar. 24, 1972; *Village Voice*, May 25, 1972.

BULLOCK, BARBARA

Sources: Phila. Division of Art. *Afro-American Artists 1800-1969.*

BULLOCK, STARMANDA

Sources: Myers, Carol L. *Black Power in the Arts*, Flint, Mich., 1970; Harley, Ralph, Jr. "Checklist of Afro-Amer. Art & Artists," *Serif*, Dec. 1970.

BUNDY, MOSES T. CROSS

Collections: Schomburg Collection, NY Public Library.
Sources: Schatz, Walter. *Directory of Afro-American Resources*, 1970.

BUNN, LEROY

Painter. Born in Rocky Mount, North Carolina in 1942.
Works: *Africa Part I*, 1970; *Africa Part II*, 1970; *Panther Flower*, 1970; *Jail Artist*, 1970.
Member: Boston Negro Artists' Assn.
Sources: Information from the artist.

BURKE, ARLENE

Painter.
Works: *Series of Portraits: #1, #2* (oil).
Exhibited: Lee Cultural Center, Phila.
Sources: Phila. Dept. of Recreation. *Love . . . and the Black Community.*

BURKE, SELMA HORTENSE

Sculptor. Born in Mooresville, North Carolina. Studied at St. Agnes Training School for Nurses, Raleigh, NC; Women's Medical College, NC; Columbia University (PhD, 1936-41); studied sculpture under Maillol, Paris; under Povolney, Vienna.
Works: *Mary Bethune; Mary Holiday; Gentle Spring; Amazonia; Temptation; Stone; Negro Woman; Edith Barome; Deborah; The Widow; Plaque of FDR; Boy's Head; Bowed Down; Study in Cedar Wood; Torso; Mr. Johnson; Torso in Limestone; Amazon* (Tuckahoe marble); *Morrhua Lusca* (NC marble).
Exhibited: Carlen Galleries, Phila., 1945; Public Library, Mooresville, NC; Julian Levy Galleries, NY, 1945; Atlanta Univ., 1945; McMillen Inc. Galleries, NY, 1941; NY Public Library; Howard Univ.; City College of NY, 1967; Amer. Negro Exposition, Chicago, 1940; Avant Garde Gallery, 1958; Modernage Art Gallery, NY, 1945 (1-man); Rainbow Sign Gallery, Berkeley, 1972.

Collections: Col. William Haywood; Mr. John Brown, Lake Placid, NY; National Archives.
Awards: Rosenwald Fellowship, 1939; Edward B. Alford, Jr. Purchase Award, Atlanta Univ., 1944; Honorary degrees in Pedagogy, Humanities, Teemer College.
Member: Pa. Council of Arts.
Sources: Greene, Carroll, Jr. "Perspective: The Black Artist in America," *Art Gallery*, Apr. 1970; "Negro Art Scores Without Double Standards," *Art Digest*, Feb. 1, 1945; Pierre-Noel, Lois Jones. "American Negro Art in Progress," *Negro History Bulletin*, Oct. 1967; Craig, Randall J. "Focus on Black Artists: A Project for Schools and Community," *School Arts*, Nov. 1970; Myers, Carol L. *Black Power in the Arts*, Flint, Mich., 1970; Spradling, Mary M., ed. *In Black & White: Afro-Americans in Print; Ebony*, Mar. 1947, pp. 32-5, Aug. 1966, p. 91; *Negro Digest*, Dec. 1945, p. 35; "Leading Negro Artists," *Ebony*, Sept. 1963; Rainbow Sign Gallery. *Black Arts Day II*, Press Release, Berkeley, 1972; Albany Institute of History & Art. *The Negro Artist Comes of Age*; Dover. *American Negro Art*; Indiana Univ. *Fine Arts & the Black American*; City College of NY. *The Evolution of Afro-American Artists 1800-1950*; "Art by Negroes," *Art Digest*, Oct. 15, 1941; Jewell, Edward A. "Chiefly Modern in Idiom," *New York Times*, June 17, 1945; "Peace Is Truman Plea at Dedication of Roosevelt Plaque," *Evening Star* (DC), Sept. 25, 1945; "Displays Her Plaque of FDR," *Washington Afro-American*, Aug. 4, 1945; DuSable Museum of African-Amer. History. *Contemporary Black Artists*, 1970 Calendar; Tanner Art Galleries. *Art of the American Negro*, 1940; McMillen Inc. Galleries. *Contemporary Negro Art*, NY, 1941; Pittsburgh Community College. *16 Black Artists*; Afro-American Slide Depository, 1971-2 Catalog; Harmon Foundation. *Select Picture List; Negro Handbook*, Chicago, 1966; Porter. *Modern Negro Art*; Harley, Ralph, Jr. "Checklist of Afro-Amer. Art & Artists," *Serif*, Dec. 1970; "Princeton Group Arts," *Crisis*, Jan. 1951; Ploski, Harry, & Ernest Kaiser. "The Black Artist," *Afro USA*, 1971; Ploski, Harry, Ernest Kaiser, & Otto Lindenmeyer. "The Black American Artist," *Reference Library of Black America*, Book 4; Walker, Roslyn. *A Resource Guide to the Visual Arts of Afro-Americans*, South Bend, Ind., 1971.

BURKES, EUGENE ALEXANDER

Painter, composer, educator. Born in Virginia, 1880. Studied at Newark School of Fine and Applied Arts.
Works: *Slave Mother; By the Cabin Door; John Brown & Frederick Douglass in Conference; Spiritual Creator; Wendell Phillips.*

Exhibited: Harmon Foundation, 1931, 1933; Newark Art Club, 1934; Alumni Assn., Newark Art School.
Collections: Oakland Art Museum.
Sources: Dover. *American Negro Art*; Harmon Foundation. *Exhibition of Productions by Negro Artists*; Harmon Foundation. *Non Jury Exhibit of Works of Negro Artists*, 1933; Harmon Foundation. *Negro Artists*, 1936; Indiana Univ. *Fine Arts & the Black American*; DuSable Museum of African-Amer. History. *Contemporary Black Artists*, 1970 Calendar; Harley, Ralph, Jr. "Checklist of Afro-Amer. Art & Artists," *Serif*, Dec. 1970; Oakland Museum Archives; Walker, Roslyn. *A Resource Guide to the Visual Arts of Afro-Americans*, South Bend, Ind., 1971.

BURNETT, CALVIN

Painter, graphic artist, educator. Born in Cambridge, Massachusetts on July 18, 1921. Studied at Massachusetts School of Art (BFA); Boston Museum School; Massachusetts College of Arts (BS); Boston University (MFA); Impressions Graphic Workshop; University Extension. Teacher at DeCordova Museum, Lincoln, Massachusetts; Massachusetts College of Art.
Works: *Trio; For This My Mother Wrapped Me Warm; Six Recent Deaths; Four Part Black Political Poem; Nineteen Black Profiles; Jennifer Lawson; They Send Me to Eat in the Kitchen When Company Comes; Subtle Slough; Nat Turner; Three Crippled Drunks; Boy With Balloons; Augusta Savage 1; Girl With Raised Arm; Recurring Dream; Double Box; Figure Seated in Moonlight; Marcus Garvey; Sisters; Head in Ellipse; Girl Waiting; Vote Victim; They That; Figure in Black; Landscape; Blues Singer; Jump Rope; Theseus & King Minos; Still Life; Nude; Portrait; Merry-Go-Round; Insect; You & Me Baby; Coffle; Blue & Gold Blues; Pink Landscape; Together; Past Shadow; Little Black Landscape; Great Day A'Coming; Fire Next Time; Double Interior; Silver Abstract; Juvenile Jailhouse; Faces in the Future; Frank Stout; Ann Rafferty; Bunowski; Cummings; Hillside; Front Hall; Shadows on a Hill; 4-Point Stairs; Figure With Globe; Jenifer;* Untitled print; *Burk Johnson* (pen & ink); *Clementine Hunter* (print).
Exhibited: WVa. State College, 1966 (1-man); Lowell State College, 1955; Weeden Gallery, 1964; Newbury Gallery, 1963; Children's Art Center, 1953, 1957; Village Studio; Gropper Gallery, Boston; Mass. Inst. of Tech., 1955; Wheelock College, Boston; Arlington (Mass.) Public Library; Cambridge Art Assn.; Lawrence Academy; Framingham State College; Smithsonian Inst. & Amer. Fed. of Arts Traveling Shows; US Dept. Traveling Show; Brooklyn Museum; Downtown Gallery; Assoc. Amer. Artists; Nat'l Academy of Design; Internat'l Print Society; Albany Inst. of Contemporary Art; Library of Congress; Barnet Aden Gallery, Washington, DC; Silvermine, Conn.; Brandeis Univ.; Harvard; Boston Negro Artists Assn.; Boston College; Natick (Mass.) Community Church; Studio Museum, Harlem; Inst. of Modern Art, Boston; Boris Mirski Gallery; Oakland Museum; Jordan Marsh, Boston; Wellesley College; Boston Public Library, 1973; Kiel Auditorium, St. Louis; San Francisco Art Assn.; Taller de Grafica, Mexico; Elma Lewis School of Fine Arts; Smith-Mason Gallery, 1971; Xavier Univ., 1963; Dickson Art Center, Los Angeles, 1966; Bumpus Gallery, Duxbury, Mass.; Nat'l Center of Afro-Amer. Artists, 1972 (1-man).
Collections: Wiggin Collection, Boston Public Library; Paul Sachs, Fogg Museum; Museum of Fine Arts, Boston; Wellesley College; Howard Univ.; Atlanta Univ.; Oakland Museum; Simmons College, Boston; Roland Hayes; Johnson Pub. Co., Chicago; Harvard; Wharton House, Phila.; Elma Lewis School, Boston; Nat'l Bezalel Museum, Jersalem; Inst. of Contemporary Art.
Awards: Atlanta Univ., 1953, 1955, 1960, 1963, 1966, 1968; Boston Printmakers, 1959, 1961, 1962, 1964; Beverley Farms Regional, Wichita, Kansas; Cambridge Art Assn., 1946, 1949, 1961; New England Print Competition, Marion, Mass. & Conn., 1960; Assoc. Amer. Artists, NYC, 1959; Jordan Marsh, 1967; Cambridge Centennial Exhibition; Germanic Museum, Cambridge, Mass.; Wharton Settlement; Busch-Reisinger Museum, Cambridge, Mass.; Howard Univ.
Member: Cambridge Art Assn.; Nat'l Conference of Artists; Boston Negro Artists Assn. (co-founder, 1963); Inst. of Contemporary Art, Boston; Board of Directors, Boston Printmakers.
Sources: *Who's Who in American Art*, 1966, 1970; Boston Museum of Fine Arts. *Afro-Amer. Artists: NY & Boston*, 1970; Roelof-Lanner, T. V., ed. *American Negro Artists*, 1970; Afro-Amer. Slide Depository; "Afro-American Issue," *Art Gallery*, April 1968; Indiana Univ. *Fine Arts & the Black American*; Univ. of Cal. *The Negro in American Art*; Smith-Mason Gallery. *National Exhibition Black Artists*, 1971; Oakland Museum Archives, Ruth Waddy Collection; Information from artist; "Philippa Schuyler," *Boston Chronicle*, June 6, 1946; "Common Ground," *Beacon Hill News*, Oct. 10, 1946, pp. 4-5; "No Birds Sing," *Christian Science Monitor*, Aug. 21, 1954, p. 8; Dames, Marshall. "Boston Arts Festival," *Boston Globe*, June 19, 1954, p. 2; "Two Girls Talking," *Provincetown Advocate*, July 30, 1964, p. 9; "March on Washington,"

Boston Globe, Aug. 29, 1963, pp. 10, 21;
"Head in Ellipse," *Lowell Sun*, April 1965;
"Black Head Front View," *Charlestown Gazette*, May 6, 1966, p. 1; "Figures on the
Grass," *Bay State Banner*, Aug. 20, 1966;
Cohen, Cathleen. "First Art Exhibition in
Roxbury," *Boston Globe*, Sept. 13, 1966; "We're
Into Something," *Boston Record American*,
July 18, 1968, p. 16; Titcomb, Charles.
"Black Artists from Boston at Brandeis,"
Harvard Summer News, 1969; Jordan, Robert.
"Black Art: Hub's Retarded Child," *Boston
Globe*, 1969; Van Almelo, Frederik. "In the
Afro-American Grain," *Tuesday*, May 26, 1971,
p. 24; *Boston Printmaker*, 1958, p. 3; *Head in
Hand*, 1962, p. 8; Assoc. Amer. Artists.
*Twenty-Fifth Anniversary National Fine Print
Competition*, Oct. 1959, p. 4; *American Grafik
Sanatlare*, 1960, p. 10; *Wichita 31st National
Graphic Arts Drawing Exhibition*, 1963; *Cambridge Art Assn. Exhibition: Hamburg*, Aug.
1965, p. 10; *Graphikaus Funt Kontinenten*,
1965, p. 63; Atlanta Univ. *Annual Exhibitions
of Painting, Sculpture & Prints by Negro Artists*, 1966, 1967; Bucknell Drawing Exhibition.
Study for Sculpture, 1966; *The Portrayal of
the Negro in American Painting*, 1967, p. 36;
Phila. Division of Art. *Afro-Amer. Artists
1800-1969*, 1969, p. 36; Spelman College.
Eleven Black Printmakers, Feb. 1970; Acts of
Art Gallery. *Rebuttal to the Whitney Museum
Exhibition*, 1971; Wright, Frederick. *Art News*,
Nov. 1946; Binger, Carl. *Atlantic*, Feb. 1961;
Brucker, Gerard. *Atlantic*, Jan. 1963; *Boston
Globe. Eastern Arts Quarterly*, 1963, pp. 21-3;
The Galleries, 1967; Housel, Mildred. *The
Connoisseur*, Mar. 1967; Univ. of Wis. *Arts
in Society*, Vol. 5, #2, 1968; Univ. of Wis.
Arts in Society, Vol. 5, #3, 1968; *Boston Arts*,
May 1970; Art Directors Club of Boston.
Directory of New England Artists & Photographers, Nov. 1947; Cultural Exchange Center.
Prints by American Negro Artists, 1965; Burnett, Calvin. *Objective Drawing Techniques*,
Reinhold Pub. Co., 1966; Atkinson, Edward J.
*Black Dimensions in Contemporary American
Art*, 1971; *National Conference of Artists
Traveling Color Slide Exhibition*, Oct. 1971;
Boston Negro Artists Assn. Calendar, 1968,
1973; Nat'l Conference of Artists. *Print Portfolio of Negro Artists*, 1963; Cambridge
(Mass.) Art Assn. Calendar, 1960, p. 1; DuSable Museum of African-Amer. History. *Contemporary Black Artists*, 1970 Calendar; Community Lecture Series. *Local Afro-American
Artists*, 1969; Johnson Pub. Co. *The JPC Art
Collection*, Chicago, Pamphlet; Xavier Univ.
*Emancipation Proclamation Centennial Nat'l
Art Exhibition*, 1963; Harley, Ralph, Jr.
"Checklist of Afro-Amer. Art & Artists," *The
Serif*, Dec. 1970; "Black Art Exhibit Opens

Sunday," *Herald*, Belmont, Mass., May 14,
1970; "Preview Party to Open Show by 13
Black Artists," *Citizen*, Belmont, Mass., May
14, 1970; Driscoll, Edgar. "Blacks Duncanson
& Bannister Honored in Fine Arts Exhibit,"
Boston Globe, Jan. 16, 1972; Gerson, Sareen
R. "Black Art NY-Hub Set for Museum of
Fine Arts," *Minuteman*, March 19, 1970;
Walsh, Rose. "Artists to Meet Public at Art
Exhibit Preview," *Record American*, May 19,
1970; "Black Artists' Work on View at Museum," *News*, Newburyport, Mass., May 16,
1970; Le Brun, Caron. "Blacks' Art on Display," *Herald Traveler*, Boston, May 26, 1970;
Paris, Jean. "Black Art Experience in Art,"
Long Island Press, Jamaica, NY, June 14,
1970; *The Negro Handbook*, Composed by
the Editors of *Ebony*, Chicago, 1966; Schatz,
Walter. *Directory of Afro-American Resources*,
1970; Myers, Carol L. *Black Power in the
Arts*, Flint, Mich., 1970; Gaither, Edmund B.
"The Evolution of the Afro-Amer. Artists,"
Artists' Proof, Vol. 2; Le Brun, Caron. "Black
Art," *Herald Traveler*, Sunday Supplement,
Boston, May 24, 1970; "At Boston Museum—
Afro-American Art," *New Bedford Sunday
Standard Times*, May 10, 1970; Boston Negro
Artists' Assn. *The Black Artist in America:
A Negro History Month Exhibition*, Boston
Public Library, 1973; *Institute of Contemporary Art*, Bulletin, Vol. 5, No. 1, 1955, p. 1;
Walker, Roslyn. *A Resource Guide to the
Visual Arts of Afro-Americans*, South Bend,
Ind., 1971.

BURNSIDE, H.E.S.

Works: *Mask (Angola) Design Concept* (oil).
Exhibited: Lee Cultural Center, Phila.
Sources: Phila. Dept. of Recreation. *Love . . .
and the Black Community*.

BURNSIDE, JACKSON, III

Painter.
Works: *Kullard Days & Sunshine* (oil); *Stateside Life* (white birch).
Exhibited: Lee Cultural Center, Phila.
Sources: Phila. Dept. of Recreation. *Love . . .
and the Black Community*.

BURR, JOHN P.

Sources: Harley, Ralph, Jr. "Checklist of Afro-Amer. Art & Artists," *Serif*, Dec. 1970; Porter. *Modern Negro Art*.

BURRELL, REUBEN

Worked in Brooklyn, New York; Portsmouth,
Virginia.
Works: *Plowing; Still Life.*
Exhibited: Atlanta Univ., 1943, 1951.
Sources: Atlanta Univ. Annuals Catalogs.

BURROUGHS, MARGARET TAYLOR GOSS

Painter, sculptor, educator, writer, illustrator, graphic artist. Born in St. Rose Parish, Louisiana, 1917. Studied at Chicago Normal School; Art Institute of Chicago (BAE, MAE); Teachers' College, Columbia University; Northwestern University; in Mexico City. Founder of Museum of Negro History, Chicago; South Side Community Art Center, Chicago; National Conference of Artists.

Works: *Sojourner Truth; Mexican Landscape; Abstraction; Head,* 1968; *Black Queen,* 1968; *Homage to Marion Perkins; Blowing Bubbles; Deserted Church; Street Scene; Mama Takes in Washing; Social Worker; Friends; Two Girls; Grief; Neighborhood.*

Exhibited: Ill. State Univ.; Winston-Salem Teachers' College; Atlanta Univ., 1942, 1943, 1945; Amer. Exposition, Chicago, 1940; Xavier Univ., 1963; Howard Univ., 1961; Hull House, Chicago, 1955; Mexico City, 1955; San Francisco Civic Museum, 1949; Ill. State Fair, 1949; Market Place Gallery, NY, 1950; Kenosha Museum, 1953; Poland, 1965; House of Friendship, Moscow, 1967; Internat'l Kook Art Exhibit, Leipzig, Germany, 1965; Fox Valley Presbyterian Church, Geneva, Wisc., 1969; Elmhurst College, 1970; Ball State Teachers' College, 1969; South Side Community Art Center, 1941, 1945; McMillen Inc. Galleries, NY, 1941.

Collections: Howard Univ.; Ala. State Normal; Atlanta Univ.; DuSable Museum of African-Amer. History, Chicago; Johnson Pub. Co.; Oakland Museum.

Member: Nat'l. Conference of Artists; Annual Lake Meadows Outdoor Arts & Crafts Fair, 1957; South Side Community Art Center; Ebony Museum of Negro History & Art, Chicago, 1961; New Crusader—Negro History Hall of Fame, 1960-2; State of Ill. Centennial of Emancipation Committee, 1963; Amer. Forum of African Studies Program, 1968; Staff of Amer. Forum for Internat'l Study at Univ. of Ghana, 1969; Staff of Amer. Forum for Internat'l Study at Univ. of West Indies, Jamaica, 1970; Chicago Council of Foreign Relations, 1970; DuSable Museum of African-Amer. History; Gov.'s Commission of the Financing of the Arts in the State of Ill., 1971.

Sources: Dover. *American Negro Art;* Roelof-Lanner, T. V., ed. *Prints by American Negro Artists;* "Afro-American Issue," *Art Gallery,* April 1968; Indiana Univ. *Fine Arts & the Black American;* Lewis/Waddy. *Black Artists on Art,* Vol. 2; DuSable Museum of African-Amer. History. *Contemporary Black Artists,* 1970 Calendar; Roucek/Kiernan. *The Negro Impact on Western Civilization;* Pierre-Noel, Lois Jones. "American Negro Art in Progress," *Negro History Bulletin,* Oct. 1967; A & T

Univ. Lyceum Program. *15 Afro-American Women;* Nat'l. Conference of Artists. *A Print Portfolio by Negro Artists;* Johnson Pub. Co. *The JPC Art Collection,* Pamphlet; Atlanta Univ. *National Conference of Negro Artists,* 1959; "Exhibition," *Scrapbook of Art & Artists of Chicago,* 1956, p. 19; Harley, Ralph, Jr. "Checklist of Afro-Amer. Art & Artists," *Serif,* Dec. 1970; Woodruff, Hale. "Negro Artists Hold 4th Annual in Atlanta," *Art Digest,* April 15, 1945; "Atlanta's Annual," *Time,* April 9, 1945; Locke, Alain. "Chicago's New Southside Art Center," *American Magazine of Art,* Aug. 1941; Xavier Univ. *Emancipation Proclamation Centennial National Art Exhibition,* 1963; Atkinson, J. Edward. *Black Dimensions in Contemporary American Art,* NY, 1971; Howard Univ. *Exhibition of Negro Artists of Chicago at Howard Univ. Gallery of Art,* 1941; Tanner Art Galleries. *Art of the American Negro,* 1940; Information from artist; South Side Community Art Center. *Chicago Collectors Exhibit of Negro Art,* 1945; South Side Community Art Center. *National Negro Art Exhibition,* Chicago, 1941; Myers, Carol L. *Black Power in the Arts,* Flint, Mich., 1970; Oakland Museum Archives, Ruth Waddy Collection; McMillen Inc. Galleries. *Contemporary Art,* NY, 1941; *Art News,* April 15, 1945, pp. 8-9; Burroughs, Margaret T. *Did You Feed My Cow?,* Follett, 1969; Burroughs, Margaret T. *Jasper the Drummin' Boy,* Follett, 1970; Randall, Dudley, & Margaret T. Burroughs, eds. *For Malcolm: Poems on the Life & Death of Malcolm X,* Broadside, 1969; Walker, Roslyn. *A Resource Guide to the Visual Arts of Afro-Americans,* South Bend, Ind., 1971.

BUSH, ELWYN

Painter, sculptor. Born May 8, 1931 in Springfield, Illinois. Studied at the Society of Arts and Crafts (1954-57).

Works: *Deep Thought; Still Life; Dr. Martin Luther King, Jr.; Young Woman; Woman in Black; Eddy; Reclining; Olga; Malcolm X; Eve; Jocelyn; The Struggle; Delight; African Queen; Hope.*

Exhibited: Detroit Institute of Arts, 1964-66; 1969; Smith-Mason Gallery, Washington, DC, 1971.

Sources: Smith-Mason Gallery. *National Exhibition Black Artists,* 1971; Afro-American Slide Depository, Catalog; Detroit Institute of Arts files.

BUSTION, NATHANIEL

Painter, ceramist. Born in Gadsden, Alabama, June 2, 1942. Studied at Colorado State University; Otis Art Institute; Belgium Ortwerp Academy.

Works: *Black Illusion; Black Experience; Two*

Figures; Black Heritage; Dutch People; Untitled.
Exhibited: Watts Summer Festival; Gallery 32; Brockman Gallery; Otis Art Institute; Panorama of Black Artists, Los Angeles, 1972; Los Angeles County Museum of Art; Los Angeles Art Associates.
Collections: Fort Collins, Colo.; Mr. Lee Gross; Mr. Richard Dowling, Pan Am Building, NY; Ebony Building, Chicago; Johnson Pub. Co.
Awards: Black Art Council Scholarship, Los Angeles; Studio Watts Fellowship, Los Angeles.
Member: Los Angeles Art Associates.
Represented by: Brockman Gallery; Westwood Gallery.
Sources: Lewis/Waddy. *Black Artists on Art,* Vol. 2; Information from artist; Johnson Pub. Co. *The JPC Art Collection,* Pamphlet.

BUTLER, JO

Painter, educator. Born in Buffalo, New York, 1937. Studied at Queens College; New York University. Art teacher at the Incarnation School, Harlem.
Works: *Blue Day Man; Untitled; Model for Larger Work.*
Exhibited: Studio Museum in Harlem, 1969.
Sources: Studio Museum in Harlem. *Harlem Artists 69.*

BUTLER, SHARYLE

Weaver. Born in Berkeley, California, 1947. Studied at California College of Arts and Crafts (BA, 1969).
Works: *Composition; Egypt.*
Exhibited: Concord Art Assn., 1969; Cal. College of Arts & Crafts, 1968, 1969; Mills College, 1970; College of Marin, 1970; Pacific Grove Art Center Gallery, 1970; Stanford Univ., 1969; Pleasant Hill Library; Opening of Model Apartments at the Martin Luther King Square, San Francisco, 1969.
Member: Art West Associated North.
Sources: Lewis/Waddy.` *Black Artists on Art,* Vol. 2; Mills College. *California Black Craftsmen,* 1970; Cal. College of Arts & Crafts. *Towards A Black Aesthetics,* Unpublished List, 1969.

CADE, WALTER

Painter. Studied at the Institute of Modern Art; Pratt Institute.
Works: *A First for 125th Street.*
Exhibited: Various stores, luncheonettes in New York City; 20th Century Creators.
Sources: *New York Post,* March 21, 1966.

CADE, WALTER, III

Mixed media. Born 1936.
Works: Untitled mixed media, 1970; *Abstraction.*

Exhibited: Whitney Museum, 1971.
Collections: Mr. Russ Thompson.
Sources: Doty. *Contemporary Black Artists in America.*

CADOO, JOYCE

Graphic artist.
Works: *Decline and Fall* (color woodcut).
Collections: Oakland Museum, Ruth Waddy Collection.
Sources: Roelof-Lanner, T. V. *Prints by American Negro Artists;* Oakland Museum Archives; Walker, Roslyn. *A Resource Guide to the Visual Arts of Afro-Americans,* South Bend, Ind., 1971.

CAGE, CURTIS

Painter.
Works: *Autumn Landscape.*
Exhibited: Harmon Foundation, College Art Assn. Touring Exhibition, 1934-35.
Collections: National Archives.
Sources: Afro-American Slide Depository, 1971-72 Catalog; Harley, Ralph, Jr. "Checklist of Afro-Amer. Art & Artists," *Serif,* Dec. 1970.

CALIFANO, J.

Collections: Schomburg Art Collection, NY Public Library.
Sources: Schatz, Walter. *Directory of Afro-American Resources,* 1970.

CAMPBELL, BENJAMIN

Painter. Born in Jamaica, British West Indies, 1935.
Works: *Composition: 8.*
Exhibited: Studio Museum in Harlem, 1969.
Sources: Studio Museum in Harlem. *Harlem Artists 69.*

CAMPBELL, ELMER SIMMS

Painter, cartoonist, illustrator. Born in St. Louis, Missouri, 1906. Studied at Art Institute of Chicago. Former illustrator for *New Yorker, Esquire, Judge.*
Works: *Creole Woman Started It; Levee Luncheon; Deep River; The Wake; Voodoo Drummer* (lithograph); *Cuties* (syndicated cartoons).
Exhibited: Minneapolis Artists Exhibit, 1924, 1925; Harmon Foundation, 1929, 1935; American Negro Exposition, Chicago, 1940; National Gallery of Art, 1929; South Side Community Art Center, Chicago, 1941; Arthur H. Newton Galleries, 1935.
Collections: Mrs. Gonzalez Motto; NY Public Library-Schomburg Collection.
Awards: Honorable Mention, American Negro Exposition, 1940; Hearst Prize ($1,000), 1936.

Sources: Carter, Elmer. "E. Simms Campbell-Caricaturist," *Opportunity*, March 1932; Brown, Sterling. *Southern Road.* NY, 1932; *More Cuties in Arms.* Phila., 1943; Dover. *American Negro Art;* Locke. *The Negro in Art;* Indiana Univ. *Fine Arts & the Black American;* Harmon Foundation. *Exhibition of Productions by Negro Artists;* Tanner Art Galleries. *Art of the American Negro*, 1940; *Esquire*, Dec. 1950, pp. 120-1; Harley, Ralph, Jr. "Checklist of Afro-American Art & Artists," *The Serif*, Dec. 1970; Porter. *Modern Negro Art;* Boning, Richard A. *Profiles of Black Americans*, NY, 1968; Porter, James. "Negro Artists Gain Recognition After Long Battle," *Pittsburgh Courier*, July 29, 1950; Ploski, Harry, Ernest Kaiser. "The Black Artist," *Afro, USA;* Ploski, Harry, Ernest Kaiser, & Otto Lindenmeyer. "The Black Artist," *Reference Library of Black America*, Book 4; "Elmer Simms Campbell, One of the Few Who Have Crashed the Color Line to Success," *Washington Tribune*, June 12, 1937; Schatz, Walter. *Directory of Afro-American Resources*, 1970; Adams, Russell. *Great Negroes Past and Present.* Chicago, 1969; South Side Community Art Center. *National Negro Art Exhibition*, Chicago, 1941; Robinson, Wilhelmena S. *Historical Negro Biographies; Current Biography*, 1941, pp. 128-9; *Ebony*, Nov. 1966, pp. 132-8; *Negro Digest*, Feb. 1945, pp. 27-30; Spradling, Mary M., ed. *In Black and White: Afro-Americans in Print;* "Cuties Artist Makes Address at Howard Univ.," (DC) *Times Herald*, March 22, 1944; "Colored Cartoonist 'Doodles' to Get Clever Gag Ideas," (DC) *Evening Star*, March 22, 1941; "Let John Henry Go," cover, *Opportunity*, March 1942; DuSable Museum of African-American History. *Contemporary Black Artists*, 1970 calendar; Brawley, Benjamin. *The Negro Genius;* Harmon Foundation. *Negro Artists*, 1935; Woodson, Carter G., Charles H. Wesley. *The Story of the Negro Retold*, p. 402; Bontemps, Arna. "Cuties By Campbell," *Negro Digest*, 1944; Smithsonian Institution. *Painting & Sculpture by American Negro Artists*, 1929; Pierre-Noel, Lois Jones. "American Negro Art in Progress," *Negro History Bulletin*, Oct. 1967; Balch, Jack. "Democracy at Work," *American Magazine of Art*, Feb. 1943, p. 66; *National Conference of Artists Journal*, Winter, 1971; Jackson, A.L., "The Onlooker: Talent Rewarded," *The Chicago Defender*, Oct. 18, 1924; "County Gentleman," *Ebony*, Aug. 1947, pp. 1-15; Walker, Roslyn. *A Resource Guide to the Visual Arts of Afro-Americans*, South Bend, Ind., 1971; "Ein Broadway—Romantiker Am Zurichsee," *Sie Und Ei*, Vol. 1, No. 31, 1939; Holbrook, Francis C. "A Group of Negro Artists," *Opportunity*, July 1923.

CAMPBELL, FREDERICK

Painter. Born in Philadelphia on January 22, 1926. Studied at Hussian School of Art (1950-52).

Works: *The Cotton Pickers; The Testimonial; Janie's Place in the Sun; Sixth Generation; Portrait of W.E.B. Dubois; Cindy; Liberals Token; Tribute to Professor Herring; No Dress* (oil); *Red Dress* (oil).

Exhibited: Barnet Aden Gallery, Washington, DC, 1967; Hampton Institute, Va., 1967; William Moor Foundation, Baltimore, 1968; Phila. Civic Center, 1968; Studio 5, NYC, 1970; State Armory, Wilmington, Del., 1971; Lee Cultural Center, Phila.

Collections: Mr. James Cuffee, NYC; Atlanta Univ.; Bew Curritteus, NYC; Hampton Institute, Va.

Member: The Woodmere Art Gallery, Phila.; The Allens Lane Art Center, Phila.

Sources: Studio 5, NYC; Information from artist; Aesthetic Dynamics. *Afro-American Images*, 1971; Harley, Ralph, Jr. "Checklist of Afro-Amer. Artists," *The Serif*, Dec. 1970; Phila. Dept. of Recreation. *Love . . . and the Black Community.*

CAMPBELL, JOHNNY

Painter, sculptor.
Works: *Head of Christ.*
Sources: *St. Louis Dispatch*, Feb. 2, 1949.

CANYON, NICHOLAS L.

Painter. Born in 1931. Self-taught.
Sources: Dover. *American Negro Art*, p. 51; Indiana Univ. *Fine Arts & the Black American;* Harley, Ralph, Jr. "Checklist of Afro-Amer. Artists," *The Serif*, Dec. 1970; Walker, Roslyn. *A Resource Guide to the Visual Arts of Afro-Americans*, South Bend, Ind., 1971.

CAPESTONY, EFRAM

Exhibited: Harlem Cultural Council, 1966.
Sources: Morrison, Allan. "New Surge in the Arts," *Ebony*, Aug. 1967; Myers, Carol L. *Black Power in the Arts*, Flint, Mich., 1970.

CARAVA, ROY DE

See: DeCarava, Roy.

CARDENAS, AGUSTIN

Sculptor.

CARDOZO, FRANCIS

Illustrator. Active in the 1950's.
Sources: Indiana Univ. *Fine Arts & the Black American; Negro Year Book;* Walker, Roslyn. *A Resource Guide to the Visual Arts of Afro-Americans*, South Bend, Ind., 1971.

CAREY, MELVIN

Graphic artist.
Works: *Hunger.*

Collections: Oakland Museum.
Sources: Roelof-Lanner, T.V., ed. *Prints by American Negro Artists;* DuSable Museum of African-Amer. History. *Contemporary Black Artists,* 1970 Calendar; Oakland Museum Archives, Ruth Waddy Collection; Walker, Roslyn. *A Resource Guide to the Visual Arts of Afro-Americans,* South Bend, Ind., 1971.

CARLIS, JOHN, JR.

Painter, book designer. Born in Chicago, 1927. Studied at the Art Institute of Chicago (1935-40).
Works: *View of Kinzua Valley; Colored Lights; Colored Animals; Green Still Life; Two Brown Ladies; String of Pearls.*
Exhibited: Dillard Univ., 1939; Amer. Negro Exposition, Chicago, 1940; Howard Univ., 1941; South Side Community Art Center, Chicago, 1941; McMillen Inc. Galleries, NY, 1941.
Sources: "Art by Negroes," *Art Digest,* Oct. 15, 1941; Tanner Art Galleries. *Art of the American Negro,* 1940; DuSable Museum of African-Amer. History. *Contemporary Black Artists,* 1970, Calendar; Locke. *The Negro in Art;* Mallett. *Index of Artists;* Howard Univ. *Exhibition of Negro Artists of Chicago at Howard Univ. Gallery of Art,* 1941; Locke, Alain. "Chicago's New South Side Art Center," *American Magazine of Art,* Aug. 1941; Lane, James W. "Afro-Amer. Art on Both Continents," *Art News,* Oct. 19, 1941; Porter. *Modern Negro Art;* Harley, Ralph, Jr. "Checklist of Afro-Amer. Art & Artists," *Serif,* Dec. 1970; South Side Community Art Center. *National Negro Art Exhibition,* Chicago, 1941; McMillen Inc. Galleries. *Contemporary Negro Art,* NY, 1941; Walker, Roslyn. *A Resource Guide to the Visual Arts of Afro-Americans,* South Bend, Ind., 1971.

CARLO, FRED

Graphic artist, sculptor.
Works: *Little Man; Sleepy Head; The Tool Shed.*
Exhibited: Amer. Negro Exposition, Chicago, 1940.
Sources: Tanner Art Galleries. *Art of the American Negro,* 1940; "Negro Art from Cleveland's Karamu House," *Art Digest,* Jan. 15, 1942.

CAROTHERS, RICE

Painter.
Works: *Four Horsemen of the Apocalypse.*
Collections: National Archives.
Sources: Afro-Amer. Slide Depository Catalog, 1971-2; Harley, Ralph, Jr. "Checklist of Afro-Amer. Artists," *The Serif,* Dec. 1970.

CARPENTER, JUNE

Painter.

Works: *African Coffure; Mother and Child* (acrylic).
Exhibited: Sunday in the Park, Boston, 1972.
Awards: 3rd prize, painting, Sunday in the Park, 1972.
Sources: Boston Negro Artists' Assn. Calendar 1973.

CARRAWAY, ARTHUR

Painter, printmaker. Born in Fort Worth, Texas in 1927. Studied at California School of Fine Arts; Academy of Advertising Art, San Francisco.
Works: *African Symbol of Wisdom; Fetish Form; Across the Hudson; Fetish Form* Series II; *Fetish Form* Series IV.
Exhibited: Los Angeles County Fair, 1953; Oakland Museum of Art, 1968; Crocker Art Gallery, Sacramento, 1958; San Francisco Art Assn. Annuals, 1953-6; San Francisco Museum of Art, 1954, 1955; The Six Gallery, San Francisco, 1955; Gump's Gallery, 1965-7; Walnut Creek Civic Arts Gallery, 1968.
Awards: Nomination as one of San Francisco's Future Leaders in the Arts by Committee for San Francisco Future, 1953; Purchase prize & 1st prize, Los Angeles County Fair, 1953; Purchase prize, Oakland Art Museum, 1968; Special scholarship for painting, 1957; San Francisco Art Festival, 1955; Cal. Society of Classical Arts Special Scholarship for Painting, 1957.
Sources: Oakland Museum. *New Perspectives in Black Art;* Indiana Univ. *Fine Arts & the Black American;* Lewis/Waddy. *Black Artists on Art;* DuSable Museum of African-Amer. History. *Contemporary Black Artists,* 1970 Calendar; Harley, Ralph, Jr. "Checklist of Afro-Amer. Art & Artists," *Serif,* Dec. 1970; Atkinson, J. Edward. *Black Dimensions in Contemporary American Art,* NY, 1971; Oakland Museum Archives; Walker, Roslyn. *A Resource Guide to the Visual Arts of Afro-Americans,* South Bend, Ind., 1971.

CARROLL, TED

Cartoonist. Worked for *New York Mirror* as Sports cartoonist.
Sources: *Ebony,* Dec. 1959, pp. 123-8; Spradling, Mary M., ed. *In Black and White: Afro-Americans in Print.*

CARSON, LINDA E.

Painter. Studied at Knoxville College.
Works: Untitled charcoal.
Exhibited: Sun Times/Daily News Gallery, Chicago, 1970.
Sources: United Negro College Fund. *Art 1970,* Chicago, 1970.

CARTER, ALBERT JOSEPH

Painter, curator. Born in Washington, DC,

1915. Studied at Howard University (BS); Columbia University Teachers' College (MA). Curator of Howard University Gallery of Art.
Works: *The Search for Truth* (oil).
Exhibited: State Armory, Wilmington, Del., 1971; DC Art Assn., 1971; Art Gallery, Dept. of Interior; District of Columbia Public Library; Aesthetic Dynamics, 1971; Howard Univ.
Awards: Teamer Religious & Educational Enterprises, honorary DHL, 1968.
Sources: Aesthetic Dynamics. *Afro-American Images,* 1971; DC Art Assn. *Exhibition '71,* Washington, DC, 1971; Brown, Marion. "The Negro in the Fine Arts," *The Negro Heritage Library,* Vol. 2.

CARTER, DONALD

Sources: DuSable Museum of African-Amer. History. *Contemporary Black Artists,* 1970 Calendar; Walker, Roslyn. *A Resource Guide to the Visual Arts of Afro-Americans,* South Bend, Ind., 1971.

CARTER, GEORGE C.

Painter, mixed media. Born in Jamaica, New York, 1931. Studied at Union College (BS); Columbia University; Pratt Institute; Northwestern University; City College of New York; Art Students League; New School for Social Research.
Works: *An American Dream; Weekend Triptych; Le Roi.*
Exhibited: Studio Museum in Harlem, 1969; Gallery 500, 1963 (1-man); Harouts, 1964 (1-man); Lever House, NY, 1969; New School for Social Research, 1961; Rhode Island School of Design, 1969; Memorial Art Gallery, Rochester, NY, 1969; San Francisco Museum of Art, 1969; Contemporary Arts Museum, Houston, 1970; NJ State Museum, Trenton, 1970; Robeson Center for the Arts & Sciences, Binghamton, NY, 1970; Univ. of Cal. at Santa Barbara, 1970.
Sources: Studio Museum in Harlem. *Harlem Artists 69;* Lever House. *Counterpoints,* NY, 1969; Ruder & Finn Fine Arts. *Contemporary Black Artists,* 1969; "Showcase for Black Artists," *Boston Sunday Globe,* July 6, 1969, p. A73; Walker, Roslyn. *A Resource Guide to the Visual Arts of Afro-Americans,* South Bend, Ind., 1971.

CARTER, GRANT

Painter.
Works: *Missouri Share-Croppers.*
Exhibited: Atlanta Univ., 1943.
Sources: Harley, Ralph, Jr. "Checklist of Afro-Amer. Art & Artists," *The Serif,* Dec. 1970; Parks, James D. "An Experiment in Painting the Local Scene," *Design,* Feb. 1946, pp. 10-12.

CARTER, HAROLD

Painter.
Works: *West African Maiden* (oil).
Exhibited: Lee Cultural Center, Phila.
Sources: Phila. Dept. of Recreation. *Love . . . and the Black Community.*

CARTER, JOSEPH S.

Painter, educator. Studied at New York University (BS in Art Education, 1934). Worked in Corona, New York.
Works: *Still Life.*
Exhibited: Harmon Foundation, 1933; Grand Central Art Galleries, 1934.
Member: Sanka Art Guild, president.
Sources: Harmon Foundation. *Negro Artists,* Catalog, 1935; Harmon Foundation. *Exhibition of Productions by Negro Artists;* DuSable Museum of African-Amer. History. *Contemporary Black Artists,* 1970, Calendar; Harley, Ralph, Jr. "Checklist of Afro-Amer. Art & Artists," *Serif,* Dec. 1970; Dover. *American Negro Art;* Oakland Museum. *New Perspectives in Black Art;* Indiana Univ. *Fine Arts & the Black American;* Walker, Roslyn. *A Resource Guide to the Visual Arts of Afro-Americans,* South Bend, Ind., 1971.

CARTER, ROBERT

Graphic artist. Born in Louisville, Kentucky, 1938.
Works: *My Black; Oh Say Can You See.*
Exhibited: Illinois Bell Telephone Traveling Show, 1971-2.
Sources: Illinois Bell Telephone. *Black American Artists/71,* 1972; Haas, Joseph. "A Big, Brilliant & Exciting Exhibition of Black Art," *Chicago Daily News,* Jan. 16-7. 1971.

CARTER, WILLIAM

Painter. Born in St. Louis, Missouri in 1909. Studied at Art Institute of Chicago (1930-1); University of Illinois (1935-6). Worked with the Illinois Art and Craft Project, Chicago (1943).
Works: *Missouri Snow; Clouds Over Kinlock; Still Life With Purple Plum; Demi-Monde; Town in Arizona; Study; West Kinlock; Forest Park; Hestus House; Peonies; Study in Grey; Barbara; Nude; Small Town Dandy; Banquet; Portrait of Rev. Joseph Branham; Portrait of Mrs. Joseph H. Branham; Bouquet; Landscape; Ballerina Takes a Bow; Ballerina; Hermits; Midwestern Landscape.*
Exhibited: Chicago Art League, 1934; Art Institute of Chicago, 1937; Hull House, Chicago, 1938; Illinois Federal Project, 1937-9; Amer. Negro Exposition, Chicago, 1940; Atlanta Univ., 1944; Howard Univ., 1941; Library of Congress, 1940; Smith College, 1943; Institute of Modern Art, Boston, 1943; South Side Community Art Center, Chicago, 1941, 1945.

Collections: Johnson Pub. Co., Chicago; Rev. & Mrs. Joseph H. Branham; Mr. & Mrs. Earl B. Dickerson; Mrs. O. H. Crosthwait.
Sources: Albany Institute of History. *The Negro Artist Comes of Age;* Locke. *The Negro in Art;* Chatfield-Taylor, Rose. "Howard U. Holds Negro Exhibit," *Washington Post,* Feb. 16, 1941; Howard Univ. *Exhibit of Negro Artists of Chicago at H.U. Gallery of Art,* 1941; Motley, Willard F. "Negro Art in Chicago," *Opportunity,* Jan. 1940; Berryman, Florence S. "Negro Artists of Chicago, George Neal Proteges, Exhibit Work Here," *Sunday Star* (Washington, DC), Feb. 23, 1941; Du-Sable Museum of African-Amer. History. *Contemporary Black Artists,* calendar, 1970; Tanner Art Galleries. *Art of the American Negro,* catalog, 1940; Afro-American Slide Depository, Catalog; "Art By Negroes," *Art Digest,* Oct. 15, 1941; "Amer. Negro Art Given Full Length Review in NY Show," *Art Digest,* Dec. 15, 1941; "Negro Art Annual," *Art Digest,* May 1, 1942; Locke, Alain. "Chicago's New Southside Art Center," *American Magazine of Art,* Aug. 1941, p. 320; J.W.L. "Negro in Art," *Art News,* Dec. 19, 1941, p. 24; "The Negro Artist Comes of Age," *Art News,* Feb. 1, 1945; "American Negro Art," *Design Magazine,* Feb. 1942, p. 28; Johnson Pub. Co. *The JPC Art Collection,* pamphlet; Porter. *Modern Negro Art;* Dover. *American Negro Art;* Harley, Ralph, Jr. "Checklist of Afro-Amer. Art & Artists," *The Serif,* Dec. 1970; Ploski, Harry, Ernest Kaiser. "The Black Artist," *Afro USA,* 1971; Ploski, Harry, Ernest Kaiser, Otto Lindenmeyer. "The Black Artist," *Reference Library of Black America,* Book 4, 1971; South Side Community Art Center. *Chicago Collectors Exhibit of Negro Art,* 1946; South Side Community Art Center. *National Negro Art Exhibition,* Chicago, 1941; South Side Community Art Center. *Opening Exhibition of Paintings by Negro Artists,* Chicago, 1941; Myers, Carol. *Black Power in the Arts,* Flint, Mich., 1970; McMillen Inc. Galleries. *Contemporary Negro Art,* NY, 1941; Walker, Roslyn. *A Resource Guide to the Visual Arts of Afro-Americans,* South Bend, Ind., 1971.

CARTER, YVONNE

Graphic artist.
Works: *Lateral Movement* (etching); *Not Yet Forgotten; Natural Movement.*
Exhibited: Smith-Mason Gallery, Washington, DC, 1971.
Collections: Oakland Museum, Ruth Waddy Collection.
Sources: Roelof-Lanner, T.V. *Prints by American Negro Artists;* Smith-Mason Gallery. *National Exhibition Black Artists 1971;* Oakland Museum Archives; Walker, Roslyn. *A Re-source Guide to the Visual Arts of Afro-Americans,* South Bend, Ind., 1971.

CARTWRIGHT, CATHERINE

Painter.
Works: *Gravity; The Nature of Man; Biafra & 116th Street; Women Waiting #3; Faces; Join Together; The Social Animal; Poly-Rhythm; Sense of Oneness; Women Waiting #7; Freedom Song; Dichotomy; Nubian Trilogy; Seat of Spirit; Patterns; Ascend; Descend; Woman Waiting #5.*
Sources: Afro-American Slide Depository, Catalog.

CARTY, LEO

Painter, printmaker, educator, illustrator of children's books. Studied at the Museum of Modern Art School; Cooper Union; Pratt Institute; School of Visual Arts; Brooklyn Community College. Born in New York City, 1931.
Works: *Funeral; Utopia; The Prophet: Marcus Garvey,* 1964.
Exhibited: Market Place Gallery; American Internat'l College, 1972 (1-man); Brooklyn Public Library, 1957 (1-man); Madison Square Garden; Marino Galleries; Fulton Art Fair.
Sources: Sheridan, Lee. "Afro-American Cultural Center To Exhibit NY Artist's Works," *Daily News,* Springfield, Mass., Nov. 9, 1972; *Market Place Gallery,* Catalog; Snyder, Anne. *50,000 Names for Jeff,* 1969; Madison Square Garden. *Art USA,* Unpublished list; Information from the artist.

CARVER, GEORGE WASHINGTON

Painter. Born 1864 near Diamond Grove Missouri. Died 1943. Taught in Art Department of Tuskegee Institute.
Works: *Yucca; Peaches; Still Life; Landscape; Roses.*
Collections: Carver Museum.
Sources: *Negro Year Book;* Indiana Univ. *Fine Arts and the Black American;* Mallett. *Index of Artists;* Afro-American Slide Depository, Catalog, 1971-2; Dover. *American Negro Art;* Walker, Roslyn. *A Resource Guide to the Visual Arts of Afro-Americans,* South Bend, Ind., 1971.

CASEY, BERNARD TERRY

See: Casey, Bernie.

CASEY, BERNIE

Painter. Born in Wyco, West Virginia in 1939. Studied at Bowling Green State University (BA; MFA, 1966). Screen actor and writer; co-founder of Negro Industrial and Economic Union; President of Community Arts Foundation; star flanker back for Los Angeles Rams.
Works: *You Can Win the Game, If It's Your*

Turn; In Little Ways; Schizophrenic Moon Folly; White Bird; Some Rainy Days; Saturday's Nightscape; Shadow in the Bright Sun; Barbara; An Excerpt From a Terry Trip; The Quiet Time (pencil dwg.), 1970; *That Saturday Morning* (pencil dwg.), 1970; *Quiet Lady* (pencil dwg.), 1970; *A.T.* (pencil dwg.), 1970; *Special Places* (pencil dwg.), 1970; *That Erotic Line* (pencil dwg.), 1970; *Nicole* (pencil dwg.), 1970; *I Remember; Soul Meditation* (pencil dwg.), 1969; *Your Brown* (pencil dwg.), 1970.
Exhibited: Ankrum Gallery, Los Angeles (two 1-man shows); John Bolles Gallery, San Francisco (two 1-man shows); La Jolla Museum of Art, 1970; Univ. of Iowa Museum of Art, 1972.
Collections: Ankrum Gallery, Los Angeles; Ms. Naomi Hirshhorn; Ms. Mary Jane Hewitt.
Sources: Indiana Univ. *Fine Arts & the Black American;* "Afro-American Issue," *Art Gallery,* April 1968; Lewis/Waddy. *Black Artists on Art,* Vol. 1; La Jolla Museum of Art. *Dimensions of Black;* DuSable Museum of African-Amer. History. *Contemporary Black Artists,* 1970 calendar; Ill. Bell Telephone. *Black American Artists/71,* Catalog; Greene, Carroll, Jr. "Afro-American Artists: Yesterday & Now," *The Humble Way,* Vol. 8, No. 3, 1968; Greene, Carroll, Jr. *Afro-American Artists: 1800-1968,* slides & commentary; Harley, Ralph L., Jr. "Checklist of Afro-American Art & Artists," *The Serif,* Dec. 1970; Atkinson, J. Edward. *Black Dimensions in Contemporary American Art,* NY, 1971; Myers, Carol L. *Black Power in the Arts,* Flint, Mich., 1970; Casey, Bernie. *My Point of View-Poems and Drawings,* Los Angeles, Bernie Casey, 1971; Walker, Roslyn. *A Resource Guide to the Visual Arts of Afro-Americans,* South Bend, Ind., 1971.

CASSELL, ALBERT I.

Architect. Born in Washington, 1895. Studied at Cornell University.
Works: Girls Dormitory, Morgan State College, Baltimore; buildings at Howard University, Washington, DC—3 women's dormitories, recitation building (Frederick Douglass Memorial Hall), power plant, Chemistry building, Library building.
Sources: Brawley, Benjamin. *The Negro Genius;* Wilson, John L. *The Negro Architect;* Robinson, Wilhelmena S. *Historical Negro Biographies;* Spradling, Mary M., ed. *In Black & White: Afro-Americans in Print;* Downing, Lewis K. "Contributions of Negro Scientists," *Crisis,* June 1939.

CATCHINGS, YVONNE PARKS

Painter. Born in Atlanta, August 17, 1935. Studied at Spelman College (AB); Columbia University (MA, 1958); Museum Practice University of Michigan (MA); Atlanta University; Wayne State University; Detroit Institute of Art (1959-60). Art teacher in Detroit secondary schools.
Works: *From New York to Jersey; War; Backyard Wash; Still Life; Through the Columns; Cafe in the Village; Riverside Church at Night; The Detroit Riot; The Resurrection; Bringing a Baby to a Sick World; Indigo #1; Flowers; Frustrated Woman in Society; Search for Peace; New Site; Stop the War; Indigo #2; The Chains Are Still There.*
Exhibited: Atlanta Univ., 1953-9, 1963; Detroit Art Teachers, 1960-1; Contemporary Studio, 1960-1; Northwestern High School, 1970; Lafayette Park Art Fair, Columbia; Tuskegee Institute.
Collections: Spelman College; Atty. & Mrs. Hobart Taylor; Col. & Mrs. Francis Davis; Carnegie Institute slide collection.
Awards: Honorable Mention, Atlanta Univ., 1955, 1957-9; Scarab Club, 1961; Jerome Award, Spelman College, 1955.
Member: National Conference of Artists; National Art Education Assn. Founders Society; Detroit Institute of Art.
Sources: Afro-American Slide Depository, catalog, 1970-1; Lewis/Waddy. *Black Artists on Art,* Vol. 2; Information from artist; *Arts and Activities,* Jan. 1960; *The Instructor,* May 1960, April 1961, Dec. 1962; *The Michigan Chronicle,* March 1971; Dover. *American Negro Art;* Nat'l Conference of Artists. *A Print Portfolio by Negro Artists,* 1963.

CATLETT, ALICE

Sculptor, painter, printmaker. Born in Washington, DC, 1915.
Exhibited: Univ. of Iowa, 1939; Downtown Gallery, 1940; Amer. Negro Exposition, Chicago, 1940; Brown Univ., 1943; Smith College Museum of Art, 1943; Institute of Modern Art, Boston, 1943; Baltimore Museum, 1944; Newark Museum, 1944; Renaissance Society, Univ. of Chicago, 1944; Barnet Aden Gallery, 1948 (1-man); Howard Univ., 1961.
Sources: "Amer. Negro Art Given Full Length Review in NY Show," *Art Digest,* Dec. 15, 1941; "The Negro Artists in America," *Amer. Contemporary Art,* April 1944; "A Tribute to the Negro People," *Amer. Contemporary Art,* Winter 1946; Harley, Ralph, Jr. "Checklist of Afro-Amer. Art & Artists," *The Serif,* Dec. 1970; Myers, Carol L. *Black Power in the Arts,* Flint, Mich., 1970.

CATLETT, ELIZABETH (Mrs. Charles White)

Sculptor, painter, printmaker. Born in Washington, DC, 1915. Studied at Howard University (AB, 1936); University of Iowa (MFA,

1940); studied under Ossip Zadkine and Grant Wood; Arts Students League; Art Institute of Chicago. Teacher of painting and sculpture at Dillard University (1940); Prairie View College; Hampton Institute; George Washington Carver School; the Jefferson School; University of Mexico.

Works: *Olmec Bather; Reclining Woman; Woman; Malcolm X Speaks for Us; Freyer; Mother and Child* (terra cotta); *Negro Woman; Sharecropper; Homage to the Panthers; Black Unity; Figure; Head of Negro Woman; The Bathers; Tired; Young Girl; Singing Head* (brown marble); *Homage to My Young Black Sisters,* 1968 (cedar).

Exhibited: Univ. of Iowa, 1939; Downtown Gallery, NYC, 1940; Amer. Negro Exposition, 1940; Atlanta Univ., 1942, 1943, 1951; Institute of Modern Art, 1943; Baltimore Museum, 1944; Newark Museum, 1944; Renaissance Society, 1944; Univ. of Chicago, 1944; Albany Institute of History & Art, 1945; Museum of Modern Art, Mexico; Brockman Gallery, Los Angeles (1-man); City College, NY, 1967; La Jolla Museum, 1970; James A. Porter Gallery, 1970; National Print Salon; National Center of Afro-Amer. Artists, 1970; Rainbow Sign Gallery, 1972; Solar Exhibition, Olympic Villa, Mexico; Cal. State Univ., 1971; Studio Museum, Harlem, 1971-2.

Collections: Museum of Modern Art; Library of Congress; Museum of Modern Art, Mexico; Univ. of Iowa; Howard Univ.; Atlanta Univ.; Mr. & Mrs. Daniel Shirmer; National Polytechnic Institute, Mexico City; DuSable Museum of African-Amer. Art & History.

Awards: 1st prize, sculpture, Amer. Negro Exposition, 1940; Acquisition Prize, National Print Salon; Olympic Village, 1968; Rosenwald Fellowship; 1st prize, sculpture, Golden Jubilee Exhibition, Chicago; 2 prizes, sculpture, Sculpture Biannuals, Mexico City; Honorable Mention, 2nd Latin Amer. Print Exhibit, Havana.

Sources: Locke. *The Negro in Art;* Dover. *American Negro Art;* Albany Institute of History & Art. *Negro Artist Comes of Age;* "Afro-American Issue," *Art Gallery,* April 1968; Indiana Univ. *Fine Arts & the Black American;* Lewis/Waddy. *Black Artists on Art,* Vol. 2; Fax, Elton C. *Seventeen Black Artists;* City College of NY. *Evolution of Afro-American Artists 1800-1950,* 1967; "Negro World's Fair," *Newsweek,* Sept. 9, 1940; La Jolla Museum of Art. *Dimensions of Black;* DuSable Museum of African-Amer. History. *Contemporary Black Artists,* 1970 Calendar; Tanner Art Galleries. *Art of the American Negro,* 1940; Howard Univ. *James A. Porter Gallery of African-American Art,* 1970; Greene, Carroll, Jr. "Perspective: The Black Artist in America," *Art Gallery,* April 1970,

p. 25; "The Negro in Art," *Art Digest,* June 1, 1944; "Negro Winners," *Art Digest,* May 1, 1946; Pierre-Noel, Lois Jones. "American Negro Art in Progress," *Negro History Bulletin,* Oct. 1967; "The Negro Artist Comes of Age," *Art News,* Feb. 1, 1945; Greene, Carroll, Jr. "Afro-Amer. Artists: Yesterday & Now," *The Humble Way,* Vol. 8, No. 3, 1968; Xavier Univ. *Emancipation Proclamation Centennial National Art Exhibition,* 1963; Greene, Carroll, Jr. *Afro-American Artists: 1800-1968,* slides; Fax, Elton C. "Four Rebels in Art," *Freedomways,* Spring 1961; Ploski, Harry, & Ernest Kaiser. "The Black Artist," *Afro USA,* 1971; "My Art Speaks for Both My Peoples," *Ebony,* Feb. 1970; *The Negro Handbook,* Composed by Editors of *Ebony,* Chicago, 1966; Schatz, Walter. *Directory of Afro-American Resources,* 1970; National Center of Afro-Amer. Artists. *Elizabeth Catlett,* 1972; Rainbow Sign Gallery. *Elizabeth Catlett,* Press Release, Berkeley, Cal., Sept. 1972; Rainbow Sign Gallery. *Black Arts Day II,* Press Release, Sept. 1972; Barnet Aden Gallery. *The Negro Woman,* 1948; Walker, Roslyn. *A Resource Guide to the Visual Arts of Afro-Americans,* South Bend, Ind., 1971.

CATLETT, FRANCIS DUNHAM

Painter, educator. Born in Hartford, Connecticut, July 3, 1908. Studied at Boston University (BA); Mills College, Oakland (MA); University of Chicago; University of California, Berkeley (MSW); San Francisco Art Institute. Assistant Professor, Social Work, Sacramento State College.

Works: *St. Thomas Sea; Eagle Lake-Lassen.*

Exhibited: Oakland Museum, Kaiser Center, 1967, 1968; San Francisco Art Commission, 1968; Chaboy College, 1968.

Sources: Oakland Museum. *New Perspectives in Black Art;* Harley, Ralph, Jr. "Checklist of Afro-American Art & Artists," *The Serif,* Dec. 1970; DuSable Museum of African-Amer. History. *Contemporary Black Artists,* 1970, calendar; Indiana Univ. *Fine Arts & the Black American;* Walker, Roslyn. *A Resource Guide to the Visual Arts of Afro-Americans,* South Bend, Ind., 1971.

CATO, ROY

Sculptor, educator. Works in Boston. Teacher of sculpture at Cambridge Center for Adult Education, 1971.

Works: *Woman II; Blue Angel; The Egyptian; Woman I.*

Exhibited: Institute of Contemporary Art, Boston, 1971; National Center of Afro-Amer. Artists, Boston; Boston Center for the Arts, 1973.

Sources: Faxon, Alicia. "Profile: Local Artist Roy Cato," *Boston Globe,* Sept. 8, 1971.

CATON, MITCHELL

Painter. Born 1930 in Chicago. Studied at Arkansas AM&N College.
Works: Untitled mural details.
Exhibited: Museum of Contemporary Arts, Chicago.
Sources: Lewis/Waddy. *Black Artists on Art*, Vol. 2.

CATTANI, ADOLPH DANTE

Works: *Female Nudes.*
Exhibited: 12th Annual Invitational Exhibition, Pyramid Club, Phila., 1952.
Sources: Drummond, Dorothy. "Coast-to-Coast," *Art Digest*, March 1, 1952.

CATTI

Painter. Born 1940.
Works: *Man, Moon, and Earth*, 1970 (synthetic polymer on canvas).
Exhibited: Whitney Museum, 1971.
Sources: Doty. *Contemporary Black Artists in America.*

CEDENIO, JUAN

Painter.
Works: *Portrait of George Cleveland Hall.*
Exhibited: South Side Community Art Center, Chicago, 1945.
Collections: Mrs. George Cleveland Hall.
Sources: South Side Community Art Center. *Chicago Collectors Exhibit of Art*, Chicago, 1945.

CHAMBERS, WILLIAM

Painter. Born in Tampa, Florida in 1932. Studied at the Art Students League, NY.
Works: *The Assassination of a Leader; Blue Boy.*
Exhibited: Studio Museum in Harlem, 1969.
Sources: Studio Museum in Harlem. *Harlem Artists 69.*

CHAMBLESS, CHARLOTTE

Painter, graphic artist, educator. Born in New Orleans. Studied at Dillard University, Louisiana (BA); Mills College, Oakland (MEd); California College of Arts & Crafts; University of California, Berkeley; University of Oregon; University of Aix Marsaille, Aix-en, Provence, France. Teacher at McClymonds High School, Oakland.
Works: *Windblown; How Wild the Wind.*
Exhibited: Oakland Museum, 1968; Henry Gallery, Univ. of Wash.; Oakland Chapter, California Art Assn., 1966, 1967.
Sources: Oakland Museum. *New Perspectives in Black Art;* Indiana Univ. *Fine Arts & the Black American;* DuSable Museum of African-Amer. History. *Contemporary Black Artists*, 1970; Harley, Ralph, Jr. "Checklist of Afro-Amer. Art & Artists," *The Serif*, Dec. 1970;

Walker, Roslyn. *A Resource Guide to the Visual Arts of Afro-Americans*, South Bend, Ind., 1971.

CHANDLER, DANA C., JR.

Painter, muralist, lecturer. Born in Lynn, Massachusetts in 1941. Studied at Massachusetts College of Art (BS, 1967).
Works: *Bobby Seale, Prisoner of War*, 1970; *Fred Hampton's Door; Martin Luther King, Jr. Assassinated*, 1970; *The Golden Prison; Land of the Free; Land of the Free #2; Nigger . . . You Are a Four Hundred Year Prisoner; LeRoi Jones—House Arrest; Death of Uncle Tom; Moses Brings the Word to His People; Rebellion '68; Challenge; Taters and Bullets; Dynamite; Death of a Bigot.*
Exhibited: Edna Stebbins Gallery, Cambridge, Mass. (1-man); Piper Gallery, Lexington, Mass. (1-man); Emerson Gallery (1-man); Gallery Amadeus, Boston (1-man); Skifin Gallery, Boston (1-man); Copley Gallery, Boston; Boston College; Rhode Island School of Design; Boston Univ.; Nat'l Center of Afro-Amer. Artists, Boston; Lawrence Cultural Art Center; 1st Church in Belmont; Rose Museum, Brandeis Univ., 1968; Studio Museum in Harlem, 1968; Boston Museum of Fine Arts, 1970; Smith-Mason Gallery, Washington, DC, 1971; Northeastern Univ.; Univ. of Mass. at Amherst; Mass. College of Art; Wheelock College; Wheaton College; WVa. State College; Clayborne's Black Arts Gallery; Unitarian Church in Beverly, Mass.; Unitarian Church, Norton, Mass.; Concord Baptist Church in Roxbury, Mass.; Community Church, Copley Square, Boston; NAACP Nat'l Convention, Boston, 1967; Professional Businessmen's Club, Roxbury, Mass.; Children's Art Center; Boston Negro Artists' Assn.
Collections: Mr. Benny Andrews.
Member: Boston Negro Artists' Assn.; Model Cities Consortium Art Program.
Sources: Boston Museum of Fine Arts. *Afro-American Artists: New York & Boston*, 1970; Lewis/Waddy. *Black Artists on Art*, Vol. 1; *Time*, April 6, 1970; *Jet*, June 1, 1971; *Muhammud Speaks*, 1969-70; *Newsweek*, Aug. 18, 1970; *Harvard Art Review*, 1969; *Who's Who in the East*, 1971; DuSable Museum of African-Amer. History. *Contemporary Black Artists*, calendar, 1970; Smith-Mason Gallery. *National Exhibition of Black Artists*, 1971; Community Lecture Series (Boston). *Local Afro-American Artists*, 1969; Bowling, Frank. "Silence: People Die Crying When They Should Love," *Arts*, Sept. 1970; Giuliano, Charles. "MFA: What the Museum is Doing for Black Art," *Boston After Dark*, March 11, 1970; "Black Art Exhibit Opens Sunday," *Herald* (Belmont, Mass.), May 14, 1970;

"Preview Party to Open Show by 13 Black Artists," *Citizen,* May 14, 1970; Hinchcliffe, Diane. "Black Art Exhibit: Future Looks a Little Brighter," *Chronicle-Citizen* (Brookline, Mass.), June 4, 1970; Sherman, Majorie. "Afro-America Gets Biggest Show," *Boston Globe,* May 18, 1970; Kramer, Hilton. "Trying to Define 'Black Art': Must We Go Back to Social Realism?," *New York Times,* May 31, 1970; "What is Black Art?," *Newsweek,* June 22, 1970; Museum of the Nat'l Center of Afro-Amer. Artists. *Taking Care of Business;* Loercher, Diana. "National Center of Afro-Amer. Artists Art & Benefit Premier," *Christian Science Monitor,* May 4, 1971; Driscoll, Edgar. "Art Show Reflects Black Rage, Pride," *Boston Globe,* April 28, 1971; "Museum to Hold Black Art Show," *Tri-Town Transcript & Pennysaver,* April 29, 1970; Gerson, Sareen R. "Black Art New York-Hub Set for Museum of Fine Arts," *Minuteman,* March 19, 1970; Ploski, Harry, & Ernest Kaiser. "The Black Artist," *Afro USA,* 1971; Berkman, Florence. "Afro-American Exhibit Fosters Understanding of Black Artists," *Times* (Hartford, Conn.), May 24, 1970; Van Almelo, Frederik. "In the American Grain," *Boston After Dark,* May 26, 1970; Walsh, Rose. "Artists to Meet Public at Art Exhibit Preview," *Record American* (Boston), May 19, 1970; "Black Show," *Times* (Gloucester, Mass.), May 16, 1970; LeBrun, Caron. "Blacks' Art on Display," *Herald Traveler* (Boston), May 26, 1970; Schwartz, Therese. "The Political Scene," *Arts,* April 1971; Paris, Jean. "Black Art Experience in Art," *Long Island Press,* June 14, 1970; Ploski, Harry, Otto Lindenmeyer, & Ernest Kaiser. "The Black Artist," *Reference Library of Black America,* Book 4, 1971; Bowling, Frank. "It's Not Enough to Say 'Black is Beautiful,'" *Art News,* April 1971; Jordan, Robert A. "Roxbury Students Build African Hut," *Boston Globe,* June 26, 1970; LeBrun, Caron. "Black Art," *Herald Traveler* (Boston), Sunday Supplement, May 24, 1970; Driscoll, Edgar. Column, *Boston Evening Globe,* May 20, 1970; Dinger, Paul. "Chandler's Revolutionary Art Puzzles Critic," *Boston Globe,* Oct. 13, 1970; Walker, Roslyn. *A Resource Guide to the Visual Arts of Afro-Americans,* South Bend, Ind., 1971; "Afro-American Artists: NY & Boston," *Prudential Center News,* March 1, 1970, p. 4.

CHANDLER, HOUSTON E.

Graphic artist. Studied at State University of Iowa (MA, MFA).
Works: *2 Masks* (beaten lead); *Mother & Child; Bust; Cock.*
Exhibited: People's Art Center, 1949.

Awards: Atlanta Univ.; Walker Art Center, Minn.; Iowa State Fair.
Sources: *St. Louis Post Dispatch,* Feb. 6, 1949; Aug. 15, 1948.

CHANDLER, JOHN EDWARD

Painter. Born in 1943 in Virginia. Studied at the High School of Music and Art, New York; New York University; New York Studio School.
Works: *Stasis 4; Solation; Kulu Se,* 1969 (acrylic); Untitled acrylic, 1969; *Garvey's Quest; B.B.P.; Otis Span,* 1971; *Audubon Wallroom,* 1971; *Red Ascending.*
Exhibited: Pan-Am Building, NY, 1969; NY Univ., 1970; Boston Museum of Fine Arts, 1970; Whitney Museum, NY, 1971-2; Gallery Museum, Saratoga, NY, 1970.
Collections: Whitney Museum, NY; Mr. Douglas Durst; Schoenfield Collection.
Sources: NY State Education Dept. *Fifteen Under Forty,* Saratoga, NY, 1970; Boston Museum of Fine Arts. *Afro-American Artists: New York & Boston,* 1970; Doty. *Contemporary Black Artists in America;* Rose, Barbara. "Black Art in America," *Art in America,* July-Dec. 1970; Whitney Museum. *Whitney Annual of Painting 1972,* catalog; NY Univ. *Eclipse,* 1969; Information from artist.

CHAPLIN, J. G.

Painter. Studied in Germany.
Works: *Macbeth Frightened by Banquo's Ghost; Emancipation; The Fool; Dream of Nebuchadnezzar.*
Collections: William H. Dorsey Collection of Afro-Americana.
Sources: *Art in America,* Jan. 1936, pp. 16-27; Brawley, Benjamin. *The Negro Genius;* DuSable Museum of African-Amer. History. *Contemporary Black Artists,* 1970 calendar; Harley, Ralph, Jr. "Checklist of Afro-Amer. Art & Artists," *The Serif,* Dec. 1970.

CHAPLIN, J. W.

Painter. Worked in 19th century in Philadelphia area. Concentrated on anti-slavery themes.
Sources: Runes/Schrickel. *Encyclopedia of the Arts,* p. 36.

CHAPPELL, JESSE

Sculptor. Studied at Claflin College.
Exhibited: Sun Times/Daily News Gallery, Chicago, 1970.
Sources: United Negro College Fund. *Art 1970,* Chicago, 1970.

CHARLES, GERALDINE

Commercial artist.
Exhibited: Harmon Foundation, 1928, 1935.
Sources: Harley, Ralph, Jr. "Checklist of Afro-Amer. Art & Artists," *The Serif,* Dec. 1970;

Harmon Foundation. *Exhibition of Productions by Negro Artists*, 1928; Harmon Foundation. *Negro Artists*, 1935; Indiana Univ. *Fine Arts & the Black American;* DuSable Museum of African-Amer. History. *Contemporary Black Artists*, calendar, 1970; Walker, Roslyn. *A Resource Guide to the Visual Arts of Afro-Americans*, South Bend, Ind., 1971.

CHASE, WILLIAM CHARLES

Graphic artist. Born in 1911 in Arkansas. Studied at Howard University. Staff artist on the *Amsterdam News*.
Works: *The Gossipers* (charcoal); *Portrait of My Mother* (charcoal).
Exhibited: Harmon Foundation, 1933.
Collections: Howard Univ.
Awards: Art Award in High School.
Sources: Harmon Foundation. *Non-Jury Exhibit of Works of Negro Artists*, 1933.

CHASE-RIBOUD, BARBARA

Sculptor, printmaker, illustrator. Born in 1939 in Philadelphia. Studied at Temple University, Philadelphia (BFA); Yale University (MFA, 1960). Lives in Paris, France.
Works: *Victorious Bullfighter; Adam and Eve; Mother and Child; The Last Supper; Bulls; Figure Volante; The Centurion; Monuments to Malcolm X; The Ultimate Sound; Time Womb; The Bullfighter.*
Exhibited: Art Alliance, 1957; 1st Spoleto Festival, 1958; Gallery L'Obelisou, Rome, 1958; Amer. Academy, Rome, 1958; Carnegie Internat'l Exhibition, 1958; Pa. Academy of Fine Arts, Phila., 1959; Wheaton Plaza Fountain, Washington, 1960; NY Architect League Show, 1965; Festival of Negro Art, Dakar, 1966; Bertha Schaefer Gallery, NY, 1970; Whitney Museum, NY, 1971; Americans of Paris, Air France, 1969; L'Oeil Ecoute, Festival of Avignon, 1969; Museum of Fine Arts, Boston, 1970; Commercial Museum, Phila., 1965; ACA Gallery, NY, 1954; Betty Parsons Gallery, NY, 1972 (1-woman); Mass. Institute of Technology, 1970 (1-woman); Le Cadron Solaire, Paris, 1966 (1-woman); Nat'l Gallery of Art, Toronto, 1971; Salon de Mai, Paris, 1971-2; Salon de la Jeune Sculpture, 1971; Salon des Nouvelles Réalitiés, 1972; Hudson River Museum, 1971; Newark Museum, 1971.
Collections: Bertha Schaefer Gallery, NY; Newark Museum; Museum of Modern Art; Phila. Art Alliance.
Awards: John Hay Whitney Foundation Fellowship, 1957-8; Phila. Art Alliance Purchase Prize, 1957; *Seventeen* Painting Prize, 1954; Nat'l Endowment for the Arts Award.
Sources: Dover. *American Negro Art;* US Committee for the 1st World Festival of Negro Arts. *Ten Negro Artists From the United States*, Dakar, Senegal, 1966; "Afro-American Issue," *Art Gallery*, April 1968; Boston Museum of Fine Arts. *Afro-American Artists/ New York & Boston*, 1970; Bertha Schaefer Gallery. *Barbara Chase-Riboud*, NY, Feb. 1970; Indiana Univ. *Fine Arts & the Black American;* Doty. *Contemporary Black Artists in America;* Last, Martin, "Reviews and Previews," *Art News*, March 1970, p. 12; "People: Barbara Chase-Riboud," *Essence*, June 1970, pp. 62, 71; Ratcliff, Carter. "New York Letter," *Art International*, May 20, 1970; DuSable Museum of African-Amer. History. *Contemporary Black Artists*, 1970, calendar; Roucek & Kiernan. *The Negro Impact on Western Civilization;* Greene, Carroll, Jr. "Perspective: The Black Artist in America," *Art Gallery*, April 1970; Rose, Barbara. "Black Art In America," *Art in America*, July-Dec. 1970; Harley, Ralph, Jr. "Checklist of Afro-American Art & Artists," *The Serif*, Dec. 1970; Brown, Marion. "The Negro in the Fine Arts," *Negro Heritage Library*, Vol. 2; Woodruff, Hale. "Artists of the 60's," *The Negro in Music and Art*, 1969; *The Negro Handbook*, composed by the editors of *Ebony*, Chicago, 1966; Nora, Francoise. "From Another Country," *Art News*, March 1972; Lansner, Fay. *Craft Horizons*, April 1972; Hunter, Sam. *American Sculpture and Painting*, Abrams, 1972; Fine, Elsa H. *The Afro-American Artist*, Holt, Rinehart-Winston, 1972; La Coste, Michael Conil. Review, *Le Monde*, May 1971; White, Charles. Review, *Village Voice*, April 15, 1971; Kramer, Hilton. Review, *New York Times*, Feb. 14, 1970; Smith, Alvin. Letter, *New York Times*, Feb. 1970; Ghent, Henri. Letter, *New York Times*, Feb. 1970; *Fine*, film. Silvermine Films, 1971; Johnson, Tom. Interview, *New York Times*, 1966; *Les Lettres Francaises*, Nov. 1966; *Paris Match*, Nov. 1966; Information from artist; Myers, Carol L. *Black Power in the Arts*, Flint, Mich., 1970; Fine, Elsa H. "Mainstream, Blackstream and the Black Art Movement," *Art Journal*, Spring 1971; Walker, Roslyn. *A Resource Guide to the Visual Arts of Afro-Americans*, South Bend, Ind., 1971; *"Afro-American Artists: NY & Boston," Prudential Center News*, March 1, 1970, p. 4.

CHAVANNE, ROSE

Sources: Harley, Ralph, Jr. "Checklist of Afro-Amer. Art & Artists," *The Serif*, Dec. 1970.

CHAVIS, KITTY

Painter. Born in New York City in 1938.
Member: Contemporary Artists Guild, NY.
Sources: Dover. *American Negro Art;* Indiana Univ. *Fine Arts & the Black American;* Harley, Ralph, Jr. "A Checklist of Afro-Amer. Art & Artists," *The Serif*, Dec. 1970; Walker,

Roslyn. *A Resource Guide to the Visual Arts of Afro-Americans,* South Bend, Ind., 1971.

CHELTENHAM, EUGENE
Graphic artist.
Works: *Roota Toot Toot . . .* (color woodcut).
Collections: Oakland Museum, Ruth Waddy Collection.
Sources: Roelof-Lanner, T.V. *Prints by American Negro Artists;* Oakland Museum Archives; Walker, Roslyn. *A Resource Guide to the Visual Arts of Afro-Americans,* South Bend, Ind., 1971.

CHRISTIAN, RUDOLPH
Studied at Lemoyne-Owen College.
Works: *Brown & Green.*
Exhibited: Sun Times/Daily News Gallery, Chicago, 1970.
Sources: United Negro College Fund. *Art 1970,* Chicago, 1970.

CHRISTMAS, EDWARD
Painter.
Sources: Myers, Carol L. *Black Power in the Arts,* Flint, Mich., 1970; "Afro-American Issue," *Art Gallery,* April 1968; Indiana Univ. *Fine Arts & the Black American;* DuSable Museum of African-Amer. History. *Contemporary Black Artists,* 1970 Calendar; Walker, Roslyn. *A Resource Guide to the Visual Arts of Afro-Americans,* South Bend, Ind., 1971.

CHRISTMAS, WALTER
Sources: Harley, Ralph, Jr. "Checklist of Afro-Amer. Art & Artists," *The Serif,* Dec. 1970.

CLARK, BENJAMIN
Painter.
Works: *Age* (oil).
Collections: Johnson Pub. Co.
Sources: Johnson Pub. Co. *The JPC Art Collection,* Pamphlet.

CLARK, CLAUDE, SR.
Painter, draftsman, educator. Born in Rockingham, Georgia, 1914. Studied at Philadelphia Museum School, Barnes Foundation, Philadelphia; Sacramento State College (BA); University of California (MA). Teacher at San Francisco State College; Merritt Campus, Peralta College, California.
Works: *Rascal; Grease Paint; Spring Flowers; Lady in the Park; The Barn; Fish Vendor; Men in Industry; Autumn Landscape; Chee Lai; Victorian Sophistication; Rain; Primitive Mill; Sponge Fisherman; Work Song; Soldering #1; On Guard; Colored Mask; Kindling; Yo Feets Too Big; The Draftsman; Desert Bouquet; Beyond the Marshes; Conversation; Decoration; Poet II; Pallbearers; The Tub; Field Dressing;*
Downbeat; The Camp; Soldering #2; Bouquet; The Attack; Pendle Hill; Upmeads; Resting; Black Orchid; Motor Boat; Homestead; The Hat; In Memoriam; Pot O' Gold; Hoeing & Planting; Southern Exposure; Guttersnipe; The Plow & the Artist; Meditation; Runner; Licolnia; Mangoes; Hillside Landscape; Coffee; Freedom Morning; Building of Tub; Cutting the Sheet; The Troubles I've Seen; Slaughter; Falling Leaves; Evening Meal; Station House; Noon; The Ignition; Near the Beach, Puerto Rico (oil).
Exhibited: Atlanta Univ., 1942-4; Sheraton Hotel, Phila., 1968; Kaiser Center Gallery Oakland, 1968; Friends School, Phila.; Wharton House, Phila.; Phila. Public Schools; NY World's Fair; Library of Congress; Oklahoma Art Center; Southside Art Center, Chicago; Pyramid Club; Academy of Fine Arts, Phila.; Brooklyn Museum; Montclair Art Museum, NJ; G Place Gallery, Washington, DC; Rhode Island School of Design; Florida Internat'l Exhibition; Sorbonne, Paris; San Juan, Puerto Rico; Mexico City; Artists Gallery, Phila. (1-man); Pendel Hill, Wallingford, Pa. (1-man); Bonestell & Roko Galleries, NYC (1-man); Colgate Univ.; Alabama Power Co.; Talladega College; Greater Urban League of Cincinnati; Denison Univ.; Riverside Jr. College, Ohio; Riverside Jr. College, Cal.; Hall of Art, Beverly Hills; E.B. Crocker Gallery, City Library of Sacramento; Ruthermore Galleries, San Francisco; City College, NY, 1967; Harlem Library, NYC; Corcoran Gallery of Art, Washington, DC, 1942; Atlanta Univ., 1951; Oakland Art Museum, 1968.
Collections: NY Public Library-Schomburg Collection; Oakland Museum.
Awards: Carnegie grant-in-aid.
Sources: Locke. *The Negro in Art;* Dover. *American Negro Art;* Albany Institute of History & Art. *Negro Artist Comes of Age;* "Afro-Amer. Issue," *Art Gallery,* April 1968; Oakland Museum. *New Perspectives in Black Art;* "Amer. Negro Art Given Full Length Review in NY Show," *Art Digest,* Dec. 15, 1941; Indiana Univ. *Fine Arts & the Black American;* City College of NY. *The Evolution of Afro-Amer. Artists 1800-1950;* DuSable Museum of African-Amer. History. *Contemporary Black Artists,* 1970; Harmon Foundation. *Select Picture List;* J.G. "Honoring Negro History," *Art Digest,* Feb. 15, 1949, p. 20; "Negro Art Scores Without Double Standards," *Art Digest,* Feb. 1, 1945; Locke, Alain. "Chicago's New Southside Art Center," *Amer. Mag. of Art,* Aug. 1941; E.K. "Negro Artists Art News,* Feb. 1949; Harley, Ralph, Jr. "Checklist of Afro-Amer. Art & Artists," *The Serif,* Dec. 1970; "Claude Clark at Roko Gallery," *Art News,* May 1946; Lockhart, Alice.

"Claude Clark," *Motive,* March 1955; Ruthermore Galleries. *Three Pictures,* San Francisco; Paterson, Lindsay. "Contemporary Artists," *The Negro in Music & Art,* 1969; *The Negro Handbook,* Composed by Editors of *Ebony,* Chicago, 1966; Schatz, Walter. *Directory of Afro-Amer. Resources,* 1970; Southside Community Art Center. *National Negro Art Exhibition,* Chicago, 1941; Myers, Carol L. *Black Power in the Arts,* Flint, Mich., 1970; Oakland Museum Archives; Walker, Roslyn. *A Resource Guide to the Visual Arts of Afro-Americans,* South Bend, Ind., 1971.

CLARK, CLAUDE LOCKHART, JR.

Painter, sculptor. Born in Philadelphia on March 28, 1945. Studied at California College of Arts & Crafts (BA, 1968); University of California, Berkeley (MA); Alfred University, New York (BA); Philadelphia Museum School of Art; Barnes Foundation; Sacramento State College.
Works: *Metamorphosis; Psycho.*
Exhibited: Oakland Museum, 1968; Chabot College, Hayward, 1967 (father-son show), 1968; Links Exhibition, 1968; Cal. State College, Hayward, 1960.
Awards: Scholarship student, Cal. College of Arts & Crafts; Sculpture Award, Ford Internat'l Competition.
Sources: Oakland Museum. *New Perspectives in Black Art;* Harley, Ralph, Jr. "Checklist of Afro-Amer. Art & Artists," *The Serif,* Dec. 1970; Walker, Roslyn. *A Resource Guide to the Visual Arts of Afro-Americans,* South Bend, Ind., 1971.

CLARK, EDWARD

Painter. Born on May 6, 1926, in New Orleans, Louisiana. Studied at the Art Institute of Chicago; L'Academie de la Grand Chaumiere.
Works: *Vetheuil; The Big Egg; Vetheuil, Early Summer; Vetheuil, Summer 1968; Vetheuil, August 1968; Vetheuil, September 1968; Blue Top; Paris Rose; Last; Blue.*
Exhibited: Gallery Creuze, Paris, 1955 & 1966 (1-man); Brata Gallery, NY, 1958 (1-man); US Embassy, Paris, 1969 (1-man); Salon d'Automne Paris, 1952; Craven Gallery, Paris, Americans in Paris, 1953; Salon Des Réalitiés Nouvelles, Paris, 1954-6; Musée des Arts Decoratifs, Paris, 1955; Salon des Ind> pendants, Paris, 1956; American Center for Students and Artists, 1956, 1969; Brata Gallery, NY, 1957; Nova Gallery, Boston, Bennington College, 1959; Modern Museum, Tokyo & Kyoto; Brata Group Show, 1960; Riverside Museum, NY, 1963; Stockholm, 1964; Morgan State College, Baltimore, 1969; Boston Museum of Fine Arts, 1970; Univ. of Texas, 1970.

Sources: Walker, Roslyn. *A Resource Guide to the Visual Arts of Afro-Americans,* South Bend, Ind., 1971; Boston Museum of Fine Arts. *Afro-American Artists: New York & Boston,* 1970; Univ. of Texas. *Afro-American Artists Abroad;* Grillo, Jean B. "Elma Lewis: A New Show A New Showplace," *Boston After Dark,* Aug. 16, 1970; Loercher, Diana. "Afro-American Artists Abroad," *Christian Science Monitor,* Aug. 1, 1970.

CLARK, GEORGE

Sculptor. Born in Sequin, Texas. Studied at Otis Art Institute.
Works: *Afro-Form.*
Exhibited: Brockman Gallery; Laguna Beach Art Assn.; Watts Summer Festival; Cal. State College at Dominguez Hills; Occidental College.
Sources: Lewis/Waddy. *Black Artists on Art,* Vol. 2; Harley, Ralph, Jr. "Checklist of Afro-Amer. Artists," *The Serif,* Dec. 1970.

CLARK, IRENE

Painter, designer, gallery director. Born in Washington, DC in 1927. Studied at Art Institute; 414 Workshop, Chicago; San Francisco Art Institute. Gallery director of Exhibit Gallery & Studio, Chicago.
Works: *Decoration; Playmates; A Mansion on Prairie Avenue; Once Upon a Time; Rolling Calf; Mother & Child,* 1970; *Family Unity,* 1971; *Keeper of the Birds,* 1960.
Exhibited: Oakland Museum, 1968; African Historical Society, 1972; South Side Art Center; Old Town Triangle Fair; North Shore Art League, Chicago; Crown Hall, Ill. Institute of Tech.; Lioga Duncan Gallery, NYC; Howard Univ.; Atlanta Univ.; Grant St. Art Fair; Walnut Creek Art Festival; Left Bank Gallery, San Francisco; San Francisco Art Festival; Chabot College; Tamapais High School, Mill Valley; Kaiser Center Gallery, NYC.
Collections: Johnson Pub. Co.; Atlanta Univ.; Oakland Museum; Ms. Therese Heyman.
Awards: John Hope Purchase Award, Atlanta Annual; 1st Atlanta Univ. Purchase Award; Lake Meadows Art Fair Award, 1960; Nat'l Competitive Award, Beaux Art Ball, Chicago.
Member: African-American Historical & Cultural Society.
Sources: Dover. *American Negro Art;* Oakland Museum. *New Perspectives in Black Art;* DuSable Museum of African Amer. History, *Contemporary Black Artists,* 1970, Calendar; Johnson Pub. Co. *The JPC Art Collection,* Pamphlet; Harley, Ralph, Jr. "Checklist of Afro-Amer. Art & Artists," *The Serif,* Dec. 1970; *Art Gallery,* April 1970; Information from the artist; Walker, Roslyn. *A Resource*

Guide to the Visual Arts of Afro-Americans, South Bend, Ind., 1971.

CLARK, NATHANIEL

Photographer.
Works: *Blood; Great Ones.*
Exhibited: Lee Cultural Center, Phila.
Sources: Phila. Dept. of Recreation. *Love . . . and the Black Community.*

CLARK, PAT

Painter.
Works: *Brian* (watercolor).
Exhibited: Boston Public Library, 1973.
Sources: "Black Art Exhibit Opens Sunday," *Herald,* Belmont, Mass., May 14, 1970; "Preview Party to Open Show by 13 Black Artists," *Citizen,* Belmont, Mass., May 14, 1970; Boston Negro Artists' Assn. *10th Anniversary Exhibition,* 1973.

CLARK, SAMUEL

Born in Birmingham, Alabama in 1927. Studied at the Art Institute of Chicago; Roosevelt University; privately with Boris Anisfeld, Charles Schoeder, Ethel Spears.
Exhibited: South Side Community Art Center (1-man); Melrose Park.
Sources: "Afro-American Issue," *Art Gallery,* April 1970; DuSable Museum of African-Amer. History. *Contemporary Black Artists,* calendar, 1970.

CLARKE, GERALDINE

Studied at Tuskegee Institute.
Works: *The Achievers.*
Exhibited: Sun Times/Daily News Gallery, Chicago, 1970.
Sources: United Negro College Fund. *Art 1970,* Chicago, 1970.

CLARKE, JOHN HENRIK

Painter, sculptor. Born in Union Springs, Alabama; grew up in Columbus, Georgia. Co-founder of the *Harlem Quarterly;* one of the original members of the Harlem Writer's Guild. Associate editor of *Freedomways* magazine.
Works: *Christ.*
Sources: David, Jay. *Black Joy,* 1971.

CLARKE, LEROY

Painter, poet. Born in Trinidad, West Indies, 1938. Artist-in-Residence, Studio Museum in Harlem.
Works: *Black Poet; Mother Guiding Light; Olabunmi; Mythical II; Now; Him; Redemption; Vernal; When Chanting Fires Leapt from My Eyes a Poem for Blackness; Junkie with Sun; I Want Word of the Dying; Tyranny Never Sleeps; Fragments of a Spiritual.*
Exhibited: Univ. of Iowa, 1971-2; Studio Museum in Harlem, 1969, 1972; Sao Paulo Biennial, 1965; Expo '67; Trinidad, 1966 (1-man); The Muse, 1971 (1-man); Phila. Civic Center; Illinois Bell Telephone, 1971.
Collections: Mr. Benny Andrews; Johnson Pub. Co.; Studio Museum in Harlem; IBM.
Sources: Information from artist; Phila. Division of Art. *Afro-American Artists 1800-1969;* Illinois Bell Telephone. *Black American Artists/71,* 1972; Studio Museum in Harlem. *Harlem Artists 69; Black Shades,* May 1972, March 1972.

CLAY, PAULINE

Painter.
Works: *Carter's Little Filling Station.*
Exhibited: Atlanta's 4th Annual Exhibition, 1945; Nelson Museum, Kansas City, 1945.
Awards: 2nd prize, oil, Missouri State Fair, 1945.
Sources: "Atlanta's Annual," *Time,* April 9, 1945; Parks, James D. "An Experiment in Painting the Local Scene," *Design,* Feb. 1946, pp. 10-12.

CLAYE, CHARLENE MARETTE

Painter. Born in Chicago, 1945. Studied at University of Bridgeport (BA, 1966); Howard University (MA, 1970).
Works: *Black Void,* 1971; *Heads of Flies,* 1969; *Fishing,* 1972; *Man is Born to Die,* 1972.
Exhibited: Spelman College, 1971; National Conference of Artists, Atlanta, 1971; Black Art Center, Houston, 1972.
Member: American Society for Aesthetics; National Conference of Artists.
Represented by: Creative Cancer Gallery, Atlanta, Georgia.
Sources: Black Art Center. "Black Beginning," Houston, 1972. Information from the artist.

CLEMENT, LOUISE

Works: *Mournful Souls; Blue Nude.*
Exhibited: State Armory, Wilmington, Del., 1971.
Sources: Phila. Division of Art. *Afro-American Artists 1800-1969;* Aesthetic Dynamics. *Afro-American Images 1971.*

CLEVELAND, LADYBIRD

Painter. Born in Cornelia, Georgia in 1927.
Sources: Dover. *American Negro Art;* Indiana Univ. *Fine Arts & the Black American;* Harley, Ralph. "Checklist of Afro-Amer. Art & Artists," *The Serif,* Dec. 1970; Walker, Roslyn. *A Resource Guide to the Visual Arts of Afro-Americans,* South Bend, Ind., 1971.

COGBURN, CECELIA

Studied at Tuskegee Institute.
Works: *Troubles in Mind.*

Exhibited: Sun Times/Daily News Gallery, Chicago, 1970.
Sources: United Negro College Fund. *Art 1970,* Chicago, 1970.

COLBERT, BENJAMIN

Painter. Born in Savannah, Georgia. Visiting teacher of art in Savannah.
Sources: Kiah, Virginia. "Black Artists," *Savannah Magazine,* April 1972.

COLEMAN, FELTON

Painter.
Works: *House on the Hill; The Revival; Southern Landscape.*
Exhibited: Dillard Univ., 1941.
Collections: National Archives.
Sources: Dillard Univ. *Arts Festival,* Catalog, 1941; Afro-American Slide Depository, Catalog, 1971-2; "Amer. Negro Artists Given Full Length Review in NY Show," *Art Digest,* Dec. 15, 1941; Harley, Ralph, Jr. "Checklist of Afro-Amer. Art & Artists," *The Serif,* Dec. 1970.

COLEMAN, FLOYD W.

Painter, graphic artist. Born in Sawyerville, Alabama on January 13, 1937. Studied at Alabama State College, Montgomery, Alabama (BA); University of Wisconsin (MS); Emory University, Atlanta; University of Chicago; University of Georgia.
Works: *Homage to Bessie Smith; Importance of Tradition; Self Portrait; Like It Is; Red Square; The Importance of Symbols; New Money; Yellow Patch; In the Park; Drawing,* 1969 (mixed media).
Exhibited: Arts Festival, Atlanta, 1968; Arts Festival Ten, Jacksonville, Fla., 1967; Mandorla Gallery, Atlanta, 1966; Wesley Foundation, Ohio State Univ., 1966; Columbus (Ga.) Museum of Arts and Crafts, 1966; Alexander Gallery, Atlanta, 1965; Louisiana State Art Commission Traveling Exhibition, 1965; Annual Southeastern Exhibition, Atlanta, 1963, 1965; Atlanta Univ., 1958-65; Castle Gallery, Atlanta, 1966; Univ. of Iowa, 1971; Minneapolis Institute of Arts, 1968; High Art Museum, Atlanta, 1969; Flint (Mich.) Institute of Arts, 1969; Everson Museum of Art, Syracuse, NY, 1969; IBM Gallery of Arts & Sciences, NY, 1969; Rhode Island School of Design, 1969; Memorial Art Gallery, Rochester, NY, 1969; San Francisco Museum of Art, 1969; Contemporary Arts Museum, Houston, 1970; NJ State Museum, 1970; Roberson Center for the Arts & Sciences, Binghamton, NY, 1970; Univ. of Cal. at Santa Barbara; Exhibition of Afro-Amer. Artists, Atlanta, Ga. 1958, 1959, 1960, 1961, 1963, 1964, 1965; Young America Exhibition, New Orleans, La., 1959; Landmarks of Milwaukee, Wisc., 1962; National Watercolor Exhibition, Peoria, Ill., 1961; 24th Annual Exhibition of Contemporary American Painting, Fla., 1962; American Drawing Annual, Norfolk Museum of Arts & Sciences, 1962; WVa. Centennial Exhibition of Painting & Sculpture, 1963; High Museum, 1964; World's Fair, NY, 1964; 4th Dixie Annual Exhibition, Montgomery Museum of Fine Arts, Ala., 1965; Rich's Salute to the Arts, Atlanta, 1966; Alabama A & M College; High Museum Art Shop, Atlanta; Gallery 44, Atlanta; Agnes Scott College, Decatur, Ga., 1968; Brooklyn College, NY, 1969; Mount Holyoke College, 1969; Six Institution's Consortium Invitational Exhibition, Greensboro, NC, 1971; Wesleyan College; Illien Gallery, Atlanta; Salon des Refuses, Atlanta; Rainbow Sign Gallery, Berkeley, 1972.
Collections: High Art Museum, Atlanta; Florida A & M Univ.; Emory Univ.; Atlanta Univ.; Spelman College; Oakland Museum.
Awards: 1st award, watercolor, Atlanta Univ. Annual, 1964; John Hope Prize, oil, Atlanta Univ. Annual, 1965; Honorable mention, painting, Savannah Arts Festival, 1968; Ford Foundation Advance Study Fellowship, 1968-70.
Member: National Conference of Artists.
Sources: Minneapolis Inst. of Arts. *30 Contemporary Black Artists;* Mandorla Gallery. *Psychedelic Art,* Atlanta, 1966; Patterson, Lindsay. *The Negro in Music and Art,* 1969; Harley, Ralph L., Jr. "Checklist of Afro-American Art & Artists," *The Serif,* Dec. 1970; Mount Holyoke College. *Ten Afro-American Artists;* Lewis/Waddy. *Black Artists on Art,* Vol. 2; Ill. Bell Telephone. *Black American Artists/71;* Roelof-Lanner, T.V., ed. *Prints by American Negro Artists;* Ruder & Finn Fine Arts. *Contemporary Black Artists;* Brooklyn College. *Afro-American Artists: Since 1950;* Myers, Carol L. *Black Power in the Arts,* Flint, Mich., 1970; Oakland Museum Archives, Ruth Waddy Collection; Rainbow Sign Gallery, *Black Arts Day II,* Press Release, Berkeley, 1972; Walker, Roslyn. *A Resource Guide to the Visual Arts of Afro-Americans,* South Bend, Ind., 1971; Driscoll, Edgar J., Jr. "Showcase for Black Artists," *Boston Sunday Globe,* July 6, 1969, p. A73.

COLEMAN, R.

Collections: NY Public Library, Schomburg Art Collection.
Sources: Schatz, Walter. *Directory of Afro-American Resources,* 1970.

COLES, DONALD E.

Painter. Born in 1947 in Philadelphia. Studied at the Philadelphia College of Art; California College of Arts and Crafts, Oakland.
Exhibited: Associated Students Art Gallery,

Oakland; San Francisco Black Art Fair; Stanford Univ., 1969; Oakland Museum, 1970.
Sources: Lewis/Waddy. *Black Artists on Art,* Vol. 1; "San Francisco," *Artforum,* Oct. 1970, p. 81; Oakland Museum. *Black Untitled,* 1970; Stanford Univ. *Prints & Drawings by California Afro-American Artists,* 1969; Walker, Roslyn. *A Resource Guide to the Visual Arts of Afro-Americans,* South Bend, Ind., 1971.

COLLIER, EDWARD T.
Ceramist. Active in the 1940's.
Exhibited: Howard Univ., 1941.
Sources: Roosevelt, Eleanor. "Negro Paintings at Howard were Inspiring," 'My Day' column, *Washington Daily News,* March 3, 1941; Harley, Ralph, Jr., "Checklist of Afro-Amer. Art & Artists," *The Serif,* Dec. 1970.

COLLIER, MARCIA JANENE
Painter, graphic artist. Born in Louisville, Kentucky, March 9, 1957.
Works: *Space Flower; Embryo I; Popeye's Sundae; Desert by Night; The Wedge; Space Hook; Hobby Horse; Night Chase; Solar.*
Exhibited: Downtown Louisville Salutes the Arts, 1971; The Louisville Defender, Expo '71, 1971; 6th Annual Student & Instructor's Show, 1972; Bob Thompson Memorial Gallery, 1972; Univ. of Louisville Black Student Union, 1972; Black Arts Festival, 1972; Metro-Shively Cultural Center-Louisville Art Workshop Merge Showing, May 1972.
Awards: Nat'l. Merit Award, 25th Annual School Traffic Safety Poster Contest, 1969; Gold Ribbon, Shawnee Jr. High School Art Exhibit; Certificate for Superior Ability and Proficiency, Shawnee Jr. High School, 1970-1; 3rd prize, Bob Thompson Memorial Gallery & Louisville Art Workshop Showing, 1972; 2nd prize for illustration of "You're a Good Man Charlie Brown," 1972; 3rd prize, Metro-Shively Cultural Center-Louisville Art Workshop, 1972.
Member: Louisville Art Workshop.
Sources: Information from artist.

COLLIER, T. WALCOTT
Painter. Born in Nashville, Tennessee in 1910.
Works: *Mother's Delight; Sue.*
Exhibited: Independent Artists in Detroit; Harmon Foundation, 1933.
Sources: Harmon Foundation. *Non Jury Exhibit of Works of Negro Artists,* 1933.

COLLINS, HUBERT
Ceramist. Studied at Studio Two, Oakland (1966-9); Merritt College, Oakland (1966-9); California State College at Hayward. Pottery Instructor, Studio II of the Arts and Crafts Division of the Oakland Recreation Department.

Works: Stoneware pots.
Exhibitions: Studio Two, Oakland Art Festival, Jack London Square, 1968-9; Cal. State College at Hayward, 1968-9; 8th Annual Hayward Area Festival of the Arts, 1969; Mills College, 1970.
Sources: Mills College Art Gallery. *California Black Craftsmen,* 1970.

COLLINS, PAUL
Painter.
Works: *Abdou; Mandingo; Boi Guéye; Yorro Bâ; Three Boys and a Boat; Bara, Douda, and Khalifa; Bassari Country; Drums; Tegou; Water Hole; Madam Crimson; La Garde Rouge; Gal; Apollo; Ammadou; Gorée; Ibrahima's Afrique; Woman of Fass; Captain Moussa; Mamsanou; On the Plains; The Unprotected; An Old Laobé; Battling Siki; Fisherman's Graveyard; Ida; Hawk; Girl of Korité; The Baobabs of Lambango; The Contemporary.*
Sources: Collins, Paul, & Tom Lee. *Black Portrait of an African Journey,* Grand Rapids, Mich., William B. Eerdsmans Pub. Co., 1971.

COLLINS, RICHARD L.
Painter, mixed media. Born in New York City on June 5, 1942. Studied at Cooper Union School; Art Student's League, New York City.
Works: *Mendecino* (collage).
Exhibited: Oakland Museum, 1968; Baker Gallery, San Francisco, 1968 (1-man); Society of Illustrators, 1960; Grant Ave. Art Fair, 1965-8.
Awards: Simmons Award, 1961.
Sources: Oakland Museum. *New Perspectives in Black Art;* Indiana Univ. *Fine Arts & the Black American;* DuSable Museum of African-Amer. History. *Contemporary Black Artists,* 1970, Calendar; Harley, Ralph, Jr. "Checklist of Afro-Amer. Art & Artists," *The Serif,* Dec. 1970; Walker, Roslyn. *A Resource Guide to the Visual Arts of Afro-Americans,* South Bend, Ind., 1971.

COLLINS, SAMUEL O.
Born 1880. Died 1932. Interested in ash can school genre, like Tanner, W. O. Thompson, May Howard Jackson, & Richard Lonsdale Brown.
Works: *Autumn; Ancient Memories.*
Sources: Porter, James. "Negro Artists Gain Recognition After Long Battle," *Pittsburgh Courier,* July 29, 1950; *Encyclopedia of the Arts,* p. 38; Thompson, W.O. "Collins & DeVillis-Two Promising Painters," *Voice of the Negro,* Dec. 1905, p. 687; Long, B.S. "Samuel Collins the Miniaturist," *Burlington Mag.,* Sept. 1910; Harley, Ralph, Jr. "Checklist of Afro-Amer. Art & Artists," *The Serif,* Dec. 1970; *1st Annual Exhibit of Books, Manuscripts, Sculptures, etc. by the Negro Library Assn.,* Aug. 7-16, 1918, Catalog.

COMPTON, LAWRENCE
See: Kolawole, W.L. Compton.

COMPTON, WILLIAM LAWRENCE
See: Kolawole, W.L. Compton.

CONCH, FRANCIS P.
Painter, graphic artist. Worked in Philadelphia.
Works: *Laughing Man; Woman.*
Exhibited: Atlanta Univ., 1944.
Sources: Harley, Ralph, Jr. "Checklist of Afro-Amer. Art & Artists," *The Serif,* Dec. 1970.

CONCHOLAR, DAN
Painter, printmaker, educator. Born in San Antonio, Texas in 1939. Studied at Phoenix College; Pasadena City College. Drawing and painting instructor at Watts Towers Art Center.
Works: *War Machine; In Your Womb; Zebra Man Coming No. 1; Zebra Man Coming No. 2; Peace* (2 greeting cards for Brockman Gallery); *Fact of Man; Series of Africa #2.*
Exhibited: Ariz. State Fair; Phoenix Art Museum; Udinotti Gallery; Brockman Gallery; Univ. of Iowa, 1972.
Awards: 1st prize, Ariz. State Fair; 1st prize, Phoenix Art Museum.
Sources: Lewis/Waddy. *Black Artists on Art,* Vol. 1; Ill. Bell Telephone. *Black American Artists/71;* Harley, Ralph, Jr. "Checklist of Afro-American Art & Artists," *The Serif,* Dec. 1970; Atkinson, J. Edward. *Black Dimensions in Contemporary American Art,* NY, 1971; Walker, Roslyn. *A Resource Guide to the Visual Arts of Afro-Americans,* South Bend, Ind., 1971.

CONLEY, MICHAEL
Studied at Tuskegee Institute.
Works: *Architectural Rendering.*
Exhibited: Sun Times/Daily News Gallery, Chicago, 1970.
Sources: United Negro College Fund. *Art 1970,* Chicago, 1970.

CONWAY, WALLACE X., SR.
Painter. Born June 11, 1920 in Washington, DC. Studied Cooper Union School of Arts and Sciences; Art Students League; American University; Catholic University; Miner Teachers College.
Works: *Ascension of Christ,* Metropolitan AME Church, Washington, DC (mural); *The Spectators; Many Faces of Black; The Gladiator; Spring.*
Exhibited: DC Dept. of Recreation Exhibition (outdoor), 1962, 1968, 1969; Dupont Theatre Galleries, 1967; Afro-American Experience, Greater Washington Youth Center, 1969; Smithsonian Institution-Anacostia Museum, 1969-71; Studio on the Canal, Princeton, NJ, 1971; Smith-Mason Gallery, Washington, DC, 1971; NJ State Museum, 1972; Princeton Youth Center, 1972; Empire State Black Arts Exhibition, Albany, NY, 1972.
Awards: Chairman, Exhibits Bureau, NJ State Museum; Appointed member, Mercer County Community College Advisory Board of Art and Design; Member, Advisory Board, Hudson Arts Festivals, Union City, NJ; Citation for Graphic Design by Gov. Cahill of NJ, 1972; Appointed Graphic Arts Consultant for NJ Support Committee for Martin Luther King, Jr. Memorial Center, 1971; Appointed Graphic Arts Consultant for the Museum for Educational Research of Amer. Black Art, Science & History, 1971-2.
Member: Communication Arts Consultant, Assn. for the Arts, NJ State Museum; DC Art Assn.
Sources: Conway, W.X. "Theatrical Display Techniques," *Signs of the Times Magazine,* 1960; *Screen Printing Magazine,* Oct. 1971; *Museum News,* Feb. 1972; "Speaking of People," *Ebony,* April 1972; DC Art Assn. *Exhibition '71,* Washington, DC, 1971; Smith-Mason Gallery. *National Exhibition of Black Artists,* 1971; Information from artist.

CONWILL, HOUSTON
Painter, sculptor. Studied at Howard University (BA, 1973).
Exhibited: Howard Univ.; Black Arts Festival, Reston, Va.; Malcolm X Park; Church of the Holy Redeemer, Washington, DC; Showcase Gallery, Washington, DC, 1973.
Sources: *Black Shades,* Vol. 3, #2.

CONWILL, KINSHASHA
(Mrs. Houston Conwill)
Painter, designer. Studied Howard University (BA, 1973).
Exhibited: Howard Univ.; Black Arts Festival, Reston, Va.; Malcolm X Park; Church of the Holy Redeemer, Washington, DC; Showcase Gallery, Washington, DC, 1973.
Sources: *Black Shades,* Vol. 3, #2.

COOKE, JULIAN ABELE
Architect. Born in Spokane, Washington, April 10, 1905. Studied at Pennsylvania State College; University of Pennsylvania. Architectural coordinator, Howard University Building Program.
Member: National Technical Assn.; Omega Psi Phi.
Sources: Furr, Arthur F. *History & Progress of Negroes in the US.*

COOPER, ARVELA O.
Painter.
Works: *Promises, Promises* (acrylic).
Exhibited: Lee Cultural Center, Phila.
Sources: Phila. Dept. of Recreation. *Love . . . and the Black Community.*

COOPER, JIMMIE

Born in North Carolina, August 3, 1936. Studied at the School of Visual Art, New York. **Sources:** New York NAACP. *A Most Memorable Showing of Creative Negro Art;* New York NAACP. *Art Exhibition of Negro Expression Sponsored by Minars Furniture,* April 1964.

COOPER, LEONARD

Painter, music teacher. Born in 1899. Worked in Salinas, California.
Works: *Rain on the Farm; Before the Rains Come.*
Exhibited: Atlanta Univ., 1943.
Sources: Dover. *American Negro Art,* p. 47; Indiana Univ. *Fine Arts & the Black American;* "Negro Winners," *Art Digest,* May 1, 1946; Harley, Ralph, Jr. "Checklist of Afro-Amer. Art & Artists," *The Serif,* Dec. 1970.

COOPER, WILLIAM ARTHUR

Painter, educator. Born in Hicksboro, North Carolina, 1895. Studied at Livingstone College; North Carolina Theological; self-taught artist. Teacher at Palmer Institute, Sedalia, North Carolina. A.M.E. Zion minister.
Works: *Louise; The Slave & His Hope; Brother; Vanishing Washer Woman; My Dad; Portrait of Grace; Self Portrait; A Serious Lady; Dean Tilley, Shaw University; A Modest Negro Beauty.*
Exhibited: Harmon Foundation, 1931, 1933, 1935; Bennett College, 1933; Duke Univ., 1935; Valentine Gallery, 1935; Howard Univ., 1932; Shaw Univ.; North Carolina College; Harmon Traveling Exhibition, 1934-5; NJ State Museum, 1935; NC Negro Artist, 1935; Texas Centennial Exposition, 1936.
Awards: Honorable Mention, painting, Harmon Exhibit, 1931; 1st prize, NC State Fair, 1934.
Sources: Harmon Foundation. *Negro Artists,* 1935; "Harmon Foundation Exhibit," *Art Digest,* Feb. 15, 1931, p. 7; Harley, Ralph, Jr. "Checklist of Afro-Amer. Art & Artists," *Serif,* Dec. 1970; "Negro Artists Paintings on Display at University," *East Tennessee News,* Knoxville, June 6, 1932; Locke. *The Negro in Art;* Afro-American Slide Depository, Catalog; Cooper. *A Portrayal of Negro Life;* Dover. *American Negro Art;* Harmon Foundation. *Exhibition of Productions by Negro Artists;* Indiana Univ. *Fine Arts & the Black American;* DuSable Museum of African-Amer. History. *Contemporary Black Artists,* 1970; Harmon Foundation. *Non-Jury Exhibit of Works of Negro Artists,* 1933; Texas Centennial Exposition. *Thumbnail Sketches of Exhibiting Artists,* 1936.

COPPEDGE, ARTHUR

Painter. Born 1938. Studied at Brooklyn College; Brooklyn Museum Art School; Art Students League.
Works: *The Studio; Uptown; Eva; Rhododendrons; Self Portrait; Untitled.*
Exhibited: Nordness Galleries, NY, 1969; Smith-Mason Gallery, 1971.
Collections: Brooklyn Museum; Benny Andrews.
Sources: Nordness Galleries. *12 Afro-American Artists-1969;* Smith-Mason Gallery. *National Exhibition Black Artists,* 1971.

CORBIN, BERESFORD ST. C.

Photographer. Born in Boston, 1919.
Works: *Smiling Faces.*
Exhibited: Boston Public Library, Egleston Square; City of Boston Employees Art Show.
Member: Boston Negro Artists' Assn.
Represented by: Boston Negro Artists' Assn.
Sources: Boston Negro Artists' Assn. yearly calendars (1973); Information from the artist.

CORTOR, ELDZIER

Painter, educator. Born in Chicago in 1915. Studied at Chicago Art Institute (1937-8); Institute of Design, Columbia University; Pratt Graphic Art Center. Teacher at South Side Community Art Center, Chicago. Worked on Illinois Federal Art Project (1938-40); Illinois Arts & Crafts Project (1940's).
Works: *The Merchants; Lady Knitting; The Wall; Study 39; A Day in May; Eviction; March Afternoon; One Alone; But to Rest a Little; Southern Gate; Southern Landscape; Americana; Loneliness; Room Number 5; Trio V; Out of the Past; Sense of Loneliness; Where Once Stood a Dwelling; Dance Composition #7; L'Abattoir #3; Affection; Two Figures on Bed; Skin Deep; March Afternoon; Environment V; Southern Souvenir #2; Brother & Sister; And So to Bed; Night Letter; Portraits of Madge Revels Cayton; Portrait of Susie Revels Cayton; Woman Washing Hair; Early Morning Promenade; Oak Table; The Woman; Classical Composition No. IV,* 1971 (oil); *Classical Study,* Nos. 30, 34, 1971 (oil); *Dance Composition No. 9,* 1972 (oil); *Environment,* 1947 (oil); *Still Life: Past Revisitated,* 1972 (oil); *Dance Composition,* Nos. 31, 34, 35, 40, 41 (etchings); *Dance Composition,* Nos. 30, 32, 1971 (drawings); *Late Night; Vision of Sunset; Day Clean.*
Exhibited: South Parkway YMCA, Chicago; Artists Gallery, 1938; Amer. Negro Exposition, Chicago, 1940; Howard Univ., 1945; South Side Community Art Center, Chicago, 1941, 1945; City College of NY, 1967; James A. Porter Gallery, 1970; Boston Museum of Fine Arts, 1970; Smith-Mason Gallery, 1971; Illinois

State Fair, 1951; Albany Institute of History & Art; Metropolitan Museum; Carnegie Institute; Nat'l Center of Afro-Amer. Artists, Boston, 1973; McMillen Inc. Galleries, NY, 1941; Studio Museum, Harlem, 1973.

Collections: Howard Univ.; Johnson Pub. Co.; Mr. Horace Revels Cayton; Dr. Earl Evans; Musée Du Peuple Haitian; Univ. of Illinois; Mr. & Mrs. Richard Rosenwald; Martha Jackson Gallery; Mr. Ben Goldstein, NY.

Awards: Amer. Negro Exposition, 2nd Prize, oils, Chicago, 1940; Carnegie Award; Bertha Aberle Florsheim Award; William H. Bartel Award; Rosenwald Fellowship; Guggenheim Fellowship for travel and painting to West Indies.

Sources: City College of NY. *The Evolution of Afro-American Artists 1800-1950;* "Afro-American Issue," *Art Gallery,* April 1968; Indiana Univ. *Fine Arts & the Black American;* Chatfield-Taylor, Rose. "Howard Univ. Holds Negro Exhibit," *Washington Post,* Feb. 16, 1941; *Exhibition of Negro Artists of Chicago at Howard Univ. Gallery of Art,* Feb. 1941; Motley, Willard F. "Negro Art in Chicago," *Opportunity,* Jan. 1940; Porter. *Modern Negro Art;* "Wins National Prize," *Chicago Daily News,* March 30, 1940; "Day Clean by Eldzier Cortor Wins the William H. Bartels Prize in Current Chicago Show," *Chicago Art Institute Bulletin,* April/May 1946, p. 52; "Nineteen Young American Artists," *Life* (Articles on Art), 1950, pp. 145-59; "Exhibition 1951 . . . wins State Fair Art Prize . . .," *Scrapbook of Art & Artists of Chicago,* 1951, pp. 8, 14, 32-3; Harley, Ralph, Jr. "A Checklist of Afro-Amer. Art & Artists," *The Serif,* Dec. 1970; DuSable Museum of African-Amer. History. *Contemporary Black Artists,* 1970, Calendar; Tanner Art Galleries. *Art of the American Negro,* 1940; Butcher, Margaret. *The Negro in American Culture,* p. 239; Roucek & Kiernan. *The Negro Impact on Western Civilization;* Howard Univ. *Festival of Fine Arts,* May 1945; Howard Univ. *James A. Porter Gallery of African American Art,* 1970; "Negro Artists," *Life,* July 22, 1946; Ploski, Harry, Ernest Kaiser, & Otto Lindenmeyer. "The Black Artist," *Reference Library of Black America,* Book 4, 1971; Ploski, Harry, & Ernest Kaiser. "The Black Artist," *Afro USA,* 1971; *The Negro Handbook,* Composed by Editors of *Ebony,* Chicago, 1966; Locke. *The Negro in Art;* Dover. *American Negro Art;* Albany Institute of History & Art. *The Negro Artist Comes of Age;* Boston Museum of Fine Arts. *Afro-American Artists: NY & Boston,* 1970; "Afro-American Artists: NY & Boston," *Prudential Center News,* March 1, 1970, p. 4; South Side Community Art Center. *Chicago Collectors Exhibit of Negro Art,* 1945; South Side Community

Art Center. *National Negro Art Exhibition,* 1941; South Side Community Art Center. *Opening Exhibition by Negro Artists,* 1940-1; Myers, Carol. *Black Power in the Arts,* Flint, Mich., 1970; Museum of the Nat'l Center of Afro-Amer. Artists. *Expanding Reality,* Boston, 1973; McMillen Inc. Galleries. *Contemporary Negro Art,* NY, 1941; Gaither, Edmund B. "The Evolution of the Afro-American Artist," *Artists Proof,* Vol. 2; Studio Museum. *Reality Expanded,* press release, Harlem, 1973; "Leading Negro Artists," *Ebony,* Sept. 1963; Walker, Roslyn. *A Resource Guide to the Visual Arts of Afro-Americans,* South Bend, Ind., 1971; Smith-Mason Gallery. *National Exhibition Black Artists,* 1971; Rollins. *They Showed the Way;* "Art by Negroes," *Art Digest,* Oct. 15, 1941; "Amer. Negro Art Given Full Length Review in NY Show," *Art Digest,* Dec. 15, 1941; Greene, Carroll, Jr. "Perspective: The Black Artist in America," *Art Gallery,* April 1970, p. 25; "The Negro in Art," *Art Digest,* June 1, 1944; "Negro Art Scores Without Double Standards," *Art Digest,* Feb. 1, 1945; Pierre-Noel, Lois Jones. "American Negro Art in Progress," *Negro History Bulletin,* Oct. 1967; "Afro-Amer. Artists 1800-1950," *Ebony,* Vol. 23, pp. 116-22; Locke, Alain. "Chicago's New Southside Art Center," *Amer. Magazine of Art,* Aug. 1941, p. 320; J.W.L. "Negro in Art," *Art News,* Dec. 19, 1941, p. 24; "Amer. Negro Art," *Design,* Feb. 1942, p. 28; Johnson Pub. Co. *The JPC Art Collection,* Pamphlet; Pearson, Ralph. *The Modern Renaissance in American Art,* NY, 1954; Haydon, Harold. "Coming of Age of Black Art," *Chicago Sun Times,* July 26, 1970; Brown, Marion. "The Negro in the Fine Arts," *The Negro Heritage Library,* Vol. 2.

COSTLEY, ANNA E.
Painter.

Works: *Bronca.*

Exhibited: Xavier Univ., 1963.

Sources: Xavier Univ. *Emancipation Proclamation Centennial National Art Exhibition,* 1963.

COUNTEE, SAMUEL
Painter. Born in Marshall, Texas, 1909. Studied at Bishop College (AB, 1934); Boston Museum School (1935-7).

Works: *I Remember the Cross; Little Brown Boy; My Guitar; Portrait of Beauty.*

Exhibited: Bishop College, 1933, 1934; Harmon Foundation, 1933, 1935; Texas Centennial, 1936; Amer. Negro Exposition, 1940; Atlanta Univ., 1940; Howard Univ., 1933, 1937; Negro Library, Houston, 1933; Smith College, 1943; Institute of Modern Art, Boston, 1943.

Awards: Boston Museum School Scholarship.

Sources: Tanner Art Galleries. *Art of the*

American Negro, 1940; Mallett. *Index of Artists;* Locke. *The Negro in Art;* Harmon Foundation. *Exhibition of Productions by Negro Artists;* Johnson Pub. Co. *The JPC Art Collection;* Harley, Ralph, Jr. "Checklist of Afro-Amer. Art & Artists," *Serif,* Dec. 1970; Indiana Univ. *Fine Art & the Black American;* DuSable Museum of African-Amer. History. *Contemporary Black Artists,* 1970, Calendar; Howard Univ. *Art of American Negro,* 1937; Brawley, Benjamin. *The Negro Genius;* Texas Centennial Exposition. *Thumbnail Sketches of Exhibiting Artists,* 1936; Harmon Foundation. *Negro Artists,* 1935; Walker, Roslyn. *A Resource Guide to the Visual Arts of Afro-Americans,* South Bend, Ind., 1971.

COUSINS, HAROLD
Sculptor.
Works: *River Man.*
Exhibited: James A. Porter Gallery, 1970; Howard Univ., 1961.
Sources: Howard Univ. *James A. Porter Gallery of African-American Art,* 1970; Harley, Ralph, Jr. "Checklist of Afro-Amer. Art & Artists," *The Serif,* Dec. 1970.

COVENEY, PAM
Photographer.
Exhibited: Addison Gallery, 1971.
Sources: James Van DerZee Institute. *The Black Photographer (1908-1970): A Survey.*

COWAN, LEE S.
Born in Pittsburgh, Pennsylvania. Studied at Carnegie-Mellon University. Helped to organize Watt Lane Art Triange which later became Group One Art Club.
Sources: Pittsburgh Community College. *16 Black Artists.*

COX, VIRGINIA
Painter. Born in Detroit, 1929.
Sources: Dover. *American Negro Art;* Indiana Univ. *Fine Arts & the Black American;* Pierre-Noel, Lois Jones. "American Negro Art in Progress," *Negro History Bulletin,* Oct. 1967; Harley, Ralph, Jr. "Checklist of Afro-Amer. Art & Artists," *Serif,* Dec. 1970; Brown, Marion. "The Negro in the Fine Arts," *Negro Heritage Library;* "Leading Young Artists," *Ebony,* April 1958; Walker, Roslyn. *A Resource Guide to the Visual Arts of Afro-Americans,* South Bend, Ind., 1971.

COXE, G. CALIMAN
Painter.
Works: *Miscegenation; From a Window.*
Exhibited: Smith-Mason Gallery, 1971.
Collections: Johnson Pub. Co.
Sources: Smith-Mason Gallery. *National Exhibition Black Artists,* 1971; Johnson Pub. Co. *The JPC Art Collection,* Pamphlet.

COXE, PHILIP A.
Painter.
Works: *Conferres of Two Worlds.*
Exhibited: Smith-Mason Gallery, 1971.
Sources: Smith-Mason Gallery. *National Exhibition Black Artists,* 1971.

CRADDOCK, THERESA
Painter. Born in Boston in 1937. Studied at Vesper George School of Art; Emmanuel College; Massachusetts College of Art.
Works: *Madison Park,* 1970; *Ghetto Song,* 1971; *Portrait* (pastel); *Portrait* (oil); *Abstract* (pen & ink).
Exhibited: Annual Internat'l Fair, 1970-1; Boston Negro Artists' Assn; Boston City Hall, 1970; Black Artist Union Exhibit; Boston Public Library, 1973.
Collections: Seaborn Scott; Esther Titcomb McLean.
Member: Black Artist Union; Boston Negro Artists' Assn.
Sources: Information from artist; "Black Art Exhibit Opens Sunday," *Herald,* Belmont, Mass., May 14, 1970; "Preview Part to Open Show by 13 Black Artists," *Citizen,* Belmont, Mass., May 14, 1970; Boston Negro Artists' Assn. *10th Anniversary Exhibition,* Boston Public Library, 1973; Boston Negro Artists' Assn. *The Black Artist in America: A Negro History Month Exhibition,* Boston Public Library, 1973.

CRAIG, RANDALL J.
Sculptor.
Works: *Woman of Walta; Black Is Black; Ashanti Woman; Wisemen at Their End; Do Not Go Gentle.*
Exhibited: State Armory, Wilmington, Del., 1971; Smith-Mason Gallery, 1971.
Sources: Phila. Division of Art. *Afro-American Artists 1800-1969;* Aesthetic Dynamics. *Afro-American Images,* 1971; Smith-Mason Gallery. *National Exhibition Black Artists,* 1971.

CRAIG, WILLIAM
Graphic artist.
Works: *Self Portrait.*
Sources: *Black Shades,* Feb. 1972, Magazine.

CRAMPTON, GLADYS E.
Painter.
Works: *Of Royal Blood* (oil).
Exhibited: Lee Cultural Center, Phila.
Sources: Phila. Dept. of Recreation. *Love . . . and the Black Community.*

CRAWFORD, CLEO
Painter. Born 1892. Died 1939 in Haverstraw, New York. Self-taught.
Works: *Christmas; Telegraph Pole.*
Exhibited: Museum of Modern Art.
Collections: National Archives.

Sources: Dover. *American Negro Art*; Indiana Univ. *Fine Arts & the Black American*; Janis, Sidney. *They Taught Themselves*, NY, Dial Press, 1942, pp. 232-5; Afro-American Slide Depository, 1971-2, Catalog; Harley, Ralph, Jr. "Checklist of Afro-American Art & Artists," *The Serif*, Dec. 1970; "American Negro Art Given Full Length Review in NY Show," *Art Digest*, Dec. 15, 1941; Walker, Roslyn. *A Resource Guide to the Visual Arts of Afro-Americans*, South Bend, Ind., 1971.

CRAWFORD, DOROTHY P.
Painter.
Works: *Bronze Girl*.
Exhibited: Atlanta Univ., 1944.
Sources: Harley, Ralph, Jr. "Checklist of Afro-American Art & Artists," *The Serif*, Dec. 1970.

CRAWFORD, HOMER
Born in New York City.
Exhibited: Richmond College, April-May 1972.
Represented by: Gloria Wiggins, 168 Brabant St., NY, 10303.
Sources: Information from artist.

CREMER, MARVA
Printmaker, painter, educator. Born in Miami, Florida in 1942. Studied at California College of Arts & Crafts (BA, 1965; BFA, 1966; MFA, 1968). Teacher at Studio I, Oakland, California; School for Emotionally Disturbed Children, East Bay Activity Center.
Works: *Do You Know What I'm Doing?; Strange Journey; Stuff of the Moon; Laugh When You're Afraid; Half a Rainbow Autistic*.
Exhibited: Western Addition Library, 1968; Oakland Museum, 1968; Gallery III, Corte Madera, 1968; Art West Associated North Walnut Creek Festival; College of the Holy Names Gallery; Cal. College of Arts & Crafts.
Collections: Oakland Museum.
Awards: William Porter Scholarship; Grace C. Richards Scholarship; scholarship student, Cal. College of Arts & Crafts, 1967.
Member: Art West Associated North.
Sources: Oakland Museum Archives; Oakland Museum. *New Perspectives in Black Art*; Lewis/Waddy. *Black Artists on Art*; Indiana Univ. *Fine Arts & the Black American*; Harley, Ralph, Jr. "Checklist of Afro-Amer. Art & Artists," *The Serif*, Dec. 1970; DuSable Museum of African-Amer. History. *Contemporary Black Artists*, 1970; Walker, Roslyn. *A Resource Guide to the Visual Arts of Afro-Americans*, South Bend, Ind., 1971.

CRICHLOW, ERNEST
Painter, illustrator, graphic artist. Born in New York City, 1914. Studied at New York University; Art Students League. Worked on New York Federal Art Project; Greensboro, North Carolina Art Project. Former Director of Society for American Culture; co-founder of Cinque Gallery, New York City.
Works: *White Fence No. 2; Mother and Child* (oil); *The Kitchen; Hairdresser; The Red Shawl; Lend Me a Hand; The Domestic;* Illustrated TWO IS A TEAM (1945), CARRIE AND THE YANKEE (1959), ENTER IN (1959); *White Fence; Lovers; White Fence No. 1; Young Boy; The Waiters; Waiting; Shoe Shine; Young Mother; Hilda; Painting of a Sculptured Head*.
Exhibited: Harlem Community Center, 1938, 1939; ACA Gallery, NYC, 1960; Federal Art Gallery, NYC; Boston Museum of Fine Arts; Newark Museum; Downtown Gallery, NYC; Roko Gallery, NYC; International Print Society, NYC; NY World's Fair; Smith College; Atlanta Univ., 1942, 1944; City College of NY 1967; State Armory, Wilmington, Del., 1971; Amer. Negro Exposition, 1940; Augusta Savage Studios, 1939; Library of Congress, 1940; Institute of Modern Art, Boston, 1943; Washington Irving High School; Rockford (Ill.) College, 1965; McMillan Inc. Galleries, NY, 1941.
Sources: Locke. *The Negro in Art;* Dover. *American Negro Art; The Negro Almanac;* Albany Institute of History & Art. *The Negro Artist Comes of Age;* Boston Museum of Fine Arts. *Afro-American Artists: NY & Boston* 1970; "Afro-American Issue," *Art Gallery* April 1968; Indiana Univ. *Fine Arts & the Black American;* Newark Museum. *Black Artists: Two Generations;* City College of NY *Evolution of Afro-American Artists 1800-1950* 1967; Chatfield-Taylor, Rose. "Negro Artist Prove Skill in DC Display," *Washington Post* Jan. 5, 1941; Aesthetic Dynamics. *Afro-American Images*, 1971; DuSable Museum of African-Amer. History. *Contemporary Black Artists*, 1970; Tanner Art Galleries. *Art of the American Negro*, 1940; Porter. *Modern Negro Art;* "Two Artists in Exhibits Downtown," *NY Amsterdam News*, May 21, 1938 Beim, Jerrold, & Ernest Crichlow. *Twelve O'Clock Whistle*, NY, Wm. Morrow, 1946 Sterling, Dorothy. *Mary Jane*, Garden City Doubleday, 1959; Lansdown, Brenda. *Galumph*, Houghton-Mifflin, 1963; Locke, Alain "Advance on the Art Front," *Opportunity*, May 1939; Harley, Ralph, Jr. "Checklist of Afro Amer. Art & Artists," *Serif*, Dec. 1970; Harmon Foundation. *Non-Jury Exhibit of Work by Negro Artists*, 1933; Newark Museum *Black Artists: Two Generations*, 1971; Afro American Slide Depository, Catalog; *Daily Worker*, June 1950, May 5, 1948, "Art by Negroes," *Art Digest*, Oct. 15, 1941, p. 11; "American Negro Art Given Full Length Review in NY Show," *Art Digest*, Dec. 15, 1941; Greene Carroll, Jr. "Perspective: The Black Artist in

America," *Art Gallery*, April 1970, p. 8; "The Negro in Art," *Art Digest*, June 1, 1944, p. 15; "Afro-American Artists 1800-1950," *Ebony*, Vol. 23, pp. 116-22; Rockford College. *Creativity and the Negro*; Bowling, Frank. "The Rupture," *Arts*, Summer 1970; Lane, James. "Afro-American Art on Both Campuses," *Art News*, Oct. 15, 1941; "The Negro Artist Comes of Age," *Art News*, Feb. 1, 1945; "Negro Artists," *Art News*, Feb. 1949, p. 47; "American Negro Art," *Design*, Feb. 1942, p. 28; Greene, Carroll, Jr. "Afro-American Artists: Yesterday & Now," *The Humble Way*, Vol. 8, No. 3, 1968; Jacobs, Jay. "The Cinque Gallery," *Art Gallery*, April 1970; Greene, Carroll, Jr. *Afro-American Artists: 1800-1968*, Slides; Brown, Marion. "The Negro in the Fine Arts," *The Negro Heritage Library*, Vol. 2; Ploski, Harry, & Ernest Kaiser. "The Black Artist," *Afro USA*, 1971; "Afro-American Art a Cultural Experience for All," *Record American*, May 19, 1970; Ploski, Harry, Otto Lindenmeyer, & Ernest Kaiser. "The Black Artist," *Reference Library of Black America*, Book 4, 1971; Myers, Carol L. *Black Power in the Arts*, Flint, Mich., 1970; McMillen Inc. Galleries. *Contemporary Negro Art*, NY, 1941; Sprading, Mary M., ed. *In Black & White: Afro-Americans in Print*; Le Brun, Caron. "Black Art," *Herald Traveler*, Sunday Supplement, Boston, May 24, 1970; "Leading Negro Artists," *Ebony*, Sept. 1963; Walker, Roslyn. *A Resource Guide to the Visual Arts of Afro-Americans*, South Bend, Ind., 1971; Crichlow, Ernest. *Paintings and Drawings*, NY, ACA Galleries, 1960.

CRISS, NORMA

Painter. Born in Montclair, New Jersey, 1942.
Works: *Four Women.*
Exhibited: Newark Museum, 1971.
Represented by: Midblock Art Service, East Orange, NJ.
Sources: Newark Museum. *Black Artists: Two Generations*, 1971.

CRITCHETT, NAOMI AZALIA

Painter, magazine illustrator. Born in Maryland. Studied at Pratt Institute of Fine Arts, and previously with Miss M. Albertson and Mrs. Mary E. Joyce.
Awards: Won contest which gave her entrance to Pratt Institute.
Sources: "Maryland Girl is to Study Art," *Afro-American* (Baltimore, Md.), Oct. 15, 1923.

CRITE, ALLAN ROHAN

Painter. Born in New Jersey in 1910. Studied at Boston Latin & English High School; Boston Museum School of Fine Arts; Massachusetts School of Art; Children's Art Center; a pupil of Charles H. Woodbury; Harvard University (BA in Extension Studies, 1968).

Works: *Children at Play; Still Life; Shaw Monument; Three Sisters-Bertha, Dorothy, Sarah; Leon & Harriet; King Street; City of God; Tyre Jumping;* Illustrated books & pamphlets such as THE CHRISTMAS MESSAGE IN PICTURES, SOME OF THE COLORED PEOPLES OF GOD; *The Magi; Settling the World's Affairs; School's Out; The Annunciation; Adoration of the Shepherds; Beneath The Cross of Saint Augustine; Drill at English High School; Impression From the Green Pastures; Neighbrohood Madonna; Sketch for Summer's Child; Young Woman; Corner Store; The Handy Street Bridge; The Last Game at Dusk; Crucifixion; Palm Sunday; Finance & Commerce.*

Exhibited: Boston Society of Independent Artists, 1929; Harmon Foundation, 1930-2, 1935; Texas Centennial, 1936; Howard Univ., 1939; Dillard Univ., 1939, 1940; Amer. Negro Exposition, Chicago, 1940; Boston Printmakers, 1948; Grace Horne Galleries, Boston, 1943; Symphony Hall, Boston, 1945; Corcoran Gallery, Washington, DC, 1939; Institute of Contemporary Art, Boston, 1939; Atlanta Univ., 1942-4; Addison Gallery, Andover, Mass.; Home Study Class, Boston, 1929; Jordan Marsh Co., Boston; Fraternity Art Exhibit, 1932; Newark Museum, 1971; James A. Porter Gallery, 1970; National Center of Afro-Amer. Artists, 1971; St. John and St. James Church, Boston, 1968.

Awards: Boston Museum School Scholarship, 1935; Boit Prize, 1935.

Collections: Boston Museum of Fine Arts School; Seabury Western Theological Seminary of American Art, Andover; Villanova College; Smith College; Mt. Holyoke; Newton College of Sacred Heart; Addison Gallery of American Art; Fitchburg Art Museum; Duncan Phillips Gallery, Washington, DC; Wiggin Collection, Boston Public Library; Boston Athenaeum.

Sources: Mallett. *Index of Artists*; Dover. *American Negro Art*; Porter. *Modern Negro Art*; Harmon Foundation. *Exhibition of Productions by Negro Artists*; "Afro-American Issue," *Art Gallery*, April 1968; Indiana Univ. *Fine Arts & the Black American*; *Who's Who in American Art*, 1940-1, 1970; Locke. *The Negro in Art*; The Newark Museum. *Black Artists: Two Generations*; "Allan Crite Exhibit in Gallery of Art," *The Hilltop*, Howard Univ., Feb. 22, 1939; DuSable Museum of Afro-Amer. History. *Contemporary Black Artists*, Calendar, 1970; Tanner Art Galleries. *Art of the American Negro*, 1940; Locke, Alain. "Advance on the Art Front," *Opportunity*, May 1939; *Were You There When They Crucified My Lord?*, Cambridge, Society of St. John the

Evangelist, 1944; *The Christmas Message in Pictures*; *Some of the Colored Peoples of God*; Porter. *Modern Negro Art*; Shorewood Reproductions Catalog. *The Art of Black America*, 1969; Bourne, Kay. "Quiet, Powerful Exhibit," *Bay State Banner*, Oct. 7, 1971; Danikian, Caron Le Brun. *Herald Traveler*, Oct. 10, 1971; Driscoll, Edgar. "Blacks Duncanson & Bannister Honored In Fine Arts Exhibit," *Boston Globe*, Jan. 16, 1972; *The Negro Handbook*, Composed by Editors of *Ebony*, Chicago, 1966; Howard Univ. *Art of the American Negro*, 1937; Harmon Foundation. *Non-Jury Exhibit of Works of Negro Artists*, 1933; Harmon Foundation. *Negro Artists*, 1935; Harmon Foundation. *Exhibit of Fine Arts*, 1930; Howard Univ. *James A. Porter Gallery of African-American Art*, 1970; "American Negro Given Full Length Review in NY," *Art Digest*, Dec. 15, 1941; Pierre-Noel, Lois Jones. "American Negro Art in Progress," *Negro History Bulletin*, Oct. 1967; "American Negro Art," *Design*, Feb. 1942, p. 28; Harley, Ralph L., Jr. "A Checklist of Afro-Amer. Art & Artists," *The Serif*, Dec. 1970; St. John & St. James Church. *Exhibition of Neighborhood Paintings & Religious Drawings & Prints by Allan Rohan Crite*, Boston, April 17, 1968; Information from the artist; Myers, Carol L. *Black Power in the Arts*, Flint, Mich., 1970; Nat'l Center of Afro-American Artists. *Our Elders: Crite & Dame*, Boston, 1971; Crite, Allan R. *All Glory: Brush Drawing Meditations on the Prayer of Consecration*, Society of St. John the Evangelist, Cambridge, Mass., 1947; Crite, Allan R. *Three Spirituals From Earth to Heaven*, Cambridge, Harvard Univ. Press, 1948; Walker, Roslyn. *A Resource Guide to the Visual Arts of Afro-Americans*, South Bend, Ind., 1971.

CROOK, VICKI

Lived in Berkeley, California.
Exhibited: Atlanta Univ., 1951.
Sources: Atlanta Univ. *10th Annual for Negro Artists*, Catalog, 1951.

CROPPER, HARVEY TRISTAN

Painter. Born in New York City in 1931. Studied at Art Students League, NY; private studies with Japanese Sumiekaki Flower Sekido; Galerie Moderne, NY.
Works: *The Unicorn's Birth*.
Exhibited: Strangnas, Sweden; Helsinki, Finland; Den Frie, Copenhagen, 1964.
Sources: Dover. *American Negro Art*; Indiana Univ. *Fine Arts & the Black American*; *Ten American Negro Artists Living & Working in Europe*; Harley, Ralph L., Jr. "Checklist of Afro-American Art & Artists," *The Serif*, Dec. 1970; Pierre-Noel, Lois Jones. "American Negro Art In Progress," *Negro History*

Bulletin, Oct. 1967; Brown, Marion. "The Negro in the Fine Arts," *The Negro Heritage Library*, Vol. 2; Walker, Roslyn. *A Resource Guide to the Visual Arts of Afro-Americans*, South Bend, Ind., 1971.

CROSTHWAIT, DAVID N., JR.

Architect.
Sources: Downing, Lewis K. "Contributions of Negro Scientists," *Crisis*, June 1939.

CROXTON, RUSHIE E.

Painter, educator. Born in Georgia. Studied at Miner Teachers College (BS); Columbia University Teachers College (MA); Catholic University.
Works: *Turmoil*.
Exhibited: Smith-Mason Gallery; Anacostia Neighborhood Museum-Smithsonian Institution, 1971; Howard Univ.; Margaret Dickey Gallery.
Awards: Fellowship, Whitney Museum Project, 1967.
Sources: DC Art Assn. *Exhibition '71*, Washington, DC, 1971.

CRUDUP, DORIS

Painter. Born in Chicago, 1933. Studied at Herzl Junior College (1950-1).
Works: *Soul Man*.
Exhibited: Los Angeles City Hall, 1968.
Sources: Lewis/Waddy. *Black Artists on Art*, Vol. 1; Walker, Roslyn. *A Resource Guide to the Visual Arts of Afro-Americans*, South Bend, Ind., 1971.

CRUMP, IRIS

Sculptor, illustrator. Born in New York City. Teacher, Fieldston School, New York City.
Exhibited: 3rd Annual Purchase Art Show, 1960; Revel Gallery; Madison Gallery; Lee Nordness Gallery; Pratt Graphic Show; CCNY, 1950.
Awards: 1st Prize, Mt. Morris Show; Art Director's Award; McCresery Award; 1st Prize, CCNY Arts Exhibit, 1950; Scholarship to CCNY, 1951; Brooklyn Museum Scholarship; Whitney Fellowship; Merrill Ingram Fellowship; Pratt Graphic Scholarship.
Sources: A & T Univ. Lyceum Program. *15 Afro-American Women*.

CRUMP, ROBERT

Sculptor, painter. Born in York, North Dakota.
Works: *Statute of Leonidas Merritt; Figures from Canterbury Tales;* Cartoons in WASHINGTON EVENING JOURNAL.
Member: WPA Art Project.
Sources: Dover. *American Negro Art*; Indiana Univ. *Fine Arts & the Black American*; Mitchell, Clarence W., Jr. "Robert Crump," *Opportunity*, Oct. 1941; Pierre-Noel, Lois

Jones. "American Negro Art in Progress," *Negro History Bulletin*, Oct. 1941; Kiah, Virginia. "Black Artists," *Savannah Magazine*, April 1972, p. 14; Porter. *Modern Negro Art*; Harley, Ralph, Jr. "A Checklist of Afro-Amer. Art & Artists," *Serif*, Dec. 1970; Walker, Roslyn. *A Resource Guide to the Visual Arts of Afro-Americans,* South Bend, Ind., 1971.

CRUMPLER, DEWEY

Painter, muralist.
Exhibited: Rainbow Sign Gallery, Berkeley, 1972.
Collections: George Washington High School, San Francisco.
Sources: Rainbow Sign Gallery. *Black Arts Day II,* Press Release, Berkeley, 1972.

CRUZ, EMILIO

Painter. Born in New York City in March 1938. Studied at Art Students League under Edwin Dickinson, George Grosz, Frank J. Reilly.
Works: *Figure Composition 1; Figure Composition 2; Figure Composition 3; Couldn't I; Them; Untitled* (oil), 1967; *Silver Umbrella* (oil); *Figure Composition 6; Darlene.*
Exhibited: Sun Gallery, Provincetown, Mass., 1959-61, 1963; Richard Grey Gallery, Chicago, 1963; Gallery of Modern Art, NY, 1965; Univ. of North Carolina, 1965; Zabriskie Gallery, NY, 1963, 1965 (1-man); *1st World Festival of Nefro Arts,* Dakar, Senegal, Africa, 1966; American Greetings Gallery, NY, 1968; Minneapolis Institute of Art, 1968; Boston Museum of Fine Arts, 1968; Nat'l Collection of Fine Arts, Washington, DC, 1968; Phila. Museum of Art, 1967; Fontana Gallery, Phila., 1967; Univ. of Cal. at Los Angeles, 1966; Rhode Island School of Design, Providence, 1966; Ithaca (NY) Museum of Art, 1966; Bowdoin College, Brunswick, Me., 1966; Martha Jackson Gallery, NY, 1966; American Federation of Arts, 1965-6; Wadsworth Athenaeum, Hartford, Conn., 1965; Steinhardt Gallery, Westbury, NY; Paula Johnson Gallery, NY; Dayton Internat'l; Germantown (Pa.) Art Assn.; Dickson Art Center, Los Angeles, 1966; High Art Museum, Atlanta, 1969; Flint (Mich.) Institute of Arts, 1969; Everson Museum of Art, 1969; IBM Gallery of Arts & Sciences, 1969; Memorial Art Gallery, Rochester, NY, 1969; San Francisco Museum of Art, 1969; Contemporary Arts Museum, 1970; NJ State Museum, 1970; Roberson Center for the Arts & Sciences, Binghamton, NY, 1970; The Art Galleries, Univ. of Cal. at Santa Barbara, 1970.
Collections: Mr. Walter Gutman; Mr. Joseph H. Hirshhorn; Ms. Martha Jackson; Ms. Virginia Zabriskie; Mr. James Michener; Mr. Meyer Shapiro; Mr. Benny Andrews.

Awards: Cintas Foundation Fellowship, 1965-6; John Hay Whitney Fellowship, 1964-5; Walter Gutman Foundation Award, 1962.
Sources: "Afro-American Issue," *Art Gallery,* April 1968; Indiana Univ. *Fine Arts and the Black American; Ten Negro Artists from the United States,* 1st World Festival, Dakar; Boston Museum of Fine Arts. *Afro-American Artists: New York & Boston,* 1970; Minneapolis Institute of Arts, *30 Contemporary Black Artists;* Morrison, Allan. "New Surge in the Arts," *Ebony,* Aug. 1967; UCLA Art Galleries. *The Negro in American Art;* American Greetings Gallery. *New Voices: 15 New York Artists;* American Federation of Arts. *Inform and Interpret;* DuSable Museum of African-American History. *Contemporary Black Artists,* calendar, 1970; Greene, Carroll, Jr. "Perspective: The Black Artist in America," *Art Gallery,* April 1970; Pierre-Noel, Lois Jones. "American Negro Art in Progress," *Negro History Bulletin,* Oct. 1967; Rose, Barbara. "Black Art in America," *Art in America,* July-Dec. 1970; Harley, Ralph, Jr. "Checklist of Afro-American Art and Artists," *The Serif,* Dec. 1970; Sherman, Marjorie. "Afro-America Gets Biggest Show," *Boston Globe,* May 18, 1970; Woodruff, Hale. "Artists of the 60's," *The Negro in Music and Art,* 1969; Walsh, Rose. "Artists to Meet Public at Art Exhibit Preview," *Record American* (Boston), May 19, 1970; "Afro-American Art a Cultural Experience for All," *Record American* (Boston), May 19, 1970; Ruder & Finn Fine Arts. *Contemporary Black Artists,* NY, 1969; Myers, Carol L. *Black Power in the Arts,* Flint, Mich., 1970; Walker, Roslyn. *A Resource Guide to the Visual Arts of Afro-Americans,* South Bend, Ind., 1971; Driscoll, Edgar, Jr. "Showcase for Black Artists," *Boston Sunday Globe,* July 6, 1969, p. A73.

CULLEN, CHARLES

Sources: Cullen, Countee. *The Black Christ & Other Poems,* NY, 1921; Cullen, Countee. *The Ballad of the Brown Girl,* NY & London, 1927; Cullen, Countee. *Copper Sun,* NY, 1927; Harley, Ralph, Jr. "Checklist of Afro-Amer. Art & Artists," *Serif,* Dec. 1970; Johnson, Charles S., ed. *Ebony and Topaz,* Black Heritage Library Collection, 1927, Illustrator.

CUMMINGS, RODERICK

Born in Pittsburgh, Pennsylvania, 1943. Studied at Carnegie-Mellon University.
Exhibited: Three Rivers Arts Festival.
Awards: Blue Ribbon, County Fair.
Sources: Pittsburgh Community College. *16 Black Artists.*

CUMMINGS, URANIA PRINCE

Painter. Born in St. Thomas, Virgin Islands

on April 21, 1889. Studied at Nisky School, Virgin Islands; Merritt College, California.
Works: *Flamboyant Tree* (oil).
Exhibited: Berkeley Art Festival, 1958-72; Pleasanton Fair, 1964; Univ. of Cal., Berkeley, 1963; Black Expo '72, San Francisco; San Francisco YMCA, 1969; Grove Recreational Center, 1959; Berkeley High School, 1972; Berkeley Adult Art School, 1969; Allen Temple Baptist Church, Oakland, 1972; Oakland Museum, 1968; South Berkeley Branch Library, 1961; Rainbow Sign Gallery, Berkeley; Almeida County Fair; Cal. State Fair; Jack-Tar Hotel, San Diego; Hobbs, New Mexico; McKinley Adult School, Berkeley; All Nations Foundation, Brotherhood Week, Los Angeles, 1965; Artist Coop, Berkeley; Chabot College, Hayward.
Awards: Senior Artist of the Year, 1972; Federated Womens Club, 1957.
Member: Berkeley Artist Coop, Arts & Crafts Chairman; Cal. State Assn. of Federated Women.
Sources: Senegal, Foster. "Grandmother, Daughter Display Artistic Talents," *The California Voice*, Sept. 23, 1971; Rainbow Sign Gallery, Berkeley; Harley, Ralph, Jr. "Checklist of Afro-Amer. Art & Artists," *The Serif*, Dec. 1970; Oakland Museum. *New Perspectives in Black Art*; Indiana Univ. *Fine Arts & the Black American*; Walker, Roslyn. *A Resource Guide to the Visual Arts of Afro-Americans*, South Bend, Ind., 1971.

CUNNINGHAM, BEN

See BABB'C.

CUNNINGHAM, CAROLYN

Sources: DuSable Museum of African-Amer. History. *Contemporary Black Artists*, 1970 Calendar; Walker, Roslyn. *A Resource Guide to the Visual Arts of Afro-Americans*, South Bend, Ind., 1971.

CUNNINGHAM, DEVON

Painter.
Works: *The Christ*.
Collections: St. Cecelia, Detroit.
Sources: Myers, Carol L. *Black Power in the Arts*, Flint, Mich., 1970.

CUNNINGHAM, FERN L.

Sculptor, educator. Born in Sitka, Alaska. Studied at Albany Institute of History and Art; Art Workshop, University of Buffalo (1966); École des Beaux Arts under Etienne Martin (1967); Boston University (1971). Teacher at Cambridge Art Center; Elma Lewis School of Fine Arts.
Works: *Save the Children* (cast concrete), 1972.

Collections: Grove Hall Branch, Boston Public Library; Martin Luther King, Jr. Center, Boston Univ.; Hamilton Hill "Drop-In" Arts & Crafts Center, Schenectady.
Sources: Museum of Nat'l. Center of Afro-Amer. Artists. *Save the Children*, 1972; Press, Robert M. "Warm Spark in Cement Sculpture," *Christian Science Monitor*, Dec. 27, 1972.

CUNNINGHAM, LUCILE

Painter.
Sources: "Afro-American Issue," *Art Gallery*, April 1968; Indiana Univ. *Fine Arts & the Black American*; DuSable Museum of African-Amer. History. *Contemporary Black Artists*, 1970 Calendar; Myers, Carol. *Black Power in the Arts*, Flint, Mich., 1970; Walker, Roslyn. *A Resource Guide to the Visual Arts of Afro-Americans*, South Bend, Ind., 1971.

CUREAU, HAROLD

Art Staff of Southern University.
Awards: Grant, Ford Foundation.
Sources: *National Conference of Artists*, Winter 1971, Journal.

CURRY, LARRY

Painter, photographer. Born 1950. Studied at Savannah State College, Savannah, Georgia; Massachusetts School of Art.
Works: Untitled oil, 1970; untitled acrylic, 1971.
Exhibited: Howard St. Youth Center, Boston; Black Artist Union; All Boys School Prep, Lenox, Mass.
Member: Boston Negro Artists' Assn.; Black Artist Union; Nat'l. Conference of Artists.
Sources: Information from the artist.

CURTIS, WILLIAM

Painter. Born in St. Louis, Missouri in 1939. Studied at Lincoln University (1957-8).
Works: *Riot: USA*.
Exhibited: Paris, 1959-61; Germany, 1963; Atlanta Univ.; Beaux Arts.
Sources: Lewis/Waddy. *Black Artists on Art*, Vol. 1.

CUYJET, HELEN CORNELE

Craftsman, designer, educator. Born in Philadelphia on Oct. 15, 1921. Studied at Temple University (AB, 1941); Columbia University (MA, 1942). Designer and manufacturer of leather accessories.
Sources: Furr, Arthur F. *History & Progress of Negroes in the US*.

DAMES, CHESTER

Painter.
Exhibited: National Center of Afro-Amer. Artists, Boston, 1971.
Collections: NY Public Library, Schomburg Collection.

Sources: Le Brun, Caron. *Herald Traveler* (Boston), Oct. 10, 1971; Harley, Ralph, Jr. "Checklist of Afro-Amer. Art & Artists," *The Serif*, Dec. 1970; Bourne, Kay. "Quiet, Powerful Exhibit," *Bay State Banner* (Mass.), Oct. 7, 1971; Schatz, Walter. *Directory of Afro-American Resources*, 1970.

DANIEL, ALBERT
Lived in Virgin Islands.
Exhibited: Atlanta Univ., 1951.
Sources: Atlanta Univ. *10th Annual for Negro Artists*, 1951.

DANIEL, MARY REED
Painter.
Works: *Integral Forms; A Friend.*
Exhibited: Rockford College, 1965.
Sources: Myers, Carol L. *Black Power in the Arts*, Flint, Mich., 1970; "Afro-American Issue," *Art Gallery*, April 1968; Indiana Univ. *Fine Arts & the Black American;* DuSable Museum of African-Amer. History. *Contemporary Black Artists*, 1970; Afro-American Slide Depository, 1971-2 Catalog; Rockford College. *Creativity and the Negro;* Harley, Ralph L., Jr. "Checklist of Afro-American Art & Artists," *The Serif*, Dec. 1970; Atkinson, J. Edward. *Black Dimensions in Contemporary American Art*, NY, 1971; Walker, Roslyn. *A Resource Guide to the Visual Arts of Afro-Americans*, South Bend, Ind., 1971.

DANIELS, RAYMOND H.
Painter. Born in New York City, 1944. Studied at the Art Workshop, La Rochelle, France (1964); Academy of Art, Nuremburg, Germany (1965).
Works: *Mongolian Warriors; Brazilian Swamps; Swahili Song; African Morning; Blues to Passion; Sun Dance; Sun Mystery; Cosmic Lake; Direction; Soul Birth; Black Power; Sex in Color; Brass a Hurt; K Hepera.*
Exhibited: Studio Museum in Harlem, 1969.
Sources: Afro-American Slide Depository, Catalog; Studio Museum in Harlem. *Harlem Artists 69.*

DARLING, AARON E.
Painter.
Works: *John Jones; Mary Richardson Jones.*
Sources: Drotning, Phillip T. *A Guide to Negro History in America*, 1968.

DATES, DWIGHT E.
Painter. Born in New York in 1940. Studied at the High School of Music & Art; Pratt Institute; Art Students League. Graphic arts instructor, Youth in Action, 1967.
Works: *Forest Aflame; Poverty or the Pill Won't Solve the Problem.*
Exhibited: Sphinx Shop (1-man), 1969; Brook-

lyn Museum, 1968; Graphic Art Institute; Studio Museum in Harlem, 1969.
Sources: Studio Museum in Harlem. *Harlem Artists 69.*

DAVIS, ALONZO JOSEPH
Painter, educator. Born in Tuskegee, Alabama in 1942. Studied at Pepperdine College; University of Southern California; University of California at Los Angeles; Otis Art Institute, Los Angeles.
Works: *Bag Series; Caution; Black Modern Dance; Heart Dance; Cultural Greetings* (greeting card for Brockman Gallery).
Exhibited: Galleria del Sol, 1970; Brockman Gallery, 1967-9; Occidental College, 1969; Gallery Negra, 1969; Laguna Beach Assn., 1968; Westside Jewish Center; Watts Summer Art Festival; Studio Museum in Harlem, 1972; Los Angeles Co. Museum, 1972; Bob Jefferson Studio, 1968; Simon Patrick Gallery, 1966; Los Angeles Art Teachers Exhibition, 1966.
Member: Black Artist Assn.; Crenshaw Neighbors, Inc.; Black Educators, Inc.; Cal. Teachers Assn.
Sources: Lewis/Waddy. *Black Artists on Art*, Vol. 2; Atkinson, J. Edward. *Black Dimensions in Contemporary American Art;* Brockman Gallery. *Black Scholar*, 1972; "Brothers Operate Art Gallery," *Southwest Wave*, Jan. 6, 1972; Harley, Ralph L., Jr. "Checklist of Afro-American Art & Artists," *The Serif*, Dec. 1970; *Wilson Library Bulletin*, April 1969.

DAVIS, BING
Born 1937 in Spartenberg, South Carolina. Studied at DePauw University; Miami University, Ohio; Dayton Art Institute.
Works: *Great American Hang-Up Series #3.*
Exhibited: Black Arts Festival, Cincinnati; Dayton Art Institute; Ohio Designers-Craftsman Show, Columbus; Univ. of Cincinnati.
Awards: Midwest Ceramics Show, 1964, 1965, 1967.
Sources: Lewis/Waddy. *Black Artists on Art*, Vol. 2; Univ. of Cincinnati. *Discovery 70*, Unpublished list.

DAVIS, CHARLES
Painter, graphic artist. Born in Evanston, Illinois, 1912. Studied at the Art Institute of Chicago; pupil of George E. Neal.
Works: *Benediction; Newsboy; Johnny Mae Sewing; Victory at Dawn; Perhaps Tomorrow; Deep Thought; My World; Perhaps; Low Cost of Living; Tycoon Toys; It Was Thanksgiving; Low Cost Housing; Nocturne to Victoria; Workers Interlude; The Blue Pitcher.*
Exhibited: South Side Settlement House, Chicago, 1937, 1938; Amer. Negro Exposition, Chicago, 1940; WPA Artists Project, Chicago;

48th Annual for Artists of Chicago & Vicinity, 1938; Fort Huachuca, Ariz., 1943; McMillen Inc. Galleries, NY, 1941; South Side Community Art Center, Chicago, 1941, 1945; Howard Univ., 1970.
Collections: Hall Library, Chicago (mural).
Member: United Amer. Artists.
Sources: Mallett. *Index of Artists;* Locke. *The Negro in Art;* Indiana Univ. *Fine Arts & the Black American;* Dover. *American Negro Art;* Porter. *Modern Negro Art;* Harley, Ralph L., Jr. "A Checklist of Afro-American Art and Artists," *The Serif,* Dec. 1970; Motley, Willard F. "Negro Art in Chicago," *Opportunity,* Jan. 1940; Howard Univ. *Exhibition of Negro Artists of Chicago at Howard University Gallery of Art,* Feb. 1-25, 1941; Tanner Art Galleries. *Art of the American Negro,* 1940; Roucek/Kiernan. *The Negro Impact on Western Civilization;* Howard Univ. *James A. Porter Gallery of African-Amer. Art,* 1970; Harmon Foundation. *Select Picture List;* "Art by Negroes," *Art Digest,* Oct. 15, 1941; "Amer. Negro Art Given Full Length Review in NY Show," *Art Digest,* Dec. 15, 1941; Locke, Alain. "Chicago's New Southside Art Center," *Magazine of Art,* Aug. 1941, p. 320; South Side Community Art Center. *Chicago Collectors Exhibit of Negro Art,* Chicago, 1945; South Side Community Art Center. *Opening Exhibition of Paintings by Negro Artists,* 1941; South Side Community Art Center. *National Negro Art Exhibition,* 1941; Myers, Carol L. *Black Power in the Arts,* Flint, Mich., 1970; *Who's Who in American Art,* 1940-1; McMillen Inc. Galleries. *Contemporary Negro Art,* NY, 1941; Walker, Roslyn. *A Resource Guide to the Visual Arts of Afro-Americans,* South Bend, Ind., 1971.

DAVIS, DALE B.

Ceramist, sculptor, educator. Born in Tuskegee, Alabama on November 11, 1945. Studied at Los Angeles City College; University of Southern California (BFA); University of California at Los Angeles (MFA). High school art instructor; Co-director of Brockman Gallery, Los Angeles.
Works: *God of Fertility & Goddess of Fertility; Age for Peace; Totem Assemblage; Untitled #2, #3; Ecology #1; Growth Process; Monk's Now.*
Exhibited: Brockman Gallery, Los Angeles, 1970, 1972; Ankrum Gallery, 1970; Mills College, 1970; Leimert Park Art Festival, 1969; Watts Summer Festival, 1969; Multipurpose Health Center, Watts; Gallery Negra; Bob Jefferson Gallery, Oakland, Cal.; Univ. of Iowa, 1971; Galeria del Sol, Santa Barbara, 1971; Harlem Studio Museum, 1972; Contemporary Black Artists, Chicago, 1971.

Collections: Multipurpose Health Center, Watts, Cal.; County Mental Hospital, Compton; KCET Television, Los Angeles; Mr. Bill Cosby; Ms. Elaine Robinson.
Represented by: Brockman Gallery.
Sources: Information from artist; Lewis/Waddy. *Black Artists on Art,* Vol. 2; Mills College. *California Black Craftsmen,* 1970; Illinois Bell Telephone. *Black American Artists/71,* 1972; Patterson, Lindsay. "Contemporary Artists," *The Negro in Music & Art,* 1969.

DAVIS, E. DeLOUIS

Painter.
Works: *Camel Back Mountain.*
Exhibited: Atlanta Univ., 1942.
Sources: Harley, Ralph, Jr. "Checklist of Afro-Amer. Art & Artists," *The Serif,* Dec. 1970.

DAVIS, JAMES

Sculptor.
Works: *Two Vases.*
Collections: National Archives.
Sources: Afro-American Slide Depository, Catalog, 1971-2.

DAVIS, M. LOUISE

Exhibited: State Armory, Wilmington, Del.
Sources: Aesthetic Dynamics. *Afro-American Images 1971.*

DAVIS, NICHOLAS

Painter. Born in New York City in 1937. Studied at Art Students League; Mexico City College.
Works: *Black Emergence; Living Eulogy; Untitled* (acrylic).
Exhibited: Phila. School District; Studio Museum in Harlem, 1969.
Sources: Phila Division of Art. *Afro-American Artists 1800-1969;* Studio Museum in Harlem. *Harlem Artists 69.*

DAVIS, NORMAN E.

Painter.
Works: *Untitled* (acrylic).
Collections: Mr. Benny Andrews.

DAVIS, RACHEL ESTWICK

Painter, educator. Studied at Howard University (BA); under James Porter; Lois Mailou Jones Studio; DC Teachers College; American University. Teacher in Washington, DC public schools.
Works: Untitled acrylic.
Exhibited: All Souls Unitarian Art Show; Margaret Dickey Gallery; Anacostia Neighborhood Museum-Smithsonian Institution, 1971.
Collections: Estate of George A. Parker; Freedmen's Hospital, Children's Ward.
Awards: William E. Brown Memorial Fund

Grant; Superior Accomplishment Award for cartoon series for Naval Research Laboratory Newsletter.
Member: DC Black Writers Workshop.
Sources: DC Art Assn. *Exhibition '71,* Washington, DC, 1971.

DAVIS, W. BRUCE

Born in Richmond, Virginia. Studied at Maryland State College (BS). Specialized art teacher, Department of Health, Education & Welfare, St. Elizabeth's Hospital.
Works: *Life Cycle.*
Exhibited: Maryland State College; Virginia Union Univ.; Univ. of Maryland; Atlanta Univ.; Salisburg State College; Wicomico Art League; Maryland Art Academy of Easton; Bank & Trust Co. Art Show; DCAA, Anacostia Neighborhood Museum-Smithsonian Institution.
Awards: 1st place, wood sculpture, Virginia Union Univ., 1964; Howard Hudson Memorial Award, Wicomico Art League; Certificate Award, Bank & Trust Co.
Sources: DC Art Assn. *Exhibition '71,* Washington, DC, 1971.

DAVIS, W.F.

Exhibited: Augusta Savage Studios, 1939.
Sources: Harley, Ralph, Jr. "Checklist of Afro-Amer. Art & Artists," *The Serif,* Dec. 1970.

DAVIS, WALTER

Painter. Born in Americus, Georgia. Studied at the Detroit Institute of Arts; New York City Community College; Abracheff School of Art, New York.
Works: *Figure With Birds; Blue Bird Music; Charlie Parker After Death; Bird Spirit; Bird Roots; Afro-Delights; East Village Sound; Bird Form #7; Circle #3; Birds in the Ark; Blue Bird West; Study #6; Black Bird Totem; Bird Form #6.*
Exhibited: Whitney Museum, NY, 1971; Sukiran Annual, Okinawa, 1957; Studio Gallery, NY, 1960; St. Marks in the Bowery, NY, 1961; Art of the New Frontier Show, NY, 1962; Logoa Duncan Gallery, NY, 1963-4; Schomburg Studio, NY, 1963-4; Dunham School of Cultural Arts, NY, 1964-5; Hall of Education, World's Fair, 1964-5; Mary McLeod Bethune Memorial Exhibit, Blumenstein's, NY, 1965; Countee Cullen Library, NY, 1966; Detroit Institute of Art, 1966-7; Detroit Public Library, 1966; Arts Extended Gallery, Detroit, 1966-71; Oakland Univ. Gallery, Rochester, Mich., 1968; American Academy of Arts & Letters, 1969; Museum of American Art, NY, 1971.
Collections: Detroit Board of Education.
Sources: "The Negro in Music and Art," from International Library Series *The Study of Negro Life and History,* 1967; "Black Perspectives," the Scholastic Black Literature Series, published in cooperation with Los Angeles City Schools, 1971, p. 16; Perreault, John. "Review," *Village Voice,* April 15, 1971, p. 21; Tall, William. "Walter Davis' Totems for Charlie Parker," *Detroit Free Press,* Aug. 15, 1971; Hakanson, Joy. "Review," *Sunday Detroit News,* Aug. 15, 1971.

DAWKINS, P.W.

Sculptor, educator.
Exhibited: Knoxville.
Sources: Texas Centennial Exposition. *Thumbnail Sketches of Exhibiting Artists,* 1936; Harley, Ralph, Jr. "Checklist of Afro-Amer. Art & Artists," *The Serif,* Dec. 1970.

DAWSON, CHARLES C.

Painter, illustrator, sculptor, newspaper artist. Born 1889 in Brunswick, Georgia. Studied at Tuskegee Institute; Art Students League, NY; Art Institute of Chicago.
Works: *The Quadroon Madonna; Brother and Sister; Searchlights; Dr. G. W. Carver; Dr. F. Patterson; The Nephew; Shrimp Fisherman; The Crisis; The Quadroon;* booklet design for National DeSaible Memorial Society Exhibit, 1933, 1934.
Exhibited: Harmon Foundation, 1929, 1933; National Gallery of Art, 1929; Howard Univ., 1932; Findlay Art Gallery, Chicago, 1933; Illinois Host House, 1933; National DeSaible Memorial Exhibit, 1933, 1934; Urban Social Work Exhibit, Century of Progress, Chicago, 1933, 1934; Smithsonian Institution, 1929; Art Institute of Chicago; Amer. Negro Exposition, 1940; South Side Community Art Center, Chicago, 1941.
Collections: Tuskegee Institute (Dioramas); Carver Museum.
Awards: Honorable mention, Harmon exhibits.
Sources: Harmon Foundation. *Exhibition of Productions by Negro Artists;* Indiana Univ. *Fine Arts & the Black American;* Art Institute of Chicago. *The Negro in Art Week,* catalog; Dawson, Charles C. *ABC of American Negroes,* 26 linoleum blocks; Harley, Ralph L., Jr. "Checklist of Afro-American Art & Artists," *The Serif,* Dec. 1970; Afro-American Slide Depository, 1971-2 catalog; Furr, Arthur F. *History and Progress of Negroes in the US;* "O, Sing A New Song," *Chicago Art Institute Scrapbook,* April 1934-May 1935, p. 42; Motley, Willard F. "Negro Art in Chicago," *Opportunity,* Jan. 1940; DuSable Museum of African-American History. *Contemporary Black Artists,* 1970 calendar; Tanner Art Galleries. *Art of the American Negro,* 1940; Harmon Foundation. *Negro Artists,* 1935; Smith-

sonian Institution. *Painting & Sculpture by American Negro Artists*, 1929; Parry, Barbara. "Painter Charles C. Dawson Has Been Finding Beauty in Black Subjects for 81 Years," *Philadelphia Inquirer Magazine*, July 19, 1971; Ploski, Harry, & Ernest Kaiser. "The Black Artist," *Afro USA*, 1971; Ploski, Harry, Ernest Kaiser, & Otto Lindenmeyer. "The Black Artist," *Reference Library of Black America*, Book 4, 1971; *The Negro Handbook*, Composed by the Editors of *Ebony*, Chicago, 1966; Troup, Cornelius V. *Distinguished Negro Georgians*, 1962; South Side Community Art Center. *National Negro Art Exhibition*, Chicago, 1941; Walker, Roslyn. *A Resource Guide to the Visual Arts of Afro-Americans*, South Bend, Ind., 1971.

DAWSON, MORRIS

Painter. Born in New York City in 1928. Studied at the Cartoonist Illustrator School, Brooklyn Museum School of Art; under Myles Cooper at Columbia University. Art Consultant in NY public schools.
Works: *Birch Tree; Aqua Life; Chief Mask (Ukumba Tribe SW Africa); Mask of Baboon (Bantu Tribe S. Africa).*
Exhibited: Columbia Univ., 1967 (1-man); Irwin Shanes Home Gallery, Brooklyn; New York World's Fair, 1965; Nyumba-Ya Sanaa Outdoor Exhibit, 1964; Studio Museum in Harlem, 1969.
Sources: Studio Museum in Harlem. *Harlem Artists 69.*

DAY, JUETTE JOHNSON

Painter, educator. Born in Richmond, Virginia. Studied at Virginia Union University (BA); Ohio State University (MFA); Columbia University; private studies under Mrs. Beatrice Riese.
Works: *Vision; Smouldering; Tenement; Cathedral; Plight.*
Exhibited: State Armory, Wilmington, Del., 1971; Smith-Mason Gallery, Washington, DC, 1971; Delver Woman's Club Art Show; Potter's House Gallery, 1971; Ohio State Univ. (1-man); College Art Assn. Traveling Exhibition.
Awards: 1st prize, Art Show of the Delver Woman's Club; Honorable mention, Washington Art Teachers Show.
Sources: Aesthetic Dynamics. *Afro-American Images 1971*; Smith-Mason Gallery. *Anniversary Exhibit*, Washington, DC, 1971; DC Art Assn. *Exhibition '71*; Harley, Ralph L., Jr. "Checklist of Afro-American Art & Artists," *The Serif*, Dec. 1970; Atkinson, J. Edward. *Black Dimensions in Contemporary American Art*, NY, 1971.

DAY, SELMA

Exhibited: Library of Congress, 1940.

Sources: Harley, Ralph, Jr. "Checklist of Afro-Amer. Art & Artists," *The Serif*, Dec. 1970.

DAY, THOMAS

Woodcarver, cabinetmaker. Born in Charleston, South Carolina, early 19th century. Studied in Washington, DC and Boston. By 1818 had workshop in North Carolina. In 1823 moved to Milton, North Carolina where he purchased Old Yellow Brick Tavern and manufactured furniture in mahogany on a large scale, using white and slave apprentices.
Sources: Dover. *American Negro Art*; Indiana Univ. *Fine Arts & the Black American*; Herring, James V. "The American Negro Craftsman," *Crisis*, April 1942; Walker, Roslyn. *A Resource Guide to the Visual Arts of Afro-Americans*, South Bend, Ind., 1971.

DAY, WILLIAM E.

Painter. Born in Dayton, Ohio in 1937. Studied at the School of Visual Arts; Art Students League, NY; University of Dayton; Dayton Art Institute.
Works: *Aunt Sarah; 118th Street; The Playground; Black Girl.*
Exhibited: Phila. School District; Studio Museum in Harlem, 1969.
Sources: Phila. Division of Art. *Afro-American Artists, 1800-1969*; Studio Museum in Harlem. *Harlem Artists 69.*

DEAN, EDMOND

Ceramist.
Works: *Cactus Vase; Flat Vase; Vase; The Cobra; Leaf Bowl; Bettle Vase; Japanese Tori; The Hunchback; Weed Pot; Gabriel's Horn; Flat Bottle; Weed Vase; Three Vases.*
Sources: Afro-American Slide Depository, Catalog, 1971-2.

DEAN, HILLIARD

Printmaker.
Works: *Strike Up The Band; Untitled D; Untitled B; A Mulatto Looking For His Home; Fisherman Lithograph.*
Collections: Nat'l Collection of Fine Arts.
Sources: Afro-Amer. Slide Depository catalog, 1971-2.

DEAN, MARY T.

Painter. Worked in Atlanta, Georgia.
Works: *Knitting; Flowers; Not Wanted.*
Exhibited: Atlanta Univ., 1942-4; Dillard Univ., 1941.
Sources: Dillard Univ. *Arts Festival*, 1941; Harley, Ralph, Jr. "Checklist of Afro-Amer Art & Artists," *The Serif*, Dec. 1970.

DeCARAVA, ROY

Painter, photographer, printmaker. Born in Harlem, New York. Studied at Cooper Union, New York; Harlem Art Center; George Wash-

ngton Carver Art School, New York (1944-5).
Photographer for *Sports Illustrated* and *Look.*
Founded Photographers' Gallery, New York;
Kamoinge Workshop, New York.
Works: *Sweet Flypaper of Life,* 1955 (Book
of photographs); *Palma; Subway.*
Exhibited: NY Serigraph Society (1-man);
Hotel Diplomat, 1948; Museum of Modern
Art, NY, 1957; Studio Museum in Harlem,
NY; Countee Cullen Branch, NY Public Library (1-man); Atlanta Univ., 1944.
Awards: Guggenheim Fellowship, 1952.
Collections: Museum of Modern Art, NY; Mr.
Benny Andrews.
Member: NY Serigraph Society; Amer. Society
of Magazine Photographers.
Sources: Fax, Elton C. *Seventeen Black Artists;* Museum of Modern Art. *Seventy Photographers Look at New York,* 1957; Studio
Museum in Harlem. *Thru Black Eyes;* Schatz,
Walter. *Directory of Afro-American Resources,*
1970; "Negro Winners," *Art Digest,* May 1,
1946; *Daily Worker (NY),* May 5, 1948; Harley, Ralph, Jr. "Checklist of Afro-American
Art & Artists," *The Serif,* Dec. 1970; DeCarava,
Roy. *Sweet Flypaper of Life,* Book of Photographs.

DeGRANGE, ELMORE

Painter.
Works: *Children Bathing; Composition; Portrait of My Father.*
Exhibited: Xavier Univ., 1963.
Sources: Xavier Univ. *Emancipation Proclamation Centennial National Art Exhibition,*
1963.

de KNIGHT, AVEL

Painter. Born in New York, 1933. Studied at
Ecole des Beaux-Arts, Paris; Pratt Institute,
New York; Grand Chaumiere, Paris.
Works: *Veiled Woman,* 1968 (oil wash on
paper); *Tombs of Samarkand* (gouache); *Mirage; Sunset; Two Heads; Mirage Painting;
Shields,* 1970; *Mirage Painting: No. 2; Desert
Stones; Mirage Painting: The Guardian; Figure;
Mirage Painting; Sea & Sky; Mediterranean;
Passage to the Sun; Fragments,* 1969 (oil on
paper); *Domes of Samarkand* (watercolor).
Exhibited: Larcada Gallery, NY, 1968; American Greetings Gallery, NY, 1968; American
Watercolor Society, NY, 1967; Butler Institute
of American Art, Youngstown, Ohio; Pa.
Academy of Fine Arts; Banfer Gallery, NY;
The Contemporaries Gallery, NY; Roko Gallery, NY; Minneapolis Institute of Arts; Whitney Museum, 1971; Univ. of Iowa, 1971-2;
High Museum of Art, Atlanta, 1969; Flint
(Mich.) Institute of Arts, 1969; Everson Museum of Art, Syracuse, NY, 1969; IBM Gallery
of Arts & Sciences, 1969; Rhode Island School
of Design, 1969; Memorial Art Gallery,
Rochester, NY, 1969; San Francisco Museum
of Art, 1969; NJ State Museum, 1970; Contemporary Arts Museum, Houston, 1970; Roberson Center for the Arts & Sciences, 1970;
Univ. of Cal., Santa Barbara, 1970.
Collections: Walker Art Center, Minneapolis;
Springfield (Mo.) Art Museum; Norfolk (Va.)
Museum of Arts & Science; Miles College,
Birmingham, Ala.; Denison (Ohio) Univ.; Metropolitan Museum of Art, NY; Massilon Art
Museum, Ohio; Larcada Gallery, NY.
Awards: Grand Prize, American Watercolor
Society, 1967; William A. Paton Prize, National Academy School of Fine Arts, NY,
1958, 1967; Ranger Fund Purchase Prize, National Academy School of Fine Arts, NY,
1958, 1964, 1966; Grumbacher Award, Audubon Artists Society, NY, 1964; Samuel F. B.
Morse Medal, National Academy School of
Fine Arts, NY, 1963; Karpick Memorial Prize,
Audubon Artists Society, 1961; Childe Hassam
Fund Purchase, American Academy of Arts
and Letters, NY, 1960; Emily Lowe Award,
American Watercolor Society, NY, 1960;
Palmer Memorial Prize, National Academy
School of Fine Arts, 1958; Cultural Exchange
Grant, NY & the USSR, 1961.
Sources: *Who's Who in American Art,* 1970;
Minneapolis Institute of Arts. *30 Contemporary Black Artists,* 1968; American Greetings Gallery. *New Voices: 15 New York Artists,* NY, 1968; "Afro-American Issue," *Art
Gallery,* April 1968; Boston Museum of Fine
Arts. *Afro-American Artists: New York &
Boston,* 1970; Doty. *Contemporary Black Artists in America;* Browne, Rosalind. "Reviews
and Previews," *Art News,* Nov. 1968, p. 13;
DuSable Museum of African-Amer. History.
Contemporary Black Artists, calendar, 1970;
Illinois Bell Telephone. *Black American Artists/71,* 1972; Afro American Slide Depository,
Catalog, 1971-2; Harley, Ralph, Jr. "Checklist of Afro-American Art and Artists," *The
Serif,* Dec. 1970; Ploski, Harry, Ernest Kaiser.
"The Black Artist," *Afro USA,* 1971; Van
Almelo, Frederik. "In the American Grain,"
Boston After Dark, May 26, 1970; Le Brun,
Caron. "Black Art on Display," (Boston)
Herald Traveler, May 26, 1970; Ploski, Harry,
Ernest Kaiser, & Otto Lindenmeyer. "The
Black Artist," *Reference Library of Black
America,* Vol. 4, 1971; Schatz, Walter. *Directory of Afro-American Resources,* NY, Bowker, 1970; Ruder & Finn Fine Arts. *Contemporary Black Artists,* 1969; Myers, Carol L.
Black Power in the Arts, Flint, Mich., 1970;
Hollingsworth, Alvin. "Wealth of Expression
in Black Artists' RISD Show," *Providence Sunday Journal,* June 29, 1969; Haas, Joseph.
"A Big, Brilliant & Exciting Exhibition of

Black Art," *Chicago Daily News,* Jan. 16-7, 1971; Walker, Roslyn. *A Resource Guide to the Visual Arts of Afro-Americans,* South Bend, Ind., 1971.

DELANEY, BEAUFORD

Painter. Born in Knoxville, Tennessee in 1910. Studied at Massachusetts Normal Art School; South Boston School of Art; Copley Society. Studied under Thomas Hart Benton; John Sloan; Don Freeman. Lives & works in Paris.

Works: *Composition; Greene St.; Minstrel; Yaddo; The Face; Spring; Figure in a Landscape; Autumn; Austin Hall; Captain Sanky; Mandy Lou; Meditation; Head of a Poet; Portrait of a Man; Snow Scene; Picnic; East River.*

Exhibited: Vendome Galleries, NY, 1941 (1-man); Artists Gallery, NY, 1948; Roko Gallery, NY, 1950-3; Salon des Réalitiés Nouvelles, Paris, 1954, 1960, 1963; Galerie Clan, Madrid, 1955; Galerie Prisme, Paris, 1956; Galerie Paul Facchetti, Paris, 1960; Centre Culturel Americain, Paris, 1961, 1969; Whitney Galleries, NY, 1930; NY Public Library, 135th St. Branch, 1932; Cooperative Art Market & Roxy Theatre, 1933; Harmon Foundation, 1933; Galerie Arnaud, Paris, 1956; Iserlohn, Germany, 1956; Bordighera, Italy, 1957; Univ. of Wisconsin, 1957; Leverkusen, Germany, 1958; Galerie Breteau, Paris, 1959, 1962; Musée des Arts Decoratifs, Paris, 1960; Lincoln Gallery, London, 1961; Musée d'Art Moderne, Paris, 1963; Musée Cantonal des Beaux-Arts, Lausanne, 1963; Galerie International d'Art Contemporain, Paris, 1964; Morgan State College, Baltimore, 1967; Univ. of Texas, 1970; Amer. Negro Exposition, 1940; 42nd St. Branch of NY Public Library, 1932; Newark Museum, 1971; McMillen Inc. Galleries, NY, 1941.

Awards: Fairfield Foundation Grant, 1964.

Collections: Whitney Museum of American Art, NY; Newark Museum; Morgan State College, Baltimore; Mr. Henry Miller; Ms. Marian Anderson; Mr. James Baldwin; Professor Richard A. Long; Mr. Julien Alvard.

Sources: Dover. *American Negro Art,* pp. 31, 50; "Afro-American Issue," *Art Gallery,* April 1968; "Delaney Remembered," *Art Gallery,* n.d.; Miller, Henry "The Amazing & Invariable Beauford Delaney," *Remember to Remember,* NY, 1947; Harmon Foundation. *Exhibition of Productions by Negro Artists;* Indiana Univ. *Fine Arts & the Black American;* Univ. Art Museum of Univ. of Texas. *Afro-American Artists Abroad;* Mallett. *Index of Artists;* Du-Sable Museum of African-Amer. History. *Contemporary Black Artists,* Calendar, 1970; Tanner Art Galleries. *Art of the American Negro,* 1940; Roucek & Kiernan. *The Negro Im-*

pact on Western Civilization; Harmon Foundation. *Non-Jury Exhibit of Works of Negro Artists,* 1933; Harmon Foundation. *Negro Artists,* 1935; Newark Museum. *Black Artists: Two Generations,* 1971; *New York Times,* May 16, 1948; *10 American Artists Living & Working in Europe,* 1964; J.G. "Honoring Negro History," *Art Digest,* Feb. 15, 1949, p. 20; "Art by Negroes," *Art Digest,* Oct. 15, 1941; "American Negro Art Given Full Length Review in NY Show," *Art Digest,* Dec. 15, 1941; Pierre-Noel, Lois Jones. "American Negro Art in Progress," *Negro History Bulletin,* Oct. 1967; E.K. "Negro Artists," *Art News,* Feb. 1949, p. 47; ". . . Paintings by Beauford Delaney . .," *Life,* Articles on Art, 1938, p. 216; "Exhibition," *Pictures on Exhibit,* Feb. 1950, p. 24; Schweicher, Curt, & Chares Dallyce. *Neues Aus Der Neuen Malerei;* Harley, Ralph L., Jr. "A Checklist of Afro-Amer. Art & Artists," *The Serif,* Dec. 1970; Grillo, Jean B. "Elma Lewis: A New Show A New Showplace," *Boston After Dark,* Aug. 16, 1970; Loercher, Diana. "Afro-American Artists Abroad," *Christian Science Monitor,* Aug. 1, 1970; Myers, Carol L. *Black Power in the Arts,* Flint, Mich., 1970; McMillen Inc. Galleries. *Contemporary Negro Art,* NY, 1941; Walker, Roslyn. *A Resource Guide to the Visual Arts of Afro-Americans,* South Bend, Ind., 1971.

DELANEY, JAMES

Painter.

Works: *The Choir.*

Collections: National Archives.

Sources: Afro-American Slide Depository, Catalog, 1971-2.

DELANEY, JOSEPH

Painter. Born in Knoxville, Tennessee in 1904. Studied at the London School of Art in Washington, DC; Art Students League in NY under Thomas Hart Benton. Worked on the New York Federal Art Project (1936-9).

Works: *The Artist; Herald Square Night; Morning Subway; Ice Skating in Central Park, NYC; Chelsea Bar; Day Times Square; 125th Street; Dr. Graham; City Life; George's Bar; Pelham Rocks; Girl at the Window; Harlem Stoop; Going Home; Night on Fifth Avenue; Revival on the Corner; St. Patrick's Day; Fish Packing, Hampton, Va.; Penn Station Troop Moving; Loby Arts Student League; Village Corner; Pigeons; Third Avenue Movie.*

Exhibited: Washington Square Shows, NYC, 1937-40; Atlanta Univ., 1942; Greenwich House, NYC, 1944; New York Federal Art Project, 1936-9; City College of NY, 1967; Amer. Negro Exposition, Chicago, 1940; Hotel Diplomat, 1948; McMillen Inc. Galleries, NY, 1941.

Collections: Arizona Collection; Metropolitan Museum; British American Galleries; Riverside Museum; National Academy of Design.
Sources: Mallett. *Index of Artists;* Locke. *The Negro in Art;* Albany Institute of History & Art. *The Negro Artist Comes of Age;* Afro-American Slide Depository, Catalog, 1970-1; *Negro Year Book;* "Afro-American Issue," *Art Gallery,* April 1968; Indiana Univ. *Fine Arts & the Black American;* City College of NY. *The Evolution of Afro-American Artists.* McMillen Inc. Galleries. *Contemporary Negro Art,* NY, 1941; DuSable Museum of African-Amer. History. *Contemporary Black Artists,* Calendar, 1970; Tanner Art Galleries. *Art of American Negro,* 1940; Harmon Foundation. *Negro Artists;* "Art by Negroes," *Art Digest,* Oct. 15, 1941; "American Negro Art Given Full Length Review in NY Show," *Art Digest,* Dec. 14, 1941; "Negro Art Scores Without Double Standard," *Art Digest,* Feb. 1, 1945; "Negro Winners," *Art Digest,* May 1, 1946; Harley, Ralph L., Jr. "Checklist of Afro-Amer. Art & Artists," *The Serif,* Dec. 1970; Patterson, Lindsay. "Contemporary Artists," *The Negro in Music & Art,* 1969; Ploski, Harry, & Ernest Kaiser. "The Black Artist," *Afro USA,* 1971; Ploski, Harry, Ernest Kaiser, & Otto Lindenmeyer. "The Black Artist," *Reference Library of Black America,* Book 4, 1971; Walker, Roslyn. *A Resource Guide to the Visual Arts of Afro-Americans,* South Bend, Ind., 1971.

DÉLÉ, BABALAIYE S.
See Pinckney, Stanley.

De LOACH, JAMES IRA
Works: *Forester B. Washington.*
Collections: Nat'l Portrait Gallery.
Sources: Afro-Amer. Slide Depository, Catalog, 1971-2; Harley, Ralph, Jr. "Checklist of Afro-Amer. Art & Artists," *Serif,* Dec. 1970.

DeLEON, HENRY
Sculptor, filmmaker. Born in Puerto Rico in 1945. Studied at Brandeis University.
Works: *Untitled* (stone); *Untitled* (wood); *Untitled* (limestone); *Negrita.*
Exhibited: Boston Museum of Fine Arts, 1970.
Awards: Deborah Joseph Cohen Memorial Award in Sculpture, 1968.
Sources: Boston Museum of Fine Arts. *Afro-American Artists: New York & Boston,* 1970.

DEMPSEY, RICHARD W.
Painter. Born in Ogden, Utah, 1909. Studied at Sacramento Junior College, California (1929-31); California College of Arts and Crafts (1932-34); Students Art Center, California (1935-40). Instructor, Corcoran Gallery of Art, Washington, DC.
Works: *Planes and Lines; Cityscape; Charles Richard Drew; View from My Room, Haiti; Impression No. 1; Death & Black; Life; Mother, Father, Self & Friends; Wife & My Future; Father, Mother, & Child; Christ in the Crowd; Summertime; Mexican Landscape; Waterhole; Design of Traffic; Fish Vendor; Market Place —Barranquilla; Children on Seawall; Georgetown; Community Facade; Midtown USA; Mexican Architectural; Carrousel; High and Dry; Golden Grove; Boats and Birds; Tropicana; Brownstones USA; Street of Memories; Mastheads; Brillent Moorings; Continuous Construction; Cape Cod Seascape; Lighthouse; Mountains; Banaistas; End of Fisherman's Day; Fortress (Cartagena); Birch Trees; Bayou; Washington, DC to NY; Jamaica Ritual; Cathedral of Trees; Fear.*
Exhibited: Linden St. Branch YWCA, Oakland, Cal., 1935 (1-man); Academy of Art, San Francisco, 1940 (1-man); Art Guild Gallery, Palo Alto, Cal., 1940 (1-man); Vera Jones Bright Gallery, San Francisco, 1940 (1-man); Centre d'Art Gallery, Port-au-Prince, Haiti, 1951 (1-man); Barnet Aden Gallery, Washington, DC, 1951 (1-man), 1955; Whyte Gallery, Washington, DC, 1953 (1-man); Dupont Theatre Gallery, Washington, DC, 1954 (1-man); Franz Bader Gallery, Washington, DC, 1955, 1959, 1962, 1968 (1-man); Luis-Angel Arango Gallery, Banco de la Republic, Colombia, South America, 1963; El Centro Artistico, La Queva, Barranquilla, Colombia, 1963; Institute of Jamaica Gallery, Kingston, 1963 (1-man); US House of Representatives, Rayburn Building, Washington, DC, 1966; Stendahl Art Galleries, Los Angeles, 1939; Mills College, Oakland, Cal., 1939; Golden Gate Internat'l Exposition, San Francisco, 1940; Times Herald Annual Exhibition, 1944; Smithsonian Institution, 1950; Howard Univ., 1950, 1955, 1958, & 1968 (1-man); Corcoran Gallery of Art, 1950, 1951; Pan Amer. Union Gallery, 1953; Obelisk Gallery, 1953; Watkins Gallery of Art, Amer. Univ., 1956; Margaret Dickey Gallery, 1958, 1959, 1963, 1964; Art Rental Gallery, Washington, DC, 1958; Madison Square Garden, NY, 1958; National Academy Gallery, NY, 1958; Amer. Academy of Arts & Letters, NY, 1958; Norton Gallery, West Palm Beach, Fla., 1958; Norfolk Museum of Arts & Science, Va., 1958; Baltimore Museum of Art, 1958; 20th Century Gallery of Art, Williamsburg, Va., 1959, 1962, 1964; United States Information Agency Traveling Show, 1959; Corcoran Gallery of Art Traveling Show, 1960; Birmingham (Ala.) Museum of Art; George Thomas Hunter Gallery of Art, Ala.; Columbus (Ga.) Museum of Arts &

Crafts; Ga. Museum of Art; Academy of the Arts, Easton, Md., 1962; Rhodes Nat'l Gallery, Salisbury, Southern Rhodesia, 1962; King George VI Art Gallery, Port Elizabeth, South Africa, 1962; High Museum, Atlanta, 1965; Telfair Academy of Arts & Sciences, Savannah, Ga., 1966; Dulin Gallery of Art, Knoxville, Tenn., 1966; Southwest Ga. Art Assn., Albany, 1966; Julius Garfinkle Gallery, Washington, DC, 1966; Oakridge (Tenn.) Gallery, 1966; George Washington Univ., 1966; Anacostia Museum of Art-Smithsonian Institution; Washington Post Outdoor Exhibition; Nat'l Museum, Valletta, Malta; Univ. of Iowa, 1971-72; James A. Porter Gallery, 1970.

Collections: Franz Bader Gallery, Washington, DC; Corcoran Gallery of Art, Washington, DC; District of Columbia Juvenile Court; Obelisk Gallery, Washington, DC; Barnet Aden Gallery, Washington, DC; Margaret Dickey Gallery, Washington, DC; District of Columbia Municipal Courts; IBM, NY; Vera Jones Bright Gallery, San Francisco; Atlanta Univ.; School of Plastic Arts, Matanzas, Cuba; Atlantica Foundation, Southern Rhodesia; Luis-Angel Arango Gallery, Bogata, Colombia; US Embassy, Bogota, Colombia; El Centro Gallery, Kingston; US State Department; American Univ.

Awards: Golden Gate Exposition, San Francisco, 1940; Times Herald Annual Exhibition, Washington, DC, 1943; Julius Rosenwald Fellowship, 1946; Corcoran Gallery of Art, 1949; Invitation to visit and paint by Government of Haiti, 1951; Atlanta Univ. Purchase Prize, 1951; Purchase Prize, Corcoran Gallery of Art, 1959; Takoma Park (Md.) Art Exhibition, 1962, 1963.

Sources: Dover. *American Negro Art;* Indiana Univ. *Fine Arts & the Black American;* DuSable Museum of African-Amer. History. *Contemporary Black Artists,* 1970 Calendar; Illinois Bell Telephone. *Black American Artists/71,* 1972; Howard Univ. *James A. Porter Gallery of African American Art,* 1970; Greene, Carroll, Jr. "Perspective: The Black Artist in America," *Art Gallery,* Apr. 1970; Pierre-Noel, Lois Jones. "American Negro Art in Progress," *Negro History Bulletin,* Oct. 1967; Information from artist; Harley, Ralph, Jr. "Checklist of Afro-Amer. Art & Artists," *Serif,* Dec. 1970; Porter, James. "Negro Artists Gain Recognition after Long Battle," *Pittsburgh Courier,* July 29, 1950; Fax, Elton. "Four Rebels in Art," *Freedomways,* Spring 1961; *The Negro Handbook,* Composed by Editors of *Ebony,* Chicago, 1966; Myers, Carol L. *Black Power in the Arts,* Flint, Mich., 1970; United States Information Agency. *American Painters,* 1959, Unpublished list; Corcoran Gallery of Art. *Paintings from the Permanent Collection,* 1960, Unpublished list; Walker, Roslyn. *A Resource Guide to the Visual Arts of Afro-Americans,* South Bend, Ind., 1971.

DENDY, J. BROOKS, III

Painter, graphic artist, educator. Studied at Tyler School of Fine Arts (BFA); Temple University (MEd, 1963); Carnegie-Mellon University (MFA, DArts). Supervisor of Drama, Division of Education, Carnegie Institute.

Works: *Poverty of Man; The View; Blue Lake; Untitled; Death to You Now and Forever More, Amen . . . Amen* series, 1970 (mixed media)—*Now I Lay Me Down to Sleep, On That Great Gettum' Day, The Rock Cried Out, My God What A Morning; Show Me That City Called David* series, 1970 (mixed media)—*The Protestant Town, The Catholic Kingdom, The Jewish Ghetto.*

Exhibited: Phila. Civic Center; Brooklyn Museum; Phila. Art Alliance; Carnegie Institute; Phila. Museum of Art; Royal College of Art, London; Polisher Foundation (1-man); Art Menagerie, Phila.; Heritage House, Phila.; Phila. Print Club; Assoc. Artists of Pittsburgh; Armand's Gallery, Dormont, Pa.; Temple Univ., 1970.

Collections: Mr. Benny Andrews.

Awards: State Dept. Award, 1960; Polisher Foundation 3 Year Scholarship.

Sources: Phila. Division of Art. *Afro-American Artists Abroad 1800-1969;* Pittsburgh Community College. *16 Black Artists;* Tyler School of Art. *Seven by Seven,* Temple Univ., 1970.

DENMARK, JAMES

Painter, sculptor, graphic artist. Born in Winter Haven, Florida, 1936. Studied at Florida A & M University, Tallahassee (BS); Pratt Institute, Brooklyn.

Works: *The Struggle; Moondog; Head Study; Militant Black Woman; Young, Black and Proud; Untitled; Mask; Afro; Head of a Black Woman* (bronze); *The Family* (collage).

Exhibited: Atlanta Univ. Annual, 1962; Lever House Gallery, NY, 1969; C. W. Post College, Brookville, NY, 1969; Nassau Community College, Garden City, NY, 1968; Pratt Neighborhood Outdoor Show, Brooklyn, 1965; Boston Museum of Fine Arts, 1968; Rhode Island School of Design, 1969; Memorial Art Gallery, Rochester, NY, 1969; San Francisco Museum of Art, 1969; Contemporary Arts Museum, Houston, 1970; NJ State Museum, 1970; Roberson Center for the Arts & Sciences, Binghamton, NY, 1970; The Art Galleries, Univ. of Cal. at Santa Barbara, 1970; Acts of Art Gallery, NY, May 1972, Nov. 1972 (1-man); Mount Holyoke College, 1969.

Collections: Mr. Benny Andrews.

Sources: Boston Museum of Fine Arts. *Afro-American Artists: NY & Boston;* Acts of Art Gallery, Catalog, 1972; Rose, Barbara. "Black Art in America," *Art in America,* July-Dec. 1970; Mount Holyoke College. *Ten Afro-American Artists,* Nov. 1969; Berkman, Florence. "Afro-American Exhibit Fosters Understanding of Black Artists," *Times,* Hartford, Conn., May 24, 1970; Baker, Kenneth. "Art in the Service of People," *Christian Science Monitor,* n.d.; Ruder & Finn Fine Arts. *Contemporary Black Artists,* NY, 1969; Walker, Roslyn. *A Resource Guide to the Visual Arts of Afro-Americans,* South Bend, Ind., 1971.

DEPEARSON, DANIEL
Studied at Clark College.
Works: *Still Life.*
Exhibited: Sun Times/Daily News Gallery, Chicago, 1970.
Sources: United Negro College Fund. *Art 1970,* Chicago, 1970.

DePILLARS, MURRY N.
Painter. Born in Chicago. Studied at Roosevelt University, Chicago.
Works: *And There Was a Call from the East . . . ; Children at Play; Fifi and Muh Deah; Aunt Jemima,* 1968 (ink).
Exhibited: Afam Studio & Gallery, Chicago; Black Aesthetics; Chicago Museum of Science & Industry; Whitney Museum, 1971.
Awards: Outstanding Art Achievement Trophy; Special Award, Governor's Island Art Show, 1968.
Sources: Lewis/Waddy. *Black Artists on Art,* Vol. 2; Doty. *Contemporary Black Artists in America;* Preston, Malcolm. "Art: Black Exhibit," *Boston Herald Traveler,* Apr. 19, 1971; DuSable Museum of African Amer. History. *Contemporary Black Artists,* 1970, Calendar; Walker, Roslyn. *A Resource Guide to the Visual Arts of Afro-Americans,* South Bend, Ind., 1971.

DERRICK, GAMALIEL
Exhibited: Harmon Foundation, 1936.
Sources: Harley, Ralph, Jr. "Checklist of Afro-Amer. Art & Artists," *Serif,* Dec. 1970.

DERZEE, JAMES VAN
Photographer. Born in Lenox, Massachusetts. Self-taught.
Works: *Black Yankees; Girl with a Rose; Soldier; The Church Bishops; Grocery Store; Ladies' Tea; Jack Johnson; Husband & Wife; Sam Langford; Nude and Fire; School Ring Games; Portrait: Female; Dancer at the Ball; Black Maja; Lady in Furs; Female Banjo Player; Nude & Ivey; Soccer Team; Bride; Policemen; Refreshment Truck on 135th Street; Dunbar Bank Staff; Dunbar Bank Guard;* *Unity & Athletic Social Club; St. Mary's School; Alpha Phi Alpha Basketball Team; Ferdinand Q. Morton; Tea Time at Walker Beauty Salon; Protest Parade; Garvey Ladies' Brigade; Marcus Garvey; Black Cross Nurses; Garvey Militia; Black Star's Yarmouth.*
Exhibited: Addison Gallery, 1971; Studio Museum in Harlem, 1972; Metropolitan Museum, NY, 1968.
Collections: Metropolitan Museum.
Sources: Schoener, Allon. *Harlem on My Mind: Cultural Capital of Black America 1900-1968;* Afro-American Slide Depository, Catalog 1971-72; McGhee, Reginald, & James Van DerZee. *The World of James Van Der-Zee: A Visual Record of Black Americans,* NY, Grove Press, 1969; James Van DerZee Institute. *The Black Photographer (1908-1970): A Survey;* Schatz, Walter. *Directory of Afro-American Resources,* 1970; *Esquire,* June 1963; *Black Shades,* Mar. 1972.

DES PRES, FRANCOIS M.T.
Works: *Southern Village.*
Exhibited: Roko Gallery, 1949.
Sources: J.G. "Honoring Negro History," *Art Digest,* Feb. 15, 1949, p. 20; E.K. "Negro Artists," *Art News,* Feb. 1949, p. 47.

DE VILLIS, CLINTON
Painter. Active c. 1912.
Works: *Sunrise; Sunset at Ronkonkoma.*
Exhibited: NY Public Library, 1921.
Collections: A.A. Schomburg Collection, NY Public Library.
Sources: *Negro Year Book;* Indiana Univ. *Fine Arts & the Black American;* Thompson, W.O. "Collins & DeVillis—Two Promising Painters," *Voice of the Negro,* Dec. 1905; Harley, Ralph, Jr. "Checklist of Afro-Amer. Art & Artists," *Serif,* Dec. 1970. Porter. *Modern Negro Art;* Porter, James A. "Negro Artists Gain Recognition after Long Battle," *Pittsburgh Courier,* July 29, 1950; *1st Annual Exhibit of Books, Manuscripts, Paintings, Sculptures, etc. by the Negro Library Assn. at Carlton Ave. YMCA,* Aug. 7-16, 1918; *Encyclopedia of the Arts,* p. 28; Walker, Roslyn. *A Resource Guide to the Visual Arts of Afro-Americans,* South Bend, Ind., 1971.

D'HUE, ROBERT RALEIGH, JR.
Painter. Born in Cleveland, Ohio in 1917. Studied for six years at Academie Royale des Beaux-Arts, Liege, Belgium (certificate and honors, 1954). Art teacher in San Diego Unified Schools.
Works: *Haze.*
Exhibited: Museum of Liege, Belgium.
Sources: Lewis/Waddy. *Black Artists on Art,* Vol. 1; Walker, Roslyn. *A Resource Guide to*

the Visual Arts of Afro-Americans, South Bend, Ind., 1971.

DICKERSON, JULIUS JAMES

Architect. Born January 20, 1922. Studied at Howard University (BArch.).
Member: National Technical Assn.; Alphi Phi Alpha.
Sources: Furr, Arthur F. *History & Progress of Negroes in the US.*

DICKERSON, KENNETH

Painter. Born in New York City, 1935. Self-taught.
Works: *Climax.*
Exhibited: Brooklyn Museum, 1970; Huntington Jewish Center, 1970; Huntington Museum, 1970; Priscilla Gower Gallery, Port Washington, LI; NY Arts Festival, Americana Hotel, NYC.
Collections: Private collection of Mr. Henry Heydenryk of The House of Heydenryk; Dr. & Mrs. Nathaniel Ross; Mr. & Mrs. William Kunstler, NY.
Sources: Lewis/Waddy. *Black Artists on Art,* Vol. 2.

DICKERSON, NAOMI

Painter, sculptor.
Works: *Grand Junction; Tundra; Standing Woman; Shape I; Desert; Still Life with Plants; Feelie; Seated Man; Flight of Two Owls; Man Leaning on Palms; Torso; Still Life with Melon; Open Range.*
Sources: Afro-American Slide Depository, Catalog, 1971-72.

DICKERSON, REBA

Works: *Cloud Calligraphers; Thy Winds.*
Exhibited: Phila. Civic Center.
Sources: Phila. Division of Art. *Afro-American Artists 1800-1969.*

DICKERSON, THOMAS, JR.

Painter.
Works: *Me . . . ; Sound & Motion; Guess What?* (oil); *Guess Who?* (oil).
Exhibited: Phila. Civic Center; Lee Cultural Center, Phila.
Sources: Phila. Division of Art. *Afro-American Artists, 1800-1969.* Phila. Dept. of Recreation. *Love . . . and the Black Community.*

DIGGS, ANDREA

Studied at Tuskegee Institute.
Works: *Leaf Forms.*
Exhibited: Sun Times/Daily News Gallery, Chicago, 1970.
Sources: United Negro College Fund. *Art 1970,* Chicago, 1970.

DIGGS, ARTHUR

Painter. Born in Columbia, Missouri, 1888.

Studied at the Art Institute of Chicago. Worked in Reinhardt Galleries.
Works: *Purple Autumn Gentians; The Red Oak;* 3 murals, Children's Home, Maywood, Ill.; *Old Shacks in Winter; A Curve in the Tracks; Winter Sunshine; Oaks & Alders; The Scintillas; Midsummer; Native Son; The Lawd and Noah; The Green Pastures; De Lawd and Moses; The Three Graces; A City of Towers; Fleeting Cumulus.*
Exhibited: Tanner Art League, 1922; Howard Univ., 1932; Chicago Art League; Art Institute of Chicago; Roosevelt High School, Gary, Ind.; Harmon Foundation, 1929, 1930; Atlanta Univ., 1943, 1944; Dillard Univ., 1941; Century of Progress, Chicago, 1933; Findlay Galleries, 1933; Salon des Refuses, 1935; Texas Centennial, 1936; Smithsonian Institution, 1929.
Collections: Roosevelt High School, Gary, Ind.; Children's Home, Maywood, Ill.
Awards: Eames MacVeagh Prize, Chicago Art League, 1929.
Member: Chicago Art League; Ill. Academy of Fine Arts.
Sources: Harmon Foundation. *Exhibition of Productions by Negro Artists;* Harmon Foundation. *Non Jury Exhibits of Works of Negro Artists,* 1933; Indiana Univ. *Fine Arts & the Black American;* Mallett. *Index of Artists; American Art Annual,* 1933; Art Institute of Chicago. *The Negro in Art Week,* Catalog; DuSable Museum of African-Amer. History. *Contemporary Black Artists,* 1970 Calendar; Dillard Univ. *Arts Festival Catalog,* 1941; Texas Centennial Exposition. *Thumbnail Sketches of Exhibiting Artists,* 1936; Harmon Foundation. *Negro Artists,* 1935; Harmon Foundation. *Exhibit of Fine Arts,* 1930; Harmon Foundation. *Select Picture List;* Smithsonian Institution. *Painting & Sculpture by American Negro Artists,* 1929; Harley, Ralph, Jr. "Checklist of Afro-Amer. Art & Artists," *Serif,* Dec. 1970; Walker, Roslyn. *A Resource Guide to the Visual Arts of Afro-Americans,* South Bend, Ind., 1971.

DILLARD, P.

Painter.
Works: *Aviator.*
Exhibited: Fort Huachuca, Ariz., 1943.
Sources: *Exhibition of the Work of 37 Negro Artists at Fort Huachuca, Ariz., 1943.*

DILLON, ERROL

Painter. Studied at Tougaloo College.
Works: *Angle in a Wheel Chair; Until Then; Abstract; Time; Adam & Eve;* Untitled acrylic; *Face Unknown.*
Exhibited: Sun Times/Daily News Gallery, Chicago, 1970.

Sources: United Negro College Fund. *Art 1970,* Chicago, 1970.

DILLON, FRANK J.

Designer, craftsman. Born in New Jersey, 1866. Studied at Oberlin (Ohio) College; Art Students League.
Works: *St. Simon Window; Landscape; Tulips; Snow Scene; Gladiolas; Grey Day; Self Portrait; Still Life—Melon; Still Life; Christ Blessing Little Children.*
Exhibited: Harmon Foundation, 1929, 1933; Dillard Univ.; 1941; NJ State Museum, 1935; Harmon Traveling Show, 1934-36; Texas Centennial, 1936; Smithsonian Institution, 1929.
Collections: St. Augustine College, Raleigh, NC.
Awards: Honorable Mention, Harmon Foundation, 1933.
Sources: Harmon Foundation. *Exhibition of Productions by Negro Artists;* Harmon Foundation. *Non-Jury Exhibits of Works of Negro Artists,* 1933; Indiana Univ. *Fine Arts & the Black American;* DuSable Museum of African Amer. History. *Contemporary Black Artists,* 1970 Calendar; Dillard Univ. *Arts Festival,* 1941; Texas Centennial Exposition. *Thumbnail Sketches of Exhibiting Artists,* 1936; Harmon Foundation. *Negro Artists,* 1935; Smithsonian Institution. *Painting & Sculpture by American Negro Artists,* 1929; Harley, Ralph, Jr. "Checklist of Afro-Amer. Art & Artists," *Serif,* Dec. 1970; Walker, Roslyn. *A Resource Guide to the Visual Arts of Afro-Americans,* South Bend, Ind., 1971.

DINDGA

See McCannon, Dindga.

DONALDSON, JEFF

Printmaker, painter, mixed media. Born in Pine Bluff, Arkansas.
Works: *For My Daddy—His Generation Praised; Black Family; Oshun, Oka, Yansan—Wives of Shango; Shango Shortys; Allah Shango; Right On Right Reverend; Amos n' Andy,* 1972; *Man-Bad Maryland Farmer; Chris Goddy, Thurman Barker, Joe Jarman, Charles Clark.*
Exhibited: National Center of Afro-American Artists, Boston, 1970, 1972; Drum and Spear Bookstore, Washington, DC, 1972; Studio Museum in Harlem, 1970-1972; Howard Univ., 1970, 1972.
Collections: Johnson Pub. Co.
Member: AFRICOBRA.
Sources: Myers, Carol L. *Black Power in the Arts,* Flint, Mich., 1970; "Afro-American Issue," *Art Gallery,* April 1968; Indiana Univ. *Fine Arts & the Black American;* DuSable Museum of African-Amer. History. *Contem-*

porary Black Artists, 1970 calendar; Johnson Pub. Co. *The JPC Art Collection,* pamphlet; Grillo, Jean B. "Where Down Home Meets Back Home," *Boston After Dark,* Sept. 1970; *Black Shades,* March 1972; Howard Univ. *Africobra I,* Catalog, 1970; Howard Univ. *Africobra II,* Catalog, 1972; Walker, Roslyn. *A Resource Guide to the Visual Arts of Afro-Americans,* South Bend, Ind., 1971.

DONAWA, EDWARD L.

Painter, sculptor. Born in Miami, 1931. Studied at the Art Students League; Columbia University.
Works: *Shadows on the Barn; Sugar Brown Baby,* 1970.
Exhibited: Studio Museum in Harlem, 1969; Berkshire Art Assn., 1972; Afro Art Alliance, Springfield, Mass., 1972; Academic Artists 23rd Annual Nat'l Exhibition, 1972; St. Luke's Hospital Women's Auxiliary Show, NY, 1970; Hammer Galleries, NY; Springfield (Mass.) Museum of Fine Arts; Amer. Internat'l College; Springfield Public Library.
Awards: 1st prize, oil, St. Luke's Hospital Women's Auxiliary Show, NY, 1970.
Member: Afro Art Alliance, Springfield, Mass.; Springfield (Mass.) Art League.
Sources: Studio Museum in Harlem. *Harlem Artists 69;* Information from artist.

DONOVAN, ELLEN

Painter, gallery director.
Exhibited: 12th Invitational Exhibition, Pyramid Club, Phila., 1952.
Sources: Drummond, Dorothy. "Coast-to-Coast," *Art Digest,* Mar. 1, 1952.

DORCH, CELESTINE JOHNSTON

Painter.
Works: *Old Camper.*
Exhibited: Atlanta Univ., 1944.
Sources: Harley, Ralph, Jr. "Checklist of Afro-Amer. Art & Artists," *Serif,* Dec. 1970.

DORSEY, HAROLD

Sculptor, painter.
Works: *Two Musicians; Homage to My Ancestors; Black Goddess; Madame Lamumba; Patrice Lamumba; Sails; Indian Summer; Colorado Landscape; Life Study #5; Crap Game; Torres; Black Man; Woman; Ball of Confusion; Still Life (White Head); Dynamics; Angela.*
Collections: Johnson Pub. Co.
Sources: Afro-Amer. Slide Depository Catalog, 1970-71; Johnson Pub. Co. *The JPC Art Collection,* Pamphlet.

DORSEY, KATHERINE

Painter.
Works: *Flowers.*

79

Exhibited: Howard Univ., 1941.
Sources: Howard Univ. *Exhibition of Negro Artists of Chicago at Howard Univ. Gallery of Art,* 1941; Harley, Ralph, Jr. "Checklist of Afro-Amer. Art & Artists," *Serif,* Dec. 1970.

DORSEY, LILLIAN A.

Painter. Born in Philadelphia, 1912. Student of Maurice Sterne (1930-32).
Works: *Teatime; My Mother; Self Portrait.*
Exhibited: Harmon Foundation, 1931; Darien Guild, 1931; Atlanta Univ., 1944; Burdick High School, Stamford, Conn.; Education Week, Stamford, Conn., 1941.
Awards: Otto H. Kahn Prize for Portraiture, Harmon Foundation, 1931.
Sources: "Harmon Foundation Exhibit," *Art Digest,* Feb. 15, 1931, p. 7; Locke. *The Negro in Art;* Harmon Foundation. *Exhibition of Productions by Negro Artists;* DuSable Museum of African-Amer. History. *Contemporary Black Artists,* 1970 Calendar; Harmon Foundation. *Non-Jury Exhibits of Works of Negro Artists,* 1933; Harmon Foundation. *Negro Artists,* 1935; "Harlem Library Shows Negro Art," *Art News,* May 20, 1933, p. 14; Harley Ralph, Jr. "Checklist of Afro-Amer. Art & Artists," *Serif,* Dec. 1970; Walker, Roslyn. *A Resource Guide to the Visual Arts of Afro-Americans,* South Bend, Ind., 1971.

DORSEY, WILLIAM

Landscape painter. Active late 19th century.
Sources: Porter. *Modern Negro Art; Negro Year Book;* Indiana Univ. *Fine Arts & the Black American;* Harley, Ralph, Jr. "Checklist of Afro-Amer. Art & Artists," *Serif,* Dec. 1970.

DOUGLAS, AARON

Painter, educator, printmaker, illustrator. Born in Topeka, Kansas in 1899. Studied at University of Kansas (AB, 1923); University of Nebraska (BFA, 1922); Columbia University Teachers College (MA); L'Academie Scandinave. Studied under Winold Reiss (1925-7); Despiau; Waroquier; Othon Frieze (Paris, 1931). Teacher of art at Lincoln High School, Kansas City; Fisk University, 1937-39. He did numerous murals, usually of allegorical scenes on historical life or cultural background of the Negro. Considered the leading painter of the "Negro Renaissance." He was in New York City 1923-25, and spent 1938 touring the South and Haiti.
Works: *Still Life with Black Bottle; Prince Peter Ehet Ngang Udo Nigeria; Power Plant, Harlem River; Alta* (mural in oils); *Man with Flowers; Nashville Skyline; Marian Anderson; Mr. Baker; Alexander Dumas; Student; Drama; Street Scene, Accra; Tower Bridge, London; Song of the Towers; An Idyll of the Deep South; Alta Douglas; Jungle Dancers; Siesta, Edwin L. Embree* (oil); *The Negro Through the Ages; Visions of Liberty; The Patrolman; Triborough Bridge*; Illustrations in books by Weldon Johnson, Countee Cullen, Langston Hughes, James W. Johnson (GOD's TROMBONES), Paul Morand (BLACK MAGIC); Illustrations in NEW NEGRO; VANITY FAIR, THEATRE ARTS, OPPORTUNITY, NEW YORK SUN, BOSTON TRANSCRIPT, AMERICAN MERCURY.
Exhibited: Harmon Foundation, 1928, 1935; Texas Centennial, 1936; Howard Univ., 1937; Baltimore Museum, 1939; Atlanta Univ., 1944; Caz-Delbos Gallery, NYC, 1933 (1-man); ACA Gallery, NYC, 1938 (1-man); Bennett College; NY Public Library; Sherman Hotel, Chicago; Art Institute of Chicago, 1932; City College of NY, 1967; Univ. of Nebraska, 1936; Brooklyn Museum; Findlay Gallery, NYC; Univ. of Kansas; Joslyn Memorial, Omaha; Gallery of Modern Art, NYC; Amer. Negro Exposition, Chicago, 1940; Dillard Univ. 1941; NJ State Museum, 1935; College Art Assn Traveling Exhibit, 1934-35; Harmon Traveling Exhibition, 1935-36; Newark Museum, 1971; 135th St. YMCA; NYC South Side Community Art Center, Chicago, 1945.
Collections: Fisk Univ.; Sherman Hotel, Chicago; NY Public Library; 135th St. YMCA, NYC; Hall of Negro Life, Texas Centennial Exposition; Bennett College; Fisk Univ. Library, murals.
Awards: Barnes Foundation Fellowship, 1928-29; Rosenwald Grant, 1931; Rosenwald Travel Grant, 1938.
Member: Kappa Alpha Psi.
Sources: Howard Univ. *Art of the American Negro,* 1937; Mallett. *Index of Artists; Who's Who in American Art; Negro Almanac;* Dover *American Negro Art,* pp. 30, 34, 37-38, 40, 48, 92, 102, 132; Johnson, Weldon. *Gods Trombones and Seven Negro Sermons in Verse* (illus.); Cullen, Countee. *Caroling Dusk* (illus.); Hughes, Langston. *Not Without Laughter* (illus.); Albany Institute of History and Art. *The Negro Artist Comes of Age;* Harmon Foundation. *Exhibition of Productions by Negro Artists;* "Afro-American Issue," *Art Gallery,* April 1968; Young. *Dictionary of American Artists, Sculptors & Engravers; Encyclopedia of the Arts;* Indiana Univ. *Fine Art & the Black American;* City College of New York. *The Evolution of Afro-American Artists 1800-1950;* Art Institute of Chicago. *The Negro in Art Week;* UCLA Art Galleries. *The Negro in Modern Art;* Baltimore Museum of Art. *Contemporary Negro,* 1939; Porter. *Modern Negro Art;* Locke. *The New Negro: An Interpretation;* Morand, Paul. *Black Magic*

Translated to the French by Hamish Miles. NY, Viking, 1929; Hughes, Langston. *Six Broadsides*, poems (illustrator); American Artists Congress. *The Negro in American Culture*, NY, 1936; Brown, Ina Corina. *The Story of the American Negro.* NY, Friendship Press, 1957; Harley, Ralph L., Jr. "A Checklist of Afro-Amer. Art & Artists," *The Serif*, Dec. 1970; Locke, Alain. "Advance on the Art Front," *Opportunity*, May 1939; Tanner Art Galleries. *Art of the American Negro*, 1940; Brawley, Benjamin. *The Negro Genius;* Dillard Univ. *Arts Festival*, 1941; Butcher, Margaret J. *The Negro in American Culture;* Roucek & Kiernan. *The Negro Impact on Western Civilization;* Texas Centennial Exposition. *Thumbnail Sketches of Exhibiting Artists*, 1936; Newark Museum. *Black Artists: Two Generations*, 1971; Afro-American Slide Depository, Catalog; *Who's Who in Colored America*, 3rd edition; Harmon Foundation. *Negro Artists*, 1935; Harmon Foundation. *Select Picture List;* "Negro Artists Reveal Genius in Trenton Show," *Art Digest*, April 15, 1935; Greene, Carroll, Jr. "Perspective: The Black Artist in America," *The Art Gallery*, April 1970, p. 19; Pierre-Noel, Lois Jones. "American Negro Art in Progress," *Negro History Bulletin*, Oct. 1967; Locke, Alain. "The Amer. Negro as Artist," *Amer. Magazine of Art*, Sept. 1931; "The Negro Artist Comes of Age," *Art News*, Feb. 1, 1945; Thurman, Wallace. "Negro Artists and the Negro," *The New Republic*, Aug. 31, 1927; Greene, Carroll, Jr. "Afro-Amer. Artists: Yesterday & Now," *The Humble Way*, Vol. 8, No. 3, 1968; Greene, Carroll, Jr. *Afro-American Artists: 1800-1968*, Slides; Boning, Richard A. *Profile of Black Americans*, NY, 1968; "Leading Negro Artists," *Ebony*, Sept. 1963, pp. 131-2; Brawley, Benjamin. *The Negro Literature & Art in the US;* Huggins, Nathan Irvin. *Harlem Renaissance;* "Six Paintings of City Life," *Arts Quarterly*, Dec. 1939; Thurman, Wallace. *Fire:* A Quarterly Devoted to the Younger Negro Artists, NY, Vol. 1, #1; Brown, Marion. "The Negro in the Fine Arts," *The Negro Heritage Library*, Vol. 2; Morsbach, Mabel. *The Negro in American Life;* Ploski, Harry, & Ernest Kaiser. "The Black Artist," *Afro USA*, 1971; Ploski, Harry, Ernest Kaiser & Otto Lindenmeyer. "The Black Artist," *Reference Library of Black America*, Book 4, 1971; *The Negro Handbook*, Composed by Editors of *Ebony*, Chicago, 1966; Atkinson, J. Edward. *Black Dimensions in Contemporary American Art*, NY, 1971; "Aaron Douglas A Distinguished Painter," *Chicago Defender*, Nov. 10, 1934; Morrow, Libbie. "Progress of Negro Race Told in Fisk Library Mural Decorations," *Banner*; "At New York Art Exhibit," *Afro-American*, March 30, 1935; Schatz, Walter. *Directory of Afro-American Resources*, 1970; South Side Community Art Center. *Chicago Collectors Exhibit of Negro Art*, Chicago, 1945; Myers, Carol L. *Black Power in the Arts*, Flint, Mich., 1970; Spradling, Mary M., ed. *In Black & White: Afro-Americans in Print*; DuSable Museum of African-Amer. History. *Contemporary Black Artists*, Calendar, 1970; *Pictorial History of Negro America*, 1956 (portrait), p. 276; Walker, Roslyn. *A Resource Guide to the Visual Arts of Afro-Americans*, South Bend, Ind., 1971; Fisk Univ. *Exhibition of Paintings*, 1948.

DOUGLASS, CALVIN

Painter, teacher. Born in Baltimore, 1931. Studied at Howard University; Philadelphia Museum School; Skowhegan (Maine) School of Painting and Sculpture; Brooklyn Museum Art School.

Works: *In; Out; Detail; Untitled.*

Exhibited: NYC Center, 1955; Brooklyn Museum, 1956; Spiral Group Exhibit, NYC, 1965; Brooklyn College, 1969; Rockford (Ill.) College, 1965; Wilson College, Chambersburg, Pa.; Univ. of Rhode Island.

Collections: Museum of African Art, Washington, DC.

Member: Spiral.

Sources: Douglass, Calvin. *Our Wonderful World*, Grolier Press; NY State Education Dept. *Fifteen Under Forty*; Rhode Island Univ. *Spiral*, Catalog, 1965; Brooklyn Museum. *Afro-American Artists: Since 1950*, 1969; Rockford (Ill.) College. *Creativity and the Negro*; Siegel, Jeanne. "Why Spiral?," *Art News*, Sept. 1966.

DOUGLASS, ROBERT M., JR.

Painter. Born 1809. Studied under Thomas Sully. Kept a study and gallery of painting and Daguerreotype in Philadelphia.

Sources: *Art in America*, Jan. 1936; *American Negro Reference Book;* Brawley, Benjamin. *The Negro Genius;* DuSable Museum of African-Amer. History. *Contemporary Black Artists*, 1970 Calendar; Roucek/Kiernan. *The Negro Impact on Western Civilization*; Kiah, Virginia. "Black Artists," *Savannah Magazine*, Apr. 1972, p. 14; Harley, Ralph, Jr. "Checklist of Afro-Amer. Art & Artists," *Serif*, Dec. 1970; Brown, Marion. "The Negro in the Fine Arts," *The Negro Heritage Library*, Vol. 2; Walker, Roslyn. *A Resource Guide to the Visual Arts of Afro-Americans*, South Bend, Ind., 1971.

DOWELL, JOHN

Graphic artist, educator. Studied at Temple University; John Herron Art Institute, Indianapolis; Tamarind Lithography Workshop, Los Angeles; University of Washington, Seattle (MFA). Assistant Professor of Art, Lithogra-

phy, and Drawing at the University of Illinois.
Works: *For the Pridgen & The Hunt; Soul Coultrane,* 1967 (etching); *White Wheel of W.H.T.,* 1967 (etching); *Yea . . . Janlee,* 1968 (etching); *Doughnut,* 1969 (lithograph); *American Sun Dream,* 1969 (lithograph); *Welll Du!!,* 1969 (lithograph); *Damn If I Know,* 1970 (lithograph); *Letter to My Betty II,* 1970 (lithograph).
Exhibited: Phyllis Kind Gallery, Chicago; Martha Jackson Gallery, NY; Venice Biennale; Temple Univ., 1970.
Collections: Museum of Modern Art; Phila. Museum of Art; Chicago Art Institute; Brooklyn Museum; Los Angeles County Museum of Art; Lessing J. Rosenwald Foundation.
Awards: Artist-in-residence, American Pavilion; Ford Foundation Grant.
Sources: Rose, Barbara. "Black Art in America," *Art in America,* July-Dec. 1970; Tyler School of Art. *Seven by Seven,* Temple Univ., 1970; Gaither, Edmund B. "The Evolution of the Afro-American Artists," *Artists Proof,* Vol. 2; Walker, Roslyn. *A Resource Guide to the Visual Arts of Afro-Americans,* South Bend, Ind., 1971.

DRAGGAN, EGBERT

Sources: Harley, Ralph, Jr. "Checklist of Afro-Amer. Art & Artists," *Serif,* Dec. 1970.

DRISKELL, DAVID CLYDE

Painter, graphic artist, educator. Born in Eatonton, Georgia, 1931. Studied at Howard University (BA); Catholic University of America (MA, 1962); Skowhegan School of Painting and Sculpture; Netherlands Institute for History of Art. Teacher at Talladega College, Alabama; Fisk University, Art Department Chairman.
Works: *African Fantasy; Still Life with Gateleg Table; Lovers; The Chain; Jonah in the Whale #2; Benin Woman; Who Me?; Festival: Thelma; Antique Chair; Maine Island; Gabriel; Mercury Black; Chieftain's Chair; Figure Winter Landscape; Partial Eclipse #2,* 1968 (woodcut); *Jonah in the Whale,* 1967 (woodcut); *Upon Return; Current Forms: Yoruba Circle; Yoruba Form #5; The Poet; Young Pine's; Portrait; Round Still Life; Compote* (woodcut); *Memory Benin; Ancestral Head; African Poet, Bakota; The Moon Does See; African Boy with Mask; African Poet #1; The Laborer; Boy with Bird; Growing Bush; Three Masks; African Landscape; Benin Woman II; African Hat; Africanization; Woman Drying Hair; Ancestral Visitation; African Sentinel; Bakota Figure; Ancestral Figure; Bakota Girl; Moon View; Self Portrait; Little David with Tree; Sea Forms; Landscape; Mountain and Tile; Young Pine's Growing.*

Exhibited: Corcoran Art Gallery; National Museum; Rhodes National Gallery, Salisbury, Southern Rhodesia; Society of Washington Artists; Talladega College; Barnet Aden Gallery; Portland Museum of Art; Smithsonian Institute; Whitney Museum, 1971; Univ. of Iowa, 1971-2; Atlanta Univ.; Carver Museum; Dupont Gallery; Fourier Gallery; Howard Univ.; Lincoln Univ.; Colby College; King George VI Gallery; Vechten Gallery; Baltimore Museum; F. Bader Gallery; Oakland Museum; Dulin Gallery; Univ. of Conn.; Fisk Univ., 1964; Dickson Art Center, 1966; Sheraton Hotel, Phila., 1968; Art in Embassies, USA, 1966; San Diego Fine Arts Gallery, 1966; White House, 1966; Cheekwood Fine Arts Center, 1968; Norfolk Museum, 1969; Brooks Memorial Gallery, 1969; VD Laskey Library, 1972; James A. Porter Gallery, 1970; Xavier Univ., 1963; National Gallery of Art, 1954; Carver Museum, 1956; Savery Art Gallery, 1957; Scarritt College for Christian Workers; Florida Presbyterian College, 1972.

Collections: Howard Univ.; Corcoran Art Gallery; Barnet Aden Gallery; Skowhegan School; Savery Art Gallery; Danforth Foundation; Atlanta Univ.; Bocour Art Collection; LeMoyne College; Smithsonian Institution; US Embassy, Denmark.

Awards: European Museum Visitation; Fisk Univ. Grant; Rockefeller Foundation Faculty Research Grant, 1967; Skowhegan Fellowship; Scholastic Award in Fine Arts, Howard Univ.; John Hope Award; Danforth Foundation; Amer. Federation of Art, 1962, 1964; Harmon Foundation, 1964; Honorable Mention, Corcoran Gallery, 1965.

Member: College Art Assn. of America; Southeastern Museum Conference; Maine Arts & Crafts Assn.; American Assn. of Museums; Nashville Artists Guild.

Sources: UCLA Art Galleries. *The Negro in Modern Art;* Dover. *American Negro Art; American Negro Reference Book;* Lewis/Waddy. *Black Artists on Art,* Vol. 1; Indiana Univ. *Fine Arts & the Black American;* "Afro-American Issue," *Art Gallery,* April 1968; Afro-American Slide Depository, Catalog; Morrison, Allan. "New Surge in the Arts," *Ebony,* Aug. 1967; Doty. *Contemporary Black Artists in America;* DuSable Museum of African-Amer. History. *Contemporary Black Artists,* 1970, Calendar; Illinois Bell Telephone. *Black American Artists/71,* 1972; Roucek/Kiernan. *The Negro Impact on Western Civilization;* Benbow, Charles. "Experience in Black Art," *St. Petersburgh Times,* April 7, 1972; Scarritt College. *David C. Driskell: Watercolors & Prints,* 1972; *Who's Who in American Art,* 1959, 1962; *Who's Who in the Southeast,* 1963; Wright, Frederick. *American Negro Art,* 1966;

UCLA Galleries. *Prints by American Negroes,* 1967; Walker, Roslyn. *A Resource Guide to the Visual Arts of Afro-Americans,* South Bend, Ind., 1971; Information from artist; Barnet Aden Gallery. *Exhibition of Paintings,* Washington, DC; Driskell, David C. *John Rhoden & Walter Williams,* Fisk Univ., 1967; Driskell, David C. *Sam Middleton & Richard Hunt,* Fisk Univ., 1968; Driskell, David C. *Elton Fax: Drawings From Africa,* Fisk Univ., 1968; Driskell, David C. *Jacob Lawrence: The Toussaint L'Ouverture Series,* Fisk Univ., 1968; Driskell, David C. *Contemporary Trends in African Art,* Fisk Univ., 1968; Plass, Margaret. "Ashanti Goldweights," *College Art Journal,* Spring 1968; Driskell, David C. *Klee, Kandinsky & Other Modern Masters From the Guggenheim Museum,* Talladega College, Ala., 1958; Driskell, David C. *Eight Young Printmakers,* Fisk Univ., 1966; Howard Univ. *James A. Porter Gallery of African-Amer. Art,* 1970; Greene, Carroll, Jr. "Perspective: The Black Artist in America," *Art Gallery,* April 1970, p. 18; Pierre-Noel, Lois Jones. "American Negro Art in Progress," *Negro History Bulletin,* Oct. 1967; Kiah, Virginia. "Black Artists," *Savannah Magazine,* April 1972; Xavier Univ. *Emancipation Proclamation Centennial National Art Exhibition,* 1963; Harley, Ralph, Jr. "Checklist of Afro-Amer. Art & Artists," *Serif,* Dec. 1970; Brown, Marion. "The Negro in the Fine Arts," *Negro Heritage Library,* Vol. 2; Patterson, Lindsay. "Contemporary Artists," *Negro in Music and Art,* 1969; Atkinson, J. Edward. *Black Dimensions in Contemporary American Art,* NY, 1971; Myers, Carol L. *Black Power in the Arts,* Flint, Mich., 1970.

DROB, PEARL

Painter.
Works: *Untitled;* series of untitled paintings in oil-tempera emulsion.
Sources: Afro-American Slide Depository Catalog.

DRYSDALE, HAROLD

Painter. Born in Harlem, New York, 1927. Self-taught.
Works: *Ife (Love); Moon God.*
Exhibited: Studio Museum in Harlem, 1969.
Sources: Studio Museum in Harlem. *Harlem Artists 69.*

DUNCANSON, ROBERT S.

Painter. Born in Cincinnati, Ohio in 1817. Died 1872.
Works: *Portrait of William Carey; Nicholas Longworth; Portrait of Bishop Payne & Family; The Land of the Lotos Eaters; Lady Macbeth; Shylock & Jessica; The Ruins of Carthage; Western Hunter's Encampment; Ellen Isle of Loch Katrine; Old Oaken Bucket; The Trial of Shakespeare; Blue Hole, Little Miami River; Uncle Tom & Little Eva; The Drunkard's Plight; Portrait of William Berthelet; Romantic Landscape; Fruit Piece; Vale of Kashmir; Water Nymphs; Valley of Lake Peipin, Minn.; Evening; Blue Hole, Little White River; Portrait of Richard Sutton Rust I,* 1858; *Landscape with Classical Ruins, Temple of Sibilla,* 1859; *Four Murals,* Front Hall, Taft Museum, Cincinnati; *Fruit Still Life,* 1849; *Blue Hole, Flood Waters, Little Miami River,* 1851; *View of Cincinnati, Ohio, from Covington, Kentucky,* 1851; *Landscape with Classical Ruins, Recollections of Italy,* 1854; *Pompeii,* 1855; *Remembrance of a Scene near Auerbach,* 1856; *Forest Landscape,* 1857; *Maiden's Rock, Lake Peipin, Minn.,* 1862; *Minihaha Falls, Minn.,* 1862; *Minenopa Falls, Minn.,* 1862; *Lancaster, New Hampshire,* 1862; *Waterfalls of Montmorency,* 1864; *Mountain Landscape with Cows & Sheep,* 1866; *Landscape with Fantastic Figures,* 1867; *Landscape with Men & Boats,* 1868; *Waiting for a Shot,* 1869; *Mountain Pool,* 1870; *Dog's Head, Scotland,* 1870; *View of St. Anne's River,* 1870; *Ellen's Isle,* 1870; *Lough Leane,* 1870; *Landscape with Indians Making Camp; River Scene; On the River Bank; Fall Fisherman; Transportation in Early Cincinnati,* 1842; *The Ox Cart,* 1842; *Watermelon & Peaches,* 1842; *Light & Shade, Ruins of Carthage,* 1845; *Winter Landscape,* 1846; *Summer Landscape,* 1846; *Portrait of Louis Benjamin Berthelet,* 1846; *Elizabeth Longworth Potter,* 1847; *Landscape with Hawk,* 1848; *The New World,* 1849; *Portrait of John Northrup,* 1850; *The Ford,* 1852; *Landscape with Shepherd,* 1852; *Colintogle's Ford,* 1867; *Morning in the Highlands,* 1868; *Woodland Pool,* 1868; *The Caves,* 1869; *Loch Long,* 1867; *Landscape with Horseman,* 1869; *Scene off Irish Coast During a Storm; Eventide,* 1871; *Landscape with View of Vesuvius & Pompeii,* 1871; *Seascape,* 1871; *River Scene with Fisherman; Mexican Landscape; The Gamblers,* 1854; *Chapultepec Castle, Mexico; Mountain Stream; Sunset Landscape with Sheep; Landscape,* 1870; *Landscape with Picknickers,* 1853; *Summer Retreat of Horace & Virgil,* 1854; *Portrait of Robert Bishop,* 1855; *Portrait of Freeman Cary,* 1855; *The Hiding of Moses,* 1855; *Portrait of Mrs. James Drew,* 1856; *Valley Pasture,* 1857; *Peaceful Valley,* 1858; *Portrait of Jessie Northrup,* 1860; *The Buffalo Hunt,* 1861; *Faith,* 1862; *Lakeside Outing,* 1863; *Niagra Falls,* 1863; *Twilight Landscape,* 1864; *Highland Scenery, The Pass of Leny,* 1866; *Landscape with Tower,* 1867.

Exhibited: Detroit Institute of Art, 1949; Boston Museum of Fine Arts, 1972; National Center of Afro-Amer. Artists, Boston, 1972; Amer. Negro Exposition, Chicago, 1940; Museum of Modern Art, 1943-4; Cincinnati Art Museum, 1955; Univ. of Cal. at Los Angeles, 1966; Public Education Assn., Rosenburg & Co., NYC, 1968; Columbus Gallery of Fine Arts, 1953; Detroit Public Library, 1932; Denver Art Museum, 1953; Indianapolis Art Museum, 1961; Flint (Mich.) Institute of Arts, 1963; Bowdoin College Museum of Art, 1971; City College of NY; Detroit Art Assn., 1876; Detroit Art Loan, 1883; Cincinnati Art Museum, 1972; Taft Museum, Cincinnati; Ohio Military Institute; Ohio Mechanics Institute; Wilberforce Univ.; Balmoral Castle, Scotland; Howard Univ., 1967; James A. Porter Gallery of African-Amer. Art, 1970.

Collections: Taft Museum, Cincinnati; Detroit Institute of Art; Ohio Military Institute; Ohio Mechanics Institute; Wilberforce Univ.; Balmoral Castle, Scotland; National Archives; Amherst (Mass.) College; Boston Museum of Fine Arts; Butler Inst. of American Art, Youngstown, Ohio; Cincinnati Historical Society; Cleveland Museum of Art; Corcoran Gallery of Art, Washington, DC; Mr. William T. Earls, Cincinnati; Mr. Henry Melville Fuller, NYC; Mr. Charles Fleischman, Cincinnati; Mr. & Mrs. Warren Griffin, Atlanta; Mrs. Theodore Haar, Jefferson City, Mo.; Hirschl Gallery, NYC; Adler Gallery, NYC; Howard Univ.; Ms. Elizabeth Jergens, Los Angeles; Mr. Ralph van Matre, Edenton, NC; Rev. & Mrs. Andrew Newman, Bellbrook, Ohio; Mr. Razlemond Parker, Washington, DC; Mr. & Mrs. Richard Rust III, Cincinnati; St. Louis Art Museum; Mr. & Mrs. Frank Stout, Mt. Healthy, Ohio; Mr. & Mrs. James R. Williams, Cincinnati; Mr. Murdock Williams, Yellow Springs, Ohio; Cincinnati Art Museum; E.H. Dwight, Utica, NY; William R. Kemper, Seattle, Wash.; Douglass Settlement House, Toledo; E.N. Pike, Detroit; Mr. & Mrs. Morris L. Mason, Montgomery, Ohio; Bernard Moeller, Cincinnati; Mr. Frank Patria, Detroit; Mr. & Mrs. James Rust, Cincinnati; Mrs. Gibson Youngblut, Cincinnati; Mr. Carroll Greene, NYC; Mr. Paul North, Columbus, Ohio; Dr. & Mrs. Stuart N. White, Tulsa, Oklahoma; Chapellier Galleries, NYC; De Vant Crissey Gallery, Marietta, Ga.; Mr. & Mrs. James Rupel, Dayton, Ohio; YWCA West End Branch, Cincinnati; Mr. Douglas Collins, Longmeadow, Mass.; Campus Martius, Marietta, Ohio; Mr. & Mrs. Robert Bates, Dayton, Ohio; Mr. David Silvetta, Richmond, Va.; Albert Healey Werner, Chicago; Glasgow Art Gallery, Scotland.

Awards: Freeman's Aid Society Scholarship; Anti-Slave League Award.

Member: Cincinnati Artists Society.

Sources: Mallett. *Index of Artists*; *Encyclopedia of Art;* Young. *Dictionary of American Artists, Sculptors & Engravers*; *Negro Almanac*; Porter, James A. "Versatile Interests of the Early Negro Artist, a Neglected Chapter in American Art History," *Art in America*, Jan. 1936; Locke. *The Negro in Art*; Indiana Univ. *Fine Arts & the Black American*; Caffin, Charles H. *The Story of American Painting*, NYC, 1907; Clark, Edna M. *Ohio Art & Artists*, Richmond, Va., 1932; *Catalog of the 2nd Annual Exhibition of Painting & Statuary by the Section of Fine Arts of the Society for the Promotion of Useful Knowledge*, Cincinnati, June 9, 1842; *Catalog of Paintings & Sculpture Exhibited at the Fireman's Fair*, Cincinnati, June 16, 1845; "An Uncle Tomitude," *Detroit Free Press*, April 21, 1853; "Land of the Lotos Eaters, Painted by Robert S. Duncanson," *Art Journal*, New Series V, London, March 1, 1866; Greve, Charles T. *Centennial History of Cincinnati & Representative Citizens*, Bibliographical Pub. Co., Chicago, 1904; Siple, Walter H. "The Taft Museum," *Bulletin of the Cincinnati Art Museum*, June 1933; Cavallo, A.S. "Uncle Tom & Little Eva, A Painting by Robert S. Duncanson," *Bulletin of the Detroit Institute of Arts*, XXX, I, 1950-1; Dwight, Edward H. "Robert S. Duncanson," *Museum Echoes*, Ohio Historical Society, June 1954; Dwight, Edward H. "Robert S. Duncanson," *Cincinnati Historical Society*, July 1955; Dover. *American Negro Art*; Rinhart, Floyd & Marion. *American Daguerrian Art*, Clarkson N. Potter, NYC, 1967; Greene, Carroll, Jr. "The Afro-American Artist," *Art Gallery*, April 1968; Cincinnati Art Museum. *Robert S. Duncanson: A Centennial Exhibition*, 1972; City College of NY. *The Evolution of Afro-American Artists 1800-1950*; Bearden, Romare, & Harry Henderson. *Six Black Masters of American Art*; Howard Univ. *Ten Afro-American Artists of the 19th Century*; Dabney, Wendell P. "Dimension," *Ebony*; Dabney, Wendell P. "Dimension," *Topaz*; *Art in America*, 1954, p. 220, 221, 235; Tanner Art Galleries. *Art of the American Negro*, 1940; Butcher, Margaret. *The Negro in American Culture*, p. 216; Roucek & Kiernan. *The Negro Impact on Western Civilization*; Porter, James A. *Modern Negro Art*, p. 43-9, 177; Porter, James A. "Robert S. Duncanson, Midwestern Romantic Realist," *Art in America*, Oct. 1951; Rogers. *Africa's Gift to America: The Afro-American in the Making & Saving of the United States*; Afro-American Slide Depository Catalog; Howard Univ. *James A. Porter Gallery of African American Art*, 1970; Harmon Foundation. *Select Picture List*; Cist, Charles. *Cincinnati in 1841*; *Western Art Union Record*, April 1850; Cist, Charles. *Cincinnati in 1851*; Fireman's Hall Gallery of Fine Arts, Catalog, Detroit, 1852; Foote, John P. *Schools* of Cincinnati; Ball's Mammouth Pictorial Tour of the United States; Cist, Charles. Sketches & Statistics of Cincinnati in 1859; Cincinnati Weekly Gazette, Oct. 22, 1862; Detroit Tribune, Dec. 26, 1872; Howe, Henry. Historical Collections of Ohio; Goss, Rev. Charles Frederick. Cincinnati the Queen City 1788-1912; Mayer, Frank Blackwell. With Pen & Pencil on the Frontier in 1851; Siple, Walter. Catalog of the Taft Museum, Cincinnati, 1939; De Chambrun, Clara Longworth. Cincinnati: The Story of the Queen City; Bauer, John I.H. Revolution & Tradition in Modern American Art; Dwight, Edward H. "Art in Early Cincinnati," The Cincinnati Art Museum Bulletin, New Series, Aug. 1953; Marshall, Fred F. The Little Miami River of 116 Years Ago; Calkins, David L. People & Events in the History of Cincinnati Negroes 1800-1969; "American Negro Art Given Full Length Review in NY Show," Art Digest, Dec. 15, 1941; Greene, Carroll, Jr. "Perspective: The Black Artist in America," Art Gallery, April 5, 1970, p. 5; Pierre-Noel, Lois Jones. "American Negro Art in Progress," The Negro History Bulletin, Oct. 1967; "Afro-American Artists," Ebony, Vol. 23, pp. 116-22; Locke, Alain. "The American Negro as Artist," American Magazine of Art, Sept. 1931; "American Negro Art," Design, Feb. 1942, p. 28; Craig, Randall J. "Focus on Black Artists: A Project for Schools & Community," School Arts, Nov. 1970, pp. 30-3; Kiah, Virginia. "Black Artist," Savannah Magazine, April 1972, p. 14; Greene, Carroll. "Afro-American Artists: Yesterday & Now," The Humble Way, Vol. 8, No. 3, 1968; Harley, Ralph, Jr. "Checklist of Afro-Amer. Art & Artists," The Serif, Dec. 1970; Greene, Carroll. Afro-American Artists: 1800-1968, slides; Shorewood Reproductions Catalogue. The Art of Black America, 1969; Porter, James. "Negro Artists Gain Recognition After Long Battle," Pittsburgh Courier, July 29, 1950; Dabney, Wendell P. "Duncanson: An American Artist Whose Color Was Forgotten," Topaz; Dabney, Wendell P. "Duncanson: An American Artist Whose Color Was Forgotten," Ebony; National Center of Afro-Amer. Artists Museum. 19th Century Afro-American Artists: Duncanson & Bannister, Jan. 13, 1972; Driscoll, Edgar. "Blacks Duncanson & Bannister Honored in Fine Arts Exhibit," Boston Globe, Jan. 16, 1972; Le Brun, Caron. "Duncanson & Bannister," Sunday Herald Traveler, Jan. 23, 1972; Sheridan, Lee. 19th Century Afro-American Exhibit Shows Black Artists in History; Setlik, Robert. "Cultural Cross Currents 19th Century Style," Patriot Ledger, Jan. 20, 1972; "Afro-American Paintings at Boston Museum," Fence Viewer, Jan. 20, 1972; "Afro-Art," Jewish Advocate, Jan. 20, 1972; "Paintings of Afro-Amer. Artists Now at Museum," Chronicle, Needham, Mass., Jan. 27, 1972; Brown, Marion. "The Negro in Fine Arts," The Negro Heritage Library, Vol. 2, Chicago; Morsbach, Mabel. The Negro in American Life, NYC; The Negro in Music & Art, NYC, 1969; Ploski, Harry A., & Ernest Kaiser. "The Black Artist," Afro USA, 1971; Ploski, Harry A., Ernest Kaiser, & Otto Lindenmeyer. "The Black Artist," Reference Library of Black America, Book 4, 1971; Adams, Russell. Great Negroes Past & Present, Chicago, 1969; DuSable Museum of African-Amer. History. Contemporary Black Artists, 1970 Calendar; Myers, Carol L. Black Power in the Arts, Flint (Mich.) Board of Education, 1970; Spradling, Mary M., ed. In Black & White: Afro-Americans in Print; Robinson, Wilhelmina S. Historical Negro Biographies, p. 77; Porter, James A. "A Further Note on Robert S. Duncanson," Art in America, Oct. 1954; Walker, Roslyn. A Resource Guide to the Visual Arts of Afro-Americans, South Bend, Ind., 1971.

DUNN, EUGENIA V.

Painter, commercial artist, printmaker. Born in Henderson, Kentucky, 1918; died on September 21, 1971. Studied at Long Island University (1967-8); under Leo Katz. Co-founder of the National Conference of Artists.
Works: Encore; Brush Fire over Arkansas; Shadows (linocut); Gosman's Dock.
Collections: Oakland Museum.
Member: National Conference of Artists (co-founder).
Sources: Dover. American Negro Art; Indiana Univ. Fine Arts & the Black American; Lewis/Waddy. Black Artists on Art, Vol. 1; Roelof-Lanner, ed. Prints by American Negro Artists; Pierre-Noel, Lois Jones. "American Negro Art in Progress," Negro History Bulletin, Oct. 1967; Journal of the National Conference of Artists, Winter 1971; National Conference of Artists. A Print Portfolio by Negro Artists; "The Art Career of Eugenia Dunn," The Illustrator, Summer 1959; Harley, Ralph, Jr. "Checklist of Afro-Amer. Art & Artists," Serif, Dec. 1970; Atkinson, J. Edward. Black Dimensions in Contemporary American Art, NYC, 1971; Oakland Museum Archives, Ruth Waddy Collection; Walker, Roslyn. A Resource Guide to the Visual Arts of Afro-Americans, South Bend, Ind., 1971.

DUNN, JOHN MORRIS

Painter, sculptor. Studied at the Boston Museum School of Art under Frederick.
Works: Bust of Himself as a Young Man; Home-made telescope; Emancipation Proclamation; Bust of the Symbol of Faith.
Exhibited: Annabelle Gardener Exhibit, Symphony Hall, Boston, 1946.

Awards: Bronze medals, Pa. Proclamation Commission, Phila.
Member: Boston Amateur Telescope Makers.
Sources: "Janitor Genius: Admirers Call John Dunn Modern Leonardo da Vinci," *Ebony*, Dec. 1952, p. 140; Spradling, Mary M., ed. *In Black & White: Afro-Americans in Print.*

DUVALL, TAIWO
Sources: NY NAACP. *Art Exhibition of Negro Expression Sponsored by Minars Furniture*, April 1964.

DUVERGER, JULIO
Painter. Born in Haiti, 1934. Studied at the Centre d'Art; Academie des Beaux Arts, Port-au-Prince, Haiti; Famous Artists School.
Works: *Still Life; Still Life-Landscape.*
Exhibited: Studio Museum in Harlem, 1969.
Sources: Studio Museum in Harlem. *Harlem Artists 69.*

DUVILLIER, KIRBY
Painter, sculptor. Born in Staten Island, New York, 1939. Studied at Syracuse University; Art Students League; Staten Island College; City College of New York.
Works: *Serenity; Collision No. 2; Theorem.*
Exhibited: Studio Museum in Harlem, 1969; Staten Island Museum, 1970.
Sources: Studio Museum in Harlem. *Harlem Artists 69*; "Black Is Bountiful," *Art Gallery*, April 1970, p. A16; Staten Island Museum. *Coalition '70*, NY, 1970, Unpublished list.

DYER, ELLIOT
Painter, sculptor, educator. Born in Little Rock, Arkansas in 1937. Studied at Philander Smith College (BA); University of Massachusetts (MAT).
Works: *Reclining Nude*, 1970; *Experiment in Color #1*, 1971; *Experiment in Color #2*, 1971; *Liberated Sister*, 1970.
Exhibited: Afro-Art Alliance Group Exhibition, Springfield, Mass., 1972; Little Rock (Ark.) YWCA, 1958; Atlanta Univ., 1957.
Awards: 1st prize, pastel, Little Rock YWCA, 1958.
Member: Afro-Art Alliance, Springfield, Mass.; Springfield Art League.
Sources: Information from the artist.

EALY, ADOLPHUS
Painter, curator. Studied at Howard University; Academie de la Grand Chaumiere, France. Curator, Barnet Aden Collection, Washington, DC.
Sources: *Black Shades*, Oct. 1970.

EARLEY, CHARLES
Painter. Born in Baltimore, 1949. Studied at the High School of Art & Design; Art Stu-

dents League; Syracuse University.
Works: *All Twenty-Eight Minus Two; Five Faces from Africa.*
Exhibited: Studio Museum in Harlem, 1969.
Sources: Studio Museum in Harlem. *Harlem Artists 69.*

EASTMOND, C. DEITRA
Photographer.
Exhibited: Addison Gallery, 1971.
Sources: James Van DerZee Institute. *The Black Photographer (1908-1970): A Survey.*

EBERHARDT, JOHN THOMAS
Architect. Born in Chattanooga, Tennessee, August 13, 1894. Studied at Howard University (BS); Tennessee State College (AB).
Member: National Technical Assn.; Omega Psi Phi.
Sources: Furr, Arthur F. *History & Progress of Negroes in the US.*

EDAW, EUGENE
Painter. Born in Scotlandville, Louisiana. Studied at Southern University; Howard University; Temple of Divine Love.
Works: *The Wall of Meditation.*
Sources: Lewis/Waddy. *Black Artists on Art*, Vol. 2; "Afro-American Issue," *Art Gallery*, April 1968; Indiana Univ. *Fine Arts & the Black American;* Myers, Carol L. *Black Power in the Arts*, Flint, Mich., 1970; Walker, Roslyn. *A Resource Guide to the Visual Arts of Afro-Americans*, South Bend, Ind., 1971.

EDMONDS, JOSEPHINE
Painter. Born in Cambridge, Massachusetts. Studied at City College of New York; Springfield (Mass.) College; George W.V. Smith Museum; Hartford Art School, University of Hartford. Art coordinator for Afro-American Cultural Center, American International College.
Works: *Fifth Atmosphere*, 1963; *Tea House*, 1966; *Brothers*, 1969; *Rappin*, 1970.
Exhibited: Longmeadow Plaza, 1963; Eastern States Exposition, 1966; Freedom National Bank, Brooklyn, 1967-70; George W.V.S. Museum, 1969; Winchester Square Library, 1970 (1-woman); Amer. Internat'l College; Springfield (Mass.) College; Our Lady of Elms College; Pratt Institute, 1972; Forbes & Wallace; Stage West; Cinema I, II, & III, Springfield, Mass.
Collections: Amer. Internat'l College; Dr. J. English, Brooklyn.
Member: Springfield (Mass.) Art League; Afro Art Alliance, Springfield, Mass. (cofounder).
Sources: Information from artist.

EDMONDS, WALTER

Works: *Nigger Removal; Pamela; Portrait of Me.*
Exhibited: Phila. Civic Center; State Armory, Wilmington, Del., 1971.
Sources: Phila. Division of Art. *Afro-American Artists 1800-1969;* Aesthetic Dynamics. *Afro-American Images,* 1971.

EDMONDSON, WILLIAM

Sculptor, stonemason. Born in Davidson County, Kentucky, 1882. Self-taught.
Works: *Preacher; Lion; Choir Girls; Sculpture of Animal; Two Birds; Mother and Child; The Angel; The Pig; Lady in Cloak.*
Exhibited: Museum of Modern Art, May 1938 (1-man); City College of NY, 1967; La Jolla Museum of Art, 1970; Newark Museum, 1971.
Collections: Mrs. Meyer Dahl-Wolfe; Galerie Osten-Kaschey, Ltd., NY; Robert Schoelkop Gallery, NY; Mrs. Iola Stetson Havestick, NY; Museum of Amer. Folk Art, NY.
Sources: Locke. *The Negro in Art;* Dover. *American Negro Art;* Indiana Univ. *Fine Arts & the Black American; Art Gallery,* April 1968; City College of NY. *The Evolution of Afro-American Artists 1800-1950;* La Jolla Museum of Art. *Dimensions of Black;* DuSable Museum of African-Amer. History. *Contemporary Black Artists,* 1970 Calendar; Newark Museum. *Black Artists: Two Generations,* 1971; Greene, Carroll, Jr. "Perspective: The Black Artist in America," *Art Gallery,* Apr. 1970; "American Negro Art Given Full Length Review in NY Show," *Art Digest,* Dec. 15, 1941; "American Negro Art," *Design,* Feb. 1942, p. 28; Art Museum to Show Stonecutter's Work," *New York Daily News,* Oct. 9, 1937; Harley, Ralph, Jr. "Checklist of Afro-Amer. Art & Artists," *Serif,* Dec. 1970; Porter. *Modern Negro Art;* Greene, Carroll, Jr. *Afro-American Artists: 1800-1968,* Slides; Nicholas Roerich Museum. *Paintings & Sculpture by Four Tennessee Primitives,* Jan. 12-Feb. 9, 1964; Genauer, Emily. "Unseen Miracles: Aesthetic Validity Marks Carvings of Self-taught Tombstone Cutter," *New York World Tribune,* Oct. 23, 1937; Myers, Carol L. *Black Power in the Arts,* Flint, Mich., 1970; Walker, Roslyn. *A Resource Guide to the Visual Arts of Afro-Americans,* South Bend, Ind., 1971.

EDOUARD, LOUISIMON

Sculptor.
Works: *Toussaint L'Ouverture.*
Exhibited: James A. Porter Gallery, 1970.
Sources: Howard Univ. *James A. Porter Gallery of American Art,* 1970.

EDWARDS, JAMES

Painter.
Works: *Swiss Memory; Trip; The Hard Road; Fantasy; Girl with White Wig; Black Venus; Jungle Flowers; Blue Balloon; Reclining Nude; Friends; Home Sweet Home; The White Kitten; Afro-American; Faces and Forms; Orange on a String; Landscape with Girl.*
Sources: Afro-American Slide Depository Catalog.

EDWARDS, MELVIN

Sculptor, educator. Born in Houston, May 4, 1937. Studied at the University of Southern California, Los Angeles (BFA); University of California at Los Angeles; Chouinard Art Institute, Los Angeles.
Works: *My Bell and One Thing,* 1966 (steel); Untitled steel, 1967; *Pyramid Up & Down Pyramid; The Yellow Way; Hard Times; Benny Andrews; Lynch Fragments,* 1960-65; *Coco; B Wire-corner; B Wire-pyramids; B Wire-womb; B Wire-chain Curtain.*
Exhibited: Amer. Greeting Cards Gallery, NY, 1968; Los Angeles Co. Museum; La Jolla (Cal.) Art Center; Atlanta Univ.; Los Angeles Contemporary Craft Council; Museum of Modern Art, NY; Cal. State College, Northridge; Fine Arts Gallery of San Diego; Walker Art Center, Minneapolis; Whitney Museum, NY; Minneapolis Institute of Art; Esther Bear Gallery, Santa Barbara; San Fernando Valley State College; Storm King Art Center, Mountainville, NY, 1972; Wabash Transit Gallery; Art Institute of Chicago, 1972; State Univ. of NY at Stonybrook, 1969; Studio Museum in Harlem, 1969; Santa Barbara Museum of Art, 1965 (1-man).
Collections: Los Angeles Co. Museum of Art; Chase Manhattan Bank, NY; Mr. Benny Andrews; Museum of Modern Art, NY; Long Beach (Cal.) Museum.
Awards: Los Angeles Co. Art Institute Fellowship; John Hay Whitney Fellowship; Los Angeles Co. Museum Grant; National Endowment for the Arts & Humanities, 1970; Santa Barbara Art Assn. Award, 1969; Long Beach Museum of Art Award, 1967.
Sources: "Afro-American Issue," *Art Gallery,* Apr. 1968; Indiana Univ. *Fine Arts & the Black American; Time,* Apr. 6, 1970 (portrait); Morrison, Allan. "New Surge in the Arts," *Ebony,* Aug. 1967; Minneapolis Institute of Art. *30 Contemporary Black Artists;* UCLA Art Galleries. *The Negro in Modern Art;* DuSable Museum of African-Amer. History. *Contemporary Black Artists,* 1970 Calendar; Werner, Alfred. "Black is Not a Color," *Art and Artists,* May 1969, pp. 14-17; Bowling, Frank. "It's Not Enough to Say 'Black Is Beautiful'," *Art News,* Apr. 1971; Bowling,

87

Frank. "Discussion on Black Art II," *Arts,* May 1969; Bloom, Janet. "5+1," *Arts,* Dec. 1969, p. 56; Harley, Ralph, Jr. "Checklist of Afro-Amer. Art & Artists," *Serif,* Dec. 1970; Storm King Art Center. *New York Artists at Storm King Art Center,* 1972; Museum of Modern Art. *Artist of Advocate,* 1970; Studio Museum in Harlem. *X to the Fourth Power,* 1969; Los Angeles Co. Museum. *Five Younger Los Angeles Artists,* 1965; Information from artist; Myers, Carol L. *Black Power in the Arts,* Flint, Mich., 1970; Fine, Elsa H. "Mainstream, Blackstream and the Black Art Movement," *Art Journal,* Spring 1971; American Greetings Gallery. *New Voices: 15 New York Artists,* NY, 1968; Minneapolis Institute of Arts. *30 Contemporary Black Artists,* 1968; Walker, Roslyn. *A Resource Guide to the Visual Arts of Afro-Americans,* South Bend, Ind., 1971.

EDWARDS, SARA

See: Mitchell, Sara Edwards Hardy.

ELDER, JOHN

Painter, public school administrator. Born in Gastonia, North Carolina. Studied at Howard University (BA, MA); New York University.
Works: *Roses Are Red* (acrylic).
Exhibited: Inspriation House, Washington, DC; Howard Univ.; Anacostia Neighborhood Museum-Smithsonian Institution.
Sources: DC Art Assn. *Exhibition '71,* Washington, DC, 1971.

ELDRIDGE, ROBERTA

Painter. Born in Everett, Massachusetts in 1920.
Works: *Blue Robe,* 1969; *Search for Completion,* 1966; *Reach for Tomorrow,* 1966; *Deception Fantasy & Truth,* 1965; *Rhythm & Forces,* 1965; *Indian Heads; Faces in the Future; The Pool at Sunset* (oil); *He Comes Again* (oil); *All Sadness Reach for Tomorrow* (oil).
Exhibited: Winterfest '66, War Memorial Auditorium, Boston; Prudential Center, Boston; Hynes Memorial Hall, Boston, 1971-72; Interworld Fair, Commonwealth Armory, Boston, 1970-71; Boston Public Library, 1973.
Awards: 1st award, wood carving, 1971 Sunday in the Park Exhibit, Boston.
Member: Boston Negro Artists' Assn.
Sources: Information from artist; Boston Negro Artists' Assn. Calendar, 1971, 1972, 1973; Boston Negro Artists Assn. *10th Anniversary Exhibition,* Boston Public Library, 1973; Boston Negro Artists' Assn. *The Black Artist in America: A Negro History Month Exhibition,* Boston Public Library, 1973.

ELLINGTON, FERDINAND W.

Commercial artist and designer. Born in 1894 in Jamaica, BWI. Studied at National Academy of Design.
Works: *Moonlight Skating; Evening Night.*
Exhibited: Harmon Foundation, 1929, 1933; Smithsonian Inst., 1929.
Sources: Harmon Foundation. *Exhibition of Productions by Negro Artists;* Indiana Univ. *Fine Arts & the Black American;* DuSable Museum of African-Amer. History. *Contemporary Black Artists,* 1970 calendar; Harmon Foundation. *Negro Artists,* 1935; Smithsonian Inst. *Painting & Sculpture by American Negro Artists,* 1929; Harley, Ralph L., Jr. "Checklist of Afro-American Art & Artists," *The Serif,* Dec. 1970; Walker, Roslyn. *A Resource Guide to the Visual Arts of Afro-Americans,* South Bend, Ind., 1971.

ELLISON, WALTER W.

Painter, craftsman, designer. Born in Eatonton, Georgia on Feb. 20, 1900. Studied at Art Institute of Chicago under Adrian Troy, Morris Topchevsky, T.K. Persley, and J.A. Pye.
Works: *Buy Bonds of By, By, Bye and Bye; Happy as a Lark; Sunny South; The Story Book* (watercolor).
Exhibited: Chicago Non-Jury Society of Artists; Navy Pier Exhibition, Chicago; Fort Huachuca, Ariz., 1943; Atlanta Univ., 1942; Amer. Negro Exposition, Chicago, 1940; Library of Congress, 1940; South Side Commun. Art Center, Chicago, 1941; Tanner Art Galleries, 1940.
Member: United Amer. Artists, Chicago.
Sources: Tanner Art Galleries. *Art of the American Negro;* Fort Huachuca, Ariz. *Exhibition of the Work of 37 Negro Artists at Fort Huachuca, Arizona,* May 16-22, 1943; Harley, Ralph, Jr. "Checklist of Afro-American Art & Artists," *The Serif,* Dec. 1970; South Side Community Art Center. *Opening Exhibition of Paintings by Negro Artists,* Chicago, 1941.

EMANUEL, HUGH

Sources: Harley, Ralph, Jr. "Checklist of Afro-Amer. Art & Artists," *The Serif,* Dec. 1970.

ENOCH, CHARLES W., JR.

Graphic artist.
Exhibited: Atlanta Univ., 1951.
Awards: Atlanta Univ., 1951.
Sources: *Atlanta University's 10th Annual for Negro Artists,* 1951.

ENSLEY, ANNETTE LEWIS

Sculptor, actress. Born in Birmingham, Alabama, 1948. Self-taught.
Works: *Bust.*

Exhibited: Los Angeles County Museum of Art, 1972; Watts Festival, 1969, 1970; Barnsdell Park City Wide Exhibitions, 1969-70.
Sources: Lewis/Waddy. *Black Artists on Art,* Vol. 1; Information from artist; Walker, Roslyn. *A Resource Guide to the Visual Arts of Afro-Americans,* South Bend, Ind., 1971.

EPTING, MARION A.
Painter, printmaker, educator. Born in Forrest, Mississippi in 1940. Studied at Otis Art Institute, Los Angeles (BFA, MFA).
Works: *Alternative; The Moon Also Rises; Poem; Distance 22—9 2—9; Hawk Family; Hiku; Klunk Boom.*
Exhibited: Southern Cal. Exposition; Los Angeles City Parks and Recreation 1st National Print Exposition; Inglewood Art League; Stanford Univ.; Occidental College; 1st National Invitational Print Exhibition; La Jolla Museum of Art, 1970; Seattle Art Museum, 1969; Portland Art Museum, 1969; San Diego Fine Arts Society, 1969; Old Bergen Art Guild; Oakland Museum; San Jose State College, 1972.
Awards: 1st place, graphics, Southern Cal. Exposition; 1st place, graphics, Los Angeles City Parks and Recreation show; Purchase prize, Northwest printmakers show.
Collections: Brockman Gallery; Johnson Pub. Co; Denison Univ.; Ball State Univ.; Mesa College, Ariz.; Seattle Art Museum; San Jose State Univ.; Otis Art Institute.
Represented by: Brockman Gallery, Los Angeles; Lakeside Studios, Lakeside, Mich.
Sources: Lewis/Waddy. *Black Artists on Art,* Vol. 1; La Jolla Museum. *Dimensions of Black;* Johnson Pub. Co. *The JPC Art Collection,* pamphlet; Harley, Ralph, Jr. "Checklist of Afro-American Art & Artists," *The Serif,* Dec. 1970; Atkinson, J. Edward. *Black Dimensions in Contemporary Art,* NY, 1971; Information from artist; San Jose State College. *Black Artists Today,* March 17-28, 1972; Walker, Roslyn. *A Resource Guide to the Visual Arts of Afro-Americans,* South Bend, Ind., 1971.

ESKRIDGE, THOMAS
Studied at Tougaloo College.
Exhibited: Sun Times/Daily News Gallery, Chicago, 1970.
Sources: United Negro College Fund. *Art 1970,* Chicago, 1970.

ESTEVES, MICHAEL KENT
Painter, graphic artist, mixed media. Born in New York City, March 31, 1947. Self-taught.
Works: *Black Cat; The Awareness; Floretta; Young Man with a Beard; The Picnic.*
Exhibited: Univ. of Iowa, 1971-72; Kalamazoo Institute of Arts, Mich., 1971; West Bronx Art League, 1972; Committee of the Arts to

Free Angela Davis, 1971; Illinois Bell Telephone, 1971.
Collections: Dewitt Reformed Church, NY; Malcolm X College, Chicago.
Member: West Bronx Art League, Inc.; Art Students League.
Sources: Illinois Bell Telephone. *Black American Artists/71,* 1972; Information from artist; West Bronx Art League, Inc.

EUBANKS, CLIFFORD, JR.
Painter. Born in Pittsburgh, June 28, 1944. Studied at Pennsylvania Academy of Fine Arts (1964-69); University of Pennsylvania (BFA, 1968-69); Barn Arts Center, Delran, New Jersey (1963).
Works: *Father and Son; Three Figures at a Table; Purple Negative; Some Flat; Self Portrait at the Spirit of Toussaint; Red and Under; Blue and Up.*
Exhibited: Brooklyn Museum, 1969; Phila. Civic Center; State Armory, Wilmington, Del., 1971; Columbia Univ., 1969.
Awards: European Travel Scholarship, 1968.
Member: Fleicher Art Memorial, Phila. (1962-63).
Sources: Loercher, Diana. "Art: Idioms of Blackness at the Elma Lewis School," *Christian Science Monitor,* July 10, 1970; Brooklyn Museum. *New Black Artists,* 1969; Phila. Division of Art. *Afro-American Artists 1800-1969;* Aesthetic Dynamics. *Afro-American Images,* 1971; Harlem Cultural Council. *New Black Artists,* 1969; Walker, Roslyn. *A Resource Guide to the Visual Arts of Afro-Americans,* South Bend, Ind., 1971.

EUBANKS, JONATHAN
Photographer. Born in Oakland, California on August 27, 1927. Studied at Oakland College (AA); University of California under Joseph Humphrey. Teacher at University of California.
Works: *Sunset; Portrait in Ebony; Abstrusities; Portrait; Wild Artichoke; Boy Playing in Water; Art Fair #1; Artichoke Flowers with White Background; Boats on the Lake.*
Exhibited: Beaux Arts Gallery, Oakland, 1966; Oakland Museum, 1968; El Cerrito; Bernal Heights; San Francisco Civic Art Center; The Pomegranate & The Coffee Gallery, San Francisco, 1966 (1-man); Univ. Ave. Arts & Crafts Coop, Berkeley, 1966.
Collections: Oakland Museum.
Awards: 2nd place, Bernal Heights Fair, 1965; General Exhibit award, Grant Ave. Art Fair, 1966; 2nd place, "People are Creative," Berkeley, 1966.
Sources: Oakland Museum Archives; Oakland Museum. *New Perspectives in Black Art;* Indiana Univ. *Fine Arts & the Black Amer-*

ican; Harley, Ralph, Jr. "Checklist of Afro-Amer. Art & Artists," *The Serif,* Dec. 1970; Walker, Roslyn. *A Resource Guide to the Visual Arts of Afro-Americans,* South Bend, Ind., 1971.

EVANS, BUFORD E.

Painter, graphic artist, mixed media. Born in Waco, Texas, 1931. Studied at Texas Southern University, Houston (BS); University of Paris.

Works: *Ghetto Voices; My Son, My Son,* 1970 (oil); *Dreams Unlimited; Man Child in a Promis-Land; Two Brothers Have I Had on Earth—One of Soul and One of Spirit; Mother and Child #IV; Soul Brother-USA; Boy with Fighting; Old Mose; Black Gothic,* 1970 (oil and graphite); *Chief's Guard; The Bold Ones; Nun; Nude with Glass; Mother and Child III; Mood V; Pier 45; When a Dream Gets Kicked Around; Another Good Shepherd; Concentrating on a Beat; Moses,* 1967 (oil); *African Princess,* 1968 (oil); *Mother and Child,* 1969 (oil); *Just Because You Have Silenced a Man, You Have Not Converted Him,* 1970 (oil); *June Teenth,* 1972 (oil); *Untitled black Christ* (stained glass), 1970.

Exhibited: Bishop College, Dallas, 1967 (1-man); Hotel Sonesta, Houston, 1967-71 (1-man); Russi Art Gallery, Conroe, Tex., 1968 (1-man); Univ. of Houston, 1968 & 1971 (1-man); McDonald Art Gallery, Houston, 1968 (1-man); House of Arts, Houston, 1969 (1-man); First Unitarian Church, Houston, 1970 (1-man); Adept Gallery, Houston, 1971 (1-man); Ramada Inn, Waco, 1971 (1-man); Paul Quinn College, Waco, 1971 (1-man); McLennan County Community College, 1972 (1-man); Blue Triangle Branch YWCA, Houston, 1965; Houston-Galveston Diocese Religious Art Exhibit, 1965; Houston Art League Dimensions I-V, 1967-71; Assistance Guild, Houston, 1967; Nassau Bay Liturgical Art Festival, 1968; Baytown Annual Art Festival, 1969; Beaux Arts Assn. Arts Festival, Houston, 1969-71; Beaumont Art Festival, 1970, 1971; Mobile Art Festival, 1970; Neches River Festival, Beaumont, Tex., 1970; Links Inc. Discovery '70, Cincinnati, 1970; Black Arts Festival, Houston, 1971; Adept Gallery, Houston, 1971; Dubose Gallery, Houston, 1971.

Collections: School Board, Detroit; Baxter Laboratories, Costa Mesa, Cal.; Paul Quinn College, Waco; Bishop College, Dallas; St. John's Episcopal Church.

Awards: Humble Cash Award, Dimension III, 1968; Honorable Mention, Baytown Art Festival, 1969; Betty McGowin Cash Award, Mobile Art Festival, 1970; Best in Show, Discovery '70, Cincinnati, 1970; 2nd & 3rd Award, Dimension IV, Houston, 1971; Outstanding

Contributions to the Arts Award, League of Women Voters.

Member: Art League of Houston; Texas Fine Arts Assn.; Contemporary Arts Assn.; Organization of Black Artists; New American Folk Gallery, Co-owner (board).

Represented by: Mrs. R.E. Evans, Houston; Gallery 7, Detroit; Adept Gallery, Houston; Dreyer Gallery, 4713 San Jancinto, Houston.

Sources: Information from the artist; Afro-American Slide Depository, Catalog; Lewis/Waddy. *Black Artists on Art;* Smithsonian Institution. *Contemporary Black Artists,* 1973; *Ebony,* Sept. 1970; *Art News,* Oct. 1968.

EVANS, CHARLES

Exhibited: Wharton House, Phila., 1942.
Sources: Harley, Ralph. "Checklist of Afro-Amer. Art & Artists," *The Serif,* Dec. 1970.

EVANS, EDGAR

Exhibited: Augusta Savage Studios, 1939.
Sources: Harley, Ralph, Jr. "Checklist of Afro-Amer. Art & Artists," *The Serif,* Dec. 1970.

EVANS, GLENN

Sculptor.
Works: *Portrait Bust; Head of a Girl; White and Green Bowl; Rose Vase (pair); Cowboy Platter; Small Brown Bowl; Red, Yellow, Green Vase.*
Exhibited: Amer. Negro Exposition, Chicago, 1940.
Sources: Tanner Art Galleries. *Art of the American Negro,* 1940.

EVANS, HELEN B.

Sculptor.
Works: *Purple Rhythm.*
Collections: Johnson Pub. Co.
Sources: Johnson Pub. Co. *The JPC Art Collection,* Pamphlet.

EVANS, MINNIE

Painter.
Sources: Walker, Roslyn. *A Resource Guide to the Visual Arts of Afro-Americans,* South Bend, Ind., 1971; Greene, Carroll, Jr. "Perspective: The Black Artist in America," *Art Gallery,* Apr. 1970, p. 21; Harley, Ralph. "Checklist of Afro-Amer. Art & Artists," *The Serif,* Dec. 1970.

EVANS, PERCY CORNELIUS

Painter. Born in 1904 in Virginia. Studied art through correspondence courses.
Works: *African Native Girl; The Bridge; The Fagot Gatherer; The Madonna.*
Exhibited: Harmon Foundation, 1933.
Sources: Harmon Foundation. *Non-Jury Exhibit of Works of Negro Artists,* 1933.

EVERSLEY, FREDERICK JOHN

Sculptor. Born in Brooklyn, New York, 1941. Studied at Carnegie Institute, Pittsburgh (BS, 1963); Institute Allende, San Miguel de Allende, Mexico.
Works: Untitled polyester resin, 1971; Untitled polyester resin, 1970; *Oblique Prism II;* Untitled acrylic sculpture.
Exhibited: Phyllis Kind Gallery, Chicago, 1970 (1-man); Whitney Museum of Amer. Art, NY, 1970 (1-man), 1970 (group); OK Harris Gallery, NY, 1970 (1-man); Jack Glenn Gallery, Corona Del Mar, Cal., 1970 (1-man); Morgan Gallery, Kansas City, Mo., 1971 (1-man); Cal. State College, Los Angeles, 1969, 1970; Limited Editions Gallery, Los Angeles, 1969; San Pedro (Cal.) Municipal Gallery, 1969; Westside Jewish Center, Los Angeles, 1969; Jewish Museum, NY, 1969; Milwaukee Art Center, 1970; San Francisco Museum of Art, 1970; La Jolla Museum of Art, 1970; Los Angeles County Museum of Art, 1970; Museum of Contemporary Art, Chicago, 1970; Joslyn Museum of Art, Omaha, Neb., 1970; Pace Gallery, NY, 1970; Cal. State College, Long Beach, 1971; Museum of Fine Arts, St. Petersburg, Fla., 1971; Oakland Museum, 1970.
Collections: Smithsonian Institution, Washington, DC; Cal. State College, Los Angeles; Oakland Museum; Milwaukee Art Center; Whitney Museum of Amer. Art, NY; John Marin Memorial Collection, NY; Univ. of Kansas.
Awards: 1st Purchase Prize, 4th Annual Cal. Small Images Exhibition, Cal. State College, Los Angeles, 1970.
Sources: Musee Rath. *8 Artistes Afro-Americains;* Rose, Barbara. "Black Art in America," *Art in America,* July/Dec. 1970; La Jolla Museum of Art. *Dimensions of Black;* Doty. *Contemporary Black Artists in America;* Seldis, Henry J. "Eversley in New York," *Los Angeles Times,* June 8, 1970; Whitney Museum of Amer. Art. *Fred Eversley: Recent Sculpture,* NY, 1970, Statement by the artist; Oakland Museum. *Pierres De Fantaisie,* Abbey Press, Oakland, Cal., Oct. 27-Nov. 29, 1970; Jewish Museum. *A Plastic Presence,* NY, Unpublished list; Los Angeles County Museum of Art. *Art & Technology,* 1970, Unpublished list; Joslyn Museum of Art. *Looking West,* Omaha, Neb., 1970, Unpublished list; Oakland Museum Archives.

EWING, ALBERTA F.

Ceramist.
Works: *Pueblo Jar; Corn on the Cob; Egyptian Jewel Jar.*
Exhibited: Amer. Negro Exposition, Chicago, 1940.
Sources: Tanner Art Galleries. *Art of the American Negro,* 1940.

FABIO, CYRIL

Sculptor. Born in St. Croix, Virgin Islands in 1921. Studied at Hampton Institute, Virginia; Meharry Medical College; University of Wichita, Kansas; California College of Arts and Crafts; Academy of Art, San Francisco; Patri School of Art, San Francisco. Studied under Robert Bednorz, Wiesbaden, Germany.
Works: *Youth Leading the Blind.*
Exhibited: San Francisco Art Festival, 1963, 1965; Cory Gallery, 1966 (1-man); Hunters Point Festival, 1967; The Negro in American Art, local division, 1968; Berkeley Art Festival, 1968; California Black Artists; College of Marin, 1970.
Sources: Lewis/Waddy. *Black Artists on Art,* Vol. 2.

FAIR, JOSEPHINE

Painter.
Works: *Still Life.*
Exhibited: Atlanta Univ., 1942.
Sources: Harley, Ralph, Jr. "A Checklist of Afro-Amer. Art & Artists," *The Serif,* Dec. 1970.

FALANA, KENNETH

Painter, printmaker. Born in Reddick, Florida in 1940. Studied at Gibbs Junior College; Florida Atlantic University; Florida A & M University.
Works: *Africa.*
Exhibited: Hollywood Art School; Diplomat Hotel Gallery; Broward County Art Teachers' Exhibit; Instructional Television Centers.
Collections: Mr. Mort Berenstein; Ms. Fran Sweeney; Mr. Carl Crawford; Mr. Walter Jordan.
Sources: Lewis/Waddy. *Black Artists on Art,* Vol. 2.

FARLEY, JAMES CONWAY

Photographer. Born 1861. Worked as photographer for *New Orleans World.*
Exhibited: 1885 Exposition.
Sources: Simmons, William J. *Men of Mark,* pp. 801-4; Spradling, Mary M., ed. *In Black & White: Afro-Americans in Print.*

FARLEY, OLIVER

Painter, sculptor.
Works: *Gordon Jones; Red Munger.*
Exhibited: Rockefeller Institute; Coliseum Art Show, NY; Studio Gallery, NYC, 1960.
Collections: Mr. Gordon Jones; Mr. Red Munger.
Sources: "Union Provides the Time, Artist Provides the Talent," *Hotel,* Nov. 14, 1960.

FARRAR, JOHN

Painter. Worked in Washington, DC.
Works: *Self Portrait; Miss Ruth Jones;*

Queenie; Waiting; Rear of Three House Houses.
Exhibited: Atlanta Univ., 1943, 1944; New Names in Negro Art, 1945; G Place Gallery, Washington, DC, 1945.
Collections: Barnet Aden Gallery, NY; Mrs. Eleanor Patterson.
Sources: Myers, Carol L. *Black Power in the Arts,* Flint, Mich., 1970; Harley, Ralph, Jr. "A Checklist of Afro-Amer. Art & Artists," *The Serif,* Dec. 1970; "Negro Art Prizes," *Art News,* May 1, 1944, p. 7; City College of NY. *The Evolution of Afro-American Artists;* "Afro-American Issue," *Art Gallery,* April 1968; Indiana Univ. *Fine Arts & the Black American;* DuSable Museum of African-Amer. History. *Contemporary Black Artists,* 1970, Calendar; Walker, Roslyn. *A Resource Guide to the Visual Arts of Afro-Americans,* South Bend, Ind., 1971.

FARRILL, OTTO

Exhibited: Harmon Foundation, 1936.
Sources: Harley, Ralph, Jr. "Checklist of Afro-Amer. Art & Artists," *The Serif,* Dec. 1970.

FARROW, WILLIAM McKNIGHT

Painter, printmaker, author, craftsman, educator. Born April 13, 1885 in Dayton, Ohio. Studied at Art Institute of Chicago under Ralph Clarkson, Karl Buehr. Art instructor at Carl Shurz Evening School and Museum; Art Institute of Chicago; Superintendent of print shop, Art Institute of Chicago, and Asst. to Curator of temporary exhibitions.
Works: *Paul Lawrence Dunbar; Christmas Eve; Mother Nature's Mirror; Dr. Daniel Hale Williams; Abraham Lincoln; Aida; A Relic; Phyllis Wheatley;* Illustrations for vocational training texts for Chicago Board of Education.
Exhibited: Amer. Negro Exposition, Chicago, 1940; Lincoln Exposition, 1915; Tanner Art League, 1922; Nat'l Gallery, 1930; Chicago Art League, 1928-45; Century of Progress, 1934; Harmon Foundation, 1928, 1930, 1931, 1935; NY Public Library; Dayton Museum; Howard Univ., 1932; Augusta Savage Studios, 1939; Art Institute, NY; Harmon Traveling Exhibs.; South Side Community Center, Chicago, 1945.
Collections: Women's Club, Western Springs, Ill.; Phillips Jr. High School, Chicago; Provident Hospital, Chicago; Stewart Community House, Chicago; Roosevelt High School, Gary, Ind.; Dunbar High School, Dayton, Ohio; Wiley College, Marshall, Tex.; Charles Ringling, Sarasota, Fla.; Pathe Phonograph Co., NY; Kimball Piano Co.; Grace Presbyterian Church, Chicago; Art Institute of Chicago.
Awards: Eames McVeagh Prize for Etching, 1928, Chicago Art League; Peterson Prize,

1929; 1st Honors, figures & still life, Lincoln Exposition, 1915.
Member: Art Institute of Chicago Alumni; Alliance of Society of Fine Arts; Chicago Art League, President; Society for Sanity in Art; YMCA, Chicago; Chicago Urban League; NAACP.
Sources: Porter. *Modern Negro Art;* Mallett. *Index of Artists; Who's Who in American Art,* 1940-1; Locke. *The Negro in Art; Who's Who in Colored America,* 3rd edition; Holbrook, Francis C. "William M. Farrow, Artist and Craftsman," *Southern Workman,* March 1925, p. 118-22; Harmon Foundation. *Exhibition of Productions by Negro Artists;* Art Inst. of Chicago. *The Negro in Art Week;* Motley, Willard F. "Negro Art in Chicago," *Opportunity,* Jan. 1940; *American Art Annual,* 1930; DuSable Museum of African-Amer. History. *Contemporary Black Artists,* 1970, Calendar; Tanner Art Galleries. *Art of the American Negro,* 1940; Harley, Ralph L., Jr. "Checklist of Afro-American Art & Artists," *The Serif,* Dec. 1970; Brawley, Benjamin. *The Negro Genius;* Harmon Foundation. *Non-Jury Exhibits of Works of Negro Artists,* 1933; Ploski, Harry, & Ernest Kaiser. "The Black Artist," *Afro USA,* 1971; Ploski, Harry, Ernest Kaiser, & Otto Lindenmeyer. "The Black Artist," *Reference Library of Black America,* Book IV, 1971; South Side Commun. Art Center. *Chicago Collectors Exhibit of Negro Art,* Chicago, 1945; Walker, Roslyn. *A Resource Guide to the Visual Arts of Afro-Americans,* South Bend, Ind., 1971.

FAX, ELTON CLAY

Painter, illustrator, author, printmaker, educator. Born in Baltimore in 1909. Studied at Claflin University; Syracuse University (BFA, 1931); and under Augusta Savage. Teacher at Claflin University (1935-6); Public Works Administration Project; Maryland Federal Art Project; Harlem Community Center.
Works: *Seth Cudjoe of Ghana; Sunny Day; Coal Hoppers; Steel Worker; Lunchtime; Self Portrait; Little Gray Eyes; Paul Du Chaillu; A Nigerian Patriarch; Bread; Ethiopia Old & New; Illustration for the Pygmies.*
Exhibited: Syracuse Univ., 1930-1; Women's Civic League, Baltimore, 1932; Harmon Foundation, 1933; Regional Public Works Admin. Project; Corcoran Gallery, 1934; Baltimore Museum, 1939; Amer. Negro Exposition, Chicago, 1940; Afro-Amer. Building, Baltimore, 1932; Baltimore YWCA, 1932; Central School of Business & Arts, NY, 1932; Nat'l Gallery of Art, 1934; Claflin Univ., 1935; Visual Arts Gallery, NY, 1970.
Collections: Dunbar High School, Baltimore.
Awards: Gold medal, Women's Civic League

Contest, Baltimore, 1932; Coretta Scott King Award for 17 BLACK ARTISTS; Louis Seley Nacal Award for Painting, 1972; Arena Players Award for Achievement in Contribution to Fine Arts in America, 1972.
Member: Nacal Committee of Salmagundi Club.
Sources: Mallett. *Index of Artists;* Locke. *The Negro in Art*; Harmon Foundation. *Exhibition of Productions by Negro Artists*; Dover. *American Negro Art;* Indiana Univ. *Fine Arts & the Black American; Daily Worker,* NY, May 5, 1948; *Who's Who in American Art,* 1970; Herring, James V. "The American Negro Craftsman & Artist," *Crisis,* April 1942; Fax, Elton. "Four Rebels in Art," *Freedomways,* Spring 1961; Fax, Elton. *West African Vignettes,* NY, Amer. Soc. of African Culture, 1967; Fax, Elton. *17 Black Artists;* Baltimore Museum. *Contemporary Negro Art,* 1939; Howard Univ. *Art of the American Negro,* 1937; DuSable Museum of African-Amer. History. *Contemporary Black Artists,* 1970, calendar; Tanner Art Galleries. *Art of the American Negro,* 1940; Brawley, Benjamin. *The Negro Genius;* Locke, Alain. "Advance on the Art Front," *Opportunity,* May 1939; Harley, Ralph, Jr. "Checklist of Afro-Amer. Art & Artists," *The Serif,* Dec. 1970; Roucek & Kiernan. *The Negro Impact on Western Civilization;* Harmon Foundation. *Negro Artists,* 1935; Pierre-Noel, Lois Jones. "American Negro Art in Progress," *Negro History Bulletin,* Oct. 1967; "Art By Negroes," *Art News,* Feb. 11, 1939; Fax, Elton. *Black & Beautiful Series,* Portfolio of 10 prints by Elton Fax; Patterson, Lindsay. *The Negro in Music and Art,* 1969; School of Visual Arts. *Black Artists 1970,* NY; Driskell, David C. *Elton Fax: Drawings from Africa,* Fisk Univ., 1968; Walker, Roslyn. *A Resource Guide to the Visual Arts of Afro-Americans,* South Bend, Ind., 1971.

FEELINGS, TOM

Painter, illustrator, writer, designer. Born in Brooklyn in 1933. Studied at School of Visual Arts, New York City. . Worked in Africa as staff illustrator for the *Africa Review.*
Works: *Motherhood; Senegalese Woman,* 1970; *A Dream Deferred,* 1960; *Woman with Headwrap, Brooklyn, NY; Young Student, Senegal; Young Girl, Ghana; Woman at Bus Stop, Senegal; Hair Straightening, Brooklyn, NY; Shoeshine Boy, Senegal; Young Woman, Ghana; A Booth at the Muslim Bazaar, NYC; Camels, Central Park Zoo, NYC; Done.*
Exhibited: Brooklyn Fulton Art Fair; Atlanta Univ.; Park Village Gallery (1-man); Market Place Gallery, NY; NAACP, NY; Morgan State College; J. Walter Thompson Advertising Agency.

Awards: Certificate of merit, Society of Illustrators.
Member: Contemporary Artists Guild, NYC.
Sources: Meglin. *On-the-Spot Drawing;* Dover. *American Negro Art;* Indiana Univ. *Fine Arts & the Black American;* Lewis/Waddy. *Black Artists on Art,* Vol. 2; DuSable Museum of African-Amer. History. *Contemporary Black Artists,* 1970, Calendar; NY NAACP. *A Most Memorable Showing of Creative Negro Art;* Harley, Ralph, Jr. "A Checklist of Afro-Amer. Art & Artists," *The Serif,* Dec. 1970. De Vore, J. "Negro Art Theme Winning: Successful Brooklynite," *Crisis,* April 1963, pp. 228-30; Metropolitan Applied Research Center. *Six Painters;* "Home Folk, America," *Monitor,* April 8, 1971; Patterson, Lindsay. "Contemporary Artists," *The Negro in Music & Art,* 1969; Spradling, Mary M., ed. *In Black & White: Afro-Americans in Print;* Dunbar, Ernest, ed. *Black Expatriates,* pp. 39-50; *Freedomways,* Spring 1962, p. 161; Atlanta Univ. *21st Annual Negro Artist Exhibition; The Tuesday Elephant* (designer, illus.); *Bola & the Oba's Drummers* (designer, illus.); *Tales of Temba* (designer, illus.); *A Quiet Place* (designer, illus.); Lester, Julius. *To Be a Slave* (designer, illus.); Walker, Roslyn. *A Resource Guide to the Visual Arts of Afro-Americans,* South Bend, Ind., 1971.

FERGUSON, CHARLES

Printmaker.
Collections: Oakland Museum, Ruth Waddy Collection.
Sources: Roelof-Lanner, T.V., ed. *Prints by American Negro Artists*; Oakland Museum Archives; Walker, Roslyn. *A Resource Guide to the Visual Arts of Afro-Americans,* South Bend, Ind., 1971.

FERGUSON, CLARENCE

Studied at Voorhees College.
Works: *A Man in Darkness.*
Exhibited: Sun Times/Daily News Gallery, Chicago, 1970.
Sources: United Negro College Fund. *Art 1970,* Chicago, 1970.

FERGUSON, PERRY

Painter. Studied at the Art Students League.
Exhibited: Simpson Gallery.
Member: Spiral.
Sources: Long Island Univ. *Spiral,* catalog; Siegel, Jeanne. "Why Spiral?," *Art News,* Sept. 1966.

FERNANDO, CHARLES

Sculptor.
Works: *Man.*
Collections: Chase Manhattan Bank.

93

FIGURES, ALFRED

Painter.
Works: *Composition; Red Sky; Composition with Curve Sign; February 1967; Untitled; The Old Korean; Design with Hors D'Oeuvre; Landscape with Rooftops; Los Angeles Riot; Patchwork #1; Composition in Red, Black & Purple; Mother Cuddling Child; Composition with Mallett; Rock and Roll Guitarist; Reflections; New Republic.*
Sources: Afro-American Slide Depository, Catalog, 1971-2.

FINLEY, GAIL

Studied at Tuskegee Institute.
Works: *Composition.*
Exhibited: Sun Times/Daily News Gallery, Chicago, 1970.
Sources: United Negro College Fund. *Art 1970,* Chicago, 1970.

FISHER, LAWRENCE

Painter. Studied at California College of Arts & Crafts (BFA, 1968).
Works: *Beautiful America; Untitled #4; Untitled #2.*
Exhibited: Oakland Museum, 1968; Lowell Columbus Group Show, Sausalito, 1968; Cal. College of Arts & Crafts.
Member: Art West Associated North.
Sources: Oakland Museum. *New Perspectives in Black Art;* Indiana Univ. *Fine Arts & the Black American;* DuSable Museum of African-Amer. History. *Contemporary Black Artists,* 1970, Calendar; Harley, Ralph, Jr. "Checklist of Afro-Amer. Art & Artists," *The Serif,* Dec. 1970; Walker, Roslyn. *A Resource Guide to the Visual Arts of Afro-Americans,* South Bend, Ind., 1971.

FISHER, RONALD

Painter.
Works: *Portrait-Ronald.*
Exhibited: Studio Museum in Harlem, 1969.
Sources: Studio Museum in Harlem. *Harlem Artists 69.*

FLANAGAN, THOMAS JEFFERSON

Painter. Began painting after his retirement from government employment at the age of 60 in Atlanta.
Works: *Fishing on the Quarters.*
Sources: Dover. *American Negro Art;* Indiana Univ. *Fine Arts & the Black American;* Harley, Ralph, Jr. "Checklist of Afro-Amer. Art & Artists," *Serif,* Dec. 1970; Brown, Marion. "The Negro in the Fine Arts," *The Negro Heritage Library,* Vol. 2; Walker, Roslyn. *A Resource Guide to the Visual Arts of Afro-Americans,* South Bend, Ind., 1971.

FLEMISTER, FRED C.

Painter, educator. Born in Atlanta, 1916. Studied at Morehouse College, under Hale Woodruff (1935-9); John Herron Art Institute, Indianapolis.
Works: *The Plotters; The Mourners; Man Viewing A Painting; Nude; Street Scene; Man With Brush; Portrait of the Artist; Self Portrait.*
Exhibited: Atlanta Univ., 1936, 1937, 1942; High Art Museum, Atlanta, 1939, 1941, 1944; Dillard Univ., 1939; Amer. Negro Exposition, Chicago, 1940; Institute of Modern Art, Boston, 1943; Albany Institute of History & Art; City College of NY, 1967; Xavier Univ., 1963; Smith College Museum of Art, 1943.
Awards: Scholarship, Herron Art Institute; 3rd Prize, High Museum, Atlanta, 1941; 1st Prize in oils, Amer. Negro Exposition, 1940; Atlanta Univ. Prize for painting.
Sources: Dover. *American Negro Art;* Albany Institute of History & Art. *The Negro Artist Comes of Age,* 1945; Locke. *The Negro in Art;* "Afro-American Issue," *Art Gallery,* April 1968; Indiana Univ. *Fine Arts & the Black American;* City College of NY. *The Evolution of Afro-American Artists 1800-1950;* DuSable Museum of African-Amer. History. *Contemporary Black Artists,* 1970, calendar; Tanner Art Galleries. *Art of the American Negro,* 1940; Dillard Univ. *Arts Festival,* 1941; "Negro Art Annual," *Art Digest,* May 1, 1942; Woodruff, Hale. "Negro Artists Hold Fourth Annual in Atlanta," *Art Digest,* April 15, 1945; *Art News,* April 15, 1945; Kiah, Virginia. "Black Artists," *Savannah Magazine,* April 1972, p. 16; Xavier Univ. *Emancipation Proclamation Centennial National Art Exhibition,* 1963; Harley, Ralph, Jr. "Checklist of Afro-Amer. Art & Artists," *The Serif,* Dec. 1970; Ploski, Harry, Ernest Kaiser. "The Black Artist," *Afro USA,* 1971; Ploski, Harry, Ernest Kaiser, Otto Lindenmeyer. "The Black Artist," *Reference Library of Black America,* Book IV, 1971; *The Negro Handbook,* composed by the editors of *Ebony,* Chicago, 1966; Myers, Carol. *Black Power in the Arts,* Flint, Mich., 1970; Walker, Roslyn. *A Resource Guide to the Visual Arts of Afro-Americans,* South Bend, Ind., 1971.

FLETCHER, ROBERT

Photographer.
Exhibited: Addison Gallery, 1971.
Sources: James Van DerZee Institute. *The Black Photographer (1908-1970): A Survey.*

FLETCHER, WILLIAM HARRIS

Painter.
Works: *The Blues.*
Exhibited: Atlanta Univ., 1944.

Sources: Harley, Ralph. "Checklist of Afro-Amer. Art & Artists," *The Serif,* Dec. 1970.

FLOOD, CURT

Painter, baseball player.
Sources: *Ebony,* July 1968, pp. 70-6; *St. Louis Post Dispatch.* Sunday Magazine, March 31, 1968; *Washington Post,* Sept. 16, 1967; Spradling, Mary M., ed., *In Black and White: Afro-Americans in Print.*

FLOWERS, ERLENE

Educator. Studied at Wayne State University; studied under Rasil Anguiou.
Exhibited: Detroit Art Teachers Show; Normacel Gallery, Detroit, 1970.
Sources: Normacel Gallery. *A Black Women Exhibit,* Detroit, 1970.

FLOWERS, JEAN

Painter.
Works: *Urban Yule.*
Exhibited: Hallmark Art Exhibition, 1954.
Sources: *St. Louis Post Dispatch,* May 7, 1954.

FLOYD, RICKT

Studied at Voorhees College.
Works: *Lust of Sunset.*
Exhibited: Sun Times/Daily News Gallery, Chicago, 1970.
Sources: United Negro College Fund. *Art 1970,* Chicago, 1970.

FLY

Sculptor.
Works: *Bat.*
Collections: Chase Manhattan Bank, NY.

FOLAYEMI, BABATUNDE

Painter. Born in New York City, 1942.
Works: *The Babaji; The Family; The Magician.*
Exhibited: Univ. of Iowa, 1971-2.
Sources: Illinois Bell Telephone. *Black American Artists/71,* 1972.

FONTAINE, B.E.

Painter.
Sources: Porter. *Modern Negro Art;* Harley, Ralph, Jr. "Checklist of Afro-Amer. Art & Artists," *The Serif,* Dec. 1970; O'Brien, Howard. "Another Artist," *Crisis,* June 1914.

FONTAINE, H.

Born in 1912?
Exhibited: Harmon Foundation, 1928, 1933.
Sources: Harmon Foundation. *Exhibition of Productions by Negro Artists;* Indiana Univ. *Fine Arts & the Black American;* Harley, Ralph, Jr. "Checklist of Afro-Amer. Art & Artists," *The Serif,* Dec. 1970; Walker, Roslyn. *A Resource Guide to the Visual Arts of Afro-Americans,* South Bend, Ind., 1971.

FORD, GEORGE

Painter.
Exhibited: Atlanta Univ., 1951.
Awards: Honorable Mention, Atlanta Univ., 1951.
Sources: Atlanta Univ. *10th Annual for Negro Artists,* 1951.

FOREMAN, DOYLE

Sculptor, educator. Born in Ardmore, California, July 7, 1933. Studied at Arizona State University (BFA, MFA); California College of Arts & Crafts. Teacher at Merrill College; University of California at Santa Cruz.
Works: *Spirit From Two Worlds; Corner; Sonoma-Baha; Spirits From All Over the World; Untitled cast bronze sculpture; Spirit from Everywhere.*
Exhibited: Oakland Museum, 1968; Johnson C. Smith Univ., Charlotte, NC, 1968; Civic Arts Gallery, Cal., 1968 (2-man); Telegraph Hill Gallery, San Francisco, 1961; Quay Gallery, San Francisco, 1964; Arlene Lind Gallery, San Francisco, 1968 (1-man); Studio I, Berkeley, 1967; Stanford Univ., 1968; Univ. of Cal. at Santa Cruz, 1971; Bechtel Internat'l Center, Stanford Univ., 1968; San Francisco Museum of Art, 1964; Civics Art Theatre Gallery, Walnut Creek; Black Arts Festival, 1968; Studio I, Berkeley.
Collections: Oakland Museum; Ariz. State Univ.
Awards: Honorable Mention, Improvement Grant-Development of Instructional Program on Art & Social Processes in Africa, 1971-72.
Sources: Oakland Museum Archives; Oakland Museum. *Black Untitled II,* 1971; Oakland Museum. *New Perspectives in Black Art;* Indiana Univ. *Fine Arts & the Black American;* Harley, Ralph, Jr. "Checklist of Afro-Amer. Art & Artists," *The Serif,* Dec. 1970; DuSable Museum of African-Amer. History. *Contemporary Black Artists,* Calendar, 1970; Studio 1: *6 Black Artists;* Walker, Roslyn. *A Resource Guide to the Visual Arts of Afro-Americans,* South Bend, Ind., 1971.

FOSTER, (MRS.) C. ROSENBERG

Weaver. Head of Dept. of Weaving, Wendell Phillips High School, Chicago, in 1920's.
Works: *Breakfast Cloth and Napkins; Dresser Scarf* (Swedish Weave); *Quilt* (Tumbling Cube Design).
Exhibited: Art Institute of Chicago, 1927.
Sources: Art Inst. of Chicago. *The Negro in Art Week,* 1927; Harley, Ralph, Jr. "A Checklist of Afro-American Art and Artists," *The Serif,* Dec. 1970.

FOSTER, LEROY

Painter.
Works: *Head; The Market, Shepherd's Bush, London; An Evening in the Garden; Wilfred; In Memory of Nog; Lady with a Blackmoor; Trois Chats; Kee and Mee; Interior; Portrait of Reginald Morris; The Actress; Summer Silhouettes; Soliloquy; Portrait of Melvin O. Jones; Beauregard and Bill; Elizabeth.*
Exhibited: Detroit Institute of Arts, 1948, 1950, 1955, 1956, 1959, 1960.
Collections: Ms. Elizabeth Wolf.
Sources: Dover. *American Negro Art*; Indiana Univ. *Fine Arts & the Black American;* Pierre-Noel, Lois Jones. "American Negro Art in Progress," *Negro History Bulletin,* Oct. 1967; Harley, Ralph, Jr. "Checklist of Afro-Amer. Art & Artists," *The Serif,* Dec. 1970; *The Negro Handbook,* Eds. of *Ebony,* Chicago, 1966; Detroit Institute of Arts files; Walker, Roslyn. *A Resource Guide to the Visual Arts of Afro-Americans,* South Bend, Ind., 1971.

FRANCISCO, EUGENE

Painter, draftsman.
Works: Mural, Fairfield State Jail.
Exhibited: Fairfield State Jail, 1961.
Sources: *New York Times,* Aug. 31, 1961.

FRANKLIN, CHARLOTTE WHITE

Painter, educator. Born in Philadelphia on April 30, 1923. Studied at Temple University; University of Guanajuato, Mexico; University of the Americas, Mexico; Escuela Nat. de Bellas Aretes, Buenos Aires; University of London, England; Institute Cultural Mex-Norteamericano, Mexico.
Works: *Corner Boys; Cera del Mercado, Mexico City; El Bulto; Bahama Food Market; Nassau Straw Market; Los Andes, Huancayo, Peru; Carnival in Rio De Janeiro; Listening to Dr. King's Dream; Tialoc, The Rain God; Paragua de Azul; Los Pobres; Street in Morocco; War Bride; Abstract in Yellow; El Pescadon (The Fishmonger); Las Mujeres del Mercado; Tegucigalpa, Honduras; Ajustando El Balto (Adjusting the Burden); Le Petit Socco, Tanger, Maron (Street Scene, Tangiers); Gli Etruschi-Temi Da Dipinti Di Tombe a Targurnia, Italia (Etruscans-Themes from Tomb Paintings in Targuinia, Italy); O Pao de Acucan, Baia de Guanabara do Rio de Janeiro (Sugar Loaf, Harbor of Rio de Janeiro); La Vista de las Andes de Huancayo, Peru (View of the Andes Mountains, Huancayo, Peru); Los Campesinos; La Navidad, Avenida Juarez, Mexico City; La Casa de Mia, Buenos Aires, Argentina; Matador; Los Peregrinos; Los Incas de los Andes; Por la Tarde; Manana porla Manana, Los Lomas de Chapultepec.*
Exhibited: Phila. Art Festival Professional Show, 1966; Del. Valley Artists Show: Amer Exhibiting Artists Assn., 1964-6; Nat'l Forum of Professional Artists Assn., 1971-2; Phila Community College, 1968; Drexel Univ., 1969 Phila. Univ. Women's Club, 1969; Lincoln Univ., Oxford, Pa., 1970; Phila. Board of Education Nat'l. Afro-Amer. Show, 1969; John Wanamaker Dept. Store Gallery, 1970; Glassboro State College, 1971; Paley Library, Temple Univ., 1971; La Salle College's Latin Amer Festival, 1971; Phila. Civic Center.
Member: Society of British Artists; Nat'l Forum of Professional Artists; Phila. Art Teachers Assn.; Phila. Women's Univ. Club; Phila. North Art Council, Inc.
Sources: La Salle College Spanish Club. *Latin American Festival*; Mahoney, Fabia. "Charlotte White Franklin: I Lide Painting," unidentified source; Amer. Assn. of Univ. Women *Oil Paintings by Charlotte White Franklin* Phila. Division of Art. *Afro-American Artists 1800-1969.*

FRANKLIN, RICHARD

Works: *Little Orphan Annie Defending th Myth of Daddy Warbucks Before the Inquisi tion.*
Sources: Greene, Carroll, Jr. "Perspective: The Black Artist in America," *Art Gallery,* April 1970; Harley, Ralph, Jr. "Checklist of Afro Amer. Art & Artists," *The Serif,* Dec. 1970 "Afro-American Issue," *Art Gallery,* April 1968; Walker, Roslyn. *A Resource Guide to the Visual Arts of Afro-Americans,* South Bend, Ind., 1971.

FRAZIER, ERNEST

Painter, photographer. Born in Sumter, South Carolina in 1942. Studied at the School of Visual Arts, New York; Kunstunwerkschule Pforzheim, Germany.
Works: *Rasolar* (synthetic polymer on canvas)
Exhibited: Caravan House Galleries, NY, 1970 1 (1-man); Whitney Museum, 1971-2; AARD Gallery, Newark, NJ, 1972 (1-man).
Collections: Mrs. Dorothy White, NY; Caravan House Galleries. NY; Whitney Museum NY; Mr. Frederick W. Jaker.
Sources: Information from artist; Doty. *Contemporary Black Artists in America*; AARD Gallery. One Color is Like One Vibration Ernest Frazier at the AARD Gallery, Carryin the Pure Spirit,* Newark, 1972; Caravan House Galleries. *Black Faces '70 by Ernest Frazier* NY, 1970.

FREELON, ALLAN R.

Painter, printmaker, educator. Born in Phil adelphia on September 2, 1895. Studied at Pennsylvania School of Industrial Art; University of Pennsylvania under Earl Horter an Hugh Breckenridge.

Works: *Gloucester Harbor; Bass Rocks; Sunny Morning, Gloucester; Sand Dunes, East Gloucester; Landscape; Nine Coming Up; Our Lady of Good Voyage; Seascape; The Studio Window; Boats and Men; Drop Forge; Icing the Boats; Autumn; Rocky Neck Road—Gloucester; Gloucester Coast.*

Exhibited: Harmon Foundation, 1928-31; Newton Galleries, NY, 1935; College Art Assn., 1935; Texas Centenary, 1936; Howard Univ., 1937, 1939; Lincoln Univ., 1937; Whitney Museum Regional Show, 1934; Amer. Negro Exposition, 1940; Phila. Civic Center; Smithsonian Institution, 1933; Moorestown (NJ) High School, 1934; John Wanamaker Stores, NY, Phila., 1934; NJ State Museum, 1935; Warwick Gallery, Phila. (1-man), 1935; Tanner Art League, 1922; Nat'l Gallery of Art, 1929, 1930, 1933; Gimbell Galleries, 1934.

Collections: Jay Cooke High School, Phila.; Gloucester (NJ) High School; Vineland, NJ Museum of Art; Lincoln (Pa.) Univ.; South Phila. Boys School.

Awards: 4-year scholarship, Pa. Museum School of Art; 1st Prize, Art League of Germantown, Pa. & Racial Commission of Phila., 935.

Member: Gloucester (Mass.) Society of Artists; North Shore Arts Assn.

Sources: Indiana Univ. *Fine Arts & the Black American*; Mallett. *Index of Artists*; Dover. *American Negro Art*; Harmon Foundation. *Exhibition of Productions by Negro Artists*; *Who's Who in American Art*, 1940-1; Locke. *The Negro in Art*; Howard Univ. *Paintings by 3 Artists*, 1940; "Paintings by 3 Artists Are Displayed," *Washington Star*, Feb. 18, 1940; Phila. Museum Division of Art. *Afro-American Artists 1800-1969*; Assn. for the Study & History of Negro Life. *Exhibition of Works by Negro Artists*, 1933; DuSable Museum of African-Amer. History. *Contemporary Black Artists*, 970, calendar; Brawley, Benjamin. *The Negro Genius*; Roucek/Kiernan. *The Negro Impact on Western Civilization*; Texas Centennial Exposition. *Thumbnail Sketches of Exhibiting Artists*, 1936; Harmon Foundation. *Negro Artists*, 1935; Harmon Foundation. *Exhibit of Fine Arts*; Smithsonian Institute. *Painting & Sculpture by American Negro Artists*, 1929; "Negro Art Scores Without Double Standards," *Art Digest*, Feb. 1, 1945; Pierre-Noel, Lois Jones. "American Negro Art in Progress," *Negro History Bulletin*, Oct. 1967; Craig, Randall. "Focus on Black Artists: A Project for Community & Schools," Nov. 1970, pp. 30-3; Porter. *Modern Negro Art*; Brown, Marion. "The Negro in the Fine Arts," *Negro Heritage Library*, Vol. 2; Ploski, Harry, & Ernest Kaiser. "The Black Artist," *Afro USA*, 1971; Ploski, Harry, Ernest Kaiser, & Otto Lindenmeyer.

"The Black Artist," *Reference Library of Black America*, Book IV, 1971; "Negro Artists Paintings on Display at University (Howard)," *East Tennessee News* (Knoxville), June 6, 1932; Holbrook, Francis C. "A Group of Negro Artists," *Opportunity*, July 1923, pp. 211-3; Walker, Roslyn. *A Resource Guide to the Visual Arts of Afro-Americans*, South Bend, Ind., 1971.

FREEMAN, ROBERT
Painter, sculptor.
Works: *Mood Indigo.*
Exhibited: Smith-Mason Gallery, 1971.
Sources: Smith-Mason Gallery. *National Exhibition Black Artists*, 1971; Smith-Mason Gallery. *Anniversary Exhibit*, May 2, 1971, Catalog.

FRYE, GEORGE
Photographer.
Exhibited: Addison Gallery, 1971.
Sources: James Van DerZee Institute. *The Black Photographer (1908-1971): A Survey*; "The Black Artist in America: A Symposium," *Metropolitan Museum of Art Bulletin*, Jan. 1969, p. 249.

FUDGE, ALVIN E.
Painter, mixed media. Born in Newark, 1948. Studied at Montclair State College, Upper Montclair, New Jersey (BA); Arts High School, Newark.
Works: *Flight of the Nirvana*, 1970 (mixed media); *Galaxy VII, Planet LX*, 1972 (mixed media construction); *Creation, In the Beginning*, 1972 (mixed media); *Universe—Creation?*, 1971 (mixed media); *Eclipse of a Moon Glacier*, 1972 (mixed media).
Exhibited: Montclair State College, 1969; Newark Museum, 1970; NAACP, Newark Branch; Mid-Block Art Gallery, East Orange, NJ, 1970; Upsala College, 1971; Newark Public Library, 1970; Rutgers Univ., 1971; Essex County College, 1970.
Collections: Mr. Samuel Miller; Mr. Donald S. McNaughton; Dr. Ruth Assarson; Dr. L. Charles Jones; Dr. Harrison Drwer.
Awards: 1st prize, Weequatic Art Festival, 1972; Best in Show Award, NAACP; Community Arts Award, 1972.
Member: Afro-Amer. Artists Alliance; Federated Art Assn. of NJ; Universal Artists; Art Exhibitions Council; Organization of Newark Educators.
Sources: Information from artist; Newark Museum. *Black Artists: Two Generations*, Newark, 1971; Montclair State College. *Ecstasy in Black Art*, Upper Montclair, NJ, 1969; NAACP. *New Things by Black Artists*, 1968; Mid-Block Art Gallery. *We're A Proud People*, East Orange, NJ, 1970; Upsala College. *Injema*, 1971; New-

ark Public Library. *Up and Coming*, 1970; Essex Co. College. *Black Artists '70*, 1970.

FUDGE, BARBABA
See Jenkins, Barbara F.

FUDGE, JOHN
Painter. Born in Newark, New Jersey, 1941.
Works: *One Instant After the Veritable Birth of Homo Sapiens*, 1970.
Exhibited: Newark Museum, 1971.
Represented by: Mid-Block Art Service, East Orange, NJ.
Sources: Newark Museum. *Black Artists: Two Generations*, 1971.

FULLER, META VAUX WARRICK
Sculptor, illustrator, writer. Born in Philadelphia on June 9, 1877. Died in 1967. Studied at Pennsylvania School of Industrial Art (1899-1904); Pennsylvania Academy of Fine Arts (1907); Academie Colarossi, Paris; Ecole des Beaux Arts, Paris (1899). Studied under Charles Grafly; Rodin; Injalbert; Gauqui; Rollard; Raphael Collin, Paris. One of the first sculptors to turn from anti-slavery concerns; most of her early works were destroyed in a fire in Philadelphia in 1910. She lived and studied in Paris for three years; wrote the poem "Departure" in 1964.
Works: *The Wretched; Water Boy; William Monroe Trotter; The Awakening of Ethiopia; The Seasons; Richard B. Harrison as "De Lawd"* (in GREEN PASTURES); *Procession of Arts & Crafts; Secret Sorrow (Man Eating His Heart); The Impenitent Thief; Peace Halting the Ruthlessness of War; Man Carrying Dead Body; Oedipus; Three Gray Women; John the Baptist; The Silent Appeal; Immigrant in America; Swing Along Chillun; Lazy Bones; Bacchante; Relief Portrait of Moorfield Storey; The Silent Sorrow; Exodus; Carrying the Dead Body; Warrick Tableau; The Refugee*, 1964; *Mother & Child; The Princess of Birds; Storytime; Three Wise Men; Statue of Jesus on the Cross*, 1962; *Emancipation Group*, 1913; *The Dancing Girl; Head of Medusa; The Thief on the Cross; Man Carrying a Dead Comrade; Bust of Chalotte Hawkins Brown*, 1965; *The Madonna of Consolation*, 1961; *The Good Shepherd; The Voice of the Cello; The Good Samaritan*; plaque of William Trent, president of Livingston College; busts & statuettes of Sammuel Coleridge-Taylor, Maxwell Hasen, & Henry Gilbert; *Spirit of Inspiration; Crusaders for Freedom* (heads of Frederick Douglass, Sojouner Truth, & Harriet Tubman); *Dark Hero; The Talking Skull; Martha Graham*.
Exhibited: Paris Salon, 1898, 1899, 1903; Jamestown Tercentenary, 1913; Harmon Foundation, 1931-3; Boston Art Club, 1930's; Guild of Arts & Crafts; Howard Univ., 1961; Art Institute of Chicago, 1927; Amer. Negro Exposition, 1940; L'Art Nouveau Gallery; Jamestown Tercentennial Exposition, 1907; Making of America Exhibit, NY, 1922; NY Emancipation Exhibit, 1931; Boston Public Library, 1922; Framingham Center Library, 1964; NY Public Library, 1921; Augusta Savage Studios, 1939; City College of NY, 1967.
Collections: Cleveland Art Museum; Schomburg Collection; Atlanta YMCA; Garfield School, Detroit; Collection of Mrs. Samuel Evans, Chicago; 135th St. Branch, NY Public Library; Moorfield Storey; Framingham Center Library, Mass.; Framingham Union Hospital; St. Andrews Episcopal Church, Framingham; Palmer Memorial Institute; San Francisco Museum of Fine Arts; Howard Univ.; Library, Livingston College, Salisbury, NC; Business & Professional Women's Club, Washington, DC.
Awards: George K. Crozier, 1st prize, modeling; Battles, 1st prize, pottery, 1904; 2nd prize, Mass. Branch of Women's Peace Party, 1915; Honorary Degree of Doctor of Letters, Livingston College, 1962; 3-year scholarship to Pa. School of Industrial Art (now Phila. College of Industrial Art); $25 prize, painting; 1-year postgraduate scholarship, sculpture; Metalwork prize, 1889; Honorable Mention, modeling, 1898; Silver Medal & $500, New Vistas in Amer. Art Exhibition, Howard Univ., 1961; Fellowship, Academy of Fine Arts.
Member: Boston Art Club; Alumni Assn., Phila. School of Industrial Art; Wellesley Society of Artists; Civic League; The Players; Zonta (only Negro Chapter President); Framingham Women's Club, Honorary Member & Chairman of Art Committee; Business & Professional Women's Club; Civic League Players; Framingham Planning Committee; Amer. Federation of Arts; Federation of Women's Clubs; Alpha Kappa Alpha, Honorary Member; Aristo Club, Boston, Honorary Member.
Sources: Mallett. *Index of Artists; Who's Who in American Art*, 1940-1; Fielding. *Dictionary of American Painters, Sculptors & Engravers*; Young. *Dictionary of American Artists, Sculptors & Engravers*; Locke. *The Negro in Art*; Dover. *American Negro Art*; Smith. *Biographical Index of American Artists*; Harmon Foundation. *Exhibition of Productions by Negro Artists; American Art Annual*, Vol. XX, XXIV; *Biographical Sketches of American Artists*; "A Sculptor," *Crisis*, Jan. 1918; Tanner Art Galleries. *Art of the American Negro*, 1940; City College of NY. *The Evolution of Afro-American Artists: 1800-1950*; Art Institute of Chicago. *The Negro in Art Week*, 1927; Brawley, Benjamin. *The Negro Genius*; Butcher, Margaret. *The Negro in American Culture*, p 220; *Current Literature*, Jan. 1908, p. 55;

Dowd. *The Negro in American Life*; Roucek & Kiernan. *The Negro Impact on Western Civilization*; *Negro Almanac*; *Encyclopedia of the Arts*; Dannett. *Negro Heritage Library, Profiles of Negro Womanhood*, Vol. II, 20th Century; Brawley, Benjamin. "Meta Warrick Fuller," *Southern Woman*, Jan. 1918; O'Donnell, William Francis. "Meta Warrick Fuller, Sculptor of Horrors," *World Today*, Nov. 1907, p. 1139-45; Bently, Florence Lewis. "Meta Warrick, a Promising Sculptor," *The Voice*, pp. 114-8; *Negro History Bulletin*, March 1939, p. 56; Herring, James V. "The Negro Sculptor," *Crisis*, Aug. 1942; Coburn, F.W. "In the World of Art," *Sunday Herald*, Oct. 8, 1922; *Framingham Evening News*, Feb. 1923; *Globe*, Nov. 27, 1921; *Framingham News*, Dec. 7, 1932; Framingham Women's Club. *Bulletin*, March 5, 1964; *Livingston College Bulletin*, May 1958; Harmon Foundation. *Negro Artists*, 1935; *Who's Who in Colored America*, 3rd Edition; Harmon Foundation. *Select Picture List*; Ovington, Mary White. *Portraits in Color*, 1927; Pierre-Noel, Lois Jones. "American Negro Art in Progress," *Negro History Bulletin*, Oct. 1967; Schuyler, George S. "The Negro Art Hokum," *The Nation*, Vol. 122, No. 31; Locke, Alain. "The American Negro As Artist," *American Magazine of Art*, Sept. 1931; Porter. *Modern Negro Art*; Harley, Ralph, Jr. "A Checklist of Afro-Amer. Art & Artists," *The Serif*, Dec. 1970; "Treasures of Mass.," *Globe*; Boning, Richard A. *Profiles of Black Americans*, NY, 1968; Porter, James A. "Negro Artists Gain Recognition After Long Battle," *Pittsburgh Courier*, July 29, 1950; Brawley, Benjamin. *The Negro Literature & Art in the US*; Kirkland, Winifred Margaretta. *Girls Who Became Artists by Winifred & Francis Kirkland*, NY, 1967; Locke, Alain. "Youth Speaks: The Artistic Vanguard," *The Survey*, March 1925; Ploski, Harry, & Ernest Kaiser. "The Black Artist," *Afro USA*, 1971; Ploski, Harry, Ernest Kaiser, & Otto Lindenmeyer. "The Black Artist," *Reference Library of Black America*, Book IV, 1971; *The Negro Handbook*, Composed by the Editors of *Ebony*, Chicago, 1966; "Negro Has Given Much to Art, Survey Shows," *Boston Traveler*, Feb. 23, 1933; Shaw, Ester Popel. "Meta Vaux Warrick Fuller—Genius," *Aframerica Woman's Journal*, Summer 1944, pp. 16-7, 23; DuSable Museum of African-Amer. History. *Contemporary Black Artists*, Calendar, 1970; Myers, Carol L. *Black Power in the Arts*, Flint, Mich., 1970; *Negro History Bulletin*, March 1939, p. 51; Spradling, Mary M., ed. *In Black & White: Afro-Americans in Print*; Walker, Roslyn. *A Resource Guide to the Visual Arts of Afro-Americans*, South Bend, Ind., 1971.

FULLER, PERRY J.
Industrial designer. Born 1916.
Works: Manufactures African masks.
Sources: *Ebony*, Dec. 1952, pp. 71-3; Spradling, Mary M., ed. *In Black and White: Afro-Americans in Print*.

FULLER, QUEENIE
Studied at Tuskegee Institute.
Works: *Composition in Grey*.
Exhibited: Sun Times/Daily News Gallery, Chicago, 1970.
Sources: United Negro College Fund. *Art 1970*, Chicago, 1970.

FUNDI, IBIBIO (Jo Austin)
Sculptor, painter, educator. Born in Boston in 1929. Studied at University of California (BA, Phi Beta Kappa, 1965; MA with distinction). Teacher in Oakland Unified Schools.
Works: *Non-Kinetic Motor for the Good Ship Lollipop; Wooden Sketch for Possible Non-Functioning Machine; The City*.
Exhibited: Univ. of Cal., Berkeley; Oakland Art Museum, 1968; Mills College; San José College, 1969; Hartnell College, 1971; San Francisco, 1972.
Collections: Univ. of Cal., Berkeley.
Awards: Genevieve McErnery Scholarship.
Member: Art West Associated North.
Sources: Oakland Museum. *New Perspectives in Black Art*; Indiana Univ. *Fine Arts & the Black American*; Lewis/Waddy. *Black Artists on Art*; Harley, Ralph, Jr. "Checklist of Afro-Amer. Arts & Artists," *The Serif*, Dec. 1970; Mills College Art Gallery. *California Black Craftsmen*; Information from artist; San José State College. *Black Arts Today*, 1969; Walker, Roslyn. *A Resource Guide to the Visual Arts of Afro-Americans*, South Bend, Ind., 1971.

GABRIEL, RAYMOND
Painter. Active in the 1940's.
Works: *Man on Donkey* (watercolor); *Market Place; Prize Fight; The Party; Restaurant; Cocoanut Palms; Recreation; Adventure; Study in Color; Improvisation*.
Exhibited: Howard Univ., 1941; South Side Community Art Center, Chicago, 1941, 1945; McMillen Inc. Galleries, NY, 1941.
Collections: Mrs. Pauline K. Reed.
Sources: South Side Community Art Center. *Chicago Collectors Exhibit of Negro Art*, 1945; Motley, Willard F. "Negro Art in Chicago," *Opportunity*, Jan. 1940; Howard Univ. *Exhibition of Negro Artists of Chicago*, 1941; Harley, Ralph, Jr. "Checklist of Afro-Amer. Art & Artists," *The Serif*, Dec. 1970; Locke, Alain. "Chicago's New Southside Art Center," *American Magazine of Art*, Aug. 1941; South Side Community Art Center. *National Negro Art*

Exhibition, 1941; South Side Community Art Center. *Opening Exhibition of Paintings by Negro Artists*, Chicago, 1941; McMillen, Inc. Galleries. *Contemporary Negro Art*, NY, 1941.

GADSON, JAMES

Sculptor.
Sources: Greene, Carroll, Jr. "Perspective: The Black Artist in America," *Art Gallery*, April 1970, p. 23.

GAFFORD, ALICE

Painter. Born 1886 in Tecumseh, Kansas. Studied at Otis Art Institute; University of California at Los Angeles; under Paul Lauritz, Dr. Glen Lukens, and Rea Sofield.
Works: *Tea Party*.
Exhibited: Charles W. Bowers Memorial Museum, Santa Ana; Long Beach Museum of Art; Howard Univ.; Pacific Coast Club, Long Beach; Los Angeles City Hall Rotunda.
Collections: Howard Univ.; Art Gallery, Washington, DC; Bowers Memorial Museum, Santa Ana; Long Beach Museum of Art; Golden State Mutual Life Insurance Co.
Sources: Lewis/Waddy. *Black Artists on Art*, Vol. 2; Harley, Ralph, Jr. "Checklist of Afro-Amer. Art & Artists," *The Serif*, Dec. 1970; Ploski, Harry, & Ernest Kaiser. "The Black Artist," *Afro USA*, 1971; Ploski, Harry, Ernest Kaiser, & Otto Lindenmeyer. "The Black Artist," *Reference Library of Black America*, Book IV, 1971.

GALBREATH, OTIS

Painter. Born in Missouri in 1898. Worked in Keokuk, Iowa.
Works: *Sweet Contentment; Old Folks at Home; Old Mission; Birch Drive*.
Exhibited: Atlanta Univ., 1943; Harmon Foundation, 1933; Wabash Dept. YMCA Nat'l Negro Exhibit, Chicago, 1934.
Collections: Nat'l Archives.
Sources: Dover. *American Negro Art*; Harmon Foundation. *Exhibit of Productions by Negro Artists*; Indiana Univ. *Fine Arts & the Black American*; DuSable Museum of African-Amer. History. *Contemporary Black Artists*, 1970, calendar; Afro-American Slide Depository, 1971-2, catalog; Harmon Foundation. *Negro Artists*, 1935; Harley, Ralph, Jr. "Checklist of Afro-Amer. Art & Artists," *The Serif*, Dec. 1970; Walker, Roslyn. *A Resource Guide to the Visual Arts of Afro-Americans*, South Bend, Ind., 1971.

GALE, WEST

Painter, professional actor, dancer. Born in New York City. Studied at Otis Art Institute in Los Angeles (1942). Has own gallery, House of Caribbean Arts; Director of Watts Summer Arts Festival (1963-6).

Sources: Lewis/Waddy. *Black Artists on Art*; Walker, Roslyn. *A Resource Guide to the Visual Arts of Afro-Americans*, South Bend, Ind., 1971.

GAMMON, REGINALD

Painter, photographer. Born in Philadelphia on March 31, 1921. Studied at Philadelphia Museum College of Art; Tyler School of Fine Arts, Philadelphia.
Works: *The Scottsboro Boys; Family Album; The Poet Inflamed; Mary Ellen; Still-Life; Chanticleer (Paul Robeson); Homage to Henry O. Tanner; Paul Lawrence Dunbar; Alienation; Rhythm of Revolt; Mississippi Landscape; Naïf Noire; Portrait of Raymond Grist; Landscape; Harlem 66; Malcolm Speaks; Nude with Cello; Freedom Now; Double Portrait (Raymond & Elaine Grist); Portrait of Annette; Nature Morte; Portrait of Leigh Whipper, Actor; Study of Carol Hudak; Girl in the Yellow Sweater; Cleo; Girl at the Window; The Dreamer (Dr. Martin Luther King); Holy Family; The Poet; The Young Jack Johnson*.
Exhibited: Brooklyn College, 1968; Minneapolis Institute of Art, 1968; Boston Museum of Fine Arts, 1970; Amer. Greeting Galleries, NY, 1968; Long Island Univ., NY; Harlem Cultural Council, NY; Smith-Mason Gallery, 1971; Gallery 7, Detroit; Sill Gallery, Ypsilanti, Mich.; Studio Museum in Harlem; Martha Jackson Gallery, NY; Staten Island Museum, NY; Phila. Civic Center; Flint Institute of Arts, Mich.; Everson Museum of Art, Syracuse, NY; Rhode Island School of Design; Memorial Art Gallery, Rochester, NY; IBM Gallery, NY; Contemporary Arts Assn., Houston, Texas; San Francisco Museum of Art; SEDF Exhibition, NY; Atlanta Univ. Annual; Lake Forest College Soul Week Exhibition, Ill.; Temple Emmanuel Annual Cultural Exhibition, NY; MUSE Children's Museum, Brooklyn; Greenwich News Theatre, NY (1-man); Saginaw (Mich.) Art Museum, 1972; Hudson River Museum, Yonkers, NY; Phila. Print Club; YMCA, NYC; CW Post College.
Collections: Chase Manhattan Fine Arts Collection, NYC; Dennison College, Ohio; Benny Andrews Collection.
Awards: 4th prize, Jazz/Art Exhibition, Detroit Art Institute, Jan. 1972.
Member: Spiral (1963-6); The Black Emergency Cultural Coalition, NYC.
Sources: "Afro-American Issue," *Art Gallery*, April 1968; Brooklyn College. *Afro-American Artists: Since 1950*, 1969; Minneapolis Institute of Arts. *30 Contemporary Black Artists*, 1968; Boston Museum of Fine Arts. *Afro-American Artists: New York & Boston*, 1970; Amer. Greetings Gallery. *New Voices: 15 New York Artists*, 1968; Long Island Univ. *The Spiral,*

catalog; Phila. Civic Center. *Afro-American Artists 1800-1969*; Indiana Univ. *Fine Arts & the Black American*; Afro-American Slide Depository, Catalog, 1971-2; DuSable Museum of African-Amer. History. *Contemporary Black Artists*, Calendar, 1970; Smith-Mason Gallery. *National Exhibition of Black Artists*, Washington, DC, 1971; Assn. for the Study of Negro Life & History. *Encyclopedia of Music and Art*; Hudson River Museum. *Contemporary American Black Artists*; "Art," *Evening News* (NY), March 11, 1968; "Art," *Staten Island Sunday Advance* (NY), May 4, 1969; "Art," *Sunday News* (NY), March 17, 1968; "Art," *New York Amsterdam News*, March 16, 1968; "Art," *New York Times*, March 10, 1968; "The Rhode Islander," *Providence Sunday Journal*, Sunday Supplement, June 29, 1969; "Art," *Huron Valley Advisor*, Nov. 4, 1970; "Art," *San Francisco Chronicle*, Nov. 27, 1969; "Art," *Sunday News* (Detroit), Nov. 14, 1971; Chase, Judith W. *Afro-American Art and Crafts*; Goldstein, Rhoda L. *Life and Culture of Black People in the US*; Greene, Carroll, Jr. "Perspective: The Black Artist in America," *Art Gallery*, April 1970; Bowling, Frank. "The Rupture," *Arts*, Summer 1970; Harley, Ralph, Jr. "Checklist of Afro-Amer. Art and Artists," *The Serif*, Dec. 1970; "Now Showing: The Black Artist," *Contact Magazine,* Sept. 1970; Patterson, Lindsay. "Contemporary Artists," *The Negro in Music and Art*, 1969; Ploski, Harry, & Ernest Kaiser. "The Black Artist," *Afro USA*, 1971; Ploski, Harry, Ernest Kaiser, & Otto Lindenmeyer. "The Black Artist," *Reference Library of Black America*, Vol. IV, 1971; Ruder & Finn Fine Arts. *Contemporary Black Artists*, 1969; Harlem Cultural Council. *Negro Artists in America*; Myers, Carol L. *Black Power in the Arts*, Flint, Mich., 1970; Hollingsworth, Alvin. "Wealth of Expression in Black Artists' RISD Show," *Providence Sunday Journal*, June 29, 1969; Gallery 7. *16 Artists*, Detroit; Saginaw Art Museum. *4 Black Artists*, Saginaw, Mich., 1972; Glueck, Grace. "America Has Black Art on Her Mind," *New York Times*, Feb. 17, 1969, p. C34; Walker, Roslyn. *A Resource Guide to the Visual Arts of Afro-Americans*, South Bend, Ind., 1971.

GANAWAY, KING DANIEL

Photographer. Born in Kentucky. Staff photographer on a Chicago newspaper. Active in the 1940's.
Works: *Spirit of Transportation* (study of the 20th Century Limited); *Indian Sand Dunes; Chicago Skyline; Old Museum; In a Park, the Swans; The Builders; The Gardener's Cart; In Town on Chicago River; The Spirit of Chicago.*
Exhibited: Harmon Foundation, 1930-1; Art Institute of Chicago, 1927; Texas Centennial, 1936; Museum of Science & Industry; NJ State Museum, 1935.
Awards: Wanamaker Prize for "Spirit of Transportation."
Sources: Harmon Foundation. *Negro Artists,* 1935; Harmon Foundation. *Exhibition of Productions by Negro Artists*; Harmon Foundation. *Exhibit of Fine Arts*; Art Institute of Chicago. *The Negro in Art Week*; Indiana Univ. *Fine Arts & the Black American*; Lloyd, Edith M. "This Negro Butler Has Become Famous as a Photographer," *American Magazine*, March 1925, pp. 56-8; DuSable Museum of African-Amer. History. *Contemporary Black Artists*, Calendar, 1970; Texas Centennial Exposition. *Thumbnail Sketches of Exhibiting Artists*, 1936; Harley, Ralph, Jr. "A Checklist of Afro-Amer. Arts & Artists," *The Serif*, Dec. 1970; Walker, Roslyn. *A Resource Guide to the Visual Arts of Afro-Americans*, South Bend, Ind., 1971.

GARDNER, JULIUS M.

Architect.
Sources: Downing, Lewis K. "Contributions of Negro Scientists," *Crisis*, June 1939.

GARDNER, KENLEY A.

Photographer.
Exhibited: Lee Cultural Center, Phila.
Sources: Phila. Dept. of Recreation. *Love . . . and the Black Community.*

GARDNER, ROBERT N.

Painter. Worked in Philadelphia.
Works: *Winter Passage* (watercolor).
Exhibited: Atlanta Univ., 1944.
Sources: Atlanta Univ. exhibition files.

GARY, JIM

Sculptor.
Works: *Universal Woman; Signs of the Times.*
Exhibited: Smith-Mason Gallery, 1971.
Sources: Smith-Mason Gallery. *National Exhibition Black Artists*, 1971.

GASKIN, FRANKLIN (FRANCO)

Painter. Born in Panama in 1933. Studied at Fine Arts School, Panama.
Works: *Black Women; Mother's Love* (oil).
Exhibited: Studio Museum in Harlem, 1969.
Sources: Studio Museum in Harlem. *Harlem Artists 69.*

GASKIN, LEROY

Sculptor, educator. Born in Norfolk, Virginia. Studied at Hampton Institute; Tyler School of Fine Arts, Temple University; Columbia University; George Washington University; Pennsylvania State University.
Works: *Sea Labyrinth; Marine Armadillo; Apostle of Non-Violence.*

Exhibited: Smith-Mason Gallery, 1971; DC Art Assn., 1971.
Sources: Smith-Mason Gallery. *National Exhibition Black Artists*, 1971; DC Art Assn. *Exhibition '71*, Washington, DC, 1971.

GASTON, RODGER W.

Painter. Worked in Cincinnati, Ohio.
Works: *Fat Boy—Resting Nude.*
Exhibited: Atlanta Univ., 1944.
Sources: Harley, Ralph, Jr. "Checklist of Afro-Amer. Art & Artists," *The Serif*, Dec. 1970.

GAVIN, CHARLES W.

Works: *Brother; Man; Structure.*
Exhibited: Phila. Civic Center.
Sources: Phila. Division of Art. *Afro-American Artists 1800-1969.*

GAYLES, GERTRUDE

Sculptor.
Works: *Shoe Shine Boy* (sculpture).
Exhibited: McMillen Inc. Galleries, NY, 1941.
Sources: "Art by Negroes," *Art Digest*, Oct. 15, 1941; McMillen Inc. Galleries. *Contemporary Negro Art*, NY, 1941.

GAYMON, RANSON Z.

Works: *The Dreamer; Fright.*
Exhibited: Phila. Civic Center.
Sources: Phila. Division of Art. *Afro-American Artists 1800-1969.*

GELABERT, FLORENCE

Sculptor.
Works: *Fudor; Piedra; Mulata; Sitmo Afrocubano.*
Collections: Nat'l Archives.
Sources: Afro-American Slide Depository, Catalog.

GENTRY, HERBERT

Painter. Born in Pittsburgh in 1921. Studied at New York University; WPA Art School; Academie de la Grande Chaumiere, Paris. Lives in Stockholm.
Works: *Come In; Autour de Nous; The Spin III; Winter in Sweden; All in a Day; Touch; All Night Long; Riding High; Stability; La Fierte.*
Exhibited: Galerie de Seine, Paris, 1949 (1-man); Burr Gallery, NY, 1953, 1957; Galerie Suzanne Bollag, Zurich, 1959; Galerie Aesthetica, Stockholm, 1960; Den Frie, Copenhagen, 1960; Kunstudstillingsbygninge, Odense, 1960; Galerie Passepartout, Copenhagen, 1961, 1963; Galerie Perron, Geneva, 1961; Galerie Rudolf Meier, Davos, Switzerland, 1962; Galerie Leger, Malmo, 1962; Galerie Moderne, Silkeborg, 1963; Lorensbergs Konstalong, Goteborg, 1963; 1966; Modern Nordisk Konstgallerie, Karlstad, 1965; Vikingsbergs Konstmuseum, Halsingborg,
1966; Vasterbottens Lans Konstforening, Umea, 1966; Galerie Marya, Copenhagen, 1967; Galerie Zodiaque, Brussels, 1967; Galerie Dr. Glas, Stockholm, 1967; Kunstforening, Finspang, 1968; Nyttokonst, Uddevalla, 1969; Klippans Kulturreservat, Malmo, 1969; Galerie Hult, Paris, 1950; Salon d'Automne, Paris, 1951; Academie de la Grande Chaumiere, Paris, 1952; Salon de Mai, Paris, 1952; Galerie Hybler, Copenhagen, 1959, 1964, 1965; Galerie Perron, Geneva, 1962; Prix Suisse, Lausanne, 1962; Moderna Museet, Stockholm, 1963; Kresten Krestensen Collection, Charlottenborg, Odense Museum, 1963; Amer. Art Gallery, Copenhagen, 1964-5; Amer. Center for Students & Artists, Paris, 1965; Konstframjandet, 1966; Folkets Husutstalln, Stockholm, 1967; Hallands Museum, Halmstad, 1968; Univ. of Texas Art Museum, 1970.
Collections: Riverside Museum, NY; Unesco, Paris; Stedelijk Museum, Amsterdam; Kresten Krestensen Collection, Copenhagen; Harmon Foundation, NY; National Museum, Stockholm; Vikingsbergs Konstmuseum, Halsingborg; Museum of African-Amer. History, Chicago; Umea Radhus, Umea; Galerie Rive Gauche, Paris; Moderna Museet, Stockholm.
Sources: Univ. of Texas Art Museum. *Afro-American Artists Abroad;* DuSable Museum of Afro-Amer. History. *Contemporary Black Artists*, Calendar, 1970; Harley, Ralph, Jr. "A Checklist of Afro-Amer. Art & Artists," *The Serif*, Dec. 1970; Grillo, Jean B. "Elma Lewis: A New Show A New Showplace," *Boston After Dark*, Aug. 16, 1970; Loercher, Diana. "Afro-American Artists Abroad," *Christian Science Monitor*, Aug. 1, 1970; Den Frie. *10 American Negro Artists Living & Working in Europe*, Copenhagen, 1964; Walker, Roslyn. *A Resource Guide to the Visual Arts of Afro-Americans*, South Bend, Ind., 1971.

GEORGES, JUSTIN

Artist-in-Residence, Studio Museum in Harlem.
Sources: *Black Shades*, March 1972.

GILCHRIEST, LORENZO

Mixed media. Born in 1938 in Thomasville, Georgia. Studied at Newark State College (BS); Pratt Institute, 1967 (MS). Assistant Professor at Towson State College, Baltimore.
Works: *George Washington Monument; Kitchen Table Piece; Male Box; Self with Flowers; USA First Families; Guided Missile; Magic Door; Centaur; Vari-drawing; Woman; Melon, Earth, Sky; The Castle; Bird in the Hand; Female Box; War Game; Girl; Melon, Chain, Grass, Sky; Eggs Act; The Flyer Open; Erotic Wall Piece; Joy Box; Erotic Box #1.*
Exhibited: Univ. of Maryland, 1968; Baltimore Annual.

Collections: Newark State College.
Awards: Grants from Fairleigh Dickenson Univ., 1962, Univ. of S. Alabama, 1970.
Members: College Art Assn.; College Univ. Designers Assn.
Sources: Afro-American Slide Depository, Catalog; Information from the artist.

GILES, PATRICIA
Painter.
Works: *Mud & Roots.*
Exhibited: Smith-Mason Gallery, 1971.
Sources: Smith-Mason Gallery. *National Exhibition Black Artists 1971.*

GILES, WILLIAM
Born in South Carolina in 1930.
Sources: Ploski, Harry, & Ernest Kaiser. "The Black Artist," *Afro USA*, 1971; Ploski, Harry, Ernest Kaiser, & Otto Lindenmeyer. "The Black Artist," *Reference Library of Black America*, Book IV, 1971.

GILL, BEATRICE
Painter. Studied at Lemoyne-Owen College.
Works: Untitled acrylic.
Exhibited: Sun Times/Daily News Gallery, Chicago, 1970.
Sources: United Negro College Fund. *Art 1970*, Chicago, 1970.

GILL, MESHACH
Painter, printmaker. Born in Virgin Islands in 1908. Studied at the Academia, Florence, Italy; National Academy of Design.
Works: *The Ethiopian; Landscape; Dr. King-The Robe.*
Exhibited: Market Place Gallery; Studio Museum in Harlem, 1969.
Sources: *Market Place Gallery,* Catalog; Studio Museum in Harlem. *Harlem Artists 69.*

GILLIAM, SAM
Painter, educator. Born in Tupelo, Mississippi, November 30, 1933. Studied at University of Louisville (BA; MA, 1961). Instructor of painting, Maryland Institute; Corcoran School of Art, Washington, DC.
Works: *Carousel Change; Tempo; Sun Sprite; Shift Again; Balance; Bush; Carousel Form III; Restore; Pace Now; Range; Sky Chord; Wash Drawing; Muse I; Alphabet II (Part II); Bow Form I; Light Depth; But Through; Rather.*
Exhibited: Studio Museum in Harlem, 1969; Martin Luther King Memorial Exhibition, Museum of Modern Art, 1969; Art for Embassies, Washington Gallery of Modern Art, 1967; Byron Gallery, NY, 1968; Jefferson Place Gallery, Washington, DC (1-man), 1965-9; Corcoran Gallery, 1969; Whitney Museum Annual, 1970; 1st World Festival of Negro Arts, Dakar,

Senegal, 1966; J.B. Speed Museum, Louisville, 1959, 1961; Pan American Union, Washington, 1964; Institute of Contemporary Art, Washington, DC, 1965; Museum of Modern Art, Buenos Aires, 1965; Univ. of Louisville, 1956; Adams-Morgan Gallery, Washington, DC, 1963, 1964; Galeria Rubbers, Buenos Aires, 1965; Michael Walls Gallery, San Francisco, 1970; Univ. of Cal., Los Angeles, 1967; Minneapolis Institute of Arts, 1968; Univ. of Iowa, 1971-2; La Jolla Museum of Art, 1970; State Armory, Wilmington, Del., 1971; Menil Foundation, Houston, Texas, 1971; Venice Biennale, Italy, 1970; Univ. Art Museum, Austin, Texas; Indian Triennale, New Delhi, India, 1971; State Univ. College at Potsdam (NY); Madison (Wisc.) Art Center; Walker Art Center, Minneapolis; Milwaukee Art Center; Albright-Knox Gallery, Buffalo, NY; Deluxe Theatre Exhibit, Houston; Columbia (SC) Museum of Art; Phillips Collection, Washington, DC; Art Institute of Chicago, 1970; Edmonton Art Gallery, Alberta, Canada; La Jolla Museum of Art; Baltimore Museum of Art; Univ. of Pa. Institute of Contemporary Art; Pa. State Univ. Museum of Modern Art, 1970; Detroit Institute of Art, 1969; Ringling Museum, Sarasota, Fla.; Corcoran Gallery of Art, Washington, DC; Whitney Museum of Amer. Art, NY; Nat'l Collection of Fine Arts, Washington, DC, 1968; Washington Gallery of Modern Art, Washington, DC; Smithsonian Institution, 1968; A.M. Sachs Gallery, NYC; UCLA Galleries, Los Angeles, 1966; Pan American Union, Washington, DC, 1964; James A. Porter Gallery, 1970; Dickson Art Center, Los Angeles, 1966; Sidney Janis Gallery, NY, 1972; Pace Gallery, NY, 1972.

Collections: Chase Manhattan Bank, NY; Museum of African Art, Washington, DC; Woodward Foundation; Museum of Modern Art; Phillips Collection; Amer. Federation of Arts, NY; Wash. Gallery of Modern Art, Washington, DC; Nat'l Collection of Fine Arts; Corcoran Gallery; Howard Univ.; George Washington Univ.; IBM; Rockefeller Collection; Carnegie Institute; Madison (Wisc.) Art Center; Walker Art Center, Minneapolis; Univ. of Iowa Museum.

Awards: Allen R. Hite Scholarship, Louisville, 1955; Nat'l Endowment for the Arts, 1966; Washington Gallery of Modern Art Fellowship, 1968-70; Guggenheim Fellowship, 1971; Longview Foundation Purchase Award, 1970; Norman Walt Harris Prize.
Member: Artist Fellow, Washington Gallery of Modern Art, 1968.
Represented by: Jefferson Place Gallery, Washington, DC; Michael Walls Gallery, San Francisco.

Sources: "Afro-American Issue," *Art Gallery,* April 1968; Indiana Univ. *Fine Arts & the Black American; Who's Who in American Art,* 1970; Detroit Institute of Arts. "10 Negroes from the U.S.," "Other Ideas," 1969; *Time,* April 6, 1970 (portrait); Minneapolis Institute of Arts. *30 Contemporary Black Artists;* La Jolla Museum of Art. *Dimensions of Art;* Illinois Bell Telephone. *Black American Artists/ 71,* 1972; Information from artist; Davis, Douglas. *The National Observer,* Aug. 4, 1969; Forgey, Ben. *Washington Star Sunday Magazine,* Oct. 12, 1969; Mellow, James. *New York Times* (Art Section), June 29; Metropolitan Museum of Art. *The Black Artist in America,* Jan. 1969; Richard, Paul. *Washington Post,* April 7, 1969; Richard, Paul. "Corcoran's Stunning Show," *Washington Post,* Oct. 4, 1969; Richard, Paul. "Local Exhibition with Internat'l Appeal," *Washington Post,* Nov. 9, 1969; Rose, Barbara. *Vogue,* Nov. 1968; Ahlander, Leslie Judd. *Art in Washington,* 1968; Canaday, John. *New York Times* (Art Section), June 1, 1968; Fields, Suzanne. "Ten Years," *Washington Free Press,* n.d.; Hudson, Andrew. *Artforum,* March 1968; Wasserman, Emily. *Artforum,* Sept. 1968; Rose, Barbara. *Art in America,* April-May 1968; Forgey, Ben. *Washington Sunday Star,* Oct. 22, 1967; Geldzahler, Henry. *Art for Embassies,* 1967; Richard, Paul. *Washington Post,* Aug. 6, 1967; Hudson, Andrew. *Washington Post,* Nov. 30, 1966; Noland, Cornelia. *The Washingtonian,* Oct. 1965; Alloway, Lawrence. "Seven US Painters," *Americas,* July 1964; Danese, Renato G. *Washington Art,* 1971; Hudson, Andrew. *Ten Washington Artists 1950-70;* Johnson, Diana. *Washington: Twenty Years,* Baltimore Museum of Art, May 1970; Prokapoff, Stephen. *Two Generations of Color Painting,* Institute of Contemporary Art; Speyer, James. *69th American Exhibition,* Institute of Chicago, Jan. 1970; Hopps, Walter. *Gilliam, Krebs, Mc-Gowin,* Corcoran Gallery of Art, 1969; Howard Univ. *James A. Porter Gallery of African American Art,* 1970; Greene, Carroll, Jr. "Perspective: The Black Artist in America," *Art Gallery,* April 1970; Pierre-Noel, Lois Jones. "American Negro Art in Progress," *Negro History Bulletin,* Oct. 1967; Rose, Barbara. "Black Art in America," *Art in America,* July-Dec. 1970; "The Black Artist in America: A Symposium," *Metropolitan Museum of Art Bulletin,* Jan. 1969, p. 245; US Committee for the 1st World Festival of Negro Arts. *Ten Negro Artists from the US,* 1966; Greene, Carroll, Jr. "Afro-Amer. Artists: Yesterday & Now," *The Humble Way,* Vol. 8, No. 3, 1968; Harley, Ralph, Jr. "A Checklist of Afro-Amer. Art & Artists," *The Serif,* Dec. 1970; Woodruff, Hale. "Artists of the '60s," *The Negro in Music & Art,* 1969; Ploski, Harry, & Ernest Kaiser "The Black Artist," *Afro USA,* 1971; Ploski Harry, Ernest Kaiser & Otto Lindenmeyer "The Black Artist," *Reference Library of Black America,* Book IV, 1971; Aesthetic Dynamics. *Afro-American Images,* 1971; DuSable Museum of African-Amer. History. *Contemporary Black Artists,* Calendar, 1970; Menil Foundation. *The Deluxe Show,* Houston, 1971; UCLA Art Galleries. *The Negro in American Art* 1967; Ruder & Finn Fine Arts. *Contemporary Black Artists,* 1969; *Art in Washington,* 1969 calendar, Acropolis Books; Myers, Carol L. *Black Power in the Arts,* Flint, Mich., 1970 Hollinsworth, Alvin. "Wealth of Expression in Black Artists' RISD Show," *Providence Sunday Journal,* June 29, 1969; Le Sueur Dorothy. "Portrait of the Artist in His Studio," *Washington Post,* Sunday Supplement, Jan. 25 1970; Univ. of Texas. *Color Forum,* Austin 1971; Walker, Roslyn. *A Resource Guide to the Visual Arts of Afro-Americans,* South Bend, Ind., 1971; Driscoll, Edgar. "Showcase for Black Artists," *Boston Sunday Globe,* July 6, 1969, p. A73; Glueck, Grace. "America Has Black Art on Her Mind," *New York Times* Feb. 27, 1969, p. C34.

GILLIAM, WALTER S.

Works: *The Dreamer; Fright.*
Exhibited: Phila. Civic Center.
Sources: Phila. Division of Art. *Afro-American Artists 1800-1969.*

GIRAU, LEISAN

Photographer.
Exhibited: Addison Gallery, 1971.
Sources: James Van DerZee Institute. *The Black Photographer (1908-1970): A Survey.*

GLENN, ROTELL

Sources: DuSable Museum of African-Amer History. *Contemporary Black Artists,* 1970 Calendar.

GLENN, SOLLACE J.

Printmaker. Born in Florida in 1905. Studied at the Art Students League, New York; Beaux Arts Institute of Design; Mural Painter Atelier.
Works: *Sea Island Rendevous; Jersey Farm Moonlight Sonata; NY State Farm (Maple Grove); Palisades Valley Farm; Portrait of Service at St. Phillip's.*
Exhibited: Baltimore Museum, 1939; Amer Negro Exposition, Chicago, 1940; Harmon Foundation, 1933; Library of Congress, 1940 Tanner Art Galleries, 1940.
Sources: Baltimore Museum. *Contemporary Negro Art,* 1939; DuSable Museum of African Amer. History. *Contemporary Black Artists* 1970, calendar; Tanner Art Galleries. *Art of*

the American Negro, 1940; Harmon Foundation. *Non-Jury Exhibit of Works of Negro Artists,* 1933; Harley, Ralph, Jr. "Checklist of Afro-Amer. Art & Artists," *The Serif,* Dec. 1970.

GLOSTER, DOROTHY L.

Painter. Born in Pittsbury, Pennsylvania. Studied at Bard College (BA); Columbia University; Art Students League (1967); Brooklyn Museum (1969); Whitney Art Resources Center (1970).

Works: *Rage Mutations; Resolution; Family Portrait.*

Exhibited: Cinque Gallery, 1971; Philharmonic Hall, 1972; Whitney Museum, 1972.

Represented by: D. Gloster Assoc., 770 Riverside Drive, NYC, 10032.

Sources: "A Foremost Afro-American Artist Discusses His Work," *African Progress Magazine,* March-April 1972; Cinque Gallery. Press Release, Nov. 1971; Whitney Museum. Press Release, 1972; Philharmonic Hall. *Promenade,* brochure, 1972.

GLOVER, ROBERT

Painter, printmaker. Born in Chicago on May 26, 1941. Studied at Wilson Junior College.

Works: *City* (linocut); *Untitled,* 1969.

Exhibited: John Wells Gallery, Chicago (1-man); South Side Community Art Center, Chicago; Lake Meadows Galleries, Chicago; Lake Meadows Art Fair, Chicago.

Collections: Oakland Museum.

Sources: Roelof-Lanner, T.V. *Prints by American Negroes;* "Afro-American Issue," *Art Gallery,* April 1968; Indiana Univ. *Fine Arts & the Black American;* Lewis/Waddy. *Black Artists on Art,* Vol. 2; DuSable Museum of African-Amer. History. *Contemporary Black Artists,* Calendar, 1970; Nat'l Conference of Artists. *A Print Portfolio by Negro Artists;* Myers, Carol L. *Black Power in the Arts,* Flint, Mich., 1970; Oakland Museum Archives, Ruth Waddy Collection; Walker, Roslyn. *A Resource Guide to the Visual Arts of Afro-Americans,* South Bend, Ind., 1971.

GOLDBOURNE, SELVIN

Painter.

Works: *Portrait of a Young Woman; Still Life; Lady in Red.*

Exhibited: Market Place Gallery.

Sources: *Market Place Gallery,* Catalog.

GOLDSMITH, WILLIAM

Painter. Studied at Knoxville College.

Works: Untitled watercolor.

Exhibited: Sun Times/Daily News Gallery, Chicago, 1970.

Sources: United Negro College Fund. *Art 1970,* Chicago, 1970.

GOMEZ, MANUEL ALBERT

Jeweler. Studied at Merritt Junior College; California College of Arts and Crafts.

Works: Natural Comb (black walnut).

Exhibited: Mills College; Oakland Public School Industrial Arts Exhibit, 1965-6; Alameda County Fair, 1969.

Awards: Honorable Mention, sculpture, 1969, Alameda County Fair.

Sources: Mills College Art Gallery. *California Black Craftsmen,* 1970.

GONZALEZ, CARMELO

Graphic artist.

Works: *Portrait of a Sculptor.*

Exhibited: James A. Porter Gallery of African-American Art, 1970.

Sources: Howard Univ. *James A. Porter Gallery of African Amer. Art,* 1970.

GONZALEZ, CHRISTOPHER F.

Sculptor. Born in Kingston, Jamaica, West Indies. Studied at Jamaican School of Arts (BFA); California College of Arts & Crafts, Oakland, California (MFA).

Exhibited: Oakland Museum, 1968, 1971; Pacific Grove Art Center, Cal., 1970.

Awards: Guest artist for a year in Denmark, 1964; All-Jamaica Art Festival Sculpture Award.

Sources: Oakland Museum. *Black Untitled II,* 1971; Pacific Grove Art Center. *California Black Artists,* 1970; *The Face of Jamaica,* traveling exhibit, 1964; *Two Jamaicans,* 1965; *Generation of Jamaican Art,* 1968.

GOOD, RICHARD L.

Photographer.

Works: *Mother's Love.*

Exhibited: Lee Cultural Center, Phila.

Sources: Phila. Dept. of Recreation. *Love . . . and the Black Community.*

GOODEN, DONALD

Studied at Claflin College.

Exhibited: Sun Times/Daily News Gallery, Chicago, 1970.

Sources: United Negro College Fund. *Art 1970,* Chicago, 1970.

GOODEN, PHYLLIS

Studied at Tuskegee Institute.

Works: *Revolution.*

Exhibited: Sun Times/Daily News Gallery, Chicago, 1970.

Sources: United Negro College Fund. *Art 1970,* Chicago, 1970.

GORALEIGH, GILBERT

Collections: NY Public Library-Schomburg Art Collection.

Sources: Schatz, Walter. *Directory of Afro-American Resources,* 1970.

GORDON, DOROTHY

Sources: Harley, Ralph, Jr. "Checklist of Afro-Amer. Artists," *The Serif,* Dec. 1970.

GORDON, PAULA

Graphic artist.
Works: *Untitled* (pencil); *One* (pencil).
Exhibited: Lee Cultural Center, Phila.
Sources: Phila. Dept. of Recreation. *Love . . . and the Black Community.*

GORDON, ROBERT GARY

Painter, mixed media.
Works: *Bronze Powder* (mixed media), 1966; *Untitled.*
Exhibited: Iolas Gallery (1-man), NY, 1968; Galeria Del Leone (1-man), Venice, 1968; Contemporary Arts Center, Cincinnati, 1968; Park Place Gallery, NY, 1966, 1967; Leo Castelli Gallery, NY, 1966, 1967; Minneapolis Institute of Arts, 1968; High Art Museum, Atlanta, 1969; Flint (Mich.) Institute of Arts, 1969; Everson Museum of Art, Syracuse, NY, 1969; IBM Gallery of Arts & Sciences, NY, 1969; Rhode Island School of Design, 1969; Memorial Art Gallery, Rochester, NY, 1969; San Francisco Museum of Art, 1969; Contemporary Arts Museum, Houston, Tex., 1970; NJ State Museum, 1970; Roberson Center for the Arts and Sciences, Binghamton, NY, 1970; Univ. of Cal. at Santa Barbara, 1970.
Collections: Mr. Hans Namuth; Mr. Harrison Rivera; Mr. Roy Lichtenstein; Mr. F. Arman; Pasadena Museum of Art; Rice Univ., Houston, Tex.
Awards: Copleu Grant, 1967; John Hay Whitney Fellowship, 1965.
Sources: Minneapolis Institute of Arts. *30 Contemporary Black Artists;* Rose, Barbara. "Black Art in America," *Art in America,* July-Dec. 1970; Ruder & Finn Fine Arts. *Contemporary Black Artists,* 1969; Myers, Carol L. *Black Power in the Arts,* Flint, Mich., 1970; Driscoll, Edgar J., Jr. "Showcase for Black Artists," *Boston Sunday Globe,* July 6, 1969, p.A73; Walker, Roslyn. *A Resource Guide to the Visual Arts of Afro-Americans,* South Bend, Ind., 1971.

GORDON, RUSSELL T.

Painter, printmaker. Born in Altoona, Pennsylvania in 1932. Studied at Pennsylvania Academy of Fine Arts; Barnes Foundation, Merion, Pennsylvania; under Hobson Pittman.
Works: *Portrait Series Nos. 1-3; Totem Pole; Kaleidoscopic Portrait; Yesterday; Today; Tomorrow; Kaleidoscopic Woman; Temptation; No Title; Kaleidoscopic Portrait Series #5; California Series #3; Portrait; Kaleidoscopic;*

Earth Mother, 1970 (etching & aquatint).
Exhibited: Pa. Academy of Fine Arts; Yale Univ. Art Gallery; Amer. Academy of Arts & Letters; Gallery of Modern Art, NY; Va. Museum of Fine Arts; Sarah Lawrence College, NY; Addison Gallery of Amer. Art; De-Cordova & Dana Museum; Deerfield Academy; Newport Art Assn.; Contemporary Museum of Art; Durlacher Brothers, NY (1-man), 1957-67; Fantasy Gallery Washington, DC, 1958; Fort Worth Art Center; Whitney Museum 1971; Univ. of Iowa, 1971-2.
Collections: Oakland Museum.
Sources: "Afro-American Issue," *Art Gallery,* April 1968; Indiana Univ. *Fine Arts & the Black American; Who's Who in American Art,* 1970; Afro-American Slide Depository, Catalog, 1971-2; Doty. *Contemporary Black Artists in America;* DuSable Museum of African-Amer. History. *Contemporary Black Artists,* 1970, Calendar; Illinois Bell Telephone. *Black American Artists/71,* 1972; Berkman, Florence. "Some Black Artists Enraged Over Whitney Exhibit," *Times,* Hartford, Conn., April 25, 1971; Atkinson, J. Edward. *Black Dimensions in Contemporary American Art,* NY, 1971; Myers, Carol L. *Black Power in the Arts,* Flint, Mich., 1970; Oakland Museum Archives; Gaither, Edmund B. "The Evolution of the Afro-American Artist," *Artists Proof,* Vol. 2; Walker, Roslyn. *A Resource Guide to the Visual Arts of Afro-Americans,* South Bend, Ind., 1971.

GORE, JOHN W.

Sources: Porter. *Modern Negro Art;* Harley, Ralph, Jr. "Checklist of Afro-Amer. Art & Artists," *The Serif,* Dec. 1970.

GORELEIGH, REX

Painter, printmaker, educator. Born in Penllyn, Pennsylvania in 1902. Studied at Howard University; University of Chicago; Andre L'Hote Academie, Paris. Studied under Xavier J. Bavile, New York. Teacher at Harlem Art Center (1936-7); WPA, Greensboro, North Carolina Art Center (1938); Palmer Memorial Institute, Sedalia, North Carolina; Princeton, New Jersey. Director of South Side Community Art Center, Chicago (1938); Studio-on-the-Canal.
Works: *The Twins; The House on Canal Road; Jungle Dance; Dune Landslide; Dean's Alley; Ploughing; Music Maestro; Young Mother; The Tomato Picker; Christ in Gethsemane* (mural); *Noon Day Chat; Misery; North Carolina Moon; Moving Sea; Landscape; Maxwell Sheet; Camp Feasting; Envy; Migrant Series—Cabins in Winter* (watercolor), *Mother & Child* (oil), *Ready for Church* (oil), *Social Hour* (oil), *Social Hour* (watercolor), *Twins* (oil); *Dying Tree* (watercolor); *End of the Day*

(oil); *Open Door* (oil); *Still Life* (watercolor); *Thrashing Wheat* (oil).

Exhibited: Society of Independent Artists, 1930-2, 1936; Anderson Galleries, NYC, 1931-2, 1936; Baltimore Museum, 1939; Amer. Negro Exposition, Chicago, 1940; Strindberg Gallery, Finland; YMCA, Greensboro, NC; Shaw Univ., Raleigh, NC; Renaissance Gallery, Washington, DC, 1971; Harmon Foundation, 1936; Augusta Savage Studios, 1939; Atlanta Univ., 1932, 1936, 1942; Trenton Museum, 1970-1; Westtown School, Pa., 1968 (1-man); Little Gallery, Princeton, NJ, 1960; NJ State Museum, Trenton, 1950; Amer. Artist Gallery, Chicago, 1943; Pyramid Club, Phila., 1942, 1948, 1949; Greensboro (NC) Public Library, 1940 (1-man); Art Gallery, Greensboro, NC, 1940; Newark Museum, 1968; Clifton Art Show, NJ, 1968; Trenton Trust Co., 1965 (1-man); Lambertville House, NJ, 1961 (1-man); Phillips Mill, New Hope, Pa., 1959; Montclair (NJ) Museum, 1950; Nat'l Center of Afro-American Artists, Boston, 1973; Studio Museum, Harlem, 1973.

Collections: Mr. & Mrs. Leonard F. Newton; Mr. & Mrs. Glenn Cullen; Mr. & Mrs. Edward A. Ring; Mr. Malcolm Peyton; Mrs. James Grigsby; Mrs. Rex Goreleigh; Mural in 1st Baptist Church, Princeton, NJ.

Awards: NJ State Council on the Arts Award for Contribution to NJ, 1971; Mini-Grant from NJ State Council on the Arts, 1971; Afro-Amer. Award for Superior public service, 1955.

Member: NJ State Council on the Arts, 1966; Princeton Historical Society, 1964; Federal Arts Projects.

Sources: Locke. *The Negro in Art;* Dover. *American Negro Art;* Indiana Univ. *Fine Arts & the Black American;* DuSable Museum of African-Amer. History. *Contemporary Black Artists,* Calendar, 1970; Smith-Mason Gallery. *Nat'l Exhibition of Black Artists,* 1971; Fax, Elton C. *Seventeen Black Artists;* Pierre-Noel, Lois Jones. "American Negro Art in Progress," *Negro History Bulletin,* Oct. 1967; "Negro Art Scores Without Double Standards," *Art Digest,* Feb. 1, 1945; Harley, Ralph, Jr. "A Checklist of Afro-Amer. Art & Artists," *The Serif,* Dec. 1970; "Princeton Group Arts," *Crisis,* Jan. 1951, pp. 19-22; Ploski, Harry, & Ernest Kaiser. "The Black Artist," *Afro USA,* 1971; Ploski, Harry, Ernest Kaiser, & Otto Lindenmeyer. "The Black Artist," *Reference Library of Black America,* Book IV, 1971; *The Negro Handbook,* Composed by Editors of *Ebony,* Chicago, 1966; Porter. *Modern Negro Art*; Albany Institute of History & Art. *The Negro Artist Comes of Age;* Chase, Judith W. *Afro-American Arts & Crafts.* South Side Community Art Center. *Chicago Collectors Exhibit of Negro Art,* 1945; Information from artist; Museum of the Nat'l Center of Afro-American Art. *Reality Expanded,* Boston, 1973; Studio Museum. *Reality Expanded,* press release, Harlem, 1973; Walker, Roslyn. *A Resource Guide to the Visual Arts of Afro-Americans,* South Bend, Ind., 1971.

GOSS, BERNARD

Painter, muralist, printmaker. Born in Sedalia, Missouri, 1913. Studied at University of Iowa (BA, 1935); Art Institute of Chicago (1935-7); Institute of Design.

Works: *Still Life; Always the Dirty Work; Slave Revolt; John Henry* (print); Murals in New Crusader's Negro History Hall of Fame, Chicago Coliseum, 1960-2; *Slave Rebellion; Seven Generations.*

Exhibited: Student Salon, Iowa, 1935; Little Gallery, Cedar Rapids, 1934; Ill. Federal Artists Project; Howard Univ., 1941; Library of Congress, 1940; Amer. Negro Exposition, 1940; South Side Community Art Center, Chicago, 1941, 1945; Tanner Art Galleries, 1940.

Awards: Honorable Mention, Student Salon, Univ. of Iowa, 1935.

Collections: Miss Fern Gayden; Mr. & Mrs. William H. Patterson.

Member: Nat'l Conference of Artists, Founder.

Sources: Locke. *The Negro in Art;* Howard Univ. *Exhibition of Negro Artists of Chicago at Howard University Gallery of Art,* 1941; Motley, Willard F. "Negro Art in Chicago," *Opportunity,* Jan. 1940; Tanner Art Galleries. *Art of the American Negro,* 1940; Nat'l Conference of Artists. *A Print Portfolio by Negro Artists;* Harley, Ralph L., Jr. "A Checklist of Afro-American Art and Artists," *The Serif,* Dec. 1970; Porter, James. *Modern Negro Art;* South Side Community Art Center. *Chicago Collectors Exhibit of Negro Art,* Chicago, 1945; South Side Community Art Center. *Opening Exhibition of Paintings by Negro Artists,* Chicago, 1941.

GOSS, MARGARET TAYLOR

See: Burroughs, Margaret Taylor Goss.

GOSS, WILLIAM THOMPSON

Commercial artist. Born in Kentucky in 1894. Studied at the Haines Institute, Augusta, Georgia; independent study in France.

Works: *Still Life; Mother and Child; Portrait; St. Patricks; Voters.*

Exhibited: Society of Independent Artists, 1932; Gordon Galleries, Detroit; Mich. State Fair, 1932; Annual Exhibition of Mich. Artists, 1933; Harmon Foundation, 1931, 1933, 1935.

Collections: Nat'l Archives.

Sources: Harmon Foundation. *Negro Artists,* 1935; Afro-Amer. Slide Depository, catalog; DuSable Museum of African-Amer. History. *Contemporary Black Artists,* 1970, calendar;

Harmon Foundation. *Exhibition of Productions by Negro Artists;* Harmon Foundation. *Non-Jury Exhibit of Works of Negro Artists,* 1933; Indiana Univ. *Fine Arts & the Black American;* Harley, Ralph, Jr. "Checklist of Afro-Amer. Art & Artists," *The Serif,* Dec. 1970; Albany Institute of History & Art. *The Negro Artist Comes of Age;* Walker, Roslyn. *A Resource Guide to the Visual Arts of Afro-Americans,* South Bend, Ind., 1971.

GRACE, DENISE Y.

Painter. Born in Baltimore, 1952.
Works: *New World Coming—Here Comes the Sun,* 1971; *Face the Nation,* 1972; *Me . . . ,* 1972 (acrylic on black velvet); *Double Image,* 1970; *Demure,* 1972; *Mother's Looking Glass,* 1972; *Moving Right Along;* Untitled mural, Wellesley Sr. High School, 1970; Untitled mural, artist's home, 1969-70.
Exhibited: Sunday in the Park, Boston; Bette's Rolls Royce, Boston; Lady Grace's Gallery, Boston, 1972; Boston Globe Annual.
Honors: United States Army Flag Day Award; Boston Museum School Scholarship.
Member: Boston Negro Artists Assn.
Sources: Boston Negro Artists Assn. Calendar, 1970; Information from the artist.

GRADY, EDWARD

Studied at Fisk University.
Works: *Karen Dreams I; Linda; Chad; Viola; Water Lilys.*
Exhibited: Sun Times/Daily News Gallery, Chicago, 1970.
Sources: United Negro College Fund. *Art 1970,* Chicago, 1970.

GRAHAM, SADIE

Painter. Born in Atlanta, 1931. Studied at the Charles McGee School of Art; under Oscar Graves, Charles McGee, Leroy Foster, and Carl Owens.
Works: *Fruit; Boy and His Ball; Fisherman; Basket; Meditation; Candy; Father and Son; Reclining Girl; Mexican Workers; Jomo; Child's World; Bottles; Mother and Child; Rag Dolls; Old Man; Head Start; Boy and Marbles; Three Boys,* 1969; *Flutist,* 1969; *Turmoil,* 1970; *Fantasy,* 1971.
Exhibited: Detroit Artists Mart, 1969; Gallery 7, 1969-70; Mich. State Fair, 1970; J.L. Hudson, 1970; Wayne State Univ., 1970; McGregor Library, 1972; Detroit Institute of Arts, 1972-3.
Collections: Mr. Robert Campbell, Detroit; Mr. Charles Primas, Detroit; Mr. Arthur Dorham, Grand Bahamas; Mr. Lorenzo Marvel, Chicago; Mr. Robert Fulton, Detroit; Nat'l Archives; Langston Univ.; Alcorn A&M Univ.
Member: Amer. Black Artist, Inc.; Merrill-

Palmer Institute; Univ. of Southern Ala. Afro-Amer. Art Studies Program.
Represented by: Detroit Artists Mart; Gallery 7; Detroit Institute of Art.
Sources: Afro-Amer. Slide Depository, catalog; Founders Society, Detroit Institute of Art. *The Art Journal,* catalog; Information from artist.

GRAMBS, BLANCHE

Collections: NY Public Library-Schomburg Art Collection.
Sources: Schatz, Walter. *Directory of Afro-American Resources,* 1970.

GRANT, WILLIAM EMMETT

Painter. Studied at Art Institute of Chicago; in Paris. Active in the 1930's.
Works: *Virginia; Mrs. G.; Green Turban.*
Exhibited: Harmon Foundation, 1929-31, 1933; Smithsonian Institution, 1929; Grand Rapids, Mich.; Muskegan, Mich.
Collections: Mural, St. Philips Church, Grand Rapids, Mich.
Sources: Harmon Foundation. *Exhibit of Fine Arts,* 1930; Harmon Foundation. *Exhibition of Productions by Negro Artists;* Harmon Foundation. *Negro Artists,* 1935; Indiana Univ. *Fine Arts & the Black American;* DuSable Museum of African-Amer. History. *Contemporary Black Artists,* Calendar, 1970; Smithsonian Institution. *Painting & Sculpture by American Negro Artists,* 1929; Harley, Ralph, Jr. "A Checklist of Afro-Amer. Art & Artists," *The Serif,* Dec. 1970; Walker, Roslyn. *A Resource Guide to the Visual Arts of Afro-Americans,* South Bend, Ind., 1971.

GRAVES, OSCAR

Sculptor, ceramist. Born May 20, 1921 in Detroit, Michigan. Studied at Cranbook Academy, 1954; Wayne State University, 1953.
Works: *Elephant; Crisis; Sea Struggle.*
Exhibited: Great Lakes Ceramic Exhibit, Chicago, Detroit, 1955-7; Detroit Institute of Arts, 1957.
Sources: Detroit Institute of Arts files.

GRAY, RUTH

Textile painter. Born in Jamaica, British West Indies, 1896.
Exhibited: Harmon Foundation, 1929.
Sources: Harmon Foundation. *Exhibition of Productions by Negro Artists;* Indiana Univ. *Fine Arts & the Black American;* Harley, Ralph, Jr. "Checklist of Afro-Amer. Art & Artists," *Serif,* Dec. 1970; Walker, Roslyn. *A Resource Guide to the Visual Arts of Afro-Americans,* South Bend, Ind., 1971.

GREEN, ANABELLE

Painter, educator. Studied at Miner Teachers College; Columbia University; Howard Univer-

108

sity; DC Teachers College; Famous Artists Correspondence Course; Corcoran School of Art.
Works: *Compassion.*
Exhibited: Garnet-Patterson Parent-Teacher Program; Zion Baptist Church; DCAA, Anacostia Neighborhood Museum-Smithsonian Institution; Margaret Dickey Gallery of Art; Smith-Mason Gallery; Oxon Hill, Md. Library; Potter's House Gallery (1-man).
Sources: DC Art Assn. *Exhibition '71,* Washington, DC, 1971.

GREEN, BOB

Studied at AM&N College. Assistant Professor of art at Lincoln University, Jefferson City, Missouri.
Sources: *National Conference of Artists,* Winter 1971, Journal.

GREEN, CARL H.

Mixed media.
Works: *Grafitti* (construction).
Exhibited: Lee Cultural Center, Phila.
Sources: Phila. Dept. of Recreation. *Love . . . and the Black Community.*

GREEN, GEORGE

Painter.
Works: *A Peep at the Library; The Barn; Still Life in Monotone; Still Life, View of Big Thompson Canyon; Out the Bathroom Window; View of the Corner in the Flour Mill.*
Exhibited: Atlanta Univ., 1944.
Sources: Harley, Ralph, Jr. "Checklist of Afro-Amer. Art & Artists," *The Serif,* Dec. 1970; Atlanta Univ. Annual Exhibition catalog, 1944.

GREEN, JAMES

Painter. Born in Chattanooga, Tennessee in 1939. Studied at Knoxville College (BS).
Works: *The Room,* 1970; *Screaming Man; Black America Rises; Flaming Forest; Crossroads; Boy; Moom; Seated Man; Self Portrait.*
Exhibited: Newark Museum, 1969, 1971, 1972; Newark Public Library, 1970; Stuart County Day School, 1970; Irvington Art Show, 1971.
Collections: Mr. Benny Andrews.
Awards: Newark Museum, 1969; Honorable Mention, Irvington Art Show, 1971.
Represented by: Mid-Block Art Service, East Orange, NJ.
Sources: Newark Museum. *Black Artists: Two Generations,* 1971; Information from artist.

GREEN, KENNETH

Photographer. Born in 1946. Studied at AA Peralta College, Oakland (1968). Staff photographer, Oakland *Tribune.*
Works: *Portrait.*
Exhibited: Oakland Museum, 1968.

Sources: Oakland Museum. *New Perspectives in Black Art;* Indiana Univ. *Fine Arts & the Black American;* Harley, Ralph, Jr. "Checklist of Afro-Amer. Art & Artists," *The Serif,* Dec. 1970.

GREEN, MELVIN

Studied at the American Art School; School of Visual Art.
Sources: NY NAACP. *A Most Memorable Showing of Negro Creative Art;* NY NAACP. *Art Exhibition of Negro Expression Sponsored by Minars Furniture,* April 1964.

GREEN, ROBERT H., JR.

Born in Okmulgee, Oklahoma, 1930. Studied at Langston University (BA, 1952); University of Tulsa, Oklahoma (MA, 1958); Mexico Art School, Juarez, Mexico. Teacher of Art, Alabama State College, Montgomery, Alabama.
Works: *There Is No Greater Love.*
Exhibited: Municipal Gallery, Springfield, Mo.; Wesleyan College, Lincoln, Neb.; Dallas Museum of Art; Oklahoma Art Center, Oklahoma City; Denver Museum of Art.
Awards: Atlanta Univ.; Topeka City Museum.
Sources: Lewis/Waddy. *Black Artists on Art;* Walker, Roslyn. *A Resource Guide to the Visual Arts of Afro-Americans,* South Bend, Ind., 1971.

GREEN, ROSE

Painter.
Exhibited: Tuskegee Institute; Atlanta Univ.
Awards: 1st prize, Tuskegee Institute Annual Exhibit; Atlanta Univ.
Sources: Ploski, Harry, & Ernest Kaiser. "The Black Artist," *Afro USA,* 1971; Ploski, Harry, Ernest Kaiser, & Otto Lindenmeyer. "The Black Artist," *Reference Library of Black America,* Book IV, 1971.

GREEN, SAMUEL L.

Painter, educator, museum curator. Curator of the Museum of Negro Art and Culture, Tuskegee Institute, Alabama.
Sources: Dover. *American Negro Art,* p. 39; Indiana Univ. *Fine Arts & the Black American;* Harley, Ralph, Jr. "A Checklist of Afro-Amer. Art & Artists," *The Serif,* Dec. 1970; Ploski, Harry, & Ernest Kaiser. "The Black Artist," *Afro USA,* 1971; Ploski, Harry, Ernest Kaiser, & Otto Lindenmeyer. "The Black Artist," *Reference Library of Black America,* 1971.

GREENE, BOB

Photographer.
Exhibited: Addison Gallery, 1971.
Sources: James Van DerZee Institute. *The Black Photographer (1908-1970): A Survey,* 1971.

GREENE, CLIFTON

Painter. Born in Bristol, Connecticut, 1948. Studied at the University of Hartford (BFA); Howard University (MFA).

Works: *Vivian* (oil); *Journey through Struggle* (oil); *In the Beginning God* (oil); *Thoughts on My Mind* (oil); *Self Portrait* (oil).

Exhibited: Push Expo, 1972; Hartford Arts Festival, 1971, 1972; Willa Hardgrow Mental Health Clinic Show, 1972; Through Young Black Eyes, 1970-2.

Collections: Hartford Chamber of Commerce; Allen Chapel Church; Mr. James Jackson.

Awards: Book Award, Hartford Arts Festival, 1971; Stax Art Award, Push Expo, 1972; Best in show, 1970, 1971, & Best in oils, 1970, Through Young Black Eyes.

Sources: Information from the artist; Berkman, Florence. "Message Differs in Black Art," *Times,* Hartford, Conn., June 15, 1970.

GREENE, DONALD O.

Painter, graphic artist. Born in Youngstown, Ohio in 1940. Studied at City College of San Francisco; San Francisco Academy of Art; California College of Arts and Crafts. Five year national art film made for educational TV; extensive experience in youth programs.

Works: *County Seat; Antelers; Untitled* (drawing).

Exhibited: Galleries throughout San Francisco Bay area; Oakland Museum Rental Gallery.

Collections: Oakland Museum.

Sources: Oakland Museum Archives; Lewis/Waddy. *Black Artists on Art,* Vol. 1; Walker, Roslyn. *A Resource Guide to the Visual Arts of Afro-Americans,* South Bend, Ind., 1971.

GREENE, LARRY C.

Photographer. Born in Philadelphia, 1945. Studied at Boston University (BA); Villanova University Law School.

Works: *Life's Window,* 1964; *Arc,* 1970; *Cone,* 1972.

Exhibited: Phila. Black Expo, 1970, 1971, 1972; Sunday in the Park, Boston, 1971, 1972; Book Festival, J. B. Hynes Auditorium, Boston, 1971, 1972; All World Celebration, Commonwealth Armory, Boston, 1971, 1972.

Collections: Phila. Black Expo Collection; Afro-Amer. Artists Collection, Germantown, Pa.

Awards: 2nd Award, Black Expo, most unusual use of media, 1964; 1st Award, Black Expo, most unusual use of media, 1970.

Member: Boston Artists Assn.; Afro-Amer. Artists, Inc.

Represented by: Boston Negro Artists Assn.

Sources: Information from the artist.

GREENE, MICHAEL B.

Graphic artist, mixed media. Born in Akron, Ohio, 1943. Studied at Karon Art Institute; San Francisco Art Institute (BFA).

Exhibited: San José City College, 1968; Oakland Museum, 1970.

Collections: Oakland Museum.

Sources: Oakland Museum Archives; "San Francisco," *Artforum,* Oct. 1970; Oakland Museum. *Black Untitled,* 1970.

GREENE, SAMUEL P.

Painter. Born in Boston, Massachusetts, 1928. Studied at the New York School of Music and Art; Vesper George Art School.

Works: *The Rice Planters,* 1968; *The Toilers,* 1972; *The Lord Is My Shepherd,* 1970; *Black Christ,* 1970; *Seascape,* 1970; *They Tilled the Fields; 400 Years and No More; Malcolm X at the Temple.*

Exhibited: Boston Negro Artists Assn. Annual, 1968-70.

Awards: 1st award, Boston Negro Artists Annual, 1968, 1969, 1970.

Member: Boston Negro Artists Assn.

Sources: Information from the artist.

GREENE, STEPHEN

Painter.

Sources: Ploski, Harry, Ernest Kaiser, & Otto Lindenmeyer. "The Black Artist," *Reference Library of Black America,* Book IV, 1971.

GREY, JOSEPH E.

Painter. Born in Lancaster, Ohio in 1927.

Works: *Bull and Fighter.*

Awards: 9th Annual Emily Lowe Competition.

Sources: Dover. *American Negro Art;* Indiana Univ. *Fine Arts & the Black American;* Pierre-Noel, Lois Jones. "American Negro Art in Progress," *Negro History Bulletin,* Oct. 1967; Harley, Ralph, Jr. "Checklist of Afro-American Art & Artists," *The Serif,* Dec. 1970; *The Negro Handbook,* composed by the editors of *Ebony,* Chicago, 1966; Walker, Roslyn. *A Resource Guide to the Visual Arts of Afro-Americans,* South Bend, Ind., 1971.

GREYSON, CONSTANCE WILLARD

Born in New Rochelle, New York in 1909. Studied at Hunter College.

Works: *Hazel: A Portrait; Donald: A Portrait; Inez: A Portrait; Self-Portrait.*

Exhibited: Harmon Foundation, 1933, 1935.

Sources: Harmon Foundation. *Negro Artists,* 1935; Harmon Foundation. *Exhibition of Productions by Negro Artists;* Harmon Foundation. *Non-Jury Exhibit of Works of Negro Artists,* 1933; Indiana Univ. *Fine Arts & the Black American;* Harley, Ralph, Jr. "A Checklist of Afro-Amer. Art & Artists," *The Serif,* Dec. 1970; DuSable Museum of African-Amer.

History. *Contemporary Black Artists,* Calendar, 1970; Walker, Roslyn. *A Resource Guide to the Visual Arts of Afro-Americans,* South Bend, Ind., 1971.

GRIFFIN, RON

Painter. Born in Chicago in 1938. Studied at Los Angeles City College; Otis Art Institute (BFA, MFA).
Works: *Untitled; The Middle Passage Series.*
Exhibited: Cal. State College, Los Angeles; Watts Art Exhibition; Citrus College; Brockman Gallery; Oakland Museum.
Awards: Watts Festival, 1971.
Collections: Oakland Museum.
Sources: Lewis/Waddy. *Black Artists on Art,* Vol. 2; Oakland Museum. *Black Untitled II,* 1971; *Art Week,* Vol. 2, No. 40; *San Francisco Chronicle,* Nov. 4, 1971; *San Francisco Examiner,* Nov. 4, 1971; Information from artist.

GRIGSBY, J. EUGENE, JR.

Painter, educator. Born in Greensboro, North Carolina, 1918. Studied at Morehouse College under Hale Woodruff (BA, 1938); Ohio State University (MA, 1940); New York University (PhD, 1963); American Artists School, New York; Philadelphia College of Art (Honorary DFA, 1964). Teacher at the Brussells World Fair, Belgium for the Museum of Modern Art (1958); Associate Professor, School of Fine Arts, Arizona State University.
Works: *Landscape; Episcopal Church; Yellow House; The Hunter; Fertility; Freedom Now; Brother; African Genesis; Study for No Vacancy; Specters; Love; Carolina Shack; Long Island Lumber; Circus Past; Girl in Green; Drop Outs; Saints & Sinners; Free Spirits; The Fallen One; Poverty Playground; Strange Figure; Freedom March; Right On; Antagonistic; Design for Mural; Madonna; Conflict; Boy; Ode to Shamba; Ominous; Cyclops I; Fusion; 2+Blue+X.*
Exhibited: Atlanta Univ., 1943, 1951; Phoenix Art Center, 1955 (1-man); Morehouse College, 1967; J.C. Smith Univ., 1966; Texas Southern Univ., 1966; Amer. Negro Exposition, Chicago, 1940; Dillard Univ., 1941; Smith-Mason Gallery, 1971.
Awards: Medallion of Merit, Gallery of Art, Washington, DC, 1966.
Sources: Dover. *American Negro Art;* Indiana Univ. *Fine Arts & the Black American;* Lewis/Waddy. *Black Artists on Art,* Vol. 1; Grigsby. "Art Education at Carver High," *Art Education Journal,* May 1954; Grigsby. "Teaching Children Art at the Brussells World Fair," *Pacific Arts Assn. Bulletin,* Fall 1958; Grigsby. *African Arts,* Heard Museum, Phoenix, Ariz.; Afro-American Slide Depository, Catalog; La Jolla Museum of Art. *Dimensions of Black;*

DuSable Museum of African-Amer. History. *Contemporary Black Artists,* 1970, Calendar; Tanner Art Galleries. *Art of the American Negro,* 1940; Dillard Univ. *Arts Festival,* 1941; Harley, Ralph, Jr. "Checklist of Afro-Amer. Art & Artists," *Serif,* Dec. 1970; *The Negro Handbook,* Composed by Editors of *Ebony,* Chicago, 1966; Myers, Carol L. *Black Power in the Arts,* Flint, Mich., 1970; Smith-Mason Gallery. *National Exhibition Black Artists,* 1971; Walker, Roslyn. *A Resource Guide to the Visual Arts of Afro-Americans,* South Bend, Ind., 1971.

GRIST, RAYMOND

Painter. Born in New York City, January 31, 1939. Studied at the Art Students League (1959); New School for Social Research (1960); Printmakers Workshop (1970); School for Visual Arts (1972).
Works: *Family Group; Landscape; Oil.*
Exhibited: 100 Flowers Gallery, 1967; Studio Museum in Harlem, 1970; Dieerste Mahlerwoche in Eisenstadt, Austria, 1969; Shooting Star Gallery, 1971 (1-man); Cinque Gallery, 1971 (1-man).
Collections: Eisenstadt Museum, Austria.
Sources: Studio Museum in Harlem. *African-American Extensions,* 1969; Afro-American Slide Depository, Catalog; Cinque Gallery. *Raymond Grist,* NY, Dec. 1971.

GROVE, JEAN DONNER

Sculptor.
Exhibited: Pyramid Club, Phila., 1952.
Sources: Drummond, Dorothy. "Coast-to-Coast," *Art Digest,* March 1, 1952; Pyramid Club. *12th Annual Invitational Exhibition,* Phila., 1952.

GUDGELL, HENRY

Sculptor. Gudgell was a slave in Missouri. His carved and whittled pieces were eventually brought to the attention of the art world and preserved.
Works: *Hardwood Stick.*
Sources: Dover. *American Negro Art;* Indiana Univ. *Fine Arts & the Black American;* Harley, Ralph, Jr. "Checklist of Afro-Amer. Art & Artists," *Serif,* Dec. 1970; Thompson, Robert. "African Influence on the Art of the United States," *Black Studies in the University,* Armistead L. Robinson, ed., pp. 127-30; Walker, Roslyn. *A Resource Guide to the Visual Arts of Afro-Americans,* South Bend, Ind., 1971.

GUILFORD, JAMES E., JR.

Painter. Born in Boston in 1911. Studied at Northeastern University; Boston Center For Adult Education.
Works: *The Brook House & Brookline Village,* 1969; *Racine Point,* 1971; *Cliffs of Gay Head,*

1971; *Sea Street Docks,* 1971; *Hot Pot Barbados,* 1971; *Lady Resting,* 1970; *Serenity,* 1968; *Eggs,* 1968; *Aruba Beach,* 1970; *Semi-Nude,* 1970; *Floral,* 1968; *The Fruit,* 1968; *Bouquet* (oil); *Chinese Boy* (oil); *Jamaicaway* (oil); *Aruba* (watercolor); *Gayhead* (oil); *Beach Scene* (oil).
Exhibited: Boston Adult Center, 1970, 1971, 1972; Boston Negro Artists Assn, 1971, 1972; Whole World Celebration, Commonwealth Armory, Boston, 1972; Boston Public Library, 1973.
Represented by: Boston Negro Artists' Assn.
Sources: Information from artist; Boston Negro Artists' Assn. *10th Anniversary Exhibition,* 1973, Boston Public Library; Boston Negro Artists' Assn. *The Black Artist in America: A Negro History Month Exhibition,* Boston Public Library, 1973.

GUNN, THEODORE D.

Painter. Born in Saugerties, New York, 1932.
Works: *Faces of the Prophets; Easter Morning,* 1970.
Exhibited: Greenwich Village Outdoor Exhibit; Countee Cullen Library, NY; Congregational Church of Long Island; Blumstein's Dept. Store, NY; Library Music Store, NY; Harlem Hospital Cultural Showcase Festival, 1967; River-View Towers, NY, 1967; Drew Hamilton Houses, 1967; Harlem Social Services Center, 1967; Collegiate School for Boys, NY, 1968; Barnard College, 1968; Community Church Art Gallery, 1969; Unitarian Church, Paramus, NJ, 1969; Amer. Internat'l College, Springfield, Mass., 1969; Black Arts Festival, New Rochelle, 1969; Abacus Gallery, Providence, RI, 1969; Muhlenberg College, Pa., 1970; Harlem Out-door Afro-Amer. Arts Festival, 1970; Bowdoin College, Me., 1970; Black Awareness Week, *The Afro-American,* Springfield, Mass., 1969; Manhattan College, 1970; Impact Africa, 1970; Brooklyn Museum, 1972; Manufacturers-Hanover Trust Co., NY, 1972; Medgar Evers College, Brooklyn, 1972; Seventh Day Adventist Church, NY (1-man); Lang and Merbin Art Gallery, NY (1-man); Summer Art Festival of Antioch Baptist Church of Brooklyn (1-man); St. James Towers (1-man); Bowery Savings Bank, NY (1-man); Roosevelt Hotel, 1965 (1-man); Board of Education District #6 Schools, 1966 (1-man); Neighborhood Board #2, NY, 1966 (1-man); Yonkers Public Library, 1966 (1-man); Kenwood Riter Dept. Store, NY; NY Bank for Savings (1-man); Afro-Amer. Arts Festival, Mt. Vernon; St. John the Baptist Church, NY; Rutgers Univ.; Madison Gallery, Brooklyn; Bowdoin Afro-Amer. Society, 1969.
Collections: Seventh Day Adventist Church, Bronx, NY.

Sources: McCarthy, Nancy. "Harlem Welfar Center is Folk Art Showcase," *Sunday News* NYC, Jan. 15, 1967; Glueck, Grace. "Harlem Initiated First Art Museum," *New York Times* Sept. 25, 1968; Glueck, Grace. "A Very Ow Thing in Harlem," *New York Times,* Nov. 15 1968; "Haitian Artists in Museum Show," *Afro-American* (NJ edition), Feb. 8, 1969 Berkley, Roy. "Harlem Uptown Art Scene," *Manhattan Tribune,* Feb. 22, 1969; Schwartz Theresa. "Black Art, White Eye," *New York Element,* March 21, 1969; Glueck, Grace "Less Downtown Uptown," *New York Times* July 20, 1969; Genauer, Emily. "Art and th Artist," *New York Post,* Aug. 2, 1969; Moore William. "Former Slaves, New Art," *Manhattan Tribune,* Aug. 16, 1969; Schjeldahl Peter. "Alive with Strength and Variety of it Passions," *New York Times,* Aug. 31, 1969 "New AIC Afro-American Cultural Cente Opens," *Springfield Union,* Mass., Sept. 29 1969; Springer, David. "Black Art: A Cul tural Bridge," *Sunday Record Call,* Paramus NJ, Nov. 2, 1969; Berkman, Florence. "Verve Vitality in Harlem Art Show," *Hartford Times* March 4, 1970; "Black Artists Reflect Trouble Culture," *New Haven Register,* April 12, 1970 Ross, David. "Junior Lake Art Show," *York towner,* Aug. 27, 1970; Community Churcl Art Gallery. "A Tribute to the Life of Dr Martin Luther King Jr.," NYC, 1969; Infor mation from the artist.

GYLBERT

Painter, mixed media, printmaker. Born i New York City, May 14, 1944. Studied a the Universidad de Mexico; Pratt Institut (BFA).
Works: *Lady in Red,* 1971 (acrylic); *20th Century Foxes,* 1971 (acrylic); *Untitled,* 197 (acrylic); *My Mommie,* 1971 (acrylic/shells) *My Man,* 1971 (acrylic); *Portrait* (acrylic).
Exhibited: Internat'l House, 1971 (3-man) Weusi Gallery, 1971; Where We at Blac Women Artists, 1972; Pax Gallery, 1972 Community Church Art Gallery, 1972; Inter nat'l Artists for the Defense of Angela Davis 1972; NY Public Theatre, 1972.
Member: Where We at Black Women Artists.
Sources: Information from artist; Where W at Black Women Artists. *Cookin & Smokin* 1972, Unpublished list; Internat'l House. *Three Afro-American Artists,* 1971, Unpublished list

HAIG, CHARLES T.

Painter.
Works: *Wabash and Thirty-Fourth Streets Dead End; View of the River; Landscape Bernard; Walter; Mulatto Nude; White Bo: Car; Late Summer.*
Exhibited: Atlanta Univ., 1944; Howard Univ. 1941; South Side Community Art Center, 1941

945; McMillen Inc. Galleries, NY, 1941.
Collections: Dr. & Mrs. Roscoe F. Singleton.
Sources: Locke, Alain. "Chicago's New Southide Art Center," Aug. 1941; "Art by Negroes," *Art Digest,* Oct. 15, 1941; Howard Univ. *Exhibition of Negro Artists of Chicago at Howard Univ. Gallery of Art,* 1941; DuSable Museum of African-Amer. History. *Contemporary Black Artists,* 1970 Calendar; Harley, Ralph, Jr. "Checklist of Afro-Amer. Art & Artists," *Serif,* Dec. 1970; South Side Community Art Center. *Chicago Collectors Exhibit of Negro Art,* Chicago, 1945; South Side Community Art Center. *National Negro Art Exhibition,* Chicago, 1941; South Side Community Art Center. *Opening Exhibition of Paintings by Negro Artists,* Chicago, 1941; McMillen Inc. Galleries. *Contemporary Negro Art,* NY, 1941.

HAILE, ALLEN
Sources: Harley, Ralph, Jr. "Checklist of Afro-Amer. Art & Artists," *The Serif,* Dec. 1970.

HAILSTALK, JOHN
Painter. Born in Virginia, 1894. Self-taught.
Works: *Little Farm; A Happy Day; Winter Day.*
Exhibited: Harmon Foundation, 1929; Smithsonian Institution, 1929.
Sources: Dover. *American Negro Art;* Harmon Foundation. *Exhibition of Productions by Negro Artists;* Indiana Univ. *Fine Arts & the Black American;* Afro-American Slide Depository, Catalog; Harmon Foundation. *Negro Artists,* 1935; DuSable Museum of African-Amer. History. *Contemporary Black Artists,* 1970 Calendar; Smithsonian Institution. *Painting & Sculpture by American Negro Artists,* 1929; Porter. *Modern Negro Art;* Harley, Ralph, Jr. "Checklist of Afro-Amer. Art & Artists," *Serif,* Dec. 1970; Walker, Roslyn. *A Resource Guide to the Visual Arts of Afro-Americans,* South Bend, Ind., 1971.

HAINES, CHARLES E.
Painter, commercial artist, educator, graphic artist. Born in Louisville, Kentucky, 1925. Studied at Indiana University (AB, MA, MFA).
Works: *The Hold City,* 1951 (oil); *Oriental Joy,* 1961 (oil/casein); *Hiroshima Images,* 1962 (oil); *Sunday Morning* (gouache); *Africa Images,* 1968 (mixed media); *African Images,* 1970 (mixed media); *The Clown,* 1952 (wood print); *Lazarus,* 1960 (pen & ink).
Exhibited: Ky. State Fair, 1951, 1955, 1956, 1961, 1963, 1970; Ind. State Fair, 1956, 1962, 1968, 1969; Art Center Assn., Louisville; Mid-States Exhibition, Evansville, Ind.; Ind. Artists Show; Atlanta Univ.
Collections: Commonwealth of Kentucky; Atlanta Univ.; Mr. Gene Sherman, Greenwich, Conn.
Awards: Ky. State Fair Grand Prize, 1961; Ind. State Fair Grand Prize, 1962; 3rd prize, Atlanta Univ.; 3rd prize, 1951, 1st & 2nd prizes, 1955, Ky State Fair; 2nd prize, Ind. State Fair, 1956.
Member: College Art Assn. of America.
Sources: Atlanta Univ. Exhibition Files; Indiana Artist Show Catalogues; Indianapolis Art Assn. Files; Information from the artist; *Ebony,* April 1957; Spradling, Mary M., ed. *In Black and White: Afro-Americans in Print.*

HALL, ALEXANDER
Painter. Worked in Atlanta, Georgia.
Works: *The Road Back.*
Exhibited: Atlanta Univ., 1943.
Sources: Atlanta Univ. Exhibition Files.

HALL, ANN
Painter. Studied at Douglass College, New Jersey; and under Aiko Yamaguchi, Tokyo, Japan.
Exhibited: Showcase Gallery, Washington, DC, 1973.
Sources: *Black Shades,* Vol. 3, #2.

HALL, CHARLES
Educator, commercial artist. Born in Anderson, South Carolina. Studied at Carnegie Mellon University (BFA). Teacher at Point Park College; Community College of Allegheny County. Staff artist at Carnegie Institute Library; Art Director, Kingsley Association.
Member: Pittsburgh Society of Artists; Assoc. Artists of Pittsburgh; Pittsburgh Council for the Arts; Board, Pittsburgh Plan for Art.
Sources: Pittsburgh Community College. *16 Black Artists.*

HALL, JAMES
Sculptor.
Works: *Number 7; Standing Figure.*
Exhibited: Tanner Art League, 1922.
Collections: National Archives.
Sources: Afro-American Slide Depository, Catalog, 1971-72; Harley, Ralph, Jr. "Checklist of Afro-Amer. Art & Artists," *The Serif,* Dec. 1970; Myers, Carol L. *Black Power in the Arts,* Flint, Mich., 1970.

HALL, JULIA
Studied at Spelman College.
Works: *Winter's Delight.*
Exhibited: Sun Times/Daily News Gallery, Chicago, 1970.
Sources: United Negro College Fund. *Art 1970,* Chicago, 1970.

HALL, WES
Painter. Born in Toledo, Ohio in 1934. Studied at Toledo Museum of Art School; University

of California, Los Angeles; Art Center School of Design; California State College (BA, 1960). Design illustrator for Vignette Films, Los Angeles.
Works: *Monumental Man; Awareness.*
Sources: Lewis/Waddy. *Black Artists on Art;* Walker, Roslyn. *A Resource Guide to the Visual Arts of Afro-Americans,* South Bend, Ind., 1971.

HALLOWAY, M. JENNELSIE WALDEN

Painter, printmaker, educator. Born in Atlanta, Georgia. Art teacher at Spelman College.
Works: *Nude; Stage; In a World Alone.*
Exhibited: Atlanta Univ., 1944.
Sources: Atlanta Univ., catalog, 1944; Woodruff, Hale. "Negro Artists Hold 4th Annual in Atlanta," *Art Digest,* Apr. 1945; *Art News,* Apr. 15, 1945, p. 8-9; Kiah, Virginia. "Black Artists," *Savannah Magazine,* Apr. 1972, p. 16.

HAMMERS, RONALD

Photographer.
Works: *4 photos* (black & white photographs).
Collections: Oakland Museum.
Sources: Oakland Museum Archives.

HAMMONS, DAVID

Painter. Born in Springfield, Illinois, 1943. Studied at Los Angeles City College; Los Angeles Trade Technical College; Chouinard Art Institute; Otis Art Institute.
Works: *Injustice Case,* 1970 (mixed media); *Print #5 (Bread); Wine Leading the Wine; Back to Black; Flag Day; America the Beautiful; American Hang Up; East Side West Side,* 1969; *A Cry from the Inside,* 1969; *Man in Grass,* 1970; *Black First, American Second,* 1970; *Sexy Sue; Spade; Stars on Sleeve; Close Your Eyes and See Black,* 1970.
Exhibited: Inglewood Library; Laguna Beach Art Assn.; Nat'l Council of Jewish Women; Los Angeles County Museum, 1971; Illinois Bell Telephone, 1971; Illinois Bell Telephone Traveling Show, 1971-72; Cal. State College, Los Angeles; Brockman Gallery (1-man).
Collections: Oakland Museum.
Sources: Lewis/Waddy. *Black Artists on Art;* Los Angeles County Museum. *Three Graphic Artists,* 1971; Illinois Bell Telephone. *Black American Artists/71,* 1972; Harley, Ralph, Jr. "Checklist of Afro-Amer. Art & Artists," *Serif,* Dec. 1970; Ploski, Harry, & Ernest Kaiser. "The Black Artist," *Afro USA,* 1971; Ploski, Harry, Ernest Kaiser, & Otto Lindenmeyer. "The Black Artist," *Reference Library of Black America,* Book 4, 1971. Atkinson, J. Edward. *Black Dimensions in Contemporary American Art,* NY, 1971; Oakland Museum Archives; Gaither, Edmund B. "The Evolution of the Afro-Amer. Artists," *Artists Proof,* Vol. 2; Young, Joseph. "Los Angeles," *Art Inter-*

national, Oct. 20, 1970, p. 74; Haas, Joseph. "A Big, Brilliant & Exciting Exhibition of Black Art," *Chicago Daily News,* Jan. 16-17, 1971; Walker, Roslyn. *A Resource Guide to the Visual Arts of Afro-Americans,* South Bend, Ind., 1971; *Time,* April 6, 1970, p. 80.

HAMPTON, CLARK

Sources: Harley, Ralph, Jr. "Checklist of Afro-Amer. Art & Artists," *The Serif,* Dec. 1970.

HAMPTON, HENRY E.

Filmmaker. President and founder of Blackside, Inc., film and television production company.
Works: Executive Producer, *"Nighttrain* (TV series); Commentator & Assoc. Producer of WGBH *Say Brother* series; Commentator for *TCB,* WNAC-TV, Boston; Producer of 2 films, Blackside, Inc.

HAMPTON, JAMES

Sculptor. Born in South Carolina, 1911. Died 1964.
Works: *Throne of the Third Heaven of the Nation's Millennium General Assembly.*
Exhibited: Abby Aldrich Museum, Williamsburg, Va.
Collections: Nat'l Collection of Fine Arts, Washington, DC.
Sources: Abby Aldrich Rockefeller Museum. *Throne of the Third Heaven of the Nation's Millennium General Assembly.*

HAMPTON, PHILLIP J.

Painter, educator, graphic artist. Born in Kansas City, Missouri, 1922. Studied at Citrus Junior College, Glendora, California; Kansas State University; Drake University; Kansas City University; Kansas City Art Institute (BFA, MFA). Teacher at Southern Illinois University.
Works: *Class Drawing; Young Girls of Savannah; The Harbinger; Bang, Abel; Sitting; Backyard Affair; The Butterfly Girls and the Now Now; Weekend Song; Boy in Alice's Now Land; Autobiography of Another Series 1970-,* unfinished, 32 pieces in progress; *A Crown of Thorns.*
Exhibited: Mid-Amer. Galleries, Kansas City, Mo., 1950 & 1952 (3-man); 44th Newport (RI) Annual Exhibit, 1955; Atlanta Univ., 1958; Telfair Academy, Savannah, Ga., 1959; National Watercolor & Print Competition, Knoxville, Tenn., 1964; Southeastern Exhibit of Prints, Jacksonville, Fla., 1964; Contemporary Southern Art Festival, Sears & Roebuck Co., Savannah, Ga., 1965; Lincoln Univ., 1966; Wellfleet Galleries, Palm Beach, Fla.; A&M Univ., 1968; Stephens College, Columbia, Mo.; Savannah Art Assn., 1969; Smith-Mason Gallery, 1971.

Collections: Kiah Gallery; Dr. & Mrs. Kenneth Payne, Compton, Cal.; Delta Sorority, Jefferson City, Mo.; Lincoln Univ.; Tuskegee Institute; Farmers & Merchants Bank, Brooklet, Ga.; Ga. Southern College, Statesboro.
Awards: 1st purchase prize, 4th Coastal Empire Arts Festival, Savannah, Ga.; 2nd prize, 1964, 2nd & 3rd prizes, 1966 & 1967, Contemporary Art Festival, Savannah, Ga. Best in Show Cash Award, Spring Art Festival, Jesup, Ga., 1967; Purchase Award, Beaux Arts Guild, Tuskegee Institute, 1967.
Member: Nat'l Conference of Artists; College Art Assn.; Amer. Federation of Art.
Represented by: Friedman's Art Store, Savannah, Ga.
Sources: Dover. *American Negro Art;* Lewis/Waddy. *Black Artists on Art;* Indiana Univ. *Fine Arts & the Black American;* "Afro-American Issue," *Art Gallery,* Apr. 1968; Information from artist; Myers, Carol L. *Black Power in the Arts,* Flint, Mich., 1970; *Who's Who in American Art,* 1952, 1970; *Dictionary of Art International; Who's Who in the South and Southwest; Who's Who in the Midwest; The Two Thousand Men of Achievement;* 1968 *Register of United States Living Artists;* Dover. *American Negro Art;* Thomas, Alma. "Phillip Hampton," *Savannah Morning News,* Magazine Section, Mar. 12, 1967; Haulbrook, James. *Search for Soul,* 1969; Atkinson, Edward. *Black Dimensions in Contemporary American Art;* Hampton, Phillip. "Modern Art—The Celebration of Man's Freedom," *Savannah State College Bulletin,* Research edition, Dec. 1966; Hampton, Phillip. "An Approach to Art for Pre-adults," *Savannah State College Bulletin,* Research edition, Dec. 1963; Hampton, Phillip. "Impressions of College Art," *Savannah State College Bulletin,* Research edition, Oct. 1956; Smith-Mason Gallery. *National Exhibition Black Artists,* 1971; DuSable Museum of African-Amer. History. *Contemporary Black Artists,* 1970 Calendar; Harley, Ralph, Jr. "Checklist of Afro-Amer. Art. & Artists," *Serif,* Dec. 1970; Morsbach, Mabel. *The Negro in American Life;* Walker, Roslyn. *A Resource Guide to the Visual Arts of Afro-Americans,* South Bend, Ind., 1971.

HAMPTON, R. H.
Painter.
Exhibited: NY Public Library, 1921; Tanner Art League, 1922.
Sources: Harley, Ralph, Jr. "Checklist of Afro-Amer. Art & Artists," *Serif,* Dec. 1970; *1st Annual Exhibit of Books, Manuscripts, Paintings, Sculptures, etc. by the Negro Library Assn. at Carlton Ave. YMCA,* Aug. 7-16, 1918.

HANEY, WILBUR
Sources: Harley, Ralph, Jr. "Checklist of Afro-

Amer. Art & Artists," *The Serif,* Dec. 1970.

HANNAH, JOEL
Sources: DuSable Museum of African-Amer. History. *Contemporary Black Artists,* 1970 Calendar.

HARDEN, MARVIN
Painter, graphic artist, educator. Born in Austin, Texas. Studied at Los Angeles City College; University of California at Los Angeles (BA, 1959, MA, 1963).
Works: *Increasingly Transparent: Red, White and Blue* (pencil); *The Uniqueness of Each Form Arises from the Fact that It Exists in Relation to Every Other Form; One Does Not Exclude Such Thoughts: They Simply Fall Away When Found to be Unnecessary; It Is the Business of Little Minds to Shrink,* 1970; *Prolong the Experience Without Jumping to Conclusions,* 1970; *Past, Present and Future Are Not, as Is Commonly Supposed, Stretched Out to Inaccessible Distances,* 1970; *There Were Trees Here Before, Now Horses, But Trees None the Less, Yet Horses Still; Perfectly Natural, Perfectly Human, & No Pulling & Stretching of Fancy Will Make It Otherwise,* 1970; *Hidden Behind Customs & Opinions: A Desire for Comfort; The Past Is Not Something Fixed and Unalterable; Poster Image; I Celebrate Topanga #10; The Field as Viewed from Here; A Fine and Private Place,* 1967 (drawing); *Little Boys Are Very Impressionable* (drawing); *Anecdotes; Some Horse Hair; I Celebrate Topanga #3; What Can One Say about a Life so Suddenly Rushed, Soonly Hushed,* 1970 (pencil); *A Fragment of the Cattle, with Buve in Mind,* 1968 (pencil on buff paper); *Melancholia #7,* 1964 (oil); *Peculiarly Subtle and Extremely Hard to Put into Words,* 1970 (pencil); *Ritual of Consumption —Delusion, Snare and Salient Flaw,* 1971 (pencil); *I Celebrate Topanga #5,* 1965 (pencil).
Exhibited: Occidental College, Los Angeles, 1968-9 (1-man); Eugenia Butler Galleries, Los Angeles, 1971 (1-man); Los Angeles Harbor College, 1971 (1-man); Brand Library Art Center, Glendale, Cal., 1971 (1-man); Whitney Museum of Amer. Art, NY, 1971 (1-man); Western Wash. State College, Bellingham, 1965; Ceeje Galleries, 1964, 1966, 1967 (1-man); Newport Pavilion Gallery; Harbor College, Los Angeles, 1966; Cal. State College, Long Beach, 1967; Lytton Center of the Visual Arts, Los Angeles, 1967, 1968; Gallery Reese Palley, San Francisco, 1969; Municipal Gallery, San Pedro, Cal., 1969; La Jolla Museum (Cal.), 1969, 1970; Nat'l Drawing Exhibition, San Francisco Museum of Art; Los Angeles City College; Cal. State College, Los Angeles, 1970; 8th Annual Southern Cal. Exhibition; Long Beach Museum of Art, 1970; Touring Exhi-

bition in the USSR organized by US State Dept., 1966; UCLA; Univ. of Cal. at Davis; San Diego Fine Arts Gallery, 1966; Oakland Art Museum, 1966; Laguna Beach Art Gallery, 1972; Minneapolis Institute of Art, 1969; High Museum of Art, Atlanta, 1969; Flint (Mich.) Institute of Art, 1969; Everson Museum of Art, Syracuse, 1969; Contemporary Arts Museum, 1970; NJ State Museum, 1969-70; IBM Gallery of Arts & Sciences, NY, 1969; Rhode Island School of Design, 1969; Memorial Art Gallery, Rochester, NY, 1969; Roberson Center for the Arts & Sciences, Binghamton, NY, 1970; The Art Galleries, Univ. of Cal. at Santa Barbara, 1970; American Express Pavilion, NY World's Fair, 1964; Southern Cal. Exposition, Del Mar, Cal.; Phila. Civic Center 1969; Westside Jewish Community Center; Los Angeles Art Assn.; Western Wash. State College; San Pedro Municipal Gallery, 1969; Irving Blum Gallery, 1972 (1-man); Univ. Art Museum, Berkeley, Cal., 1971; Rath Museum, Geneva, 1971; Los Angeles County Museum, 1969; 16th All City Art Festival, Los Angeles, 1968.

Collections: Whitney Museum of Amer. Art, NY; The Berkeley Museum; The Museum of Modern Art, NY; Metromedia, Inc., Los Angeles; Westside Jewish Community Center; San Diego Jewish Community Center; Dr. Leon O. Banks; Ms. Eugenia Butler; Mr. Connor Everts; Ms. Naomi Hirshhorn; Mr. Josine Ianco; Mr. Ben Sakofuchi; Ms. Roslind Wholden.

Awards: 1st Prize, Univ. of Judaism Invitational Art Exhibition, Los Angeles, 1969; San Diego Jewish Community Center, 1st Purchase Prize, 1966; Downey Museum, Honorable Mention, 1965; Westside Jewish Community Center, Purchase Prize, 1964; Graduate Art Council Award, UCLA Art Council; Teaching Assistantship in Art, UCLA; Annual All Univ. of Cal. Art Exhibit, 1964; Honorary Art Society, UCLA, 1959; Los Angeles City College, Academic Honor Student, 4 semesters.

Sources: "Afro-American Issue," *Art Gallery*, Apr. 1968; Indiana Univ. *Fine Arts and the Black American;* Afro-American Slide Depository, Catalog; Minneapolis Institute of Arts. *30 Contemporary Black Artists;* Long Beach Museum of Art. *8th Annual Southern California Exhibition,* 1970; San Francisco Museum of Art. *1970 National Drawing Exhibition,* 1969; La Jolla Museum. *The California Landscape Then and Now,* 1969; San Pedro Municipal Gallery. *Familiar Objects,* 1969; Lytton Center of the Visual Arts. *Mini Things,* Los Angeles, 1968; Lytton Center of the Visual Arts. *4th Annual California Print Exhibition and Young Talent in Graphics,* Los Angeles, 1967; Newport Pavilion Gallery. *Collector's Show '66,* 1966; Laguna Beach Art Gallery.

Artists Prints—Southern California, 1972; UCLA Art Galleries. *The Negro in American Art;* DuSable Museum of African-Amer. History. *Contemporary Black Artists,* calendar, 1970; Musée Rath. *8 Artistes Afro-Americains,* Geneve; Harley, Ralph, Jr. "Checklist of Afro-American Art and Artists," *The Serif,* Dec. 1970; Atkinson, J. Edward. *Black Dimensions in Contemporary American Art,* NY, 1971; Ruder & Finn Fine Arts. *Contemporary Black Artists,* NY, 1969; Myers, Carol L. *Black Power in the Arts,* Flint, Mich., 1970; Information from artist; Walker, Roslyn. *A Resource Guide to the Visual Arts of Afro-Americans,* South Bend, Ind., 1971.

HARDIE, ARTHUR

Painter. Born in New York in 1930. Studied at the Art Students League, New York. Lives and works in Stockholm.
Works: *Christ.*
Exhibited: Den Frie, Copenhagen; NY Public Library, 1950, 1952; YWCA Gallery, 1952; Gallery Aestetica, 1964.
Sources: Den Frie. *10 American Negro Artists Living & Working in Europe,* Catalog, 1964; Harley, Ralph, Jr. "A Checklist of Afro-Amer. Art & Artists," *The Serif,* Dec. 1970; Dunbar, Ernest, ed. *Black Expatriates,* pp. 201-6; Spradling, Mary M., ed. *In Black & White: Afro-Americans in Print.*

HARDISON, BUIST

Studied at Fisk University.
Works: *Heard Sound; Who Us?; Requiem; And We Spoke of Jai-B; Conversation with Duke E and Count B.*
Exhibited: Sun Times/Daily News Gallery, Chicago, 1970.
Sources: United Negro College Fund. *Art 1970,* Chicago, 1970.

HARDISON, INGE

Sculptor, painter, educator. Teacher at Hunter College, High School Art Department; Haryou Act Anti-Poverty Program.
Works: *Mother and Child; Negro Giants of History.*
Collections: Mt. Sinai Hospital, NYC.
Member: Black Academy of Arts & Letters (co-founder).
Sources: A&T Univ. Lyceum Program. *15 Afro-American Women.*

HARDRICK, JOHN WESLEY

Painter. Born in Indianapolis, 1891. Studied at John Herron Art Institute; under William Forsyth, Otto Stark.
Works: *Marguerite; Doris; Civil War Veteran; Jesus of Nazareth; Aunty; Little Brown Girl; Col. Ward; Evans Woollen; Portrait of Mrs. W.E. Brown; Portrait of K.K. McComb; Sy-*

donia; Hallie Mas; Self Portrait; A Portrait; Betty; Two Boys Fishing; Hetty; Judge X; Civil War Veteran.

Exhibited: Harmon Foundation, 1927-31, 1933; Chicago Art Institute, 1932; Amer. Negro Exposition, Chicago, 1940; Smithsonian Institution, 1929.

Awards: Bronze Award, Harmon Foundation, 1927; Outstanding Work & Outstanding Portrait Size Awards, Ind. State Exhibition, 1933.

Member: Ind. Art Assn.

Sources: Tanner Art Galleries. *Art of the American Negro,* 1940; *Who's Who in American Art,* 1940-41; Locke. *The Negro in Art;* Harmon Foundation. *Exhibition of Productions by Negro Artists;* Benezit. *Dictionnaire Des Peintres, Sculpteurs, Dessinateurs et Graveurs,* 1948; Dover. *American Negro Art;* Mallett. *Index of Artists;* Indiana Univ. *Fine Arts & the Black American;* Chicago Art Institute. *The Negro in Art Week;* Harmon Foundation. *Non-Jury Exhibit of Works of Negro Artists,* 1933; Harmon Foundation. *Negro Artists,* 1935; Harmon Foundation. *Exhibit of Fine Arts,* 1930; DuSable Museum of African-Amer. History. *Contemporary Black Artists,* 1970 Calendar; Harmon Foundation. *Select Picture List;* Smithsonian Institution. *Painting & Sculpture by American Negro Artists,* 1929; FLK. "American Negroes as Artists," *Survey,* Sept. 1, 1928, pp. 648-9; "Harlem Library Shows Negro Art," *Art News,* May 20, 1933, p. 14; "The Young Sailor," *Chicago Art Institute Scrapbook,* Nov. 1929/Sept. 1930, p. 139; Harley, Ralph, Jr. "Checklist of Afro-Amer. Art & Artists," *Serif,* Dec. 1970; *The Negro Handbook,* Composed by Editors of *Ebony,* Chicago, 1966; Schatz, Walter. *Directory of Afro-American Resources,* 1970; Roberts, Evangeline. "Praise Work of Two Young Ind. Artists," *Chicago Defender,* Aug. 16, 1924; Walker, Roslyn. *A Resource Guide to the Visual Arts of Afro-Americans,* South Bend, Ind., 1971.

HARLESTON, EDWIN AUGUSTUS

Painter, muralist. Born in Charleston, South Carolina, 1882; died May 5, 1931. Studied at Atlanta University (AB, 1904); Boston Museum of Fine Arts School (1906-12); Harvard University. Pioneer in Negro portraiture.

Works: *Portrait Study; Magnolia Gardens; The Pool; Entrance to Magnolia Gardens; Old Church; Old Lady with Bandana; Old War Veteran; A Charlestonian; The Artist's Father; Head of a Child; The Old Servant; The Bible Student; Pierre S. Dupont; Murals, Fisk Univ. Library; The Servant; Portraits of Mr. & Mrs. Jesse Binga; Lady with African Shawl; Old Colonel; The Doughboy; The Veteran; Oil Portrait: Mrs. Harleston; Portrait of Aaron Douglas.*

Exhibited: Harmon Foundation, 1928, 1931, 1936; Texas Centennial, 1936; Howard Univ., 1935, 1937; City College of NY, 1967; National Gallery of Art, 1930, 1933; Downtown Gallery, 1942; South Side Community Art Center, Chicago, 1941, 1945.

Collections: Fisk Univ.; Howard Univ.; Nat'l Archives; Mr. William P. Harrison.

Awards: Amy E. Spingarn Prize, *Crisis;* Harmon Foundation, 1931.

Sources: Dover. *American Negro Art;* Locke. *The Negro in Art;* Harmon Foundation. *Exhibition of Productions by Negro Artists;* Indiana Univ. *Fine Arts & the Black American;* City College of NY. *The Evolution of Afro-American Artists 1800-1950;* Chicago Art Institute. *The Negro in Art Week,* 1932; Winslow, Vernon. "Negro Art and the Depression," *Opportunity,* Feb. 1941; Allison, Madeline G. "Harleston: Who Is E.A. Harleston?," *Opportunity,* Jan. 1924; *Chicago Institute Scrapbook,* Aug. 1927/Mar. 1928, p. 62; Harley, Ralph, Jr. "Checklist of Afro-Amer. Art & Artists," *Serif,* Dec. 1970; Porter. *Modern Negro Art;* Afro-American Slide Depository, Catalog, 1971-72; Assn. for the Study of Negro Life & History. *Exhibition of Works by Negro Artists,* 1933; Howard Univ. *Art of the American Negro,* 1937; Brawley, Benjamin. *The Negro Genius;* Texas Centennial Exposition. *Thumbnail Sketches of Exhibiting Artists,* 1936; Roucek/Kiernan. *The Negro Impact on Western Civilization; Who's Who in Colored America,* 3rd edition; Harmon Foundation. *Negro Artists,* 1935; Harmon Foundation. *Select Picture List;* "Harmon Foundation Exhibit," *Art Digest,* Feb. 15, 1931, p. 7; "American Negro Art Given Full Length Review in NY Show," *Art Digest,* Dec. 15, 1941; Pierre-Noel, Lois Jones. "American Negro Art in Progress," *Negro History Bulletin,* Oct. 1967; *American Magazine of Art,* Sept. 1931; Greene, Carroll, Jr. *Afro-American Artists: 1800-1968,* Slides; Porter, James. "Negro Artists Gain Recognition after Long Battle," *Pittsburgh Courier,* July 29, 1950; Brawley, Benjamin. *The Negro Literature & Art in the US;* Brown, Marion. "The Negro in the Fine Arts," *The Negro Heritage Library,* Vol. 2; Ploski, Harry, Ernest Kaiser. "The Black Artist," *Afro USA,* 1971; Ploski, Harry, Ernest Kaiser, & Otto Lindenmeyer. "The Black Artist," *Reference Library of Black America,* Book 4, 1971; DuSable Museum of African-Amer. History. *Contemporary Black Artists,* 1970 Calendar; "Race Artist to Paint Portrait of Rich Doner," *Afro-American,* Baltimore, Nov. 15, 1924; South Side Community Art Center. *Chicago Collectors Exhibit of Negro Art,* 1945; South Side

Community Art Center. *National Negro Art Exhibition*, 1941; Walker, Roslyn. *A Resource Guide to the Visual Arts of Afro-Americans*, South Bend, Ind., 1971.

HARMON, BERNARD

Works: *An American Landscape; Stars and Stripes Forever; Untitled.*
Exhibited: Phila. Civic Center.
Sources: Phila. Division of Art. *Afro-American Artists 1800-1969.*

HARPER, ROBIN

Painter.
Works: *Jack Johnson* (acrylic).
Collections: Johnson Pub. Co.
Sources: Johnson Pub. Co. *The JPC Art Collection,* Pamphlet.

HARPER, WILLIAM A.

Painter. Born December 27, 1873 near Cayuga, Canada. Died March 27, 1910 in Mexico City. Studied at Art Institute of Chicago (1895-1901, 2nd honors); studied under H.O. Tanner in Paris (1903-1907).
Works: *Landscape; Autumn Landscape; Afternoon at Montigny.*
Exhibited: Art Institute of Chicago, 1905, 1910; Fortnightly Club, 1908; Municipal Art League, Chicago, 1905, 1908; Howard Univ., 1970.
Awards: 1st Prize, Fortnightly Club.
Member: Western Artists Assn.; Assn. of Chicago Artists.
Collections: Providence Hospital; Mr. Charles Burkholder; Mr. Walter J. Sherwood; Mr. Max Keitz; Mrs. R. S. Brooke.
Sources: Mallett. *Index of Artists;* Locke. *The Negro In Art;* Dover. *American Negro Art;* Art. Inst. of Chicago. *The Negro in Art Week,* catalog; *Encyclopedia of the Arts; American Art Annual,* 1908; Ploski, Harry, ed. *Negro Almanac,* p. 626; Mich. State Library. *Biographical Sketches of Artists;* Indiana Univ. *Fine Arts & the Black American;* Butcher, Margaret J. *The Negro in American Culture,* p. 219; Afro-American Slide Depository, 1971-2 Catalog; Howard Univ. *James A. Porter Gallery of African-American Art,* 1970; DuSable Museum of African-American History. *Contemporary Black Artists,* calendar, 1970; Pierre-Noel, Lois Jones. "American Negro Art in Progress," *The Negro History Bulletin,* Oct. 1967; Brawley, Benjamin. *The Negro in Literature & Art in the US;* "William A. Harper," *Art Institute of Chicago Scrapbook,* Aug. 1900/ March 1901, p. 144; "Chicago Art Echoes," *American Art News,* Feb. 25, 1905; Bentley, Florence L. "William A. Harper," *Voice of the Negro,* Feb. 1906, p. 85; "William A. Harper," *Art Institute of Chicago Bulletin,* July 1910, p. 11; "The Showing of Mr. Harper's Work Was Interesting," *Art Institute of Chicago Bulletin,* Oct. 1910, p. 20; "William Harper," *Art Institute of Chicago Scrapbook,* Aug. 1927/Mar. 1928, p. 43; Harley, Ralph, Jr. "Checklist of Afro-American Art & Artists," *The Serif,* Dec. 1970; Porter, James A. "Negro Artists Gain Recognition After Long Battle," *Pittsburgh Courier,* July 29, 1950; Brown, Marion. "The Negro in the Fine Arts," *Negro Heritage Library,* Vol. 2; Ploski, Harry, Ernest Kaiser. "The Black Artist," *Afro USA,* 1971; Ploski, Harry, Ernest Kaiser, Otto Lindenmeyer. "The Black Artist," *Reference Library of Black America,* Book 4, 1971; Myers, Carol L. *Black Power in the Arts.* Flint, Mich., 1970; Spradling, Mary M., ed. *In Black & White: Afro-Americans in Print;* Holbrook, Francis C. "A Group of Negro Artists," *Opportunity,* July 1923, pp. 211-3; Walker, Roslyn. *A Resource Guide to the Visual Arts of Afro-Americans,* South Bend, Ind., 1971.

HARRELL, HUGH

Printmaker, sculptor. Born in Hampton, Virginia, July 22, 1926. Studied at Hampton Institute; Brooklyn Museum School.
Works: *Janie; Trope* (metal & cement); *Calloused Soul* (plaster); *The Junkie.*
Exhibited: Brooklyn Museum, 1969; Columbia Univ., 1969.
Collections: Oakland Museum.
Sources: Roelof-Lanner, T.V., ed. *Prints by American Negro Artists;* Brooklyn Museum. *New Black Artists,* 1969; Patterson, Lindsay, comp. "Contemporary Artists," *The Negro in Music and Art,* 1969; Oakland Museum Archives, Ruth Waddy Collection; Harlem Cultural Center. *New Black Artists,* 1969; Walker, Roslyn. *A Resource Guide to the Visual Arts of Afro-Americans,* South Bend, Ind., 1971.

HARRINGTON, HENRY "OL"

Sources: Porter. *Modern Negro Art;* Harley, Ralph, Jr. "Checklist of Afro-Amer. Art. & Artists," *The Serif,* Dec. 1970.

HARRINGTON, OLIVER WENDELL

Painter, cartoonist, illustrator, scene designer. Born in Valhalla, New York, 1913. Studied at the National Academy of Design; Yale University (BFA, 1938). Worked on WPA project; art editor of *The Peoples Voice.*
Works: Cover design, *Opportunity,* Dec. 1942; Illustrated *Hezekiah Horton.*
Sources: Harley, Ralph, Jr. "Checklist of Afro-Amer. Art & Artists," *Serif,* Dec. 1970; Dover. *American Negro Art;* "America's Socio-Artist," *Opportunity,* Dec. 1942; DuSable Museum of African-Amer. History. *Contemporary Black Artists,* 1970 Calendar; "Deep South," *Life,* 1940, p. 62 (Articles on Art Issue); Tarry, Ellen. *The Runaway Elephant,* NY, 1950;

Walker, Roslyn. *A Resource Guide to the Visual Arts of Afro-Americans,* South Bend, Ind., 1971.

HARRIS, CLARENCE
Exhibited: Pyramid Club, Phila., 1952.
Sources: Drummond, Dorothy. "Coast-to-Coast," *Art Digest,* Mar. 1, 1952, p. 12; Pyramid Club. *12th Annual Invitational Exhibition,* Phila., 1952.

HARRIS, DOUG
Photographer.
Works: *Saffi's Decision.*
Sources: Rose, Barbara. "Black Art in America," *Art in America,* July/Dec. 1970.

HARRIS, GILBERT S.
Painter. Born in 1931.
Works: *Nude.*
Exhibited: 9th Annual Emily Lowe Competition.
Awards: Emily Lowe Competition.
Sources: Indiana Univ. *Fine Arts & the Black American;* Dover. *American Negro Art;* Pierre-Noel, Lois Jones. "American Negro Art in Progress," *Negro History Bulletin,* Oct. 1967; Harley, Ralph, Jr. "Checklist of Afro-Amer. Art & Artists," *Serif,* Dec. 1970; Brown, Marion. "The Negro in the Fine Arts," *The Negro Heritage Library,* Vol. 2; Walker, Roslyn. *A Resource Guide to the Visual Arts of Afro-Americans,* South Bend, Ind., 1971.

HARRIS, JACK
Photographer.
Exhibited: Addison Gallery, 1971.
Sources: James Van DerZee Institute. *The Black Photographer (1908-1970): A Survey.*

HARRIS, JOHN TAYLOR
Painter, educator. Born in Philadelphia, 1908. Studied at Philadelphia College of Art (BAA, 1943); Temple University (MA). Teacher at Wharton Settlement, Philadelphia; Cheyney State College.
Works: *Portrait; Character Study; Portrait of Dr. James Duckrey, Former President of Cheyney State College,* 1967.
Exhibited: Pa. Academy of Fine Arts; Atlanta Univ.; Morgan State College; Harmon Foundation, 1933; Lea Contest Exhibit, 1931; Industrial Art School, 1928-32; Citizens Republican Club, 1931; YWCA, Phila., 1932-33; Whittier Centre, Phila., 1932; Wharton Settlement, 1931, 1943; Pittsburgh YMCA, 1960.
Collections: Nat'l Archives; Cheyney State College; Mercy Hospital, Phila.
Member: Alumni Assn., Phila Museum School of Industrial Arts; Chester County Art Assn.; Nat'l Conference of Artists; Phila. College of Art Alumni Assn.

Sources: Mallett. *Index of Artists;* Lewis/Waddy. *Black Artists on Art;* Indiana Univ. *Fine Arts & the Black American;* Harmon Foundation. *Exhibition of Productions by Negro Artists; Who's Who in American Art,* 1940-41; Harmon Foundation. *Non-Jury Exhibit of Works of Negro Artists,* 1933; Afro-American Slide Depository, Catalog, 1971-72; Harmon Foundation. *Negro Artists,* 1935; DuSable Museum of African-Amer. History. *Contemporary Black Artists,* 1970 Calendar; Harley, Ralph, Jr. "Checklist of Afro-Amer. Art & Artists," *Serif,* Dec. 1970; Pa. Academy of Fine Arts. *Watercolor Show,* 1934; James, John. *Storyland,* Missouri, Illustrator; Information from artist; Walker, Roslyn. *A Resource Guide to the Visual Arts of Afro-Americans,* South Bend, Ind., 1971.

HARRIS, OBLETON
Painter. Worked in Chicago and Detroit.
Works: *Marble Game; Self Portrait; Gathering Storm; Mother; Uncle Jim.*
Exhibited: Atlanta Univ., 1942-4.
Sources: Harley, Ralph, Jr. "Checklist of Afro-Amer. Art & Artists," *The Serif,* Dec. 1970.

HARRIS, ROMAINE
Ceramist. Active in 1960's.
Sources: *Negro Yearbook;* Indiana Univ. *Fine Arts & the Black American;* Walker, Roslyn. *A Resource Guide to the Visual Arts of Afro-Americans,* South Bend, Ind., 1971.

HARRIS, SCOTLAND
Printmaker.
Works: *Jazz Player* (woodcut); *Nude #3.*
Collections: Oakland Museum.
Sources: Roelof-Lanner, T.V., ed. *Prints by American Negro Artists;* Patterson, Lindsay, comp. "Contemporary Artists," *The Negro in Music and Art,* 1969; Oakland Museum Archives, Ruth Waddy Collection; Walker, Roslyn. *A Resource Guide to the Visual Arts of Afro-Americans,* South Bend, Ind., 1971.

HARRIS, THOMAS LISTON
Painter. Active in 1950's.
Sources: Dover. *American Negro Art;* Indiana Univ. *Fine Arts & the Black American;* DuSable Museum of African-Amer. History. *Contemporary Black Artists,* 1970 Calendar; Harley, Ralph, Jr. "Checklist of Afro-Amer. Art & Artists," *Serif,* Dec. 1970; Walker, Roslyn. *A Resource Guide to the Visual Arts of Afro-Americans,* South Bend, Ind., 1971.

HARRIS, WARREN
Painter, sculptor.
Works: *Recreation; Tugboat; Old Factories; Broadway Junction; Fulton Street on Sunday;*

Self-Portrait; Brooklyn Bridge; Southern Shadows; River Scene; Shipyard Activity; Grandfather; Approaching the Bridge; Boy in Overcoat; Jackie; Repose; Brooklyn Landscape; Head of a Child; Mattie; Warren, Jr.
Exhibited: West 135th St. Branch, NY Public Library (1-man); School of Visual Arts, 1970; Atlanta Univ.
Collections: Nat'l. Archives.
Awards: 1st prize, Atlanta Univ. 9th Annual Exhibit.
Sources: Afro-American Slide Depository, 1971-72 Catalog; *Amsterdam News,* Nov. 11, 1950; Harley, Ralph, Jr. "Checklist of Afro-Amer. Art & Artists," *Serif,* Dec. 1970; Brown, Evelyn S. "The Harmon Awards," *Opportunity,* Mar. 1933; Patterson, Lindsay. "Contemporary Artists," *The Negro in Music and Art,* 1969; Myers, Carol L. *Black Power in the Arts,* Flint, Mich., 1970; School of Visual Arts. *Black Artists 1970*; Mashek, Joseph. "Morris Louis, Rubin Gallery; Michael Steiner, Marlborough Gallery; Black Artists, Visual Arts Gallery," *Artforum,* Sept. 1970, pp. 79-80.

HARRISON, STARLIGHT
Painter. Self-taught.
Exhibited: Mr. Lincoln Gordon, Detroit, 1966; Normacel Gallery, Detroit, 1970 (1-woman).
Sources: Normacel Gallery, Detroit. *A Black Women Art Exhibit,* July 19, 1970.

HART, AGNES
Collections: NY Public Library-Schomburg Art Collection.
Sources: Schatz, Walter. *Directory of Afro-American Resources,* 1970.

HATCHER, GILBERT H.
Painter. Born in Augusta, Georgia, 1924. Self-taught.
Works: *Violent Water; Serenity; The Sax Player; Oreneco Sailboat; Atures Paric Landscape; Atowe; Convetti; Blue and White Study; Island Port; Non Objective Dropping; Hill Top House; Out of the Mist; Asian Monks; Floral Study #10; Town House; Winding Road; The Poodle; Blue Bolts; Red and Yellow Study; Maze; Untitled; Paddy Toilers; Beyond the Horizon; Gold Paddy,* 1965; *Spring Frolic,* 1967; *House in the Field,* 1965.
Exhibited: 22 West, 1964 (1-man); Charles Mann Gallery, 1966; Studio Museum in Harlem, 1969; Wells Gallery; Lisbon Art Show; Carver One Man Show, Beth Shalom, White Plains, NY; Tyringham Gallery, Tanglewood, NY; Huntington Hartford Museum of Modern Art; Harlem Research Center, 1967-68; Madison Gallery, City College of NY; Carnegie Institute; Hartford Univ.; Yale Univ.; Muhlenberg College, Allentown, Pa.
Collections: Atlanta Univ.; Mr. Roy Campa-

nella; Mr. Andrew Hilton; Ms. Rose Morgan; Los Angeles Museum; Nat'l. Archives; Langston Univ.; Alcorn A&M; Six Month Gallery, New Rochelle.
Awards: 1st prize, any subject, Atlanta Univ., 1965; 1st prize, landscape, Atlanta Univ., 1967.
Represented by: Charles Z. Mann Gallery, NYC.
Sources: Afro-American Slide Depository, Catalog; Studio Museum in Harlem. *Harlem Artists 69; New York Post,* May 2, 1966, Dec. 17, 1966; "Art News," *Newsweek,* April 1966; *Jet,* May 26, 1966; *NY Amsterdam News,* June 7, 1969; *Atlanta Daily World,* Mar. 30, 1965; Information from artist.

HATHAWAY, ISAAC SCOTT
Sculptor, ceramist, educator. Born on April 4, 1874, in Lexington, Kentucky. Studied at Chandler College, Lexington, Kentucky; Pittsburg College, Pittsburg, Kansas; New England Conservatory of Music. Head of Ceramics Department, Alabama State Teachers College, Montgomery.
Works: *Bust of Mary McLeod Bethune; Bust of Dr. Charles Drew.* Major works are portrait busts, the most famous of which are those of Frederick Douglass, Paul Laurence Dunbar and Booker T. Washington. He was commissioned to design memorial coins issued to honor Booker T. Washington and George Washington Carver.
Member: Ceramic Society; ATA American Assn. for the Advancement of Science.
Sources: *Negro Yearbook;* Indiana Univ. *Fine Arts & the Black American*; Furr, Arthur F. *History & Progress of Negroes in the US*; *Jet,* April 4, 1968, p. 11; Spradling, Mary M., ed. *In Black & White: Afro-Americans in Print*; *Negro Almanac,* p. 626; *Afro-American,* May 18, 1935; "Isaac Scott Hathaway: Artist & Teacher," *Negro History Bulletin,* Jan. 1958, p. 74; Ploski, Harry, & Ernest Kaiser. "The Black Artist," *Afro USA,* 1971; Ploski, Harry, Ernest Kaiser, & Otto Lindenmeyer. "The Black Artist," *Reference Library of Black America,* Book 4, 1971; Walker, Roslyn. *A Resource Guide to the Visual Arts of Afro-Americans,* South Bend, Ind., 1971.

HATHAWAY, ISAIAH
Works: *Dunbar; C.C. Spaulding; C.G. Woodson; M.C. Bethune; P.L. Dunbar; H.C. Trenholm; T.M. Campbell; N. Dett; W. Dawson; G.W. Carver; B.T. Washington & G.W. Carver; Hand of I.H. Hathaway; F.D. Bluford; Dr. E.C. Morris; Douglass; Mrs. Hathaway; I.H. Hathaway; Gen. B.O. Davis, St.; Dr. J.E. Walker; B.T. Washington; Dunbar.*
Collections: I.H. Hathaway Museum.
Sources: Afro-American Slide Depository, Catalog, 1971-72.

HAUPT, THEODORE J.

Collections: NY Public Library-Schomburg Art Collection.
Sources: Schatz, Walter. *Directory of Afro-American Resources*, 1970.

HAWELL, SAMUEL

Studied at Claflin College.
Exhibited: Sun Times/Daily News Gallery, Chicago, 1970.
Sources: United Negro College Fund. *Art 1970*, Chicago, 1970.

HAWKINS, EUGENE

Printmaker. Born in Los Angeles, 1933. Studied at Los Angeles City College; Los Angeles State College. Art director, Jazz Festival, Hollywood Bowl.
Works: *Take Note* (linocut); *To Find Nothing* (drawing).
Exhibited: Dickson Art Center, Los Angeles, 1966.
Collections: Oakland Museum.
Awards: Freedom Foundation Award; John Hay Whitney Fellowship, 1965.
Sources: Roelof-Lanner, T.V., ed. *Prints by American Negro Artists*; "Afro-American Issue," *Art Gallery*, April 1968; Indiana Univ. *Fine Arts & the Black American*; UCLA Art Galleries. *The Negro in American Art*; DuSable Museum of African-Amer. History. *Contemporary Black Artists*, 1970 Calendar; Harley, Ralph, Jr. "Checklist of Afro-Amer. Art & Artists," *Serif*, Dec. 1970; Oakland Museum Archives; Myers, Carol L. *Black Power in the Arts*, Flint, Mich., 1970; Walker, Roslyn. *A Resource Guide to the Visual Arts of Afro-Americans*, South Bend, Ind., 1971.

HAWKINS, MARCELLUS

Exhibited: NY Public Library, 1921.
Sources: Porter. *Modern Negro Art*; Harley, Ralph, Jr. "Checklist of Afro-Amer. Art & Artists," *The Serif*, Dec. 1970.

HAYDEN, FRANK

Sculptor, mosaicist, educator. Born in Memphis, Tennessee on June 10, 1934. Studied at Xavier University (BFA, 1957); Notre Dame University (MFA, 1959); Iowa State University (1959); Munich Art Academy (1959-60); Royal Academy, Copenhagen; Academy of Fine Arts, Stockholm (1967-8); Studied under Ivan Mestrovic; Heinrich Kirchner; Mogens Boggeld. Teacher of graphic arts at Xavier University (1961); Professor of Art at Southern University, Baton Rouge, Louisiana (1961-).
Works: *Frank; David; Group I; Adam & Eve; Where; Flight; Dam's Evenings; Protest; Family; Love Ring; Waiting; King; Dancer's Out; Why; In the Garden; Hands; Stations of the Cross;* 12 ft. relief of *Christ;* 5 ft. relief of *Madonna & Child;* 5 ft. mahogany corpus for crucifix; 8 ft. figure of *St. Joseph;* 7 ft. figure of *Madonna & Child;* 4 ft. relief of *The Annunciation;* 5 ft. figure for fountain *Christ of Living Waters;* 4 ft. relief of crucifixion; *The Nativity;* Baptismal Font, 5 ft. crucifix, 3 ft. relief of *Mary & Joseph;* 6 ft. figure of the *Holy Family;* 4 ft. cross; 5 ft. relief, *Commandments;* 5 ft. figure for reflection pool, *Christ of Living Waters;* 6 ft. figure of *Risen Christ.*
Exhibited: Xavier Univ., 1957, 1964 (1-man); South Bend Art Center, 1958 (1-man); Xavier Artists' Guild Show, 1959 (1-man); Young American 1959 Artists' Show, New Orleans; St. Paul's Church, Baton Rouge, La., 1962 (1-man); Southern Univ., Baton Rouge, La., 1962, 1967 (1-man); Old State Capitol Show, 1961-5; Vatican Pavilion, World's Fair, NY, 1965; Contemporary Christian Art Gallery, NY, 1965-6; Baton Rouge Gallery, 1966-7; La. State Univ. Union, 1967 (1-man); Catholic Life Center, Baton Rouge, La., 1967 (1-man); St. Pious X Church, Baton Rouge, La., 1967 (1-man).
Collections: St. John Fisher Church, Chicago; St. John Vianny School, North Lake, Ill.; St. Michael's Chapel, Torresdale, Pa.; St. Joseph Minor Seminary, Covington, La.; Mr. John L. Bartolomeo, AIA, Chicago; Father Judge Mission Seminary, Monroe, Va.; St. Paul's Church, Baton Rouge, La.; Immaculate Conception Church, Baton Rouge, La.; St. Mathilda's Church, Eunice, La.; St. Joseph's Cathedral, Baton Rouge, La.; Wesleyan Methodist Church, La. State Univ. Campus, Baton Rouge; St. Aloysius Church, Baton Rouge, La.; St. Benedict's Church, Grambling, La.
Awards: 4 yr. scholarship, Xavier Univ.; Henry Bynam Achievement Award; Xavier Univ. Service Award; Mother M. Agatha Award; graduate scholarship, Notre Dame Univ.; Assistantship, Iowa State Univ.; Fulbright Fellowship, Munich Academy of Art, 1959-60; Fulbright Fellowship Renewal offered for 2nd yr., 1960-1; Henrik Kaufman Award, 1963-4; Southern Fellowship Fund Grant for study in Stockholm, 1967-8; "The Ten Outstanding Young Catholics in America" roster, *Sign Magazine*, 1961; listed in "Outstanding Young Men in America," 1967.
Member: College Art Assn. of America; Amer. Society of Aesthetics.
Sources: Information from artist; Hayden, Frank. *Sketches in Black & White*, Branden Press, 1967; Afro-American Slide Depository, catalog; Johnson Pub. Co. *The JPC Art Collection*, Pamphlet; La. State Univ. *Exhibition of Sculpture*, 1965.

HAYDEN, KITTY L.

Painter. Born in Marlin, Texas, 1942. Studied

at Dorsey High School Adult Classes; B.J. Shyffer Workshop, Los Angeles.
Works: *Blue Landscape; Pink Landscape.*
Sources: Lewis/Waddy. *Black Artists on Art*; Walker, Roslyn. *A Resource Guide to the Visual Arts of Afro-Americans*, South Bend, Ind., 1971.

HAYDEN, PALMER C.

Painter. Born in Wide Water, Virginia, 1893. Studied at Cooper Union; Boothbay Colony, Maine, under Asa G. Randall; under M. Clivett LeFevre in Brittany, France (1927-32).
Works: *Faun Au Crepescule; Mother Goose Stories; Red Shoes; No Easy Riders; Fork of the Road at Midnight; Mitchie Stadium West Point; Baltimore; Baptizing Day; Fetiche et Fleurs; When Tricky Sam Shot "Father" Lamb; St. Servan, France; The Schooners; The Janitor Who Paints; Le Quai à Port Louis; Berry Pickers; Port Louis; Still Life—Fruits & Flowers; Midsummer Night in Harlem; The Carrousel; Cavalry Stables at Versailles; Back Yards; Brittany Marine; Café St. Servan, Paris; Concarneau; Cabanes des Pecheurs; Fishermen of Brittany; Raccoon up a Persimmon Tree; Picking up the Paper; Old Man Milking Cow; Fishing Boats & Houses; School Child; Blue Nile; At Haverstraw, NY; Auray-Balcaux Dr. Piches; Basin Street; The Cove; Portland, Maine; Along the Sheepscot River; Boothbay Harbor; St. Patrick's Cathedral; Virginia Teamster; Song & Dance Boy; Steers in Sage; Old Soldier Lost His Bet; The Blues Singer; Flotte de Peche; Le Matin; When John Was a Baby; Ballad of John Henry; Where'd You Git Them High Top Shoes; A Home in Brittany.*
Exhibited: Baltimore Museum, 1939; Howard Univ., 1937; Independent Artists in NY; Colonial Exposition, Paris; Cooperative Art Market, 1933; Harmon Foundation, 1928-33; Texas Centennial, 1936; Commodore Hotel, 1934; Civic Club, NY, 1926; Galeries Bernheim Jeune, 1937 (1-man); Roerich Museum, 1934; Amer. Negro Exposition, Chicago, 1940; Atlanta Univ., 1940, 1944; Whitney Museum; City College of NY, 1967; Smithsonian Institution, 1929, 1933; Newark Museum, 1971; Art Center, NYC, 1933; Harmon Foundation Traveling Show, 1934-35.
Collections: Fisk Univ.; Atlanta Univ.; Oakland Museum.
Awards: Harmon Gold Award in Fine Arts, 1926; Rockefeller Prize, 1933.
Sources: Baltimore Museum of Art. *Contemporary Negro*, 1939; Howard Univ. *Art of the American Negro*, 1937; Indiana Univ. *Fine Arts & the Black American*; Mallett. *Index of Artists*; Locke. *The Negro in Art*; Albany Institute of History & Art. *The Negro Artist Comes of Age*; Harmon Foundation. *Exhibition of Productions by Negro Artists*; Dover.

American Negro Art; "Afro-American Issue," *Art Gallery*, April 1968; Brawley, Benjamin. *The Negro Genius*; Texas Centennial Exposition. *Thumbnail Sketches of Exhibiting Artists*, 1936; City College of NY. *The Evolution of Afro-American Artists 1800-1950*; La Jolla Museum of Art. *Dimensions of Black*; Assn. for the Study of Negro Life & History. *Exhibition of Works by Negro Artists*, 1933; Tanner Art Galleries. *Art of the American Negro*, 1940; Locke, Alain. "Advance on the Art Front," *Opportunity*, May 1939; Harley, Ralph, Jr. "Checklist of Afro-Amer. Art & Artists," *Serif*, Dec. 1970; Porter. *Modern Negro Art*; Butcher, Margaret Just. *The Negro in American Culture*, p. 232; Harmon Foundation. *Negro Artists*, 1935; Harmon Foundation. *Exhibit of Fine Arts*, 1930; Harmon Foundation. *Non-Jury Exhibit of Works of Negro Artists*, 1933; Newark Museum. *Black Artists: Two Generations*, 1971; DuSable Museum of African-Amer. History. *Contemporary Black Artists*, 1970 Calendar; Harmon Foundation. *Select Picture List*; Smithsonian Institution. *Painting & Sculpture by American Negro Artists*, 1929; *Art Digest*, Mar. 1, 1933; "Amer. Negro Artists Given Full Length Review in NY Show," *Art Digest*, Dec. 15, 1941; Pierre-Noel, Lois Jones. "American Negro Art in Progress," *Negro History Bulletin*, Oct. 1967; Wolf, Ben. "Negro Art Scores without Double Standards," *Art Digest*, Feb. 1, 1945; *Apollo*, Feb. 1968, p. 141; "Harlem Library Shows Negro Art," *Art News*, May 20, 1933; Craig, Randall J. "Focus on Black Artists: A Project for Schools & Community," *School Arts*, Nov. 1970, pp. 30-33; Porter, James A. "Negro Gains Recognition after Long Battle," *Pittsburgh Courier*, July 29, 1950; Brawley, Benjamin. *The Negro in Literature & Art in the US*; Brown, Marion. "The Negro in the Fine Arts," *The Negro Heritage Library*, Vol. 2; Bearden, Romare. *The Negro Artist and Modern Art*, 1934; Ploski, Harry, & Ernest Kaiser. "The Black Artist," *Afro USA*, 1971; Ploski, Harry, Ernest Kaiser, & Otto Lindenmeyer. "The Black Artist," *Reference Library of Black America*, Book 4, 1971; *The Negro Handbook*, Composed by Editors of *Ebony*, Chicago, 1966; "Negro Artists Paintings on Display at University (Howard)," *East Tennessee News*, Knoxville, June 6, 1932; "Exhibition of Work by Negro Artists," *Afro-American Presbyterian*, Feb. 23, 1933; Myers, Carol L. *Black Power in the Arts*, Flint, Mich., 1970; Oakland Museum Archives, gift of the Harmon Foundation; Robinson, Wilhelmina S. *Historical Negro Biographies*, p. 201; Spradling, Mary M., ed. *In Black & White: Afro-Americans in Print*; "Leading Negro Artists," *Ebony*, Sept. 1963; Walker, Roslyn. *A Resource Guide to the Visual Arts of*

Afro-Americans, South Bend, Ind., 1971; Brown, Evelyn S. "Negro Achievement Revealed by Harmon Award," *Opportunity,* Jan. 1927; Brady, Mary. "An Experience in Inductive Service," *Opportunity,* May 1931, pp. 142-3; Fisk Univ. *The John Henry Series & Paintings Reflecting the Theme of Afro-American Folklore,* Feb./March 1970.

HAYDEN, WILLIAM
Painter, educator. Born in Lexington, North Carolina, 1916. Studied at Morehouse College (AB, 1939); under Hale Woodruff. Teacher at Atlanta University.
Works: *Checker Players; Boy in Blue Shirt; Saturday Night Function.*
Exhibited: Atlanta Univ., 1938; Dillard Univ., 1938, 1939; Baltimore Museum, 1939; Amer. Negro Exposition, Chicago, 1940; Xavier Univ., 1963.
Sources: Locke. *The Negro in Art*; Baltimore Museum of Art. *Contemporary Negro,* 1939; Tanner Art Galleries. *Art of the American Negro,* 1940; DuSable Museum of African-Amer. History. *Contemporary Black Artists,* 1970 Calendar; Xavier Univ. *Emancipation Proclamation Centennial National Art Exhibition,* 1963; Walker, Roslyn. *A Resource Guide to the Visual Arts of Afro-Americans,* South Bend, Ind., 1971.

HAYDON, MADELINE
Sources: DuSable Museum of African-Amer. History. *Contemporary Black Artists,* 1970 Calendar.

HAYES, DOROTHY
Graphic designer, painter, commercial artist.
Works: *An Exhibition System #1; Invitation to Takashimava #1; Book Jacket; 4th of July Project; White on White—A Counting Device; 8+8 Brochures, Nos. 1-5; Brochure for Two Fine Artists; Poster: Problem in Typographic Design; Problem in Typographic Design: Trick or Treat; Type Talks ATA #1, #2, #3; Book of Poems; Black Artists in Graphics Communication #1; Francesca #1; Poster: No More War; Design for Alphabet Book; Design for Stationery; Promotion Piece.*
Sources: Afro-American Slide Depository, Catalog; Jackson, Dorothy. "The Black Experience in Graphic Design," *Print,* Nov./Dec. 1968.

HAYES, OSCAR
Sources: DuSable Museum of African-Amer. History. *Contemporary Black Artists,* 1970 Calendar.

HAYES, VERTIS
Painter. Born in Atlanta, 1911. Self-taught in art, but later studied under Jean Charlot in New York (1934-35). Head of Federal Art Center, Memphis, Tennessee (1938-39); teacher at Le Moyne College, Memphis (1939-40).
Works: *Hunting Scene; The Trailer; Burial at Mt. Moriah; Juke Joint; Tourist Cabins; The Scales; Rustle of Spring 1941.*
Exhibited: Rabouin Gallery; Fisk Univ., 1938; Artists School, NY, 1938; Atlanta Univ., 1931, 1942, 1944; Baltimore Museum, 1939; Amer. Negro Exposition, Chicago, 1940; NY Federal Artists Project, Mural Division, 1936-38; Harlem Hospital, NY; Harmon Foundation, 1936; Dillard Univ., 1941.
Collections: Harlem Hospital.
Sources: Locke. *The Negro in Art;* Dover. *American Negro Art;* Indiana Univ. *Fine Arts & the Black American;* Tanner Art Galleries. *Art of the American Negro,* 1940; Dillard Univ. *Arts Festival,* 1941; Porter. *Modern Negro Art;* Harley, Ralph L., Jr. "A Checklist of Afro-American Art and Artists," *The Serif,* Dec. 1970; Locke, Alain. "Advance on the Art Front," *Opportunity,* May 1939; Walker, Roslyn. *A Resource Guide to the Visual Arts of Afro-Americans,* South Bend, Ind., 1971.

HAYNIE, WILBUR
Painter. Born in Camden, Arkansas, 1929. Studied at Wiley College, Texas (1958-59); Dallas County Museum of Fine Arts (1948-49); School of Allied Arts, Glendale, California (1949-50); Otis Art Institute, Los Angeles (MFA, 1959).
Exhibited: Downey Museum of Art; Ankrum Gallery, 1965; Dallas County Museum, 1948; Los Angeles Art Assn., 1954, 1965; Otis Art Institute, 1957; San Diego State College, 1958; Long Beach (Cal.) Festival, 1965; Laguna Beach Internat'l Art Exhibit; Annual Newport (Cal.) Harbor Exhibition, 1958, 1960, 1963, 1965; Barnsdall Park, Los Angeles, 1960-65; Amer. Friends Service Committee, Pasadena, 1963-67; UCLA Art Galleries, 1966-67; Univ. of Cal., Davis, 1966-67; Fine Arts Gallery of San Diego, 1966-67; Oakland Museum, 1966-67; Watts Art Festival, 1969; Dickson Art Center, 1966.
Collections: Fine Arts Patrons of Newport Harbor; Otis Art Institute; Pasadena Art Museum.
Awards: Purchase Award, Newport Harbor Exhibition, Cal., 1958; Honorable Mention, 13th All City Art Festival, Los Angeles; Honorable Mention, Topanga Plaza Art Exhibit, 1965; Honorable Mention, Long Beach 4th Annual Exhibition, 1966; Scholarship, Otis Art Institute (1953-58); Jose Drudis Foundation, 1957; 2nd prize, Watts Art Festival, 1969.
Sources: Seldis, Henry J. *Los Angeles Times Calendar,* Sept. 24, 1966, Dec. 23, 1962; UCLA Art Galleries. *The Negro in American Art;* "Afro-American Issue," *Art Gallery,* Apr. 1968;

Indiana Univ. *Fine Arts & the Black American;* DuSable Museum of African-Amer. History. *Contemporary Black Artists,* 1970 Calendar; Musée Rath. *8 Artistes Afro-Americains;* Seldis, Henry J. *Artforum,* Feb. 1963; Carr, Jack. *Pasadena Independent Star News,* Sunday Supplement, Dec. 13, 1964; *Los Angeles Times Calendar,* Feb. 28, 1965; Seldis, Henry J. *Los Angeles Times,* Oct. 25, 1965; Harley, Ralph, Jr. "Checklist of Afro-Amer. Art & Artists," *Serif,* Dec. 1970; Atkinson, J. Edward. *Black Dimensions in Contemporary American Art,* NY, 1966; Myers, Carol L. *Black Power in the Arts,* Flint, Mich., 1970; Walker, Roslyn. *A Resource Guide to the Visual Arts of Afro-Americans,* South Bend, Ind., 1971.

HAYWOOD, G. T.
Sources: Harley, Ralph, Jr. "Checklist of Afro-Amer. Art & Artists," *The Serif,* Dec. 1970.

HAZARD, BENJAMIN W.
Sculptor, painter, graphic artist, curator. Born in Newport, Rhode Island on May 30, 1940. Studied at Vallejo Junior College (1963-64); California College of Arts & Crafts (BFA with distinction, 1968); University of California at Berkeley (MA, 1969).
Works: *Self-Portrait; Medal of Honor; Black Impressions; Wipeout; Bird With Dead Mate; Gold Medal* (acrylic); *Our Window* (lithograph); *Two Cars* (lithograph); *6th of Vacab's Children Montanya* (lithograph); *Big Iron* (lithograph); *The Struggle* (lithograph); *One Is Black; Like Father, Like Son.*
Exhibited: La Jolla Museum of Art; Univ. of Iowa, 1971, 1972; Oakland Museum, 1968; Alamo Gallery, Benicia, 1967; Lowell Colbus Gallery, Sausalito, 1967; Cal. State College, Hayward, 1968; Chabot College, San Leandro, 1968; Conta Costa College, San Pablo, 1968; Berkeley Art Center, 1969; Lobby Gallery, Chicago, 1969; Carl Van Der Voorst Galleries, 1969; St. Mary's College, Moraga, 1969; Worth Ryder Gallery, Univ. of Cal., 1969; Walnut Creek Art Center, 1969; Univ. of Nevada, 1969, 1970; The Art Store Gallery, Reno, 1969; The Nevada Art Gallery, Reno, 1969; Cal. College of Arts & Crafts, 1969; Juried San Francisco Art Festival, 1969; Expo 70, Osaka, Japan, 1970; Univ. of Cal. at San Diego, 1970; American Paintings, Va., 1970; Quay Gallery, San Francisco, 1970; Oakland Art Museum, 1970; Palace of Fine Arts, San Francisco, 1969-72; Bell Telephone Traveling Exhibit, 1971-72; Richmond (Cal.) Art Center, 1972; Books Galleries, Vallejo; Fidelity Savings & Loan, San Francisco; Merrit Campus, Peralta College, Oakland; Tanner Gallery, Oakland; all Art West Associated North Shows.
Collections: Oakland Museum.

Awards: Joseph P. Berger Award, 1965; 1st award, Vallejo Art Exhibit, 1964-65; Cal. College of Arts & Crafts Scholarship, 1967-68; Ford Award, 1969.
Member: Junior Center for Arts & Sciences, Oakland; Rogues' Gallery (board of directors); Oakland Youth Foundation (board of directors); Cal. Humanities Assn. (board of directors); Guild for Cultural & Ethnic Affairs, Oakland Museum; Art West Associated North.
Represented by: Van Der Voorst Galleries, San Francisco.
Sources: Oakland Museum. *New Perspectives in Black Art;* Indiana Univ. *Fine Arts & the Black American;* La Jolla Museum of Art. *Dimensions of Black;* Ill. Bell Telephone. *Black American Artists/71,* 1972; Harley, Ralph, Jr. "Checklist of Afro-Amer. Art & Artists," *The Serif,* Dec. 1970; Oakland Museum Archives; DuSable Museum of African-Amer. History. *Contemporary Black Artists,* 1970; Blum, Walter. "A Look At Three Black Artists," *San Francisco Sunday Examiner & Chronicle,* Sunday Supplement, June 14, 1970; "Afro-American Issue," *Art Gallery,* April 1968; Walker, Roslyn. *A Resource Guide to the Visual Arts of Afro-Americans,* South Bend, Ind., 1971.

HECTOR, JUNE
Painter, designer. Worked in Atlanta.
Works: *Wild Flowers.*
Sources: Dover. *American Negro Art; American Negro Reference Book,* p. 771; Indiana Univ. *Fine Arts & the Black American;* Harley, Ralph, Jr. "Checklist of Afro-Amer. Art & Artists," *Serif,* Dec. 1970; Brown, Marion. "The Negro in the Fine Arts," *The Negro Heritage Library,* Vol. 2; "Afro-American Issue," *Art Gallery,* April 1968; Walker, Roslyn. *A Resource Guide to the Visual Arts of Afro-Americans,* South Bend, Ind., 1971.

HEGOMIN, ANZOLA D. LAIRD
Educator. Born in Tennessee. Studied at University of Chicago; Michigan State Normal College.
Exhibited: St. Louis Public Library, 1929; Harmon Foundation, 1931.
Sources: Harmon Foundation. *Negro Artists,* 1935; DuSable Museum of African-Amer. History. *Contemporary Black Artists,* 1970 Calendar; Harley, Ralph, Jr. "Checklist of Afro-Amer. Art & Artists," *Serif,* Dec. 1970.

HELITON, BOB
Photographer. Born 1934 in Houston, Texas. Studied at Texas Southern University; Pratt Institute, Los Angeles College of Design; New York Institute of Photography; Famous Photographers School.
Exhibited: Expo '70, Santa Monica, Cal.
Collections: Studio Watts Workshop; Custom

Print Shop; NY Institute of Photography; Holman Methodist Community Center.
Sources: Lewis/Waddy. *Black Artists on Art,* Vol. 2.

HELM, REGINALD
Sources: Myers, Carol L. *Black Power in the Arts,* Flint, Mich., 1970; DuSable Museum of African-Amer. History. *Contemporary Black Artists,* 1970 Calendar; "Afro-American Issue," *Art Gallery,* Apr. 1968; Indiana Univ. *Fine Arts & the Black American;* Walker, Roslyn. *A Resource Guide to the Visual Arts of Afro-Americans,* South Bend, Ind., 1971.

HENDERSON, AARON F.
Studied at Tuskegee Institute.
Works: *Black Women Don't Hide No Mo.*
Exhibited: Sun Times/Daily News Gallery, Chicago, 1970.
Sources: United Negro College Fund. *Art 1970,* Chicago, 1970.

HENDERSON, DION
Born 1941 in Detroit, Michigan. Studied at University of Washington; Burnley School of Professional Art, Seattle; Famous Artist School.
Works: *React to White Reactions; For the Brothers and Sisters Murdered.*
Exhibitions: The Friend Center Garfield Faculty Show; Mercer Island Arts Festival; Univ. of Wash.; Olympic Hotel; Burien Art Festival; Bellevue Arts and Crafts Festival; Quinta del Sordo Gallery.
Sources: Lewis/Waddy. *Black Artists on Art,* Vol. 2.

HENDERSON, ESELEAN
Sculptor, ceramist.
Works: *Windbell; Pot with Lid.*
Collections: Johnson Pub. Co.
Sources: DuSable Museum of African-Amer. History. *Contemporary Black Artists,* 1970 Calendar; Johnson Pub. Co. *The JPC Art Collection,* Pamphlet.

HENDERSON, LEROY
Photographer.
Exhibited: Addison Gallery, 1971.
Sources: James Van DerZee Institute. *The Black Photographer (1908-1970): A Survey.*

HENDERSON, LEROY W.
Printmaker.
Works: *Lift Us, We Pray* (linocut).
Collections: Oakland Museum.
Sources: Roelof-Lanner, T.V., ed. *Prints by American Negro Artists;* Oakland Museum Archives, Ruth Waddy Collection; Walker, Roslyn. *A Resource Guide to the Visual Arts of Afro-Americans,* South Bend, Ind., 1971.

HENDERSON, MARTHA
Painter. Born in Mt. Vernon, New York,

October 10, 1925. Studied under Dr. Long, advisor to Norman Rockwell. Coordinator, Merabash Museum.
Works: *Trumansburg, New York; First United States Army Headquarters on Governors Island, NY; Stolen; Interlaken, New York; Okinawa, Still Life; Mt. Vernon, New York.*
Exhibited: Tri-county Exhibit, Trumansburg, NY, 1964; US Army Exhibit, NY, 1967; Private Exhibit, Geneva, NY, 1968; Interlaken, NY Local, 1968; US Army Exhibit, Okinawa, 1963; US Army Exhibit, Ausburg, Germany, 1969.
Awards: 1st prize, Honorable mention, Trumansburg, NY; Honorable mention & cash award, US Army Exhibit, Governors Island, NY; 2nd prize & Honorable mention, Interlaken, NY; 1st prize, US Army Exhibit, Okinawa; Honorable mention, US Army Exhibit, Ausburg, Germany.
Member: Tri-county Art Society, NY; Art Assn. of NJ.
Represented by: Mr. Mark Henderson, Jr.
Sources: Information from artist.

HENDERSON, NAPOLEON
Weaver. Born in Chicago.
Works: *Blanket; Doodle; Cool Ade Icicles; Untitled; Bakota.*
Exhibited: Howard Univ., 1970, 1972; Nat'l Center of Afro-Amer. Artists, 1970, 1972; Studio Museum in Harlem, 1970, 1972.
Member: AFRICOBRA.
Sources: DuSable Museum of African Amer. History. *Contemporary Black Artists,* 1970 Calendar; *Black Shades,* Feb. 1972; Grillo, Jean B. "Where Down Home Meets Back Home," *Boston After Dark,* Sept. 1970; Howard Univ. *AFRICOBRA I,* Catalog, 1970; Howard Univ. *AFRICOBRA II,* Catalog, 1972.

HENDERSON, VERNITA
Jeweler. Studied at Columbia College of Theatrical Arts, Los Angeles; Richmond, California Art Center; Studio Craftsmen.
Works: Silver & jadeite ring.
Exhibited: Mills College, 1970.
Member: Art West Associated North; El Sobrante Art Guild.
Sources: Mills College. *California Black Craftsmen,* 1970.

HENDERSON, WILLIAM
Painter, filmmaker. Born in Marshall, Missouri, 1943. Studied at San Francisco Art Institute (BFA-painting, MFA-filmmaking, 1970).
Works: *Castration; Non Violent; The Great Masturbator; Revolution,* 1970 (synthetic polymer on canvas); *The Smile,* 1968 (oil); *The Last Supper,* 1970 (film); *Dufus,* 1970 (film); *Hog,* 1970 (film); *Mother's Day,* 1970 (film); *Money,* 1970 (film); *King David,* 1970 (film);

What Daddy Can Do, 1972 (film); *It's a Jungle,* 1972 (film); *Down Hear,* 1972 (film); *Portrait of Hindu* (oil).
Exhibited: San Francisco Art Institute, 1968; Whitney Museum, 1969-70 (1-man); Quay Gallery, San Francisco, 1970; College of Marin, 1970; Oakland Museum, 1970; Whitney Museum, 1971; Union Art Gallery, Univ. of Cal., 1971; San Francisco Art Institute, 1970 (film show); Ann Arbor Film Festival, Univ. of Michigan, 1970, 1971; Nevada City, Cal., 1970 (film show); San Francisco Museum of Art, 1970 (film show); Museum of Modern Art, 1971 (film show).
Collections: Oakland Museum.
Awards: 1968-70 Summer Scholarships, Skowhegan, Maine.
Sources: Information from artist; *San Francisco Examiner-Chronicle,* Nov. 23, 1969, Feb. 1, 1970, Mar. 6, 1970; *Oakland* (Cal.) *Times,* May 1970; *Berkeley Post,* May 14, 1970; *Hayward* (Cal.) *Review,* May 19, 1970; Doty. *Contemporary Black Artists in America; Artforum,* Dec. 1969; Lewis/Waddy. *Black Artists on Art,* Vol. 2; Oakland Museum Archives; *Fremont* (Cal.) *Argus,* May 1970; "San Francisco," *Art Forum,* Oct. 1970, p. 81; Oakland Museum. *Black, Untitled,* 1970.

HENDRICKS, BARKLEY LEONARD

Painter, photographer. Born in Philadelphia, April 16, 1945. Studied at Yale University School of Art (MFA, 1972); Pennsylvania Academy of the Fine Arts (1963-67).
Works: *Erection; Miss T; Sister Lucas; Brown Sugar Vine,* 1970 (oil & synthetic polymer/canvas); *Black on Black on Black; Robin's Red Breasts; J.S.B. III.*
Exhibited: Whitney Museum, NY, 1971; Contemporary Black Artists in America, 1971; Carnegie Institute, 1971; USA, 1971-72; Glassboro (NJ) State College, 1971; Amer. Academy of Fine Arts & Letters, NY, 1971; Nat'l. Institute of Arts & Letters, 1971-72; Provident Nat'l Bank, Phila., 1971; Yale Univ., 1970-72; Nat'l Academy of Design, NY, 1969-71; Phila. Civic Center, 1969-70; Phila. Museum of Art, 1970; Phila. Art Alliance, 1968-71; Butler Institute of Amer. Art, Youngstown, Ohio, 1967; Kenmore Galleries, Phila., 1966-72; Pa. Academy of Fine Arts, 1967-72; Woodmere Art Gallery, Phila., 1964, 1969; Kenmore Galleries, Phila., 1970 (1-man); Messiah College, Grantham, Pa., 1970; State Armory, Wilmington, Del., 1971.
Collections: Phila. Museum of Art; Pa. Academy of the Fine Arts; Uris Collection; Cornell Univ.; Wichita State Univ.; Mr. Richardson Dilworth, former mayor of Phila.; Dr. & Mrs. Michael Katzev, Oberlin, Ohio; Dr. & Mrs. John T. Williams, Phila.; Mr. Michael

Straight, Chairman, Nat'l. Council on the Arts, Washington, DC; Mrs. Frank Lamey, Wilmington, Del.; Dr. & Mrs. Gordon Moore, Boston.
Awards: Richard & Hilda Rosenthal Award, Nat'l. Institute of Arts & Letters, 1972; Teaching Assistantship, Yale Univ., 1971-72; Childe Hassim Purchase Award, Amer. Academy of Arts & Letters, 1971; Sengstacke Publication Award for Photography, Carnegie Institute, 1971; 2nd prize, National Academy of Design, 1971; Caroline Gibson Granger Prize, PAFA Fellowship Exhibition, 1969; Honorable Mention, Amer. Exhibiting Artists, 1966; J. Henry Scheidt Traveling Scholarship, 1967; William Emlen Cresson European Traveling Scholarship, 1966; Half-tuition scholarship, 1964-66.
Represented by: Kenmore Galleries, 122 S. 18th St., Phila.
Sources: Whitney Museum. *Contemporary Black Artists in America;* Phila. Division of Art. *Afro-American Artists 1800-1969;* Aesthetic Dynamics. *Afro-American Images,* 1971; Doty. *Contemporary Black Artists in America;* Afro-American Slide Depository, Catalog, 1971-72; Craig, Randall J. "Focus on Black Artists: A Project for Schools and Community," *School Arts,* Nov. 1970, pp. 30-33.

HENRIGUZ, STEPHANIE

Studied at Oakwood College.
Exhibited: Sun Times/Daily News Gallery, Chicago, 1970.
Sources: United Negro College Fund. *Art 1970,* Chicago, 1970.

HENRY, RICHARD

Photographer.
Exhibited: Addison Gallery, 1971.
Sources: James Van DerZee Institute. *The Black Photographer (1908-1970): A Survey.*

HENRY, ROBERT

Painter.
Exhibited: BlackMan's Art Gallery, San Francisco.
Sources: Juba Solo & The Artists of the BlackMan's Art Gallery. *Permanent Home of the BlackMan's Art Gallery,* Cal.

HERBERT, ERNEST

Ceramist. Born in Los Angeles, 1932. Studied at Pasadena City College; Chouinard Art Institute; Otis Art Institute; Trade Technical College; Richards, Rubens, and Moore.
Works: *Black Anchor;* Stoneware pots.
Exhibited: Los Angeles County Art Assn., 1968, 1969 (1-man); Mills College; Pasadena Art Museum, 1956; Pasadena Art Festival, 1961; Downy Art Museum, 1962; Brooklyn Museum, 1962.
Awards: Long Beach Art Show, 1968; Santa

Monica Art Show, 1969; Descanso Gardens, 1969; Los Angeles Art Assn., 1971; Brooklyn Museum, 1962.
Sources: Lewis/Waddy. *Black Artists on Art,* Vol. 2; Mills College. *California Black Craftsmen,* Oakland, Cal., 1970.

HERRING, JAMES
Artist, educator. Inaugurated the art department and gallery at Howard University where he taught. Director of Howard University.
Sources: Dover. *American Negro Art;* Brawley, Benjamin. *The Negro Genius;* DuSable Museum of African-Amer. History. *Contemporary Artists,* 1970 Calendar.

HEWITT, MARK
Painter, graphic artist.
Works: *Spirit of the 366th; Slave Girl* (print); *Fort Devens 1943.*
Exhibited: Atlanta Univ., 1943, 1944.
Collections: Atlanta Univ.
Awards: 1st Atlanta Univ. Purchase Prize, 1944.
Sources: *Art News,* Apr. 15, 1945, pp. 8-9; "Negro Annual," *Art Digest,* Apr. 15, 1943; Woodruff, Hale. "Negro Artists Hold 4th Annual in Atlanta," *Art Digest,* Apr. 15, 1945.

HICKS, ALFRED
Painter.
Works: *Industrialscape; Fragment of a Dream.*
Exhibited: Market Place Gallery.
Sources: *Market Place Gallery,* Catalog.

HICKS, FANNIE
Sources: Porter. *Modern Negro Art;* Harley, Ralph, Jr. "Checklist of Afro-Amer. Art & Artists," *The Serif,* Dec. 1970.

HICKS, LEON N.
Printmaker, educator. Born in Deerfield, Florida, 1933. Studied at Kansas State University (BS); State University of Iowa (MA, MFA); Stanford University; La Romita School of Art, Italy, 1966. Teacher at Lincoln University, Jefferson City, Missouri.
Works: *Apogee; Black Boy; Appalachian Sequela #6; Little Bird; New Faces, Series #3.*
Exhibited: Des Moines Annual Exhibit; Amer. Graphic Workshops, Cincinnati Art Museum; 9th Annual Arts Guild Exhibition; Tuskegee Institute; Academy of Design, NY; Northwest Printmakers Internat'l Exhibition, Seattle; Nat'l Conference of Artists.
Collections: Mr. Benny Andrews; Oakland Museum.
Sources: Myers, Carol L. *Black Power in the Arts,* Flint, Mich., 1970; "Afro-American Issue," *Art Gallery,* Apr. 1968; Indiana Univ. *Fine Arts & the Black American;* Lewis/ Waddy. *Black Artists on Art;* Roelof-Lanner,

T.V., ed. *Prints by American Negro Artists;* DuSable Museum of African-Amer. History. *Contemporary Black Artists,* 1970 Calendar; Oakland Museum Archives, Ruth Waddy Collection; Walker, Roslyn. *A Resource Guide to the Visual Arts of Afro-Americans,* South Bend, Ind., 1971.

HIEBER, VIVIAN
Active in 1960's.
Sources: Walker, Roslyn. *A Resource Guide to the Visual Arts of Afro-Americans,* South Bend, Ind., 1971; Myers, Carol L. *Black Power in the Arts,* Flint, Mich., 1970; "Afro-Amer. Issue," *Art Gallery,* April 1968; Indiana Univ. *Fine Arts & the Black American;* DuSable Museum of African-Amer. History. *Contemporary Black Artists,* 1970 Calendar.

HILL, CLIFTON THOMPSON
Painter, commercial artist. Born in Virginia in 1902. Studied commercial and mechanical drawing in his spare time between odd jobs. Worked at Cooper Union and in the studio of Winold Reiss.
Works: *Vie-The Struggle for Superiority; Home Again; Ashes & Cinders.*
Exhibited: Harmon Foundation, 1929, 1930, 1933; Smithsonian Institution, 1929.
Sources: Indiana Univ. *Fine Arts & the Black American;* Harmon Foundation. *Exhibition of Productions by Negro Artists;* Harmon Foundation. *Negro Artists,* 1935; Harmon Foundation. *Exhibit of Fine Arts,* 1930; DuSable Museum of African-Amer. History. *Contemporary Black Artists,* Calendar, 1970; Smithsonian Institution. *Painting & Sculpture by American Negro Artists,* 1929; Harley, Ralph, Jr. "A Checklist of Afro-Amer. Art & Artists," *The Serif,* Dec. 1970; Walker, Roslyn. *A Resource Guide to the Visual Arts of Afro-Americans,* South Bend, Ind., 1971.

HILL, DAVID
Studied at Tougaloo College.
Works: *The Watcher; Dimension of Love.*
Exhibited: Sun Times/Daily News Gallery, Chicago, 1970.
Sources: United Negro College Fund. *Art 1970,* Chicago, 1970.

HILL, GEORGE T.
Works: *Home Again.*
Collections: Nat'l Archives.
Sources: Afro-American Slide Depository, catalog.

HILL, HECTOR
Painter, educator. Born 1934 in New York City. Died 1963 in Cuba of swimming mishap while there with his students for the summer. Studied at Music & Art High School, NYC;

San Bernadino State College (Calif.); Louvre Drawing Seminars; Brooklyn Museum of Art, 1957-8.

Exhibited: Marino Gallery, 1958; 1st Assembly District Democratic Club, 1961; Market Place Gallery, 1961; Ligoa Duncan Gallery, 1962.

Sources: *Negro Almanac*, p. 626; Ploski, Harry, & Ernest Kaiser. "The Black Artist," *Afro USA*, 1971; Ploski, Harry, Ernest Kaiser, & Otto Lindenmeyer. "The Black Artist," *Reference Library of Black America*, Book IV, 1971; Spradling, Mary M., ed. *In Black & White: Afro-Americans in Print.*

HILL, HUGH
Photographer.

Exhibited: Addison Gallery, 1971.

Sources: James Van DerZee Institute. *The Black Photographer (1908-1970): A Survey.*

HILL, REBA DICKERSON
Painter.

Works: *Study in Copper and Brass Barriers; The Proud Ones; Sounds of Silence.*

Exhibited: State Armory, Wilmington, Del., 1971; Smith-Mason Gallery, 1971.

Sources: Aesthetic Dynamics. *Afro-American Images 1971*; Smith-Mason Gallery. *National Exhibition Black Artists 1971.*

HILL, TONY
Ceramist. Born in St. Joseph, Missouri, 1907. Studied at the University of Kansas (1928); University of Chicago Graduate School; University of California under Glenn Lukens.

Works: Clay ashtray; lamp & figurine; 3-piece cluster of nut & fruit dishes; lamp, bowl, & ashtray; ashtray & lamp; hand-painted bowl; trough bowl & African figurines (ebony); flower bowl.

Sources: "Ceramics by Tony Hill," *Ebony*, Nov. 1946, pp. 31-35.

HINES, FELRATH
Painter. Born in Indianapolis, Indiana, 1918. Studied at Pratt Institute, Brooklyn, 1962; New York University, 1953-55; Art Institute of Chicago, 1944.

Works: *Blue Painting; Sunburst; Red Painting; Beyond; Blue Moon; Morning* (oil on canvas), 1968; *Afternoon* (oil on canvas), 1968; *Untitled; Landscape.*

Exhibited: Parma Galleries, New York, 1960, 1962; Herron Museum of Art, Indianapolis, 1959; Riverside Museum, NY, 1959; John Heller Gallery, NY, 1955; Provincetown, Mass. Annual; Nordness Galleries, NY, 1969; Hudson River Museum, Yonkers; Minneapolis Institute of Arts, 1968; High Museum of Art, Atlanta, Ga., 1969; Flint (Mich.) Institute of Arts, 1970; Everson Museum of Art, Syracuse, NY, 1970; IBM Gallery of Arts & Sciences, 1970;

Rhode Island School of Design, 1969; Memorial Art Gallery, Rochester, NY, 1969; San Francisco Museum of Art, 1969; Contemporary Arts Museum, Houston, 1970; New Jersey State Museum, 1970; Roberson Center for the Arts & Sciences, 1970; The Art Galleries, Univ. of Calif. at Santa Barbara.

Collections: Dr. & Mrs. Fred Olsen; Mr. John Kern; Mr. Marc Moyens; Chase Manhattan Bank, NY.

Member: *Spiral.*

Sources: Boston Museum of Fine Arts. *Afro-American Artists: New York and Boston*, 1970; Nordness Galleries. *12 Afro-American Artists*, 1969; Minneapolis Institute of Arts. *30 Contemporary Black Artists*, 1969; Hudson River Museum. *Contemporary American Black Artists*, Yonkers; L.I. Univ. *Spiral*, catalog; Greene, Carroll, Jr. "Perspective: The Black Artist in America," *The Art Gallery*, April 1970; Siegel, Jeanne. "Why Spiral," *Art News*, Sept. 1966, pp. 48-50; Harley, Ralph, Jr. "Checklist of Afro-American Art and Artists," *The Serif*, Dec. 1970; Kramer, Hilton. "Is Politics Submerging Black Art?," *Courier Journal & Times* (Louisville, Ky.), June 7, 1970; Ploski, Harry, & Ernest Kaiser. "The Black Artist," *Afro USA*, 1971; Paris, Jean. "Black Art Experience in Art," *Long Island Press*, Jamaica, NY, June 14, 1970; Ploski, Harry, Ernest Kaiser, & Otto Lindenmeyer. "The Black Artists," *Reference Library of Black America*, Vol. IV, 1971; Ruder & Finn Fine Arts. *Contemporary Black Artists*, 1969; Myers, Carol L. *Black Power in the Arts*, Flint, Mich., 1970; Hollingsworth, Alvin. "Wealth of Expression in Black Artists' RISD Show," *Providence Sunday Journal*, June 29, 1969; Walker, Roslyn. *A Resource Guide to the Visual Arts of Afro-Americans*, South Bend, Ind., 1971; Driscoll, Edgar J., Jr. "Showcase for Black Artists," *Boston Sunday Globe*, July 6, 1969, p. A73; Glueck, Grace. "America Has Black Art on Her Mind," *New York Times*, Feb. 27, 1969, p. C34.

HOBBS, G.W.
Painter, Methodist minister. Worked during the late 18th century in Baltimore, Maryland, painting portraits.

Works: *Portrait of Richard Allen.*

Sources: Dover. *American Negro Art*, p. 22; Indiana Univ. *Fine Arts & the Black American*; Harley, Ralph, Jr. "A Checklist of Afro-Amer. Art & Artists," *The Serif*, Dec. 1970; Walker, Roslyn. *A Resource Guide to the Visual Arts of Afro-Americans*, South Bend, Ind., 1971.

HODGE, SONNY
Sources: Brown, Marion. "The Negro in the Fine Arts," *The Negro Heritage Library*, Vol. 2.

HOFFMAN, IRWIN

Sources: Salpeter, Harry. "About Irwin Hoffman," *Coronet*, IV, Oct. 1938; Harley, Ralph, Jr. "Checklist of Afro-Amer. Art & Artists," *The Serif*, Dec. 1970; Benet, Stephen V. "Rivers of America . . . illustrations by eminent artists," *Philadelphia Art Alliance Bulletin VIII-IX*, March 1943.

HOFFMAN, THELMA

Painter. Born in Washington, DC, 1946. Self-taught.
Exhibited: Afro Art Alliance Exhibits.
Member: Afro Art Alliance, Springfield, Mass.
Sources: Information from the artist.

HOLDER, GEOFFREY

Painter. Born in Port-of-Spain, Trinidad in 1930. Studied at Queen's Royal College.
Exhibited: Public Library in Trinidad; Barone Gallery, 1957 (1-man).
Awards: Guggenheim Fellowship, 1957.
Collections: Trinidad Hilton Hotel; Univ. of the West Indies.
Sources: Dover. *American Negro Art*, p. 47; Indiana Univ. *Fine Arts & the Black American; Shorewood Reproductions. The Art of Black America;* Catalog; *Current Biography*, 1957, pp. 263-4; *Ebony*, Oct. 1955, p. 78; *Ebony*, July 1960, pp. 38-43; Spradling, Mary M., ed. *In Black & White: Afro-Americans in Print;* "Afro-American Issue," *Art Gallery*, April 1968; Walker, Roslyn. *A Resource Guide to the Visual Arts of Afro-Americans*, South Bend, Ind., 1971.

HOLDER, ROSCOE

Works: *Girl in White; Martiniquan Beauty; Back View; East Indian Vendors; Oistin Barbados; Espanol; Point Cumana Hills; Dance Group; Fruit Vendors; Landscape With Huts.*
Collections: National Archives.
Sources: Myers, Carol L. *Black Power in the Arts*, Flint, Mich., 1970; Afro-American Slide Depository, Catalog, 1971-72; Harley, Ralph. "Checklist of Afro-Amer. Art & Artists," *The Serif*, Dec. 1970.

HOLLAND, CHARLES

Sources: Porter. *Modern Negro Art;* Harley, Ralph, Jr. "Checklist of Afro-Amer. Art & Artists," *The Serif*, Dec. 1970.

HOLLINGSWORTH, ALVIN C.

Painter, illustrator, educator, art director. Born in New York City, 1931. Studied at Art Students League; City College of New York (BA 1956, MA 1959). Currently Ph.D. candidate at New York University. Has taught at the High School of Art and Design, NYC; Is Art Director of the Lincoln Institute of Psycho-therapy Art Gallery; has been artist-teacher at the Scarsdale Studio Workshop. He was teacher-in-charge of the art project "Turn On" for the New York Board of Education, instructor at USDAN Center for Creative and Permanent Arts. He is currently Assistant Professor of Art at Hostos Community College.

Works: *City Images; Waiting; Flower Girl; Lonely Woman; Black Madonna; A Place In The Sun; Rumble; The Artist; Hallelujah; Madonna and Child; Folklore; Chance 1970; Blue Triptych; No Colored; Composition #2; Cry City #2; Inner Reflections; Mogul's Wife; The Prophet; Family Tree; Trapped; Head; The City; Black Guernica; Tenement Madonna; The Walls Have Eyes; Deserted Landscape; Lonelyscape; Yellow Landscape; Moodscape; Familiarscape; Sunscape; Figured Landscape; Seascape Rouge; Red Sun; Muted Landscape with Figure; Tranquil Landscape; Regatta; Landscape Balance; Grey Landscape; Landscape with Mood White; Green Sky with Boats; Spanish Landscape; Cool Landscape; Butte; Tree; Mood Rouge; Midwestern Landscape; Arctic Landscape; Crystal Lakescape; Beachscape; Bullscape; Greenscape; Woman Allegory; Prophet and the City; Woman No. 3; Natives; Chance; Adrift; Family Tree #1; Family Tree #2; The Prophet at the Marsh; The Wall; Psychedelic Sun; Psychedelic Orange; Trip; Mountain Top; Natives; Prophet with Bull; Prophet Viewing the Sea; Red Desert; Vista Azul; Love; The Field; All-Allegory; Prophet's Trek; Verde Landscape; He Stood on the Dock.*

Exhibited: American Greetings Gallery, NY, 1968; Lever House, NY, 1969; Boston Museum of Fine Arts, 1970; 45th Annual Newport Art Assn. Show, 1956; Jewish Museum, NY, 1957; Bodley Gallery, NY, 1958; Ward Eggleston Gallery, NY, 1960; Emily Lowe Award Exhibit, NY, 1963; Spiral Group, NY, 1964; Sixth Annual Arts Festival, Temple Emanu-El, Yonkers, NY; Urban Show, New School Art Gallery, 1965, 1966; Oakland (Calif.) Museum, 1967; Lake Forrest College (Ill.), 1967; Nassau Community College (L.I., NY), 1968; Riverside Museum, NY, 1968; Teaneck Library, Teaneck, NJ, 1968; Nat'l. Academy Annual, NY, 1969; Coalition '70, Staten Island Museum, NY, 1970; Hudson River Museum, Yonkers, NY; Terry Dintenfass Gallery, NY (1-man), 1965; Loeb Center, NYU, 1967; Harbor Gallery, Cold Spring Harbor, L.I., NY, 1969, 1970, 1972; Koltnow Gallery, NY, 1967; Museum of African Art, Washington, D.C., 1964; The Brooklyn Museum, 1961; Phila. Civic Center Museum; Whitney Museum, 1971; Smith-Mason Gallery, Washington, DC, 1971; San Francisco Museum; The Studio Museum in Harlem, NY,

1970; City Center Gallery, NY (1-man); Herve Galleries, NY (1-man); Monede Galleries, NY (1-man); Minneapolis Institute of Arts, 1968; High Museum of Art, Atlanta, 1969; Flint Institute of Arts (Mich.), 1969; Everson Museum of Art, Syracuse, NY, 1969; IBM Gallery of Arts & Sciences, NY, 1969; Rhode Island School of Design, 1969; Memorial Art Gallery, Rochester, NY, 1969; Contemporary Arts Museum, Houston, Tex., 1970; New Jersey State Museum, Trenton, 1970; Roberson Center for the Arts and Sciences, 1970; Art Galleries, Univ. of Calif. at Santa Barbara, 1970; Metropolitan Museum of Art, NY, 1969; Fleishem Gallery, 1958; ANTA Theatre, 1967.

Awards: Phi Beta Kappa, CCNY, 1956; Alumni Award, City College, Exhibition, 1957; Technicrafts Graphic Arts Competition, 1958; Bodley Gallery Nat'l. Drawing Competition, 1958; Emily Lowe Award, 1963; Whitney Fellowship, 1964; Artists of the Year Award, New York Univ., 1967; Award of Distinction, Smith-Mason Gallery, Washington, D.C., 1971; Museum of African Art, Washington, D.C.; Brooklyn Museum; General Electric Co., Metropolitan Museum, NY; Johnson Publications; Chase Manhattan Bank, NY; IBM.

Member: Art Students League; Artists Equity; Spiral.

Sources: Dover. *American Negro Art;* Roelof-Lanner T.V., ed. *Prints by American Negro Artists;* Boston Museum of Fine Arts. *Afro-American Artists, New York & Boston,* 1970; Indiana Univ. *Fine Arts and the Black American;* Afro-American Slide Depository, Catalog, 1970; NY State Education Dept. *Fifteen under Forty;* Minneapolis Institute of Arts. *30 Contemporary Black Artists;* Lever House. *Counterpoints,* NY, 1967, 1969; American Greetings Gallery. *New Voices: 15 New York Artists,* NY, 1968; Metropolitan Museum of Art. *Inner World of Black Artists,* NY, 1969; Ruder & Finn Fine Arts. *Contemporary Black Artists,* 1969; UCLA Art Galleries. *The Negro in American Art;* Doty. *Contemporary Black Artists in America;* Terry Dintenfass Gallery. *Al Hollingsworth,* New York, n.d.; Hammond, Sally. "Al Hollingsworth: An Art to it All," *New York Post,* Jan. 10, 1970; Harbor Gallery, Cold Spring Harbor, NY. *Hollingsworth,* 1969; Smith-Mason Gallery. *National Exhibition Black Artists,* Washington, D.C., 1971; DuSable Museum of African American History. *Contemporary Black Artists,* calendar, 1970; *Manhattan East,* Jan. 12, 1961; L. I. Univ. *Spiral;* Miller, Earl. *Rhode Island School of Design Bulletin,* June 1969; "What makes Alvin run," *Art Gallery,* April 1970; Greene, Carroll, Jr. "Perspective: The Black Artist in America," *The Art Gallery,* April

1970; Siegel, Jeanne. "Why Spiral?," *Art News,* Sept. 1966; Johnson Publishing Co. *The JPC Art Collection;* Harley, Ralph, Jr. "Checklist of Afro-American Art and Artists," *The Serif,* Dec. 1970; Metropolitan Applied Research Center (MARC). *Six Painters;* Spengler, David. "It's Hard Not to Be Awed by Artist Al Hollingsworth," *The Record,* Hackensack, New Jersey, June 25, 1970; Patterson, Lindsay. "Contemporary Artists," *The Negro in Music and Art,* 1969; Ploski, Harry, Ernest Kaiser. "The Black Artist," *Afro USA,* 1971; Ploski, Harry, Ernest Kaiser, Otto Lindenmeyer. "The Black Artist," *Reference Library of Black America,* Book IV, 1971; *The Negro Handbook,* comp. by Editors of *Ebony,* Chicago, 1966; Harbor Gallery. *The Prophet and Other Paintings by Hollingsworth,* Cold Spring Harbor, N.Y., 1970; Harbor Gallery. *Landscapes and Other Paintings by Hollingsworth,* Cold Spring Harbor, N.Y., 1972; "Art," *Long Island Press,* May 14, 1972; "Art: Moody Motif," *Newsday,* May 25, 1972; Coombs, Orde. "People: Al Hollingsworth: Portrait of the Artist as Believer," *Essence,* Feb. 1971; Hollingsworth, A.C. *I'd Like the Goo-Gen-Heim,* Reilly & Lee, 197?; "Hollingsworth Art in Harlem Exhibit," *The Voice,* Oct. 2, 1970; Delaney, Barry Leo. "Hollingsworth a one-man culture force," *Staten Island Sunday Advance,* Nov. 15, 1970; Bearden, Romare. "Hollingsworth on Exhibit at Studio," *N.Y. Amsterdam News,* Oct. 17, 1970; Hall, Dorothy. "Alvin Hollingsworth," *Park East (N.Y.),* Oct. 22, 1970; "Art Depicts Spiritual Man," *The New York Times,* Jan. 3, 1971; Myers, Carol L. *Black Power in the Arts,* Flint, Mich., 1970; "The Editors Bless: Artist Al Hollingsworth," *Show,* Mar. 1970; Riverside Museum. *Eight Plus Eight,* 1969; Hollingsworth, Alvin. "Wealth of Expression in Black Artists' RISD Show," *Providence Sunday Journal,* June 29, 1969; "Leading Negro Artists," *Ebony,* Sept. 1963; Driscoll, Edgar J., Jr. "Showcase for Black Artists," *Boston Sunday Globe,* July 6, 1969, p. A73; "Harlem," *High,* Dec. 1957; Walker, Roslyn. *A Resource Guide to the Visual Arts of Afro-Americans,* South Bend, Ind., 1971.

HOLLINSWORTH, FRED P.

Painter.

Active in the 1940's in Chicago.

Works: *Heating Stove; Abstraction; Evangelist Tent; Still Life* (watercolor); *Tent Meeting; Table Arrangement of Fruit; The Lagoon; Sheep Herding.*

Exhibited: Atlanta Univ., 1942; Howard Univ., 1941; Library of Congress, 1940; Amer. Negro Exposition, Chicago, 1940; Dillard Univ., 1941; South Side Community Art Center, Chicago, 1941.

Sources: *Exhibition of Negro Artists of Chicago at Howard Univ. Gallery of Art,* Feb. 1941; Library of Congress. *Catalog of the Exhibition of Oils, Watercolors, Prints & Drawings,* Wash., D.C., Dec. 1940; Porter. *Modern Negro Art;* Harley, Ralph, Jr. "A Checklist of Afro-Amer. Art & Artists," *The Serif,* Dec. 1970; Tanner Art Galleries. *Art of the American Negro,* 1940; Dillard Univ. *Arts Festival,* 1941; "Art by Negroes," *Art Digest,* Oct. 15, 1941; Locke, Alain. "Chicago's New Southside Art Center," *American Magazine of Art,* Aug. 1941; South Side Community Art Center. *National Negro Art Exhibition,* 1941; South Side Community Art Center. *Opening Exhibition of Paintings by Negro Artists,* Chicago, 1941; McMillen Inc. Galleries. *Contemporary Negro Art,* NY, 1941.

HOLMES, EDDIE

Painter. Born in Newark, New Jersey 1948.
Works: *The Gods Make Love,* 1970; *Black Experiences,* 1970; *Mood of Anguish,* 1968; *Pride,* 1969.
Exhibited: Newark Museum, 1971.
Sources: Newark Museum. *Black Artists: Two Generations,* 1971.

HOLMES, HENRY

Printmaker. Born in Atlanta in 1906. No formal art training.
Works: *Head of a Negro; My Daughter; Study of Negro.*
Exhibited: Harmon Foundation, 1933; 135th St. Branch of NY Public Library.
Sources: Harmon Foundation. *Non-Jury Exhibit of Works of Negro Artists,* 1933.

HOLT, BARBARA R.

Photographer. Born in Boston, Massachusetts in 1933. Studied under Harry Emerson, Boston.
Works: *The Embrace* (black & white); *Acapulco Bay at Midnight* (color print); *Mother and Child* (color print); *Boy and Wall* (black & white).
Exhibited: Boston Negro Artists Assn. Annual, 1971, 1972; Boston Globe Festival, 1971; Internat'l. Festival, Boston, 1971, 1972; Northeastern Univ. Afro Institute; Kresgee Auditorium, MIT, 1972; Columbia Univ., 1972; Harvard Univ., 1972.
Member: Boston Negro Artists Assn.
Represented by: Holt Photo Lab and Studio, Boston; Internat'l. Children's Shop, Market and Bow Sts., Portsmouth, New Hampshire, 03801.
Sources: Information from the artist.

HOOKS, EARL J.

Painter, ceramist, educator. Born in Baltimore on August 2, 1927. Studied at Howard University (BA); Catholic University, Washington, D.C.; Rochester Institute of Technology; School of American Craftsmen, 1954-55. Teacher at Shaw University, Raleigh, North Carolina; Gary, Indiana; Indiana University, Northwest Campus; Fisk University.

Works: *Louis Armstrong; Current Forms; Slide Untitled; Ceramics Form for Flowers; Crucifixion; Primordinal Landscape; Punch Bowl; Head of a Boy; Bloom 1; Female Form #1; Just Friends; Head; Mark III; Seed Form; Female Form #2; Ballad Singer; The Family; The Fatigued Warrior; Woman; Spore; Bird Form; Flying Pigtails.*

Exhibited: Smithsonian Institution, Wash., D.C., 1954, 1963; Howard Univ. (1-man); Miami Nat'l., Fla., 1954-55, 1958; Atlanta Univ.; Rochester Memorial Art Gallery, 1954; American House, NYC, 1954; Young American Show, 1954; John Herron Art School, 1957, 1959; Washington Art Center, South Bend, Ind., 1956-57; Robert North Gallery, Chicago; Chicago Art Institute, 1957; Barnet Aden Gallery, Wash., D.C.; Evanston Community Art Center; Smithsonian Institution Traveling Show, 1957-58; 21st Syracuse Biennial, Everson Museum, NY, 1961; 23rd Syracuse Biennial, Everson Museum, 1963; Invitational, Howard Univ., 1961; 9th Internat'l Invitational, Smithsonian Institution, 1963; Invitational, Syracuse Biennial Show, 1964-66; Oak Park Library; Indiana Univ.; Internat'l Minerals & Chemicals Exhibition, Skokie, Ill.; Fort Wayne (Ind.) Museum, 1965; Talledega (Ala.) College, 1968; Louisville Art Workshop, 1969; Studio 22, Fisk Univ. Faculty Art Show, 1969, Chicago; Invitational Chicago Public Library, 1969; South Central Craft Show, 1969; MTSU, Murfreesboro, Tenn.

Awards: 2nd prize, John Herron Art School, 1959; 1st prize, Indiana Univ.; 3rd prize, De Pauw Univ.; Purchase Prize, South Bend Art Center.

Member: President, Midwest Potters & Sculptors, Chicago; treasurer & exhibition chairman, Midwest Designer Craftsmen; Exhibition "A" Gallery, Chicago; vice-president, Gary (Ind.) Artists League.

Sources: Dover. *American Negro Art,* p. 141; Indiana Univ. *Fine Arts & the Black American;* Afro-American Slide Depository, catalog; Fisk Univ. Art Galleries. *3 Afro-Americans,* 1969; Pierre-Noel, Lois Jones. "American Negro Art in Progress," *Negro History Bulletin,* Oct. 1967; Fax, Elton. *Seventeen Black Artists;* "Exhibition," *Scrapbook of Art & Artists of Chicago,* 1959, p. 92, 125; Harley, Ralph, Jr. "A Checklist of Afro-Amer. Art & Artists," *The Serif,* Dec. 1970; Walker, Roslyn. *A Resource Guide to the Visual Arts of Afro-Americans,* South Bend, Ind., 1971.

HOOPER, ELVOYCE

Photographer. Born in 1946. Studied at Merritt Campus, Peralta College.
Works: *Untitled*; *Untitled* (portrait); *Chance.*
Exhibited: Oakland Museum, 1968.
Collections: Oakland Museum.
Member: President, Black Photography Club, Merritt College.
Sources: Oakland Museum. *New Perspectives in Black Art*; Indiana Univ. *Fine Arts & the Black American*; Harley, Ralph, Jr. "Checklist of Afro-Amer. Art & Artists," *The Serif*, Dec. 1970; Oakland Museum Archives; Walker, Roslyn. *A Resource Guide to the Visual Arts of Afro-Americans*, South Bend, Ind., 1971.

HORTON, HELEN TAYLOR

Painter, graphic artist. Born in Washington, DC, 1913. Studied privately with Professor H. Dodson (1932-33); at New England Conservatory (1939-40); Northeastern University (1970-72).
Works: *Muir Woods*, 1971 (acrylic); *Sausalito*, 1967 (acrylic); *African Village*, 1972 (acrylic); *Winter Stillness*, 1972 (acrylic); *Cypress and Sunset Across the Bay*, 1972 (acrylic); *For over Egg Rock*, 1972 (acrylic).
Exhibited: Sunday in the Park, Boston, 1970-72.
Member: Boston Negro Artists Assn.
Represented by: Boston Negro Artists Assn.
Sources: Information from the artist.

HORTON, ISABEL

Painter.
Works: *Construction Workers.*
Exhibited: Dillard Univ., 1941.
Sources: Dillard Univ. *Arts Festival*, Catalog, 1941.

HOUSLEY, JESSIE MAY

Commercial artist, printmaker, educator. Born in St. Louis, Missouri in 1908. Studied at Summer Teacher's College; Art Institute of Chicago. Worked as teacher; fashion illustrator; commercial artist.
Works: *Bacchanlis* (lithograph); *Girl at Window; Meditation; Mischievous.*
Exhibited: Harmon Foundation, 1929, 1933; Art Alliance of St. Louis, 1929; Black & White Exhibit, 1930; Art Students League, 1931; Smithsonian Institution, 1929.
Awards: 1st prize, black & white, Art Alliance of St. Louis, 1929.
Sources: Harmon Foundation. *Exhibition of Productions by Negro Artists*; Harmon Foundation. *Non-Jury Exhibit of Works of Negro Artists*, 1933; Indiana Univ. *Fine Arts & the Black American;* Smithsonian Institution. *Painting & Sculpture by American Negro Artists*, 1929; Harley, Ralph, Jr. "A Checklist of Afro-Amer. Art & Artists," *The Serif*, Dec. 1970;

Walker, Roslyn. *A Resource Guide to the Visual Arts of Afro-Americans*, South Bend, Ind., 1971.

HOUSTON, LANORA

Painter, graphic artist, sculptor, ceramist.
Works: *Mask* (charcoal); *Bowl* (red clay); *Three Points* (red clay); *Woman* (oil); *The Lime* (acrylic); *Vase* (sandstone).
Sources: Afro-American Slide Depository, catalog.

HOWARD, CONSTANCE

Painter.
Exhibited: Atlanta Univ. 10th Annual for Negro Artists, 1951.
Awards: Honorable mention, Atlanta University, 1951.
Sources: Atlanta Univ. *10th Annual for Negro Artists*, 1951.

HOWARD, HUMBERT L.

Painter. Born in Philadelphia in 1915. Studied at Howard University; University of Pennsylvania; Barnes Foundation; studied aesthetic philosophy under Dr. Paul Ziff, University of Pennsylvania, 1961-62.
Works: *Women Dressing; What's Happening; Black Orpheus; Two Figures; Show Girl; The Gardener's House; Crucifixion; The Yellow Cup; Landscape with Red Figures; Still Life on Landscape.*
Exhibited: Pa. Academy of Fine Arts (1-man); Phila. Art Alliance; Dubin Galleries, Phila.; Pyramid Club, Phila.; Newman Galleries, Phila.; Donovan Gallery, Phila.; William Penn Memorial Museum Exhibit, 1971; Internat'l Academy of Arts & Letters, Rome; Fort Huachuca, Arizona, 1943; McCleaf Gallery, Phila., 1971; Phila. Civic Center Museum; Smith-Mason Gallery, 1971; Library of Congress, 1940; Howard Univ., 1959; Graber Art Gallery, 1968; Congregation Adath Jeshwrun, 1968.
Collections: Pa. Academy of The Fine Arts; Howard Univ.; Phila. Civic Center Museum; Phila. Stern School; Library of Congress; Stanley Bernstein Collection.
Member: Member of Omega Psi Phi Fraternity; Artist Equity Assn.; Art Faculty, Cheltenham Art Center; Peale Club; Phila. Art Alliance; Faculty, Allens Lane Art Center; Amer. Foundation for Negro Affairs Commission on Cultural & Performing Arts.
Sources: Lewis/Waddy. *Black Artists on Art*, Vol. 2; Dover. *American Negro Art*; "Afro-American Issue," *Art Gallery*, April 1968; Information from artist; Phila. Division of Art. *Afro-American Artists: 1800-1969*; Afro-American Slide Depository, catalog, 1971-72; Smith-Mason Gallery. *National Exhibition Black Artists 1971*; DuSable Museum of African-Amer. History. *Contemporary Black Artists*, Calendar,

1970; New York City College. *Afro-American Exhibition*, 1967; *Who's Who in America*, 1969; Saunders, Jack. *100 Years After the Emancipation*; Grafly, Dorothy. *Art in Focus*; Smith, R. Robert. *Philadelphia Artists*, 1957; *Living Philadelphia Artists*, 1956; Green Hill in Lower Merion Gallery. *Exhibition Notice*, 1969; Drummond, Dorothy. "Coast-to-Coast," *Art Digest*, Mar. 1, 1952; Pierre-Noel, Lois Jones. "American Negro Art in Progress," *Negro History Bulletin*, Oct. 1967; Harley, Ralph, Jr. "A Checklist of Afro-Amer. Art & Artists," *The Serif*, Dec. 1970; "Oils by Humbert Howard Go on Exhibit Nov. 5," *Philadelphia Art Alliance Bulletin*, Nov. 1958, pp. 7-8; Green Hill in Lower Merion Gallery. *Humbert Howard: Exhibition*, Sept. 1969; Howard Univ. *Humbert Howard: Paintings*, April 1959; *The Negro Handbook*, Composed by Editors of *Ebony*, Chicago, 1966; Myers, Carol L. *Black Power in the Arts*, Flint, Mich., 1970; "Leading Negro Artists," *Ebony*, Sept. 1963; Walker, Roslyn. *A Resource Guide to the Visual Arts of Afro-Americans*, South Bend, Ind., 1971.

HOWARD, JOHN

Painter, educator. Born in Alcorn, Mississippi in 1912. Teacher of art education at Arkansas A&M College.
Works: *Old Woman with a Letter; Arkansas Landscape; The Violin.*
Exhibited: Atlanta Univ., 1944; Exhibition of Arkansas Art, 1946.
Sources: Dover. *American Negro Art*; Indiana Univ. *Fine Arts & the Black American*; Harley, Ralph, Jr. "A Checklist of Afro-Amer. Art & Artists," *The Serif*, Dec. 1970; Patterson, Lindsay. "Contemporary Artists," *The Negro in Music & Art*; Walker, Roslyn. *A Resource Guide to the Visual Arts of Afro-Americans*, South Bend, Ind., 1971.

HOWARD, KENNETH

Painter.
Works: *Two Ideas* (oil).
Collections: Johnson Pub. Co.
Sources: Johnson Pub. Co. *The JPC Art Collection*, Pamphlet.

HOWELL, RAYMOND

Painter, mixed media. Born in Oakland, California on September 7, 1927. No formal art education.
Works: *The Brown Painting; Proud Tradition; Final Solution; Man from San Miguel; Pursuit; In a Dark House; Social Readjustment; From a Great Past; The Brown Family.*
Exhibited: Boston Art Festival; Cape Cod Art Assn.; The Palace of the Legion of Honor; Emporium Gallery, Arizona; Gump's, San Francisco; Shore Gallery, Boston; Galerie de Tours, San Francisco; Heritage Gallery, Los Angeles; Maxwells Gallery, San Francisco; Gilberts Gallery, San Francisco; The Kaiser Center, Oakland; Los Angeles Internat'l Black Art Show; Oakland Art Museum; Black American Artists/71, Travel Show; Black American Artists/71, Kalamazoo Institute of Arts, Mich.; The Charles & Isabel Eaton Collection of Amer. Paintings Exhibition, Univ. of N. Carolina; Richmond Art Center, California; Hayward State, Calif.; Sonoma State, Calif.
Awards: First Superb Black Arts Show, Univ. of California, 1st prize, 1970; Berkeley Art Festival, Calif., 1st prize, Graphics, 1968; Berkeley Art Festival, Calif., 1st prize, Photography, 1967.
Collections: Oakland Art Museum; Fine American Art Calendar Collection; Harold Zellerbach; Nat "King" Cole; Miss Zsa Zsa Gabor; Mr. & Mrs. Gilbert Anyon; Mr. & Mrs. Robert Bell; Julius Fleischmann Collection; Mr. & Mrs. Maxwell Soroken.
Represented by: Gilberts Galleries, San Francisco.
Sources: Information from artist; *Artform; Black Arts; American Artists; San Francisco Magazine*; Lewis/Waddy. *Black Artists on Art*; Illinois Bell Telephone. *Black American Artists/71*, Catalog; Oakland Museum Archives; Walker, Roslyn. *A Resource Guide to the Visual Arts of Afro-Americans*, South Bend, Ind., 1971.

HOWELL, WILLIAM L.

Graphic designer, art director. Born in Jefferson City, Tennessee, on September 12, 1942. Studied at Philadelphia College of Art, 1960-62. Art Director, New Lafayette Theatre, New York.
Works: *Gates of the Ghetto, Freedom of the Sea; Twelve Seeds of Truth-Weusi; From Whence We Came; Poster for Pamoja Gallery; Child in Thought; Judy; Circle of Truth; Condition of Time; Learning; Thinking of Our Children; Family Tree; The Oppressors; The Beginning; The Junkie; The Indian; Molecular Motion; Growth of a New Life.*
Exhibited: School of Visual Arts, NY; Brooklyn Museum, 1969; Columbia Univ., 1969; Elma Lewis School of Fine Arts, Dorchester, Mass., 1970; Univ. of Florida Art Gallery, Gainesville, 1970; Millikin Univ. Kirkland Gallery, Decatur, Illinois, 1970; Reading Public Museum & Art Gallery, Pa., 1971; Illinois Bell Telephone Traveling Show, Chicago, 1971; Univ. of Rochester; Pan Am Building Gallery, NY, 1970; Gallery 303, NY, 1970; Pratt Institute, NY; Boston Museum of Fine Arts; Rhode Island School of Design, Providence, 1970; Studio Museum, NY, 1970; Public Library of Newark, NJ, 1970; Univ. of the State of NY, Albany, 1970; Mobile Art Gallery, Langan

Park, Ala., 1971; Pensacola Art Center, Florida, 1971; Missouri State College, Springfield, 1971; Studio Five, NY; Nyumba Ya Sanaa Gallery, NY, 1971-72; Hunter College, NY, 1972; Ile-Ife Museum of Afro-American Culture, Phila., 1972; Univ. of Iowa, 1972.
Collections: Mr. Whitman Mayo, NY; Mr. Robert McBeth; Ms. Martha Charles, NY; Mr. Ed Bullins, NY; Ms. Hattie Gossett, NY; Mr. Ollie Johnson, NY; Ms. Diane Lacey, NY; Mr. Herbert Allen, NY; The New Lafayette Theatre, NY; Nyumba Ya Sanaa Gallery, NY; Mr. James Greene, NY; Mr. & Mrs. James Caldwell, NY; Mr. Robin Davis, NY; Ms. Martha Lewis, NY; Ms. Jacqueline Teamor, Phila.; Ile-Ife Museum of Afro-American Culture, Phila.
Awards: 1st prize, Atlantic City Art Exhibit; 2nd prize, Huntington Art Fair.
Member: Weusi Nyumba Ya Sanaa Art Gallery, Harlem.
Sources: *Print*, Nov.-Dec. 1968; Illinois Bell Telephone. *Black American Artists/71*, 1972; *Ebony Magazine*, 1969; *New York Times*, 1970; *Time Magazine*, 1970; *Taking Care of Business*, 1971; *Amsterdam News*, 1971; *Black Theatre Magazine*, 1970-71; *Philadelphia Bulletin*, 1972; *Print Magazine*, 1971; *Tuesday Magazine*, 1970; Information from artist; Jackson, Dorothy. "The Black Experience in Graphic Design," *Print*, Nov.-Dec. 1968; Loercher, Diana. "National Center of Afro-American Artists Art & Benefit Premier," *Christian Science Monitor*, May 4, 1971; Driscoll, Edgar, Jr. "Art Show Reflects Black Rage, Pride," *Boston Globe*, April 28, 1971; Drysdale, Susan. "Black Arts: Alive & Struggling in America," *Christian Science Monitor*; Brooklyn Museum. *New Black Artists*; Boston Museum of Fine Arts. *Afro-American Artists: New York & Boston*, 1970; Mashek, Joseph. "Black Artists, Visual Arts Center," *Artforum*, Sept. 1970, p. 80; School of Visual Arts. *Black Artists 1970*; Loercher, Diana. "Art: Idioms of Blackness at the Elma Lewis School," *Christian Science Monitor*, July 10, 1970.

HUBBARD, JEAN PAUL

Sources: Harley, Ralph, Jr. "Checklist of Afro-Amer. Art & Artists," *The Serif*, Dec. 1970.

HUDSON, ALFONZO

Painter, educator. Born in Philadelphia, Pennsylvania on August 7, 1927. Studied at Pennsylvania Academy of Fine Arts. Art instructor at Philadelphia Recreation Cultural Division.
Works: *Mr. Valé; Fruit & Copper; Black Youth; Golden Youth; Marilyn; Black Nude.*
Exhibited: Afro-Amer. Artist, 1971-72; Carnegie Institute Division of Education; Inner City Art Festival, 1971-72; Nat'l Forum of Professional Artists, 1972; Lee Cultural Center, Phila.
Awards: Prize, anatomy, Pa. Academy of Fine Arts; Scholarship student, Graduate, Pa. Academy of Fine Arts.
Member: Fellowship, Pa. Academy of Fine Arts; Nat'l Forum of Professional Artists.
Sources: Information from artist; Phila. Dept. of Recreation. *Love . . . and the Black Community*.

HUDSON, BILL

Sources: Grillo, Jean B. "Elma Lewis: A New Show A New Showplace," *Boston After Dark*, Aug. 16, 1970.

HUDSON, CHARLES

Sources: NY N.A.A.C.P. *Art Exhibition of Negro Expression Sponsored by Minars Furniture*, April 1964.

HUDSON, HENRY

Painter. Born in Georgia, 1908. Studied at Yale University School of Fine Arts; Howard University.
Works: *Christ before Pilate* (oil).
Exhibited: Howard Univ., 1937, 1932-34; P.W.A.P. Art Exhibit; Corcoran Gallery, Washington, D.C., 1934; Texas Cent., 1936; Harmon Exhibition, 1936.
Collections: Howard Univ. Physical Education Dept.; P.W.A.P. 2 murals (Pied Piper).
Sources: Howard Univ. *Art of the American Negro*, Catalog, 1937; Texas Centennial Exposition. *Thumbnail Sketches of Exhibiting Artists*, 1936; Harley, Ralph, Jr. "Checklist of Afro-Amer. Art & Artists," *The Serif* Dec. 1970.

HUDSON, JULIEN

Portrait painter. Born in 1830. Active during early 19th century in New Orleans.
Works: *Colonel Jean Michel Fortier, Jr.; Self Portrait.*
Exhibited: Howard Univ., 1967.
Sources: Dover. *American Negro Art*, p. 21; Indiana Univ. *Fine Arts & the Black American;* Louisiana. *A Guide to the State*, 1941; Porter. *Modern Negro Art*, 1943, p. 47; DuSable Museum of African-Amer. History. *Contemporary Black Artists*, Calendar, 1970; Harley, Ralph, Jr. "A Checklist of Afro-Amer. Art & Artists," *The Serif*, Dec. 1970; Myers, Carol L. *Black Power in the Arts*, Flint, Mich., 1970; Walker, Roslyn. *A Resource Guide to the Visual Arts of Afro-Americans*, South Bend, Ind., 1971.

HUDSON, ROSE

Mixed media. Studied at Oakwood College.
Works: Untitled clay collage.
Exhibited: Sun Times/Daily News Gallery, Chicago, 1970.

Sources: United Negro College Fund. *Art 1970,* Chicago, 1970.

HUE, ROBERT RALEIGH de
See: D'Hue, Robert Raleigh, Jr.

HUFFMAN, CYNTHIA
Painter.
Works: *Nude.*
Exhibited: Atlanta Univ., 1942.
Sources: Harley, Ralph, Jr. "Checklist of Afro-Amer. Art & Artists," *The Serif,* Dec. 1970.

HUGHES, MANUEL
Painter. Born in 1938. Studied at University of Missouri (BFA, MFA).
Works: *Group 1,* 1970 (oil); Untitled series of oils; *Guardians; The Chitlin' Eater.*
Exhibited: Whitney Museum, 1971; Univ. of Iowa, 1971-72; Mid-America III, City Art Museum, St. Louis, 1970; Butler Art Institute, 1970; *Salon 71/72,* Wardnasse Gallery, 1971-72; *Black American Artists/71;* Carnegie Institute, 1971-72.
Collections: Whitney Museum of Amer. Art, NY; City Art Museum, St. Louis; Morton May Collection, St. Louis; Bell Telephone Co. NYC.
Represented by: Wardnasse Gallery, NYC.
Sources: St. Louis Public Library. *Words & Drawings of Manuel Hughes,* 1972; Doty, Robert. *Contemporary Black Artists in America,* 1972; *Art Journal,* Vol. 31, No. 3, 1972, p. 330; Illinois Bell Telephone. *Black American Artists/71.*

HUGHES, RICHARD
Painter.
Sources: *The Negro Handbook,* Composed by Editors of *Ebony,* Chicago, 1966.

HULSINGER, GEORGE E.
Painter.
Works: *Cleveland by the Rapid; Intersection.*
Exhibited: Atlanta Univ., 1942.
Sources: Harley, Ralph, Jr. "Checklist of Afro-Amer. Art & Artists," *Serif,* Dec. 1970; "Negro Art from Cleveland's Karamu House," *Art Digest,* Jan. 15, 1942; Beckett, Henry. "Zell Ingram, Painter of 'America's Most Tragic Figure,' Talks about Mothers," *New York Post,* Jan. 13, 1942.

HUMPHREY, MARGO
Printmaker, painter. Born in Oakland, California in 1942. Studied at Merritt Junior College; California College of Arts & Crafts.
Works: *Zebra Series; Some Fields Have More Flowers Than Grass; The New Garden; I'm Not Really Listening; A Second Time in Blackness; The Queen Anne and Her Contents; The Day After; The Persistent Reflection; Back to Earth; Black Doll; Untitled; Some Hearts Are Hard to Hearts.*
Exhibited: Casa de Ena Gallery, 1965 (1-woman); Western Addition Library, San Francisco, 1968; Lytton Savings & Loan Assn. Show, 1968; Oakland Museum, 1968; Oakland Flower Show, 1964; Western Addition Art West Associated North Exhibit, 1968; Jack London Art Festival.
Collections: Oakland Museum; Art West Associated North.
Awards: Scholarship student to Cal. College of Arts & Crafts; Golden State Ins. Co. Purchase Award, 1968; Circle-Lets Award, 1968; Berkeley Post Award, 1st Prize (1-woman show, 1965).
Sources: *Negro Year Book;* Indiana Univ. *Fine Arts & the Black American;* Lewis/Waddy. *Black Artists on Art;* Oakland Art Museum. *New Perspectives in Black Art;* DuSable Museum of African-Amer History. *Contemporary Black Artists,* 1970; Harley, Ralph, Jr. "Checklist of Afro-Amer. Art & Artists," *The Serif,* Dec. 1970; Oakland Museum Archives; Walker, Roslyn. *A Resource Guide to the Visual Arts of Afro-Americans,* South Bend, Ind., 1971.

HUNSTER, THOMAS WATSON
Painter.
Exhibited: Memorial Exhibition, Howard Univ., 1951.
Sources: Porter. *Modern Negro Art;* Pierre-Noel, Lois Jones. "American Negro Art in Progress," *Negro History Bulletin,* Oct. 1967; Harley, Ralph, Jr. "Checklist of Afro-Amer. Art & Artists," *Serif,* Dec. 1970; Roucek & Kiernan. *The Negro Impact on Western Civilization.*

HUNT, RAYMOND
Painter. Born in Montclair, New Jersey, 1947.
Works: *Good Company,* 1970; *Who?,* 1970; *Be Calm,* 1971; *May Follows,* 1971.
Exhibited: Newark Museum, 1971.
Represented by: The Art Gallery, Elizabeth, New Jersey.
Sources: Newark Museum. *Black Artists: Two Generations,* 1971.

HUNT, RICHARD HOWARD
Sculptor, educator, printmaker. Born in Woodlawn, Chicago on September 12, 1925. Studied at Junior School of Art Institute of Chicago; Art Institute of Chicago, 1953-57 (BAE). Instructor of art at Art Institute of Chicago, 1960-61; University of Illinois, 1960-62; Chouinard Art School of California Institute of Arts, Los Angeles, 1964-65; Yale University, 1964; Purdue University, 1965.
Works: *Construction D,* 1965; *Hero Construction,* 1958; *Extending Horizontal Forms,* 1958; *Construction with Branching Forms,* 1961; *Medium Expansive Construction,* 1957; *Minor Monument, #1, 2, 3, 5,* 1963; Glider, 1966;

Expansive Construction, 1960; *Growth Form,* 1966-68; *Play,* 1967-69; *John Jones Memorial,* 1968; *Loyola Centennial Sculpture,* 1969; *Cross & Candelabra,* 1970; *Man on a Vehicular Construction,* 1956; *Unicycle Built for Two,* 1956; *Arachne,* 1956; *Icarus,* 1956; *Standing Figure,* 1956; *Sky Form #2,* 1957; Untitled welded steel, 1957; *Wing Bloom,* 1957; *Construction,* 1958; *Double Disk* (welded steel), 1958; *Planar Form Construction,* 1958; *Organic Form #4,* 1959; *Construction,* 1960; *Extended Form,* 1960; *Forms Carried Aloft, #2,* 1960; *Wall Piece with Extending Form,* 1960; *Wall Piece with Hanging Forms,* 1960; *Antique Study After Nike,* 1961; *Organic Construction #9,* 1961; *Linear Spatial Theme,* 1962; *Organic Construction with Branching Forms,* 1962; *Fragmented Figure Construction,* 1963; *Antique Study,* 1964; *Hybrid Form,* 1964; *The Chase,* 1965; *Kneehorn,* 1965; *Winged Hybrid #3,* 1965; *Coil,* 1966; *Natural Form,* 1968; *Pyramidal Complex,* 1966; *Rock Form,* 1966; *Wall Piece,* 1966; *Pegasus,* 1967; *Large Natural Form,* 1968; *Study for Play, #1-3,* 1968; *The Chase, Second Version,* 1969; *Little Pegasus,* 1969; *Hybrid Form #1, Alternate Version,* 1970; *Hybrid Form, #2,* 1970; *Hybrid Form #3, Alternate Version,* 1970; Maquette for *St. Matthew's Cross,* 1970; *Hybrid Form #4,* 1971; *Oppressed Forms; Running Hybrid;* Drawings: *Warrior,* 1957; Untitled, casein & pencil, 1959; Untitled pencil, 1961; Untitled pencil & ink wash, 1961; Prints: *Prometheus,* 1956; *Crucifix Figure,* 1957; Untitled lithograph, 1956; Untitled lithograph from *Details,* 1965; Untitled lithograph, 1969; *Outgrowth.*

Exhibited: Art Institute of Chicago, 1955-66; Museum of Modern Art, NY, 1957, 1959, 1960, 1968, 1969; Whitney Museum of Amer. Art, NY, 1958, 1962, 1966, 1964, 1970; Navy Pier, Lake Michigan, 1957; Contemporary Arts Museum, Houston, 1957; Amer. Federation of the Arts traveling exhibition, 1958-59; Alan Gallery, NY, 1958, 1960, 1961, 1962, 1963 (1-man); Carnegie Institute, 1958, 1961; Henry Durand Institute, Lake Forest College, Ill.; Stewart Rickard Gallery, San Antonio, 1958 (1-man); Galerie Claude Bernard, Paris, 1960; Cincinnati Art Museum, 1961; Holland-Goldowsky Gallery, Chicago, 1961; Seattle World's Fair, 1962; Newark Museum, 1962; Wisconsin Union Galleries, 1962; Solomon R. Guggenheim Museum, NY, 1962; Krannert Art Museum, Univ. of Ill., Urbana, 1962; Parke-Bernet Galleries, NY, 1963-64; B.C. Holland Gallery, Chicago, 1963, 1966 (1-man); Yale Univ. School of Art & Architecture, 1964, 1966; Wesleyan College, Macon, Ga., 1964 (1-man); Univ. of Tulsa, Okla., 1964 (1-man); Felix Landau Gallery, Los Angeles, 1965 (1-man); Arkansas Art Center, Little Rock, 1965; Rockford (Ill.) College, 1965; Stewart Rickford Gallery, San Antonio, 1965 (2-man); Occidental College, Los Angeles, 1965; Univ. of Notre Dame Art Gallery, 1966; Ohio State Univ. School of Art, Columbus, 1966 (1-man); "1st World Festival of Negro Arts," Dakar, Senegal, 1966; Dickson Art Center, Univ. of Calif., Los Angeles, 1966; Cleveland Art Museum, 1967 (1-man); Univ. of Ill. Dept. of Art, 1967; B.C. Holland, Chicago, 1968, 1970; Hemisfair, San Antonio, 1968; Fisk Univ. Ballentine Hall Art Gallery, 1968; Ill. Sesquicentennial, Barat College, Drake Galleries, Lake Forest, 1968; Dorsky Gallery, NY, 1968, 1969 (1-man); Museum of Contemporary Art, Chicago, 1968; Minneapolis Institute of Art, 1968; Johnson C. Smith Univ., Charlotte, N.C., 1968; Ill. State Museum, Springfield, 1968; Metropolitan Museum of Art, NY, 1969; Grand Rapids Art Museum, 1969; Indiana Univ. Art Museum, 1969; Southern Ill. Univ. Mitchell Gallery, 1970 (1-man); Living Art Center, Dayton, Ohio, 1970 (1-man); Museum of Modern Art Traveling Exhibition, 1970; Janet Wallace Fine Arts Center, Macalester College, St. Paul, Minn., 1970 (1-man); Univ. of Neb. Art Galleries, 1970; Boliou Gallery, Carleton College, Northfield, Minn., 1970 (1-man); Milwaukee Art Center, 1967; Israel Museum, Jerusalem, 1965; Baltimore Museum; Des Moines Art Center.

Awards: Scholarship, Chicago Public School Art Society, 1953; Mr. & Mrs. Frank G. Logan Prize, 1956, 1961, 1962; James Nelson Raymond Foreign Travel Fellowship, 1957; Pauline Palmer Prize, 1957; Walter H. Campana Memorial Prize, 1962; John Simon Guggenheim Memorial Fellowship, 1962; Humanities & the Arts of the Ford Foundation Fellowship, 1965.

Collections: Art Institute of Chicago; Whitney Museum of Amer. Art, NY; Museum of Modern Art, NY; Israel Museum, Jerusalem; Milwaukee Art Center; Chicago Circle Campus, Univ. of Ill.; La. State Univ., Baton Rouge; Ridgewood High School, Norridge, Ill.; John J. Madden Mental Health Clinic, Hines, Ill.; Loyola Univ., Chicago; St. Matthew's Methodist Church, Chicago; Mr. & Mrs. C. Howard Hunt, Chicago; Albright-Knox Art Gallery, Buffalo, NY; Mr. & Mrs. Victor W. Ganz, NY; Felix Landau, Los Angeles; Mr. & Mrs. Edwin A. Bergman, Chicago; Mrs. Sidney R. Yates, Chicago; Richard Brown Baker, NY; Mr. & Mrs. Eugene D. Spertus, Evanston, Ill.; Lori Manilow, Chicago; Cleveland Museum of Art; William R. Clarke, Chicago; Mr. & Mrs. Harold Zweig, Chicago; Mr. & Mrs. Max Hess Weinberg, Glencoe, Ill.; Mr. & Mrs. Gifford Phillips, Santa Monica, Cal.; Mr. & Mrs. David C. Ruttenberg, Chicago; Mr. & Mrs. B.C. Holland, Chicago; George M. Irwin,

Quincy, Ill.; Mr. & Mrs. Bernard Nath, Highland Park, Ill.; Metropolitan Museum of Art, NY; Mr. & Mrs. Paul W. Saltzman, Chicago; Mr. & Mrs. Samuel Dorsky, Great Neck, NY; Margo Coleman, Chicago; Mr. & Mrs. Ralph I. Goldenberg, Highland Park, Ill.; Mr. & Mrs. Joseph Randall Shapiro, Oak Park, Ill.; Mr. & Mrs. Edgar B. Miller, Chicago; Dr. & Mrs. Lionel O. Friedman, NY; Mr. & Mrs. Silas Seandel, NY; New Jersey State Museum, Trenton; Nelson Gallery, Atkins Museum, Kansas City, Mo.; Dorsky Galleries, Ltd., NY; Martin Unterman, Evanston, Ill.; Mrs. Louis G. Davidson, Chicago; Joseph H. Hirshhorn; Johnson Pub. Co.; Mr. Howard Lipman; Guggenheim Museum; Oakland Museum.

Member: Art Students' League, Chicago; Nat'l Council on the Arts.

Sources: Ashton, Dore. *Modern American Sculpture;* Albright-Knox Art Gallery. *Contemporary Art: Acquisitions,* 1959-1961; Dover. *American Negro Art;* Ashton, Dore. "Art: Welding New Forms," *New York Times,* September 30, 1958; Bruner, Louise. "Black Art," *The Blade* (Toledo), Sept. 13, 1970; Burckhardt, Edith. "Richard Hunt," *Art News* (New York), Nov. 1958; Burroughs, Margaret. "To Make a Poet Black," *The Art Gallery,* April 1968; Burton, Scott. "Richard Hunt," *Art News,* Summer 1968; Campbell, Lawrence. "Richard Hunt," *Art News,* Summer 1969; Danieli, Fidel A. "Los Angeles," *Artforum,* Feb. 1965; Feldman, Anita. "Richard Hunt," *Arts Magazine,* Summer 1969; "Fifty-six Painters and Sculptors," *Art in America,* August 1964; Ghent, Henri. "Richard Hunt," *School Arts,* April 1969; Glueck, Grace. "Negroes' Art Is What's In Just Now," *New York Times,* Feb. 1969; Greene, Carroll, Jr. "The Afro-American Artist," *The Art Gallery,* April 1968; Greene, Carroll, Jr. "Afro-American Artists, Yesterday and Now," *The Humble Way,* 1968; Greene, Carroll, Jr. "Perspective: The Black Artist in America," *The Art Gallery,* April 1970; Halstead, Whitney. "Chicago," *Artforum,* June 1966; Henning, Edward B. "In Pursuit of Content," *Cleveland Museum of Art Bulletin,* October 1963; "He Seeks the 'Soul' in Metal," *Ebony,* April 1969; Johnston, Jill. "Richard Hunt, Yutaka Ohashi and Nathan Oliveira," *Art News,* April 1962; Key, Donald. "Richard Hunt," *Art Scene,* November 1967; Kramer, Hilton. "Month in Review," *Arts Magazine,* June 1959; Kramer, Hilton. "Art," *The Nation,* March 23, 1963; Kramer, Hilton. "Sculpture above the Fashions," *New York Times,* May 18, 1968; Kramer, Hilton. "Art: A Bounty of Modern Sculpture," *New York Times,* April 19, 1969; Lanes, Jerrold. "Current and Forthcoming Exhibitions," *Burlington Magazine,* June 1969; Lee, Sher-

man E. "Year in Review, 1962," *Cleveland Museum of Art Bulletin,* Nov. 1962; Lee, Sherman E. "The Year in Review for 1969," *Cleveland Museum of Art Bulletin,* Jan. 1970; Raynor, Vivien. "Yutaka Ohashi, Richard Hunt, Nathan Oliveira," *Arts Magazine,* April 1962; "A Red-Hot Hundred," *Life,* September 14, 1962; Sawin, Martica. "Richard Hunt," *Arts Magazine,* Nov. 1958; Schjeldahl, Peter. "A Triumph Rather Than a Threat," *New York Times,* April 27, 1969; Schjeldahl, Peter. "New York Letter," *Art International,* Oct. 1969; S., L. H. "Richard Hunt," *Art News,* April 1963; Schulze, Franz. "Art News from Chicago," *Art News,* Jan. 1964; Schwartz, Donald M. "Portrait of the Artist as a Lonely Man," *Chicago Sun-Times Magazine,* August 14, 1966; Speyer, A. James. "Art News from Chicago," *Art News,* March 1957; "Stuffed Moose & Stacked Tibias," *Time,* Dec. 1, 1967; The Museum of Modern Art. *The Sculpture of Richard Hunt;* "Afro-American Issue," *Art Gallery,* Apr. 1968; Indiana Univ. *Fine Arts & the Black American;* Roelof-Lanner, T.V. *Prints by American Negro Artists;* "Art," *Time Magazine,* Apr. 6, 1970; Minneapolis Institute of Art. *30 Contemporary Black Artists; Who's Who in American Art,* 1970; Illinois Bell Telephone. *Black American Artists/71,* Chicago, 1972; Roucek & Kiernan. *The Negro Impact on Western Civilization;* Afro-American Slide Depository, catalog, 1971-72; DuSable Museum of African-American History. *Contemporary Black Artists,* calendar, 1970; Werner, Alfred. "Black is not a Colour," *Art & Artists,* May 1969, pp. 14-17; Pierre-Noel, Lois Jones. "American Negro Art in Progress," *Negro History Bulletin,* Oct. 1967; Rockford College. *Creativity & the Negro;* "The Black Artist in America: A Symposium," *Metropolitan Museum of Art Bulletin,* Jan. 1969, p. 245; *Art Journal,* Vol. 31, No. 3, 1972, p. 330; Johnson Pub. Co. *The JPC Art Collection;* "Dewar's Profiles: Richard Hunt," *Boston Globe,* Nov. 12, 1970; "Best Chicago Art, Jury Decides," *Scrapbook of Art & Artists of Chicago,* 1956, p. 31; "Steel Boom No. 10," *Scrapbook of Art & Artists of Chicago,* 1957, pp. 38, 42, 47; Harley, Ralph, Jr. "A Checklist of Afro-Amer. Art & Artists," *The Serif,* Dec. 1970; Boning, Richard A. *Profiles of Black Americans,* NY, 1968; Brown, Marion. "The Negro in the Fine Arts," *The Negro Heritage Library,* Vol. 2; Drotning, Phillip T. *A Guide to Negro History in America,* 1968; Woodruff, Hale. "Artists of the 60's," *The Negro in Music & Art,* 1969; Ploski, Harry, & Ernest Kaiser. "The Black Artist," *Afro USA,* 1971; Ploski, Harry, Ernest Kaiser & Otto Lindenmeyer. "The Black Artist," *Reference Library of Black America,* Book IV, 1971; *The Negro Handbook,* Composed by

Editors of *Ebony*; Atkinson, J. Edward. *Black Dimensions in Contemporary American Art*, NY, 1971; Schatz, Walter. *Directory of Afro-American Resources*, Bowker, 1970; Adams, Russell. *Great Negroes Past & Present*, Chicago, 1969; *1st World Festival of Negro Art*, Dakar, Senegal; Ruder & Finn Fine Arts. *Contemporary Black Artists*, NY, 1969; Brooklyn College. *Afro-American Artists: Since 1950*, 1969; Myers, Carol L. *Black Power in the Arts*, Flint, Mich., 1970; Oakland Museum Archives, Ruth Waddy Collection; Fine, Elsa H. "Mainstream & the Black Art Movement," *Art Journal*, Spring 1971; "Leading Negro Artists," *Ebony*, Sept. 1963; Menil Foundation. *The Deluxe Show*, Houston, 1971; *Black Shades*, Mar. 1972; Art Institute of Chicago. *Annual Exhibition by Artists of Chicago & Vicinity*; Driskell, David C. *Sam Middleton & Richard Hunt*, Fisk Univ., 1968; Walker, Roslyn. *A Resource Guide to the Visual Arts of Afro-Americans*, South Bend, Ind., 1971; Alan Gallery. *Sculpture*, NY, 1958; Glueck, Grace. "America Has Black Art on Her Mind," *New York Times*, Feb. 27, 1969, p. C34.

HUNT, YVONNE PARKS

Painter, designer, educator. Born in Atlanta, Georgia, 1930.
Sources: Dover. *American Negro Art*; Indiana Univ. *Fine Arts & the Black American*; Harley, Ralph, Jr. "Checklist of Afro-Amer. Art & Artists," *The Serif*, Dec. 1970; Walker, Roslyn. *A Resource Guide to the Visual Arts of Afro-Americans*, South Bend, Ind., 1971.

HUNTER, CLEMENTINE

Painter. Born c. 1880 on Little Eva Plantation near New Orleans, Louisiana. Began painting in 1930's after a life of cotton picking, and serving as cook in kitchen of Melrose Plantation which was a haven for many artists of the time.
Works: *Saturday Night; Uncle Tom; Grandfather; Christ on Cross; Crucifixion.*
Exhibited: Delgado Art Museum, New Orleans, 1955; La. State Library, permanent exhibition; La Jolla Museum of Art.
Sources: "The Primitive Art of Clementine Hunter," *Ebony*, May 1969, pp. 144-147; La Jolla Museum of Art. *Dimensions of Black.*

HUNTER, NATHANIEL, JR.

Sculptor. Born 1939. Lives in New York.
Works: *Afro-American Queen*, 1970 (mixed media); *Child With Stick.*
Exhibited: Whitney Museum, NY, 1971; Smith-Mason Gallery, 1971.
Sources: Doty. *Contemporary Black Artists in America*; Smith-Mason Gallery. *National Exhibition Black Artists 1971.*

HURLEY, ARNOLD J.

Painter, educator. Born in Boston in 1944. Studied at Boston Museum School of Fine Arts; Boston University; Tufts University (BS, Art education).
Works: *Self Portrait*, 1964 (oil); *German Art Book*, 1965 (oil); *View Girl*; *Rays of Truth* (oil); *Watermelon Man* (oil).
Exhibited: Milton Academy, 1967; Canton Public Library, Canton, Mass., 1965; Jordan Marsh Co., Boston, 1964-5; Rhode Island Arts Festival, Providence, 1965; Northeastern Univ., 1966; Doll & Richards Gallery, Boston, 1966; Tufts Univ. Afro-Amer. Center, Medford, Mass., 1967; Stevens Gallery, Rockport, Mass., 1965-7; The Collectors Gallery, Camden, Me., 1966-7; Nat'l Center of Afro-Amer. Artists, Boston, 1971; Sunday-in-the-Park, Boston, 1968-72; Boston Public Library, 1973; The Gallery, Columbus Ave., Boston, 1973.
Collections: Hallmark Cards, Inc.; The Strathmore Paper Co., Springfield, Mass.; John McCormick School; James Timility School, Boston; Martin Luther King School, Boston; private collections.
Awards: Ford Foundation Grant, 1964; Scholastic Magazine Scholarship, 1964; Hallmark Honor Prize, 1964; Strathmore Award, 1964; New England School of Art Scholarship, 1964; Dorchester Women's Club Scholarship, 1964; Museum of Fine Arts Scholarship, Boston, 1965-6; Kerygma Foundation Grant, 1966; Mary O. H. Longstreth Scholarship, 1965-7; Dana Pond Prize, 1966-7.
Member: Boston Negro Artists Assn.; Martha's Vineyard Artists Assn.; Copley Society of Boston; Cambridge Artists Assn.
Sources: "Black Art Exhibit Opens Sunday," *Herald*, Belmont, Mass., May 14, 1970; "Preview Party to Open Show by 13 Black Artists," *Citizen*, Belmont, Mass., May 14, 1970; Boston Negro Artists Assn. *10th Anniversary Exhibition*, Boston Public Library, 1973, unpublished list.

HUTCHINS, SYLVIA

Painter.
Works: *Portrait* (oil); *Woman* (pastel); *God Ears* (oil); *Masai: from East Africa* (oil).
Exhibited: Boston Public Library, 1973.
Sources: Boston Negro Artists Assn. *10th Anniversary Exhibition*, 1973.

HUTSON, BILL

Painter. Born in San Marcos, Texas in 1936. Studied at University of New Mexico; Los Angeles City College; San Francisco Academy of Art; studied under Frank N. Ashley in California in 1960-1 and in Amsterdam. Lives and works in France and Italy.
Works: *Head of a Poet; Saga of the First Creation Crossing a Bone Path North by*

Northeast; Motive Method; Summerscape; Biafra; La France; Homage to Dr. Martin Luther King; Motion of the Grist; Regarding Outside; Drawing Wash.

Exhibited: Prism Gallery, San Francisco, 1960- (1-man); Artists Cooperative Gallery, San Francisco, 1962; Gallery Krikhaar, Amsterdam, 1964; Stedlijk Museum, Apeldoorn, 1964; Bolles Gallery, San Francisco, 1962; Gallery De Haas, Rotterdam, 1967; USIS London, 1966; Mickery Gallery, Amsterdam, 1967-8; Salon de Juvisy, France, 1968; Galerie R. Cazenave, Paris, 1968; Morgan State College, Baltimore, 1969; Bolles Gallery, San Francisco, 1960; San Francisco Museum of Arts, 1961; San Francisco Arts Festival, 1961-2; Amer. Center for Students & Artists, Paris, 1969; Univ. of Texas Art Museum, 1970; Newark Museum, 1971; Nat'l Center of Afro-American Artists, 1970.

Collections: Nat'l Gallery of South Australia; Morgan State College, Baltimore; Boymans Museum, Rotterdam; Bolles Gallery, San Fransisco; Maxwell Galleries, San Francisco Arts Festival; Amer. Center for Students & Artists, Paris; Bertha Schaeffer Gallery, NY; Bodley Gallery, NY; Chase Manhattan Bank, NY; French & Co., NY; Grand Central Galleries, NY; Lee Nordness Gallery, NY; Midtown Galleries, NY; Terry Dintenfass Gallery.

Awards: Harold L. Zellerbach Prize, San Francisco, 1960; Emanuel Walter Bequest Purchase Award, San Francisco Museum of Art, 1961; Mr. & Mrs. William T. Brantman Prize, San Francisco, 1962; Art of All Faiths Purchase Award, San Francisco, 1962.

Sources: Newark Museum. *Black Artists: Two Generations*, 1971; The Univ. Art Museum of the Univ. of Texas. *Afro-American Artists Abroad*; San Francisco Museum of Art. *25th Annual Drawing, Print, Sculpture Show*, 1961; Walker, Roslyn. *A Resource Guide to the Visual Arts of Afro-Americans*, South Bend, Ind., 1971.

HYKS, STERLING VANCE

Sources: "Negro Art from Cleveland's Karamu House," *Art Digest*, Jan. 1, 1942; Porter. *Modern Negro Art*; Harley, Ralph, Jr. "Checklist of Afro-Amer. Art & Artists," *The Serif*, Dec. 1970.

INGRAM, EDITH

Painter, mixed media. Born in Penlan, Virginia in 1921. Studied at Brockton Art Center, Massachusetts.

Works: *Underwater Fantasies*, 1970 (mixed media); *Sailboat*, 1970 (tissue paper collage); *Autumn Haze*, 1971 (oil collage); *Caribbean Sunset*, 1971 (acrylics); *Quiet Moments; Landscape* (oil); *Seascape.*

Exhibited: Boston Hub Theatre, 1971-2; Newport Art Festival, 1971; South Shore Art Festival, 1970-1; Rockland Art Festival, 1970-1; Boston Negro Artists Assn., 1969-72; Holbrook Art Workshop, 1970; Brockton Art Center, 1971; Randolph Turner Library, 1969-71; Boston Public Library, 1973.

Awards: 1st prize, Holbrook Art Workshop, 1970; 1st prize, Randolph Art Assn., 1971; 1st prize, Popular Prize, Boston Negro Artists Assn., 1970-1.

Member: Boston Negro Artists Assn.

Represented by: Boston Negro Artists Assn.

Sources: Boston Negro Artists Assn. Calendar, 1973; Boston Negro Artists Assn. *10th Anniversary Exhibition*, Boston Public Library, 1973; Boston Negro Artists Assn. *The Black Artist in America: A Negro History Month Exhibition*, Boston Public Library, 1973; "Black Art Exhibit Opens Sunday," *Herald*, Belmont, Mass., May 14, 1970; "Preview Party to Open Show by 13 Black Artists," *Citizen*, Belmont, Mass., May 14, 1970; Information from artist.

INGRAM, ZELL

Painter, graphic artist. Born in Cleveland, 1910. Studied at the Cleveland School of Art; Art Students League, New York.

Works: *Girl before Mirror; Seated Nude; Kneeling Figure; Torso; Figure Composition; Dixie Mother; Conversation.*

Exhibited: Amer. Negro Exposition, Chicago, 1940; Newark Museum, 1971; Boston Museum of Fine Arts, 1970.

Sources: Boston Museum of Fine Arts. *Afro-American Artists: NY & Boston*, 1970; Tanner Art Galleries. *Art of the American Negro*, 1940; Newark Museum. *Black Artists: Two Generations*, 1971; "Negro Art from Cleveland's Karamu House," *Art Digest*, Jan. 15, 1942; Bowling, Frank. "The Rupture," *Arts*, Summer 1970; Porter. *Modern Negro Art*; Harley, Ralph, Jr. "Checklist of Afro-Amer. Art & Artists," *The Serif*, Dec. 1970; Grillo, Jean B. "Black Art—White Museum," *Phoenix*, May 23, 1970; Paris, Jean. "Black Art Experience in Art," *Long Island Press*, Jamaica, NY, June 14, 1970; Le Brun, Caron. "Black Art," *Herald Traveler*, Sunday Supplement, Boston, May 24, 1970; Beckett, Henry. "Zell Ingram, Painter of 'America's Most Tragic Figure,' Talks about Mothers," *New York Post*, Jan. 13, 1942.

IRONS, SUE

Sculptor, educator. Born September 18, 1943 in Chicago. Studied at Pasadena State College, California, 1961; California State College, Los Angeles (BA, 1966); Weseda University, Tokyo, Japan, 1966-7; California State College, Los Angeles (MA, 1971). Art instructor at Pasadena Art Museum; Fine Arts Community Workshop, Pasadena, California.

Works: *Water Composition* Series—Nos. I-V, 1970-1.
Exhibited: Cal. State College, Los Angeles; Gallery-Central 1015, Pasadena, Cal. (3-man); Watts Health Center Art Exhibit, Los Angeles; Musée Rath, Geneva, Switzerland.
Awards: Purchase prize, Watts Festival Art Exhibit, 1970.
Sources: Musée Rath. *8 Artistes Afro-Americains.*

IRVIS, K. LEROY
Sculptor. Born in Saugerties County, New York. Studied at New York State Teachers College (AB); University of New York (MA); University of Pittsburgh (received LLB, summa cum laude). Assistant District Attorney, 1957-1963; Secretary of public relations, Urban League of Pittsburgh; Majority Caucus Chairman, 1965-66; Minority Whip, 1967-68; Majority Leader, 1969-70.
Exhibited: William Penn Memorial Museum, Harrisburg.
Sources: *Pittsburgh Press*, Sunday, Feb. 23, 1969; Pittsburgh Community College. *16 Black Artists.*

IVORY, ALICE E.W.
Sculptor.
Works: *Little Giant Sable; Little Turkey Gobbler.*
Exhibited: Smith-Mason Gallery, 1971.
Sources: Smith-Mason Gallery. *National Exhibition Black Artists 1971.*

JACKSON, A. E.
Painter. Active in the 1960's.
Sources: "Afro-American Issue," *Art Gallery*, April 1968; Indiana Univ. *Fine Arts & the Black American*; DuSable Museum of African-Amer. History. *Contemporary Black Artists*, Calendar, 1970; Harley, Ralph, Jr. "A Checklist of Afro-Amer. Art & Artists," *The Serif*, Dec. 1970; Myers, Carol L. *Black Power in the Arts*, Flint, Mich., 1970; Walker, Roslyn. *A Resource Guide to the Visual Arts of Afro-Americans*, South Bend, Ind., 1971; Links. *Discovery '70.*

JACKSON, BURT
Works: *To the Front; Evening at Home.*
Exhibited: Amer. Negro Exposition, Chicago, 1940.
Sources: Tanner Art Galleries. *Art of the American Negro*, Catalog, 1940.

JACKSON, CLIFFORD
Painter. Born in Paterson, New Jersey in 1927. Studied at the American Art School in New York; New York's Art Students League. Lives and works in Stockholm.
Works: *Semana Santa Procession.*
Exhibited: Gallerie Hybler, Copenhagen, 1957; Gallery Brinken, Stockholm, 1958; Gallery Ugglan, Strangnas, 1961; Galerie Marya, Copenhagen, 1962; Gallery Brinken, Stockholm, 1963; City Center Gallery, NY; Regina Gallery, NY; ACA Gallery, NY; Roko Gallery; D Contemporary Gallery, Atlantic City, NJ; Angora Gallery, Helsinki; Den Frie-Oslo Plads-Copenhagen, 1964.
Awards: New School for Social Research, 1955; Skowhegan School of Painting & Sculpture; John Hay Whitney Fellowship, 1957.
Sources: *10 American Negro Artists Living & Working in Europe*, Catalog, 1964; Harley, Ralph, Jr. "Checklist of Afro-Amer. Art & Artists," *The Serif*, Dec. 1970.

JACKSON, FLORINE TEAL
Painter, educator, mixed media. Born in Hartford, Connecticut.
Works: *We Disagree*, 1948 (oil); *The Dancers*, 1950.
Exhibited: American Internat'l College, Springfield, Mass., 1972; Wadsworth Atheneum, 1972.
Awards: Hartford *Courant* Award, 1951; Hartford *Times* Art Commentary of Art Exhibit, 1962.
Member: Conn. Art Assn.; Through Young Black Eyes Art Assn.
Sources: Information from artist; *National Scholastic Art Magazine*, Dec. 1950; *Seventeen*, Dec. 1950.

JACKSON, GERALD
Painter; electric light artist. Born in Chicago, 1936.
Works: *Aries; Duocoin Tapestry; Homage to Chicago in Light; 136 in Three Parts.*
Exhibited: Boston Museum of Fine Arts, 1970; Newark Museum, 1971.
Collections: Mr. Allen Stone, NYC.
Awards: Brooklyn Museum Scholarship, 1963-4.
Sources: Boston Museum of Fine Arts. *Afro-American Artists: New York & Boston*, 1970; Perry, Regina A. Anthology (in process); Newark Museum. *Black Artists: Two Generations*, 1971; Le Brun, Caron. "Black Art," *Herald Traveler*, Sunday Supplement, May 24, 1970.

JACKSON, HARLAN
Painter.
Works: *Camp #1.*
Exhibited: State Armory, Wilmington, Del. 1971; James A. Porter Gallery, 1970; Howard Univ., 1961.
Sources: "News of Harlan Jackson," *San Francisco Art Assn. Bulletin*, Jan. 1949, p. 5; Roucek & Kiernan. *The Negro Impact on Western Civilization*; Howard Univ. *James A. Porter Gallery of African-American Art*, 1970; Harley, Ralph, Jr. "A Checklist of Afro-Amer. Art & Artists," *The Serif*, Dec. 1970.

JACKSON, HARRY

Exhibited: Wharton House, Phila., 1942.
Sources: Harley, Ralph, Jr. "Checklist of Afro-Amer. Art & Artists," *The Serif*, Dec. 1970.

JACKSON, HIRAM

Painter.
Works: *Rest Period; Life Class; R.B. Foster; St. Mitchell; C. Richardson; Background Music; Ethnic Beauty; W. B. Jason; W.H. Payne; I. E. Page; Dr. C. W. Florence; Dr. S. D. Scruggs; Abe Lincoln in Illinois; Nude with African Sculpture; Seated Nude; Dr. E. E. Dawson; N. B. Young; Color in Motion; Dr. W. C. Daniel.*
Sources: Afro-American Slide Depository, Catalog; Newark Museum. *Black Artists: Two Generations*, 1971.

JACKSON, J.D.

Painter.
Works: *Climax* (oil).
Collections: Johnson Pub. Co.
Sources: Johnson Pub. Co. *The JPC Art Collection*, Pamphlet.

JACKSON, JAY PAUL

Illustrator, cartoonist. Born in Oberlin, Ohio, September 10, 1905. Studied at Ohio Wesleyan College (1925-6); Chicago Art Institute; Los Angeles Art Institute; under Norman Rockwell.
Collections: *Negro Digest; Ebony.*
Member: Amer. Newspaper Guild; NAACP.
Sources: Furr, Arthur F. *History & Progress of Negroes in the US.*

JACKSON, JOHN SPENCER

Sources: Porter. *Modern Negro Art*; Harley, Ralph, Jr. "Checklist of Afro-Amer. Art & Artists," *The Serif*, Dec. 1970.

JACKSON, KATHERINE

Painter. Worked in Tallahassee, Florida.
Works: *Miss Brown America; Baby Asters.*
Exhibited: Atlanta Univ., 1943.
Sources: Atlanta Univ. Exhibition files.

JACKSON, MARTIN

Painter.
Works: *Sorcerer's Apprentice.*
Exhibited: Pyramid Club, Phila., 1962.
Sources: *Art Digest*, March 1, 1952, review of Pyramid show; Pyramid Club. *12th Annual Invitational Exhibition at Pyramid Club*, Phila., 1962.

JACKSON, MAY HOWARD

Sculptor, educator. Born in Philadelphia in 1877. Died July 12, 1931, Long Beach, Long Island. Studied at J. Liberty Tadd's Art School in Philadelphia; Pennsylvania Academy of Fine Arts.
Works: *Mulatto Mother; Enigma; Brotherhood; Kelly Miller*; busts of Francis J. Grimke, Dean Kelly Miller, W.E.B. DuBois.
Exhibited: Corcoran Art Gallery, 1915; Nat'l Academy of Design, 1916; Harmon Foundation, 1927, 1928; NY Emancipation Exposition, 1913.
Collections: Howard Univ.; Dunbar High School, Washington, DC; St. Thomas' Church, Phila.
Awards: Scholarship (4 yrs.), Pa. Academy of Fine Arts; Harmon Foundation Award for Sculpture, 1928.
Sources: Mallett. *Index of Artists*; *American Art Annual*, Vol. 29, 1932 (obit.); *Encyclopedia of the Arts*, p. 38; *Dictionary of American Artists, Sculptors, & Engravers*; Dover. *American Negro Art*, pp. 289, 231, 235; *Negro Almanac*; Locke. *The Negro in Art*; Brawley, Benjamin. *The Negro Genius*; Butcher, Margaret. *The Negro in American Culture*, p. 221; Roucek & Kiernan. *The Negro Impact on Western Civilization*; Harmon Foundation. *Negro Artists*, 1935; Harmon Foundation. *Select Picture List*; DuSable Museum of African-Amer. History. *Contemporary Black Artists, Calendar*, 1970; Furr, Arthur F. *History & Progress of Negroes in the US*; Pierre-Noel, Lois Jones. "American Negro Art in Progress," *Negro History Bulletin*, Oct. 1967; Locke, Alain. "The American Negro as Artist," *American Magazine of Art*, Sept. 1931; Craig, Randall J. "Focus on Black Artists: A Project for School & Community," *School Arts*, Nov. 1970, pp. 30-3; Porter. *Modern Negro Art*; Harley, Ralph, Jr. "A Checklist of Afro-Amer. Art & Artists," *The Serif*, Dec. 1970; Porter, James. "Negro Artists Gain Recognition After Long Battle," *Pittsburgh Courier*, July 29, 1950; Brawley, Benjamin. *The Negro Literature & Art in the US*; Ploski, Harry, & Ernest Kaiser. "The Black Artist," *Afro USA*, 1971; Ploski, Harry, Ernest Kaiser, & Otto Lindenmeyer. "The Black Artist," *Reference Library of Black America*, Book 4, 1971; Myers, Carol L. *Black Power in the Arts*, Flint, Mich., 1970; Walker, Roslyn. *A Resource Guide to the Visual Arts of Afro-Americans*, South Bend, Ind., 1971; Bennet, Mary. "The Harmon Awards," *Opportunity*, Feb. 1969, pp. 47-8; Holbrook, Francis. "A Group of Negro Artists," *Opportunity*, July 1923, pp. 211-3.

JACKSON, OLIVER L.

Painter, educator. Born in St. Louis, Missouri. Studied at Illinois Wesleyan University, Bloomington, Illinois (BFA); University of Iowa (MFA). Teaching in Black Studies at Sacramento State College, Sacramento, California.
Exhibited: Downstairs Gallery, St. Louis, Mo. (1-man); "Art in the Embassies Program,"

Washington, DC; Contra Costa College, San Pablo, Cal.; Compton Jr. College, Compton, Cal.; Richmond (Cal.) Art Center.
Collections: Univ. of Ill., Urbana.
Sources: Oakland Museum. *Black Untitled II*, 1967.

JACKSON, OWEN T.

Sources: Harley, Ralph, Jr. "Checklist of Afro-Amer. Art & Artists," *The Serif*, Dec. 1970.

JACKSON, ROBERT

Painter.
Works: *St. Francis; Despair; Dead Child; Young Negro Worker.*
Exhibited: Amer. Negro Exposition, Chicago, 1940; Dillard Univ., 1941; James A. Porter Gallery of African-Amer. Art, 1970.
Sources: Tanner Art Galleries. *Art of the American Negro*, 1940; Dillard Univ. *Arts Festival*, 1941; Howard Univ. *James A. Porter Gallery of African-Amer. Art*, 1970; "The New York Negro: Portrait Studies are Made by Robert M. Jackson," *Sunday Star*, Washington, DC, Oct. 20, 1940.

JACKSON, SUZZANE

Painter. Born in St. Louis in 1944. Studied at San Francisco State College; Otis Art Institute; primarily self-taught.
Works: *Untitled; Grandparents*, 1970; *Escaped*, 1970.
Exhibitions: Two-woman & Sapphire Gallery; Cal. State College at Los Angeles; Palm Springs Desert Museum; Pasadena City College; Watts Tower Art Center; Pasadena Fine Arts Workshop; Mark Taper Forum, Los Angeles; Gallery 32, Los Angeles.
Collections: Palm Springs Desert Museum; Joseph Hirshhorn Collection; Ankrum Gallery; Ms. Naomi Hirshhorn; Mr. Bernie Casey; Mr. Bill Cosby; Mr. & Mrs. Ron Rifkin; Mr. & Mrs. Nelson Wheeler.
Sources: Lewis/Waddy. *Black Artists on Art*, Vol. 2; Oakland Museum. *Black Untitled II*, 1971; Cal. State College. *Two Generations of Black Artists*, Los Angeles, list.

JACKSON, WILLIAM

Photographer.
Works: *Mudflat.*
Collections: NY Public Library, Schomburg Collection; Oakland Museum.
Sources: Schatz, Walter. *Directory of Afro-American Resources*, 1970; Oakland Museum Archives.

JAMES, BEN

Ceramist. Studied at Laney College, Oakland, California; University of California Extension, San Francisco.
Works: Stoneware plate & jar.
Exhibited: Mills College, Oakland, 1970; Laney College, 1969; San Leandro Chamber of Commerce, 1969; Alameda Public Library; Art Inn Gallery, 1968.
Sources: Mills College. *California Black Craftsmen*, 1970.

JAMES, BOB

Painter.
Works: *Avatar*, 1971; *Kojo*, 1971; *Lioness*, 1965.
Exhibited: Newark Museum, 1971.
Sources: Newark Museum. *Black Artists: Two Generations*, 1971.

JAMES, CATHERINE

Painter.
Works: *Tribes & Forms of the Anglo Saxon Syndrome.*
Exhibited: Smith-Mason Gallery, 1971.
Sources: Smith-Mason Gallery. *National Exhibition Black Artists*, 1971.

JAMES, FREDERICK

Sources: Harley, Ralph, Jr. "Checklist of Afro-Amer. Art & Artists," *Serif*, Dec. 1970; "Two Artists in Exhibits Downtown," *NY Amsterdam News*, May 21, 1938; William Rockhill Nelson Gallery of Art. *Five Kansas City Artists*, Kansas City, April 1948.

JAMES, WILMER

Printmaker. Active in 1960's.
Works: *Untitled* (serigraph).
Collections: Oakland Museum.
Sources: Roelof-Lanner, T.V. *Prints by American Negro Artists*; Oakland Museum Archives, Ruth Waddy Collection.

JANVIER, LOISE

Born in Haiti. Studied at Foyer des Arts Plastiques, Port-au-Prince, Haiti.
Works: *Jardin des Enfants.*
Exhibited: Studio Museum in Harlem, 1969.
Awards: 2nd prize, Sao Paulo (Brazil) Biennial, 1964.
Sources: Studio Museum in Harlem. *Harlem Artists 69.*

JARRELL, JAE

Textile artist, designer. Born in Cleveland, Ohio.
Works: *Black Family; Suit w 1; Shirt & Beret w 2; Knit Suit m 1; Knit Suit m 2; Dashiki & Pants; Outfit c 1; Outfit c 2.*
Exhibited: Nat'l Center of Afro-Amer. Artists, 1970, 1972; Howard Univ., 1970, 1972; Studio Museum in Harlem, 1970, 1972.
Member: AFRICOBRA.
Sources: Grillo, Jean B. "Where Down Home Meets Back Home," *Boston After Dark*, Sept. 1970; *Black Shades*, Feb. 1972; Howard Univ. *Africobra I*, Catalog, 1970; Howard Univ. *Africobra II*, Catalog, 1972.

JARRELL, WADSWORTH A.
Painter. Born in Albany, Georgia.
Works: *Black Family; Compared to What; Tightening the Game; This Time Baby; The Other Side; Cool Ade Lester; Boss Couple; Poster: Cool Ade Rhythm.*
Exhibited: Howard Univ., 1970, 1972; Nat'l Center of Afro-Amer. Artists, 1970, 1972; Studio Museum in Harlem, 1970, 1972.
Member: AFRICOBRA.
Sources: DuSable Museum of African-Amer. History. *Contemporary Black Artists,* 1970, Calendar; *Black Shades,* Feb. 1972; Grillo, Jean B. "Where Down Home Meets Back Home," *Boston After Dark,* Sept. 1970; Howard Univ. *Africobra I,* Catalog, 1970; Howard Univ. *Africobra II,* Catalog, 1972.

JARVIS, ANTONIO J.
Painter, illustrator, cartoonist, commercial artist. Born in the Virgin Islands, 1901. Studied at Columbia University (1933).
Works: *Cha Cha Peddlar; Lauritz;* Illustrations for government folders.
Exhibited: Harmon Foundation, 1933; *Opportunity* Contest, 1927.
Awards: Award, *Opportunity* Contest, 1927.
Sources: Harmon Foundation. *Exhibition of Productions by Negro Artists;* Indiana Univ. *Fine Arts & the Black American;* Mallett. *Index of Artists;* Harmon Foundation. *Non-Jury Exhibit of Works of Negro Artists,* 1933; Harmon Foundation. *Negro Artists,* 1935; DuSable Museum of African-Amer. History. *Contemporary Black Artists,* 1970, Calendar; Walker, Roslyn. *A Resource Guide to the Visual Arts of Afro-Americans,* South Bend, Ind., 1971.

JEFFERSON, ARCHIE
Works: *Montantalus.*
Sources: Patterson, Lindsay. "Contemporary Artists," *The Negro in Music and Art,* 1969.

JEFFERSON, BOB
Jeweler, studio designer. Born in New Orleans, 1943. Studied at Southern University, Baton Rouge; Oakland City College; self-taught jeweler.
Works: 14K gold ring and rutilated quartz & blue bronze pearl & mexican opal; Pendant; *Horny #1* (silver, jade, pearls, & feathers); *Horny #2* (gold gilt, jade, & opals); *Horny #3* (gold gilt, pearls, & moonstones).
Exhibited: Berkeley Art Festival, 1967; San Francisco Art Festival, 1968, 1969; Johnson Wax Collection, 1969; Mills College; Oakland Museum, 1971.
Collections: Oakland Museum.
Awards: Berkeley & San Francisco Art Festivals; Oakland Museum Purchase Prize.
Sources: Mills College. *California Black Craftsmen,* 1970; Nordness, Lee. *Objects: USA;* Oakland Museum. *The Metal Experience,* 1971.

JEFFERSON, DONZLEIGH HENDRICKS
Painter, sculptor. Born in Nashville, Tennessee, 1912. Studied at Fisk University.
Exhibited: Harmon Foundation, 1928.
Sources: Harmon Foundation. *Exhibition of Productions by Negro Artists;* Harmon Foundation. *Negro Artists,* 1935; DuSable Museum of African-Amer. History. *Contemporary Black Artists,* 1970, Calendar; Harley, Ralph, Jr. "Checklist of Afro-Amer. Art & Artists," *Serif,* Dec. 1970.

JEFFERSON, HENRY HOMER
Architect, civil engineer. Born in Houston, Texas. Studied at Howard University (BS); University of Pennsylvania.
Member: Omega Psi Phi.
Sources: Furr, Arthur F. *History & Progress of Negroes in the US.*

JEFFERSON, JANICE
Painter. Born in 1948. Studied at Oakland City College.
Works: *The Sea Crab* (acrylic).
Exhibited: Oakland Museum, 1968.
Sources: Oakland Museum. *New Perspectives in Black Art;* Indiana Univ. *Fine Arts & the Black American;* Walker, Roslyn. *A Resource Guide to the Visual Arts of Afro-Americans,* South Bend, Ind., 1971.

JEFFERSON, JOHN H.
Painter. Born in Yonkers, New York in 1926. Studied at Pratt Institute.
Works: *White Witch Hall of Jamaica, W.I.; Martinique Beauty.*
Exhibited: Studio Museum in Harlem, 1969.
Sources: Studio Museum in Harlem. *Harlem Artists 69.*

JEFFERSON, LOUISE E.
Painter.
Works: *Savoy Ballroom Dancers; Blues Singer.*
Exhibited: Baltimore Museum of Art, 1939; Amer. Negro Exposition, Chicago, 1940.
Sources: Baltimore Museum of Art. *Contemporary Negro,* 1939; Tanner Art Galleries. *Art of the American Negro,* 1940; DuSable Museum of African-Amer. History. *Contemporary Black Artists,* 1970, Calendar; Greene, Carroll, Jr. "Perspective: The Black Artist in America," *Art Gallery,* April 1970, p. 23; Harley, Ralph, Jr. "Checklist of Afro-Amer. Art & Artists," *Serif,* Dec. 1970.

JEFFRIES, ROSALIND
Painter. Born 1938 in New York City. Studied at Hunter College; Columbia University.
Works: Untitled painting: *Composition #3.*

143

Exhibits: Hotel Ivoire Art Gallery, Abidjan, Ivory Coast, West Africa, 1966; Lafayette College, Pa., 1968; Jackson State College, Miss., 1970.
Sources: Lewis/Waddy. *Black Artists on Art,* Vol. 2; Patterson, Lindsay. "Contemporary Artists," *The Negro in Music and Art,"* 1969.

JENKINS, BARBARA F.

Painter, mixed media. Born in Newark, New Jersey.
Works: *Boy in a Fantasy Rodeo,* 1970; *Corridors,* 1968; *Escapes 1,* 1970; *Ghetto Nigger,* 1971; *Corridors of the Soul,* 1970; *Boy on a Sea Horse in Fantasy Rodeo,* 1971; *Suburban Nigger,* 1971; *Zodiac Series,* 1972; *Musicians Series,* 1972; *Jammin,* 1972.
Exhibited: Newark Museum, 1970-2; Newark Public Library, 1970-2; NY State Museum, 1971; Montclair State College, 1971; NC State College, 1971; East Orange City Hall, NJ, 1970-2; City Hall, Orange, NJ, 1969-72.
Collections: Newark Museum; Urban League; Mid-Block Art Service; Del. State College; Paterson City Hall.
Awards: Purchase Award, Newark Museum; Purchase Award, Paterson City Hall; 2nd prize, Paterson Art Show; 3rd prize, Newark Public Library.
Represented by: Mid-Block Art Service, East Orange, NJ; Maxine Singleton.
Sources: Newark Museum. *Black Artists: Two Generations,* 1971; Information from artist.

JENKINS, CHARLES

Painter, graphic artist, commercial artist. Born in Waterbury, Connecticut. Studied at Butera School of Art, Boston.
Exhibited: Eastfield Mall Cinema, 1969 (2-man); Amer. Internat'l College, Springfield; Afro-Art Alliance Exhibitions.
Collections: Malcolm X College, Chicago.
Member: Afro-Art Alliance, Springfield, Mass.
Sources: Information from the artist.

JENKINS, FLORIAN

Painter. Born in Newark, New Jersey, 1940.
Works: *A Matter of Identity,* 1970; *The Wonder of It All,* 1970; *Ghetto Heiroglyphs,* 1968; *Ed,* 1970; murals, Dartmouth College, 1972; mural, Abraham Clark High School, 1971.
Exhibited: Newark Museum, 1971; Dartmouth College; Newark Public Library; Del. State College; Montclair State College; Trenton State Museum.
Collections: Newark Public Library; Newark Museum; Paterson Bank.
Represented by: Mid-Block Art Service.
Sources: Newark Museum. *Black Artists: Two Generations,* 1971; Information from the artist.

JENNINGS, JAMES N.
Sources: DuSable Museum of African-Amer. History. *Contemporary Black Artists,* 1970, Calendar.

JENNINGS, PERSIS
Painter. Worked in Hampton, Virginia.
Works: *Mother and Child.*
Exhibited: Atlanta Univ., 1944.
Sources: Harley, Ralph, Jr. "Checklist of Afro-Amer. Art & Artists," *The Serif,* Dec. 1970.

JENNINGS, VENDA SEALS
Painter, educator. Studied at Lincoln University (BS); University of Southern California; Catholic University.
Works: *Man from Sierra Leone; To Market; Ouch.*
Exhibited: Smith-Mason Gallery, 1971; DCAA, Anacostia Neighborhood Museum-Smithsonian Institution, 1971.
Sources: Smith-Mason Gallery. *National Exhibition Black Artists,* 1971; DC Art Assn. *Exhibition '71,* Washington, DC, 1971.

JENNINGS, WILMER
Painter, printmaker, educator, designer, jeweler. Born in Atlanta, 1910. Studied at Morehouse College (BS, 1931); under Hale Woodruff; Rhode Island School of Design.
Works: *Rendez-Vous; Dead Tree; The Land, Blind Alley; Boat House; Boat Station; Coal Storage; Hand Line; Lazy Bones; Man and Mule; Oil Tanks; Providence Houses; Still Life; Tug Boat; Head of a Girl.*
Exhibited: Art Institute of Chicago, 1939; Baltimore Museum; NY World's Fair, 1939; Harmon Foundation, 1933, 1935; Amer. Negro Exposition, Chicago, 1940; Atlanta Univ., 1942; NJ State Museum, 1935; Library of Congress, 1940; Texas Centennial, 1936; Harmon College Art Assn., 1934-5; Harmon Traveling Exhibit, 1935-6; Newark Museum, 1971.
Collections: Atlanta High School (mural); Public Works Art Project; Newark Museum; Nat'l Archives.
Awards: Honorable Mention, Amer. Negro Exposition, Chicago, 1940.
Sources: Mallett. *Index of Artists;* Dover. *American Negro Art;* Tanner Art Galleries. *Art of the American Negro;* Locke. *The Negro in Art;* Baltimore Museum of Art. *Contemporary Negro,* Catalog; Locke, Alain. "Advance on the Art Front," *Opportunity,* May 1939; Harley, Ralph, Jr. "Checklist of Afro-Amer. Art & Artists," *Serif,* Dec. 1970; Texas Centennial Exposition. *Thumbnail Sketches of Exhibiting Artists,* 1936; Newark Museum. *Black Artists Two Generations,* 1971; Afro-American Slide Depository, Catalog, 1971-2; Harmon Foundation. *Negro Artists,* 1935; DuSable Museum of

African-Amer. History. *Contemporary Black Artists,* 1970, Calendar; "Amer. Negro Art Given Full Length Review in NY Show," *Art Digest,* Dec. 15, 1941; "Negro Winners," *Art Digest,* May 1, 1946; Porter, James. "Negro Artists Gain Recognition after Long Battle," *Pittsburgh Courier,* July 29, 1950; *The Negro Handbook,* Composed by Editors of *Ebony,* Chicago, 1966; Walker, Roslyn. *A Resource Guide to the Visual Arts of Afro-Americans,* South Bend, Ind., 1971.

JESSUP, GEORGIA MILLS

Painter, educator. Born in Washington, DC. Studied at Howard University (BFA); American University; DC Teachers College; Catholic University (MFA). Artist-in-residence, Anacostia Neighborhood Museum-Smithsonian Institution.
Works: *Peace and Love.*
Exhibited: 1939 World's Fair; Howard Univ.; Heritage Art Gallery; Franklin School; Channell Galleries; Olde Towne Gallery; Potter's House Gallery (1-man); Margaret Dickey Gallery; Teacher-Artists, DC Armory Show; Georgetown Gallery; Sidwell Friends School; Congregation Beth El; Anacostia Neighborhood Museum-Smithsonian Institution; Museum of Natural History, Smithsonian Institution; Ontario Gallery; DC Teachers College; Norfolk Museum of Arts & Sciences; Catholic Univ.; Penn Women's Show.
Collections: Medical Arts Center; Jonson-Robnson Clinic; Honorable T.M. Beale; Mrs. Gayord, British Embassy; Late Honorable Arthur B. Christopher; Mrs. Jeanne Dixon.
Awards: Whitney Foundation Project, summer of 1967.
Sources: DC Art Assn. *Exhibition '71,* Washington, DC, 1971; Congregation Beth El. *Art-st Equity Show,* Washington, DC, Unpublished List.

JOHNS, WILLIAM N.

Graphic artist.
Works: *Going to Church* (silkscreen).
Collections: Oakland Museum.
Sources: Oakland Museum Archives, gift of the Harmon Foundation.

JOHNSON, BARRY C.

Sculptor. Born in New York City in 1948. Studied at the High School of Art & Design.
Works: *The Dolphins.*
Exhibited: Studio Museum in Harlem, 1969.
Sources: Studio Museum in Harlem. *Harlem Artists 69.*

JOHNSON, BESSIE VIOLA

Artist; composer; specialized in portraiture. Born in Burlington, Iowa, December 12, 1878. Studied at Hawksworth Art School (7 years).

Member: NAACP; Negro Business League; Chicago Art League.
Sources: *Who's Who in Colored America,* 3rd edition.

JOHNSON, CORNELIUS W.

Painter, commercial artist. Born in Texas, 1905. Studied at Mechanical Arts High School, St. Paul; Art Institute of Chicago; Art Students League, New York.
Works: *My Girl.*
Exhibited: Regal Theatre, Chicago, 1931; South Center Dept. Store, Chicago, 1932; Open Art Exhibition, Chicago, 1932; Harmon Foundation, 1933.
Sources: Harmon Foundation. *Exhibition of Productions by Negro Artists;* Indiana Univ. *Fine Arts & the Black American;* Mallett. *Index of Artists;* Harley, Ralph, Jr. "Checklist of Afro-Amer. Art & Artists," *Serif,* Dec. 1970; Walker, Roslyn. *A Resource Guide to the Visual Arts of Afro-Americans,* South Bend, Ind., 1971.

JOHNSON, DANIEL LaRUE

Sculptor, painter. Born in Los Angeles, 1938. Studied at Chouinard Art School; California Institute of Arts, Los Angeles (BFA); under Alberto Giacometti in Paris.
Works: *Homage to Rene D'Harnoncourt; Yesterday; Death of Tarzan; Eve; Study for a Church Altar; Bob Ornette; The Boy Wonder Dejohnette; Orbits Revisited; Miles Infinite; Big Red; Untitled; Monk; Wendell.*
Exhibited: Chouinard Art School, Los Angeles, 1956 (1-man); Pasadena Community Center, 1953 (1-man); Rolf Nelson Gallery, Los Angeles, 1964; Dwan Gallery, Los Angeles, 1964; Friegen Palmer Gallery, Los Angeles, 1964; Atlanta Univ. Annual, 1963, 1965; Howard Univ. Annual, 1963; San Francisco Art Institute, 1963; Long Beach (Cal.) Museum of Art, 1962; Pasadena Art Museum, 1962; Whitney Museum Annual, 1969; French & Company, 1970 (1-man); Jewish Community Center, Los Angeles; La Jolla Museum of Art, 1962, 1970; Dickson Art Center, 1966; Museum of Modern Art; High Museum, Atlanta; Minneapolis Institute of Art.
Collections: Pasadena Art Museum; Museum of Modern Art, NYC; Chouinard Art School; Cal. Institute of the Arts, Los Angeles; Mrs. John D. Rockefeller, II, NY; Gov. Nelson Rockefeller, NY; Mrs. Bliss Parkinson, NY; Mr. Joseph H. Hirshhorn, NY; French & Co., Inc., NYC; Jewish Community Center; Mr. James Baldwin; Ms. Lena Horne; Dr. & Mrs. Leon O. Banks; Mr. Benny Andrews.
Awards: Guggenheim Memorial Fellowship, 1965-6; John Hay Whitney Foundation Fellowship, 1963-4; Stanton Fellowship, 1961-2; Allied Art Committee Grant.

Sources: Minneapolis Institute of Art. *30 Contemporary Black Artists;* Coffin, Patricia. "Black Artist in a White Art World," *Look,* Jan. 7, 1969, pp. 66-69; *Time,* April 6, 1970, Portrait; "Afro-American Issue," *Art Gallery,* April 1968; Indiana Univ. *Fine Arts & the Black American;* Boston Museum of Fine Arts. *Afro-American Artists: NY & Boston,* 1970; UCLA Art Galleries. *The Negro in American Art;* La Jolla Museum of Art. *Dimension of Black;* DuSable Museum of African-Amer. History. *Contemporary Black Artists,* 1970, Calendar; Greene, Carroll, Jr. "Perspective: The Black Artist in America," *Art Gallery,* April 1970; Bowling, Frank. "The Rupture," *Arts,* Summer 1970; Bowling, Frank. "It's Not Enough to Say 'Black Is Beautiful'," *Art News,* April 1971; Bowling, Frank. "Discussion on Black Art II," *Arts,* May 1969; Harley, Ralph, Jr. "Checklist of Afro-Amer. Art & Artists," *Serif,* Dec. 1970; "What Is Black Art?," *Newsweek,* June 22, 1970; Ploski, Harry, & Ernest Kaiser. "The Black Artist," *Afro USA,* 1971; Berkman, Florence. "Afro-Amer. Exhibit Fosters Understanding of Black Artists," *Times,* Hartford, May 24, 1970; Van Almelo, Frederik. "In the American Grain," *Boston After Dark,* May 26, 1970, p. 24; *Arts,* Summer 1970; Paris, Jean. "Black Art Experience in Art," *Long Island Press,* Jamaica, NY, June 14, 1970; Ploski, Harry, Ernest Kaiser, & Otto Lindenmeyer. "The Black Artist," *Reference Library of Black America,* Book 4, 1971; Schatz, Walter. *Directory of Afro-American Resources,* 1970; Le Brun, Caron. "Black Art," *Herald Traveler,* Sunday Supplement, Boston, May 24, 1970; Walker, Roslyn. *A Resource Guide to the Visual Arts of Afro-Americans,* South Bend, Ind., 1971; Glueck, Grace. "America Has Black Art on Her Mind, *New York Times,* Feb. 27, 1969, p. C34.

JOHNSON, EUGENE H.

Painter.
Works: *The Storm.*
Exhibited: South Side Community Art Center, 1945.
Collections: Mrs. Eugene Johnson.
Sources: South Side Community Art Center. *Chicago Collectors Exhibit of Negro Art,* 1945.

JOHNSON, EUNICE

Painter. Worked in Topeka, Kansas in 1940's.
Works: *Back Yard.*
Exhibited: Atlanta Univ., 1943.
Sources: Atlanta Univ. Exhibition Files.

JOHNSON, EVELYN ELIZABETH

Born in Boston in 1909. Studied at Boston University.
Works: *French Medieval Manuscript.*

Exhibited: Harmon Foundation, 1933; Boston Univ.
Sources: Harmon Foundation. *Non-Jury Exhibit of Works of Negro Artists,* 1933.

JOHNSON, EVERETT

Sources: Porter. *Modern Negro Art;* Harley, Ralph, Jr. "Checklist of Afro-Amer. Art & Artists," *The Serif,* Dec. 1970.

JOHNSON, GEORGE H. BEN

Painter, illustrator. Born in Richmond, Virginia, 1888. Studied at Hampton Institute, Virginia; Landon School, Cleveland, Ohio; Columbia University.
Works: *Paupers & Princes; A Virginia Flower Vendor; Business Competition; Frederick Douglass with President Lincoln; Idyl of Virginia Mountains; Abandoned Is the Little Brown House; A Pause at the Plough in the Virginia Mountains; The Church above the Railroad; Blitzkrieg, Homo Sapiens, Call Me Savage Said the Great Ape; Blushing; A Fall Evening; Still Life; The Sycamore; Atheotes, Ethiopian Writer, 2122 BC.*
Exhibited: Atlanta Univ., 1942-4; Amer. Negro Exposition, Chicago, 1940; Dillard Univ. 1941; Richmond Public Library, 1926; YMCA, Indianapolis, 1930; Smithsonian Institution, 1929; Richmond Academy of Arts, 1934; Imperial Galleries, London; Va. Museum of Fine Arts; Whitney Museum, NY; Harmon Foundation, 1933, 1939; Tanner Art League, 1922; 135th St. Branch, NY Public Library, 1934; Central YWCA, 1935.
Collections: Speed Memorial Museum, Louisville, Ky.; Valentine Museum, Richmond, Va.
Awards: 2nd prize, 1936, 1st prize, 1937, Cross Alumni Assn., Boothbay Harbor, Maine.
Member: South Streets Art League; Albemarle Art League; Amer. Institute of Architects.
Sources: Indiana Univ. *Fine Arts & the Black American;* Harmon Foundation. *Exhibition of Productions by Black Artists;* Harmon Foundation. *Non-Jury Exhibits of Works of Negro Artists,* 1933; Harmon Foundation. *Negro Artists,* 1935; *Who's Who in American Art,* 1940-1; Mallett. *Index of Artists;* Harley, Ralph, Jr. "Checklist of Afro-Amer. Art & Artists," *Serif,* Dec. 1970; Tanner Art Galleries. *Art of the American Negro,* 1940; Dillard Univ. *Arts Festival,* Catalog, 1935; DuSable Museum of African-Amer. History. *Contemporary Black Artists,* 1970, Calendar; Smithsonian Institution. *Painting & Sculpture by American Negro Artists,* 1929; Walker, Roslyn. *A Resource Guide to the Visual Arts of Afro-Americans,* South Bend, Ind., 1971.

JOHNSON, GERTRUDE

Born in Connecticut, 1911. Self-taught.
Works: *Vase of Geraniums*

Exhibited: Harmon Foundation, 1930, 1933.
Sources: Harmon Foundation. *Exhibition of Productions by Negro Artists;* Indiana Univ. *Fine Arts & the Black American;* Harmon Foundation. *Negro Artists,* 1935; Harmon Foundation. *Exhibit of Fine Arts,* 1930; DuSable Museum of African-Amer. History. *Contemporary Black Artists,* 1970, Calendar; Harley, Ralph, Jr. "Checklist of Afro-Amer. Art & Artists," *Serif,* Dec. 1970.

JOHNSON, GLADYS L.
Textile artist. Active in 1930's.
Exhibited: Harmon Foundation, 1928, 1933.
Sources: Harmon Foundation. *Exhibition of Productions by Negro Artists;* Indiana Univ. *Fine Arts & the Black American;* Harmon Foundation. *Negro Artists,* 1935; DuSable Museum of African-Amer. History. *Contemporary Black Artists,* 1970, Calendar; Harley, Ralph, Jr. "Checklist of Afro-Amer. Art & Artists," *Serif,* Dec. 1970; Walker, Roslyn. *A Resource Guide to the Visual Arts of Afro-Americans,* South Bend, Ind., 1971.

JOHNSON, GRACE MOTT
Exhibited: Augusta Savage Studios, 1939.
Sources: "Animal Sculpture," *Amer. Magazine of Art,* Feb. 1923; "Grace Mott Johnson Wins Sculpture Prize," *El Palacia,* April 1936, p. 94; Harley, Ralph, Jr. "Checklist of Afro-Amer. Art & Artists," *The Serif,* Dec. 1970.

JOHNSON, HERBERT
Painter.
Works: *One Direction* (oil).
Exhibited: Oakland Museum, 1968.
Sources: Oakland Museum. *New Perspectives in Black Art;* Indiana Univ. *Fine Arts & the Black American;* DuSable Museum of African-Amer. History. *Contemporary Black Artists,* 1970, Calendar; Harley, Ralph, Jr. "Checklist of Afro-Amer. Art & Artists," *The Serif,* Dec. 1970; Walker, Roslyn. *A Resource Guide to the Visual Arts of Afro-Americans,* South Bend, Ind., 1971.

JOHNSON, JEANNE
Painter. Born in Harlem, New York, 1940.
Works: *Nigerian Brother,* 1970; *Bobby,* 1970; *Two Girls,* 1968.
Exhibited: Newark Museum, 1971.
Sources: Newark Museum. *Black Artists: Two Generations,* 1971.

JOHNSON, JOSEPH
Painter. Born in Ohio. Self-taught.
Works: *Death of a Young Poet; Ulysses and the Sirens; Marius Contemplates Ruins of Carthage.*
Exhibited: NY Public Library, 1950 (1-man).
Sources: *New York Times,* Sept. 18, 1950.

JOHNSON, KAREN
Painter, graphic artist, mixed media. Born in San Francisco, March 24, 1948. Studied at San Francisco Art Institute.
Works: *A Son Dies-His Mother's Hands* (pencil); *Change,* 1969 (acrylic); *The Edge of Revolution,* 1970 (collage with acrylic); *Series of Songs,* 1972; *Return from 'They All Look Alike to Me',* 1972 (serigraph); Posters—*Bessie Smith, Montage of a Dream Deferred, Two Hunters, Kwame Nkrumah, Julius Nyere.*
Exhibited: The Marcus Book Store, 1971, 1972; Golden Gate College, 1972; Rainbow Sign Gallery, 1971; Black Expo, San Francisco, 1972; San Francisco Art Institute, 1972; In the Street, 1972.
Collections: Julian & Raye Richardson Collection; Mr. & Mrs. D.V. Welcher, Jr.
Sources: Information from artist; Marvin X. *The Black Bird,* San Francisco, Julian Richardson & Assoc., Illustrator; Poster series published by Julian Richardson & Assoc., San Francisco.

JOHNSON, LARRY
Printmaker.
Works: *Rev. Martin Luther King* (print).
Exhibited: Boston Public Library, 1973.
Sources: Boston Negro Artists Assn. *The Black Artist in America: A Negro History Month Exhibition,* Boston Public Library, 1973; "Black Art Exhibit Opens Sunday," *Herald,* Belmont, Mass., May 14, 1970; "Preview Party to Open Show by 13 Black Artists," *Citizen,* Belmont, Mass., May 14, 1970.

JOHNSON, LeROY
Works: *American Summer.*
Exhibited: Phila. Civic Center.
Sources: Phila. Division of Art. *Afro-American Artists 1800-1969.*

JOHNSON, LESTER
Painter. Born September 28, 1937 in Detroit. Studied at Wayne State University; self-taught artist.
Works: *Traumerei,* 1970 (polymer); *Black Fox; Ten For Miles; John Coltrane; Point of Departure; Nefertiti; Exit; Composition 18; The Impending Darkness; Composition 20; The Recession; Quiet Village; Warm Night; Transition 2; Brief Bridges.*
Exhibited: Whitney Museum, NY, 1971; Smith-Mason Gallery, Washington, DC, 1971; Detroit Institute of Arts, 1970; Flint (Mich.) Community Schools, 1970.
Awards: John S. Newberry Prize; Mrs. Albert Kahn prize, Detroit Institute of Arts.
Collections: Johnson Pub. Co.
Sources: Doty. *Contemporary Black Artists in America;* Smith-Mason Gallery. *National Ex-*

hibition of Black Artists, 1971; Flint Community Schools (Mich.). *Black Reflections*; Johnson Pub. Co. *The JPC Art Collection*, Pamphlet; Myers, Carol L. *Black Power in the Arts*, Flint, Mich., 1970; Detroit Institute of Arts files; Preston, Malcolm. "Art: Black Exhibit," *Boston Herald Traveler*, April 19, 1971.

JOHNSON, MALVIN GRAY

Painter, commercial artist. Born in Greensboro, North Carolina on January 28, 1896. Died October 4, 1934. Studied at National Academy of Design, New York under F.C. Jones.

Works: *The Red Cloth; Climbing up the Mountain; Negro Masks; Domestic; Over Harlem Rooftops; Girl Reading; All Day Nesting; Cow & Calf; Ezekiel; Landscape; Old Horse; Platform Dance; Pigs; Rail Fence; Raking Hay; Southern Landscape: Nos. 1-5; Masks; Turkeys; Meditation; Thinin' Corn; Swing Low Sweet Chariot; Negress; Fruit Vendor; Still Life; Portrait of Wilson Lamb; Woman Washing; Harmony; Brothers; Self-Portrait; Portrait of a Soldier; Turkeys at Roast; Uncle Joe; Caterpillar; Come Up Sometime; Convict Labor; Elks; Pully Lines; Red Roads; Sailor; Squash; Picking Beans; Rain Squall; Turkey Roost; Brothers; Harmony; Picking Cotton; All Day Meeting; The Old Mill; Henderson; Ill Wind; The Bakers; The Letter; Millie; Ermia; Dixie Madonna; River Boat; Toussaint l'Ouverture; After The Storm; Backyard Snow Scene; Backyard; The Ploughman; Flowers; Seated Figure; Rain; Millie; Head of a Child; Mighty Day.*

Exhibited: Harmon Foundation, 1928, 1929, 1931, 1933, 1935; Anderson Galleries, 1931; Salon of Americans, 1934; Corcoran Gallery, 1934; Roerich Museum, 1934; Texas Centennial, Dallas, 1936; Howard Univ. Gallery of Art; Baltimore Museum, 1939; Amer. Negro Exposition, 1940; Art Institute of Boston, 1943; Washington Square Outdoor Exhibit, 1932; Jumble Shop, 1932; Cooperative Art Market, 1933; NJ State Museum, Trenton, 1935; Arthur U. Newton Galleries, 1935; Library of Congress, 1940; Sheraton Hotel, Phila., 1968; Newark Museum, 1971; Smithsonian Institution, 1929.

Collections: Whitney Museum; Harmon Collection; Howard Univ. Gallery of Art; Nat'l Collection of Fine Arts, Washington, DC; Fisk Univ.; Public Works Administration Projects; Nat'l Archives; NY Public Library, Schomburg Collection; Oakland Museum.

Awards: Otto H. Kahn Prize, Harmon Foundation, 1928.

Member: Society of Independent Artists; NY Artists Project; Public Works Administration Project.

Sources: Mallett. *Index of Artists;* Dover. *American Negro Art*, pp. 31, 45; Young. *Dictionary of American Artists, Sculptors & Engravers;* Locke. *The Negro in Art; American Art Annual,* 1933; Harmon Foundation. *Exhibition of Productions by Negro Artists;* City College of NY. *The Evolution of the Afro-American Artist: 1800-1950;* Herring, James V. "The American Negro Craftsman & Artist," *Crisis,* April 1942; Baltimore Museum of Art. *Contemporary Negro,* 1939; Howard Univ. *Art of the American Negro,* 1937; Tanner Art Galleries. *Art of the American Negro,* 1940; Roucek & Kiernan. *The Negro Impact on Western Civilization;* Texas Centennial Exposition. *Thumbnail Sketches of Exhibiting Negro Artists,* 1936; Newark Museum. *Black Artists: Two Generations,* 1971; Afro-American Slide Depository, catalog; Harmon Foundation. *Exhibit of Fine Arts;* Locke, Alain. "Advance on the Art Front," *Opportunity,* May 1939; "Swing Low, Sweet Chariot Will Be Popular," *Art Digest,* Jan. 1929, pp. 5-6; Porter, James A. *Modern Negro Art;* Porter, James A. "Malvin Gray Johnson, Artist," *Opportunity,* April 1935, pp. 117-8; "Self-Portrait of the Late Malvin Gray Johnson," *Opportunity,* May 1939, p. 134; Harley, Ralph L., Jr. "A Checklist of Afro-Amer. Art & Artists," *The Serif,* Dec. 1970; Brawley, Benjamin. *The Negro Genius;* Butcher, Margaret. *The Negro in American Culture,* pp. 236-7; Harmon Foundation. *Negro Artists,* 1935; Harmon Foundation. *Select Picture List;* Smithsonian Institution. *Painting & Sculpture by American Negro Artists,* 1929; "Harmon Foundation Spreads Public Appreciation of Negro Art," *Art Digest,* June 1, 1935; Greene, Carroll, Jr. "Perspective: The Black Artist in America," *Art Gallery,* April 1970, p. 7; "American Negro Art Given Full Length Review in NY Show," *Art Digest,* Dec. 15, 1941; Pierre-Noel, Lois Jones. "American Negro Art in Progress," *Negro History Bulletin,* Oct. 1967; Locke, Alain. "The American Negro As Artist," *American Magazine of Art,* Sept. 1931; "Baltimore: Art by Negroes," *Art News,* Feb. 11, 1939; "The Negro Artist Comes of Age," *Art News,* Feb. 1, 1945; Locke, Alain. "Negro Art in America," *Design* Magazine, Dec. 1942, pp. 12-3; "American Negro Art," *Design* Magazine, Feb. 1942, p. 28; Boning, Richard A. *Profiles of Black Americans,* NY, 1968; Porter, James. "Negro Artists Gain Recognition After Long Battle," *Pittsburgh Courier,* July 29, 1950; Brawley, Benjamin. *The Negro in Literature & Art in the US;* "Six Paintings of City Life," *Arts Quarterly,* Dec. 1939, pp. 13-9; Brown, Marion. "The Negro in Fine Arts," *The Negro Heritage Library,* Vol. 2; *The Negro in Music & Art,* NY, 1969; Winslow, Vernon. "Negro Art & the Depression," *The Negro in Music & Art; The Negro Handbook,* Composed by Editors of *Ebony,* Chicago, 1966; Schatz,

Walter. *Directory of Afro-American Resources*, 1970; Adams, Russell. *Great Negroes Past & Present*, Chicago, 1969; DuSable Museum of African-Amer. History. *Contemporary Black Artists*, Calendar, 1970; Oakland Museum Archives, gift of the Harmon Foundation; Robinson, Wilhelmina S. *Historical Negro Biographies*, p. 216; Spradling, Mary M., ed. *In Black & White: Afro-Americans in Print*; Porter, James A. "Malvin Gray Johnson: An Appreciation," *Opportunity*, March 1935; Bennet, Mary. "The Harmon Awards," *Opportunity*, Feb. 1969, pp. 47-8; Walker, Roslyn. *A Resource Guide to the Visual Arts of Afro-Americans*, South Bend, Ind., 1971.

JOHNSON, MARIE E.

Mixed media, educator, consultant. Born in Baltimore, April 10, 1920. Studied at Morgan State College (BA, 1952); San José State College (MA, 1968); Stanford University (1968-9); Coppin State Teachers College (1940). Art instructor at California College of Arts & Crafts; consultant to Oakland Museum of Art (1954-72).
Works: *Construction; Dark Refuge; How Long; Early Militant; Black Americana; Precious Lord; Getting It Together; Family; The Mother; Soul Food; Woman With Flowers; Dream Deferred; Dilemma; Mrs. Jackson; Now; Cell; The Sister; Warning; Glimpses; The Window; Family* (collage).
Exhibited: Nat'l Academy; Allied Artists of America Annual, NYC; San Francisco Art State Fair; Oakland Art Museum, 1967, 1968; Northwood & Polaris Buildings, Fairbanks, Alaska (1-man); San José State College, 1962, 1968 (1-man); Labaudt Gallery, San Francisco (1-man); San Francisco Women Artists Annual, 1970; Hunters Point Art Festival, 1968; Univ. of Cal., 1967; San José Art League, 1956-71; San José City College, 1964; William Sawyer Gallery, San Francisco, 1971; Brockman Gallery, Los Angeles; Glide Memorial Church, San Francisco; Foothill College, 1967; San José Art Center, 1966; Horse's Mouth, Saratoga, Cal., 1964; Lucien Labaudt Gallery, 1964; First Nat'l Bank, San Jose, 1957; Ladd Air Force Base, Fairbanks, Alaska, 1954; San Francisco Artists Cooperative; Quill Gallery, San Francisco; all Art West Associated North Shows.
Collections: San José State College; Oakland Museum; Salinas Savings & Loan Co.; Johnson Pub., Chicago; San José City College; San Francisco Art Commission; 1st Nat'l Bank, San Jose; Morton Salt Co., Chicago; Palo Alto Unitarian Church.
Awards: Honorable Mention, New Perspectives in Black Art, Oakland Museum, 1968; Non-purchase Award, Cal. State Fair, 1962; 1st

award, mixed media, San Jose Art League Regional Show, 1971; Purchase Award, San Francisco Art Commission, 1969; Purchase Award, San José State College, 1968; 1st award, San José Art League, 1965; Grand prize & 1st prize, Town & Country Village, San José, 1965; Purchase Award, Palo Alto Unitarian Church, 1965; Purchase Award, San José City College, 1964; Grand prize, Hale's Art Fair, 1964; 1st prize, 1st Unitarian Church, San José, 1959; 1st award, Andrew Hill Art Festival, Town & Country Village, 1962; 2 1st awards, Valley Fair Art Festival; 2nd Grand Award, Santa Clara County Fair; 2 2nd awards, 2 3rd awards, Hart's Street Show, 1961; 2 1st awards, San Thomas Estates Show; 1st prize, San Jose Art League.
Member: Art West Associated North; San Francisco Women Artists; United College Professors; Black Arts Council, Los Angeles.
Represented by: Brockman Gallery, Los Angeles; William Sawyer Gallery, San Francisco.
Sources: Oakland Museum. *New Perspectives in Black Art*; Indiana Univ. *Fine Arts & the Black American*; Lewis/Waddy. *Black Artists on Art*; Afro-Amer. Slide Depository, Catalog; Information from the artist; *Black World*, Dec. 1972 ("Family" on cover); *San José Mercury*, 1964, March 1965; *East San José Sun*, May 1967; DuSable Museum of African-Amer. History. *Contemporary Black Artists*, 1970, Calendar; Johnson Pub. Co. *The JPC Art Collection*, Pamphlet; Oakland Museum Archives; Blum, Walter. "A Look at Three Black Artists," *San Francisco Sunday Examiner & Chronicle*, Sunday Supplement, June 14, 1970; Walker, Roslyn. *A Resource Guide to the Visual Arts of Afro-Americans*, South Bend, Ind., 1971.

JOHNSON, MILTON

Painter, illustrator, book designer, printmaker, educator. Born in Milwaukee, 1932. Studied at Milwaukee Layton School of Art; Minneapolis Institute of Art; School of the Museum of Fine Arts, Boston. Teacher at the Museum School, Boston.
Works: *Another Birthday*, 1969; *Ellie and Children*, 1967-8; *Limited* (woodcut); *Untitled* (woodcut).
Exhibited: Brandeis Univ., 1969; Boston Museum of Fine Arts, 1970; Atlanta Univ.; Mobile (Ala.) Artists Assn. Painting Annual, 1952.
Collections: Oakland Museum; Wiggin Collection, Boston Public Library.
Awards: Traveling Fellowship, Museum School of Fine Arts, Boston.
Sources: Boston Museum of Fine Arts. *Afro-American Artists: NY & Boston*, 1970; Roelof-Lanner, T.V., ed. *Prints by American Negro Artists*; *Newsweek*, June 22, 1970; Boston Community Lecture Series. *Local Afro-American*

Artists, 1972; Brandeis Univ. *Three Boston Black Artists: Milton Johnson, Richard Yarde, & Al Smith,* Nov. 1971; Oakland Museum Archives, Ruth Waddy Collection; "At Boston Museum—Afro-American Art," *New Bedford Sunday Standard Times,* May 10, 1970; Walker, Roslyn. *A Resource Guide to the Visual Arts of Afro-Americans,* South Bend, Ind., 1971.

JOHNSON, RAY
Mixed media. Founding director of the NY Correspondence School of Art.
Exhibited: Willard Gallery, NYC, 1965 (1-man).
Sources: Glueck, Grace. "What Happened? Nothing," *New York Times,* April 11, 1965.

JOHNSON, RICHARD
Painter.
Works: 100 ft. murals in a nightclub located on Market St., near Broadway.
Sources: *St. Louis Post Dispatch.*

JOHNSON, SARGENT CLAUDE
Sculptor, ceramist, printmaker. Born in Boston on October 7, 1888. Died in San Francisco on October 10, 1967. Studied at California School of Fine Arts; Boston School of Fine Arts; A.W. Best School of Art, San Francisco. Studied under Benjamino Bufano; Ralph Stackpole.
Works: *Sammy* (terracotta); *Hippo; Vera; Esther; Chester; Hippopotamus; Mask; Terra Cotta Figure; Forever Free; Boys Head; Girls Head; Negro Woman; Divine Love* (etching); *Elephant; Primitive Boy; The Politician; The Lovers; Mother & Child; Bound; Statue for Court of Pacific-Inca Indian & Llama; Mask of a Girl; Dorothy C.; White & Black; Lenox Avenue; Bound; Pearl; P.W.A.; Anderson; Copper Mask #3; Forever True; Elizabeth Gee,* 1925 (porcelain, ceramic); *Head of a Negro Woman* (terracotta); *Head of a Negro Girl; Copper Mask,* 1935; *Negro Mother,* 1935 (copper); redwood panel for California School for the Blind, 1937; *Neptune's Daughter,* 1939 (plaster cast); mosaic of tile on balcony at Maritime Museum, San Francisco, 1939; George Washington High School Athletic Field frieze, 1942 (cast stone); *Teapot,* 1941 (ceramic); *Singing Saint,* 1940 (lithograph); trivets (polychrome porcelain enamel on steel); plate (polychrome porcelain enamel on steel); *The Bull* (polychrome enamel on steel); *Secure,* 1949 (carved polychrome wood); *Enigma,* 1961 (carved polychrome redwood); plate (ceramic); *Defiant.*
Exhibited: Harmon Foundation, 1926, 1928, 1933, 1935; Harmon Foundation Traveling Exhibition of Negro Art, 1927, 1931; Wadsworth Atheneum, Hartford, Conn.; Butler Art Institute, Youngstown, Ohio; Herron Art Institute,

Indianapolis; J.B. Speed Memorial Museum, Louisville, Ky.; Fisk Univ., Nashville; Spelman College, Atlanta; Nat'l. Gallery of Art, Washington, DC; Cleveland Art Center; Municipal Art League, Chicago; City Art Museum, St. Louis, 1929; Oakland Municipal Art Gallery, 1930, 1931; Howard Univ., 1937, 1939; San Francisco Art Assn., 1929, 1935, 1936, 1938, 1952; Palace of Fine Arts, San Francisco, 1940; Albany Institute of History and Art, NY, 1945; San Francisco Museum of Art, 1945; Jack Tar Hotel, San Francisco, 1964; Kaiser Center Gallery, Oakland Museum, 1967; San Francisco Public Library, 1969; Art Center, NYC, 1933; James A. Porter Gallery, 1970; Syracuse, NY, 1946, 1947; San Francisco Annual Art Festivals, 1948, 1949, 1953; Eric Locke Galleries, San Francisco, 1959; M.H. de Young Museum, San Francisco, 1965; UCLA Fine Arts Gallery, 1966; San Francisco Negro Historical Society, 1967; Chabot College, Hayward, Cal., 1968; La Jolla Museum, 1970.

Collections: San Francisco Museum of Art; Mrs. E.R. Alexander, NYC; Adolph Loewi & Alan Bement, NYC; Federal Arts Project, Northern Cal.; Fine Arts Gallery of San Diego; Oakland Museum; Nat'l Collection of Fine Arts, Washington, DC; San Francisco Afro-American Historical & Cultural Society; Smithsonian Institution Archives of American Art; Matson Navigation Co.; Matson (SS Monterey); Richmond (Cal.) City Hall; George Washington High School Athletic Field; Fisk Univ.; Howard Univ.; Mr. & Mrs. William Abbensenth; Mr. & Mrs. Ray Allen; Mr. Roger Boas, San Francisco; Ms. Mildred Cotabish; Mr. Charles M. Goodwin; Dr. & Mrs. Jack Gordon; Paul Gordon; Mr. Bob G. Hanson; Mr. & Mrs. Leslie C. Hilty; Mr. Henri Lenoir; Mr. & Mrs. Norman S. Lezin; Mrs. John Magnani; Mr. Peter Magnani; Mr. & Mrs. Arthur C. Painter; Mr. Mathew Pemberton; Mr. & Mrs. Lawrence L. Pitt; Mr. & Mrs. Leonard Polakoff; Ms. Helen Dinwiddie Pray; Dr. & Mrs. E. Fritz Schmerl; Mrs. Ansley Salz; Mr. Richard Simmons; Mrs. Robert Gordon Sproul; Mr. & Mrs. Hunter D. Wells; Dr. Reidar Wennesland; Mr. Alan Williams; Mr. & Mrs. Frank Wooley; M.H. de Young Museum; Mr. Daniel Baker; Mr. & Mrs. Paul Desch; Mr. & Mrs. Romeo Tessano; Mrs. Russell H. Tansey; California School for the Blind, Berkeley; Maritime Museum in Aquatic Park, San Francisco; Nathan Dohrmann & Co.; Sunnydale Housing Project Childcare Center, San Francisco.

Awards: Medals for Sculpture, San Francisco Art Assn., 1925, 1931, 1935; Harmon Foundation prize of $150, 1933; Bronze Award, 1937, 1939; 1st prize, Cal. Legion of Honor, 1931; Robert C. Ogden Prize, 1933; 3rd prize, sculpture, Amer. Negro Exposition, Chicago, 1940;

Artists Fund Prize, lithograph, 1938; Abraham Rosenberg Scholarship, 1944, 1949; Harmon Bronze Award in Fine Arts, 1929; 1st prize, Harmon Foundation, $250, 1928.
Member: San Francisco Art Assn. (council board, 1934).
Sources: Mallett. *Index of Artists*; Dover. *American Negro Art*; *Who's Who in American Art*, 1940-1; *The American Art Annual*, 1933; San Francisco Museum of Art. *Art of Our Time*, Jan. 18-Feb. 5, 1945; Porter. *Modern Negro Art*; Locke. *The Negro in Art*; Locke. *Negro Art: Past and Present*; Albany Institute of History and Art. *The Negro Artist Comes of Age*; Harmon Foundation. *Negro Artists, An Illustrated Review of Their Achievements;* La Jolla Museum of Art. *Dimensions of Black*, 1970; Harmon Foundation catalogs, 1926-35; Schnier, Jacques. *Sculpture in Modern America*, Univ. of Cal. Press, 1948; Thiel, Yvonne G. *Artists & People*, Philosophical Library, Inc., NY, 1959; *American Magazine of Art*, Sept. 1931, May 1930, 1931; *Life*, July 1946; Montgomery, Evangeline. *Sargent Johnson*, Oakland Museum, 1971; Afro-American Slide Depository, Catalog; UCLA Art Galleries. *The Negro in American Art*; Baltimore Museum of Art. *Contemporary Negro*, 1939; Tanner Art Galleries. *Art of the American Negro*, 1940; "Sculpture in Wood," *San Francisco Art Assn. Bulletin*, Oct. 1934; "Inca Indian & Llama," *San Francisco Art Assn. Bulletin*, Dec. 1938; "Odds & Ends," *San Francisco Art Assn. Bulletin*, March 1945; Harley, Ralph, Jr. "A Checklist of Afro-American Art & Artists," *The Serif*, Dec. 1970; Locke, Alain. "Advance on the Art Front," *Opportunity*, May 1939; Butcher, Margaret J. *The Negro in American Culture*, pp. 234, 239. Brawley, Benjamin. *The Negro Genius*; Texas Centennial Exposition. *Thumbnail Sketches of Exhibiting Artists*, 1936; *Who's Who in Colored America*, 3rd edition; Howard Univ. *James A. Porter Gallery of African-American Art*, 1970; Harmon Foundation. *Exhibit of Fine Arts*, 1930; Harmon Foundation. *Select Picture List; New York Times*, Jan. 5, 1930; *Art Digest*, March 1, 1933, March 15, 1939; San Francisco Museum of Art. *Opening Exhibitions*, catalog, Jan. 1935; San Francisco Museum of Art. *Quarterly Bulletin*, Nov. 4, 1954; *Western Arts*, March 1926; *San Francisco Housing Project*, July 1946; *American Artist*, Jan. 1949; Salinger, Jehanne Bietry. "Sargent Johnson: We Call Him Ours," *Opera & Concert*, Jan. 1949; Palace of Fine Arts. *Calif. Art Today*, San Francisco, 1940; *Cal. Arts & Architecture*, May 1931; *Bayviewer*, Aug. 1967, p. 3; *Black Dialogue*, #3, 1968; Varda, Jean. *Cosmopolitan*, Dec. 1963; *San Francisco 7th Annual Art Festival*; Eric Locke Galleries. *2nd Annual Outdoor Exhibition*, Oct. 1959; Hagan, Robert. "The Walls They Left Behind," *San Francisco*, April 1964; San Francisco School of Fine Arts. *51st Annual Exhibition of San Francisco Art Assn.*, 1929; Palace of Legion of Honor. *53rd Annual Exhibition of San Francisco Art Assn.*, 1931; San Francisco Museum of Art. *56th Annual Exhibition of San Francisco Art Assn.*, 1936; San Francisco Museum of Art. *71st Annual Exhibition of San Francisco Art Assn.*, 1952; *Sunday Mirror*, San Diego, Aug. 2, 1935, p. 4; *Washington Post*, June 1, 1930; "Sculptor at 2 Cadell Place," *The Post*, Berkeley, Nov. 6, 1965; "Artist in Touch with the People," *People's World*, San Francisco, Feb. 2, 1950; "Sargent Johnson Sculptor," *Our World*, July 1946; DuSable Museum of African-Amer. History. *Contemporary Black Artists*, Calendar, 1970; Furr, Arthur F. *History & Progress of Negroes in the US*; "Harmon Foundation Exhibit," *Art Digest*, Feb. 15, 1931, p. 7; *Art Digest*, Vol. 4; "Harmon Foundation Spreads Public Appreciation of Negro Art," *Art Digest*, June 1, 1935; Pierre-Noel, Lois Jones. "American Negro Art in Progress," *Negro History Bulletin*, Oct. 1967; F.L.K. "American Negroes as Artists," *The Survey*, Sept. 1, 1928, pp. 648-9; Locke, Alain. "The American Negro as Artist," *American Magazine of Art*, Sept. 1931; "Harmon Awards Announced," *Art News*, Feb. 8, 1930, p. 17; "Baltimore: Art by Negroes," *Art News*, Feb. 11, 1939; Craig, Randall J. "Focus on Black Artists: A Project for Schools & Community," *School Arts*, Nov. 1970, pp. 30-3; Porter, James A. "Negro Artists Gain Recognition After Long Battle," *Pittsburgh Courier*, July 29, 1950; Ploski, Harry, & Ernest Kaiser. "The Black Artist," *Afro USA*, 1971; Ploski, Harry, Ernest Kaiser, & Otto Lindenmeyer. "The Black Artist," *Reference Library of Black America*, Book 4, 1971; *The Negro Handbook*, Composed by Editors of *Ebony*, Chicago, 1966; "Exhibition of Work by Negro Artists," *Afro-American Presbyterian*, Feb. 23, 1933; Arvey, Verns. "Sargent Johnson," *Opportunity*, July 1939, pp. 213-4; Robinson, Wilhelmina S. *Historical Negro Biographies*, p. 216; *Negro History Bulletin*, March 1939, pp. 51-2; Spradling, Mary M., ed. *In Black & White: Afro-Americans in Print*; "The San Francisco Collector," *M.H. De Young Memorial Museum Catalog*, Sept./Oct. 1965; *San Francisco Chronicle*, Jan. 5, 1930, p. 7; April 20, 1930, p. D5; March 12, 1933, p. D3; Oct. 6, 1935, p. D3; March 18, 1940, p. 24; March 17, 1940, p. 8; June 12, 1940, p. 14; June 26, 1940, p. 14; Nov. 14, 1940, p. 1; Nov. 19, 1940, p. 1; Nov. 20, 1940, p. 12; Nov. 23, 1940, p. 9; Nov. 25, 1940, p. 12; Nov. 27, 1940, p. 7; Nov. 16, 1944; Nov. 30, 1944, p. 9; Feb. 27, 1948, p.

17; Oct. 12, 1967 (obit.); Oakland Museum. *Sargent Johnson: Retrospective*; Oakland Museum Archives; USIS. "The Negro in American Art," *Topic*, 1966, #5; Walker, Roslyn. *A Resource Guide to the Visual Arts of Afro-Americans*, South Bend, Ind., 1971.

JOHNSON, THELMA BEATRICE

Painter. Born in 1912 in Washington. Self-taught.

Works: *At Play; Man With Violin.*

Exhibited: Oregon Federation of Colored Women, 1929-31; Spanish Exhibition, Washington High School, 1930-1; Harmon Foundation, 1933.

Sources: Harmon Foundation. *Non-Jury Exhibit of Works of Negro Artists*, 1933.

JOHNSON, WILLIAM HENRY

Painter, graphic artist. Born in Florence, South Carolina, 1901. Studied at National Academy of Design, New York; Cape Cod School of Art, under Charles Hawthorne; in Paris and Southern France. Teacher at Harlem Art Center, Federal Art Project (1930-40).

Works: *Looking from My Balcony; Sun Setting over Fishing Boats; A Dane; Untitled; Street in Tunis; Lofoten Island; Christ Crucified; Young Man in Vest; Descent from the Cross; On a John Brown Flight; Volunteer Workers; Jacobia Hotel, Florence; Come unto Me Little Children; Booker T. Washington; Convalescence from Somewhere; Mt. Calvary; Jesus and the Three Marys; Flowers to the Teacher; Kerteminde Harbor, Denmark; Self Portrait; Jim; Jitterbugs II; War Voyage ca.; Training for War; Sun Setting over Fishing Port, Kerteminde; Garden, Kerteminde; Lillies; Sonny; Crucifixion; Jim; Mother and Child; Landscape; Landscape with Sun Setting; Red Cross Service Station; Off To Market; Portrait (Danish Boy); Seaside, Kerteminde; Ezekiel Saw The Wheel; Lis Sis; Portrait of Youth; Study of A Man of Letters; Portrait of an Elderly Dane; Vielle Maison; Cagnes Sur Mer; Trees and Mountains; Landscape, Kerteminde; Untitled Folk Scene; Mountain Stream; Norway Landscape, Flowering Trees; Street in Florence, South Carolina; Danish Landscape; Lom Kirke, Norway; Sarah; Viaduct Road, Cagnes; K.P.; 3 Great Abolitionists: A. Lincoln, F. Douglass, & J. Brown; Commodore Perry At the North Pole; Portrait With Sun Flower; Street Scene With Churches; Off to War; Jitter Bugs VI; Street Musicians; Fright; The Town Simpleton; Street People; Holcha; Night Bride; Refugee; Farm Couple at Wall; Lame Man; Mosque; Sitting Model.*

Exhibited: Artists Gallery, NY, 1939 (1-man); Harlem Art Center, NY, 1940; Alma Reed Gallery, NY, 1941; Wakefield Gallery, NY,

1943-4; Marquette Gallery, NY, 1944; NY Public Library, 135th St. Branch, 1946; Paris, 1927; Nice, 1928-9; Harmon Foundation, NY, 1930-3; Florence, SC, 1930; Marquette, Mich., 1930; Copenhagen, 1931-3; Esbjerg, Denmark, 1934; Auhus, Denmark, 1934; Oslo, Norway, 1935; Volda, Norway, 1936; Aalesund, Norway, 1936; Tromsoe, Norway, 1938; Gavle Museum, Sweden, 1938; Copenhagen, 1947; National Museum, Stockholm; Trondhjem Museum, Norway, 1937; Howard Univ.; Fisk Univ.; Morgan State College, Baltimore; Smithsonian Institution; Spelman College, Atlanta; Phila. Civic Center; State Armory, Wilmington, Del., 1971; Amer. Negro Exposition, Chicago, 1940; Harmon Traveling Exhibition, 1935-6; Harmon College Art Traveling Exhibition, 1934-5; Texas Centennial, 1936; Newark Museum, 1971; James A. Porter Gallery, 1970; Tuskegee Institute, 1971.

Collections: Oakland Museum, Nat'l Gallery.

Awards: Gold Medal, Harmon Foundation, 1930 (for the 1929 series); Cannon Prize; Hallgarten Prize, Nat'l Academy of Design.

Member: United Amer. Artists.

Sources: Tanner Art Galleries. *Art of the American Negro*, 1940; Howard Univ. *Art of the American Negro*, 1937; *American Art Annual*; Locke. *The Negro in Art*; Albany Institute of History & Art. *The Negro Artist Comes of Age;* Dover. *American Negro Art;* Harmon Foundation. *Exhibition of Productions by Negro Artists;* "Afro-American Issue," *Art Gallery*, April 1968; Indiana Univ. *Fine Arts & the Black American;* Newark Museum. *Black Artists: Two Generations;* City College of NY. *The Evolution of Afro-American Artists 1800-1950;* Univ. of Texas Art Museum. *Afro-American Artists Abroad;* "Johnson One-Man Show Opens in New York May 4," *Crisis*, April 1941; "Tempera Paintings by Johnson Shown in New York," *Opportunity*, 1943; Phila. Division of Art. *Afro-American Artists 1800-1969;* Assn. for the Study of Negro Life & History. *Exhibition of Works by Negro Artists*, 1933; Harley, Ralph L., Jr. "A Checklist of Afro-American Art and Artists," *The Serif*, Dec. 1970; Locke, Alain. "Advance on the Art Front," *Opportunity*, May 1939; Porter. *Modern Negro Art;* "Is William H. Johnson, Negro Prize Winner, Blazing a New Trail," *Art Digest*, Jan. 1930, p. 13; Landy, Jacob. "William H. Johnson: Expressionist Turned Primitive," *Journal of the American Assn. of Univ. Women*, March 1958; *William H. Johnson, An Artist of the World Scene*. NY, The Harmon Foundation, n.d. Available through Materials on Negro Artists, Dept. of Art, Fisk Univ.; Brawley, Benjamin. *The Negro Genius;* Butcher, Margaret J. *The Negro in American Culture*, pp. 229, 236-7; Roucek/Kiernan. *The*

Negro Impact on Western Civilization; Harmon Foundation. *Non-Jury Exhibit of Works of Negro Artists,* 1933; Texas Centennial Exposition. *Thumbnail Sketches of Exhibiting Artists,* 1936; Newark Museum. *Black Artists: Two Generations,* 1971; Afro-American Slide Depository, Catalog, 1971-2; Harmon Foundation. *Negro Artists,* Catalog, 1935; Howard Univ. *James A. Porter Gallery of African Amer. Art,* 1970; Harmon Foundation. *Exhibit of Fine Arts,* 1930; DuSable Museum of African-Amer. History. *Contemporary Black Artists,* 1970, Calendar; Harmon Foundation. *Select Picture List; New York Times,* Jan. 5, 1930; *Art Digest,* Vol. 4; "Art by Negroes," *Art Digest,* Oct. 15, 1941; "Amer. Negro Art Given Full Length Review in NY Show," *Art Digest,* Dec. 15, 1941; Greene, Carroll, Jr. "Perspective: The Black Artist in America," *Art Gallery,* April 1970, p. 9; Pierre-Noel, Lois Jones. "American Negro Art in Progress," *Negro History Bulletin,* Oct. 1967; Locke, Alain. "The Amer. Negro As Artist," *Amer. Magazine of Art,* Sept. 1931; "Harmon Awards Announced," *Art News,* Feb. 8, 1930; "Harlem Library Shows Negro Art," *Art News,* May 20, 1933, p. 14; "The Artist Comes of Age," *Art News,* Feb. 1, 1945; "American Negro Art," *Design,* Feb. 1942, p. 28; Craig, Randall J. "Focus on Black Artists: a Project for Schools and Community," *School Arts,* Nov. 1970, pp. 30-3; Greene, Carroll, Jr. "Afro-Amer. Artists: Yesterday & Now," *The Humble Way,* Vol. 8, No. 3, 1968; Greene, Carroll, Jr. *Afro-American Artists: 1800-1968,* Slides; Grillo, Jean B. "Elma Lewis: A New Show A New Showplace," *Boston After Dark,* Aug. 16, 1970; Loercher, Diana. "Afro-Amer. Artists Abroad," *Christian Science Monitor,* Aug. 1, 1970; Brown, Marion. "The Negro in the Fine Arts," *The Negro Heritage Library,* Vol. 2; Ploski, Harry, Ernest Kaiser. "The Black Artist," *Afro USA,* 1971; Ploski, Harry, Ernest Kaiser, & Otto Lindenmeyer. "The Black Artist," *Reference Library of Black America,* Book 4, 1971; *The Negro Handbook,* Composed by Editors of *Ebony,* Chicago, 1966; Oakland Museum Archives, gift of the Harmon Foundation; McMillen Inc. Galleries. *Contemporary Negro Art,* NY, 1941; Hampton (Va.) Institute. *W.H. Johnson,* 1968; Walker, Roslyn. *A Resource Guide to the Visual Arts of Afro-Americans,* South Bend, Ind., 1971.

JOHNSTON, CELESTINE GUSTAVA

Art educator. Born in 1911 in Pittsburgh. Studied at Boston University. Teacher at Episcopal City Mission, Boston.
Works: *Miss Virginia Tucker.*
Exhibited: Harmon Foundation, 1930.
Sources: Harley, Ralph, Jr. "Checklist of Afro-Amer. Art & Artists," *Serif,* Dec. 1970; Harmon Foundation. *Exhibition of Productions by Negro Artists;* Indiana Univ. *Fine Arts & the Black American;* Harmon Foundation. *Exhibit of Fine Arts,* 1930; Walker, Roslyn. *A Resource Guide to the Visual Arts of Afro-Americans,* South Bend, Ind., 1971.

JOHNSTON, JOSHUA

Painter. Born 1765. Died 1830. Dates of activity 1796-1824. Negro slave from Baltimore whose talent won him privilege of devoting his time to portrait painting as early as 1800. Believed to have served painting apprenticeship under Peale Family or their contemporaries.
Works: *Mrs. John Moale and Her Granddaughter; The McCormick Family; Mrs. Andrew Beckford Bankson and Child; Benjamin Franklin Yoe and Son; In the Garden; Portrait of a Cleric; The Westwood Children; Father and Son; Mother and Daughter; Edward and Sarah Rutter; Portrait of Charles Herman Wilmans; Portrait of John Spear Smith; Portrait of May B. Smith; Portrait of Mary McCurdy and Daughters; Portrait of Mrs. West and Mary Ann West.*
Exhibited: Peale Museum, Baltimore, 1948; Pa. Academy of Fine Arts; Metropolitan Museum, NY, 1961; Walker Art Center, Minneapolis, 1962; Columbus (Ohio) Gallery of Fine Arts, 1962; City Art Museum of St. Louis, 1962; Municipal Art Gallery, Los Angeles, 1962; deYoung Museum, San Francisco, 1962; Atlanta Art Assn. Galleries, 1962; Va. Museum of Fine Arts, Richmond, 1963; Cincinnati Art Museum, 1963; Art Institute of Chicago, 1963; Carnegie Institute, 1963; Dallas Museum of Fine Arts, 1963; Rochester Memorial Art Gallery, 1963; Milwaukee Art Center, 1963; Isaac Delgado Museum, New Orleans, 1963; Baltimore Museum, 1963; Phila. Museum, 1963; Museum of Fine Arts, Boston, 1964; Detroit Institute of Arts, 1964.
Collections: Historical Society; Museum of Early Southern Decorative Arts, Winston-Salem, N.C.; Bowdoin College; Frick Gallery, NY; Metropolitan Museum of Art; Smithsonian Institution; Edgar and Bernice Garbisch.
Sources: City Univ. of NY. *Evolution of Afro-American Artists: 1800-1950;* Bearden, Romare & Harry Henderson. *Six Masters of American Art;* Howard Univ. *Ten Afro-American Artists of the 19th Century,* Washington, D.C., 1967; Porter. *Modern Negro Art; American Negro Reference Book;* Young, William. *Dictionary of American Artists, Sculptors and Engravers,* 1968; Locke. *The Negro in Art;* Dover. *American Negro Art;* Indiana Univ. *Fine Arts and the Black American;* Pleasants, J. Hall. "Joshua Johnston, the First Negro Portrait Painter,"

Maryland Historical Magazine, June 1942; Roucek, Joseph, Thomas Kiernan. *The Negro Impact on Western Civilization,* 1970; Afro-American Slide Depository, 1971-2 Catalog; Harmon Foundation. *Select Picture List;* Greene, Carroll, Jr. "Perspective: The Black Artist in America," *Art Gallery,* April 1970; Pierre-Noel, Lois Jones. "American Negro Art in Progress," *Negro History Bulletin,* Oct. 1967; "Afro-American Artists 1800-1950," *Ebony,* Vol. 23, p. 116-122; "Negro Portrait Painter," *Hobbies,* July 1943; Hunter, Jr., Wilbur Harve. "Joshua Johnston: 18th Century Negro Artist," *American Collector,* Feb. 1948; Craig, Randall J. "Focus on Black Artists: A Project for Schools and Communities," *School Arts,* Nov. 1970; Greene, Carroll, Jr. "Afro-American Artists: Yesterday & Now," *The Humble Way,* Vol. 8, No. 3, 1968; The James McCormick Family," *Life,* 1940; "Mrs. John Moale & Ellin North Moale Lent by Roswell P. Russell," *Baltimore Municipal Museum Bulletin,* Dec. 15, 1941; Harley, Ralph, Jr. "Checklist of Afro-American Art & Artists," *The Serif,* Dec. 1970; Greene, Carroll, Jr. *Afro-American Artists 1800-1968,* Slide Catalog; Brown, Marion. "The Negro in the Fine Arts," *Negro Heritage Library,* Vol. 2; Schatz, Walter. *Directory of Afro-American Resources,* 1970; DuSable Museum of African Amer. History. *Contemporary Black Artists,* 1970; Scarborough, Katherine. "An Early Negro Portrait Artist," *Negro History Bulletin,* Feb. 1968; *101 Masterpieces of American Primitive Painting from the Collection of Edgar William & Bernice Chrysler Garbisch,* NY, Doubleday, 1961; Walker, Roslyn. *A Resource Guide to the Visual Arts of Afro-Americans,* South Bend, Ind., 1971.

JOHNSTON, WILLIAM EDWARD

Painter, mosaic artist. Born in Salem, Ohio, June 12, 1917. Studied at Alabama State College (BS, 1963); Rochester Institute of Technology (MFA, 1970); Auburn University; John Herron Art Institute (diploma). Chairman, Art Department, Mississippi Valley State College.
Works: *Black Madonna,* 1972; *Mosaic* (glass tesserae); *Constructions* (shaped canvases).
Exhibited: Atlanta Univ., 1951, 1956, 1957, 1963; Tuskegee Institute, 1960; Tribune Tower, Chicago, 1962; Stillman College, 1963; Delta State College, Cleveland, Miss., 1967; Frontal Images-Municipal Gallery, Jackson, Miss., 1967; Masur Museum, Monroe, La., 1969; Rochester Institute of Technology, 1970; Univ. of Cincinnati, 1970; Carnegie Institute, 1971; Haiti Gallery, Rochester, NY, 1972; 100 American Craftsmen Show, Lockport, NY, 1972; 15th Annual Delta Art Show, 1972.

Collections: John Herron Gallery, Indianapolis, Ind.
Awards: Tuskegee Institute, 2nd Purchase Award.
Sources: Information from artist.

JOINER, LEMUEL
Sources: Harley, Ralph, Jr. "Checklist of Afro-Amer. Art & Artists," *The Serif,* Dec. 1970.

JONES, ALLEN
Sources: Porter. *Modern Negro Art;* Harley, Ralph, Jr. "Checklist of Afro-Amer. Art & Artists," *The Serif,* Dec. 1970.

JONES, ARCHIE JOSEPH
Active in the 1930's.
Exhibited: Harmon Foundation, 1933.
Sources: Harmon Foundation. *Exhibition of Productions by Negro Artists;* Indiana Univ. *Fine Arts & the Black American;* Harley, Ralph, Jr. "A Checklist of Afro-Amer. Art & Artists," *The Serif,* Dec. 1970; DuSable Museum of African-Amer. History. *Contemporary Black Artists,* 1970, Calendar; Walker, Roslyn. *A Resource Guide to the Visual Arts of Afro-Americans,* South Bend, Ind., 1971.

JONES, ARTHUR
See: Jones, Lawrence Arthur.

JONES, ARZIE
Painter.
Works: *Etoile de Hollande.*
Exhibited: Atlanta Univ., 1942.
Sources: Atlanta Univ. exhibition files; Harley, Ralph, Jr. "Checklist of Afro-Amer. Art & Artists," *The Serif,* Dec. 1970.

JONES, BARBARA
Printmaker. Born in Chicago.
Works: *Heritage; High Priestess; Stop Genocide; Unite; Rise & Take Control; Your Brother's Keeper; Black Family; I'm Better Than You Maryland Farmers; Land Where My Father Die.*
Exhibited: Howard Univ., 1970, 1972; National Center of Afro-Amer. Artists, Boston, 1970, 1972; Studio Museum in Harlem, 1970, 1972.
Member: AFRICOBRA.
Sources: *Black Shades,* Feb. 1972; Grillo, Jean B. "Where Down Home Meets Back Home," *Boston After Dark,* Sept. 1970; Howard Univ. *AFRICOBRA II,* 1972; Atkinson, J. Edward. *Black Dimensions in Contemporary American Art.*

JONES, BEATRICE RUTH
Sources: DuSable Museum of African-Amer. History. *Contemporary Black Artists,* 1970, Calendar.

JONES, BENJAMIN

Painter, mixed media, sculptor, educator. Born in Paterson, New Jersey, 1941. Studied at Paterson State College (BA, 1963); Pratt Institute (1966); New York University (MFA, 1966). Teacher at Jersey City State College.

Works: *Ameer, Truth and the Universe; Five Black Face Images; High Priestess of Soul; Malcolm; African Panorama; Black Universe,* 1970; *Untitled (6 arms),* 1970; *Five Black Faces; Mask; Leg; Head; Huey; Black Mask I; Black Mask II; Eldridge; Man & His History* (mixed media).

Exhibited: Studio Museum, Harlem; Weusi Nyumba Ya Sanaa Gallery, Harlem; Newark Museum, 1971; Boston Museum, 1970; Museum of Modern Art, 1972; Howard Univ., 1972; Smith-Mason Gallery, 1971; City College of NY.

Collections: Newark Museum; Howard Univ.; Johnson Pub. Co., Chicago.

Sources: Information from artist; Boston Museum of Fine Arts. *Afro-American Artists: NY & Boston,* 1970; Newark Museum. *Black Artists: Two Generations;* Smith-Mason Gallery. *National Exhibition of Black Artists,* 1971; Studio Museum (Harlem). *Ben Jones & Joe Overstreet,* 1971; Bowling, Frank. "The Rupture," *Arts,* Summer 1970; Rose, Barbara. "Black Art in America," *Art in America,* July-Dec. 1970; Johnson Pub. Co. *The JPC Art Collection,* Pamphlet; City College of NY. *New Black Artists;* Museum of Nat'l Center of Afro-Amer. Artists. *Taking Care of Business;* Loercher, Diana. "National Center of Afro-Amer. Artists Art & Benefit Premier," *Christian Science Monitor,* May 4, 1971; Driscoll, Edgar. "Art Show Reflects Black Rage, Pride," *Boston Globe,* May 28, 1971; Locke, Alain. "Advance on the Art Front," *The Negro in Music and Art,* 1969; Ploski, Harry, & Ernest Kaiser. "The Black Artist," *Afro USA,* 1971; Walsh, Rose. "Artists to Meet Public at Art Exhibit Preview," *Record American,* May 19, 1970; *Arts,* Summer 1970; "Afro-American Art a Cultural Experience for All," *Record American,* May 19, 1970; Ploski, Harry, Ernest Kaiser, & Otto Lindenmeyer. "The Black Artist," *Reference Library of Black America,* Book 4, 1971; Fine, Elsa H. "Mainstream, Blackstream and the Black Art Movement," *Art Journal,* Spring 1971; Le Brun, Caron. "Black Art," *Herald Traveler,* Sunday Supplement, Boston, May 24, 1970; *Black Shades,* Mar. 1972; "Afro-American Artists: NY & Boston," *Prudential Center News,* March 1, 1970, p. 4.

JONES, DEXTER

Exhibited: 12th Annual Invitational Exhibition, Pyramid Club, Phila., 1952.

Sources: Drummond, Dorothy. "Coast-to-Coast," *Art Digest,* March 1, 1952, p. 12.

JONES, DORIS

Painter.
Works: *Color* (oil); *Still Life* (oil); *Flowers* (oil).
Exhibited: Boston Public Library, 1973.
Sources: Boston Negro Artists' Assn. *10th Anniversary Exhibition,* Boston Public Library, 1973; Boston Negro Artists' Assn. *The Black Artist in America: A Negro History Month Exhibition,* Boston Public Library, 1973.

JONES, FREDERICK A.

Exhibited: Tanner Art League, 1922.
Sources: Harley, Ralph, Jr. "Checklist of Afro-Amer. Art & Artists," *The Serif,* Dec. 1970.

JONES, FREDERICK D., JR.

Painter, printmaker. Born in Chicago, 1914.
Works: *Wash Day; Magnolia Seed; Girls After Bath; Girl in Turban; Daughter of Eve.*
Exhibited: Atlanta Univ., 1942, 1943; Xavier Univ., 1963.
Collections: Atlanta Univ.
Awards: Atlanta Univ. Purchase Award, 1943.
Sources: Dover. *American Negro Art,* pp. 45, 52, 53; "Afro-American Issue," *Art Gallery,* April 1968; Indiana Univ. *Fine Arts & the Black American;* DuSable Museum of African-Amer. History. *Contemporary Black Artists,* 1970, Calendar; "Negro Annual," *Art Digest,* April 15, 1942; "Negro Annual," *Art News,* April 15, 1943; Xavier Univ. *Emancipation Proclamation Centennial National Art Exhibition,* 1963; Harley, Ralph, Jr. "A Checklist of Afro-Amer. Art & Artists," *The Serif,* Dec. 1970; Myers, Carol L. *Black Power in the Arts,* Flint, Mich., 1970; Walker, Roslyn. *A Resource Guide to the Visual Arts of Afro-Americans,* South Bend, Ind., 1971.

JONES, GAIL

Studied at Cass Technical High; Western Michigan University; Wayne State University; Charles McGee School.
Exhibited: New Breed Studio, Detroit, 1968 (1-woman); AAA Art Gallery, Detroit; Biro Gallery, Detroit; Gallery International, Acapulco; Souza Gallery, Mexico City; CBC Broadcasting Co., Bermuda; G.Q. Modern Shop, Detroit; Normacel Gallery, Detroit, 1970.
Awards: Krajenke Buick Scholarship.
Sources: Normacel Gallery. *A Black Women Art Exhibit,* Detroit, 1970.

JONES, GEORGE

Painter.
Collections: Mr. Benny Andrews.

JONES, HENRY BOZEMAN

Painter, graphic designer, author. Born in Philadelphia, 1889. Studied at Philadelphia School of Pedagogy under William M. Chase, Cecilia Beaux, H. H. Breckenridge, and Thomas Anshutz.

Works: *Moonlight & Houses; Guardian of the Wood; Stone Giants at Night; September Haze; Wolf Brethren; Spruce in Snow; Caves of the Trolls; Shulz Farm; Wind Scales; Head of a Negro Woman; The Moon Was Gracious; Elizabeth; The Voodoo Tree; Miss Frances Waters; Raymond Rourke; Banks of Chaloon; Portrait of the Artist; Biddie.*

Exhibited: Harmon Foundation, 1929, 1933; Howard Univ., 1937; Smithsonian Institution, 1929; Rumph Gallery, 1928; Warwick Galleries, 1930-4; Print Club, 1932, 1934, 1935; YWCA, 1929-33; Sketch Club, 1932; Reed Galleries, 1934; NJ State Museum, 1935.

Collections: Singerly School, Walter G. Smith School, Harrison School, & Martha Washington School, all in Phila.; Steel Works, Gary, Ind.; Lincoln Univ.; St. Thomas Church, Phila.; Douglas School, Wilmington, Del.

Awards: Internat'l House, 1929.

Sources: Harmon Foundation. *Exhibition of Productions by Negro Artists;* Harmon Foundation. *Non-Jury Exhibit of Works of Negro Artists,* 1933; Harmon Foundation. *Negro Artists,* 1935, Catalog; Harmon Foundation. *Exhibit of Fine Arts,* 1930; Indiana Univ. *Fine Arts & the Black American;* Mallett. *Index of Artists; Who's Who in American Art,* 1940-1; *American Art Annual,* 1933; Howard Univ. *Art of the American Negro,* 1937; DuSable Museum of African-Amer. History. *Contemporary Black Artists,* 1970, Calendar; Smithsonian Institution. *Painting & Sculpture by American Negro Artists,* 1929; Harley, Ralph, Jr. "Checklist of Afro-Amer. Art & Artists," *Serif,* Dec. 1970; Ploski, Harry, Ernest Kaiser, & Otto Lindenmeyer. "The Black Artist," *Reference Library of Black America,* Book 4, 1971; "Negro Artists Paintings on Display at Univ. (Howard)," *East Tennessee News,* Knoxville, Tenn., June 6, 1932; Walker, Roslyn. *A Resource to the Visual Arts of Afro-Americans,* South Bend, Ind., 1971.

JONES, JAMES EDWARD

Painter, educator. Born in Paducah, Kentucky. Studied at Philadelphia College of Art (BFA); University of Pennsylvania (MFA).

Works: *The Uncola; Bandbridge; Window; Circles; May Town; Landscape; Bound Brook; King William; Summer I; Door I; Night Tide; Sun-Sol-Uno; Spring; Home Again; East Orange; Seasons Discovered; Centerings* (acrylic series).

Exhibited: Goucher College; Morgan State College; Wilmington (Del.) Society of Fine Arts; Baltimore Museum of Art; Gallery One; Gallery of Internat'l. Art; Coppin State College; Ontario Gallery, Washington, DC; Denison Univ., Granville, Ohio; Baltimore Arts Festival; Loyola 4th Annual Invitational; Katzensteins Gallery, Luthersville, Md.; Michelsons Gallery, Washington, DC; CPHA Exhibition; Studio 116; Parish Hall Gallery; Studio 13, Phila.; Phila Art Alliance; Heritage House, Phila.; Trapezium, Mt. Washington, Md.; Spelman College, Atlanta; McDonogh School Summer Show-Cleveland Memorial Gallery; Courtney & Jones Paint Exhibition; Phila. College of Art; Univ. of Pa., Phila.; Calvert Savings & Loan Assn.; Corcoran Museum of Art, Washington, DC; Black Printmakers Exhibition; Univ. of South Alabama; Jerry Gilden Gallery, Pikesville, Md., 1972 (1-man); Elizabethtown College, Pa.; Townhouse Gallery; Arena Players; McDonogh School (2-man); Karamu House, Cleveland; Parker & Jones Studio 116; Md.; Univ. of Md., 1972; Parish Hall Gallery; Jonade Gallery, Baltimore, 1972.

Collections: Studio 13, Phila.; Gallery 1, Baltimore; Gallery of Internat'l Art, Baltimore; Mikelson Gallery, Washington, DC; Trapezium Gallery of Art, Mt. Washington, Md.; Katzensteins Gallery of Art, Luthersville, Md.; Jerry Gilden Gallery, Pikesville, Md.; Morgan State College, Baltimore; McDonogh (Md.) School; Karamu House, Cleveland; Univ. of South Alabama.

Awards: Stewart Art Award of NJ, 1956; Phila. College of Art Scholarship, 1957-60; Phila. College of Art Fellowship, 1960-61; Univ. of Pa. Fellowship, 1961-62; Thorton Oakley Creative Achievement Award, 1962; Morgan State College Grant for Research, 1963, 1968.

Member: Amer. Society for Aesthetics; Amer. Assn. of Univ. Professors; Phila. Print Club; Baltimore Museum of Art; Phila. College of Art Alumni; Univ. of Pa. Alumni; Hunterdon County Art Center, NJ; Amer. Federation of Teachers; Museum of Natural History, NJ; Amer. Crafts Council.

Represented by: Jerry Gilden Gallery, Pikesville, Md.; Katzensteins, Luthersville, Md.

Sources: Afro-Amer. Slide Depository, Catalog; Information from artist.

JONES, LAWRENCE ARTHUR

Painter, graphic artist, educator. Born in Lynchburg, Virginia, December 25, 1910. Studied at Dillard University (BA, 1939); Art Institute of Chicago; University of Mississippi (MA, 1971); Tallers Graficas, Mexico. Teacher of art at Dillard University, New Orleans; Fort Valley State College, Georgia; Jackson

State Teachers' College, Mississippi (1949); University of Mississippi.

Works: *Workman; Fisher Family; Landscape; The Sun Do Moves—The Earth Square; Street Scene New Orleans; Triptych: Past, Present, Future; The Rape of Ethiopia; Many Years of Growth.*

Exhibited: Chicago Hull House Gallery, 1938; Dillard Univ., 1939; Fort McClellan, Ala., 1942; Dunbar & EC Glass High School Show, Lynchburg, Va., 1952; New Orleans YMCA, 1959; Centennial Show of Black Progress, Chicago, 1964; Black Amer. Show of Graphic Arts, Western Europe & Russia, 1944; Deposit Guaranty Bank, Jackson, Miss., 1968; Univ. of Miss., 1971; Chase Plaza Hotel, 1972; Carver High School, Raymond, Miss., 1972; Atlanta Univ., 1942, 1944, 1946; Amer. Negro Exposition, Chicago, 1940; Emancipation Proclamation Show, Chicago; Augusta Savage Studios, 1939.

Collections: Service Club, Fort McClellan.

Awards: Rosenwald Fellowship, 1940, 1947; Emancipation Proclamation Show, New Orleans; 1st place blue ribbon award, Emancipation Show, Chicago; Class Honors in Painting, Art Institute of Chicago, 1946; Carnegie Fellowship, 1948; Academic Fellowship, Univ. of Miss., 1971; Karl Douglas Trophy, Centennial of Negro Progress, 1964.

Member: Nat'l. Conference of Artists; Miss. Art Assn.; Nat'l. Art Educational Assn.

Sources: Tanner Art Galleries. *Art of the American Negro,* 1940; Fax, Elton C. *Seventeen Black Artists;* Xavier Univ. *Emancipation Proclamation Centennial National Art Exhibition,* 1963; Harley, Ralph, Jr. "A Checklist of Afro-Amer. Art & Artists," *The Serif,* Dec. 1970; Information from the artist; Furr, Arthur F. *History & Progress of Negroes in the US.*

JONES, LEON

Painter. Born in Montclair, New Jersey.

Works: *Girl with a Ring,* 1970.

Exhibited: Newark Museum, 1971.

Represented by: Midblock Art Service, East Orange, NJ.

Sources: Newark Museum. *Black Artists: Two Generations,* 1971.

JONES, LOIS MAILOU

Painter, designer, illustrator, educator. Born in Boston, 1906. Studied at High School of Practical Arts, Boston; Boston Museum of Fine Arts School (1923-7); Boston Normal Art School (1926-7, certificate); Harvard Summer School (1927); Columbia University Summer School; Columbia University Teachers College; Howard University (AB in Art Education); Designers Art School, Boston (1927-8); Academie Julian, Paris (1937-8); Ecole des Beaux Arts, Paris (1937-8); studied in Rome; pupil of Philip Hale, Jules Adler, and Joseph Berges. Associated with Professor Herring at Howard University. Associate Professor of Design, Howard University, 1930-present; Head, Art Department, Palmer Memorial Institute, Sedalia, NC, 1928-30; Director, Children's Saturday Morning Art Class, Washington, DC.

Works: *Barnum and Bailey Circus; Place du Terte à Montmartre; Old Houses; 7th Street; Apple Time; Jennie; Still Life and Portrait; Banjo Player; Evening at Menemsha; Mme. Evanti as Rosina; The Pink Table Cloth; The Janitor; Menemsha; Vieille Rue de Montmartre; Lavoir sur la Sein, Paris; Rue St. Michel, Paris; Petites Barques sous le Pont Marie; Notre Dame de Paris; Pont Marie, Paris; Les Enfants Jouant dans un Square Parisien; Dans le Jardin du Luxembourg—Paris; Le Cafe Denfert-Rochereau—Paris; La Mosque; Sous le Pont; Old Mill, Fretin, France; La Mere; Jeanne-Martiniquaise; Le Chapeau Rose; Apple Time; Les Pommes Vertes; Still Life with Clover; An Artist Lived Here; Turnells' Flying Horses, Oak Bluffs, Mass.; Liberian Decoration; Trois Vieux Copains, Paris; Mob Victim; Still Life with Lobsters; Quarry on the Hudson; Japanese Garden; The Fountain; The Arbor; Fetiche with an Orchid; Barbara; Menemsha Shacks, Mass.; Menemsha Bright; Mary-Jean; The White Cliff; Still Life with Thistles; Eusebia Cosme; 36th Street; Georgetown; Docked; Philome & Robert in Haiti; Ascent of Ethiopia; Negro Youth; Three Old Companions; Old House Near Frederick, Va.; Boasts at Theoule, France; Tete De Negre; Les Fetiches; La Rue Norvins, Montmartre; Le Jardin de Cluny; Les Barques sous le Pont Marie II; Sue; Portrait of John Panorama of Chilmark Village; Circus; Liberian Abstraction; Paula and Mirza; Marechiaro; Changing Tide; The Lion House; Through the Coal Yard; Speracedes, France; Voodoo Worshippers; Rue Chevalier de la Barre, Paris; Hotel Colber, Paris; Ande; Haitian Scene; Marche Haiti, 1965 (acrylic); The Fishing Village; Across the Lagoon; South Carolina Farm; Negro Cabin; After the Storm; Sunset; Zinnias; The Doorway; The Betel Chewer; Brother Brown; Japanese Student; Edgartown Harbor; Twin Boats; Niagara Falls; Up Stream; Study from a Tapestry; Still Life with Green Apples; Artists Kitchen; Challenge; Letitia and Patrick; Vendeuses de Tissue, Haiti; Indian Shops, Gayhead, Mass.; Hudson; Zenobia; Still Life; Bazar du Quai; Sea Goddess; The Blue Masque; Veve Vodou II; Haiti Vodou IV; Milkmaids, Kenscoff, Haiti; Fertilite; Paris Rooftops; Rue Mont Cenis, Montmartre; Rue Galande, Paris; Le Pettis Bateaux Marchande.*

Exhibited: Salon des Artistes Francais, Paris, 1938-9; Corcoran Gallery of Art, 1939, 1951, 1968; Nat'l Academy of Design, 1942, 1944, 1949, 1951, 1969; Pa. Academy of Fine Arts, 1934-6, 1938-9; College Art Assn. Travelling Exhibition, 1934; Harmon Foundation, 1930-1; Trenton Museum; Texas Centennial, 1936; Galerie de Paris, 1938; Nat'l Gallery of Art, Washington, DC; Baltimore Museum of Art, 1939-40, 1944; Albany Institute of History & Art, 1945; Amer. Negro Exposition, Chicago, 1940; Barnet Aden Gallery, Washington, DC, 1946; Smith College; Vose Gallery, Boston, 1939 (1-man); Institute of Modern Art, Boston, 1943; Whyte Gallery, Washington, DC, 1941-4, 1948; San Francisco Art Museum; Seattle Art Museum; Boston Public Library; Atlanta Univ.; Hampton Institute; Watkins Gallery, Amer. Univ., Washington, DC; Goucher College, Md.; Fisk Univ.; United Nations Club, Washington, DC, 1950; Dupont Theatre Gallery, Washington, DC, 1951; Grand Central Art Gallery, NY; ACA Galleries, NY, 1952; Soulanges Gallerie, Paris (1-man); State Armory, Wilmington, Del., 1971; Smithsonian Institution, 1933; Galleries Charpentier, 1938; Tanner Art Galleries, 1940; Amer.-British Art Center, 1944; Amer. Watercolor Society, 1942, 1944, 1946, 1964; Phillips Collection, Washington, DC, 1941-2, 1944-5; Washington Art Guild, 1929-58; Society of Washington Artists, 1938-43, 1945-6, 1959-65; Washington Watercolor Society, 1931-6, 1939-65; Whyte Gallery (1-man); Haiti, 1954 (1-man); Salisbury, Rhodesia Museum, 1960; Galerie International, NYC, 1961, 1968 (both 1-man); Howard Univ., 1936, 1937 (1-man), 1961, 1963 (1-man), 1967-8, 1945, 1972; Grumbacher Travelling Exhibition, 1966-9; Dillard Univ., 1941; James A. Porter Gallery, 1970; Smith-Mason Gallery, 1971; Georgetown Public Library; Pan Amer. Union, Washington, DC; Centre D'Art, Haiti; Southern Univ., New Orleans; Lincoln Univ.; Xavier Univ., 1963; Boston Museum of Fine Arts, 1970, 1973 (1-man).

Collections: Phillips Collection, Washington, DC; IBM; Brooklyn Museum; Internat'l Fair Gallery, Izmir, Turkey; Univ. of Punjab, Pakistan; Palais National, Haiti; Atlanta Univ.; Howard Univ.; WVa. State College; Rosenwald Foundation; Retreat for Foerign Missionaries, Washington, DC, mural; Corcoran Gallery of Art; Barnet Aden Gallery; Galeries International, NY; Walker Art Center, Minneapolis; Bowdoin College; American Embassy, Luxembourg; 135th St. Branch, NY Public Library; Johnson Pub. Co., Chicago.

Awards: Boston Museum of Fine Arts School Prize, 1926; Prizes, National Museum, Washington, DC, 1947, 1954, 1960, 1964; Prizes, Corcoran Gallery, 1949, 1951; Robert Woods Bliss Landscape Prize in Oil Painting, Corcoran Gallery, 1941; 1st prize, Corcoran Gallery, 1953; Prizes, Atlanta Univ., 1942, 1952, 1955, 1960; 1st award, oil, Atlanta Univ., 1949; Haitian Government Decoration & Order for Achievement in Art, 1954; Lubin Award, 1954; Washington Society of Artists Award, 1962; Award for National and International contributions as an artist & teacher, Assn. for Presentation & Preservation of the Arts, 1968; Honorable Mention, Amer. Negro Exposition, 1940; Foreign Fellowship, General Education Board, 1937-8; 1st prizes, oil, National Museum, 1940, 1948.

Member: Vineyard Haven (Mass.) Artists Guild; Amer. Artists Congress; Society of Independent Artists, France; Amer. Watercolor Society; Washington Art Guild; Washington Watercolor Club; Art Directors Club; Society of Washington Artists; Fellow, Royal Society of the Arts, London; Artists Equity Assn.; National Conference of Artists.

Sources: Mallett. *Index of Artists;* Albany Institute of History & Art. *The Negro Artist Comes of Age;* Locke. *The Negro in Art;* Locke. *Negro Art Past and Present;* Dover. *American Negro Art;* Harmon Foundation. *Exhibition of Productions by Negro Artists;* "Afro-American Issue," *Art Gallery,* April 1968; Lewis/Waddy. *Black Artists on Art,* Vol. 1; *Who's Who in American Art,* 1940-1, 1970, 1944; Indiana Univ. *Fine Arts & the Black American;* Afro-Amer. Slide Depository, Catalog; Aesthetic Dynamics. *Afro-American Images,* 1971; Assn. for the Study of Negro Life & History. *Exhibition of Works by Negro Artists,* 1933; Baltimore Museum of Art. *Contemporary Negro,* Catalog, 1939; "Howard University Gallery," *Sunday Star,* DC, Dec. 7, 1941; "Saturday Morning Art Class," *Negro History Bulletin,* April 1942, p. 158; "Lois Mailou Jones," *Negro History Bulletin,* April 1939; "Mural Painting 'Light'," *Howard Univ. Bulletin,* July 1940, pp. 16-7; Phila Division of Art. *Afro-American Artists 1800-1969;* Brawley, Benjamin. *The Negro Genius;* Dillard Univ. *Arts Festival,* Catalog, 1941; Harmon Foundation. *Non-Jury Exhibit of Works of Negro Artists,* 1933; Harmon Foundation. *Negro Artists,* Catalog, 1935; Howard Univ. *Festival of Fine Arts,* May 1945; Porter. *Modern Negro Art;* DuSable Museum of African-Amer. History. *Contemporary Black Artists,* Calendar, 1970; *Lois Mailou Jones Peintures 1937-1951,* Tourcoing, France, Presses Georges Frere, 1952; McBrown, G. P. *The Picture Poetry Book,* Washington, DC, Assoc. Pub., 1935 (illustrator); Newsome, Effie Lee. *Gladiola Garden,* Washington, DC, Assoc. Pub., 1940 (illustrator); Herring, James V. "The American Negro Craftsman and Artist," *Crisis,* April 1942; Lewis/Waddy. *Black Artists on Art,* Vol. 1; Tanner Art Galleries. *Art of the American Negro,* 1940; Locke, Alain. "Advance on the Art Front," *Opportunity,* May 1939; Harley, Ralph L., Jr. "A Checklist of Afro-Amer. Art and Artists," *The Serif,* Dec. 1970; Brown, Evelyn S. "The Harmon Awards," *Opportunity,* March 1933; Roucek/Kiernan. *The Negro Impact on Western Civilization;* Texas Centennial Exposition. *Thumbnail Sketches of Exhibiting Artists,* 1936; Howard Univ. *James A. Porter Gallery of African American Art,* 1970; Harmon Foundation. *Exhibit of Fine Arts,* 1930; Smith-Mason Gallery. *National Exhibition Black Artists,* 1971; Harmon Foundation. *Select Picture List;* Woodson, Carter G., Charles H. Wesley. *The Story of the Negro Retold,* p. 402; Furr, Arthur F. *History and Progress of Negroes in the US;* "Harmon Foundation," *Art Digest,* Feb. 15, 1931, p. 7; Greene, Carroll, Jr. "Perspective: The Black Artist in America," *Art Gallery,* April 1970, p. 19; "Negro Art Annual," *Art Digest,* May 1, 1942; Pierre-Noel, Lois Jones. "American Negro Art in Progress," *Negro History Bulletin,* Oct. 1967; Wolf, Ben. "Negro Art Scores Without Double Standards," *Art Digest,* Feb. 1, 1945; Porter, James A. "Negro Art on Review," *Amer. Magazine of Art,* Jan. 1934; Bowling, Frank. "The Rupture," *Arts,* Summer 1970; A & T Univ. Lyceum Program. *15 Afro-American Women;* Kiah, Virginia. "Black Artists," *Savannah Magazine,* April 1972, p. 16; *National Conference of Artists,* Winter 1971, Journal; Johnson Pub. Co. *The JPC Art Collection,* Pamphlet; Barnet Aden Gallery. *Lois Mailou Jones,* April-May 1946; Greene, Carroll, Jr. "Afro-Amer. Artists: Yesterday & Now," *The Humble Way,* No. 3, Vol. 8, 1968; Xavier Univ. *Emancipation Proclamation Centennial National Art Exhibition,* 1963; "Black Art: What Is It?" *Art Gallery,* April 1970; Greene, Carroll. *Afro-American Artists: 1800-1968,* Slides; Boning, Richard A. *Profiles of Black Americans,* NY, 1969; Brown, Marion. "The Negro in the Fine Arts," *The Negro Heritage Library,* Vol. 2; *The Negro in Music and Art,* NY, 1969; Ploski, Harry, & Ernest Kaiser. "The Black Artist," *Afro USA,* 1971; Walsh, Rose. "Artists to Meet Public at Art Exhibit Preview," *Record American,* May 19, 1970; "Black Artists Work on View at Museum," *News,* Newburyport, Mass., May 16, 1970; Le Brun, Caron. "Blacks' Art on Display," *Herald Traveler,* Boston, May 26, 1970; Paris, Jean. "Black Art Experience in Art," *Long Island Press,* Jamaica, NY, June 14, 1970; Ploski, Harry, Ernest Kaiser, & Otto Lindenmeyer. "The Black Artist," *Reference Library of Black America,* Book 4, 1971; *The Negro Handbook,* Composed by Editors of *Ebony,* Chicago, 1966; Atkinson, J. Edward. *Black Dimensions in Contemporary American Art,* NY, 1971; "Negro Artists Paintings on Display at University (Howard)," *East Tennessee News,* Knoxville, June 6, 1932; Jones, Lois M. "An Artist Grows Up in America," *Aframerican Woman's Journal,* Summer-Fall 1942, p. 23; Schatz, Walter. *Directory of Afro-American Resources,* 1970; Myers, Carol L. *Black Power in the Arts,* Flint, Mich., 1970; Robinson, Wilhelmena S. *Historical Negro Biographies,* p. 217; *Ebony,* Nov. 1968; Spradling, Mary M., ed. *In Black & White: Afro-Americans in Print;* Boston Museum of Fine Arts. *Afro-American Artists: NY & Boston,* 1970; "At Boston Museum—Afro-American Art," *New Bedford Sunday Standard Times,* May 10, 1970; Pierre-Noel, Lois Jones. "American Negro Art in Progress," *Negro History Bulletin,* Oct. 1967; Boston Museum of Fine Arts. News Release, *Reflective Moments: Lois Mailou Jones,* Mar. 1973; *Black Shades,* Mar. 1972; Walker, Roslyn. *A Resource Guide to the Visual Arts of Afro-Americans,* South Bend, Ind., 1971.

JONES, MARK
Painter.
Works: *The Cousins;* Untitled oil.
Collections: Johnson Pub. Co.
Sources: Johnson Pub. Co. *The JPC Art Collection,* Pamphlet.

JONES, PETER
Photographer.
Exhibited: Addison Gallery, 1971.
Sources: James Van DerZee Institute. *The Black Photographer (1908-1970): A Survey.*

JONES, ROBERT EDMOND
Sculptor, printmaker. Born in Lynchburg, Virginia in 1913. Studied at Hull House; Art Institute of Chicago.
Collections: Negro History Hall of Fame, Chicago Coliseum.
Member: Nat'l Conference of Artists, co-founder.
Sources: "Afro-American Issue," *Art Gallery,* April 1968; Indiana Univ. *Fine Arts & the Black American;* DuSable Museum of African-Amer. History. *Contemporary Black Artists,* 1970 Calendar; Nat'l Conference of Artists. *A Print Portfolio by Negro Artists;* Harley, Ralph, Jr. "A Checklist of Afro-Amer. Art & Artists," *The Serif,* Dec. 1970; Myers, Carol. *Black Power in the Arts,* Flint, Mich., 1970; "Negro Students Hold Their Own Art Exhibition," *New York Herald Tribune,* Feb. 15, 1935; Walker, Rosyln. *A Resource Guide to the Visual Arts of Afro-Americans,* South Bend, Ind., 1971.

JONES, STEPHANIE

Painter.
Works: *Howard McCallebb* (oil).
Collections: Mr. Benny Andrews.

JONES, TED

Painter, printmaker, mixed media. Studied at University of Montana. Assistant Professor of Art, Tennessee State.
Works: *Two Women; Bird Man; Man Searching for Peace; Willie "Blood" Brown; Open-Season on Panthers; Contemplating Monk; Grass USA; Man Grasping for a Pinch of Space; In the Name of The Lord; Night Mountain Scape; Wall Paper Sky; Landscape Composition with Red Sky and Collage; Horned Toad Frog; Horse and Rider; Landscape with Yellow Sky; Great Southern Landscape.*
Sources: Countee Cullen Branch, NY Public Library. *Ted Jones, Avant Garde Artist,* n.d.; Afro-Amer. Slide Depository, Catalog, 1971-2; *National Conference of Artists Journal,* Winter 1971.

JONES, TONNIE O.

Sculptor, painter. Born in Palo Alto, California, 1943. Self-taught.
Works: *Revelation of Kings,* 1970 (pine); *Order of Man,* 1965 (pine); *Call for Unity,* 1968 (oak); *Fatimah,* 1969 (oak); *Unknown,* 1970 (oak); *Three Faces,* 1971; *Number 7,* 1967; *Quest,* 1972 (rosewood); *Alpha Centaur,* 1972; *Monument to James Baldwin,* 1972 (black walnut); Untitled oil; *The Sacrifice; Untitled* (wood).
Exhibited: Univ. of Iowa, 1971-2; Pan Am Building, 1968; Brooklyn Museum, 1969; Columbia Univ.; Boston Museum of Fine Arts, 1970; Illinois Bell Telephone; Westchester (Pa.) State College, 1973.
Collections: Brooklyn Museum; Jean Faulkner; Phila. RIGHT, West Mill Creek Housing.
Represented by: McCleaf Gallery, 1713 Walnut St., Phila., Pa. 19103.
Sources: Sherman, Marjorie. "Afro-America Gets Biggest Show," *Boston Globe,* May 18, 1970; Walsh, Rose. "Artists to Meet Public at Art Exhibit Preview," *Record American,* May 19, 1970; Canaday, John. Review of Brooklyn Museum show, *New York Times,* Oct. 8, 1969; Rose, Barbara. "Black Art In America," *Art in America,* July-Dec. 1970; Baker, Kenneth. "Art in the Service of the People," *Christian Science Monitor,* n.d.; Information from the artist; Le Brun, Caron. "Black Art," *Herald Traveler,* Sunday Supplement, Boston, May 24, 1970; *Black American Artists/71,* 1972; Le Brun, Caron. "Blacks' Art on Display," *Herald Traveler,* Boston, May 26, 1970; Brooklyn Museum. *New Black Artists,* 1969; Boston Museum of Fine Arts. *Afro-American Artists: NY & Boston,* 1970;

Loercher, Diana. "Art: Idioms of Blackness at the Elma Lewis School," *Christian Science Monitor,* July 10, 1970; "Afro-American Artists: NY & Boston," *Prudential Center News,* March 1, 1970, p. 4; Walker, Roslyn. *A Resource Guide to the Visual Arts of Afro-Americans,* South Bend, Ind., 1971; Harlem Cultural Center. *New Black Artists.*

JORDAN, JACK

Sculptor, painter, graphic artist, educator. Born in Wichita Falls, Texas, in 1925. Studied: Langston University (BA, 1948); Iowa University (MA, 1949); University of Iowa (MFA, 1953). Teacher in Art Department of Langston University; Professor of Art at Southern University, New Orleans. Appointed to State of Louisiana Commission of Creative and Performing Arts.
Works: *Madonna and Child; The Musician; Diana and Apollo; Going Home* (linocut); *Struggle for Freedom; Cinderella was a Soul Sister* (marble); *African Drummer* (bronze); *Bourbon Street* (graphics); *Black Artists* (graphics); *Black 20c Madonna* (painting); *Ghetto Madonna; Black Eve; Soul Music; Black Crucifixion; Negro, Banjo and Soul; Black Messiah; And God Said, Let There Be Woman; Adam and Eve; Black Slave Girl; Swinging Ghetto Child; Old Black Shepherd; Black Combo; Black Lovers; Black Self; Black Seated Madonna; Girls in Waiting; Ghetto Children; Female and Kids; Crowing Rooster; Integration; Immaturity; Revolution; Matrimony; Anatomy of a Fowl; Black Contestants; Fred Too? Yes; My Dream; Charlie Selling Papers; Contemplation; Tomorrow's Hope; Third Generation; Black Guardian; Two Afro-Americans; Abstract Lovers; I Had A Dream of Africa; Brainwashed Figures; Black is Beautiful; Woman at Mirror; Cousins; Seated Black Female; Black Father & Son; Oblation Fetish; Fetish Fecundity; Oblation; Mythology of the Black Man; Mask; Ghetto Family; Trichinosis; Christ Crowned With Thorns; Negro Girl Skipping Rope; Soul Family.*
Exhibited: Smith-Mason Gallery, 1971; Savannah State College, 1971; Xavier Univ., 1963; Howard Univ., 1961.
Collections: Oakland Museum.
Sources: Dover. *American Negro Art;* "Afro-American Issue," *Art Gallery Magazine,* April 1968; Indiana Univ. *Fine Arts & the Black American;* Roelof-Lanner, T.V., ed. *Prints by American Negro Artists;* Nat'l Conference of Artists. *A Print Portfolio by Negro Artists;* Lewis/Waddy. *Black Artists on Art;* Afro-American Slide Depository, Catalog; Smith-Mason Gallery. *National Exhibition Black Artists,* 1971; *National Conference of Artists.* Journal, Winter 1971; Pierre-Noel, Lois Jones.

"American Negro Art in Progress," *Negro History Bulletin*, Oct. 1967; Xavier Univ. *Emancipation Proclamation Centennial National Art Exhibition*, 1963; Harley, Ralph, Jr. "A Checklist of Afro-Amer. Art & Artists," *The Serif*, Dec. 1970; *Art Gallery*, April 1970; Ploski, Harry, & Ernest Kaiser. "The Black Artist," *Afro USA*, 1971; Ploski, Harry, Ernest Kaiser, & Otto Lindenmeyer. "The Black Artist," *Reference Library of Black America*, Book IV, 1971; Atkinson, J. Edward. *Black Dimensions in Contemporary American Art*, NY, 1971; Myers, Carol. *Black Power in the Arts*, Flint, Mich., 1970; Oakland Museum Archives, Ruth Waddy Collection; DuSable Museum of African-Amer. History. *Contemporary Black Artists*, 1970 Calendar; Walker, Roslyn. *A Resource Guide to the Visual Arts of Afro-Americans*, South Bend, Ind., 1971.

JORDAN, KENNETH
Commercial artist. Born in Chicago, April 23, 1940. Studied at Pratt Institute (BFA).
Works: *One; Three.*
Exhibited: Cinque Gallery, NY; City College of NY; Brooklyn Community Gallery.
Collections: Cinque Gallery, NY.
Sources: Brooklyn Museum. News Release, July 25, 1972; Information from artist.

JORDAN, LOUIS JOSEPH
Painter.
Works: *West Side Winter; Pure Oil Building; Gloomy.*
Exhibited: Amer. Negro Exposition, Chicago, 1940; Dillard Univ., 1941.
Sources: Tanner Art Galleries. *Art of the American Negro*, 1940; Dillard Univ. *Arts Festival*, 1941; "Afro-American Issue," *Art Gallery*, April 1968; Indiana Univ. *Fine Arts & the Black American*; DuSable Museum of African-Amer. History. *Contemporary Black Artists*, 1970 Calendar; Myers, Carol. *Black Power in the Arts*, Flint, Mich., 1970.

JOSEPH, CLIFF
Painter, art therapist. Born in Panama, 1927. Studied at Pratt Institute (BFA).
Works: *Blackboard; My Country Right or Wrong; Superman; The Bystanders; The Mothers of Armageddon; The Game; Egg from the Eagle's Nest; Heirs to the Kiss of Judas; The Playpen*, 1968; *The Militant*, 1966; *An American Speaks*, 1966; *Southern Comfort*, 1965; *The Fire the Next Time*, 1965; *The Separatists*, 1966; *Palm Sunday*, 1960; *The Dead Negotiate the Peace*, 1966; *The Superman*, 1966; *Pterodactyl*, 1966; *Isaiah II:4*, 1966; *Something for the Censors*, 1966; *The Window*, 1960; *Summa Camp*, 1955; *Ballet (red shoes)*, 1953; *Carousel*, 1956; *Self Portrait*, 1952.
Exhibited: Spencer Memorial Church, Brooklyn, 1969 (1-man); Christ Congregational Church, Silver Springs, Md., 1967 (1-man); Union Presbyterian Church, Schenectady, NY, 1967 (1-man); Fuld Neighborhood House, Newark, 1967 (1-man); The Aspects Gallery, NY, 1966 (1-man); Hunter College, 1969; Riverside Museum, NY, 1968, 1969; Central Atlantic Conference, Hood College, 1968; Albert Einstein College of Medicine, 1966; Phila. Civic Center Museum; Boston Museum of Fine Arts, 1970; Rhode Island School of Design, 1969; Memorial Art Gallery, Rochester, NY, 1969; San Francisco Museum of Art, 1969; Contemporary Arts Museum, Houston, 1970; NY State Museum, 1970; Roberson Center for the Arts & Sciences, Binghamton, NY, 1970; Univ. of Cal. at Santa Barbara Art Galleries, 1970; Ruder & Finn Fine Arts, 1969; Nat'l Center for Afro-Amer. Artists, Boston, 1971; Good Shepherd Faith Presbyterian Church, NY, 1964; 1st Presbyterian Church, Rutherford, NJ, 1964; 1st Presbyterian Church, Franklin Lakes, NJ, 1964; Armonk Methodist Church, NY, 1965; Harlem on Canvas Exhibit, NY, 1967; No. Ave. Presbyterian Church, New Rochelle, NY, 1968; Bernard W. Baruch College, NY, 1970; Currier Gallery, Manchester, NH, 1971; Univ. of NH; Acts of Art Gallery, NY, 1971; Manhattan Country School, 1972; Countee Cullen Library, 1972; Pratt Institute, 1972; Black Expo, NY, 1972; Afro-Amer. Studios, NY, 1972; Ghost Ranch, New Mexico, 1967 (1-man); Church of the Redeemer Presbyterian, Washington, DC, 1967 (1-man); Church of the Pilgrims Presbyterian, Washington, DC, 1967 (1-man); Univ. Ecumenical Ministry at Oregon State, 1970; 1st Congregational Church, Williamstown, Mass., 1970 (1-man); Westbeth Galleries, NY, 1972 (1-man).
Member: Amer. Assn. of Art Therapists; Black Emergency Cultural Coalition.
Sources: Boston Museum of Fine Arts. *Afro-American Artists: NY & Boston*, 1970; Phila. Division of Art. *Afro-American Artists 1800-1969*; Bowling, Frank. "The Rupture," *Arts*, Summer 1970; Craig, Randall J. "Focus on Black Artists: A Project for Schools and Community," *School Arts*, Nov. 1970, pp. 30-3; Berkman, Florence. "Some Black Artists Irate Over Whitney Exhibit," *Times*, Hartford, Conn., April 25, 1971; Hinchcliffe, Diane. "Black Art Exhibit: Future Looks a Little Brighter," *Chronicle-Citizen*, Brookline, Mass., June 4, 1970; Bourne, Kay. "Black Artists Shown At Museum," *Bay State Banner*, Mass., May 28, 1970; Museum of the Nat'l Center of Afro-Amer. Artists. *Taking Care of Business*; Loercher, Diana. "National Center of Afro-American Artists and Art Benefit Premier," *Christian Science Monitor*, May 4, 1971; Driscoll, Edgar. "Art Show Reflects Black Rage,

Pride," *Boston Globe*, April 28, 1971; "Now Showing: The Black Artist," *Contact*, Sept. 1970; Berkman, Florence. "Afro-American Exhibit Fosters Understanding of Black Artists," *Times*, Hartford, Conn., May 24, 1970; Le Brun, Caron. "Blacks' Art on Display," *Herald Traveler*, Boston, May 26, 1970; Ruder & Finn Fine Arts. *Contemporary Black Artists*, 1969; Information from the artist; Riverside Museum. *Eight Plus Eight*, 1969; Le Brun, Caron. "Black Art," *Herald Traveler*, Sunday Supplement, Boston, May 24, 1970.

JOSEPH, RONALD

Painter. Born in St. Kitts, British West Indies, 1910. Studied at Art Students League.
Works: *Card Players; Family; Interior; Introspect; Park Avenue Market; Mood; Violin; Family Group.*
Exhibited: Harlem Art Center, 1938, 1939; Baltimore Museum, 1939; Columbia Univ., 1939; Amer. Negro Exposition, Chicago, 1940; Albany Institute of History & Art, 1945; Mc-Millen Inc. Galleries, NY, 1941; Augusta Savage Studios, 1939; Library of Congress, 1940; City College of NY, 1967.
Collections: Nat'l Archives.
Sources: Indiana Univ. *Fine Arts & the Black American*; Locke. *The Negro in Art*; Afro-American Slide Depository, Catalog, 1971-2; Albany Institute of History & Art. *The Negro Artist Comes of Age*; City College of NY. *The Evolution of Afro-American Artists 1800-1950*, 1967; Baltimore Museum. *Contemporary Negro Art*, 1939; Locke, Alain. "Advance on the Art Front," *Opportunity*, May 1939; Harley, Ralph, Jr. "A Checklist of Afro-Amer. Art & Artists," *The Serif*, Dec. 1970; Porter. *Modern Negro Art*; DuSable Museum of African-Amer. History. *Contemporary Black Artists*, 1970, Calendar; "Art by Negroes," *Art Digest*, Oct. 15, 1941; "American Negro Artists Given Full Length Review in NY Show," *Art Digest*, Dec. 15, 1941; "American Negro Art," *Design Magazine*, Feb. 1942, p. 28; McMillen Inc. Galleries. *Contemporary Negro Art*, NY, 1941; "Afro-American Issue," *Art Gallery*, April 1968; Myers, Carol. *Black Power in the Arts*, Flint, Mich., 1970; Walker, Roslyn. *A Resource Guide to the Visual Arts of Afro-Americans*, South Bend, Ind., 1971.

JOSEPH, THEOPHILUS

Painter.
Sources: "Charwoman's Son," *Time,* June 24, 1929.

JOYMER, CHARLES E.

Painter.
Works: *Freedom Last 1970.*
Exhibited: Smith-Mason Gallery, 1971.
Sources: Smith-Mason Gallery. *National Exhibition Black Artists 1971.*

JOYNER, LEMUEL M.

Painter.
Works: *Judgment.*
Sources: Atkinson, J. Edward. *Black Dimensions in Contemporary American Art*, NY, 1971.

JUNIER, ALLAN G.

Painter. Born in Milwaukee, Wisconsin. Studied at Wisconsin Art Academy (MFA, 1951). Chief Medical Illustator, VAH, Tuskegee Institute, Alabama.
Exhibited: Kittler Galleries, NY, 1972; 1st Nat'l Bank, Birmingham, Ala., 1972; Montgomery Museum of Art, 1972; Tuskegee Institute, 1972.
Awards: 1st Prize, Biological Photographic Assn. in Color Medical Photography; 2nd Prize, AU Show, Oil Painting; 1st Award, Layton Art Annual Show, Milwaukee, Wisc.
Sources: Pierre-Noel, Lois Jones. "American Negro Art in Progress," *Negro History Bulletin*, Oct. 1967; Information from the artist.

KAHLER, ROSE

Sources: Harley, Ralph, Jr. "Checklist of Afro-Amer. Art & Artists," *The Serif*, Dec. 1970.

KANE, DORIS T.

Painter. Born in Harlem, New York, 1931. Studied at City College of New York (BS, 1956); Art Students League; Columbia University; New School for Social Research.
Works: *The Deadly Eyes Are Stars.*
Exhibited: Studio Museum in Harlem, 1969.
Sources: Studio Museum in Harlem. *Harlem Artists 69.*

KANE, JOHN

Sources: Harley, Ralph, Jr. "Checklist of Afro-Amer. Art & Artists," *The Serif*, Dec. 1970.

KAVE, MARGARET

Painter.
Exhibited: Smith-Mason Gallery, 1971.
Sources: Smith-Mason Gallery. *Anniversary Exhibit*, 1971.

KECK, CHARLES

Sculptor.
Sources: *The Negro Handbook*, Composed by Editors of *Ebony*, Chicago, 1966.

KEENE, CHARLES

Exhibited: Harmon Foundation, 1936.
Sources: Harley, Ralph, Jr. "Checklist of Afro-Amer. Art & Artists," *The Serif*, Dec. 1970.

KEENE, PAUL F., JR.

Painter, educator. Born in Philadelphia on August 8, 1920. Studied at Philadelphia Museum School of Art; Tyler School of Fine Arts; Academie Julien, Paris (BFA, BSC Ed., MFA); Temple University; University of Pennsylvania; Graphic Sketch Club; Philadelphia Industrial

Art School. Past Assistant Professor of Painting at Philadelphia Museum School of Art; Chairman of Fine Arts Department, Bucks County Community College.

Works: *Let's Go See Snake Mary; The World of Dr. Buzzard; The Cabinet of Dr. Buzzard; The Root Man; The Prophet #2 Rootman Series; The Prophet #1 Rootman Series; Carnage; Lament for Ignalio Sanchez Mejias-Triptych Panel #3; Plaza de Toros #16; The Chess Masters; The Torture Machine; The Shooting Gallery; Lament for Ignalio Sanchez Mejias-Triptych Panel #2; Chicken Woman; Garden of Shango; Country Choir; Man With Drum; Contemplations of a Vindictive Society; Anastasis; Black Gothic; Procession #3; The Dying Society; The Mirror; Assassins; Death Calls on the Rootman; Death Comes to the Rootman.*

Exhibited: Art in America—New Talent, 1954; Contemporary Gallery, Atlantic City; 1015 Gallery, Wyncote, Pa.; Roko Gallery, NY, 1968; Pa. Academy of Art Annual, 1952-3, 1968-9; 1st Biennale Internat'l of Marine Art, Genoa, Italy, 1951; Art Alliance, Phila., 1966; Johnson C. Smith Univ., Charlotte, NC, 1968; San Jose State College, Cal., 1969; La Salle College, Phila., 1969; Institute of Modern Art, Boston, 1943; James A. Porter Gallery, 1970; Phila. Civic Center Museum; Master Series, Carnegie Library, 1969-70; Phila. Pyramid Club, 1952; Smith College Museum of Art, 1943; Howard Univ., 1961; Temple Univ., 1970; Colgate Univ.

Collections: Mr. Morton P. Rome, Phila.; Mr. John Hay Whitney, NY; Hirshhorn Collection, NY; Pa. Academy of Fine Arts; Tucson Museum; Tyler School of Fine Arts, Phila.; Dallas Museum; Bowdoin College; Morgan College; Phila. Museum, Pa. Collection; Howard Univ.

Awards: Whitney Fellowship Alumni Award, Temple Univ., 1970; Alumni Award, Phila. College of Art, 1972; John H. Whitney Fellowship, 1952-3.

Member: Pa. Academy of Fine Arts, professional member.

Sources: Dover. *American Negro Art*; Phila. Division of Art. *Afro-American Artists 1800-1969*; *Art Digest*, March 1, 1962, p. 12, review of Pyramid show; "Afro-Amer. Issue," *Art Gallery*, April 1968; Afro-Amer. Slide Depository, catalog; Lewis/Waddy. *Black Artists on Art*, Vol. 2; Howard Univ. *James A. Porter Gallery of African-Amercan Art*, 1970; Du-Sable Museum of African-Amer. History. *Contemporary Black Artists*, 1970, Calendar; "American Negro Given Full Length Review in NY Show," *Art Digest*, Dec. 15, 1941; "Black Art: What Is It?," *Art Gallery*, April 1970; Tyler School of Art. *Seven by Seven*, Temple Univ., 1970; Myers, Carol. *Black Power in the Arts*, Flint, Mich., 1970; Information from artist; Drummond, Dorothy. "Coast-to-Coast," *Art Digest*, March 1, 1952; Pierre-Noel, Lois Jones. "American Negro Art in Progress," *Negro History Bulletin*, Oct. 1967; Harley, Ralph, Jr. "A Checklist of Afro-Amer. Art & Artists," *The Serif*, Dec. 1970; "Paul Keene to Show His Oil Paintings," *Philadelphia Art Alliance Bulletin*, Nov. 1957; Brown, Marion. "The Negro in Fine Arts," *The Negro Heritage Library*, Vol. 2; Walker, Roslyn. *A Resource Guide to the Visual Arts of Afro-Americans*, South Bend, Ind., 1971.

KEITH, WILLIAM

Painter, sculptor. Born in Harlem, New York in 1929. Studied at the Newark School of Fine & Industrial Arts; School of Visual Arts.

Works: *Collision; Fishing Boat Harbor.*

Exhibited: Studio Museum in Harlem, 1969; Harlem Art Gallery; Portrait Gallery; Hudson Guild; NY Public Library.

Sources: Studio Museum in Harlem. *Harlem Artists 69.*

KELLY, ANDREW TAYLOR

Photographer. Born in 1894 in Texas. Has no formal training in art. Worked as an apprentice in a photographic studio.

Works: *Reverend E.R. Carter; June Gideon; Priestly; Sims.*

Exhibited: Harmon Foundation, 1933.

Sources: Harmon Foundation. *Non-Jury Exhibit of Works of Negro Artists,* 1933.

KEMP, KENNETH

Sources: Harley, Ralph, Jr. "Checklist of Afro-Amer. Art & Artists," *The Serif*, Dec. 1970.

KENNEDY, HARRIET F.

Sculptor, painter, mixed media. Born in Cambridge, Massachusetts in 1939. Studied at Museum School of Fine Arts, Boston (1960-5); Boston University (1965); Northeastern University (BFA).

Works: *Women in the Pool; Vietnam Lament* (pastel); Untitled watercolor; *Head of Michael,* 1970 (bronze sculpture); *Ancestral Memory,* 1971 (bronze); *Claudia* (mixed); *Sand, Sea & Sky* (oil); *Shadows in the Grass* (oil); *US Highway: Road to Destruction* (mixed); *Abstract* (watercolor).

Exhibited: Boston Museum of Fine Arts, 1970; Smith-Mason Gallery, 1971; Mass. Institute of Tech.; Amer. Internat'l College, Springfield, Mass.; Boston Public Library, 1973; Medford Public Library, Mass.; Cambridge Art Assn.; Boston Negro Artists Assn.; Palmer Gallery, Cambridge, Mass.; Input-Output Corp., Cambridge, Mass.; Boston Art Institute; NJ State Art Museum; Atlantic Union College.

Collections: Mrs. Aaron Kennedy, Mass.

Awards: Boit Award, Boston Museum School; Smith-Mason Gallery Award, sculpture, 1971; Best in Show, 1st prize, drawing, Medford Public Library, Mass., 1971; 1st prize, sculpture, Medford Public Library, Mass., 1970; Award of distinction, drawing, Medford 57th Anniversary Exhibition, Mass., 1969.
Member: Boston Negro Artists Assn.; Cambridge Art Assn.; Medford Arts Council; Barbados Arts Council.
Sources: Boston Museum of Fine Arts. *Afro-Amer. Artists New York/Boston*, 1970; Smith-Mason Gallery. *National Exhibition Black Artists*, 1971; DuSable Museum of African-Amer. History. *Contemporary Black Artists*, 1970, Calendar; Goodman, Ellen. "What Black Artists Are Doing & Why," *Boston Globe*, June 18, 1970, p. 28; "Afro-Amer. Art a Cultural Experience for All," *Record American*, May 19, 1970; Information from artist; Boston Negro Artists Assn. *10th Anniversary Exhibition*, Boston Public Library; Boston Negro Artists Assn. *The Black Artist in America: A Negro History Month Exhibition*, Boston Public Library, 1973.

KENNEDY, JAMES E.

Painter, sculptor, educator. Born in Jackson, Mississippi in 1933. Studied at Ohio State University (BS, MA).
Works: *Gather Ye Rosebuds While Ye May; Landscape; The Marble Shooters; Reclining Nude; The Alice; The Piano Player; Purgatory; Finite; American Cover-Up; Getting There; The Tempest; Seated Girl; Self-Portrait; Pelvis; The Revolution; From the Roots the Promise of the Future; Head; The Society.*
Exhibited: Atlanta Univ. Nat'l Competition, 1960, 1961; Eastern Shore Annual, 1967; Beaux Arts Show, Mobile, Ala., 1962-3.
Collections: Johnson Pub. Co.; Dr. Kurt Tauss, Mobile, Ala.; Mr. Johnny D. Shelwood, Mobile, Ala.
Awards: Samuel H. Kress Foundation Grant; 1st award, Eastern Shore Art Gallery, 1966; 1st & 3rd awards, Beaux Arts Show, Mobile, Ala., 1963; 1st & 2nd awards, Beaux Arts Show, Mobile, Ala., 1962.
Member: College Art Assn.; Nat'l Conference of Artists; Afro-American Slide Depository at Univ. of So. Ala., co-founder.
Sources: Afro-American Slide Depository, catalog; Johnson Pub. Co. *The JPC Art Collection*, Pamphlet; Information from the artist; Conlon, James E., & James E. Kennedy. "An Afro-American Slide Project," *Art Journal*, Winter 1970-1, pp. 164-5.

KENNER, DANIEL

Graphic artist.
Sources: *St. Louis Post Dispatch*, Jan. 18, 1951.

KERSEY, JOSEPH

Sculptor, painter, educator. Born in Chicago, 1909.
Works: *Young Girl; St. Francis; Backyards, Chicago; City Callers; Mountain; Landscape; The Old Tree* (watercolor); *Anna* (sculpture); *Girl's Head; Study of a Lady; Three Witch Doctor Bedes; Scout Trees; Trees, Lonely Trees; Baby George* (sculpture); *Etta* (sculpture); *After The Invasion* (watercolor); *We Are Not Alone* (watercolor); *Kittens* (sculpture); *Spiritual Singer* (sculpture); *Ellen Jane* (sculpture); *Clyde Winkfield* (sculpture).
Exhibited: Chicago Artists, 1938; Federal Arts Project, 1939; Amer. Negro Exposition, 1940; Atlanta Univ., 1942; Howard Univ., 1941; Library of Congress, 1940; South Side Community Art Center, Chicago, 1941; McMillen Inc. Galleries, NY, 1941.
Collections: Johnson Pub. Co.
Awards: Honorable mention, Amer. Negro Exposition, 1940.
Sources: Mallett. *Index of Artists*; Dover. *American Negro Art*; Indiana Univ. *Fine Arts & the Black American*; Locke. *The Negro in Art*; Tanner Galleries. *Art of the American Negro,* 1940; Roosevelt, Eleanor. "Negro Paintings at Howard were Inspiring," in "My Day" column, *Washington Daily News*, March 3, 1941; Howard Univ. *Exhibition of Negro Artists of Chicago at Howard Univ. Gallery of Art*, Feb. 1941; DuSable Museum of African-Amer. History. *Contemporary Black Artists,* 1970, Calendar; "Art by Negroes," *Art Digest*, Oct. 15, 1941; "American Negro Art Given Full Length Review in NY Show," *Art Digest*, Dec. 15, 1941; Locke, Alain. "Chicago's New Southside Art Center," *American Magazine of Art*, Aug. 1941; Johnson Pub. Co. *The JPC Art Collection*, Pamphlet; Porter. *Modern Negro Art*; Harley, Ralph, Jr. "A Checklist of Afro-Amer. Art & Artists," *The Serif*, Dec. 1970; South Side Community Art Center. *National Negro Art Exhibition*, Chicago, 1941; South Side Community Art Center. *Opening Exhibition of Paintings by Negro Artists*, Chicago, 1941; McMillen Inc. Galleries. *Contemporary Negro Art*, NY, 1941; Walker, Roslyn. *A Resource Guide to the Visual Arts of Afro-Americans*, South Bend, Ind., 1971.

KEY, VIVIAN SCHUYLER

Designer. Born in 1906. Studied at Pratt Institute, 1926. Worked as assistant director at Lincoln Settlement House, Brooklyn; worked at Glen Cove Settlement Houses on Long Island.
Works: Covers for CRISIS magazine; *Evelyr (Dimple) Little.*
Exhibited: Harmon Foundation, 1931, 1933, 1930.

Awards: Amy E. Spingarn Award, 1927.
Sources: Harmon Foundation. *Exhibition of Productions by Negro Artists*; Harmon Foundation. *Negro Artists*, 1935; Harmon Foundation. *Exhibit of Fine Arts*, 1930; Indiana Univ. *Fine Arts & the Black American*; DuSable Museum of African-Amer. History. *Contemporary Black Artists*, 1970, Calendar; Harley, Ralph, Jr. "A Checklist of Afro-Amer. Art & Artists," *The Serif*, Dec. 1970; "Negro Artists Paintings on Display at University (Howard)," *East Tennessee News*, Knoxville, Tenn., June 6, 1932; Walker, Roslyn. *A Resource Guide to the Visual Arts of Afro-Americans*, South Bend, Ind., 1971.

KHAREM, OMAR
Photographer.
Exhibited: Addison Gallery, 1971.
Sources: James Van DerZee Institute. *The Black Photographer (1908-1970): A Survey.*

KIAH, VIRGINIA JACKSON
Painter, educator, museum director. Studied at Teachers College, Columbia University (BS, MA); University of Pennsylvania; New York Art Students League; Philadelphia Museum School of Art; under Frank Vincent Dumond; Robert Brackman. Founder-Director of the Kiah Museum.
Works: *Congressman Adam Powell; Dr. Mary McLeod Bethune; Carol Brice; Finley Wilson; Judge Thomas Griffith; Karl E. Downs; Mary Nottingham Smith; Carl Murphy; Dr. Lillie M. Jackson; Keiffer A. Jackson; Bishop John Bowen; Bishop Edgar Love; Richard Allen; Mrs. Susie Love; President Dwight D. Eisenhower; Rev. Simon Williamson; Rev. W. W. Allen; Rev. J.R. Butler; Rev. A.J. Payne; Rev. W.W. Payne; George Murphy; Charles Houston; Mrs. Sarah Fernandis; Mrs. Susie Love; Dr. D.W. Hargis; Mrs. D.W. Hargis; Miss Ida Cummings; Mrs. William Harcum; Mother of Rev. Lillian Thompson; Raphael Kiah; Mrs. Constantine Wharton; Mrs. Hattie Carter; Mrs. Mary Patterson; Mrs. Augusta Chissel; Rev. William Garnet; Frederick Douglass; Old Man; Rev. R. Lewis; Masculinity; Aunt Esther; Mrs. Jennie Taylor; J.N. Francis; Saint Louis Ponder; Mrs. Alice Simmons; Dr. Kathrine D. Barry; Mrs. Alice McCoy; Mrs. Margaret Davis Bowen; Mrs. Abbie Johnson; Bennie Warshaw; Mrs. Herman Sartor; Mrs. Alice Dennis; Julian Weitz; Capt. Frank Spencer; Dr. Calvin S. Kiah; 5th Avenue & 59th, NY; Boy with Safety Pin; Full Fighter; Feeding Time; Dejection; The Threat; Clarence Keiffer & Michael Mitchell; James Luten; Mrs. Lillie Harris; Dr. Tola Harris; Mrs. Matilda Harris; Mrs. Gertie Lizzamore; Mrs. Eva Renfrow; Karlene; Anna Lucasta; Godmother West*

(watercolor); Little Boy Head Study (pencil); Little Girl Head Study (pencil); So Pale; Mrs. Ursala Murrell; Rev. B.C. Roberson; Rev. W. Wainwright; Mrs. Thomas Dyett; Rev. Harry Hoosier; Mrs. Thomas Griffith; Mrs. Margaret Carline; Mr. Alfred Evans; Mother of Ursala Murrell; Sacred Birth; Rudolph Bolden Renfrow.
Exhibited: Kiah Museum, 1971; Phila. Republican Club, 1929; Phila. Museum, 1930-1; Baltimore Museum of Art, 1935; NY Baptist Ministers' Conference, 1936 (1-woman); Art Students League, 1937; Eggleston Galleries, NYC, 1947; Telfair Museum, Savannah; Savannah State College, 1963 (1-woman); Winston-Salem (NC) Civic Center, 1969; Southern Regional Art Show, Williamsburg, Va., 1969; Charlestown (SC) Civic Center, 1970; Tuskegee Institute, 1971; Carnegie Institute, 1971.
Collections: NAACP, Baltimore; Morgan Christian Center, Baltimore; Freedom House, Baltimore; Apostolic Faith Church, Baltimore; Attys. Clarence & Juanita Mitchell; Morgan State College; Morningstar Baptist Church, Baltimore; Old St. George's Methodist Church, Phila.; Mr. John Harris, Phila.; Mrs. Esther White, Phila.; Carver State Bank, Savannah; Kiah Museum; Mrs. Evanel Terrell, Savannah; Ga. State Univ.; Mr. & Mrs. Calvin L. Kiah; Tompkins High School; St. Mary's Elem. School; Matilda Harris School; Abbysinia Baptist Church, NYC; 7th Ave. Baptists, NYC; Gulfpride, Miss. Methodist Retreat; Downs Methodist Church, Oakland, Cal.; Holman Methodist Church, Los Angeles; Marian Downs Smith, Los Angeles; Mary Smith High School, Pungoteague, Va.; Eisenhower Museum, Independence, Kansas.
Awards: 4th prize, Paulette Goddard-Anna Lucasta Portrait Painting Contest, sponsored by Columbia Motion Pictures Corp.; 1st & 2nd prizes in 3rd & 4th yrs. at Phila. Museum School of Art; Phila. Museum scholarships, 1929, 1930; 2nd prize, Md. Women's Civic League, 1932; State of Md. Scholarships, 1948, 1949; Columbia Univ. Teachers College Award, 1949; YMCA Achievement Award, Savannah, 1955; Nat'l Conference of Artists Distinctive Merit Award, 1960-2, 1970-2, 1968; Asbury Methodist Church Achievement Award, 1966; DuSable High School Art Club Award, 1968; Links Distinctive Merit Award, 1966; Margaret Burroughs Achievement Award, 1970.
Sources: Information from artist; *Journal of the Nat'l Conference of Artists*, Winter 1971; Raut. "Profile: Mrs. Virginia J. Kiah—Artists, Kiah Museum," *Savannah Magazine*, Jan. 1971; Kiah, Virginia. "Black Artists," *Savannah Magazine*, April 1972, p. 16; WVa. State College. *Journal of the Nat'l Conference of Artists*, 1968.

165

KILLIAN, DARLYNE ATKINSON

Painter, sculptor, textile designer, metalworker, educator. Born in Brenham, Texas, October 9, 1928. Studied at Spelman College (AB, 1948); University of Georgia (MEd, 1968).
Works: *Untitled Batik; Koko the Knockkneed Clown;* Copper jars; *Orange Eaters.*
Exhibited: Witte Museum, 1964; Washington High Evening School Graduation Reception, 1967.
Collections: Mr. W.T. Leaphart; Dr. and Mrs. J.D. Atkinson; Mrs. W.H. Killian, Sr.
Member: Nat'l Conference of Artists; Georgia Assn. of Art Educators; Nat'l Art Education Assn.
Sources: Information from artist; "Increasing Perceptual Sensitivity and Aesthetic Awareness of a Group of Middle School Pupils Through the Use of Three Dimensional Media," *Research and Development,* Atlanta Public Schools, Nov. 11, 1968.

KING, ANDRE

Sources: DuSable Museum of African-Amer. History. *Contemporary Black Artists,* 1970, Calendar.

KING, HENRI UMBAJI

Painter.
Works: *Uhuru; Flowers; Incantation to God: Yemonja; Back Porch, U.S.A.; Seven Points South; The Ascension; The Casbah; Senegalese Mother or the Red M'Bou Bou; Sacred Mother and Child; Mosque du Senegal; Black Repose; Integrated; Bubble Dancers; Bride of Shango; The Family; After the Fall; Josifo, Jajili and Jisu; Lady and Waiter; Mama, Baba and Mwana.*
Collections: Johnson Pub. Co.
Sources: Afro-American Slide Depository, Catalog; Johnson Pub. Co. *The JPC Art Collection,* Pamphlet.

KING, HERMAN

Active in 1960's.
Sources: "Afro-American Issue," *Art Gallery,* April 1968; Indiana Univ. *Fine Arts & the Black American;* DuSable Museum of African-Amer. History. *Contemporary Black Artists,* 1970, Calendar; Walker, Roslyn. *A Resource Guide to the Visual Arts of Afro-Americans,* South Bend, Ind., 1971.

KING, JAMES DeWITT

Sculptor. Born in Chicago, 1941. Studied at Goethe Institute, Germany; University of Vienna; University of Chicago.
Works: *Al Fatiha; The Dancer No. 2.*
Exhibited: Univ. of Iowa, 1971-2.
Collections: Merrill-Palmer Institute.
Sources: Ill. Bell Telephone. *Black American Artists/71,* 1972; Myers, Carol L. *Black Power in the Arts,* Flint, Mich., 1970.

KING, JOHN F.

Painter, educator, graphic artist. Born in Lower Peachtree, Alabama in 1937. Studied at Alabama State University (BS, 1961); San Jose State University (MA, 1968).
Works: *The Joker,* 1971 (oil); *King of Spades,* 1971 (oil); *Queen of Spades,* 1972 (oil); *Self Portrait,* 1972 (pastel); *Five Black Sisters,* 1972 (oil); *Natural Woman,* 1972 (ink).
Exhibited: Japan, 1957; Atlanta Art Exhibit, 1958-64; Beaux Art League, Mobile, Ala., 1961; Ankrum's Gallery-Contemporary II, Los Angeles, 1966; Moterrey Jazz Festival, 1968; Sacramento State Univ., 1969, 1970; Black Affair Gallery, Sacramento, 1970; Jennifer Paul's Gallery, Sacramento, 1971.
Awards: 2nd & 3rd prizes, Japan exhibit, 1957; 2nd place, oil, Beaux Art League, Mobile, Ala., 1961.
Sources: Information from the artist.

KINNEY, RICHARD

Printmaker. Active in 1960's.
Works: *Spring* (color woodcut).
Collections: Oakland Museum.
Sources: Roelof-Lanner, T.V., ed. *Prints by American Negro Artists;* Oakland Museum Archives; Walker, Roslyn. *A Resource Guide to the Visual Arts of Afro-Americans,* South Bend, Ind., 1971.

KINNON, E'LOIS

Photographer.
Exhibited: Addison Gallery, 1971.
Sources: James Van DerZee Institute. *The Black Photographer (1908-1970): A Survey.*

KITCHIN, BENJAMIN SPURGEON

Painter, sculptor, designer. Born in Jamaica in 1892. Worked in Jamaica as a marble cutter; employed by BMT in Brooklyn where he designed many of their safety slogans and placards.
Works: *Hunger; Modern Venus.*
Exhibited: Harmon Foundation, 1931, 1933.
Collections: Church of the Redeemer, Kingston, British West Indies.
Sources: Dover. *American Negro Art;* Harmon Foundation. *Exhibition of Productions by Negro Artists;* Harmon Foundation. *Negro Artists,* 1935; Indiana Univ. *Fine Arts & the Black American;* DuSable Museum of African-Amer. History. *Contemporary Black Artists,* 1970, Calendar; Walker, Roslyn. *A Resource Guide to the Visual Arts of Afro-Americans,* South Bend, Ind., 1971.

KNIGHT, AVEL de

See: deKnight, Avel.

KNIGHT, B. NATHANIEL

Painter. Born 1942.

Works: *Rhythm of My People, II,* 1970 (oil & enamel on canvas).
Exhibited: Whitney Museum, 1971.
Sources: Doty. *Contemporary Black Artists in America.*

KNIGHT, GWENDOLYN

Sculptor, painter. Born in Barbados, West Indies. Studied at Howard University School of Fine Arts; New School for Social Research; Skowhegan (Maine) School of Painting and Sculpture.
Works: *Dorothy II* (painting); *Young Man* (sculpture); *Girl in Chair.*
Exhibitions: New School for Social Research; Workshop Gallery, West Hempstead, NY; Amer. Society of African Culture, Lagos, Nigeria; Forum Gallery, NY; Dillard Univ., 1941.
Sources: Lewis/Waddy. *Black Artists on Art,* Vol. 2; Dillard Univ. *Arts Festival,* Catalog, 1941.

KNIGHT, ROBERT

Painter, illustrator, graphic artist. Born in Newark, New Jersey on December 1, 1944. Studied at Newark School of Fine and Industrial Art; Cooper Union.
Works: *Ancient Lovers,* 1970; *Space Walk,* 1971; *Black Child's Eyes; Natural Woman; Visitation.*
Exhibited: Pentagon, Washington, DC; Smithsonian Institution, 1968; YM-YWCA, West Orange, NJ, 1968; Stuart Gallery, NJ, 1971; NJ Artists, 1968; Newark Museum, 1968, 1971.
Collections: Office of the Chief of Military History, Dept. of Art, Washington, DC; Historical Dept., Fort Eustis, Va.; Newark Museum; Battin High School, NJ; Dr. Earl LeRoy Wood, MD, NJ; Mr. & Mrs. William Bartle, NJ; Newark Public Library.
Awards: 3 yr. scholarship, Newark School of Fine & Industrial Art; Full scholarship, Cooper Union, NYC; Scholastic Achievement Award, Newark School of Fine & Industrial Art; 1st prize, graphics, Wayne, NJ; Certificate of Achievement, Dept. of Army; 1st prize, Newark Community Outdoor Exhibit, 1968.
Sources: Newark Museum. *Black Artists: Two Generations,* 1971; *Newark Chamber of Commerce Magazine,* Aug. 1971, Spring/Summer 1969; *US History for High School,* Laidlaw Bros., Div. of Doubleday, River Forrest, Ill.; *Combat Artist Exhibition,* Washington, DC.

KNIGLE, GWENDOLYN

Exhibited: Augusta Savage Studios, 1939.
Sources: Harley, Ralph, Jr. "Checklist of Afro-Amer. Art & Artists," *The Serif,* Dec. 1970.

KNOX, COLUMBUS

Works: *Charging Warriors.*
Exhibited: Phila. Civic Center.

Sources: Phila. Division of Art. *Afro-American Artists 1800-1969.*

KNOX, SIMMIE

Exhibited: State Armory, Wilmington, Del., 1971.
Sources: Aesthetic Dynamics. *Afro-American Images,* 1971, Catalog.

KOLAWOLE, WILLIAM LAWRENCE COMPTON

Painter, graphic artist, sculptor. Born in Beaumont, Texas, August 20, 1931. Studied at California School of Fine Arts. Lives and works in Paris and Munich.
Works: *Homage to Thelonius Monk; Untitled; Oil I; Oil III; Untitled etching; Motion Art* series, 1970; Untitled goache, 1970; *Zeichnung; Radierung; Stahlskulptur,* 1950.
Exhibited: Xavier Univ., 1963; Galerie L55, Paris, 1973; San Francisco Museum of Art, 1950, 1953, 1955; Lucien Labaudt Art Gallery, San Francisco, 1955 (1-man); The Gallery 6, 1955 (1-man), Regional Show, 1955; Action Painters of Northern Cal., Los Angeles, 1955; Camino Gallery, NY, 1956; Parma Gallery, NY, 1957; Market Place Gallery, NY, 1959, 1960 (1-man); Commercial Museum, Phila., 1960; Americana Hotel, NY, 1963; Family Savings, Los Angeles, 1964 (1-man); Ankrum Gallery, Los Angeles, 1965; Print-Show in Worms, Mainz, Frankfurt, & Stuttgart, 1966; Haus der Kunst, Munich, 1966, 1968; Galerie Schrag, Nuremburg, 1967 & 1968 (1-man); Goethe House, Lagos, Nigeria, 1967 (3-man); Print-Show, Worms, Kunstverein 1967; Print-Show, Munich, Frankfurt, Ludwigshafen, 1967-8; Kleine Galerie, Munich, 1968 (1-man); Municipal Museum of Treves, 1969; Galerie Dürr, 1969 (1-man); Galerie-Atelier 67, Ulm, 1969 (1-man); Galerie Soulange, Paris, 1969; Morgan State College, 1970; Univ. of Texas, 1970; Nat'l Center of Afro-Amer. Artists, Boston, 1970; Cité International Des Arts, Paris, 1971; Märk. Museum der Stadt Witten, 1971 (1-man); Internationale Kunst-und Informationemess, Cologne, 1971; Studio Kausch, Kassel, 1972 (1-man); Galerie Dürr, Munich, 1972 (1-man); Galerie Werne 70, Bochum, 1972; Galerie Dimitrios, Amsterdam, 1972 (1-man).
Awards: Academic honors, 3-year scholarship student, Cal. School of Fine Arts; *San Francisco Chronicle* Certificate of Merit for Sculpture, 1949; Certificate of Excellence Exhibit, sculpture, 1949; *Scholastic Magazine,* 1949; Bank Prize, painting, San Francisco Art Assn., 1954; Cash prize, San Francisco Museum of Art, 1953.
Member: San Francisco Art Assn.
Sources: Dover. *American Negro Art,* p. 50;

Roelof-Lanner, T.V. *Prints by American Negro Artists;* Indiana Univ. *Fine Arts & the Black American;* Harley, Ralph, Jr. "Checklist of Afro-Amer. Art & Artists," *Serif,* Dec. 1970; Walker, Roslyn. *A Resource Guide to the Visual Arts of Afro-Americans,* South Bend, Ind., 1971; Kolawole, L.C. *Motion Art,* Galerie L55, Paris, 1973; Frankenberg. *Der Blaue Mohr,* Chris-Verlag, Munich, Germany, 1968; Xavier Univ. *Emancipation Proclamation Centennial National Art Exhibition,* 1963; Brown, Marion. "The Negro in the Fine Arts," *The Negro Heritage Library,* Vol. 2; Lewis/Waddy. *Black Artists on Art,* Vol. 1; Univ. of Texas. *Afro-American Artists Abroad;* Grillo, Jean B. "Elma Lewis: A New Show in a New Showplace," *Boston After Dark,* Aug. 16, 1970; Loercher, Diana. "Afro-American Artists Abroad," *Christian Science Monitor,* Aug. 1, 1970; Market Place Gallery. *Contemporary Artists,* NY, 1970; Commercial Gallery. *The American Negro Artist Looks at Africa,* Phila., 1960; Americana Hotel. *Negroes on the American Scene,* NY, 1963.

KUMALE, SIDNEY
Active in 1960's.
Sources: Myers, Carol. *Black Power in the Arts,* Flint, Mich., 1970; "Afro-American Issue," *Art Gallery,* April 1968; Indiana Univ. *Fine Arts & the Black American;* DuSable Museum of African-Amer. History. *Contemporary Black Artists,* 1970, Calendar; Walker, Roslyn. *A Resource Guide to the Visual Arts of Afro-Americans,* South Bend, Ind., 1971.

LAGRONE, OLIVER
Sculptor, educator, poet. Studied at Cranbrook Academy of Art; Howard University.
Works: *Philosopher; Woman Wringing Sheets; Masl-African Motif; The Dancer; Albert Schweitzer; Man Shaping Elements; Black Resolve; Oedipus Reckless; Frederick Douglass; George Washington Carver; Woman Combing Hair; Father & Son; Charles A. Hill; Portrait of a Young Artist; Harriet Tubman; Sojourner Truth.*
Collections: Dr. & Mrs. John Chavis; Mr. & Mrs. Alfred Keats.
Sources: Myers, Carol. *Black Power in the Arts,* Flint, Mich., 1970; Harley, Ralph, Jr. "A Checklist of Afro-Amer. Art & Artists," *The Serif,* Dec. 1970; Afro-American Slide Depository, catalog; "Howard Univ. Boy Undertaker While Seeking Art Fame," *Washington Daily News,* April 21, 1938.

LAGRONE, R. E.
Painter, graphic artist. Worked in Tuskegee, Alabama.
Works: *Brown Man Who Fly; Captain Charles B. Hall* (portrait of 1st Negro to shoot down a German plane); *Strange Fruit.*
Exhibited: Atlanta Univ., 1944.
Sources: Atlanta Univ., *Annual Exhibition for Negro Artists,* 1944.

LAIRD, ANZOLA D.
Painter, educator. Born in Tennessee. Studied at University of Chicago; Michigan State Normal College.
Exhibited: Harmon Foundation, 1931, 1933; St. Louis Public Library.
Sources: Harmon Foundation. *Exhibition of Productions by Negro Artists;* Indiana Univ. *Fine Arts & the Black American;* Harley, Ralph, Jr. "A Checklist of Afro-Amer. Art & Artists," *The Serif,* Dec. 1970; Walker, Roslyn. *A Resource Guide to the Visual Arts of Afro-Americans,* South Bend, Ind., 1971.

LAM, WILFREDO
Painter.
Works: *Exodo.*
Exhibited: James A. Porter Gallery, 1970; Rockford (Ill.) College, 1965.
Sources: Howard Univ. *James A. Porter Gallery of African American Art,* 1970; Rockford College. *Creativity and the Negro.*

LAMA, OMAR
Painter.
Works: *Fertility God* (watercolor).
Collections: Johnson Pub. Co., Chicago.
Sources: Johnson Pub. Co. *The JPC Art Collection,* Pamphlet.

LANDEN, EDWARD
Exhibited: San Francisco Art Assn., 1946.
Sources: Harley, Ralph, Jr. "Checklist of Afro-Amer. Art & Artists," *The Serif,* Dec. 1970.

LANE, ARTIS
Painter.
Works: *Portrait of Fannie Jackson Coppin; Portrait of Langston Hughes; Portrait of Garrett A. Morgan; Portrait of Edward (Duke) Ellington; Portrait of Blanche K. Bruce; Portrait of Alain Leroy Locke; Portrait of Theodore K. Lawless; Portrait of Benjamin Mays; Portrait of James P. Beckworth; Portrait of Benjamin O. Davis, Sr.; Portrait of Clarence Reed White; Portrait of Rosa Parks; Portrait of Gov. George Romney; Portrait of C. E. Wilson.*
Collections: Mr. George Romney; Mr. Henry Ford; Brockman Gallery.
Sources: Pierre-Noel, Lois Jones. "American Negro Art in Progress, *Negro History Bulletin,* Oct. 1967; Brockman Gallery. *Black History in Calendar Form* (illustrations), Los Angeles, 1973.

LANE, DOYLE
Ceramist, muralist. Born in New Orleans in

1925. Studied at Los Angeles City College (AA, 1953); East Los Angeles City College; University of Southern California. Glaze technician, L.H. Butcher Co.; studio craftsman.
Works: *Enameled Plaque; Earthenware Pot; Earthenware Pots; Earthenware Bud Pots; Landscape #9; Red Abstraction, 1965* (ceramic plaque); Untitled tile mural; Untitled ceramic fountain; Untitled ceramic mural; *Gold Ark Mural Wall;* Untitled ceramic wall mural.
Exhibitions: Brockman Gallery, 1968; Ankrum Gallery, 1967, 1968; Cal. Design, Pasadena Art Museum, 1956, 1957; Oakland Museum; Mills College.
Collections: Oakland Museum; Mutual Savings & Loan, Pasadena, Cal.; Lutheran Nursing Home & Health Center, Alhambra, Cal.; Equitable Savings & Loan, Canoga Park; Pantry Foods, Pasadena, Cal.; Miller Robinson, Santa Fe Springs, Cal.; Temple B'nai David, Southfield, Mich.
Sources: Nordness, Lee. *Objects, USA,* NY, Viking Press, 1970, p. 87; Lewis/Waddy. *Black Artists on Art,* Vol. 2; Mills College Art Gallery. *California Black Craftsmen,* 1970; Oakland Museum Archives.

LANKFORD, JOHN ANDERSON

Architect, structural engineer, educator. Born in Potosi, Montana, 1874. Studied at Lincoln University (1889-96); Tuskegee Institute (1896-8); Architectural Designing and Mechanical Engineering School, Scranton, Pennsylvania; Frelinghuysen University, Washington, DC (1917-21). Planned and designed churches and school buildings in West and South Africa and in Central and South America.
Member: Tuskegee Club, Washington, DC; President, vice president, & director, Musulit Club; Board of Directors, YMCA, Washington, DC; Trustee, Board, Frelinghuysen Univ.; Trustee, Metropolitan AME Church; NAACP.
Sources: *Who's Who in Colored America,* 3rd edition; Wilson, John L. *The Negro Architect,* pp. 25, 30; Downing, Lewis K. "Contributions of Negro Scientists," *Crisis,* June 1939.

LARK, RAYMOND

Painter, graphic artist. Born in Philadelphia, June 16, 1939. Studied at Philadelphia Museum School of Art; Dobbins Vocational, Philadelphia; Temple University, Philadelphia; Los Angeles Technical College.
Works: *Howard H. McGee; Sweet Peaches; Nogachi & Chocolate Baby; Little Willy; Nothing But Work; Bernard's Shoes; Old Man Harvey and the Chickens; Bernard's Daddy.*
Exhibited: Governor's Mansion, NY, 1967; Nader's Art Gallery, Port-Au-Prince, Haiti; Santa Barbara Museum of Art; Philip E. Freed Gallery of Fine Arts, Chicago; NJ State Museum; Cape Cod Art Assn. Gallery, Hyannis, Mass.; San Diego Museum; Diplomat Hotel, Hollywood Beach, Fla.; Stanford Univ. Museum of Art; Ambassador Hotel, Dalzell Hatfield Galleries, Los Angeles; Smith-Mason Gallery, Washington, DC, 1971; Los Angeles City Hall Gallery; Charles W. Bowers Memorial Museum, Santa Ana, Cal.; La Mirada City Hall, Cal.; Lyzon Galleries, Nashville, Tenn.; La Jolla City Hall; Ball State Univ. Art Gallery, Muncie, Ind.; Compton (Cal.) College; Cal. Museum of Science & Industry, Los Angeles; WayUp Gallery, Hermosa Beach, Cal.; Western Wash. State College, Bellingham, Wash.; Cal. Lutheran College, Thousand Oaks, Cal.; Gasparian Gallery, Los Angeles; Arthur's Gallery of Masterpieces and Jewels, Beverly Hills, Cal.; Art Event of the Year, 1966; South Bay Art Fair, Redondo Beach, Cal., 1965; La Cienega Art Festival, Los Angeles, 1965, 1966; Immanuel's Art Exhibition, Los Angeles, 1967-8; Florenz's Art Show, Hollywood, Cal.
Awards: Chosen to represent the US, Art Event of the Year, 1966; 1st Prize, Immanuel's Art Exhibition, 1966, 1967; 1st Prize, Florenz's Art Show.
Member: Art West Associated (President, 1968-70); Internat'l Platform Assn.
Sources: Lewis/Waddy. *Black Artists on Art,* Vol. 1; *Los Angeles Times* Calendar, 1967-8; Smith-Mason Gallery. *National Exhibition Black Artists,* 1971; *Who's Who in American Art,* 1973; *Dictionary of International Biography,* Vol. 9, 1972-3; *Who's Who in the West,* 13th ed., 1971-2; *Outstanding Young Men of America,* 1972; *Who's Who in California,* 8th ed., 1971-2; Contemporary Crafts, Inc. *A Portfolio of Prints by Raymond Lark,* Los Angeles; Lewis, Samella S. *Art African America,* NY, Harcourt, Brace, 1973; *Who's Who in the Arts,* Jayell Pub. Co., 1973-4; "The Art of Raymond Lark of California," *Miami Herald,* Jan. 1969; "Drawings and Paintings by Raymond Lark," *Westways Magazine,* Nov. 1968; "International Graphic Art Masters," *Coast FM & Fine Arts Magazine,* Jan. 1970; Walker, Roslyn. *A Resource Guide to the Visual Arts of Afro-Americans,* South Bend, Ind., 1971.

LATIMER, GLENNA MONTAGUE

Exhibited: NY Public Library, 1921.
Sources: "Two one-man shows by Virginia Artists," *Museum Bulletin III,* April 1942; Colt, T.C., Jr. "Glenna Montague Latimer . . . 'Evenin',"* Virginia Artists Series No. 19, pp. 77-80; Harley, Ralph, Jr. "Checklist of Afro-Amer. Art & Artists," *The Serif,* Dec. 1970.

LATIMER, LEWIS HOWARD

Graphic designer, inventor. Born 1848; died 1928.

169

Sources: Haber, Louis. *Black Pioneers of Science & Invention; Negro Almanac*, p. 637; Spradling, Mary M., ed. *In Black & White: Afro-Americans in Print.*

LATIMER, LOUIS R.

Painter. Active in 1920's.
Sources: Holbrook, Francis. "Louis R. Latimer: Painter & Illustrator," *Southern Workman*, Dec. 1924, pp. 551-3; Walker, Roslyn. *A Resource Guide to the Visual Arts of Afro-Americans*, South Bend, Ind., 1971; Holbrook, Francis. "A Group of Negro Artists," *Opportunity*, July 1923, p. 211.

LAVEDO

Collections: NY Public Library-Schomburg Art Collection.
Sources: Schatz, Walter. *Directory of Afro-American Resources*, 1970.

LAWE, JOSEPH

Designer. Born in New York City in 1931. Studied at Pratt Institute, New York (BID, 1959). Formerly with Raymond Loewy-William Snaith design office, now heading his own design office in New York.
Exhibited: World Festival of Negro Arts, Dakar, Senegal, 1966.
Awards: Industrial Designers Society of America Medallion for outstanding product & graphic design, 1959; NY State Fisher Body Craftsman's Guild Award, 1949; Raymond Loewy Award, for excellence in the field of product design, 1949.
Sources: *First World Festival of Negro Arts*, Dakar, Senegal, 1966; *10 Artists from the United States*, designed catalog; Indiana Univ. *Fine Arts & the Black American;* DuSable Museum of African-Amer. History. *Contemporary Black Artists*, 1970, Calendar; Pierre-Noel, Lois Jones. "American Negro Art in Progress," *Negro History Bulletin*, Oct. 1967; Walker, Roslyn. *A Resource Guide to the Visual Arts of Afro-Americans*, South Bend, Ind., 1971.

LAWRENCE, CAROL

Painter. Born in Prairie View, Texas.
Works: *Pops; Manhood.*
Exhibited: Howard Univ., 1972; Nat'l Center of Afro-American Artists, Boston, 1970.
Member: AFRICOBRA.
Sources: *Black Shades*, Feb. 1972; Grillo, Jean B. "Where Down Home Meets Back Home," *Boston After Dark*, Sept. 1970; Howard Univ. AFRICOBRA II, 1972.

LAWRENCE, JACOB

Painter, illustrator, educator. Born in Atlantic City, New Jersey, 1917. Studied at the Art Workshop under Charles Alston and Henry Bannarn; Harlem Art Center and American Artists School (1937-9); Harlem Workshop (1932). Teacher at Pratt Institute.
Works: *The Life of Toussaint L'Ouverture* (941 tempera panels); *The Life of Frederick Douglass*, 1938 (40 tempera panels); *The Life of Harriet Tubman*, 1939 (40 tempera panels); *The Negro Migration Northward in the World War* (tempera panels); *The Artist Speaks; Life of John Brown; Pool Parlor; Mass Meeting; Ambulance Call; Tombstones; John Brown Leaves Harper's Ferry for Twelve House, No. 20; Street Scene; John Brown Took to Guerilla Warfare, No. 11; John Brown, after Long Meditation, Planned to Fortify Himself Somewhere in the Mountains, No. 13; Praying Ministers; The Builder*, 1971; *The Ordeal of Alice*, 1963; *This Is Harlem*, 1942; *Nigerian Meat Market; The Watchmaker; Clown; Battling Slaves; Coming Home; Anchor and Chart; Prayer; Roosters; Family; Study for Three Red Hats; Antiquities* (gouache); *Firewood; Pool Game*, 1970 (gouache); *Trees; Strike; Rent Strike; Builders No. 1; Migrations of the Negro* (60 panel series); *The Library; Funeral Sermon; Blind Beggars; The Shoe Maker; Frederick Douglass* (33 panel series); *4 Men; 10 Fugitives; Chess on Broadway; Lullaby; 2 Rebels; Invisible Man among Scholars; And the Migrants Kept Coming; Street Shadows*, 1959; *They Were Poor; The Migration; Taboo; Street Orator; Clinic; Rain; The Green Table; Reflections; Harlem Series; Sidewalk Drawings; Home Chores; Cabinet Makers; Radio Repairs; Seamstress; War Series; Catfish Row; Summer Street Scene; The Wedding; Depression; In the Garden; Slums; Square Dance; Sedation; Vaudeville; Comedy & Tragedy; The Concert; Night after Night; Struggle: From the History of the American People; Cafe Comedian; Dominoes; Library II; Builders 3; Playland; Forward 1967; Pool Room; Builders No. 2* (gouache).
Exhibited: Alston-Bannarn Studios, 1935-7; Harlem Art Center, 1936-9; Detroit Museum, 1938; Harlem YMCA, 1938 (1-man); Dillard Univ., 1938; Fisk Univ., 1938; Brooklyn College, 1938; Baltimore Museum, 1939; Amer. Negro Exposition, 1940; NY Federal Art Project, 1938-40; Atlanta Univ., 1944; Museum of Modern Art; Ford Foundation Retrospective Exhibit; Amer. Society of African Culture; Downtown Gallery (1-man); Terry Dintenfass Gallery; Metropolitan Museum; Artists for Victory Exhibition; Chicago Art Institute; Traveling Expedition to Nigeria; Johnson Wax Exhibition World Tour; State Dept. Exhibition, Pakistan, 1963; Alan Gallery, NY; Phillips Memorial Gallery, Washington, DC; Morgan State College, 1965; Brandeis Univ., 1965; 1st World Festival of Negro Arts, Dakar, Senegal, 1966; Boston Museum of Fine Arts, 1970;

Portland Museum of Art, 1943, 1945, 1947, 1950, 1953; Boston Institute of Modern Art, 1945; NJ State Museum, Trenton, 1947; Nat'l. Center of Afro-Amer. Artists, 1970; Univ. of Texas, 1970; Whitney Museum, 1971; State Armory, Wilmington, Del., 1971; Univ. of Iowa, 1971-2; Newark Museum, 1971; James A. Porter Gallery, 1970; Dartmouth College, 1968; Allegheny College, Meadowville, Pa., 1961; Xavier Univ., 1963; Amer. Academy of Arts & Letters, Nat'l. Institute of Arts & Letters, 1972.

Collections: Museum of Modern Art; Metropolitan Museum of Art; Phillips Collection; Art Faculty, Art Students League; New School for Social Research; Addison Gallery of Amer. Art, Phillips Academy, Andover, Mass.; Ala. Polytechnic Institute; Albright-Knox Gallery, Buffalo; Atlanta Univ.; Baltimore Museum of Art; Brooklyn Museum; Container Corp. of Amer.; Detroit Institute of Art; George Washington Carver School; Harmon Foundation; Howard Univ.; Internat'l Business Machines Corp.; Museum of Modern Art, Sao Paulo, Brazil; NJ State Museum; Phillips Memorial Gallery, Washington, DC; Portland Museum of Art, Ore.; Rhode Island School of Design; Southern Ill. Univ.; Univ. of Ariz.; Va. Museum of Fine Arts, Richmond; Cornell Univ.; Whitney Museum; Roland P. Murdock Collection of the Wichita Art Museum; Worcester Art Museum, Mass.; Spelman College, Atlanta; Morgan State College, Baltimore; Joseph H. Hirshhorn Collection; Nat'l. Archives; Johnson Pub. Co.; Newark Public Library.

Awards: Rosenwald Fellowship, 1940-2; Guggenheim Foundation Fellowship, 1946; Chapelbrook Foundation Fellowship, 1954; 2nd prize, Amer. Negro Exposition, Chicago, 1939; 6th purchase prize, Artists for Victory, Metropolitan Museum, 1942; Silver Medal, Art Institute of Chicago, 1948; 1st prize, Brooklyn Society of Artists, 1948; Honorable Mention, Brooklyn Museum, 1952; Purchase Prize, Atlanta Univ., 1948; Amer. Artists School Scholarship; Amer. Academy of Arts & Letters Grant, 1953; Purchase Prize, Metropolitan Museum of Art; Spingarn Medal, NAACP, 1970.

Member: Artists Equity Assn.; Nat'l Institute of Arts & Letters.

Sources: Mallett. *Index of Artists*; Albany Institute of History & Art. *The Negro Artist Comes of Age*; Locke. *The Negro in Art*; Locke. *Negro Art Past and Present*; *Negro Almanac*; *Who's Who in American Art*, 1966, 1970; *Fortune*, Nov. 1941; "Negro Artists," *Life*, July 22, 1946; *Christian Science Monitor*, Dec. 6, 1947; Dover. *American Negro Art*; "Afro-American Issue," *Art Gallery*, April 1968; Afro-American Slide Depository, 1971-2, catalog; Baur, John I. H., ed. *New Art in*

America, 1957, pp. 272-5; Larkin, Oliver W. *Art and Life in America*, 1949; Eliot, Alexander. *300 Years of American Painting*, 1957; Bethers, Ray. *Pictures, Painters and You*, 1948, pp. 240-1; Gruskin, Alan D. *Painting in the USA*, 1946; Hughes, Langston. *One Way Ticket*, 1948, Illustrator; Puma, Fernando. *Modern Art Looks Ahead*, 1947; Richardson, E. P. *Painting in America*; Richardson, Ben Albert. *Great American Negroes*, 1956, pp. 102-10; Rodman, Selden. *Conversations With Artists*, 1957; Downtown Gallery. *Harlem*, 1943; Downtown Gallery. *John Brown*, 1945; Univ. of Illinois. *Contemporary American Painting and Sculpture*, 1955; Phillips Gallery. *Three Negro Artists: Horace Pippin, Jacob Lawrence, Richmond Barthé*, Washington, DC, 1946-7; "And the Migrants Kept Coming," *South Today*, Spring 1942; "American Abroad," *Magazine of Art*, Jan. 1947; "American Struggle," *Vogue*, July 1957; "Arizona Art Collection," *Life*, Feb. 18, 1946, "Art," *Time*, Dec. 22, 1947, April 11, 1949, Feb. 2, 1953; Jan. 14, 1957; "Artist in Harlem," *Vogue*, Sept. 15, 1943; Denvir, Bernard. "Negro Art in the United States," *London Forum*, Christmas 1947; Evans, Walker. "In the Heart of the Black Belt," *Fortune*, Aug. 1948; "First Generation of Negro Artists," *Survey Graphic*, March 1939; Fitzsimmons, James. "Lawrence Documents," *Art Digest*, Nov. 1, 1950; Frankfurter, Alfred M. "Artists for Victory Exhibition: The Paintings," *Art News*, Jan. 1, 1943; Gibbs, Jo. "Lawrence Uses War for New Sermon in Paint," *Art Digest*, Dec. 15, 1947; Greene, Marjorie E. "Jacob Lawrence," *Opportunity*, Winter 1945; "John Brown's Body," *Newsweek*, Dec. 24, 1945; "The Negro Sympathetically Rendered by Lawrence," *Art News*, Feb. 18, 1939; "Life of Toussaint," *Art Digest*, Dec. 15, 1940; McCausland, Elizabeth. "Jacob Lawrence," *Magazine of Art*, Nov. 1945; "Effective Protest by Lawrence of Harlem," *Art Digest*, May 15, 1943; Saarinen, Aline B. "An Artist Reports on the Troubled Mind," *New York Times Magazine*, Oct. 15, 1944; Valente, Alfredo. "Jacob Lawrence," *Promenade*, Dec. 1947; "Saga of John Brown," *Art Digest*, Dec. 15, 1945; Amer. Federation of Arts. *Jacob Lawrence*, 1960; Minneapolis Institute of Arts. *30 Contemporary Black Artists*; Newark Museum. *Black Artists: Two Generations*, 1971; Boston Museum of Fine Arts. *Afro-American Artists: NY & Boston*, 1970; Nat'l. Center of Afro-Amer. Artists. *Five Famous Black Artists*, 1970; Indiana Univ. *The American Scene 1900-1970*; Aesthetic Dynamics. *Afro-American Images*, 1971; Univ. of Texas. *Afro-American Artists Abroad*; Cummings, Paul. *A Dictionary of Contemporary American Artists*; Finkelstein, Sidney. *Realism in Art*;

Goodrich, Lloyd, & John, Il Baur. *American Art of Our Century*; McCurdy, Charles, ed. *Modern Art . . . A Pictorial Anthology*; Halpert, Edith Gregor. *The Downtown Gallery*; Newmeyer, Sarah. *Enjoying Modern Art*; Nordness, Lee, ed. *Art: USA: Now*; Pearson, Ralph M. *The Modern Renaissance in American Art*; Richardson, E. P. *Painting in America, The Story of 450 Years*; "Home Forum," *Christian Science Monitor*, April 24, 1972; "Exhibition of Paintings by Jacob Lawrence," *Opportunity*, July 1943; Devree, Howard. "Jacob Lawrence Show at Downtown Gallery," *New York Times*, May 16, 1943; *New York Times Book Review*, June 10, 1948, Illustrator of "Children Go to School"; "Harlem in Color," *Newsweek*, April 1943; Bearden, Romare, & Harry Henderson. *Six Masters of American Art*; "Bright Sorrow," *Time*, Feb. 24, 1961; Baltimore Museum of Art. *Contemporary Negro*, 1939; Locke, Alain. "Advance on the Art Front," *Opportunity*, May 1939; Crocker Art Gallery. *Notes*, Sacramento, Sept./Oct. 1943; Museum of Modern Art. "Paintings by Leading Negro Artists Shown at Museum of Modern Art," NY, press release; "Negro Migration Depicted," *Afro-American*, Oct. 8, 1944; "Lawrence: Quiet Spokesman," *Art News*, Oct. 15, 1944; "Lawrence's Migration of the Negro to the North During World War I," *Art Digest*, Nov. 1, 1944; "New Series of Tempera Paintings, Downtown Gallery," *Pictures on Exhibit*, Dec. 1947, p. 20; Harley, Ralph, Jr. "Checklist of Afro-Amer. Art & Artists," *Serif*, Dec. 1970; "Kibitzers," *Pictures on Exhibit*, Nov. 1949, p. 5; "Exhibition," *Pictures on Exhibit*, Nov. 1950, pp. 27, 33; "Tratta di Negri," *Emporium*, Dec. 1950, p. 286; "Lawrence and Fox in Joint Exhibit," *Philadelphia Art Alliance Bulletin*, Jan. 1955, p. 8; "Exhibition at the Alan Gallery, NY," *Pictures on Exhibit*, Jan. 1957, p. 4; "America's Struggle, Three Paintings by Jacob Lawrence," *Vogue*, July 1957; Canaday, John. "Art: Scanning America of 19th Century," *New York Times*, Nov. 1, 1969, p. 29; Fisk Univ. *The Toussaint L'Ouverture Series by Jacob Lawrence*, 1968; Glueck, Grace. "NY Gallery Notes: Who's Minding the Easel?," *Art in America*, Jan./Feb. 1968; Lee, Virginia. "Jacob Lawrence—Story Teller," *Northwest Art News & Views*, March/April 1970, pp. 16-21; "Pictures of Harlem by Jacob Lawrence," *Springfield Sunday Union & Republican*, May 16, 1943, p. E6; Pomeroy, Ralph. "Reviews & Previews," *Art News*, Jan. 1968, p. 15; Doty. *Contemporary Black Artists in America*; Porter. *Modern Negro Art*; "The American Negro," scrapbook of clippings from *Christian Science Monitor*, Schomburg Collection, NYC, 1943; Butcher, Margaret J. *The Negro in American Culture*, p. 239;

Illinois Bell Telephone. *Black American Artists/71*, 1972; Roucek/Kiernan. *The Negro Impact on Western Civilization*; Howard Univ. *Festival of Fine Arts*, 1945; Howard Univ. *James A. Porter Gallery of African-American Art*, 1970; DuSable Museum of African-Amer. History. *Contemporary Black Artists*, 1970, Calendar; *New York Times*, April 4, 1948; *Daily Worker*, May 5, 1948; Dartmouth College. *6 Black Artists*, 1968; Werner, Alfred. "Black Is Not a Colour," *Art & Artists*, May 1969, pp. 14-7; Greene, Carroll, Jr. "Perspective: The Black Artist in America," *Art Gallery*, April 1970, p. 19; "American Negro Art Given Full Length Review in NY Show," *Art Digest*, Dec. 15, 1941; "The Negro in Art," *Art Digest*, June 1, 1944; "Negro Art Scores without Double Standards," *Art Digest*, Feb. 1, 1945; Pierre-Noel, Lois Jones. "American Negro Art in Progress," *Negro History Bulletin*, Oct. 1967; "Afro-Amer. Artists 1800-1950," *Ebony*, Vol. 23, pp. 116-22; Fax. *Seventeen Black Artists*; Wechsler, Lawrence. "The Negro Sympathetically Rendered," *Art News*, Feb. 18, 1939; "Art by Negroes," *Art News*, Feb. 11, 1939; "Negro Art Show," *Art News*, July 1, 1944, p. 6; "The Negro Comes of Age," *Art News*, Feb. 1, 1945; "An Introduction to the Negro in American History," *Arts*, Sept./Oct. 1969, p. 58; "American Negro Art," *Design*, Feb. 1942, p. 28; "The Black Artist in America: A Symposium," *Metropolitan Museum of Art Bulletin*, Jan. 1969, p. 245; Kiah,, Virginia. "Black Artists," *Savannah Magazine*, April 1972, p. 14; Johnson Pub. Co. *The JPC Art Collection*, Pamphlet; Greene, Carroll, Jr. "Afro-American Artists: Yesterday & Now," *The Humble Way*, Vol. 8, No. 3, 1968; Xavier Univ. *Emancipation Proclamation Centennial National Art Exhibition*; "Black Art: What Is It?," *Art Gallery*, April 1970; Driscoll, Edgar, Jr. "Exhibit Features Black Artists," *Boston Globe*, Feb. 16, 1970, p. 17; Greene, Carroll, Jr. *Afro-American Artists: 1800-1968*, Slides; Boning, Richard A. *Profiles of Black Americans*, NY, 1968; "Leading Negro Artists," *Ebony*, Sept. 1963, pp. 131-2; Shorewood Reproductions. *The Art of Black America*, 1969; Brown, Evelyn S. "The Harmon Awards," *Opportunity*, March 1933; Fax, Elton C. "Four Rebels in Art," *Freedomways*, Spring 1961; Giuliano, Charles. "Five Black Artists," *Boston After Dark*, March 4, 1970; "Winthrop Students Visit Arts Center," *Bay State Banner*, March 19, 1970; Loercher, Diana. "Black Artists Exhibition Reveals Visual Eloquence," *Christian Science Monitor*, March 2, 1970; Haydon, Harold. "Coming of Age of Black Art," *Chicago Sun Times*, July 26, 1970; Sherman, Marjorie. "Afro-America Gets Biggest Show," *Boston Globe*, May 18, 1970; Bourne,

Kay. "Black Artists Shown at Museum," *Bay State Banner*, May 28, 1970; Driscoll, Edgar. "Blacks Duncanson & Bannister Honored in Fine Arts Exhibit," *Boston Globe*, Jan. 16, 1972; Brown, Marion. "The Negro in the Fine Arts," *The Negro Heritage Library*, Vol. 2; Morsbach, Mabel. *The Negro in American Life*; Ploski, Harry, & Ernest Kaiser. "The Black Artist," *Afro USA*, 1971; Walsh, Rose. "Artists to Meet Public at Art Exhibit Preview," *Record American*, May 19, 1970; Le Brun, Caron. "Blacks' Art on Display," *Herald Traveler*, Boston, May 26, 1970; Paris, Jean. "Black Art Experience in Art," *Long Island Press*, Jamaica, NY, June 14, 1970; Ploski, Harry, Ernest Kaiser, & Otto Lindenmeyer. "The Black Artist," *Reference Library of Black America*, Book 4, 1971; *The Negro Handbook*, Composed by Editors of *Ebony*, Chicago, 1966; Schatz, Walter. *Directory of Afro-American Resources*, 1970; Adams, Russell. *Great Negroes Past and Present*, Chicago, 1969; Ruder & Finn Fine Arts. *Contemporary Black Artists*, 1969; Myers, Carol L. *Black Power in the Arts*, Flint, Mich., 1970; South Side Community Art Center. *Exhibition of Book Illustrations by Jacob Lawrence, Charles Sebree, Vernon Winslow*, Chicago, 1941; Spradling, Mary M., ed. *In Black & White: Afro-Americans in Print*; *Negro History Bulletin*, Oct. 1957, p. 18; Robinson, Wilhelmena S. *Historical Negro Biographies*, p. 222; Hollingsworth, Alvin. "Wealth of Expression in Black Artists' RISD Show," *Providence Sunday Journal*, June 29, 1969; Preston, Malcolm. "Art: Black Exhibit," *Boston Herald Traveler*, April 19, 1971; "Exhibition of Paintings by Jacob Lawrence," *Opportunity*, July 1943; Amer. Academy of Arts & Letters and Nat'l. Institute of Arts & Letters. *Paintings by Members*, 1972; Smithsonian Institution. *Ten Negro Artists From the United States*, 1966; Walker, Roslyn. *A Resource Guide to the Visual Arts of Afro-Americans*, South Bend, Ind., 1971; Barnet Aden Gallery. *The Life of John Brown*, Washington, DC, 1946; Driscoll, Edgar, Jr. "Showcase for Black Artists," *Boston Sunday Globe*, July 6, 1969, p. A73.

LAWSON, ADELAIDE J.

Exhibited: Tanner Art League, 1922.
Sources: Saylor, Gregory. "Adelaide Lawson," *Art Review I*, April 1922, p. 24; Harley, Ralph, Jr. "Checklist of Afro-Amer. Art & Artists," *The Serif*, Dec. 1970.

LAWSON, CLARENCE

Sculptor. Born in Beaumont, Texas in 1909. Studied at Art Institute of Chicago (1933-8); and in Europe.
Works: *Green Apples, Oranges & Objects; Self-Portrait; Patron of the Arts; Water Boy;* *Portrait of a Girl; I'm Hep; Canteen Girl; The Prophet; Maylayan Village; Design for Wooden Door; Primitive; Nude Woman; Portrait #1.*
Exhibited: Art Institute of Chicago Student Exhibits, 1937, 1939; Amer. Negro Exposition, 1940; Atlanta Univ., 1942, 1944; Howard Univ., 1941; South Side Community Art Center, Chicago, 1941; Tanner Art Galleries, 1940.
Awards: Travel Fellowship to Europe, 1938-40; Honorable Mention, Atlanta Univ., 1944.
Sources: Locke. *The Negro in Art*; *Negro Yearbook*; Indiana Univ. *Fine Arts & the Black American*; Howard Univ. *Exhibition of Negro Artists of Chicago at Howard Univ. Gallery of Art*, 1941; Brawley, Benjamin. *The Negro Genius*; DuSable Museum of African-Amer. History. *Contemporary Black Artists*, 1970, Calendar; Locke, Alain. "Chicago's New Southside Art Center," *American Magazine of Art*, Aug. 1941, p. 374; *Chicago Art Institute Scrapbook*, LXXI, 1937-8, p. 144; Harley, Ralph, Jr. "A Checklist of Afro-Amer. Art & Artists," *The Serif*, Dec. 1970; Tanner Art Galleries. *Art of the American Negro*, 1940; South Side Community Art Center. *National Negro Art Exhibition*, Chicago, 1941; Walker, Roslyn. *A Resource Guide to the Visual Arts of Afro-Americans*, South Bend, Ind., 1971.

LAWSON, YVONNE

Works: *Washington, D.C.; Johannesburg, South Africa.*
Exhibited: Smith-Mason Gallery, 1971.
Sources: Smith-Mason Gallery. *National Exhibition Black Artists 1971.*

LAWTON, BETTY

Painter, educator. Studied at University of Northern Iowa (BA); District of Columbia Teachers College; under Lucille Roberts. Art & Production Director, World Confederation of Organizations of the Teaching Profession; Publications Assistant, International City Management Association.
Works: *Adaptation of a Winter Scene.*
Exhibited: Margaret Dickey Gallery; Zion Baptist Church; DCAA, Anacostia Neighborhood Museum-Smithsonian Institution.
Sources: DC Art Assn. *Exhibition '71*, Washington, DC, 1971.

LAZARD, LUCNER

Painter. Born in Haiti, 1928. Studied at the Centre d'Art; Foyer des Arts Plastiques, Port-au-Prince, Haiti; École des Arts Modernes, Paris.
Exhibited: Studio Museum in Harlem, 1969; Zegri Gallery, 1961 (1-man).
Sources: Studio Museum in Harlem. *Harlem Artists 69.*

LEE, BERNARD

Painter.
Works: *3-D* (acrylic).
Exhibited: Lee Cultural Center, Phila.
Sources: Phila. Dept. of Recreation. *Love . . . and the Black Community.*

LEE, BERTINA

Sources: Porter. *Modern Negro Art*; Harley, Ralph, Jr. "Checklist of Afro-Amer. Art & Artists," *The Serif*, Dec. 1970.

LEE, CLIFFORD

Painter. Active in 1960's.
Works: *Guitars; Louis Armstrong; Trapeze.*
Exhibited: Rockford College, Ill., 1965; Oak Park Library.
Collections: Johnson Pub. Co.; Mr. Herbert Nipson; Sears-Vincent Price Art Gallery.
Sources: "Afro-American Issue," *Art Gallery*, April 1968; Indiana Univ. *Fine Arts & the Black American*; Rockford College. *Creativity & the Negro*; Johnson Pub. Co. *The JPC Art Collection*, Pamphlet; DuSable Museum of African-Amer. History. *Contemporary Black Artists*, 1970, Calendar; Myers, Carol. *Black Power in the Arts*, Flint, Mich., 1970; Walker, Roslyn. *A Resource Guide to the Visual Arts of Afro-Americans*, South Bend, Ind., 1971.

LEE, HARVEY W., JR.

Painter, educator. Born in St. Louis, Missouri in 1925. Studied at Bradley University (BFA and MA); Syracuse University.
Works: *And They Did Not Believe*, 1955 (oil); *Reflections of an Age Long Past*, 1959 (casein); *Sailboats*, 1960 (oil); *Portrait of a Friend*, 1960 (oil & casein); *Still Life*, 1965 (oil); *Trio*, 1965 (oil); *Seascape*, 1951 (oil).
Exhibited: Artagon Show, Peoria, Ill.; YWCA Exhibition of Negro Art, Peoria, Ill., 1950; Bradley Univ., 1951 (2-man); Univ. of Ohio, 1952; Dinner Key Auditorium, Miami, Fla., 1952; Stetson Univ., 1953-6; Atlanta Univ., 1952.
Collections: Atlanta Univ. Collection of Negro Artists.
Awards: Bachelor of Fine Arts Degree Cum Laude, 1944; Atlanta Univ. Award for Best Landscape Painting, 1952; 1st Prize for Best Figure Painting, Stetson Univ., 1953; 1st Prize for Best Portrait Painting, Stetson Univ., 1954; 1st Prize for Best Landscape Painting, Stetson Univ., 1955 & 1956; Syracuse Methodist Faculty Fellowship Fund, 1964-5; United Negro College Fund (IBM Fellowship Fund), Summers, 1965-6.
Sources: Information from the artist.

LEE, JAMES

Printmaker, painter. Born 1927.
Works: *Cleo II.*

Exhibited: Whitney Museum, 1971.
Member: Michigan Assn. of Printmakers.
Sources: Doty. *Contemporary Black Artists in America*; Myers, Carol L. *Black Power in the Arts*, Flint, Mich., 1970.

LEE, NANNO

Painter, educator. Born in St. Louis, Missouri. Studied at Stowe Teachers College (BA); Howard University; District of Columbia Teachers College; Catholic University.
Works: *Las Mananitas; Purple Enlightenment; Glo.*
Exhibited: State Armory, Wilmington, Del., 1971; Smith-Mason Gallery, 1971; Benning Branch Library; DCAA, Anacostia Neighborhood Museum-Smithsonian Institution.
Sources: Aesthetic Dynamics. *Afro-American Images 1971*; Smith-Mason Gallery. *Anniversary Exhibit*, 1971; DC Art Assn. *Exhibition '71*, Washington, DC, 1971.

LEE, SIDNEY ELLISON

Painter.
Works: *Peanut Wizard.*
Exhibited: Atlanta Univ., 1942.
Sources: Harley, Ralph, Jr. "Checklist of Afro-Amer. Art & Artists," *The Serif*, Dec. 1970; Atlanta Univ. *Annual Exhibition for Negro Artists*, 1942.

LEE-SMITH, HUGHIE

Painter. Born in Eustis, Florida, 1915. Studied at the Cleveland Institute of Art; Wayne State University (BS, 1953); Art School of the Detroit Society of Arts and Crafts; John Huntington Polytechnic Institute. Worked for Ohio Federal Art Project (1938-9); teacher of art, Claflin University, Orangeburg, South Carolina (1939-40); organized an exhibit of Negro artists in the Midwest (1943); worked on "History of the Negro in the Navy."
Works: *Portrait of a Sailor; Unusual Landscape; Landscape #4; Negro Boy; Man with Balloon; Discussion on the Roof; Man Standing on His Head*, 1970 (oil); *Aftermath; Impedimenta; Festival's End; Boy on Roof; The Bridge; Interval; Artists Life No. 1; Artists Life No. 2; Waste Land; The Other Side* (oil); Detail for sketch of *Black Heroes; Drawing; Girl with Towel; The Juggler* (oil); *Man in Boat* (oil); *Old Man and Youth*, 1958 (oil); *Posture* (oil); *The Rehearsal*, 1959 (oil); *River's Edge* (oil); *Two Girls* (oil); *Girl With Balloon; End of the Festival; Rocky Beach; Children at Play; The Kite; The Piper; Little Diana; Two Boys and a Girl.*
Exhibited: Buck Hills (Pa.) Art Assn.; South Side Community Art Center, 1945 (1-man); Snowden Gallery, Chicago, 1945; Ten Thirty Galleries, Cleveland, 1950; Detroit Artists Market, 1952, 1958, 1961, 1966; Garelick Gal-

ery, Detroit, 1953; Anna Werbe Galleries, Detroit, 1954; Forsythe Gallery, Ann Arbor, 1954, 1966; Howard Univ., 1955, 1958; Univ. of Mich.; Wayne State Univ.; USIA Traveling Show, USSR, 1950; Petite Gallery (Janet Nessler), NYC, 1958 (1-man), 1960, 1962; Grand Central Art Galleries, NYC, 1969; Univ. of Chicago, 1969; JL Hudson Co., Detroit, 1971; Arwin Galleries, Detroit, 1971; Museum of Modern Art; Boston Museum; San Francisco Museum; Cleveland Museum; Detroit Institute of Art; Brooklyn Museum; Phila. Civic Center; Albany Institute; Albright Art Gallery; Denver Museum; Dayton Art Institute; Cincinnati Art Museum; NJ State Museum; Contemporary Arts Museum, Houston; Memorial Art Gallery, Rochester, NY; Munson-Williams-Proctor Institute, Utica, NY; Rhode Island School of Design; Pittsburgh Institute of Art; Butler Art Gallery; Grand Rapids Art Gallery; USIA Traveling Show, Mexico & South America, 1950's; Roberson Center for the Arts & Sciences, Binghamton, NY; Univ. of Cal., Santa Barbara; Provincetown Art Festival; NYC Center Gallery; Art: USA, 1959; 1st Metropolitan Exhibition; Swarthmore College; Muskingum College, New Concord, Ohio; Atlanta Univ.; Nat'l. Academy of Design; La Jolla Museum of Art, 1970; Whitney Museum, 1971; James A. Porter Gallery, 1970; Nat'l. Center of Afro-Amer. Artists, Boston, 1973; Studio Museum, Harlem, 1973.

Collections: Atlanta Univ.; Detroit Institute of Arts; Art School of the Detroit Society of Arts & Crafts; Lagos Museum, Nigeria; Squibb & Sons; Amer. Natural Gas Service Co.; Mahogany Corp.; US Navy Art Center; Univ. of Mich.; Wayne State Univ.; Howard Univ.; Mr. & Mrs. Stanley Akers; Parrish Museum, Southampton, Long Island, NY; Johnson Pub. Co.; Mrs. William Clay Ford; Mr. & Mrs. Harry Nessler; Mrs. Edsel Ford; Mr. Malcolm Forbes; Arwin Galleries; Mr. Richard Clarke; Mr. Donald Byrd; Mr. & Mrs. Aaron Liebenson; Col. Francis J. Marlen; Mr. Arnold Rhodes; Mr. Maurice Seton.

Awards: Cleveland Museum—3rd prize, freehand drawing, 1938, Honorable mention, linoprint, 1938, 3rd prize, lithography, 1939, 2nd prize, lithography, 1940; Purchase Prize, Atlanta Univ., 1943; Detroit Institute of Art—Anthony Maiuello Prize, oil, 1951, Wineman Prize, oil, 1952, 2nd Popular Prize, oil, 1952, Founders Prize, oil, 1953, Winkleman Foundation Prize, oil, 1955, Roundtable Prize, oil, 1955; Mich. State Fair—4th prize, oil, 1952, 2nd prize, oil, 1953, 3rd prize, oil, 1954; Popular Prize, oil, Kirk-in-the-Hills Exhibit, 1954; Purchase Prize, Mich. Academy of Science, Arts & Letters, 1956; Emily Lowe Award, 1957; Clarke Prize, oil, 1959, Purchase Prize, 1963, Nat'l Academy of Design; Allied Artists Prize, 1958; Honorable mention, City Center Gallery, NYC, 1959; 1st Purchase Prize, Amer. Society of African Culture, 1960.

Member: Nat'l Academy of Design; Mich. Academy of Sciences, Arts & Letters; Artists Equity Assn.; Allied Artists of Amer.; Grand Central Art Galleries; The Players.

Represented by: Grand Central Art Galleries, NYC; Detroit Artists Market; Arwin Galleries, Detroit; Forsythe Gallery, Ann Arbor, Mich.

Sources: Locke. *The Negro in Art*; Locke. *Negro Art Past & Present*; Detroit Institute of Arts files; Dover. *American Negro Art*; "Afro-American Issue," *Art Gallery*, April 1968; Oakland Art Museum. *New Perspectives in Black Art*; *Who's Who in America*; *Who's Who in the East*; *Who's Who in American Art*; *Dictionary of International Biographies*; Albany Institute of History & Art. *The Negro Artist Comes of Age*; Information from artist; Porter. *Modern Negro Art*; Indiana Univ. *Fine Arts & the Black American*; La Jolla Museum of Art. *Dimensions of Black*; Doty. *Contemporary Black Artists in America*; Tanner Art Galleries. *Art of the American Negro*, 1940; Howard Univ. *James A. Porter Gallery of African-American Art*, 1970; "Negro Art from Cleveland's Karamu House," *Art Digest*, Jan. 15, 1942; Johnson Pub. Co. *The JPC Art Collection,* Pamphlet; Greene, Carroll, Jr. "Afro-American Artists: Yesterday & Now," *The Humble Way*, Vol. 8, No. 3, 1968; "Black Art: What Is It?," *Art Gallery*, April 1970; Harley, Ralph, Jr. "A Checklist of Afro-Amer. Art & Artists," *The Serif*, Dec. 1970; Greene, Carroll, Jr. *Afro-American Artists: 1800-1968*, Slides; Haydon, Harold. "Coming of Age of Black Art," *Chicago Sun Times*, July 26, 1970; Ploski, Harry, & Ernest Kaiser. "The Black Artist," *Afro USA*, 1971; Walsh, Rose. "Artists to Meet Public At Art Exhibit Preview," *Record American*, May 19, 1970; Le Brun, Caron. "Blacks' Art on Display," *Herald Traveler*, Boston, May 26, 1970; Paris, Jean. "Black Art Experience in Art," *Long Island Press*, Jamaica, NY, June 14, 1970; Ploski, Harry, Ernest Kaiser, & Otto Lindenmeyer. "The Black Artist," *Reference Library of Black America*, Book 4, 1971; *The Negro Handbook*, Composed by the Editors of *Ebony*, Chicago, 1966; City College of NY. *The Evolution of Afro-American Artists 1800-1950*; Phila. Division of Art. *Afro-American Artists 1800-1969*; Butcher, Margaret. *The Negro in American Culture*, p. 240; DuSable Museum of African-Amer. History. *Contemporary Black Artists*, 1970, calendar; Flint (Mich.) Community Schools. *Black Reflections*; Greene, Carroll, Jr. "Perspective: The Black Artist in America," *Art Gallery*, April 1970, p. 19; "Negro

175

Annual," *Art Digest*, April 15, 1943; Pierre-Noel, Lois Jones. "American Negro Art in Progress," *Negro History Bulletin*, Oct. 1967; Lee-Smith, Hughie. "Howard Univ.'s On-campus Murals," *Art Gallery*, April 1970; Shorewood Reproductions Catalog. *The Art of Black America*, 1969; Sherman, Marjorie. "Afro-America Gets Biggest Show," *Boston Globe*, May 18, 1970; Brown, Marion. "The Negro in the Fine Arts," *The Negro Heritage Library*, Vol. 2; Patterson, Lindsay. "Contemporary Artists," *The Negro in Music and Art*, 1969; Ruder & Finn Fine Arts. *Contemporary Black Artists*, NY, 1969; South Side Community Art Center. *Chicago Collectors Exhibit of Negro Art*, Chicago, 1945; Myers, Carol L. *Black Power in the Arts*, Flint, Mich., 1970; Museum of the Nat'l. Center of Afro-Amer. Artists. *Reality Expanded*, Boston, 1973; Boston Museum of Fine Arts. *Afro-American Artists: NY & Boston*, 1970; Studio Museum. *Reality Expanded*, Press Release, Harlem, 1973; "Leading Negro Artists," *Ebony*, Sept. 1963; Walker, Roslyn. *A Resource Guide to the Visual Arts of Afro-Americans*, South Bend, Ind., 1971; Driscoll, Edgar, Jr. "Showcase for Black Artists," *Boston Sunday Globe*, July 6, 1969, p. A73; Howard Univ. *Exhibition of Paintings*, 1955.

LEND, CARL V.
Collections: NY Public Library-Schomburg Art Collection.
Sources: Schatz, Walter. *Directory of Afro-American Resources*, 1970.

LEON, HENRY De
See: LeLeon, Henry

LEONARD, A.W.
Painter.
Works: *Bringing Home The Sheep; The Harvest Time; Cardinal & Flowers; After the Flight.*
Exhibited: Xavier Univ., 1963.
Sources: Xavier Univ. *Emancipation Proclamation Centennial National Art Exhibition*, 1963.

LEONARD, LEON LANK, SR.
Painter, sculptor, educator. Born in Waco, Texas, 1922. Studied at Texas College (AB); University of Denver School of Art (BFA).
Works: *African Laborer; The Coffle*, 1969; *Fetish—Mother and Child; Pride of Eight; Still Life Blue; Negro Statesman; Eternal; Bottles and Apples; Ancient Warrior; Black Nun; Doris; Los Prazos in La Tierra; Torso in Landscape; Boy Playing with Wheel; Foster Boy; Crown of Thorns; Nieve Fish; Dr. George Washington Carver; Primitive People's Conversation #1; Black Christ; Perchmouth; Black Prophet* (marble); *The Mardi Gras; African*

Mother and Child; Knotted Barrier; Afro-Boy #2; Three Wisemen; Conspirators; Dancers; Cyclist Coming through a Mudhole; La Cara Del Copa; Brain Pain; Science Innovation; Leonard's Soliloquy; Africa's Black Pilgrimage; Namable; Los Tres Reys Magos; Adam and Eve; The White Gold Cocks Compromising; La Cruz; La Cruz #2; Disintegration of Fire Works; Waterboon—Riot.
Exhibited: Univ. of Iowa, 1971-2; Xavier Univ., 1963; Atlanta Univ., 1956-70; Witte Museum, 1958; Expo, San Francisco, 1972; Ill. Bell Telephone, 1970-1; Internat'l Black Arts, Los Angeles, 1968; Hemisfair, San Antonio, 1968; Carnegie Institute, 1970; Watercolor USA, 1971; Black Expo, 1972; Cal. State Exposition, Sacramento, 1972; All City Outdoor Show, Los Angeles, 1969; Santa Ana Museum, 1972; Whittier (Cal.) College, 1972; Dominguez College.
Collections: Johnson Pub. Co.; Atlanta Univ.; Prairie View A&M College; Rev. Harold Perry; Mr. Bill Cosby; Council House of Jewish Women, Los Angeles; Mr. Sugar Ray Robinson.
Member: Texas Watercolor Society; Art West Assoc. North; Cal. Nat'l. Watercolor Society.
Represented by: Heritage Gallery; Dazell Hatfield Gallery; Black Artists Council; Art West Assoc. North; Brockman Gallery.
Sources: Dover. *American Negro Art*, p. 51; Indiana Univ. *Fine Arts & the Black American*; Harley, Ralph, Jr. "Checklist of Afro-Amer. Art & Artists," *Serif*, Dec. 1970; Information from artist; *Who's Who in American Art*, 1960, 1972; *Ebony*, April 1958; Afro-American Slide Depository, Catalog; Illinois Bell Telephone. *Black American Artists/71*, 1972; Johnson Pub. Co. *The JPC Art Collection*, Pamphlet; Xavier Univ. *Emancipation Proclamation Centennial National Art Exhibition*, 1963; Haas, Joseph. "A Big, Brilliant & Exciting Exhibition of Black Art," *Chicago Daily News*, Jan. 16-7, 1971; Walker, Roslyn. *A Resource Guide to the Visual Arts of Afro-Americans*, South Bend, Ind., 1971.

LEPER, EDWARD
Sculptor.
Sources: *The Negro Handbook*, Composed by Editors of *Ebony*, Chicago, 1966.

LEVINE, EMMA AMOS
See: Amos, Emma

LEWIS, EDMONIA
Sculptor (first Negro woman sculptor). Born in Albany, New York c. 1845 of mixed Indian parentage. Studied at Oberlin College and was trained in the studio of Edmund Brackett of Boston. She specialized in portrait busts and symbolic groups. She left Boston and went to

Rome to continue her study of sculpture under the patronage of the Story family.

Works: *Unknown Woman,* 1867 (marble); *Hiawatha,* 1868 (marble); *Minnehaha; Old Indian Arrow Maker and His Daughter,* 1872 (marble); *Freedwoman; Bust of a Woman; Medallion Head of John Brown; Col. Robert Gould Shaw; Charles Sumner; Abraham Lincoln; Henry Wadsworth Longfellow; James McCune Smith; William Lloyd Garrison; Hagar,* 1871; *The Marriage of Hiawatha; The Departure of Hiawatha and Minnehaha; Madonna & Child,* 1867; *Morning of Liberty (Forever Free); Awake; Hygeia,* Harriet Hunt Mausoleum, Mt. Auburn Cemetery, Cambridge, Mass.; *Death of Cleopatra; Hagar in the Wilderness; Madonna & the Infant Christ;* Busts of Wendell Phillips, Harriet Hosmer, Charlotte Cushman, John Brown, Charles Sumner, Longfellow, & Lincoln; *Baby's Waking; Asleep,* 1871; *Asleep,* 1872; *Wooing of Hiawatha,* 1867; *Poor Cupid.*

Exhibited: Soldiers Aid Fair, Boston, 1864; Farwell Hall Exhibit, Chicago, 1870; Phila. Semi-Centennial, 1876; Commissions for Harvard College; Howard Univ., 1967; Amer. Negro Exposition, 1940; Ind. Univ.; Mich. State Univ.; City College of NY, 1969; South Side Community Art Center, Chicago, 1945; San Francisco Art Assn., 1873; Vassar College, 1972.

Collections: Frederick Douglass Institute of Negro Arts & History, Washington, DC; Harvard College Library; Fogg Museum; San José (Cal.) Public Library; Mr. & Mrs. Benjamin J. Duster; Mr. Jimmy Ricau; Kennedy Gallery, NY.

Sources: Murray, Freeman. *Emancipation & the Freed in American Sculpture;* Gerdts, William. *American Sculpture: the Collection of James A. Ricau,* 1964; H.W. "Lady Artists in Rome," *Art Journal,* London, Jan. 1966, p. 177; *20th Century Dictionary of Notable Americans,* Vol. VI, 1904; Bullard, Laura. "Edmonia Lewis," *The Revolution,* NY, April 20, 1871; Brawley, Benjamin. *The Negro Genius;* Tanner Art Galleries. *Art of the American Negro,* 1940; Butcher, Margaret. *The Negro in American Culture,* p. 216; Dowd. *The Negro in American Life;* Roucek & Kiernan. *The Negro Impact on Western Civilization;* Afro-American Slide Depository, Catalog, 1971-2; Rollins. *They Showed the Way;* Haley, James T. *Afro-American Encyclopedia,* 1896; Furr, Arthur F. *History & Progress of Negroes in the US,* Vol. 1-9; Greene, Carroll, Jr. "Perspective: The Black Artist in America," *Art Gallery,* April 1970, p. 7; Pierre-Noel, Lois Jones. "American Negro Art in Progress," *Negro History Bulletin,* Oct. 1967; *Apollo,* Feb. 1968, p. 141; Locke, Alain. "The American Negro As Artist," *American Magazine of Art,* Sept. 1931; Porter, James A. "Versatile Interests of the Early Negro Artist: A Neglected Chapter of American Art History," *Art in America,* Washington, DC, Vol. 24, 1936; Craig, Randall J. "Focus on Black Artists: A Project for Schools & Community," *School Arts,* Nov. 1970, p. 30-3; Kiah, Virginia. "Black Artists," *Savannah Magazine,* April 1972, p. 14; Greene, Carroll, Jr. "Afro-American Artists: Yesterday & Now," *The Humble Way,* Vol. 8, No. 3, 1968; Tuckerman, Henry T. *Book of the Artists,* Nov. 1882; Harley, Ralph, Jr. "A Checklist of Afro-American Artists," *The Serif,* Dec. 1970; Boning, Richard A. *Profiles of Black Americans,* NY, 1969; Brawley, Benjamin. *The Negro in Literature & Art in the US; 1st Annual Exhibit of Books, Manuscripts, Paintings, Sculpture Etc. by the Negro Library Assn. at the Carlton Ave. YMCA,* Aug. 7-16, 1918; Brown, Marion. "The Negro in the Fine Arts," *The Negro Heritage Library,* Vol. 2; Morsbach, Mabel. *The Negro in American Life;* Ploski, Harry, & Ernest Kaiser. "The Black Artist," *Afro USA,* 1971; Ploski, Harry, Ernest Kaiser, & Otto Lindenmeyer. "The Black Artist," *Reference Library of Black America,* Book IV, 1971; *The Negro Handbook,* Composed by the Editors of *Ebony,* Chicago, 1966; "Negro Has Given Much to Art, Survey Shows," *Boston Traveler,* Feb. 23, 1933; Adams, Russell. *Great Negroes, Past & Present,* Chicago, 1969; Edmonia Lewis Papers; "Women in the Arts," *Ebony,* Aug. 1966, pp. 90-4; Cikovsky, Nicolai, Jr., Marie H. Morrison, & Carol Ockman. *The White, Marmorean Flock,* Vassar College Art Gallery, Poughkeepsie, NY, 1972; Myers, Carol L. *Black Power in the Arts,* Flint, Mich., 1970; *The Aldine, II,* Aug. 1969, p. 76; Brown, William Wells. *The Rising Son,* Boston, 1874, pp. 465-8; Dannett, Sylvia G. L. *Profiles on Negro Womanhood,* Yonkers, NY, 1965, Vol. 1, pp. 118-23; *The Freedman's Record, II,* 1866, p. 67; Majors, Monroe A. *Noted Negro Women, Their Triumphs and Activities,* Chicago, 1893, p. 27; Montesano, Philip M. "The Mystery of the San José Statues," *Urban West,* 1968, pp. 25-7; *The Negro History Bulletin, II,* March 1939, p. 51; *New National Era, II,* May 4, 1871, p. 1; *Progressive American Coloured Weekly,* NY, Dec. 28, 1876; Wyman, Lillian B. C., & Arthur C. *Elizabeth Buffum Chace, 1806-1899, Her Life and Its Environment,* Boston, 1914; Blodgett, Geoffrey. "John Mercer Langston and the Case of Edmonia Lewis: Oberlin, 1862," *Journal of Negro History,* July 1968, p. 201; Mallett. *Index of Artists;* Fielding. *Dictionary of American Painters, Sculptors & Engravers;* Chase/Post. *History of Sculpture;* Taft. *History of American Sculpture;*

Mich. State Library. *Biographical Sketches of American Artists*; Indiana Univ. *Fine Arts & the Black American;* Locke. *The Negro in Art;* Dover. *American Negro Art; Negro Almanac; Encyclopedia of Art; Freedman's Record,* Jan. 1867; *Art in America,* Jan. 1936, pp. 16-29; *Apollo,* Feb. 1968, p. 141-2; Clement. *Women in the Fine Arts;* Clement/Hutton. *Artists of the 19th Century;* Thorp, M.F. *The Literary Sculptors;* City College of NY. *The Evolution of Afro-American Artists: 1800-1950;* Art Institute of Chicago. *The Negro in Art Week,* 1927; Howard Univ. *Ten Afro-American Artists of the 19th Century;* Locke. *Negro Art, Past & Present;* Porter. *Modern Negro Art;* Thieme, Ulrich, & Felix Becker. *Allgemeines Lexikon Der Buildenden Kuenstler;* Walker, Roslyn. *A Resource Guide to the Visual Arts of Afro-Americans,* South Bend, Ind., 1971; Benezit. *Dictionaire Des Peintres, Sculpteurs, Dessinateurs Et Graveneurs,* Librairie Grund, France, 1948; DuSable Museum of African-Amer. History. *Contemporary Black Artists,* Calendar, 1970; *Pictoral History of Negroes in America,* Crown Pub., 1956, p. 77 (portrait).

LEWIS, EDWIN E.

Painter. Born in Philadelphia. Teacher at Howard University.
Sources: Dover. *American Negro Art;* Harley, Ralph, Jr. "Checklist of Afro-Amer. Art & Artists," *The Serif,* Dec. 1970; Walker, Roslyn. *A Resource Guide to the Visual Arts of Afro-Americans,* South Bend, Ind., 1971.

LEWIS, FLORA CARNELL

Painter. Born in Atchison, Kansas in 1903. Self-taught in art.
Works: *Christ and the Woman at the Well; Farm Life; Interpretation of Sin Surrounding the Churches.*
Exhibited: Mo. State Fair, 1939; Museum of Modern Art, NY.
Awards: 1st Prize, Mo. State Fair, 1939.
Sources: Janis, Sidney. *They Taught Themselves,* NY, Dial Press, 1942, pp. 208-12; Museum of Modern Art. *Unknown American Painters;* "When Is Art Art?," editorial, *Art Digest,* Oct. 15, 1939; Janis, Sidney. "Reply to 'When Is Art Art?'," *Art Digest,* Nov. 1, 1939; Indiana Univ. *Fine Arts & the Black American;* Harley, Ralph, Jr. "Checklist of Afro-Amer. Art & Artists," *The Serif,* Dec. 1970; Walker, Roslyn. *A Resource Guide to the Visual Arts of Afro-Americans,* South Bend, Ind., 1971.

LEWIS, HARRY C.

Painter.
Works: *Three Sisters-Canadian Rockies.*
Exhibited: Harmon Foundation, 1933.

Sources: Harmon Foundation. *Non-Jury Exhibit of Works of Negro Artists,* 1933.

LEWIS, HENRY JACKSON

Cartoonist. Born in 1847. Co-Founder, *The Freeman,* first illustrated Negro newspaper.
Sources: *Jet,* April 13, 1967; Spradling, Mary M., ed. *In Black and White: Afro-Americans in Print.*

LEWIS, JAMES E.

Sculptor, draftsman, illustrator, painter, educator. Born in Phenix, Virginia in 1923. Studied at Pennsylvania College of Art; Temple University (MFA, 1950); Yale University (1954-5). Teacher at Pennsylvania College of Art; Professor of Art at Morgan State College, Baltimore.
Works: *Portrait of Frederick Douglass; Study for Sculpture; Study of Senufo Helmet Mask; Portrait Drawing; Portrait of Dwight O.W. Holmes; Portrait of Carl Murphy; Portrait of Theodore McKeldin;* Untitled bronze sculpture of Frederick Douglass; *Portrait of Charles Key; Portrait of Dr. Edward N. Wilson;* Untitled sculpture depicting historical involvement of tht Negro soldier in the wars involving the USA, 1968; *An Ambiguous Image of Ralph Ellison.*
Exhibited: Phila. Civic Center Museum; Howard Univ., 1961, 1970; Nat'l. Center of Afro-Amer. Artists, Boston, 1970; Atlanta Univ.; Baltimore Museum of Art; Enoch Pratt Free Library, Baltimore (1-man); Federal Plaza, Baltimore; Fellowship House, Phila.; Gallery I, Baltimore; Goucher College; Johns Hopkins Univ.; Morgan State College; Peale Museum of Art, Baltimore; Phila. Academy of Art; Phila. College of Art; Phoenix Galleries, Baltimore; Print Club of Phila.; Pyramid Club, Phila.; Towson State College; The Wharton Center, Phila.
Collections: Morgan College, Baltimore; Cherry Hill Jr. High School, Baltimore; Assn. of Colored Womens Clubs; Douglass High School, Baltimore; Broadway Median Park, Baltimore; Baltimore County Library, Towson; St. Paul's School for Boys.
Awards: Ford Foundation Fellowship, 1954; Carnegie Grant in Art, 1939-41; Faculty Medal for highest average in the Arts, Dunbar High School, 1942.
Member: Md. Fine Arts Commission, 1962; Baltimore City Commission for Historical & Architectural Preservation; Amer. Society of African Culture; Barnet Aden Gallery of Art, Washington, DC (Board, 1965-9); Baltimore City Ballett Co. Board, 1968; College Arts Assn.; Eastern Arts Assn.; Amer. Federation of Arts; Md. Art Assn.; College Language Assn.; Amer. Assn. of Museums; Artist Equity; Deutche-Afrika-Gesellschaft; Centre for Af-

rican & Amer. Studies, Atlanta Univ. (Associate Fellow); Greater Baltimore Arts Council (board).

Sources: Information from artist; Lewis, James E. "Senoufo Firespitter Masks," *African Forum: Journal of the Amer. Assn. of African Culture*, Dec. 1969; Dover. *American Negro Art*, p. 38; Indiana Univ. *Fine Arts & the Black American*; Phila. Division of Art. *Afro-American Artists 1800-1969*; Howard Univ. *James A. Porter Gallery of African American Art*, 1970; Fax, Elton C. *Seventeen Black Artists*; Harley, Ralph, Jr. "A Checklist of Afro-Amer. Art & Artists," *The Serif*, Dec. 1970; Lewis, James E. "Traditional African Art & Its Influences," *Baltimore Bulletin of Education*, Vol. 45, No. 203, 1968-9; Scarupa, Henry. "James E. Lewis: Making Visible the Invisible Artist," *Sunday Sun*, March 19, 1972; "Where Three Cultures Meet," *Washington Post*, May 14, 1972; Cheek, King, Jr. "Black Students, Black Studies & Black Colleges," *Chronicle of Higher Education*, Nov. 1971 (Illus.); Lewis, James E. "A College Art Study Collection," *Maryland Art Assn. Journal*, Spring 1966; Lewis, James E. "A College Art Study Collection," *Museum News*, Baltimore Museum of Art, June 1965; *College Language Assn. Journal*, Vol. 13, No. 3, cover; Walker, Roslyn. *A Resource Guide to the Visual Arts of Afro-Americans*, South Bend, Ind., 1971.

LEWIS, LARRY

Painter. Born in Selma, Alabama in 1927. Studied drawing briefly with a local art teacher; essentially self-taught.
Works: *Composition No. 25; La Ronde; Danson.*
Exhibited: Studio Museum in Harlem, 1969.
Collections: Chase Manhattan Bank, NY.
Sources: Studio Museum in Harlem. *Harlem Artists 69;* Ploski, Harry, Ernest Kaiser, & Otto Lindenmeyer. "The Black Artist," *Reference Library of Black America*, Book IV, 1971.

LEWIS, MURPHY A.

Painter.
Works: *Frederick Douglass* (oil); Untitled oil.
Exhibited: Boston Public Library, 1973.
Sources: Boston Negro Artists Assn. *10th Anniversary Exhibition*, Boston Public Library, 1973; Boston Negro Artists Assn. *The Black Artist in America: A Negro History Month Exhibition*, Boston Public Library, 1973.

LEWIS, NORMAN

Painter. Born in New York City in 1909. Studied at Columbia University; under Augusta Savage, Raphael Soyer, Vaclav Vytacil, Angela Streater. Taught art at Harlem Art Center, Federal Art Project (1936-9).

Works: *Card Players; Landscape; Figure on Chair; Figure at Table; Four Figures; Procession; Jumping Jive; White Plains; Cathedral; Cafe; Migrating Birds; Street Scene; Arrival & Departure; Heroic Evening; Carnavale I; Carnavale II; The Yellow Hat; Every Atom; Let's Get Ourselves Together; Togetherness I, II, III; Subway Musician; Bon Fine; Friends; Roof Tops; New World a Coming; Louie; Eats; Hunger.*

Exhibited: Harlem Artists Guild, 1936, 1937; Harlem Art Center, 1937-9; Amer. Artists School, 1938; Harlem YWCA, 1938; Fisk Univ., 1939; Baltimore Museum, 1939; Amer. Negro Exposition, Chicago, 1940; Atlanta Univ., 1942; Willard Gallery, NY, 1949; Albany Institute of History & Art, 1945; Mary Washington College, 1959; Metropolitan Museum of Art; Whitney Museum of Art; Art Institute of Chicago; Boston Museum of Fine Arts, 1970; Arden Gallery, Washington, DC; Brooklyn Museum; Museum of Modern Art; Baltimore Museum of Art; Munson-Williams Proctor Institute, Utica, NY; Corcoran Gallery; Phila. Civic Center Museum; State Armory, Wilmington, Del., 1971; Musée de Peinture et de Sculpture, Grenoble, France; Ghana Nat'l Museum, Accra, Ghana; Venice Bienale; Newark Museum, 1971; Minneapolis Institute of Arts; Nordness Galleries, NY, 1969; City College of NY, 1967; Hudson River Museum, Yonkers, NY; Rockford (Ill.) College, 1965; South Side Community Art Center, Chicago, 1945; McMillen Inc. Galleries, NY, 1941; Howard Univ., 1971; Studio Museum in Harlem, 1971; Nat'l Center for Afro-Amer. Artists, Boston, 1971.

Collections: Addison Gallery of Amer. Arts; Museum of Modern Art, NY; Munson-Williams Proctor Institute, Utica, NY; Art Institute of Chicago; Mr. & Mrs. John D. Rockefeller, NY; Arden Gallery, Washington, DC; Mr. Benny Andrews; IBM; Manufacturers Hanover Bank, NYC; Mrs. Edward Ellihu Root; Time-Life Building; St. Albens High School, Long Island, mural; Mrs. Daniel Goldberg.

Awards: Carnegie Institute Award, 1955; Amer. Academy of Arts & Letters, 1970; Nat'l Institute of Arts & Letters, 1971.

Member: Spiral.

Sources: Locke. *The Negro in Art;* Locke. *Negro Art: Past & Present;* Albany Institute of History & Art. *Negro Artist Comes of Age;* Indiana Univ. *Fine Arts & the Black American;* Dover. *American Negro Art;* "Afro-American Issue," *Art Gallery*, April 1968; Boston Museum of Fine Arts. *Afro-American Artists: NY & Boston*, 1970; Nordness Galleries. *12 Afro-American Artists*, NY, 1969; Minneapolis Institute of Art. *30 Contemporary*

Black Artists; Newark Museum. *Black Artists: Two Generations,* 1971; City College of NY. *Evolution of Afro-American Artists 1800-1950,* 1967; Phila. Division of Art. *Afro-American Artists 1800-1969;* Aesthetic Dynamics. *Afro-American Images,* 1971; Baltimore Museum of Art. *Contemporary Negro,* 1939; Tanner Art Galleries. *Art of the American Negro,* 1940; Porter. *Modern Negro Art;* "Norman Lewis," *Munson-Williams Proctor Institute Bulletin,* Utica, Feb. 1952; "Exhibition, New York," *Pictures on Exhibit,* Dec. 1952, p. 28; "Blending," *Munson-Williams Proctor Institute Bulletin,* Oct. 1955; Locke, Alain. "Advance on the Art Front," *Opportunity,* May 1939; Harley, Ralph, Jr. "A Checklist of Afro-Amer. Art & Artists," *The Serif,* Dec. 1970; DuSable Museum of African-Amer. History. *Contemporary Black Artists,* 1970, Calendar; Hudson River Museum. *Contemporary American Black Artists;* Long Island Univ. *Spiral,* catalog; J.G. "Honoring Negro History," *Art Digest,* Feb. 15, 1949, p. 20; "Art by Negroes," *Art Digest,* Oct. 15, 1941; Greene, Carroll, Jr. "Perspective: The Black Artist in America," *Art Gallery,* April 1970, p. 25; "American Negro Art Given Full Length Review in NY Show," *Art Digest,* Dec. 15, 1941; "The Negro in Art," *Art Digest,* June 1944; Pierre-Noel, Lois Jones. "American Negro Art in Progress," *Negro History Bulletin,* Oct. 1967; Wolf, Ben. "Negro Art Scores Without Double Standards," *Art Digest,* Feb. 1, 1945; "Afro-American Artists 1800-1950," *Ebony,* Vol. 23, pp. 116-22; Rockford College. *Creativity & the Negro;* Rose, Barbara. "Black Art in America," *Art in America,* July/Dec. 1970; "The Negro Artist Comes of Age," *Art News,* Feb. 1, 1945; Siegel, Jeanne. "Why Spiral?," *Art News,* Sept. 1966; "American Negro Art," *Design Magazine,* Feb. 1942, p. 28; Jacobs, Jay. "The Cinque Gallery," *Art Gallery,* April 1970; Greene, Carroll, Jr. *Afro-American Artists: 1800-1968,* Slides; "Leading Negro Artists," *Ebony,* Sept. 1963, pp. 131-2; Mt. Holyoke College. *Ten Afro-American Artists,* Nov. 1969; Metropolitan Applied Research Center. *Six Painters;* "Museum of Fine Arts to Hold Black Show," *Chronicle,* Ipswich, Mass., April 30, 1970; "Museum of Fine Arts to Hold Black Art Show," *Tri-Town Transcript & Pennysaver,* April 29, 1970; Brown, Marion. "The Negro in the Fine Arts," *The Negro Heritage Library,* Vol. 2; Ploski, Harry, & Ernest Kaiser. "The Black Artist," *Afro USA,* 1971; Ploski, Harry, Ernest Kaiser, & Otto Lindenmeyer. "The Black Artist," *Reference Library of Black America,* 1971; Berkman, Florence. "Afro-American Exhibit Fosters Understanding of Black Artists," *Times,* Hartford, Conn., May 24, 1970; Schwartz, Therese. "The Political Scene," *Arts,* NY,

April 1970; Paris, Jean. "Black Art Experience in Art," *Long Island Press,* Jamaica, NY, June 14, 1970; *The Negro Handbook,* Composed by Editors of *Ebony,* Chicago, 1966; Ruder & Finn Fine Arts. *Contemporary Black Artists,* NY, 1969; South Side Community Art Center. *Chicago Collectors Exhibit of Negro Art,* 1945; Myers, Carol. *Black Power in the Arts,* Flint, Mich., 1970; McMillen Inc. Galleries. *Contemporary Negro Art,* NY, 1941; Hollingsworth, Alvin. "Wealth of Expression in Black Artists' RISD Show," *Providence Sunday Journal,* June 29, 1969; Walker, Roslyn. *A Resource Guide to the Visual Arts of Afro-Americans,* South Bend, Ind., 1971; Glueck, Grace. "America Has Black Art on Her Mind," *New York Times,* Feb. 27, 1969, p. C34; Driscoll, Edgar, Jr. "Showcase for Black Artists," *Boston Sunday Globe,* July 6, 1969, p. A73.

LEWIS, OLLIE

Sources: Harley, Ralph, Jr. "Checklist of Afro-Amer. Art & Artists," *The Serif,* Dec. 1970; Keelan, Henry. "Voice in the Wilderness," *Afro American,* Nov. 6, 1945.

LEWIS, MRS. PERCY

Painter.
Exhibited: Mo. State Fair, 1939.
Awards: Painting prize at Mo. State Fair, Aug. 1939.
Sources: Lewis, Mrs. Percy. "Farm Life by Mrs. Percy Lewis," *Arts Quarterly,* Sept. 1939.

LEWIS, RICHARD

Painter, illustrator. Born in Avondale, Pennsylvania. Studied at the Philadelphia Museum College of Art. Illustrator & author of children's books.
Sources: Scott, Ann Herbert. *Big Cowboy Western,* 1965; Scott, Ann Herbert. *A Summer Adventure.*

LEWIS, ROBERT H.

Painter.
Works: *Self Portrait; Welcome News; Portrait of Mrs. Gale.*
Sources: Porter. *Modern Negro Art;* Harley, Ralph, Jr. "Checklist of Afro-Amer. Art & Artists," *The Serif,* Dec. 1970; *1st Annual Exhibit of Books, Manuscripts, Paintings, Sculptures, etc. by the Negro Library Assn. at Carlton Ave. YMCA,* 1918, Catalog.

LEWIS, SAMELLA S.

Painter, graphic artist, author, sculptor, educator. Born in New Orleans. Studied at Hampton Institute (BS); Ohio State University (MA & PhD); New York University; Tung-Hai University, Taiwan. Teacher, School of Humanities and Fine Arts, California State College. Co-editor of *Black Artists on Art.*

Works: *Burning Bush; Banyon; Canefield; Royal Sacrifice; Tropical Landscape; Migrants; Family.*
Exhibited: La Jolla Museum of Art, 1970; State Armory, Wilmington, Del., 1971; James A. Porter Gallery, 1970; Brockman Gallery; Ankrum Gallery; Rainbow Sign Gallery, Berkeley, 1972; Whitney Museum, NY, 1971.
Collections: Baltimore Museum of Fine Arts; Va. Museum of Fine Arts; High Museum, Atlanta; Ohio Union Gallery; Pa. State Univ.; Atlanta Univ.; Denison Univ.; Hampton Institute; Boys College, Aman, Jordan; Mrs. Mary Jane Hewitt; Oakland Museum; Mr. Henry Simon; Ms. Susan Langer; Mr. Frank Sieberlisy, Jr.; Ohio Univ.; Ohio State Univ.
Awards: Delta Sigma Theta Scholarship, Dillard Univ.; Carr Scholarship, State Univ. of Iowa; Hampton Institute Art Scholarship; Amer. Univ. Scholarship, Ohio State Univ.; Fulbright Grant for Far Eastern Research & Travel; NY State Ford Foundation Grant; NDEA Post Doctoral Grant.
Sources: Rainbow Sign Gallery. *Black Arts Day II*, Press Release, Berkeley, 1972; Lewis/Waddy. *Black Artists on Art;* Aesthetic Dynamics. *Afro-American Images,* 1971; Howard Univ. *James A. Porter Gallery of African-American Art,* 1970; DuSable Museum of African-Amer. History. *Contemporary Black Artists,* 1970, calendar; Greene, Carroll, Jr. "Perspective: The Black Artist in America," *Art Gallery,* April 1970, p. 10; Harley, Ralph, Jr. "Checklist of Afro-Amer. Art & Artists," *Serif,* Dec. 1970; Glueck, Grace. "Black Show under Fire at the Whitney," *New York Times,* Jan. 31, 1971; Oakland Museum Archives; Walker, Roslyn. *A Resource Guide to the Visual Arts of Afro-Americans,* South Bend, Ind., 1971.

LEWIS, THOMAS R.

Jeweler, designer, silversmith and silver manufacturer. Studied at Rhode Island School of Design. Worked for 6 years with a jewelry manufacturer, then started own business.
Works: Jewelry for L'Overture Co. of NYC—pins, insignias, emblems.
Member: New England Manufacturing Jewelers & Silversmiths Assn.
Sources: "Thomas R. Lewis—Master Craftsman," unidentified magazine article, *Mary O. Williamson Scrapbook #2,* Howard Univ.

LIAUTAUD, G.

Exhibited: Rockford (Ill.) College, 1965.
Sources: Rockford College. *Creativity and the Negro.*

LIGHTFOOT, ELBA

Painter. Born in Evanston, Illinois, 1910. Studied at Northwestern University; Art Students League, New York.

Works: *Self Portrait; Portrait of a Child;* Murals, Federal Art Project, 1936-8.
Exhibited: Art Students League, NY, 1936; Harlem Art Center, 1937-9; ACA Gallery, NY, 1938; Harlem YMCA, 1938; Amer. Negro Exposition, Chicago, 1940; Atlanta Univ., 1942; Dillard Univ., 1941; Augusta Savage Studios, 1939; Library of Congress, 1940; Tanner Galleries, 1940; Harmon Foundation.
Collections: Nat'l Archives.
Sources: Locke. *The Negro in Art;* Tanner Art Galleries. *Art of the American Negro,* 1940; Dillard Univ. *Arts Festival,* 1941; Afro-Amer. Slide Depository, Catalog, 1971-2; Harmon Foundation. *Select Picture List;* "American Negro Given Full Length Review in NY Show," *Art Digest,* Dec. 15, 1941; Harley, Ralph, Jr. "Checklist of Afro-Amer. Art & Artists," *The Serif,* Dec. 1970; Walker, Roslyn. *A Resource Guide to the Visual Arts of Afro-Americans,* South Bend, Ind., 1971.

LINDSEY, RICHARD WILLIAM

Painter, graphic artist. Born in North Carolina in 1904. Studied at National Academy of Design.
Works: *Swing; Birth of Jazz; A Daughter of Africa; Fulton Market; Lake Taxi; The Music Man; Back Yard; The Baptism; Zinnias.*
Exhibited: Harmon Foundation, 1928, 1929, 1931, 1933; Herron Art Institute, Indianapolis; Baltimore Museum, 1939; Amer. Negro Exposition, Chicago, 1940; 135th St. Branch, NY Public Library, 1935; Atlanta Univ., 1942; Smithsonian Institution, 1929.
Collections: Nat'l Archives.
Awards: Art Assn. Prize, Herron Institute, Indianapolis.
Sources: Harley, Ralph, Jr. "A Checklist of Afro-Amer Art & Artists," *The Serif,* Dec. 1970; DuSable Museum of African-Amer. History. *Contemporary Black Artists,* 1970, Calendar; Harmon Foundation. *Negro Artists,* 1935; Harmon Foundation. *Exhibition of Productions by Negro Artists;* Harmon Foundation. *Non-Jury Exhibit of Works by Negro Artists,* 1933; Indiana Univ. *Fine Arts & the Black American;* Baltimore Museum of Art. *Contemporary Negro,* 1939; Tanner Art Galleries. *Art of the American Negro,* 1940; Afro-American Slide Depository, catalog, 1971-2; Smithsonian Institution. *Painting & Sculpture by American Negro Artists,* 1929; Walker, Roslyn. *A Resource Guide to the Visual Arts of Afro-Americans,* South Bend, Ind., 1971.

LINTON, HENRY

Painter.
Works: *Alone.*
Sources: Harley, Ralph, Jr. "Checklist of Afro-Amer. Art & Artists," *The Serif,* Dec. 1970;

Atkinson, J. Edward. *Black Dimensions in Contemporary American Art,* NY, 1971.

LIPPMAN, ROMEYN VAN VLECK

Painter, educator. Born in Sag Harbor, New York, 1892. Studied at Tuskegee School of Architecture (AB); Cornell University; Boston University.
Works: *Wilderness,* 1936 (watercolor); *Early Morning—Wharf Scene; Gabriel; Hunger Marchers; Tobacco; Mount of Dreams; Eternal,* 1954; *Baptismal,* 1949; *Revival,* 1953; *The Church,* 1961.
Exhibited: Institute of Modern Art, Boston, 1943; Harmon Foundation, 1933, 1935; Amer. Negro Exposition, Chicago, 1940; NJ State Fair, 1935; Smith College Museum of Art, 1943; Art Center, NY, 1933; NY Public Library, 1933; Howard Univ., 1933; NJ State Museum, 1935; Museum of Fine Arts, San Diego, Cal., 1935; Texas Centennial, Dallas, 1936; Boston Public Library; WVa. State Teachers College; Boston Arts Festival, 1962; Forthnightly Club, Summit, NJ; 20th Century Club, Boston; Boston Museum of Fine Arts, 1950; Tanner Art Galleries, 1940.
Collections: Atlanta Univ.
Awards: Nat'l. Urban League Certificate of Recognition, 1949; Music Festival Award, Boston, 1955.
Member: Society of Independent Artists of New England.
Sources: Harmon Foundation. *Exhibition of Productions by Negro Artists;* Dover. *American Negro Art;* Indiana Univ. *Fine Arts & the Black American;* Tanner Art Galleries. *Art of the American Negro,* 1940; Afro-Amer. Slide Depository, Catalog, 1971-2; Harmon Foundation. *Negro Artists,* 1935; Harley, Ralph, Jr. "Checklist of Afro-American Art & Artists," *The Serif,* Dec. 1970; Information from artist; Walker, Roslyn. *A Resource Guide to the Visual Arts of Afro-Americans,* South Bend, Ind., 1971.

LIS, EDWARD

Exhibited: Phila. Invitational Exhibition, Pyramid Club, 1952.
Sources: Drummond, Dorothy. "Coast-to-Coast," *Art Digest,* March 1, 1952; Pyramid Club. *12th Annual Invitational Exhibition,* Phila., 1952.

LLORENS, JOSEPH P.

Painter, graphic artist, photographer, sculptor, educator. Born in Detroit. Studied at Wayne State University (BS & MEd); University of California at Berkeley.
Exhibited: Russell-Sullivan Art Festival, Detroit, 1959; Art Teachers Show, Scarab Club, Detroit, 1962-3; Wayne State Univ., 1964; Northeastern High School, Detroit, 1964; Univ.

of the Pacific, Stockton, Cal., 1969, 1970 (2-man), 1970 (1-man); College of Marin, 1969; College of Notre Dame, Belmont, Cal., 1970; Univ. of Florida, 1972; Santa Fe Arts Festival, Santa Fe Community College, Gainesville, Fla., 1972.
Member: Detroit Art Teachers Club; Detroit Federation of Teachers; Art Education Alumni Assn., Wayne State Univ.; College of Alumni Assn., Wayne State Univ.; Amer. Assn. of Univ. Professors; Photographic Assn. of America; Amer. Forum for Internat'l Study (Board, 1970-1).
Sources: Llorens, Joseph P. "Black Man," *African Art,* College of Marin Art Gallery, 1969; Llorens, Joseph P. A Book of Poetry and Essays—African '69, untitled, in preparation; Wayne State Univ. *Art as a Social Protest,* 1964; Univ. of the Pacific. *Comments,* Exhibition of the Work of Black & Mexican-Amer. Artists, 1969; Univ. of the Pacific. *Africa: A Photographic Essay,* 1970; Univ. of the Pacific. *Black Man,* 1970; College of Notre Dame. *Africa: A Photographic Essay,* Belmont, Cal., 1970; Yonge Laboratory School, Univ. of Florida. *Black Art,* 1972; Information from artist.

LLOYD, TOM

Electronic sculptor, art consultant, educator. Born in New York City on January 13, 1929. Studied at Pratt Institute under Gottlieb, McNeil, Guston, & Nakian; Brooklyn Museum, 1961; under Peter Agostini. Instructor of Light Media, Sarah Lawrence College, Bronxville, NY, 1969-; Three Dimensional Design Instructor, Cooper Union, 1969-; Art Consultant, Group Services Agencies and Education Division, Lincoln Hospital, New York, 1966; Director, Painting and Sculpture, Adult Creative Arts Workshop, Department of Parks, Office of Cultural Affairs, New York City, 1967-.
Works: *Mantara,* 1965; *Moskee,* 1967; *Majora; Rivaco; Moussakoo,* 1968 (glass, metal, electric circuitry); *Puncheono; Phinuala; Milrotho; Veleuro; Saskatoon; Amstel; Clavero; Objects On Wall of Artists Studio; Resawan; Light Sculpture.*
Exhibited: Studio Museum, NY, 1968 (1-man); Amel Gallery, NY (1-man); American Greetings Gallery, NY, 1968; Electronic Refractions II, Studio Museum, NY, 1968; Museum of Modern Art, 1967; Wadsworth Atheneum, Hartford, Conn., 1966; Art Electric, Galerie Ileana Sonnabend, Paris, 1966; Contemporary Arts Museum, Houston, 1966; Walker Art Center, Minneapolis, 1966; Carpenter Center Gallery, Harvard Univ., 1965; Institute of Contemporary Art, Boston, 1965; Amel Gallery, NY, 1965; C.W. Post College, Greenvale, NY, 1969; Waddell Gallery, NYC; Univ. of Cal.

at Los Angeles, 1969; Phoenix Art Museum, 1969; Howard Wise Gallery, NY, 1968; Boston Museum of Fine Arts, 1970; Minneapolis Institute of Arts, 1968; Phila. Civic Center Museum, 1971.
Collections: Chrysler Art Museum, Provincetown, Mass.; Mr. Howard Lipman, NY; Mr. Peter Meltzer, NY; Mr. Bert Stern, NY; Mr. & Mrs. Bertram Amel, NY; Mr. & Mrs. Victor Friedman, NY; Mr. & Mrs. Victor Linn, NY.
Sources: *Negro Yearbook; Who's Who in American Art,* 1970; Indiana Univ. *Fine Arts & the Black American;* Boston Museum of Fine Arts. *Afro-American Artists: NY & Boston,* 1970; Afro-American Slide Depository, Catalog; American Greetings Gallery. *New Voices: 15 NY Artists,* 1968; Phila. Division of Art. *Afro-American Artists 1800-1969;* Studio Museum. *Electronic Refractions II,* 1968; Galerie Ileana Sonnabend. *Art Electric,* Paris, 1966; Houston Contemporary Arts Museum. *Light in Art,* 1966; Harvard Univ. Carpenter Center. *Light as a Creative Medium,* 1965; Institute of Contemporary Art. *Art Turned On,* Boston, 1966; Amel Gallery. *A New World of Fascination,* NY, 1965; Minneapolis Institute of Arts. *30 Contemporary Black Artists,* 1968; Doty. *Contemporary Black Artists in America;* DuSable Museum of African-Amer. History. *Contemporary Black Artists,* 1970, Calendar; Greene, Carroll, Jr. "Perspective: The Black Artist in America," *Art Gallery,* April 1970; Rose, Barbara. "Black Art in America," *Art in America,* July/Dec. 1970; "The Black Artist in America: A Symposium," *Metropolitan Museum of Art Bulletin,* Jan. 1969, p. 245; "Black Art: What Is It?," *Art Gallery,* April 1970; Harley, Ralph, Jr. "A Checklist of Afro-Amer. Art & Artists," *The Serif,* Dec. 1970; "What Is Black Art?," *Newsweek,* June 22, 1970; Ploski, Harry & Ernest Kaiser. "The Black Artist," *Afro USA,* 1971; Ploski, Harry, Ernest Kaiser, & Otto Lindenmeyer. "The Black Artist," *Reference Library of Black America,* 1971; Le Brun, Caron. "Black Art on Display," *Herald Traveler,* Boston, May 26, 1970; Paris, Jean. "Black Art Experience in Art," *Long Island Press,* Jamaica, NY, June 14, 1970; Ruder & Finn Fine Arts. *Contemporary Black Artists;* Myers, Carol L. *Black Power in the Arts,* Flint, Mich., 1970; Hollingsworth, Alvin. "Wealth of Expression in Black Artists' RISD Show," *Providence Sunday Journal,* June 29, 1969; Le Brun, Caron. "Black Art," *Herald Traveler,* Sunday Supplement, Boston, May 24, 1970; Glueck, Grace. "America Has Black Art on Her Mind," *New York Times,* Feb. 27, 1969, p. C34; Walker, Roslyn. *A Resource Guide to the Visual Arts of Afro-Americans,* South Bend, Ind., 1971.

LOCKARD, JON ONYE

Painter.
Works: *Rev. Dr. Martin Luther King Jr.; The Black Messiah; Interruption; Plea For A Second Chance.*

LOEHLE, BETTY

Exhibited: Atlanta Artists Club.
Sources: *National Conference of Artists,* Winter 1971, Journal.

LOGAN, JUARI

Sculptor.
Works: *Bird in Flight; Girl with Balloon.*
Exhibited: Smith-Mason Gallery, 1971.
Sources: Smith-Mason Gallery. *National Exhibition Black Artists 1971.*

LOGUEN, GERRITT

Sources: Porter. *Modern Negro Art;* Harley, Ralph, Jr. "Checklist of Afro-Amer. Art & Artists," *The Serif,* Dec. 1970.

LONGSHORE, WILLIE F.

Painter, educator. Born in Roanoke, Alabama, 1933. Studied Miami University (BFA, 1956); Kent State University (MA 1963). Art instructor at Lincoln University, Jefferson City, Missouri.
Works: *Gloria.*
Exhibited: Ohio Museum, 1960-8; Lima (Ohio) May Show, 1963; College & univ. galleries in US.
Awards: 1st Prize, painting, Lima (Ohio) Museum May Show, 1963.
Sources: Lewis/Waddy. *Black Artists on Art,* Vol. 1; *Western Artist Magazine,* May 1965, 2-page reproduction of paintings; Walker, Roslyn. *A Resource Guide to the Visual Arts of Afro-Americans,* South Bend, Ind., 1971.

LOONEY, BEN EARL

Collections: NY Public Library-Schomburg Art Collection.
Sources: Schatz, Walter. *Directory of Afro-American Resources,* 1970.

LOPER, EDWARD L., JR.

Painter. Born in Wilmington, Delaware, 1916. Received private criticism from N.C. Wyeth, Walter Pyle, and David Reyam.
Works: *12 St. Gardens; After the Bath; Mother and Child; Vacant Lot; The Creek; Wuarry; McCauley St.; Under the Highline; Angry City; St. Pierre Revisited; Primitive; Behind the Tracks; Bird Bath; Cold Evening; Across the Railroad Tracks; 34 St. Pierre St.; February 8; Brandywine Boats; Rue Sous le Cape.*
Exhibited: Del. Artists Annual, 1937; Whyte Gallery, Washington, 1938; Amer. Negro Exposition, Chicago, 1940; Phila., 1944; Institute of Modern Art, Boston, 1943; Howard High

School, 1939; Fort Huachuca, Ariz., 1943; Atlanta Univ., 1941-2; State Armory, Wilmington, Del., 1971; Tanner Art Galleries, 1940; Newark Museum, 1971; Howard Univ., 1961; James A. Porter Gallery, 1970; Smith-Mason Gallery, 1971; Library of Congress, 1940; Smith College, 1943.
Collections: Atlanta Univ.; Aesthetic Dynamics, Wilmington, Del.
Awards: Honorable Mention, Del. Annual, 1938; Popular prize, Whyte Gallery, 1938; Purchase Prize, Del. Annual, 1938; Purchase Prize, Atlanta Univ., 1942; Yarnall Albott prize, Phila., 1944.
Sources: Chatfield-Taylor, Rose. "Negro Artists Prove Skill in D.C. Display," *Washington Post*, Jan. 5, 1941; Winslow, Vernon. "Negro Art & the Depression," *Opportunity*, Feb. 1941; Aesthetic Dynamics. *Afro-American Images*, 1971; Tanner Art Galleries. *Art of the American Negro*, 1940; Howard Univ. *Festival of Fine Arts*, 1945; Howard Univ. *James A. Porter Gallery of African American Art*, 1970; Smith-Mason Gallery. *National Exhibition of Black Artists*, 1971; DuSable Museum of African-Amer. History. *Contemporary Black Artists*, 1970, Calendar; "Negro Art Annual," *Art Digest*, May 1, 1942; Pierre-Noel, Lois Jones. "American Negro Art in Progress," *Negro History Bulletin*, Oct. 1967; "Under the High Line," *Wilmington Society of the Fine Arts Bulletin*, Oct. 1948; Harley, Ralph, J. "A Checklist of Afro-Amer. Art & Artists," *The Serif*, Dec. 1970; Ploski, Harry, & Ernest Kaiser. "The Black Artist," *Afro USA*, 1971; Ploski, Harry, Ernest Kaiser & Otto Lindenmeyer. "The Black Artist," *Reference Library of Black America;* Indiana Univ. *Fine Arts & the Black American;* Locke. *The Negro in Art*; Albany Institute of History & Art. *The Negro Artist Comes of Age;* Dover. *American Negro Art*; Newark Museum. *Black Artists: Two Generations*, 1971; Walker, Roslyn. *A Resource Guide to the Visual Arts of Afro-Americans*, South Bend, Ind., 1971.

LORD, FRANCISCO P.

Exhibited: Augusta Savage Studios, 1939.
Sources: Harley, Ralph, Jr. "Checklist of Afro-Amer. Art & Artists," *The Serif*, Dec. 1970.

LOUIS, ROSEMARY

Painter.
Works: *Still Life with Fruit; Still Life With Brass Kettle.*
Exhibited: Amer. Negro Exposition, Chicago, 1940.
Sources: Tanner Art Galleries. *Art of the American Negro*, 1940.

LOVE, EDWARD

Sculptor. Born 1936 in Los Angeles. Studied at Los Angeles City College; University of Southern California; California State College at Los Angeles; University of Uppsala, Sweden.
Works: *Genesis; All My Fathers; All My Mothers.*
Exhibited: Uppsala, Sweden, 1968; Black Focus, Reston, Va., 1969; Howard Univ.; Smith-Mason Gallery, 1971.
Collections: Golden State Mutual, Los Angeles; Mr. W.S. Chapman, Los Angeles; Uppsalastad, Sweden.
Sources: Lewis/Waddy. *Black Artists on Art*, Vol. 2; Smith-Mason Gallery. *National Exhibition Black Artists 1971.*

LOVEJOY, ROBERT

Studied at Clark College.
Works: *The Headhunter.*
Exhibited: Sun Times/Daily News Gallery, Chicago, 1970.
Sources: United Negro College Fund. *Art 1970*, Chicago, 1970.

LOVING, ALVIN, JR.

Painter, educator. Born in Detroit, 1935. Studied at University of Illinois (BFA, 1963); University of Michigan (MFA, 1965).
Works: *Untitled; Septahedron Red, Black, White, Septahedron 32; Cube Orange Black Violet Cube 26; Cube Blue Cube II; Septahedron Green & White; Cube Yellow; Septahedron Modular; Cube Orange Off White Black; Septahedron Orange Variation; Three Piece Modular; Septahedron Violet Septahedron; Cube with Blue Off White Bowery; Cube Orange Black Pink (Name) Trouble Maker; Red Deptahedron (Name) I Just Love Red; Septahedron Red Green Orange 14th Street; Red Septahedron 11th Street; Three Piece Triangular Modular Three Solid Questions; Time Trip One; Cube No. 15*, 1960 (acrylic).
Exhibited: Brooklyn College, 1969; Detroit Institute of Art, 1968; NY State Univ. at Stonybrook; Whitney Museum, 1971; Gertrude Kasle Gallery, Detroit; Eastern Mich. State Univ., 1968; Univ. of Mich.; NC College, Durham; Birmingham (Mich.) Invitational; Bloomfield (Mich.) Invitational; Grosse Point (Mich.) Invitational; Chicago Area Show; National Acrylic Show.
Collections: Univ. of Illinois; NC College; Whitney Museum; Gertrude Kasle Gallery, Detroit; Univ. of Mich.; Detroit Institute of Arts; William Ziler Gallery, NY.
Awards: Teaching Fellowship, Univ. of Mich., 1963; Teaching Fellowship, Rackham School of Graduate Studies, Univ. of Mich., 1964.
Sources: "Afro-American Issue, *Art Gallery*, April 1968; Indiana Univ. *Fine Arts & the Black American;* Boston Museum of Fine Arts. *Afro-American Artists: NY & Boston*, 1970;

Afro-American Slide Depository, Catalog; Myers, Carol L. *Black Power in the Arts,* Flint, Mich., 1970; Doty. *Contemporary Black Artists in America;* Ashton, Dore. "New York Commentary," *Studio International,* April 1970; Perret, George A. "In the Museums," *Arts,* Feb. 1970; Ratcliff, Carter. "New York," *Art International,* April 20, 1970; Whitney Museum of Amer. Art. *Alvin Loving,* 1969; DuSable Museum of African-Amer. History. *Contemporary Black Artists,* 1970, Calendar; Bowling, Frank. "It's Not Enough to Say 'Black Is Beautiful'," *Art News,* April 1971; Bloom, Janet. "5+1," *Arts,* Dec. 1969/Jan. 1970, p. 56; Sherman, Marjorie. "Afro-America Gets Biggest Show," *Boston Globe,* May 18, 1970; "Museum of Fine Arts to Hold Black Art Show," *Chronicle,* Ipswich, Mass., May 30, 1970; "What Is Black Art?," *Newsweek,* June 22, 1970; "Museum of Fine Arts to Hold Black Art Show," *Tri-Town Transcript & Penny-Saver,* April 29, 1970; Kramer, Hilton. "Is Politics Submerging Black Art?," *Courier Journal & Times,* Louisville, Ky., June 7, 1970; Walsh, Rose. "Artists to Meet Public at Art Exhibit Preview," *Record American,* May 19, 1970; Baker, Kenneth. "Art in the Service of People," *Christian Science Monitor,* n.d.; Paris, Jean. "Black Art Experience in Art," *Long Island Press,* Jamaica, NY, June 14, 1970; Brooklyn College. *Afro-American Artists: Since 1950,* 1969; Menil Foundation. *The Deluxe Show,* Houston, 1971; Walker, Roslyn. *A Resource Guide to the Visual Arts of Afro-Americans,* South Bend, Ind., 1971.

LOVING, MICHAEL VINCENT

Painter, educator. Studied at Central State College, Wilberforce, Ohio; Eastern Michigan University, Ypsilanti.
Works: *Wall of Pride.*
Sources: Myers, Carol L. *Black Power in the Arts,* Flint, Mich., 1970.

LOVING, SHARON

Painter, ceramist. Studied at Central State College, Wilberforce, Ohio; University of Michigan.
Sources: Myers, Carol L. *Black Power in the Arts,* Flint, Mich., 1970.

LOY, RAMON

Painter. Born in Havana, Cuba, 1896. Studied at the School of Fine Arts, Havana; Academy Fernando, Madrid (1912); in Paris (1912-4).
Works: *Los Maragueres.*
Exhibited: Havana, 1911; Seville Exposition, 1920; Riverside Museum, NYC, 1939; 1-man shows in Havana, 1923, 1924, 1927; Mexico City, 1937.
Collections: Nat'l. Archives.

Awards: Gold Medal, Seville Exposition, 1920.
Sources: Locke. *The Negro in Art;* Afro-Amer. Slide Depository, Catalog, 1971-2; Harley, Ralph, Jr. "Checklist of Afro-Amer. Art & Artists," *Serif,* Dec. 1970.

LUCAS, EMMETT W.

Painter, commercial artist. Born in Washington, DC, in 1928. Studied at Howard University; Corcoran School of Art.
Exhibited: Spectrum Gallery, 1970 (1-man), 1972 (1-man); Neighbors Inc. Annual Show, Washington, DC, 1970; Smithsonian, 1969.
Member: Society of Federal Artists and Designers; DC Art Assn.
Represented by: Spectrum Gallery, 3033 M St., NW, Washington, DC.
Sources: Information from the artist.

LUCAS, LEROY

Photographer.
Exhibited: Addison Gallery, 1971.
Sources: James Van DerZee Institute. *The Black Photographer (1908-1970): A Survey.*

LUCKETT, WILLIAM E.

Painter.
Works: *Chicago Builds a Subway.*
Exhibited: Atlanta Univ., 1942.
Sources: Atlanta Univ. Exhibition Files; Harley, Ralph, Jr. "Checklist of Afro-Amer. Art & Artists," *The Serif,* Dec. 1970.

LUTZ, JOHN C.

Painter. Born in Hickory, North Carolina, 1908. Largely self-taught; studied at Cincinnati Art Academy.
Works: Murals, Ohio Federal Art Project, 1935-8; Murals, Harriet Beecher Stowe School; *Figure.*
Exhibited: Cincinnati Museum, 1938; Federal Art Gallery, Cleveland, 1939; Amer. Negro Exposition, 1940; Fort Huachuca, Ariz., 1943; Library of Congress, 1940.
Collections: Cincinnati Art Museum; Harriet Beecher Stowe School, Cincinnati.
Member: Creative Negro Artists.
Sources: Locke. *The Negro in Art; Who's Who in American Art,* 1940-1; Tanner Art Galleries. *Art of the American Negro,* 1940; Harley, Ralph, Jr. "Checklist of Afro-Amer. Art & Artists," *Serif,* Dec. 1970; Walker, Roslyn. *A Resource Guide to the Visual Arts of Afro-Americans,* South Bend, Ind., 1971.

LYNCH, JOHN ROY

Photographer. Born 1847; died 1939. Served as US Congressman, Mississippi; Speaker, Mississippi House of Representatives.
Sources: Adams, Russell L. *Great Negroes Past & Present;* Robinson, Wilhelmena. *Historical Negro Biographies;* Simmons, William J.

Men of Mark, p. 1042; *Ebony*, Feb. 1966, p. 130; Spradling, Mary M., ed. *In Black & White: Afro-Americans in Print*.

McALPINE, J.E.
Ceramist.
Works: *Mask of Ce Ce.*
Collections: Nat'l. Archives.
Sources: Afro-Amer. Slide Depository, Catalog, 1971-2.

MacALPINE, SAMUEL E.
Painter. Born in Alabama, 1892. Studied at Morris Brown University (AB, 1918).
Works: *Deserted; Majestic Solitude; Cece-Mask from Life.*
Exhibited: Harmon Foundation, 1928, 1933; Nat'l Negro Exposition, Chicago, 1933-4; South Side Community Art Center, Chicago, 1945.
Collections: Mr. & Mrs. Benjamin Feldon.
Member: Chicago Art League.
Sources: Harley, Ralph, Jr. "Checklist of Afro-Amer. Art & Artists," *Serif*, Dec. 1970; DuSable Museum of African-Amer. History. *Contemporary Black Artists*, Calendar, 1970; Harmon Foundation. *Negro Artists*, 1935, catalog; Harmon Foundation. *Exhibition of Productions by Negro Artists*; Harmon Foundation. *Non-Jury Exhibit of Works of Negro Artists*, 1933; Indiana Univ. *Fine Arts & the Black American*; South Side Community Art Center. *Chicago Collectors Exhibit of Negro Art*, Chicago, 1945; Walker, Roslyn. *A Resource Guide to the Visual Arts of Afro-Americans*, South Bend, Ind., 1971.

McBRIDE, WILLIAM
Born in Algiers, Louisiana in 1942. Studied at Art Institute of Chicago; under George Neal. Manages decorative arts studio.
Exhibited: Art Institute of Chicago.
Member: South Side Community Art Center, Chicago.
Sources: DuSable Museum of African-Amer. History. *Contemporary Black Artists*, 1970, Calendar; *Art Gallery*, April 1970.

McCALLEBB, HOWARD
Painter, graphic artist.
Works: *Composition; Composition Improvisation.*
Collections: Mr. Benny Andrews.

McCANNON, DINDGA
Painter, printmaker. Born in Harlem, New York. Studied printmaking under Abdullah Aziz and at the Bob Blackburn Workshop; studied painting under Charles Alston, Richard Mayhew, P. Connor, and at Nyumba Ya Sanaa Galleries.
Works: *The Last Farewell*; Illustrations for

two children's books by Ed White, OMAR and THE LITTLE RUSTIFARRON.
Exhibited: Harlem Outdoor Art Show, 1964-71; Village Outdoor Art Show, 1964-8; Mount Morris Park; Countee Cullen Library; Johnson Pub. Co., Chicago, 1972; Nyumba Ya Sanaa, 1969-72; Acts of Art Gallery, NYC, 1970-2 (1-woman); Studio X (1-woman).
Collections: Johnson Pub. Co.
Sources: Acts of Art Gallery, NYC.

McCLELLAN, OLLIE
Assistant to Sargeant Johnson, 15th St. U.M.E. Church (1935).
Sources: Harley, Ralph, Jr. "Checklist of Afro-Amer. Art & Artists," *The Serif*, Dec. 1970.

McCLOUD, CARROL
Photographer.
Exhibited: Addison Gallery, 1971.
Sources: James Van DerZee Institute. *The Black Photographer (1908-1970): A Survey.*

McCLUNEY, EDWARD, JR.
Printmaker, educator. Studied at Virginia State College (BA); University of Massachusetts (MFA). Teacher at Virginia State College; University of Massachusetts; Massachusetts College of Art.
Works: *Howard; Mower*, 1970 (etching); *Sitters*, 1969 (etching); *Leaving Home.*
Collections: Johnson Pub. Co.
Sources: Le Brun, Caron. "Black Art," *Herald Traveler*, Sunday Supplement, Boston, May 24, 1970; Johnson Pub. Co. *The JPC Art Collection*, Pamphlet; Boston Museum of Fine Arts. *Afro-American Artists: NY & Boston*, 1970; "At Boston Museum—Afro-American Art," *New Bedford Sunday Standard Times*, May 10, 1970; "Afro-American Artists: NY & Boston," *Prudential Center News*, March 1, 1970, p. 4.

McCULLOUGH, ANNA
Born in Chicago. Studied at Chicago Art Institute; under Margaret Burroughs.
Exhibited: Atlanta Univ.; Lake Meadows Art Fair, Chicago.
Sources: "Afro-American Issue," *Art Gallery*, April 1968; Indiana Univ. *Fine Arts & the Black American*; Nat'l. Conference of Artists. *A Print Portfolio by Negro Artists*; Myers, Carol L. *Black Power in the Arts*, Flint, Mich., 1970.

McCULLOUGH, GERALDINE HAMILTON
Sculptor, printmaker, educator. Born in Edinburg, Arkansas. Studied at Art Institute of Chicago (1945-8); DePaul University; University of Chicago; Northwestern University; University of Illinois. Teacher at Wendell Phillips High School, Chicago (1950-64); Rosary College, River Forest, Illinois.

Works: *Phoenix* (welded steel & copper); *Black Diamond* (color woodcut); *War Dance*; *Chaka*; *Black Knight Rides Unicorn*; *Babel*; *Moment*; *Project Totem*; *Clown with Atomic Toy*; *On the Periphery*; *Pawn*; *Chaka: Empty Crown*; *Requiem to an Elm*; *The Bishop*; *Confrontation*; *Flower Child*; *Tomb Figure*; *Judges*; *Tower of Babel*; *Riveter*; *Escape from the Box*; *The Last Christian*; *Toad Hall*; *Baroque*; *Cloud over Hiroshima*; *Icarus*; *April Mourning*; *Aquarius Clockplaque*; *Toad Hall-Front*; *Surveyor*; *Bessie Smith*; *View from the Moon*; *Specimen*; *Atomic Rose*; *Chess Set*; *Appolonian Fall*; *The Moment*; *Crucifix*; *The Oracle*.
Exhibited: Pa. Academy of Fine Arts, 1964; Phila. Civic Center Museum; Univ. of Iowa, 1971-2; Atlanta Univ.; Howard Univ.; Ontario E. Gallery (1-man); Brooklyn Museum; Spelman College; Univ. of Wisc.; Schenectady Museum; Univ. of Chicago; 2nd Invitational Contemporary Crafts Show; Mount Holyoke College; Atlanta Univ., 1959-61; 327 Gallery, Albany, NY, 1960; Hyde Park Art Center, 1962; McCormick Place-Negro Centennial, 1963; Munson-Williams Proctor Institute, Utica, NY, 1963; Gilman Gallery, Chicago, 1965; Rockford (Ill.) College, 1965; Rosary College; Brooklyn College, 1969.
Collections: Oakland Museum; Howard Univ.; Dr. Louis River, Oak Park, Ill.; Ms. Kimberly McCullough, Cambridge, Mass.; Atty. Miller, Evanston, Ill.; Mr. George D. Widner; Concordia College, River Forest, Ill.; Schenectady Museum; D. James Cunningham; Dr. Ronald Rasmussen; Mr. & Mrs. Bolotin; Mrs. Erna Landburg; Mr. Otto Neigubr; Mr. James Klein; Mr. Robert Stricker; Muriel Ziek Foundation; Mr. Eric Nussbaum; Dr. Daniel James; Mr. & Mrs. Perel; Gilman Gallery, Chicago; Johnson Pub. Co.
Awards: Basic-Excellence Award, Chicago Art Institute; John D. Steinbecker Scholarship, Chicago Art Institute; 1st prize, Atlanta Univ.; Commission, Howard Univ.; George D. Widner Memorial Gold Medal for Sculpture, 1964; Pa. Academy of Fine Arts; 1st prize, Chicago Art Institute Alumna, 1966.
Member: Chicago Art Editors; Amer. Craftsmen's Council; National Art Educators Assn.; Perspective; Art Institute of Chicago Alumni.
Sources: Phila. Division of Art. *Afro-American Artists: 1800-1969*; *Negro Almanac*; "Afro-American Issue," *Art Gallery*, April 1968; Indiana Univ. *Fine Arts & the Black American*; Roelof-Lanner, ed. *Prints by American Negro Artists*; Dannett. *Negro Heritage Library: Profiles of Negro Womanhood*, Vol. II, 20th Century, pp. 46-54; Johnson Pub. Co. *The JPC Art Collection*, Pamphlet; Oakland Museum Archives, Ruth Waddy Collection;

Pa. Academy of Fine Arts. *159th Annual Exhibition*, 1964; Spelman College. *Eleven Black Printmakers*; Afro-American Slide Depository, Catalog; *Direct Metal Sculpture*; "La Revue Moderne," *Des Arts et le Vie*, 1965, Paris; *Prize Winning Sculpture*, 1966; *American Negro Heritage Library*, 1967; *Chicago Magazine*, Winter 1969; *Carnegie Institute Series*, 1969; *Afro-American Women in Art*, Negro Heritage, 1969; Illinois Bell Telephone. *Black American Artists/71*, 1972; "A Gold Medal for Talent," *Ebony*, June 1964, p. 118; DuSable Museum of African-Amer. History. *Contemporary Black Artists*, 1970, Calendar; Rockford (Ill.) College. *Creativity and the Negro*; Ploski, Harry, & Ernest Kaiser. "The Black Artist," *Afro USA*, 1971; Ploski, Harry, Ernest Kaiser, & Otto Lindenmeyer. "The Black Artist," *Reference Library of Black America*, Book IV, 1971; *The Negro Handbook*, Composed by Editors of *Ebony*, Chicago, 1966; Adams, Russell. *Great Negroes Past & Present*, Chicago, 1969; Myers, Carol. *Black Power in the Arts*, Flint, Mich., 1970; Brooklyn College. *Afro-American Artists: Since 1950*, 1969; Spradling, Mary M., ed. *In Black & White: Afro-Americans in Print*; Walker, Roslyn. *A Resource Guide to the Visual Arts of Afro-Americans*, South Bend, Ind., 1971.

McDOWELL, EDWARD T.
Sculptor. Born in the British West Indies, 1883.
Exhibited: Harmon Foundation, 1929.
Sources: Harmon Foundation. *Exhibition of Productions by Negro Artists*; Indiana Univ. *Fine Arts & the Black American*; Harley, Ralph, Jr. "Checklist of Afro-Amer. Art & Artists," *Serif*, Dec. 1970; Walker, Roslyn. *A Resource Guide to the Visual Arts of Afro-Americans*, South Bend, Ind., 1971.

McDOWELL, TANYA
Studied at Spelman College.
Works: *Landscape*
Exhibited: Sun Times/Daily News Gallery, Chicago, 1970.
Sources: United Negro College Fund. *Art 1970*, Chicago, 1970.

MACEIRA, GEORGE
Sources: NY NAACP. *Art Exhibition of Negro Expression Sponsored by Minars Furniture*, April 1964.

McGAUGH, LAWRENCE
Painter. Born in Newton, Kansas on October 11, 1940. Studied at Peralta College, California.
Works: *Sleeping Man; World Scape; Landscape.*
Exhibited: Oakland Museum, 1968.

Sources: DuSable Museum of African-Amer. History. *Contemporary Black Artists*, 1970, Calendar; Oakland Museum. *New Perspectives in Black Art*; Indiana Univ. *Fine Arts & the Black American*; Lewis/Waddy. *Black Artists on Art*, Vol. 1; Harley, Ralph, Jr. "Checklist of Afro-Amer. Art & Artists," *The Serif*, Dec. 1970; Walker, Roslyn. *A Resource Guide to the Visual Arts of Afro-Americans*, South Bend, Ind., 1971.

McGEE, CHARLES

Painter. Born in Clemson, South Carolina on December 15, 1924. Studied at Detroit Society of Arts and Crafts, 1947-57; Escuela Massana, 1968; Barcelona School of Graphics, 1968.
Works: *Despondency; About to Receive; Dark Patterns; Nude; Untitled No. 1*, 1969 (charcoal); *Reclining Nude; Hope; The Window; Despondence; African Market; Ritual; Soul Circle No. 1; Untitled Drawing No. 2; Spring; Date's Eve; Study in Nature; The Viscera; Deep Slumber; Preparation; Barbara; Why?; Dignity; Confections; Opus in Blues; Sustenance; Grapes & Pears; Lemons; Horse; The Jungle; Tin Horn; Black to Move; Equilibrium; Reflections; Nuns; Rag Doll; African Queen; Shoppers.*
Exhibited: Biannual Pa. Academy of Fine Art Show; Butler Institute of Amer. Art; Five Main Galleries of Detroit Show, Flint Museum, Mich.; Atlanta Univ.; Howard Univ. (1-man); Wayne State Univ.; Detroit Artist Market; Phila. Civic Center Museum; Whitney Museum, NY, 1971; Brooklyn Museum, 1969; State Armory, Wilmington, Del., 1971; Univ. of Iowa, 1971-2; Univ. of Cal.; Nordness Galleries, NYC; La Jolla Museum of Art, 1970; James A. Porter Gallery, 1970; Columbia Univ., 1969.
Collections: Willisted Museum, Windsor, Canada; Detroit Institute of Arts; Howard Univ.; Atlanta Univ.; Henry Ford II; Edsel B. Ford; American Embassy, Lima, Peru; Mr. & Mrs. Hobart Taylor; Senator & Mrs. Phillip Hart, Mich.; Mr. & Mrs. James A. Porter; Detroit Museum of Arts.
Awards: 1st prize, Atlanta Univ.; 1st prize, Annual Mich. State Fair Exhibit.
Sources: UCLA Art Galleries. *The Negro in American Art*, 1967; Phila. Civic Center. *Afro-American Artists 1800-1969*; Doty. *Contemporary Black Artists in America;* Illinois Bell Telephone. *Black American Artists/71*, 1972; DuSable Museum of African-Amer. History. *Contemporary Black Artists*, 1970, Calendar; Nordness Galleries. *12 Afro-American Artists*, 1969; La Jolla Museum of Art. *Dimensions of Black;* Howard Univ. *James A. Porter Gallery of African-American Art*, 1970; "Afro-American Issue," *Art Gallery*, April 1968; Indiana

Univ. *Fine Arts & the Black American*; Brooklyn Museum. *New Black Artists*, 1969; Aesthetic Dynamics. *Afro-American Images*, 1971; Pierre-Noel, Lois Jones. "American Negro Art in Progress," *Negro History Bulletin*, Oct. 1967; Harley, Ralph, Jr. "A Checklist of Afro-Amer. Art & Artists," *The Serif*, Dec. 1970; Brown, Marion. "The Negro in the Fine Arts," *The Negro Heritage Library*, Vol. 2; Myers, Carol. *Black Power in the Arts*, Flint, Mich., 1970; Loercher, Diana. "Art: Idioms of Blackness at the Elma Lewis School," *Christian Science Monitor*, July 10, 1970; Howard Univ. *New Vistas in American Negro Art*; Walker, Roslyn. *A Resource Guide to the Visual Arts of Afro-Americans*, South Bend, Ind., 1971.

McGEE, FRANCIS

Sculptor.
Works: *Blue Vase; Yellow, Green Vase; Blue, Green Vase.*
Exhibited: Amer. Negro Exposition, Chicago, 1940.
Sources: Tanner Art Galleries. *Art of the American Negro*, 1940.

McGHEE, ALLIE

Painter. Born in Charleston, West Virginia, August 21, 1941.
Works: *Man Experiment; The Praying Packerwood; He Was Only Seven Years; Clutch the Heart and Chain the Man.*
Exhibited: Univ. of Iowa, 1971-2; Detroit Institute of Arts, 1969.
Sources: Illinois Bell Telephone. *Black American Artists/71*, 1972; Detroit Institute of Arts files.

McGHEE, REGINALD

Photographer.
Exhibited: Addison Gallery, 1971.
Sources: "The Black Artist in America: A Symposium," *Metropolitan Museum of Art Bulletin*, Jan. 1969, p. 245; James Van DerZee Institute. *The Black Photographer (1908-1970): A Survey.*

McILVAINE, DON

Painter, educator, gallery director, graphic artist. Studied at Howard University; Newark Academy of Arts.
Works: *The Wall of Respect; The Black Man's Dilemma* (mural); *Black Laborer; Into the Mainstream* (mural).
Exhibited: Art & Soul Gallery, Chicago.
Sources: "Object: Diversity, *Time*, April 6, 1970, p. 80; Jones, Mary Lou. "Until the Walls Fall Down, Paint Them," *Chicago Tribune*, Sunday Supplement, Jan. 17, 1971, pp. 46-52. Walker, Roslyn. *A Resource Guide to the Visual Arts of Afro-Americans*, South Bend, Ind., 1971.

McIVER, SUSIE MARIBEL

Painter, printmaker. Born in North Carolina in 1906. Studied at Columbia University.
Works: *Wall Hanging* (block print); *Wall Hanging: Pied Piper; Wall Hanging: Painted Life.*
Exhibited: Harmon Foundation, 1933-5; Cooper Union, 1930-2; Columbus Hill Community Center, NY, 1932.
Awards: Cooper Union Silver Medal, 1930; 1st prize, bronze medal, 1931; silver medal, 1932.
Sources: Harmon Foundation. *Exhibition of Productions by Negro Artists;* Harmon Foundation. *Non-Jury Exhibit of Works by Negro Artists,* 1933; Harmon Foundation. *Negro Artists,* 1935; Indiana Univ. *Fine Arts & the Black American;* DuSable Museum of African-Amer. History. *Contemporary Black Artists,* 1970, Calendar; Harley, Ralph, Jr. "A Checklist of Afro-Amer. Art & Artists," *The Serif,* Dec. 1970; Walker, Roslyn. *A Resource Guide to the Visual Arts of Afro-Americans,* South Bend, Ind., 1971.

MACK, JOHN

Sources: Harley, Ralph, Jr. "Checklist of Afro-Amer. Art & Artists," *The Serif,* Dec. 1970.

MACK, JOSEPH L.

Painter.
Works: *Four Freedoms* (study for a mural); *Pieta; Composition #1.*
Exhibited: Museum of Modern Art, 1943; Xavier Univ., 1963.
Sources: "Young Negro Art Impresses NY," *Art Digest,* Oct. 15, 1943; Lowenfeld, Viktor. "Negro Art in America," *Design,* Sept. 1944, pp. 20-1; Xavier Univ. *Emancipation Proclamation Centennial National Art Exhibition,* 1963.

McKAY, EDWARD R.

Painter, illustrator. Born in Lillington, North Carolina. Studied at Morgan State College (BS); Howard University.
Works: *Primitive Lovers.*
Exhibited: Morgan State College; Howard Univ.; DCAA, Anacostia Neighborhood Museum-Smithsonian Institution.
Sources: DC Art Assn. *Exhibition '71,* Washington, DC, 1971.

McKENZIE, C. G.

Textile designer. Active in 1930's.
Exhibited: Harmon Foundation, 1928.
Sources: Harmon Foundation. *Exhibition of Productions by Negro Artists;* Indiana Univ. *Fine Arts & the Black American;* Harley, Ralph, Jr. "Checklist of Afro-Amer. Art & Artists," *Serif,* Dec. 1970; Walker, Roslyn. *A Resource Guide to the Visual Arts of Afro-Americans,* South Bend, Ind., 1971.

MACKEY, HOWARD HAMILTON

Architectural designer, educator, painter, printmaker. Born in Philadelphia, 1901. Studied at University of Pennsylvania (BArch., 1924; MArch., 1937). Professor of Architecture, Howard University; University of Maryland Housing Advisor.
Works: *Collegiate Spires* (lithograph); *English Towers; Nomad; Quaint Old Normandy.*
Exhibited: Art Institute of Chicago, 1930; Corcoran Gallery, Washington, DC; Washington Watercolor Club, 1931; Howard Univ., 1929 (1-man); Harmon Foundation, 1933; Amer. Institute of Architects, 1930, 1933.
Member: Amer. Institute of Architects; Nat'l. Technology Assn.
Sources: Indiana Univ. *Fine Arts & the Black American; AIA Membership Directory,* 1956; Harmon Foundation. *Exhibition of Productions by Negro Artists;* Harmon Foundation. *Non-Jury Exhibit of Works of Negro Artists,* 1933; Harmon Foundation. *Negro Artists,* 1935; DuSable Museum of African-Amer. History. *Contemporary Black Artists,* 1970, Calendar; Harley, Ralph, Jr. "Checklist of Afro-Amer. Art & Artists," *Serif,* Dec. 1970; Downing, Lewis K. "Contributions of Negro Scientists," *Crisis,* June 1939; Walker, Roslyn. *A Resource Guide to the Visual Arts of Afro-Americans,* South Bend, Ind., 1971.

McKINNEY, THOMAS A.

Works: *Our World Today.*
Exhibited: Phila. Civic Center.
Sources: Phila. Division of Art. *Afro-American Artists 1800-1969.*

MACKLIN, ANDERSON

Printmaker. Active in 1960's.
Works: *At Noon Time* (etching); *Girl with Rag Doll.*
Collections: Johnson Pub. Co.; Oakland Museum.
Sources: Roelof-Lanner, T.V., ed. *Prints by American Negro Artists;* Johnson Pub. Co. *The JPC Art Collection,* Pamphlet; Oakland Museum Archives, Ruth Waddy Collection.

McLAREN, ELENOR

Graphic artist, craftsman, educator. Born in Ohio in 1906. Studied at University of Cincinnati; Art Academy of Cincinnati.
Exhibited: Harmon Foundation, 1928.
Sources: Harley, Ralph, Jr. "A Checklist of Afro-Amer. Art & Artists," *The Serif,* Dec. 1970; Indiana Univ. *Fine Arts & the Black American;* Harmon Foundation. *Exhibition of Productions by Negro Artists;* Harmon Foundation. *Negro Artists,* 1935; DuSable Museum of African-Amer. History. *Contemporary Black Artists,* 1970, Calendar; Walker,

Roslyn. *A Resource Guide to the Visual Arts of Afro-Americans,* South Bend, Ind., 1971.

McLAURIN, SAMUEL C.

Painter, draftsman. Born in Holyoke, Massachusetts in 1954. Graduate of Technical High School, 1972.
Works: *Togetherness,* 1972 (charcoal); *See No Exit,* 1972 (oil); *Self Portrait* (charcoal); *Black Moses* (acrylic).
Exhibited: Springfield College, 1969, 1970, 1972; Amer. Internat'l College, 1969, 1970, 1972; Dunbar Community Center, Mass., 1970, 1971; Black Harambee, 1970, 1971.
Awards: 1st prize, Black Harambee, 1970.
Represented by: Afro Art Alliance Organization.
Sources: Information from the artist.

McLEAN, BARRINGTON

Painter, educator. Born in 1938. Studied at University of Panama; California College of Arts & Crafts (BFA).
Works: *Untitled #18* (oil).
Exhibited: Oakland Museum, 1968; Studio 1, Berkeley.
Awards: Scholarship student, Cal. College of Arts & Crafts, 1965.
Member: Artist Equity Assn.; Art West Associated North.
Sources: Oakland Museum. *New Perspectives in Black Art;* Indiana Univ. *Fine Arts & the Black American;* Harley, Ralph, Jr. "Checklist of Afro-Amer. Art & Artists," *The Serif,* Dec. 1970; Studio 1. *6 Black Artists;* Walker, Roslyn. *A Resource Guide to the Visual Arts of Afro-Americans,* South Bend, Ind., 1971.

MACLIN, ELAINE

Studied at Tuskegee Institute.
Works: *Landscape with Apple.*
Exhibited: Sun Times/Daily News Gallery, Chicago, 1970.
Sources: United Negro College Fund. *Art 1970,* Chicago, 1970.

McMATH, ALEXANDER S.

Painter, educator. Born in Clinton, South Carolina in 1945. Studied at Morehouse College (BA, 1968); University of California at Berkeley (MA & MFA).
Works: *Prelude to a Kiss,* 1967 (acrylic); *Untitled,* 1971 (acrylic).
Exhibited: Creative Cancer Art Gallery, Atlanta, 1972 (1-man); Acts of Art Gallery, NY, 1971; Univ. of Cal., 1971 (1-man); Atlanta Univ.; Gibbes Art Museum, Charleston, SC.
Collections: Atlanta Univ.; Gibbes Art Museum, Charleston, SC.
Awards: 1st prize, Atlanta Univ., 1967; John Hope Prize for best landscape, 2nd prize watercolors, Atlanta Univ., 1969; Anna Wheeler Scholarship, Univ. of Cal., 1970-1; 1st place Purchase Award, Gibbes Art Gallery, 1971; Eismer Prize, Art Dept., Univ. of Cal., 1970-1.
Member: Nat'l. Conference of Artists; College Art Assn. of America.
Represented by: Creative Cancer Art Gallery, Atlanta.
Sources: Information from the artist.

McMICHAEL, EDDIE

Studied at Morehouse College.
Works: *Space and Revolution.*
Exhibited: Sun Times/Daily News Gallery, Chicago, 1970.
Sources: United Negro College Fund. *Art 1970,* Chicago, 1970.

McMILLAN, JAMES A.

Painter, graphic artist. Born in North Carolina, 1941. Studied at the Industrial School for Crippled Children, Boston; Boston Museum School.
Works: *A Brief Glimpse of Sanity,* 1968 (etching); *When Six Is Nine,* 1970 (etching); *Woman on a Sofa* (oil); *Self Portrait,* 1971 (watercolor); *Manifestations,* 1972 (oil); *The Firmament* (watercolor); *Solid Interpretation* (watercolor); *Untitled* watercolor; *Self Study* (watercolor); *New Light with Sailboat; Nude #3; Saxophonist; Brief Sanity; Reflections* (watercolor); *Cosmos* (watercolor).
Exhibited: Professional & Businessmen's Club, 1968; Cambridge Art Assn., 1970; Nat'l Center of Afro-Amer. Artists, 1971; Old West Church, Boston, 1971; Boston Museum School, 1970; Gallery Renaissance, Portsmouth, NH, 1973; Boston Public Library, 1973.
Collections: Dr. & Mrs. J. Sidney Stillman; Dr. & Mrs. Yale Perry; Mr. & Mrs. Warren Webber.
Awards: Mary Perry Scholarship, Industrial School for Crippled Children, 1960; Dana Chandler Scholarship, 1968.
Member: Boston Negro Artists Assn.
Represented by: Boston Negro Artists Assn.
Sources: Information from artist; Boston Negro Artists Assn. *The Black Artist in America: A Negro History Month Exhibition,* Boston Public Library, 1973; Boston Negro Artists Assn. 1973 Calendar; Boston Negro Artists Assn. *10th Anniversary Exhibition,* Boston Public Library, 1973; Spradling Mary M., ed. *In Black & White: Afro-Americans in Print; Ebony,* Sept. 1969, pp. 70-4; *Record American,* Boston, June 29, 1968.

McNEELEY, GARY

Painter.
Exhibited: People's Art Service Center, St. Louis.

Sources: Balch, Jack. "Democracy at Work," *Amer. Magazine of Art*, Feb. 1943, p. 66.

McNEIL, JAMES

Printmaker. Active in 1960's.
Works: *Pregnant Mother* (woodcut).
Collections: Oakland Museum.
Sources: Roelof-Lanner, T.V., ed. *Prints by American Artists;* Oakland Museum Archives, Ruth Waddy Collection.

McNEIL, WILLIAM

Painter, sculptor, printmaker, educator. Born in Austin, Texas in 1935. Studied at Chouinard Art Institute (BFA, 1963); University of Southern California (teaching credential, 1966; MS, 1968). Art instructor in Los Angeles public schools.
Works: *Libera Nos A Malo.*
Exhibited: Los Angeles Art Assn. Print Show, 1965; Brand Library of Art & Music, Glendale, Cal., 1965; Frye Art Museum, Seattle (1-man); The Ryder Gallery, Los Angeles (1-man).
Collections: Oakland Museum.
Awards: Outstanding Fine Arts Major, voted by Faculty of Chouinard Art Institute.
Sources: Lewis/Waddy. *Black Artists on Art,* Vol. 1; Roelof-Lanner, T.V. *Prints by American Negro Artists;* Oakland Museum Archives, Ruth Waddy Collection; Walker, Roslyn. *A Resource Guide to the Visual Arts of Afro-Americans,* South Bend, Ind., 1971.

McNEILL, LLOYD G.

Painter, printmaker, musician, sculptor. Born in Washington, DC, 1935. Studied at Morehouse College (BA); Howard University (MFA); École des Beaux Art, Paris.
Works: *Yolk; Two Figures;* Untitled ink on paper, 1970; *Three for Peace; Sun-Ra; Miles; Wes Montgomery; Excelsior No. 9;* With Lou Stovall, 6 silkscreens, 1969—*Six Characters in Search of an Author, Bicycledelic on the Ellipse Day, Feed Kids, The Conversation of Patrolman O'Connor,* & *Improvisations by Harold Clayton.*
Exhibited: Phila. Civic Center; Barnet Aden Gallery; Atlanta Arts Festival; La Grange College; Atlanta Univ. (1-man); Howard Univ.; Dartmouth College; Green Mountain Jr. College; Spelman College; Whitney Museum, 1971; James A. Porter Gallery, 1970; Dickson Art Center, 1966; Gallery of Modern Art, Washington.
Collections: Mr. William B. Jaffe, NY; Spelman College; Dartmouth College; Atlanta Art Museum; King and Queen of Sikkim; Le Havre Museum, France; Nat'l Collection of Fine Arts.
Awards: 1st prize, watercolor, Annual South-west Art Exhibit, Washington, DC; 2nd prize, oil, 1st Annual Buchanan Art Exhibit, Rockville, Md.; Grant-in-aid, Atlanta Arts Festival.
Sources: UCLA Art Galleries. *The Negro in American Art;* Phila. Division of Art. *Afro-American Artists 1800-1969;* Doty. *Contemporary Black Artists in America;* Corcoran Workshop. *Lloyd McNeill: New Drawings,* Washington, DC, 1970; Afro-Amer. Slide Depository, Catalog, 1971-2; Howard Univ. *James A. Porter Gallery of African American Art,* 1970; DuSable Museum of African-Amer. History. *Contemporary Black Artists,* 1970, Calendar; Mahal, H.E. "Approaches to Inhumanity," *Art Gallery,* April 1970; Pierre-Noel, Lois Jones. "American Negro Art in Progress," *Negro History Bulletin,* Oct. 1967; Mahal, H.E. "Interviews: Four Afro-Amer. Artists," *Art Gallery,* April 1970; Harley, Ralph, Jr. "Checklist of Afro-Amer. Art & Artists," *Serif,* Dec. 1970; Myers, Carol. *Black Power in the Arts,* Flint, Mich., 1970; "Afro-Amer. Issue," *Art Gallery,* April 1968; Indiana Univ. *Fine Arts & the Black American;* Walker, Roslyn. *A Resource Guide to the Visual Arts of Afro-Americans,* South Bend, Ind., 1971.

MAJORS, WILLIAM

Painter, printmaker, educator. Born in Indianapolis in 1930. Studied in Herron School of Art, Indianapolis, 1953-5; Cleveland School of Art, Ohio, 1956-8; BFA, 1960. Teacher at Herron Museum of Art, 1958-60; Jewish Community Center, Indianapolis, 1958-9; Indianapolis Public Schools, 1960-1; Art School of Museum of Modern Art, NYC, 1964-5; Orange Community College, Middletown, New York, 1965.
Works: *Ecclesiastes* (from portfolio *"Etchings from Ecclesiastes"*); *Big Blue #4; Arno I; Ecclesiastes VII; Liberation.*
Exhibited: Boston Arts Festival, 1956-7; Drawing Annual, Ball State Teachers College, 1954-6, 1959; Museum of Modern Art, NY, 1963; Drawing Society of America, Gallery of Modern Art, NY, 1965; 1st World Festival of Negro Arts, Dakar, Senegal, 1966; American Greetings Gallery, NY, 1968; Society of Arts, Fredrikstad, Norway, 1967; Phila. Art Alliance, 1967; Internat'l Triennial of Colored Graphics, Grenchen, Switzerland, 1967; Univ. of Cal. at Los Angeles, 1966, 1967; Weyhe Gallery, NY, 1966; 2nd Biennial of Printmaking, Santiago, Chile, 1965; ACA Gallery, NY, 1962; John Herron Museum, Indianapolis, 1957, 1958; Brooklyn Museum; Cleveland Museum; Dickson Art Center Gallery, 1966.
Collections: Brooklyn Museum; Museum of Modern Art, NY; Metropolitan Museum of Art; John Herron Art Museum, Indianapolis; US Information Agency, Washington, DC;

Smithsonian Institution; Library of Congress; Internat'l Graphic Arts Society, NY; Everson Museum of Art, Syracuse, NY; Mr. David Rockefeller, NY; Chase Manhattan Bank, NY; Mr. Benny Andrews.
Awards: John Hay Whitney Foundation Fellowship, 1960-1; Ingram Merrill Foundation Grant, 1967; Grand prize, 1st World Festival of Negro Art, Dakar, Senegal; Louis Comfort Tiffany Foundation Grant, 1965.
Sources: *Who's Who in American Art,* 1970; Indiana Univ. *Fine Arts & the Black American;* "Afro-American Issue," *Art Gallery,* April 1968; American Greetings Gallery, NY. *New Voices: 15 NY Artists,* 1968; UCLA Art Galleries. *The Negro in American Art,* 1967; *First World Festival of Negro Arts,* Dakar, Senegal, 1966, catalog; Afro-American Slide Depository, 1971-2, catalog; DuSable Museum of African-Amer. History. *Contemporary Black Artists,* 1970, Calendar; Minneapolis Institute of Art. *30 Contemporary Black Artists,* 1968; Rhode Island Univ. *Spiral,* catalog; Siegel, Jeanne. "Why Spiral?," *Art News,* Sept. 1966; Werner, Alfred. "Black Is Not a Colour," *Art & Artists,* May 1969, pp. 14-7; Greene, Carroll, Jr. "Perspective: The Black Artist in America," *Art Gallery,* April 1970; Harley, Ralph, Jr. "A Checklist of Afro-Amer. Art & Artists," *The Serif,* Dec. 1970; *The Negro Handbook,* Composed by Editors of *Ebony,* Chicago, 1966; Schatz, Walter. *Directory of Afro-American Resources,* 1970; Myers, Carol. *Black Power in the Arts,* Flint, Mich., 1970; Hollingsworth, Alvin. "Wealth of Expression in Black Artists' RISD Show," *Providence Sunday Journal,* June 29, 1969; Walker, Roslyn. *A Resource Guide to the Visual Arts of Afro-Americans,* South Bend, Ind., 1971.

MALIK, LATIF A.
Painter.
Works: *Mother Africa; Genocide* (oil).
Exhibited: Studio Museum in Harlem, 1969.
Sources: Studio Museum in Harlem. *Harlem Artists 69.*

MALLORY, HOWARD
Painter, ceramist.
Exhibited: Howard Univ., 1970, 1972; Studio Museum, 1970, 1972; National Center of Afro-Amer. Artists, 1970, 1972.
Member: AFRICOBRA.
Sources: "Afro-American Issue," *Art Gallery,* April 1968; Indiana Univ. *Fine Arts & the Black American;* DuSable Museum of African-Amer. History. *Contemporary Black Artists,* 1970, Calendar; *Black Shades,* Feb. 1972; Myers, Carol L. *Black Power in the Arts,* Flint, Mich., 1970; Howard Univ. *AFRICOBRA I,* Catalog, 1970; Howard Univ. *AFRICOBRA II,* Catalog, 1972; Walker, Roslyn. *A Resource*

Guide to the Visual Arts of Afro-Americans, South Bend, Ind., 1971.

MALONE, JAMES H.
Painter, mixed media, cartoonist, commercial artist.
Works: *Hand-Me-Downs; Afro-Mod; Ghetto Headlines; Street Corner; Swing Low Ghetto Church; Down the Street; White Ghetto; East Side of Town; Riot: 1967; Soul Sister; Bus Stop; 12th St., Detroit; Up the Street; Me; Black & White Ghetto; Whites Moved Out; Medal of Honor; Sunday Go Meetin; Soul Sister No. 1; Twelfth Street—Business as Usual.*
Exhibited: Scarab Club, Detroit, 1972.
Sources: *Black Shades,* Oct. 1972; Afro-Amer. Slide Depository, Catalog.

MANCUSO, FRANK
Painter.
Exhibited: 12th Annual Invitational Exhibition, Pyramid Club, Phila., 1952.
Sources: Drummond, Dorothy. "Coast-to-Coast," *Art Digest,* Mar. 1, 1952, p. 12.

MANN, DAVID
Painter, educator. Born in Los Angeles in 1927. Studied at Art Students League, New York; University of Mexico, Mexico City; Art Center School, Los Angeles; Merchant Marine Academy. Art instructor at Los Angeles Teen Posts.
Works: *The Sink.*
Exhibited: DeYoung Museum; San Francisco All-City Art Festival, 1960; Seattle Biennial Show, 1962; Watts Summer Art Festival, Ecumenical Center at Univ. of Southern Cal.; Univ. of Cal. at Los Angeles & Berkeley; Palos Verde (Cal.) Galleria; Dickson Art Center, 1966.
Sources: Lewis/Waddy. *Black Artists on Art;* Indiana Univ. *Fine Arts & the Black American;* "Afro-Amer. Issue," *Art Gallery,* April 1968; DuSable Museum of African-Amer. History. *Contemporary Black Artists,* 1970, Calendar; UCLA Art Galleries. *The Negro in American Art;* Harley, Ralph, Jr. "A Checklist of Afro-Amer. Art & Artists," *The Serif,* Dec. 1970; Myers, Carol. *Black Power in the Arts,* Flint, Mich., 1970; Walker, Roslyn. *A Resource Guide to the Visual Arts of Afro-Americans,* South Bend, Ind., 1971.

MARGNI, SEMAJE
Sculptor, ceramist, educator, industrial and interior designer. Born in Washington, DC, 1941. Studied at Hampton Institute (BS); Corcoran Gallery of Art.
Works: *Apollo 10.*
Exhibited: 20th Century Gallery; Hampton Institute; Corcoran Gallery of Art; Outdoor Art Fairs, President's Park; Adams-Morgan Out-

door Art Fair; Meridian Hill Outdoor Art Fair; Capital Area Art Exhibition, Smithsonian Institution; Bowie State Teachers College; DCAA, Anacostia Neighborhood Museum-Smithsonian Institution; Washington Gallery of Art.
Awards: Honorable Mention, ceramics, 20th Century Gallery; 1st prize, sculpture, Outdoor Art Fair; Honorable Mention, ceramics, Capital Area Art Exhibition, Smithsonian Institution; Honorable Mention, ceramics, Outdoor Art Fair.
Sources: DC Art Assn. *Exhibition '71,* Washington, DC, 1971.

MARSHALL, EDWARD
See: Marshall, Harold Edward.

MARSHALL, FRANK
Painter. Born in Bronx, New York, 1943.
Works: *Dream City,* 1969.
Exhibited: Newark Museum, 1971.
Represented by: Mid-Block Art Service, East Orange, NJ.
Sources: Newark Museum. *Black Artists: Two Generations,* 1971.

MARSHALL, HAROLD EDWARD
Born in Charleston, South Carolina, 1899. Studied at Clinton College (degree in pharmacy); Meharry College (degree in dentistry). Self-taught artist.
Works: *Kutter; Head of a Soldier.*
Exhibited: Harmon Foundation, 1930.
Sources: Harley, Ralph, Jr. "Checklist of Afro-Amer. Art & Artists," *Serif,* Dec. 1970; Indiana Univ. *Fine Arts & the Black American;* Harmon Foundation. *Exhibition of Productions by Negro Artists;* Harmon Foundation. *Exhibit of Fine Arts,* 1930; Walker, Roslyn. *A Resource Guide to the Visual Arts of Afro-Americans,* South Bend, Ind., 1971.

MARSHALL, HENRY
Painter.
Works: *What Am I; Where to Now.*
Exhibited: Smith-Mason Gallery, 1971.
Sources: Smith-Mason Gallery. *National Exhibition Black Artists,* 1971.

MARTIN, ALFRED JAMES
Painter.
Works: *Jazz.*
Exhibited: Museum of Modern Art, NY, 1943.
Sources: "Young Negro Art Impresses NY," *Art Digest,* Oct. 15, 1943.

MARTIN, IONIS B.
Painter. Born in Chicago in 1936. Studied at Fisk University (BA, 1957); University of Hartford (MA, 1968).
Works: *Birches,* 1971 (oil & perlrex); *New Justice—Enter Spring,* 1971 (oil); *Wood Nymphs Delight,* 1972 (acrylic).

Exhibited: Hartford Arts Festival, 1970-2; "Through Young Black Eyes Art Exhibit," Hartford, 1969-72; William Hardgrow Clinic Art Exhibit, NY, 1972; Amer. Internat'l College, Springfield, Mass., 1970-2.
Collections: Mr. John Carter, San José, Cal.; Dr. Russell Martin, Bloomfield, Ga.; Atty. Howard Klebanoff, Hartford.
Awards: Judge—1970 Scholastic Art Awards, *Hartford Courant*'s Club of the Year Competition, 1972; WRCH Radio Distinguished Service Award, 1972.
Member: Artists Collective; Greater Hartford Arts Council; Greater Hartford Arts Festival Steering Committee; Artists Studio Workshop (president), Hartford.
Sources: Barrett, Betty. "Arts Festival Will Groove on Constitution Plaza," *Hartford Courant,* May 16, 1971; "Club Contest Judges Selected," *Hartford Courant,* July 23, 1972; Information from the artist.

MARTIN, PEARL S.
Painter.
Works: *The Bull Fight* (oil).
Exhibited: Xavier Univ., 1963.
Sources: Xavier Univ. *Emancipation Proclamation Centennial National Art Exhibition,* 1963.

MARTIN, PHILIP
Painter, graphic artist.
Works: *Leah; Abstraction.*
Exhibited: Market Place Gallery.
Sources: *Market Place Gallery,* Catalog.

MARTINO, ANTONIO
Painter.
Exhibited: 12th Annual Invitational Exhibition, Pyramid Club, Phila., 1952.
Sources: Pyramid Club. *12th Annual Invitational Exhibition,* Phila., 1952; Drummond, Dorothy. "Coast-to-Coast," *Art Digest,* Mar. 1, 1952.

MARTINO, GIOVANNI
Painter.
Exhibited: 12th Annual Invitational Exhibition, Pyramid Club, Phila., 1952.
Sources: Drummond, Dorothy. "Coast-to-Coast," *Art Digest,* March 1, 1952, p. 12; Pyramid Club. *12th Annual Invitational Exhibition,* Phila., 1952.

MARTINO, MARIE
Painter.
Exhibited: 12th Annual Invitational Exhibition, Pyramid Club, Phila., 1952.
Sources: Drummond, Dorothy. *Coast-to-Coast, Art Digest,* March 1, 1952, p. 12; Pyramid Club. *12th Annual Invitational Exhibition,* Phila., 1952.

MASDEU, HORACIO T.

Painter. Born in Manhattan, New York, 1939. Self-taught artist.
Works: *The Dive.*
Exhibited: Studio Museum in Harlem, 1969.
Sources: Studio Museum in Harlem. *Harlem Artists 69.*

MASON, EFFIE

Sculptor. Active 1930's.
Exhibited: Harmon Foundation, 1928.
Sources: Harmon Foundation. *Exhibition of Productions by Negro Artists;* Indiana Univ. *Fine Arts & the Black American;* Harley, Ralph, Jr. "Checklist of Afro-Amer. Art & Artists," *Serif,* Dec. 1970; Walker, Roslyn. *A Resource Guide to the Visual Arts of Afro-Americans,* South Bend, Ind., 1971.

MASON, HELEN H.

Educator, painter. Born in Boston. Studied at Massachusetts School of Art.
Exhibited: League of Neighbor's Bazaar; Harmon Foundation, 1928, 1933, 1935.
Sources: Harmon Foundation. *Negro Artists,* 1935; DuSable Museum of African-Amer. History. *Contemporary Black Artists,* 1970, Calendar; Harley, Ralph, Jr. "A Checklist of Afro-Amer. Art & Artists," *The Serif,* Dec. 1970.

MASON, INEZ

Painter. Worked in New York City. Deceased.
Sources: Dover. *American Negro Art;* Indiana Univ. *Fine Arts & the Black American;* Harley, Ralph, Jr. "Checklist of Afro-Amer. Art & Artists," *Serif,* Dec. 1970; Walker, Roslyn. *A Resource Guide to the Visual Arts of Afro-Americans,* South Bend, Ind., 1971.

MASON, PHILLIP LINDSAY

Painter, graphic artist, educator. Born in St. Louis in 1939. Studied at California College of Arts & Crafts.
Works: *Blues People; Odetta; Native Son; The Deathmakers; Manchild in the Promised Land,* 1969 (synthetic polymer); *With Everything on My Mind,* 1968 (lithograph); *So Many Things I Might Have Done, But Clouds Got in My Way,* 1968 (lithograph); *Black Orpheus & the Butterfly* (oil); *Black Family; Soul-er Eclipse* (acrylic); *Any Moment Now We Shall Disappear Leaving Only Space to Mark the Place Where We Have Been.*
Exhibited: Oakland Art Museum; La Jolla Museum of Art, 1970; Whitney Museum, NYC, 1971.
Collections: Oakland Museum.
Sources: *Sepia Magazine,* Oct. 1968; Lewis/Waddy. *Black Artists on Art,* Vol. 1; La Jolla Museum of Art. *Dimensions of Black;* Doty. *Contemporary Black Artists in America;* Rose, Barbara. "Black Art in America," *Art in Amer-*
ica, July-Dec. 1970; Oakland Museum Archives; Blum, Walter. "A Look at Three Black Artists," *San Francisco Sunday Examiner & Chronicle,* Sunday Supplement, June 14, 1970; Preston, Malcolm. "Art: Black Exhibit," *Boston Herald Traveler,* April 19, 1971; Mason, Phillip. *A Delicate Balance of Soul,* book of paintings and poetry, In progress, 1973; *Black Shades,* Vol. 3, #2; Walker, Roslyn. *A Resource Guide to the Visual Arts of Afro-Americans,* South Bend, Ind., 1971.

MATANCERO, R.

Exhibited: Tanner Art League, 1922.
Sources: Harley, Ralph, Jr. "Checklist of Afro-Amer. Art & Artists," *The Serif,* Dec. 1970.

MATHEWS, LESTER

Painter. Assistant to Sargent Johnson, 15th St. U.M.E. Church (1935).
Exhibited: Mural, Negro Community Center, San Francisco, 1934.
Sources: Harley, Ralph, Jr. "Checklist of Afro-Amer. Art & Artists," *The Serif,* Dec. 1970.

MATHIS, JAMES

Painter.
Works: *Nude; Indian; Kilimanjaro; Still Life; Tonight; Reflections; Abstract Form; Yellow Bird; African Princess; Louise; Women with Jug; The Wind; Still Life; City Scape; Princess Emma; Flight; Mother & Child.*
Sources: Afro-American Slide Depository, Catalog, 1971-2.

MAXWELL, WILLIAM

Ceramist, sculptor, mixed media, jeweler, educator. Born in Los Angeles, 1934. Studied at California State College (BA; MA, 1966); under Hudson Roysher. Teacher at California State College; All Nations Settlement House; Los Angeles State College.
Works: *Texture—La Corrida; Jomo #1;* 14k. gold bracelet & sterling silver earrings; sterling silver ring & forks.
Exhibited: Ankrum Gallery, Los Angeles; Pasadena Science and Industry Museums; Mills College, 1970.
Member: Southern Cal. Designer Craftsmen.
Sources: Lewis/Waddy. *Black Artists on Art,* Vol. 1; Mills College. *California Black Craftsmen,* 1970; Walker, Roslyn. *A Resource Guide to the Visual Arts of Afro-Americans,* South Bend, Ind., 1971.

MAYES, GORDON

Painter.
Works: *Target; The Fence; On the Beach.*
Exhibited: Newark Museum, 1971.
Sources: Newark Museum. *Black Artists: Two Generations,* 1971.

MAYES, MARIETTA "BETTY"

Painter, educator, mixed media. Born in Newark, New Jersey, 1939. Studied at Jersey City State College (BA).

Works: *Tusi Princess and Child*, 1970-1; *Tusi Princess*, 1970; *Luo Chief*, 1971 (mixed media); *Watusi*, 1969; *Wife of Mangebetu Chief*, 1970.

Exhibited: Newark Museum, 1971; Newark Arts Festival, 1970; Newark Library, 1970-1; Jersey City State College, 1971; Young Men, Young Women's Hebrew Assn., West Orange, NJ, 1972.

Sources: West Orange (NJ) Young Men, Young Women's Hebrew Assn. *Black Expressions in Art*, 1972, Unpublished list; *Newark Sunday News*, Aug. 30, 1970, April 5, 1970, Sept. 6, 1970; *Life*, Oct. 14, 1970; Newark Public Library. *Experimental Artist League Group*, 1971, Unpublished list; Newark Museum. *Black Artists: Two Generations*, 1971; "Black Perspectives," *Scholastic Black Literature Series*, Murray & Thomas; Information from artist.

MAYHEW, RICHARD

Painter. Born in Amityville, New York, 1924. Studied at Brooklyn Museum Art School; Art Students League; Pratt Institute.

Works: *Across the Marsh; Echo; Equinox; Essence II; Ever; Flute Solo; Hill Grove; Image; Intermission; July; June; March Serenade; West; Field; Thorn Bush; Time and Space; Here, There, Everywhere; Mystique; Foot Hills; North by Northwest; Birth; Dr. G.W. Carver; Counterpoint; Eclipse; October; Surge; Gorge; Intermezzo; Sonata in D Minor; Marshland; Nature Solitude; Northeast Wind; Nuance; Opus #1; Progression; Ridge; Rockland; Sonorous; Spring '72; Tempo 2; Then; Through the Woods; Tree Landscape; Vibrations.*

Exhibited: The Contemporaries, NY, 1967 (1-man); Durlacher Brothers Gallery, NY, 1964, 1966 (1-man); Sutherland Gallery, Boston, 1963 (1-man); Morris Gallery, NY, 1957 (1-man); Amer. Academy of Arts & Letters; Brooklyn Museum; Butler Institute of Amer. Art, Youngstown, Ohio; Chicago Art Institute; Gallery of Modern Art, NY; National Academy of Design; New School for Social Research; Pa. Academy; Carnegie Institute; Univ. of Illinois; UCLA Art Gallery; Morris Gallery; Washington Irving Gallery; City College of NY, 1967; Boston Museum of Fine Arts, 1970; Univ. of Iowa, 1971-2; Newark Museum, 1971; Dartmouth College, 1968; Rockford College (Ill.), 1965; Whitney Museum of Amer. Art; Rhode Island School of Design, 1969; Memorial Art Gallery, Rochester, NY, 1969; San Francisco Museum of Art, 1969; Contemporary Arts Museum, Houston, 1970; NJ State Museum, 1970; Roberson Center for the Arts and Sciences, Binghamton, NY, 1970; Univ. of Cal. at Santa Barbara, 1970; Minneapolis Institute of Arts, 1968; High Museum of Art, Atlanta, 1969; Flint (Mich.) Institute of Arts, 1969; Everson Museum of Art, Syracuse, 1969; IBM Gallery of Arts & Sciences, NY, 1969.

Collections: Whitney Museum of Amer. Art; Olsen Foundation, Conn.; Brooklyn Museum; Evansville Museum; Ball State Teachers College, Ind.; Albion College, Mich.; Midtown Galleries, NY; Mr. Benny Andrews.

Awards: MacDowell Colony Fellowship, 1958; John Hay Whitney Fellowship, 1958; Ingram Merrill Foundation Award, 1960; Tiffany Foundation, 1963; Nat'l. Institute of Arts and Letters Grant, 1965; Childe Hassam Purchase Award, 1963-4; Ford Foundation Purchase Award, 1962; Henry Ward Ranger Purchase Prize, 1964; Benjamin Altman Award, Nat'l. Academy of Design, 1970.

Sources: *Who's Who in American Art*, 1970; Indiana Univ. *Fine Arts & the Black American*; Boston Museum of Fine Arts. *Afro-American Artists: New York/Boston*, 1970; City College of NY. *Evolution of Afro-American Artists 1800-1950*, 1967; UCLA Art Galleries. *The Negro in American Art*; Illinois Bell Telephone. *Black American Artists/71*, 1972; Newark Museum. *Black Artists: Two Generations*, 1971; Afro-American Slide Depository, Catalog; Carnegie Institute. *Pittsburgh International*; Ruder & Finn Fine Arts. *Contemporary Black Artists*, NY, 1969; Midtown Galleries. *Richard Mayhew: Exhibition of Paintings*, 1969, 1971; DuSable Museum of African-Amer. History. *Contemporary Black Artists*, 1970, calendar; Minneapolis Institute of Art. *30 Contemporary Black Artists*, 1968; Dartmouth College. *6 Black Artists*, 1968; Rhode Island Univ. *Spiral*, catalog; Greene, Carroll, Jr. "Perspective: The Black Artist in America," *Art Gallery*, April 1970; Rockford College. *Creativity and the Negro*, Ill.; Bowling, Frank. "The Rupture," *Arts*, Summer 1970; Greene, Carroll, Jr. "Afro-American Artists," *The Humble Way*, No. 3, Vol. 8, 1968; Greene, Carroll, Jr. *Afro-American Artists: 1800-1968*, Slides; Harley, Ralph, Jr. "Checklist of Afro-American Artists," *The Serif*, Dec. 1970; New School for Social Research. *Landscape in Recent American Painting*, Feb.-March 1963; Berkman, Florence. "Afro-American Exhibit Fosters Understanding of Black Artists," *Times* (Hartford, Conn.), May 24, 1970; Van Almelo, Frederik. "In the American Grain," *Boston After Dark*, May 26, 1970, p. 24; Schwartz, Therese. "The Political Scene," *Arts*, April 1971; Paris, Jean. "Black Art Experience in Art," *Long Island Press*

(Jamaica, NY), June 14, 1970; Myers, Carol L. *Black Power in the Arts*, Flint, Mich., 1970; Walker, Roslyn. *A Resource Guide to the Visual Arts of Afro-Americans*, South Bend, Ind., 1971; Driscoll, Edgar, Jr. "Showcase for Black Artists," *Boston Sunday Globe*, July 6, 1969, p. A73.

MAYNARD, VALERIE J.

Printmaker. Director, Print Workshop, Studio Museum in Harlem.
Works: *Rufus.*
Exhibited: Studio Museum in Harlem, 1972.
Collections: Johnson Pub. Co.
Sources: Johnson Pub. Co. *The JPC Art Collection*, Pamphlet; *Black Shades*, Mar. 1972.

MAYO, CLARENCE, JR.

Studied at Shaw University.
Works: *Peephole.*
Exhibited: Sun Times/Daily News Gallery, Chicago, 1970.
Sources: United Negro College Fund. *Art 1970*, Chicago, 1970.

MAYO, STEPHEN

Painter. Born in New York in 1937. Self-taught.
Works: *Margie; Untitled 1965; Untitled 1967; Untitled 1968.*
Exhibited: Studio Museum in Harlem, 1969.
Collections: Johnson Pub. Co.
Sources: Johnson Pub. Co. *The JPC Art Collection*, Pamphlet; Studio Museum in Harlem. *Harlem Artists 69.*

MEEKS, LEON

Mixed media, chemorphic artist, photographer, architectural designer, jeweler, educator. Born in Brooklyn, New York, 1940. Studied at Pratt Institute; Mechanics Institute; New York University.
Works: *The Abstract Beauty of Earth; Moon Spilling Over; Crust of the Moon; Blue Side of the Moon; Study of the Moon #17; Study of the Moon #20.*
Exhibited: Studio Museum in Harlem, 1969; Columbia Univ., 1969 (1-man); Barnard College, 1969 (1-man); Spelman College, Atlanta, 1970 (1-man); Talladega College, Ala., 1970 (1-man); The Asia House, NY, 1971 (1-man); 9th Street Studio, Inc., NY, 1972 (1-man); National Boutique Fashion Show, 1972 (jewelry); Robert Lebron Gallery, NY, 1969; Madison Gallery, NY, 1969; Nyumba Ya Sanaa Gallery, NY, 1969; Greenwich Gallery, NY, 1969; Waverly Gallery, NY, 1969; Loeb Student Center, NY Univ., 1969; Martha Jackson Gallery, NY, 1972; Bedford Stuyvesant Restoration Corp., NY Council Benefit Show, 1972; Ad Hoc Committee for the Schomburg Collection Benefit Show, 1972.

Collections: Johnson Pub. Co.; Chase Manhattan Bank, NY; IBM Corp.; NY Community Training Institute, Inc.
Sources: Johnson Pub. Co. *The JPC Art Collection*, pamphlet; Studio Museum in Harlem. *Harlem Artists 69;* Ploski, Harry, Ernest Kaiser, & Otto Lindenmeyer. "The Black Artist," *Reference Library of Black America*, Book IV, 1971; Information from artist.

MEEKS, RENELDA

Studied at Tuskegee Institute.
Works: *Landscape.*
Exhibited: Sun Times/Daily News Gallery, Chicago, 1970.
Sources: United Negro College Fund. *Art 1970*, Chicago, 1970.

MELTER, CARL

Exhibited: Den Frie-Oslo Plads, Copenhagen, 1964.
Sources: Harley, Ralph, Jr. "Checklist of Afro-Amer. Art & Artists," *The Serif*, Dec. 1970.

MEO, YVONNE COLE

Sculptor, printmaker. Born in Seattle, Washington. Studied at University of California, Los Angeles (BA); California State College (MA); under Dr. Glenn Lukens, Francis de Erdeley, Herbert Jepson; and independently in Mexico.
Works: *No Way Out; Going My Way; Automation; Strings* (print); *Mother & Child.*
Exhibited: Ankrum Gallery; Oakland Museum; Print shows in Leipzig, Germany, & USSR; Westwood Art Assn.; Fisk Univ. (1-man); Safety Savings & Loan, Los Angeles; United Design Assoc., Beverly Hills.
Collections: Oakland Museum, Ruth Waddy Collection.
Awards: Los Angeles Regional Art Exhibit, 1968, citation & 1st Prize.
Sources: Lewis/Waddy. *Black Artists on Art,* Vol. 1; Roelof-Lanner, T.V., ed. *Prints by American Negro Artists; Artforum*, 1965; Nat'l Conference of Artists. *A Print Portfolio by Negro Artists; Art Gallery*, April 1970; Patterson, Lindsay. "Contemporary Artists," *The Negro in Music & Art*, 1969; Oakland Museum Archives; Walker, Roslyn. *A Resource Guide to the Visual Arts of Afro-Americans,* South Bend, Ind., 1971.

MERRIWEATHER, ROBERT

Painter. Born in Detroit, Michigan. Studied at Detroit Institute of Arts; Meizinger Art School.
Works: *Woodland*, 1967 (pen & ink).
Awards: 2nd place, Dr. J. Carter Woodson Award.
Collections: Albany, NY; Detroit; Lansing, Mich.

Sources: Flint Community Schools. *Black Reflections;* Myers, Carol L. *Black Power in the Arts,* Flint, Mich., 1970.

MEYER, HELGA

Collections: NY Public Library-Schomburg Art Collection.
Sources: Schatz, Walter. *Directory of Afro-American Resources,* 1970.

MICHEAUX, OSCAR

Filmmaker.
Works: *The Homesteader; Symbol of the Unconquered; Within the Gates; Body & Soul; In God's Step Children; Scar of Shame.*
Sources: Kagan, Norman. "Black American Cinema," *Cinema,* Vol. 6, No. 2.

MICKENS, CHARLES

Painter. Born in Beaver Dam, Virginia. Studied at Howard University; King-Smith School of Creative Art, Institute of Contemporary Arts; Washington School of Drafting; New York Institute of Art; under Alma Thomas and Lois Mailou Jones. Special assistant, Office of Exhibits, Smithsonian Institution.
Works: *The Well.*
Exhibited: Howard Univ.; King-Smith School of Creative Art; Neighbors, Inc.; DCAA, Anacostia Neighborhood Museum-Smithsonian Institution.
Sources: DC Art Assn. *Exhibition '71,* Washington, DC, 1971.

MIDDLETON, ARTHUR

Sources: Harley, Ralph, Jr. "Checklist of Afro-Amer. Art & Artists," *The Serif,* Dec. 1970.

MIDDLETON, SAMUEL M.

Painter, printmaker, mixed media. Born in 1927 in New York City. Studied at the Instituto Allende at San Miguel de Allende in Mexico. Lives and works in Amsterdam.
Works: *Mexican Boy; Rage; Rehearsal; Music; Holland; Lithograph (Oriental); Collage; Portfolio of Poems; Relaxin; Theatre Piece.*
Exhibited: Galerie Excelsior, Mexico City, 1957 (1-man); Assoc. Artists Studio, New Orleans, 1957, 1959; Sunken Meadow Foundation, NY, 1958; Contemporary Arts, NY, 1958, 1960, 1962; Galerie Silo, Madrid, 1960; Galerie Passepartout, Copenhagen, 1961; Svea Galeriet, Stockholm, 1961; Galerie Parnass, Wupperta, 1962; Galerie Delta, Rotterdam, 1962; Galerie Arta, The Hague, 1963, 1964; De Beyerd, Breda, 1963; Groninger Museum, Groningen, 1963; De Blauwe Hand, Harlingen, 1963; Galerie Les Contemporains, Brussels, 1964; Schiedam, 1964; Magdalene Sothman, Amsterdam, 1964, 1966; Galerie Cauberg, Valkenburg, 1964; Kunstzaal Barteljoris, Haar-lem, 1964; Bas Grafiek, Amsterdam, 1965; Galerie Modern, Silkeborg, 1965; De Knipscheer, Laren, 1965; Court Gallery, Copenhagen, 1965; Galerie de Jong Bergers, Maastricht, 1966; Galerie Falazik, Bochu, 1966; Kunstcentrum 't Venster, Rotterdam, 1966; Galerie Westing, Odense, 1966; Leids Academisch Kunstcentrum, Leiden, 1966; Galerie 14, Aarhus, Denmark, 1966; Stedelijk Museum, Amsterdam, 1966; Galeria El Patio, San Miguel, Mexico, 1957; Marino Art Gallery, NY, 1957; Art USA '58, NY, 1958; Nat'l. Arts Club, NY, 1958; Artists Gallery, NY, 1958; Whitney Museum of Amer. Art, NY, 1958-62; Brooklyn Museum, NY, 1959-61; Univ. of Illinois Biennial, 1959-61; Kaplinger Gallery, New Orleans, 1959; Sunken Meadow Foundation, NY, 1959; Morse Gallery of Art, Winter Park, Fla., 1959; Columbus Gallery of Fine Arts, Ohio, 1960; Young Americans, 1960; Museum of Modern Art, Saõ Paulo, Brazil, 1960; 11 Americans in Spain, Madrid, 1960; Art Center, Summit, NJ, 1961; Collectie Sandberg, Amsterdam, 1962; Amer. Art Gallery, Copenhagen, 1963-64; Galerie Pijnenborg, Eindhoven, 1963; 10 Americans, Copenhagen, 1964; Galerie Al-veka, The Hague, 1965; Prent 190, Amsterdam, 1965; Galerie Pictural Groningen, 1966; Fodor Museum, Amsterdam, 1966; Galerie Moderne, Silkeborg, Denmark, 1966; 11 Moderne Kunstenaars, Horsens, Denmark, 1966; 7 Kunstenaars, Kasteel Zwaulwenburg, 1966; Amer. Center for Students & Artists, Paris, 1969; Univ. of Texas Art Museum, 1970; James A. Porter Gallery, 1970.
Collections: Bache & Co., Rockefeller Center, NY; Besjakov Collection, Copenhagen; Borenstein Collection, New Orleans; Buchsbaum Collection, The Hague; Sandberg Collection, Stedelijk Museum, Amsterdam; Stuyvesant Collection; Kley Collection, Dortmund; De Beyerd Collection, Breda; Groninger Museum, Groningen; Dr. Groot Collection, Groningen; Hammerstrand Collection, Stockholm; Hellwig Collection, Stockholm; Howard Univ.; Prof. Kurt Herberts, Wuppertal; Igell Collection, Stockholm; Mr. Rolf Jahrling, Wuppertal; John Hay Whitney Foundation, NY; Nat'l Gallery of South Australia; Omme Collection, Silkeborg, Denmark; Museum of Modern Arts, Haifa; Pijnenborg Collection, Eindhoven; Benno Premsela, Amsterdam; Mr. Vincent Price, Chicago; Sonnenberg Collection, Rotterdam; Springhornhof Falazik, Neuenkirchen; Stedelijk Museum, Amsterdam; Swedish-Amer. Line, Stockholm; Whitney Museum of Amer. Art, NY; Univ. of Texas.
Awards: Scholarship, Koinonia Foundation, 1957; John Hay Whitney Foundation Fellowship, 1959; Ford Foundation Purchase Award,

1961; Instituto Allende, Mexico, 1956.
Sources: Dover. *American Negro Art;* Indiana Univ. *Fine Arts & the Black American;* Art Museum, Univ. of Texas. *Afro-American Artists Abroad;* Howard Univ. *James A. Porter Gallery of African American Art,* 1970; *10 American Negro Artists Living & Working in Europe,* catalog, 1964; "Exhibition at the Excelsior Gallery, Mexico City," *Pictures on Exhibit,* Feb. 1957, p. 57; Harley, Ralph, Jr. "A Checklist of Afro-Amer. Art & Artists," *The Serif,* Dec. 1970; "Samuel Middleton: Painter-Printmaker," *Material on Negro Achievement;* Grillo, Jean B. "Elma Lewis: A New Show A New Showplace," *Boston After Dark,* Aug. 16, 1970; Brown, Marion. "The Negro in Fine Arts," *The Negro Heritage Library,* Vol. 2; Myers, Carol. *Black Power in the Arts,* Flint, Mich., 1970; Driskell, David C. *Sam Middleton & Richard Hunt,* Fisk Univ., 1968; Whitney Museum. *Fifteen under Forty,* NY, 1962; Walker, Roslyn. *A Resource Guide to the Visual Arts of Afro-Americans,* South Bend, Ind., 1971.

MILLER, AARON

Painter. Most of works were church murals similar in style to the Renaissance painters.
Sources: *American Negro Reference Book,* p. 769; Brown, Marion. "The Negro in the Fine Arts," *The Negro Heritage Library,* Vol. 2; *Ebony,* June 1952, pp. 66-7; Spradling, Mary M., ed. *In Black & White: Afro-Americans in Print.*

MILLER, ALGERNON

Sculptor. Born in New York City in 1945. Studied at the High School of Art and Design, New York; School of Visual Arts, New York; New School for Social Research, New York.
Works: *Reflections: Sun and Moon Altarasun; Moon-Birth; Third World Tree,* 1970 (painted wood); *Cryptonite; Ibis.*
Exhibited: Boston Museum of Fine Arts, 1970; Whitney Museum, NY, 1971; Univ. of Iowa, 1971; Illinois Bell Telephone Traveling Show, 1971-2.
Awards: John Meyers Scholarship, New School for Social Research.
Sources: Boston Museum of Fine Arts. *Afro-American Artists: New York & Boston,* 1970; Doty. *Contemporary Black Artists in America;* Illinois Bell Telephone. *Black American Artists/71;* "Afro-American Artists: NY & Boston," *Prudential Center News,* March 1, 1970, p. 4.

MILLER, BENJAMIN

Born in Aliquippa, Pennsylvania in 1934. Studied at the University of Denver; Carnegie-Mellon University (BA). Teacher at Westinghouse High School; Office of Cultural Affairs,

City of Pittsburgh; pre-college program, Carnegie-Mellon University.
Exhibited: Pittsburgh Playhouse; Pittsburgh Plan for Art; Skibo Hall; Carnegie-Mellon Univ.; Watt Lane Art Society; Group One (1-man).
Sources: Pittsburgh Community College. *16 Black Artists.*

MILLER, DON

Painter. Born in Jamaica, West Indies in 1923.
Works: *Children of Rio Bueno,* 1967-8; *Congo Mother & Child.*
Exhibited: Newark Museum, 1971.
Collections: Random House, Macmillan; Negro Heritage Library; Crowell-Collier; Grolier; Doubleday; Houghton Mifflin.
Represented by: Mid-Block Art Service, East Orange, NJ.
Sources: Newark Museum. *Black Artists: Two Generations,* 1971.

MILLER, EARL B.

Painter, educator, mixed media. Born in Chicago in 1930. Studied at Roosevelt College, Chicago; Illinois Institute of Technology, Chicago; Pratt Institute; Brooklyn Museum School; Art Students League, NY; Akademie der Bildenden Kunste, Germany.
Works: *American Flyer; Stellar; Games; African Flyer; Space Figure; Diamonds & Silver; Blue Diamond Munich; Probe I; Asian Flyer I; Lightfle; Tone Poems With 2 Blue Squares; March 2; Accordion Flyer.*
Exhibited: Akademie der Bildenden Kunste, Munich; Univ. of Pa.; Bulart Foundation Annual, 1961; Phoenix Gallery, NY; Hudson Park Buvlic Library Gallery, NYC; Municipal Building Gallery; Residence of Dr. Robert Georg Liersch, Imbari Cultural Representative, Germany, 1964; Marino Art Gallery, NY, 1958; Jersey City (NJ) Museum, 1959; Commercial Museum, Phila.; Greenwich Society of Artists, Conn., 1961; Cape Cod Art Assn., Mass.; El Capricho Gallery, Spain, 1962; Stadt Wolfsburg, Germany, 1963; Salon Bosio, Monaco; Den Frie, Copenhagen, Denmark, 1964; Spiral Gallery, NY, 1965; Annual Festival of Arts, San Francisco; Long Island Univ., 1966; Temple Emanuel, Yonkers, NY; Prospect Park, Brooklyn, NY; Museum of Modern Art, NY, 1967; Minneapolis Institute of Arts, 1968-70; Brooklyn College; Studio Museum in Harlem, 1970; Univ. of Washington School of Art Faculty Painting & Sculpture; Alaska Methodist Univ., Anchorage, 1958; Macon Library, Brooklyn; Town Hall, Marbella, Spain, 1962; Art Students League, NY; Marino Art Gallery, 1958; Ivory Tower Gallery, Los Angeles, 1961; Redondo Beach Gallery, Cal.; Salon Bosio, Monte Carlo, 1963; YMCA, Munich, 1963.
Collections: Municipal Building Gallery, Spain;

Danish Labor Union, Denmark; Museum of Modern Art; Chase Manhattan Bank, NYC; Univ. of South Ala., Afro-American Slide Depository; Los Angeles County Art Museum; Nat'l Archives; Langston Univ.; Alcorn A&M Univ.; Mr. Benny Andrews.

Awards: 1958 Grand Concourse Award for Painting, Art Students League of NY, 1959; 1st prize, tempera painting, Jersey City Museum Annual; Tuition scholarship, Akademie der Bildenden Kunste; Bavarian Culture Ministry; Nat'l Institute of Arts & Letters, 1970; Univ. of Washington Research Fund Award, 1972; Scholarship, Brooklyn Museum Art School.

Member: Spiral.

Sources: "Afro-American Issue," *Art Gallery*, April 1968; Indiana Univ. *Fine Arts & the Black American*; Afro-Amer. Slide Depository, Catalog; DuSable Museum of African-Amer. History. *Contemporary Black Artists*, Calendar, 1970; Callahan, Fran. "Nothing Bohemian About Artist Miller," *Times Reporter*, Aug. 7, 1968; *Rhode Island School of Design Alumni Bulletin*, June 1969; *Vermont Academy Bulletin*, Sept. 1968; Long Island Univ. *Spiral*, catalog; *10 American Negro Artists*, Copenhagen, 1964; Minneapolis Institute of Arts. *30 Contemporary Black Artists*; McDarrah, Fred W. *The Artists World*, 1961; Brooklyn College. *Afro-American Artists Since 1950*, 1969; Driscoll, Edgar, Jr. "Showcase for Black Artists," *Boston Sunday Globe*, July 6, 1969; Werner, Alfred. "Black is Not a Colour," *Art and Artists*, May 1969; Siegel, Jeanne. "Why Spiral?," *Art News*, Sept. 1966; Ploski, Harry, & Ernest Kaiser. "The Black Artist," *Afro USA*, 1971; Ploski, Harry, Ernest Kaiser, & Otto Lindenmeyer. "The Black Artist," *Reference Library of Black America*, Book IV, 1971; Lever House. *Counterpoints*, NY, 1969; American Greetings Gallery. *New Voices: 15 New York Artists*, NY, 1968; Ruder & Finn Fine Arts. *Contemporary Black Artists*, NY, 1969; Myers, Carol L. *Black Power in the Arts*, Flint, Mich., 1970; Walker, Roslyn. *A Resource Guide to the Visual Arts of Afro-Americans*, South Bend, Ind., 1971.

MILLER, EVA HAMLIN

Painter, designer of stained glass, sculptor, educator. Born in Brooklyn, New York. Studied at Yonkers School of Design, New York; Pratt Institute (BFA, 1940); Columbia University (MA, 1945); New York University; Art Students League, New York; sculpture under Hugo Rebus at Columbia University; painting with Villa Schiffanoia, Graduate School of Fine Arts, Florence, Italy. Associate Professor of Art, North Carolina A&T State University, Greensboro, North Carolina.

Works: Stained glass window, St. James Presbyterian Church, 1961; *Luba Mask*; *Sight of Sound*; *This Land of Ours*.

Collections: Univ. of NC, Durham; Johnson Pub. Co.; Amer. Federal Savings Bank.

Sources: Lewis/Waddy. *Black Artists on Art*; A&T Univ. Lyceum Program. *15 Afro-American Women*; Johnson Pub. Co. *The JPC Art Collection*, Pamphlet; *Artists/USA 1972-1973*, Feasterville, Pa., 1972, p. 125.

MILLER, GUY

Sculptor. Born in 1909.

Works: *Street Corner; Congo Beauty*.

Sources: Dover. *American Negro Art*; Indiana Univ. *Fine Arts & the Black American*; Harley, Ralph, Jr. "Checklist of Afro-Amer. Art & Artists," *Serif*, Dec. 1970; Walker, Roslyn. *A Resource Guide to the Visual Arts of Afro-Americans*, South Bend, Ind., 1971.

MILLER, JUANITA

Works: *Paula; Untitled*.

Exhibited: Phila. Civic Center Museum.

Sources: Phila. Division of Art. *Afro-American Artists 1800-1969*.

MILLER, JULIA BOOKER

Painter, educator. Born in Lynn, North Carolina, 1940. Studied at Rutgers University, Newark, New Jersey (BA).

Works: *The Awakening*, 1970; *Afro Man*, 1968; *Forgotten Images*, 1971; *Focus II*, 1972; *Woman*, 1972; *Guitar Man*, 1969.

Exhibited: Stuart Gallery, Princeton, NJ; NJ Council on the Arts Traveloan Exhibit; Newark Museum, 1971; NJ State Museum, 1972; Midblock Art Service, NJ; Newark Public Library, 1972; Black Artists, Short Hills, NJ, 1972; Art on the Plaza, West Orange, NJ, 1968; Julia Booker Miller Exhibits, Tryon, NC, 1969; 1969 Annual NJ Juried Exhibition, Trenton State Museum; Black Motion Troupe Exhibits, NJ colleges.

Collections: Newark Museum.

Member: Linden Art Assn.

Represented by: Midblock Art Service, East Orange, NJ.

Sources: Newark Museum. *Black Artists: Two Generations*; City College of NY. *The Evolution of Afro-American Artists 1800-1950*, 1967; *The Linden (NJ) Leader*, Dec. 30, 1971; *The Tryon Daily Bulletin*, Tryon, NC; *The Trentonian*, Trenton, NJ, Oct. 21, 1970; Information from artist.

MILLER, LARRY

Sculptor.

Exhibited: 12th Annual Invitational Exhibition, Pyramid Club, Phila., 1952.

Sources: Drummond, Dorothy. "Coast-to-Coast," *Art Digest*, March 1, 1952.

MILLES, CHARLES

Painter. Active in 1960's.
Works: *Mural on Orchard Park Wall.*
Sources: "Object: Diversity," *Time*, April 6, 1970, p. 80; Walker, Roslyn. *A Resource Guide to the Visual Arts of Afro-Americans*, South Bend, Ind., 1971.

MILLINGS, SAMUEL

Graphic artist.
Works: *House on a Hilltop; Miss; Line Movement; The Egoist; The Angry God; Portrait Study Aurelia; A Study of the Raven; The Remorseful; Head of A Wise Man; The Profile; Portrait Study; Human Equals Destruction; The Escapist; Sobbing.*
Collections: Nat'l Archives.
Sources: Myers, Carol L. *Black Power in the Arts*, Flint, Mich., 1970; Harley, Ralph, Jr. "Checklist of Afro-Amer. Art & Artists," *The Serif*, Dec. 1970; Afro-American Slide Depository, Catalog, 1971-2.

MILLS, P'LLA

Painter. Born in Connersville, Indiana in 1918. Died in 1964. Studied at the Chicago Art Institute; with Carlton Ball at University of Southern California.
Exhibited: Heritage Gallery; Los Angeles Art Assn.; Paramount Studios.
Sources: Ploski, Harry, & Ernest Kaiser. "The Black Artist," *Afro USA*, 1971; Ploski, Harry, Ernest Kaiser, & Otto Lindenmeyer. "The Black Artist," *Reference Library of Black America*, Book IV, 1971; Bennet, Lerone, Jr. "The Negro Woman," *Ebony*, Sept. 1963.

MILTON, SAMUEL D.

Exhibited: Tanner Art League, 1922.
Sources: Harley, Ralph, Jr. "Checklist of Afro-Amer. Art & Artists," *The Serif*, Dec. 1970.

MINNER, ROSETTA DOTSON

Painter.
Works: *Circles of Confusion* (oil).
Collections: Johnson Pub. Co.
Sources: Johnson Pub. Co. *The JPC Art Collection*, Pamphlet.

MITCHELL, CHARLES E.

Printmaker. Studied at Sturbridge School; Exchange Student at École de Chateau, Corcelles s/ Chavornay, Switzerland; Corcoran School of Art; Maryland Institute, College of Art.
Works: *Moisi* (silkscreen).
Exhibited: Neighbors, Inc. Art Show; Rahway City Library; Holy Comforter Church; Elizabeth City Univ.; DCAA, Anacostia Neighborhood Museum-Smithsonian Institution; Loyola Univ.
Sources: DC Art Assn. *Exhibition '71*, Washington, DC, 1971.

MITCHELL, CLIFFORD

Painter, graphic artist, architect, sculptor, photographer, mixed media. Born in Birmingham, Alabama, 1925. Studied at Tuskegee Institute (BS, 1949); Hartford Art School (BFA, 1958).
Works: *Brick and Plaster*, 1968 (mixed media); *Tank Weld*, 1967 (oil & collage); *Comment*, 1971 (ink & wash); *Poem Painting—Ghost City*, 1972 (woodcut); *Ancient Pottery*, 1959; *Who's to Know*; *Tribute to Wiley's Work*; *Man Builds*; *Directional* (collage); *Politico*; *Of Art and Human Nature*; *Mother Earth*; *Summer Cottages*; *Cathedrals*; *Real Estate*; *Orange City*; *European Motif*; *The Examiner*; *Black, White and Gray*.
Exhibited: New Britain (Conn.) Museum of Amer. Art, 1968 (1-man); Amer. Internat'l College, 1969 (1-man); Hartford Jewish Community Center Gallery, 1971 (1-man); Augsburg College, Minneapolis, 1972; George Walter Vincent Smith Art Museum, Springfield, Mass., 1959 (1-man); Panoras Art Gallery, NYC, 1960 (1-man); Silvermine Guild of Artists, New Canaan, Conn., 1961 (1-man); Korvette Art Gallery, Hartford, 1962 (1-man); Northwestern Conn. Community College, Winsted, 1971 (1-man); Amer. Watercolor Society, NYC; Audubon Artists, NYC; Conn. Academy of Fine Arts; Conn. Watercolor Society; Silvermine Guild of Artists; Springfield Art League; New Haven Arts Festival; Boston Arts Festival; Waterbury (Conn.) Arts Festival; Slater Memorial Museum, Norwich, Conn.; Lyman Allyn Museum, New London, Conn.; Hartford Art School, Univ. of Hartford; Mystic (Conn.) Art Assn.; Ceceile Art Gallery, NYC, 1959; Eastern States Art Exhibition, Springfield, Mass.; Gallery on the Green, Canton, Conn.; Galerie 8, Erie, Pa.; Art Directions Galleries, NYC; Trinity College, Hartford; Univ. of Conn.; Decatur Art Center; Stamford (Conn.) Museum; Museum of Art, Science & Industry, Bridgeport, Conn.; Conn. College; Hartford Arts Festival; Vasso Gallery, New Canaan, Conn., 1973 (1-man).
Collections: New Britain (Conn.) Museum of Amer. Art; Hartford Arts Festival Collection; Univ. of Conn. School of Pharmacy, Storrs, Conn.; Stamford (Conn.) Museum & Nature Center; Low Haywood School, Stamford; Burgdorf Health Center, Hartford; James E. Cook Elem. School, St. Louis.
Awards: Donald F. White Award, architecture, Tuskegee Institute, 1948; Ruth Cheney Goodwin Memorial Award, design & painting, Hartford Art School, 1957; Faculty Award, painting, Hartford Art School, 1958; Conn. Watercolor Society—Honorable Mention, 1958, 1959, 1962, Carling Prize, 1969, Past President's Prize, 1970; Springfield Art League—1st prize, 1959,

1968, Albert Steiger Award, 1966, 1969; Silvermine Guild of Artists—Treadway Award, 1959, Larry Aldrich Award, 1960, Laura M. Gross Memorial Award, 1964; Two Best in Show Awards, oil & watercolor, New Haven Arts Festival, 1959; 3rd prize, First Inter-Amer. Exhibit, Ceceile Art Gallery, 1959; Conn. Artists Show Award, 1965; Mystic (Conn.) Art Assn. Show, Honorable Mention, 1965; Doublas Watercolor Award, Canton (Conn.) Gallery Anniversary Show, 1966; Honorable Mention, William Pitt Courtyard Show, Darien, Conn., 1966; Honorable Mention, Waterbury Arts Festival, 1969; Hartford Arts Festival Purchase Award, 1971.
Member: Conn. Academy of Fine Arts; Silvermine Guild of Artists; Conn. Watercolor Society (past pres.); Amer. Institute of Architects; Nat'l Society of Interior Designers (past pres.); Springfield (Conn.) Art League.
Represented by: Silvermine Guild of Artists, New Canaan, Conn.
Sources: Information from the artist; Goldenthal, Jolene. "An Architect Turns Artist," *Hartford Courant*, Nov. 1971; "Works by Mitchell on Exhibit at Local Museum," *New Britain* (Conn.) *Herald*, April 6, 1968; "AIC Presents 1-Man Show of Architect," *Springfield* (Mass.) *Daily News*, April 23, 1969; "Art League Prizes Awarded," *Springfield Union*, Nov. 12, 1968, picture caption; *Who's Who Among Students in Amer. Universities & Colleges*, 1957-8; Slater Memorial Museum. "12 New England Artists," Norwich, Conn.; Lyman Allyn Museum. "Drawings by New England Artists," New London, Conn.; Springfield Museum of Fine Arts. *50th Anniversary, Springfield Art League*, Nov. 9-24, 1968, Springfield, Mass.; Vasso Gallery. *Many Moods of Clifford Mitchell*, New Canaan, Conn., 1973.

MITCHELL, CORRINE

Painter, educator. Studied at Saint Paul's Episcopal College; Virginia State College (BS); George Washington University.
Works: *Smog; Green Pastures; Man Hurrying Home.*
Exhibited: Smith-Mason Gallery, 1971; Rahway City Library; Holy Comforter Espiscopal Church; Neighbors, Inc. Art Show; Va. State College; DCAA, Anacostia Neighborhood Museum-Smithsonian Institution; Md. State Teacher's Gallery.
Collections: Johnson Pub. Co.
Sources: Smith-Mason Gallery. *National Exhibition Black Artists*, 1971; DC Art Assn. *Exhibition '71*, Washington, DC, 1971; Johnson Pub. Co. *The JPC Art Collection*, Pamphlet.

MITCHELL, EVELYN

Painter.

Works: *Preview to Cubism; Things Falling Apart* (acrylic).
Exhibited: Smith-Mason Gallery, 1971.
Sources: Smith-Mason Gallery. *National Exhibition Black Artists*, 1971.

MITCHELL, HENDRICK E.

Painter.
Works: *Winter Fern.*
Exhibited: Smith-Mason Gallery, 1971.
Sources: Smith-Mason Gallery. *National Exhibition Black Artists*, 1971.

MITCHELL, JAMES MARCUS, SR.

Painter, curator. Born in Nashville, Tennessee on July 28, 1921. Studied at Harvard Business School; Naval Electronics Schools; Boston University; Fogg Museum, Cambridge, Massachusetts; Tennessee State University. Curator and Director of Programs, Museum of Afro-American History, Boston; Former Director of Boston Negro Artists Association Workshops.
Works: *Emerging Forth; Attacks; Searching . . . Searching; Early Morn; Black is Beautiful; Endless Journey; Miguel's World; Vibration* (oil); *Boats of Senegal* (watercolor); *Polish Village Square* (oil); *Self Portrait* (oil); *Crispus Attucks Monument, Boston Common* (oil).
Exhibited: Atlanta Univ., 1962; Freedom House & Touraine, 1963; Boston Public Library, 1964, 1973; Boston Negro Artists Assn., 1964; Kerygma Art Exhibit, Sturbridge, Mass., 1967; Internat'l Book Exhibition, Leipzig.
Collections: Johnson Pub. Co., Chicago; Museum of Afro-Amer. History, Boston.
Awards: NAACP 10th Anniversary Award, 1969; Brotherhood Award, Nat'l Conference of Christians & Jews for Museum Program, 1971; Howard Truman Scholarship, Boston Univ., 1967, 1968; Senior Fellowship, Nat'l Endowment for the Humanities, Museum Management, 1970-1.
Member: Boston Negro Artists Assn. (cofounder); Visitors Committee, Dept. of Public Education, Museum of Fine Arts, Boston; Nat'l Conference of Artists; Boston Public Library (assoc. member); Smithsonian Inst. (assoc. member); NAACP; Assn. for the Study of Negro Life & History.
Sources: Levine, Jo Ann. "Proud Trail," *Christian Science Monitor*, Feb. 14, 1967; Taylor, Robert. "Black History Comes to Life," *Boston Globe*, 1968; Le Brun, Caron. "A Museum of Negro History," *Sunday Herald-Traveler*, Dec. 8, 1968; Titcomb, Caldwell. *Harvard Graduate* publication, 1967; Kay, Jane Holtz. "Artists as Social Reformers," *Art in America*, Jan.-Feb. 1969, p. 44; *Harvard Art Review*, Winter 1968-9; Killens, John. "A Travelers Guide to Two Cities: Boston and New Orleans," *Redbook*, July 1969; *Boston*

Public Library Bulletin, Feb. 1964-71; Burnett, Calvin. *Objective Drawing Techniques* (illus.); Boston Negro Artists Assn. Calendar, 1968-73; Mitchell, James Marcus, Sr. "Influence of Dakar Festival on Boston," *The Beacon*, Internat'l Institute, Boston, Dec. 1966; "Black Heritage Trail," Educational Slide-tape, 1971; "19th Century Afro-American Artists," Educational Slide-tape; "54th Massachusetts Regiment," Educational Slide-tape, 1972; "Say, Brother," Channel 2, 1st show; "Negro Freedom Trail," Channel 4, 1967; "Black Freedom Trail," Black Journal, 1967; "Catch 44," Channel 44, April 1972; DuSable Museum of African-Amer. History. *Contemporary Black Artists*, 1970, Calendar; Johnson Pub. Co. *The JPC Art Collection*, Pamphlet; *Art Gallery*, April 1970; "Black Art Exhibit Opens Sunday," *Herald*, Belmont, Mass., May 14, 1970; "Preview Party to Open Show by 13 Black Artists," *Citizen*, Belmont, Mass., May 14, 1970; Boston Negro Artists Assn. *10th Anniversary Exhibition*, Boston Public Library, 1973; Boston Negro Artists Assn. *The Black Artist in America: A Negro History Month Exhibition*, Boston Public Library, 1973.

MITCHELL, SARA EDWARDS HARDY

Painter, educator. Born in Wilkes-Barre, Pennsylvania in 1920. Studied at Howard University (AB, 1942); Radcliffe College (MA, 1946).
Works: *Promise; Gehenna; One of the Gifts; The Void, The Foundation, The Sea; Tribute to the Greatest Power; Pointers for Patriots; The Blackman is a Mirror; Amoeba in the Beginning; The Unicorn is Free; Now Adam and Eve; Butterfly; Had We Loved, We Wouldn't Be Lost; The Void #2; Tree; Message from Andrew; Private Home; Is It Too Late to Understand—To Be Understood—Too Late to Love; Purple Thistle; Pink Flowers; The Red Lily; The Young Princess; The Black Princess.*
Exhibited: Gallery 47, NY, 1972 (1-woman); Nat'l. Assn. of Black Women Artists Exhibits, 1970; 1969 North Shore Art Assn., NY; Metropolitan Savings Bank, Brooklyn, 1970; Westchester Art Assn., 1969; Painters and Sculptures Show, Newark, 1971; Nat'l. Academy of Art, 1970.
Member: Nat'l. Assn. of Women Artists.
Sources: Afro-American Slide Depository, Catalog; Information from the artist.

MOHR, NICHOLASA

Printmaker.
Works: *Reflection Memoriter; Epitaph.*
Collections: Johnson Pub. Co.
Sources: Johnson Pub. Co. *The JPC Art Collection*, Pamphlet.

MONROE, ARTHUR

Painter, educator. Born in New York City in 1935. Studied at City College of New York; Brooklyn Museum School; University of California at Berkeley; Pratt Institute. Lecturer at University of California at Berkeley; San Francisco Art Institute.
Works: *Andean Wall; Nico-Mexican Boy; In Memorium; Eastern Star; Peruvian Glyphs; Yoruba Motif; Dreams of Tinker Machine; Languages of the Moon; Drawings Based on Conibo People of the Amazon.*
Exhibited: Univ. of Iowa, 1971-2; Seattle World's Fair, 1961; Cellini Gallery, San Francisco, 1968; Art West Assoc. North, San Francisco, 1970; Exhibition of Dr. Wennesland's Collection, San Francisco, 1971; Oakland Museum, 1971; Univ. of Santa Clara, Cal., 1971; Vorpal Gallery, San Francisco, 1971; Southern Ill. Univ., 1972; Dr. Wennesland's Bequest, Cathedral School College, 1972; Ill. Bell Telephone, 1972.
Collections: Cathedral School, Christiansand, Norway; Oakland Museum; Santa Clara Univ.; Dr. Reidar Wennesland; Mrs. Cacacae; Mr. William Cholous; Ernst Tie Co.
Awards: Pratt Institute Scholarship, 1947; Brooklyn Museum School Scholarship, 1956.
Member: Assoc. Councils of the Arts, NY; Kenya Museum, Kenya, Africa; Univ. of Cal. Art Museum Council.
Sources: Ill. Bell Telephone. *Black American Artists/71*, 1972; *Art Workers Newsletter*, Nat'l Art Workers Community, Vol. 1, No. 4; *San Francisco Chronicle*, March 28, 1971, March 29, 1971, April 24, 1971; *Oakland Tribune*, May 30, 1971; Information from artist; Oakland Museum Archives; Vorpal Galleries, catalog, San Francisco, 1971; Haas, Joseph. "A Big, Brilliant & Exciting Exhibition of Black Art," *Chicago Daily News*, Jan. 16-7, 1971.

MONTGOMERY, EVANGELINE J.

Photographer, jeweler, weaver, printmaker, sculptor. Born in New York City on May 2, 1933. Studied at Los Angeles City and State Colleges with Mary Jane Leland; California College of Arts and Crafts (BFA, 1969). Black Art Consultant (Organizing exhibits and researching).
Works: *Cast Bronze Incense Burner; The Pipe on 7th St. in D.C. #3; The Sculpture on 7th St. in D.C. #1; Beauty on 7th St. in D.C.; Sculpture on 7th St. in D.C. #4; Untitled cast bronze box; Beauty on 7th St. in D.C. #2* (photograph); *3 Cast Bronze Caskets-Incense Burners.*
Exhibited: Design West, 1962; All Metal Art Guild Shows, 1968, 1969; Graphic Art Show, 1966; Metal Art Guild, 1970-2; 19 Cal. Black Craftsmen Traveling Show, 1970; So. Ill. Univ.,

1971; Edwardsville, Ill., 1972; Bowie State College, Feb. 1973 (1-woman); 10-man photograph exhibit, Berkeley Art Center, 1969; Oakland Museum, 1968, 1971; Los Angeles City & State Colleges; Kappa Pi Nat'l Honorary Art Assn.; Los Angeles State College Community Exhibits; Barnsdall Park Arts & Crafts Center, 1955-60; Cambridge (Mass.) Adult Center, 1964-5; Rainbow Sign Gallery, Berkeley, 1972.
Collections: Oakland Museum; So. Ill. Univ.; Mr. Hudson Roysher; Ms. Mary Jane Hewitt; Ms. Betty LaDuke.
Awards: Merit Award, jewelry, San Francisco Art Festival, 1968; Purchase Award, 2 photographs, Oakland Museum, 1968.
Member: Art West Associated North (founder); Metal Arts Guild of Cal.; Nat'l. Conference of Artists; Contemporary Art Comm., Oakland Museum Art Guild; Kappi Pi.
Sources: Oakland Museum. *The Metal Experience,* 1971; Oakland Museum. *New Perspectives in Black Art;* Indiana Univ. *Fine Arts & the Black American;* Lewis/Waddy. *Black Artists on Art,* Vol. 1; Mills College Art Gallery. *California Black Craftsmen,* 1970; DuSable Museum of African-Amer. History. *Contemporary Black Artists,* 1970, Calendar; Information from artist; *Los Angeles Times,* Home Section, June 1961 & 1962; Kaiser Center Gallery. "Art West Associated North Exhibit," Catalog forward; *19 Black Craftsmen Catalog,* 1971; Harley, Ralph, Jr. "Checklist of Afro-Amer. Art & Artists," *The Serif,* Dec. 1970; Glueck, Grace. "Black Show Under Fire at the Whitney," *New York Times,* Jan. 31, 1971; Montgomery, Evangeline J. "Black Art Scene," column, *The Bayviewer;* Rainbow Sign Gallery. *Black Arts Day II,* Press Release, Berkeley, 1972; Walker, Roslyn. *A Resource Guide to the Visual Arts of Afro-Americans,* South Bend, Ind., 1971.

MONTGOMERY, LORRAINE S.

Works: *Roberta; Old New Orleans Woman.*
Exhibited: Smith-Mason Gallery, 1971.
Sources: Smith-Mason Gallery. *National Exhibition Black Artists 1971.*

MOODY, RONALD C.

Painter, sculptor. Born in Kingston, Jamaica in 1900. Studied at Kensington Museum School.
Works: *Lilith; Midonz; Le Repos; A Mask; Annie; A Ripple; Madame de Muns; Wohin; Une Tete; L'Homme; Viscountess d'Almocaden; Reclining Figure; Helene; St. John;* untitled boy's head; *Portrait of Miss Elsie Cohen; Small Head Rosenwood; Torso.*
Exhibited: Adams Gallery, London, 1935; Walker Art Gallery, Liverpool, 1937; G. Billiet Paris, 1937; Van Lier Gallery, Amsterdam,

1938; Salon de Tuileries, 1938; Amer. Negro Exposition, 1940; Baltimore Museum, 1939.
Collections: Nat'l. Archives.
Sources: Locke. *The Negro in Art;* Baltimore Museum of Art. *Contemporary Negro,* 1939; Locke, Alain. "Advance on the Art Front," *Opportunity,* May 1939; "A Seated Figure," *Opportunity,* May 1939, p. 134; Harley, Ralph, Jr. "A Checklist of Afro-Amer. Art & Artists," *The Serif,* Dec. 1970; Tanner Art Galleries. *Art of the American Negro,* 1940; Afro-Amer. Slide Depository, catalog, 1971-2; DuSable Museum of African-Amer. History. *Contemporary Black Artists,* 1970, Calendar; Harmon Foundation. *Select Picture List.*

MOODY, TED

Painter. Born in Philadelphia, 1947. Studied at Pennsylvania Academy of Fine Arts.
Works: *Wall; Flag; Ballet.*
Exhibited: Brooklyn Museum, 1969.
Sources: Brooklyn Museum. *New Black Artists,* 1969; Loercher, Diana. "Art: Idioms of Blackness at the Elma Lewis School," *Christian Science Monitor,* July 10, 1970; Walker, Roslyn. *A Resource Guide to the Visual Arts of Afro-Americans,* South Bend, Ind., 1971.

MOORE, FRANK

Painter.
Sources: Dover. *American Negro Art;* Harley, Ralph, Jr. "Checklist of Afro-Amer. Art & Artists," *Serif,* Dec. 1970; NY NAACP. *Art Exhibition of Negro Expression Sponsored by Minars Furniture,* April 1964; Walker, Roslyn. *A Resource Guide to the Visual Arts of Afro-Americans,* South Bend, Ind., 1971.

MOORE, JAMES

Studied at Voorhees College.
Works: *Aquarius.*
Exhibited: Sun Times/Daily News Gallery, Chicago, 1970.
Sources: United Negro College Fund, *Art 1970,* Chicago, 1970.

MOORE, LONNIE

Painter.
Works: *After School; My Choice.*
Exhibited: Fort Huachuca, Ariz., 1943; South Side Community Art Center, Chicago, 1941.
Sources: Fort Huachuca. *Exhibition of the Works of 37 Negro Artists,* 1943; Locke, Alain. "Chicago's New Southside Art Center," *American Magazine of Art,* Aug. 1941; Southside Community Art Center. *National Negro Art Exhibition,* Chicago, 1941.

MOORE, OSCAR

Born in White Plains, New York, 1916. Self-taught.
Works: *Dr. Martin Luther King.*

Exhibited: Colgate Gallery, NY; Studio Museum in Harlem, 1969.
Sources: Studio Museum in Harlem. *Harlem Artists 69.*

MOORE, ROBERT

Painter, sculptor, printmaker, educator. Born in Philadelphia in 1921. Studied at Philadelphia College of Art (BFA in Ed., 1950); Tyler School of Fine Arts, Temple University (MFA, 1958).
Works: *Monuments; Landscape; Embryonic; Regal Hunter; Phoenix Retold,* 1972 (wood & plastic); *Slaves of Morpheus,* 1965 (oil); *Modern Gladiators,* 1958 (plaster); *Nativity,* 1965 (lithograph); *Allegorical Pilgrimage,* 1965 (lithograph); *Gothic Campus,* 1965 (lithograph).
Exhibited: Phila. Civic Center Museum; State Armory, Wilmington, Del., 1969, 1971; Phila. College of Art, 1947-9; Phila. Art Alliance, 1967; Lee Cultural Center, Phila., 1972; Temple Univ., 1957-8; Cheyney State Teachers College, 1958 (1-man); Westminster College, 1969; Del. Art Center, 1956-7; Warehouse Gallery, Arden, Del., 1958; Univ. of Del.; Univ. of Chicago, 1965 (2-man); Chester County Art Assn. Center, Westchester, Pa., 1961.
Awards: John Hay Fellowship, Whitney Foundation, 1964-5; US Office of Education Fellowship, 1966, 1968; Artist of the Year Award, 1970; Christ in Christmas Committee, Council of Churches in Wilmington & Newcastle County; 1971 Teacher of the Year Award, Wilmington Public Schools.
Member: Aesthetic Dynamics, Wilmington; Phila. Art Teachers Assn.
Sources: Phila. Division of Art. *Afro-American Artists, 1800-1969;* Aesthetic Dynamics. *Afro-American Images,* 1971, Catalog; Moore, Robert. "Trends in Art Education," *Journal of the National Art Education Assn.,* Jan. 1968; Phila. Dept. of Recreation. *Love . . . and the Black Community.*

MOORE, RON

Draftsman. Born in 1944 in Washington, D.C. Studied at University of Cincinnati; Pasadena City College; California State College at Los Angeles.
Exhibited: Santa Barbara Small Image Show; Gallery 32, Los Angeles (1-man).
Sources: Lewis/Waddy. *Black Artists on Art,* Vol. 2.

MOORE, SABRA

Painter.
Works: Untitled acrylic.
Sources: Ghent, Henri. "The Community Art Gallery," *Art Gallery,* April 1970; Walker, Roslyn. *A Resource Guide to the Visual Arts of Afro-Americans,* South Bend, Ind., 1971.

MOORE, WILBERT

Born in Harlem in 1938. Self-taught.
Works: *Window Still Life With Knife; Girl.*
Exhibited: Studio Museum in Harlem, 1969.
Sources: Studio Museum in Harlem. *Harlem Artists 69.*

MOOREHEAD, LEEDELL

Painter, educator. Born in Pine Bluff, Arkansas in 1927. Teacher at Florida A&M University.
Works: *Across the Tracks.*
Sources: Dover. *American Negro Art;* Indiana Univ. *Fine Arts & the Black American;* Harley, Ralph, Jr. "A Checklist of Afro-Amer. Art & Artists," *The Serif,* Dec. 1970; Walker, Roslyn. *A Resource Guide to the Visual Arts of Afro-Americans,* South Bend, Ind., 1971.

MOORHEAD, SCIPIO

Painter. Slave of the Reverend John Moorhead of Boston. Worked in late 18th century. Was first Negro artist in colonial America to receive formal training. Attracted interest of Phillis Wheatley who wrote and dedicated a poem entitled "To S.M., A Young African Painter, on Seeing His Works."
Works: *Aurora; Damon & Pythias.*
Sources: Dover. *American Negro Art;* Brawley, Benjamin. *The Negro Genius;* Indiana Univ. *Fine Arts & the Black American;* Harley, Ralph, Jr. "A Checklist of Afro-Amer. Art & Artists," *The Serif,* Dec. 1970; Porter, James A. "Versatile Interests of the Early Negro Artist: A Neglected Chapter of American Art History," *Art in America,* Jan. 1936, p. 19; Rogers. *Africa's Gift to America: The Afro American in the Making & Saving of The United States;* DuSable Museum of African Amer. History. *Contemporary Black Artists* 1970, Calendar; Kiah, Virginia. "Black Artists," *Savannah Magazine,* April 1972, p. 14; Brawley, Benjamin. *The Negro in Literature & Art in the US;* Brown, Marion. "The Negro in the Fine Arts," *The Negro Heritage Library,* Vol. 2; Myers, Carol. *Black Power in the Arts,* Flint, Mich., 1970; Walker, Roslyn. *A Resource Guide to the Visual Arts of Afro Americans,* South Bend, Ind., 1971.

MORGAN, GERTRUDE

Works: *Revelation 18.*
Exhibited: La Jolla Museum of Art, 1970.
Sources: La Jolla Museum of Art. *Dimensions of Black.*

MORGAN, NORMA GLORIA

Printmaker, painter. Born in New Haven, Connecticut in 1928. Studied at Hans Hoffman School of Fine Arts, New York; Art Students League, New York; Whitney School of Art

Stanley Hayters Atelier 17. Lives and works in England.

Works: *Middle Dene Farm; Badenock, Iverness; Character Study; David in the Wilderness; Dark Heights; A Cave Interior; Dunstanburgh Castle; Alf, Man of the Moors; An Upland Rain; Glen in Badenoch; Dartmoor; A Cave Interior* (engraving), 1967; *Wild; Moor Demon; Tired Traveler.*

Exhibited: NY Cultural Center (Fairleigh-Dickinson Univ.), 1970; Washington, DC Watercolor Club; Ball State Teachers College; Internat'l Exhibition of Graphic Arts, Yugoslavia, 1957; Museum of Modern Art Internat'l Exhibition, Kassel, Germany, 1959; *Art in America* Magazine show, 1959; Art USA, 1961; Brooklyn Museum, 1965; First World Festival of Negro Arts, Dakar, Senegal, 1966; NY World's Fair, 1965; Woodstock Gallery, London; Society of NJ Painters, Sculptors, & Graphic Artists; Lever House, NYC, 1969; Whitney Museum, 1971; Market Place Gallery; Keighley Museum, Yorkshire, England, 1965; Prints From 20 Nations, Yugoslavia, 1965; Amer. Prints Today, 1959; Contemporary Graphic Arts, 1960; Assn. of Amer. Artists Galleries, 1962; Royal Society of Watercolour Painters, 1962; US State Dept. Show, USSR, 1963; Audubon Annual, 1964; Institute of Graphic Arts, 1964; Smithsonian Institute; Pachita Crespi Gallery, NY, 1954.

Collections: DuSable Museum of African-Amer. History; Victoria & Albert Museum, London; Montclair (NJ) Museum; Boston Museum of Fine Arts; Arts Council of Great Britain, London; Leeds Museum, England; Glasgow Museum, Scotland; Cliffe Council Art Gallery & Museum Keighley; Library of Congress Pennell Collection; Lessing Rosenwald Collection; James Weldon Johnson Collection; Museum of Modern Art; Nat'l Gallery of Art, Washington, DC; Walker Art Centre; Phila. Museum; City Art Museum, St. Louis; Brooks Memorial Art Gallery; Howard Univ.; Gov. Nelson Rockefeller; Assn. of Amer. Artists; Internat'l Graphic Art Society; John Hay Whitney Foundation, NY; Pa. Academy of Fine Arts; Smithsonian Institution; Society of Amer. Graphic Artists, NY; Chase Manhattan Bank, NY; Oakland Museum.

Awards: John Hay Whitney Fellowship, 1951; Louis Comfort Tiffany Foundation Grant, 1962; John F. Lee Stacey Foundation Grant, 1961; 1st prize, Phila. Museum, 1955; Washington Watercolor Club Annual Exhibition, Bainbridge Prize, 1959; Gold Medal, Graphics Award, Nat'l Academy of Arts & Letters, 1963; Gold Medal, Amer. Arts Professional League, Smithsonian Institution, 1963; Gold Medal of Honor, NJ Society of Painters, Sculptors & Graphic Artists, 1967; Academic Artists Prize, Springfield, Mass.; David Rose Award.

Member: Society of Amer. Graphic Arts; Knickerbocker Artists, NYC; Assoc. Amer. Artists.

Sources: Dover. *American Negro Art;* "Afro-American Issue," *Art Gallery,* April 1968; Roelof-Lanner, T.V., ed. *Prints by American Negro Artists;* Newark Museum. *Black Artists: Two Generations,* 1971; *Dictionary of International Biographies;* Information from artist; Morgan, Norma Gloria. "Imaginative Painting," *The Artist,* March 1964; *International Who's Who in Art & Antiques,* London, 1972; *Who's Who in American Art,* 1970; UCLA Art Galleries. *The Negro in American Art;* Doty. *Contemporary Black Artists in America;* Roucek/Kiernan. *The Negro Impact on Western Civilization;* Afro-Amer. Slide Depository, catalog, 1971-2; DuSable Museum of African-Amer. History. *Contemporary Black Artists,* 1970, Calendar; *Market Place Gallery,* catalog; *New York Courier,* Feb. 27, 1965; *10 American Negro Artists Living & Working in Europe,* catalog, 1964; Greene, Carroll, Jr. "Perspective: The Black Artist in America," *Art Gallery,* April 1970, p. 14; Pierre-Noel, Lois Jones. "American Negro Art in Progress," *Negro History Bulletin,* Oct. 1967; Fax, Elton C. *Seventeen Black Artists;* A & T Univ. Lyceum Program. *15 Afro-American Women; 10 Negro Artists from the US,* catalog, 1966; Harley, Ralph, Jr. "A Checklist of Afro-Amer. Art & Artists," *The Serif,* Dec. 1970; *The Negro Handbook,* Composed by Editors of *Ebony,* Chicago, 1966; Schatz, Walter. *Directory of Afro-American Resources,* 1970; "Women in the Arts," *Ebony,* Aug. 1966, pp. 90-4; Pachita Crespi Gallery. *Paintings,* NY, 1954; Walker, Roslyn. *A Resource Guide to the Visual Arts of Afro-Americans,* South Bend, Ind., 1971; Myers, Carol. *Black Power in the Arts,* Flint, Mich., 1970; Oakland Museum Archives, Ruth Waddy Collection; Morgan, Norma Gloria. *Engravings & Imaginative Paintings;* Ball State Teachers College. *Drawing Annual;* Museum of Modern Art. *Documenta II: Art Science 1945,* Kassel, Germany, 1959; Art in America Magazine. *New Talent,* catalog, 1959; Brooklyn Museum. *15th National Print Exhibition,* 1965.

MORRIS, BENJAMIN THOMAS

Sculptor. Born in Boston, 1938.

Works: *The Family; The Sun, Moon, and Earth; Princess,* 1971; 14 other untitled works.

Exhibited: Elements, Cambridge, Mass., 1972.

Member: New England Sculptors; Boston Negro Artists' Assn.

Sources: Information from the artist.

MORRIS, FRANKLIN WILLIAM

Designer. Born in Philadelphia, November 9, 1918. Studied at the Pennsylvania Museum School of Industrial Art (1940); Temple University (BS); School of Fine Arts (1941-2); Harvard University Graduate School of Design (1946-7); Boston University (MA).
Member: Nat'l Assn. of Housing Officials; Amer. Institute of Planners; NAACP Urban League; Alpha Phi Alpha.
Sources: "Preview Party to Open Show by 13 Black Artists," *Citizen,* Belmont, Mass., May 14, 1970; Furr, Arthur F. *History & Progress of Negroes in the US;* "Black Art Exhibit Opens Sunday," *Herald,* Belmont, Mass., May 14, 1970.

MORRIS, FREDERICK A.

Painter.
Works: *Angela* (acrylic).
Exhibited: Smith-Mason Gallery, 1971.
Sources: Smith-Mason Gallery. *National Exhibition Black Artists 1971.*

MORRIS, LENWOOD

Painter.
Exhibited: Harmon Foundation, 1936.
Sources: Roucek & Kiernan. *The Negro Impact on Western Civilization;* Harley, Ralph, Jr. "Checklist of Afro-Amer. Art & Artists," *The Serif,* Dec. 1970.

MORRIS, WILLIE JAMES

Works: *Fire Setters; S.S. Manhattan.*
Exhibited: Harmon Foundation, 1933.
Sources: Harmon Foundation. *Non-Jury Exhibit of Works of Negro Artists,* 1933.

MORRISON, KEITH

Painter, printmaker, educator. Born in Jamaica, West Indies on May 20, 1942. Studied at Art Institute of Chicago (MFA). Associate Professor of Art at University of Illinois.
Works: *Silhouette; The Ocean is Green at Port Maria; Prevalence of Ritual.*
Exhibited: Univ. of Iowa, 1971-2; Smith-Mason Gallery, 1971; 25th Ill. Invitational, 1972; Art Institute of Chicago, 1968, 1971; Illinois Bell Tel., 1972; Univ. of Chicago; Ill. Institute of Technology; Cornell Univ.; Columbia Univ.; Sheraton Hotel, Phila., 1968.
Collections: Fisk Univ.; DuSable Museum, Liberia; Horanvich Collection.
Awards: Danforth Assoc.
Member: Nat'l Society of Artists; College Art Assn. of America.
Represented by: Humkin, Chicago; Phyllis Kond, Chicago.
Sources: Information from artist; Muzarts. *Valid Humanities Concept,* 1970; "Jacob Lawrence's Toussaint L'Ouverture," *Art Scene,* 1969; Fisk Univ. *The Probing Line of Richard Hunt,* 1968; Univ. of Chicago. *The Black Experience,* 1971; *Chicago Sun Times,* 1971; Jamaica Gleaner, newspaper, 1969; Harley, Ralph, Jr. "A Checklist of Afro-Amer. Art & Artists," *The Serif,* Dec. 1970; Myers, Carol. Black Power in the Arts, Flint, Mich., 1970; Smith-Mason Gallery. *National Exhibition Black Artists,* 1971.*

MORRISSEAU, CAROLE

Painter, educator. Studied at Central State University, Ohio; Charles McGee School.
Works: *Lynne; Tangerine Sky; Joe, the Clown; Women in Red; Subterranean Light; Reclining Nude; Shirley; Sphzitt; Epiphany; Afro; Market Woman; Still Life; The Stranger; Study of a Black Man; Girl with a Scarab Ring.*
Exhibited: Normacel Gallery, Detroit; Detroit Afro-Amer. 1968 Biennial Art Teacher Exhibition; Wayne State Univ.
Awards: 2nd prize, Detroit Afro-Amer. 1968 Biennial Art Teacher Exhibition; Honorable mention, Black Exhibit, Wayne State Univ.
Sources: Afro-American Slide Depository, Catalog, 1971-2; Normacel Gallery. *A Black Women Art Exhibit,* Detroit, 1970.

MORROW, PAULA D.

Studied at Tougaloo College.
Works: *Face.*
Exhibited: Sun Times/Daily News Gallery, Chicago, 1970.
Sources: United Negro College Fund, *Art 1970,* Chicago, 1970.

MORSE, ALICE

Sources: Harley, Ralph, Jr. "Checklist of Afro-Amer. Art & Artists," *The Serif,* Dec. 1970.

MORSE, GEORGE B.

Painter. Born in Jacksonville, Florida in 1902. Studied at the School of Applied Arts in Battle Creek, Michigan.
Works: *Negro Girl; Slum Area Back Yard Under Winter Snow; Three Girls Walking in the Rain.*
Exhibited: Hospital for Special Surgery, 1950.
Sources: *New York Times,* June 3, 1950.

MORTON, KENNETH

Painter. Born in New York City, 1930. Studied at City College of New York.
Works: *Kwei-Swei,* 1966 (oil); *Europa 66,* 1965 (oil); *Untitled,* 1966 (oil); *Mozartians* or *The Johnson Family,* 1971 (oil); *Landscape I,* 1965 (oil); *Grey Mountain.*
Exhibited: Greenwich Village Outdoor Art Show, Spring 1961; Brata Gallery, NY, 1964; Lerner Misrachi Gallery, NY.
Collections: Dana Atcherly Pavillion, Medical

Center, NY; Sloan-Kettering Memorial Hospital, NY.
Awards: Ford Foundation Grant, 1965; Scholarship in Fine Arts, Anco Wood Foundation for Fine Arts, 1967.
Sources: Lerner Misrachi Gallery. *Summer of '72,* NYC; Information from the artist.

MOSELY, JIMMIE LEE

Painter, printmaker, educator, sculptor, mixed media. Born in Lakeland, Florida in 1927. Studied at Texas Southern University (BA, 1952); Pennsylvania State University (MA, 1955). Director of Art Education at Maryland State College; President of National Conference of Artists.
Works: *Migration #2; Noah's Ark; Skyline; Composition from Styrofoam; Stained Glass; Migration #1; Humanity; Waiting to Vote; Collage Composition; Boats at Deal Island; Red Sun; Mineral Cavern; Private Devotion; Black Sophistication; Three Witches from Macbeth; Right Triangles; Hungry Hands; Nymphs & Little Girls; Collage with Nymphs; Contemplation; Protest; Waiting for Freedom; Wild Volcano; Korean Prisoners.*
Exhibited: Phila Civic Center Museum; Smith-Mason Gallery, 1971; Jonade Gallery, Baltimore, 1971; Xavier Univ., 1963; Atlanta Univ.; Illinois State Univ.; Nelson Gallery, Kansas City, Mo.; Atkins Museum, Kansas City, Mo.
Collections: Johnson Pub. Co.; Atlanta Univ. Art Gallery; Illinois State Univ.; DuSable Museum, Chicago.
Awards: 1st prize, Atlanta Univ.; Xavier Univ.; Nat'l Conference of Artists.
Sources: Smith-Mason Gallery. *National Exhibition Black Artists,* 1971; DuSable Museum of African-Amer. History. *Contemporary Black Artists,* 1970, Calendar; "Afro-American Issue," *Art Gallery,* April 1968; Indiana Univ. *Fine Arts & the Black American;* Lewis/Waddy. *Black Artists on Art;* Roelof-Lanner, T.V., ed. *Prints by American Negro Artists;* Afro-American Slide Depository, catalog; Pierre-Noel, Lois Jones. "American Negro Art in Progress," *Negro History Bulletin,* Oct. 1967; *National Conference of Artists,* Journal, Winter 1971; Johnson Pub. Co. *The JPC Art Collection,* pamphlet; Xavier Univ. *Emancipation Proclamation Centennial National Art Exhibition, 1963; Artists/USA 1972-3,* Feasterville, Pa., 1972, p. 131; Atkinson, J. Edward. *Black Dimensions in Contemporary American Art,* NY, 1971; Myers, Carol. *Black Power in the Arts,* Flint, Mich., 1970; Walker, Roslyn. *A Resource Guide to the Visual Arts of Afro-Americans,* South Bend, Ind., 1971.

MOSLEY, THADDEUS G.

Born in New Castle, Pennsylvania in 1926.

Studied at the University of Pittsburgh (BA).
Works: *Revolutionist; Jazz Bird; Animal Form.*
Exhibited: Assoc. Artists; Three Rivers Arts Festival; Westermoreland Co. Museum; William Penn Museum, Harrisburg; Homewood Black Arts Festival; Crestas Black Culture Show; Kingsley Assn., Carnegie Institute (1-man).
Sources: Pittsburgh Community College. *16 Black Artists;* "Black Pour Out Soul, Pride at Their Art Show," *Pittsburgh Press,* Feb. 23, 1969.

MOSS, LOTTIE WILSON

Sources: Porter. *Modern Negro Art;* Harley, Ralph, Jr. "Checklist of Afro-Amer. Art & Artists," *The Serif,* Dec. 1970.

MOTLEY, ARCHIBALD J., JR.

Painter. Born in New Orleans in 1891. Studied at Art Institute of Chicago under Karl Buehler, Norton & Krehbiel.
Works: *Portrait of My Mother; Octoroon Girl; Parisian Scene; Barbecue; Black Belt; Chicken Shack; Gettin' Religion; Jockey Club, Paris; United States Mail; Mending Socks; Old Snuff Dipper; Stomp; Aline-An Octoroon; Waganda Charm Makers; Suncopation; Mulattress; The Jockey Club; The Plotters; Parisian Scene; The Picnic; Sharks; Saturday Night; The Liar; The Picnic at the Grove; Blues; A Surprise in Store; Sunday Afternoon; Carnival.*
Exhibited: Harmon Foundation, 1929, 1931; Guggenheim Fellows Exhibit, 1931, 1933; Amer. Scandanavian Exhibit, 1931; Ill. Academy of Fine Arts, 1931; Art Institute of Chicago, 1932, 1934; Toledo Museum, 1934; Corcoran Gallery, Washington, 1934; Dallas Exposition, 1936; Howard Univ., 1937, 1938, 1945; Baltimore Museum, 1939; Amer. Negro Exposition, 1940; South Side Community Art Center, Chicago, 1940, 1941; Library of Congress, 1940; College Art Traveling Exhibition, 1942; New Galleries, NYC, 1928 (1-man); City College of NY, 1967; La Jolla Art Museum, 1970; Smithsonian Institution, 1933; Chicago Women's Club, 1931, 1933; Texas Centennial, 1936; JAP, 1970.
Collections: Harmon Collection; Howard Univ. Art Gallery; Wood River Post Office; Evansville State Hospital; Chicago Public Library; Ryerson School, Chicago; Nichols School, Evanston, Ill.; Doolittle School, Chicago; Nat'l Archives; NY Public Library, Schomburg Collection.
Awards: Harmon Collection Gold Medal; Frank J. Logan Medal, 1925; J.N. Eisendrath Prize, 1925; Guggenheim Fellowship, 1929.
Sources: Mallett. *Index of Artists;* Locke. *The Negro in Art;* Dover. *American Negro Art; American Art Annual,* 1933; *Who's Who in*

American Art, 1940-1; Albany Institute of History & Art. *The Negro Artist Comes of Age;* Harmon Foundation. *Exhibition of Productions by Negro Artists;* "Afro-American Issue," *Art Gallery,* April 1968; Indiana Univ. *Fine Arts & the Black American;* Afro-American Slide Depository, catalog; City College of NY. *The Evolution of Afro-American Artists 1800-1950;* La Jolla Museum of Art. *Dimensions of Black;* Herring, James V. "The American Negro Craftsman & Artist," *Crisis,* 1942; Howard Univ. *Art of the American Negro,* 1937; Brawley, Benjamin. *The Negro Genius;* Walker, Roslyn. *A Resource Guide to the Visual Arts of Afro-Americans,* South Bend, Ind., 1971; Bennett, Mary. "The Harmon Awards," *Opportunity,* Feb. 1929, pp. 47-8; Butcher, Margaret. *The Negro in American Culture,* p. 236-7; "Archibald J. Motley," *Opportunity,* April 1928; Roucek & Kiernan. *The Negro Impact on Western Civilization;* Texas Centennial Exposition. *Thumbnail Sketches of Exhibiting Artists,* 1936; Howard Univ. *Festival of Fine Arts,* 1945; Howard Univ. *James A. Porter Gallery of African American Art,* 1970; Harmon Foundation. *Negro Artists,* 1935; DuSable Museum of African-Amer. History. *Contemporary Black Artists,* Calendar, 1970; Smithsonian Institution. *Paintings & Sculpture by American Negro Artists,* 1929; Furr, Arthur F. *History & Progress of Negroes in the US;* "American Negro Art Given Full Length Review in NY Show," *Art Digest,* Dec. 15, 1941; Greene, Carroll, Jr. "Perspective: The Black Artist in America," *Art Gallery,* April 1970, p. 19; Pierre-Noel, Lois Jones. "American Negro Art in Progress," *Negro History Bulletin,* Oct. 1967; *Apollo,* Feb. 1968, p. 141; Porter, James A. "Negro Art on Review," *American Magazine of Art,* Jan. 1934; Locke, Alain. "The American Negro as Artist," *American Magazine of Art,* Sept. 1931; Locke, Alain. "Negro Art in America," *Design Magazine,* Dec. 1942, p. 12-3; Craig, Randall J. "Focus on Black Artists: A Project for Schools & Community," *School Arts,* Nov. 1970, p. 30-3; Greene, Carroll, Jr. "Afro-American Artists: Yesterday & Now," *The Humble Way,* Vol. 8, No. 3, 1968; Greene, Carroll, Jr. *Afro-American Artists: 1800-1968,* slides; Brawley, Benjamin. *The Negro Literature & Art in the US; Who's Who in Colored America,* 7th Edition, 1950; *The Negro Yearbook,* 11th Edition; Haydon, Harold. "Coming of Age of Black Art," *Chicago Sun Times,* July 26, 1970; Brown, Marion. "The Negro in Fine Arts," *The Negro Heritage Library,* Vol. 2; *The Negro in Music & Art,* NY, 1969; Motley, Willard F. "Negro Art in Chicago," *The Negro in Art & Music,* 1969; Ploski, Harry, & Ernest Kaiser. "The Black Artist," *Afro USA,* 1971; Ploski, Harry, Ernest Kaiser, & Otto Lindenmeyer. "The Black Artist," *Reference Library of Black America,* Book IV, 1971; *The Negro Handbook,* Composed by Editors of *Ebony,* Chicago, 1966; "Views Finished Product," *Chicago Defender,* Feb. 20, 1932; "Negro Artists Paintings on Display at Univ. (Howard)," *East Tennessee News,* Knoxville, June 6, 1932; Schatz, Walter. *Directory of Afro-American Resources,* 1970; South Side Community Art Center. *National Negro Art Exhibition,* Chicago, 1941; Myers, Carol L. *Black Power in the Arts,* Flint, Mich., 1970; South Side Community Art Center. *Opening Exhibit of Paintings by Negro Artists,* Chicago, 1941; Spradling, Mary M., ed. *In Black & White: Afro-Americans in Print;* Robinson, Wilhelmina S. *Historical Negro Biographies,* p. 20; Porter. *Modern Negro Art;* "Mr. and Mrs. Frank C. Logan Medal to Motley for 'A Mulattress'," *Chicago Art Institute Bulletin,* XIX, March 1925, p. 36; "Joseph N. Eisendroth Prize to Motley for 'Syncopation'," *Chicago Art Institute Bulletin,* XIX, March 1925, p. 36; Mannes, Mary A. "Gallery Notes," *Creative Art,* II, April 1928; Jewell, Edward Aldari. "A Negro Artist Plumbs the Negro Soul," *New York Times Magazine,* March 25, 1928; "Octoroon Girl," *Art Digest,* III, mid-Jan. 1929, p. 6; *Chicago Art Institute Scrapbooks,* LVI (Jan. 1929-Nov. 1929), LV (Feb. 1928-Jan. 1929), LXXI (Oct. 1937-Aug. 1938); "Top Negro Artist Works in Factory Job," *Scrapbook of Art and Artists of Chicago,* 1956, p. 121; Harley, Ralph L., Jr. "A Checklist of Afro-American Art and Artists," *The Serif,* Dec. 1970; Assn. for the Study of Negro Life & History. *Exhibition of Works by Negro Artists,* 1933, Catalog; Baltimore Museum of Art. *Contemporary Negro,* 1939; Tanner Art Galleries. *Art of the American Negro,* 1940.

MUCK, JOSEPH

Painter.
Exhibited: Museum of Modern Art, 1943.
Sources: "Young Negro Art Impresses New York," *Art Digest,* Oct. 15, 1943.

MULZAC, HUGH

Sources: *A Star to Steer By,* An Autobiography, NY, 1960; Harley, Ralph, Jr. "Checklist of Afro-Amer. Art & Artists," *The Serif,* Dec. 1970.

MURRAY, GEORGE

Exhibited: Augusta Savage Studios, 1939.
Sources: Harley, Ralph, Jr. "Checklist of Afro-Amer. Art & Artists," *The Serif,* Dec. 1970.

MURRELL, SARA

Studied under Charles Alston; Henry Bannarn.

Exhibited: Harmon Foundation, 1936; Augusta Savage Studios, 1939.
Sources: Locke, Alain. "Advance on the Art Front," *Opportunity,* May 1939; Brawley, Benjamin. *The Negro Genius;* Harley, Ralph, Jr. "A Checklist of Afro-Amer. Art & Artists," *The Serif,* Dec. 1970; DuSable Museum of African-Amer. History. *Contemporary Black Artists,* 1970, Calendar.

MYLES, GLENN

Exhibited: Studio 1, Berkeley.
Sources: Studio 1. *6 Black Artists,* n.d.

MYLES, MILTON

Sources: Harley, Ralph, Jr. "Checklist of Afro-Amer. Art & Artists," *The Serif,* Dec. 1970.

NALL, GUS

Painter. Active in 1960's.
Sources: "Afro-American Issue," *Art Gallery,* April 1968; Indiana Univ. *Fine Arts & the Black American;* Myers, Carol. *Black Power in the Arts,* Flint, Mich., 1970; DuSable Museum of African-Amer. History. *Contemporary Black Artists,* 1970, Calendar; Walker, Roslyn. *A Resource Guide to the Visual Arts of Afro-Americans,* South Bend, Ind., 1971.

NASH, TEIXERA

Painter. Active in 1960's.
Sources: "Afro-American Issue," *Art Gallery,* April 1968; Indiana Univ. *Fine Arts & the Black American;* Myers, Carol. *Black Power in the Arts,* Flint, Mich., 1970; DuSable Museum of African-Amer. History. *Contemporary Black Artists,* 1970, Calendar; Walker, Roslyn. *A Resource Guide to the Visual Arts of Afro-Americans,* South Bend, Ind., 1971.

NEAL, CECIL

Works: *The Dilemma of Three Artists.*
Exhibited: Atlanta Univ., 1945.
Sources: Woodruff, Hale. "Negro Artists Hold Fourth Annual in Atlanta," *Art Digest,* April 15, 1945.

NEAL, FRANK

Painter, dancer. Studied at Art Institute of Chicago; and in Mexico. Founder, president & chief designer for Tray House.
Works: *Basket Carrier; Woman in White; Inspiration; Southern Express; Girl in Blue* (watercolor); *Opening Number* (watercolor); *One Hot Day* (watercolor); *Hat Makers; Departure; Young Man; Still Life; Jose; Idle Hour; Wash Women of Haiti; Despondent; White Church; The Cock Fight.*
Exhibited: Howard Univ., 1941, 1970; South Side Community Art Center, Chicago, 1941; Atlanta Univ., 1943; McMillen Inc. Galleries, NY, 1941; deYoung Museum, San Francisco,

1943 (1-man); Internat'l. Print Society, NY, 1943, 1944 (1-man); Albany Institute of History and Art, 1945.
Awards: 1st Prize, watercolor, Atlanta Univ., 1943.
Sources: South Side Community Art Center. *National Negro Art Exhibition,* Chicago, 1941; South Side Community Art Center. *Opening Exhibition of Paintings by Negro Artists,* Chicago, 1941; Howard Univ. *Exhibition of Negro Artists of Chicago at Howard Univ. Gallery of Art,* Feb. 1-25, 1941; Albany Institute of History and Art. *The Negro Artist Comes of Age,* 1945; Dover. *American Negro Art;* Indiana Univ. *Fine Arts & the Black American;* Howard Univ. *James A. Porter Gallery of African American Art,* 1970; *New York Times,* May 11, 1955; *Daily Worker,* July 6, 1958; "Art by Negroes," *Art Digest,* Oct. 15, 1941; Locke, Alain. "Chicago's New Southside Art Center," *American Magazine of Art,* Aug. 1941; "Negro Art Prizes," *Art News,* May 1, 1944; Harley, Ralph, Jr. "Checklist of Afro-American Art & Artists," *The Serif,* Dec. 1970; McMillen Inc. Galleries. *Contemporary Negro Art,* NY, 1941; Walker, Roslyn. *A Resource Guide to the Visual Arts of Afro-Americans,* South Bend, Ind., 1971.

NEAL, GEORGE

Painter. Lived in Chicago. Active in 1940's.
Works: *Portrait of Ann; After the Bath; Still Life* (watercolor); *The Hat* (watercolor); *The Mask; Across the Street.*
Exhibited: Howard Univ., 1941; South Side Community Art Center, Chicago, 1941.
Collections: William McBride, Jr.
Sources: *Exhibition of Negro Artists of Chicago at Howard Univ. Gallery of Art,* Feb. 1941; Roosevelt, Eleanor. "Negro Paintings at Howard Were Inspiring," in 'My Day' column, *Washington Daily News,* March 3, 1941; South Side Community Art Center. *National Negro Art Exhibition,* Chicago, 1941; Locke, Alain. "Chicago's New Southside Art Center," *Magazine of Art,* Aug. 1941, p. 320.

NEAL, GEORGE E.

Painter, educator. Born in Chicago in 1906. Died in Chicago in 1938.
Works: *The Red House; Young Girl in Pink Turban; Portrait.*
Exhibited: Amer. Negro Exhibition, 1940; Baltimore Museum, 1939; Howard Univ., 1941; South Side Community Art Center, Chicago, 1945.
Sources: Dover. *American Negro Art;* Indiana Univ. *Fine Arts & the Black American;* Tanner Art Galleries. *Art of the American Negro,* 1940; *Daily Worker,* July 6, 1958; Harley, Ralph, Jr. "A Checklist of Afro-Amer. Art &

Artists," *The Serif*, Dec. 1970; South Side Community Art Center. *Chicago Collectors Exhibit of Negro Art*, 1945; Walker, Roslyn. *A Resource Guide to the Visual Arts of Afro-Americans*, South Bend, Ind., 1971.

NEAL, HAROLD

Born in Duquesne, Pennsylvania in 1930. Studied at Carnegie-Mellon University.
Exhibited: Pittsburgh Plan for Art; Arts & Crafts Center; Carnegie Institute; Flowerhouse Gallery, Ohio; Ligonier Art Show; Pittsburgh Playhouse (1-man); Dayton Ohio Gallery; Art Gallery, Kaufmann's.
Sources: Pittsburgh Community College. *16 Black Artists*; Myers, Carol L. *Black Power in the Arts*, Flint, Mich., 1970.

NEAL, ROBERT L.

Painter. Born in Atlanta, 1916. Studied at Morehouse College; under Hale Woodruff.
Works: *Three Trees; Butterfly on a Skull; Southern Hills; Georgia Landscape; Hill Hand; Project Workers.*
Exhibited: Baltimore Museum of Art, 1939; Amer. Negro Exposition, Chicago, 1940; Dillard Univ., 1939, 1941; Tanner Art Galleries, 1940; Atlanta Univ., 1937; High Art Museum, Atlanta, 1939.
Awards: 2nd prize, Tri-County Exhibit, High Art Museum, 1939.
Sources: Baltimore Museum of Art. *Contemporary Negro*, 1939; Tanner Art Galleries. *Art of the American Negro*, 1940; Dillard Univ. *Arts Festival*, 1941; DuSable Museum of African-Amer. History. *Contemporary Black Artists*, 1970, Calendar; Harley, Ralph, Jr. "A Checklist of Afro-Amer. Art & Artists," *The Serif*, Dec. 1970; Albany Institute of History & Art. *The Negro Artist Comes of Age*; Locke. *The Negro in Art*; Walker, Roslyn. *A Resource Guide to the Visual Arts of Afro-Americans*, South Bend, Ind., 1971.

NEALS, OTTO

Sculptor, painter, photographer. Born in Lake City, South Carolina, December 11, 1931. Self-taught. Illustrator for US Government.
Works: *Great Expectations; Out of the Wilderness; Crocodile; Ancestry; A New Sun Will Rise.*
Exhibited: Studio Museum in Harlem, 1971; Brooklyn Museum, 1969; Howard Univ., 1971; Lincoln Univ., 1970; Marino Galleries, NYC, 1960; Yale Univ.; Clyde Mack Gallery; Countee Cullen Library; Weusi Nyumba Ya Sanaa, NY, 1972.
Collections: Former Zambian Ambassador to UN, Hon. J.W. Mulkita; Mrs. W.E.B. DuBois; Prime Minister Forbes Burnham, Guyana.
Represented by: Nyumba Ya Sanaa Gallery, 158 W. 132nd St., NYC.

Sources: Information from artist; *Ebony*, 1971; Mendes, Helen. *African Heritage Cookbook*, Macmillan, 1971; *Black Shades*, Feb. 1972; Jan. 1972.

NEALY, CHARLES

Ceramist.
Works: *Vase & Box.*
Collections: Nat'l Archives.
Sources: Afro-American Slide Depository, Catalog, 1971-2.

NED

Slave artist, carver.
Sources: Walker, Roslyn. *A Resource Guide to the Visual Arts of Afro-Americans*, South Bend, Ind., 1971; Rutledge, Anna Wells. "Ned, A Negro Woodcarver," *Transactions American Philosophical Society*, XXXIX, 1949, p. 144; Harley, Ralph, Jr. "Checklist of Afro-Amer. Art & Artists," *The Serif*, Dec. 1970; Dover. *American Negro Art.*

NEFERTITI

Graphic artist, mixed media.
Works: *Ecology III* (mixed media); *L'homme avec un livre* (linocut); *Metamorphosis* (oil); *The Merrygoround* (linocut); *Biafra* (pen & ink).
Exhibited: Boston Public Library, 1973.
Sources: Boston Negro Artists Assn. *10th Anniversary Exhibition*, Boston Public Library, 1973.

NELSON, CECIL D., JR.

Painter. Worked in Tuskegee, Alabama.
Works: *Green Corn and White Roofs; Tragedy in One Scene.*
Exhibited: Atlanta Univ., 1944.
Collections: Atlanta Univ.
Awards: John Hope Purchase Award for best landscape, Atlanta Univ., 1944.
Sources: "Negro Art Prizes," *Art News*, May 1, 1944, p. 7; Harley, Ralph, Jr. "Checklist of Afro-Amer. Art & Artists," *The Serif*, Dec. 1970.

NEWMAN, HERBERT

Sculptor.
Works: *Alligator; Crown in Confusion; Decayed Bull's Head; Hand's of Bird Wings.*
Exhibited: Xavier Univ., 1963.
Sources: Xavier Univ. *Emancipation Proclamation Centennial National Art Exhibition,* 1963.

NEWSOME, ROBERT

Sculptor. Born in Monmouth, Illinois on May 3, 1926. Studied at Monmouth College; Berkeley Evening School.
Works: *Hornblower.*
Exhibits: Oakland Museum, 1968; Oakland Museum Sculptor's Show, 1957; Berkeley Nat'l Audubon Society Convention, Sacramento, 1966; Harwood Anderson Gallery, Berkeley,

1965; Kaiser Center, 1967; Chabot College, Hayward, 1968; Bella Vista Elem. School, Oakland, 1968; Bay Area Afro-Amer. Art Exhibition, LINKS, Inc., 1968; Oakland Jr. College, 1968.
Awards: Blue Ribbon Award, sculpture, Berkeley Art Festival, 1960.
Sources: Oakland Museum. *New Perspectives in Black Art*; Indiana Univ. *Fine Arts & the Black American*; DuSable Museum of African-Amer. History. *Contemporary Black Artists*, 1970; Harley, Ralph, Jr. "Checklist of Afro-Amer. Art & Artists," *The Serif*, Dec. 1970; Walker, Roslyn. *A Resource Guide to the Visual Arts of Afro-Americans*, South Bend, Ind., 1971.

NICHOLS, GREGORY
Graphic artist. Studied at Shaw University.
Exhibited: Sun Times/Daily News Gallery, Chicago, 1970.
Sources: United Negro College Fund. *Art 1970*, Chicago, 1970.

NICHOLS, JOHN
Printmaker.
Works: *Message From Home; Margaret* (etching).
Collections: Mr. Benny Andrews.

NIXON, WILLIAM D.
Exhibited: Tanner Art League, 1922.
Sources: Harley, Ralph, Jr. "Checklist of Afro-Amer. Art & Artists," *The Serif*, Dec. 1970.

NJAROGE TAWA
See: Tawa, Njaroge.

NOEL, FREDERICK R.
Painter. Studied at Glassboro State College; Columbia University (MA); Escuela des Artes Plasticas, Guadalajara, Mexico; Academie de la Grande Chaumiere Paris, France.
Exhibited: Teachers Union Gallery, 1962 (1-man); Inwood Heights, 1964 (1-man); Young Adult Institute, 1965 (1-man); Riverside Drive Park, 1967.
Sources: "Frederick R. Noel: Exhibition of Oil Paintings & Drawings," Jan. 26, 1968.

NOISETTE, WILLIAM S.
Exhibited: Phyllis Wheatley YMCA, Washington, DC, 1935.
Sources: "Second Exhibit of Noisette's Paintings Opens on 28th," *Afro-Amer.*, Oct. 26, 1935; "Painting in One Man Display," *Norfolk Journal & Guide*, Nov. 9, 1935; Harley, Ralph, Jr. "Checklist of Afro-Amer. Art & Artists," *The Serif*, Dec. 1970.

NOMMO, ISAAC
Painter. Born 1940 in Atlanta, Texas. Self-taught.

Works: *Allah U Akbar*.
Exhibitions: Albina Art Center, 1969; Portland State Univ., 1970; The Bush House Museum of Art, Salem, 1970; The More Bookstore, San Francisco, 1967; Portland Art Museum, 1970.
Collections: Mr. & Mrs. J. Rand; Mr. Steve Allen; Albina Art Center; Portland State Univ.
Sources: Lewis/Waddy. *Black Artists on Art*, Vol. 2.

NORMAN, MABEL
Studied at Oakwood College.
Exhibited: Sun Times/Daily News Gallery, Chicago, 1970.
Sources: United Negro College Fund. *Art 1970*, Chicago, 1970.

NORWOOD, TONY
Graphic artist.
Works: *Elephant* (serigraph).
Exhibited: Lee Cultural Center, Phila.
Sources: Phila. Dept. of Recreation. *Love . . . and the Black Community*.

NTIRO, SAM J.
Painter.
Works: *Carrying Poles; Chagga Home; Clearing Building Site; Maize Harvest*.
Collections: Chase Manhattan Bank, NY.

NUGENT, RICHARD BRUCE
Illustrator, writer, actor. Born in Washington.
Works: Illustrations for THE NEW NEGRO, EBONY, TOPAZ; *Gabun Head*.
Exhibited: Harmon Foundation, 1931, 1936.
Collections: Nat'l Archives.
Sources: Harmon Foundation. *Exhibition of Productions by Negro Artists*; Harmon Foundation. *Negro Artists*, 1935; Indiana Univ. *Fine Arts & the Black American*; Afro-American Slide Depository, Catalog, 1971-2; DuSable Museum of Afro-Amer. History. *Contemporary Black Artists*, 1970 Calendar; Harley, Ralph, Jr. "A Checklist of Afro-Amer. Art & Artists," *The Serif*, Dec. 1970; Walker, Roslyn. *A Resource Guide to the Visual Arts of Afro-Americans*, South Bend, Ind., 1971.

OFFORD, CARL
Painter, novelist.
Exhibited: Roko Gallery, 1928.
Sources: E.K. "Negro Artists," *Art News*, Feb. 1949, p. 47.

OGELSBY, ALLISON
Painter. Born in Atlanta, Georgia in 1905. Studied at Detroit School of Fine Arts.
Works: *The Poor Shall Never Cease; Contrast; Picknicking; Return from the Night Shift; The Bread Line; Conducting the Orchestra; Gang Warfare; Self-Portrait*.
Exhibited: Harmon Foundation, 1930-1, 1933; Michigan State Fair, 1928, 1932; Pen & Palette,

Detroit, 1929-32; Detroit Institute of Art, 1930; Smithsonian Institution, 1930; John Reed Club, 1933; Atlanta Univ., 1942, 1944; Texas Centennial Exposition, 1936.
Collections: Nat'l Archives.
Sources: Indiana Univ. *Fine Arts & the Black American*; Harmon Foundation. *Exhibition of Productions by Negro Artists*; Harmon Foundation. *Exhibit of Fine Arts*, 1930; Harmon Foundation. *Negro Artists*, 1935; Harley, Ralph, Jr. "A Checklist of Afro-Amer. Art & Artists," *The Serif*, Dec. 1970; Afro-American Slide Depository, catalog; Texas Centennial Exposition. *Thumbnail Sketches of Exhibiting Artists*, 1936; Harmon Foundation. *Non-Jury Exhibit of Works of Negro Artists*, 1933; DuSable Museum of African-Amer. History. *Contemporary Black Artists*, 1970, Calendar; Walker, Roslyn. *A Resource Guide to the Visual Arts of Afro-Americans*, South Bend, Ind., 1971.

OGUNJAMI, SUSANNE

Painter. Born in Nigeria, Africa, member of the Ebo tribe. Studied in Jamaica, West Indies; Columbia University Teachers College (BS, 1927; MA, 1928).
Works: *Full Bloom Magnolia.*
Exhibited: Nat'l Archives; Harmon Foundation, 1928; NY State Museum, 1935; Delphic Studio, NY, 1935 (1-woman).
Sources: Harmon Foundation. *Select Picture List*; Harmon Foundation. *Negro Artists*, 1935; Afro-American Slide Depository, catalog; DuSable Museum of African-Amer. History. *Contemporary Black Artists*, 1970, Calendar.

OLDEN, GEORGE

Graphic artist. Born 1921. Graphic Arts Director for CBS Television Network; director of his own studios in New York City.
Works: *Emancipation Proclamation* postage stamp.
Sources: *Ebony*, Nov. 1960, pp. 79-85; *Jet*, Aug. 17, 1967, p. 11; Pierre-Noel, Lois Jones. "American Negro Art in Progress," *Negro History Bulletin*, Oct. 1967; Spradling, Mary M., ed. *In Black & White: Afro-Americans in Print*, 1971.

OLDS, ELIZABETH

Collections: NY Public Library-Schomburg Art Collection.
Sources: Schatz, Walter. *Directory of Afro-American Resources*, 1970.

OLIVER, LYN

Painter.
Works: *Mother & Child* (pastel); *The Hunter* (pastel); *Chief* (pastel); *Monkey Man* (pastel).
Exhibited: Boston Public Library, 1973.
Sources: Boston Negro Artists Assn. *10th Anniversary Exhibition*, Boston Public Library, 1973.

OLNEY, DANIEL

Sources: "Frieze Shows Progress of Race," *Washington Star*, Oct. 11, 1936; Harley, Ralph, Jr. "Checklist of Afro-Amer. Art & Artists," *The Serif*, Dec. 1970.

OLUGEBEFOLA, ADEMOLA

Painter, graphic artist, mixed media, designer. Born in St. Thomas, Virgin Islands, October 2, 1941. Studied at Nyumba Ya Sanaa Academy of Arts and Studies.
Works: *Manifestation; The Coming of Allah; Evolution; The Prophecy; Orionic Etchings; Burden of Injustice; Black Family; Africa; Emerging Spirit; Unity Chant; Untitled; Olori My Son.*
Exhibited: Nyumba Ya Sanaa, 1970; Pamoja Gallery, NYC; Malcolm X, 1969; Harlem Gallery, 1969 (1-man); Brooklyn Museum, 1969; Malikah Gallery, 1966; 22 West, 1965; Bestu Gallery, 1964-5; Karibu Galleries, 1965-6; Pyramid Galleries, 1968-9; Uptown Gallery, 1969; Clyde Mack Gallery, 1967; Studio Museum in Harlem, 1970-1; Corcoran Gallery, Washington, DC; Bowery Bank, 1966; NY Bank for Savings, 1967; Carver Federal Savings, 1970; Visual Art Gallery, 1970; Countee Cullen Gallery; Acts of Art Gallery, 1971; Burpee Art Gallery, Rockford, Ill.; Quincy (Ill.) Art Club; Peoria (Ill.) Art Guild; Sloan Galleries of Amer. Painting, Valparaiso, Ill.; Ill. State Museum, Springfield; Afro-Arts Gallery, White Plains, NY; James Weldon Johnson Theatre Center, NY, 1969; Lincoln Improvement Center, 1966; Omo Ife Festival, 1969; Rockland Palace; NY Hilton Hotel; Internat'l House, 1969; African-Amer. Festival, 1970; Professional Negro Businesswomen Assn., 1969; Woodstock Hotel, 1966; Truth Coffee Shop Gallery; Univ. of Iowa, 1971-2; Harlem Outdoor Art Festival, 1964-72; Bul Arts Festival, 1965; Winston Salem State Univ., 1970; NY Institute of Technology, 1969; Univ. of Pittsburgh, 1971; Lincoln Univ., Pa., 1969; Bronx Community College, 1969; Boston Univ., 1970; Hartford Univ., 1970; Amer. Internat'l College, 1970; Urban Center, NY, 1970; Ill. Univ., 1971; Store Front Museum, Queens, NY, 1972.
Collections: Afro-Arts Cultural Center, Northern Ill. Univ.; Bennett College.
Awards: 1st prize, Harlem Outdoor Festival; 3rd prize, graphics, Westchester Show.
Member: Smithsonian Institution; St. Croix Arts Council; Studio Museum; Harlem Cultural Council.
Represented by: Nyumba Ya Sanaa Gallery; Acts of Art Gallery; Osiris Enterprises, Chicago.

Sources: Information from artist; Illinois Bell Telephone. *Black American Artists/71*, 1972; Greene, Carroll, Jr. "Perspective: The Black Artist in America," *Art Gallery*, April 1970, p. 14; Rose, Barbara. "Black Art in America," *Art in America*, July/Dec. 1970; Harley, Ralph, Jr. "Checklist of Afro-Amer. Art & Artists," *Serif*, Dec. 1970; Atkinson, J. Edward. *Black Dimensions in Contemporary American Art*, NY, 1971; Haas, Joseph. "A Big, Brilliant & Exciting Exhibition of Black Art," *Chicago Daily News*, Jan. 16-7, 1971; *Black Shades*, Oct. 1972; *Liberator Magazine*, March 1965; *National College Board Review*, Spring 1969; *National Magazine,* Sept. 1969; Fuja, Abayomi, Comp. *Fourteen Hundred Cowries & Other Tales From Africa*, William Morrow, 1971, Illustrator; *We A Baddd People & It's A New Day*, Detroit, Broadside Press; Walker, Roslyn. *A Resource Guide to the Visual Arts of Afro-Americans*, South Bend, Ind., 1971.

OMARIAMA

Graphic artist. Born in Halls, Tennessee.
Works: *Black Jesus; Unite or Perish.*
Exhibited: Nat'l Center of Afro-Amer. Artists, 1970.
Sources: Grillo, Jean B. "Where Down Home Meets Back Home," *Boston After Dark*, Sept. 1970.

O'NEAL, KENNETH RODERICK

Painter. Born in Missouri, July 30, 1908. Studied at the University of Iowa.
Works: *A Lake; A Portrait of a Child.*
Exhibited: Harmon Foundation, 1933; Iowa Memorial Union, Iowa City, 1929-30.
Collections: Nat'l Archives.
Sources: Harmon Foundation. *Non-Jury Exhibit of Works of Negro Artists*, 1933; Afro-Amer. Slide Depository, Catalog, 1971-2; Harmon Foundation. *Negro Artists*, 1935; Furr, Arthur F. *History & Progress of Negroes in the US;* Harley, Ralph, Jr. "A Checklist of Afro-Amer. Art & Artists," *The Serif*, Dec. 1970; Indiana Univ. *Fine Arts & the Black American;* DuSable Museum of African-Amer. History. *Contemporary Black Artists*, 1970, Calendar; Walker, Roslyn. *A Resource Guide to the Visual Arts of Afro-Americans,* South Bend, Ind., 1971.

OSBORN, JOHN P.

Painter. Born in Toronto, Canada. Self-taught.
Works: *Emerging Masses; The Eyes of the Soul.*
Exhibited: Studio Museum in Harlem, 1969.
Sources: Studio Museum in Harlem. *Harlem Artists 69.*

OSBORNE, CHARLES H.

Painter. Born in Savannah in 1875. Studied at the Boston Art Club; Eric Pape School.
Works: *A Market in the West Indies; Concentration.*
Exhibited: Atlanta Univ., 1944; Harmon Foundation, 1933.
Sources: Harmon Foundation. *Non-Jury Exhibit of Works of Negroes*, 1933; Harley, Ralph, Jr. "Checklist of Afro-Amer. Art & Artists," *Serif*, Dec. 1970; Walker, Roslyn. *A Resource Guide to the Visual Arts of Afro-Americans,* South Bend, Ind., 1971; "Our Young Negro Artists," *Opportunity,* Jan. 1923; Holbrook, Francis C. "A Group of Negro Artists," *Opportunity,* July 1923, p. 211.

OSIFO, PAUL O.

Sources: DuSable Museum of African-Amer. History. *Contemporary Black Artists, 1970,* Calendar.

OUBRÉ, HAYWARD L.

Sculptor, painter, printmaker, educator. Born in New Orleans, Louisiana. Studied at Dillard University (BA); University of Iowa (MFA). Chairman of Art Department at Winston-Salem State College.
Works: *Conflict; Manikins; Roof Top Virtuoso; Crescendo; Prodigal Son; Pensive Family; Above the City; You Are Cannon Fodder; Self Portrait; Young Horse; Mother & Child; Ram; Prophet; Lunar Robot; Wilted; Within These Portals; A Day's Harvest; Transition; Oubre Series; Equilibrium; Fragmented Profiles; Space Rhythm; Atomic Energy; Enigmatic Countenance; Verily I Say Unto You; Crown of Thorns.*
Exhibited: Walker Art Center, Minneapolis; John & Mable Ringling Museum, Sarasota, Fla.; Northwest Printmakers Exhibit, Seattle; Isaac Delgado Museum, New Orleans; Art Directions Gallery; Carver Museum; Tuskegee Institute; Xavier Univ., 1963.
Awards: Honorable Mention, Atlanta Univ.'s 10th Annual for Negro Artists, 1951.
Sources: Pierre-Noel, Lois Jones. "American Negro Art in Progress," *Negro History Bulletin,* Oct. 1967; Kiah, Virginia. "Black Artists," *Savannah Magazine,* April 1972, p. 16; Xavier Univ. *Emancipation Proclamation Centennial National Art Exhibition,* 1963; Harley, Ralph, Jr. "A Checklist of Afro-Amer. Art & Artists," *The Serif,* Dec. 1970; Bearden, Romare. "The Negro Artist & Modern Art," *Opportunity,* Dec. 1934; Patterson, Lindsay. "Contemporary Artists," *The Negro in Music & Art,* 1969; *The Negro Handbook,* Composed by Editors of *Ebony,* Chicago, 1966; DuSable Museum of African-Amer. History. *Contemporary Black Artists,* 1970, Calendar; Afro-American Slide Depository, catalog; Dover.

213

American Negro Art; Lewis/Waddy. *Black Artists on Art*; Walker Art Center. *A New Direction in Intaglio*; *Design Magazine*, 1962, 1968; Indiana Univ. *Fine Arts & the Black American*; Myers, Carol. *Black Power in the Arts*, Flint, Mich., 1970; Walker, Roslyn. *A Resource Guide to the Visual Arts of Afro-Americans*, South Bend, Ind., 1971.

OUTLAW, SIMON
Works: *Planes in Black and White.*
Sources: Patterson, Lindsay. "Contemporary Artists," *The Negro in Music and Art,* 1969.

OUTTERBRIDGE, JAMES
Sculptor.
Works: *East Side, West Side* (metal collage).
Collections: Oakland Museum.
Sources: Oakland Museum Archives.

OUTTERBRIDGE, JOHN WILFRED
Sculptor, photographer, painter. Born in Greenville, North Carolina, 1933. Studied at American Academy of Art, Chicago; Chicago Art Academy; Art Center School of Design, Los Angeles; Agricultural and Technical University, Greensboro, North Carolina. Teacher at California State College; Pasadena Art Museum; Pasadena Museum of Art Summer Workshops.
Works: *Mogo Ghetto; Reclining Figure; Birth Process; No Time for Jiving; The Great American Eagle; Containment Series: Let Us Tie Down the Loose Ends; Mood Ghetto; The Old Folks.*
Exhibited: Long Beach Museum; Watts Festival of Arts Annual; Brockman Gallery, Los Angeles (1-man); San José State College; Univ. of Cal., Los Angeles; Ankrum Gallery, Los Angeles; Gallery 32, Los Angeles; Pasadena Artists Assn.; Westwood Art Assn.; La Jolla Museum of Art, 1970; Galeria Del Sole; Oakland Museum; Mills College, Oakland; Rainbow Sign Gallery, Berkeley, 1972.
Awards: 2nd prize, Pasadena Artists Assn., 1967; Best in Show & 1st prize, contemporary sculpture, Westwood Art Assn.
Member: Black Artists Assn., Los Angeles; Black Arts Council, Los Angeles.
Sources: Lewis/Waddy. *Black Artists on Art,* Vol. 1; Mills College. *California Black Craftsmen,* 1970; La Jolla Museum of Art. *Dimensions of Black*; Atkinson, J. Edward. *Black Dimensions in Contemporary American Art,* NY, 1971; Outterbridge, John Wilfred. Film on the Pasadena Paint In; Rainbow Sign Gallery. *Black Arts Day II,* Press Release, Berkeley, 1972; *Time,* April 6, 1970; Walker, Roslyn. *A Resource Guide to the Visual Arts of Afro-Americans,* South Bend, Ind., 1971.

OVERR, CARL
Sources: Harley, Ralph, Jr. "Checklist of Afro-Amer. Art & Artists," *The Serif,* Dec. 1970.

OVERSTREET, JOSEPH
Painter. Born in Conehatta, Mississippi in 1934. Studied at California School of Arts and Crafts; University of California (BFA).
Works: *Jazz in 4/4 Time; Keep on Keeping On; Alpha & Omega; Ungawa-Black Power; Crawling; Benin Triptych; Three; He & She; Ancestral Tomb for Mr. White; Music.*
Exhibited: Boston Museum of Fine Arts, 1970; Brooklyn Museum, 1969; Univ. of Iowa, 1971-2; Newark Museum, 1971; Studio Museum in Harlem, 1971, 1969; Columbia Univ., 1969; Ill. Bell Telephone.
Collections: Studio Museum in Harlem, NY; Chase Manhattan Bank, NY.
Sources: Brooklyn Museum. *New Black Artists,* 1969; Newark Museum. *Black Artists: Two Generations,* 1971; Boston Museum of Fine Arts. *Afro-American Artists: NY & Boston,* 1970; Ill. Bell Telephone. *Black American Artists/71,* 1972; Studio Museum in Harlem. *Ben Jones & Joe Overstreet,* 1971; Studio Museum in Harlem. *Harlem Artists 69;* Bowling, Frank. "The Rupture," *Arts,* Summer 1970; Rose, Barbara. "Black Art in America," *Art in America,* July/Dec. 1970; Reed, Ishmael. "The Black Artist: Calling a Spade a Spade," *Arts,* May 1967; Sherman, Marjorie. "Afro-America Gets Biggest Show," *Boston Globe,* May 18, 1970; "Museum of Fine Arts to Hold Black Art Show," *Chronicle,* Ipswich, Mass., April 30, 1970; "Afro-American Artists: NY & Boston," *Prudential Center News,* March 1, 1970, p. 4; "Museum of Fine Arts to Hold Black Art Show," *Tri-Town Transcript & Pennysaver,* April 29, 1970; Brown, Marion. "The Negro in Fine Arts," *The Negro Heritage Library,* Vol. 2; Walsh, Rose. "Artists to Meet Public at Art Exhibit Preview," *Record American,* May 19, 1970; Ploski, Harry, & Ernest Kaiser. "The Black Artist," *Afro USA,* 1971; Ploski, Harry, Ernest Kaiser, & Otto Lindenmeyer. "The Black Artist," *Reference Library of Black America,* Book IV, 1971; "San Francisco," *Artforum,* Dec. 1970, p. 85; Fine, Elsa H. "Mainstream, Blackstream & the Black Art Movement," *Art Journal,* Spring 1971; "Museum of Fine Arts to Hold Black Art Show," *Chronicle,* Belmont, Mass., April 28, 1970; Walker, Roslyn. *A Resource Guide to the Visual Arts of Afro-Americans,* South Bend, Ind., 1971.

OWENS, MAUDE IRWIN
Painter, illustrator. Born in 1900. Studied at Philadelphia Graphic Sketch Club.
Works: *Fusion; Girl with Russian Doll; Il-*

lustrations for CRISIS; Fresco for Polish Catholic Church, Phila.
Exhibited: Harmon Foundation, 1929-30; Smithsonian Institution, 1929.
Collections: Nat'l Archives; Polish Catholic Church, Phila.
Sources: Harmon Foundation. *Exhibition of Productions by Negro Artists;* Harmon Foundation. *Negro Artists,* 1935; Harmon Foundation. *Exhibit of Fine Arts,* 1930; Indiana Univ. *Fine Arts & the Black American;* DuSable Museum of African-Amer. History. *Contemporary Black Artists,* 1970, Calendar; Smithsonian Institution. *Painting & Sculpture by American Negro Artists,* 1929; Harley, Ralph, Jr. "A Checklist of Afro-Amer. Art & Artists," *The Serif,* Dec. 1970; Walker, Roslyn. *A Resource Guide to the Visual Arts of Afro-Americans,* South Bend, Ind., 1971.

PADGETT, JAMES
Painter. Studied at Howard University.
Exhibited: Howard Univ. (thesis show), 1972.
Sources: *Black Shades,* Mar. 1972.

PAIGE, ALVIN
Painter, sculptor. Born in 1934.
Works: *Man Symbol Machine;* untitled white styrofoam figure; *The Ring; Dandelion; Money Screen.*
Exhibited: Canadian Pavilion, Expo '67; Royal Crown Cola Display, Moscow Trade Fair.
Collections: Mr. Melvin Belli; Dr. Paul P. Gregory; the late Nat King Cole; Saratoga Springs Gallery.
Sources: *Ebony,* Jan. 1969, pp. 72-7; Spradling, Mary M., ed. *In Black & White: Afro-Americans in Print;* Paige, Alvin. *Money;* Paige, Alvin. *Why.*

PAJAUD, WILLIAM E.
Painter, printmaker. Born in New Orleans on August 3, 1925. Studied at Chouinard Art Institute, Los Angeles; Xavier University (BA).
Works: *Collards; Hustlin' the Hustler; After Hours Club; After the Party* (lithograph); *Derby Hat; Family Circle; Friday Afternoon* (lithograph); *O.C.'s Honey* (lithograph); *Wash Day* (lithograph); *I'll Be a Woman Tomorrow* (lithograph); *Main Street Mission* (lithograph).
Exhibited: Los Angeles County Art Museum; Crocker Gallery, Sacramento, Cal.; deYoung Museum, San Francisco; Esther Robles Gallery, Los Angeles (1-man); Univ. of Iowa, 1972; Pasadena Art Museum; Orange County Art Exhibit; Los Angeles County Art Exhibit; Atlanta Univ.; Wisconsin Univ.; Claremont Colleges; Chapman College; City College of Los Angeles; Cal. Watercolor Society; Joseph Massa Gallery (1-man); Emerson Gallery (1-man); Heritage Gallery (1-man).
Collections: Atlanta Univ.; Amer. Artists

Group; Mr. Norton Simon; Mr. Norman O. Houston; Mr. Harry Karl; Mr. Sammy Cahn; Mr. George A. Beavers, Jr.; Mr. William Goldberg; Mrs. Arthur Bernstein; Mr. T.M. Doheny; Mr. Charles C. Coiner; Mr. James Bellows; Dr. Richard Simms.
Awards: Atlanta Univ. Annual; Westside Jewish Community Center Annual; Chrysler Scholarship, Chouinard Art Institute.
Member: Society of Graphic Designers; Cal. Watercolor Society; Los Angeles Art Assn.
Represented by: Heritage Gallery, Los Angeles.
Sources: Lewis/Waddy. *Black Artists on Art,* Vol. 1; Illinois Bell Telephone. *Black American Artists/71;* Atkinson, J. Edward. *Black Dimensions in Contemporary American Art,* NY, 1971; San José State College. *Black Arts Today,* Mar. 1972; Haas, Joseph. "A Big Brilliant & Exciting Exhibition of Black Art," *Chicago Daily News,* Jan. 16-17, 1971; Pajaud, William. *My People,* portfolio of lithographs, Los Angeles, Heritage Gallery, 1970; Walker, Roslyn. *A Resource Guide to the Visual Arts of Afro-Americans,* South Bend, Ind., 1971.

PALM, DENISE
Painter. Born 1951 in Philadelphia. Studied at El Camino Junior College, Los Angeles.
Works: *Struggle; Three Asses.*
Exhibitions: Chicago West Gallery, 1970.
Sources: Lewis/Waddy. *Black Artists on Art,* Vol. 2.

PALMER, WILLIAM
Born in Pulaski, Tennessee in 1936. Studied at the Art Institute of Pittsburgh.
Exhibited: Greece.
Sources: Pittsburgh Community College. *16 Black Artists.*

PANKEY, AUBREY
Painter, composer, singer. Born in Pittsburgh.
Sources: Dover. *American Negro Art;* Indiana Univ. *Fine Arts & the Black American.*

PAPPAS, JAMES G.
Painter. Born 1937. Studied at State University of New York at Buffalo; Albright Art School in Buffalo. Teacher at the State University of New York at Buffalo; Chairman, Cultural Section, Model Cities Program in Buffalo.
Works: *Inner and Outer Forms; Untitled; Eastern Impressions.*
Exhibitions: Unitarian Universalist Church, Erie, Pa.; Pan-African Writers Conference, State Univ. of NY, Buffalo; 6 from the City, Buffalo.
Awards: Shirley Lindsey Curr Award, Rochester, NY; Univ. of Buffalo Foundation Award.
Sources: NY State Education Department. *Fifteen under Forty.*

PARENZUELA, C.M.
Collections: NY Public Library-Schomburg Art Collection.
Sources: Schatz, Walter. *Directory of Afro-American Resources,* 1970.

PARHAM, ALONZO
Sources: DuSable Museum of African-American History. *Contemporary Black Artists,* Calendar, 1970.

PARHAM, HILTON L. JR.
Painter, illustrator. Born in Medford, Massachusetts in 1930. Studied at Vesper George School of Art, 1956-59.
Works: *Peaceful,* 1968 (oil & acrylics); *Let It Burn,* 1970 (oil & acrylics); *Winter Scene,* 1968 (oil); *The Fishermen,* 1960 (pen & ink); *Winter Farm;* Untitled illustration.
Exhibited: Holiday Inn, Cambridge, Mass., 1968; Museum of Science, Boston, 1970, 1972; Internat'l Fair, Boston, 1971, 1972; Boston Negro Artists Assn., 1971, 1972; Boston Public Library, 1973.
Awards: Museum of Science Merit Award, multi-colored pictorial art, 1970, 1972.
Member: Boston Negro Artists Assn.
Represented by: Boston Negro Artists Assn.
Sources: Information from artist; Boston Negro Artists Assn. Calendar, 1973; Boston Negro Artists Assn. *10th Anniversary Exhibition,* Boston Public Library, 1973; Boston Negro Artists Assn. *The Black Artist in America: A Negro History Month Exhibition,* Boston Public Library, 1973.

PARISH, NORMAN
Sources: DuSable Museum of African-American History, *Contemporary Black Artists,* Calendar, 1970.

PARK, MARGO
Sources: "Evelyn Ambrosine Romney by Margo Park," *New York Herald,* April 29, 1923; Harley, Ralph, Jr. "Checklist of Afro-Amer. Art & Artists," *The Serif,* Dec. 1970.

PARKER, ABRAHAM
Studied at Lemoyne-Owen College.
Works: *Memphis-Arkansas Bridge.*
Exhibited: Sun Times/Daily News Gallery, Chicago, 1970.
Sources: United Negro College Fund. *Art 1970,* Chicago, 1970.

PARKER, LEROY
Graphic artist.
Works: Untitled (pencil).
Collections: Oakland Museum.
Sources: Oakland Museum Archives.

PARKER, WARREN
Painter.

Works: *J.C.; Under Bama Skies; Untitled; Sophia III; Miles; Corner of an Atelier; Frenzy; Singer N'Things; Yusef; Richie; Up Against the Wall; Leroi; Self Portrait; Sophia II; Sophia I.*
Sources: Afro-Amer. Slide Depository, Catalog.

PARKS, CHRISTOPHER
Works: *Uptown.*
Awards: 1st prize, Del. Art Museum; 1st prize, Academy Artists League; Helen Foster Barnett Prize, Pa. Academy of Fine Arts; Allied Artists of America Award; Samuel F. Breese Morse Medal, Nat'l Academy of Design.
Sources: *Artists/USA,* 1972-3, Feasterville, Pa., 1972, p. 144.

PARKS, GORDON
Photographer, illustrator, author. Born in Kansas, November 30, 1912. Two year assignment with *Life & Time,* 1950-2.
Works: *Photography.*
Collections: Museum of Modern Art, NYC; Metropolitan Museum, NYC.
Member: NY Newspaper Guild.
Sources: Indiana Univ. *Fine Arts & the Black American;* Afro-Amer. Slide Depository, Catalog, 1971-2; Furr, Arthur. *History & Progress of Negroes in the US;* Rockford (Ill.) College. *Creativity and the Negro;* Boning, Richard A. *Profiles of Black Americans,* NY, 1969; Morsbach, Mabel. *The Negro in American Life;* Schatz, Walter. *Directory of Afro-American Resources,* 1970; Adams, Russell. *Great Negroes Past & Present,* 1969; Robinson, Wilhelmena S. *Historical Negro Biographies,* p. 243; *Ebony,* July 1946, p. 25; *Negro Digest,* Jan. 1944, pp. 41-2; *Parade,* June 23, 1968; Spradling, Mary M., ed. *In Black & White: Afro-Americans in Print; Gordon Parks: A Poet and his Camera,* NY, Viking Press, 1968; *Gordon Parks, W. Eugene Smith, John Szarkowski & Walter Rosenblum in a Symposium Speaking Out on "Photographic Style,"* April 1, 1963, New School for Social Research, NY; Parks, Gordon. *Whispers of Intimate Things,* NY, Viking Press, 1971; Parks, Gordon. *Born Black,* Lippincott, 1971, Illustrator; Parks, Gordon. *Choice of Weapons,* Harper-Row, 1966; Parks, Gordon. *In Love,* Lippincott, 1971, Illustrator; Parks, Gordon. *Learning Tree,* Harper-Row, 1963; Walker, Roslyn. *A Resource Guide to the Visual Arts of Afro-Americans,* South Bend, Ind., 1971.

PARKS, JAMES DALLAS
Painter, printmaker, sculptor, educator. Born in St. Louis, Missouri, August 25, 1907. Studied at Bradley University (BS); University of Iowa (MA, 1943); under Philip Guston and Jean Charlot. Head of Art Department, Lin-

coln University, Jefferson City, Missouri. Co-founder of the National Conference of Artists; National chairman, 1961-2.
Works: *Vision of Early Presidents of Lincoln University,* 1951 (oil mural panel); *Artists Model,* 1958; *Reveries; The Knockout* (lithograph); *Dilemma* (oil); *View over Monterrey, Mexico; Still Life of Mug and Old Shoe; Portrait of Florence; Reveries in a Beer Tavern; Portrait of a Brown Girl; Portrait of a Mulatto Girl; Still Life, Wine Jug and Book; Autumn Scene; Westphalia, Mo.; A Glass of Wine and You; Old Church, Mexico City; The Artist's Wife; Missouri Village; Old Mill; Mask & A Matisse.*
Exhibited: Harmon Foundation, 1929; St. Louis Museum, 1946; Atlanta Univ., 1944-6, 1957-8; Missouri State Fair, 1946, 1928; Kansas City Museum, 1950; WVa. State, 1959 (1-man); Savannah State, 1967 (1-man); Tuskegee Institute, 1967 (1-man); Alabama State, 1966 (1-man); Lincoln Univ. (1-man); Joslyn Museum, Omaha, Neb.; St. Louis Central Library, 1928-31; Langston Univ., 1932; Xaxier Univ., 1963; Howard Univ., 1961.
Collections: Howard Univ.; Atlanta Univ.; Texas Southern Univ.; Lincoln Univ. (mural); Dunbar School, Kansas City; Springfield (Mo.) Art Museum; Univ. of Iowa (thesis collection).
Awards: 2nd prize, painting, 1st prize, sculpture, Mo. State Fair, 1945; Honorable Mention, Atlanta Univ., 1944; 1st prize, watercolor, Nat'l Conference of Artists, 1964, 1965; Honorable Mention, oil, Nat'l Conference of Artists, 1969; Honorable Mention, lithograph, Kansas City Art Institute, 1943.
Member: Nat'l Conference of Artists; College Art Assn. of America; Missouri College Art Education Assn.
Sources: Dover. *American Negro Art;* Patterson, Lindsay, comp. *Negro in Music and Art;* Atkinson, J. Edward. *Black Dimensions in Contemporary American Art,* 1971; *Encyclopedia of Black America,* McGraw Hill; *Who's Who in the Mid-West; International Blue Book;* "Afro-American Issue," *Art Gallery,* April 1968; Indiana Univ. *Fine Arts & the Black American;* Lewis/Waddy. *Black Artists on Art,* Vol. 1; Information from artist; Harmon Foundation. *Non-Jury Exhibit of Works of Negro Artists,* 1933; Afro-Amer. Slide Depository, Catalog, 1971-2; DuSable Museum of African-Amer. History. *Contemporary Black Artists,* 1970, Calendar; Pierre-Noel, Lois Jones. "American Negro Art in Progress," *Negro History Bulletin,* Oct. 1967; *National Conference of Artists,* Winter 1971, Journal; Xavier Univ. *Emancipation Proclamation Centennial National Art Exhibition;* Harley, Ralph, Jr. "Checklist of Afro-Amer. Art & Artists," *Serif,* Dec. 1970; *Art Gallery,* April 1970; Myers, Carol

L. *Black Power in the Arts,* Flint, Mich., 1970; Walker, Roslyn. *A Resource Guide to the Visual Arts of Afro-Americans,* South Bend, Ind., 1971.

PARKS, LOUISE ADELE
Painter, mixed media. Born July 5, 1945. Studied at Pratt Institute (BFA); Hunter College, New York City.
Works: *Tapestry #3; Tapestry #4.*
Exhibited: Hunter College, NYC, 1969; Bowdoin College, Brunswick, Me., 1970; Cinque Gallery, NYC (1-woman); Franklin & Marshall College, Lancaster, Pa., 1970 (1-woman); Boston Museum of Fine Arts, 1970.
Sources: NY State Education Dept. *Fifteen Under Forty;* Boston Museum of Fine Arts. *Afro-American Artists: NY & Boston,* 1970; Le Brun, Caron. "Blacks' Art on Display," *Herald Traveler,* Boston, May 26, 1970; Schwartz, Therese. "The Political Scene," *Arts,* April 1971.

PARKS, LUCILLE G.
Painter, educator. Born in Buffalo, New York, June 30, 1924. Studied at Springfield College, Massachusetts; self-taught artist.
Works: *Confrontation,* 1972 (oil); *Biafra,* 1970 (watercolor); *Woman,* 1971 (oil); *Grant Us Lord,* 1971 (oil); *Toadstools,* 1972 (oil); *Seascape,* 1970 (oil); *Joy* (oil); *Mis'ry,* 1971 (oil); *Seabreeze,* 1973 (oil); *Waterfall,* 1970 (oil).
Exhibited: Cinema 3, Springfield, Mass., 1971; Stage West Theater, Springfield, Mass., 1972; NH College, 1972; Amer. Internat'l College, Springfield, Mass., 1972; Afro-Art Alliance exhibits, 1972.
Member: Afro-Art Alliance, Springfield, Mass.
Sources: Information from artist.

PARKS, SAMUEL DALLAS
Exhibited: Atlanta Univ., 1944.
Sources: Harley, Ralph, Jr. "Checklist of Afro-Amer. Art & Artists," *Serif,* Dec. 1970.

PARRY, F.
Sources: Harley, Ralph, Jr. "Checklist of Afro-Amer. Art & Artists," *The Serif,* Dec. 1970.

PATTERSON, MINNIE
Painter.
Works: *Norwegian Blanket; Norwegian Landscape.*
Exhibited: Art Inst. of Chicago, 1927.
Sources: Art Inst. of Chicago. *The Negro in Art Week,* 1927.

PATTON, KATHERINE
Sources: "Katherine Patton Receives First Prize in Negro Art Exhibit," *California Eagle,* Dec. 2, 1937; Harley, Ralph, Jr. "Checklist of Afro-Amer. Art & Artists," *The Serif,* Dec. 1970.

PATTON, SHARON F.
Printmaker.
Works: *Cosmos 2.*
Collections: Johnson Pub. Co.
Sources: Johnson Pub. Co. *The JPC Art Collection,* Pamphlet.

PAYNE, JOHN (B.)
Painter, sculptor, graphic artist, educator. Born in Pontotoc, Mississippi in 1932. Studied at Beloit College, Wisconsin (BA, 1959); University of Wisconsin (MS, 1961; MFA, 1969); University of Kansas (1965-6).
Works: *Now Black Woman,* 1969 (wood); *Take Me as I Am Pig Tails 'N' All,* 1969 (wood); *Come Together Ova Me,* 1970 (wood); *Nicht Mehr Flhen (No More Fleeing),* 1961; *Folk Singer,* 1961 (serigraph); *With Each Birth A New Hope,* 1958 (steel).
Exhibited: Beloit College, 1959 (1-man), 1968 (1-man), 1959; Univ. of Wisconsin, 1961 (1-man), 1969; Langston Univ., 1961 (1-man); Bazza Gallery, Okla., 1962 (1-man); Southern Univ., New Orleans, 1964 (1-man), 1967; Baton Rouge Gallery, 1967-71 (1-man), 1970, 1971, 1968; La. State Univ., 1968 (1-man); La. Institute of Interior Design, Baton Rouge, 1970; Stillman College, Ala., 1970 (1-man); Unitarian Chapel, Baton Rouge, 1971; Atlanta Univ., 1959, 1963-6; Milwaukee State Fair, 1961; Okla. Arts Center, 1962; Okla. City Univ. Traveling Show, 1962; Mulvane Arts Museum, Topeka, 1962; La. State Art Commission Annual, 1963, 1964; Masur Museum, Monroe, La., 1964; Art Commission Annual, Baton Rouge, 1966; Adventures in Art Gallery, New Orleans, 1966; Kansas Univ., 1966; Internat'l Exhibition of African Peoples Art, Los Angeles, 1968; Univ. of Cincinnati; Fidelity Nat'l Bank, Baton Rouge, 1971.
Collections: Beloit College; Beloit State Bank; Univ. of Wisc.; Union College; Loyola Univ.; Stillman College; Atlanta Univ.; Kansas Univ.; La. Nat'l Bank; Fidelity Nat'l Bank; Southern Univ.; Baton Rouge Gallery; La. State Univ.
Awards: Morse Foundation Grants, 1958-9; Southern Fellowship Foundation Grant, 1968; Top award, Wisc. State Fair, 1961; Best in show, All Wisc. Show, 1961; 2nd awards, graphics, 1964, watercolor, 1965, sculpture, 1966, Atlanta Univ.; Outstanding Young Man in America, 1964, 1971; Judge, Crete Annual Art Exhibit, 1972; Judge, Scholarship Annual for Talented Area High School Art Students, 1972; Jurist, Park Forest (Chicago) Art Annual, 1972.
Member: College Art Assn.; Nat'l Endowment for Humanities (Director, 1972).
Represented by: Tri-Arts Gallery, Beloit, Wisc.; Graphics Gallery, Baton Rouge; Adventures in Art Gallery, New Orleans.

Sources: Howard Univ. *American Negro Artists,* revised edition, 1970; Kansas Univ. *National/International Casting Conference,* 1966, Unpublished list; Univ. of Wisc. *Twelve Black American Artists,* 1969, Unpublished list; Univ. of Cincinnati. *Discovery 1970,* Alms Gallery, 1970, Unpublished list; Information from artist; *Who's Who in Art,* 1965; *Dictionary of International Biographies,* 1972.

PEACOCK, CLARENCE·
Painter. Self-taught. Worked in New York City.
Sources: Dover. *American Negro Art*; Indiana Univ. *Fine Arts & the Black American*; Harley, Ralph, Jr. "Checklist of Afro-Amer. Art & Artists," *Serif,* Dec. 1970; Walker, Roslyn. *A Resource Guide to the Visual Arts of Afro-Americans,* South Bend, Ind., 1971.

PEARSON, JULI
Painter.
Works: *The Honorable Raymond Pace Alexander* (oil).
Exhibited: Lee Cultural Center, Phila.
Sources: Phila. Dept. of Recreation. *Love . . . and the Black Community.*

PECK, SANDRA
Sculptor.
Works: *Black Madonna.*
Collections: Johnson Pub. Co.
Sources: Johnson Pub. Co. *The JPC Art Collection,* Pamphlet.

PENA, ALBERTO
Painter, educator. Born in Havana, Cuba in 1900. Deceased. Educated at San Alesandro Academy; Pennsylvania Academy of Fine Arts.
Exhibited: Club Atenas, Havana, 1934; Modern Cuban Art, Mexico City, 1937; Havana, 1935, 1937.
Awards: Cresson Scholarship, Pa. Academy of Fine Arts.
Sources: Mallett. *Index of Artists*; Locke. *The Negro in Art*; Harley, Ralph, Jr. "Checklist of Afro-Amer. Art & Artists," *The Serif,* Dec. 1970.

PENNINGTON, T. MAURICE
Painter, illustrator, cartoonist, photographer. Born July 31, 1923 in Louisville, Kentucky. Studied at Atlanta School of Art.
Exhibited: Atlanta Univ., 1959-67; Clark College, 1966; Tuskegee Institute, 1963-4; Piedmont Park Arts Festival, 1957-71; High Museum, Atlanta, 1971; Macon Museum of Art, 1972.
Member: Nat'l Conference of Artists.
Sources: Kiah, Virginia. "Black Artists," *Savannah Magazine,* April 1972, p. 16; Information from artist.

PERKINS, ANGELA L.
Painter. Born in Chicago, 1948. Studied at Los Angeles City College (AA); self-taught artist.
Works: *Design.*
Exhibited: Watts Summer Festival, 1967, 1968; Art-West Associated, Inc.; Independent Square Qualifying Exhibit, 1968.
Sources: Lewis/Waddy. *Black Artists on Art*, Vol. 1; Walker, Roslyn. *A Resource Guide to the Visual Arts of Afro-Americans*, South Bend, Ind., 1971.

PERKINS, MARION M.
Sculptor. Born 1908 in Marche, Arkansas. Died 1961. Studied under Cy Gordon.
Works: *Man of Sorrow*; *Don Quixote*; *Head of a Girl* (plaster); *Head of a Boy*; *Mother and Child.*
Exhibited: Art Institute of Chicago; Howard Univ.; Evanston (Ill.) Country Club; Hull House, Chicago; Amer. Negro Exposition, Chicago, 1940; Rockford College (Ill.), 1965; Xavier Univ., 1963; South Side Community Art Center, Chicago, 1945.
Collections: Art Institute of Chicago; Mr. & Mrs. John Gray.
Awards: Art Institute of Chicago Purchase Award, 1951.
Sources: Dover. *American Negro Art*; Indiana Univ. *Fine Arts & the Black American*; Albany Institute of History & Art. *The Negro Artist Comes of Age*; Howard Univ. *Exhibition of Negro Artists of Chicago at the Howard Univ. Gallery of Art*, 1941; Tanner Art Galleries. *Art of the American Negro*, 1940; Rockford College. *Creativity and the Negro*; Xavier Univ. *Emancipation Proclamation Centennial National Art Exhibition*, 1963; Harley, Ralph, Jr. "Checklist of Afro-American Art & Artists," *The Serif*, Dec. 1970; "Man of Sorrows," *Pictures on Exhibit*, June 1951, pp. 6-7; "Exhibition," *Art Institute of Chicago Scrapbook*, LXXXVI, 1951, p. 15; "Prize Winners . . . 55th Annual Chicago & Vicinity Show . . .," *Art Institute of Chicago Scrapbook*, LXXXVI, 1951, pp. 52, 56-9; Boning, Richard A. *Profiles of Black Americans*, NY, 1969; Steele, Victoria. "Marion Perkins—Worker-Artist," *Masses & Mainstream*, Aug. 1952, p. 17; "Marion Perkins: Hiroshima in Sculpture," *Masses & Mainstream*, Aug. 1952; Drotning, Phillip T. *A Guide to Negro History in America*, 1968, p. 57; Ploski, Harry, & Ernest Kaiser. "The Black Artist," *Afro USA*, 1971; Ploski, Harry, Ernest Kaiser, & Otto Lindenmeyer. "The Black Artist," *Reference Library of Black America*, Book 4, 1971; *The Negro Handbook*, composed by the editors of *Ebony*, Chicago, 1966; Schatz, Walter. *Directory of Afro-American Resources*, 1970; Adams, Russell. *Great*

Negroes Past & Present, Chicago, 1969; South Side Community Art Center. *Chicago Collectors Exhibit of Negro Art*, Chicago, 1945; Myers, Carol L. *Black Power in the Arts*, Flint, Mich., 1970; Spradling, Mary M., ed. *In Black & White: Afro-Americans in Print.*

PERRY, CYNTHIA
Painter. Worked in Atlanta.
Works: *Pastel.*
Exhibited: Atlanta Univ., 1944.
Sources: Atlanta Univ. Catalog, 1944.

PERRY, FREDERICK
Painter.
Works: *Landscape* (oil wash on watercolor); *Street Scene*; *Dance Group.*
Exhibited: Baltimore Museum, 1939; Amer. Negro Exposition, Chicago, 1940; Augusta Savage Studios, 1939.
Collections: Nat'l Archives.
Sources: Afro-Amer. Slide Depository, Catalog; Baltimore Museum of Art. *Contemporary Negro Art*, 1939; Tanner Art Galleries. *Art of the American Negro*, 1940; DuSable Museum of African-Amer. History. *Contemporary Black Artists*, 1970, Calendar; "Amer. Negro Art Given Full Length Review in NY Show," *Art Digest*, Dec. 15, 1941; Harley, Ralph, Jr. "Checklist of Afro-Amer. Art & Artists," *Serif*, Dec. 1970; Myers, Carol L. *Black Power in the Arts*, Flint, Mich., 1970.

PERRY, L. A., JR.
Collections: Mr. Benny Andrews.

PERRY, MICHAEL KAVANAUGH
Painter, printmaker. Born in Los Angeles in 1940. Studied at Otis Art Institute (BFA; MFA, 1967). Art instructor at Albany State College, Albany, Georgia.
Works: *Walking, Standing, Walking* (intaglio).
Exhibited: Otis Art Institute; Independence Square Qualifying Show; Los Angeles City Hall, 1968.
Collections: Golden State Mutual Life Insurance Co.
Sources: Lewis/Waddy. *Black Artists on Art*, Vol. 1; Walker, Roslyn. *A Resource Guide to the Visual Arts of Afro-Americans*, South Bend, Ind., 1971.

PETERS, JOY BALLARD
Painter, educator. Studied at Howard University (AB); DC Teachers College.
Works: *Man's Escape; Lines in Space; All in the Mind.*
Exhibited: State Armory, Wilmington, Del., 1971; Howard Univ.; Jr. Scholastic Show; YWCA; DC Recreation Outdoor Show; Margaret Dickey Gallery; DCAA, Anacostia Neighborhood Museum-Smithsonian Institution; Import Gallery.

Sources: Aesthetic Dynamics. *Afro-American Images*, 1971; DC Art Assn. *Exhibition '71*, Washington, DC, 1971.

PETERSON, BARBARA

Born in Pittsburgh, Pennslyvania, 1940. Studied at Carnegie-Mellon University. Art consultant, Anna B. Heldman Center.
Works: *New Forest IV*.
Exhibited: Halfway Art Gallery; Mercyhurst College, Erie; Smith-Mason Gallery, 1971.
Sources: Pittsburgh Community College. *16 Black Artists*; Smith-Mason Gallery. *National Exhibition Black Artists 1971*.

PHILLIPIS, JOHN

Glass painter. Born in Canada, 1892.
Exhibited: Harmon Foundation, 1928.
Sources: Harmon Foundation. *Exhibition of Productions by Negro Artists*; Indiana Univ. *Fine Arts & the Black American*; Walker, Roslyn. *A Resource Guide to the Visual Arts of Afro-Americans*, South Bend, Ind., 1971.

PHILLIPS, ALVIN TURTEL

Painter.
Works: *Family Group* (oil).
Collections: Johnson Pub. Co.
Sources: Johnson Pub. Co. *The JPC Art Collection*, Pamphlet.

PHILLIPS, BERTRAND D.

Painter, graphic artist, educator. Born in Chicago, 1938. Studied at the Art Institute of Chicago (BFA); Northwestern University (MFA).
Works: *On the Death of Emmet Till; Canine Onslaught; Man Child; Faces; Power to the People; Sheol; For God and Country; Blue Soul; Stars, Bars and Bones; Wet Nurse; Liberation; Vigilance; Figure with Dove; The Organizer; Peace; Tender Warriors; Break Through; Black and White*, 1969; *Black Experience*, 1971; *Existence Black*, 1972.
Exhibited: Kover Gallery, Chicago, 1969; Univ. of Chicago, 1971; Southern Ill. Univ., 1972.
Awards: George C. Brown Foreign Traveling Fellowship, Art Institute of Chicago, 1961; Ponte Dell'Arte, Art Institute of Chicago, 1961.
Member: Nat'l Conference of Artists.
Sources: Afro-Amer. Slide Depository, Catalog, 1971-2; Information from artist.

PHILLIPS, HARPER TRENHOLM

Painter, educator. Born in Courtland, Alabama, 1928. Professor of Art, Grambling (Louisiana) College.
Works: *Lullabye; Fisherman; Winter Equinox; Coavus; Spring 1960; Space Impaction; Avalanche; Discernment*.
Exhibited: WVa. State College, 1968; Xavier Univ., 1963; Howard Univ., 1961, 1970.

Awards: Best in show, WVa. State College, 1968.
Sources: Harley, Ralph, Jr. "Checklist of Afro-Amer. Art & Artists," *Serif*, Dec. 1970; Dover. *American Negro Art*; Indiana Univ. *Fine Arts & the Black American*; Roucek/Kiernan. *The Negro Impact on Western Civilization*; Howard Univ. *James A. Porter Gallery of African Art*, 1970; Pierre-Noel, Lois Jones. "American Negro Art in Progress," *Negro History Bulletin*, Oct. 1967; *Journal of the National Conference of Artists*, 1968; Xavier Univ. *Emancipation Proclamation Centennial National Art Exhibition*, 1963; Brown, Marion. "The Negro in the Fine Arts," *The Negro Heritage Library*, Vol. 2; Walker, Roslyn. *A Resource Guide to the Visual Arts of Afro-Americans*, South Bend, Ind., 1971.

PHILLIPS, JAMES

Painter. Artist-in-Residence, Studio Museum in Harlem.
Exhibited: Howard Univ., 1972.
Sources: *Black Shades*, Mar. 1972; Oct. 1972.

PHIPPS, EDGAR EUGENE

Photographer. Born in Kingston, British West Indies, 1887.
Works: *Central Park Lane—Evening; Harlem Dancer; Ready for School; Untitled Figure Study; Art Class; Central Park—West 106th St.; Martinque Lady; Mother; The Sister*.
Exhibited: Harmon Foundation, 1933; Buckingham Palace, England.
Collections: Nat'l Archives.
Sources: Indiana Univ. *Fine Arts & the Black American*; Harmon Foundation. *Exhibition of Productions by Negro Artists*; Afro-Amer. Slide Depository, Catalog, 1971-2; Harmon Foundation. *Non-Jury Exhibit of Works of Negro Artists*, 1933; Harmon Foundation. *Negro Artists*, 1935; DuSable Museum of African-Amer. History. *Contemporary Black Artists*, 1970 Calendar; Walker, Roslyn. *A Resource Guide to the Visual Arts of Afro-Americans*, South Bend, Ind., 1971.

PICKIL, ALEXANDER

Painter. Lived and worked in New Orleans.
Sources: Porter. "Versatile Interests of the Early Negro Artist: A Neglected Chapter of American Art History," *Art in America*, Jan. 1936; Desdunes, R. L. *Nos Hommes et Notre Histoire*; Harley, Ralph, Jr. "Checklist of Afro-Amer. Art & Artists," *The Serif*, Dec. 1970; Walker, Roslyn. *A Resource Guide to the Visual Arts of Afro-Americans*, South Bend, Ind., 1971.

PIERCE, DELILAH WILLIAMS

Painter, educator. Born in Washington, DC, March 3, 1904. Studied at Howard Universit

(BS); Teachers College, Columbia University (MA); University of Pennsylvania; New York University; Chicago University; Museum of Modern Art, People's Art Center, NYC; Louis Jones-Celine Tabary Studio, Washington, DC; James L. Wells Studio, Washington, DC; Ralph Pearson Studio, Nyack, NY; Jack Perlmutter Studio, Washington, DC; DC Teachers College; Old Sculpin Gallery, Edgartown, Massachusetts. Assistant Professor of Art Education, DC Teachers College.

Works: *Waterfront; Daffodils; The Piers; Gay Head Cliffs; Tradesmen-Africa; Long Bridge, Washington, DC; Tradersmen, Khartoum, Sudan; Sails; Dawn-A New Day-On the Nigger; Jetty-Keeper of the Shore, Nantucket Sound; The Illumination, Lantern Patterns; Supplications.*

Exhibited: Smith-Mason Gallery, 1971; State Armory, Wilmington, Del., 1971; Margaret Dickey Gallery, 1949-69; Artists Mart, 1963, 1965, 1968, 1970, 1972; Corcoran Gallery, 1949; Baltimore Museum; NJ State Museum, Trenton; Atlanta Univ.; Howard Univ.; NC State College; Catholic Univ., Washington, DC; Hampton (Va.) Institute; Barnet Aden Gallery, Washington, DC; 20th Century Gallery, Williamsburg, Va.; Amer. Federation of Art, NYC; Martha's Vineyard Island Show; Collectors Corner; Amer. Art League, Smithsonian Institution; Anacostia Museum-Smithsonian Institution; Alain Locke Show, Negro College Fund; Washington Watercolor Society; Aesthetic Dynamics; Society of Washington Artists; DC Teachers College; Lois Jones Studio, 1949-51; Corcoran Traveling Show, 1960-1; DuPont Theatre Gallery; Rehoboth Art League; Northern Va. Hadassa Show; James A. Porter Gallery, Howard Univ., 1970.

Collections: Howard Univ.; DC Teachers College; Eugene Clark Elementary School; Smith-Mason Gallery; Anacostia Neighborhood Museum.

Awards: AFA Purchase Award, 1964; Smith-Mason Gallery Citation, 1971; Agnes Meyer Summer Fellowship, 1962; Phi Delta Kappa Achievement Award for Outstanding Service & Achievement in Art & Art Education.

Member: Artists Equity Assn.; Nat'l Conference of Artists; Society of Washington Artists; Washington Watercolor Assn.; DC Art Assn.; NAEA; Martha's Vineyard Art Assn.; Artists' Mart; AAUW Art Committee.

Represented by: Artists' Mart, Georgetown, Washington, DC; Smith-Mason Gallery, Washington, DC.

Sources: Dover. *American Negro Art*; Indiana Univ. *Fine Arts & the Black American*; Smith-Mason Gallery. *National Exhibition Black Artists*, 1971; Aesthetic Dynamics. *Afro-American Images*, Wilmington, Del., 1971; Pierre-Noel, Lois Jones. "Amer. Art in Progress," *Negro History Bulletin*, Oct. 1967; *Washington Artists Today Directory*; *Who's Who in American Art*; Atkinson, J.E. *Black Dimensions in Contemporary American Art*; DC Art Assn. *Exhibition '71*, Washington, DC, 1971; A&T Univ. Lyceum Program. *15 Afro-American Women*; Harley, Ralph, Jr. "Checklist of Afro-Amer. Art & Artists," *Serif*, Dec. 1970; *The Negro Handbook*, Composed by Editors of *Ebony*, Chicago, 1966; DeNauw, Lois. "Mrs. Pierce's Art Shows Progression over 20 Years," *Alexandria Gazette*, June 12, 1969; Margaret Dickey Gallery. *Exhibition of Paintings*, Washington, DC, 1959; Walker, Roslyn. *A Resource Guide to the Visual Arts of Afro-Americans*, South Bend, Ind., 1971.

PIERCE, ELIJAH

Sculptor, carver, painter. Born in 1892 near Baldwin, Mississippi. Self-taught.

Works: *The Barber Shop and the Fight Against Evil; Birds; Birthday Flowers; Crucifixion; Death on the Level; Father Time Racing; Funeral, 1933; Highway; Horse Racing; Human Society; I Am the Vine, You are the Branches; Image of Man; Jesse Owen's Love of Sport; Joe Louis—Four Champions; John Crying in the Wilderness; Jonah and the Whale; Mary Sits at Jesus' Feet; Monday Morning Gossip; Noah's Ark; Pearl Harbor; Presidents and Convicts; Redemption; Sad Bad Day; Seeking Gold in the West; Sport; Straining at a Gnat and Swallowing a Camel; The Twenties; The White Church; When Joe Became Champ; Your Life is a Book.*

Exhibited: Ohio State Univ., 1971; Univ. of Illinois, 1972; Museum of Modern Art, 1972; Bernard Danenberg Galleries, NY, 1972.

Collections: Mr. Boris Gruenwald; Dr. Gerhard Martin.

Sources: *Elijah Pierce: Painted Carvings*, NY, Bernard Danenberg Galleries, 1972; Ohio State Univ. *Elijah Pierce Carvings*, Columbus, Oct. 18-29, 1971; Krannert Art Museum. *Carvings*, Univ. of Illinois, Urbana, Dec. 12-Jan. 2, 1972; Museum of Modern Art. *Untitled III*, NY, Feb. 3-Mar. 15, 1972.

PIERCE, HAROLD

Painter. Born in Nowatla, Oklahoma, 1914.
Works: *Debbie.*
Sources: Dover. *American Negro Art*; Indiana Univ. *Fine Arts & the Black American*; Harley, Ralph, Jr. "Checklist of Afro-Amer. Art & Artists," *Serif*, Dec. 1970; Walker, Roslyn. *A Resource Guide to the Visual Arts of Afro-Americans*, South Bend, Ind., 1971.

PIERRE, PHILIP LEO

Industrial designer. Born in Trinidad.
Works: *Portrait of Miss Maggie Hunter.*

Exhibited: Harmon Foudation, 1931.
Collections: Nat'l Archives.
Sources: Harmon Foundation. *Exhibition of Productions by Negro Artists*; Indiana Univ. *Fine Arts & the Black American*; Afro-Amer. Slide Depository, Catalog; Harmon Foundation. *Negro Artists*, 1935; DuSable Museum of African-Amer. History. *Contemporary Black Artists*, 1970, Calendar; Walker, Roslyn. *A Resource Guide to the Visual Arts of Afro-Americans*, South Bend, Ind., 1971.

PIERRE-NOEL, LOIS MAILOU JONES
See: Jones, Lois Mailou.

PIGATT, ANDERSON J.
Sculptor. Born in Baltimore, 1928. Self-taught.
Works: *Slave Girl; Sugar Hill Rose; King of Kings—Solomon; America the Beautiful; Khodeja; The Vision of Revelations; Message from the Mountain (We Are United); One Leg of Alabama.*
Exhibited: Brooklyn Museum, 1969; Columbia Univ., 1969.
Sources: Brooklyn Museum. *New Black Artists*, 1969; Walker, Roslyn. *A Resource Guide to the Visual Arts of Afro-Americans*, South Bend, Ind., 1971.

PILLARS, MURRAY De
See: DePillars, Murray.

PINCKNEY, STANLEY (BABALAIYE S. DÉLÉ)
Painter, mosaicist. Born in Boston, 1940. Studied at The Famous Artists School, Westport, Connecticut; School of the Museum of Fine Arts, Boston, 1967. Has travelled and studied in Africa.
Works: *Benin Triptych*, 1969 (mosaic).
Exhibited: Boston Museum of Fine Arts, 1970.
Collections: Nat'l Center of Afro-Amer. Artists, Boston.
Awards: 5th yr. traveling scholarship, School of the Museum of Fine Arts, Boston.
Sources: Boston Community Lecture Series. *Local Afro-American Artists*, 1972; Le Brun, Caron. "Blacks' Art Display," *Herald Traveler*, Boston, May 26, 1970; Paris, Jean. "Black Art Experience in Art," *Long Island Press*, Jamaica, NY, June 14, 1970; Boston Museum of Fine Arts. *Afro-American Artists: NY & Boston*, 1970; "Afro-American Artists: NY & Boston," *Prudential Center News*, March 1, 1970, p. 4.

PINDELL, HOWARDENA
Painter. Born 1943.
Works: Untitled, 1970 (synthetic polymer on canvas).
Exhibited: Whitney Museum, NY, 1971.

Sources: Doty. *Contemporary Black Artists in America.*

PINKNEY, JERRY
Illustrator, designer. Born in Philadelphia in 1939. Studied at Philadelphia Museum College of Art.
Works: *Paraders* (pencil); *Mushroom*, 1970 (pen & ink); *Owl & Skunk*, 1969 (watercolor & pencil); Advertising & promotional work for Klopman Fabrics, Boston Globe, Sheraton Hotels, Borden Co., Thom McAn, Pan Am.
Exhibited: NY Illustrators Show; Brandeis Univ., 1969; Boston Museum of Fine Arts, 1970; Nat'l Center of Afro-Amer. Artists, 1969; American Institute of Graphic Arts; NY Art Directors Show; NJ Art Directors Show; Boston Art Directors Show; Providence Art Directors Show.
Awards: AIGA Award; NY Illustrators; NY, NJ, Providence & Boston Art Directors Shows.
Member: Kaleidoscope (co-founder).
Sources: Boston Community Lecture Series. *Local Afro-American Artists*, 1969; Le Brun, Caron. "Blacks' Art on Display," *Herald Traveler*, Boston, May 26, 1970; Trofimuk, Ann. *Babushka and the Pit*, Houghton & Mifflin, Illus.; Saleh, Harold J. *Even Tiny Ants Must Sleep*, McGraw Hill, Illus.; Green, Lila. *Folk Tales & Fairy Tales of Africa*, Silver Burdett Co., Illus.; Shaw, Thelma. *Juano & the Wonderful Fresh Fish*, Addison & Wesley Co., Illus.; Traudl. *Kostas the Rooster*, Lothrop, Lee & Shepherd Co., Illus.; Dale, Ralph Alan. *Shoes, Pennies & Rockets*, LW Singer Co., Illus.; Sobol, Ken. *Sizes & Shapes*, McGraw Hill, Illus.; Spellman, John. *The Beautiful Jay & Other Tales of India*, Little Brown, Illus.; Sobol, Ken. *The Clock Museum*, McGraw Hill, Illus.; Powell, Fern. *The Porcupine & the Tiger*, Lothrop, Lee & Shepard, Illus.; Garshin, V.M. *The Traveling Frog*, McGraw Hill, Illus.; Fletcher, Helen. *The Year Around Book*, McGraw Hill, Illus.; McCall, Adeline. *This is Music*, Illus.; Information from artist; Boston Museum of Fine Arts. *Afro-American Artists: NY & Boston*, 1970; "Afro-American Artists: NY & Boston," *Prudential Center News*, March 1, 1970, p. 4; Brandeis Univ. *12 Black Artists From Boston*, 1969.

PIOUS, ROBERT SAVON
Commercial artist, painter. Born in Mississippi, 1908. Studied at Art Institute of Chicago; National Academy of Design. Worked as artist for *Bronzeman Magazine* and for *Opportunity*.
Works: *Portrait of a Singer; A Penny, Please; Call for Duty; Harriet Tubman; Portrait of a Doctor; Portrait of Augusta Savage; Toward Freedom; Portrait of a Writer; Portrait of Ronald Hayes; Negro in Congress; The Slave Shys.*

Exhibited: Urban League, 1932; Harlem Businessmen's League; Harmon Foundation, 1930-1, 1933; Amer. Negro Exposition, Chicago, 1940; NY Federal Art Project, 1936-9; Atlanta Univ., 1942; City College of NY, 1967; Smithsonian Institution, 1930; Harmon Foundation-College Art Assn. Touring Exhibition, 1934-5; Harlem Art Committee, 1935; Augusta Savage Studios, 1939.

Collections: Nat'l Archives; Smithsonian Institution.

Awards: Spingarn Prize for Drawing, Harmon Foundation, 1933; Scholarship to Nat'l Academy of Design; Nat'l Poster Competition Prize.

Sources: City College of NY. *Evolution of Afro-American Artists 1800-1950*, 1967; Locke. *The Negro in Art*; Harmon Foundation. *Exhibition of Productions by Negro Artists*; "Afro-American Issue," *Art Gallery*, April 1968; Indiana Univ. *Fine Arts & the Black American*; Afro-Amer. Slide Depository, Catalog, 1971-2; Tanner Art Galleries. *Art of the American Negro*, 1940; Harmon Foundation. *Non-Jury Exhibit of Works of Negro Artists*, 1933; Texas Centennial Exposition. *Thumbnail Sketches of Exhibiting Artists*, 1936; Harmon Foundation. *Negro Artists*, 1935; Harmon Foundation. *Exhibit of Fine Arts*, 1930; DuSable Museum of African-Amer. History. *Contemporary Black Artists*, 1970, Calendar; Harmon Foundation. *Select Picture List*; "Harmon Foundation Exhibit," *Art Digest*, Feb. 15, 1931; "Harlem Library Shows Negro Art," *Art News*, May 20, 1933; *Modern Negro Art*, NY, 1969; Harley, Ralph, Jr. "Checklist of Afro-Amer. Art & Artists," *Serif*, Dec. 1970; "At New York Art Exhibit," *Afro-American*, March 30, 1935; Myers, Carol L. *Black Power in the Arts*, Flint, Mich., 1970; Walker, Roslyn. *A Resource Guide to the Visual Arts of Afro-Americans*, South Bend, Ind., 1971.

PIPER, ROSE

Painter. Studied at Art Students League.
Works: *Grievin' Hearted; Empty Red Blues.*
Exhibited: Atlanta Univ., 1948; Roko Gallery (1-man); ACA Gallery; Xavier Univ., 1963.
Awards: Rosenwald Fellowships, 1946, 1947.
Sources: *New York Times*, April 4, 1948; J.G. "Honoring Negro History," *Art Digest*, p. 20; E.K. "Negro Artists," *Art News*, Feb. 1949, p. 47; Xavier Univ. *Emancipation Proclamation Centennial National Art Exhibition*, 1963.

PIPPIN, HORACE

Sculptor, primitive painter. Born in West Chester, Pennsylvania, February 22, 1888. Died July 6, 1946. Completed his first painting at 43 years of age. A WWI injury immobilized his right hand, which he manipulated across the canvas with his left. He was given his first 1-man show after a painting placed in the window of a shoe repair shop was noticed by Dr. Christian Brinton who was walking past with the noted illustrator N.C. Wyeth.

Works: *End of the War; John Brown Going to His Hanging; Lilies; Flowers with Red Chair; John Brown Reading His Bible; The Den; Cabin in the Cotton; Gas Alarm Outpost: Argonne Sector; The Barracks; Domino Players; Victorian Interior; A Chester County Art Critic; Self Portrait; Crucifixion; Sunday Morning Breakfast; The Milk Man of Goshen; Saturday Night Bath; After Supper, West Chester; Mr. Prejudice; Holy Mountain IV; Crossing the Junction; The Blue Tiger; The Buffalo Hunt; Landscape; Christ Crowned with Thorns; The Warped Table; Amish Letter Writer; Roses with Red Chair; West Chester Courthouse; Birmingham Meeting House III; Red, Yellow and White Roses; The Wash; Woman of Samaria; The Ending of the War: Starting Home; Victory Vase; Saying Prayers; Harmonizing; Abe Lincoln's First Book; Quaker Mother and Child; Interior; Love Letter; Summer Flowers; The Hoe Cake; Man on a Bench; Marian Anderson Singing; Victory Garden; Portrait of Marion Anderson; Birmingham Meeting House in Late Summer 1940; Water Boy; Woman Taken in Adultery; Shell Hole and Observation Balloon; Christ; Dogfight over the Trenches; Night's Call.*

Exhibited: West Chester Community Center, 1937; Carlen Galleries, Phila., 1940- (permanent dealer); Bignou Gallery, NY, 1940; Museum of Modern Art, 1938; Amer. Negro Exposition, Chicago, 1940; Arts Club of Chicago, 1941; San Francisco Museum of Art, 1942; Downtown Galleries, NY, 1941; Carnegie Institute, 1944; Atlanta Univ., 1944; Knoedler Galleries, 1947; Walker Art Center, c. 1950; City College of NY, 1967; Newark Museum, 1971; Howard Univ., 1945; James A. Porter Gallery, 1970; South Side Community Art Center, Chicago, 1941.

Collections: Albright-Knox Gallery, Buffalo, NY; Barnes Foundation, Phila.; Pa. Academy of Fine Arts; Phillips Memorial Gallery, Washington, DC; Nat'l Archives; Boston Museum of Fine Arts; Whitney Museum, NYC; Wichita Museum, Kansas; Rhode Island Museum; Encyclopedia Britannica Collection; Mr. Charles Laughton; Ms. Violet de Mazia; Mrs. Edmund C. Evans; Museum of Modern Art, NYC; Metropolitan Museum of Art, NYC; Archives of Amer. Art.

Awards: Honorable Mention, Carnegie Institute, 1944; J. Henry Scheidt Memorial Prize.

Sources: Mallett. *Index of Artists;* Locke. *The Negro in Art;* Locke. *Negro Art Past and Present; Negro Almanac; Who's Who in Amer-*

ican Art, 1940-1; *Art Digest*, Feb. 15, 1940; *Dictionary of American Artists, Sculptors & Engravers;* Albany Institute of History & Art. *The Negro Artist Comes of Age;* Rodman, Selden. *Horace Pippin, A Negro Painter in America*, Quadrangle Press, 1947; Carnegie Institute. *Hicks, Kane, Pippin*, 1966, catalog; Dover. *American Negro Art;* Indiana Univ. *Fine Arts & the Black American;* Afro-Amer. Slide Depository, Catalog; *Art Journal*, Winter 1971/72, p. 141; Nat'l Center of Afro-Amer. Artists. *Five Black Artists*, Feb./March 1970; City College of NY. *Evolution of Afro-American Artists 1800-1950*, 1967; DuSable Museum of African-Amer. History. *Contemporary Black Artists*, Calendar, 1970; "Afro-American Art: 1800-1950," *Ebony*, Feb. 1968, pp. 116-22; South Side Community Art Center. *National Art Exhibition*, Chicago, 1941; Janis, Sidney. *They Taught Themselves*, Dial Press, NY, 1942, pp. 187-9; Myers, Carol L. *Black Power in the Arts*, Flint, Mich., 1970; Spradling, Mary M., ed. *In Black & White: Afro-Americans in Print;* "Afro-American Art a Cultural Experience for All," *Record American*, Boston, May 19, 1970; Paul L. Baruch, Inc. Calendar, 1951; Walker, Roslyn. *A Resource Guide to the Visual Arts of Afro-Americans*, South Bend, Ind., 1971; Ford. *Pictorial Folk Art; Time*, April 6, 1970, p. 82; Phillips Memorial Gallery. *Three Negro Artists*, Washington, DC, 1946; Carlen Galleries. *Catalogue of Exhibition*, Phila., 1940; Klein. "Art the Hard Way," *Friday Magazine*, Jan. 17, 1941; "Primitive Pippin," *Time*, Jan. 29, 1940; "Ex-Porters Show an Art Sensation," *Philadelphia Record*, Jan. 21, 1940; Bearden, Romare, Harry Henderson. *Six Black Masters of American Art;* La Jolla Museum of Art. *Dimensions of Black;* Locke, Alain. "Advance on the Art Front," *Opportunity*, May 1939; Porter. *Modern Negro Art;* Woods, Joseph W. "Modern Primitive: Horace Pippin," *Crisis*, June 1946, p. 178-9; "Pippin, Negro Primitive, Given Memorial Show at Knoedler Galleries," *Art Digest*, Oct. 1, 1947, p. 16; "Horace Pippin, A Negro Painter in America, by S. Rodman," Review, *Magazine of Art*, May 1948, p. 202; Geldzahler, Henry. *American Paintings in the Twentieth Century*, NY, Metropolitan Museum of Art, 1965; Harley, Ralph L., Jr. "A Checklist of Afro-American Art and Artists," *The Serif*, Dec. 1970; Tanner Art Galleries. *Art of the American Negro*, 1940; Roucek & Kiernan. *The Negro Impact on Western Civilization;* Newark Museum. *Black Artists: Two Generations*, 1971; Howard Univ. *Festival of Fine Arts*, 1945; Howard Univ. *James A. Porter Gallery of African American Art* 1970; Harmon Foundation. *Select Picture List;* "Negro Primitive Finds Peace After War," *Art Digest*, Oct. 1, 1949; "Amer. Negro Artists Given Full Length Review in NY Show," *Art Digest*, Dec. 15, 1941; Greene, Carroll, Jr. "Perspective: The Black Artist in America," *Art Gallery*, April 1970, p. 21; "The Negro in Art," *Art Digest*, June 1, 1944; "Negro Art Scores Without Double Standards," *Art Digest*, Feb. 1, 1945; Pierre-Noel, Lois Jones. "American Negro Art in Progress," *Negro History Bulletin*, Oct. 1967; Woodruff, Hale. "Negro Artists Hold Fourth Annual in Atlanta," *Art Digest*, April 15, 1945; Locke, Alain. "Chicago's New Southside Art Center," *Amer. Mag. of Art*, Aug. 1941; JWL. "Negro in Art," *Art News*, Dec. 19, 1941, p. 24; "Negro Art Show," *Art News*, July 1, 1944, pp. 6-7; "The Negro Artist Comes of Age," *Art News*, Feb. 1, 1945; "Amer. Negro Art," *Design*, Feb. 1942, p. 28; Greene, Carroll, Jr. "Afro-Amer. Artists: Yesterday & Now," *The Humble Way*, Vol. 8, No. 3, 1968; Driscoll, Edgar, Jr. "Exhibit Features Black Artists," *Boston Globe*, Feb. 16, 1970, p. 17; Greene, Carroll. *Afro-American Artists: 1800-1968*, Slides; Boning, Richard A. *Profiles of Black Americans*, NY, 1969; Shorewood Reproductions Catalogue. *The Art of Black America*, 1969; "Winthrop Students Visit Arts Center," *Bay State Banner*, March 19, 1970; Loercher, Diana. "Black Artists Exhibition Reveals Visual Eloquence," *Christian Science Monitor*, March 2, 1970; Loercher, Diana. "Afro-American Center & Museum of Fine Arts Form Alliance," *Christian Science Monitor*, May 20, 1970; Bourne, Kay. "Black Artists Shown at Museum," *Bay State Banner*, May 28, 1970; Driscoll, Edgar. "Blacks Duncanson & Bannister Honored in Fine Arts Exhibit," *Boston Globe*, Jan. 16, 1972; Faxon, Alicia. "Afro-American Exhibits Museum of Fine Arts," *Journal*, Concord, Mass., Jan. 20, 1972; Brown, Marion. "The Negro in the Fine Arts," *The Negro Heritage Library*, Vol. 2; Morsbach, Mabel. *The Negro in American Life;* Ploski, Harry, Ernest Kaiser. "The Black Artist," *Afro, USA*, 1971; Driscoll, Edgar, Jr. "Museum, Black Center Join Hands," *Boston Globe*, n.d.; "Black Art Program Joint Effort," *Times*, Peabody, Mass., June 12, 1970; Paris, Jean. "Black Art Experience in Art," *Long Island Press*, Jamaica, NY, June 14, 1970; Ploski, Harry, Ernest Kaiser, Otto Lindenmeyer. "The Black Artist," *Reference Library of Black America*, Book 4, 1971; *The Negro Handbook*, Composed by Editors of Ebony Chicago, 1966; Schatz, Walter. *Directory of Afro-American Resources*, 1970; Adams, Russell. *Great Negroes Past & Present*, 1969; Horace Pippin Papers.

PITTS, BETTY J.

Painter. Born 1940. Studied State University of New York at Buffalo.
Works: *Going Home; Still Life-Red, Blue and White.*
Exhibited: Smith-Mason Gallery, 1971.
Sources: NY State Education Dept. *Fifteen Under Forty;* Smith-Mason Gallery. *National Exhibition Black Artists 1971.*

POGUE, STEPHANIE E.

Graphic artist, educator. Born in Shelby, North Carolina, September 27, 1944. Studied at Syracuse University; Howard University (BFA); Cranbrook Academy of Art, Bloomfield Hills, Michigan. Assistant Professor of Art, Fisk University.
Works: *After Kadmus; Untitled; Jonah in the Whale; Garden of Eden: The Wall; Job; Carnival.*
Exhibited: Fisk Univ., 1966; Rhode Island College; Young Printmakers, Art Assn. of Indianapolis; Rubiner Gallery, Royal Oak, Mich., 1967; Univ. of North Dakota; Mich. Assn. of Printmakers, London Arts Gallery, Detroit; Okla. Art Center, 1968; State Univ. College at Potsdam, NY; Talladega (Ala.) College; Arts Festival, Jarvis Christian College, Hawkins, Tex.; Afro-Amer. Arts Festival, St. Augustine College, Raleigh, NC; Lane College, Jackson, Tenn., 1969; Univ. of Oregon, Eugene; Fisk Faculty Exhibition, Louisville Art Workshop; Studio 22, Chicago; Central Southern Exhibition, Parthenon, Nashville, Tenn.; Phoenix Gallery, Berkeley, Cal.; Univ. of Va., Charlottesville, 1970; Shaw Univ., Raleigh, NC; Lambuth College, Jackson, Tenn.; Illinois Bell Telephone; Kansas State College; Peabody College, Nashville, Tenn.; Whitney Museum, NYC; Xavier Univ. (1-woman); Carnegie Institute, 1972; Austin Peay State Univ., Clarksville, Tenn.; Alabama State Univ., 1972; Univ. of Wisconsin; Mount Holyoke College; Sheraton Hotel, Phila., 1968.
Collections: Miss Mary Walker Phillips, NYC; Univ. of North Dakota; Fisk Univ.; Mr. Harold Blumenthal, Chicago; Whitney Museum, NYC; Xavier Univ.; Tennessee Arts Commission, Nashville; Univ. of the South, Swanee, Tenn.
Awards: Outstanding Graduate in Art at Howard Univ., 1963-6.
Sources: Doty. *Contemporary Black Artists in America;* Illinois Bell Telephone. *Black American Artists/71,* 1972; Harley, Ralph, Jr. "Checklist of Afro-Amer. Art & Artists," *Serif,* Dec. 1970; Studio 22. *Three Plus One,* Chicago.

POINDEXTER, VERNON STEPHENSEN

Commercial artist, illustrator. Born in Roanoke County, Virginia, November 28, 1918.
Studied at the Art Students League.
Exhibited: ACA Gallery, NY; Library of Congress; Brooklyn Museum; Phila. Print Club; Nat'l Academy Gallery, NY.
Awards: Library of Congress Award.
Sources: *NY Daily Worker,* May 5, 1948; Furr, Arthur F. *History & Progress of Negroes in the US.*

POPE, ALVIN

Printmaker. Active in 1960's.
Works: *Girl* (serigraph).
Collections: Oakland Museum, Ruth Waddy Collection.
Sources: Roelof-Lanner, T.V., ed. *Prints by American Negro Artists;* Oakland Museum Archives.

POPE, CELESTINE JOHNSTON

Educator, painter. Born in Pittsburgh, 1911. Studied at Boston University. Teacher at Episcopal City Mission, Boston; Palmer Memorial Institute, Sedalia, North Carolina; Hillside Park School.
Exhibited: Harmon Foundation, 1930; Smithsonian Institution, 1930.
Awards: 1st prize, Ivory Soap Contest, 1934.
Sources: Harmon Foundation. *Negro Artists,* 1935; DuSable Museum of African-Amer. History. *Contemporary Black Artists,* 1970, Calendar; Harley, Ralph, Jr. "Checklist of Afro-Amer. Art & Artists," *Serif,* Dec. 1970.

PORTER, JAMES, A.

Painter, educator, art historian. Born in Baltimore, 1905, died 1971. Studied at Howard University (BS); Teachers College, Columbia University; Art Students League of New York; Sorbonne, Paris; New York University (MA); pupil of Dimitri Romanovsky. Professor of Art, Howard University. Illustrated *Opportunity Magazine.*
Works: *On a Cuban Bus; Portrait of F.A. as Harlequin; Portrait of a Haitian Girl; Fish Vendors; Homage to Baga; Tempest; The Niger; Bal (Mardi Gras); Man with Ukelele; Mrs. M; By Lamp Light; The Shattered Mirror; Self Portrait #1; Spanish Man with Ribbon; Self Portrait # 2; African Rebirth; Charcoal Portrait; Primitive Bathers; Cement Elevators; Boy Reading; Portrait; American Legionnaire; Blue Landscape; The Farmer and His Wife; Portrait of Dr. Alexander; Girl Knitting; The Purple Vase; The Red Beret; Portrait of Constance; The Secret; Nude; Dorothy Porter; Haitian Market Woman; Cuban Bus; Young Negro; Still Life-Dahlias; The Wharves; Woman Holding a Jug; My Mother; Mr. Cyril Bow; Sarah; An American Family; The Riot; Still Life with Mushrooms; Portrait of Artist's Mother; Bronze Figure; Professor George Morton Lightfoot; Portrait of a Woman; My Sister.*
Exhibited: Harmon Foundation, 1928-30,

1933; Amer. Watercolor Society, 1932; Phila. Watercolor Society; National Gallery of Art, 1933; Corcoran Gallery, Washington, DC; Museum of Modern Art, NYC; Institute of Contemporary Art, Boston; Smith College Museum; New School for Social Research; South Side Community Art Center, Chicago; Baltimore Museum of Art; Pa. Academy of Fine Arts; Dallas Exposition, 1936; Howard Univ., 1945, 1937, 1939; Harlem Art Center; Amer. Negro Exposition, 1940; Atlanta Univ., 1942, 1944; Montclair Women's Club; Detroit Museum of Fine Arts; NJ State Museum, Trenton, 1935; Fine Arts Gallery of San Diego; Oakland Art Museum; Phila. Civic Center; State Armory, Wilmington, Del., 1971; James A. Porter Gallery, 1970; Smith-Mason Gallery, 1971; Smithsonian Institution, 1929, 1933.

Collections: Howard Univ.; Lincoln Univ., Mo.; Harmon Foundation; IBM; Hampton Institute, Va.; National Archives.

Awards: Schomburg Portrait Prize, 1933; Honorable Mention, Harmon Foundation, 1929; Scholarship Institute of Internat'l Education (Sorbonne); stipendiary, Rockefeller Foundation, 1935, 1945; Research Grant, *Washington Evening Star*; Fellow, Belgian-American Art Seminar; Achievement in Art, Pyramid Club, Phila.

Member: Internat'l Congress on African Art and Culture; Amer. Federation of Arts; Arts Council of Washington, DC.

Sources: City College of NY. *Evolution of Afro-American Artists 1800-1950,* 1967; Mallett. *Index of Artists; Who's Who in American Art,* 1940-1; *American Art Annual,* 1933; Locke. *The Negro in Art;* Albany Institute of History & Art. *The Negro Artist Comes of Age;* Dover. *American Negro Art;* Harmon Foundation. *Exhibition of Productions by Negro Artists;* "Afro-American Issue," *Art Gallery,* April 1968; *Art Digest,* April 15, 1935, p. 19; Afro-American Slide Depository, Catalog; "Howard University Gallery," *Sunday Star* (DC), Dec. 7, 1941; Phila. Division of Art. *Afro-American Artists 1800-1969;* Herring, James V. "The American Negro Craftsman and Artist," *Crisis,* April 1942; Aesthetic Dynamics. *Afro-American Images,* 1971; Howard Univ. *Art of the American Negro,* Catalog, 1937; Assn. for the Study of Negro Life & History, 1933, Catalog; Brawley, Benjamin. *The Negro Genius;* Tanner Art Galleries. *Art of the American Negro,* Catalog, 1940; Butcher, Margaret. *The Negro in American Culture,* pp. 236-8; Harmon Foundation. *Non-Jury Exhibit of Works of Negro Artists,* 1933; Texas Centennial Exposition. *Thumbnail Sketches of Exhibiting Artists,* 1936; Howard Univ. *Festival of Fine Arts,* 1945; Harmon Foundation. *Negro Artists,* 1935; Howard Univ. *James A. Porter Gallery of African-American Art,* 1970; Harmon Foundation. *Exhibit of Fine Arts,* 1930; Smith-Mason Gallery. *National Exhibition Black Artists,* 1971; DuSable Museum of African-Amer. History. *Contemporary Black Artists,* Calendar, 1970; Harmon Foundation. *Select Picture List;* Woodson, Carter G., Charles H. Wesley. *The Story of the Negro Retold,* p. 402; Smithsonian Institution. *Painting & Sculpture by Amer. Negro Artists,* 1929; *Art Digest,* March 1, 1933, p. 18; "Negro Artists Reveal Genius in Trenton Show," *Art Digest,* April 15, 1935; Greene, Carroll, Jr. "Perspective: The Black Artist in America," *Art Gallery,* April 1970, p. 6; Pierre-Noel, Lois Jones. "American Negro Art in Progress," *Negro History Bulletin,* Oct. 1967; Wolf, Ben. "Negro Art Scores Without Double Standards," *Art Digest,* Feb. 1, 1945; Porter, James A. "Negro Art on Review," *Amer. Magazine of Art,* Jan. 1934; "Harlem Library Shows Negro Art," *Art News,* May 20, 1933, p. 14; Kiah, Virginia. "Black Artists," *Savannah Magazine,* April 1972, p. 14; Logan, Rayford. "The Negro & Modern Art," *The New Negro Thirty Years Afterward,* Washington, DC, 1956, pp. 48-56; Porter. *Modern Negro Art;* Hambley, Wilfred Dyson. *Talking Animals,* Washington, DC, 1949; "The Transcultural Affinities of African Negro Art," *Presence Africaine,* 1958; "150 Years of Afro-Amer. Art," *Negro in American Art,* Los Angeles, 1967, pp. 5-12; Harley, Ralph, Jr. "Checklist of Afro-Amer. Art & Artists," *The Serif,* Dec. 1970; Greene, Carroll. *Afro-American Artists: 1800-1968,* Slides; *The Negro in Music and Art,* NY, 1969; Ploski, Harry, Ernest Kaiser. "The Black Artist," *Afro USA,* 1971; Ploski, Harry, Ernest Kaiser, & Otto Lindenmeyer. "The Black Artist," *Reference Library of Black America,* Book 4, 1971; *The Negro Handbook,* Composed by Editors of *Ebony,* Chicago, 1966; "James A. Porter, Howard Tutor, Gets High Award for Painting," *Washington Tribune,* Feb. 24, 1933; "Negro Artists Paintings on Display at University (Howard)," *East Tennessee News,* Knoxville, Tenn., June 6, 1932; "Exhibition of Work by Negro Artist," *Afro-American Presbyterian,* Feb. 23, 1933; Myers, Carol L. *Black Power in the Arts,* Flint, Mich., 1970; Porter, James A. "Four Problems in the History of Negro Art," *Journal of Negro History,* Vol 27, 1942; Porter, James A. "Versatile Interest of the Early Negro Artists," *Art in America,* 1936; Porter. *Modern Negro Art;* Barnet Aden Gallery. *Recent Paintings and Drawings,* Washington, DC, 1948; Walker, Roslyn. *A Resource Guide to the Visual Arts of Afro Americans,* South Bend, Ind., 1971.

PORTER, WYNDHAM

Illustrator. Studied at the School of Industrial Art.
Awards: 3rd prize, Honorable Mention, Art Instruction Annual Talent Contests; 2nd prize, American Relief for Korea Poster Contest; 2 Gold Keys, American Relief Contest; 2nd place, Society of Illustrators Annual Art Exhibit.
Sources: NY NAACP. *A Most Memorable Showing of Creative Negro Art;* NY NAACP. *Art Exhibition of Negro Expression Sponsored by Minars Furniture,* April 1964.

POTTER, LARRY

Painter. Born in New Jersey. Studied at Cooper Union Art School NY; Graphic Workshop, NY. Lives and works in Paris.
Works: *The Age of Black.*
Exhibited: 44th St. Gallery, NY; Galerie St.-Luc, Paris; Galerie Librairie Anglaise, Paris.
Sources: *10 American Negro Artists Living & Working in Europe,* Catalog, 1964.

POWELL, GEORGETTE SEABROOK

Born in Charleston, South Carolina. Studied at Harlem Art Workshop; Cooper Union Art School; Turtle Bay Music School (Art Therapy); Department of Agriculture Graduate School; DC Teachers College; Washington School of Psychiatry. Recreation specialist, Area C Community Mental Health Center.
Works: *Tropical Panorama; Grandmother's Birthday; Tropical Motif.*
Exhibited: Smith-Mason Gallery, 1971; NJ State Museum; Atlanta Univ.; Dillard Univ.; Smithsonian Institution; Margaret Dickey Gallery; Sidwell Friends School; Georgetown Presbyterian Church; Arts Club of Washington, DC; Outdoor community & organizational art shows; DCAA, Anacostia Neighborhood Museum-Smithsonian Institution; Carnegie Institute, Pittsburgh.
Collections: Harmon Art Foundation; Johnson Pub. Co.
Awards: 1st prize, Cooper Union; 1st prize, Dillard Univ.; 1st prize, Amer. Art League; Outstanding Performance Award, DC Public Health Dept.
Sources: Smith-Mason Gallery. *National Exhibition Black Artists,* 1971; D.C. Art Assn. *Exhibition '71,* Washington, DC, 1971; Johnson Pub. Co. *The JPC Art Collection,* Pamphlet; *Artists/USA,* 1972-1973, Feasterville, Pa., 1972 p. 149.

POWELL, GEORGIANA J.

Painter, sculptor, graphic artist, illustrator. Born in Boston in 1936. Studied at Boston University. Medical illustrator at New England Center Hospital.

Works: *On the Rocks,* 1961 (acrylic); *Red Bass,* 1963 (acrylic); *Bonds of Friendship,* 1964 (pastel); *Musician,* 1965 (acrylic); *Design-in-Color,* 1966 (acrylic); *Freighter,* 1966 (acrylic); *Main Coast,* 1966 (acrylic); *Sails,* 1967 (acrylic); *H-Design,* 1968 (acrylic); *Wings,* 1969 (steel); *Torch,* 1970 (steel); *The Ducks,* 1971 (pen & ink); *Little Boys,* 1971 (pen & ink); *Ducks* (print).
Exhibited: Unitarian Laymens League Art Exhibit, Boston, 1961; Emancipation Proclamation Centennial, 1963; Roslindale Library, 1964; Boston Public Library, 1964, 1965, 1973; Memorial Library, Boston, 1964; West Roxbury Council of United Church Women, Boston, 1964; St. Paul AME Church, Cambridge, Mass., 1964; Founders Day of the League of Women for Community Service Exhibition, 1965; Internat'l Book Exhibit, Leipzig, Germany, 1965; Historical Exhibition for Peoples Baptist Church, 1965; West Medford Community Center, 1966; Chester Park, Boston, 1966; Boston Negro Artists Assn., 1966; Professional & Businessmen Club, Boston, 1967; Robbins Library, Arlington, Mass., 1967; Mass. Ave. Baptist Church, Cambridge, Mass., 1967; Old Stout Meeting House, 1967; Unitarian Parish Hall, Newburyport, Mass., 1970; Black & White Conference, Amherst, NH, 1970; Tufts Univ., 1970; First Unitarian Church, Belmont, Mass., 1970; Salem State College, 1970; Gordon College, Wenham, Mass., 1971; Regis College, Weston, Mass., 1971; *Boston Globe* Book Festival, 1971; Whole World Celebration, Commonwealth Armory, Boston, 1971; NAACP Convention, 1963.
Awards: 2nd prize, Annual Creative Arts Show, Unitarian Laymens League, 1961; 2nd place, NAACP regional convention exhibit; Peace Cup, Women's Internat'l League for Peace & Freedom.
Member: Boston Negro Artists Assn. (treasurer); Cambridge Art Assn.
Sources: DuSable Museum of African-Amer. History. *Contemporary Black Artists,* 1970; *Art Gallery,* April 1970; St. Paul AME Church. *Fine Art Block Printing Demonstration, History & Examples,* Cambridge, Mass., Nov. 1, 1964; Information from the artist; Boston Negro Artists Assn. *10th Anniversary Exhibition,* 1973.

POWELL, JUDSON

Sculptor, painter, musician, actor. Born in Philadelphia, 1932. Studied at Brooklyn College, New York; Pratt Institute, New York; University of Southern California.
Works: *66 Signs of Neon* (wood).
Exhibited: Univ. of Southern Cal.; "Watts Renaissance of the Arts"; Markham Junior High School, Los Angeles; Dickson Art Center, 1966.

Sources: "Afro-American Issue," *Art Gallery*, April 1968; Indiana Univ. *Fine Arts & the Black American;* UCLA Art Galleries. *The Negro in American Art;* DuSable Museum of African-Amer. History. *Contemporary Black Artists,* 1970, calendar; Harley, Ralph, Jr. "Checklist of Afro-Amer. Art & Artists," *Serif,* Dec. 1970; Myers, Carol L. *Black Power in the Arts,* Flint, Mich., 1970; Walker, Roslyn. *A Resource Guide to the Visual Arts of Afro-Americans,* South Bend, Ind., 1971.

POWELL, KAREN McCLELLAN

Graphic artist, painter. Born in New York, June 30, 1945. Studied at Fisk University (BA); University of Chicago (MFA). Executive vice-president of K. Powell and Associates, graphic designers.
Sources: Information from artist.

POWELL, PAULINE

Painter. Worked in Oakland in 1890's.
Collections: Oakland Museum.
Sources: Porter. *Modern Negro Art;* Harley, Ralph, Jr. "Checklist of Afro-Amer. Art & Artists," *The Serif,* Dec. 1970.

PRES, FRANCOIS M.T. des

See: des Pres, Francois M.T.

PRESSLEY, DANIEL

Sculptor. Born in Wasamasaw, South Carolina, 1918. Self-taught.
Works: *When the Sharecropper's Daughter Do a Dance; The Hate Snake at the Garden Gate (Adam in Harlem); Sweet and Bitter Street; Flying Guitar; Down by the Riverside; The After Hour Devil and the Soul Swingers.*
Exhibited: Brooklyn Museum, 1969; Columbia Univ., 1969.
Sources: Brooklyn Museum. *New Black Artists,* 1969; Loercher, Diana. "Art: Idioms of Blackness at the Elma Lewis School," *Christian Science Monitor,* July 10, 1970; Walker, Roslyn. *A Resource Guide to the Visual Arts of Afro-Americans,* South Bend, Ind., 1971.

PRICE, LESLIE

Painter, graphic artist, educator. Born in New York City, October 2, 1945. Studied at the School of Visual Arts, New York; Pratt Institute, Brooklyn; Mills College, Oakland, California.
Works: *Dedicated to My Ancestors Past, Present & Future; There's A Void during the Day-A Void during the Night; Reflections on Being Black in New York; Black Madonna with Rainbow Sun; Oil and Water Don't Mix-But They Do; Om; Purnsa; Rebirth Universal.*
Exhibited: Oakland Museum; College of Marin; Pacific Grove Art Center, Cal.; Museum—A Project of Living Arts, Inc., NY;

Group One, NY; Univ. of Iowa, 1971-2; Illinois Bell Telephone, Chicago, 1971; Black Figures in History, Berkeley, Cal., 1972.
Collections: Mr. J. Wolkman S. Winer; W&N of Table Mountain Ranch; Oakland Museum; Mills College; Illinois Bell Telephone; *Ebony Magazine*; Johnson Pub. Co.
Awards: $1000 painting grant.
Member: Art West Associated North; Rennaissance Universal.
Sources: Oakland Museum. *Black, Untitled,* 1970; Lewis/Waddy. *Black Artists on Art,* Vol. 2; Illinois Bell Telephone. *Black American Artists/71,* 1972; Johnson Pub. Co. *The JPC Art Collection,* Pamphlet; "San Francisco," *Art Forum,* Oct. 1970, p. 81.

PRICE, RAMON B.

Mixed media, educator. Born in Chicago. Studied at the Art Institute of Chicago (BAE); under Margaret Burroughs. Program Director, South Side Community Art Center, Chicago.
Sources: DuSable Museum of African-Amer. History. *Contemporary Black Artists,* Calendar, 1970; *Art Gallery,* April 1970; Myers, Carol L. *Black Power in the Arts,* Flint, Mich., 1970; "Afro-American Issue," *Art Gallery,* April 1968; Indiana Univ. *Fine Arts & the Black American;* Walker, Roslyn. *A Resource Guide to the Visual Arts of Afro-Americans,* South Bend, Ind., 1971.

PRICE, SHIRLEY

Graphic artist.
Works: Cover drawing, *Black Shades,* Vol. 3, #2.
Sources: *Black Shades,* Vol. 3, #2.

PRIDE, WILMOT

Painter.
Works: *The Prophet.*
Exhibited: Atlanta Univ., 1944.
Sources: Exhibition catalog, Atlanta Univ., 1944.

PRIMUS, NELSON A.

Painter; specialized in portraits and religious themes. Born in Hartford, Connecticut. In 1858 became apprenticed to George Francis, and also studied under Mrs. Elizabeth Gilbert Jerome. In 1864 moved to Boston and established himself as a portrait and carriage painter. Known to have still been in Boston as late as 1895.
Works: *Christ Being Lowered from the Cross.*
Collections: Mr. Blair E. Hutson, Martinez, Cal.
Sources: Porter. *Modern Negro Art;* French. *Art & Artists in Connecticut,* p. 155; Groce/Wallace. *Dictionary of Artists in America 1564-1860,* NY Historical Society; Runes, Dagobert, & Harry Schrickel, eds. *Encyclopedia*

of the Arts, NY, 1946; Mallett. *Index of Artists;* Harley, Ralph, Jr. "Checklist of Afro-Amer. Art & Artists," *Serif,* Dec. 1970; Young, William, ed. & comp. *A Dictionary of American Artists, Sculptors & Engravers,* Cambridge, 1968.

PRINCE, ARNOLD

Sculptor, educator. Born in Basseterre, St. Kitts, British West Indies, 1925. Studied at the Art Students League of New York (1957-61); North Adams State College, Massachusetts.
Works: *The Earth; The Widow; Portrait of Sandy Wittenberg; Limestone Head; The Virgin Limestone; Portrait of Connie; Thought-Marble; Thought; The Virgin; Torso-Green; Dancer's Torso; Job; Mother and Child,* 1965 (red oak); *Carnival; Job-Marble; Mother and Child,* 1969 (black cherry); *Vest Pocket Parks* (direct cement); *Lions,* 1972 (direct cement).
Exhibited: Barbados Museum, 1949; British Council Inter-Island Art Exhibitions, 1949-53; St. Thomas Public Library, 1955; Phoenix Gallery, NY, 1961-2; Internat'l Art Gallery, 1961; Arlington (Pa.) Museum, 1961; Jersey City Museum, 1961; St. Marks on the Bauverie Episcopal Church, 1963; Chelsea Art Show, St. Peters Episcopal Church, NY, 1964; Temple Emmanuel, NY, 1964; Capricorn Gallery, NY, 1966; Lever House, NY, 1967; Norwich Univ., Vt., 1969; Sculptor's Guild, NY, 1969, 1970, 1972; North Adams State College, Mass., 1971.
Collections: Art Students League, NY.
Awards: Von Schlegel Scholarship, Art Students League, 1959; Monitor Scholarship, 1958.
Member: Sculptor's Guild, NYC.
Represented by: Sculptor's Guild, NYC.
Sources: Afro-Amer. Slide Depository, Catalog; Patterson, Lindsay, comp. "Contemporary Black Artists," *The Negro in Music and Art,* 1969; Information from artist; *Village Voice,* Dec. 2, 1965, Dec. 9, 1965; *Long Island Newsday,* April 13, 1965; *New York Herald Tribune,* May 23, 1961.

PRINCE, KENNETH

Printmaker.
Works: *Man and Boy* (etching); *31st and Ellis* (etching); *Nude* (aquatint); *Head Study* (etching); *Backyard* (etching).
Exhibited: South Side Community Art Center, Chicago, 1941.
Sources: Locke, Alain. "Chicago's New Southside Art Center," *Amer. Mag. of Art,* Aug. 1941; South Side Community Art Center. *National Negro Art Exhibition,* Chicago, 1941.

PRINGLE, BRYANT

Sources: "Amer. Negro Art Given Full Length

Review in NY Show," *Art Digest,* Dec. 15, 1941.

PRIOLEAU, SIMON D.

Works: *Bored.*
Exhibited: Phila. Civic Center.
Sources: Phila. Division of Art. *Afro-American Artists 1800-1969.*

PROCTOR, RALPH

Born in Pittsburgh, Pennsylvania. Studied at Lincoln University; Austin State College. Worked in Marketing and Public Relations, H.J. Heinz Co.; Producer, Black Horizons, WQED. Travelled extensively to develop plans for Black Studio Museum and Theatre in Pittsburgh.
Sources: Pittsburgh Community College: *16 Black Artists.*

PROPHET, NANCY ELIZABETH

Sculptor. Born in Warwick, Rhode Island in 1890. Studied at Rhode Island School of Design; École des Beaux Arts, Paris. Taught at Spelman College, Atlanta; Atlanta University.
Works: *Silence; Discontent; Congolais; Head in Ebony; Head of a Negro.*
Exhibited: Harmon Foundation, 1930, 1931, 1936; Whitney Sculpture Biennial, 1935, 1937; Paris August Salons, 1925, 1926.
Collections: Whitney Museum, NY; Rhode Island School of Design; National Archives.
Member: Le Salon d'Automne; Le Salon des Artistes Francais.
Sources: Mallett. *Index of Artists;* Locke. *The Negro in Art;* Dover. *American Negro Art;* Porter. *Modern Negro Art;* Afro-American Slide Depository, Catalog; *American Art Annual,* 1933; *Who's Who in American Art,* 1940-1; Indiana Univ. *Fine Arts & the Black American;* Harmon Foundation. *Exhibition of Productions by Negro Artists;* Brawley, Benjamin. *The Negro Genius;* Cullen, Countee. "Elizabeth Prophet: Sculptress," *Opportunity,* 1930; Roucek & Kiernan. *The Negro Impact on Western Civilization;* Harmon Foundation. *Negro Artists,* 1935; Harmon Foundation. *Exhibit of Fine Arts,* 1930; DuSable Museum of African-Amer. History. *Contemporary Black Artists,* calendar, 1970; Harmon Foundation. *Select Picture List; Art Digest,* Aug. 1, 1932; Pierre-Noel, Lois Jones. "American Negro Art in Progress," *Negro History Bulletin,* Oct. 1967; Harley, Ralph, Jr. "Checklist of Afro-American Art & Artists," *The Serif,* Dec. 1970; Ploski, Harry, & Ernest Kaiser. "The Black Artist," *Afro USA,* 1971; Ploski, Harry, Ernest Kaiser, & Otto Lindenmeyer. "The Black Artist," *Reference Library of Black America,* Book IV, 1971; *Negro History Bulletin,* March 1939, p. 52; Spradling, Mary M., ed. *In Black & White: Afro-Americans in Print;* Walker, Ros-

lyn. *A Resource Guide to the Visual Arts of Afro-Americans*, South Bend, Ind., 1971.

PRYCE, EDWARD L.

Sculptor, muralist, painter, landscape architect. Born May 26, 1914, in Lake Charles, Louisiana. Studied: Tuskegee Institute, Alabama (BS); Ohio State University (BLA); University of California, Berkeley (MLA).
Works: Tuskegee Institute Chapel Mural, 1968; Tuskegee Institute Engineering Building Bas-Relief, 1970; Atlanta University Purchase, 1968.
Exhibited: Atlanta Univ.; Tuskeegee Institute.
Collections: Atlanta Univ.; Tuskegee Institute.
Awards: Atlanta Univ. Sculpture Award, 1968.
Sources: Information from artist.

PRYOR, JESSE

Painter.
Works: *Brown's Filling Station.*
Exhibited: Dillard Univ., 1941.
Sources: Dillard Univ. *Arts Festival*, Catalog, 1941.

PRYOR, WILLIAM

Sculptor. Born 1949 in Fayetteville, Georgia. Studied at Morehouse College; Atlanta School of Art.
Works: *Yomoko.*
Exhibited: Student Exhibition, Atlanta School of Art, 1970; Phipps Plaza, 1970; Citizens Trust Bank, 1971.
Collections: Johnson Pub. Co.
Sources: Lewis/Waddy. *Black Artists on Art*, Vol. 2; Johnson Pub. Co. *The JPC Art Collection*, Pamphlet.

PUGHSLEY, RALPHINE

Studied at Tuskegee Institute.
Works: *Umbrella.*
Exhibited: Sun Times/Daily News Gallery, Chicago, 1970.
Sources: United Negro College Fund. *Art 1970*, Chicago, 1970.

PULLEY, MARY

Sources: DuSable Museum of African-Amer. History. *Contemporary Black Artists*, 1970, Calendar.

PURIFOY, NOAH

Sculptor. Born in Snow Hill, Alabama, 1917. Studied at Alabama State Teachers College; Atlanta University School of Social Service; Chouinard Art Institute, Los Angeles.
Works: *Humpty Dumpty Sat on the World; City at Night; Mechanical Man; Sir Watts; Untitled mixed media, 1970; Untitled-Twelve Holes; Six Birds Flew by My Window; Niggers Ain't Gona Never Be Nothing, All They Want to Do Is Drink & Fuck; A Two Room Apartment; Signs of Neon;* Untitled (copper, brass, & tin); Untitled construction.

Exhibited: Univ. of Cal. at Santa Cruz Faculty Show; Nordness Galleries, NYC; Long Beach Museum; Lang Art Gallery, Claremont, Cal.; Brockman Gallery, Los Angeles; Watts Renaissance of the Arts, Los Angeles; Negro Art, Traveling Exhibition, Cal.; Pasadena Museum; Orlando Galleries, Encino, Cal.; Muncipal Art Galleries, Barnsdall Park, Los Angeles; Bowman Mann Galleria, Los Angeles; Univ. of Southern Cal.; Whitney Museum, NY, 1971; Univ. of Iowa, 1971-2; Los Angeles County Museum; Oakland Museum; Illinois Bell Telephone; Huntington Galleries, Tenn.; Dickson Art Center, 1966.
Collections: Cowell College, Santa Cruz; Oakland Museum.
Member: Joined for the Arts, Inc., Chairman.
Sources: Lewis/Waddy. *Black Artists on Art*, Vol. 2; Nordness Galleries. *12 Afro-American Artists*, 1969; "Afro-American Issue," *Art Gallery*, April 1968; Indiana Univ. *Fine Arts & the Black American*; UCLA Art Galleries. *The Negro in American Art*; Doty. *Contemporary Black Artists in America*; Illinois Bell Telephone. *Black American Artists/71*, 1972; Information from artist; *Junk Art Magazine*, Pub. by 66 Signs of Neon; DuSable Museum of African-Amer. History. *Contemporary Black Artists*, 1970, Calendar; Harley, Ralph, Jr. "Checklist of Afro-Amer. Art & Artists," *Serif*, Dec. 1970; Oakland Museum. *The Metal Experience*, 1971; Myers, Carol L. *Black Power in the Arts*, Flint, Mich., 1970; Oakland Museum Archives; Preston, Malcolm. "Art: Black Exhibit," *Boston Herald Traveler*, April 19, 1971; Haas, Joseph. "A Big, Brilliant & Exciting Exhibition of Black Art," *Chicago Daily News*, Jan. 16-17, 1971.

PURNELL, EDWARD J.

Works: *Two Figures; Nude Figure.*
Exhibited: Phila. Civic Center.
Sources: Phila. Division of Art. *Afro-American Artists 1800-1969.*

PURVIANCE, FLORENCE V.

Painter, educator. Born in Baltimore. Studied at University of Pennslyvania; Columbia University; Pennsylvania State College. Art Supervisor, Baltimore public schools.
Works: *Hills; Backyards; Roofs.*
Exhibited: Baltimore Museum, 1938-40.
Sources: DuSable Museum of African-Amer. History. *Contemporary Black Artists*, 1970, Calendar; Harley, Ralph, Jr. "Checklist of Afro-Amer. Art & Artists," *Serif*, Dec. 1970; Locke, Alain. "Advance on the Art Front," *Opportunity*, May 1939; Locke. *The Negro in Art*; Baltimore Museum of Art. *Contemporary Negro*, 1939, Catalog; Walker, Roslyn. *A Resource Guide to the Visual Arts of Afro-Americans*, South Bend, Ind., 1971.

PUSEY, MAVIS

Printmaker, painter. Born in Jamaica, West Indies, 1931. Studied at the Art Students League, New York.
Works: *Untitled; Resonante; London's Night; Foggy Day; Low Tide; Eric; Nexus; Janeyo; Sea View; Paris Mai-Juin; Urison; Zphae; Carome; Frozen Vibration; Unave; Impact on Vibration; Recarte; Deiyqea.*
Exhibited: Art Students League, NY; Treasure Gallery, NJ; Whitney Museum, NY, 1971; Dickson Art Center, 1966; Univ. of Cal., Los Angeles, 1966.
Collections: Mr. Will Barnet; Mr. Henry Sternberg, NY; Mrs. Rosina Lucash, NJ; Mrs. D.S. Cohen, Cal.; Mr. E.H. Fletcher, Buenos Aires, Argentina; Mrs. Jack Dryfus, NY; Mr. Ed Aimone, Reno, Nevada; Oakland Museum.
Sources: "Afro-Amer. Issue," *Art Gallery,* April 1968; Indiana Univ. *Fine Arts & the Black American*; Roelof-Lanner, T.V., ed. *Prints by American Negro Artists*; Afro-Amer. Slide Depository, Catalog; UCLA Art Galleries. *The Negro in American Art*; Doty. *Contemporary Black Artists in America*; DuSable Museum of African-Amer. History. *Contemporary Black Artists*, 1970, Calendar; Harley, Ralph, Jr. "Checklist of Afro-Amer. Art & Artists," *Serif*, Dec. 1970; Myers, Carol L. *Black Power in the Arts*, Flint, Mich., 1970; Oakland Museum Archives, Ruth Waddy Collection; Walker, Roslyn. *A Resource Guide to the Visual Arts of Afro-Americans*, South Bend, Ind., 1971.

PYBURN, DON

Printmaker. Active 1960's.
Works: *Mathew Henson* (linocut).
Collections: Oakland Museum.
Sources: Roelof-Lanner, T.V. *Prints by American Negro Artists*; Oakland Museum Archives, Ruth Waddy Collection; Walker, Roslyn. *A Resource Guide to the Visual Arts of Afro-Americans*, South Bend, Ind., 1971.

RAE, JOHN

Sources: Harley, Ralph, Jr. "Checklist of Afro-Amer. Art & Artists," *The Serif*, Dec. 1970.

RAGLAND, PHILLDA

Photographer.
Sources: *Ebony*, March 1969, pp. 112-20; Spradling, Mary M., ed. *In Black & White: Afro-Americans in Print.*

RAGUIB, HAKIM

Photographer.
Exhibited: Addison Gallery, 1971
Sources: James Van DerZee Institute. *The Black Photographer (1908-1970): A Survey.*

RAHMAN, ABDUL

Painter. Studied at the School of Industrial Art, New York.
Exhibited: Carver Federal Bank; Manor Craft Gallery; Unique Gift Shop; Al-Shar-Art-Salon; Club 720; Club Hide A-Way; Smalls Paradise; Universal Art Studio.
Sources: NY NAACP. *A Most Memorable Showing of Creative Negro Art*; NY NAACP. *Art Exhibition of Negro Expression Sponsored by Minars Furniture*, April 1964.

RAMOS BLANCO, TEODORO

See: Blanco, Teodoro Ramos.

RAMSES, AKHENATEN, V.

Sculptor.
Works: *Upheaval.*
Exhibited: Lee Cultural Center, Phila.
Sources: Phila. Dept. of Recreation. *Love . . . and the Black Community.*

RANGE, THOMAS

Sources: DuSable Museum of African-Amer. History. *Contemporary Black Artists*, 1970, Calendar.

RAWLINGS, FRANK H.

Painter. Born in St. Paul, Minnesota in 1924. Self-taught.
Works: *Attacked.*
Sources: Dover. *American Negro Art*; Indiana Univ. *Fine Arts & the Black American*; Harley, Ralph, Jr. "A Checklist of Afro-Amer. Art & Artists," *The Serif*, Dec. 1970; Walker, Roslyn. *A Resource Guide to the Visual Arts of Afro-Americans*, South Bend, Ind., 1971.

RAY, GERTRUDE

Painter, graphic artist. Born in Hancock, Massachusetts, 1921. Self-taught.
Exhibited: Afro-Art League Exhibitions; Stage West, West Springfield, Mass.; George W. Vincent Art Museum; Eastfield Mall.
Member: Springfield (Mass.) Art League.
Sources: Information from the artist.

RAYFIELD

Architect.
Sources: Wilson, John L. *The Negro Architect.*

REASON, PATRICK HENRY

Printmaker, draftsman. Born in 1817. Died in 1850. Studied at New York Free School.
Works: *Kneeling Slave; Granville Sharp; DeWitt Clinton; James Williams; Am I Not a Woman & a Sister; Henry Bibb; James McCune Smith; John Brown; The Truth Shall Make You Free; Miniature of Kneeling Slave;* Frontispiece, Charles C. Andrew's HISTORY OF THE AFRICAN FREE SCHOOLS.
Exhibited: Howard Univ., 1967.

Collections: Mrs. James A. Porter; Howard Univ. Negro Collection.
Member: Anti-Slavery Society.
Sources: Dover. *American Negro Art*; Porter. "Versatile Interests of the Early Negro Artists: A Neglected Chapter of American Art History," *Art in America*, Vol. 24, 1926; Delaney, Martin R. *The Condition, Elevation, Emigration & Destination of the Colored People of the US*, 1852; Indiana Univ. *Fine Arts & the Black American*; Stauffer, David M. *American Engravers Upon Copper & Steel*, NY, Grolier Club, 1907; Porter. *Modern Negro Art*; Howard Univ. *Ten Afro-American Artists of the 19th Century*; Brawley, Benjamin. *The Negro Genius*; Roucek & Kiernan. *The Negro Impact on Western Civilization*; Greene, Carroll, Jr. "Perspective: The Black Artist in America," *Art Gallery*, April 1970, p. 5; Kiah, Virginia. "Black Artists," *Savannah Magazine*, April 1972, p. 14; Harley, Ralph, Jr. "A Checklist of Afro-Amer. Art & Artists," *The Serif*, Dec. 1970; *1st Annual Exhibit of Books, Manuscripts, Paintings, Sculptures etc. by the Negro Library Assn. at Carlton Ave. YMCA*, Aug. 1918; Myers, Carol. *Black Power in the Arts*, Flint, Mich., 1970; DuSable Museum of African-Amer. History. *Contemporary Black Artists*, 1970, Calendar; Walker, Roslyn. *A Resource Guide to the Visual Arts of Afro-Americans*, South Bend, Ind., 1971.

REDDICK, LARRY
Painter.
Works: *Untitled* (watercolor).
Exhibits: Lee Cultural Center, Phila.
Sources: Phila. Dept. of Recreation. *Love . . . and the Black Community*.

REDDIX, ROSCOE C.
Painter, mixed media, educator. Born in New Orleans in 1933. Studied at Southern University of New Orleans (BA); Indiana University (MS); Xavier University.
Works: *Afro-American Girl; Adolescent Dilemma; With Hair Like Lamb's Wool; Eviction; Blues People; Flowers for the Teacher; The Guitar Player; Adam & Eve; Syncopated Pattern; Three Major Movements; A Portrait of the Artist's Father; A Portrait of the Artist's Sister; Let Not Your Heart Be Troubled; Study in Blue-Green; Portrait of William G. Brown.*
Exhibited: Indiana Univ.; Professional Artist Show, State of Louisiana; Black Artists Show, Dilliard Univ.; Atlanta Univ. Annual Show; Civil Liberties Union, Savannah, Ga.; Expo '72, Chicago; Southern Univ., New Orleans, 1972; Savannah State Univ.; NJ State Museum.
Collections: Southern Univ., New Orleans; Education Building, Louisiana State Capital.
Member: Nat'l Conference of Artists.

Sources: Afro-American Slide Depository, Catalog, 1971-2; Lewis/Waddy. *Black Artists on Art*, Vol. 2; Smith-Mason Gallery. *National Exhibition Black Artists*, 1971; Information from the artist; Civil Liberties Union. *National Conference of Artists Show*, Savannah, Ga.

REDWOOD, JUNIUS
Painter. Born in Columbus, Ohio in 1917.
Works: *Night Scene*, 1941; *Infinitus XXV*.
Exhibited: Newark Museum, 1971; NY Museum of Modern Art; State Univ. of Albany, NY; Long Island Art Teachers Assn.; Acts of Art Gallery, NYC.
Collections: Museum of Modern Art, NYC.
Sources: *Artists/USA 1972-1973*, Feasterville, Pa., 1972, p. 154; Newark Museum. *Black Artists: Two Generations*, 1971; "Young Negro Art Impresses NY," *Art Digest*, Oct. 15, 1943; *Art News*, Nov. 15, 1943, p. 22; *The Negro Handbook*, Composed by Editors of *Ebony*, Chicago, 1966; Schatz, Walter. *Directory of Afro-American Resources*, 1970.

REED, JAMES REUBEN
Painter. Born in 1920.
Works: *Depressed*.
Sources: Dover. *American Negro Art*; Indiana Univ. *Fine Arts & the Black American*; Harley, Ralph, Jr. "A Checklist of Afro-Amer. Art & Artists," *The Serif*, Dec. 1970; Walker, Roslyn. *A Resource Guide to the Visual Arts of Afro-Americans*, South Bend, Ind., 1971.

REED, JERRY
Painter. Born 1949 in Los Angeles, California. Studied at Pomona College; Fisk University.
Works: *My Land*.
Exhibited: Watts Summer Festival, 1968.
Sources: Lewis/Waddy. *Black Artists on Art*, Vol. 2.

REEVES, CATHY
Graphic artist. Studied at Shaw University.
Works: Untitled line drawing.
Exhibited: Sun Times/Daily News Gallery, Chicago, 1970.
Sources: United Negro College Fund. *Art 1970*, Chicago, 1970.

REID, DAN TERRY
Painter. Born in Chicago. Studied at Howard University; Wicker School of Fine Arts, Detroit; Art Institute of Chicago.
Works: *Portrait of a Woman* (pastel); *Portrait of Dean Kelly Miller; West Side Alley; Portrait.*
Exhibited: Harmon Foundation, 1931, 1933; Chicago Outdoor Show, 1934; West Side Alley PWAP, 1934; Harmon College Art Assn. Traveling Exhibition, 1934-5; Texas Centennial, 1936; South Side Community Art Center, Chicago, 1945.

Awards: 1st prize, 3rd Annual All-Negro Showing of Chicago Artists' Guild.
Sources: Harmon Foundation. *Exhibition of Productions by Negro Artists*; Harmon Foundation. *Negro Artists*, 1935; Indiana Univ. *Fine Arts & the Black American*; Howard Univ. *Art of the American Negro*, 1937; Texas Centennial Exposition. *Thumbnail Sketches of Exhibiting Artists*, 1936; DuSable Museum of African-Amer. History. *Contemporary Black Artists*, 1970, Calendar; Harley, Ralph, Jr. "A Checklist of Afro-Amer. Art & Artists," *The Serif*, Dec. 1970; "Six Paintings of City Life," *Arts Quarterly*, Dec. 1939, pp. 13-9; South Side Community Art Center. *Chicago Collectors Exhibit of Negro Art*, Chicago, 1945; Walker, Roslyn. *A Resource Guide to the Visual Arts of Afro-Americans*, South Bend, Ind., 1971.

REID, DONALD A.

Exhibited: Harmon Foundation, 1931, 1933; Chicago Artists Outdoor Show, 1934; Westside Gallery, 1934; PWAP Exhibition, Washington & Richmond, 1934; Harmon Foundation-College Art Assn. Touring Exhibition, 1934-5.
Sources: Harley, Ralph, Jr. "Checklist of Afro-Amer. Art & Artists," *The Serif*, Dec. 1970.

REID, DONALD REDEVERS

Born in British Guiana in 1902. Studied at Art Students League, NYC, and under private instruction.
Works: *Still Life—Fruits & Flowers; Mr. J. Long; Miss Hester Boerun; An Old Gentleman; City Island Landscape; Mr. Oliver Fosler; Rudolph; Still Life—Apples, Beets, Etc.; George Washington Bridge.*
Exhibited: 135th St. Branch, NY Public Library; Art Students League; Harmon Foundation, 1931, 1933; Amer. Negro Exposition, 1940.
Collections: NY Public Library-Schomburg Collection.
Awards: Honorable Mention, Amer. Negro Exposition, 1940.
Sources: Harmon Foundation. *Exhibition of Productions by Negro Artists*; Harmon Foundation. *Non-Jury Exhibit of Works of Negro Artists*, 1933; Harmon Foundation. *Negro Artists*, 1935; Indiana Univ. *Fine Arts & the Black American*; Tanner Art Galleries. *Art of the American Negro*, 1940; DuSable Museum of African-Amer. History. *Contemporary Black Artists*, 1970, Calendar; Schatz, Walter. *Directory of Afro-American Resources*, 1970.

REID, O. RICHARD

Portrait painter. Born in Eaton, Georgia on February 27, 1898. Studied at Pennsylvania Academy of Fine Arts.
Works: *Mr. H.L. Mencken; Portrait of a Man.*

Exhibited: Society of Independent Artists, Anderson Gallery, NYC; Harmon Foundation, 1928-31; Independent Artists League; Urban League, NY; Howard Univ., 1932.
Collections: Nat'l Archives; NY Public Library-Schomburg Collection.
Member: Graphic Sketch Club, Phila.
Sources: Harmon Foundation. *Exhibition of Productions by Negro Artists*; Harmon Foundation. *Select Picture List*; Indiana Univ. *Fine Arts & the Black American*; *Who's Who in Colored America*, 3rd Edition; City College of NY. *The Evolution of Afro-American Artists, 1800-1950*; "O. Richard Reid, Portraitist," *Opportunity*, Feb. 1928; DuSable Museum of African-Amer. History. *Contemporary Black Artists*, 1970, Calendar; Harley, Ralph, Jr. "A Checklist of Afro-Amer. Art & Artists," *The Serif*, Dec. 1970; Schatz, Walter. *Directory of Afro-American Resources*, 1970; Walker, Roslyn. *A Resource Guide to the Visual Arts of Afro-Americans*, South Bend, Ind., 1971.

REID, ROBERT

Painter, mixed media, educator. Born in Atlanta, 1924. Studied at Clark College, Atlanta (1941-3); Art Institute of Chicago (1943-6); Parson School of Design, NYC (1948-50). Teacher at Rhode Island School of Design.
Works: *Agon II; Gloria-Artist's Wife; Black Beach, House with Figure; Two Beach Houses; Beach Rock; House with Falling Figure; Figure 8 After; Follow the Leader; A Falling #2,* 1970 (oil & collage); *Falling Figures Green; Business Figures; A Falling #6; Small Beach House with Figures; Beach Game #2; Beach Houses with 6 Figures; Z; Nella's Beach; Figures Seen from the Sea #1; Figures on a Beach Rock; Falling Figure #3; Midwest Landscape #1; Midwest Landscape #2.*
Exhibited: Grand Central Moderns, 1965 (1-man), 1966, 1967; City College of NY; Baruch College; Lehigh Univ., 1969; Beson Gallery, Bridgehampton, NY, 1970; Summit (NJ) Art Center, 1970; Alonzo Gallery, 1970, 1972; NC Central Univ. at Durham, 1972; NYC Center Gallery, 1959; James Gallery, NYC, 1961; Mortimer Brandt Gallery, 1962; Osborne Gallery, 1963; Barnard College, 1965; 1st World Festival of Negro Artists, Dakar, Senegal, 1965; Bucknell Univ., 1965; UCLA Art Galleries, 1966; Amer. Academy of Arts & Letters, 1967-9; Arts in the American Embassies State Dept. Program, 1967; Minneapolis Institute of Arts; Studio Museum in Harlem, 1968-9; Ill. Bell Telephone, 1972; Lobby Gallery, Chicago; Univ. of Wisc.; Sloan Galleries, Valparaiso, Ind.; Peoria (Ill.) Art Guild; Burpee Gallery, Rockford, Ill.; Davenport (Iowa) Municipal Gallery; St. Paul's College, Lawrenceville, Cal.; Whitney Museum, 1971; New-

ark Museum, 1971; Univ. of Iowa, 1971-2; Dickson Art Center, 1966; US Information Service, Washington, DC, 1971.
Collections: Myers College, Birmingham, Ala.; Museum of African Art, Washington, DC; Laura Musser Museum, Muscatine, Iowa; Notre Dame Univ.; Cornell Univ.; Syracuse Univ.; Univ. of Pa.; Lehigh Univ.; Drew Univ.; Newark Museum.
Sources: *Who's Who in American Art*, 1970; "Afro-American Issue," *Art Gallery*, April 1968; Indiana Univ. *Fine Arts & the Black American*; *Ten Negro Artists From the United States*, 1966; Afro-American Slide Depository, Catalog, 1971-2; *Pictures on Exhibit*, Feb. 1972; Information from artist; *Art News*, Feb. 1972 (review); Newark Museum. *Black Artists: Two Generations*, 1971; Whitney Museum. *Black Artists in America*; Minneapolis Institute of Arts. *30 Contemporary Black Artists*, 1968; Studio Museum in Harlem. *Contemporary Black Artists*, 1968-9; *Arts*, Feb. 1972 (review of show at Alonzo Gallery); Canaday, John. "Robert Reid," *New York Times*, March 4, 1972 (Alonzo Gallery show); UCLA Art Galleries. *The Negro in American Art*; Doty. *Contemporary Black Artists in America*; Illinois Bell Telephone. *Black American Artists/71*, 1972; DuSable Museum of African-Amer. History. *Contemporary Black Artists*, 1970, Calendar; Harley, Ralph, Jr. "Checklist of Afro-Amer. Art & Artists," *The Serif*, Dec. 1970; Woodruff, Hale. "Artists of the 60's," *The Negro in Music and Art*, 1969; *First World Festival of Negro Artists*, Dakar, Senegal, 1966, Catalog; Ruder & Finn Fine Arts. *Contemporary Black Artists*, NY, 1969; Myers, Carol L. *Black Power in the Arts*, Flint, Mich., 1970; Amer. Academy of Arts & Letters. *Childe Hassam Fund Show*, 1967; Minneapolis Institute of Art. *30 Contemporary Black Artists*; Bucknell Univ. *Bucknell Univ. Drawing Annual*, 1965; Walker, Roslyn. *A Resource Guide to the Visual Arts of Afro-Americans*, South Bend, Ind., 1961.

REID, WILLIAM

Painter. Born in Raleigh, North Carolina in 1927. Self-taught.
Exhibited: Watts Summer Festival, Los Angeles, 1968.
Sources: Lewis/Waddy. *Black Artists on Art*, Vol. 1; Walker, Roslyn. *A Resource Guide to the Visual Arts of Afro-Americans*, South Bend, Ind., 1971.

REISS, WINOLD

Painter.
Works: *The Brown Madonna; Alain Locke; Jean Toomer; Countee Cullen; Paul Robeson as Emporer Jones; Roland Hayes; African Phantasies: Awakening; From the Tropic Isles;*

Elise Johnson McDougald; Mary McLoed Bethune; W.E. Burghardt DuBois; The Librarian; The School Teacher.
Sources: Locke, Alain. *The New Negro.*

RENWICK, GLADYS W.

Painter. Born in St. Louis in 1905.
Exhibited: Boston Museum of Fine Arts, 1954; NY Academy of Design; Phila. Academy of Art, 1957; Atlanta Univ., 1951; Chester City Federal Savings & Loan, 1960; Lincoln Univ., 1950, 1966; Beach Theatre, Cape May, 1961; Post House, NY; Bird Cage Gallery, NY.
Collections: Atlanta Univ.; Lincoln Univ.
Awards: Watercolor Award, Atlanta Univ., 10th Annual for Negro Artists, 1951.
Member: Acts of Art Gallery, NYC.
Sources: Atlanta Univ. Annual, 1951, Catalog; Information from artist.

REYNEAU, BETSY GRAVES

Collections: Smithsonian Institution, Nat'l Gallery.
Sources: Schatz, Walter. *Directory of Afro-American Resources*, 1970.

REYNOLDS, CARITA

Works: *Man.*
Collections: Johnson Pub. Co.
Sources: Johnson Pub. Co. *The JPC Art Collection*, Pamphlet.

RHODEN, JOHN

Sculptor. Born in Birmingham, Alabama on March 13, 1918. Studied at Columbia University School of Painting and Sculpture; under Hugo Robus, Oronzio Maldareli, Richmond Barthé, William Zorach.
Works: *Sand Painting; Topeng; Glass Galaxy, Invictus; Female Figure; Blue Eyes (Indonesian Legend); Paytoemahtamo, An American Indian Legend; Population Explosion*, 1963 (teak).
Exhibited: Fisk Univ.; Frick Museum; Brooklyn College, 1969; Atlanta Univ. Annuals; Metropolitan Museum; Pa. Academy of Fine Arts; Art Institute of Chicago; Boston Museum of Fine Arts, 1970; Whitney Museum, 1971; Nat'l Academy of Arts & Letters; Amer. Academy of Arts & Letters; Schneider Galleria, Rome; Fairweather-Harden Gallery, Chicago; Saidenberg Gallery, NYC; Audubon Annual; British-Amer. Gallery; Univ. of Ill. Annual; Howard Univ. Museum; Amer. Academy, Rome; Camino Gallery; Brooklyn College; Univ. of Pittsburgh, 1971.
Collections: Sheraton Hotel, Phila.; Harlem Health Clinic; Harlem Hospital; Metropolitan Hospital; Clifton Sr. High School, Baltimore; Stockholm Museum; Mr. Samuel Marx; Mr. Wallace K. Harrison; Mr. G. David Thompson Heinz Collection, Pittsburgh; Delaware Museum; Mr. Carl Milles; Steinberg Collection.

Awards: Julius Rosenwald Fellowship, 1947-8; Prix de Rome Fellowship, 1952-4; Guggenheim Fellowship, 1961; Fulbright Fellowship; Rockefeller Grant; Honorarium & Medal Pro Sculptura Egregia, Howard Univ.; 1st prize, Atlanta Univ. Annual, 1955; Tiffany Award; 1st prize, sculpture, Columbia Univ. (3 times); Painters & Sculptors Society of NJ Award; James A. Porter Gallery, 1970; Xavier Univ., 1963.
Member: Municipal Art Society (life member); Amer. Society of Contemporary Artists.
Sources: Roucek/Kiernan. *The Negro Impact on Western Civilization*; Howard Univ. *James A. Porter Gallery of African-American Art*, 1970; Pierre-Noel, Lois Jones. "American Negro Art in Progress," *Negro History Bulletin*, Oct. 1967; Kiah, Virginia. "Black Artists," *Savannah Magazine*, April 1972, p. 16; Sherman, Marjorie. "Afro-America Gets Biggest Show," *Boston Globe*, May 18, 1970; Patterson, Lindsay. "Contemporary Artists," *The Negro in Music & Art*, 1969; Walsh, Rose. "Artists to Meet Public at Art Exhibit Preview," *Record American*, May 19, 1970; "Museum of Fine Arts to Hold Black Art Show," *Chronicle*, Belmont, Mass., April 28, 1970; "Museum of Fine Arts to Hold Black Art Show," *Chronicle*, Ipswich, Mass., April 30, 1970; "Museum of Fine Arts to Hold Black Art Show," *Tri-Town Transcript & Pennysaver*, April 29, 1970; "Black Artists Work on View at Museum," *News*, Newburyport, Mass., May 16, 1970; Le Brun, Caron. "Black's Art on Display," *Herald Traveler*, Boston, May 26, 1970; Xavier Univ. *Emancipation Proclamation Centennial National Art Exhibition*, 1963; Dover. *American Negro Art*; Boston Museum of Fine Arts. *Afro-American Artists: NY & Boston*, 1970; Doty. *Contemporary Black Artists in America*; Univ. of Pittsburgh. *An Exhibition of Sculpture by John Rhoden*, 1971; Brooklyn College. *Afro-American Artists: Since 1950*, 1969; Myers, Carol. *Black Power in the Arts*, Flint, Mich., 1970; "Leading Negro Artists," *Ebony*, Sept. 1963; Driskell, David C. *John Rhoden & Walter Williams*, Fisk Univ., 1967; *Who's Who in American Art*, 1970.

RHODES, JOHN W.

Sculptor.
Exhibited: Howard Univ., 1961.
Sources: *The Negro Handbook*, Composed by Editors of *Ebony*, Chicago, 1966; Dover. *American Negro Art*; Harley, Ralph, Jr. "A Checklist of Afro-Amer. Art & Artists," *The Serif*, Dec. 1970; "Sculpture Exhibitions 1955," *Scrapbook of Art & Artists of Chicago*, 1955, p. 6.

RIBOUD, BARBARA CHASE

See: Chase-Riboud, Barbara.

RICHARD, BRUCE NUGENT

Exhibited: Harmon Foundation, 1931.
Sources: Harley, Ralph, Jr, "Checklist of Afro-Amer. Art & Artists," *The Serif*, Dec. 1970.

RICHARD, WILLIAM D.

Born in Ogden, Utah, September 14, 1909. Studied at Sacramento Junior College; California School of Arts and Crafts; Student's Art Center; Kathrin Gans Studio; under Morris Logan, Sydney Lemos, Raymond Strong.
Exhibited: Oakland (1-man); San Mateo; San Francisco; Los Angeles; Seattle; Detroit; Washington, DC; Alexandria, Va.; Atlanta.
Sources: Furr, Arthur F. *History & Progress of Negroes in the US.*

RICHARDS, FRENCHIE

Sources: NY NAACP. *Art Exhibition of Negro Expression Sponsored by Minars Furniture*, April 1964.

RICHARDSON, BEN

Muralist.
Works: *Geist und Leben.*
Sources: Harrison, W.E. "The Achievement of Ben Richardson," *Opportunity*, Feb. 1938, pp. 43-5; "Murals Done at Howard," *Boston Chronicle*, Oct. 16, 1937; "Art on Sale to Aid Children," *Scrapbook of Art & Artists of Chicago*, 1963, p. 36; Harley, Ralph, Jr. "A Checklist of Afro-Amer. Art & Artists," *The Serif*, Dec. 1970.

RICHARDSON, EARLE WILTON

Painter. Born in New York City, 1913. Died December 18, 1935. Studied at the National Academy of Design.
Works: *Portrait of a Negro Girl; Study for Mural; Decorative Drawing; Virgin.*
Exhibited: Harmon Foundation, 1933-5; Corcoran Gallery, 1934; Howard Univ., 1937; Amer. Negro Exposition, Chicago, 1940; NY Federal Art Project, 1934-45; Urban League; City College of NY, 1967; Texas Centennial, 1936; Harmon Foundation College Art Assn. Touring Exhibition, 1934-5.
Awards: Alan Bement Prize, portrait, Harmon Foundation, 1933; Wanamaker Contest, Nat'l Academy of Design.
Sources: City College of NY. *The Evolution of Afro-American Artists 1800-1950*; Harmon Foundation. *Non-Jury Exhibit of Works of Negro Artists*, 1933; Texas Centennial Exposition. *Thumbnail Sketches of Exhibiting Artists*, 1936; Harmon Foundation. *Negro Artists*, 1935; Harmon Foundation. *Exhibition of Productions by Negro Artists*; DuSable Museum of African-Amer. History. *Contemporary Black Artists*, 1970, Calendar; "Harlem Library Shows Negro Art," *Art News*, May 20, 1933, p. 14; Porter. *Modern Negro Art*; Harley, Ralph, Jr.

"A Checklist of Afro-Amer. Art & Artists," *The Serif*, Dec. 1970; "Exhibition of Work by Negro Artists," *Afro-American Presbyterian*, Feb. 23, 1933; Schatz, Walter. *Directory of Afro-American Resources*, 1970; Locke. *The Negro in Art*; Mallett. *Index of Artists*; Afro-American Slide Depository, catalog, 1971-2; Walker, Roslyn. *A Resource Guide to the Visual Arts of Afro-Americans*, South Bend, Ind., 1971.

RICHARDSON, ED
Illustrator, commercial artist. Born in Springfield, Massachusetts, 1927. Studied at Rhode Island School of Design; under Thurston Munson.
Works: Illustrator of Merriam Webster dictionaries.
Exhibited: Norwich (Conn.) Rose Festival.
Sources: Information from the artist.

RICHARDSON, HARRY S.
Sculptor, craftsman. Studied at Cleveland Institute of Art (BFA, 1952).
Works: *Birds*, wrought silver and ebony feet and tail, Cream and Sugar.
Exhibitions: Cleveland and Youngstown Museums; San Francisco 21st Annual Festival; Art Assn. of the Philippines Annual; Mead's Gallery, San Francisco; Academy of Sciences, Golden Gate Park, San Francisco; Coffee Cantata, San Francisco; Gumps, San Francisco; Mills College.
Member: Artist Equality Assn.; San Francisco Gem and Mineral Society; Metal Arts Guild.
Sources: Mills College Art Gallery. *California Black Craftsmen*, 1970.

RICHARDSON, WILLIAM H.
Works: *Donna*.
Exhibited: Smith-Mason Gallery, 1971.
Sources: Smith-Mason Gallery. *National Exhibition Black Artists*, 1971.

RICHBERG, ALEXANDER
Studied at Voorhees College.
Works: *Black Jesus*.
Exhibited: Sun Times/Daily News Gallery, Chicago, 1970.
Sources: United Negro College Fund. *Art 1970*, Chicago, 1970.

RICHIE, HAROLD
Sculptor in papier-mâché. From Terre Haute, Indiana.
Works: Papier mâché figures & displays for Internat'l Float Masters, South Boston, Va.
Sources: "Harold Ritchie," *The Negro History Bulletin*, Feb. 1940.

RICHMOND, CATHERINE B.
Works: *Translucents*.

Exhibited: Smith-Mason Gallery, 1971.
Sources: Smith-Mason Gallery. *National Exhibition Black Artists*, 1971.

RICHTER, LILLIAN
Collections: NY Public Library-Schomburg Art Collection.
Sources: Schatz, Walter. *Directory of Afro-American Resources*, 1970.

RICKS, PERCY
Painter, educator. Born in Washington, DC in 1923. Teacher at Samuel Fliesher Art Memorial, Philadelphia.
Works: *Crescendo; Time Swiftly Passes; The Fire Next Time; Krishna Consciousness; Tenement House*.
Exhibited: Boston Museum of Fine Arts, 1970; Howard Univ., 1961; Phila. Civic Center Museum; State Armory, Wilmington, Del., 1971; James A. Porter Gallery, 1970; Smith-Mason Gallery, 1971.
Sources: Dover. *American Negro Art*; Boston Museum of Art. *Afro-American Artists: NY & Boston*, 1970; Aesthetic Dynamics. *Afro-American Images*, 1971; Indiana Univ. *Fine Arts & the Black American*; Phila. Division of Art. *Afro-American Artists 1800-1969*; Harley, Ralph, Jr. "A Checklist of Afro-Amer. Art & Artists," *The Serif*, Dec. 1970; Howard Univ. *James A. Porter Gallery of African-American Art*, 1970; Smith-Mason Gallery. *National Exhibition Black Artists*, 1971; Walker, Roslyn. *A Resource Guide to the Visual Arts of Afro-Americans*, South Bend, Ind., 1971.

RICKSON, GARY A.
Painter, writer, musician. Born August 12, 1942. Studied at Moorish Science Temple Inc.
Works: *Segregation, B.C.; Something That Lives, Moves; Capitalism in Organic Brown; Eastward Through the West Gate; Africa is the Beginning; The Key is to See; To Africa With Love; The Essence of Man; Sol's Fish Market; Somebody's Always; The Wall of Humanity; Beautiful People Coming Together; Red, Black, Green; Self Discipline; The Sane Society; The End* (oil).
Exhibited: Museum of Fine Arts, Boston, 1970; Boston Public Library, 1973.
Awards: Outstanding Roxbury Citizen's Award; Nat'l Endowment Federal Grant ($7,500).
Sources: "Black Art Exhibit Opens Sunday," *Herald*, Belmont, Mass., May 14, 1970; "Preview Party to Open Show By 13 Black Artists," *Citizen*, May 14, 1970; Hinchcliffe, Diane. "Black Art Exhibit: Future Looks a Little Brighter," *Chronicle-Citizen*, Brookline, Mass., June 4, 1970; "Museum of Fine Arts to Hold Black Art Show," *Chronicle*, Belmont, Mass., April 28, 1970; "Museum of Fine Arts to Hold Black Art Show," *Chronicle*, Ipswich, Mass.,

April 30, 1970; "Museum of Fine Arts to Hold Black Art Show," *Tri-Town Transcript & Pennysaver*, April 29, 1970; Gerson, Sareen R. "Black Art NY-Hub Set for Museum of Fine Arts," *Minuteman*, March 19, 1970; Lewis/ Waddy. *Black Artists on Art*, Vol. 1; DuSable Museum of African-Amer. History. *Contemporary Black Artists*, 1970, Calendar; Bowling, Frank. "It's Not Enough to Say 'Black Is Beautiful'," *Art News*, April 1971; Le Brun, Caron. "Black Art," *Herald Traveler*, Sunday Supplement, Boston, May 24, 1970; Boston Negro Artists Assn. *The Black Artist in America: A Negro History Month Exhibition*, Boston Public Library, 1973; Boston Museum of Fine Arts. *Afro-American Artists: NY & Boston*, 1970.

RIDDLE, JOHN T.

Printmaker, sculptor. Born in Los Angeles, California in 1933. Studied at Los Angeles City College; California State College at Los Angeles (BA, MA).

Works: *Billy Rene; Street Trial; Telescope-USA; Attica; The Operation; Sargent Berker; Kent State; Patriots Parade; Saturday Morning.*
Exhibitions: Ankrum Gallery, 1970; Brockman Gallery, 1968; Brand Library & Art Center; Watts Art Festival, 1965-71; Cal. State College, Retrospective in Black; Univ. of Iowa, 1971-2; Heritage Gallery, 1969; San José State College, 1972.
Awards: 3 1st prizes, Watts Festivals; Honorable Mention, 1970 All City Art Exhibit; Emmy Award, So. Cal. Sector, for "Renaissance in Black," KNBC-TV, 1971.
Collections: Mr. Bill Cosby; Mr. Sidney Poitier; Ms. Joan Kirkerby; Mr. Charles White; Golden State Mutual Life Insurance Co.; Oakland Museum.
Member: Black Arts Council, Los Angeles.
Represented by: Claude Booker, Los Angeles.
Sources: Oakland Museum Archives, Ruth Waddy Collection; Lewis/Waddy. *Black Artists on Art*, Vol. 2; Roelof-Lanner, T.V., ed. *Prints by American Negro Artists*; Illinois Bell Telephone. *Black American Artists/71*; Atkinson, J. Edward. *Black Dimensions in Contemporary American Art*, 1971; San José State College. *Black Arts Today*, March 1972, list.

RIDLEY, GREGORY D., JR.

Sculptor, painter, educator. Born in Smyrna, Tennessee in 1925. Studied at Fisk University; A&I State University; Tennessee State University (BS); University of Louisville (MA). Teacher of art at Grambling College, Louisiana.

Works: *Series of Masks*, 1954-5; *The Prophet Noah; Ode to Mrs. Bethune; Civil War Series* (copper), 1960-; *Prophet; Old Grey Prophet;* *Egyptian Mask; Prophet #10; Mother & Child; Ngere Mask; Fetish Mask; Mask; Clown; Birds; Civil War; Heads; Fetish God & Oriental Sun; Mod Mod Night; Black Gilles; Black Princess; Bushungo Totems; Black Power; The Klan; Quiet Dignity; Birds; Girl with Parrots; Masks; String Dancers; Lobster.*
Exhibited: Boston Museum of Fine Arts, 1970; Univ. of Iowa, 1971-2; Smith-Mason Gallery, 1971; Xavier Univ., 1963; Sheraton Hotel, Phila., 1968; Fisk Univ., 1945-72; Atlanta Univ.; Summer Festival of Art Exhibition of Amer. Vet's Society of Artists, NYC.
Collections: Fisk Univ.; Winston-Salem State College.
Awards: Top Award, Summer Festival Art Exhibit of Amer. Vet's Society of Artists, NYC.
Member: Nat'l Conference of Artists (founder).
Represented by: Different Strokes, NYC.
Sources: Boston Museum of Fine Arts. *Afro-American Artists: New York & Boston*, 1970; Illinois Bell Tel. *Black American Artists/71*, 1972; Smith-Mason Gallery. *National Exhibition Black Artists 1971*; Xavier Univ. *Emancipation Proclamation Centennial National Art Exhibition*, 1963; *The Art Gallery Magazine*, April 1970; Atkinson, J. Edward. *Black Dimensions in Contemporary Art*, NY, 1971; Harley, Ralph, Jr. "A Checklist of Afro-American Art & Artists," *The Serif*, Dec. 1970; Dover, Cedric. *American Negro Art*, 1961; Fax. *17 Black Artists*; Information from the artist; Myers, Carol L. *Black Power in the Arts*, Flint, Mich., 1970.

RIGBY, GWENDOLYN

Studied at Tuskeegee Institute.
Works: *Black and White.*
Exhibited: Sun Times/Daily News Gallery, Chicago, 1970.
Sources: United Negro College Fund. *Art 1970*, Chicago, 1970.

RIGG, MARGARET

Mixed media.
Works: *The King & The Queen.*
Exhibited: Fla. Creates, 1971-2; Univ. of Turku, Finland; Yamada Gallery, Kyoto, Japan; Trend House, Tampa, Fla.; Botolph Group Gallery, Boston; Wash. Fed. Gallery, Miami; Nashville Artists Guild; Fla. Artist Group Annuals; Contemporary Gallery, St. Petersburg; Krannert Art Museum, Urbana, Ill.; Ringling Museum Rental-Sales Gallery, Sarasota, Fla.; CBS-TV, May 1968; Fla. Gulf Coast Art Center.
Sources: *Artists/USA 1972-1973*, Feasterville, Pa., 1972, p. 157.

RILEY, ANITA B.

Sculptor, painter. Born in New Bedford, Mas-

sachusetts, 1928. Studied at Swain School of Design.
Works: *Emergence.*
Exhibited: Temple Univ. Paley Library, 1971; Phila. Civic Center Museum; Holyoke College, 1972; Woodmere Gallery, 1970; Storrelli Gallery, 1972.
Member: Art Alliance of Phila.; Artists Equity, Phila.
Sources: Phila. Division of Art. *Afro-American Artists 1800-1969; Essence,* Feb. 1973; Information from the artist.

RINGGOLD, FAITH

Painter, educator. Born in New York City in 1934. Studied at City College of New York (BS, 1955; MFA, 1959).
Works: *Mommy & Daddy; Soul Baby; Flag for the Moon: Die Nigger; The Flag is Bleeding; Party Time; American Art Poster; Ego; God Bless America; Cocktail Party; Man; Love Black Life; Us, Black America; Artist & Model; Big Black; Nigger; US Postage Stamp; Black Poser; Charley; The American Spectrum; Hide Little Children,* 1965 (oil); *Soul Sister,* 1968 (oil).
Exhibited: State Armory, Wilmington, Del., 1971; Univ. of Iowa, 1971-2; Carroll Reece Museum, Johnson City, Tenn.; Martin Luther King, Jr. Exhibition, NY Museum of Modern Art; Harlem Cultural Council; Mertopolitan Applied Research Corp., NYC; Lever House Gallery, NYC; Nat'l Academy of Art; Phila. Civic Center Museum; NC A&T Univ.; Martha Jackson Gallery, NY, 1970; NY Shakespeare Festival Public Theater, 1970; Ill. Bell Telephone, Chicago, 1971-2; Ill. State Museum, Springfield, 1971-2; Sloane Galleries, Valparaiso, Ind., 1971-2; Peoria (Ill.) Art Guild, 1971-2; Burpee Gallery, Rockford, Ill., 1971-2; Davenport (Ind.) Municipal Gallery, 1971-2; Kalamazoo (Mich.) College, 1971-2; Museum of the Nat'l Center of Afro-Amer. Artists, Boston, 1971; Univ. of NH, 1971; Currier Gallery of Art, Manchester, NH, 1971; Bank St. College, NYC, 1971; Acts of Art Gallery, NYC, 1971; NY Cultural Center, 1971; Gedok at Kunsthaus, Hamburg, Germany, 1972; Finch College, 1971; Spectrum Gallery, NYC, 1967, 1970 (1-woman); NY State Dept. of Education, 1971 (1-woman); La. State Univ., 1972 (1-woman); Rutgers Univ., 1973 (1-woman).
Collections: Chase Manhattan Bank, NYC; Museum of Modern Art; NY State Council for the Arts; Bank St. College of Education, NYC; Mr. Melvin Van Peebles; Dr. Benjamin Mays.
Member: Women Students & Artists for Black Art Liberation.
Sources: Aesthetic Dynamics. *Afro-American Images,* 1971; Ill. Bell Telephone. *Black Amer-*

ican Artists/71, 1972; "Afro-American Issue," *Art Gallery,* April 1968; Indiana Univ. *Fine Arts & the Black American;* Afro-American Slide Depository, catalog; DuSable Museum of African-Amer. History. *Contemporary Black Artists,* 1970, Calendar; Greene, Carroll, Jr. "Perspective: The Black Artist in America," *Art Gallery,* April 1970; Rose, Barbara. "Black Art in America," *Art in America,* July/Dec. 1970; A&T Univ. Lyceum Program. *15 Afro-American Women;* "Black Art: What Is It?," *Art Gallery,* April 1970; Harley, Ralph, Jr. "A Checklist of Afro-Amer. Art & Artists," *The Serif,* Dec. 1970; Greene, Carroll, Jr. *Afro-American Artists: 1800-1968,* slides; Metropolitan Applied Research Center. *Six Painters;* Spectrum Gallery. *Faith Ringgold-American People: Recent Paintings,* NYC, 1968; Museum of Afro-Amer. Artists. *Taking Care of Business;* Loercher, Diana. "Nat'l Center of Afro-Amer. Artists & Benefit Premiere," *Christian Science Monitor,* May 4, 1971; Driscoll, Edgar, Jr. "Art Show Reflects Black Rage, Pride," *Boston Globe,* April 28, 1971; Patterson, Lindsay. "Contemporary Artists," *The Negro in Music & Art;* Schwartz, Therese. "The Political Scene," *Arts,* NY, April 1971; Fax, Elton. *17 Black Artists,* 1970; Schwartz, Barry. *Humanism in 20th Century Art,* Praeger Press, 1972; Tigh, Donald. *What's Happening,* a communications reader, Winthrop Pub., 1971; Smithsonian-Artists Protest Movement. *Archives of American Art,* tape; "Heavenly City," *Educreative Systems,* NYC, record; Myers, Carol. *Black Power in the Arts,* Flint, Mich., 1970; Prothman Assn., catalog of slides, Baldwin, NY; Information from the artist; Educational Dimensions Corp., catalog of slides, Great Neck, NY; Walker, Roslyn. *A Resource Guide to the Visual Arts of Afro-Americans,* South Bend, Ind., 1971.

RINGLE, BRYANT

Printmaker.
Works: *Arc Welder* (lithograph).
Exhibited: Library of Congress, 1940; South Side Community Art Center, 1941.
Sources: Harley, Ralph, Jr. "Checklist of Afro-Amer. Art & Artists," *The Serif,* Dec. 1970; South Side Community Art Center. *National Negro Art Exhibition,* Chicago, 1941.

RIVERS, HAYWOOD BILL

Painter. Born in Morven, North Carolina on May 8, 1922. Studied at Art Students League, New York (1946-9); École du Musée du Louvre, Paris (1949-52).
Works: *Quilting Party; The Tailor Shop; Le Village; Card Game; Central Park; Eclipse I-III; Invisible Man; Self-Portrait; Exit; Green Painting; Barnyard; Woman Smoking Pipe;*

Barber Shop; Dance Around a Flower; Op; The Circus; Globe.
Exhibited: Baltimore Museum, 1948 (1-man); Baltimore Museum Annual, 1948; Carnegie Internat'l, 1949; Le Salon des Jeunes Peintres, Paris, 1950; Le Salon d'Hiver, Paris, 1950; Le Salon de Mai, Paris, 1950; Le Salon de L'art Libre, Paris, 1950; Amer. Embassy Show, Paris, 1950; City College of NY, 1967; Stout State Univ., Wisc., 1970; Boston Museum of Fine Arts, 1970; Rebuttal to the Whitney Museum Exhibition, 1971; Newark Museum, 1971.
Collections: Baltimore Museum; Le Musée d'Art Moderne, Paris; Col. Harry N. Abrams; Mr. Robert K. Haas; Miss Lillie Dache; Miss Gertrude Berg; Mr. Robert Rosenwald; Col. William Keighley; Mr. Charles Van Renseler; Mr. Donald McIntosh; Mr. & Mrs. Herman Voichcick; NY Public Library-Schomburg Art Collection.
Awards: Md. State Scholarship to study art, 1946-9; Gretchen H. Hutzler Award, 1948; John Hay Whitney Fellowship, 1952; Baltimore Museum Annual, 1948; Julius Rosenwald Fellowship, 1948.
Sources: "Afro-American Issue," *Art Gallery*, April 1968; Afro-American Slide Depository, Catalog; Indiana Univ. *Fine Arts & the Black American*; City College of NY. *Evolution of Afro-American Artists: 1800-1950*, 1967; Stout State Univ. *Eleven NY Area Black Artists*, 1970; Hudson River Museum. *Contemporary American Black Artists*, 1970; Boston Museum of Fine Arts. *Afro-American Artists: NY & Boston*, 1970; Newark Museum. *Black Artists: Two Generations*; *Rebuttal to the Whitney Museum Exhibition*, NY, 1971; Information from the artist; DuSable Museum of African-Amer. History. *Contemporary Black Artists*, 1970, Calendar; Bowling, Frank. "The Rupture," *Arts*, Summer 1970; Harley, Ralph, Jr. "A Checklist of Afro-Amer. Arts & Artists," *The Serif*, Dec. 1970; Kramer, Hilton. "Trying to Define 'Black Art'; Must We Go Back to Social Realism," *New York Times*, May 31, 1970; Kramer, Hilton. "Is Politics Submerging Black Art?," *Courier-Journal & Times*, Louisville, Ky., June 7, 1970; Schatz, Walter. *Directory of Afro-American Resources*, 1970; Myers, Carol. *Black Power in the Arts*, Flint, Mich., 1970; Le Brun, Caron. "Black Art," *Herald Traveler*, Sunday Supplement, Boston, May 24, 1970.

ROACH, REV. ARTHUR

Painter. Born in Perth Amboy, New Jersey, 1935. Studied at Newark State College; Newark School of Fine and Industrial Arts; School of Visual Arts; Collegiate Bible Institute.
Works: *Wounded Feelings*, 1970; *Solitude*, 1966; *Suspicion*, 1970; *A Mother's Dilemma*, 1965.

Exhibited: Newark Museum, 1971; YM-YWHA, West Orange, NJ; Purdue Univ., 1972; NJ Artist; Newark Community Art Show, 1969.
Collections: Newark Museum.
Awards: 2nd Prize, Community Art Show of Newark, 1969.
Sources: Information from artist; Newark Museum. *Black Artists: Two Generations*, 1971; Young Men-Young Women's Hebrew Assn. *Black Expression in Art*, West Orange, NJ, 1972.

ROBERTS, DONALD H.

Painter.
Exhibited: Atlanta Univ., 1951; Boston Museum of Fine Arts, 1970.
Awards: $125 Award for watercolor, Atlanta Univ., 1951.
Sources: Boston Museum of Fine Arts. *Afro-American Artists: New York & Boston*, 1970; Atlanta Univ. *10th Annual for Negro Artists*, 1951, catalog.

ROBERTS, LUCILLE D.

Painter, educator. Born in Hyattsville, Maryland. Studied at Howard University (AB); University of Michigan (MFA); Catholic University, Washington, DC; Parsons School of Design, New York City; under Jack Perlmutter in Washington, DC; New York University. Assistant Professor of Fine Arts at District of Columbia Teachers College.
Works: *Emergence; Black is Beautiful; Nasai Woman; Black Heritage; Black Madonna.*
Exhibited: Society of Washington Artists; Smithsonian Institution; Hampton Institute; Washington Gallery of Art; Dickey Gallery, Washington, DC; Teachers College, 1968; Smith-Mason Gallery, 1971; 1st World Festival of Negro Arts, Dakar, Senegal; James A. Porter Gallery of Afro-Amer. Art, 1971.
Awards: Agnes Meyer Fellowship, 1963; *Evening Star* Award, Society of Washington Artists, 72nd Annual Show, 1966; paintings on loan to the US State Department's "Art in the Embassies Program" in the US Embassies in Pakistan & Taiwan.
Sources: Lewis/Waddy. *Black Artists on Art*; Smith-Mason Gallery. *National Exhibition Black Artists*, 1971; Pierre-Noel, Lois Jones. "American Negro Art in Progress," *Negro History Bulletin*, Oct. 1967; A&T Univ. Lyceum Program. *15 Afro-American Women*; *National Conference of Artists*, Winter 1971, Journal; Harley, Ralph, Jr. "Checklist of Afro-Amer. Art & Artists," *The Serif*, Dec. 1970; Atkinson, J. Edward. *Black Dimensions in Contemporary American Art*, NY, 1971; Walker, Roslyn. *A Resource Guide to the Visual Arts of Afro-Americans*, South Bend, Ind., 1971.

ROBERTS, SOLOMON

Photographer.
Exhibited: Addison Gallery, 1971.
Sources: James Van DerZee Institute. *The Black Photographer (1908-1970): A Survey.*

ROBERTS, WALTER L.

Architect. Helped prepare engineering drawings to show at the New York World's Fair, c. 1939.
Sources: "Walter L. Roberts," *Opportunity,* Dec. 1938, biography.

ROBERTSON, DONALD J.

Painter. Born in Mt. Vernon, New York in 1933. Studied at School of Visual Arts, New York; National Academy of Design.
Works: *Resurrection; Civilization; The Mask,* 1971; *Oh Say, Can You See?,* 1972; *Father & Son,* 1971; *The Family,* 1972.
Exhibited: Smith-Mason Gallery, 1971; River View Galleries, NY; Studio Workshop Gallery, NY; Mary Tucker Gallery, NY; Six-Month Gallery, New Rochelle, NY; Acts of Art Gallery, NY; Northpoint Gallery, LI; Sindin-Harris Gallery, Hartsdale, NY; Afro-Leito Gallery, White Plains, NY; Duchess Community College, Poughkeepsie, NY; Carnegie Institute; Nat'l Print-Drawing-Photography Show.
Collections: Dr. Charles Hamilton; Mr. Eddie C. Moore; Mr. Courtney Brown; Dr. Harold Najac; Mr. Charles Williams; Mr. Frank Furman.
Awards: Nat'l Academy of Design scholarship; 1st prize, Washington Sq. Outdoor Show.
Member: New Rochelle Artists Guild; Mt. Vernon Artists Guild; Mamaroneck Artists Guild.
Represented by: Afro-Leito Gallery, White Plains, NY.
Sources: Smith-Mason Gallery. *Nat'l Exhibition Black Artists,* 1971; Acts of Art Gallery. *Rebuttal to the Whitney Nat'l Black Arts Show,* 1971; Information from the artist.

ROBINSON, CHARLES ARAL

Commercial artist. Born in Pennsylvania in 1905. Studied in New York; Canada; Buffalo. No formal art training.
Works: *Plantation Scene.*
Exhibited: Harmon Foundation, 1924, 1929, 1930; Studio 1, Berkeley.
Sources: Studio 1. *6 Black Artists,* n.d.; Indiana Univ. *Fine Arts & the Black American;* Harmon Foundation. *Exhibition of Productions by Negro Artists;* Harmon Foundation. *Negro Artists,* 1935; Harmon Foundation. *Exhibition of Fine Arts,* 1930; DuSable Museum of Afro-Amer. History. *Contemporary Black Artists,* Calendar, 1970; Harley, Ralph, Jr. "A Checklist of Afro-Amer. Art & Artists," *The Serif,*

Dec. 1970; Walker, Roslyn. *A Resource Guide to the Visual Arts of Afro-Americans,* South Bend, Ind., 1971.

ROBINSON, HILYARD ROBERT

Architect, designer. Born in Washington, DC, 1899. Studied at Pennsylvania Museum of Industrial Arts (1917); University of Pennsylvania; Columbia University (BArch, 1924; MArch, 1931); University of Berlin (1931-2). Former head of Department of Architecture, Howard University. Senior and Consulting Architect, Government Housing Agencies (1934-5, 1939).
Works: Women's dorm, Columbia Univ.; Langston Terrace, Washington, DC, 1937 (Assoc. Architect); Logan Homes, Public Housing Project, Ypsilanti, Mich., 1943; Chester (Pa.) Recreation Center, 1944; Logan Homes, Public Housing Project & Public School, Dundalk, Md., 1957; School of Engineering & Architecture, Howard Univ., 1952; Men's Dorm, Hampton (Va.) Institute, 1954.
Exhibited: Harmon Foundation, 1928.
Awards: 1st, 2nd, 4th Cash Prizes & Medal, *Magazine of Architecture,* 1928; 2nd prize, Washington Board of Trade, 1943; Diploma of Merit, Washington Board of Trade, 1952.
Sources: Indiana Univ. *Fine Arts & the Black American;* Harmon Foundation. *Exhibition of Productions by Negro Artists;* Brawley, Benjamin. *The Negro Genius;* Harley, Ralph, Jr. "Checklist of Afro-Amer. Art & Artists," *Serif,* Dec. 1970; Wilson, John. *The Negro Architect,* pp. 25-6; Robinson, Wilhelmena S. *Historical Negro Biographies,* p. 243-4; Spradling, Mary M., ed. *In Black & White: Afro-Americans in Print; American Architects Directory,* 1962; Downing, Lewis K. "Contributions of Negro Scientists," *Crisis,* June 1939; Walker, Roslyn. *A Resource Guide to the Visual Arts of Afro-Americans,* South Bend, Ind., 1971.

ROBINSON, IRENE

Studied at Tuskegee Institute.
Works: *Head.*
Exhibited: Sun Times/Daily News Gallery, Chicago, 1970.
Sources: United Negro College Fund. *Art 1970,* Chicago, 1970.

ROBINSON, J. H. D.

Painter. Active 1930's. Studied part time at Brooklyn Art School; Art Students League, NY; New York University; College Art Association Courses.
Works: *Stevedore; Landscape With Red Truck.*
Exhibited: Harmon Foundation, 1931, 1935; 135th St. Branch, NY Public Library; Amer. Negro Exposition, Chicago, 1940; Roerich Museum, 1934; Society of Independent Artists, 1935; Harmon-College Art Traveling Exhibit,

1934-5; Texas Centennial, 1936; WPA, 1934; Atlanta Univ., 1944.
Sources: Harmon Foundation. *Negro Artists*, 1935; Harmon Foundation. *Exhibition of Productions by Negro Artists*, 1931; Indiana Univ. *Fine Arts & the Black American*; Tanner Art Galleries. *Art of the American Negro*, 1940; Texas Centennial Exposition. *Thumbnail Sketches of Exhibiting Artists*, 1936; DuSable Museum of African-Amer. History. *Contemporary Black Artists*, 1970, calendar; Harmon Foundation. *Select Picture List*; Harley, Ralph, Jr. "Checklist of Afro-Amer. Art & Artists," *The Serif*, Dec. 1970; Walker, Roslyn. *A Resource Guide to the Visual Arts of Afro-American Artists*, South Bend, Ind., 1971.

ROBINSON, JOHN D.

Works: *Mr. & Mrs. Barton.*
Exhibited: Xavier Univ., 1963.
Sources: Xavier Univ. *Emancipation Proclamation Centennial National Art Exhibition*, 1963.

ROBINSON, JOHN N.

Painter. Born in Washington, DC, 1912. Largely self-taught.
Works: *Spring Landscape; Outdoor Art Fair; Pete and Blanche; My Grandparents; Anacostia Hills.*
Exhibited: Atlanta Univ., 1944.
Sources: Dover. *American Negro Art*; Indiana Univ. *Fine Arts & the Black American*; Atlanta Univ., catalog, 1944; Pierre-Noel, Lois Jones. "American Negro Art in Progress," *Negro History Bulletin*, Oct. 1967; *The Negro Handbook*, Composed by Editors of *Ebony*, Chicago, 1966; Walker, Roslyn. *A Resource Guide to the Visual Arts of Afro-Americans*, South Bend, Ind., 1971.

ROBINSON, JULIAN C.

Exhibited: Henry Goode Art Studio, Los Angeles, 1938.
Sources: "Posthumous Art Exhibit Thrills Los Angeles," *California Eagle*, June 30, 1938; Harley, Ralph, Jr. "Checklist of Afro-Amer. Art & Artists," *The Serif*, Dec. 1970.

ROBINSON, LEO

Painter. Studied at Howard University; Cranbrook Academy of Art (MFA).
Works: *Lemming Series No. 3 (No Jesus, This Is)* (acrylic).
Exhibited: James A. Porter Gallery, 1970; Barnet Aden Gallery, Washington; Howard Univ.; Smithsonian Institution; Dreyer Gallery, Houston; Fisk Univ.; G. Washington Univ.; Washington Gallery of Modern Art; Talladega College (1-man); Dartmouth College; Sheraton Hotel, Phila., 1968.
Awards: Skowhegan (Me.) School of Painting & Sculpture; Savery Gallery of Talladega College; Dartmouth College; Howard Univ.
Sources: Howard Univ. *James A. Porter Gallery of African-American Art*, 1970; Boston Community Lecture Series. *Local Afro-American Artists*, Catalog, 1969; Pierre-Noel, Lois Jones. "American Negro Art in Progress," *Negro History Bulletin*, Oct. 1967; Harley, Ralph, Jr. "Checklist of Afro-Amer. Art & Artists," *The Serif*, Dec. 1970.

ROBINSON, LEON H., III

Painter. Born 1947. Studied at Boston University.
Works: *Spanish Woman*, 1973 (encaustic); *Self-Portrait*, 1972 (encaustic); *Karen*, 1972 (charcoal); *Self-Portrait Looking Out*, 1972 (wash & pencil).
Exhibited: Boston Univ., 1972.
Sources: Information from artist.

ROBINSON, PETER L., JR.

Painter. Born in Washington, DC in 1922. Studied at Howard University (BA). Visual Information Officer for Office of Manned Space Flight, National Aeronautics & Space Administration.
Works: *El Toro; Amorphous Cloud; Three Brothers; Autumn Fields.*
Exhibited: State Armory, Wilmington, Del., 1971; James A. Porter Gallery, 1970; Smith-Mason Gallery, 1971; Corcoran Gallery of Art; Collectors' Corner; Artists' Mart; Atlanta Univ.; Barnet Aden Gallery; Potter's House Gallery; Howard Univ.; DCAA, Anacostia Neighborhood Museum-Smithsonian Institution.
Awards: Works selected by the State Dept. for "Art for Embassies Program" for US embassies in Costa Rica & Ceylon.
Sources: Aesthetic Dynamics. *Afro-American Images*, 1971; Howard Univ. *James A. Porter Gallery of African-American Art*, 1970; Smith-Mason Gallery. *National Exhibition Black Artists*, 1971; Pierre-Noel, Lois Jones. "Amer-Negro Art in Progress," *Negro History Bulletiin*, Oct. 1967; DC Art Assn. *Exhibition '71*, Washington, DC, 1971, Catalog; Harley, Ralph, Jr. "Checklist of Afro-Amer. Art & Artists," *The Serif,* Dec. 1970.

ROBINSON, RUDOLPH

Photographer.
Exhibited: Addison Gallery, 1971.
Sources: James Van DerZee Institute. *The Black Photographer (1908-1970): A Survey.*

ROBINSON, T. H. D.

Painter.
Works: *Hi; Portrait; Landscape with Red Trunk.*

Collections: Nat'l Archives.
Sources: Afro-Amer. Slide Depository, Catalog, 1971-2.

ROBYNSON, BERNIE HAYNES

Graphic artist. Born in Paris, Kentucky, 1900. Studied at Knoxville College; YMCA School of Art; National Academy of Art; Associated Art School; Art Students League; National Academy of Design; under Mort Burger, Charles Hinton, Augusta Savage.
Works: *Christmas Cards; Christmas Morn; Cose I Do; John Henry; Serenade.*
Exhibited: Harmon Foundation, 1933; 135th St. Branch, NY Public Library; Teachers College Library, Columbia Univ., 1932; Art Students Club, NYC.
Sources: "Successful Commercial Artist Would Paint Portraits," *Amsterdam News,* n.d.; "The Negro in Art," *New York Evening Journal;* Harmon Foundation. *Non-Jury Exhibit of Works of Negro Artists,* 1933; Harley, Ralph, Jr. "Checklist of Afro-Amer. Art & Artists," *Serif,* Dec. 1970.

RODGERS, HERBERT

Sources: "Cordozo High Presents Students' Art Works," *Afro-American,* Dec. 1, 1934; Harley, Ralph, Jr. "Checklist of Afro-Amer. Art & Artists," *The Serif,* Dec. 1970.

ROGERS, BARBARA

Studied at Spelman College.
Works: *Still Life.*
Exhibited: Sun Times/Daily News Gallery, Chicago, 1970.
Sources: United Negro College Fund. *Art 1970,* Chicago, 1970.

ROGERS, BRENDA

Painter, educator. Born in Los Angeles, California in 1940. Studied at the University of Southern California (BS, 1963).
Works: *Flower Pot; Friends.*
Exhibited: Simon Rodia Festival of Arts.
Collections: Multipurpose Health Center.
Awards: Merit Award, Simon Rodia Festival, 1967; Purchase Award, Multipurpose Health Center, 1967.
Sources: Lewis/Waddy. *Black Artists on Art;* Walker, Roslyn. *A Resource Guide to the Visual Arts of Afro-Americans,* South Bend, Ind., 1971.

ROGERS, CHARLES D.

Painter, printmaker. Born in Cherokee, Oklahoma in 1935. Studied at California State College (BA, 1963).
Works: *Child; An Adaptation from the Theme of The Prodigal Son by Murtillo* (woodcut).
Exhibited: Art-West Assoc. shows; Dooto's Music Center; Security Pacific Nat'l Bank, 1964; Univ. of Cal., Los Angeles; Soviet Union.
Collections: Oakland Museum, Ruth Waddy Collection.
Sources: Roelof-Lanner, T.V., ed. *Prints by American Negro Artists;* Lewis/Waddy. *Black Artists on Art,* Vol. 1; Oakland Museum Archives; Walker, Roslyn. *A Resource Guide to the Visual Arts of Afro-Americans,* South Bend, Ind., 1971.

ROGERS, GEORGE

Sculptor. Born August 10, 1930 in Rutledge, Alabama. Studied at Cleveland Institute of Art (1955-9); Cranbrook Academy (1959-60).
Works: *Hanging Forms; Wall Composition; Sailing; Study for Fountain; Station West; For Growing Fountain Study; Structure Theme; The Global; Cloud Movement; Outer Stream; The Tunnel; Modulars #1; The Tunnel; Crucifixion; The Global.*
Exhibited: Waden Gallery, Cleveland, 1959; Detroit Institute of Arts, 1960, 1971; Cranbrook Academy, 1959.
Sources: Afro-American Slide Depository, catalog; Detroit Institute of Arts files.

ROGERS, LESLIE

Cartoonist, illustrator. Worked for the *Chicago Defender.*
Exhibited: Art Institute of Chicago, 1927.
Sources: Art Inst. of Chicago. *The Negro In Art Week,* 1927.

ROLAND, ARTHUR

Painter.
Works: *Right On; Untitled* (oil on velvet); *The Baptism; Meditation; The Family; Suspicious; Solitude; The Whisper; Fruit Market; Last Supper; Innocence; Mother and Child; Sheba; Thumb Sucking; Judas; Ain't; Guitar Player; Ena Ne Abofra; Backwood Playground; Cold Turkey.*
Exhibited: Smith-Mason Gallery, 1971.
Collections: Johnson Pub. Co.
Sources: Afro-American Slide Depository, catalog; Smith-Mason Gallery. *National Exhibition Black Artists,* 1971; Johnson Pub. Co. *The JPC Art Collection,* Pamphlet.

ROLLINS, BERNARD

Painter.
Works: *Di Bau Cu.*
Sources: Lewis/Waddy. *Black Artists on Art,* Vol. 2.

ROLLINS, HENRY C.

Sculptor. Born 1937. Studied at Rhode Island School of Design.
Works: *The Sum,* 1968; *Blue Totem,* 1970 (painted bronze).
Exhibited: Whitney Museum, 1968; 1971; Oakland Museum, 1970.

Sources: Myers, Carol L. *Black Power in the Arts,* Flint, Mich., 1970; DuSable Museum of African-Amer. History. *Contemporary Black Artists,* 1970, calendar; "Afro-American Issue," *Art Gallery,* April 1968; Indiana Univ. *Fine Arts & the Black American;* "San Francisco," *Artforum,* Oct. 1970, p. 81; Doty. *Contemporary Black Artists in America;* Oakland Museum. *Black, Untitled,* 1970; Walker, Roslyn. *A Resource Guide to the Visual Arts of Afro-Americans,* South Bend, Ind., 1971.

ROLLINS, ONEY
Sources: DuSable Museum of African-Amer. History. *Contemporary Black Artists,* 1970, calendar.

ROLLO, HERMAN
Painter.
Collections: Mr. Benny Andrews.

RONALD, JOSEPH
See: Joseph, Ronald.

ROQUETTE, MANSION
Sources: Indiana Univ. *Fine Arts & the Black American.*

ROSE, ARTHUR
Sculptor.
Works: *The Praying Parson; Don Quixote; The Port of Charleston; Madonna & Child; The Family.*
Exhibited: Smith-Mason Gallery, 1971; The Parthenon, Nashville, Tenn.; Guild of SC Artists.
Collections: Johnson Pub. Co.; SC Arts Commission; Indiana Univ., Bloomington.
Sources: Smith-Mason Gallery. *National Exhibition Black Artists,* 1971; Johnson Pub. Co. *The JPC Art Collection,* Pamphlet; Harley, Ralph, Jr. "Checklist of Afro-Amer. Art & Artists," *The Serif,* Dec. 1970; Atkinson, J. Edward. *Black Dimensions in Contemporary American Art,* NY, 1971.

ROSS, DAVID
Painter, sculptor.
Works: *Boudoir; Missouri Landscape; The Bushman* (plaster); *Head of a Negro; Solace; Missouri Hills.*
Exhibited: Howard Univ., 1941; Amer. Negro Exposition, Chicago, 1940; South Side Community Art Center, 1941, 1945.
Collections: Hon. & Mrs. Louis B. Anderson, Chicago.
Sources: *Exhibition of Negro Artists of Chicago at Howard University Gallery of Art,* Feb. 1941; Tanner Art Galleries. *Art of the American Negro,* 1940; Harley, Ralph, Jr. "Checklist of Afro-Amer. Art & Artists," *The Serif,* Dec. 1970; South Side Community Art Center. *Collectors Exhibit of Negro Art,* Chicago, 1945; South Side Community Art Center. *Opening Exhibition of Paintings by Negro Artists,* Chicago, 1941.

ROSS, J.C.
Sources: Harley, Ralph, Jr. "Checklist of Afro-Amer. Art & Artists," *The Serif,* Dec. 1970.

ROSS, JOSEPH B., JR.
Painter, educator. Born in Washington, DC, 1943. Studied at Howard University (BA); University of Maryland (MA).
Works: *Outlook on Life; Shade for a New Image; Watching an Eclipse; Rising of a New Morn; My Main Man with Flower; Evil Is Watching; Looking at T?V? Screen; Ghost Tree; Red Tree Blooming; Honey Tree and Me; Flower Tree Blooms; Little Boss Man Coming; Looking for a Better World; Fruit of the Moon; Striking a Regal Pose; A Rainy Day But I'm Happy; Strange Fruit Repeated* (synthetic polymer on canvas); *Waiting for a Dryer.*
Exhibited: Whitney Museum, 1970, 1971; Univ. of Iowa, 1971-2; Illinois Bell Telephone Traveling Show, 1971-2; "Four Black Artists," Washington, DC, 1972; Atlanta Univ., 1969; Black Printmaking Exhibition, 1969; Black Artist Exhibition, Chicago, 1970.
Collections: Fisk Univ.; Howard Univ.
Awards: Nat'l Society of Arts & Letters Grant, 1968-9.
Member: Nat'l Conference of Artists; College Art Assn.; DC Art Assn.
Sources: Afro-American Slide Depository, catalog; Doty. *Contemporary Black Artists in America.* Illinois Bell Telephone. *Black American Artists/71,* 1972; Information from artist; Haas, Joseph. "A Big, Brilliant & Exciting Exhibition of Black Art," *Chicago Daily News,* Jan. 16-7, 1971.

ROSS, KENNETH
Painter.
Collections: Mr. Benny Andrews.

ROSS, M. L.
Painter. Worked in Topeka, Kansas.
Works: *Cotton Gin and Press.*
Exhibited: Atlanta Univ., 1944.
Sources: Atlanta Univ. catalog; Harley, Ralph, Jr. "Checklist of Afro-Amer. Art & Artists," *The Serif,* Dec. 1970.

ROSS, WILLIAM
Sources: Porter. *Modern Negro Art;* Harley, Ralph, Jr. "Checklist of Afro-Amer. Art & Artists," *The Serif,* Dec. 1970.

ROUSSEVE, NUMA
Painter.
Works: *Nude; At Work; Reading; End of the*

Day-Evaluation; Hunk of Bread and a Bottle of Wine; Far Pacific Horizons; Still Life; Tulips; Eldest Son; The Seated Man; Nude; Reclining Nude; Seated Woman.
Sources: Afro-American Slide Depository, Catalog.

ROWLAND, NANCY

Works: *Sunset.*
Sources: Harley, Ralph, Jr. "Checklist of Afro-Amer. Art & Artists," *The Serif,* Dec. 1970; Atkinson, J. Edward. *Black Dimensions in Contemporary American Art,* NY, 1971.

RUDOLPH, SA

Photographer.
Exhibited: Addison Gallery, 1971.
Sources: James Van DerZee Institute. *The Black Photographer (1908-1970): A Survey.*

RUSSELL, JEWELL

Mixed media. Studied at Tougaloo College.
Works: Untitled rag & paint collage.
Exhibited: Sun Times/Daily News Gallery, Chicago, 1970.
Sources: United Negro College Fund. *Art 1970,* Chicago, 1970.

RUSSELL, JOHN

Photographer. Born 1931, Los Angeles, California. Studied at Fred Artcher School of Photography; Art Center School of Design; University of Southern California.
Works: *After Mass Only the Lights Turned On;* Untitled photograph.
Sources: Lewis/Waddy. *Black Artists on Art,* Vol. 2.

RUSSELL, WINFRED JONATHAN

Painter, illustrator. Born in Virginia. Studied at School of the Boston Museum of Fine Arts.
Works: Illustrations for magazines and newspapers.
Exhibited: Harmon Foundation, 1928, 1935; Independents Exhibit; New Art Circle; 135th St. Branch, NY Public Library; Texas Centennial, 1936.
Collections: NY Public Library-Schomburg Art Collection.
Sources: DuSable Museum of African-Amer. History. *Contemporary Black Artists,* 1970, calendar; Harmon Foundation. *Exhibition of Productions by Negro Artists;* Harmon Foundation. *Negro Artists,* 1935; Indiana Univ. *Fine Arts & the Black American;* Texas Centennial Exposition. *Thumbnail Sketches of Exhibiting Artists,* 1936; Porter. *Modern Negro Art;* Harley, Ralph, Jr. "Checklist of Afro-Amer. Art & Artists," *The Serif,* Dec. 1970; Schatz, Walter. *Directory of Afro-American Resources,* 1970; Walker, Roslyn. *A Resource Guide to the Visual Arts of Afro-Americans,* South Bend, Ind., 1971.

RYDER, MAHLER B.

Mixed media, jazz musician. Born in 1937. Studied at College of Fine & Applied Arts, Ohio State University (1954-8); Art Students League (1965-6); School of Visual Arts, NY (1966-7).
Works: *Collages I, II, III, IV; East Meets West; The Great American Bus; The Great American Subway; Different Strokes; 2nd Class; 10:30; Malcolm; 21; Bantu; RMD Enclosure; Lotta Roots; Special K's; Collages V-IX.*
Exhibited: Satori Studio, NY, 1965 (1-man); Riverside Museum, 1968; Ruder & Finn, 1969; Boston Museum of Fine Arts, 1970; Whitney Museum, 1971; Amer. Greetings Gallery, NY, 1968; Art Students League; Lever House, NY, 1966-8; Minneapolis Institute of Arts, 1968; High Museum of Art, Atlanta, 1969; Flint (Mich.) Institute of Arts, 1969; Everson Museum of Art, 1969; IBM Gallery of Arts & Sciences, NY, 1969; Rhode Island School of Design, 1969; Memorial Art Gallery, Rochester, NY, 1969; San Francisco Museum of Art, 1969; Contemporary Arts Museum, Houston, 1970; NJ State Museum, 1970; Roberson Center for the Arts & Sciences, Binghamton, NY, 1970; Art Galleries, Univ. of Cal. at Santa Barbara, 1970; Pan Am Building, NYC, 1968; NYC Univ.; 30 Contemporary Black Artists National Traveling Show.
Collections: Wisconsin State Univ.; Columbus Gallery of Fine Arts, Ohio; Chaim Gross Foundation; Emil J. Arnold; Late Senator Robert F. Kennedy.
Awards: Ford Foundation Grant, 1964-6.
Sources: "Afro-American Issue," *Art Gallery,* April 1968; Indiana Univ. *Fine Arts & the Black American;* Boston Museum of Fine Arts. *Afro-American Artists: New York/Boston,* 1970; Univ. of South Alabama. Afro-Amer. Slide Depository, Catalog; Doty. *Contemporary Black Artists in America;* DuSable Museum of African-Amer. History. *Contemporary Black Artists,* 1970, calendar; Minneapolis Institute of Art. *30 Contemporary Black Artists,* 1968; Bourne, Kay. "Black Artists Shown at Museum," *Bay State Banner* (Mass.), May 28, 1970; Ruder & Finn Fine Arts. *Contemporary Black Artists,* 1969; American Greetings Gallery. *New Voices: 15 New York Artists,* 1968; Riverside Museum. *8+8,* 1968; Myers, Carol L. *Black Power in the Arts,* Flint, Mich., 1970; Walker, Roslyn. *A Resource Guide to the Visual Arts of Afro-Americans,* South Bend, Ind., 1971.

SAADIE

See: Graham, Sadie.

SAAR, BETYE

Painter, graphic artist, mixed media, educator. Born in Los Angeles in 1926. Studied at Pasadena City College; University of California (BFA); Long Beach State College; University of Southern California; San Fernando State College; Valley State College, California. Artist, teacher-in-residence at Hayward State College, California.

Works: *The Astrologer's Window; The Mystic Window; The Jewel of Gemini; Samsara; Whitney's Way,* 1970 (mixed media); *Time,* 1970 (mixed media); *Sambo's Banjo; Gelede; 10 Mojo Secrets; Black Girl's Window; The Vision of El Cremo; Africa; The View from the Sorcerer's Window.*

Exhibited: Kozlow Gallery; Long Beach State College Drawing Exhibit; Riverside Art Assn. Art Exhibit; Miracle Mile of Art Gallery; 2nd Annual All-Cal. Print Exhibit; Contemporary I & II Art Exhibits; Los Angeles Outdoor Art Exhibit; Art on Paper, NC; 5th Annual Mercynurst Nat'l Exhibit, Pa.; 20th Nat'l Exhibition of Prints, Washington, DC; Nat'l Black & White Print Exhibit, Kansas; Los Angeles County Art Museum; San Francisco Legion of Honor Museum; Northwest Printmakers, Seattle, Wash.; Library of Congress; Whitney Museum, 1971; Lang Art Gallery, Scripps College, Claremont, Cal.; La Jolla Museum, 1970; Whitney Sculpture Annual, 1970; Multi-Cul, Los Angeles, 1972; Los Angeles County Museum of Art, 1972; Cal. College of Arts & Crafts, 1970; Boston Museum of Fine Arts, 1968; NY, Museum of Modern Art, 1968; Lytton Center of Visual Arts, Los Angeles, 1968; Santa Barbara Museum of Art, 1970; Oakland Museum, 1969; San Francisco Museum of Art, 1969; Fine Arts Gallery of San Diego; Minneapolis Institute of Art, 1968; High Museum, Atlanta; NJ State Museum, 1968; Contemporary Arts Museum, Houston, 1968; 3rd Biennial Nat'l Invitational Print Exhibit; Dickson Art Center, 1966.

Collections: Los Angeles County Museum; Univ. of Mass.; Oakland Museum.

Awards: 1st prize, graphics 1965, Honorable mention, 1966, Miracle Mile of Art Exhibit, Hollywood; 1st prize, Los Angeles Area Print Exhibit; Purchase Prize, Los Angeles Outdoor Art Exhibit; Cash Award, Contemporary II Art Competition, Los Angeles, 1972; Purchase Prize, 5th Cal. Small Images Exhibition, Los Angeles; 1st prize, graphics, Pasadena Artist Society, 1969; 1st prize, graphics, Watts Summer Festival, Los Angeles, 1969; 1st prize, small image exhibit, Westwood Art Assn., Cal., 1969; 1st prize, graphics, Contemporary Los Angeles Exhibit, 1965; 2nd prize, Contemporary Los Angeles Exhibit, 1965.

Sources: Oakland Museum. *Black Untitled II,* 1971; UCLA Art Galleries. *The Negro in American Art;* American Negro Artist. *Prize Winning Graphics,* 1965; Roelof-Lanner, T.V., ed. *Prints by American Negro Artists;* "Afro-American Issue," *Art Gallery,* April 1968; Indiana Univ. *Fine Arts & the Black American;* Lewis/Waddy. *Black Artists on Art;* Doty. *Contemporary Black Artists in America;* Information from artist; Los Angeles Fine Arts & FM. *Black Talent Speaks,* Jan. 1967; Seldis, J., & William Wilson. "Art Walk," *Los Angeles Times,* May 12, 1972; DuSable Museum of African-Amer. History. *Contemporary Black Artists,* 1970, calendar; Minneapolis Institute of Art. *30 Contemporary Black Artists,* 1968; Flint (Mich.) Community Schools. *Black Reflections;* Greene, Carroll, Jr. "Perspective: The Black Artist in America," *Art Gallery,* April 1970; Harley, Ralph, Jr. "Checklist of Afro-Amer. Art & Artists," *The Serif,* Dec. 1970; Ruder & Finn Fine Arts. *Contemporary Black Artists,* NY, 1969; Myers, Carol L. *Black Power in the Arts,* Flint, Mich., 1970; Oakland Museum Archives; Walker, Roslyn. *A Resource Guide to the Visual Arts of Afro-Americans,* South Bend, Ind., 1971.

SAINT CLAIR, IRVIN

Worked in Washington, DC.
Exhibited: Atlanta Univ., 1951.
Sources: Harley, Ralph, Jr. "Checklist of Afro-Amer. Art & Artists," *The Serif,* Dec. 1970.

ST. JOHN, ROLAND

Graphic artist.
Works: *Northeast Wind; The Temple Dance; Night; Mother Earth; The Rainbow.*
Exhibited: Baltimore Museum of Art, 1939.
Sources: Baltimore Museum of Art. *Contemporary Negro Art,* 1939; DuSable Museum of African-Amer. History. *Contemporary Black Artists,* 1970, calendar; Harley, Ralph, Jr. "Checklist of Afro-Amer. Art & Artists," *The Serif,* Dec. 1970.

SALLEE, CHARLES L., JR.

Painter, graphic artist. Born in Oberlin, Ohio, 1913. Studied at Western Reserve University; John Huntington Polytechnic Institute; Cleveland Museum School of Art. Teacher at Playhouse Settlement; Kennard Junior High School, Cleveland. Worked on Federal Art Project, 1936-7.

Works: *Jitterbug; Mrs. Forbs; Bedtime; Lilly; Girl with Geraniums; Nude Back; Flowers on Red Table; Lillian; Bertha* (aquatint); *Swingtime; The Post Setters.*
Exhibited: Howard Univ., 1937; Internat'l Watercolor Show; Annual May Show, Cleveland, 1937-9; Amer. Negro Exposition, 1940; Atlanta Univ., 1942; South Side Community Art Center, Chicago, 1941.
Collections: Sunny Acres Hospital, Cleveland; US Nat'l Museum, Washington.

Sources: *Negro Yearbook;* Howard Univ. *Art of the American Negro,* 1937; DuSable Museum of African-Amer. History. *Contemporary Black Artists,* 1970, Calendar; "Negro Art from Cleveland's Karamu House," *Art Digest,* Jan. 15, 1942; Porter. "Negro Gains Recognition after Long Battle," *Pittsburgh Courier,* July 29, 1950; Beckett, Henry. "Zell Ingram, Painter of 'America's Most Tragic Figure,' Talks about Mothers," *New York Post,* Jan. 13, 1942; Mallett. *Index of Artists;* Locke. *The Negro in Art;* Porter. *Modern Negro Art;* Harley, Ralph, Jr. "Checklist of Afro-Amer. Art & Artists," *Serif,* Dec. 1970; Tanner Art Galleries. *Art of the American Negro,* 1940; Patterson, Lindsay. *The Negro in Music and Art,* NY, 1969; South Side Community Art Center. *National Negro Art Exhibition,* Chicago, 1941; Walker, Roslyn. *A Resource Guide to the Visual Arts of Afro-Americans,* South Bend, Ind., 1971.

SAMPLER, MARIAN
Painter.
Sources: Harley, Ralph, Jr. "Checklist of Afro-Amer. Art & Artists," *The Serif,* Dec. 1970; Atkinson, J. Edward. *Black Dimensions in Contemporary American Art,* NY, 1971.

SANDERS, SAMELLA
Painter. Worked in New Orleans.
Works: *Stimulant; Grace; Sharecroppers.*
Exhibited: Atlanta Univ., 1943, 1944.
Sources: Atlanta Univ. Annual Exhibition Catalogs; *Design,* Sept. 1944, pp. 20-1; Harley, Ralph, Jr. "Checklist of Afro-Amer. Art & Artists," *The Serif,* Dec. 1970.

SANFORD, WALTER
Works: *Susan and Friend; Seated Nude; Sun Ritual; Malcolm X; Martin Luther King, Jr.; We Will Count Nothing But Money.*
Collections: Johnson Pub. Co.
Sources: Dover. *American Negro Art;* Indiana Univ. *Fine Arts & the Black American;* DuSable Museum of African-Amer. History. *Contemporary Black Artists,* 1970, calendar; Johnson Pub. Co. *The JPC Art Collection,* pamphlet; Harley, Ralph, Jr. "Checklist of Afro-Amer. Art & Artists," *The Serif,* Dec. 1970; *The Negro Handbook,* composed by the editors of *Ebony,* 1966; Walker, Roslyn. *A Resource Guide to the Visual Arts of Afro-Americans,* South Bend, Ind., 1971.

SATCHELL, ERNEST
Printmaker. Active in 1960's in New Orleans.
Works: *Working in the Field* (woodcut).
Collections: Oakland Museum, Ruth Waddy Collection.
Sources: Roelof-Lanner, T.V., ed. *Prints by American Negro Artists;* Oakland Museum

Archives; Walker, Roslyn. *A Resource Guide to the Visual Arts of Afro-Americans,* South Bend, Ind., 1971.

SAUNDERS, RAYMOND
Painter, mixed media. Born in Pittsburgh in 1934. Studied at Carnegie Institute of Technology (BFA); Pennsylvania Academy of Fine Arts; Barnes Foundation, Merion, Pennsylvania; University of Pennsylvania; California College of Arts and Crafts (MFA).
Works: *Gumdrops; And Leave the Driving to Us; Ohhowiwish; Theycomedownfromthe northtoget; Juicy Fruit; Don'taskmeidon'tknow; Titled; Algiers; Hollywood; Bill Jones Mother is a Hore; Bea is Now 15, Her Baby is 15 Months Old; Dr. Jesus; Plenda Love; I Didn't Want to Get Started Having Babies, But After I Got Started, There Wasn't Anything I Could Do About It; La Chambre; Memory; 28 Works; Mother & Child; Ain't America Beautiful; American Goodies; One to Go & Then 9 Months; 2,3,4,5et; Marie's Bill,* 1970 (oil); *Play God,* 1970 (pencil); *Made in Japan,* 1970 (pencil); *7.5.6.3.,* 1970 (pencil); *1st Grade Reader, D. & J.,* 1970 (pencil); *Light Up,* 1970 (pencil); *Puff; Jewsdon'tgotoheavenwargames; Ornette'stimeintheredsq.; Targetpractice; The Red Star; Ifyou'reonvacationfromtheUSAplease cometoourofficewemayhaveabonusforyou; Big Moma Plenty; Post No Bills; Miss America; General Electric Lady; Chris Columbus?; Blue Chip Stamps; Landscape; See America 1st; A-1; Happy Birthday; Thoreau; Conquering Fashions; R.S.V.P.; Cardinal; Tops; Ain't Nobody Got Nothing; Going Home; Still Life; Mr. Charlie Gets 4 Stars for Being a Nigger; Three; Mexican Doorway; Si; An American Dream,* 1967 (oil/collage).
Exhibited: San Francisco Museum of Art, 1961; Pa. Academy of Fine Arts, 1962-7; New School Art Gallery, 1963, 1964, 1967; UCLA Traveling Exhibition, 1966-7; NY Museum of Modern Art, 1968; Phila. Art Museum, 1968; St. Paul (Minn.) Art Center, 1968; Whitney Museum, 1969, 1971; Minneapolis Institute of Art, 1968-70; Amer. Academy of Arts & Letters, NYC, 1969; Roberson Gallery for the Arts & Sciences, Binghamton, NY, 1970; Carnegie Internat'l, 1970; Boston Museum of Fine Arts, 1970; Terry Dintenfass Gallery, NYC, 1962, 1964, 1966, 1967, 1969; Dartmouth College, 1969; Lehigh Univ., 1970; La Jolla Museum of Art, 1970; State Armory, Wilmington, Del.; James A. Porter Gallery, 1970; Univ. of Iowa, 1971-2; Brooklyn College, 1969; Dickson Art Center, 1966; Pittsburgh Playhouse; Cal. College of Arts & Crafts; Cheltenham Annual.
Collections: Whitney Museum; Howard Univ.; Addison Gallery of Amer. Art; Univ. of Texas;

James A. Michner Collection; Cal. College of Arts & Crafts; Nat'l Institute of Arts & Letters; Pa. Academy of Fine Arts; Allentown Art Museum, Pa.; Terry Dintenfass, Inc., NY; Mr. Benny Andrews.

Awards: Nat'l Scholastic Scholarship, 1953; 1st prize, Thoron Oil Painting Award, 1956; Cresson European Traveling Scholarships, 1956; Prizes in Oil Painting, Pa. Academy of Fine Arts,, Univ. of Pa., 1955-7; San Francisco Award, San Francisco Annual, 1960; 1st prize, Pittsburgh Playhouse Invitational, 1959, 1963; Nat'l Institute of Arts & Letters Award, 1963; Ford Foundation Purchase Award, 1964; Prix de Rome, 1964-5; Lee (Phila.) Cultural Center, 1968; Pa. Academy of Fine Arts-1st prize, watercolor, 1955, 1st prize, figure drawing, 1954; Bakins Prize, 1956; Schwabacker-Frey Award, 1961.

Sources: Aesthetic Dynamics. *Afro-American Images/71,* 1972; NY State Education Dept. *Fifteen Under Forty;* Myers, Carol. *Black Power in the Arts,* Flint, Mich., 1970; "Afro-Amer. Issue," *Art Gallery,* April, 1968; Boston Museum of Fine Arts. *Afro-American Artists: NY & Boston;* Afro-Amer. Slide Depository, catalog, 1971-2; Indiana Univ. *Fine Arts & the Black American;* Information from artist; UCLA Art Galleries. *The Negro in American Art;* Doty. *Contemporary Black Artists in America;* La Jolla Museum of Art. *Dimensions of Black;* Bowles, Jerry. "In the Galleries," *Arts,* Feb. 1969; Ives, Colta Feller. "In the Galleries," *Arts,* May 1967; Saunders, Raymond. "Letters," *Arts,* May 1967; Ill. Bell Telephone. *Black American Artists/71,* 1972; Howard Univ. *James A. Porter Gallery of African American Art,* 1970; Beaumont-May Gallery. *Ray Saunders,* 1972; DuSable Museum of African-Amer. History. *Contemporary Black Artists,* 1970, Calendar; Minneapolis Institute of Art. *30 Contemporary Black Artists,* 1968; Dartmouth College. *6 Black Artists,* 1968; Werner, Alfred. "Black is Not a Colour," *Art & Artists,* May 1969, pp. 14-7; Greene, Carroll, Jr. "Perspective: The Black Artist in America," *Art Gallery,* April 1970; Andrews, Benny. "The Emergency Cultural Coalition," *Arts,* Summer 1970, p. 18; Harley, Ralph, Jr. "A Checklist of Afro-Amer. Art & Artists," *The Serif,* Dec. 1970; Mt. Holyoke College. *Ten Afro-American Artists,* Nov. 1969; New School for Social Research Art Center. *Landscapes in Recent American Painting,* 1963; "Introducing New Talent," *Art Voices from Around the World,* Oct. 1962, p. 24; Atkinson, J. Edward. *Black Dimensions in Contemporary American Art,* 1971; Ruder & Finn Fine Arts. *Contemporary Black Artists,* 1969; Brooklyn College. *Afro-American Artists: Since 1950,* 1969; Hol-

lingsworth, Alvin. "Wealth of Expression in Black Artists' RISD Show,", *Providence Sunday Journal,* June 29, 1969; *Who's Who in American Art;* San Francisco Museum of Art; *California Annual,* 1961; Pa. Academy of Fine Arts. *Fellowship Annuals,* catalogs, 1962-7; St. Paul Art Center. *Drawing USA,* Minn., 1968; Whitney Museum. *Whitney Museum Annual,* NYC, 1969; Walker, Roslyn. *A Resource Guide to the Visual Arts of Afro-Americans,* South Bend, Ind., 1971; Glueck, Grace. "America Has Black Art on Her Mind," *New York Times,* Feb. 27, 1969, p. C34.

SAUNDERS, SAMELLA
Painter.
Works: *Sharecroppers.*
Sources: Lowenfeld, Viktor. "New Negro Art in America," *Design Magazine,* Sept. 1944.

SAUNDERS, VINCENT
Born in Chicago in 1916. Studied at Fisk University; under Aaron Douglas; Margaret Burroughs Workshop, Chicago.
Sources: DuSable Museum of African-Amer. History. *Contemporary Black Artists,* 1970, calendar; *Art Gallery,* April 1970.

SAVAGE, AUGUSTA CHRISTINE
Sculptor, educator, art center director. Born in Green Cove Spring, Florida in 1900. Died on March 27, 1962. Studied at Tallahassee State Normal School; Cooper Union; Grande Chaumiere, Paris (1934-5); Academy of Fine Arts, Rome; Woman's Art School. Studied under H.A. McNeil; Felix Beeneteau, Paris. Director of Harlem Community Art Center. Opened private art studios in Harlem.
Works: *The Harp; Lift Every Voice and Sing; The Chase; Prima Donna; Black Woman; Gamin; Lenore; Faun.*
Exhibited: Harmon Foundation, 1928, 1930-1; Architecture League, 1934; Nat'l Assn. of Woman Painters, 1934; YWCA, Harlem, 1934; Argent Galleries, NY, 1935, 1938; Traveling Exhibits, 1938-9; Amer. Negro Exhibition, 1940; City College of NY, 1967; Sesqui-Centennial, Phila.; 135th St. Public Library, NYC; Douglas High School, Baltimore; Grande Chaumiere, Paris; Salon D'Antoinne, Paris; Sociate Des Artistes Francais, Paris; Le Salon, Paris; Grand Palais Des Champs Elysees Ave. Alexander III, Paris; James A. Porter Gallery, 1970; YMCA, 135th St., NYC; South Side Community Art Center, Chicago.
Collections: Morgan State College; Nat'l Archives; NY Public Library-Schomburg Collection.
Awards: Rosenwald Fellowship for study in Paris, 1930-2; Carnegie Grant to open art gallery in Harlem; Julius Rosenwald Fellowship, 1929-31.

Member: Nat'l Assn. of Woman Painters & Sculptors (1st Negro to be accepted).
Sources: Mallett. *Index of Artists;* Locke. *The Negro in Art; Negro Almanac; Architectural Forum,* Feb. 1938; *Art Digest,* April 15, 1935; *Art News,* May 27, 1939; *Who's Who in American Art,* 1940-1; City College of NY. *The Evolution of Afro-American Artists: 1800-1950,* 1967; Bearden, Romare, & Harry Henderson. *Six Black Masters of American Art;* Tanner Art Galleries. *Art of the American Negro,* 1940; Brawley, Benjamin. *The Negro Genius;* Butcher, Margaret. *The Negro in American Culture,* p. 238; Roucek & Kiernan. *The Negro Impact on Western Civilization;* Afro-Amer. Slide Depository, catalog, 1971-2; *Who's Who in Colored America,* 3rd Edition; Howard Univ. *James A. Porter Gallery of African-American Art,* 1970; Harmon Foundation. *Exhibit of Fine Arts,* 1930; Harmon Foundation. *Select Picture List;* Woodson, Carter, Charles H. Wesley. *The Story of the Negro Retold,* p. 403; "The Negro Artists Reveal Genius in Trenton Show," *Art Digest,* April 15, 1935; Greene, Carroll, Jr. "Perspective: The Black Artist in America," *Art Gallery,* April 1970; Pierre-Noel, Lois Jones. "American Negro Art in Progress," *Negro History Bulletin,* Oct. 1967; Locke, Alain. "The American Negro as Artist," *American Magazine of Art,* Sept. 1931; "American Negro Art," *Design Magazine,* Feb. 1942; Kiah, Virginia. "Black Artists," *Savannah Magazine,* April 1972, p. 14; Harley, Ralph, Jr. "Checklist of Afro-Amer. Art & Artists," Dec. 1970; "Sculptress Gives Views on Art of the Negro," *Black Dispatch,* Sept. 26, 1936; "Realization," *Chicago Art Institute Scrapbook LXVIII,* Feb.-Aug. 1936, p. 36; "Negro Art to be at World's Fair," *Iowa Bystander,* Dec. 16, 1937; Sculpture by Augusta Savage . . ," *Life* (n.d.), pp. 216-8; "Photo of Artist & Sculptural Group," *Opportunity,* May 1939; Greene, Carroll, Jr. *Afro-American Artists: 1800-1968,* slides & text; Ploski, Harry, Ernest Kaiser. "The Black Artist," *Afro USA,* 1971; Ploski, Harry, Ernest Kaiser, Otto Lindenmeyer. "The Black Artist," *Reference Library of Black America,* Book IV, 1971; "At New York Art Exhibit," *Afro-American,* March 30, 1936; "Negro Students Hold Their Own Art Exhibition," *New York Herald Tribune,* Feb. 15, 1935; Schatz, Walter. *Directory of Afro-American Resources,* 1970; DuSable Museum of African-Amer. History. *Contemporary Black Artists,* 1970, calendar; Allen, Cleveland G. "Our Young Artists," *Opportunity,* June 1923; "Ban on Negress Artist is Criticised in France," *New York Times,* May 3, 1923; "Barred from French Fine Art School," *Afro-American* (Baltimore, Md.), April 27, 1923; "Negro Divine Raps Ban on Girl Artist," *New York City World,* April 30, 1923; "Afro-American Art: 1800-1950," *Ebony,* Feb. 1968, pp. 116-22; South Side Community Art Center. *Chicago Collectors Exhibit of Negro Art,* Chicago, 1945; Myers, Carol L. *Black Power in the Arts,* Flint, Mich., 1970; Spradling, Mary M., ed. *In Black and White: Afro-Americans in Print;* Robinson, Wilhelmena S. *Historical Negro Biographies,* p. 248; *Current Biography,* 1941, pp. 752-4; *Ebony,* Aug. 1966, pp. 90-4; *Negro History Bulletin,* March 1939, p. 51; Holbrook, Francis C. "A Group of Negro Artists," *Opportunity,* July 1923; Walker, Roslyn. *A Resource Guide to the Visual Arts of Afro-Americans,* South Bend, Ind., 1971.

SAVAIN, PETION

Painter.
Works: *Black Madonna; Country Market.*
Exhibited: Atlanta Univ., 1942.
Sources: Atlanta Univ. Annual catalog, 1942; Harley, Ralph, Jr. "Checklist of Afro-Amer. Art & Artists," *The Serif,* Dec. 1970.

SAWYER, ANN

Painter. Born in Johnstown, Pennsylvania in 1914.
Works: *I Gotta Right.*
Sources: Dover. *American Negro Art;* Indiana Univ. *Fine Arts & the Black American;* Harley, Ralph, Jr. "Checklist of Afro-Amer. Art & Artists," *The Serif,* Dec. 1970.

SAWYER, ANNA M.

Painter.
Works: *Leonore.*
Collections: Nat'l Archives.
Sources: Afro-Amer. Slide Depository, Catalog; Harley, Ralph, Jr. "Checklist of Afro-Amer. Art & Artists," *The Serif,* Dec. 1970.

SCHULMAN, M.

Collections: NY Public Library-Schomburg Art Collection.
Sources: Schatz, Walter. *Directory of Afro-American Resources,* 1970.

SCHUYLER, G.S.

Sources: Harley, Ralph, Jr. "Checklist of Afro-Amer. Art & Artists," *The Serif,* Dec. 1970.

SCOTT, BETTY

Painter, printmaker.
Exhibited: Drum & Spear Bookstore, Washington, DC, 1972.
Sources: *Black Shades,* Feb. 1972.

SCOTT, HAROLD C.

Born in 1907 in Alabama.
Works: *Water Boy.*
Exhibited: Harmon Foundation, 1933; Pen & Pallette Exhibit; YMCA; Annual Recreational Dept. Art Exhibit; Brewster Community Cen-

ter; Annual Students Exhibit in Detroit.
Awards: 1st prize, soap carving contest.
Sources: Harmon Foundation. *Non-Jury Exhibit of Works of Negro Artists,* 1933.

SCOTT, HENRY WILLIAM

Graphic artist. Born in 1876 in Texas.
Works: *The Cathedral At Rheims.*
Exhibited: Harmon Foundation, 1933; Phyllis Wheatley Branch, YWCA.
Sources: Harmon Foundation. *Non-Jury Exhibit of Work of Negro Artists,* 1933.

SCOTT, JOHN TARRELL

Painter, graphic artist, mixed media. Born in New Orleans, Louisiana on June 30, 1940. Studied at Xavier University (BFA); Michigan State University (MFA). Assistant Professor of Fine Arts, Xavier University of Louisiana.
Works: *Vanity-Monze 21; Kenneth Harris; Window; Tarrell; My Lonely Self; America, America; Head of Christ; Behold the Lamb III; Monk; Child's Toy; Bishop; Jonah II; Four Evangelists; Vetoed; Peter; Self Portrait; Out One Bag & In Another; Black; Midnight Brotherhood; Jonah & the Whale.*
Exhibited: Univ. of Iowa; "Young American," Xavier Univ., 1959; Orleans Gallery, 1966; Hibernia Nat'l Bank, 1966; Louisiana State Univ. Drawing & Private Show, 1966; Florida A&M Univ., 1968; Our Lady of Holy Cross College, 1969; Experience Gallery, 1971; Laemmle Fine Arts Theatres, 1971; Kalamazoo Institute of Art, 1971; Fisk Univ., 1971.
Collections: All Girls Academy, Minneapolis, Minn.; Louisiana State Univ.; Fisk Univ.; Florida A&M Univ.; Sisters of the Blessed Sacrament, Va.; St. Joseph School, Ill.; Methodist Church, Ala.; Napels County Civic Center, Fla.; Xavier Univ. Student Center, New Orleans; Methodist Church, Mich.; The Maji Shop, New Orleans; St. Phillip's Church, New Orleans; St. Angela Merici Church, La.; Johnson Pub. Co., Chicago.
Awards: 1st prize, Louisiana State Univ. Drawing & Private Show; Psi Kappa Psi Honor Society; Liturgical Arts Society; Assistantship & fellowship, Mich. State Univ.
Represented by: Brockman Gallery Los Angeles, Cal.; Studio 8, New Orleans, La.
Sources: Gallery Press Releases, Brockman Gallery; Afro-Amer. Slide Depository, Catalog, 1971-2; Illinois Bell Telephone. *Black American Artists/71,* 1972; Johnson Pub. *The JPC Art Collection,* Pamphlet.

SCOTT, JOSEPHINE

Painter. Worked in Atlanta.
Works: *Flower.*
Exhibited: Atlanta Univ., 1943.
Sources: Atlanta Univ. catalog.

SCOTT, OLIVER PATRICK

Works: *Do You Know Mr. Jones; No More.*
Exhibited: State Armory, Wilmington, Del., 1971.
Sources: Aesthetic Dynamics, *Afro-American Images,* 1971, Catalog.

SCOTT, WILLIAM EDOUARD

Painter, illustrator, muralist. Born in Indianapolis on March 11, 1884. Studied at Art Institute of Chicago (1904-8); Julian and Colarossi Academies in Paris under H. O. Tanner.
Works: *La Pauvre Voisine; Jean Baptiste de Saible; The Lord Will Provide; Local Color-Haiti; Calabash for Market; When the Tide is Out; Haitian Man; Blind Sister Mary; Mexican Scene; Lead Thou Me On; Castillian Blood; Portrait of Mr. W. Ellis Stewart; Vacation Time; Her First Communion; The Fort Napoleon Could Not Take; Christmas Dinner; La Misere; La Connoisserue; A Rainy Night in Etaples; The Potter of Gonnives; Port-au-Prince, Haiti; Booker T. Washington; Old Age; Sunday Morning, Port-au-Prince, Haiti; Lead Kindly Light; The Turkey Market; Haitian Scene;* Mural decoration for the Century of Progress Exposition, Chicago.
Exhibited: Royal Academy, London, 1912; Autumn Salon, Paris; Salon la Tourquet; Art Institute of Chicago; Cincinnati Museum; San Diego Museum; Los Angeles Museum; Port-au-Prince, 1931 (1-man); Johannesburg, Africa; Harmon Foundation, 1928, 1931, 1933; Harmon College Traveling Art Exhibit, 1934-5; Findlay Galleries, Chicago, 1935; Amer. Negro Exposition, 1940; Murals for public buildings in Indiana, West Virginia, YMCA, NYC; Art Institute of Chicago, 1932; Smithsonian Institution, 1933; Salon des Beaux Arts, Toquet; New Jersey State Museum, 1935; Texas Centennial, 1936; Howard Univ., 1945; James A. Porter Gallery, 1970; South Side Community Art Center, Chicago, 1941, 1945.
Collections: Mural decorations, Evanston, Ill.; Herron Art Institute, Indianapolis; Ind. Court House, Fort Wayne; Lafayette, Ind. Court House; Ill. State House; Murals in schools in Institute, WVa. & Charlestown, WVa.; 1st Presbyterian Church, Chicago; *Chicago Defender* Newspaper Lobby; Binga State Bank, Chicago; Anthony Hotel, Fort Wayne, Ind.; Ill. Nat'l Bank, Edwardsville; South Park M.E. Church, Chicago; Paris Salon; Royal Academy, London; 1st Nat'l Bank & high school, Michigan City, Ind.; Peoples Finance Corp. Bank, St. Louis; John Shoop School, Chicago; Betsy Ross Jr. High School, Chicago; Government of Argentina; Port-au-Prince, Haiti; Truly Park, Davis Sq., Stanford Fieldhouse, Chicago; Cook County Juvenile Court, Chicago; YMCA, Indianapolis; YMCA, 135th St., NYC; Municipal

Tuberculosis Sanitarium, Chicago; City Hospital, Indianapolis; Murals in Pilgrim Baptist Church, Chicago; Bethesda Baptist Chuch, Chicago; Metropolitan Community Center, Chicago; Nat'l Archives; Judge Albert G. George; NY Public Library, Schomburg Art Collection; Dr. & Mrs. S.W. Smith.

Awards: Frederick Manus Brand Prize, Art Institute of Chicago (twice); Harmon Gold Medal, 1927; Rosenwald Fellow, 1931; Jesse Binga Prize, 1931; James McVeagh Prize, 1931; Municipal Art League Traveling Scholarship; Legion of Honor, Gov't of Haiti; 1st prize, Indiana State Fair, 1914.

Member: Hoosier Salon; Alumni Assn., Art Institute of Chicago; Chicago Art League.

Sources: Mallett. *Index of Artists*; Dover. *American Negro Art*; Locke. *Negro in Art*; Young. *Dictionary of American Artists, Sculptors & Engravers*; *Who's Who in American Art*, 1940-1; *American Art Annual*, 1933; Brawley, Benjamin. *The Negro Genius*; Holbrook, Francis C. "William Edouard Scott," *Southern Workman*, Feb. 1924, pp. 72-5; Albany Institute of History & Art. *Negro Artist Comes of Age*; Harmon Foundation. *Exhibition of Productions by Negro Artists;* "Afro-Amer. Issue," *Art Gallery*, April 1968; Indiana Univ. *Fine Arts & the Black American*; Afro-Amer. Slide Depository, catalog; City College of NY. *The Evolution of Afro-American Artists 1800-1950*; Art Institute of Chicago. *The Negro in Art Week*, 1927; Porter, James A. "Negro Art on Review," *American Magazine of Art*, Jan. 1934; Locke, Alain. "The American Negro As Artist," *American Magazine of Art*, Sept. 1931; "Harlem Library Shows Negro Art," *Art News*, May 20, 1933, p. 14; Greene, Carroll. *Afro-American Artists: 1800-1968*, slides; Porter, James A. "Negro Artists Gain Recognition After Long Battle," *Pittsburgh Courier*, July 29, 1950; Brawley, Benjamin. *The Negro in Literature & Art in the US*; *1st Annual Exhibit of Books, Manuscripts, Paintings, Sculptures etc. by the Negro Library Assn. at Carlton Ave. YMCA*, 1918; Locke, Alain. "Youth Speaks: The Artistic Vanguard," *The Survey*, March 1925; Brown, Marion. "The Negro in Fine Arts," *The Negro Heritage Library*, Vol. 2; Patterson, Lindsay, comp. *The Negro in Music & Art*, 1969; Motley, Willard F. "Negro Art in Chicago," *The Negro in Music & Art*, 1969; Ploski, Harry, & Ernest Kaiser. "The Black Artist," *Afro USA*, 1971; Ploski, Harry, Ernest Kaiser, & Otto Lindenmeyer. "The Black Artist," *Reference Library of Black America*, Book IV, 1971; "Negro Artists Paintings on Display at University (Howard)," *East Tennessee News*, Knoxville, June 6, 1932; "Negro Has Given Much to Art, Survey Shows," *Boston Traveler*,

Feb. 23, 1933; Schatz, Walter. *Directory of Afro-American Resources*, 1970; DuSable Museum of African-Amer. History. *Contemporary Black Artists*, Calendar, 1970; Herring, James V. "The American Negro Craftsman & Artist," *Crisis*, April 1942; Porter. *Modern Negro Art*; Winslow, Vernon. "Negro Art & the Depression," *Opportunity*, Feb. 1941; "Art," *Crisis*, Feb. 1911, p. 10; *Crisis*, Jan. 1914, p. 114; "The Cross of Calvary," *Chicago Defender*, May 12, 1934; Fielding. *Dictionary of American Painters, Sculptors & Engravers*; Harley, Ralph, Jr. "A Checklist of Afro-Amer. Art & Artists," *The Serif*, Dec. 1970; Motley, Willard F. "Negro Art in Chicago," *Opportunity*, Jan. 1940; Assn. for the Study of Negro Life & History. *Exhibition of Works by Negro Artists*, 1933; Howard Univ. *Art of the American Negro*, 1937; Butcher, Margaret. *The Negro in American Culture*, p. 219; Roucek & Kiernan. *The Negro Impact on Western Civilization*; Harmon Foundation. *Non-Jury Exhibit of Work of Negro Artists*, 1933; Texas Centennial Exposition. *Thumbnail Sketches of Exhibiting Artists*; Howard Univ. *Festival of Fine Arts*, 1945; Harmon Foundation. *Negro Artists*, 1935; Howard Univ. *James A. Porter Gallery of African-American Art*, 1970; *Who's Who in Colored America*, 3rd Edition; Furr, Arthur F. *History & Progress of Negroes in the US*; Pierre-Noel, Lois Jones. "American Negro Art in Progress," *Negro History Bulletin*, Oct. 1967; South Side Community Art Center. *National Negro Art Exhibition*, Chicago, 1941; Myers, Carol L. *Black Power in the Arts*, Flint, Mich., 1970; *Jet*, March 17, 1966, p. 11; "A Young Artist," *Crisis*, March 1913, p. 221; Walker, Roslyn. *A Resource Guide to the Visual Arts of Afro-Americans*, South Bend, Ind., 1971.

SCURLOCK, ADDISON W.
Photographer.

Sources: "One of Washington's Best Studios Is Negro Owned," *Tuskegee Messenger*, Jan. 31, 1931.

SEABROOK, GEORGETTE
Painter. Born in New York City in 1916. Studied at Cooper Union Art School.

Works: *Emilie; Southern Flower Vendors.*

Exhibited: Amer. Negro Exposition, Chicago, 1940; Atlanta Univ.; YMCA Art Group, 1933; Harlem Art Workshop Exhibition, 1933; Harlem Art Committee, 137th St. Branch YWCA; NJ State Museum, Trenton, 1935; Harmon Foundation, 1936; Amer. Artists Congress; Wanamaker Art Gallery, 1938; Augusta Savage Studios, 1939; Library of Congress, 1940.

Collections: NY Public Library-Schomburg Art Collection.

Sources: Pierre-Noel, Lois Jones. "American

Negro Art in Progress," *Negro History Bulletin*, Oct. 1967; Brown, Marion. "The Negro in the Fine Arts," *The Negro Heritage Library*, Vol. 2; Schatz, Walter. *Directory of Afro-American Resources*, 1970; *Negro Yearbook*; Indiana Univ. *Fine Arts & the Black American*; Porter. *Modern Negro Art*; Harley, Ralph, Jr. "Checklist of Afro-Amer. Art & Artists," *The Serif*, Dec. 1970; Locke, Alain. "Advance on the Art Front," *Opportunity*, May 1939; Harmon Foundation. *Negro Artists*, 1935; DuSable Museum of African-Amer. History. *Contemporary Black Artists*, Calendar, 1970; Walker, Roslyn. *A Resource Guide to the Visual Arts of Afro-Americans*, South Bend, Ind., 1971.

SEALEY, ROY

Architect.

Sources: *Ebony*, Aug. 1950, pp. 32-4; Spradling, Mary, ed. *In Black & White: Afro-Americans in Print*.

SEARLES, CHARLES R.

Painter, educator. Born in Philadelphia, 1937. Studied at Fleicher Art Memorial; Pennsylvania Academy of Fine Arts.

Works: *Departure*, 1971; *Nigerian Street Traders*, 1972; *Back Porch*, 1969; *Up Against the Wall*; *Land*; *Front Porch*; *Festival in the Park*, 1972; *Idle Hours*; *Doris*; *Untitled*; *Victim*; *On the Corner*; *Four No More*; *Sitting on the Porch*; *In Front of the Store*; *Coming Down*; *Pat*; *When Do We Leave?*; *Come with Me to That Place*; *Brothers from the Land*; *The Back Lot*; *News Stand*; *Pirate Jenny*; *Brothers*; *News*, 1970.

Exhibited: Brooklyn Museum, 1969; Phila. Civic Center; State Armory, Wilmington, Del., 1971; Whitney Museum, 1971; Columbia Univ., 1969; Reading Museum, 1970; Univ. of Florida, 1970; Phila. Museum of Art, 1970; Studio Museum, Harlem, 1971.

Collections: Pa. Academy of Fine Arts; Mr. Herbert A. Allen, NY.

Awards: Cresson Memorial Traveling Award, 1971, & Ware Memorial Traveling Award, 1972, Pa. Academy of Fine Arts.

Member: Phila. North Arts Council (board); Pa. Academy of Fine Arts (Exhibition Committee).

Sources: Doty. *Contemporary Black Artists in America*; Brooklyn Museum. *New Black Artists*, 1969; Afro-Amer. Slide Depository, Catalog; Phila. Division of Art. *Afro-American Artists 1800-1969*; Aesthetic Dynamics. *Afro-American Images*, 1971; Preston, Malcolm. "Art: Black Exhibit," *Boston Herald Traveler*, April 19, 1971; Whitney Museum. *Contemporary Black American Artists*, 1971; *New York Times*, April 6, 1971; *Tuesday Magazine*, Feb. 1970; *Philadelphia Bulletin*, May 16, 1971;

Philadelphia Daily News, May 8, 1971; *Who's Who in American Art*, 1973; Information from the artist; Loercher, Diana. "Art: Idioms of Blackness at the Elma Lewis School," *Christian Science Monitor*, July 10, 1970; Walker, Roslyn. *A Resource Guide to the Visual Arts of Afro-Americans*, South Bend, Ind., 1971.

SEBREE, CHARLES

Painter, illustrator. Born in Madisonville, Kentucky in 1914. Studied at the Art Institute of Chicago. Worked for Illinois Federal Art Project (Easel Division), 1936-8.

Works: *The Clown; Seated Nude; Seated Woman in Red; Heads of Two Old Women; Primitive Boy; Head of a Girl; New York Hat; Portrait of a Girl; Woman & Lemons; Head of Woman; Ritual Woman; Still Life;* Illustrations for Countee Cullen's book, THE LOST ZOO; *Solitude; War Talk in Turkey; Dance; The Double Headed Hoolnkas; Ethiopia's Awakening; Bruin Bear; Two Marias; Woman on the Balcony; Refugee; Christ Child; Costume; Angel Thinking; Good Friday; Cape Train; Michael Monkey* (The Lost Zoo); *The Ha Ka Ha* (The Lost Zoo); *The Sleepamitemore; The Wakeup World at Three O'Clock; Harlem Saltimbanques; To Dream of Pearls; Moses; Head of Cora; The Flutist; Girl with Flowers; Lamenting; Garcon Bleu; Pink Turban; Memory of Giotto.*

Exhibited: Internat'l Watercolor Society, 1935; Katharine Kuh Gallery, Chicago, 1936; Federal Art Project Gallery, Chicago, 1937; Breckenridge Gallery, 1938; Grace Horne Gallery, Boston, 1939; Amer. Negro Exposition, Chicago, 1940; Institute of Modern Art, Boston, 1943; City College of NY, 1967; Howard Univ., 1941; James A. Porter Gallery, 1970; Roko Gallery, 1949; South Side Community Art Center, Chicago, 1945, 1941; McMillen Inc. Galleries, NY, 1941.

Collections: Renaissance Society Collection; Univ. of Chicago; Thornton Wilder Collection; McBride Collection, Chicago; Nat'l Archives; NY Public Library-Schomburg Art Collection; Atlanta Univ.-Countee Cullen Collection; Ms. Gertrude Abercrombie; Miss Stella Dubow; Mr. William McBride; Mr. & Mrs. Jack Rogin; Mrs. Arthur Lowenstein; Mr. William Halperin; Mr. Norman MacLeish.

Sources: Dover. *American Negro Art*; Locke. *Negro in Art*; Albany Institute of History & Art. *Negro Artist Comes of Age*; Indiana Univ. *Fine Arts & the Black American*; Afro-Amer. Slide Depository, catalog; City College of NY. *Evolution of Afro-American Artists, 1800-1950*, 1967; *Exhibition of Negro Artists of Chicago at Howard Univ. Gallery of Art*, Feb. 1941; Motley, Willard F. "Negro Art in Chicago," *Opportunity*, Jan. 1940; Watson,

Jane. "New Gallery of Art to Open Today," *Washington Post*, March 28, 1943; Herring, James V. "The American Negro Craftsman & Artist," *Crisis*, April 1942; Porter. *Modern Negro Art*; *Chicago Art Institute Scrapbook*, June/Nov. 1938, p. 170; Harley, Ralph,, Jr. "A Checklist of Afro-Amer. Art & Artists," *The Serif*, Dec. 1970; Howard Univ. *James A. Porter Gallery of African-American Art*, 1970; DuSable Museum of African-Amer. History. *Contemporary Black Artists*, 1970, Calendar; Harmon Foundation. *Select Picture List*; J.G. "Honoring Negro History," *Art Digest*, Feb. 15, 1949, p. 20; "Art by Negroes," *Art Digest*, Oct. 15, 1941; Cullen, Countee. *Lost Zoo*, Illus.; McMillen Inc. Galleries. *Contemporary Negro Art*, NY, 1941; "American Negro Artists Given Full Length Review in NY Show," *Art Digest*, Dec. 15, 1941; "The Negro in Art," *Art Digest*, June 1, 1944; Pierre-Noel, Lois Jones. "American Negro Art in Progress," *Negro History Bulletin*, Oct. 1967; Locke, Alain. "Chicago's New Southside Art Center," *Magazine of Art*, Aug. 1941, p. 320; E.K. "Negro Artists," *Art News*, Feb. 1949, p. 47; Greene, Carroll, Jr. *Afro-American Artists: 1800-1968*, slides; Brown, Marion. "The Negro in the Fine Arts," *The Negro Heritage Library*, Vol. 2; Patterson, Lindsay. "Contemporary Artists," *The Negro in Music & Art*, 1969; Bearden, Romare. *The Negro Artist & Modern Art*, 1934; Ploski, Harry, & Ernest Kaiser. "The Black Artist," *Afro USA*, 1971; Ploski, Harry, Ernest Kaiser, & Otto Lindenmeyer. "The Black Artist," *Reference Library of Black America*, Book IV, 1971; *The Negro Handbook*, Composed by Editors of *Ebony*, Chicago, 1966; Schatz, Walter. *Directory of Afro-American Resources*, 1970; South Side Community Art Center. *Chicago Collectors Exhibit of Negro Art*, 1945; South Side Community Art Center. *National Negro Art Exhibition*, Chicago, 1941; Myers, Carol. *Black Power in the Arts*, Flint, Mich., 1970; South Side Community Art Center. *Opening Exhibition of Paintings by Negro Artists*, Chicago, 1941; South Side Community Art Center. *Exhibition of Book Illustrations by Jacob Lawrence, Charles Sebree, Vernon Winslow*, Chicago, 1941; Walker, Roslyn. *A Resource Guide to the Visual Arts of Afro-Americans*, South Bend, Ind., 1971.

SEJOURNE, BERNARD

Painter. Born in Port-Au-Prince, Haiti, 1947. **Works:** *Ti-Fi (Little Girl)*, 1971; *Fleurs Fannées*, 1971; *You and I*, 1971.
Exhibited: Newark Museum, 1971.
Sources: Newark Museum. *Black Artists: Two Generations*, 1971.

SEKOTO, C.

Painter.
Works: *African Portrait* (oil); *Street Scene* (watercolor).
Collections: Oakland Museum.
Sources: Oakland Museum Archives, gift of the Harmon Foundation.

SELF, HOWRHU

Studied at Tuskegee Institute.
Works: *Why*.
Exhibited: Sun Times/Daily News Gallery, Chicago, 1970.
Sources: United Negro College Fund. *Art 1970*, Chicago, 1970.

SENGTACKE, BOBBY

Photographer.
Sources: Fisk Univ. Art Galleries. *3 Afro-Americans*, Catalog, 1969; Harley, Ralph, Jr. "Checklist of Afro-Amer. Art & Artists," *The Serif*, Dec. 1970.

SEWELL, HELEN

Works: *The Truant*.
Awards: Logan Purchase Prize, 1927.
Sources: "The Mr. & Mrs. Frank G. Logan purchase prizes to . . . Helen Sewell for 'Truant'," *Chicago Art Institute Bulletin*, XXI March 1927, p. 38; Hughes, Langston. *The Dream Keeper & Other Poems*," NY, 1932; Harley, Ralph, Jr. "Checklist of Afro-Amer. Art & Artists," *The Serif*, Dec. 1970.

SHANDS, FRANKLIN McKENZIE

Painter.
Works: *Jungle Gal; Southern Mud; Back Way*
Exhibited: Atlanta Univ., 1942.
Sources: "Negro Winners," *Art Digest*, May 1 1946; Harley, Ralph, Jr. "Checklist of Afro-Amer. Art & Artists," *The Serif*, Dec. 1970.

SHARPE, FRANK

Painter, printmaker. Born in Columbia, South Carolina on May 6, 1942. Studied at Pratt Institute; Benedict College, Columbia, South Carolina. Artist/Adjunct Lecturer at Bronx College, New York.
Works: *Man: Business Meeting; Man: On the Stoop at 143 Lenox Ave.; Man: Cocktail Thrower; Man: Amnesty; Man: Outlook Woman: In the Paril; Woman: On the Street Corner; Woman: A Week of Dreams; City Three on the Block; City: Window; City Police Line; City: No Place to Play; City World by Itself; More Blood on the Chain World: Bureaucratic; World: Sing of On Voice; World: Strategy for Change; Man X the Name; Man-King's Mountain; Search World: The 11th Hour; Malcolm, John, Martin Man: A Friend With Two Faces; Man: The Forgotten Secret; World: Exit; Woman: Smile*

Girl Smile; Peace, Love, Hate; Thoughts; World: Out of Space; City: Warning; World: On the 8th Day; World: Underworld; Black o Brown; City: Dusk to Dawn.
Exhibited: Whitney Museum, NY, 1971; Smith-Mason Gallery, 1971; Amer.-German Artist 1966/1967, Hanau, Germany; Wilson College, Pa., 1968; Brooklyn Museum, 1970; Prints & Graphics, 1970, Phila.; Black Artists, Brooklyn Public Library, 1969; Amer. Federation of Artists, 1971-2; Lincoln Penison Univ., 1971; Cinque Gallery, NY, 1971 (1-man); Little Carnegie Theatre, NY, 1971 (1-man); Cinque Gallery, 1972.
Collections: Bibliothèque Nationale, Paris, France; Print Shop; Amsterdam, Holland; Far Gallery, NYC.
Awards: Contemporary Black Artists.
Member: Amer. Federation of Arts.
Represented by: Far Gallery; Brownstone Galery, NYC; Cinque Gallery.
Sources: Afro-Amer. Slide Depository, Catalog, 1971-2; Doty. *Contemporary Black Artists in America*; Cinque Gallery. *Recent Prints: Frank Sharpe*, 1971; Smith-Mason Gallery. *National Exhibition Black Artists*, 1971; Information from the artist; Whitney Museum. *Contemporary Black Artists in America*; Amer. Federation of Art. *The Indignant Eye*, Catalog, 1971; *World Magazine*, Nov. 21, 1970; Pratt Institute. *Soulism*, Brooklyn Museum Catalog.

SHEARER, TEDDY

Graphic artist, cartoonist. Born in 1920. Studied at the Art Students League.
Works: *Lindy Hop; Most Landladies; Jam Session; For Drinkers Only; Flash!; The Hilltop.*
Sources: Minor, Marcia. "Pen and Life in Motion," *Daily Worker*, Sept. 7, 1938.

SHELTON, CHRISTOPHER

Sculptor, painter. Born in New Orleans, Louisiana, 1933.
Works: *Air Afrique #3 (For Carol)*, 1971.
Exhibited: Newark Museum, 1971.
Sources: Newark Museum. *Black Artist: Two Generations*, 1971.

SHELTON, MICHAEL

Painter.
Works: *Rage; Erotic Fancy; Time & Space Series; Man; Black Madonna* (mixed).
Exhibited: Phila. Civic Center Museum; State Armory, Wilmington, Del., 1971; Lee Cultural Center, Phila.
Sources: Phila. Civic Center Museum. *Afro-American Artists 1800-1969*; Aesthetic Dynamics. *Afro-American Images*, 1971, Catalog; Phila. Dept. of Recreation. *Love . . . and the Black Community.*

SHENCK, SIDNEY

Painter.
Collections: Mr. Benny Andrews.

SHISHIR, DAVID

Studied at Tuskegee Institute.
Works: *Village Morning.*
Exhibited: Sun Times/Daily News Gallery, Chicago, 1970.
Sources: United Negro College Fund. *Art 1970*, Chicago, 1970.

SHULKIN, ANATOL

Exhibited: Midtown Galleries, 1938.
Sources: "Exhibition in New York," *Chicago Art Center Bulletin,* V, Jan. 1927; "Anatol Shulkin. "The Fruit Basket," *Magazine of Art*, Nov. 1938; Harley, Ralph, Jr. "Checklist of Afro-Amer. Art & Artists," *The Serif*, Dec. 1970.

SILLS, THOMAS

Painter. Born in Castalia, North Carolina on August 20, 1914. Self-taught. An ex-laborer who took up 'brushless' painting about 1954 in New York City.
Works: *Composition; Drawing #2; My Home; Summer; Earth; Mirror; The Storm; She; Pleasant; Return*, 1970 (oil); *Africa; The South; Red Berries; Sea; Land; Summer Field; Feminine*, 1968 (oil).
Exhibited: Betty Parsons Gallery, NY, 1955, 1957, 1959, 1961 (1-man); Paul Kantor Gallery, Los Angeles, 1962; Bodley Gallery, NY, 1964, 1967, 1969, 1972; Artists Annual, Stable Gallery, NY, 1955; New School for Social Research, NY, 1956; Artists Group, Camino Gallery, NY, 1956; Whitney Museum, 1959-60; Univ. of Colo.; Fairleigh-Dickinson Univ., 1964; Dord Fitz Gallery, Amarillo, Texas; Museum of Modern Art, NY, 1969; Brooklyn College Student Art Center Gallery, 1969; Phila. Civic Center Museum, 1969; Wilson College, Chambersberg, Pa., 1968; Creighton Univ., Omaha, Neb., 1967; Mt. Holyoke College, 1969; Ruder & Finn Fine Arts, NYC, 1969; Boston Museum of Fine Arts, 1970; State Armory, Wilmington, Del., 1971; Minneapolis Institute of Art, 1968.
Collections: Bodley Gallery, NYC; Fordham Univ., NY; Whitney Museum, NY; Museum of Modern Art, NY; Finch College Museum, NY; Rose Museum, Brandeis Univ.; Syracuse Univ. Museum; Sheldon Memorial Gallery, Lincoln, Neb.; Williams College Museum, Williamstown, Mass.; Phoenix Art Museum, Ariz.; Norfolk Museum of Arts and Sciences, Va.; Los Angeles County Museum; Univ. of Ill. Krannert Art Museum; Rockefeller Univ., NY; Hofstra Univ., NY; Fisk Univ.; San Francisco Museum; Ciba-Geigy; Johnson Pub. Co.; Chase Manhattan Bank, NY; Betty Parsons;

Jeanne Reynal; Mr. & Mrs. William Copley; Mr. & Mrs. Ben Mildwoff; Ms. Ethel Schwabacher; Mr. & Mrs. George Wittenborn.
Awards: William & Norma Copley Foundation Award, 1957.
Sources: Dover. *American Negro Art*; Boston Museum of Fine Arts. *Afro-American Artists: NY & Boston*, 1970; *Who's Who in American Art*, 1970; Information from artist; Museum of Modern Art. *The New American Painting & Sculpture, The First Generation*, NYC, 1969; Schatz, Walter. *Directory of Afro-American Resources*, 1970; Ruder & Finn Fine Arts. *Contemporary Black Artists*, 1969; Brooklyn College. *Afro-American Artists: Since 1950*; Myers, Carol L. *Black Power in the Arts*, Flint, Mich., 1970; Walker, Roslyn. *A Resource Guide to the Visual Arts of Afro-Americans*, South Bend, Ind., 1971; Driscoll, Edgar, Jr. "Showcase for Black Artists," *Boston Sunday Globe*, July 6, 1969, p. A73; Phila. Civic Center Museum. *Afro-American Artists Exhibition*, 1969; Campbell, Lawrence. "The Flowering of Thomas Sills," *Art News*, March 1972; Aesthetic Dynamics. *Afro-American Images*, 1971; Doty. *Contemporary Black Artists in America*; Bodley Gallery. *Thomas Sills*, NY, 1970; Henry, Gerrit. "Reviews and Previews," *Art News*, March 1970; Kantor Gallery. *Thomas Sills*, Beverly Hills, Cal., 1962; Minneapolis Institute of Art. *30 Contemporary Black Artists*, 1968; Greene, Carroll, Jr. "Perspective: The Black Artist in America," *Art Gallery*, April 1970; Jacobs, Jay. "Now I'm Boss," *Art Gallery*, April 1970; Bowling, Frank. "The Rupture," *Arts*, Summer 1970; Johnson Pub. Co. *The JPC Art Collection*, pamphlet; "Black Art: What Is It?," *Art Gallery*, April 1970; "Exhibition at the Betty Parsons Gallery," *Pictures on Exhibit*, Vol. 30, No. 5; Harley, Ralph, Jr. "Checklist of Afro-Amer. Art & Artists," *The Serif*, Dec. 1970; Mount Holyoke College. *Ten Afro-American Artists*, 1969; Kramer, Hilton. "Is Politics Submerging Black Art?," *Courier-Journal & Times* (Louisville, Ky.), June 7, 1970; Patterson, Lindsay. "Contemporary Artists," *The Negro in Music & Art*, 1969; Van Almelo, Frederik. "In the American Grain," *Boston After Dark*, May 26, 1970, p. 24; Paris, Jean. "Black Art Experience in Art," *Long Island Press* (Jamaica, NY), June 14, 1970.

SIMMONS, JOHN W.

Painter, photographer. Born in 1950. Studied at Fisk University.
Works: *Free Flight and Stained Glass; Earl Hooks; Chicago; Nashville, Tennessee; San Francisco, California; Los Angeles, California; New York, New York.*
Exhibited: Nat'l. Students Union Assn. (2-

man); Fisk Univ., 1969-71; Tenn. State Museum, 1972 (1-man).
Collections: Fisk Univ.
Awards: Sengstacke Publication Award, *Chicago Daily Defender*, 1971.
Sources: Information from artist; Tenn. State Museum. *An Exhibit of Contemporary Photographs*, 1972.

SIMMS, CARROLL HARRIS

Painter, sculptor, educator, jeweler. Born in Bald Knob, Arkansas in 1924. Studied at Hampton Institute (1944-5); University of Toledo (1945-7); Toledo Museum School of Art (1945-8); Cranbrook Academy of Art, Bloomfield Hills, Michigan (BA, 1950; MFA, 1961); Wayne University, Detroit (1949-50); Slade School of Art, University of London (1954-6); Royal College of Art, London (1955); Central School of Arts and Crafts, London (1954-5); The British Museum (1955-6); Swedish Institute, Stockholm (1964); Morris Singer Bronze Art Foundry, London (1955-6); Institute of African Studies, University of Ibadan, Nigeria (1968-9). Teacher in Art Department of Texas Southern University, Houston.
Works: *Christ & the Lambs; Angels; The Miracles of Christ; Two Corners* (oil); *Weaver* (bronze); *African Queen Mother; Old Couple Seated on a Stump Fishing*, 1952 (bronze); *Whale*, 1953 (aluminum); *Water Angels*, 1960 (plexiglass); *Water Angels*, 1956 (bronze); *Doves & the Sacrament*, 1958 (stained glass); *Jonah & the Whale*, 1959 (bronze fountain); *Woman with a Bird*, 1959 (bronze); *Longshoremen*, 1957 (plexiglass mural); *Adam & Eve*, 1958 (stained glass); *Leopard*, 1957 (bronze); *Fertility*, 1957 (plexiglass mural); *Monkeys Reaching for the Moon*, 1964 (plexiglass mural); *Man & the Universe*, 1961 (aluminum); *Twelve Sculptural Free-Form Mosaic Ashtrays* (stoneware).
Exhibited: Toledo Museum of Fine Arts, 1948-50; Syracuse Museum, 1949; Wichita Museum, 1949; Detroit Art Institute, 1949-50; Atlanta Univ., 1950-2; Houston Museum of Fine Arts, 1950, 1952-4; Toledo Museum of Fine Arts, 1951 (1-man); State Capitol Building, Austin, 1951; Boston Contemporary Museum, 1952; Galleries of the Cranbrook Museum Invitational, 1952-3; Dallas Museum, 1952-3; Whitty Memorial Museum, 1953; Contemporary Arts Museum, Houston, 1953; Galleries of the Royal Society of British Artists, London, 1955; Galleries of the Slade Society, London, 1955; Galleries of the Internat'l Institute of Education, 1957; Amer. Institute of Design & The Amer. Institute of Decorators Annual Exhibition, Cocoanut Grove, Fla., 1957-60; Wellington Art Galleries, NY, 1958; Ford Foundation Invitational, Fort Worth Art Center, 1958,

1959; Invitational, The Town Gallery, Toledo, 1959; Invitational, Phillip Johnson & Lipchitz Shrine, New Harmony, Ind., 1960; Beaumont Museum Invitational, 1960; Amer. Society of African Culture, Galleries of the Univ. of Pa., 1960; Houston Baptist College (2-man), 1965; Invitational, Amer. Institute of Architects, Rice Univ., 1965, 1966, 1967; Invitational, Denver Museum, 1967; Invitational Negro Culture Exhibition; Texas Hemisfair, 1968; Sculpture, Eliza Johnson Home for Aged Negroes, Houston, 1951-2; Aluminum Fountain, Houston, 1953; Bronze Fountain, Houston, 1956.

Collections: Eliza Jones Home for Aged Negroes, Houston; Mrs. Kenneth Dale Owen, Houston; Phillip Johnson & Lipchitz Shrine, New Harmony, Ind.; Dr. A.W. Beal, Houston; Phillip Reichenback, Houston; Longshoreman's Temple, Houston; Boynton Methodist Church, Houston; George Washington Carver High School, Houston; F.B. Prince, Houston; New Veterinary Clinic of Dr. F. McWillam, Houston; Texas Southern Univ.; St. Oswald's Church, Tile Hall, Coventry, England; Texas Capitol State Room; Univ. of Houston.

Awards: 1st award, sculpture, Toledo Museum of Fine Arts, 1949, 1950; 1st award, silk-screen, Dallas Museum of Fine Arts, 1951; 1st award, jewelry, Dallas Museum of Fine Arts, 1953; Purchase award, Cranbrook Museum of Art, 1953; Fulbright Fellowship, 1954-6; Southern Fellowship Fund Grant, 1968-9.

Member: Amer. Society of African Culture; Institute of African Culture, Univ. of Ibadan, Nigeria (assoc.); Institute of Internat'l Education; Slade Society, London; Texas Assn. of College Teachers; Texas Commission on the Arts & Humanities.

Sources: Dover. *American Negro Art*; Indiana Univ. *Fine Arts & the Black American*; Harley, Ralph, Jr. "A Checklist of Afro-Amer. Art & Artists," *The Serif*, Dec. 1970; "Two-Man Show: Lippold-Simms," *The Christian Science Monitor*, 1952; "Two-Man Show: Lippold-Simms," *The Toledo Blade*, 1952; "Annual Art Exhibition of Young Contemporaries," *British Art News*, film, 1955; Weinberger. *Jewelry Making a Creative Expression*, NY, 1954; "Carroll H. Simms Only Fulbright Art Scholar in Britain in 1954-55," *International News Bulletin*, 1957; "Coventry: The New Coventry Cathedral-Tile Hill St. Oswald's Church," *The Architectural Review*, 1957; "New Church Dedicated to St. Oswald at Tile Hill, *Coventry: Christ & the Lambs Crucifix*," *The London Times*, 1957; *Institute of International Education News Bulletin*, Dec. 1957, pp. 28-30; "Longshoreman's Plex-i-glass Mural," *Longshoreman's National News Bulletin*, 1958; "The Art Dept. at Texas Southern Univ.," *American Artists Magazine*, 1959;

"Texas Sculptors: Fort Worth Art Center," *American Federation of Artists Bulletin*, 1959; Internat'l Library of Negro Life & History. *The Negro in Music & Art*, 1965; "Title II Program, The Negro Legacy," *Denver Museum News Bulletin*, 1967; "Exhibition of Sculpture Hemisfair 1968," *Institute of Texas Culture*, 1968; Patterson, Lindsay. "Contemporary Artists," *The Negro in Music & Art*, 1969; Chase, Judith. *Catalog of Slide Lectures on Afro-American History and Art*, the Audio-Visual Library of the Old Slave Mart Museum of Charleston, SC, 1970; Chase, Judith W. *Afro-American Art and Crafts*, Van Nostrand Reinhold Co., NY, 1971; Information from the artist; Dallas Museum. *Annual Exhibition of Texas Artists*, 1952, 1953; Dallas Museum. *Annual Exhibition of Texas Crafts*, 1952, 1953; Walker, Roslyn. *A Resource Guide to the Visual Arts of Afro-Americans*, South Bend, Ind., 1971.

SIMMS, CHARLES
Painter.
Works: *The Spirit; Portrait; Crucifixion; Beauty in Nature.*
Exhibited: Xavier Univ., 1963.
Sources: Xavier Univ. *Emancipation Proclamation Centennial National Art Exhibition*, 1963.

SIMMS, ERNEST W.
Sculptor.
Works: *Unity & Strength* (wood); *Untitled* wood; *4 Heads, Kings of Antiquity* (wood).
Exhibited: Boston Public Library, Feb. 1973.
Member: Boston Negro Artists Assn.
Sources: Boston Negro Artists Assn. *The Black Artist in America: A Negro History Month Exhibition*, Boston Public Library, Feb. 1973.

SIMMS, SAMUEL
Painter.
Works: *The Hammer Man.*
Exhibited: Amer. Negro Exposition, Chicago, 1940.
Sources: Tanner Art Galleries. *Art of the American Negro*, Catalog, 1940.

SIMON, JEWEL W.
Painter, sculptor, printmaker. Born in Houston, Texas on July 28, 1911. Studied at Atlanta University (BFA summa cum laude); Atlanta School of Art (BFA); Colorado University; under Hale Woodruff, Alice Dunbar, Lois Hellman. First Negro graduate of the Atlanta School of Art.
Works: *Neon City; The Tusi Princess; Paula-Paulina; Teen Enigma; The Eternal Hills; Jealousy; Foolish Fellow; Coat Hanger Medley; Apparition; Still Life; Knob Hill; Dance of the Paper Dolls; Lick; City Scape; Friendly Tea; Red, White and Blue; Urban Renewal; Pov-*

erty's Play Pen; Possible Dream; City Patterns; Madonna of the "Inner City"; Long Wait; Net Menders; Crosspatch; Blue Veins; Bowl of Flowers; A City Growing; Tea Time; Landscape; From the Mound; Galactic Dance; Drip Magic; Awaking Birds; Reach; Swamp Fishing; Walk Together Children; Spider; Lonesome Journey; Hidden Danger; Dead Trees; Hand of Fate; Ship of State; Bee Log; Guess (sculpture); Smile of Pride; Flower Arrangement; The Early Birds; Nude; Cloud Calligraphy; February Lace.

Exhibited: Houston, Texas, 1934-9; Atlanta Univ., 1943-73; Wayne State Univ., Detroit, 1952; Tuskegee Arts Festival, 1953-4; West Hunter Library, 1953 (1-woman); Houston Fine Arts Museum, 1957; "Art USA," NY, 1958; Howard Univ. Invitational, 1960; Adair's Art Gallery, W. Peachtree, 1963 (1-woman); High Museum, Atlanta, 1964-7, 1971; NY World's Fair, 1965; Brand Library of Music & Art; Los Feliz Jewish Community Center, 1965; UCLA Art Galleries, 1966-7; Oakland Museum, 1966-7; Art Comes to Hunter St., 1966-7; Emory Univ. Art Show, 1967; Experiment in Friendship, Moscow, 1966-7; West Va. State College, 1968; Methodist-Wesleyan Service Guild, 1968; Atlanta Jewish Community Center, 1968, 1971 (1-woman); Augusta Richmond Library, 1969; Atlanta Artists Club, Merit Members, 1971 (2-woman); Xavier Univ., 1963; Dickson Art Center, 1966; Herren's Restaurant Gallery, 1969, 1971-2; Rich's Inc., 1969; Stillman College, Tuscaloosa, Ala., 1970; Citizen's Trust Co., 1970; Jackson (Miss.) State College, 1970; Creative Cancer Gallery, 1971-2; Carnegie Institute, 1971; Ga. Institute of Technology Student Center, 1972; Dekalb College, Clarkston; Coan Elementary School, 1972.

Collections: Atlanta Univ.; Clark College; Nat'l Archives Slide Collection; Carnegie Institute; Chicago Univ.; Univ. of Maryland; Univ. of South Ala.

Awards: Bronze Woman of the Year in Fine Arts, 1950; Distinguished Service Awards; Plaque for Distinction, Atlanta Univ. Alumni Assn.; Atlanta Univ.—2nd prize, sculpture, 1949, 1955, 2nd prize, watercolor, 1953, honorable mention, watercolor, 1954, 1st prize, watercolor, 1957, 1962, 1968, honorable mention, sculpture, 1957, 1st prize, sculpture, 1964, honorable mention, print, 1964, honorable mention, oil, 1964, 1967; John Hope Prize, oil, 1966.

Member: Nat'l Conference of Artists; Atlanta Artists Club; High Museum, Atlanta; Church Women United; Girls Club of America, Board of Directors; Amer. Assn. of Univ. Women.

Represented by: Creative Cancer Gallery.

Sources: Dover. American Negro Art; Afro-Amer. Slide Depository, catalog; Indiana Univ. Fine Arts & the Black American; Lewis/Waddy. Black Artists on Art, Vol. 1; Roelof-Lanner, T.V., ed. Prints by Negro Artists; Registry of Living Artists, Cal.; Registry of Georgia Artists; "Afro-American Issue," Art Gallery, April 1968; Information from artist; Bowen, Alma. "Library Opens First Painting Exhibit," The Daily Times, Gainesville, Ga.; Atkinson, J. Edward. Black Dimensions in Contemporary Art; DuSable Museum of African-Amer. History. Contemporary Black Artists, 1970, Calendar; Pierre-Noel, Lois Jones. "American Negro Art in Progress," Negro History Bulletin, Oct. 1967; National Conference of Artists, Winter 1971; Kiah, Virginia. "Black Artists," Savannah Magazine, April 1972; Xavier Univ. Emancipation Proclamation Centennial National Art Exhibition, 1963; Harley, Ralph, Jr. "A Checklist of Afro-Amer. Art & Artists," The Serif, Dec. 1970; Art Gallery, April 1970; Brown, Marion. "The Negro in the Fine Arts," The Negro Heritage Library, Vol. 2; Myers, Carol. Black Power in the Arts, Flint, Mich., 1970; High Museum. End of the Year Show, Atlanta, 1964, 1965, 1967; UCLA Art Galleries. Negro in American Art; High Museum. Exhibit of Georgia Artists, 1971; Ga. Institute of Technology. Negro History Celebration, 1972; Walker, Roslyn. A Resource Guide to the Visual Arts of Afro-Americans, South Bend, Ind., 1971.

SIMON, WALTER AUGUSTUS

Painter, educator. Born in Brooklyn, New York, 1913. Art Teacher, Paterson State College, Paterson, New York.

Works: Looking Over the Terrace; Apartment on Washington Street; String Dance; Caroline Linguen.

Exhibited: Atlanta Univ., 1951.

Collections: Nat'l Archives.

Awards: Highest Cash Prize, Atlanta Univ.

Sources: Dover. American Negro Art; Indiana Univ. Fine Arts & the Black American; Art Digest, April 15, 1951, p. 13; Afro-Amer. Slide Depository, Catalog; Time, April 9, 1951; Harley, Ralph, Jr. "Checklist of Afro-Amer. Art & Artists," The Serif, Dec. 1970; Walker, Roslyn. A Resource Guide to the Visual Arts of Afro-Americans, South Bend, Ind., 1971; "Walter Simon: The Socialization of a Negro Artist," Phylon, Atlanta Univ., 1954, pp. 372-92.

SIMONS, RICHARD

Studied at Oakwood College.

Exhibited: Sun Times/Daily News Gallery, Chicago, 1970.

Sources: United Negro College Fund. Art 1970, Chicago, 1970.

SIMPSON, JOHN

Sculptor.
Works: *Baby and Doll; Wild Boar; Renene; Crucifix.*
Exhibited: Phila. Civic Center Museum; State Armory, Wilmington, Del., 1971.
Sources: Phila. Civic Center. *Afro-American Artists 1800-1969;* Aesthetic Dynamics. *Afro-American Images,* 1971, Catalog.

SIMPSON, KENN

Painter, educator. Studied at Howard University (AB); Catholic University (MFA); DC Teachers College (Teaching Certificate); American University; New York University; under Jack Perlmutter. Teacher, Roosevelt High School; instructor at Smith-Mason Gallery; serving his 2nd term as president of the DC Art Association.
Works: *The Me; Gainsborough; Quiet Lights; Two Musicians; Soul Qualities; The Talking Theatre; Bobby's Band Room; Sensations; Wes; Band Room; Waterfront; Eddie; Market Place; Thing; Cello; Boston; Early Morning Shady Side; Columbia Sunset; Produce; Tight.*
Exhibited: State Armory, Wilmington, Del., 1971; Smith-Mason Gallery, 1971; Society of Washington Artists; Hampton Institute; Howard Univ.; Catholic Univ.; DCAA, Anacostia Neighborhood Museum-Smithsonian Institution; Lycoming College; Cosmos Club; Museum of Natural History, Smithsonian Institution; Ontario Gallery; Margaret Dickey Gallery (1-man); DC Teachers College; Shaw Univ.; Ala. State A&M Institute; National Collection of Fine Arts, DC; Carnegie Institute; NJ State Museum; Univ. of Pittsburgh; Bowie State College (1-man); Shady Grove; Prince Georges County Library; DC Central Library.
Collections: Shaw Univ.; Ala. State A&M Institute; DC Juvenile Court; Anacostia Neighborhood Museum-Smithsonian Institution.
Awards: Special commendation, DC Public School Board; 2nd prize, oils, Outdoor Art Fair sponsored by DC Recreation Dept. & *The Washington Post;* honorable mention, Howard Univ. Art Show; painting selected to be the 1st in the collection of Ford Foundation funded gallery at Shaw Univ.; Max Roach Award, Carnegie Institute, 1971-2.
Member: DC Art Assn.; Nat'l Conference of Artists; Corcoran Gallery; Neighborhood Arts Council.
Represented by: Smith-Mason Gallery.
Sources: DC Art Assn. *Exhibition '71,* Washington, DC, 1971; Aesthetic Dynamics. *Afro-American Images,* 1971; Smith-Mason Gallery. *National Exhibition Black Artists,* 1971; Margaret Dickey Gallery of Art. *Kenn Simpson-Paintings,* 1969; The Little Gallery, Bowie State College. *Kenn Simpson's Linocuts;* Information from the artist.

SIMPSON, MERTON D.

Painter, collector of African Art. Born in Charleston, South Carolina, 1928. Studied at Cooper Union; New York University; under William Halsey, Robert Motherwell.
Works: *Landscape Symphony; Untitled; Harlem Passage; Confrontation Ia; Confrontation IV; Confrontation IIa; Confrontation I; Confrontation II; Nude; Oriental Fable; Confrontation VI; Confrontation XXa; Confrontation XXaa; Confrontation XXVI; Confrontation XX; Confrontation XXIIa; Confrontation XXIIIa; Confrontation XXIV; Confrontation Poems; Confrontation Duet I; Reflection; Outer Push #1 & #2; Garden; Floating Forms; Sky Party #1 & #2; Poem: Nos. 1-8* (tempera); *Quartet: Nos. 1-4; Landscape: Nos. 1-8; Seascape: Nos. 1-7; Composition: Nos. 1-3.*
Exhibited: Chatham College, Pa.; Fairleigh Dickinson College, NY; Contemporary Arts Gallery, NYC; Barone Gallery, NYC; Guggenheim Museum; Metropolitan Museum of Art; Brooklyn Museum; National Gallery, Paris; Bertha Schaefer Gallery, NY; Oakland Art Museum, 1952; Atlanta Univ., 1950, 1951, 1956; Intercultural Club, 1951; City College of NY, 1967; Nat'l. Museum of Japan; Univ. of Michigan; Fisk Univ., 1969; Barnet Aden Gallery, Washington, DC; Afro-Amer. Exhibit, NY; Alfredo Valente Gallery, 1964; Gibbes Art Gallery; Red Cross Exchange Exhibit, France, Japan, 1950.
Collections: Guggenheim Museum; Howard Univ.; Merton Simpson Gallery; Gov. Nelson Rockefeller; Gen. Dwight D. Eisenhower; Duke Ellington; James J. Sweeney Collection; Scott Field Museum, Chicago; Atlanta Univ.; Gibbes Art Gallery; Ms. Helen Rubenstein; Stanley Marcus; Mr. Alexander Bing; Gen. Nathan F. Twining; Mr. Henry Luce, Jr.; Mr. Arthur Cohen; Prime Minister Nkrumah, Ghana; Mr. Frederick Ossorio; Mr. Gustave Schindler; Dr. Werner Muensterberger; Dr. Renato Almansi; Univ. of Mass.; Fisk Univ.; Columbia (SC) Museum of Art.
Awards: SC Cultural Fund Fellowship, 1951; John Hope Landscape Award, 1951.
Member: Spiral.
Sources: Dover. *American Negro Art;* "Afro-American Issue," *Art Gallery,* April 1968; *Art Digest,* April 15, 1951; Indiana Univ. *Fine Arts & the Black American;* City College of NY. *The Evolution of Afro-American Artists: 1800-1950;* Brown, Evelyn S. "The Harmon Awards," *Opportunity,* March 1933; Harley, Ralph, Jr. "Checklist of Afro-Amer. Art & Artists," *Serif,* Dec. 1970; Fisk Univ. *3 Afro-Americans,* 1969; DuSable Museum of African-Amer. History. *Contemporary Black Artists,* 1970, Calendar; *New York Times,* April 1, 1951; *Time,* April 9, 1951; Greene, Carroll,

Jr. "Perspective: The Black Artist in America," *Art Gallery,* April 1970, p. 19; Pierre-Noel, Lois Jones. "American Negro Art in Progress," *Negro History Bulletin,* Oct. 1967; Siegel, Jeanne. "Why Spiral?," *Art News,* Sept. 1966; "American Negro Art," *Design,* Feb. 1942, p. 28; Alfredo Valente Gallery. *Oils & Temperas by Merton D. Simpson,* NY, Jan. 1964; Patterson, Lindsay, comp. "Contemporary Artists," *The Negro in Music and Art,* 1969; *The Negro Handbook,* Composed by Editors of *Ebony,* Chicago, 1966; Information from artist; Myers, Carol L. *Black Power in the Arts,* Flint, Mich., 1970; Fine, Elsa H. "Mainstream, Blackstream and the Black Art Movement," *Art Journal,* Spring 1971; "Leading Negro Artists," *Ebony,* Sept. 1963; *Who's Who in American Art,* 1970; Walker, Roslyn. *A Resource Guide to the Visual Arts of Afro-Americans,* South Bend, Ind., 1971.

SIMPSON, WILLIAM H.

Painter. Born c. 1818, Buffalo, New York. Died 1872 in Boston. Apprentice-errand boy to painter Matthew Wilson. Moved to Boston 1854 where he became renowned as portrait painter.
Works: *Charles Sumner; John T. Hilton; Jeremiah Loguen; Caroline Loguen.*
Exhibited: Howard Univ., 1945, 1967; Downtown Gallery, 1942.
Collections: Howard Univ.; Nat'l Archives; Masonic Lodge, Boston.
Sources: Brawley, Benjamin. *The Negro Genius;* Dover. *American Negro Art; Encyclopedia of the Arts;* Young, William. *Dictionary of American Artists, Sculptors, and Engravers; Art in America,* Vol. 24, pp. 16-27; Locke. *The Negro in Art;* Indiana Univ. *Fine Arts & the Black American;* City College of NY. *The Evolution of Afro-American Artists, 1800-1950;* Howard Univ. *Art of the American Negro,* 1937; Roucek & Kiernan. *The Negro Impact on Western Civilization;* Howard Univ. *Festival of Fine Arts,* 1945; Afro-American Slide Depository, 1971-2 Catalog; Howard Univ. *James A. Porter Gallery of African American Art,* 1970; DuSable Museum of African-American History. *Contemporary Black Artists,* 1970, Calendar; Greene, Carroll, Jr. "Perspective: The Black Artist in America," *Art Gallery,* April 1970, p. 4; Brown, William W. *The Rising Sun,* Boston, 1874; Harley, Ralph, Jr. "Checklist of Afro-American Art & Artists," *The Serif,* Dec. 1970; Myers, Carol L. *Black Power in the Arts,* Flint, Mich., 1970; Robinson, Wilhelmena S. *Historical Negro Biographies;* Spradling, Mary M., ed. *In Black & White: Afro-Americans in Print;* Walker, Roslyn. *A Resource Guide to the Visual Arts of Afro-Americans,* South Bend, Ind., 1971.

SIMUEL, RHOMEYN M.

Painter. Born in Oxford, North Carolina in 1931. Self-taught.
Works: *Sundown.*
Exhibited: Studio Museum in Harlem, 1969.
Sources: Studio Museum in Harlem. *Harlem Artists 69.*

SINGLETARY, MICHAEL

Painter. Born in New York City, 1949. Studied at the High School of Art & Design; New School of Social Research; Art Students League; Vermont Academy, Vermont, New York.
Works: *Blues Woman; Negro Gothic, Black Metamorphosis: Waiting for Next; Oscar Robertson; Waiting Room.*
Exhibited: Smith-Mason Gallery, 1971; Studio Museum in Harlem, 1969.
Collections: Mr. Benny Andrews.
Sources: Smith-Mason Gallery. *National Exhibition Black Artists,* 1971; Studio Museum in Harlem. *Harlem Artists 69.*

SKEETE, RICHARD D., JR.

Painter, educator. Born in Boston. Studied at Massachusetts College of Art (BS); Boston University (MEd); Cebu College, Cebu, Philippine Islands; North Carolina College; Agricultural & Technical College of North Carolina; DC Teachers College. Art Department Chairman, Northwestern Senior High School, Prince Georges County, Maryland.
Works: *Constellation.*
Exhibited: Roxbury Neighborhood House; Shaw House; Hayes Taylor YMCA; Susie B. Dudley YWCA; DCAA, Anacostia Neighborhood Museum-Smithsonian Institution.
Sources: DC Art Assn. *Exhibition '71,* Washington, DC, 1971.

SLADE, MARGARET LOUISE

Painter, graphic artist. Born in Newark, New Jersey, July 25, 1949. Studied at Newark School of Fine & Industrial Arts. Graphic designer at Essex County College.
Works: *The Imam; Liberty and Justice for All; Three Faces of Me; Lady in Paisley Print; Stale Bread; Mommy's Slip & Daddy's Underwear.*
Exhibited: Rutgers Univ., Newark, 1968; Blazor Anti-Poverty Art Festival, Newark, 1969; Jack & Jill Annual, Newark; Newark School of Fine & Industrial Arts, 1969, 1971; Seton Hall Univ. Soul Weekend, South Orange, NJ, 1969; Washington Park Outdoor Exhibit, Newark, 1969; Midblock Art Gallery, East Orange, NJ, 1970; Carson Art Gallery, East Orange, NJ, 1971; National Police Week Poster Contest, Newark, 1971; Newark Public Library, 1971; Newark Museum, 1971; Harris Gallery, 1971 (1-woman).

Collections: Slides at Spelman College, Atlanta and at Elias Boudinot School, Elizabeth, NJ.
Awards: 2nd prize, Blazor Anti-Poverty Art Festival, 1969; 2nd prize, Newark School of Fine & Industrial Arts, 1970, 1st prize, 1971.
Sources: Information from artist; *Junior Scholastic Magazine,* NY, 1970; Newark Museum. *Black Artists: Two Generations,* 1971; *La Revue Des Arts Et La Vie,* Paris (date to be announced).

SLATER, VAN
Printmaker. Born in Arkansas, 1937. Studied at Los Angeles City College; University of California at Los Angeles.
Works: *Barber Shop; Sapphire; Eula Seated* (woodcut).
Exhibited: Prints, Traveling Invitational, 1965-7; Soviet Union Exhibition of Amer. Negro Artists, 1966-7; Amer. Negro Artists, Univ. of Cal., 1966-7; Watts Festival, 1970; Compton College, 1970; Emerald Gallery; Diplomat Hotel, Hollywood, Fla., 1970; Brand Library of Art & Music, Glendale, Cal.; Assoc. Students Lounge, UCLA; Los Feliz Jewish Community Center; Dickson Art Center, 1966.
Collections: Oakland Museum, Ruth Waddy Collection.
Member: Los Angeles County Art Assn.
Sources: Oakland Museum Archives; DuSable Museum of African-Amer. History. *Contemporary Black Artists,* 1970, Calendar; Lewis/Waddy. *Black Artists on Art,* Vol. 2; UCLA Art Galleries. *The Negro in American Art;* "Afro-American Issue," *Art Gallery,* April 1968; Indiana Univ. *Fine Arts & the Black American;* Roelof-Lanner, T.V. *Prints by American Negro Artists;* Harley, Ralph, Jr. "Checklist of Afro-Amer. Art & Artists," *Serif,* Dec. 1970; Myers, Carol L. *Black Power in the Arts,* Flint, Mich., 1970; Walker, Roslyn. *A Resource Guide to the Visual Arts of Afro-Americans,* South Bend, Ind., 1971.

SLAVE OF THOMAS FLEET
Made prints to illustrate the ballads and small books of his master, Thowas Fleet, a Boston printer.
Sources: Porter, James A. "Early Negro Artists: A Neglected Chapter of American Art History," *Art in America,* Jan. 1936, pp. 19-20; Thomas, Isaiah. *History of Printing in America.*

SLEET, MONETA J., JR.
Photographer. Born 1926. Staff photographer for *Ebony.*
Awards: Pulitzer Prize (1st member of black press to win this award).
Sources: *Crisis,* May 1970, p. 187; *Ebony,* June

1969, p. 147; Spradling, Mary M., ed. *In Black & White: Afro-Americans in Print.*

SLOAN, LOUIS B.
Mixed media.
Works: *Late Summer; Gathering Storm over Philadelphia; Conshohocken Quarry; Apple Tree; Self Portrait of a Landscape; Backyards.*
Exhibited: Phila. Civic Center; State Armory, Wilmington, Del., 1971.
Collections: Pa. Academy of Fine Arts.
Sources: Phila. Civic Center. *Afro-American Artists 1800-1969;* Aesthetic Dynamics. *Afro-American Images 1971;* Afro-American Slide Depository, Catalog, 1971-2; Craig, Randall J. "Focus on Black Artists: a Project for Schools and Community," *School Arts,* Nov. 1970, pp. 30-3.

SMITH, ALBERT ALEXANDER
Painter, graphic artist. Born in New York City, September 17, 1896. Died 1940. Studied at the Ethical Culture Art School; National Academy of Design. Employed as a musician in Paris, painting in spare time.
Works: *Street in Rome, Italy; Music; Cartoons Music; Chartres, France; Le Port Honfleur; Market Place, Nice, France; Old Man River; Selling Pigs, Normandy; Spanish Road; Street Scene; The Laugh; Friends; Ethiopian Music; Bilboa Spain; Pont Neuf; The Roman Forum; Dancing Time; Darktown Strutters; Beggars in Spain; Bell Tower; Feeding Time; Picking Cotton; Side Street; Weighing Cotton; Generations;* Portraits of Frederick Douglass, Paul Lawrence Dunbar, Booker Washington, Toussaint L'Ouverture; *Etching of Alexander S. Pushkin; The Concierge, France; Street in Cannes, France; The Workers; Down Home; The Martyr; Black & White; Ponte Vecchio; Laughter; Beggars in Church, Madrid; Church of St. Andres, Spain; Courbevoie, France-Sunday Outing.*
Exhibited: Ethical Culture School, 1928; 135th St. Branch, NY Public Library, 1921 (1-man); Veterans Exhibit, Paris, 1932; Harmon Foundation, 1928-31, 1933, 1935-6; Baltimore Museum, 1939; Amer. Negro Exposition, Chicago, 1940; Boston Museum of Fine Arts, 1932; Paris, 1938; Art Institute of Chicago, 1927; Harlem Art Committee, 137th St. Branch YWCA, NY; NJ State Museum, 1935; Harmon-College Art Traveling Exhibition, 1934-5; Harmon Traveling Exhibition, 1935-6; Texas Centennial, 1936; Smithsonsian Institution, 1929; Tanner Art League, 1922; South Side Community Art Center, 1945.
Collections: Harmon Foundation; NY Public Library, Schomburg Collection; Nat'l Archives.
Awards: Suydam Medal, 1917 & 1919, and Chaloner Prize, 1919, National Academy of Design; Harmon Foundation Award, 1929;

Amy E. Spingarn Prize, *Crisis;* Tanner Gold Medal, 1916; Scholarship to Ethical Cultural Art School, DeWitt Clinton High School, NY, 1911; Wolfe Scholarship, Ethical Cultural Art School; 3 Honorable Mentions, draftsmanship, Nat'l Academy of Design.
Sources: Dover. *American Negro Art;* Harmon Foundation. *Exhibition of Productions by Negro Artists;* Locke. *Negro in Art;* Indiana Univ. *Fine Arts & the Black American;* "Negro Artists," *Crisis,* Dec. 1926; Afro-Amer. Slide Depository, Catalog; City College of NY. *The Evolution of Afro-American Artists 1800-1950;* McGleughlin, Jean. "Albert Alexander Smith," *Opportunity,* July 1940; DuSable Museum of African-Amer. History. *Contemporary Black Artists,* 1970, Calendar; Review, Salon of Assn. of Amer. Professional Painters in Paris, *La Revue Moderne,* July 15, 1938; Art Institute of Chicago. *The Negro in Art Week,* 1927; Baltimore Museum of Art. *Contemporary Negro,* 1939; Tanner Art Galleries. *Art of the American Negro,* 1940; Brawley, Benjamin. *The Negro Genius;* Butcher, Margaret. *The Negro in American Culture,* p. 232; Dowd. *The Negro in American Life;* Harmon Foundation. *Non-Jury Exhibit of Works of Negro Artists,* 1933; Texas Centennial Exposition. *Thumbnail Sketches of Exhibiting Artists,* 1936; Harmon Foundation. *Negro Artists,* 1935; *Who's Who in Colored America,* 3rd Edition; Harmon Foundation. *Exhibit of Fine Arts,* 1930; Harmon Foundation. *Select Picture List; New York Times,* Jan. 5, 1930; Smithsonian Institution. *Painting & Sculpture by American Negro Artists,* 1929; "Harmon Exhibit Foundation," *Art Digest,* Feb. 15, 1931, p. 7; *Art Digest,* Vol. 4; Pierre-Noel, Lois Jones. "American Negro Art in Progress," *Negro History Bulletin,* Oct. 1967; "Harmon Awards Announced," *Art News,* Feb. 8, 1930; "Harlem Library Shows Negro Art," *Art News,* May 20, 1933, p. 14; Harley, Ralph. "Checklist of Afro-Amer. Art & Artists," *The Serif,* Dec. 1970; Porter, James. "Negro Artists Gain Recognition After Long Battle," *Pittsburgh Courier,* July 29, 1950; *1st Annual Exhibit of Books, Manuscripts, Paintings, Sculptures, Etc. by the Negro Library Assn.,* Aug. 1918; "Albert A. Smith, Artist Returns from Europe," Unidentified newspaper clipping, Tuskegee Institute; Schatz, Walter. *Directory of Afro-American Resources,* 1970; Allen, Cleveland G. "Our Young Artists," *Opportunity,* June 1923; South Side Community Art Center. *Chicago Collectors Exhibit of Negro Art,* Chicago, 1945; Walker, Roslyn. *A Resource Guide to the Visual Arts of Afro-Americans,* South Bend, Ind., 1971.

SMITH, ALFRED J.
Painter, muralist. Born in Boston. Studied at Boston University (1966). Active in Boston's "Summerthing" program, 1969.
Works: *Impressions of Karma,* 1970 (oil).
Exhibited: Brandeis Univ., 1969; Boston Museum of Fine Arts, 1970; Studio Museum in Harlem, 1969-70.
Sources: Boston Museum of Fine Arts. *Afro-American Artists: NY & Boston,* 1970; Van Almelo, Frederik. "In the American Grain," *Boston After Dark,* May 26, 1970, p. 24; Le Brun, Caron. "Blacks' Art on Display," *Herald Traveler,* Boston, May 26, 1970; "Afro-American Artists: New York & Boston," *Prudential Center News,* Boston, June 1, 1970.

SMITH, ALVIN
Painter, illustrator, educator, mixed media. Born in Gary, Indiana on November 27, 1933. Studied at University of Iowa (BA); University of Illinois; Kansas City Art Institute; New York University; Columbia University Teachers College. Lecturer in Art Education at Queens College, Flushing, New York.
Works: *Flow II; To the Beckmans; Remnants of a Dream; Yellow Dream,* 1971; *Rites of Spring,* 1971; *Indiana Fugue,* 1971; *J.C. at Chappaqua: No. 2,* 1971; *My Lai,* 1971; *7th Avenue Juggernaut,* 1971; *Orangeburg: In Memoriam,* 1971; *Dreams are Made of the Dreamer,* 1969; *Dog Days,* 1970; *Thermopylae; Vow: II,* 1968 (mixed media construction).
Exhibited: Toledo Museum, 1961, 1962; Amer. Academy of Arts & Letters, Childe Hassam Exhibit, NYC, 1968; Brooklyn College, 1969; Community Gallery, Brooklyn Museum, 1969, 1970; Mt. Holyoke College, Mass., 1969 (1-man); The Dayton Art Institute & Museum, Ohio, 1961, 1962; Columbia Univ. Teachers College, 1966-7; The Living Arts Center, Dayton, Ohio, 1969; Atlanta Univ., 1962; Contemporary Arts Inc. Gallery, NYC, 1962; NY Univ., 1963; The Dulin Gallery, Knoxville, Tenn., 1964; Purdue Univ., Lafayette, Ind., 1964; Ruth Sherman Gallery, NYC, 1964; Nat'l Academy Galleries, NYC, 1965; Queens College Art Education Faculty Show, Flushing, NY, 1968; Gallery Museum, Saratoga, NY, 1970; William Rockhill Art Museum; Sioux City Art Center; Musée Rath, Geneva, Switzerland, 1971.
Collections: Atlanta Univ.; The Dayton (Ohio) Museum; The Living Arts Center, Dayton, Ohio; Columbia Univ. Teachers College; Univ. of Minn., Kerlan Collection; Mt. Holyoke College; Public Library, Gary, Ind.; Tougaloo College, Miss.; Mr. Russ Thompson.
Awards: 4 purchase awards, Dayton Art Institute, 1961-6; Purchase Prize, The Living Arts Center, 1969; Purchase Award, Columbia Univ.; Dow Award, 1967; Purchase Award, Mt. Holyoke College, 1969; Painting Award,

The Chicago Tribune, 1954; Purchase Award, 4 awards, Atlanta Univ., 1962-7.
Member: Charter member, Advisory Committee, Community Gallery of The Brooklyn Museum; Nat'l Art Education Assn.; Internat'l Society for Education Through Art; Phi Delta Kappa—Education Honor Fraternity.
Sources: Musée Rath. *8 Artistes Afro-Americains,* Genève, 1971; *La Revue Moderne,* Paris, Sept. 1965; *Who's Who in American Art,* 1966; *Who's Who in the East,* 1968; "A Triumph Rather Than a Threat," *New York Times,* April 27, 1969; *Art International Magazine,* Oct. 1969; *Art Gallery,* April 1970; "Not Judicious," Art Mailbag, *The New York Times,* April 19, 1970; *Art in America,* Sept./Oct. 1970; *Dictionary of International Biographies,* 1971, London, 7th Edition; Rose, Barbara. "Black Art in America," *Art in America,* July/Dec. 1970; Ghent, Henri. "The Community Art Gallery," *Art Gallery,* April 1970; Mt. Holyoke College. *Ten Afro-American Artists,* Nov. 1969; *3 Boston Black Artists: Milton Johnson, Al Smith & Richard Yarde,* Nov. 1971; Le Brun, Caron. "Black Art," *Herald Traveler,* Sunday Supplement, Boston, May 24, 1970; NYC Dept. of Education. *Fifteen Under Forty;* Wojciechowska, Maia. *Shadow of a Bull,* NY, Atheneum (Illus.); Wojciechowska, Maia. *Odyssey of Courage,* NY, Atheneum (Illus.); Pederson, Elsa. *Fisherman's Choice,* NY, Atheneum (Illus.); Krumgold, Joseph. *Henry Three,* NY, Atheneum (Illus.); Felton, Harold. *William Phips & the Treasure Ship,* NY, Dodd/Mead (Illus.); Stuart, Norma. *Marassa & Midnight,* NY, McGraw-Hill (Illus.); Rice, Inez. *A Tree this Tall,* NY, William Morrow (Illus.); Bonham, Frank. *The Mystery of the Fat Cat,* NY, EP Dutton Co. (Illus.); Bonham, Frank. *The Nitty Gritty,* NY, EP Dutton Co. (Illus.); McCain, Murray. *The Boy Who Walked off the Page,* NY, EP Dutton Co. (Illus.); Calson, Natalie Savage. *Marchers for the Dream,* NY, Harper & Row (Illus.); Sprague, Gretchen. *A Question of Harmony,* NY, Dodd/Mead, Cover design; Sprague, Gretchen. *White in the Moon,* NY, Dodd/Mead, Cover design; Barry, Lucy. *Stage Struck Secretary,* NY, William Morrow, Cover design; Information from artist; Brooklyn College. *Afro-American Artists: Since 1950;* Brooklyn College. *15 Artists,* NYC, 1969; Dayton Art Institute & Museum. *Southern Ohio Exhibitions,* 1961, 1962; Atlanta Univ. *Atlanta Univ. Annual,* 1962, 1966-7; Toledo Museum. *44th Toledo Area Artists Annual,* 1962; Dulin Gallery. *1st National Watercolor Exhibition,* Knoxville, Tenn., 1964; Wesleyan College. *National Exhibition of Prints & Drawings,* Macon, Ga., 1964; Purdue Univ. *National Exhibition of Small Paintings,*

Lafayette, Ind., 1964; Ruth Sherman Gallery. *Talent Search,* NYC, 1964; Nat'l Academy Galleries. *Audubon Artists,* NYC, 1965; Brooklyn Museum. *Allusions: 2nd Annual Exhibit,* 1970; Walker, Roslyn. *A Resource Guide to the Visual Arts of Afro-Americans,* South Bend, Ind., 1971.

SMITH, ARENZO
Born 1939 in Pittsburgh, Pennsylvania. Studied at Philadelphia Musuem College of Art.
Works: *#3.*
Exhibitions: Gallery 32, 1970.
Sources: Lewis/Waddy. *Black Artists on Art,* Vol. 2.

SMITH, ARTHUR
Jeweler. Born in 1923 in Brooklyn, New York. Studied at Cooper Union; Hewitt Museum of Design, New York.
Works: *Neckpiece; Bangle Bracelet; Pin.*
Exhibited: Museum of Contemporary Crafts, NY; Nordness Galleries, NY; Oberlin College; Univ. of Minnesota; Bennington College.
Collections: Museum of Contemporary Crafts; Staten Island Museum; Walker Art Center, Minneapolis.
Sources: Nordness Galleries. *12 Afro-American Artists,* 1969; Nordness, Lee. *Objects: USA; Sunday News,* Oct. 11, 1953 (Manhattan-Bronx Section).

SMITH, BEUFORD
Photographer.
Exhibited: Addison Gallery, 1971.
Sources: James Van DerZee Institute. *The Black Photographer (1908-1970): A Survey.*

SMITH, BUSE T.
Sources: DuSable Museum of African-Amer. History. *Contempory Black Artists,* 1970, Calendar.

SMITH, CARL R.
Sculptor. Born in 1931. Self-taught.
Works: *Mother and Child; Untitled; Father and Son; The Moon.*
Exhibited: Studio Museum in Harlem, 1969; Phila. Civic Center; Halfway Art Gallery; Pittsburgh Plan for Art.
Sources: Studio Museum in Harlem. *Harlem Artists 69;* Phila. Civic Center. *Afro-American Artists 1800-1969;* Pittsburgh Community College. *16 Black Artists.*

SMITH, CELESTE M.
Sources: "Excelsior," *Crisis,* Jan. 1929; Harley, Ralph, Jr. "Checklist of Afro-Amer. Art & Artists," *The Serif,* Dec. 1970.

SMITH, CHARLES L.A.
Exhibited: Wharton House, Phila., 1942.

Sources: Harley, Ralph, Jr. "Checklist of Afro-Amer. Art & Artists," *The Serif,* Dec. 1970.

SMITH, DOLPHUS
Work: *Devil Fish.*
Exhibited: Phila. Civic Center.
Sources: Phila. Civic Center. *Afro-American Artists 1800-1969.*

SMITH, E.S.
Exhibited: Harmon Foundation, 1929.
Sources: Harley, Ralph, Jr. "Checklist of Afro-Amer. Art & Artists," *The Serif,* Dec. 1970.

SMITH, ERIC
Mixed media. Studied at Tougaloo College.
Works: Untitled collage.
Exhibited: Sun Times/Daily News Gallery, Chicago, 1970.
Sources: United Negro College Fund. *Art 1970,* Chicago, 1970.

SMITH, FRANK E.
Printmaker, ceramist, educator. Born in Chicago, 1935. Ceramics instructor, Sterling School, Brooklyn.
Works: *City* (linocut); *Subway 1; Dream Street.*
Exhibited: Studio Museum in Harlem, 1969.
Collections: Oakland Museum.
Sources: Roelof-Lanner, T.V. *Prints by American Negro Artists;* Studio Museum in Harlem. *Harlem Artists 69;* Oakland Museum Archives, Ruth Waddy Collection.

SMITH, GAYLORD
Educator, painter. Born in New York City. Studied at the Art Students League; Famous Artist Painting Course. Teacher, Abraham Lincoln Community Center.
Exhibited: Abraham Lincoln Center; John Russwurm School; Waltam School of Creative Arts; The Empire Bank; The Ritz-Annette; 135th St. & 5th Ave.
Sources: NY NAACP. *Art Exhibition of Negro Expression Sponsored by Minars Furniture,* April 1964; *Sepia Magazine; City College Workshop Weekly News Letters.*

SMITH, GEORGE
Painter, sculptor. Born in Buffalo, New York in 1941. Studied at North Carolina A & T; Florida A&M; San Francisco Art Institute; Hunter College.
Works: *Freedom Drummer; Homage to a Black Bag; Black Jack; The Immortal; Crocodile & the Head Hunter #2; Untitled #8; Self Portrait; Sculpture.*
Exhibited: Oakland Museum, 1968; Newark Museum, 1971; Reese Palley Gallery, NYC, 1970; Hunter College, 1970.
Collections: Mr. Benny Andrews; Reese Palley Gallery, NYC; Mr. & Mrs. John Carlos; Mr. & Mrs. Tommie Smith.
Sources: Oakland Art Museum. *New Perspectives in Black Art;* Indiana Univ. *Fine Arts & the Black American;* Newark Museum. *Black Artists: Two Generations,* 1971; Harley, Ralph, Jr. "Checklist of Afro-Amer. Art & Artists," *The Serif,* Dec. 1970; Lewis/Waddy. *Black Artists on Art,* Vol. 2; DuSable Museum of African-Amer. History. *Contemporary Black Artists,* 1970, Calendar; Walker, Roslyn. *A Resource Guide to the Visual Arts of Afro-Americans,* South Bend, Ind., 1971.

SMITH, H.A. HAMMOND
Exhibited: Tanner Art League, 1922.
Sources: "Restoration of Paintings," *Chicago Art Institute Bulletin,* July 1913; "Died Late in August 1927," *Museum News,* Chicago, Sept. 15, 1927; Harley, Ralph, Jr. "Checklist of Afro-Amer. Art & Artists," *The Serif,* Dec. 1970.

SMITH, HELEN FRANCIS
Exhibited: Harmon Foundation, 1928.
Sources: "Among the Artists," *Amer. Art News,* Oct. 1905; Harley, Ralph, Jr. "Checklist of Afro-Amer. Art & Artists," *The Serif,* Dec. 1970.

SMITH, HELEN HENRIETTA
Commercial artist, painter, educator. Born in Boston. Studied at Massachusetts School of Art.
Works: *Clothesline* (watercolor); *Hickory Trees; Leghorns; Oaks.*
Exhibited: Harmon Foundation, 1928, 1933; League of Neighbors' Bazaar.
Sources: Harmon Foundation. *Exhibition of Productions by Negro Artists;* Indiana Univ. *Fine Arts & the Black American;* Harmon Foundation. *Non-Jury Exhibit of Works of Negro Artists,* 1933; Harley, Ralph, Jr. "Checklist of Afro-Amer. Art & Artists," *Serif,* Dec. 1970; Walker, Roslyn. *A Resource Guide to the Visual Arts of Afro-Americans,* South Bend, Ind., 1971.

SMITH, HOWARD
Born 1928 in Moorestown, New Jersey. Studied at Pennsylvania Academy of Fine Arts, Philadelphia.
Works: Untitled design multiples.
Exhibited: Amos Anderson Museum, Helsinki, Finland.
Collections: Turku Museum, Finland; Museum of Modern Art, NY; Mr. Benny Andrews.
Sources: Lewis/Waddy. *Black Artists on Art,* Vol. 2.

SMITH, HUGHIE LEE
See: Lee-Smith, Hughie.

SMITH, JANET

Painter, graphic artist.
Works: *Nude sketches* (pen & ink); *Seated Woman; A Young Girl; Geneva Seated; Happy; Her Back; Thinking; Woman in Space; Geneva; Fraulein; Venus; Geneva Sleeping; Nude Study; Reclining Nude; Meditation; Still Life Study.*
Sources: Afro-American Slide Depository, Catalog.

SMITH, JESSIE

Painter. Born in St. Louis, Missouri, 1910.
Works: *African Woman and Baby; Still Life #1; Mother & Baby; Imagination; Black and Proud; African Stroll; Flowers; In the Country; African Carver; The Family; Deserted Street; The Cocks; Jomo Kenyatta; The Heads; Praying Girl; Christ Healing the Cripple,* 1971.
Exhibited: Russell Woods Show, 1964; Scarab Club; Detroit Institute of Art; Grosse Pointe Memorial Church; Wayne State Univ., 1969; Harlem Art Gallery Square; St. Clair (Mich.) Art Show, 1972; Cobo Hall Water Front Show, 1971; Detroit Artists Mart, 1972.
Collections: Mount Carmel Mercy Hospital; Vernon Chapel, AME Church.
Sources: Afro-American Slide Depository, Catalog; *Detroit Free Press,* Sept. 26, 1971; Information from the artist.

SMITH, JOHN

Photographer.
Exhibited: Howard Univ., 1972.
Sources: *Black Shades,* Oct. 1972.

SMITH, JOHN HENRY

Sculptor. Born 1879. Self-taught.
Works: *Self-Portrait* (granite); *Family* (ceramic sculpture); *Tough Boy* (ceramic on bronze); *Clarence; Surprise; Rachel; Mr. Churchill.*
Exhibited: Society of Independent Artists, NY, 1938; Barzensky Galleries.
Collections: Nat'l Archives.
Sources: *Negro Yearbook;* Indiana Univ. *Fine Arts & the Black American;* Harley, Ralph, Jr. "Checklist of Afro-American Art & Artists," *The Serif,* Dec. 1970; *Ebony,* Dec. 1954, pp. 58-61; "John Smith: Janitor & Sculptor," *Ebony,* Feb. 1950, pp. 65-7; Myers, Carol L. *Black Power in the Arts,* Flint, Mich., 1970; Spradling, Mary M., ed. *In Black & White: Afro-Americans in Print;* Walker, Roslyn. *A Resource Guide to the Visual Arts of Afro-Americans,* South Bend, Ind., 1971.

SMITH, MARVIN PENTZ

Painter. Born in Nicholasville, Kentucky, 1910. Studied at Art Students League, New York; under Augusta Savage; under Fernand Leger, Paris; Universities Nice, France.
Works: *Greenwood Lake; WPA Worker No. 172; Self Portrait.*
Exhibited: Harlem Community Art Center, 1938; Amer. Negro Exposition, Chicago, 1940; Lexington Colored Fair; Augusta Savage Studios, 1939.
Awards: 3rd prize, oil, Amer. Negro Exposition, Chicago, 1940.
Member: Negro Actors Guild, NY.
Sources: Locke. *The Negro in Art;* Dover. *American Negro Art;* Indiana Univ. *Fine Arts & the Black American;* Tanner Art Galleries. *Art of the American Negro,* 1940; Harmon Foundation. *Non-Jury Exhibit of Works of Negro Artists,* 1933; Harley, Ralph, Jr. "Checklist of Afro-Amer. Art & Artists," *Serif,* Dec. 1970; Furr, Arthur F. *History & Progress of Negroes in the US;* Walker, Roslyn. *A Resource Guide to the Visual Arts of Afro-Americans,* South Bend, Ind., 1971.

SMITH, MARY E.

Painter.
Works: *Jean and Doris.*
Exhibited: Amer. Negro Exposition, Chicago, 1940.
Sources: Tanner Art Galleries. *Art of the American Negro,* 1940.

SMITH, MORGAN SPARKS

Photographer. Studied at Gardener WPA (1930-4). Official Photographer, *NY Amsterdam News, Pittsburgh Courier.*
Exhibited: Augusta Savage Studios, 1939.
Collections: Urban League; *Ebony.*
Sources: Furr, Arthur F. *History & Progress of Negroes in the US;* Harley, Ralph, Jr. "Checklist of Afro-Amer. Art & Artists," *The Serif,* Dec. 1970.

SMITH, MURCIE

Sources: DuSable Museum of African-Amer. History. *Contemporary Black Artists,* 1970, Calendar.

SMITH, PHILLIPPE G.

Sculptor. Born in Haiti, 1934. Studied at the Foyer des Arts Plastiques, Port-au-Prince, Haiti; Art Students League.
Works: *Space Age; The Eighth Day; The Birth; The Mad Man; The Meditations; Inspired Artist; L'Obsede.*
Exhibited: Phila. Civic Center; Studio Museum in Harlem, 1969.
Sources: Phila. Civic Center. *Afro-American Artists 1800-1969;* Studio Museum in Harlem. *Harlem Artists 69.*

SMITH, RALPH

Works: *Benny Andrews.*
Collections: Mr. Benny Andrews.

SMITH, S.A.

Educator. Studied at Los Angeles City College; California State College at Long Beach. Art Instructor at Metropolitan Arts Complex.
Exhibited: Normacel Gallery, Detroit, 1970.
Sources: Normacel Gallery. *A Black Women Art Exhibit,* Detroit, 1970.

SMITH, VINCENT DaCOSTA

Painter, printmaker. Born in Brooklyn, New York, 1929. Studied at the Art Students League; Brooklyn Museum Art School; Pratt Institute; Skowhegan (Maine) Art School; under Robert Blackburn, Roberto Lamonica, Krista Reddy, and Robert Cale.
Works: *Repairing a Bombed Church; What's Happening Baby?; Peace and Freedom Party; 90 Gates Avenue; Molotov Cocktail; The People Cry Out; Sharecropper's Shack; For My People; The Voices Are Stilled; Apple Pie for the Kids; Blood on the Forge; Amnesty (Attica); Let It Be Like Men; And When I Saw the Lie; Black Family; The Supper,* 1970 (oil & sand on canvas); *Beef Steaks; Right On; The Super; Wailing the Blues; The Effigy; Home; Marcus Garvey (Black Moses); Young Sculptor; Black Caucus; Mississippi Delta; First Day of School; Mississippi Incident.*
Exhibited: ACA Gallery, NYC, 1955; Roko Gallery, NYC, 1955; Brooklyn Museum, NYC, 1955; Market Place Gallery, Harlem, 1956-7; Marinio Gallery, NYC, 1956-8; Lorraine Hansberry Exhibit, Brooklyn, 1964; Black Arts Repertory Theater, 1965; Harlem Council on the Arts, 1966; Negro Arts Festival, Yonkers, NY, 1964; CORE, NYC, 1966; CORE, National Academy of Design, 1967; Art for Mayor Lindsay, 1969; New Lots Library, 1966; Teaneck Public Library, NJ, 1969; Skowhegan Annual, 1968-9; Studio Museum in Harlem, 1969 (1-man); Fisk Univ., 1970 (1-man); Univ of Iowa; Artists of SEDF; Harlem Research Center; Collective Gallery, NYC; Larcada Gallery, NYC: Nat'l Institute of Arts & Letters, 1968; Wilson College, Pa., 1968; Nassau Community College; C.W. Post College, 1969; Long Island Univ., 1968; Lever House Gallery, NYC, 1969; NY Community College, 1969; Pratt Graphic Center, 1972-3; Brooklyn College, 1969; National Arts Club, NYC, 1966; Contemporary Arts Gallery, NYC, 1966; Barnard College, 1968; Univ. of Hartford, Conn., 1970; Muhlenberg College, Pa., 1970; College of Mount St. Vincent, Riverdale, NY, 1970; Rye (NY) Reading Room Gallery, 1969; Illinois Bell Telephone, 1971-2; Finch College, 1971; Boston Museum of Fine Arts, 1970; Hall of Springs Museum, 1970; Hudson River Museum, Yonkers, NY, 1970-1; Newark Museum, 1971; Illinois State Univ., 1971; Smith-Mason Gallery, Washington, DC, 1971; NJ State Museum, Trenton, 1972; Seton Hall Univ., 1971; Internat'l Artists for Angela Davis, 1972; Whitney Museum Art Resources Center, 1971 (1-man); Spelman College, 1971; Metropolitan Applied Research Center, Inc., 1972; Whitney Museum, 1971.
Collections: Judge Thomas Jones, NYC; Imanu Amiri Baraka; Mr. Larry Neal; Mrs. Theodore Kheel; Westinghouse; Chase Manhattan Bank, NYC; Newark Museum; Fisk Univ.; Spelman Univ.; Malcolm X Univ.; Krisna Reddy; IBM; Larcada Gallery, NYC; Mr. Benny Andrews.
Awards: Scholarship, Skowhegan School of Painting & Sculpture, 1955; John Hay Whitney Fellowship, 1959; Nat'l Institute of Arts & Letters, 1968; Cultural Council Foundation, 1971; Artist-in-Residence, Smithsonian Conference Center, Elkridge, Md., 1967.
Sources: Boston Museum of Fine Arts. *Afro-American Artists: NY & Boston,* 1970; NY State Education Dept. *Fifteen Under Forty;* Information from artist; Scholastic Book Services. *Black Perspectives,* 1972; Atkinson, Edward J. *Black Dimensions in Contemporary American Arts,* 1971; *Afro-American Encyclopedia,* 1971; *African Progress Magazine,* 1972; Doty. *Contemporary Black Artists in America;* Larcada Gallery. *Oils and Drawings by Vincent Smith,* NY, 1967; Schafran, Lynn A. "Reviews and Previews," *Art News,* Sept. 1968; Illinois Bell Telephone. *Black American Artists/71,* 1972; Newark Museum. *Black Artists: Two Generations,* 1971; Smith-Mason Gallery. *National Exhibition Black Artists,* 1971; Bowling, Frank. "The Rupture," *Arts,* Summer 1970; Ploski, Harry, & Ernest Kaiser. "The Black Artist," *Afro USA,* 1971; Ploski, Harry, Ernest Kaiser, & Otto Lindenmeyer. "The Black Artist," *Reference Library of Black America,* Book 4, 1971; Brooklyn Museum. *Afro-American Artists: Since 1950,* 1969; Haas, Joseph. "A Big, Brilliant & Exciting Exhibition of Black Art," *Chicago Daily News,* Jan. 16-7, 1971.

SMITH, WALTER W.

Designer, commercial artist. Born in Pennsylvania. Studied at Carnegie Institute of Technology; studied art privately.
Works: *April Blizzard; Snowing.*
Exhibited: Harmon Foundation, 1930; Atlanta Univ., 1944; Buffalo Academy of Fine Arts; St. Louis Museum; Corcoran Gallery; Independent Artists, NY.
Sources: Harmon Foundation. *Exhibition of Productions by Negro Artists;* Indiana Univ. *Fine Arts & the Black American;* Harmon Foundation. *Exhibit of Fine Arts,* 1930; Harley, Ralph, Jr. "Checklist of Afro-Amer. Art & Artists," *Serif,* Dec. 1970; Walker, Roslyn.

A Resource Guide to the Visual Arts of Afro-Americans, South Bend, Ind., 1971.

SMITH, WILLIAM E.

Graphic artist, painter. Born in Chattanooga, Tennessee, 1913. Studied at Cleveland School of Art; John Huntington Art Institute, Cleveland; Playhouse Settlement art classes under Richard R. Beatty; Chouinard Art Institute, Los Angeles.

Works: *Pay Day,* 1938 (linocut); *Native Son,* 1938 (linocut); *Poverty and Fatigue,* 1968 (linocut); *We Shall Overcome,* 1968 (linocut); *Corner Politics,* 1970 (oil); *Harriet Tubman Underground Railroad,* 1970 (oil); *Negro Girl,* 1969 (oil); *A Young Lad; Leaning Chimneys; Back Yard; Depressed; Stable Boy; Goin' Fishing; Anderson; Blues; War Fatigue; Sunset* (casein); *Sleeping Madonna; War Orphan* (oil); *I Too Have a Dream; The Merry-Go-Round; Young and Wise; Sweet Slumber; Native Son; The Lamp Post.*

Exhibited: Cleveland May Show, 1935-9; Dayton Art Institute, 1939; Conn. Academy of Fine Arts, 1938; Amer. Negro Exposition, 1940; Assoc. Amer. Artists Galleries, 1942; Cleveland Museum of Art, 1935-41; Library of Congress, 1943; Atlanta Univ., 1942, 1969; Nat'l Academy of Design, NYC, 1966-8; Oakland Museum, 1968; Denver Art Museum; Frye Museum, Seattle; Benedict Art Gallery, Chicago (1-man); Lyman Brothers Gallery, Indianapolis (1-man); YMCA, Los Angeles (1-man); Florenz Gallery, Los Angeles (1-man).

Collections: Library of Congress; Cleveland Museum of Art; Howard Univ.; Golden State Insurance Co., Los Angeles; Oakland Museum.

Awards: Certificate of Merit, Cleveland Museum of Art; 1st prize, Val-Verde (Cal.) Art & Hobby Show.

Member: Art West Associated, Los Angeles; Karamu Artists.

Sources: *The Art Gallery,* April 1970; Porter. *Modern Negro Art;* Harley, Ralph, Jr. "Checklist of Afro-Amer. Art & Artists," *The Serif,* Dec. 1970; Porter, James. "Negro Artists Gain Recognition After Long Battle," *Pittsburgh Courier,* July 29, 1950; Roelof-Lanner, T.V. *Prints by American Negro Artists;* Locke. *The Negro in Art;* Atlanta Univ. catalogue, 1942; Tanner Art Galleries. *Art of the American Negro,* 1940; Oakland Museum. *New Perspectives in Black Art,* 1968; *Who's Who in the West,* 11th & 12th editions, 1968-9; *Dictionary of International Biographies,* London, 1971; *Personalities of the West and Midwest,* 1971; Oakland Museum Archives, Ruth Waddy Collection; Afro-Amer. Slide Depository, Catalog, 1971-2; Walker, Roslyn. *A Resource Guide to the Visual Arts of Afro-Americans,* South Bend, Ind., 1971.

SMITH, WILLIAM L.

Painter.

Exhibited: Harmon Foundation, 1928.

Sources: Harmon Foundation. *Exhibition of Productions by Negro Artists;* Indiana Univ. *Fine Arts & the Black American;* "Arabesque Panels Dome of the Buffalo Savings Bank," *Architectural League of NY Yearbook & Catalogue,* LXII, 1927, p. 88; Harley, Ralph, Jr. "Checklist of Afro-Amer. Art & Artists," *Serif,* Dec. 1970; Walker, Roslyn. *A Resource Guide to the Visual Arts of Afro-Americans,* South Bend, Ind., 1971.

SMITH, WILLIAM W.

Painter, graphic artist.

Works: *Autumn; Ships at Dock; The Ghost Train—Private Jennings.*

Exhibited: Atlanta Univ., 1944.

Sources: "Negro Art from Cleveland's Karamu House," *Art Digest,* Jan. 15, 1942; Atlanta Univ. *Third Annual Exhibition of Paintings, Sculpture, & Prints by Negro Artists,* 1944; Harley, Ralph, Jr. "Checklist of Afro-Amer. Art & Artists," *Serif,* Dec. 1970.

SMITH, ZENOBIA

Painter.

Works: *Untitled; Untitled #2.*

Exhibited: Smith-Mason Gallery, 1971.

Collections: Johnson Pub. Co.

Sources: Smith-Mason Gallery. *National Exhibition Black Artists,* 1971; Johnson Pub. Co. *The JPC Art Collection,* Pamphlet.

SMOCK, SUE M.

Sculptor.

Works: *Priestess Orosun.*

Exhibited: James A. Porter Gallery, 1970.

Sources: Howard Univ. *James A. Porter Gallery of African-American Art,* 1970; Musel, Robert. "Painting Racist, says Black," *Boston Globe,* July 14, 1970; Patterson, Lindsay. "Contemporary Artists," *The Negro in Music and Art,* 1969.

SMOOTE, JIM S.

Works: *Watermelons; Three Sisters.*

Collections: Johnson Pub. Co.

Sources: Johnson Pub. Co. *The JPC Art Collection,* Pamphlet.

SNEED, JAMES

Exhibited: Harlem Cultural Council, 1966.

Member: Creative Artists Studio.

Sources: Morrison, Allan. "New Surge in the Arts," *Ebony,* Aug. 1967; NY NAACP. *A Most Memorable Showing of Negro Creative Art;* NY NAACP. *Art Exhibition of Negro Expression Sponsored by Minars Furniture,*

April 1964; Myers, Carol L. *Black Power in the Arts,* Flint, Mich., 1970.

SNOWDEN, ALICE B.

Exhibited: Tanner Art League, 1922.
Sources: Harley, Ralph, Jr. "Checklist of Afro-Amer. Art & Artists," *The Serif,* Dec. 1970.

SNOWDEN, SYLVIA

Graphic artist. Active in 1960's.
Works: *Mountain Man* (etching).
Collections: Oakland Museum.
Sources: Roelof-Lanner, T.V. *Prints by American Negro Artists;* Oakland Museum Archives, Ruth Waddy Collection; Walker, Roslyn. *A Resource Guide to the Visual Arts of Afro-Americans,* South Bend, Ind., 1971.

SOARES, LAURA

Printmaker.
Works: *Summer* (serigraph).
Collections: Oakland Museum.
Sources: Oakland Museum Archives, Ruth Waddy Collection; Walker, Roslyn. *A Resource Guide to the Visual Arts of Afro-Americans,* South Bend, Ind., 1971; Roelof-Lanner, T.V., ed. *Prints by American Negro Artists.*

STOCKWELL, CARROLL

Painter. Born in 1943. Studied at the Corcoran School of Art, Washington, DC.
Works: *Stop Light; Composition; Twelve Noon; Mirror Composition #9; Crisis of the 60s.*
Exhibited: Corcoran Gallery of Art; Barnet Aden Gallery, Washington, DC; Nordness Galleries, NYC; State Armory, Wilmington, Del., 1971-2.
Sources: "Afro-American Issue," *Art Gallery,* April 1968; Indiana Univ. *Fine Arts & the Black American;* Nordness Galleries. *12 Afro-American Artists,* 1969; Aesthetic Dynamics. *Afro-American Images,* 1971; DuSable Museum of African-Amer. History. *Contemporary Black Artists,* 1970, Calendar; Greene, Carroll, Jr. "Perspective: The Black Artist in America," *Art Gallery,* April 1970; Greene, Carroll, Jr. "Afro-Amer. Artists: Yesterday & Now," *The Humble Way,* Vol. 8, No. 3, 1968; Harley, Ralph, Jr. "Checklist of Afro-Amer. Art & Artists," *Serif,* Dec. 1970; Greene, Carroll, Jr. *Afro-American Artists: 1800-1968,* Slides; Myers, Carol L. *Black Power in the Arts,* Flint, Mich., 1970; Walker, Roslyn. *A Resource Guide to the Visual Arts of Afro-Americans,* South Bend, Ind., 1971.

SOLOWEY, BEN

Exhibited: 12th Annual Invitational Exhibition, Pyramid Club, Phila., 1952.
Sources: Drummond, Dorothy. "Coast-to-Coast," *Art Digest,* March 1, 1952, p. 12.

SOUTHHALL, M.A.

Exhibited: Tanner Art League, 1922.
Sources: Harley, Ralph, Jr. "Checklist of Afro-Amer. Art & Artists," *The Serif,* Dec. 1970.

SPANN, DALE H.

Painter.
Works: *Crisscross; Black Youth.*
Exhibited: Smith-Mason Gallery, 1971.
Sources: Smith-Mason Gallery. *National Exhibition Black Artists,* 1971.

SPEARS, CHARLES, JR.

Born in North Carolina, 1902. Self-taught.
Works: *A Veteran of the Argonne.*
Exhibited: Harmon Foundation, 1930, 1935.
Sources: DuSable Museum of African-Amer. History. *Contemporary Black Artists,* 1970, Calendar; Harmon Foundation. *Exhibition of Productions by Negro Artists;* Indiana Univ. *Fine Arts & the Black American;* Harmon Foundation. *Negro Artists,* 1935; Harmon Foundation. *Exhibit of Fine Arts,* 1930; Harley, Ralph, Jr. "Checklist of Afro-Amer. Art & Artists," *Serif,* Dec. 1970; Walker, Roslyn. *A Resource Guide to the Visual Arts of Afro-Americans,* South Bend, Ind., 1971.

SPENCER, ELLA D.

Works: *A Marine; Landscape.*
Exhibited: NY Public Library, 1921.
Sources: Porter. *Modern Negro Art;* Harley, Ralph, Jr. "Checklist of Afro-Amer. Art & Artists," *The Serif,* Dec. 1970; *1st Annual Exhibit of Books, Manuscripts, Paintings, Sculpture, Etc. by the Negro Library Assn.,* Aug. 1918.

SPENCER, GEORGE

Painter.
Exhibited: Museum of Modern Art, 1943.
Sources: "Young Negro Art Impresses NY," *Art Digest,* Oct. 15, 1943.

SPROUT, FRANCES ALLEN

Painter.
Works: *Azo* (acrylic).
Collections: Johnson Pub. Co.
Sources: Johnson Pub. Co. *The JPC Art Collection,* Pamphlet.

SPRUELL, MOLLYE

Studied at Bennet College.
Works: *The Chapel.*
Exhibited: Sun Times/Daily News Gallery, Chicago, 1970.
Sources: United Negro College Fund. *Art 1970,* Chicago, 1970.

SQUIER, JERRY

Works: *Allegory IV.*
Sources: *Artists/USA* 1972-3, Feasterville, Pa., 1972, p. 176.

STAATS, FLORENCE

Mixed media, educator. Born in Newark, New Jersey, November 18, 1940. Studied at Parsons School of Design; New York University (BS); Pratt Institute (MFA).
Exhibited: Jersey City Public Library, Negro History Exhibition, 1968; Montclair Museum Annual, 1960-1; Newark Museum, 1960, 1969; Painters & Sculptors Society of NY, 1961; NJ League of Contemporary Artists, 1961; Ahda Artzt Gallery, NY, 1961; Drawing USA, St. Paul, Minn., 1963; Kaymar Gallery, NYC & Cape Cod; Treasure Gallery Annual, Bellville, NJ, 1966; Nutley Museum, 1967-8; Temple Menorah Annual, 1967-8; Sterington House Artist of the Month, Montclair, NJ, 1968 (1-woman); Midblock Art Gallery, East Orange, NJ, 1968; Newark Public Library, 1968; Angry Arts Program Cover Design Contest, 1968; New Brunswick Community Center, 1968; Newark Museum, Black Motion Art Exhibition Touring Show—Trenton State College, Essex County College, Montclair State College; NJ State Council on the Arts, 1969-70; Art Centre of the Oranges, 1970; Mid-Hudson Art Show, New Paltz, NY, 1970; Pratt Graduate Gallery (thesis exhibit), 1970; Stuart Art Gallery, Princeton, NJ, 1971; NJ State Museum, 1972.
Collections: Mr. Sam Miller, Director, Newark Museum; Mr. & Mrs. John J. Melcher, Ridgewood, NJ; Mrs. Irene Carpenter, Westfield, NJ; Mr. & Mrs. Norma Levine, London; Miss Susan Wolfe, NYC; Mr. & Mrs. S. Fidel, Bloomfield, NJ; Mr. Raul Cardinal, San Juan, Puerto Rico; Ms. Annette Mizne, Milan, Italy; Mr. Dan Ainseley, Los Angeles.
Awards: Best in show, New Brunswick Community Center, 1968; Best in show, Mid-Hudson Art Show.
Member: College Art Assn. of America; Amer. Craftsmen Council; Nat'l Art Assn. of America.
Represented by: Necessary Objects, High Falls, NY.
Sources: Wragg Chase, Judith. *Afro-American Art & Craft,* Van Nostrand Reinhold Co., 1971; NJ State Museum, Bureau of Exhibits, Cultural Center, West State St., Trenton, NJ; Old Slave Mart Museum, 6 Chalmers St., Charleston, SC; Newark Public Library. *Up & Coming,* March/May 1968, Unpublished list.

STAATS, TERESSA SIMPSON

Painter, educator. Born in Alabama, 1894. Studied at Tuskegee Institute; Columbia University; New Jersey School of Fine and Industrial Arts.
Works: *Boats on the Delaware; Speedboat; Sun Flowers; Hand Sculpture; Still Life-Flow-ers; Still Life-Sun Flowers; Delaware River; Factory Buildings.*
Exhibited: Nat'l Federation of Women's Clubs, 1934; Harmon Foundation, 1933, 1938; Atlanta Univ., 1942-4; Trenton State Fair, 1934; Bowie State Normal School, 1935; NJ Museum, 1935.
Awards: Honors at Nat'l Federation of Colored Women's Clubs, 1934.
Sources: Harmon Foundation. *Exhibition of Productions by Negro Artists;* Indiana Univ. *Fine Arts & the Black American;* Harmon Foundation. *Non-Jury Exhibit of Works of Negro Artists,* 1933; Harmon Foundation. *Negro Artists,* 1935; DuSable Museum of African-Amer. History. *Contemporary Black Artists,* 1970, Calendar; Harley, Ralph, Jr. "Checklist of Afro-Amer. Art & Artists," *Serif,* Dec. 1970; Walker, Roslyn. *A Resource Guide to the Visual Arts of Afro-Americans,* South Bend, Ind., 1971.

STAFFORD, BEATRICE

Painter.
Works: *Landscape.*
Exhibited: Atlanta Univ., 1943.
Sources: Atlanta Univ. Exhibition Files.

STALLINGS, CHARLES W.

Painter, printmaker, sculptor, educator. Born in Gary, Indiana, 1919. Teacher, Morgan State College, Baltimore.
Exhibited: Atlanta Univ., 1951.
Collections: Morgan State College, Baltimore.
Awards: $200 prize, Atlanta Univ., 1951.
Sources: Dover. *American Negro Art;* Indiana Univ. *Fine Arts & the Black American;* Roucek/Kiernan. *The Negro Impact on Western Civilization;* Pierre-Noel, Lois Jones. "American Negro Art in Progress," *Negro History Bulletin,* Oct. 1967; Harley, Ralph, Jr. "Checklist of Afro-Amer. Art & Artists," *Serif,* Dec. 1970; *Some Aspects of the Evolution of Negro College in America as Depicted by the Execution of a Mural,* Ann Arbor, Univ. Microfilms, 1955; Walker, Roslyn. *A Resource Guide to the Visual Arts of Afro-Americans,* South Bend, Ind., 1971.

STANFORD, FERN

Painter. Born in Philadelphia, 1943. Studied at the Museum of the University of Pennsylvania; Museum of the American Indian, New York.
Works: *Fern & Iaishia; Roy Toy.*
Exhibited: Studio Museum in Harlem, 1969.
Sources: Studio Museum in Harlem. *Harlem Artists 69.*

STATEN, DOUGLAS

Exhibited: Southside Community Art Center, Chicago (1-man).

Sources: Harley, Ralph, Jr. "Checklist of Afro-Amer. Art & Artists," *The Serif,* Dec. 1970.

STEADWELL, MRS. GERTRUDE ANNA

Born in 1909 in Connecticut. Self-taught artist.
Works: *A Jar of Goldenglow; Orville Steadwell Jr.*
Exhibited: Harmon Foundation, 1933.
Sources: Harmon Foundation. *Non-Jury Exhibit of Work of Negro Artists,* 1933.

STEINBERG, CARL

Sources: Steinberg, Carl. *All in Line,* Drawings, NY, 1945; Steinberg, Carl. *The Art of Living,* Drawings, NY, 1949; Steinberg, Carl. *The Passport,* Drawings, NY, 1954; Harley, Ralph, Jr. "Checklist of Afro-Amer. Art & Artists," *Serif,* Dec. 1970.

STEPHENS, DAVID

Sculptor.
Exhibited: Sheraton Hotel Phila., 1968.
Sources: Rose, Barbara. "Black Art In America," *Art in America,* July-Dec. 1970; Harley, Ralph, Jr. "Checklist of Afro-Amer. Art & Artists," *The Serif,* Dec. 1970.

STEPHENS, FRANK L.

Painter, illustrator, commercial artist. Born in Augusta, Georgia, February 16, 1932. Studied at the Philadelphia College of Art; Hussian School of Art. Library Graphics Manager, Free Library of Philadelphia.
Works: *Miss Mary;* Works for Amer. Airlines, Amer. Library Assn., Commission on Human Relations, Franklin Institute, Legal Intelligencer, Pa. Library Assn., Phila. Bar Assn., Phila. Court Administration, Library Public Relations Assn. of Greater Phila., Microdoc Inc., Spielman Label Co., Sceptre Films Inc., Quality Graphics Systems, McKay Assoc.
Awards: City of Phila. Citation, Employee of the Year, Free Library of Phila., 1970; Nat'l Civil Service League Award, Free Library of Phila., 1970; Award of Esteem, US Naval Supply Depot, 1964; Honorable Mention, Library Public Relations Council, design of book lists, 1962-3; Artist Guild of Del. Valley —Gold medal, best black & white illustration of the year, 1970, Award of Excellence, 1970; Graphic Arts Assn. of Del. Valley— Bronze medal, poster design, 1971, Award for Excellence in Design & Craftsmanship, 1969, Gold medal, best of the year award, design of programs & announcements, 1968, Gold medal, best of the year award, design of invitation, 1967; 18 departmental awards for design excellence & craftsmanship, 1965-71.
Member: Chairman, Germantown High School Home & School Assn., Public Relations Committee; Philobiblon Club; Artist Guild of Del. Valley.
Sources: Information from artist.

STEPHENS, LEWIS

Painter. Born in Atlantic City, New Jersey, 1931.
Works: *Country.*
Sources: Indiana Univ. *Fine Arts & the Black American;* Dover. *American Negro Art;* Harley, Ralph, Jr. "Checklist of Afro-Amer. Art & Artists," *Serif,* Dec. 1970; Walker, Roslyn. *A Resource Guide to the Visual Arts of Afro-Americans,* South Bend, Ind., 1971.

STEPHENSON, ERIK W. A.

Painter. Born in St. James, Jamaica, 1943. Studied at Jamaica School of Art; Art Students League of New York; Edinburgh College of Art.
Works: *To Phylo—Changes; Self-Portrait, Mezzatendencies; To Ave—Come Tripping as We Go on Light Fantastic Toe.*
Exhibited: Brooklyn Museum, 1969; Columbia Univ., 1969.
Sources: Brooklyn Museum. *New Black Artists,* 1969; Loercher, Diana. "Art: Idioms of Blackness at the Elma Lewis School," *Christian Science Monitor,* July 10, 1970; Walker, Roslyn. *A Resource Guide to the Visual Arts of Afro-Americans,* South Bend, Ind., 1971.

STEPTOE, JOHN

Painter, illustrator. Born in Brooklyn, New York in 1950.
Sources: *Stevie,* Harper & Row, NY, 1969.

STETH, RAYMOND

Graphic artist.
Works: *Reggie; Sidewalk Quartet; Debris Despair; Patron St. Derelict and Apostolic.*
Exhibited: Fort Huachuca, Ariz., 1943; Library of Congress, 1940; South Side Community Art Center, Chicago, 1941.
Sources: Ft. Huachuca. *Exhibition of the Work of 37 Negro Artists,* Ariz., 1943; Locke, Alain. "Chicago's New Southside Art Center," *Amer. Mag. of Art,* Aug. 1941; JWL. "Negro in Art," *Art News,* Dec. 19, 1941, p. 24; South Side Community Art Center. *National Negro Art Exhibition,* Chicago, 1941.

STEVENS, DAVID E.

Painter.
Exhibited: State Armory, Wilmington, Del. 1971.
Sources: Aesthetic Dynamics. *Afro-American Images 1971.*

STEVENS, JOHN

Sculptor, mixed media. Born in Detroit, 1935. Studied at San Francisco Academy of Art under D. Faralla, Lundy Siegriest, and Tony Delap.

Works: *Silver Saddle.*

Exhibited: San Francisco Annual Art Festival; Oakland & Richmond Art Centers; New Mission Gallery; San Francisco Art Center; 20th Century West Galleries Ltd., NYC; Fred Hobbs Gallery, San Francisco; Dickson Art Center, 1966.

Sources: DuSable Museum of African-Amer. History. *Contemporary Black Artists,* 1970, Calendar; UCLA Art Galleries. *The Negro in American Art;* "Afro-American Issue," *Art Gallery,* April 1968; Indiana Univ. *Fine Arts & the Black American;* Harley, Ralph, Jr. "Checklist of Afro-Amer. Art & Artists, *Serif,* Dec. 1970; Myers, Carol L. *Black Power in the Arts,* Flint, Mich., 1970; Walker, Roslyn. *A Resource Guide to the Visual Arts of Afro-Americans,* South Bend, Ind., 1971.

STEVENS, NELSON

Painter, graphic artist, educator. Born in Brooklyn, New York, 1938. Studied at Ohio University (BFA, 1962); Kent State University (MFA, 1969).

Works: *Kings and Queens of Jihad; Sister of Jihad; St. Malcolm—King of Jihad; Being and Becoming; Brother of Jihad; After All Is Said and Done; New Breed: Gemini; The Brothers Carry a Brother; The Brother Who Knows; Our Nation Calls,* 1971; *Towards Identity,* 1970; *Trilogy; A Different King of Man;* Cover design, NOMMO, by Paul Harrison; Album cover design for Archie Shepp's *The Cry of My People.*

Exhibited: Nat'l Center of Afro-Amer. Artists, 1970, 1972; Studio Museum in Harlem, 1970, 1972; Howard Univ., 1970, 1972; Karamu House, Cleveland, 1972 (1-man); Kent State Univ., 1972; Neighborhood Art Center, Akron, Ohio, 1972; Florida A&M.

Collections: Kent State Univ.; Northern Ill. Univ.; Karamu House, Cleveland; Fisk Univ.; Dr. Jimmy Jones, Chicago.

Member: AFRICOBRA; College Art Assn.; Nat'l Conference of Artists.

Sources: Afro-American Slide Depository, Catalog; Lewis/Waddy. *Black Artists on Art,* Vol. 2; Grillo, Jean B. "Where Down Home meets Back Home," *Boston After Dark,* Sept. 1970; Information from artist; *Black Shades,* Feb. 1972; Howard Univ. *AFRICOBRA I,* Catalog, 1970; Howard Univ. *AFRICOBRA II,* Catalog, 1972.

STEWARD, FRANK

Exhibited: Museum of Modern Art, 1943.

Sources: "Young Negro Art Impresses NY," *Art Digest,* Oct. 15, 1943.

STEWART, CAMALETE

Sources: Harley, Ralph, Jr. "Checklist of Afro-Amer. Art & Artists," *The Serif,* Dec. 1970.

STEWART, WILLIAM

Painter.

Works: *Across the Tracks* (watercolor); *Side Street* (watercolor).

Exhibited: South Side Community Art Center, Chicago, 1941.

Sources: South Side Community Art Center. *National Negro Art Exhibition,* Chicago, 1941.

STIDHAM, EDWARD

Portrait painter. Active in late 19th century.

Sources: *Negro Yearbook;* Indiana Univ. *Fine Arts & the Black American;* Porter. *Modern Negro Art;* Harley, Ralph, Jr. "Checklist of Afro-Amer. Art & Artists," *Serif,* Dec. 1970; Walker, Roslyn. *A Resource Guide to the Visual Arts of Afro-Americans,* South Bend, Ind., 1971.

STILL, JOSEPH

Sources: Harley, Ralph, Jr. "Checklist of Afro-Amer. Art & Artists," *The Serif,* Dec. 1970.

STINSON, DONALD R.

Craftsman, educator. Studied at the School of Arts & Crafts, Frankfurt, Germany (1953-4); Barnsdall Art Center, Los Angeles (1960-2). Teacher at Simon Rodia's.

Works: Enamels on copper, wall hanging; *She in the Watermelon Path* (enamel on copper).

Exhibited: Madonna Festival, 1st Wilshire Methodist Church, Los Angeles; Barnsdall All City Watts Festival; Mills College; Oakland Museum, 1971.

Member: Black Art Council; Art West Associated, Los Angeles.

Sources: Mills College. *California Black Craftsmen,* 1970; Oakland Museum. *The Metal Experience,* 1971.

STONE, ANITA

Works: *The Organization.*

Sources: Boston Negro Artists' Assn. Calendar, 1973.

STONER, ELMER

Cartoonist. Active in 1950's.

Sources: *Negro Yearbook;* Indiana Univ. *Fine Arts & the Black American;* Porter, James. "Negro Artists Gain Recognition after Long Battle," *Pittsburgh Courier,* July 29, 1950; Walker, Roslyn. *A Resource Guide to the Visual Arts of Afro-Americans,* South Bend, Ind., 1971.

STONER, OLIVE

Exhibited: NY Public Library, 1921.

Sources: "Meet Miss Stoner," *Philadelphia Art Alliance Bulletin,* Nov. 1941; Harley, Ralph,

Jr. "Checklist of Afro-Amer. Art & Artists," *The Serif*, Dec. 1970.

STOVALL, LOU
Printmaker.
Works: *Have You Pursued the Muse Diligently*, 1969 (silkscreen); With Lloyd McNeill, 6 silkscreens, 1969—*Six Characters in Search of an Author, Bicycledelic on the Ellipse Day, The Three Penny Opera; Feed Kids; The Conversion of Patrolman O'Connor; Improvisations by Harold Clayton.*
Collections: Nat'l. Collection of Fine Arts.
Sources: Afro-Amer. Slide Depository, Catalog, 1971-2.

STOWERS, ANTHONY
Exhibited: Studio 1, Berkeley.
Sources: Studio 1. *6 Black Artists*, n.d.

STRANGE, EDITH GRIMES
Painter, educator, mixed media. Born in Virginia. Studied at Howard University (BA); American University (MA); DC Teachers College.
Works: *Hope; Highlights & Shadows.*
Exhibited: Smith-Mason Gallery, 1971; Corcoran Gallery, Washington, DC; Howard Univ.; Collectors' Corner; Margaret Dickey Gallery; DCAA, Anacostia Neighborhood Museum—Smithsonian Institution.
Awards: 2 collages selected by US State Dept. for "Art for Embassies Program" & placed in US Embassies in Malta & Luxembourg.
Sources: Smith-Mason Gallery. *National Exhibition Black Artists*, 1971; DC Art Assn. *Exhibition '71*, Washington, DC, 1971.

STREAT, THELMA JOHNSON
Painter. Born in Yakima, Washington, 1912. Studied at the Art Museum School, Portland (1934-5); University of Oregon (1933-6).
Works: *Mother and Baby on Desert; Rabbit Man*, 1941; *Africa; Confirmation; Legless Seaman.*
Exhibited: de Young Museum, 1941; Raymond & Raymond Galleries, NYC, 1942; San Francisco Museum of Art; Amer. Contemporary Gallery, 1943; Little Gallery, Beverly Hills, 1943; Art Institute of Chicago, 1943; Newark Museum, 1971; Amer. Negro Exposition, Chicago, 1940; South Side Community Art Center, Chicago, 1945.
Collections: Museum of Modern Art; Mrs. Walter Paepcke; Mrs. Sara Drucker.
Sources: Albany Institute. *Negro Artist Comes of Age*; Indiana Univ. *Fine Arts & the Black American*; The Newark Museum. *Black Artists: Two Generations*, 1971; "Painter's Death of a Black Sailor Attracts Attention," *Black Dispatch*, Dec. 1943; Harley, Ralph, Jr. "Checklist of Afro-Amer. Art & Artists," *The Serif*,

Dec. 1970; Ploski, Harry, & Ernest Kaiser. "The Black Artist," *Afro USA*, 1971; Ploski, Harry, Ernest Kaiser, & Otto Lindenmeyer. "The Black Artist," *Reference Library of Black America*, Book 4, 1971; *The Negro Handbook*, Composed by Editors of *Ebony*, Chicago, 1966; Tanner Art Galleries. *Art of the American Negro*, 1940; South Side Community Art Center. *Chicago Collectors Exhibit of Negro Art*, Chicago, 1945; Walker, Roslyn. *A Resource Guide to the Visual Arts of Afro-Americans*, South Bend, Ind., 1971; "At 17 Her Painting Won Prize . . .," *Silhouette Magazine*, 1939.

STRICKLAND, EDWARD
Sources: *Daily Worker* (NY), June 12, 1950.

STRICKLAND, JAMES
Painter, mixed media, sculptor. Born in Detroit. Studied at the Accademia Di Belle Arte, Rome; Academie De La Grande Chaumiere, Paris.
Works: *Linda; Manha de Carnival; Etude #3; Bahia; Andalusia; Red Line #2; Moorish Spain #3; Azure; Senorita; Range; White Collage; Red Line #1; Moorish Spain #1; Etude #1; Moorish Spain #2; Moorish Spain #4; Etude #2.*
Sources: Afro-American Slide Depository, Catalog; Myers, Carol L. *Black Power in the Arts*, Flint, Mich., 1970.

STRICKLAND, LARRY J.
Painter.
Works: *Jomo Kenyetta.*
Exhibited: Smith-Mason Gallery, 1971.
Sources: Smith-Mason Gallery. *National Exhibition Black Artists*, 1971.

STRICKLAND, WILLIAM
Ceramist, weaver, educator. Born in Pittsburgh, Pennsylvania. Studied at the University of Pittsburgh; Indiana University under Frank Ross; Carnegie Institute under Ronald Kosinski. Director, Manchester Craftsmen's Guild; teacher, Upward Bound Program, Alliance, Ohio.
Sources: Pittsburgh Community College. *16 Black Artists.*

STRIDER, MAURICE
Painter, educator, photographer. Born in Lexington, Kentucky, 1913. Studied at Fisk University (AB); University of Kentucky (MA); University of Cincinnati; Southern University.
Works: *Still Life; Cloths; Approaching Storm; Clouds over Georgia; Ready for the Road; Portrait of Mother; The Crucifixion; Portrait of Juliette Derricotte*, 1934 (oil); *The Carnival*, 1959 (oil); *Chadian Fantasy*, 1971 (acrylic/oil); *Burial of Whitney Young, Jr.*, 1971 (color photo); *Carnival Time.*

Exhibited: Fisk Univ., 1934; Morehead State Univ., 1970; Carnegie Institute, 1971; Southern Ill. Univ., 1972; Ill. State Univ., 1973.
Collections: Atlanta Univ.; Fisk Univ.; Dr. Fred Tillis, Univ. of Mass.
Awards: John Hope Purchase Award, Atlanta Univ.; Goode Publishing Co. Award, Texas; Chicago *Defender* Award, newswriting to improve race relations, 1973; Jury, National Scholastic Art Awards; Southern Education Foundation Fellowship, Univ. of Ky.
Member: Kappa Pi Art Fraternity; National Conference of Artists; Eastern Kentucky Art Education Assn. (secretary-treasurer); Advisory Board, Ky. Educational TV Commission.
Sources: Information from artist; Afro-American Slide Depository, Catalog; Strider, Maurice. *Blueprint to Success*, Slides.

STRINGFELLOW, ALLEN
Sources: DuSable Museum of African-Amer. History. *Contemporary Black Artists*, 1970, Calendar.

STROUD, RICHARD
Painter, educator. Born in Tarrytown, New York, 1940. Studied at the National Academy of Design; Brooklyn Museum School of Art; New School of Social Research (BA); School of the Museum of Fine Arts, Boston. Teacher at the DeCordova Museum, Lincoln, Mass.; Emerson College, Boston; School of the Museum of Fine Arts, Boston; Student Center Art Studio, Massachusetts Institute of Technology.
Works: *Two Snapshots*, 1970 (oil); *Sheep in Wolf's Clothes*, 1970 (casein); *Gunas-Magic Tortoise*, 1970 (oil); *Wolf in Sheep's Clothes*.
Exhibited: Rose Art Museum, Brandeis Univ., 1969; Studio Museum in Harlem; Boston Museum of Fine Arts, 1970; Gallery 7; Franconia College; Brookline (Mass.) Public Library.
Sources: Community Lecture Series: *Local Afro-American Artists*, 1969; Andrews, Benny. "The Black Emergency Cultural Coalition," *Arts*, Summer 1970, p. 20; Sherman, Marjorie. "Afro-America Gets Biggest Show," *Boston Globe*, May 18, 1970; "Museum of Fine Arts to Hold Black Art Show," *Chronicle*, Ipswich, Mass., April 30, 1970; "Museum of Fine Arts to Hold Black Art Show," *Tri-Town Transcript & Pennysaver*, April 29, 1970; Gerson, Sareen R. "Black Art New York-Hub Set For Museum of Fine Arts," *Minuteman*, March 19, 1970; Walsh, Rose. "Artists to Meet Public at Art Exhibit Preview," *Record American*, Boston, May 19, 1970; Boston Museum of Fine Arts. *Afro-American Artists: NY & Boston*, 1970.

STROY, DENNIS
Sculptor.

Works: *Soul Sister & Mate.*
Sources: Greene, Carroll, Jr. "Perspective: The Black Artist in America," *Art Gallery*, April 1970, p. 23; Harley, Ralph, Jr. "Checklist of Afro-Amer. Art & Artists," *The Serif*, Dec. 1970; Walker, Roslyn. *A Resource Guide to the Visual Arts of Afro-Americans*, South Bend, Ind., 1971.

STUBBS, JESSE C.
Commercial artist. Born in Tennessee. Studied at Roger Williams College; Art Institute of Chicago.
Works: *Girl in Pink.*
Exhibited: Harmon Foundation, 1930; Pen & Palette Club, 1934; Smithsonian Institution, 1930.
Sources: Indiana Univ. *Fine Arts & the Black American*; Harmon Foundation. *Exhibition of Productions by Negro Artists*; Harmon Foundation. *Negro Artists*, 1935; Harmon Foundation. *Exhibit of Fine Arts*, 1930; DuSable Museum of African-Amer. History. *Contemporary Black Artists*, 1970, Calendar; Harley, Ralph, Jr. "Checklist of Afro-Amer. Art & Artists," *Serif*, Dec. 1970; Walker, Roslyn. *A Resource Guide to the Visual Arts of Afro-Americans*, South Bend, Ind., 1971.

STUCKEY, MARY L.
Works: *Mary.*
Exhibited: Phila. Civic Center Museum.
Sources: Phila. Civic Center. *Afro-American Artists 1800-1969*.

STULL, ROBERT
Ceramist, educator. Born in Springfield, Ohio in 1935. Studied at Ohio State University (BS, 1962; MA, 1963). Teacher at the University of Michigan.
Works: *Vase with Lid and Loop Handle; Movin.*
Awards: Fulbright Fellowship, 1965-7.
Collections: Johnson Pub. Co.
Sources: Nordness, Lee. *Objects: USA*; Johnson Pub. Co. *The JPC Art Collection*, Pamphlet. Myers, Carol L. *Black Power in the Arts*, Flint, Mich., 1970.

STUYVESANT, BEDFORD
Art designer.
Sources: "The Design Works of Bedford Stuyvesant," *Interior Mag.*, Sept. 1970, p. 12.

STYLES, FREDDIE
Painter.
Works: *Neon Fantasy*; Untitled watercolor.
Collections: Johnson Pub. Co.
Sources: Johnson Pub. Co. *The JPC Art Collection*, Pamphlet.

SUGGS, ELDRIDGE, III
Painter. Born 1939. Studied at Michigan State University, Lansing, Michigan; Hunter College,

New York City; Pratt Institute, New York City; Hofstra University, Hempstead, New York; University of Hawaii, Honolulu, Hawaii.
Works: *John Henery; Feeling Groovy; Don Quixote; Artist in His Chapeau; Illusive Runner; Judge Be My Character; Dignity.*
Exhibited: Greenwich Village Art Show, NYC, 1967, 1969; Convent of the Sacred Heart, NYC, 1969; Brooklyn Museum, 1970; Hewlitt East Rockaway Jewish Center, 1970; Westbury (RI) Public Library, 1970 (1-man); Phila. Civic Center, 1969.
Awards: Brooklyn Museum Graphics Award; Honorable Mention, graphics, Greenwich Village Art Show; Traveling Award, Greenwich Village Art Show.
Sources: NY State Education Dept. *Fifteen Under Forty*; Phila. Civic Center. *Afro-American Artists 1800-1969.*

SWEATING, EARLE

Exhibited: August Savage Studios, 1939.
Sources: Harley, Ralph, Jr. "Checklist of Afro-Amer. Art & Artists," *The Serif*, Dec. 1970.

SWEETNEY, BERNARD

Sculptor.
Works: *The Old King.*
Exhibited: Xavier Univ., 1963.
Sources: Xavier Univ. *Emancipation Proclamation Centennial National Art Exhibition*, 1963.

TANDY, JEWEL

Architect.
Sources: Wilson, John L. *The Negro Architect.*

TANDY, VERTNER W.

Architect. Born in New York City, 1885. Studied at Tuskegee Institute; Cornell University (1905-8); Chandler School, Lexington, Kentucky.
Works: Designed House for Madam C.J. Walker on Hudson River; St. Phillips Church, NYC; Home of Imperial Elks.
Member: Alpha Phi Alpha, co-founder.
Sources: Brawley, Benjamin. *The Negro Genius*; *Who's Who in Colored America*, 3rd edition; Wilson, John L. *The Negro Architect*; Downing, Lewis K. "Contributions of Negro Scientists," *Crisis*, June 1939.

TANKSLEY, ANN

Painter, educator. Studied at Carnegie Institute of Technology, Pittsburgh, Pennsylvania (BFA). Free-lance artist for Tanksley-Bazzone Studios.
Works: *Imprisoned; Smothering Mother.*
Exhibited: Kaufman Gallery, Pittsburgh; Hewlett Gallery; Devon Gallery.
Collections: Johnson Pub. Co.
Member: Where We At.
Sources: Johnson Pub. Co. *The JPC Art Collection*, Pamphlet; Acts of Art. Catalog, NY,

1972; A&T Univ. Lyceum Program. *15 Afro-American Women.*

TANN, CURTIS E.

Designer, craftsman. Studied at Cleveland School of Art; Cleveland Polytechnic Institute; Chouinard Art Institute, Los Angeles. Director, Simon Rodia's at Watts Tower Arts Center.
Works: Twenty inch boat shaped bowl.
Exhibited: Mills College.
Sources: Mills College Art Gallery. *California Black Craftsmen*, 1970; "Negro Art From Cleveland's Karamu House," *Art Digest*, Jan. 15, 1942; Porter. *Modern Negro Art*; Harley, Ralph, Jr. "Checklist of Afro-Amer. Art & Artists," *The Serif*, Dec. 1970.

TANNER, HENRY OSSAWA

Painter, illustrator, photographer, educator. Born in Pittsburgh on June 21, 1859. Died in Etaples, Normandy, France on May 25, 1937. Studied at Pennsylvania Academy of Fine Arts under Thomas Eakins; Julien Academy. Studied under Jean-Paul Laurens; Benjamin Constant; Gerome. Teacher of drawing at Clark University, Atlanta, Georgia for two years. Went to Paris in 1891, and returned to the United States only once after that.
Works: *Destruction of Sodom & Gomorrah; The Wailing Wall; Annunciation; The Banjo Lesson; Christ & Nicodemus; Christ Walking on Water; The Flight into Egypt; Daniel in the Lion's Den; Disciples Healing the Sick; Return from the Crucifixion; Etaples Fisher Folk; Moonlight Hebron; Sunlight Tangier; Abraham's Oak; Two Disciples at the Tomb; Christ & His Mother; The Governor's Palace; The Good Shepherd; Flight from Egypt; Angel Appearing Before the Wise Men; Lions in the Desert; Head of a Jew in Palestine; Moses in the Bullrushes; Gateway-Tangier; Christ & Disciples; Still Life Study of Fruit; War Hospital Church; Tanner; Savings; War Hospital Church-France; The Sabot Maker; American Red Cross Canteen at the Front-Toul; American Red Cross Canteen at the Front-Intersection Roads in France; The Lion's Head, Country Road at Twilight; The Storm; Bishop Hartzell; A Lion at Home; The Resurrection of Lazarus; The Bagpipe Lesson; Moses & the Burning Bush; Jews Wailing at the Wall of Solomon; Christ & His Disciples on the Road to Bethany; The Mothers of the Bible; The Five Virgins; The Return of the Holy Women, Christ at the Home of Mary & Martha; The Holy Family; Christ Walking on the Sea; Christ at the Home of Lazarus; Return from Calvary; Palace of Justice, Tangier; Arch; Christ with the Elders; Capsized Fishing Boats Brittany; The Nativity; Mr. & Mrs. Atherton Curtis; Gate in Tangier; Study of a Young Man; Study of a Negro Man; Mountain Land*

scape, *Highlands, North Carolina; A Man Sitting in a Chair; Return Home; Kansas City, Kansas; The Canyon; Study for Raising of Lazarus; Study for Mary; Study for the Annunciation; Study for Christ & Nicodemus on a Rooftop; The Savior; Study for Portrait of Mr. Atherton Curtis; Head of a Woman in Jerusalem; Head of a Disciple; Salome with Head of John the Baptist; Street Scenes (Man Leading Calf); American Red Cross WWI; And He Disappeared Out of Sight; Study for Mary Returning From the Crucifixion; Study for the Disciple Peter; Study of a Model; The Young Sabot Maker; Raising of Lazarus; Nicodemus; Disciples at Emmaus; The Disciples at the Tomb; The Wise & The Foolish Virgins; Judas; The Thankful Poor; Boy & Sheep Lying Under Tree,* 1881; *Sand Dunes in Sunset, Atlantic City,* 1893; *Les Invalides,* 1896; *Portrait of the Artist's Mother,* 1897; *Mother of Henry O. Tanner; Portrait of the Artist's Father,* 1897; *Profile of Woman's Head,* 1899; *Christ & Nicodemus on a Rooftop,* 1899; *The Three Marys,* 1905; *Study for Disciple Kneeling at the Tomb; Study for Disciple Kneeling at the Tomb, the Head; The Two Disciples at the Tomb (Disciples Kneeling); Study for Portrait of Mrs. Atherton Curtis; Portrait of Mr. & Mrs. Atherton Curtis with Still Life; Flight into Egypt (at the Inn); Portrait,* 1910; *Hand; Portrait of Henry Boddinton; Head of a Disciple; Burning of Sodom; Flight from Sodom & Gomorrah; Walls of Tangier in Moonlight,* 1914; *American Red Cross Canteen, Toul, France, World War I,* 1918; *Intersection of Roads, Neufchateau, World War I,* 1918; *A.R.C. Canteen, World War I,* 1918; *Fisherman Returning at Night,* 1930; *Fisherman's Return; Return from the Cross,* 1930; *The Good Shepherd (Atlas Mountains Morocco),* 1930; *He Healed the Sick,* 1930; *Little Girls with Deer; The Music Lesson.*

Exhibited: Salon des Artistes Francais, Paris, 1894-1924; 12th Annual Exhibition of the Phila. Art Club, 1900; Exhibition of the Society of Amer. Artists, 1904; Anglo-Amer. Art Exhibition, London, 1914; NY Public Library, 1921; Vose Galleries, Boston, 1921; Tanner Art League, Dunbar H.S., Washington, DC, 1922; Nat'l Arts Club Galleries, NYC, 1927; Amer. Artists' Professional League, Simonson Galleries, Paris, 1933; Century of Progress, Chicago, 1933-4; Phila. Art Alliance, 1945; UCLA Art Galleries, 1966; City College of NY; Harlem Cultural Council; NY Urban League, 1967; Xavier Univ., 1963; Paris Salon, 1895; Pa. Academy of Fine Arts, 1888, 1889, 1906, 1898; Methodist Headquarters, Cincinnati, 1890; Nat'l Academy of Design, NYC, 1891; Earse's Galleries, Phila., 1892-3; Salon of the Societé des Artistes Francais, Paris,

1900; Universal Exposition, Paris, 1900; Pan Amer. Exposition, Buffalo, NY, 1901; Louisiana Purchase Exposition, 1904; Carnegie Institute Annual Exhibition, Pittsburgh, 1905, 1908; Art Institute of Chicago, 1906; Amer. Art Galleries, NYC, 1908; Thurber's Gallery, Chicago, 1911; Knoedler's Gallery, NYC, 1913; Panama-Pacific Exposition, San Francisco, 1915; Museum of History Science & Art, Los Angeles, 1920; Grand Central Art Galleries, NYC, 1920-30, 1967, 1968; Morgan State College, Baltimore, 1967; Spelman College, Atlanta, 1969; Smithsonian Institution, 1969-70; Univ. of Texas Art Museum, 1970; Phila. Civic Center, 1970; St. Louis Exposition, 1905; Nat'l Arts Club Gallery, NYC, 1967; Howard Univ., 1945, 1967, 1970; Luxembourg Gallery; Rose Art Gallery, 1970.

Collections: Louvre, Paris; Carnegie Institute, Pittsburgh; Pa. Academy of Fine Arts; French Government; Luxembourg; Wilstach Collection; Chicago Art Institute; Los Angeles Art Gallery; Des Moines Art Gallery; Phila. Museum of Art, Fairmount Park; Mrs. Sadie T.M. Alexander, Phila.; Amer. Nat'l Red Cross, Washington, DC; Mr. & Mrs. Edwin S. Barrie, Greenwich, Conn.; Isaac Delgado Museum of Art, New Orleans; Frederick Douglass Institute, Washington, DC; Mr. & Mrs. Norman Robbins; Fisk Univ. Dept. of Art, Nashville; Grand Central Art Galleries, NYC; Mr. Carroll Greene, Jr., Washington, DC; Hampton (Va.) Institute; High Museum of Art, Atlanta; Howard Univ. Gallery of Art; Hyde Collection, Glens Falls, NY; Mrs. Salim Lewis, NYC; Los Angeles County Museum of Art; Mr. Thomas Loguidice, NYC; Mrs. Marcia M. Mathews, Atlanta; Milwaukee Art Center; Houston Museum of Fine Arts; Mr. Warren M. Robbins, Washington, DC; Mr. Merton D. Simpson, NYC; Spelman College, Atlanta; Mr. Jesse O. Tanner, Paris; Mr. Haig Tahjian, NYC; Metropolitan Museum of Art; NY Public Library, Schomburg Collection; Atlanta Univ. Library.

Awards: Honorable mention, Salon des Artistes Francais, Paris, 1896; 3rd Class Medal, French Gov't, Salon des Artistes Francais, Paris, 1897; 2nd Medal, Universal Exposition, Paris, 1900; 2nd Medal, Pan-Amer. Exposition, Buffalo, NY, 1901; St. Louis Exposition, 1904; 2nd Medal, Salon des Artistes Francais, Paris, 1906; Chosen to exhibit each year, Salon des Artistes Francais, Paris, 1895-1924; Place of Honor, Salon des Artistes Francais, Paris, 1908; Chevalier, Legion of Honor, French Gov't, Paris, 1923; Nat'l Arts Club Bronze Medal, Exhibition of Arts Clubs Galleries, NYC, 1927.

Member: Knight, Legion of Honor; Associate, Nat'l Academician; Paris Society of Amer.

Painters, 1909; Amer. Art Assn., Paris, 1897; Amer. Art Club, Paris, 1891; Amer. Artists Professional League, European chapter, 1930; Nat'l Academy of Design, NYC; Societé Artistique de Picardie, president; Societé Internationale Peinture et Sculpture, Paris.

Sources: Univ. of Texas Art Museum. *Afro-American Artists Abroad*; *Negro Almanac*; *American Negro Reference Book*; Indiana Univ. *Fine Arts & the Black American*; Dover. *American Negro Art*; Mathews, Marcia M. *Henry Ossawa Tanner: American Artist*, Univ. of Chicago, 1969; Locke. *The Negro in Art*; Lester, W.R. "Henry O. Tanner, Exile for Art's Sake," *Alexandra's Magazine*, Dec. 15, 1908, p. 69; Scarborough, W.S. "Henry O. Tanner," *Southern Workman*, Dec. 1902; Smith, Lucy E. "Some American Painters in Paris," *The American Magazine of Art*, March 1927, p. 14; Isham, Samuel. *The History of American Painting*, p. 417; Porter, James A. "Henry O. Tanner," *The Negro Caravan*, NYC, Dryden, 1942; Larkin, Oliver W. *Art & Life in America*, Winston, 1966; Afro-Amer. Slide Depository, catalog; City College of NY. *Evolution of the Afro-American Artist: 1800-1950*; Phila. Civic Center. *Afro-American Artists 1800-1969*; Herring, James V. "The American Negro Craftsman," *Crisis*, April 1942; Baldwin, E.F. "Negro Artist of Unique Power," *Outlook*, April 7, 1900; Thompson, Vance. "American Painters in Paris," *Cosmopolitan*, May 1900, pp. 18-20; Wesley, Chas. "Henry O. Tanner, the Artist—An Appreciation," *Howard Univ. Record*, April 1902, pp. 661-70; Walker, Roslyn. *A Resource Guide to the Visual Arts of Afro-Americans*, South Bend, Ind., 1971; Thompson, Vance. "Salon of 1908," *New York American*, May 1, 1908; "The Story of the Artist's Life," *World's Work*, Jan.-Feb. 1909, pp. 1661-6, June-July, pp. 11769-75; "Henry O. Tanner's Biblical Pictures," *Fine Arts Journal*, March 1911, pp. 163-6; "Notes: Henry O. Tanner," *Chicago Art Institute Bulletin*, July 1911, p. 11; Barton, William E. "An American Painter of the Resurrection," *Advance*, March 20, 1913, p. 2011; MacChesney, C.T. "A Poet Painter of Palestine," *International Studio*, July 1913; "Henry O. Tanner," *Aesthetics*, July 1914, p. 61; Fauset, Jessie. "Henry Ossawa Tanner," *Crisis*, April 1923, pp. 255-8; "Henry Tanner 77 Dies in Paris, Was American Negro Painter," *New York Herald Tribune*, May 25, 1937; Porter, James A. "Henry O. Tanner," in *The Negro Caravan* by Sterling Brown; "Work of Henry Ossawa Tanner," *Carnegie Magazine*, Nov. 1945, p. 157; Locke, Alain. "Henry Ossawa Tanner, 1859-1937," *Philadelphia Art Alliance Bulletin*, Oct. 1945; Canaday, John. "Poor Deal for a Good Man," *New York*

Times, Nov. 19, 1967; Campbell, Lawrence. "Henry Ossawa Tanner at Grand Central," *Art News*, Sept. 1968; Bearden, Romare, & Harry Henderson. *Six Black Masters of American Art*; Howard Univ. *Festival of Arts*, 1945; Howard Univ. *Art of the American Negro*, 1937; Brawley, Benjamin. *The Negro Genius*; Butcher, Margaret J. *The Negro in American Culture*, p. 217; MacChesney, Clara T. "A Poet Painter of Palestine," *International Studio*, July 1913; Dowd. *The Negro in American Life*; Roucek & Kiernan. *The Negro Impact on Western Civilization*; Howard Univ. *James A. Porter Gallery of African-American Art*, 1970; *Who's Who in Colored American*, 3rd Edition; Rollins. *They Showed the Way*; Harmon Foundation. *Select Picture List*; "Paintings of Major Black Artists Found," *Boston Globe*, Nov. 26, 1970; Furr, Arthur F. *History & Progress of Negroes in the US*, Vol. 1-9; "American Negro Art Given Full Length Review in NY Show," *Art Digest*. Dec. 15, 1941; Cartwright, W. Aubrey. *Guide to Art Museums in the United States, East Coast-Washington to Miami*, 1958; Edouard-Joseph. *Dictionaire Biographique Des Artistes Contemporains 1910-1930*, 1934. Fielding, Mantle. *Dictionary of American Painters, Sculptors, & Engravers*; Hourticq, Louis. *Harper's Encyclopedia of Art*; Huddleston, Sisley. *Bohemian Literary & Social Life in Paris*; Levy, Florence N., ed. *Who's Who in Art*; McGlauflin, Alice Coe, ed. *Who's Who in American Art*; Mallet. *Index of Artists*; Porter. *Modern Negro Art*; Young, William, ed. *A Dictionary of American Artists, Sculptors & Engravers*; Barrie, Erwin. S. *Exhibition of Paintings: Henry Ossawa Tanner*; Bhalla, Hans, & Edmund Barry Gaither. *Henry O. Tanner, An Afro-American Romantic Realist 1859-1937*; Greene, Carroll, Jr. *The Evolution of Afro-American Artists: 1800-1950*; Greene, Carroll, Jr., & Warren Robbins. *Tanner Graphics & Watercolors*; Locke, Alain. *Memorial Exhibition of Paintings by Henry O. Tanner*; Morris, Harrison S. *Illustrated Catalogue of Religious Paintings by Mr. Henry O. Tanner*; Porter, James A. *The Negro in American Art: 150 Years of Afro-American Art*; Porter, James A. *Ten Afro-American Artists in the 19th Century*; "An Afro-American Painter Who Has Become Famous in Paris," *Current Literature*, Oct. 1908, p. 405; "Annunciation; Painting," *Century*, April 1900, p. 815; Burroughs, Bryson. "A Characteristic Painting of the Resurrection," *Advance*, March 20, 1913, p. 2011; Caffin, Charles H. "Exhibition of the Society of American Artists," *The International Studio*, Vol. XXII, pp. 261-2; Canaday, John. "Negroes in Art: An Exhibition Examines 250 Years of Pictoral Social History," *New York Times*,

May 24, 1969; Cole, Helen. "Henry O. Tanner, Painter," *Brush & Pencil*, June 1900, pp. 97-107; Collins, William B. "Negro's Oil Painting Is Featured Work at Museum Yule Exhibit," *Philadelphia Courier*, Dec. 15, 1967; "Field Notes (obit.): Henry Tanner Dies," *Magazine of Art*, July 1937, p. 456; Ghent, Henri. "Art Mailbag: White is Not Superior," *New York Times*, Dec. 8, 1968; Greene, Carroll, Jr. "Afro-American Artists: Yesterday & Now," *The Humble Way*, Quarterly, 1968; Greene, Carroll, Jr. "The Afro-American Artist: A Background," *Art Gallery*, April 1968, pp. 12-25; Mathews, Marcia M. "Henry Ossawa Tanner, American Artist," *South Atlantic Quarterly*, Autumn 1966, pp. 1-10; "News & Comment: The Negro In Art," *Magazine of Art*, April 1942, p. 147; Rich, Daniel Catton. "Fifty Years at Chicago," *Magazine of Art*, Dec. 1939, pp. 704-9, 722-4; Taylor, A.E. "The American Colony of Artists in Paris," *The International Studio*, June 1912, pp. 280-9; Wuerpel, "American Artists Assn. of Paris," *Cosmopolitan*, Feb. 1896; Wyer, Raymond. "Art Collecting & Psychology," *International Studio*, June 1916, pp. 121-6; Grafly, Dorothy. "Henry O. Tanner," *Pictures on Exhibit*, Oct. 1945, pp. 14-15; "Honoring Tanner," *Art Digest*, Oct. 1, 1945; "In the Galleries: Henry O. Tanner, N.A.," *Arts*, June/Summer 1968, p. 58; "Tanner: An Appreciation," *Journal of Negro History*, Oct. 1938; "Tanner: Negro Painter," *Current Literature*, Oct. 1908; Paris, Jeanne. "Tanner Show on Tuesday," *Long Island Press*, June 2, 1968; Frederick Douglass Institute. *The Art of Henry O. Tanner (1859-1937)*; Greene, Carroll, Jr. "Perspective: The Black Artist in America," *Art Gallery*, April 1970, pp. 7, 10; Pierre-Noel, Lois Jones. "American Negro Art in Progress," *Negro History Bulletin*, Oct. 1967; Schuyler, George S. "The Negro Art Hokum," *The Nation*, Vol. 122, No. 31; *Apollo*, Feb. 1968, p. 141; Locke, Alain. "The American Negro As Artist," *American Magazine of Art*, Sept. 1931; J.P. "Henry Ossawa Tanner," *Art News*, Dec. 1967; M.B. "An Introduction to the Negro in American History," *Arts*, Sept./Oct. 1969, p. 58; "American Negro Art," *Design Magazine*, Feb. 1942, p. 28; Craig, Randall J. "Focus on Black Artists: A Project for Schools & Communities," *School Arts*, Nov. 1970, pp. 30-3; Kiah Virginia. "Black Artists," *Savannah Magazine*, April 1972, p. 14; Kiah, Virginia. *Emancipation Proclamation Centennial National Art Exhibition*, 1963; "The Art of Henry O. Tanner," *Ebony*, Oct. 1969; Harley, Ralph, Jr. "A Checklist of Afro-Amer. Art & Artists," *The Serif*, Dec. 1970; Greene, Carroll, Jr. *Afro-American Artists: 1800-1968*, slides; Boning, Richard A. *Profiles of Black Americans*, NY, 1969; Porter, James A. "Negro Artists Gain Recognition After Long Battle," *Pittsburgh Courier*, July 29, 1950; Brawley, Benjamin. *The Negro in Literature & Art in the US*; Locke, Alain. "Youth Speaks: The Artistic Vanguard," *The Survey*, March 1925; Grillo, Jean B. "Elma Lewis: A New Show A New Showplace," *Boston After Dark*, Aug. 16, 1970; Loercher, Diana. "Afro-American Artists Abroad," *Christian Science Monitor*, Aug. 1, 1970; "Preview Party to Open Show by 13 Black Artists," *Citizen*, Belmont, Mass., May 14, 1970; Faxon, Alicia. "Afro-American Museum of Fine Arts," *Journal*, Concord, Mass., Jan. 20, 1972; Brown, Marion. "The Negro in Fine Arts," *The Negro Heritage Library*, Vol. 2; Morsbach, Mabel. *The Negro in American Life*; Drotning, Philip T. *A Guide to Negro History in America*, 1968; *The Negro in Music & Art*, NY, 1969; Ploski, Harry, Ernest Kaiser, & Otto Lindenmeyer. "The Black America," *Reference Library of Black America*, Book IV, 1971; "At New York Art Exhibit," *Afro-American*, March 30, 1935; "Negro Has Given Much to Art, Survey Shows," *Boston Traveler*, Feb. 23, 1933; Schatz, Walter. *Directory of Afro-American Resources*, 1970; Adams, Russell. *Great Negroes Past & Present*, Chicago, 1969; Brown, Edgar G. "Art Work of Henry Tanner, Keystone State Product, Commanding Attention," *Pittsburgh Courier*, March 22, 1924; "Tanner Exhibits Paintings," *New York Times*, Jan. 29, 1924; "Henry O. Tanner Is Making Exhibit of Paintings in NY," *New York Age*, Feb. 2, 1924; Allen, Cleveland G. "The Paintings of Henry O. Tanner," *New York News*, Feb. 9, 1924; Myers, Carol L. *Black Power in the Arts*, Flint, Mich., 1970; Butler, Joseph T. "The American Way With Art," *The Connoisseur*, March 1971; Spradling Mary M., ed. *In Black & White: Afro-Americans in Print*; Robinson, Wilhelmina S. *Historical Negro Biographies*, pp. 128-9; Simmons, William J. *Men of Mark*, pp. 180-4; *Ebony*, Oct. 1969, p. 60; *Negro Digest*, Feb. 1970, p. 51; Butler, Joseph T. "Art of Henry O. Tanner: Exhibition Tour Crosses the US," *Connoisseur*, March 1971; Henry Ossawa Tanner Papers; DuSable Museum of African-Amer. History. *Contemporary Black Artists*, Calendar, 1970; Smithsonian Institution. *The Art of Henry O. Tanner*, Washington, DC, 1969; Dinger, Paul. "Chandler's Revolutionary Art Puzzles Critic," *Boston Globe*, Oct. 13, 1970; *Carnegie Magazine*, Nov. 1945; Thompson, Vance. "Salon of 1908," *New York American*, May 1, 1908; Spelman College. *Henry O. Tanner, An Afro-American Romantic Realist 1859-1937*, Atlanta, Ga.

TANNER, JAMES

Ceramist, glassblower. Born 1941, Jacksonville, Florida. Studied at Florida A & M University of Wisconsin (MS); School of Contemporary Art, Colorado (MFA). Teacher of glassblowing and ceramics at Mankato State College, Mankato, Minnesota.
Works: Red Plate, 1968 (blown glass); Untitled vases.
Exhibited: Nordness Galleries, NY; 18th Nat'l Decorative Arts and Ceramics Exhibition; Toledo Glass Nat'l Exhibit II.
Sources: Nordness Galleries. *12 Afro-American Artists,* 1969; Nordness, Lee. *Objects: USA.*

TAPLEY, MELVIN

Graphic artist.
Exhibited: Atlanta Univ., 1951.
Awards: Honorable Mention, Atlanta Univ., 1951.
Sources: Atlanta Univ. catalog.

TATE, IVEN

Painter. Born in 1908.
Works: *Artist at Work.*
Exhibited: Ford Motor Company.
Awards: $50.00 for painting "Artist at Work.
Sources: *New York Times,* April 26, 1956.

TATE, MARY LEE

Painter. Born in Kentucky. Studied at University of Cincinnati (BA); Cincinnati Art Academy; University of Chicago.
Works: *Summer; Twilight; A Mountain Trail; In the Canyon; Morning Mist.*
Exhibited: Harmon Foundation, 1928-31; NY Public Library, 1921; Smithsonian Institution, 1930.
Sources: Indiana Univ. *Fine Arts & the Black American;* Harmon Foundation. *Exhibition of Productions by Negro Artists;* Harmon Foundation. *Negro Artists,* 1935; Harmon Foundation. *Exhibit of Fine Arts;* DuSable Museum of African-Amer. History. *Contemporary Black Artists,* 1970, calendar; Harmon Foundation. *Select Picture List;* Harley, Ralph, Jr. "Checklist of Afro-Amer. Art & Artists," *The Serif,* Dec. 1970; Walker, Roslyn. *A Resource Guide to the Visual Arts of Afro-Americans,* South Bend, Ind., 1971.

TATE, RALPH

Sculptor.
Works: Various sculptures from drawings of the late President John F. Kennedy.
Exhibited: Anacostia Neighborhood Museum-Smithsonian Institution, 1967; Schaefer Gallery, NY; Wanamaker Dept. Store, Phila.
Sources: "Artist Sculptures JFK Doodles," *Ebony,* Oct. 1969.

TAWA, NJAROGE

Born in Philadelphia, 1932.
Works: *Saturday Movie; The Good Death of a White Woman.*
Exhibited: Clyde Mack Gallery; Harlem Gallery; Afro-Amer. Studio for Acting & Speech, NY.
Sources: Studio Museum. *Harlem Artists,* Harlem, 1969; Harlem Art Gallery. *Harlem Gallery Presents Dark Faces: An Exhibition of Paintings by Njaroge Tawa.*

TAYES, U. S. S. GRANT

Painter. Born in Missouri in 1885. Worked in Jefferson City, Missouri.
Works: *Miss Cammerron—Old Time Baptism; Self Portrait from Mirror; Mrs. Ada Browne; Mrs. Louise Caldwell; The Grouch; Erastus Wells; Marie—A Child's Portrait.*
Exhibited: Harmon Foundation, 1930, 1933, 1935; Atlanta Univ., 1944; St. Louis Public Library, 1929-33; St. Louis Art Guild; Art League; Urban League; Lincoln Univ. (Mo.).
Sources: Harmon Foundation. *Exhibit of Fine Arts,* 1930; Harmon Foundation. *Negro Artists,* 1935; Harmon Foundation. *Exhibition of Productions by Negro Artists;* Harmon Foundation. *Non-Jury Exhibition of Works of Negro Artists,* 1933; Atlanta Univ. *Annual Exhibition for Negro Artists,* 1944; Indiana Univ. *Fine Arts & the Black American;* DuSable Museum of African-Amer. History. *Contemporary Black Artists,* 1970, calendar; Harley, Ralph, Jr. "Checklist of Afro-Amer. Art & Artists," *The Serif,* Dec. 1970; Walker, Roslyn. *A Resource Guide to the Visual Arts of Afro-Americans,* South Bend, Ind., 1971.

TAYLOR, BETTY B.

See: Blayton, Betty.

TAYLOR, BILL

Sculptor.
Works: *Dancer.*
Exhibited: Smith-Mason Gallery, 1971.
Sources: Smith-Mason Gallery. *National Exhibition Black Artists 1971;* Myers, Carol L. *Black Power in the Arts,* Flint, Mich., 1970.

TAYLOR, CARLTON

Painter.
Works: *Evolution or We Shall Overcome.*
Exhibited: Oakland Museum, 1968.
Sources: Harley, Ralph, Jr. "Checklist of Afro-Amer. Art & Artists," *The Serif,* Dec. 1970; Oakland Museum. *New Perspectives in Black Art,* 1968; Indiana Univ. *Fine Arts & the Black American;* DuSable Museum of African-Amer. History. *Contemporary Black Artists,* 1970, calendar; Walker, Roslyn. *A Resource Guide to the Visual Arts of Afro-Americans,* South Bend, Ind., 1971.

TAYLOR, CLARENCE

Sources: DuSable Museum of African-American History. *Contemporary Black Artists,* Calendar, 1970.

TAYLOR, DELLA BROWN

Ceramist, poet, educator. Born in Charleston, West Virginia in 1922. Studied at West Virginia State College; Boston University (MA, 1945); Boston Museum School of Art; Massachusetts College of Art; McGill French Summer School. Professor of Art, West Virginia State College; art critic for *Charleston Gazette* and *Gazette/Mail.*
Exhibited: Boston Museum of Fine Arts; Art Exhibit for Dedication of Charleston Civic Center; Kanawha County Centennial Exhibition; 31st Allied Artists Exhibition.
Awards: 1st prize, ceramics, Kanawha Co. Centennial Exhibition; 1st prize, ceramics, 31st Allied Artists Exhibition.
Member: Amer. Craftsman's Council; Nat'l Conference Artists.
Sources: Lewis/Waddy. *Black Artists on Art,* Vol. 1; *National Conference of Artists,* Winter 1971, Journal; Walker, Roslyn. *A Resource Guide to the Visual Arts of Afro-Americans,* South Bend, Ind., 1971.

TAYLOR, ELMER D.

Sculptor.
Works: *I Win . . . You Lose . . . They Lose.*
Exhibited: Smith-Mason Gallery, 1971.
Sources: Smith-Mason Gallery. *National Exhibition Black Artists,* 1971.

TAYLOR, JAMES EDWARD

Painter. Born in New York on April 3, 1940. President of Attitudes in Fashion Inc. and AIS Inc.
Exhibited: Nyumba Ya Sanaa Gallery, 1964-70.
Member: Weusi Nyumba Ya Sanaa Gallery, NY; Academy of Arts & Sciences; Board, Massive Economic Neighborhood Development Inc. of Harlem.
Sources: Nyumba Ya Sanaa Gallery, NY.

TAYLOR, JEAN

Painter. Born in Roselle, New Jersey. Studied at Jersey City State College (BA); Pratt Institute; Art Students League; Univ. of Ghana (Summer of 1969); DC Teachers College.
Works: *Children of Abdulai Amusah; Untitled.*
Exhibited: Smith-Mason Gallery, Washington, DC, 1971; DC Teachers College; United Planning Organization; DC Artists Assn.; Anacostia Neighborhood Museum-Smithsonian Institution; Exposure '69 Art Show.
Sources: Smith-Mason Gallery. *National Exhibition Black Artists,* 1971; DC Art Assn. *Exhibition '71,* Washington, DC, 1971.

TAYLOR, LAWRENCE

Sculptor, free-lance artist. Private studies under Margaret Burroughs, S. Gordon. Staff artist for Ebony Museum of Negro History and Art, Chicago.
Exhibited: South Side Community Art Center.
Sources: "Afro-Amer. Issue," *Art Gallery,* April 1968, April 1970; Indiana Univ. *Fine Arts & the Black American;* DuSable Museum of African-Amer. History. *Contemporary Black Artists,* 1970, calendar; Walker, Roslyn. *A Resource Guide to the Visual Arts of Afro-Americans,* South Bend, Ind., 1971.

TAYLOR, MARGARET

Sources: Harley, Ralph, Jr. "Checklist of Afro-Amer. Art & Artists," *The Serif,* Dec. 1970.

TAYLOR, MARY ALICE

Works: *Indian Summer.*
Exhibited: Phila. Civic Center Museum.
Sources: Phila. Civic Center. *Afro-American Artists 1800-1969.*

TAYLOR, R. R.

Architect, educator. Teacher at Tuskegee Institute.
Works: Buildings on the campus of Tuskegee Institute.
Sources: Wilson, John L. *The Negro Architect,* pp. 25, 30; Downing, Lewis K. "Contributions of Negro Scientists," *Crisis,* June 1939.

TAYLOR, RAYMOND

Sources: Harley, Ralph, Jr. "Checklist of Afro-Amer. Art & Artists," *The Serif,* Dec. 1970.

TAYLOR, ROD A.

Sculptor, ceramist. Born in Washington, DC in 1932. Studied at Virginia State College; American University (graduate work in sculpture); Howard University; Catholic University; Virginia Union University.
Exhibited: Smithsonian Institution; Corcoran Art Gallery, 1965; Catholic Univ., 1967; Howard Univ., 1967; Smith-Mason Gallery, Washington, DC, 1965; The Little Art Gallery, Raleigh, NC, 1968; Saratoga Springs Art Fair; Atlanta Univ. Annuals; Scan Art Fair, Washington, DC, 1966.
Awards: 1st Prize, Saratoga Springs Art Fair, 1964; 3rd prize, sculpture, Creative Crafts Exhibition, Smithsonian Institution, 1964; Honorable mention, Smithsonian Institution, 1964; 1st Prize, Atlanta Univ. Annual Show, 1965.
Sources: Lewis/Waddy. *Black Artists on Art,* Vol. 1; Walker, Roslyn. *A Resource Guide to the Visual Arts of Afro-Americans,* South Bend, Ind., 1971.

TAYLOR, THERON
Photographer.
Exhibited: Addison Gallery, 1971.
Sources: James Van DerZee Institute. *The Black Photographer (1908-1970): A Survey.*

TAYLOR, WILLIAM HENRY
Painter. Born in Alabama in 1908.
Works: *Bronze Figure; Bronze Head; A Spanish Castle; Sunset; Sunset, Fall & Forest Stream.*
Exhibited: Ala. State Teachers College, 1932; Harmon Exhibit, 1928, 1933, 1935; State Armory, Wilmington, Del., 1971.
Sources: Indiana Univ. *Fine Arts & the Black American;* Harmon Foundation. *Exhibition of Productions by Negro Artists;* Harmon Foundation. *Non-Jury Exhibit of Negro Artists, 1933;* Harmon Foundation. *Negro Artists, 1935;* Aesthetic Dynamics. *Afro-American Images,* 1971; DuSable Museum of African-Amer. History. *Contemporary Black Artists,* 1970, calendar; Harley, Ralph, Jr. "Checklist of Afro-Amer. Art & Artists," *The Serif,* Dec. 1970; Walker, Roslyn. *A Resource Guide to the Visual Arts of Afro-Americans,* South Bend, Ind., 1971.

TAYLOR, ZACHARY
Graphic artist. Studied at Tougaloo College.
Works: Untitled etching; *Football.*
Exhibited: Sun Times/Daily News Gallery, Chicago, 1970.
Sources: United Negro College Fund. *Art 1970,* Chicago, 1970.

TEKLE, AFEWERK
Works: *African Movement.*
Exhibited: James A. Porter Gallery, 1970.
Sources: Howard Univ. *James A. Porter Gallery of African-American Art,* 1970.

TEMPLE, HERBERT
Painter, graphic artist.
Works: *Malcolm X.*
Collections: Johnson Pub. Co.
Sources: Johnson Pub. Co. *The JPC Art Collection,* Pamphlet.

TERRY, EVELYN P.
Graphic artist. Born 1946.
Works: *Black Flag,* 1970 (etching).
Exhibitions: Whitney Museum, NY, 1971.
Sources: Doty. *Contemporary Black Artists in America.*

TERRY, LOUISE B.
Sources: Harley, Ralph, Jr. "Checklist of Afro-Amer. Art & Artists," *The Serif,* Dec. 1970.

TESSEMA, MEMO
Printmaker.
Works: *Fisherman* (woodcut).

Collections: Oakland Museum, gift of the Harmon Foundation.
Sources: Oakland Museum Archives.

THOMAS, ALMA W.
Painter, educator, gallery director. Born in Columbus, Georgia on September 22, 1896. Studied at Howard University (BS); Columbia University (MA); American University, Washington, DC (1950-60); European Tour of the Art of Western Europe under the guidance of Tyler School of Fine Arts, Temple University, Philadelphia; Miner Teachers Normal School, Washington, DC. Vice-president of Barnet Aden Gallery, Washington, DC; teacher at Shaw Junior High School, Washington, DC.
Works: *Atmosphere I,* 1970; *Atmosphere II,* 1970; *New Galaxy,* 1970; *Dances with Flower Beds; Fall's Beginning; The Wind Flirts with my Autumn Flowers; Lunar Rendevous; Spring Flowers in Washington, D.C.; Spring-Delightful Flower Bud; Breeze Sway with Fall Flowers; Snoopy Sees a Sunrise on Earth; The Wind, Sunshine & Flowers; Blue Abstraction; Spring's Burst of Love; Alma's Stripes; The Azaleas, Spring Display; Wind Dancing, with Flowers; Arboretum Azaleas Extravaganza,* 1968 (acrylic).
Exhibited: Howard Univ. Gallery of Art, 1966 (retrospective); Boston Museum of Fine Arts, 1970; Nordness Galleries, NYC; La Jolla Museum of Art, 1970; State Armory, Wilmington, Del., 1971; Whitney Museum, 1971; James A. Porter Gallery, 1970; Anacostia Neighborhood Museum-Smithsonian Institution; Nat'l Collection of Fine Arts, Smithsonian Institution; Ringling Museum of Art; Baltimore Museum; Corcoran Gallery of Art; Wesleyan Univ. Center for the Arts; Carnegie Institute; United Negro College Exhibition, DC Art Assn.; Jackson State College; Aesthetic Dynamics; Society of Washington Artists; Franz Bader Art Gallery (1-woman); Margaret Dickey Gallery; DuPont Theatre Art Gallery; two college arts traveling exhibits; Amer. Univ., Washington, DC (2-woman); Ill. Bell Telephone, 1971; A & T Univ. Lyceum Program.
Collections: Howard Univ.; George Washington Gallery of Art; Corcoran Gallery; Manuel L. Myers; La Jolla Museum; Cal. Corporate Collection; Nat'l Collection of Fine Arts, Smithsonian Institution; Nordness Galleries, NY; Franz Bader Gallery.
Awards: Selected from Corcoran area show for traveling exhibition; Mayor Washington's office, White House; chosen for "Art in Washington 1970" appointment calendar; works selected by the State Dept's "Art for Embassies Program"; 1st prize, watercolor, Community Art Show; 3rd prize, Howard Univ. Art Purchase; 1st prize, Outdoor Art Fair; Honorable mention,

Metropolitan Area Show; Honorable mention, Barnet Aden Gallery; George Washington Univ. Art Show.

Sources: Dover. *American Negro Art;* Boston Museum of Fine Arts. *Afro-American Artists: New York & Boston,* 1970; Nordness Galleries. *12 Afro-American Artists,* 1969; La Jolla Museum of Art. *Dimensions of Black;* Aesthetic Dynamics. *Afro-American Images,* 1971; Doty. *Contemporary Black Artists in America;* Illinois Bell Telephone. *Black American Artists/71;* Howard Univ. *James A. Porter Gallery of African-Amer. Art,* 1970; DuSable Museum of African-Amer. History. *Contemporary Black Artists,* 1970, calendar; Greene, Carroll, Jr. "Perspective: The Black Artist in America," *Art Gallery,* April 1970; Mahal, H. E. "Approaches to Inhumanity," *Art Gallery,* April 1970; Pierre-Noel, Lois Jones. "American Negro Art in Progress," *Negro History Bulletin,* Oct. 1967; A & T Univ. Lyceum Program. *15 Afro-American Women;* DC Art Assn. *Exhibition '71,* Washington, DC; Mahal, H.E. "Interviews: Four Afro-Amer. Artists," *Art Gallery,* April 1970; Harley, Ralph, Jr. "Checklist of Afro-Amer. Art & Artists," *The Serif,* Dec. 1970; Greene, Carroll, Jr. *Afro-American Artists: 1800-1968,* slides & text; Grillo, Jean B. "Black Art—White Museum," (Boston) *Phoenix,* May 23, 1970; Atkinson, J. Edward. *Black Dimensions in Contemporary American Art,* NY, 1971; Myers, Carol L. *Black Power in the Arts,* Flint, Mich., 1970; *Art in Washington,* 1970 Calendar, Acropolis Books; *Who's Who in American Art,* 1970; Anacostia Neighborhood Museum-Smithsonian Institution. *16 Washington Artists;* Carnegie Institute. *The Master Artists 1970 Series;* Walker, Roslyn. *A Resource Guide to the Visual Arts of Afro-Americans,* South Bend, Ind., 1971.

THOMAS, ANNA BELL

Painter, teacher of domestic arts.

Works: *Norwegian Farm Scene; Chinese Stencil for all over design; Pillow Top printed with Chinese stencil.*

Exhibited: Chicago Art Institute, 1927.

Sources: Art Inst. of Chicago. *The Negro in Art Week,* 1927.

THOMAS, ELAINE F.

Craftsman, museum director, curator, educator. Studied at Tuskegee Institute (BS, magna cum laude, 1945); Northwestern University (1944); Black Mountain College, North Carolina (1945); New York University (MA, 1949); Mexico City College (1956); Berea College, Kentucky (1961); University of Paris (*Casa,* 1966). Director and curator of George Washington Carver Museum, Tuskegee Insti-

tute; Chairman, Art Instruction, College of Arts and Sciences, Tuskegee Institute.

Works: *Octamerous; Blue Silence; The Eiffel Tower; The Green Wall; The Sacred Light.*

Exhibited: Festival of Arts, St. Paul, Minn.; Mexico City Watercolor Show, 1956; Beaux Arts Guild, 1957-68; Religious Art Show, Auburn, Ala., 1966; Tuskegee Institute, 1956, 1962, 1966, 1967, 1968, 1972 (2-woman); Art Faculty Show, Birmingham, 1966; Univ. of Fla. Traveling Exhibition Region 6; Festival of Negro Arts, Miami, 1968; Winston-Salem Univ., 1970 (1-woman); Univ. of Cincinnati, 1969; Museum of Fine Arts, Montgomery, Ala., 1968, 1972; Talladega College, Ala., 1972.

Awards: Bodden Fellowship, NY Univ., 1948-9; Rosenwald Fellowships, 1944, 1945; Distinguished Participation Award, Amer. Artists Professional League, 1968; Beaux Arts Festival Award.

Member: Amer. Assn. of Museums; Amer. Assn. of Univ. Professors; Amer. Craftsmen's Council; College of Art Assn.; Nat'l Art Education Assn.; Nat'l Conference of Artists; Beaux Arts Guild; Alpha Kappa Mu Honor Society; Ala. Art League.

Sources: *Who's Who in American Education,* Vol. 20, 1961-2, Vol. 23, 1967-8; *Who's Who of American Women,* 1st Edition, 1958-9; *Artists/USA,* 1970-1; *Internat'l Who's Who in Art & Antiques,* London, 1971; Thomas, Elaine F. "Some American Negro Artists," *Some Aspects of Black Culture,* West Ga. College Studies in the Social Sciences, Vol. 8, No. 1, Carrollton, Ga., June 1969; Thomas, Elaine F. "Think on These Things," *The Chapel Bulletin,* Tuskegee Institute, Ala., Oct. 13, 1968.

THOMAS, LARRY ERSKINE

Painter. Born in Baltimore, Maryland, 1917. Studied at Walter Vincent Smith Museum; Massachusetts State College; Oakwood Junior College; Art Students League; Jean Morgan School of Art; Cairo Museum; Haile Selassie I University, Addis Ababa, Ethiopia. Program Manager, Anacostia Neighborhood Museum-Smithsonian Institution.

Works: *Quest for Black; Africa-The Source; Design #5.*

Exhibited: State Armory, Wilmington, Del., 1971; Internat'l Exposition, Ethiopia; "Silver Jubilee" Exposition, Ethiopia; Eastern Market Internat'l Group; Smith-Mason Gallery; "This is Africa," Anacostia Neighborhood Museum-Smithsonian Institution; "16 Washington Artists," Anacostia Neighborhood Museum-Smithsonian Institution; Wesleyan Univ.; United Mutual Galleries (1-man); Public Library, Springfield, Mass.; USIA, "This is Ethiopia," Ethiopia; US Dept. of State; Cedar Lane Uni-

tarian Church; Inaugural Exhibition, Bennett College Student Union.
Collections: His Imperial Majesty Haile Selassie I, Emperor of Ethiopia; the late Duke of Harar, Leul Makonnen, Ethiopia; the late President Dwight D. Eisenhower; McLaughlin Research Corp.; Howard Univ. original Centennial Calendar; Haile Selassie I Univ., Ethiopia; Ship's Lounge of the M.S. Mussilloyd, Rotterdam, Netherlands; Office of Protocol, US Dept. of State; Anacostia Museum-Smithsonian Institution.
Awards: Gold Medal, Silver Jubilee, Internat'l Exposition, Ethiopia, for A. Bessie & Co., Ltd. Pavillion Mural.
Sources: DC Art Assn. *Exhibition '71*, Washington, DC, 1971; Aesthetic Dynamics. *Afro-American Images*, 1971; DuSable Museum of African-Amer. History. *Contemporary Black Artists*, 1970, Calendar; Greene, Carroll, Jr. "Perspective: The Black Artist in America," *Art Gallery*, April 1970, p. 23; Harley, Ralph, Jr. "A Checklist of Afro-Amer. Art & Artists," *The Serif*, Dec. 1970; Greene, Carroll, Jr. *Afro-American Artists: 1800-1968*, slides.

THOMAS, WILFRED
Painter.
Collections: Mr. Benny Andrews.

THOMAS, WILLIAM O.
Painter. Owner of The BlackMan's Art Gallery.
Sources: Albright, Thomas. "The BlackMan's Art Gallery," *Art Gallery*, April 1970.

THOMPSON, A.M.
Painter.
Works: *South Boston; Fenway; Landscape.*
Sources: *1st Annual Exhibit of Books, Manuscripts, Paintings, Sculptures etc. by the Negro Library Assn.*, 1918, Catalog.

THOMPSON, CONRAD
Painter. Born in Mobile, Alabama. Studied at Howard University (BA). Director of Naval Ship Engineering Center, Management Information Center, & Graphics Support Facility in Prince Georges Center.
Works: *Dude; Fish Fry.*
Exhibited: Smith-Mason Gallery, 1971; Woodward & Lothrop; Collectors' Corner; Howard Univ.; Smithsonian Institution; Dept. of Agriculture; Dept. of Commerce; DCAA, Anacostia Neighborhood Museum-Smithsonian Institution.
Sources: Smith-Mason Gallery. *National Exhibition Black Artists*, 1971; DC Art Assn. *Exhibition '71*, Washington, DC, 1971.

THOMPSON, JAMAL
Painter.
Exhibited: Cinque Gallery, NY, 1972.
Sources: *Black Shades*, Feb. 1972.

THOMPSON, LOVETT
Sculptor, jeweler, craftsman, painter. Born in Georgia. Self-taught.
Works: *The Junkie*, 1970 (wood).
Exhibited: Rose Art Museum, Brandeis Univ.; Studio Museum in Harlem, 1969-70; Boston Museum of Fine Arts, 1970; Nat'l Center of Afro-Amer. Artists, 1969.
Sources: *Newsweek*, June 22, 1970; Boston Community Lecture Series. *Local Afro-American Artists*, 1969; Bourne, Kay. "Black Artists Shown at Museum," *Bay State Banner*, May 28, 1970.

THOMPSON, MILDRED
Painter, sculptor. Studied in Hamburg, Germany. Lives in Germany.
Works: *Coney Island; The Emperor's Nightingale; One Sunday Afternoon; Allegro; The Sun Also Rises; For People Who Live on An Island; The Rail; Closed for the Summer; Ski-Jump; Adagio; My Window; Coltrane's Meditation; Bridge Crossing; Red, Red, Red; Red Piano; Ventilation; Afro 36; Through a Glass Darkly; Coming Through.*
Exhibited: Howard Univ., 1961, 1970.
Sources: Dover. *American Negro Art*; *American Negro Reference Book*; Indiana Univ. *Fine Arts & the Black American*; Roucek & Kiernan. *The Negro Impact on Western Civilization*; Howard Univ. *James A. Porter Gallery of African-American Art*, 1970; Harley, Ralph, Jr. "Checklist of Afro-Amer. Art & Artists," *The Serif*, Dec. 1970; Schatz, Walter. *Directory of Afro-American Resources*, 1970; Afro-Amer. Slide Depository, 1971-2, catalog; *The Negro Handbook*, composed by editors of *Ebony*, Chicago, 1966; Walker, Roslyn. *A Resource Guide to the Visual Arts of Afro-Americans*, South Bend, Ind., 1971.

THOMPSON, MOZELLE
Painter. Born in Pittsburgh, Pennsylvania. Died 1970. Studied at Parson School of Design in New York. Illustrator of children's books.
Sources: *Ebony*, Feb. 1949, p. 57; Spradling, Mary M., ed. *In Black & White: Afro-Americans in Print*; Weldon, James. *Lift Every Voice & Sing*, 1970.

THOMPSON, ROBERT
Painter. Born in Louisville, Kentucky on June 26, 1937. Died in Rome on May 30, 1966. Studied at Boston University; University of Louisville, Kentucky (1955-8); Boston Museum School (1955).
Works: *Ascension to the Heavens; Untitled Diptych; Satyr and the Maiden; This House Is Mine; The Frog & The Princess; Wagadu II; Enchanted Rider; Two Nuns; Turkey Catch; Still Life; Self Portrait; Portrait of a Musician;*

The Bathers; Sun and His Wives-Wagadu; Expulsion and Nativity; Crucifixion; Le Passage; Leroy (Jones) and Barbara in the Cedar (Bar); Portrait of Carol; Four Moods; Reclining Figure; A Caprice; Tree; The Bey; The Judgement; Family Portrait; Bird Ritual; The Spinning, Spinning, Turning, Directing; Descent From the Cross; Le Debut; Tribute to an American Indian; Queen of Sheba's Visit to King Solomon; The Bird Nester; Saint Matthew's Description of the End of the World; Nudes with Birds; Bacchanale I; Fantasy; Well; Untitled 1958; Untitled 1959; Self Portrait in the Studio; Head; Green Nude; Untitled 1963; Nativity; Angel; Perseus and Andromeda; Nymph & Satyr; Portrait of Allen (Ginsberg); Portrait of Nina Simone; Diana the Huntress; Pieta; The Recliners; Five Cows with Blue Nude; Le Jeu; Homage to Nina Simone; Figure; Death of the Infant Bethel; La Promenade; The Swing; Winter or the Flood; Lady Godiva; Blue Daphne; The Probable Death of Didone; The Restoring; Unfinished Resurrection; Judgement of Paris, 1964; *The Hairdresser,* 1962-3; *Dr. Bird,* 1962; *Reclining Nude,* 1966; Untitled sketch, 1965; Untitled ink on paper, 1966; *The Land of Cockaigne (after Bruegel),* 1965; *Flagellation; Ecco & Narcissus,* 1965 (oil).

Exhibited: Donald Morris Gallery, Detroit, 1970 (1-man); J.B. Speed Art Museum, Louisville, Ky., 1971 (1-man); Provincetown (Mass.) Art Festival, 1958; Univ. of Ariz., 1964; Chicago Art Institute, 1964; CORE Shows, NY, 1964, 1965; Dayton Art Institute, Ohio, 1964; Fairleigh Dickinson Univ., NJ, 1964; Yale Univ., 1964; Bennett College, Millbrook, NY, 1965; The New School, NY, 1965, 1969; Rockford (Ill.) College, 1965; J.B. Speed Art Museum, Louisville, Ky., 1965; Long Island Univ., 1966; Downtown Salutes the Arts Show, NY, 1966; Gallery 12, NY, 1967; Brooklyn College, 1969; Phila. Art Alliance, 1969; Mt. Holyoke College, 1969; Musée Rath, Paris; Arts in Louisville, 1958; Zabriskie Gallery, NY; Delancey St. Museum, NY, 1960; New City Gallery, NY; Superior St. Gallery, Chicago, 1961; Amer. Students & Artists Center, Paris; El Cosario Gallery, Ibiza, Spain, 1963; Amer. Federation of Arts Traveling Shows, 1960-1, 1963-4; Martha Jackson Gallery, 1963, 1965, 1968; Ellison Gallery, Ft. Worth; Felix Landau Gallery, Los Angeles; Boston Museum of Fine Arts, 1970; La Jolla Museum of Art, 1970; The Drawing Shop, NY, 1963 (1-man); Richard Gray Gallery, Chicago, 1964, 1965 (1-man); Paula Johnson Gallery, NY, 1964 (1-man); Donald Morris Gallery, Detroit, 1965 (1-man); East End Gallery, Provincetown, Mass., 1965 (1-man); Wollman Hall.

Collections: Joseph H. Hirshhorn Collection; Harry Abrams Collection; Albright-Knox Gallery; Chrysler Museum, Provincetown, Mass.; Mr. Myer Shapiro; Mr. Horace Richter; Mr. Joseph Shapiro; Mr. Walter Cutman; Mr. John Gillman; Mr. Walter P. Chrysler; Mr. Lewis Merril; Ms. Martha Jackson; Mr. David Anderson, NYC; Mint Museum of Art; Felix Landau Gallery, Los Angeles; Mr. Benny Andrews; Mr. John Powers; Container Corp. of America; Martha Jackson Gallery, NY; Mrs. Jeanne Siegal, NY; Mrs. Dorothy Reskind, NY; Mr. Sam Dorsky, NY; Mr. Larry Rivers, NY; Mr. Lester Johnson, NY; Amer. Federation of Art, NY; Miles College, Birmingham, Ala.; Dayton (Ohio) Art Institute; Mr. Bob Thompson.

Awards: Walter Gutman Foundation Grant, 1961; John Hay Whitney Fellowship, 1962-3. **Sources:** Indiana Univ. *Fine Arts & the Black American*; UCLA Art Galleries. *The Negro in American Art*; Boston Museum of Fine Arts. *Afro-American Artists: NY & Boston,* 1970; New School Art Center. *Bob Thompson*; La Jolla Museum of Art. *Dimensions of Black*; Wolman Hall. *Bob Thompson*; Musée Rath. *8 Artistes Afro-Americains*; Bowling, Frank. "Critique Discussion on Black Art," *Arts,* 1969; Harley, Ralph, Jr. "A Checklist of Afro-Amer. Art & Artists," *The Serif,* Dec. 1970; Mt. Holyoke College. *Ten Afro-American Artists,* Nov. 1969; Walker, Roslyn. *A Resource Guide to the Visual Arts of Afro-Americans,* South Bend, Ind., 1971; Bourne, Kay. "Black Artists Shown at Museum," *Bay State Banner,* May 28, 1970; "What is Black Art?," *Newsweek,* June 22, 1970; Kramer, Hilton. "Is Politics Submerging Black Art?," *Courier-Journal & Times,* Louisville, Ky., June 7, 1970; Brown, Marion. "The Negro in the Fine Arts," *The Negro Heritage Library,* Vol. 2; Ploski, Harry, & Ernest Kaiser. "The Black Artist," *Afro USA,* 1971; Ploski, Harry, Ernest Kaiser, & Otto Lindenmeyer. "The Black Artist," *Reference Library of Black America,* Book IV, 1971; Walsh, Rose. "Artists to Meet Public at Art Exhibit Preview," *Record American,* May 19, 1970; Paris, Jean. "Black Art Experience in Art," *Long Island Press,* Jamaica, NY, June 14, 1970; J.B. Speed Art Museum. *Memorial Exhibit,* Ky., 1971; Univ. of Arizona. *Bird in Art,* 1964; The New School. *Portraits in American Art World,* NY, 1965; J.B. Speed Art Museum. *A Survey of American Art,* 1965; Long Island Univ. *43 Artists From 18 Nations,* 1966; Brooklyn College. *Afro-American Artists: Since 1950,* 1969; Greene, Carroll, Jr. "Perspective: The Black Artist in America," *Art Gallery,* April 1970; Rockford College. *Creativity & the Negro*; Rose, Barbara. "Black Art in America," *Art in America,* July/Dec. 1970; *Art Journal,* April 1969; Driscoll,

Edgar. *Boston Evening Globe*, May 20, 1970; Gallery 12. *Memorial Exhibit*, NY, 1969.

THOMPSON, ROBERTA

Painter. Born in Pasco, Washington in 1928. Self-taught in art.
Works: *Nigerian Princess*, 1958.
Exhibited: Bay Area Art Fairs, San Francisco; BlackMan's Art Gallery; Oakland Museum, 1968.
Sources: Oakland Art Museum. *New Perspectives in Black Art*, 1968; Indiana Univ. *Fine Arts & the Black American*; Lewis/Waddy. *Black Artists on Art*, Vol. 2; Harley, Ralph, Jr. "Checklist of Afro-Amer. Art & Artists," *The Serif*, Dec. 1970; Walker, Roslyn. *A Resource Guide to the Visual Arts of Afro-Americans*, South Bend, Ind., 1971.

THOMPSON, RUSS

Painter. Born in Kingston, Jamaica, 1922. Studied at the Pratt Institute; Carlyle College; New York School of Modern Photography.
Works: *Cloud Flowers; My Breath Is One with the Clouds; The Acrobats; Relatives; Thoreau; Clothes to the Body; America-America; Hanging Garden; Poor Room, Rich Room; Epigram a Bromide; Passage*, 1969 (wood, epoxy, iron).
Exhibited: Museum of Modern Art; Brooklyn Museum Fence Show, 1968; Nordness Galleries, NY; Phila. Civic Center; Ruder & Finn Fine Arts, 1969; Smithsonian Institution; Mount Holyoke College, 1969; Boston Museum of Fine Arts, 1970; Rhode Island School of Design, 1969; Memorial Art Gallery, Rochester, NY, 1969; San Francisco Museum of Art, 1969; Contemporary Arts Museum, Houston, 1970; NJ State Museum, 1970; Roberson Center for the Arts & Sciences, Binghamton, NY, 1970; Art Galleries, Univ. of Cal. at Santa Barbara, 1970; Plaza Hotel, NYC; Westchester Art Society Gallery; Nassau Community College; Brooklyn Public Library; Allentown (Pa.) Art Festival; Quinnipiac College; Parrish Art Museum; NY State Pavillion; Huntington Township Art League.
Collections: Frederick Douglass Institute, Washington, DC; Spiro & Levinson Corp.; Mr. William Haber; Mr. & Mrs. B. Friedman; Mr. & Mrs. Samuel J. Rosen; Mr. David Scribner; Unigraphic Corp.; Mr. Benny Andrews; Jeanne Paris; Mr. & Mrs. Joseph Strauss.
Awards: Westchester Art Society; Mitchell College, Conn.; Brooklyn Museum; Armonk Library Show Award; Bedford Hills Library Show Award.
Sources: Boston Museum of Fine Arts. *Afro-American Artists: New York/Boston*, 1970; Nordness Galleries. *12 Afro-American Artists*,

1969; Mount Holyoke College. *Ten Afro-American Artists*, 1969; Ghent, Henri. "The Community Art Gallery," *Art Gallery*, April 1970; Paris, Jean. "Black Art Experience in Art," *Long Island Press*, Jamaica, NY, June 14, 1970; Ruder & Finn Fine Arts. *Contemporary Black Artists*; Brooklyn College. *Afro-American Artists: Since 1950*, 1969; Walker, Roslyn. *A Resource Guide to the Visual Arts of Afro-Americans*, South Bend, Ind., 1971.

THOMPSON, W.O.

Painter.
Works: *Summer Hues: A Bit of New York from the Palisades; Floral Melodie; Roses; Speeding Up the Big Lifeboat; Easy Mark & Mr. Mark; Pencil Impressions; Dandelions in Yellow.*
Sources: *1st Annual Exhibit of Books, Manuscripts, Paintings, Sculptures, etc. by the Negro Library Assn. at Carlton Ave. YMCA*, 1918; Roucek & Kiernan. *The Negro Impact on Western Civilization*; Porter. *Modern Negro Art*; Harley, Ralph, Jr. "Checklist of Afro-Amer. Art & Artists," *The Serif*, Dec. 1970; Porter. "Negro Artists Gain Recognition After Long Battle," *Pittsburgh Courier*, July 29, 1950.

THOMPSON, WILLIAM

Painter.
Works: *Portrait of Bishop Loguen.*
Sources: "Afro-Amer. Artists 1800-1950," *Ebony*, Vol. 23, pp. 116-22.

THOMPSON, WILSON E.

Printmaker. Born in Birmingham, Alabama. Studied at Wayne State University; University of Michigan.
Works: *Landscape* (silkscreen).
Sources: Flint (Mich.) Community Schools. *Black Reflections.*

THORNE, CARLTON

Exhibited: Tanner Art League, 1922.
Sources: Harley, Ralph, Jr. "Checklist of Afro-Amer. Art & Artists," *The Serif*, Dec. 1970.

THORNELL, ROBERT

Painter.
Works: *Boy #1* (pen & ink); *Family* (watercolor); Untitled pastel; *Three Figures* (oil).
Exhibited: Boston Public Library, 1973.
Sources: Boston Negro Artists Assn. *10th Anniversary Exhibition*, Boston Public Library, 1973; Boston Negro Artists Assn. *The Black Artist in America: A Negro History Month Exhibition*, Boston Public Library, 1973.

THORPE, CARLTON

Painter.
Works: *Old Shacks* (watercolor).
Exhibited: Atlanta Univ., 1942; Tanner Art League, 1944; NY Public Library, 1921.

Sources: Atlanta Univ. Catalog, 1942; Harley, Ralph, Jr. "Checklist of Afro-Amer. Art & Artists," *The Serif*, Dec. 1970.

THORWALD

Sources: DuSable Museum of African-Amer. History. *Contemporary Black Artists*, Calendar, 1970.

THRASH, DOX

Painter, printmaker, co-inventor of carborundum print-process. Born in 1893 in Griffin, Georgia. Studied art through correspondence school until 1909. After the war, he studied at the Art Institute of Chicago (1919-22) under Seyffert, Naughton, and Poole. Also studied black and white media under Earl Horter of Graphic Sketch Club, Philadelphia. Worked on Pennsylvania Federal Art Project (1939-40).

Works: *Achievement; Life; Mary Lou; Monday Morning Wash; Scare Crow; Sunday Morning; Parsket Dredge; Life; Octoroon; Boats at Night; Saturday Night; Rugged Homes; Cabin Days; Coal Yard; Glory Be; Big Deal; Ebony Joe; Abstraction; Marylou; Charlot; Second Thought; Morning; Harmonica Blues; Deacon's Well; Languid Garil; Repose; Demolition; Old Barns; Surface Mining.*

Exhibited: Graphic Sketch Club, 1933, 1934, 1935; Federal Art Project Exhibit, Corcoran Gallery, 1935; Carnegie Institute, 1937, 1938; Pa. Academy of Fine Arts, 1934, 1935, 1938, 1939; NY World's Fair, 1939, 1940; Amer. Negro Exposition, 1940; Atlanta Univ., 1942; Phila. Civic Center Museum; Newark Museum, 1971; Baltimore Museum, 1939; James A. Porter Gallery, 1970; South Side Community Art Center, Chicago, 1941.

Collections: Nat'l Archives.

Sources: Locke. *Negro in Art*; Dover. *American Negro Art*; Indiana Univ. *Fine Arts & the Black American*; Afro-Amer. Slide Depository, Catalog; The Newark Museum. *Black Artists: Two Generations*; Phila. Civic Center. *Afro-American Artists 1800-1969*; DuSable Museum of African-Amer. History. *Contemporary Black Artists*, Calendar, 1970; South Side Community Art Center. *National Negro Art Exhibition*, Chicago, 1941; "Originator Describes New Copper Etching Process at Howard University," *Evening Star*, Washington, DC, Jan. 31, 1942; Locke, Alain. "Advance on the Art Front," *Opportunity*, May 1939; Hood, Richard. "Carborundum Tint, a New Printmakers Process," *Magazine of Art*, Nov. 1938, p. 643; "Art of the Month," *Arts in Philadelphia*, March 1939, p. 13; "Printers Hail WPA Artists Carborundum," *Chicago Defender*, Dec. 28, 1940; "Local Artist to Feature His New Print Technique," *Philadelphia Art Alliance Bulletin*, May 1944; Harley, Ralph, Jr. "A Checklist of Afro-Amer. Art and Artists," *The Serif*, Dec. 1970; Tanner Art Galleries. *Art of the American Negro*, Catalog, 1940; Harmon Foundation. *Non-Jury Exhibit of Works of Negro Artists*, 1933; Howard Univ. *James A. Porter Gallery of African-American Art*, 1970; Pierre-Noel, Lois Jones. "American Negro Art in Progress," *Negro History Bulletin*, Oct. 1967; Locke, Alain. "Chicago's New Southside Art Center," *Amer. Mag. of Art*, Aug. 1941; J.W.L. "Negro in Art," *Art News*, Dec. 19, 1941, p. 24; Kiah, Virginia. "Black Artists," *Savannah Magazine*, April 1972, p. 14; Porter, James. "Negro Artists Gain Recognition After Long Battle," *Pittsburgh Courier*, July 29, 1950; Walker, Roslyn. *A Resource Guide to the Visual Arts of Afro-Americans*, South Bend, Ind., 1971.

THREADGILL, ROBERT

Painter. Born in Salisbury, North Carolina, 1930. Studied at Pratt Institute (BFA).

Works: *Mister Davis; Tom's Landing; Lovers; Charlie Jones; Marilyn; Sunny; Jimmy's Death; The Chess Player; The Musician; Lee-Lee; Ike's Corner; The Messiah; Monday Morning; Nan II; The Miners; Sylvester* (oil).

Exhibited: Acts of Art Gallery, NYC, 1972 (1-man), 1973 (1-man); Raymond Duncan Gallery, Paris, 1966; Lincoln Institute, 1967 (1-man); Ligoa Duncan Gallery, NY, 1965.

Collections: Nat'l Archives; Los Angeles Museum; Acts of Art Gallery, NYC.

Awards: Ligoa Duncan Acadamea Foundation Award, 1965.

Represented by: Acts of Art Gallery, 15 Charles St., NYC.

Sources: Afro-Amer. Slide Depository, Catalog; Information from artist; Acts of Art Gallery. *Threadgill: An Exhibition of Paintings & Drawings by Bob Threadgill*, 1973.

THURSTON, NEPTUNE

Painter, graphic artist. Slave who in his master's copper shop drew likenesses on the head of casks. Gilbert Stuart saw his work & remarked that if he had an instructor he would make quite a celebrated artist.

Sources: Rogers. *Africa's Gift to America: The Afro-American in the Making and Saving of the United States*; Porter, James A. "Versatile Interests of the Early Negro Artist," *Art in America*, Jan. 1936, p. 19.

TIBERINO, ELLEN POWELL

Painter.

Works: *Another Study of Poucne; Yvonne and Stephani; Another Study of Uncle Buddy & The Kids; Portrait of the Artist.*

Exhibited: Phila. Civic Center Museum; State Armory, Wilmington, Del., 1971.

Sources: Phila. Civic Center. *Afro-American*

Artists 1800-1969; Aesthetic Dynamics. *Afro-American Images*, 1971, Catalog.

TILLMAN, D. NORMAN

Commercial artist. Born in Pennsylvania in 1899. Studied at the Pennsylvania Academy of Fine Arts; and under private instruction.
Works: *Ruby; Still Life; The Green Smock; Mother Klivans; Dr. William H. Hudnut; Mrs. Henry Butler; The Sphinx-A Character Study; Life Study of George L. Johnson, Tenor; Character Study; An Artist's Niece.*
Exhibited: Cleveland YMCA, 1934; Fine Arts Building, Cleveland, 1935 (1-man); Harmon Foundation, 1928-31; Amer. Negro Exposition, Chicago, 1940; Smithsonian Institution, 1929; Interracial Committee Exhibition, 1933.
Member: Mahoning Society of Painters, Youngstown.
Sources: Harley, Ralph, Jr. "Checklist of Afro-Amer. Art & Artists," *The Serif*, Dec. 1970; Indiana Univ. *Fine Arts & the Black American*; Harmon Foundation. *Exhibition of Productions by Negro Artists*; Harmon Foundation. *Negro Artists*, 1935; Harmon Foundation. *Exhibit of Fine Arts*, 1930; Tanner Art Galleries. *Art of the American Negro*, 1940; DuSable Museum of African-Amer. History. *Contemporary Black Artists*, 1970, calendar; Smithsonian Institution. *Painting & Sculpture by American Negro Artists*, 1929; Walker, Roslyn. *A Resource Guide to the Visual Arts of Afro-Americans*, South Bend, Ind., 1971.

TINSLEY, DALLAS B.

Born in Louisville, Kentucky in 1941. Studied at Grambling College in Louisiana; under Gregory Ridley and Harper Phillips.
Collections: Mr. Fred Bond; Mr. Alton Greenwade; Ms. Joy Ella Bolware; Mr. Raymond Kelley; Mr. Randolph Tinsley; Ms. Gladys Brewster.
Sources: "Afro-Amer. Issue," *Art Gallery*, April 1970.

TOMPKINS, EVELYN

Born in Georgia in 1882. Studied at YWCA Art School; Fawcett Art School, Newark, New Jersey.
Works: *Bellows.*
Exhibited: Harmon Foundation, 1928, 1933, 1935; Exposition of Women's Arts and Industries, Brooklyn YWCA; Harlem Art Committee, 137th St. Branch, YWCA, 1935; NJ State Museum, 1935.
Sources: Harley, Ralph, Jr. "Checklist of Afro-Amer. Art & Artists," *The Serif*, Dec. 1970; Harmon Foundation. *Exhibition of Productions by Negro Artists*, 1928; Harmon Foundation. *Non-Jury Exhibit of Works of Negro Artists*, 1933; Harmon Foundation. *Negro Artists*, 1935; Indiana Univ. *Fine Arts & the Black*

American; DuSable Museum of African-Amer. History. *Contemporary Black Artists*, 1970, calendar; Walker, Roslyn. *A Resource Guide to the Visual Arts of Afro-Americans*, South Bend, Ind., 1971.

TOODLES, JOHN E.

Born in Washington, DC in 1893. No formal art education.
Works: *The Sea; Washers in the Sea; The Leaning Tower.*
Exhibited: Harmon Foundation, 1929-30, 1933; YMCA Exhibit, Indianapolis; YMCA Exhibit, New Orleans; Smithsonian Institution, 1929.
Sources: Harley, Ralph, Jr. "Checklist of Afro-Amer. Art & Artists," *The Serif*, Dec. 1970; Smithsonian Institution. *Painting & Sculpture by American Negro Artists*, 1929; Indiana Univ. *Fine Arts & the Black American*; Harmon Foundation. *Exhibition of Productions by Negro Artists*, 1928; Harmon Foundation. *Non-Jury Exhibit of Works of Negro Artists*, 1933; Harmon Foundation. *Exhibit of Fine Arts*, 1930; DuSable Museum of African-Amer. History. *Contemporary Black Artists*, 1970, calendar; Walker, Roslyn. *A Resource Guide to the Visual Arts of Afro-Americans*, South Bend, Ind., 1971.

TOONE, LLOYD

Mixed media. Born in Chase City, Virginia in 1940. Studied at Hampton Institute (BS, Art Education); City College of New York (MFA); Manhattan College (MA, Special Education, 1972).
Works: *Snow Job; Struggle for Identity; Take the Cash and Let the Credit Go; Dark Images I; Life; The Natural Look; High, The Woman's Got Sole.*
Exhibited: Ruder & Finn Fine Arts, NY, 1969; Boston Museum of Fine Arts, 1970; Phila. Civic Center Museum; Firehouse Gallery, Nassau Community College, Garden City, NY, 1969; C.W. Post College, Brookville, NY, 1969; Rhode Island School of Design, Providence, 1969; Internat'l House, NY, 1970-1; River View Galleries, NY, 1971; Acts of Art Gallery, NY, 1971; Pascacs Valley Chapter of Hadassah, Westwood, NJ; Great Neck Library, Great Neck, NY, 1972; Dutchess Community College, NY, 1972.
Collections: C.W. Post College; New Hampshire College.
Awards: C.W. Post College Purchase Award.
Represented by: Acts of Art Gallery, 15 Charles St., NYC.
Sources: UCLA Art Galleries. *The Negro in American Art*; Boston Museum of Fine Arts. *Afro-Amer. Artists: NY & Boston*, 1970; Phila. Civic Center. *Afro-Amer. Artists 1800-1969*; Information from artist; Rhoda Goldstein. *Life & Culture of Black People in the USA*; *50*

Contemporary Black Artists, catalog; Acts of Art Gallery. *Rebuttal to the Whitney Museum Exhibit*, 1971; *Art News*, April 1972; "Afro-Amer. Issue," *Art Gallery*, April 1972; *New York Times*, Sunday, April 23, 1972; Ruder & Finn Fine Arts. *Contemporary Black Artists*, NY, 1969; Great Neck Library. *Show of Contemporary Afro-American Artists*, 1972.

TOOREY, LOUISE B.
Collections: NY Public Library-Schomburg Art Collection.
Sources: Schatz, Walter. *Directory of Afro-American Resources*, 1970.

TORRES, JOHN, JR.
Sculptor. Born in New York City, 1939. Studied at Maryland State College (1956-7); Michigan State University (1958-9); New School for Social Research (1959-62); Brooklyn Museum School (1963-4); Art Students League of New York (1959-69); Rhode Island School of Design (BFA, 1972); studios of Arnold Prince, Seymour Lipton and William Zorach; studied under John Hovannes.
Works: *Kate*, 1970 (alabaster); *Magic Stones & Totem Pole; The Monument; Horse Sketch.*
Exhibited: Whitney Museum, 1971; Rhode Island School of Design; La Casa de la Cultura, Toluca, Mexico.
Collections: Mr. & Mrs. J. Weinberg.
Awards: Ford Foundation Grant for Vermont Summer; Edward MacDowell Colony Fellowships, 1964-7, 1971; Ford Foundation Scholarship; Scholarships for Drawing, New School for Social Research; Nora Kubic Grant for Independent Studio Work; Purchase Prize, Nat'l Assn. of the Arts; Pearlson-Sturgis Grant, studio work; Lindsay Trust Grant, Black Art Student Recruitment; *Boston Globe* Grant; Wyman Foundation Grant; Nat'l Endowment for the Arts Grant, "Discover Graphics"; Artist in the Schools Grant for Barrow, Alaska; Ford/AIA Grant to Educate Architects.
Member: Art Students League; Slamagundi Club of NY.
Sources: Information from the artist; Torres, John. *Magic Stones & Totem Poles*, 1967; "Afro-American Issue," *Art Gallery*, April 1968; Indiana Univ. *Fine Arts & the Black American*; Doty. *Contemporary Black Artists in America*; DuSable Museum of African-Amer. History. *Contemporary Black Artists*, 1970, calendar; Fax, Elton C. *Seventeen Black Artists*; Berkman, Florence. "Some Black Artists Irate Over Whitney Exhibit," *Times*, Hartford, Conn., April 25, 1971; *Encyclopedia of Black Cultural Contributions*; *Sepia Magazine*, July 1968; *New York Post*, March 11, 1968; *Life*, July 1963; Myers, Carol. *Black Power in the Arts*, Flint, Mich., 1970; Walker, Roslyn.

A Resource Guide to the Visual Arts of Afro-Americans, South Bend, Ind., 1971.

TOWNS, ELAINE
Painter. Born in Los Angeles in 1937. Studied at University of California, Los Angeles (BA, 1960; MS, 1962).
Works: *Leaping Figures.*
Exhibited: Los Angeles County Museum, 1960; Safety Savings & Loan Assn., 1961; Masters Exhibit, Univ. of Cal., 1962; James Phelan Traveling Exhibit, 1963; Exposicion de Artistas Becarios Fulbright, Madrid, 1964; Exhibition of Prints by Amer. Negro Artists sponsored by the Institute of Soviet-Amer. Relations in the Soviet Union, 1966-7; Los Angeles Schools Artmobile Exhibit, 1968-9; Long Beach Museum of Fine Arts, 1961; Univ. of Ga., 1963; Brockman Gallery, 1970.
Awards: Fulbright Grant to Spain, 1963-4.
Sources: Lewis/Waddy. *Black Artists on Art*, Vol. 1; Brockman Gallery. *Elaine Towns*, catalog, May 1972; Walker, Roslyn. *A Resource Guide to the Visual Arts of Afro-Americans*, South Bend, Ind., 1971.

TOWNSEND, THURMOND
Sources: Porter. *Modern Negro Art*; Harley, Ralph, Jr. "Checklist of Afro-Amer. Art & Artists," *The Serif*, Dec. 1970.

TRASK, P.
Sources: Harley, Ralph, Jr. "Checklist of Afro-Amer. Art & Artists," *The Serif*, Dec. 1970.

TRAVIS, WILLIAM
Sculptor.
Works: *None; Untitled.*
Exhibited: State Armory, Wilmington, Del., 1971.
Sources: Aesthetic Dynamics. *Afro-American Images*, 1971, Catalog.

TRAYLOR, BILL
Painter. Ex-slave who started painting at 87. His work resembled primitive art in early caves.
Sources: Rankin, Allen. "The Lost 10,000 Years," *Colliers*, June 22, 1946, p. 67.

TROY, ADRIAN
Painter, illustrator. Born in Hull, England in 1901.
Exhibited: Phillips Memorial Gallery, Washington, DC; Internat'l Watercolor Annual, Art Institute of Chicago, 1938; World's Fair, NY, 1939; Fort Huachuca, Ariz., 1943.
Member: Amer. Artists Congress; Chicago Society of Artists.
Collections: Evansville State Hospital; Univ. of Ill.; Chicago Normal College.
Sources: Mallett. *Index of Artists*; *Who's Who in American Art*, 1940-1; *Magazine of Art*,

Sept. 1938; Fort Huachuca, Ariz. *Exhibit of Works of 37 Negro Artists*, 1943.

TRUESDAL, BEVERLY J.
Studied at Bennett College.
Works: *A & T Power Plant.*
Exhibited: Sun Times/Daily News Gallery, Chicago, 1970.
Sources: United Negro College Fund. *Art 1970*, Chicago, 1970.

TUCKER, DAVID B.
Painter. Worked in Louisville, Kentucky.
Works: *Jacob's Dream; The Land of Milk and Honey.*
Exhibited: Atlanta Univ., 1944.
Sources: Atlanta Univ. catalog, 1944; Harley, Ralph, Jr. "Checklist of Afro-Amer. Art & Artists," *The Serif*, Dec. 1970.

TUCKER, JEROME
Photographer.
Exhibited: Addison Gallery, 1971.
Sources: James Van DerZee Institute. *The Black Photographer (1908-1970): A Survey.*

TUCKER, WILLIE
Painter.
Works: *Brown & Orange* (acrylic).
Collections: Johnson Pub. Co.
Sources: Johnson Pub. Co. *The JPC Art Collection*, Pamphlet.

TULL, CHARLENE
Painter, draftsman. Born 1945 in Chicago, Illinois. Studied at University of Bridgeport; University of Paris; under John Biggers and James Porter.
Works: Untitled pencil drawing; *Heads of Flies.*
Collections: Mr. & Mrs. Rouzeberry; Miss Phyllis Brown; Mr. & Mrs. Charles Osler.
Sources: Lewis/Waddy. *Black Artists on Art*, Vol. 2.

TUNSTALL, RUTH NEAL
Painter, printmaker, educator. Born in Denver, Colorado, January 23, 1945. Studied at the Children's Art Classes, Detroit Museum of Art; The Gallery, Detroit; Tarkio College, Missouri; Delta College, Bay City, Michigan; Saginaw (Michigan) Valley College; Detroit Society of Arts and Crafts Art School; University of Colorado, Extension Division, Denver; University of Buffalo (BA); University of Dallas (MA). Instructor at the Davis Art Center, Davis, California.
Works: *When It Rains It Pours*, 1970; *White America*, 1970; *Drawing #4*, 1969; *Sunrise/Moon-Sun*, 1970; *Moon-Sun*, 1970; *Black America*, 1970; *Suns of the World*, 1970; *Sun of the Cosmos*, 1970; *Naturalscape*, 1970; *Population/Birth Control and Ecology*, 1970;

Sun/in/Trees, 1970; *Winter*, 1970; *Self Portrait*, 1970; *Orange Shun/Sun*, 1970.
Exhibited: 1st Methodist Church, Dallas, 1967 (1-man), 1969; Univ. of Dallas, 1969, 1970; Prints & Drawings, Univ. of Buffalo, NY, 1965; Prints 66, Detroit Society of Arts & Crafts, 1966; Studio 23, Bay City, Mich., 1966, 1967; Delta College, Bay City, Mich., 1966; Annual Regional Art Exhibition, Univ. of Mich., Ann Arbor, 1967, 1968; Detroit Society of Arts & Crafts Art School, 1967; 5th Annual Area Spring Show, Saginaw (Mich.) Museum; Saginaw Area Artists' Exhibition, Saginaw (Mich.) Museum, 1968; Mt. Holyoke College, 1968; NAACP Life Membership Committee, Bay City, Mich., 1968 (3-man); Dan Danciger Jewish Community Center, Fort Worth, Texas, 1969; Senior Show, Univ. of Dallas, 1969; Atlanta Univ., 1970; Women's Club of Dallas, 1971.
Collections: Mr. & Mrs. Charles Alberg, Dallas; Mr. Harry Hawkins, Denver, Colo.; Mr. & Mrs. Charles DuBus, Dallas; Mr. & Mrs. Ronald Branch, Dallas; Mrs. Duncan C. Grant, Davis, Cal.; Dr. Lucille H. Tunstall, Dallas.
Awards: 1st prize, watercolor, Saginaw (Mich.) Museum, 1966, 1968; 1st prize, Graphic Exhibit, Studio 23, Bay City, Mich., 1965-7; Best-in-show, Area Exhibit, Studio 23, Bay City, Mich., 1967; Award in graphics, Atlanta Univ., 1970; Graduate Art Scholarship, Univ. of Dallas, 1969-70; Art Travel Scholarship to Europe, Univ. of Dallas, 1970.
Sources: Musée Rath. *8 Artistes Afro-Americains.*

TURNER, CLYDE A.
Painter. Worked in Philadelphia.
Works: *Interior; Self Portrait.*
Exhibited: Atlanta Univ., 1944.
Sources: Atlanta Univ. catalog, 1944.

TURNER, MRS. CLYDE
Graphic artist. Worked in Philadelphia.
Works: *Three Boys.*
Exhibited: Atlanta Univ., 1944.
Sources: Atlanta Univ. catalog, 1944.

TURNER, NOLAND
Studied at Lemoyne-Owen College.
Exhibited: Sun Times/Daily News Gallery, Chicago, 1970.
Sources: United Negro College Fund. *Art 1970*, Chicago, 1970.

TURNER, ROLAND
Commercial artist. Born 1931.
Works: *Street Corner.*
Member: Contemporary Arts Guild, NY.
Sources: Dover. *American Negro Art*; Indiana Univ. *Fine Arts & the Black American*; Har-

ley, Ralph, Jr. "Checklist of Afro-Amer. Art & Artists," *The Serif*, Dec. 1970; Walker, Roslyn. *A Resource Guide to the Visual Arts of Afro-Americans*, South Bend, Ind., 1971.

TWIGGS, LEO

Painter. Born in St. Stephen, South Carolina in 1934. Studied at Claflin College; New York University; Art Institute of Chicago; University of Georgia. Professor of Art at South Carolina State College.

Works: *Martyrs #1; Martyrs #2; Martyrs #3; Blue Wall; Down Home Landscape; Alone; Commemoration #2; Commemoration #3; Henry Lee's World; Alma Mater; In the Evening; The Swing; Veteran; First Child; Wild Flowers; Homage to Brother Andrew.*

Exhibited: Univ. of Cincinnati School of Art & Design; Nat'l. Conference of Artists, Atlanta; Lincoln Univ., Mo.; Columbia Museum of Art, Columbia, SC; Mint Museum, Charlotte, NC; Smith-Mason Gallery, Washington, DC, 1971; Univ. of Ga., Athens; Indiana Univ.

Collections: Spring Mills Inc., Lancaster, SC; Wachovia Bank & Trust of NC; Atlanta Univ.; Afro-Amer. Slide Depository; Johnson Pub. Co.; Amer. Craftsmen Council.

Sources: Lewis/Waddy. *Black Artists on Art*, Vol. 2; Afro-Amer. Slide Depository, 1971-2, catalog; Smith-Mason Gallery. *National Exhibition Black Artists 1971*, Washington, DC; *Journal of the Nat'l Conference of Artists*, Winter 1971; Johnson Pub. Co. *The JPC Art Collection*, pamphlet; Harley, Ralph, Jr. "Checklist of Afro-Amer. Art & Artists," *The Serif*, Dec. 1970; *Artists USA, 1972-1973*, Feasterville, Pa., 1972; Atkinson, J. Edward. *Black Dimensions in Contemporary American Art*, NY, 1971.

TYLER, ALFRED J.

Painter. Born in Chicago in 1933. Studied at Art Institute of Chicago; La Escuela Nacional de Artes Plasticas, Mexico City. Artist for S.M. Edison Chemical Company.

Works: *Dioula Woman of Trechville; Mother and Child.*

Exhibited: Museum of Science & Industry, Chicago; La Petite Gallery, Evanston, Ill. (1-man); Malcolm X Community College (1-man); South Side Community Art Center's Traveling Show; Lincoln Congregational Church (1-man); Oak Park (Ill.) Library.

Collections: Univ. of Ill. Black Studies Program; Kendal College, Evanston, Ill.; State of Ill. Centennial Collection, Springfield; DuSable Museum of African-Amer. History, Chicago; Johnson Pub. Co., Chicago; Sexton Elementary School.

Awards: Leaders Cleaners Art Contest Prize.

Sources: Lewis/Waddy. *Black Artists on Art*, Vol. 2; DuSable Museum of African-Amer.

History. *Contemporary Black Artists*, 1970, calendar; Johnson Pub. Co. *The JPC Art Collection*, pamphlet; "Afro-Amer. Issue," *Art Gallery*, April 1968, April 1970; Indiana Univ. *Fine Arts & the Black American*; Myers, Carol. *Black Power in the Arts*, Flint, Mich., 1970; Walker, Roslyn. *A Resource Guide to the Visual Arts of Afro-Americans*, South Bend, Ind., 1971.

TYLER, ANNA

Painter, printmaker. Born in 1933 in Chicago, Illinois. Studied at Art Institute of Chicago; La Esmeralda, Mexico City.

Works: *Blackness of Winter*; untitled monoprint; *Tumbleweed*; *Landscape* (monoprint).

Exhibited: Nat'l. College of Education, Evanston, Ill. (1-man); Museum of Science & Industry, Chicago; Afam Studio-Gallery; Oak Park Public Library.

Collections: State of Ill.; Centennial Collection, Springfield; DuSable Museum of African-Amer. History, Chicago; Johnson Pub. Co., Chicago.

Sources: Lewis/Waddy. *Black Artists on Art*, Vol. 2; DuSable Museum of African-Amer. History. *Contemporary Black Artists*, 1970; Johnson Pub. Co. *The JPC Art Collection*, pamphlet; Stone, Dennis. "Negro Artists from Illinois at the Oak Park Public Library," *Art Scene*, n.d.

TYLER, WALTER

Exhibited: Wharton House, Phila., 1942.

Sources: Harley, Ralph, Jr. "Checklist of Afro-Amer. Art & Artists," *The Serif*, Dec. 1970.

TYNER, EILEEN

Sources: DuSable Museum of African-Amer. History. *Contemporary Black Artists*, 1970, Calendar.

TYNER, OSMAN

Born in Philadelphia in 1940. Self-taught.

Works: *Black Woman's Head; Survival.*

Exhibited: Studio Museum in Harlem, 1969.

Sources: Studio Museum in Harlem. *Harlem Artists 69.*

UPSHUR, BERNARD

Woodcutter. Born 1936. Studied at Maryland State College; Hunter College, New York; New York University; Fordham University; South East Asia Program, India.

Works: *Africa Reborn; Brooklyn Bridge.*

Exhibitions: Univ. of Md., Eastern Shore (1-man).

Collections: Mr. Bill Fagan, Nat'l Humanities Foundation; Dr. J. T. Williams, Princess Anne, Md.

Sources: Lewis/Waddy. *Black Artists on Art*, Vol. 2.

URQUHART, JOHN

Sources: Harley, Ralph, Jr. "Checklist of Afro-Amer. Art & Artists," *The Serif*, Dec. 1970.

VAGENAS, NICHOLAS

Painter. Born in Manchester, New Hampshire. Self-taught.
Works: *A Machinist; Black Power.*
Exhibited: Studio Museum in Harlem, 1969.
Sources: Studio Museum in Harlem. *Harlem Artists 69.*

VALENTINE, JEAN

Painter.
Works: *Waiting; Relating.*
Exhibited: Smith-Mason Gallery, 1971.
Sources: Smith-Mason Gallery. *National Exhibition of Black Artists*, 1971.

VAN, LUTHER

Painter. Born in Savannah, Georgia in 1937. Studied at the High School of Music and Art; New School for Social Research; Art Students League.
Works: *Agony in the Ballroom; Growing Up in Urantia with One Eye On the Light; Mind Over Matter.*
Exhibited: Boston Museum of Fine Arts, 1970.
Sources: Boston Museum of Fine Arts. *Afro-American Artists: NY & Boston*, 1970; Bowling, Frank. "The Rupture," *Arts*, Summer 1970.

VANCE, FLORESTEE

Painter. Born 1940 in Ferriday, Louisiana. Studied at Chicago Teachers College; Illinois Institute of Technology; University of Ghana; University of Science and Technology, Ghana.
Works: *Indian Headdress.*
Exhibitions: Club Gallery, 1970; Dixie Square Art Fair, 1970; Englewood Art Fair, 1970; Afam Art Gallery, 1970.
Sources: Lewis/Waddy. *Black Artists on Art*, Vol. 2.

VAN DER MARCK, JAN

Sources: "Black Art: What is It?," *Art Gallery*, April 1970; Harley, Ralph, Jr. "Checklist of Afro-Amer. Art & Artists," *The Serif*, Dec. 1970.

VAUGHAN, RAZRE

Sources: DuSable Museum of African-Amer. History. *Contemporary Black Artists*, 1970, Calendar.

VAUGHAN, ROYCE

Painter, photographer, mixed media, filmmaker, sculptor, graphic artist. Born in Cleveland, Ohio in 1930. Studied at Princeton University (BA, Art History); San Francisco State College (BA, Art, 1967). Project Director of ABLE (The Arts and Business Experiences), San Francisco State College.
Works: *Glad Rags; Charlie; The Boys; Backyard Valley; Blue Haze; Keep America Clean; Color Round; The Nebular Hypothesis; Gesture Study; The Critic; My Favorite Nude; Autumn Muscle; Insist on Name Brands; Plastic Dashboard Jesus; Something Bad Wrong; A Rose is a Rose; Stop When Swinging; Favored Lady; Suppose God's Black?; Malcolm Spoke; Triptych for San Francisco Black Historical Society; Negro Workers and Builders.*
Exhibited: Art Assoc., 1957; San Francisco Black Historical Society, 1967; San Francisco State College, 1967; Oakland Art Museum, 1968.
Collections: Mr. Donald Brundage; Oakland Museum; San Francisco Art Commission; C.J. Wellington, MD; Jack D. Noyes, MD; Black Historical & Cultural Society.
Awards: Purchase Award, Oakland Art Museum; Purchase Award, San Francisco Art Museum; Danforth Fellowship to Univ. of Cal., 1958; Gold Seal, San Francisco Art Institute; 4 Year Scholarship, Princeton Univ.; Ford Foundation Grant, 1970.
Sources: Oakland Art Museum. *New Perspectives in Black Art;* Indiana Univ. *Fine Arts & the Black American;* Lewis/Waddy. *Black Artists on Art*, Vol. 1; Afro-Amer. Slide Depository, 1971-2, catalog; Harley, Ralph, Jr. "Checklist of Afro-Amer. Art & Artists," *The Serif*, Dec. 1970; Atkinson, J. Edward. *Black Dimensions in Contemporary American Art*, 1971; Information from artist; Oakland Museum Archives.

VAUGHN, ALMA

Painter. Born in Williamsburg, Virginia in 1922. Studied at Spelman College, Atlanta, under Hale Woodruff.
Works: *Spring Landscape; Rocks, Trees; Landscape.*
Exhibited: Institute of Modern Art, Boston, 1943; Atlanta Univ., 1943; Smith College, 1943.
Sources: DuSable Museum of African-Amer. History. *Contemporary Black Artists*, 1970, calendar; Atlanta Univ. *Annual for Negro Artists*, 1943; Harley, Ralph, Jr. "Checklist of Afro-Amer. Art & Artists," *The Serif*, Dec. 1970.

VAUGHN, LOUIS OLIVER

Born in New York in 1910. Studied at the National Academy of Design.
Works: *Portrait of an Art Student; Still Life.*
Exhibited: Harmon Foundation, 1933; Assoc. Art Students, 1933; 135th St. Branch, NY Public Library, 1933; YMCA, 1934; Harmon-College Traveling Exhibition, 1934-5; Harlem Art Committee, 137th St. Branch YWCA, 1935.
Sources: Harley, Ralph, Jr. "Checklist of

Afro-Amer. Art & Artists," *The Serif,* Dec. 1970; Harmon Foundation. *Exhibition of Productions by Negro Artists;* Harmon Foundation. *Non-Jury Exhibit of Works of Negro Artists;* Harmon Foundation. *Negro Artists,* 1935; Indiana Univ. *Fine Arts & the Black American;* DuSable Museum of African-Amer. History. *Contemporary Black Artists,* 1970, Calendar; Walker, Roslyn. *A Resource Guide to the Visual Arts of Afro-Americans,* South Bend, Ind., 1971.

VAVAK, JOSEPH
Born in Vienna, Austria, May 4, 1899. Studied at Art Institute of Chicago; Art Students League, New York; and L'hote Studio.
Works: *At Work.*
Exhibited: Fort Huachuca, Ariz., 1943; Chicago Society of Artists, 1935.
Awards: Gold Medal, Chicago Society of Artists, 1935.
Sources: *Who's Who in American Art,* 1940-1; Fort Huachuca. *Exhibition of Works of 37 Negro Artists,* Ariz., 1943.

VENABLE, JAMES
Works: *Soul Musician.*
Sources: Boston Negro Artists' Assn. Calendar, 1973.

VICKERS, ROBERT
Painter.
Works: *Terminal Tower.*
Exhibited: James A. Porter Gallery of African-Amer. Art, 1970; Howard Univ., 1961.
Sources: Howard Univ. *James A Porter Gallery of African-American Art,* 1970; Harley, Ralph, Jr. "Checklist of Afro-Amer. Art & Artists," *The Serif,* Dec. 1970.

VICTORY, GEORGE M.
Painter. Born in Savannah, Georgia in 1878. Self-taught in art. Worked in Philadelphia.
Works: *Schuylkill River.*
Exhibited: Carlen Galleries, Phila.; Institute of Modern Art, Boston, 1943; Smith College, 1943.
Collections: Nat'l Archives.
Sources: Harley, Ralph, Jr. "Checklist of Afro-Amer. Art & Artists," *The Serif,* Dec. 1970; "Amer. Negro Artists Given Full Length Review in NY Show," *Art Digest,* Dec. 15, 1941; Afro-Amer. Slide Depository, 1971-2, catalog; DuSable Museum of African-Amer. History. *Contemporary Black Artists,* 1970, calendar.

VILLIS, CLINTON De
See: De Villis, Clinton.

WACASEY, WILLIAM
Studied at Art Institute in Chicago and Detroit.
Sources: Jackson, Dorothy. "The Black Ex-

perience in Graphic Design," *Print,* Nov./Dec. 1968.

WADDY, RUTH G.
Printer, printmaker, editor. Born in Lincoln, Nebraska, 1909. Studied at Los Angeles City College; Los Angeles County Otis Art Institute; University of Minnesota; Famous Artists Home Study Course. Founder of Art West Associated North; collected prints for *Prints by American Negro Artists;* co-editor of *Black Artists on Art.*
Works: *Matter of Opinion* (linocut); *Pastoral; Daisies; The Fence; The Key; Untitled; Baluba Boy,* 1964 (oil); *Untitled #1,* 1966 (oil); *Soccer in Tobabo,* 1970 (oil); *Two Sons,* 1970 (oil); *Carpenter Ants,* 1963 (linoleum print); *Pomegranates,* 1964 (linoleum print); *Cybernetics,* 1964; *Boss Lady,* 1965; *Titillated Society; Intermission,* 1966; *Self-portrait; Mother & Child #1,* 1967; *Mother & Child #2; The Fence,* 1968; *The Key; All the World's Their Stage; Untitled Series B; Yes I Know But I'm Still Here; The White Hat,* 1970; *The Exhorters.*
Exhibited: Rainbow Sign Gallery, Berkeley, 1972; Jimmy Crawford's Frame Shop, Los Angeles, 1964; Safety Savings & Loan Assn., Los Angeles, 1965; Internationale Buchkunst-Aussellung, Leipzig, 1965; Los Felis Jewish Community Center, Los Angeles, 1965; Jewish Women's Council House, Black Dialogue, 1968-9; AWAN Negro History Week, Los Angeles City Hall, 1963-9; Oakland Art Museum; Graphik aus Funt Kintinenten, Leipzig; Brand Library of Art & Music, Glendale, Cal.; Assoc. Students Lounge, UCLA Art Center, 1966; Friendship Houses in Moscow, Leningrad, Alma Ata, & Baku, USSR, 1966; Independence Square, Los Angeles, 1969 (1-woman).
Collections: Howard Univ.; Oakland Museum; Brand Library of Art & Music, Glendale, Cal.; Golden State Insurance Co., Los Angeles; Slide Collection, Metropolitan Museum.
Awards: Nat'l Assn. of College Women Award, Los Angeles, 1963; Nat'l Conference of Artists Certificate of Merit, 1968; Ruth Waddy Testimonial & Cash Award, 1972.
Member: Art West Assoc. North, Los Angeles; Nat'l Conference of Artists; Black Arts Council, Los Angeles.
Sources: *Los Angeles Times,* July 9, 1966; *Who's Who in the West,* 13th & 14th Editions; *International Biographical Dictionary,* 1973-4; "Afro-Amer. Issue," *Art Gallery,* April 1968, April 1970; Indiana Univ. *Fine Arts & the Black American;* Lewis/Waddy. *Black Artists on Art;* Roelof-Lanner, T.V., ed. *Prints by American Negro Artists;* Oakland Museum. *New Perspectives in Black Art,* 1968; Roucek/Kiernan. *The Negro Impact on Western Civilization;* DuSable Museum of African-

289

Amer. History. *Contemporary Black Artists,* 1970, Calendar; Harley, Ralph, Jr. "Checklist of Afro-Amer. Art & Artists," *Serif,* Dec. 1970; Information from artist; Myers, Carol L. *Black Power in the Arts,* Flint, Mich., 1970; Oakland Museum Archives; Walker, Roslyn. *A Resource Guide to the Visual Arts of Afro-Americans,* South Bend, Ind., 1971.

WADE, EUGENE

Sources: DuSable Museum of African-Amer. History. *Contemporary Black Artists,* 1970, Calendar.

WADE, JAMES MARCONI

Architect. Born in Philadelphia, June 15, 1908. Studied at the University of Pennsylvania. **Member:** Nat'l Technical Assn.; General Alumni Assn., Univ. of Pa.; Club T. Square. **Sources:** Furr, Arthur F. *History & Progress of Negroes in the US.*

WADE, JOHN

Mixed media, educator. Studied at Philadelphia College of Art; Temple University (MEd, MFA). Instructor of Art, Temple University. **Works:** *Black and White; Landscape 7; Metamorphosis; Metamorphosis #5; Ikon #2; Eclipse,* 1969-70 (mixed media); *Ikon #1,* 1970 (mixed media); *Diptych,* 1969 (mixed media); *Untitled,* 1970 (mixed media). **Exhibited:** Phila. Civic Center; State Armory, Wilmington, Del., 1971; Temple Univ.; Phila. Festival of Arts, 1967; Allens Lane Art Center; New England Regional Exhibition; Woodmere Gallery; Phila. Art Teachers Assn. **Collections:** Woodmere Gallery. **Awards:** Honorable mention, Phila. Festival of Arts, 1967; 1st prize, painting, Allens Lane Art Center; Silvermine Award, New England Regional Exhibition, 1970; Woodmere Gallery Purchase Prize. **Sources:** Phila Civic Center. *Afro-American Artists 1800-1969;* Aesthetic Dynamics. *Afro-American Images,* 1971, Catalog; Tyler School of Art. *Seven by Seven,* Temple Univ., 1970.

WAH, BERNARD

Painter. Born in Haiti, in 1939. Studied at the Centre de Ceramique, Port-Au-Prince, Haiti; Grande Chaumiere, Paris, France. **Works:** *African Night.* **Exhibited:** Calfou Art Centre, Haiti, 1964; Studio Museum in Harlem, 1969. **Sources:** Studio Museum in Harlem. *Harlem Artists 69.*

WAITHE, VINCENT

Born in Trinidad, West Indies. Studied at Bennette College, England; American Art School. **Sources:** NY NAACP. *A Most Memorable*

Showing of Creative Negro Art; NY NAACP. *Art Exhibition of Negro Expression Sponsored by Minars Furniture,* April 1964.

WALDEN, JENNELSIE

See: Holloway, M. Jennelsie Walden.

WALKER, ALEX

Graphic designer. Studied at Pratt Institute. **Sources:** Jackson, Dorothy. "The Black Experience in Graphic Design," *Print,* Nov./Dec. 1968.

WALKER, ANNIE

Painter. Born in Alabama in 1855. Died in 1929. Studied at the Academie Julien, Paris; Cooper Union for Advancement of Science and Art. **Works:** *Portrait of a Woman; La Parisienne; Une Petite Parisienne; The Turk.* **Exhibited:** Paris Salon, 1896; Howard Univ. 1937, 1950, 1952, 1967, 1970. **Collections:** Howard Univ. Gallery of Art. **Sources:** Howard Univ. *Ten Afro-Amer. Artists of the 19th Century;* Howard Univ. *Art of the American Negro,* catalog, 1937; Howard Univ. *James A. Porter Gallery of African-Amer. Art,* 1970; Howard Univ. *Exhibition of Graphic Arts & Drawings by Negro Artists,* 1950; Harley, Ralph, Jr. "Checklist of Afro-Amer. Art & Artists," *The Serif,* Dec. 1970; Myers, Carol. *Black Power in the Arts,* Flint, Mich., 1970.

WALKER, CRANSTON OLIVER

Works: *Suggestive Drag.* **Exhibited:** Phila. Civic Center Museum. **Sources:** Phila. Civic Center. *Afro-American Artists 1800-1969.*

WALKER, EARL

Painter. Born in Indianapolis, Indiana, 1911. Studied at the South Side Settlement House (1933-7). Worked in the Illinois Federal Art Project (1937-40). **Works:** *Cornerstone; Landscape; Street Scene #1; Street Scene #2; Reminiscing; Ten Below Zero; Snow Scene* (oil). **Exhibited:** Art Craft Guild, Chicago, 1937; Federal Project Gallery, 1938; Amer. Negro Exposition, 1940; Fort Huachuca, Ariz., 1943; Howard Univ., 1941; Library of Congress, 1940; South Side Community Art Center, 1941. **Sources:** Tanner Art Galleries. *Art of the American Negro,* 1940; Locke. *The Negro in Art;* Fort Huachuca. *Exhibition of the Work of 37 Negro Artists,* Ariz., 1943; Howard Univ. *Exhibition of Negro Artists of Chicago at Howard Univ. Gallery of Art,* 1941; Motley, Willard F. "Negro Art in Chicago," *Opportunity,* Jan. 1940; Porter. *Modern Negro Art;* Harley, Ralph, Jr. "Checklist of Afro-Amer.

Art & Artists," *Serif,* Dec. 1970; DuSable Museum of African-Amer. History. *Contemporary Black Artists,* 1970, Calendar; Locke, Alain. "Chicago's New Southside Art Center," *American Magazine of Art,* Aug. 1941, p. 373; South Side Community Art Center. *National Negro Art Exhibition,* 1941; South Side Community Art Center. *Opening Exhibition of Painting by Negro Artists,* Chicago, 1941.

WALKER, GEORGE

Painter. Studied at Howard University.
Works: *Back Yard With Clothes Line* (oil).
Exhibited: Howard Univ., 1937; Nat'l Gallery of Art, Washington.
Sources: Howard Univ. *Art of the American Negro,* 1937.

WALKER, GRAYSON

Exhibited: Harmon Foundation, 1936.
Sources: Harley, Ralph, Jr. "Checklist of Afro-Amer. Art & Artists," *The Serif,* Dec. 1970.

WALKER, J. S.

Painter.
Works: *Kitchen Interior.*
Exhibited: Atlanta Univ., 1943.
Sources: Atlanta Univ. Catalog, 1943.

WALKER, LAWRENCE (LARRY)

Painter, educator. Born in Franklin, Georgia, October 22, 1935. Studied at Wayne State University (BS, MA). Associate Professor of Art, University of the Pacific, Stockton, California.
Works: *Children of Society* (charcoal); *Last Rites of the American Sex Here; But Related to What?; My Thoughts, My Ideas; Children of Society 14; Children of Society 17; Growth I; Microscape I; Untitled; In Search of the Promised Land; Combat Rhythms; Help Me Lord; Probe I; Struggle; Woman First Class; Viscid Plasticity; On the Threshold of the Promised Land; Night Sleeping into the Landscape; Black Man on the Threshold of Freedom,* 1969 (acrylic); *Children of Society #9,* 1968 (charcoal).
Exhibited: Smith-Mason Gallery, 1971; Univ. of the Pacific; Pioneer Museum; Haggin Galleries; Detroit Board of Education; Merced Art Assn.; Mich. Artists Annual; Smithsonian Institution; Amer. Watercolor Society Annuals; Nat'l Academy Gallery; Springfield Art Museum, Mo.; Wichita (Kan.) Centennial Nat'l Art Exhibit; Artists Contemporary Gallery, 1971; Wayne State Univ., 1956, 1963, 1965, 1969; Scarab Club, Detroit, 1958, 1961, 1963-4; Detroit Art Teachers Annuals, 1958, 1960-3; Mich. Watercolor Society Annuals, 1961, 1963-4; Washington Watercolor Assn., 1963-4; Delta Art Assn. Annuals, Antioch, Cal., 1964-9, 1971, 1972; Unitarian Fall Art Festival, Stockton, Cal., 1964-9, 1971-2; Lodi (Cal.) Art Assn. Annuals, 1965-6, 1970-2; Lodi (Cal.) Art Center, 1965 (1-man); Weatherspoon Gallery, Greensboro, NC, 1965; Lodi Grape Festival, 1965-6; San Joaquin Co. Fair, Stockton, 1965-9; Mother Lode Nat'l Art Exhibition, Sonora, Cal., 1966-8; Cal. State Fair, Sacramento, 1966-7; Northern Cal. Art Annual, Sacramento, 1966-7, 1971; 12th Annual West Coast Oil Painting Exhibition, Seattle, 1966; Max 24, Nat'l Small Painting Show, LaFayette, Ind., 1966; Kingsley Art Annual, Sacramento, 1966; Watercolor USA, Springfield, Mo., 1968-9; Ventura Forum of the Arts, Cal., 1968; Cal. Exposition, Sacramento, 1971-2; Central Cal. Art League Exhibition, Modesto, 1972; Contemporary Studios, Detroit, 1962 (1-man); Arts Extended Gallery, Detroit, 1964 (1-man), 1972; Stanislaus State College, Turlock, Cal., 1967; Gold Hill Art Gallery, Va. City, Nev., 1967 (1-man); Modesto Jr. College, 1967; State Savings & Loan Assn., Stockton, 1968 (1-man); Stockton Public Library, 1969 (1-man); Stockton Fine Arts Gallery, 1972 (1-man); Rainbow Sign Gallery, Berkeley, 1973 (1-man); Anna Werbe Gallery, Detroit, 1959; Saginaw Art Museum, 1958; Univ. of Mich., 1962; Mich. Academy of Arts, Sciences & Letters, 1963; Mich. State Fair, 1962; Harlequinn House Gallery, Stockton, 1966 Detroit Artists Mart, 1962-4; Grinnel Galleries, Detroit, 1962-5; Fresno Art Center, 1968, 1971; Stanford Univ., 1969; College of Marin, 1970; Oakland Museum; NJ State Museum, 1972; Richmond (Cal.) Art Center, 1972; Sacramento State College, 1972; Athenian School, Danville, Cal., 1972; Friends School, Detroit, 1972; Collections Gallery, Sacramento, 1972.
Collections: Univ. of the Pacific; Pioneer Museum; Haggin Art Galleries; Washington, DC offices of Cal. Congressman John McFall; Detroit Board of Education; Merced Art Assn., Cal.; Dr. Weldon West, Stockton; Provost Berndt Kilker, Stockton; Gunji Watanabe, Stockton; Prof. Faye Coleman, Stockton; A. Lee Munson, NY; Oakland Museum; Delta Memorial Hospital, Antioch; Lorree's Bookkeeping & Income Tax Service, Stockton; Dr. Malcolm Moule, Stockton; Ms. Katie Walker, Washington, DC; Mr. Jerry Olson, Eureka, Cal.; Mr. Andrew White, Cincinnati.
Awards: Univ. of the Pacific Summer Grant, 1970; Certificates of Award, Wayne State Univ. Student Annual, 1955-6; Mich. Watercolor Society Prize, Mich. Artists Exhibit, 1957, 1962; Scarab Club—Honorable mention, watercolor, 1958, 3rd prize, watercolor, 1963, 1st prize, graphics, 1964; Detroit Art Teachers Annual—3rd prize, watercolor, 1958, 1st prize, watercolor, 1960 & 1963, 2nd prize, oil, 1960,

1st prize, sculpture, 1961; Delta Art Assn. Annual—2nd prize, drawing, 1964, honorable mention, 1965 & 1967, Purchase Award, 1967, 1st prize, graphics, 1972; Unitarian Fall Arts Festival—drawing award, 1964, oil award, 1965, Ben Day Oil Award, 1966, graphics award, 1967, painting award, 1971, 1st prize, painting, 1972; Lodi Art Assn. Annual—3rd prize, watercolor, 1965 & 1970, E. Surdex Graphics Award, 1970, mixed media award, 1970; Honorable mentions, oil, 1965, watercolor, 1966, Lodi Grape Festival; 1st prize, oil, 1966, honorable mention, acrylic, 1966, Mother Lode Nat'l Art Exhibit; San Joaquin County Fair—2nd prize, oil, 1966 & 1967, 3rd prize, watercolor, 1966 & 1967, Honorable mention, drawing, 1967 & 1968, 1st prize, oil, 1968, 3rd prize, oil, 1968, 1st prize, drawing, 1969, 2nd prize, acrylic, 1969, Honorable mention, watercolor, 1969; Stockton Art League Annuals—Frank Quinn Award, 1967, West Purchase Award, 1967, Honorable mention, 1968, Museum Purchase Award, 1967, Jack Whipple Award for Contemporary Painting, 1969, Juror's Entry, 1970, Earl & Neva Rowland Award for Small Painting, 1972; B.H. Armstrong Cash Award, Watercolor USA, 1969; Juror's Entry, Central Cal. Art League Exhibit, 1972; Honorable mention, Cal. State Exposition, 1972.
Sources: Lewis/Waddy. *Black Artists on Art,* Vol. 1; Afro-Amer. Slide Depository, Catalog; "Fantasy, Form, & Fun," *School Arts Magazine;* Oakland Museum. *Black Untitled II,* 1971; Smith-Mason Gallery. *National Exhibition of Black Artists,* 1971; *Personalities of the West and Mid-West,* 1973; Information from artist; Oakland Museum Archives; Walker, Roslyn. *A Resource Guide to the Visual Arts of Afro-Americans,* South Bend, Ind., 1971.

WALKER, STEVE
Graphic artist.
Works: *Little Boy; Little Girl.*
Collections: Johnson Pub. Co.
Sources: Johnson Pub. Co. *The JPC Art Collection,* Pamphlet.

WALKER, WILLIAM
Painter. Born in Birmingham, Alabama. Studied at the Columbus Gallery School of Art.
Works: *Peace and Salvation Wall of Understanding; Wall of Respect; Wall of Dignity; Wall of Pride; Harriet Tubman Memorial Wall; Wall of Truth; Wall of Love.*
Exhibited: Columbus Gallery of Fine Arts.
Awards: Earl C. Derby Award for Figure Portraits.
Sources: Lewis/Waddy. *Black Artists on Art,* Vol. 2; DuSable Museum of African-Amer.

History. *Contemporary Black Artists,* 1970, Calendar; Harley, Ralph, Jr. "Checklist of Afro-Amer. Art & Artists," *Serif,* Dec. 1970; Dover. *American Negro Art;* Indiana Univ. *Fine Arts & the Black American;* Myers, Carol L. *Black Power in the Arts,* Flint, Mich., 1970; Walker, Roslyn. *A Resource Guide to the Visual Arts of Afro-Americans,* South Bend, Ind., 1971; *Time,* April 6, 1970, p. 80.

WALTON, RAYMOND
Painter.
Works: *Negro Fisherman.*
Exhibited: Atlanta Univ., 1942.
Sources: Atlanta Univ. catalog, 1942; Harley, Ralph, Jr. "Checklist of Afro-Amer. Art & Artists," *The Serif,* Dec. 1970.

WALTS, FRANK
Sources: Harley, Ralph, Jr. "Checklist of Afro-Amer. Art & Artists," *The Serif,* Dec. 1970.

WANGBOJE, SOLOMON IREIN
Illustrator, educator. Studied at New York University.
Sources: Doob, Leonard W. *A Crocodile Has Me By the Leg,* African Poems, 1966.

WARBOURG, EUGENE
Sculptor. Born in New Orleans, 1825. Died in 1861. Studied in France.
Works: *John Young Mason; Le Premier Baiser; Le Pecheur;* bas-reliefs of Uncle Tom from Harriet Beecher Stowe's novel.
Exhibited: Paris Exposition, 1887; Howard Univ., 1967.
Collections: Virginia Historical Society.
Sources: Howard Univ. *Ten Afro-American Artists of the 19th Century;* Desdunes, Rodolph. *Nos Hommes Et Notre Histoire,* 1911; Dover. *American Negro Art,* 1960; Porter. *Modern Negro Art;* Indiana Univ. *Fine Arts & the Black American;* Rogers. *Africa's Gift to America: The Afro-American in the Making & Saving of the US;* Brawley, Benjamin. *The Negro Genius;* Greene, Carroll, Jr. "Perspective: The Black Artist in America," *Art Gallery,* April 1970, p. 6; Kiah, Virginia. "Black Artists," *Savannah Magazine,* April 1972, p. 14; Harley, Ralph, Jr. "Checklist of Afro-Amer. Art & Artists," *Serif,* Dec. 1970; Myers, Carol L. *Black Power in the Arts,* Flint, Mich., 1970; Walker, Roslyn. *A Resource Guide to the Visual Arts of Afro-Americans,* South Bend, Ind., 1971.

WARBURG, DANIEL
Sculptor, tombstone carver, engraver. Born in New Orleans. Worked at A. Weiblen Marble Works, New Orleans.
Works: *Holcombe Memorial,* New Orleans.
Sources: Indiana Univ. *Fine Arts & the Black*

American; Dover. *American Negro Art;* Brawley, Benjamin. *The Negro Genius;* DuSable Museum of African-Amer. History, *Contemporary Black Artists,* 1970, Calendar; Desdunes, Rodolph. *Nos Hommes Et Notre Histoire,* 1911; Harley, Ralph, Jr. "Checklist of Afro-Amer. Art & Artists," *Serif,* Dec. 1970; Walker, Roslyn. *A Resource Guide to the Visual Arts of Afro-Americans,* South Bend, Ind., 1971.

WARD, CAROLE

Jeweler, educator. Born in Phoenix City, Alabama, 1943. Studied at San José State College; Sorbonne, Paris; University of California. Teacher in California high schools (1968-70).
Works: *Ring, Silver; Three Cast Silver Necklaces.*
Exhibited: Pleasant Hill Art Invitational; Mills College, Oakland, 1970; San José State College; CAEA Exhibit, Triton Gallery; Rainbow Sign Gallery, Berkeley, 1972.
Collections: Ms. Sarah Fabio.
Sources: Lewis/Waddy. *Black Artists on Art,* Vol. 2; Mills College. *California Black Craftsmen,* 1970; Rainbow Sign Gallery. *Black Arts Day II,* Press Release, Berkeley, 1972; Contemporary Crafts, Inc. *Black Craftsmen of California,* Slides.

WARD, DENISE D.

Exhibited: Lee Cultural Center, Phila.
Sources: Phila. Dept. of Recreation. *Love . . . and the Black Community.*

WARD, HERBERT

Sculptor. Many of his works showed the African native. He had a large collection of African art and sculpture which he gave to the Smithsonian Institute.
Sources: "Sculpture by Herbert Ward," *American Magazine of Art,* April 1922; "Soul of the black: Mr. Ward's bronzes," *Independent,* May 1, 1913; "The Real African. Illustrations from sculpture by Mr. Ward," *Scribner's,* Oct. 1910.

WARD, RUTH

Printmaker. Born in Germany. Studied in Germany; Corcoran School of Art, Washington, DC; Pratt Graphics Center, New York City.
Exhibited: Showcase Gallery, Washington, DC, 1973.
Sources: *Black Shades,* Vol. 3, #2.

WARE, EVELYN L.

Painter, educator. Born in Washington, DC. Studied at New York University; Catholic University; DC Teachers College; University of Maryland; University of Ghana at Accra.
Works: *Trek to Elmira; Still Life with Masks.*
Exhibited: Smith-Mason Gallery, 1971; DC Teachers College; Washington Artists in South-

west; DCAA, Anacostia Neighborhood Museum-Smithsonian Institution.
Awards: DC Youth Commission Award for participation in youth workshops at St. Martin's Catholic Church.
Sources: Smith-Mason Gallery. *National Exhibition Black Artists 1971;* DC Art Assn. *Exhibition '71,* Washington, DC, 1971.

WARING, LAURA WHEELER
(Mrs. Walter E. Waring)

Painter, illustrator, educator. Born in Hartford, Connecticut, 1887. Died February 3, 1948. Studied at the Pennsylvania Academy of Fine Arts (1918-24); Grand Chaumiere, Paris (1924-5). Teacher at Cheyney (Pennsylvania) State Teachers College; Director in charge of Negro Art Exhibits at Philadelphia Exposition.
Works: *Alonzo Aden; W.E. Burghardt DuBois; James Weldon Johnson; Mother and Daughter; Anna Washington Derry; Dr. George E. Haynes; Jessie R. Faucet; Harry Burleigh; Marion Anderson; Sadie Alexander; Dr. John Turner; Raymond Alexander; Portrait of Alonzo Aden; Colonel Arthur Whittle, NYC; Portrait; Still Life with Flowers; Waterfront; Gold Earrings; Portrait of John P. Turner; Frankie; Informal Portrait; Portrait Study; Portrait of a Child; Russian Ballet; 2nd Luxembourg Gardens; Afternoon Tea; Ratcliffe Northern Lights; Heirlooms.*
Exhibited: Phila. Civic Center; Harmon Foundation, 1927-8, 1930-1; Art Institute of Chicago, 1933; Pa. Academy of Fine Arts, 1935, 1938; Howard Univ., 1937, 1939; Amer. Negro Exposition, Chicago, 1940; Corcoran Gallery, Washington, DC; NY Watercolor Exhibition; Smithsonian Institution, 1933; Texas Centennial, 1936.
Collections: Nat'l Archives; Smithsonian Institution, Nat'l Portrait Gallery.
Awards: Gold Award, Harmon Foundation, 1927; Creason Traveling Scholarship.
Sources: *Negro Almanac;* Dover. *American Negro Art;* Locke. *The Negro in Art;* Harmon Foundation. *Exhibition of Productions by Negro Artists;* Indiana Univ. *Fine Arts & the Black American;* City College of NY. *The Evolution of Afro-American Artists 1800-1950;* Phila. Division of Art. *Afro-American Artists 1800-1969;* Tanner Art Galleries. *Art of the American Negro,* 1940; Brawley, Benjamin. *The Negro Genius;* Ploski, Harry, Ernest Kaiser, & Otto Lindenmeyer. "The Black Artist," *Reference Library of Black America,* Book 4, 1971; "Negro Artists' Paintings on Display at University (Howard)," *East Tennessee News,* Knoxville, June 6, 1932; Schatz, Walter. *Directory of Afro-American Resources,* 1970; DuSable Museum of African-Amer. History. *Contemporary Black Artists,*

1970, Calendar, 1970; *Ebony,* Aug. 1966, p. 90; Spradling, Mary M., ed. *In Black & White: Afro-Americans in Print;* Howard Univ. *In Memoriam: An Exhibition of Paintings,* Washington, DC, 1949; Walker, Roslyn. *A Resource Guide to the Visual Arts of Afro-Americans,* South Bend, Ind., 1971; "Howard University Gallery: Paintings by 3 Artists are Displayed," *Washington Star,* Feb. 18, 1940; Assn. for the Study of Negro Life & History. *Exhibition of Works by Negro Artists,* 1933; Howard Univ. *Art of the American Negro,* 1937; Butcher, Margaret. *The Negro in American Culture,* p. 232; Roucek & Kiernan. *The Negro Impact on Western Civilization;* Texas Centennial Exposition. *Thumbnail Sketches of Exhibiting Artists,* 1936; Harmon Foundation. *Negro Artists,* 1935; Harmon Foundation. *Exhibit of Fine Arts,* 1930; Harmon Foundation. *Select Picture List;* Pierre-Noel, Lois Jones. "American Negro Art in Progress," *Negro History Bulletin,* Oct. 1967; FLK. "American Negroes As Artists," *The Survey,* Sept. 1, 1928, pp. 648-9; "Wallace Pays Tribute to Dr. Carver as He Presents Portrait," *Washington Star,* May 3, 1944; "Portrait of 7 Washington Negroes in National Museum Display of Leaders," *Washington Star,* May 28, 1944; "They Are Leaders," *Detroit Free Press,* Oct. 15, 1944; "Negro Art Shown in Two Exhibits . . ," *New York Times,* Nov. 6, 1945; "White & Negro Hostesses to Greet Public at Art Show," *Milwaukee Journal,* Jan. 2, 1946; "Noted Negroes in Art Exhibit," *Chicago Herald American,* Jan. 27, 1946; "Negro History Week Exhibit to Open Sunday," *Chicago Tribune,* Jan. 27, 1946; "Historical Group to Honor Leading American Negroes," *Chicago Sun,* Jan. 27, 1946; "Portrait Show in Southport Ends on '22nd Famous Negroes'," *News,* Feb. 14, 1946; *Portraits of Outstanding Americans of Negro Origin,* NY; Harley, Ralph, Jr. "Checklist of Afro-Amer. Art & Artists" *The Serif,* Dec. 1970; Greene, Carroll, Jr. *Afro-American Artists: 1800-1968,* Slides; Porter, James A. "Negro Artists Gain Recognition After Long Battle," *Pittsburgh Courier,* July 29, 1950; Brawley, Benjamin. *The Negro in Literature & Art in the US;* Negro Library Assn. *1st Annual Exhibit of Books, Manuscripts, Paintings, Sculpture, Etc. by the NLA at Carlton Ave. YMCA,* 1918; Brown, Marion. "The Negro in the Fine Arts," *The Negro Heritage Library,* Vol. 2; Ploski, Harry, & Ernest Kaiser. "The Black Artist," *Afro USA,* 1971.

WARREN, MASOOD ALI
Sculptor.
Works: *Pfc. Redd.*
Exhibited: Atlanta Univ., 1944.
Sources: Atlanta Univ. catalog, 1944.

WARREN, WILBERT
Painter, sculptor.
Works: *Young Spooner; Matthew Henson; Thomas P. Bomar.*
Exhibited: Amer. Negro Exposition, Chicago, 1940.
Sources: Tanner Art Galleries. *Art of the American Negro,* Catalog, 1949.

WARRICK, META VAUX
See: Fuller, Meta Warrick Vaux.

WASHINGTON, CAROL
Works: *The Bull.*
Sources: Boston Negro Artists' Assn., Calendar, 1973.

WASHINGTON, HENRY
Painter, printmaker. Born in Boston, 1923. Studied at the Vesper George School of Art; Harvard University; School of the Boston Museum of Fine Arts; Boston State College.
Works: *Christ Sitting on a Curb,* 1970 (oil); *Snail on Rocks* (oil); *White Dandelion* (oil); *Assassination of Dr. Martin Luther King* (oil); *Martin Deleney* (print).
Exhibited: Boston Negro Artists' Assn. Tour; Sunday-in-the-Park Exhibition, Boston; Boston Public Library, 1973.
Member: Boston Negro Artists' Assn.
Represented by: Boston Negro Artists' Assn.
Sources: DuSable Museum of African-Amer. History. *Contemporary Black Artists,* 1970, Calendar; "Black Art Exhibit Opens Sunday," *Herald,* Belmont, Mass., May 14, 1970; Information from artist; Boston Negro Artists' Assn. *10th Anniversary Exhibition,* Boston Public Library, 1973.

WASHINGTON, JAMES
Painter, sculptor. Born in Mississippi in 1911.
Works: *Nesting Bird; Mexican Market; Sitting Bird;* untitled sculpture.
Exhibited: Tanner Art League, 1922; Faingarton Galleries, San Francisco.
Collections: Oakland Museum.
Sources: Dover. *American Negro Art; The Negro Handbook,* Composed by Editors of *Ebony,* Chicago, 1966; *Who's Who in American Art,* 1970; Oakland Museum Archives; Harley, Ralph, Jr. "A Checklist of Afro-Amer. Art & Artists," *The Serif,* Dec. 1970.

WASHINGTON, JOHN E.
Exhibited: Howard Univ., 1932.
Sources: Harley, Ralph, Jr. "Checklist of Afro-Amer. Art & Artists," *The Serif,* Dec. 1970.

WASHINGTON, MARY PARKS
Painter, mixed media, educator. Born in Atlanta. Studied at Spelman College (AB, 1946); under Hale Woodruff; Art Students League

under Reginald Marsh; University of Mexico.
Works: *Black Soul; Hope, Construction.*
Exhibited: Oakland Museum of Art, 1968.
Collections: Johnson Pub. Co., Chicago.
Sources: Johnson Pub. Co. *The JPC Art Collection,* Pamphlet; Oakland Art Museum. *New Perspectives in Black Art;* Indiana Univ. *Fine Arts & the Black American;* Lewis/Waddy. *Black Artists on Art;* DuSable Museum of African-Amer. History. *Contemporary Black Artists,* 1970, Calendar; Harley, Ralph, Jr. "Checklist of Afro-Amer. Art & Artists," *Serif,* Dec. 1970; Walker, Roslyn. *A Resource Guide to the Visual Arts of Afro-Americans,* South Bend, Ind., 1971.

WASHINGTON, ORA
Printmaker.
Works: *Still Life.*
Exhibited: Atlanta Univ., 1944.
Sources: Atlanta Univ. catalog, 1944.

WASHINGTON, TIMOTHY
Painter, graphic artist, mixed media. Born in Los Angeles, 1946. Studied at Chouinard Art School (BFA, 1969).
Works: *Liberty* (engraving on aluminum); *Introduction to Life,* 1969; *Introductory Title,* 1969; *Raw Truth,* 1970; *Exist,* 1970; *Inquisitive Presentation,* 1970; *Precaution,* 1970; *Why Poverty,* 1970; *Parakeets.* 1970; *One Nation under God,* 1970; *Ghetto,* 1970; *Silent Majority; Viet Nam.*
Exhibited: Los Angeles County Museum, 1971; Santa Barbara Museum of Art, 1971; Univ. of Iowa, 1971-2; Oakland Museum, 1971.
Awards: Scholarship to Chouinard Art School.
Sources: Oakland Museum. *The Metal Experience,* 1971; Illinois Bell Telephone. *Black American Artists/71,* 1972; Young, Joseph E. *Three Graphic Artists,* Los Angeles Co. Museum, 1971.

WATERS, PAUL
Painter. Born in Philadelphia, 1936. Studied at Goddard College, Painfield, Vermont; Harvard University; Bank Street College; self-taught artist. Director of Community Affairs, Newark Museum.
Works: *Family Time; Formula Dream Survival Kit #5; Survival Committee; Syllables of Survival; Abbreviated Dream Survival Plan.*
Exhibited: Boston Museum of Fine Arts, 1970; Newark Museum, 1971.
Collections: Mr. Samuel Miller, East Orange, NJ; Rev. William J. Schneider, Cambridge, Mass.
Sources: Boston Museum of Fine Arts. *Afro-American Artists: NY & Boston,* 1970; Newark Museum. *Black Artists: Two Generations;*

School Arts, Dec. 1971; Information from artist; Driscoll, Edgar. *Boston Evening Globe,* May 20, 1970.

WATERS, RICHARD
Painter, commercial artist. Born in Boston, 1936. Self-taught.
Works: *Tut-Ankh-Amen,* 1969 (latex on canvas).
Exhibited: Boston Museum of Fine Arts, 1970.
Sources: Boston Museum of Fine Arts. *Afro-American Artists: NY & Boston,* 1970; Bowling, Frank. "The Rupture," *Arts,* Summer 1970; Gerson, Sareen R. "Black Art NY-Hub Set for Museum of Fine Arts," *Minuteman,* March 19, 1970; "Afro-American Art a Cultural Experience for All," *Record American,* Boston, May 19, 1970.

WATKINS, GWEN
Educator. Studied at Xavier University, New Orleans; Wayne State University; University of Michigan. Art Instructor at Metropolitan Arts Complex.
Exhibited: Ann Arbor, 1967 (1-woman); Stouffers, Northland, 1968 (1-woman); Normacel Gallery, Detroit, 1970.
Sources: Normacel Gallery. *A Black Women Art Exhibit,* Detroit, 1970.

WATKINS, JAMES
Painter. Born in Macon, Georgia, 1925. Studied at the Society of Arts and Crafts, Detroit, Michigan (1949-52).
Works: *Widow Woman; Deserted; Guitar Blues.*
Exhibited: 16th-22nd Atlanta Univ. Annuals; Akron Art Institute (1-man); Beaux Art Guild, Tuskegee, Ala.; Xavier Univ., 1963.
Awards: Atlanta Univ. Annuals.
Sources: Indiana Univ. *Fine Arts & the Black American;* Dover. *American Negro Art;* Lewis/Waddy. *Black Artists on Art,* Vol 1; Xavier Univ. *Emancipation Proclamation Centennial National Art Exhibition,* 1963; Atkinson, J. Edward. *Black Dimensions in Contemporary American Art,* 1971; Walker, Roslyn. *A Resource Guide to the Visual Arts of Afro-Americans,* South Bend, Ind., 1971.

WATLINGTON, MAXINE
Graphic artist. Educator. Studied at Bennett College for Women; Howard University (BFA); Positano Art Workshop, Positano, Italy; Washington School of Psychiatry; DC Teachers College.
Works: *Germain* (pen & ink).
Exhibited: Bennett College; Howard Univ.; DCAA, Anacostia Neighborhood Museum-Smithsonian Institution.
Sources: DC Art Assn. *Exhibition '71,* Washington, DC, 1971.

WATSON, HOWARD N.

Painter. Born in Pottsfield, Pennsylvania on May 19, 1929. Studied at Philadelphia State University; Philadelphia College of Art.
Works: Calendars for City of Phila., RCA, IVB Bank; Mural for Archdiocese of Phila.; *Backyard; The El.*
Exhibited: Amer. Watercolor Shows; Allied Artists of America Shows; Audubon Artist Shows; Knickerbocker Artist Shows; Phila. Civic Center Museum; Lee Cultural Center, Phila.
Collections: Amer. Watercolor Society; Phila. Watercolor Club; Knickerbocker Artists of America; Allied Artists of America.
Awards: 3M Printing Job of the Year, 1969; Best of the Show, Del. Graphics Show.
Member: Amer. Watercolor Society; Phila. Watercolor Club; Knickerbocker Artists of America.
Represented by: Phila. Watercolor Newman Galleries; FAR Gallery, NYC; Sandpiper Gallery, Stoneharbor, NJ.
Sources: *Who's Who in the East.* "Afro-American Issue," *Art Gallery,* April 1968; Indiana Univ. *Fine Arts & the Black American;* Phila. Civic Center. *Afro-American Artists 1800-1969;* DuSable Museum of African-Amer. History. *Contemporary Black Artists,* 1970, Calendar; Myers, Carol L. *Black Power in the Arts,* Flint, Mich., Board of Education; Phila. Dept. of Recreation. *Love . . . and the Black Community.* Walker, Roslyn. *A Resource Guide to the Visual Arts of Afro-Americans,* South Bend, Ind., 1971.

WATSON, LINDA

Painter.
Works: *Family Portrait* (oil); *Unsettled* (poster paint).
Exhibited: Lee Cultural Center, Phila.
Sources: Phila. Dept. of Recreation. *Love . . . and the Black Community.*

WATSON, RENA

Painter.
Works: *There I am in the Midst of It* (acrylic).
Exhibited: State Armory, Wilmington, Del., 1971.
Sources: Aesthetic Dynamics. *Afro-American Images 1971.*

WATSON, RENEE A.

Painter.
Works: *Deserted Street.*
Exhibited: Smith-Mason Gallery, 1971.
Sources: Smith-Mason Gallery. *National Exhibition Black Artists 1971.*

WAYTT, RICHARD

Painter. Born 1955 in Lynwood, California. Studied Chouinard Art Institute, Los Angeles; University of California at Los Angeles; Studio Watts; Watts Tower Art Center; Otis Art Institute.
Works: *Brain-Washed.*
Exhibitions: Jewish Welfare Community Center; Watts Summer Art Festival, 1964-70; Festival in Black, 1970; Security Pacific Traveling Exhibition.
Awards: Golden State Mutual Life Insurance Scholarship; Los Angeles Jr. Chamber of Commerce; Student division, Watts Summer Art Festival, 1968 & 1971 Chalk-In.
Sources: Lewis/Waddy. *Black Artists on Art,* Vol. 2.

WEAVER, CLAUDE

See: Weaver, Lamar.

WEAVER, (CLAUDE) LAMAR

Painter. Born in Atlanta, Georgia, 1918. Studied at Morehouse College under Hale Woodruff.
Works: *Newcomer; Autumn Scene; Blues in the Night; Emperor Jones.*
Exhibited: Atlanta Univ., 1938-9; 1942-3; Dillard Univ., 1938; Amer. Negro Exposition, 1940.
Sources: Locke. *The Negro in Art;* Tanner Art Galleries. *Art of the American Negro,* 1940; Harley, Ralph, Jr. "Checklist of Afro-Amer. Art & Artists," *The Serif,* Dec. 1970; Walker, Roslyn. *A Resource Guide to the Visual Arts of Afro-Americans,* South Bend, Ind., 1971.

WEAVER, LEROY C.

Painter.
Works: *Red Hills; Across the Track; Harvest Time.*
Exhibited: Atlanta Univ., 1942, 1943.
Sources: Atlanta Univ. Exhibition Files; Harley, Ralph, Jr. "Checklist of Afro-Amer. Art & Artists," *The Serif,* Dec. 1970.

WEAVER, PAMELA

Studied at Tuskegee Institute.
Works: *Pattern Yourself after No One.*
Exhibited: Sun Times/Daily News Gallery, Chicago, 1970.
Sources: United Negro College Fund. *Art 1970,* Chicago, 1970.

WEAVER, STEPHANIE

Artist-in-Residence, Studio Museum in Harlem.
Sources: *Black Shades,* March 1972.

WEEDEN, LULA

Painter.
Works: *Still Life; Back Yard.*
Exhibited: Atlanta Univ., 1943.
Sources: Atlanta Univ. catalog, 1943.

WEEKS, JAMES

Painter.

Works: *The Musician.*
Sources: Brown, Marion. "The Negro in the Fine Arts," *The Negro Heritage Library,* Vol. 2.

WEINSTOCK, CAROLE

Collections: NY Public Library-Schomburg Art Collection.
Sources: Schatz, Walter. *Directory of Afro-American Resources,* 1970.

WELL, THEODORE

Painter.
Works: *Dewdrop; Rear View of Belleview; Self Portrait.*
Exhibited: State Armory, Wilmington, Del., 1971.
Sources: Aesthetic Dynamics. *Afro-American Images 1971.*

WELLS, ALBERT

Painter. Born in Charlotte, North Carolina, 1918. Studied at Morehouse College under Hale Woodruff.
Works: *Winter in Georgia; The Bottoms; Autumn; Georgia Landscape; Gathering Firewood; End of Winter; Railroad Bridge.*
Exhibited: Institute of Modern Art, Boston, 1943; Atlanta Univ., 1942, 1944; Amer. Negro Exposition, Chicago, 1940; Dillard Univ., 1941; Smith College, 1943.
Sources: Harley, Ralph, Jr. "Checklist of Afro-Amer. Art & Artists," *Serif,* Dec. 1970; Locke. *The Negro in Art;* Tanner Art Galleries. *Art of the American Negro,* 1940; Dillard Univ. *Arts Festival,* 1941, Catalog.

WELLS, DAVID STEPHENS

Sources: Harley, Ralph, Jr. "Checklist of Afro-Amer. Art & Artists," *The Serif,* Dec. 1970.

WELLS, FRIENDLY

Born in Georgia, 1913. Specialized in portraits of well-known personalities.
Sources: Wallace, Beverly. "Drugstore Porter Spends Spare Moments with Art," *Macon Telegraph,* May 5, 1935.

WELLS, J.C.

Exhibited: Tanner Art League, 1922.
Sources: Harley, Ralph, Jr. "Checklist of Afro-Amer. Art & Artists," *The Serif,* Dec. 1970.

WELLS, JAMES LESESNE

Painter, printmaker, educator. Born in Atlanta, 1902. Studied at Lincoln University; National Academy of Design under Frank Nankerville; Florida Industrial and Collegiate Institute; Teachers' College, Columbia University (BS).
Works: *Baptism of Christ; Fishermen of Galilee; Christ and the Fishermen; Bathsheba; Tropical Fruit; Farmer; Primitive Boy; Sister; Girl by the Window; Lonely Ones; Girl and Flowers; Landscape with House; African Fetish II; African Fantasy; Industry; Tam O'Shata; Rebecca at the Well; Christ Washing the Feet of the Disciple; The Escape of the Spies from Canaan; Flight into Egypt; Entry into Jerusalem; Barry Place; Street Scene; East River; Shipyard; Interlude; The Good Samaritan; Bridge Fantasy; The Wanderers; The Plowman; Baptism of Christ; Red Sailboats; Boy's Head; The Temptation of Eve; Phaeton; Dance of Salome; By the Roadside; The Road; Waterfront; Negro Worker; Builders; Landscape; Jerusalem; Tulip Garden; Brown Crucifixion; Green Apples; Jonah and the Whale; And on They Marched; Visiting; Composition; Bridges and Viaducts; The Ascension; The Vision of St. Paul; Girl Sleeping; Fisherman; The Expulsion from Eden; The Fisherman's Daughter; Crossroads; Leda and the Swan; Bronze Diana; Symbols of Freedom; Day's End; Icarus; St. Francis; Girl with Sunflowers; River Boat; Tobias and the Angel; Thomas Circle, Washington, DC; Adam and Eve; Crucifixion; Dupont Circle, Washington, DC; Reflections; The Adoration; Sea Shell and Fish; Journey to Calvary; Bridge at Night; St. Francis and the Birds; The Burning Bush* (wood engraving).
Exhibited: Howard Univ., 1937, 1945; Delphic Studios, 1932 (1-man); Downtown Gallery, NY; Brooklyn Museum, 1932 (1-man); College Art Assn. Traveling Show; National Block Print Society; Phillips Memorial Gallery, Washington, DC; New Age Gallery; Artists Mart; Collectors' Corner; Washington Printmaker Annuals; Society of Amer. Graphic Artists; African Traveling Exhibition of Paintings & Prints by Internat'l Group; Phila. Museum; Tyler Museum, Phila.; Fisk Univ. (2-man); Spelman College, Atlanta Univ., JD Rockefeller Jr. Fine Arts Building; Art Center, NYC, 1933; Harmon Foundation, 1931, 1933; Weyhe Gallery, NY; Phila. Print Club; Dydensing Gallery, NY; Dallas Exposition; Baltimore Museum; Albright-Knox Art Gallery, Buffalo; State Armory, Wilmington, Del., 1971; Smithsonian Institution; Amer. Negro Exposition, Chicago, 1940; NY Public Library, 1921; Montclair YWCA, 1930; Barnet Aden Gallery, 1932 (1-man); Studio House, Washington, DC, 1935; NJ State Museum, Trenton, 1935; Smith College, 1943; Institute of Modern Art, Boston, 1943; Sheraton Hotel, Phila., 1968; Texas Centennial, 1936; James A. Porter Gallery, 1970; Smith-Mason Gallery, 1971.
Collections: Hampton (Va.) Institute; Phillips Memorial Gallery, Washington, DC; National Archives; Valentine Museum, Richmond, Va.; Univ. of Kansas; Carl Van Vectan Gallery of Art, Fisk Univ.; J.D. Rockefeller Jr. Fine Arts

Building, Spelman College, Atlanta Univ.; Smithsonian Institution.

Awards: Harmon Gold Award, 1931; George E. Haynes Prize, 1935; Honorable Mention, 6th Annual Area Exhibit, Corcoran Gallery; 2nd prize, Federations of Churches Exhibit; George F. Muth Prize, Washington Watercolor Club; 1st prize, graphic arts, Washington Area Religious Art Exhibition; Honorable Mention, Society of Amer. Artists.

Member: Alpha Phi Alpha.

Sources: Howard Univ. *Art of the American Negro,* 1937; *Who's Who in American Art,* 1940-1; Dover. *American Negro Art;* Harmon Foundation. *Exhibition of Productions by Negro Artists;* "Afro-American Issue," *Art Gallery,* April 1968; Indiana Univ. *Fine Arts & the Black American;* Roelof-Lanner, T.V., ed. *Prints by American Negro Artists;* Locke. *The Negro in Art;* Afro-American Slide Depository, Catalog, 1971-2; City College of NY. *The Evolution of Afro-American Artists 1800-1950;* "Howard University Gallery," *Sunday Star,* Washington, DC, Dec. 7, 1941; Herring, James V. "The American Negro Craftsman and Artist," *Crisis,* April 1942; Aesthetic Dynamics. *Afro-American Images,* 1971; Assn. for the Study of Negro Life & History. *Exhibitions of Works by Negro Artists,* 1933; Brawley, Benjamin. *The Negro Genius;* Tanner Art Galleries. *Art of the American Negro,* 1940; Porter. *Modern Negro Art;* Locke, Alain. "Advance on the Art Front," *Opportunity,* May 1939; Harley, Ralph, Jr. "Checklist of Afro-Amer. Art & Artists," *Serif,* Dec. 1970; Butcher, Margaret. *The Negro in American Culture,* pp. 236-7; Roucek/Kiernan. *The Negro Impact on Western Civilization;* Harmon Foundation. *Non-Jury Exhibit of Negro Artists,* 1933; Texas Centennial Exposition. *Thumbnail Sketches of Exhibiting Artists,* 1936; Howard Univ. *Festival of Fine Arts,* 1945; Harmon Foundation. *Negro Artists,* 1935; Howard Univ. *James A. Porter Gallery of African American Art,* 1970; *Who's Who in Colored America,* 3rd edition; Smith-Mason Gallery. *National Exhibition of Black Artists,* 1971; DuSable Museum of African-Amer. History. *Contemporary Black Artists,* 1970, Calendar; Harmon Foundation. *Select Picture List;* Woodson, Carter G., & Charles H. Wesley. *The Story of the Negro Retold,* p. 402; "Harmon Foundation Exhibit," *Art Digest,* Feb. 15, 1931, p. 7; *Art Digest,* March 1, 1933; Greene, Carroll, Jr. "Perspective: The Black Artist in America," *Art Gallery,* April 1970, p. 11; Pierre-Noel, Lois Jones. "American Negro Art in Progress," *Negro History Bulletin,* Oct. 1967; Porter, James A. "Negro Art on Review," *American Magazine of Art,* Jan. 1934; Locke, Alain. "The American Negro as Artist," *American Magazine of Art,* Sept. 1931; "Harlem Library Shows Negro Art," *Art News,* May 20, 1933, p. 14; DC Art Assn. *Exhibition '71,* Washington, DC, 1971; Howard Univ. *Paintings & Prints by James L. Wells,* 1965; Spelman College. *Paintings & Prints by James L. Wells,* Series # 2, 1966; Kiah, Virginia. "Black Artist," *Savannah Magazine,* April 1972, p. 16; Porter, James. "Negro Artists Gain Recognition After Long Battle," *Pittsburgh Courier,* July 29, 1950; Brown, Marion. "The Negro in the Fine Arts," *The Negro Heritage Library,* Vol. 2; Ploski, Harry, & Ernest Kaiser. "The Black Artist," *Afro USA,* 1971; Ploski, Harry, Ernest Kaiser, & Otto Lindenmeyer. "The Black Artist," *Reference Library of Black America,* Book 4, 1971; *The Negro Handbook,* Composed by Editors of *Ebony,* Chicago, 1966; "Exhibition of Work by Negro Artists," *Afro-American Presbyterian,* Feb. 23, 1933; Myers, Carol L. *Black Power in the Arts,* Flint, Mich., 1970; *Art in Washington,* 1970 Calendar, Acropolis Books; Walker, Roslyn. *A Resource Guide to the Visual Arts of Afro-Americans,* South Bend, Ind., 1971.

WELTON, ROLAND

Painter. Born in San Francisco, 1919. Studied at the Art Students League, New York City; Otis Art Institute, Los Angeles; Chouinard Institute of Fine Arts.

Exhibited: Art West Assoc., Los Angeles City Hall, since 1962; Prints by Negro Artists Exhibition, Institute of Soviet-Amer. Relations in the Soviet Union, 1966-7.

Sources: Lewis/Waddy. *Black Artists on Art,* Vol. 1; Walker, Roslyn. *A Resource Guide to the Visual Arts of Afro-Americans,* South Bend, Ind., 1971.

WEST, EDWARD

Photographer.

Exhibited: Addison Gallery, 1971.

Sources: James Van DerZee Institute. *The Black Photographer (1908-1970): A Survey.*

WEST, FRANK G., JR.

Painter.

Exhibited: Atlanta Univ., 1951.

Awards: Honorable mention, Atlanta Univ., 1951.

Sources: Atlanta Univ. Exhibition Catalog, 1951.

WEST, THEORIS

Painter, graphic artist.

Works: *News, It's My Daddy; The Family; And Nobody Was Doing Nothing* (pencil).

Exhibited: Smith-Mason Gallery, 1971; Lee Cultural Center, Phila.

Sources: Smith-Mason Gallery. *National Exhi-*

bition of Black Artists, 1971; Phila. Dept. of Recreation. *Love . . . and the Black Community.*

WHITAKER, V.G.
Painter.
Works: *Grandma.*
Exhibited: Atlanta Univ., 1942.
Sources: Atlanta Univ. catalog, 1942.

WHITE, AEDINA
Sources: Porter. *Modern Negro Art*; Harley, Ralph, Jr. "Checklist of Afro-Amer. Art & Artists," *The Serif*, Dec. 1970.

WHITE, AMOS
Ceramist, educator. Born in Montgomery, Alabama. Studied at Alabama State College (BS, 1958); University of Southern California (1961).
Exhibited: General Motors Fisher Body Design Exhibition, 1951-2; Designer-Craftsman USA, Museum of Contemporary Crafts, NYC; Design West, Cal. Museum of Science & Industry, 1960; Contemporary Design, San Diego County Exposition, Del Mar, Cal.; 18th Nat'l Decorative Arts & Ceramics Exhibit, Wichita, Kan., 1964; Kuhn-White Exhibit, LeMoyne Art Foundation Gallery (2-man); Tallahassee, Fla., 1965; Fla. State Fair of Fine Arts, Tampa; Deshaes-White Exhibit, Univ. of Jacksonville, Fla., 1967 (2-man); Ala. State College, Montgomery, 1968.
Awards: State Award for Design & Craftsmanship in Automotive Styling & Model Construction, 1951; Honorable Mention, ceramic demonstration, Los Angeles County Home Show, 1961.
Member: Amer. Craftsmen's Council (state representative).
Sources: Lewis/Waddy. *Black Artists on Art*, Vol. 1; Walker, Roslyn. *A Resource Guide to the Visual Arts of Afro-Americans*, South Bend, Ind., 1971.

WHITE, BENNY
Painter, sculptor, graphic artist. Born October 31, 1937 in Detroit. Studied at the Society of Arts and Crafts (1961-4).
Works: *African Nude; Miss America; Whitney, Celest and Elma Bell; My Daughter Cindie; Susan; Jackie; The Way There; African Girl Sitting; My Daughter Lisa; Ilene; Sheila; Christopher from God; They Are All The Same Under God; Combustion; God's Temple of Light; Untitled; Self Portrait; Paulette; Mary Ann; Benita; Jetta; African Girl Fishing; The End of the World; Future Scape No. 1.*
Exhibited: Detroit Institute of Arts.
Sources: Afro-American Slide Depository, 1971-2, catalog; Detroit Institute of Arts files.

WHITE, CHARLES
Painter, graphic artist, educator. Born in Chicago on April 2, 1918. Studied at the Art Institute of Chicago; Art Students League, New York; Taller de Grafica, Mexico. Teacher at Otis Art Institute, Los Angeles; Southside Art Center, Chicago (1939-40); Workshop School of Art (1950-3); Artist-in-residence, Howard University (1945).
Works: *Cat's Cradle; Go Not Silently into the Night; Harvest; Head; In Memoriam; John Brown; Birmingham Totem; Sojourner Truth & Booker T. Washington; Saturday's Child; This Is My Brother; General Moses; Frederick Douglass; Mother Courage; Wanted Poster Series #6; Fellow Worker Won't You March with Us; Through the Years of Poverty a Passionate Tune Was Born; Wanted Poster Series #14; J'Accuse #8; Native Son #2; Contributions of the American Negro to Democracy; Woman of Sorrow; Blues Singer; Soldier; Songs; Sojourner; Open Gate; Walk Together; Work; Portfolio #10; Birth of Spring; Go Tell It on the Mountain; Let the Light Enter; Mayibuye Afrika; Awaken from the Unknowing; Move on up a Little Higher; Portfolio #6—I Have a Dream; Sarah; Maternity; Dawn; Exploding Star; Expectancy; Centralia Madonna; Solid as a Rock; The Preacher; Juba; Nat Turner, Yesterday, Today & Tomorrow; Two Alone; Nobody Knows My Name; Lobers; Nocturne; Paper Shelter; Spirituals; Three Round Heads; There Were No Crops This Year; Mahalia Jackson; Let's Walk Together; Frederick Douglass Lives Again; Women; Roots (ink); Now I Lay Down My Heavy Load; Micah (linocut); I'm on My Way to Canaan (charcoal); Fatigue; To a Dark Girl; Uhurah; Two Shall Live as One; Silent Song (Meditation).*
Exhibited: ACA Gallery, NY, 1941; Palace of Culture, Warsaw, 1967; Howard Univ., 1967; Morgan State College, 1967; Fisk Univ., 1968; Univ. of Dayton, 1968; Central State College, 1968; Wilberforce College, 1968; Wright State Univ., 1968; Dayton Art Institute, 1968; Otis Art Institute, 1968; Kunstnernes Hus, Oslo, 1968; Pushkin Museum, Moscow, 1968; Hermitage Museum, Leningrad, 1968; Heritage Gallery, Los Angeles, 1968, 1971; Jackson State College, 1968; Florida A&M Univ., 1968; Johnson C. Smith Univ., 1968; Dartmouth College, 1968; Charles M. Bowers Museum, Santa Ana, 1969; Boston Museum of Fine Arts, 1969; Bowdoin College, 1969; Ludwigshafen am Rheim, Germany, 1969; Chaffey College, Cal., 1969; Riverside Art Assn., 1969; Claremont College, 1969; Wisconsin Univ., 1969; Univ. of Cal., 1969, 1970; Flint (Mich.) Community Schools, 1969; Southern Oregon College, 1966, 1969; New School of NY, 1969;

La Jolla Museum of Art, 1970; Chico State College, 1970; National Center of Afro-Amer. Artists, Boston, 1970; Forum Gallery, NYC, 1970; City College of Los Angeles, 1970; Chapman College, 1970; Intergraphik, Berlin, 1970; Pratt Graphics Center, 1970; Pasadena City College, 1970; Utah State Univ., 1970; Spelman College, 1970; Atlanta Univ., 1970; Los Angeles County Museum of Art, 1971; Whitney Museum of Amer. Art, 1968, 1971; Honolulu Academy of Arts, 1971; Krannert Art Museum, 1971; Santa Barbara Museum, 1971; Monterey Penninsula Museum of Art, 1971; Internationale Buchkunst-Ausstellungin, Leipzig, 1971; Illinois Bell Telephone, 1971; Kalamazoo Institute of Arts, 1971; National Academy of Design, 1972; James A. Porter Gallery, 1970; Roko Gallery, 1949; South Side Community Art Center, Chicago, 1941; Baltimore Museum; Art Institute of Chicago; Brooklyn Museum; Library of Congress; Smith College; Institute of Contemporary Art, Boston; Newark Museum; Amer. Academy of Arts & Letters; Metropolitan Museum of Art; Smithsonian Institution; State Armory, Wilmington, Del., 1971; Tanner Art Galleries, Chicago, 1940; Univ. of Iowa, 1971-2; San Francisco Museum of Art, 1946; NYU, 1949; Univ. of Southern Cal., 1958; Univ. of Utah, 1958; Internat'l Exhibit of Art, Germany, 1959; Occidental College, 1964; Univ. of Judaism, 1964; Rockford (Ill.) College, 1965; Univ. of Cal., Los Angeles, 1966; Scripps College, 1966; Assn. pour la Rencontre des Cultures, Paris, 1966; Oakland Art Museum, 1966; Fine Arts Gallery of San Diego, 1966; 1st World Festival of Negro Arts, Dakar, Senegal, 1966; Karlovy Vary, Czechoslovakia, 1967; Institute of Modern Art, Boston, 1943; Univ. of Chicago, 1944; Long Beach Museum of Art, 1959; Budapest, Hungary, 1967; City of Los Angeles 16th Art Show, 1968.

Collections: Atlanta Univ.; Howard Univ.; Oakland Museum; Tuskegee Institute (murals); Hampton (Va.) Institute (murals); Whitney Museum; Amer. Federation of Arts; Academy of Arts & Letters; Long Beach Museum of Art; Library of Congress; Taller de Grafica, Mexico City; Deutsche Academie der Kunste, Berlin; Dresden Museum of Art; Joseph H. Hirshorn Collection; Government of Ghana; Barnet Aden Gallery, Washington, DC; Brown Pharmaceutical Co.; Golden State Insurance Co.; IBM; National Archives; George Cleveland Branch, Chicago Public Library (murals); Charles White Collection; Syracuse Univ.; Metropolitan Museum of Art; Mr. & Mrs. Peter Pollack; Mr. & Mrs. John Gray; NY Public Library; Heritage Gallery; Mr. Harry Belafonte; Fisk Univ.; Los Angeles State Univ.; Central State Univ.; Dayton (Ohio) Board of Education; Estate of Nat King Cole; Estate of Lorrain Hansberry; Mr. Sidney Poitier; *Ebony Magazine*; Mr. Gordon Parks; Boston Black United Front Foundation; Bakersfield College; Flint (Mich.) Community Schools; Illinois Bell Tel. Co.; Mr. William Cosby, Jr.; Mr. Berry Gordy, Jr.

Awards: Art Institute of Chicago Scholarship, 1937; Nat'l Scholastic Award, 1937; Amer. Negro Exposition, Chicago, 1940; Julius Rosenwald Fellowship, 1941-3; Edward B. Alfred Award, 1946; Atlanta Univ. Purchase Award, 1946, 1959, 1951, 1961; Nat'l Institute of Arts & Letters Grant, 1952; Metropolitan Museum of Art, 1952; Atlanta Univ. Award, 1953; John Hay Whitney Fellowship, 1955; Gold Medal, Internat'l Show, Germany, 1960, 1965; Purchase award, Howard Univ., 1961; Childe Hassam Award, Amer. Academy of Art, 1965; City Council Award, Los Angeles, 1968; Doctor of Arts, Columbia Univ., 1969; Tamarind Fellowship, 1970; Assoc., Nat'l Academy of Design, 1971.

Member: Executive Board, Black Academy of Arts & Letters; Otis Art Assoc.; Alumni Assn., Art Institute of Chicago; Nat'l Conference of Artists; Pasadena Society of Artists; Advisor'' Comm., USC Medical Center; Nat'l Academy of Design; Board of Directors, Nat'l Center of Afro-Amer. Artists.

Sources: Information from artist; Locke. *The Negro in Art;* Albany Institute of History & Art. *The Negro Artist Comes of Age;* Porter. *Modern Negro Art;* Larkin, Oliver W. *Art & Life in America,* NY, Rinehart & Co., 1949; Dover. *American Negro Art;* Millier, Arthur. "An Incurable Romantic," *Los Angeles Magazine,* Jan. 1964; Heritage Gallery. *Portfolio 6/Charles White,* 1964; Porter, James, & B. Horowitz. *Images of Dignity,* Los Angeles, Ward Ritchie Press, 1967; Newark Museum. *Black Artists: Two Generations,* 1971; Chatfield-Taylor, Rose. "Howard Univ. Holds Negro Exhibit," *Washington Post,* Feb. 16, 1941; UCLA Art Galleries. *The Negro in America;* La Jolla Museum of Art. *Dimensions of Black;* Aesthetic Dynamics. *Afro-American Images,* 1971; Doty. *Contemporary Black Artists in America;* ACA Gallery. *Charles White,* NY, 1950; ACA Gallery. *Charles White,* NY, 1953; ACA Gallery. *Charles White,* NY, 1958; ACA Gallery. *Charles White,* NY, 1961; Amer. Negro Exposition. *Art of the American Negro;* Howard Univ. *James A. Porter Gallery of African-American Art,* 1970; DuSable Museum of African-Amer. History. *Contemporary Black Artists,* 1970, Calendar; Harmon Foundation. *Select Picture List; New York Times,* April 1, 1951; *Daily Worker,* NY, May 5, 1948, June 12, 1950; Robinson, Louie. "Charles White: Portrayer of Black Dignity," *Ebony,*

July 1967; City College of NY. *The Evolution of Afro-American Artists: 1800-1950,* 1967; Sterling/Logan. *Four Took Freedom,* Doubleday Co., 1967 (illus.); Saunders, Earl W. *Workers With Youth Magazine,* Vol. 27, No. 10; Saunders, Earl W. *The Church School Magazine,* Vol. 21, No. 8, 1968; Jefferson, Louise E. *Contemporary Art by Afro-Americans,* NY, Friendship Press, 1968; Drimmer, Melvin. *Black History,* Doubleday & Co., 1968 (cover illus.); Borgese, Elizabeth. *The Center Magazine,* July 1968; Heritage Gallery. *I Have a Dream Portfolio: Charles White,* 1969; Heritage Gallery. *Wanted Poster Series, Portfolio,* 1970; *Long Island Press,* April 1970; *Art Digest,* April 15, 1951; *Art News,* April 1970; *Who's Who in the West,* 1970, 1971; Atkinson, J. Edward. *Black Dimensions in Contemporary American Art,* 1971; Pratt Graphic Center. *1971 Annual of Prints;* Fax. *17 Black Artists,* 1971; Larkin. *Art and Life in America;* Wright, Sarah E., & Lucy Smith. *Give Me a Child,* Phila., Kraft Pub. Co., 1952; *Portfolio of Six Drawings—The Art of Charles White,* NY, New Century Pub., 1953; Mugnaini, Joe, & Janice Lovoos. *Drawing—A Search for Form,* Reinhold, 1966; Young, Joseph E. *Three Graphic Artists: Charles White, David Hammons, Timothy Washington,* Los Angeles County Museum, 1971; "Afro-American Issue," *Art Gallery,* April 1968; Indiana Univ. *Fine Arts & the Black American;* Afro-American Slide Depository, catalog; Nat'l Center of Afro-Amer. Artists. *Five Black Artists,* 1970; *Negro Almanac;* Motley, Willard F. "Negro Art in Chicago," *Opportunity,* Jan. 1940; "Negro Paints Story of Race in America," *New York Times,* June 27, 1943; Harley, Ralph, Jr. "A Checklist of Afro-Amer. Art & Artists," *The Serif,* Dec. 1970; "Working on Hampton Mural," *Chicago Defender,* Feb. 20, 1943; "Negro Paints Story of Race in America—Mural by C. W. White Unveiled at Hampton Institute," *New York Times,* June 26, 1943; Tanner Art Galleries. *Art of the American Negro,* 1940; Illinois Bell Telephone. *Black American Artists/71,* 1972; Roucek/Kiernan. *The Negro Impact on Western Civilization;* Howard Univ. *Charles White: Drawings,* 1967; Rollins. *They Showed the Way;* Redding, Saunders. *The Negro;* Dartmouth College. *6 Black Artists,* 1968; Flint Community Schools. *Black Reflections;* J.G. "Honoring Negro History," *Art Digest,* Feb. 15, 1949, p. 20; Greene, Carroll, Jr. "Perspective: The Black Artist in America," *Art Gallery,* April 1970, p. 19; "American Negro Art Given Full Length Review in NY Show," *Art Digest,* Dec. 15, 1941; "Young Negro Art Impresses New York," *Art Digest,* Oct. 15, 1943; "The Negro In Art," *Art Digest,* June 1, 1944; Woodruff, Hale. "Negro Artists Hold 4th Annual in Atlanta," *Art Digest,* April 15, 1945; "Negro Winners," *Art Digest,* May 1, 1946, p. 11; Pierre-Noel, Lois Jones. "American Negro Art in Progress," *Negro History Bulletin,* Oct. 1967; "Afro-American Artists 1800-1950," *Ebony,* Vol. 23, pp. 116-23; Rockford (Ill.) College. *Creativity and the Negro;* Locke, Alain. "Chicago's New Southside Art Center," *Magazine of Art,* Aug. 1941, p. 320; "The Negro Artist Comes of Age," *Art News,* Feb. 1, 1945; E.K. "Negro Artists," *Art News,* Feb. 1949; Kiah, Virginia. "Black Artists," *Savannah Magazine,* April 1972, p. 14; Johnson Pub. Co. *The JPC Art Collection;* Xavier Univ. *Emancipation Proclamation Centennial National Art Exhibition,* 1963; Driscoll, Edgar, Jr. "Exhibit Features Black Artists," *Boston Globe,* Feb. 16, 1970, p. 17; Greene, Carroll, Jr. *Afro-American Artists: 1800-1968,* Slides; Fax, Elton C. "Four Rebels in Art," *Freedomways,* Spring 1961; Giuliano, Charles. "Five Black Artists," *Boston After Dark,* March 4, 1970; "Winthrop Students Visit Arts Center," *Bay State Banner,* March 19, 1970; Loercher, Diana. "Black Artists Exhibition Reveals Visual Eloquence," *Christian Science Monitor,* March 2, 1970; Haydon, Harold. "Coming Age of Black Art," *Chicago Sun Times,* July 26, 1970; Faxon, Alicia. "Afro-American Exhibit Museum of Fine Arts," *Journal,* Concord, Mass., Jan. 20, 1972; Brown, Marion. "The Negro in the Fine Arts," *The Negro Heritage Library,* Vol. 2; Morsbach, Mable. *The Negro in American Life;* Woodruff, Hale. "Artists of the 60's," *The Negro in Music and Art,* 1969; Ploski, Harry, & Ernest Kaiser. "The Black Artist," *Afro USA,* 1971; Ploski, Harry, Ernest Kaiser, & Otto Lindenmeyer. "The Black Artist," *Reference Library of Black America,* Book 4, 1971; *The Negro Handbook,* Composed by Editors of *Ebony,* Chicago, 1966; Schatz, Walter. *Directory of Afro-American Resources,* 1970; South Side Community Art Center. *Chicago Collectors Exhibit of Negro Art,* 1945; South Side Community Art Center. *National Negro Art Exhibition,* Chicago, 1941; Myers, Carol L. *Black Power in the Arts,* Flint, Mich., 1970; Oakland Museum Archives; South Side Community Art Center. *Opening Exhibition of Paintings by Negro Artists,* Chicago, 1941; Gaither, Edmund B. "The Evolution of the Afro-American Artists," *Artists Proof,* Vol. 2; *Freedomways,* Winter 1962; *Portfolio of Six Drawings: The Art of Charles White,* New Century Pub., NY, 1953; *Black Heritage Series: Black American Artists of Yesterday & Today,* George A. Pflaum Pub., 1969; *Drum Major,* Southern Christian Leadership Council, Winter 1971; *Portfolio 10/Charles White,* Los Angeles, Pro-Artis Pub., 1961; Howard Univ. *Exhibition of Negro Artists of Chicago at Howard,* 1941; Murray & Roberts. *Black Perspectives,* Scholastic Book Services, 1972, pp. 24, 155; *Graphic Arts Council of the Los Angeles County Museum,* Vol. 5; Adams, Russell L. *Great Negroes Past & Present;* Spradling, Mary M., ed. *In Black & White: Afro-Americans in Print;* Preston, Malcolm. "Art: Black Exhibit," *Boston Herald Traveler,* April 19, 1971; "Leading Negro Artists," *Ebony,* Sept. 1963; Patterson, Lindsay. *The Negro in Music & Art,* 1967; Finkelstein, Sidney. *Realism in Art,* NY, Internat'l Pub., 1954; Robinson, Louie. "Charles White: Portrayer of Black Dignity," *Ebony,* July 1967; Walker, Roslyn. *A Resource Guide to the Visual Arts of Afro-Americans,* South Bend, Ind., 1971.

WHITE, CHARLOTTE

Painter.
Works: *Mother & Child.*
Exhibited: Atlanta Univ., 1944.
Sources: Atlanta Univ. catalog; Harley, Ralph, Jr. "Checklist of Afro-Amer. Art & Artists," *The Serif,* Dec. 1970.

WHITE, DONALD FRANCIS

Architect, civil engineer, educator. Born in Cicero, Illinois, May 28, 1908. Studied at the University of Michigan (MS, 1934). Instructor of Architecture, Prairie View State College.
Member: Omega Psi Phi.
Sources: Furr, Arthur F. *History & Progress of Negroes in the US.*

WHITE, ELIZABETH CATLETT

See: Catlett, Elizabeth (Mrs. Charles White).

WHITE, ERIC

Photographer.
Exhibited: Addison Gallery, 1971.
Sources: James Van DerZee Institute. *The Black Photographer (1908-1970): A Survey.*

WHITE, FRANKLIN

Painter. Born 1943.
Works: *Oreo; The Red Cap,* 1970 (oil); *Eggs 'n Bacon.*
Exhibited: State Armory, Wilmington, Del., 1971; Whitney Museum, 1971; James A. Porter Gallery, 1970.
Sources: Aesthetic Dynamics. *Afro-American Images 1971;* Doty. *Contemporary Black Artists in America;* Howard Univ. *James A. Porter Gallery of African American Art,* 1970.

WHITE, GEORGE

Painter. Born in 1920. Studied under Frederic Taubes.
Works: *Aspiration; Moses on Mt. Sinai; Jesus Healing a Blind Man; Noah's Ark.*

Exhibited: Central Presbyterian Church Annual, Haverstraw, NY.
Collections: Haverstraw (NY) Presbyterian Church; National Bank of Haverstraw (NY); Haverstraw (NY) Trust Co.
Sources: Ross, Don. "Factory Hand Has a Deft Touch as a Painter," *New York Tribune,* April 18, 1955.

WHITE, J. PHILIP

Painter. Born in 1939. Studied at State University of New York at New Paltz.
Works: *Good Neighbors; Deity.*
Exhibited: Gallery One, Hillsdale, 1968; RPI Black Arts Festival, 1969; State Univ. of NY at New Paltz, 1970 (1-man).
Awards: 1st prize, CAL Exhibition, Hillsdale, 1968.
Sources: NY State Education Dept. *Fifteen Under Forty.*

WHITE, JACK

Sculptor. Born in New York City, 1940. Studied at the New School for Social Research; Art Students League.
Works: *Deodate; Untitled #3; Black Study 101; Hail Afro; Should I Take to the Streets; Sweet Soul Music; Kenyatta's Corner; Beat of Soul; Another Hot Summer; Wilderness; Mau Mau; Still Life; Nude; Faces, the Devil & the Deep Blue Sea; Communications.*
Exhibited: Ruder & Finn Gallery, NYC, 1969; Boston Museum of Fine Arts, 1970; Manhattan Counterpoints; Lever House, NY; Minneapolis Institute of Art; Nordness Galleries, NYC, 1969; High Museum of Art, Atlanta; Flint (Mich.) Institute of Arts, 1969; Everson Museum of Art, Syracuse, NY, 1969; IBM Gallery of Arts & Sciences, NY, 1966; Rhode Island School of Design, 1969; Memorial Art Gallery, Rochester, NY, 1969; Contemporary Arts Museum, 1970; San Francisco Museum of Art, 1969; NJ State Museum, 1970; Roberson Center for the Arts & Sciences, Binghamton, NY, 1970; Univ. of Cal., Santa Barbara, 1970.
Collections: Mr. & Mrs. Edgar Gemmel; Mr. & Mrs. Boris Orstrovsky; Mr. Karl Brussell; Mr. Will Inman; Mr. & Mrs. H. Lyman.
Awards: MacDowell Art Colony Fellowship; Allen B. Tucker Memorial Fellowship.
Sources: "Now Showing: The Black Artist," *Contact,* Sept. 1970; Walsh, Rose. "Artists to Meet Public at Art Exhibit Preview," *Record American,* May 19, 1970; "Black Artists Work on View at Museum," *News,* Newburyport, Mass., May 16, 1970; Ploski, Harry, Ernest Kaiser, & Otto Lindenmeyer. "The Black Artist," *Reference Library of Black America,* Book 4, 1971; Harley, Ralph, Jr. "Checklist of Afro-Amer. Art & Artists," *Serif,* Dec. 1970; Nord-

ness Galleries. *12 Afro-American Artists,* 1969; Minneapolis Institute of Art. *30 Contemporary Black Artists,* 1968; Greene, Carroll. "Perspective: The Black Artist in America," *Art Gallery,* April 1970; "Afro-American Issue," *Art Gallery,* April 1968; Indiana Univ. *Fine Arts & the Black American;* Boston Museum of Fine Arts. *Afro-American Artists: NY & Boston;* Bowling, Frank. "The Rupture," *Arts,* Summer 1970; Kramer, Hilton. "Is Politics Submerging Black Art?," *Courier Journal & Times,* Louisville, Ky., June 7, 1970; Afro-Amer. Slide Depository, Catalog; DuSable Museum of African-Amer. History. *Contemporary Black Artists,* 1970, Calendar; Ruder & Finn Fine Arts. *Contemporary Black Artists,* 1969; Myers, Carol L. *Black Power in the Arts,* Flint, Mich., 1970; Hollingsworth, Alvin. "Wealth of Expression in Black Artists' RISD Show," *Providence Sunday Journal,* June 29, 1969; Le Brun, Caron. "Black Art," *Herald Traveler,* Sunday Supplement, Boston, May 24, 1970; Walker, Roslyn. *A Resource Guide to the Visual Arts of Afro-Americans,* South Bend, Ind., 1971.

WHITE, SARAH

Sources: Harley, Ralph, Jr. "Checklist of Afro-Amer. Art & Artists," *The Serif,* Dec. 1970.

WHITE, WILLIAM

Painter.
Works: *African Metamorphosis.*
Exhibited: Howard Univ., 1961.
Sources: *Negro Reference Book,* p. 772; Harley, Ralph, Jr. "Checklist of Afro-Amer. Art & Artists," *The Serif,* Dec. 1970; Brown, Marion. "The Negro in the Fine Arts," *The Negro Heritage Library,* Vol. 2.

WHITNEY, STANLEY

Painter, educator. Born in Philadelphia, 1946. Studied at Kansas City Art Institute (BFA); Yale University (MFA).
Works: *Echo #7.*
Exhibited: Univ. of Iowa, 1971-2; Illinois Bell Telephone, Chicago, 1969; Yale Art Gallery, May 1972; Yale at Norfolk, Aug. 1972; Univ. of Rhode Island, 1972 (1-man).
Collections: Ms. Susan Lewis, NYC; Ms. Lois Lane, NYC; Barkley Hedricks, New London, Conn.
Awards: Yale Univ. Scholarship; Kansas City Art Institute Scholarship.
Sources: Illinois Bell Telephone. *Black American Artists/71,* 1972; Information from artist.

WHITTAKER, MILLER F.

Architect.
Sources: Downing, Lewis K. "Contributions of Negro Scientists," *Crisis,* June 1939.

WHITTEN, JACK

Painter, educator. Born in Bessemer, Alabama, 1939. Studied at Tuskegee Institute; Southern University, Baton Rouge; Cooper Union, New York (BFA). Teacher at Pratt Institute.
Works: *Psychic Square 1; First Frame,* 1971.
Exhibited: Allan Stone Gallery, 1970 (1-man); Whitney Museum, 1969.
Collections: Chase Manhattan Bank, NY.
Awards: Whitney Fellowship, 1964.
Sources: Ploski, Harry, Ernest Kaiser, & Otto Lindenmeyer. "The Black Artist," *Reference Library of Black America,* Book 4, 1971; Myers, Carol L. *Black Power in the Arts,* Flint, Mich., 1970; Ploski, Harry, Ernest Kaiser. "The Black Artist," *Afro USA,* 1971; Brown, Marion. "The Negro in the Fine Arts," *The Negro Heritage Library,* Vol. 2; Bloom, Janet. "5+1," *Arts,* Dec. 1969/Jan. 1970, p. 56; Bowling, Frank. "It's Not Enough to Say 'Black Is Beautiful'," *Art News,* April 1971; "Afro-American Issue," *Art Gallery,* April 1968; Indiana Univ. *Fine Arts and the Black American;* DuSable Museum of African-Amer. History. *Contemporary Black Artists,* 1970; Walker, Roslyn. *A Resource Guide to the Visual Arts of Afro-Americans,* South Bend, Ind., 1971.

WHYTE, GARRETT

Painter.
Works: *All That Labor* (casein); *Of Love, Life Earth . . . Unity"; Where Are We Going; Rose of Sharon; They Went North.*
Exhibited: Oak Park Library; Smith-Mason Gallery, 1971.
Collections: Johnson Pub. Co.
Sources: Oak Park Library. *Exhibit of Black Art,* n.d.; "Soldier-Artist Finished Mural at Camp," *Norfolk Journal & Guide,* Aug. 22, 1942; "Afro-American Issue," *Art Gallery,* April 1968; Indiana Univ. *Fine Arts & the Black American;* Smith-Mason Gallery. *National Exhibition Black Artists,* 1971; DuSable Museum of African-Amer. History. *Contemporary Black Artists,* 1970, Calendar; Johnson Pub. Co. *The JPC Art Collection,* Pamphlet; Harley, Ralph, Jr. "Checklist of Afro-Amer. Art & Artists," *Serif,* Dec. 1970; Atkinson, J. Edward. *Black Dimensions in Contemporary American Art,* 1971; Myers, Carol L. *Black Power in the Arts,* Flint, Mich. 1970; Walker, Roslyn. *A Resource Guide to the Visual Arts of Afro-Americans,* South Bend, Ind., 1971.

WICKHAM, REGINALD

Photographer. Born 1931.
Works: *Harlem March,* 1968 (photograph); *Tenement,* 1970 (photograph).
Exhibited: Whitney Museum, 1971; Addison Gallery, 1971.

Sources: Doty. *Contemporary Black Artists in America;* James Van DerZee Institute. *The Black Photographer (1908-1970): A Survey.*

WIGFALL, BENJAMIN LEROY

Painter, graphic artist. Born in 1930. Studied at the State University of Iowa; Yale-Norfolk Summer School, Norfolk, Connecticut; Yale School of Design, New Haven, Connecticut.
Works: *Burning #1; Burning #3; Shape Theme.*
Exhibited: Amer. Federation of Arts Traveling Exhibition, 1951-3; Norfolk Museum of Arts & Sciences; Jewish Community Center of Newport, Conn.; Addison Gallery, Andover, Mass.; Nat'l Rehabilitation Service Exhibition; Va. Museum of Fine Arts; Brooklyn Museum, 1955; State Univ. of Iowa, 1954; Lever House, NYC; Yale Univ. Graphics Dept. (1-man).
Collections: Hampton (Va.) Institute.
Awards: 1st prize, Va. Artists Show, 1951; Purchase Prize, Hampton (Va.) Institute, 1953; Purchase Prize, Va. Artists Show, 1951; Fellowships from Va. Museum of Fine Arts, 1949, 1951-3; Fellowship, Men's Council of Hampton Institute, 1952; General Education Board Fellowship, 1953-4; Yale-Norfolk Summer Art School Fellowship, 1954; Fellowship, Yale School of Design, 1954-5.
Sources: NY State Education Dept. *Fifteen Under Forty.*

WIGGINS, EDGAR ALBERT

Draftsman. Born in Chicago, 1904. Studied at the School of United Arts.
Exhibited: Harmon Foundation, 1928.
Sources: Harmon Foundation. *Exhibition of Productions by Negro Artists;* Indiana Univ. *Fine Arts & the Black American;* Walker, Roslyn. *A Resource Guide to the Visual Arts of Afro-Americans,* South Bend, Ind., 1971.

WIGGINS, GLORIA

Painter. Born in New York City, January 17, 1933.
Works: *Oil on Velvet.*
Exhibited: Mariners Harbor Art Festival, 1967, 1970; Harlem Art Festival, 1968-9; Staten Island Community College, 1969-71; Olatunji Center for African Culture, 1968-9; Richmond College, 1971-2; Sailors SNUG Harbor, 1969.
Collections: President of the 24th UN Session; Dr. Nathaniel Richardson, Asst. Sec. of State, Liberia; Mr. Lewis Michaux; Dr. Thomas Matthews; Babatunde Olatunji.
Awards: Resident Artist Award, Staten Island Community College, 1971.
Sources: Information from artist.

WIGGINS, MICHAEL

Painter, graphic artist. Born in Brooklyn, New York, July 29, 1954.

Exhibited: Brooklyn Museum, 1968; Mariners Harbor Art Festival, 1967; Harlem Art Festival, 1969; Olatunji Center for African Culture, 1969.
Collections: President W.S. Tubman, Liberia.
Awards: Sklenar Art Award, best in show, 1967; 3rd prize, PS 18, NY; 2nd place, Pininzolo Art Award, 1969.
Represented by: Gloria Wiggins, 168 Brabant Ave., Staten Island, NY.
Sources: Information from artist.

WIGGINS, TERESA

Graphic artist. Born in New York City, March 16, 1956.
Exhibited: Mariners Harbor Art Festival, 1967; PS 44, NY, 1969.
Awards: Pininzolo Art Award, 1st place, 1969.
Represented by: Gloria Wiggins, 168 Brabant Ave., Staten Island, NY.
Sources: Information from artist.

WIGGS, BERTIE

Painter. Born in North Carolina. Studied at Hampton Institute Nursing School; Junior Blair College.
Works: *A Soul's Ghost.*
Exhibited: Oxon Hill Library; DC Public Library; DCAA, Anacostia Neighborhood Museum-Smithsonian Institution.
Awards: Ford Dupont Christmas Award, 2 years.
Sources: DC Art Assn. *Exhibition '71,* Washington, DC, 1971.

WIGGUN, EDGAR ALBERT

Born in Chicago in 1904.
Exhibited: Harmon Foundation, 1928.
Sources: Harley, Ralph, Jr. "Checklist of Afro-Amer. Art & Artists," *The Serif,* Dec. 1970.

WILDER, JOHN BRANTLEY

Works: *Las Casitas; Look Who's Looking; Pointed Hat.*
Exhibited: Phila. Civic Center.
Sources: Phila Civic Center. *Afro-American Artists 1800-1969.*

WILHOIT, EUGENE FRANKLIN

Born in Virginia in 1906.
Works: *Daniel Haynes, The Actor; Black & Tan.*
Exhibited: Harmon Foundation, 1933.
Sources: Harmon Foundation. *Non-Jury Exhibit of Works of Negro Artists,* 1933.

WILKIE, EARL A.

Mixed media.
Works: *In Search of a Primeval Past; Touch Me Softly With Love; Brown Lady Brown Lady; Study in Black called Malcolm; In There; Blues Men; Totem.*

Exhibited: Phila Civic Center; State Armory, Wilmington, Del., 1971.
Sources: Phila. Civic Center. *Afro-American Artists 1800-1969;* Aesthetic Dynamics. *Afro-American Images,* 1971.

WILKINS, DEBORAH
Graphic artist.
Works: *Heads.*
Represented by: Blackman's Art Gallery, San Francisco.
Sources: *Black Shades,* Vol. 3, #2.

WILKINS, TIMOTHY
Painter, mixed media, sculptor. Born in Norfolk, Virginia on December 23, 1943. Studied at Pratt Institute; under John Rudge.
Works: *Self Portrait With Tear; Square Face; Accident; People on 5th Ave.; Phantasy Landscape; No. 30; Carnival.*
Exhibited: Starker Art Gallery, Provincetown, Mass., 1967; Flynn Gallery, NY, 1969; Acts of Art Gallery, NY, 1971.
Collections: Baron Peter Szorwoski; Mr. Walter P. Chrysler, Jr.; Mr. Sydney Rafael; Mr. Malcolm Harkness Mills; Ms. May Callas Jester; Prof. Tom Pelzel, Santa Barbara; Mr. Philippe Arnaud, Nantes, France; Prof. Paul Oppenheimer, Columbia Univ.; Prof. Burr Wallen, Princeton Univ.; Kippy Forbes (*Forbes Magazine*); Mr. Charles Muenchinger.
Awards: Guest instructor, Metropolitan Museum of Art, 1971.
Represented by: Burr Wallen, 328 E. 85th St., Apt. 5B, NY; Nigel Jackson, Director, Acts of Art Gallery, 15 Charles St., NY.
Sources: *Sixth Street Notebooks.*

WILKINS, WILBIRT M.
Exhibited: Wharton House, Phila., 1942.
Sources: Harley, Ralph, Jr. "Checklist of Afro-Amer. Art & Artists," *The Serif,* Dec. 1970.

WILKINSON, HILDA
Sources: Myers, Carol L. *Black Power in the Arts,* Flint, Mich., 1970; Herring, James V. "The American Negro Craftsman and Artist," *The Crisis,* April 1942; *The Negro in Music and Art,* NY, 1969.

WILLIAM, SAM
Sources: Myers, Carol L. *Black Power in the Arts,* Flint, Mich., 1970; DuSable Museum of African-Amer. History. *Contemporary Black Artists,* Calendar, 1970.

WILLIAMS, ALFREDUS
Primitive painter. Born 1875. Began painting late in life. First exhibited in 1940's.
Exhibited: Merino Galleries, NYC.
Sources: Dover. *American Negro Art;* Indiana Univ. *Fine Arts & the Black American;*

Harley, Ralph, Jr. "Checklist of Afro-Amer. Art & Artists," *Serif,* Dec. 1970; Walker, Roslyn. *A Resource Guide to the Visual Arts of Afro-Americans,* South Bend, Ind., 1971.

WILLIAMS, ANTHONY
Painter, educator. Born November 21, 1935 in Detroit. Teacher at the Society of Arts and Crafts.
Works: *Dancer; Dawn.*
Exhibited: Detroit Institute of Arts.
Sources: Detroit Institute of Arts files.

WILLIAMS, AUGUSTUS DuPONT
Born in Alabama in 1915.
Works: *In the Morning; Painting Inside Bottle; The Windy Day.*
Exhibited: Harmon Foundation, 1933.
Sources: Harmon Foundation. *Non-Jury Exhibit of Works of Negro Artists,* 1933.

WILLIAMS, CEOLA
Painter. Born in Jacksonville, Florida. Studied at Washington School of Art.
Works: *Sunset; Mid-Spring.*
Exhibited: Studio Museum in Harlem, 1969.
Collections: Johnson Pub. Co.
Sources: Johnson Pub. *The JPC Art Collection,* Pamphlet; Studio Museum in Harlem. *Harlem Artists 69.*

WILLIAMS, DOUGLAS
Sculptor. Active in 1960's.
Works: *Snail Bird; Mask.*
Exhibited: Oak Park Library.
Collections: Johnson Pub. Co.
Sources: "Afro-American Issue," *Art Gallery,* April 1968; Indiana Univ. *Fine Arts and the Black American;* DuSable Museum of African-Amer. History. *Contemporary Black Artists,* 1970, Calendar; Johnson Pub. Co. *The JPC Art Collection,* Pamphlet; Myers, Carol L. *Black Power in the Arts,* Flint, Mich., 1970.

WILLIAMS, GERALD
Painter. Born in Chicago.
Works: *Nation Time; Black Family; I Am Somebody; Nationhood; Wake Up.*
Exhibited: Howard Univ., 1970, 1972; National Center of Afro-Amer. Artists, 1970, 1972; Studio Museum in Harlem, 1970, 1972.
Collections: Johnson Pub. Co.
Member: AFRICOBRA.
Sources: *Black Shades,* Feb. 1972; Johnson Pub. Co. *The JPC Art Collection,* pamphlet; Grillo, Jean B. "Where Down Home Meets Back Home," *Boston After Dark,* Sept. 1970; Howard Univ. *Africobra II,* 1972.

WILLIAMS, HOBIE
Educator. Born in Bainbridge, Georgia. Studied at Fort Valley State College, Georgia (BS);

University of Wisconsin (MS in Art Education); Pennsylvania State University; Tyler School of Fine Arts, Temple University; University of Pittsburgh. Assistant Professor of Art, Florida A&M University.
Works: *Barnyard Chief; Flight 2 Departing.*
Exhibited: Hortt Exhibition, Fla.; Beaux Arts Exhibition, Tuskegee Institute; Xavier Univ., 1963; Atlanta Univ.
Awards: Honorable Mention, Hortt Memorial Exhibition; Atlanta Univ.
Sources: Pittsburgh Community College. *16 Black Artists;* Xavier Univ. *Emancipation Proclamation Centennial National Art Exhibition, 1963.*

WILLIAMS, HUGHAN

Painter. Born in 1953. Studied at Springfield (Mass.) Public Library in George Walter Vincent's children's art course; Manson House; Famous Artists School, Connecticut; Boston Art Institute.
Exhibited: Springfield College; American Internat'l College, Springfield; Valley Bank.
Member: Afro-Art Alliance, Springfield, Mass.
Sources: Information from the artist.

WILLIAMS, JAMES

Sculptor. Born in 1921.
Sources: "James Williams, 16 Year Old Jr. High School Sculptor & Some of His Completed Works," *Washington Tribune,* April 24, 1937.

WILLIAMS, JOANN

Painter, graphic artist, sculptor. Studied at Wayne State University (BS).
Works: *Confrontation; Nude; Nude in Blue; Green Mist; Still Life; Old Woman; Song of Despair; Michael; Sculpture #2; Guitarist; Unwed Mother; Mardi Gras; Stairway to Despair.*
Exhibited: Detroit Institute of Arts, 1968; Wayne State Univ.; Biro Gallery, Detroit; Normacel Gallery, Detroit, 1970.
Member: Mich. Watercolor Society.
Sources: Afro-American Slide Depository, Catalog; Normacel Gallery. *A Black Women Art Exhibit,* Detroit, 1970.

WILLIAMS, JOSÉ

Printmaker. Born in Birmingham, Alabama, 1934. Studied at the University of Illinois (BFA, 1972); Chicago Teachers College (1959-61); American Academy of Art (1955-7).
Works: *63rd Street.*
Exhibited: Wiebolt Dept. Store, Chicago, 1967 (1-man); Atlanta Univ., 1967; Anshe Emet Day School, Chicago, 1968; Baskin Clothing Co., Chicago, 1969; Millikin Univ., Decatur, Ill., 1969; South Side Community Art Center,

Chicago, 1971; Ill. State Univ., 1971; Black Expo, Chicago, 1971; Sears Roebuck Stores, Chicago & Gary, Ind., 1972; Frances Parker High School, Chicago, 1972.
Collections: Johnson Pub. Co.
Member: Nat'l Conference of Artists; Afam Gallery, founder; House of Afam, advisor; South Side Art Center, director.
Sources: "Afro-American Issue," *Art Gallery,* April 1968; Indiana Univ. *Fine Arts & the Black American;* DuSable Museum of African-Amer. History. *Contemporary Black Artists,* 1970, Calendar; Johnson Pub. Co. *The JPC Art Collection,* Pamphlet; *Freedom Unlimited,* Aug. 1970; *Sheboygan Press,* Jan. 9, 1971; *Chicago Tribune,* Dec. 12, 1971; *Chicago Daily Defender,* Feb. 24, 1972; Millikin Univ. *For Souls Only,* Decatur, Ill., May 1969; Ill. State Univ. *Midwest University Students Drawing & Print Exhibition,* March/April 1971; Information from artist; Myers, Carol L. *Black Power in the Arts,* Flint, Mich., 1970; Walker, Roslyn. *A Resource Guide to the Visual Arts of Afro-Americans,* South Bend, Ind., 1971.

WILLIAMS, JOSEPH

Painter.
Works: *Evening Falls.*
Exhibited: Dillard Univ., 1941.
Sources: Dillard Univ. *Arts Festival,* Catalog, 1941.

WILLIAMS, LAETITIA EVELYN

Painter, graphic artist. Born in New York. Studied at Nebraska University Teachers College; Columbia University. Instructor of Fine and Practical Arts, Bethune Cookman College.
Works: *Eucalyptus; Florida Dawn; The Iris.*
Exhibited: Harmon Foundation, 1933; Broadmore Art Academy; Teachers College, Columbia Univ.; Bethune Cookman College.
Sources: Harmon Foundation. *Non-Jury Exhibit of Works of Negro Artists,* 1933.

WILLIAMS, LAURA G.

Painter. Born in Philadelphia, 1915. Studied at the College of San Mateo (1960-5); under Richard Bowman at Redwood City, California (1965-8).
Works: *Figure; Red Figure; Untitled* (Acrylic).
Exhibited: Oakland Art Museum, 1968.
Awards: Honorable Mention, Oakland Museum, 1968.
Sources: Oakland Art Museum. *New Perspectives in Black Art;* Indiana Univ. *Fine Arts & the Black American;* Lewis/Waddy. *Black Artists on Art,* Vol. 1; Harley, Ralph, Jr. "Checklist of Afro-Amer. Art & Artists," *Serif,* Dec. 1970; Walker, Roslyn. *A Resource Guide to the Visual Arts of Afro-Americans,* South Bend, Ind., 1971.

WILLIAMS, LILLIAN

Painter.
Works: *Study in Blue.*
Exhibited: Atlanta Univ., 1944.
Sources: Atlanta Univ. catalog, 1944; Harley, Ralph, Jr. "Checklist of Afro-Amer. Art & Artists," *The Serif,* Dec. 1970.

WILLIAMS, LORRAINE

Painter.
Works: *Women of Mitta; Siesta.*
Exhibited: McMillen Inc. Galleries, NY, 1941.
Sources: McMillen Inc. Galleries. *Contemporary Negro Art,* NY, 1941.

WILLIAMS, LOUIS

Painter.
Works: *Urban Renewal* (acrylic).
Exhibited: Smith-Mason Gallery, 1971.
Sources: Smith-Mason Gallery. *National Exhibit Black Artists,* 1971.

WILLIAMS, LOUISE

Painter, sculptor. Born in Pittsburgh in 1913. Studied at Wayne State University; Charles McGee School; Society of Arts & Crafts.
Works: *What Price Violence* (acrylic); *Deflection 100* (acrylic); *Two Biafran Boys* (charcoal); *Formae Differentiae* (acrylic); *Gre; Piano Man; End of the Road; Generation Gap; Benne; The Masses; Storm Center; Shapes of Colors; Skyline; Market in Guadeloupe; Meleni; The Music Makers; The Proposal; Angry Sea; Warm Tomes or Pomegranates.*
Exhibited: Detroit Institute of Arts, 1969; Scarab Club, Detroit, 1969, 1972; Mt. Clemons, Mich., 1972; Russel Woods Festival; Afro-Amer. Museum, 1969, 1970; Children's Museum; Wayne State Univ.; Normacel Gallery, Detroit, 1970.
Awards: 2nd prize, Russel Woods Festival; 3rd prize, Afro-Amer. Museum; Army Special Service Award & Cash Prize.
Sources: Information from artist; Normacel Gallery. *A Black Women Art Exhibit,* Detroit, 1970; Afro-Amer. Slide Depository, Catalog, 1971-2.

WILLIAMS, PAUL REVERE

Architect. Born in Los Angeles, February 18, 1894. Studied at University of Southern California; Institute of Design; Polytechnic High School; Beaux Arts Institute of Design.
Works: Fraternity & sorority houses in Los Angeles; House for Lon Chaney; House for Corinne Griffith; Hollywood YMCA; West Coast Co. Theatre; House for Senator Flint; House for Victor Rosetti; Los Angeles International Airport (Assoc. Architect); Saks 5th Ave West; J. Sloane, Inc.; Haggerty's Beverly Hills; Negro Memorial, Washington, DC (Director of Plans); UCLA Botany Building, 1958; Marina Del Ray Jr. High School, Los Angeles, 1960.
Awards: Spingarn Medal, 1953; 3 National Awards; 4 Western Awards; Los Angeles Award for Creative Plan, 1955.
Member: Board of Directors, YMCA; Los Angeles Urban League; West Side Improvement Assoc.; NAACP; American Institute of Architects; City Planning Commission; Unity Finance Co.; Los Angeles Art Commission; Howard Univ. Trustees; Meharry Medical College Trustees; Cal. Redevelopment Commission & State Housing Commission.
Sources: Brawley, Benjamin. *The Negro Genius; Who's Who in Colored America,* 3rd edition; Furr, Arthur F. *History & Progress of Negroes in the US;* Rockford College. *Creativity and the Negro;* Harley, Ralph, Jr. "Checklist of Afro-American Art & Artists," *The Serif,* Dec. 1970; Boning, Richard A. *Profiles of Black Americans,* NY, 1968; Wilson, John L. *The Negro Architect,* pp. 25, 30; Williams, Paul R. *Small Homes of Tomorrow;* Williams, Paul R. *New Homes for Today;* Robinson, Wilhelmena A. *Historical Negro Biographies; Current Biography,* 1941, pp. 920-2; *Ebony,* Feb. 1946, p. 25; *Ebony,* March 1949, pp. 43-8; Spradling, Mary, ed. *In Black and White: Afro-Americans in Print;* Williams, Paul R. "If I Were Young Today," *Ebony,* Aug. 1963; Downing, Lewis K. "Contributions of Negro Scientists," *Crisis,* June 1939; *American Institute of Architects Directory,* 1956.

WILLIAMS, MABLE

Exhibited: NY Public Library, 1921.
Sources: Harley, Ralph, Jr. "Checklist of Afro-Amer. Art & Artists," *The Serif,* Dec. 1970.

WILLIAMS, RHODA

Painter.
Works: *Voter Registration; Pink Styx; Shades; Study in Black and White #9; Golden Black; The Grass Roots; Frolic; Scorpio 1970; Crab Grass; Memorial March; Black Gothic; Little Buddha Black; Orange Kicks; Moody Soul Suspension; Wise Ole Odd Chile; Us Kids in White Plains, Say What?*
Sources: Afro-American Slide Depository, Catalog, 1971-2.

WILLIAMS, RICHARD MILBY

Painter. Active in 1930's.
Works: *Portrait of Charles Lindbergh.*
Exhibited: Harmon Foundation, 1931.
Collections: Roosevelt High School, Chicago.
Member: Charter member, Chicago Art League.
Sources: Harmon Foundation. *Exhibition of Productions by Negro Artists;* Indiana Univ.

Fine Arts & the Black American; Harmon Foundation. *Negro Artists,* 1935; DuSable Museum of African-Amer. History. *Contemporary Black Artists,* 1970, Calendar; Harley, Ralph, Jr. "Checklist of Afro-Amer. Art & Artists," *Serif,* Dec. 1970; Walker, Roslyn. *A Resource Guide to the Visual Arts of Afro-Americans,* South Bend, Ind., 1971.

WILLIAMS, SIMEON SIR HENRY

Educator. Born in Kentucky, 1888. Studied at Wilberforce University; Cincinnati Academy of Fine Arts.
Works: *Owonoco.*
Exhibited: Harmon Foundation, 1930.
Sources: Harmon Foundation. *Exhibition of Productions by Negro Artists;* Indiana Univ. *Fine Arts & the Black American;* Harmon Foundation. *Exhibit of Fine Arts,* 1930; Walker, Roslyn. *A Resource Guide to the Visual Arts of Afro-Americans,* South Bend, Ind., 1971; Harley, Ralph, Jr. "Checklist of Afro-Amer. Art & Artists," *Serif,* Dec. 1970.

WILLIAMS, THEOPOLUS

Sources: The Scribes, St. Louis. *Sing, Laugh, Weep,* St. Louis, 1944; Harley, Ralph, Jr. "Checklist of Afro-Amer. Art & Artists," *The Serif,* Dec. 1970.

WILLIAMS, TODD

Sculptor. Born in Savannah, Georgia, 1939. Studied at the School of Visual Arts, New York (1961-5).
Works: *Coney Island; Who's Afraid of Virginia Woolf?; Tondo; Fusion; Autumn,* 1970 (painted wood).
Exhibited: School of Visual Arts, 1964-5; "Colored Sculpture," circulated by the Amer. Federation of Arts, 1965-6; 1st World Festival of Negro Arts, Dakar, Senegal, 1966; Whitney Museum, 1971; Dickson Art Center, 1966.
Awards: John Hay Whitney Foundation Fellowship, 1965; Visual Arts Scholarship; J. Clawson Mills Fellowship.
Sources: Doty. *Contemporary Black Artists in America;* "Afro-American Issue," *Art Gallery,* April 1968; Indiana Univ. *Fine Arts & the Black American;* Smithsonian Institution. *10 Negro Artists from the United States;* Morrison, Allan. "New Surge in the Arts," *Ebony,* Aug. 1967; UCLA Art Galleries. *The Negro in American Art;* DuSable Museum of African-Amer. History. *Contemporary Black Artists,* 1970, Calendar; Harley, Ralph, Jr. "Checklist of Afro-Amer. Art & Artists," *Serif,* Dec. 1970; Woodruff, Hale. "Artists of the 60's," *The Negro in Music and Art,* 1969; Myers, Carol L. *Black Power in the Arts,* Flint, Mich., 1970; Walker, Roslyn. *A Resource Guide to the*

Visual Arts of Afro-Americans, South Bend, Ind., 1971.

WILLIAMS, VIVIAN

Painter.
Works: *Kimbolton Stream; Canine Friends; Frog in Cabbage; Rocking Chair; Dresden Stream; Deserted Farm; Sollento; Venice; Band Shell; Coopendale Mill; Basilica Pompin; Chappaquiddick Beach; Odds and Ends; Our Land; Roof Tops; Menemsha Bight; Side Canal.*
Sources: Afro-American Slide Depository, Catalog, 1971-2.

WILLIAMS, WALTER

Painter, printmaker. Born in Brooklyn, New York, 1920. Studied at Brooklyn Museum Art School (1951-5).
Works: *Boy with Roots,* 1968 (oil on plywood); *Southern Landscape,* 1964 (oil & collage on board); *Fighting Cock; Poultry Market.*
Exhibited: Roko Gallery, NY, 1954, 1962, 1963 (all 1-man); Gallery Noa Poa, Copenhagen, 1956 (1-man); Texas Southern Univ., 1962 (1-man); Mexican-North Amer. Cultural Institute, Mexico City, 1963 (1-man); Gallery Brinken, Stockholm, 1965 (1-man); Studio 183, Sydney, Australia, 1965 (1-man); The Little Gallery, Phila., 1966 (1-man); Gallery Marya, Copenhagen, 1967 (1-man); Fisk Univ., Nashville, 1967-8, 1969 (1-man); Jackson (Miss.) State College, 1969 (1-man); Berea (Ky.) College (1-man); Whitney Museum, 1955, 1958, 1963; Portland Museum of Art, 1958; Instituto Nacional de Dellas Artes, Mexico, 1958; Brooklyn Museum, 1963; Musée d'art et d'histoire, Geneve, Suisse, 1965; Pa. Academy, 1966; Ala. Academy of Arts, 1966; White House, Washington, DC, 1966; UCLA Galleries, 1966; Rochester Memorial Art Gallery; Dartmouth College, NH, 1967; Albright-Knox Museum, Buffalo, 1967; Everson Gallery, Syracuse Univ., 1967; New Britain (Conn.) Museum of Amer. Art, 1967; Talladega (Ala.) College, 1968; Jarvis Christian College, Hawkins, Tex., 1968; 50 Years of Afro-Amer. Art, Phila.; Xavier Univ., Cincinnati, 1969; Lane College, Jackson, Tenn.; Shaw Univ., Raleigh; Smithsonian Institution; Brooks Memorial Art Gallery, Tenn.; Black Amer. Artists, Ill. Bell traveling show, 1971; Stephens College, Columbus, Mo., 1968; St. Augustine College, Raleigh; Utica College, NY; Univ. of Cincinnati, 1969.
Collections: Metropolitan Museum of Art; Nat'l Gallery of Art, Washington, DC; Cincinnati Art Museum; Whitney Museum; Walker Art Center, Minneapolis; Riverside Museum, NY; Texas Southern Univ., Houston; Mexican Amer. Institute, Mexico City; Brooklyn Museum; Phila. Museum of Art; Syracuse

Univ.; Lowe Art Center, NY; School of Fine Arts, Pa.; Univ. of Ga.; Tucson (Ariz.) Public Schools; Oberlin College, Ohio; Bellarmine College Library, Ky.; Dartmouth College; Print Council of America, NYC; Skowhegan (Me.) School of Painting & Sculpture; Howard Univ.; Smithsonian Institution; Hon. William Benton; Mr. Nelson Rockefeller; Univ. of Redlands, Cal.

Awards: John Hay Whitney Fellowship, 1955; National Institute of Arts & Letters Grant, 1960; Silvermine Award, 1963; Scholarship, Skowhegan School of Maine.

Sources: Information from the artist; UCLA Art Galleries. *The Negro in American Art;* Dover. *American Negro Art;* Illinois Bell Telephone. *Black American Artists/71,* 1972; Dartmouth College. *6 Black Artists,* 1968; *10 American Negro Artists Living & Working in Europe,* 1964; Shorewood Reproductions Catalogue. *The Art of Black America,* 1969; Harley, Ralph, Jr. "Checklist of Afro-Amer. Art & Artists," *The Serif,* Dec. 1970; "The Black Artist in America: A Symposium," *Metropolitan Museum of Art Bulletin,* Jan. 1969, pp. 243-8; Haas, Joseph. "A Big, Brilliant & Exciting Exhibition of Black Art," *Chicago Daily News,* Jan. 16-17, 1971; Driskell, David C. *John Rhoden & Walter Williams,* Fisk Univ., 1967; Myers, Carol L. *Black Power in the Arts,* Flint, Mich., 1970; Walker, Roslyn. *A Resource Guide to the Visual Arts of Afro-Americans,* South Bend, Ind., 1971.

WILLIAMS, WALTER J., JR.

Painter, illustrator, mixed media. Born in Biloxi, Mississippi, 1922. Studied at Meinzinger Art School; Society of Arts and Crafts, Detroit.

Works: *Man's Scar; To Nowhere; Le Jazz Hot; Blues and Rain; Carib Holiday; Mama; A Girl Cries; The Blues; Mama and the Kitten; American Jazz; Still Life 1933; Billy Boy; Reclining Nude,* 1950 (oil); *Nymph,* 1950-65 (oil); *Poppies,* 1960 (oil); *Bridge,* 1966 (mixed media); *Bass Player,* 1956 (oil); *Carnival,* 1968 (oil); *Old & Young,* 1970 (pastel); *Blind Musician,* 1955 (oil); *Hager* (oil & casein); *Carnival New Orleans* (oil); *Cleo* (acrylic); *Bless the Child* (pastel); *Ethiopian Princess* (pastel); *Corner Bar; The Winners* (pastel); *Young Mother* (pastel); *Butterfly* (oil/ink); *Hannibal* (pastel); *The Bird* (oil & sand).

Exhibited: Toledo Museum, 1969; Grand Rapids Museum, 1970; Detroit Institute of Arts Museum, 1968; Atlanta Univ.; Wayne State Univ., 1969; Scarab Club, Detroit, 1968; Rackham Memorial Museum, Detroit; Rackham Memorial Museum, Ann Arbor, Mich., 1967-9; Univ. of Fla.; Mich. Artists Annual Detroit; Mich. State Fair; Invitational, Mich.

State Fairgrounds, Detroit; Pontiac Cultural Arts Center; Lester Arwin Gallery, Detroit; Detroit Artists Market; Hannamura Gallery, Detroit; Bloomfield Hills (Mich.) Annual; Lafayette Park Outdoor Exhibition, Detroit.

Collections: Johnson Pub. Co., Chicago; Dr. Robert L. Perkins, Detroit; Mr. & Mrs. Al Keats, Detroit; Detroit Receiving Hospital; Mr. & Mrs. David Stalker; Mr. & Mrs. Howard Sims, Detroit; Mr. & Mrs. Charles Diggs, Jr.; Mr. David Harold, Jr., Detroit; Councilman William T. Patrick, Jr., Detroit; Mr. & Mrs. Frank Holman, Malibu Beach, Cal.; West Point Military Academy; Mr. & Mrs. Peter Labuzan, New Orleans; Mr. & Mrs. Eugene Chaires, Detroit; Dr. DeRoven, Detroit; Mr. Sammy Davis, Jr., Cal.; Mrs. Edith Shifflet, Detroit; Mr. Preston Bright, Detroit; Mrs. Connolly Majorca.

Awards: Arts Festival, Wayne State Univ., Detroit, 1969; 3 1st prizes, Russell Woods Outdoor Exhibition, Detroit, 1967-9; Mich. Society of Engineers, Rackham Memorial, Detroit, 1967.

Member: Mich. Academy of Arts, Science & Letters; Detroit Society for the Advancement of Culture & Education (executive board, visual arts coordinator, art director); Contemporary Studio (past president & board chairman).

Sources: Information from the artist; Afro-American Slide Depository, Catalog; Johnson Pub. Co. *The JPC Art Collection,* Pamphlet; Detroit Institute of Arts files.

WILLIAMS, WILLIAM T.

Printmaker, painter, educator. Born in Cross Creek, North Carolina, 1942. Studied at New York City Community College (AAS, 1962); Pratt Institute (BFA, 1966); Yale University (MFA, 1968).

Works: *Untitled* (etching); *In the Middle of the Day; Overkill; Doctor Buzzard Meets Saddle Head; Sweets Crane; Stacked; It's the Time of the Mind in the Middle of the Day* (acrylic).

Exhibited: Waterford Public Library, Conn.; Hillcrest Inn, Ogunquit, Me.; Wilkes College, Wilkes-Barre, Pa.; Terra Mar Yacht Club, Saybrook, Conn.; Mystic Art Assn.; Mitchell College, New London, Conn.; Indianapolis Museum of Art, 1972; Utah Museum of Fine Arts, 1972; Museum of Modern Art, 1969, 1972; Whitney Museum, 1969, 1971, 1972; Reese Palley, NY, May 1971, Mar. 1971 (1-man); DeMenil Foundation, Houston, 1971; Kolner Konstmarkt, Germany, 1971; Rice Univ., 1971; L'Art Vivant Aux États-Unis, Fondation Maeght, St. Paul, France, 1970; Critics Choice Traveling Exhibition, 1969-70; Amer. Embassy, Moscow, 1969-70; State Univ. at Stonybrook, 1969; Larry Aldrich Museum,

Ridgefield, Conn., 1969; Studio Museum, Harlem, 1969; 652 Broadway, NYC.
Collections: Museum of Modern Art; Univ. of Maine; State of NY, Albany Mall; Chase Manhattan Bank; Fisk Univ.; Whitney Museum; Menil Foundation, Rice Univ.; Charles Cowles; Russell Cowles; A. Stern, NYC; John Jacobson, NYC; John DeMenil, Houston; Harry Abrams Publishers; Gottesman Plaza, NYC.
Awards: AWS Traveling Exhibition; Soc. of North Amer. Artists; Nat'l Endowment for the Arts Traveling Grant, 1966; Nat'l Endowment for the Arts, 1970.
Sources: Roelof-Lanner, T.V., ed. *Prints by American Negro Artists;* Shapiro, David. "652 Broadway," *Art News,* Apr. 1971; Bowling, Frank. "It's Not Enough to Say 'Black Is Beautiful,'" *Art News,* Apr. 1971; Jones, Walter. "Critique to Black Artists," *Arts Magazine,* Apr. 1970, p. 16; Bowling, Frank. "Discussion on Black Art-II," *Arts Magazine,* May, 1969; Bloom, Janet. "5+1," *Arts,* Dec. '69/Jan. '70, p. 56; "The Black Artist in America: A Symposium," *Metropolitan Museum of Art Bulletin,* Vol. 27, No. 5, Jan. 1969, p. 245; *Artists/USA 1972-1973,* Feasterville, Pa., 1972; Bowling, Frank. "Problems of Criticism," *Arts Magazine,* Vol. 46, No. 7; Sandler, Irving. "Visiting Artists," New York State Council on the Arts, 1972; Indianapolis Museum of Art. *Painting and Sculpture Today 1972;* Ashton, Dore. "Drawings by New York Artists," Utah Museum of Fine Arts, 1972; Menil Foundation. *Deluxe Show,* Houston, Texas, 1971; "Canvasses Brimming with Color," *Life Magazine,* Sept. 24, 1971; Tucker, Marsha. "The Structure of Color," Whitney Museum of Amer. Art, Apr. 1971; Childs, Charles. "Some American History," Rice Univ., Apr. 1971; "The Downtown Scene," *New York Times,* Mar. 13, 1971; "William T. Williams Artist," *Bay State Banner,* Boston, Aug. 20, 1970; Jones, Walter. "Two Black Artists," *Arts Magazine,* Apr. 1970; "Begin with a Lot," *Industrial Magazine,* Apr. 1970; Ashton, Dore. "Young Abstract Painters: Right On!," *Arts Magazine,* Feb. 1970; Jewish Museum. *Using Walls,* 1970; Sandler, Irving. *Critic's Choice 1969-70,* New York State Council of the Arts; Mellow, James R. "The Black Artist; The Black Community; The White Art World," *New York Times,* June 29, 1970; "X to the 4th Power," *Arts Magazine,* Sept. 1969; Schjeldahl, Peter. "A Triumph Rather Than a Threat," *New York Times,* Aug. 17, 1969; Potter, Margaret. *American Contemporary Art,* American Embassy, Moscow; Information from the artist; Brooklyn College. *Afro-American Artists: Since 1950,* 1969.

WILLIAMS, YVONNE

Painter. Born in New York City, 1945. Studied at the Brooklyn Museum School of Art; School of Visual Arts, New York.
Works: *Drawings; Sketches of American Life.*
Exhibited: Boston Museum of Fine Arts, 1970.
Sources: Boston Museum of Fine Arts. *Afro-American Artists/NY & Boston,* 1970; Baker, Kenneth. "Art in the Service of the People," *Christian Science Monitor;* Paris, Jean. "Black Art Experience in Art," *Long Island Press,* Jamaica, NY, June 14, 1970; Le Brun, Caron. "Black Art," *Herald Traveler,* Sunday Supplement, Boston, May 24, 1970; "Afro-American Artists: NY & Boston," *Prudential Center News,* March 1, 1970, p. 4.

WILLIAMSON, DONNA M.

Painter, commercial artist. Born in Cleveland, 1944. Studied at Paier School of Art, Hamden, Connecticut.
Sources: Information from the artist.

WILLIAMSON, STAN

Painter, calligrapher, book designer. Born in Chicago in 1911.
Works: *Houses in Chicago; Old Dwellings; Glass Objects.*
Sources: Dover. *American Negro Art;* "Afro-Amer. Issue," *Art Gallery,* April 1968; Indiana Univ. *Fine Arts & the Black American;* DuSable Museum of African-Amer. History. *Contemporary Black Artists,* 1970, calendar; Harley, Ralph, Jr. "Checklist of Afro-Amer. Art & Artists," *The Serif,* Dec. 1970; *The Negro Handbook,* composed by the editors of *Ebony,* Chicago, 1966; Myers, Carol. *Black Power in the Arts,* Flint, Mich., 1970; Walker, Roslyn. *A Resource Guide to the Visual Arts of Afro-Americans,* South Bend, Ind., 1971.

WILLIS, ROBERT

Painter.
Works: *Their Only Freedom; The Musicians.*
Exhibited: Atlanta Univ., 1942.
Awards: Honorable Mention for "The Musicians."
Sources: Atlanta Univ. *Annual for Negro Artists,* 1942; *New York Times,* April 4, 1948; *Art News,* April 15, 1945; Harley, Ralph, Jr. "Checklist of Afro-Amer. Art & Artists," *The Serif,* Dec. 1970.

WILSON, A. B.

Painter. Active in mid-19th century. Painted historical subjects and religious themes.
Awards: Daniel A. Payne for Best Historical or Scriptual painting.
Sources: DuSable Museum of African-Amer. History. *Contemporary Black Artists,* 1970, calendar.

WILSON, CHARLES RODGER

Sources: DuSable Museum of African-Amer. History. *Contemporary Black Artists,* 1970, Calendar.

WILSON, CHARLIENNE

Awards: Honorable mention.
Sources: *Dowagiac* (Mich.) *Daily News,* Sept. 8, 1951.

WILSON, CHESTER

Painter.
Sources: Reed, Ishmael. "The Black Artist: Calling a Spade a Spade," *Arts,* May 1967.

WILSON, ED

Sculptor, illustrator. Born in Baltimore, Maryland on March 28, 1925. Studied at University of Iowa (BA, 1950, MA, 1951); University of North Carolina, 1961. Chairman, Dept. of Art and Art History, State University of New York at Binghamton.
Works: *Minority Man; Cybele; Trio; Figure Study I; Figure Study II; Landscape Form; Hera; Maquettes for John F. Kennedy Memorial Sculpture.*
Exhibited: Univ. of Iowa, 1951, 1954; NC A & T College, Greensboro, NC, 1955; NC Artists Annual, Raleigh, NC, 1955; Duke Univ., Durham, NC, 1956; Madison Square Garden, NY, 1958; 10th Silvermine Guild of Artists, Inc. Exhibit, New Canaan, Conn., 1959; Chapel Hill (NC) Art Gallery, 1959; Detroit Institute of Arts, 1959; Cecile Art Gallery, NY, 1959; Pa. Academy of Fine Arts, Phila., 1960; Allied Arts of Durham, Inc. (NC), 1960; Univ. of NC, Greensboro, 1961-2; Howard Univ., 1961, 1970; NC Museum of Art, Raleigh, 1961-2; Md. Artists Exhibition, Baltimore Museum, 1956, 1962; Piedmont Purchase Exhibition, Mint Museum, Charlotte, NC, 1962; Munson-Williams-Proctor Museum, Utica, NY, 1965, 1968; UCLA Art Galleries, 1966; Fine Arts Gallery of San Diego, 1967; Oakland Art Museum, 1967; Colgate Univ., Hamilton, NY, 1967; State Univ. of NY at Binghamton, 1966; State Univ. of NY at Albany, 1968; Ithaca College, 1968; Acts of Art Gallery, NY, 1971; Minneapolis Institute of Arts, 1968; High Museum, Atlanta, Ga., 1969; Flint Institute of Arts, Mich., 1969; Everson Museum, Syracuse, 1969; IBM Gallery, 1969; Rhode Island School of Design, 1969; San Francisco Museum of Art, 1969; Contemporary Arts Assn., 1970; NJ State Museum, 1970; Harpur College (1-man); Harlem School of the Arts, NY, 1960; Phila. Civic Center Museum.
Collections: Howard Univ.
Awards: Carnegie Research Grant; 1st Award, Sculpture, Cecile Art Gallery, NY, 1959; 1st Purchase Prize in Sculpture, Howard Univ.,

1961; State Univ. of NY Fellowship Grants for Sculpture, 1966, 1968.
Member: College Art Assn. of America (Bd. of Directors since 1970); State Univ. of NY Council of Art Department Chairman (Vice-Chairman, 1969).
Sources: Dover. *American Negro Art;* "Afro-Amer. Issue," *Art Gallery,* April 1968; Indiana Univ. *Fine Arts & the Black American;* Phila. Civic Center. *Afro-American Artists 1800-1969;* UCLA Art Galleries. *The Negro in American Art;* Howard Univ. *James A. Porter Gallery of African-American Art,* 1970; DuSable Museum of African-Amer. History. *Contemporary Black Artists,* 1970, calendar; Minneapolis Institute of Arts, *30 Contemporary Black Artists,* 1968; Craig, Randall J. "Focus on Black Artists: A Project for Schools and Community," *School Arts,* Nov. 1970, pp. 30-3; Harley, Ralph, Jr. "Checklist of Afro-Amer. Art & Artists," *The Serif,* Dec. 1970; Ruder & Finn Fine Arts. *Contemporary Black Artists,* 1969; Myers, Carol. *Black Power in the Arts,* Flint, Mich., 1970; Walker, Roslyn. *A Resource Guide to the Visual Arts of Afro-Americans,* South Bend, Ind., 1971.

WILSON, ELLIS

Painter. Born in Mayfield, Kentucky, 1899. Studied at Art Institute of Chicago.
Works: *Lunch Hour; Fisherman; Warriors #2; Jeremiah; Noonday Report; Watermelon Vendors; Cameon; Old Charleston Houses; Southern Fantasy; Rosie Junior; Lumber Jacks; Mothers with Children; Brownstones in Winter; Bird Vender; Paysannes; St. Marc, Haiti; Pension; Children at Sundown; Sisters; Chair Vendors; Tropical Island; Sailors; Assembling; Reptiles; Altar Boy; Nostalgia; Machine Shop; Burr Bench; Fisherwoman; Field Workers; To Market; Four Sisters; After the Flood; Harlem Tenements; Communion; Hopi Indian; Jeunne Fille; Lady with a Fan; Moroccan; Mother with Three Daughters; Marchandes; African Students; Promenade; Peasants; Mules; Alhambra; Locker Room; Plantation Life; Tropical Harvest; Peasant Funeral; Defense Porters; End of the Day; Shore Leave; Welding; Souvenier; Mules #2; Pigs with White Bands; Pink Fish; Repairing; Street Play; At the Band Saw; Magic Lanterns; Going Shrimping; Summer Magic; Cooling Cylinders; Factory Workers; Harvest; Charleston Sisters; Furnace Workers; Old Charleston Market; Bathers; Fishmen's Wives; An Artist; Night; Two Alone; Harlem Barbershop.*
Exhibited: Harmon Foundation; Howard Univ.; Dillard Univ.; Atlanta Univ.; Detroit Museum; Amer. Negro Exposition, 1940; NY World's Fair, 1939; G Place Gallery, Washington, DC; Albany Museum; Barnet Aden Gallery, Wash-

ington, DC, 1949; Contemporary Arts, NY, 1948, 1951; 135th St. NY Public Library; African Art Center, NY; Washington Square Exhibit, 1932; City College of NY, 1967; Augusta Savage Studios, 1939; James A. Porter Gallery, 1970; Roko Gallery, 1949; McMillen Galleries, NY, 1941.
Collections: NY Public Library, Schomburg Collection.
Awards: Guggenheim Fellowship, 1944; Charles S. Peterson Prize for African poster.
Sources: Albany Institute of History & Art. *Negro Artist Comes of Age; Contemporary Arts Catalog,* 1948, 1951; Dover. *American Negro Art;* Afro-Amer. Slide Depository, 1971-2, catalog; Harmon Foundation. *Exhibition of Productions by Negro Artists;* "Afro-American Issue," *Art Gallery,* April 1968; Indiana Univ. *Fine Arts & the Black American;* City College of NY. *Evolution of Afro-American Artists 1800-1950,* 1967; "Home Forum," *Christian Science Monitor,* April 24, 1972; Tanner Art Galleries. *Art of the American Negro,* 1940; Bier, Justus. "Ellis Wilson," *Courier Journal,* April 30, 1950; Brown, Evelyn S. "The Harmon Awards," *Opportunity,* March 1933; Harley, Ralph, Jr. "Checklist of Afro-Amer. Art & Artists," *Serif,* Dec. 1970; Harmon Foundation. *Non-Jury Exhibit of Works of Negro Artists,* 1933; Harmon Foundation. *Exhibit of Fine Arts,* 1930; DuSable Museum of African-Amer. History. *Contemporary Black Artists,* 1970, Calendar; Harmon Foundation. *Select Picture List; New York Times,* May 16, 1948; "Honoring Negro History," *Art Digest,* Feb. 15, 1949, p. 20; "Art by Negroes," *Art Digest,* Oct. 15, 1941; Greene, Carroll, Jr. "Perspectives: The Black Artist in America," *Art Gallery,* April 1970; "American Negro Art Given Full Length Review at NY Show," *Art Digest,* Dec. 15, 1941; Pierre-Noel, Lois Jones. "American Negro Art in Progress," *Negro History Bulletin,* Oct. 1967; Woodruff, Hale. "Negro Artists Hold 4th Annual in Atlanta," *Art Digest,* Apr. 15, 1945; "Negro Winners," *Art Digest,* May 1, 1946; *Art News,* April 15, 1945, pp. 8-9; "The Negro Artist Comes of Age," *Art News,* Feb. 1, 1945; Greene, Carroll, Jr. *Afro-American Artists: 1800-1968,* Slides; "Six Paintings of City Life," *Arts Quarterly,* Dec. 1939; Patterson, Lindsay, comp. "Contemporary Artists," *The Negro in Music and Art,* 1969; *The Negro Handbook,* Composed by Editors of *Ebony,* Chicago, 1966; Schatz, Walter. *Directory of Afro-American Resources,* 1970; Myers, Carol L. *Black Power in the Arts,* Flint, Mich., 1970; McMillen Inc. Galleries. *Contemporary Negro Art,* NY, 1941; "Leading Negro Artists," *Ebony,* Sept. 1963; Walker, Roslyn. *A Resource Guide to the Visual Arts of Afro-Americans,* South Bend, Ind., 1971.

WILSON, FRED

Sculptor, printmaker. Born in Chicago in 1932. Studied at Mt. San Antonio Junior College; LaVerne College; Fresno State College; Los Angeles State College.
Works: *Protection; Woman of the World; Three in One* (woodcut).
Collections: Oakland Museum, Ruth Waddy Collection.
Sources: Roelof-Lanner, T.V., ed. *Prints by American Negro Artists;* Lewis/Waddy. *Black Artists on Art,* Vol. 2; Oakland Museum Archives.

WILSON, GEORGE L.

Painter. Born in Windsor, North Carolina in 1930. Studied at the Art Institute of Pittsburgh; School of Visual Arts; National Academy School of Fine Arts.
Works: *Pondering; Quiet Moments; Tender Care; Mother & Child; Youthful Attitude.*
Exhibited: Smith-Mason Gallery, 1971; Uptown Gallery, NY, 1964; Harlem's 1st Outdoor Show; Carl Van Vechten Gallery; Fisk Univ.; NY Bank for Savings; Bowery Savings Bank; Brooklyn Museum; Oakland Museum; Nat'l Academy of Art Galleries; Studio Museum in Harlem, 1969.
Collections: Johnson Pub. Co., Chicago.
Awards: Emily Lowe Award 1963; Leolive Tucker Award at Harlem's 1st Outdoor Art Show.
Sources: Harley, Ralph, Jr. "Checklist of Afro-Amer. Art & Artists," *The Serif,* Dec. 1970; Smith-Mason Gallery. *Nat'l Exhibition Black Artists 1971; Amsterdam News,* Oct. 10, 1964; Johnson Pub. Co. *The JPC Art Collection,* pamphlet; Patterson, Lindsay. "Contemporary Artists," *The Negro in Music and Art,* 1969; Studio Museum in Harlem. *Harlem Artists '69.*

WILSON, GLADYS LUCILLE

Born in 1906 in Texas. Studied at the University of Chicago; Columbia University (MA); Art Institute of Chicago.
Works: *Portrait-Dr. Tigay; Still Life.*
Exhibited: Harmon Foundation, 1933; Art League of Chicago, 1928.
Sources: Harmon Foundation. *Non-Jury Exhibit of Works of Negro Artists,* 1933.

WILSON, JOHN

Painter, printmaker, illustrator, educator. Born in Boston in 1922. Studied at Museum School of Fine Arts, Boston (1944); Tufts University (1947); The Fernand Leger School, Paris (1949); The Institute Politecnico, Mexico City (1952); Esmerelda School of Art, Mexico

City; La Escuela de las Artes Del Libro, Mexico City (1954-5). Teacher at Pratt Institute 1958; Boston University.

Works: *Girl* (pastel); *Portrait* (oil); *Beach Scene* (pastel); *Father & Child*, 1965 (color lithograph); *Black Soldier; Roxbury Landscape; African Princess; My Brother; Deliver Us From Evil; Black Industrial Workers; Adolescence; Mother & Child; Trabajador; Incident*, 1952 (fresco mural); *Portrait of Claire; City Child; Roxbury Rooftops; Escapees* (lithograph).

Exhibited: Albany Institute, 1945; Library of Congress Nat'l Print Exhibit; Library of Congress Internat'l Print Exhibit; Inst. of Modern Art, Boston; Boris Mirski Art Gallery; Addison Gallery; Pepsi-Cola Annual; Society of Amer. Etchers, Engravers, Lithographers & Woodcutters, Cincinnati Museum; Boston Printmakers Annual; Art Wood Gallery; Exchange Exhibit of Amer. Prints, Italy; Brooklyn Museum; 10th Annual South Shore Art Festival; Joseph Gropper Gallery; Nat'l Academy of Design; Metropolitan Museum of Art; Museum of Modern Art; Atlanta Univ., 1943, 1944, 1951; Boston Museum of Fine Arts, 1970; Smith College; Albany Museum; Downtown Gallery, NYC; Wellesley College; Andover-Newton Theological Seminary; Carnegie Institute; New Names in Negro Art; City College of NY, 1967; Newark Museum, 1971; Simmons College; Detroit Inst. of Arts; Bibliothèque Nationale, Paris, 1952; Musée des Beaux-Arts, Rouen, 1952; Traveling Exhibit of Contemporary Amer. Prints, Dijon & Lyons; Boston Printmakers Annual; Rose Art Museum, Brandeis Univ.; Boston Univ. School of Fine & Applied Arts; Amer. Internat'l College, Springfield, Mass., 1971 (1-man); Boston Public Library, 1973.

Collections: Museum of Modern Art; Schomburg Collection, NYC; Atlanta Univ.; Mexico City; Boston Public Library; Smith College; Carnegie Inst.; Bezalel Museum, Jerusalem; Florence Heller School of Social Work, Brandeis Univ.; Howard Univ.; Tufts Univ.; Dept. of Fine Arts, French Gov't; Mr. & Mrs. Lawrence Wortzel; Rose Art Museum, Brandeis Univ.; 1st National Bank, Boston; Wiggin Collection, Boston Public Library.

Awards: John Hay Whitney Fellowship, 1950-1; James William Paige Traveling Fellowship, Boston Museum School, 1946; Atlanta Univ. Annuals; John Hope Purchase Award, Atlanta, 1944; Print Award, Atlanta, 1951; Popular prize, Boston Museum of Modern Art; Institute of Internat'l Education Grant, 1951.

Member: Boston Museum of Fine Arts (Art Faculty); Nat'l Center of Afro-Amer. Artists, Roxbury, Mass. (board of directors); Elma Lewis School of Fine Arts (board).

Sources: *Who's Who in American Art*; Boston Museum of Fine Arts. *Afro-American Artists, New York & Boston*, 1970; Roelof-Lanner, T.V. *Prints by American Negro Artists*; Dover. *American Negro Art*; Albany Inst. *Negro Artist Comes of Age*; "Afro-Amer. Issue," *Art Gallery*, April 1968; Indiana Univ. *Fine Arts & the Black American*; Newark Museum. *Black Artists: Two Generations*, 1971; City College of NY. *The Evolution of Afro-Amer. Artists 1800-1950*; Boston Negro Artists Assn. *10th Anniversary Exhibition*, 1973; Roucek & Kiernan. *The Negro Impact on Western Civilization*; Fax, Elton C. *Seventeen Black Artists*; DuSable Museum of African-Amer. History. *Contemporary Black Artists*, Calendar, 1970; Boston Community Lecture Series. *Local Afro-American Artists*, 1969; "Negro Annual," *Art Digest*, June 1, 1944; Pierre-Noel, Lois Jones. "American Negro Art in Progress," *Negro History Bulletin*, Oct. 1967; Wolf, Ben. "Negro Art Scores Without Double Standards," *Art Digest*, Feb. 1, 1945; Woodruff, Hale A. "Negro Artists Hold Fourth Annual in Atlanta," *Art Digest*, April 15, 1945; "Atlanta's Annual," *Time*, April 9, 1945; "Negro Annual," *Art News*, April 15, 1943; *Art News*, April 15, 1945, pp. 8-9; "Negro Art Prizes," *Art News*, May 1, 1944; Harley, Ralph, Jr. "Checklist of Afro-Amer. Art & Artists," *The Serif*, Dec. 1970; "Black Art Exhibit Opens Sunday," *Herald*, Belmont, Mass., May 14, 1970; "Preview Party to Open Show by 13 Black Artists," *Citizen*, Belmont, Mass., May 14, 1970; Sherman, Marjorie. "Afro-America Gets Biggest Show," *Boston Globe*, May 18, 1970; "Museum of Fine Arts to Hold Black Art Show," *Chronicle*, Ipswich, Mass., April 20, 1970; "Museum of Fine Arts to Hold Black Art Show," *Tri-Town Transcript & Pennysaver*, April 29, 1970; Ploski, Harry, & Ernest Kaiser. "The Black Artist," *Afro USA*, 1971; Walsh, Rose. "Artists to Meet Public at Art Exhibit Preview," *Record American*, May 19, 1970; "Black Artists Work on View in Museum," *News*, Newburyport, Mass., May 16, 1970; Baker, Kenneth. "Art in Service of People," *Christian Science Monitor*; Grillo, Jean B. "Black Artists: Three Views," *Phoenix*; Le Brun, Caron. "Blacks' Art on Display," *Herald Traveler*, Boston, May 26, 1970; Paris, Jean. "Black Art Experience in Art," *Long Island Press*, Jamaica, NY, June 14, 1970; Ploski, Harry, Ernest Kaiser, & Otto Lindenmeyer. "The Black Artist," *Reference Library of Black America*, Book IV, 1971; *The Negro Handbook*, Composed by the Editors of *Ebony*, Chicago, 1966; Atkinson, J. Edward. *Black Dimensions in Contemporary American Art*, 1971; Schatz, Walter. *Directory of Afro-American Resources*, 1970; George, Jean C. *Spring*

313

Comes to the Ocean, Thomas Y. Crowell, NYC, 1965 (Illustrator); Wilson, Julia. *Becky*, Thomas Y. Crowell, NYC, 1967 (Illustrator); Lexau, Joan. *Striped Ice Cream*, JB Lippincott Co., NYC, 1968 (Illustrator); Oliver, Willis. *New Worlds of Reading*, Harcourt, Brace & World, Inc., 1959 (Illustrator); Jordan, June. *Who Look At Me*, Thomas Y. Crowell, NYC, 1969 (Illustrator); Faxon, Alicia. "John Wilson: Reality is Not a Fad," *Boston Sunday Globe*, Sept. 5, 1971; *Boston Univ. Journal*, Vol. 17, No. 1, 1969; *Boston Univ. Journal*, Vol. 20, Nos. 2 & 3, 1972; Information from the artist; Boston Negro Artists Assn. Calendar, 1973; Myers, Carol L. *Black Power in the Arts*, Flint, Mich., 1970; Gaither, Edmund B. "The Evolution of the Afro-Amer. Artists," *Artists Proof*, Vol. 2; Le Brun, Caron. "Black Art," *Herald Traveler*, Sunday Supplement, Boston, May 24, 1970; "Leading Negro Artists," *Ebony*, Sept. 1963; Boston Negro Artists Assn. *The Black Artist in America: A Negro History Month Exhibition*, Boston Public Library, 1973; Walker, Roslyn. *A Resource Guide to the Visual Arts of Afro-Americans*, South Bend, Ind., 1971.

WILSON, JOHN LOUIS

Architect, draftsman. Born in New Orleans in 1899. Studied at New Orleans University; Columbia University School of Architecture. Opened own architectural office.
Exhibited: Harmon Foundation, 1928, 1935; New Orleans Univ., 1930; Atlanta Univ., 1944.
Member: Alpha Phi Alpha.
Sources: Harmon Foundation. *Exhibition of Productions by Negro Artists*; Indiana Univ. *Fine Arts & the Black American*; Harmon Foundation. *Negro Artists*, 1935; *Who's Who in Colored America*, 3rd edition; Harley, Ralph, Jr. "Checklist of Afro-Amer. Art & Artists," *The Serif*, Dec. 1970; Walker, Roslyn. *A Resource Guide to the Visual Arts of Afro-Americans*, South Bend, Ind., 1971.

WILSON, KARAN ROSE

Painter, educator. Born in Hartford, 1944. Studied at University of Hartford (BFA).
Works: *High Yeller*, 1970 (polymer acrylic); *Black and Blue*, 1971 (polymer acrylic); *Sister Tawney*, 1972 (polymer acrylic); *Pink Meat*, 1970 (polymer acrylic).
Exhibited: Univ. of Hartford, 1971; Hartford Civic & Arts Festival, 1971; Wadsworth Atheneum, 1971, 1972; Amer. Internat'l College, 1971, 1972.
Collections: Mrs. Charles Egler, Norfolk, Conn.
Awards: Adult Artists Award, graphics, "Through Young Black Eyes," Hartford, 1971.
Sources: Information from the artist; *Springfield* (Mass.) *Daily News*, Sept. 21, 1971.

WILSON, RICHARD

Sources: "Black Artists Work on View at Museum," *News*, Newburyport, Mass., May 16, 1970.

WILSON, ROGER

Active in 1960's.
Works: *Out of Opaque Emanates Black Pride.*
Collections: Johnson Pub. Co.
Sources: "Afro-American Issue," *Art Gallery*, April 1968; Indiana Univ. *Fine Arts & the Black American*; Johnson Pub. Co. *The JPC Art Collection*, Pamphlet; Myers, Carol L. *Black Power in the Arts*, Flint, Mich., 1970.

WILSON, STANLEY CHARLES

Sculptor, graphic artist, illustrator, weaver, educator. Born in Los Angeles in 1947. Studied at Otis Art Institute (BFA, MFA). Professor of Art, Southwestern College, San Diego, California.
Works: *Woven Bird Ritual Form; Shaman; Woven Shield; Fetish Form; Woven Female Bird Fetish Form.*
Exhibited: Brockman Gallery, Los Angeles; Municipal Art Gallery, San Pedro; Otis Art Institute Gallery; Los Angeles Co. Museum of Art; Galeria del Sol, Santa Barbara, 1972; Pacific Grove Art Center, 1972.
Awards: 2nd Place, published illustration; Honorable mention, Citus Award, Watts Art Festival, 1971; 2nd Place Drawing award, Allied Arts Council, San Bernadino; Honorable mention, Smirnoff Co. Drawing Award.
Collections: Otis Art Institute; Michael El Grodsky, Los Angeles; Phyl & Bill Roper Designs, Los Angeles; Mr. & Mrs. Charles White, Altadena, Cal.; Brockman Gallery.
Member: Amer. Assn. of Univ. Professors; NAEA; Amer. Crafts Council; Otis Art Alumni.
Sources: Lewis/Waddy. *Black Artists on Art*, Vol. 2; Meilach, Dona. *Creating Art With Textiles*, NY; Perry, Dr. Regina. *Afro-American Artist* (in preparation); Brockman Gallery. *Drawn Lithographs by Stanley Charles Wilson*, portfolio, Los Angeles.

WILSON, SUZANNE

Active in 1930's.
Exhibited: Harmon Foundation, 1928.
Sources: Harmon Foundation. *Exhibition of Productions by Negro Artists*; Indiana Univ. *Fine Arts & the Black American*; Harley, Ralph, Jr. "Checklist of Afro-Amer. Art & Artists," *The Serif*, Dec. 1970.

WIMBERLY, FRANK

Painter, mixed media. Born in Pleasantville, New Jersey. Studied at Howard University under Lois Mailou Jones, James Porter, James Wells.

Works: *Sketches; Framboise; Grey Tune; Reverence; Yard; Grass; Nat's New Tune; For Trane; Cookie I; The Good-natured Noodle; Blue Cool; Three and Sea; The Other Day; 11th & Madison.*
Exhibited: Museum of Modern Art, NY; Acts of Art Gallery, NY.
Sources: Afro-Amer. Slide Depository, Catalog; Acts of Art, Catalog, May 1972, NY.

WINBUSH, LeROY
Painter.
Works: *Forty-seventh Street.*
Exhibited: Amer. Negro Exposition, Chicago, 1940.
Sources: Tanner Art Galleries. *Art of the American Negro*, Catalog, 1940.

WINDER, EARL THEODORE
Architect. Born in Alexandria, Virginia on June 5, 1903. Studied at Howard University (BS). Specialist in designing school buildings.
Member: Nat'l Technical Assn.; Phi Beta Sigma.
Sources: Furr, Arthur. *History & Progress of Negroes in the US.*

WINKFIELD, CLYDE
Sculptor. Active in 1940's.
Works: *Head; Oriental Woman; Spiritual Singer.*
Exhibited: Howard Univ., 1941.
Sources: "Art Flowers in Poverty," *Washington Daily News*, Feb. 21, 1941; Howard Univ. *Exhibition of Negro Artists of Chicago at Howard University Gallery of Art*, 1941.

WINN, OSCARETTA
Painter.
Works: *Life of a Ballet Dancer* (watercolor); *Still Life* (watercolor).
Exhibited: South Side Community Art Center, Chicago, 1941.
Sources: South Side Community Art Center. *National Negro Art Exhibition*, Chicago, 1941; South Side Community Art Center. *Opening Exhibition of Paintings by Negro Artists*, Chicago, 1941.

WINSLOW, ARTHUR G.
Painter. Born in Indiana. Studied at Purdue University; and under Maurice Utrillo.
Works: *Elk Mountain in Snow Storm.*
Exhibited: Harmon Foundation, 1930-1; Smithsonian Institution, 1930; South Side Community Art Center, 1941.
Sources: Harmon Foundation. *Exhibition of Productions by Negro Artists*; Harmon Foundation. *Exhibit of Fine Arts*, 1930; Indiana Univ. *Fine Arts & the Black American*; Locke, Alain. "Chicago's New Southside Art Center," *American Magazine of Art*, Aug. 1941; Harley,

Ralph, Jr. "Checklist of Afro-Amer. Art & Artists," *The Serif*, Dec. 1970; Walker, Roslyn. *A Resource Guide to the Visual Arts of Afro-Americans*, South Bend, Ind., 1971.

WINSLOW, EUGENE
Painter. Worked in New Orleans.
Works: *Pickin' Cotton* (watercolor).
Exhibited: Atlanta Univ., 1944.
Sources: Atlanta Univ. catalog, 1944.

WINSLOW, HAROLD
Painter. Worked in Mexico.
Works: *Sharecroppers Migration, No. 2.*
Exhibited: Atlanta Univ., 1944.
Sources: Atlanta Univ. catalog, 1944; Harley, Ralph, Jr. "Checklist of Afro-Amer. Art & Artists," *The Serif*, Dec. 1970.

WINSLOW, VERNON
Painter, illustrator. Born in Dayton, Ohio.
Works: *Hamburger Hut; Tribute to Marian; Hunter Street Barber Shop; Anderson; Southern Mother;* Illustrations for *Country Life Stories.*
Exhibited: Atlanta Univ., 1942, 1943, 1944; South Side Community Art Center, Chicago, 1941; Albany Institute of History and Art, 1945; Fort Huachuca, Ariz., 1943.
Collections: Atlanta Univ.
Awards: Atlanta Univ., 2nd Purchase Award, 1944.
Sources: South Side Community Art Center. *National Negro Art Exhibition*, Chicago, 1941; South Side Community Art Center. *Exhibition of Book Illustrations by Jacob Lawrence, Charles Sebree, Vernon Winslow*, Chicago, 1941; Harley, Ralph, Jr. "Checklist of Afro-American Art & Artists," *The Serif*, Dec. 1970; Indiana Univ. *Fine Arts & the Black American*; Albany Institute of History and Art. *The Negro Artist Comes of Age*; Winslow, Vernon. "Negro Art and the Depression," *Opportunity*, Feb. 1941; "Fort Huachuca, Arizona Art Show," *Art Digest*, Aug. 1, 1943; Locke, Alain. "Chicago's New Southside Art Center," *American Magazine of Art*, Aug. 1941; Fort Huachuca. Exhibition of the *Works of 37 Negro Artists*, Ariz., 1943.

WINSTON, RICHARD
Painter, mixed media. Born in Orange, New Jersey, 1927.
Works: *Knapp's Farm*, 1966 (mixed media).
Exhibited: Arnot Art Gallery, 1956; Cameron Gallery, 1965; Winston Gallery, 1965-6; Elmira College, 1966; Fairfield Univ., 1970; Sacred Heart Univ., 1970; World Art Gallery, 1972; Sacred Heart Academy, 1972; Westport Bank & Trust, 1972; Washington Square Outside Art Show, Greenwich Village, NY; New Haven Regional Center Art Gallery, 1972.

315

Collections: Honorable Nelson A. Rockefeller, NY.
Awards: Oscar Award, Elmira Art Club.
Member: Conn. Classic Art, Inc.; Boston Negro Artists Assn.
Represented by: Bel Gallery; Post Arts Center Galleries.
Sources: Information from the artist.

WISSIN, EDGAR

Sources: Harley, Ralph, Jr. "Checklist of Afro-Amer. Art & Artists," *The Serif,* Dec. 1970.

WOOD, CLARENCE

Painter, mixed media.
Works: *Molecular Motion: Nos. 1-4; Neutrino 19; Planus IV; Planus III; Molecular Motion #41* (mixed media).
Exhibited: Lee Cultural Center, Phila.
Sources: Information from William Howell; Phila. Dept. of Recreation. *Love . . . and the Black Community.*

WOOD, JAMES A.

Painter.
Works: *The Mound; Low-Cost Housing; The Road Through the Hills.*
Exhibited: Atlanta Univ., 1942, 1943; Dillard Univ., 1941.
Sources: Atlanta Univ. catalogs; Dillard Univ. *Arts Festival,* Catalog, 1941.

WOOD, LIONEL

Sources: DuSable Museum of African-Amer. History. *Contemporary Black Artists,* 1970, Calendar.

WOODARD, BEULAH

Painter, sculptor. Born in Ohio in 1895. Died in 1964. Studied at Los Angeles Art School; Otis Art Institute.
Exhibited: Los Angeles County Museum; Municipal Museum, Munich, Germany, 1964; Office of *California News,* 1935.
Sources: Harley, Ralph, Jr. "Checklist of Afro-Amer. Art & Artists," *Serif,* Dec. 1970; Ploski, Harry, & Ernest Kaiser. "The Black Artist," *Afro USA,* 1971; Ploski, Harry, Ernest Kaiser, & Otto Lindenmeyer. "The Black Artist," *Reference Library of Black America,* Book 4, 1971; "Art Should Inspire Us Says Woman Artist of Los Angeles," *Californian News,* Feb. 22, 1935.

WOODRUFF, HALE A.

Painter, printmaker, muralist, educator, lecturer. Born in Cairo, Illinois, August 26, 1900. Studied at the John Herron Art Institute, Indianapolis; Fogg Art Museum, Harvard University; Académie Scandinave, Paris; Académie Moderne, Paris. Studied fresco painting in Mexico with Diego Rivera (1936). Studied with H. O. Tanner in Paris. In 1931 became instructor of art at Atlanta University where he developed a large number of young artists, including Wilmer Jennings, William Hayden, Robert Neal, Lamar Weaver, Albert Wells and Lawrence A. Jones. In 1938 commissioned to do Amistad Murals for the Savery Library of Talladega College. In 1941 initiated annual art shows for Negro artists at Atlanta University, where he was Art Director (1931-45). Professor of Art Education, New York University (1945-68; Emeritus, 1968).
Works: *The Yellow Bird; Totem; Sunday Promenade; American Land of Many Moons; Countee Cullen; Returning Home; The Teamsters Place; Girls Skipping; Old Woman Peeling Apples; Washer Woman; Old Street, Paris; Bridge near Avallon, France; Poor Man's Cotton; Vignettes; Mississippi Wasteland; Galaxy; Landscape; Leda; Shrine II; Trio; Shrines in a Landscape; Night Forms; Atlanta Landscape; Autumn Impression; Card Players; A Day in June; Still Life; Two Old Women; Onai De Monte Bells; Armed Mutiny; Pont Neuf; Despair; Georgia Landscape; Medieval Chartres; Quei de Monte Belle; By Parties Unknown,* 1938 (woodcut); *The Road from Chateau Neuf; Old House Tops, Paris; Landscape with Green Sun; Celestial Gate; Ancestral Memory; The Little Boy; Provencal Landscape; Studio Still Life on a Table; Woman by the Sea; Prehistoric Figurations; Red Landscape; Accents; Monolithic Torso; Primordinal Landscape; Unknown Landscape; The Amistad Mutiny,* 1939 (mural); *Founding of Talladega,* 1939 (mural); *History of California,* 1949 (mural); *The Art of the Negro,* 1950-1 (mural); *Caprice; Young Girl; An Old Woman; Georgia Woodland; Little Schoolhouse; Head of an Old Man; Blind Musician; Three Musicians; Rain and Fog in the Rockies; Suzetta; Mountain Tops; Country Church; Promenade; Relics; Trusty on a Mule; View of Atlanta; Foot Washing; I Know the Lord Laid His Hands on Me; The Banjo Player; Country Home; Africa and the Bull; Along the Eure at Chartres; Old Farmhouse in the Beauce Valley.*
Exhibited: John Herron Art Institute, Indianapolis, 1923-4, 1926; Art Institute of Chicago, 1927; Harmon Foundation, 1928-9, 1931, 1933, 1935; Downtown Gallery, NY, 1929, 1931; Valentine Gallery, 1931; Pacquereau Gallery, France, 1930; Ferargil Gallery, 1931; High Museum, Atlanta, 1935, 1938; Baltimore Museum, 1939; Amer. Negro Exposition, Chicago, 1940; Bertha Schaefer Gallery, NY, 1958; Grace Horne Galleries, Boston, 1944; Atlanta Univ., 1951; NY World's Fair, 1939; Art Center, NYC; Univ. of Southern Ill.; 1956; Univ. of NC, 1955; City Col-

lege of NY, 1967; Whitney Museum, NY; Internat'l House, NY; Galeries Jeune Peinture, Paris; Los Angeles Art Museum; San Diego Art Museum; Boston Museum of Fine Arts; St. Louis Art Museum; Howard Univ.; Nat'l Center of Afro-Amer. Artists; Va. Museum; Raleigh (NC) Museum; Pyramid Club, Phila.; Riverside Museum, NYC; Kansas City Art Museum; L'Elan, Inc., NYC; Internat'l Print Society, NYC (1-man); Bertha Schaefer Gallery, NYC (1-man); State Museum of NC, Raleigh (1-man); Univ. of NC, Chapel Hill & Greenesboro (1-man); Eastern Mich. State Teachers College, Ypsilanti (1-man); Univ. of Southern Ill., Carbondale (1-man); Hampton (Va.) Institute (1-man); Univ. of Mich., Ann Arbor (1-man); Tuskegee Institute, Ala. (1-man); Kansas City Art Institute (1-man); NY Univ., 1967; Texas Centennial, 1936; Newark Museum, 1971; James A. Porter Gallery, 1970; Smithsonian Institution, 1929; Rockford (Ill.) College, 1965; Xavier Univ., 1963.

Collections: Newark Museum; IBM; Atlanta Univ.; Howard Univ.; Spelman College, Atlanta; NY Univ.; Library of Congress; Lincoln Univ.; Harmon Foundation; Jackson College; NY State Univ. at Oneonta; Howard Jr. High School, Atlanta; Talladega College; Nat'l Archives; Bertha Schaefer Gallery, NYC; Golden State Insurance Co., Los Angeles; Johnson Pub. Co.

Awards: Purchase Prize, Atlanta Univ., 1951; Bronze Medal, Harmon Foundation, 1926; Honorable Mention, Harmon Foundation; 1st prize, High Museum, Atlanta; 2nd & 3rd awards, Diamond Jubilee Exposition, Chicago; Julius Rosenwald Fellowship, 1943-5; Great Teacher Award, NY Univ., 1966; Honorary doctorate, Morgan State College, Baltimore, 1968.

Member: NJ Society of Artists; Society of Mural Painters; Committee on Art Education, Museum of Modern Art, NYC; NY State Council on the Arts.

Sources: Pearson, Ralph M. *Experiencing Pictures,* Simon & Schuster, 1931; Johnson Pub. Co. *The JPC Art Collection,* Pamphlet; Mallett. *Index of Artists;* Dover. *American Negro Art;* Locke. *The Negro in Art;* Albany Institute of History & Art. *The Negro Artist Comes of Age; Who's Who in American Art,* 1940-1; Harmon Foundation. *Exhibition of Productions by Negro Artists,* 1933; "Afro-American Issue," *Art Gallery,* April 1968; *Art Digest,* April 15, 1951; Harmon Foundation. *Exhibit of Fine Arts by American Negro Artists,* 1930; Boston Museum of Fine Arts. *Afro-American Artists: NY & Boston,* 1970; Afro-Amer. Slide Depository, catalog, 1971-2; Nat'l Center of Afro-Amer. Artists. *Five Black Artists,* Feb./March 1970; City College of NY.

The Evolution of Afro-American Artists 1800-1950; Loeb Student Center, NY Univ. *Hale Woodruff;* Locke, Alain. "Hale Woodruff," *Amer. Mag. of Art,* Jan. 1934; McGill, Ralph. "Hale Woodruff," *Atlanta Constitution,* Dec. 1935; Locke, Alain. *Negro Art Past and Present,* 1936; Pearson, Ralph M. "Hale Woodruff," *Forum Magazine,* June 1940; Pearson, Ralph M. *New Art Education,* Harpers; UCLA Art Galleries. *The Negro in American Art;* Art Institute of Chicago. *Negro in Art Week,* 1927; Herring, James V. "The American Negro Craftsman and Artist," *Crisis,* April 1942; Porter. *Modern Negro Art;* Harley, Ralph, Jr. "Checklist of Afro-Amer. Art & Artists," *Serif,* Dec. 1970; Baltimore Museum of Art. *Contemporary Negro,* 1939; Howard Univ. *Art of the American Negro,* 1937; Tanner Art Galleries. *Art of the American Negro,* 1940; Brawley, Benjamin. *The Negro Genius;* Butcher, Margaret. *The Negro in American Culture,* pp. 232, 234, 236-7; Roucek/Kiernan. *The Negro Impact on Western Civilization;* Texas Centennial Exposition. *Thumbnail Sketches of Exhibiting Artists,* 1936; Newark Museum. *Black Artists: Two Generations,* 1971; Harmon Foundation. *Negro Artists,* 1935; Howard Univ. *James A. Porter Gallery of African American Art,* 1970; Harmon Foundation. *Exhibit of Fine Arts,* 1930; DuSable Museum of African-Amer. History. *Contemporary Black Artists,* 1970, Calendar; Harmon Foundation. *Select Picture List; New York Times,* April 1, 1951; Woodson, Carter G., & Charles H. Wesley. *The Story of the Negro Retold,* p. 402; Rhode Island Univ. *Spiral,* Catalog; Smithsonian Institution. *Painting & Sculpture by American Negro Artists,* 1929; "Amer. Negro Review in NY Show," *Art Digest,* Dec. 15, 1941; Greene, Carroll, Jr. "Perspective: The Black Artist in America," *Art Gallery,* April 1970, p. 19; "Fort Huachuca, Arizona Art Show," *Art Digest,* Aug. 1, 1943; "Negro Artist Annual," *Art Digest,* March 1, 1944; "The Negro in Art," *Art Digest,* June 1, 1944; Pierre-Noel, Lois Jones. "American Negro Art in Progress," *Negro History Bulletin,* Oct. 1967; Wolf, Ben. "Negro Art Scores without Double Standards," *Art Digest,* Feb. 1, 1945; *Art Digest,* April 15, 1946; "Afro-Amer. Artists 1800-1950," *Ebony,* Vol. 23, pp. 116-22; Porter, James A. "Negro Art on Review," *Amer. Mag. of Art,* Jan. 1934; "First Negro National, Atlanta Univ.," *Magazine of Art,* May 1942, p. 185; Locke, Alain. "The Amer. Negro as Artist," *Amer. Mag. of Art,* Sept. 1931; Locke, Alain. "Chicago's New Southside Art Center," *Amer. Mag. of Art,* Aug. 1941; Rockford (Ill.) College. *Creativity and the Negro;* "The Negro Artist Comes of Age," *Art News,* Feb. 1, 1945; Siegel, Jeanne.

"Why Spiral?," *Art News*, Sept. 1966; "The Black Artist in America: A Symposium," *Metropolitan Museum of Art Bulletin*, Jan. 1969, p. 245; Craig, Randall J. "Focus on Black Artists: A Project for Schools & Community," *School Arts*, Nov. 1970, pp. 30-3; Kiah, Virginia. "Black Artists," *Savannah Magazine*, April 1972, p. 14; Greene, Carroll, Jr. "Afro-Amer. Artists: Yesterday & Now," *The Humble Way*, Vol. 8, No. 3, 1968; Xavier Univ. *Emancipation Proclamation Centennial National Art Exhibition*, 1963; Driscoll, Edgar, Jr. "Exhibit Features Black Artists," *Boston Globe*, Feb. 16, 1970, p. 17; Greene, Carroll, Jr. *Afro-American Artists: 1800-1968*, Slides; Fuller, Hoyt W. "World Festival of Negro Art," *Ebony*, July 1966; "Leading Negro Artists," *Ebony*, Sept. 1963, pp. 131-5; Shorewood Reproductions Catalogue. *The Art of Black America*, 1969; Brawley, Benjamin. *The Negro in Literature & Art in the US*; Gibson, Martha Jane. "The Amistad in Play & Murals," *Arts Quarterly*, June 1939, pp. 8-14; "Six Paintings of City Life," *Arts Quarterly*, Dec. 1939, pp. 13-9; Giuliano, Charles. "Five Black Artists," *Boston After Dark*, March 4, 1970; "Winthrop Students Visit Arts Center," *Bay State Banner*, March 19, 1970; Loercher, Diana. "Black Artists Exhibition Reveals Visual Eloquence," *Christian Science Monitor*, March 2, 1970; "Museum of Fine Arts to Hold Black Art Show," *Chronicle*, Ipswich, Mass., April 30, 1970; "Museum of Fine Arts to Hold Black Art Show," *Tri-Town Transcript & Pennysaver*, April 29, 1970; Brown, Marion. "The Negro in the Fine Arts," *The Negro Heritage Library*, Vol. 2; Morsbach, Mabel. *The Negro in American Life*; Patterson, Lindsay, comp. "The Contemporary Artist," *The Negro in Music and Art*, NY, 1969; Winslow, Vernon. "Negro Art & the Depression," *The Negro in Music and Art*; Ploski, Harry, & Ernest Kaiser. "The Black Artist," *Afro USA*, 1971; Walsh, Rose. "Artists to Meet Public at Art Exhibit Preview," *Record American*, May 19, 1970; Le Brun, Caron. "Blacks' Art on Display," *Herald Traveler*, Boston, May 26, 1970; Schwartz, Therese. "The Political Scene," *Arts*, April 1971; Ploski, Harry, Ernest Kaiser, & Otto Lindenmeyer. "The Black Artist," *Reference Library of Black America*, Book 4, 1971; *The Negro Handbook*, Composed by the Editors of *Ebony*, Chicago, 1966; Schatz, Walter. *Directory of Afro-American Resources*, 1970; "Black Beaux-Arts," *Time*, Sept. 21, 1942, p. 74; Roberts, Evangeline. "Praise Work of Two Young Ind. Artists," *Chicago Defender*, Aug. 16, 1924; South Side Community Art Center. *Chicago Collectors Exhibit of Negro Art*, Chicago, 1945; Myers, Carol L. *Black Power in the Arts*, Flint, Mich., 1970; Gaither, Edmund

B. "The Evolution of the Afro-American Artists," *Artists Proof*, Vol. 2; Robinson, Wilhelmena S. *Historical Negro Biographies*, p. 263; *Negro Almanac*, p. 631; Spradling, Mary M., ed. *In Black & White; Afro-Americans in Print*; Le Brun, Caron. "Black Art," *Herald Traveler*, Sunday Supplement, Boston, May 24, 1970; Walker, Roslyn. *A Resource Guide to the Visual Arts of Afro-Americans*, South Bend, Ind., 1971; Fine, Elsa H. "The Afro-American Artist: A Search for Identity," *Art Journal*, Fall 1969; Gallagher, Buell G. "Talladega Library: Weapon Against Caste," *Crisis*, April 1939.

WOODS, JAMES

Painter, educator. Active in 1960's.
Sources: Indiana Univ. *Fine Arts & the Black American;* Walker, Roslyn. *A Resource Guide to the Visual Arts of Afro-Americans*, South Bend, Ind., 1971; Harley, Ralph, Jr. "Checklist of Afro-Amer. Art & Artists," *Serif*, Dec. 1970.

WOODS, KEITH

Studied at Oakwood College.
Exhibited: Sun Times/Daily News Gallery, Chicago, 1970.
Sources: United Negro College Fund. *Art 1970*, Chicago, 1970.

WOODS, RIP

Printmaker, mixed media, painter. Born in Idabel, Oklahoma in 1933.
Works: *No. 5* (oil); *Un Beso de Amor* (drawing); *Appreciation Series* (stuffed fabric); *Appreciation Series 044; Appreciation Series 0033*.
Exhibited: Univ. of Iowa, 1971-2.
Sources: Afro-Amer. Slide Depository, catalog; Ill. Bell Telephone. *Black American Artists/71*.

WOODS, ROOSEVELT

Painter, educator. Born in Idabel, Oklahoma in 1932. Studied at Arizona State University (BS, MA).
Works: *Intergroup Meeting; Materials and Me; The Brothers.*
Exhibited: Phoenix Art Museum; Main Street Galleries, Scottsdale, Ariz.; Arizona State Univ.; Dickson Art Center, 1966.
Sources: Walker, Roslyn. *A Resource Guide to the Visual Arts of Afro-Americans*, South Bend, Ind., 1971; Myers, Carol. *Black Power in the Arts*, Flint, Mich., 1970; Harley, Ralph, Jr. "Checklist of Afro-Amer. Art & Artists," *The Serif*, Dec. 1970; DuSable Museum of African-Amer. History. *Contemporary Black Artists*, 1970, calendar; Dover. *American Negro Art;* Indiana Univ. *Fine Arts & the Black American;* UCLA Art Galleries. *The Negro in American Art.*

WOODSON, SHIRLEY

Painter.
Works: *Biafra Cries—The Thrill is Gone; Study for Aretha; Aretha the Queen #1; B.B. The King; Martha's Vandellas; Dreams; Joy, Grief and the Artist; Biafran Study; The Court; The King's Dream; Flight into Egypt; Ethiopian Pastoral; Mr. Jack Johnson; Still Life with Blouses; Beach Sun.*
Sources: Patterson, Lindsay. "Contemporary Artists," *The Negro in Music and Art,* 1969; Afro-Amer. Slide Depository, catalog, 1971-2.

WORMLEY, C.K.

Exhibited: Tanner Art League, 1922.
Sources: Harley, Ralph, Jr. "Checklist of Afro-Amer. Art & Artists," *The Serif,* Dec. 1970.

WORTHAM, HARRY

Sculptor, ceramist.
Works: Vase; box.
Collections: Nat'l Archives, Washington, DC.
Sources: Afro-Amer. Slide Depository, catalog, 1971-2.

WORTHAM, HENRY

Ceramist.
Works: *Cowboys.*
Collections: Nat'l Archives, Washington, DC.
Sources: Afro-Amer. Slide Depository, catalog, 1971-2.

WRENTZ, GEORGE, III

Painter, graphic artist, architect. Born in Valdosta, Georgia, 1941. Studied at Miami Dade Junior College, Florida A & M University; International Professional College.
Exhibited: Miami Public Library, 1972; Univ. of Miami, 1971, 1972; Theater of Afro-Arts, 1971, 1972; Coral Gables High, 1971, 1972; Miami Black Arts, 1971, 1972; Perrine Art Center, 1971; St. Paul A & M Church, 1972.
Collections: Univ. of Miami; Miami Black Arts; Theater of Afro-Arts.
Awards: Links Tea Award; Award of Honor, Carver High; Graphic award, Carver High.
Represented by: Miami Black Arts; Theater of Afro-Arts.
Sources: Information from the artist.

WRIGHT, BERNARD

Painter, sculptor. Born in Pittsburgh, Pennsylvania in 1938. Self-taught.
Works: *Three Women.*
Exhibited: Extensively in the Los Angeles area; Soviet Union with the "Graphics of American Negro Artists Exhibit" sponsored by the Soviet-American Relations Committee.
Sources: Lewis/Waddy. *Black Artists on Art,* Vol. 1; Walker, Roslyn. *A Resource Guide to the Visual Arts of Afro-Americans,* South Bend, Ind., 1971.

WRIGHT, DMITRI

Painter. Born in Newark, New Jersey on October 17, 1948. Studied at Newark School of Fine & Industrial Arts; Brooklyn Museum; Cooper Union.
Works: *Seated Nude,* 1971; *Black Couple in Bed Looking at TV,* 1971; *Bev and Frank,* 1971.
Exhibited: Newark Museum, 1969, 1971, 1972; Brooklyn Museum Little Gallery, 1971; Blum Gallery, 1971; Millowbrook Mill Art Show.
Collections: Newark Museum; Newark Library; Urban Life Center, Columbia, Md.
Awards: Max Beckman Memorial Scholarship; Graduated with honors, Newark School of Fine Arts; 1st Prize, NSFIA; 1st Prize, Gallery 9; 1st Prize, drawing, Fairleigh Dickinson; 1st Prize, graphics, Millowbrook Mill Art Show.
Sources: Newark Museum. *Black Artists: Two Generations,* 1971; *Scholastic Magazine,* Black Literature Series.

WRIGHT, ESTELLA V.

Sculptor.
Works: *James Hubert Blake; Noble L. Sissle.*
Collections: City Museum, NYC.
Sources: Afro-Amer. Slide Depository, Catalog, 1971-2.

WRIGHT, GEORGE

Sculptor.
Works: *Bronze Bag.*
Exhibited: Rockford (Ill.) College, 1965; Walker Art Center, Minneapolis; Minneapolis Institute of Arts; Museum of Contemporary Crafts, NY.
Sources: Greene, Carroll, Jr. "Perspective: The Black Artist in America," *Art Gallery,* April 1970; Rockford College. *Creativity and the Negro;* Harley, Ralph, Jr. "Checklist of Afro-Amer. Art & Artists," *The Serif,* Dec. 1970.

WRIGHT, LEON

Painter.
Works: *Landscape; Still Life.*
Exhibited: South Side Community Art Center, Chicago, 1945; Amer. Negro Exposition, Chicago, 1940.
Collections: Mr. R. Thomas Hale.
Sources: South Side Community Art Center. *Chicago Collectors Exhibit of Negro Art,* Chicago, 1945; Tanner Art Galleries. *Art of the American Negro,* Catalog, 1940.

WRIGHT, ROSCOE C.

Sources: Harley, Ralph, Jr. "Checklist of Afro-Amer. Art & Artists," *The Serif,* Dec. 1970.

WYLEY, FRANK A.

Painter, printmaker. Born in Long Beach, Mississippi in 1905.
Works: *Beggars Silhouettes; Gossip; Mother and Child; Shadows of the City; The Family.*

WYNN

Exhibited: Atlanta Univ., 1942-4; Dillard
Univ., 1941; Xavier Univ., 1963; Texas Centennial, 1936.
Sources: Dillard Univ. Arts Festival, 1941;
Atlanta Univ. *Annual for Negro Artists*, catalogs, 1942-4; Xavier Univ. *Emancipation
Proclamation Centennial National Art Exhibition*, 1963; Harley, Ralph, Jr. "Checklist of
Afro-Amer. Art & Artists," *The Serif*, Dec.
1970; "Afro-Amer. Issue," *Art Gallery*, April
1970.

WYNN, DANIEL R.
Painter.
Works: *Aftermath; Man in the Park.*
Exhibited: Smith-Mason Gallery, 1971.
Sources: Smith-Mason Gallery. *National Exhibition Black Artists 1971.*

WYNNE, CASSANDRA B.
Painter.
Works: *Black Men* (oil & acrylic).
Exhibited: Lee Cultural Center, Phila.
Sources: Phila. Dept. of Recreation. *Love . . .
and the Black Community.*

YANCEY, TERRANCE L.
Painter, graphic artist. Born in Boston, 1944.
Studied at the Museum School, Boston Museum of Fine Arts.
Works: *The Birds Are Coming*, 1961 (watercolor); *The Dragon*, 1961 (watercolor); *Still
Life of Flowers*, 1961 (watercolor); *Animals
in the Park*, 1961 (watercolor); *Portrait of
John*, 1961 (pencil); *In the Park*, 1961 (pen
& ink); *Thanksgiving*, 1961 (watercolor);
Christmas Scene, 1961 (watercolor); *Fisherman*, 1962 (watercolor); *Portrait of Jean*,
1962 (pencil); *Still Life of Fruit*, 1962 (watercolor); *My Dog*, 1962 (watercolor); *Classroom*, 1962 (pencil); *Safety Poster*, 1962
(watercolor); *Red Cross Poster*, 1962 (watercolor); *Camping Out*, 1962 (watercolor); *The
Whale*, 1962 (watercolor); *Portrait of a Girl*,
1962 (pastel); *Landscape*, 1962 (watercolor);
Clean Up Boston Poster, 1962 (watercolor);
Still Life of Fruit, 1963 (oil); *Portrait of Lois*,
1963 (pastel); *Fire in the Night*, 1963 (watercolor); *John*, 1963 (block print); *The End of
the World*, 1963 (pencil); *Camp Is on Fire*,
1964 (watercolor); *Landscape*, 1964 (watercolor); *Going Fishing*, 1964 (pastel); *Storm
at Sea*, 1964 (watercolor); *Still Life of Fruit*,
1964 (watercolor); *Black Santa Claus*, 1964
(watercolor); *Winter Scene*, 1964 (watercolor);
Mother Portrait, 1965 (oil); *Still Life*, 1965
(oil); *Grocery Store*, 1965 (watercolor); *Landscape*, 1965 (pen & ink); *Mount Calvary*, 1965
(watercolor); *Seascape*, 1965 (oil); *Portrait of
Barbara*, 1965 (pencil); *Straw Painting*, 1965
(watercolor); *Pussywillow*, 1965 (scratchboard); *Portrait of Thompson*, 1966 (pencil);

Portrait of Harris, 1966 (pencil); *Portrait of
Adams*, 1966 (pencil); *Landscape*, 1966 (oil);
Coming Back from the Rice Paddies, 1966
(oil); *In Korea*, 1966 (charcoal); *Seascape*,
1966 (oil); *Portrait of Jones*, 1966 (pencil);
Children at Play, 1966 (charcoal); *Wooden
Statue*, 1966 (charcoal); *Boys Flying a Kite*,
1966 (charcoal); *Still Life—Fruit*, 1966 (watercolor); *Coat-of-Arms*, 1967 (oil); *Self-Portrait*,
1967 (oil); *Children of Korea*, 1967 (charcoal); *Statue of the Goddess*, 1967 (charcoal);
Charcoal Drawing of Papason, 1967; *Portrait
of Father*, 1967 (oil); *Landscape*, 1967 (oil);
Portrait of Johnson, 1967 (pencil); *Portrait of
Harrison*, 1967 (pencil); *The Northern Lights*,
1968 (mixed); *Insects*, 1968 (watercolor); *Action at the DMZ*, 1968 (watercolor); *Modern
Art*, 1968 (watercolor); *Still Life*, 1968 (pencil); *Still Life*, 1969 (mixed); *Camping*, 1969
(oil); *Still Life of Flowers*, 1970 (oil); *Sailing*,
1970 (oil); *Winter Scene*, 1971 (oil); *Dr. C.
Eric Lincoln*, 1972 (pastel); *Bishop Richard
Allen*, 1971 (pastel); *Still Life*, 1972 (watercolor); *Still Life*, 1972 (oil); *Confusion*, 1972
(oil); *Earth Quake*, 1972 (pencil); *Straw Painting*, 1972 (watercolor).
Exhibited: Boston Univ., 1963; John Hancock
Building, Boston, 1963; Copper Center, Boston, 1963; MIT, 1963; Memorial Library,
1964; Roslindale Library, Mass., 1964; Boston
Public Library, 1964, 1965; Roxbury YMCA,
Boston, 1964; St. Paul AME Church, Cambridge, Mass., 1965; St. Bartholomew Church,
Cambridge, Mass., 1965; People's Baptist
Church Historical Exh., 1965; Estelle's, 1965;
West Medford Community Center, 1966; Chester Park, Boston, 1966; Robbins Library, Arlington, Mass., 1967; Mass. Ave. Baptist
Church, Cambridge, Mass., 1967; Old South
Meeting House, Boston, 1967; Freedom House,
Boston, 1968; Roxbury Cinema, Boston, 1968;
Northeastern Univ., 1968; APAC of Roxbury
& Dorchester Planning Action Council, 1968;
Kennebunk (Me.) 1st Church, 1968; Univ. of
Mass., 1968; Charles Street Church, Boston,
1969; City Hall, Boston, 1969, 1970, 1972;
Black Stone Park; Lewenberg Jr. High, 1970;
Martin Luther King Middle School, 1970;
Unitarian Parish Hall, Newburyport, Mass.,
1970; Black & White Conference, Amherst &
NH; Tufts Univ., 1970; Jordan Marsh, Boston,
1970; 1st Church, Unitarian, Belmont, Mass.,
1970; Salem State College, 1970; Gordon College, Wenham, Mass., 1971; Regis College,
Weston, Mass., 1971; Boston *Globe* Annual,
Hynes Civic Auditorium, 1971; Internat'l Institute's Whole World Celebration, Commonwealth Armory, Boston, 1971; Hynes Auditorium Boat Show, 1972; Black Academy, NYC,
1972; Boston Art Institute, 1972; Boston Five
Cent Saving Bank, 1972.

Collections: Prudential Building, Boston; Mrs. UpChurch; Mr. Lincoln; Mr. John Thomas; Mr. James Harris; Mr. John Eagle; Mr. Lawrence Mend; Tennis Jones; Mr. Chong, Korea; Mr. Lee, Korea; Mr. Peck, Korea; Mr. Kim, Korea; Mrs. Juanita Smith; Dr. C. Eric Lincoln; Mrs. Bowing; Mr. Ronald Squire.
Awards: Safety Poster Award, 1961, 1962; Red Cross Poster Award, 1961-3; Boston *Globe* Scholastic Art Award, 1st prize, 1961-5; *Boston Globe* Gold Achievement Key, 1962; Clean Up Boston Poster Award, 1962, 1963; 1st award, Boston Negro Artists Assn.; 2nd award, Sunday in the Park, Boston.
Member: Boston Negro Artists Assn.; Art Directors Club of Boston.
Sources: "Black Art Exhibit Opens Sunday," *Herald*, Belmont, Mass., May 14, 1970; "Preview Party to Open Show by 13 Black Artists," *Citizen*, Belmont, Mass., May 14, 1970; Information from the artist.

YARDE, RICHARD

Painter, educator. Born in Boston, 1939. Studied at the School of the Museum of Fine Arts, Boston; Boston University (BFA, 1962; MFA, 1964). Teacher at Boston University.
Works: *The Stoop*, 1969-70 (oil); *The Wait* (oil); *The Stoop II; The Red Door; The Fence; The Demonstrator; Passage; Back; Mirror I; Mirror II; Edgar and I* (watercolor); *The Corner* (watercolor); *Door, Panel, Reflection*.
Exhibited: Fort Wright College, Spokane, 1968 (1-man); Boston City Hall, 1969; Brandeis Univ., 1969; Boston Museum of Fine Arts, 1970; Nat'l Center of Afro-Amer. Artists, Boston, 1971; Studio Museum, Harlem; Rose Art Museum, 1970; Thayer Academy, 1972; Boston Univ.; Institute of Contemporary Art; Rhode Island Arts Festival; Emancipation Proclamation Centennial; Boston Public Library, 1973; Carl Siembab Gallery; Yaddo; Windsor School, Boston.
Collections: Boston Univ.; Fort Wright College, Spokane; 1st Nat'l Bank of Boston; Windsor School, Boston.
Awards: Blanche E. Colman Award, painting, 1971; Invitation to Yaddo Corp., 1964, 1966, 1970; McDowell Colony, 1968, 1970; Artist-in-residence, Harlem Art Project, 1968; Grand Prize, Boston Univ., 1962; summer study in Ibadan, Nigeria.
Sources: Boston Museum of Fine Arts. *Afro-American Artists: NY/Boston*, 1970; List from Thayer Academy; Information from artist; *Art Gallery*, Spring 1969; *Art News*, Sept. 1969; Brandeis Univ. *Twelve Black Artists From Boston*, 1969; Boston Community Lecture Series. *Local Afro-American Artists*, 1969; Koethe, John. "Boston—Black Is Political,"

Art News, Oct. 1970; "Museum of Fine Arts to Hold Black Art Show," *Chronicle*, Ipswich, Mass., May 30, 1970; Nat'l Center of Afro-Amer. Artists. *3 Boston Black Artists: Milton Johnson, Al Smith, & Richard Yarde*, 1971; "Museum of Fine Arts to Hold Black Art Show," *Tri-Town Transcript & Pennysaver*, April 29, 1970; Grillo, Jean B. "Black Artists: Three Views," *Phoenix*, Boston; Le Brun, Caron. "Black Art," *Herald Traveler*, Sunday Supplement, Boston, May 24, 1970.

YATES, CHARLES E.

Printmaker. Born in Tennessee in 1940. Studied at University of Pennsylvania Graduate School of Fine Arts.
Works: *Self-Portrait* (etching); *Karma; Once a Dark Continent; Parabolic Reflection*.
Exhibited: Phila. Civic Center Museum; Brand Library of Art & Music, Glendale, Cal.; Assoc. Students Lounge, UCLA; Los Feliz Jewish Community Center; Dickson Art Center, Univ. of Cal.
Collections: Oakland Museum, Ruth Waddy Collection.
Awards: Cleveland Mueseum School of Art Prize.
Sources: Harley, Ralph, Jr. "Checklist of Afro-Amer. Art & Artists," *The Serif*, Dec. 1970; DuSable Museum of African-Amer. History. *Contemporary Black Artists*, 1970, calendar; Aesthetic Dynamics. *Afro-American Images*, Wilmington, Del., 1971; "Afro-Amer. Issue," *Art Gallery*, April 1968; Indiana Univ. *Fine Arts & the Black American*; Roelof-Lanner, T.V., ed. *Prints by American Negro Artists*; Phila. Civic Center. *Afro-American Artists 1800-1969*; UCLA Art Galleries. *The Negro in American Art*; Oakland Museum Archives; Myers, Carol. *Black Power in the Arts*, Flint, Mich., 1970; Walker, Roslyn. *A Resource Guide to the Visual Arts of Afro-Americans*, South Bend, Ind., 1971.

YEARGANS, HARTWELL

Painter, printmaker. Born 1925.
Works: *Folksinger* (color linocut); *Mexican Zoo; Blues for Miss Anne; Freedom Now; Three Dancers; Sunbathers; Fragments of a Nightmare; Green and Mortality; Doubt, Discord, and Regret; Quartet; 8th St. & 6th Ave.; Indigenous Cultures; Bass Player; El Sol Mexicano; Royal Couple; Even Adam; Drought Victims*.
Exhibited: Whitney Museum, 1971
Collections: Oakland Museum.
Sources: "Afro-American Issue," *Art Gallery*, April 1968; Indiana Univ. *Fine Arts & the Black American*; Roelof-Lanner, T.V., ed. *Prints by American Negro Artists*; Afro-Amer. Slide Depository, Catalog; Doty. *Contemporary*

Black Artists in America; DuSable Museum of African-Amer. History. *Contemporary Black Artists*, 1970, Calendar; Book Mart Art Gallery. *Exhibition of Graphics by Hart Yeargans*, Montreal, Mansfield, Oct. 1967; Myers, Carol L. *Black Power in the Arts*, Flint, Mich., 1970; Oakland Museum Archives, Ruth Waddy Collection; Walker, Roslyn. *A Resource Guide to the Visual Arts of Afro-Americans*, South Bend, Ind., 1971.

YEARGANS, JAMES CONROY

Studied at the National Academy of Design.
Works: *No Room at the Hotel; Hope; Drum; Rapture; Three Graces I; Caprice; Sun Plan; Three Graces II; Wide River; Zimbabroe Dream; Space Portrait; Flickers; Ember; Dana Whorl; Ibo Views.*
Exhibited: Newark Museum; San Francisco Museum of Art; Rhode Island Museum; ACA Gallery; McGill Univ., Montreal.
Member: Spiral Group.
Sources: Duo Gallery. *Recent Paintings by James Conroy Yeargans*, May 23-June 9, 1961; Siegel, Jeanne. "Why Spiral?," *Art News*, Sept. 1966; Long Island Univ. *Spiral* catalog.

YORK, ERNEST

Painter, educator. Teacher at Morgan State College.
Collections: Morgan State College.
Sources: York, Ernest. "What I Want to Be," *Occupations*, Dec. 1951, p. 206.

YOUNG, BERNARD

Mixed media.
Works: *Tang & Culture* (mixed).
Exhibited: Lee Cultural Center, Phila.
Sources: Phila. Dept. of Recreation. *Love . . . and the Black Community.*

YOUNG, BETTY

Painter, graphic artist. Born in Brooklyn, New York, September 1, 1946. Studied at City College of New York (BA); City University of New York Graduate Center. College assistant, Queens College, SEEK Program.
Works: *Little Brother; Ghetto Music; Lady Day; Little Herders; Rhythm Changes; Dialogue;* Calligrapher hand-printed citations for the Vocat'l Guidance & Workshop Center Annuals, 1967-72.
Exhibited: High School of Music & Art, 1962-5; Project Ethnoscope, Illustration for *Urban Review* article; Children's Aide Society Show, 1967; Nyumba Ya Sanaa Gallery, 1967-71; Vocat'l Guidance & Workshop Center Annual, 1967-72; Holyoke College, 1972.
Awards: *Scholastic Magazine* Award for Art, 1965.
Sources: Information from artist; *Urban Review*, NY; NY Teachers College. *Ascension of Earth Child.*

YOUNG, CHARLES A. (CHUCK)

Painter, printmaker, educator. Born in New York City, November 17, 1930. Studied at New York University (MA in Art). Professor and Chairman of Art Department, Federal City College, Washington, DC.
Works: *Two Figures in Totem; Madonna; Warriors; Mechanical Landscape; Untitled #5; Tennessee Remembrance; Break Through; Frolic in Nature; In Harmony; Image USA; Formal Encasement; Dashiki Madonnas; Figure in Totem; Four Totems; Ghetto Mother and Daughter; Nature in Flight; Lust Tondo; Floral Tribute.*
Exhibited: Fayetteville (NC) State Univ., 1960-2 (3 1-man shows); Tenn. A&I State Univ., 1964 (1-man); Voice of America, Washington, DC, 1965 (1-man); Unitarian Church, Nashville, Tenn., 1965 (1-man); Tyco Gallery, Nashville, 1966 (1-man); Smith-Mason Gallery, Washington, DC, 1969 (1-man); Agra Gallery, Washington, DC, 1972 (1-man); Hampton Institute, 1951; Richmond (Va.) Museum of Art, 1952; NY Univ., 1959; Honeycutt Art Exhibition, Fayetteville, NC, 1962; Weatherspoon Gallery, Greensboro, NC, 1962; NC Artists Open Exhibition (Ashville), 1963; Parthenon Gallery of Art, Nashville, 1967; Fisk Univ., 1969; Wilmington, Del., 1971; Smith-Mason Gallery, Washington, DC, 1971; NJ State Museum, Trenton, NJ, 1972; Sheraton Hotel, Phila., 1968.
Collections: Scottish Bank, Fayetteville, NC; Fisk Univ.; Fayetteville State Univ.; Tenn. A&I State Univ., Nashville; Kennedy Institute, Washington, DC; Tyco Gallery, Nashville; Smith-Mason Gallery, Washington, DC.
Awards: Annual Art Exhibition, Fayetteville, NC, 1st & 2nd prizes, 1962.
Societies: College Art Assn.; Nat'l Art Workers Community; Nat'l Education Assn.; DC Commission on the Arts.
Sources: *Dictionary of International Biography*, 1970; *Who's Who in American Education*, 1967; *1968 Register of United States Living Artists*; Atkinson, Edward. *Black Dimensions in Contemporary Art*; Lewis/Waddy. *Black Artists on Art*, Vol. 2; Harley, Ralph, Jr. "Checklist of Afro-Amer. Art & Artists," *Serif*, Dec. 1970; Greene, Carroll, Jr. "Perspective: The Black Artist in America," *Art Gallery*, April 1970, p. 18; Smith-Mason Gallery. *National Exhibition Black Artists 1971.*

YOUNG, CLARENCE EDWARD

Works: *A Loud Sound of Silence.*
Sources: Patterson, Lindsay. "Contemporary Artists," *The Negro in Music and Art*, 1969.

YOUNG, KENNETH

Painter. Born in Louisville, Kentucky in 1933.
Works: *Moon Spots; Night Asham; Riot; Red Dance; Upper Egypt.*
Exhibited: State Armory, Wilmington, Del., 1971; Univ. of Iowa, 1972; A.M. Sachs Gallery.
Collections: Johnson Pub. Co., Chicago.
Sources: Indiana Univ. *Fine Arts & the Black American*; Aesthetic Dynamics. *Afro-American Images*, Wilmington, Del., 1971; Ill. Bell Telephone. *Black American Artists/71*; Rose, Barbara. "Black Art in America," *Art in America*, July-Dec. 1970; Johnson Pub. Co. *The JPC Art Collection*, pamphlet; Walker, Roslyn. *A Resource Guide to the Visual Arts of Afro-Americans*, South Bend, Ind., 1971.

YOUNG, MILTON

Painter, sculptor. Born in Houston, Texas in 1935. Studied at Los Angeles City College; California State College, Los Angeles (BFA).
Works: *Utilities Of; Machine Culture Body Odor; Midwestern Cyclopedia Talking at You; Four Letter Existence; Goodbye Ovulation; Pray Just in Case; Sweet, Sweet Abby; One Plus One #16; Variable Timing Fuse; Mills of Your Female Thing; Pass it On; Shadows of Your Gable; Come Live in the Sun; Once Sweet Abby; Hello Ovulation; Fresh Egg in Search of a Sperm; Nancy's World; Superman and His Peppers; Sunday at Borel Powerhouse; Jesus Fish.*
Exhibited: Brockman Gallery; Ankrum Gallery, 1970; Los Angeles Annual Art Exhibition; Univ. of Iowa, 1972; UCLA Art Gallery, 1971; Los Angeles Co. Museum, 1965; Ill. Bell Telephone, 1971; Los Angeles Tower Gallery, 1969.
Collections: Mr. & Mrs. Albert Cruse; Mr. Sam Thomas; Mr. Thomas J. Stanley Mullin; Malcolm X College, Chicago.
Member: Los Angeles Art Assn.
Sources: Illinois Bell Telephone. *Black American Artists/71*; Afro-Amer. Slide Depository, catalog; Lewis/Waddy. *Black Artists on Art*, Vol. 2; *Good Housekeeping Magazine*, Feb. 1967; *Art Week*, March 1970, April 1972; *Art International*, Vol. 14, 1970; *Coast Magazine*, Sept. 1971; Information from the artist.

YOUNG, TOMMY

Painter, sculptor, composer. Active in the 1970's.
Works: Cover Design, THE MASK, April 1970.
Sources: "Portfolio Art," *The Mask*, Poverty Press, Los Angeles, April 1970, pp. 17-20.

ZIMMERMAN, ELYN

Born 1945.
Works: *#110*, 1970 (synthetic polymer on canvas).
Exhibited: Whitney Museum, 1971.
Sources: Doty. *Contemporary Black Artists in America.*

ZUBER, BARBARA

Born in Philadelphia. Studied at Yale University School of Fine Arts (BFA).
Works: *Jump Rope.*
Collections: Johnson Pub. Co.
Sources: A&T Univ. Lyceum Program. *15 Afro-American Women*; Johnson Pub. Co. *The JPC Art Collection*, Pamphlet.

Bibliography

For simplification, sources have been separated into four categories: books, exhibition catalogues, magazines and newspapers. Sources relevant to only one artist are listed in that artist's sources, and do not appear here.

BOOKS

Adams, Agatha Boyd. *Contemporary Negro Arts.* Chapel Hill: Univ. of North Carolina Press, c. 1948.

Adams, Russell. *Great Negroes Past and Present.* Chicago: Afro-American Publishing Co., 1969.

Alabama: A Guide to the Deep South, compiled by workers of the Writer's Program of the WPA, Alabama. New York: Richard R. Smith, 1941.

American Art Annual. Washington, D.C.: American Federation of Arts, 1898-.

American Artists' Congress. *First American Artists' Congress Against War and Fascism.* New York, 1936.

American Institute of Architects. *American Architects Directory.* Eds. 1-3. New York: R.R. Bowker, 1956-70.

The American Negro Reference Book, edited by John P. Davis. Negro Heritage Library. Yonkers, N.Y.: Educational Heritage, Inc., 1966.

Appleton's Cyclopedia of American Biography, edited by James G. Wilson and John Fiske. New York: D. Appleton and Co., 1888. Reprint. Detroit: Gale Research Co., 1968.

Aptheker, Herbert, ed. *Documentary History of the Negro People In the United States.* 2 vols., 2nd ed. New York: Citadel Press, 1964.

Arnold, John W. *Art and Artists of Rhode Island.* Providence: Rhode Island Citizen's Assn., 1905.

Artists/USA 1972-1973. Feasterville, Pa.: Artists/USA Inc., 1972.

Art of the Americas from Before Columbus to the Present Day: A Pictorial Survey. Reprinted from *Art News Annual,* No. 18. New York: Simon and Schuster, 1948.

Atkinson, J. Edward, comp. and ed. *Black Dimensions In Contemporary American Art.* New York: New American Library, 1971.

Bardolph, Richard. *The Negro Vanguard.* New York, 1959. Reprint. Westport, Conn.: Negro Universities Press.

Barr, Alfred, ed. *Painting and Sculpture In the Museum of Modern Art.* New York: Museum of Modern Art, 1942.

Bartran, Margaret. *A Guide to Color Reproductions.* Metuchen, N.J.: Scarecrow Press, Inc., 1971.

Baur, John I. H., ed. *New Art In America: 50 Painters of the 20th Century.* Greenwich, Conn.: New York Graphic Society, 1957.

Bearden, Romare, and Harry Henderson. *Six Black Masters of American Art.* New York: Zenith Books, 1972.

Benezit, Emmanuel. *Dictionnaire Des Peintres, Sculpteurs, Dessinateurs Et Graveurs.* Librairie Grund, France, 1948.

Bergman, Peter M. *The Chronological History of the Negro In America.* New York, Evanston, London: Harper and Row, 1969. A Bergman Book.

Bethers, Ray. *Pictures, Painters and You.* New York: Pitman Publishing Corp., 1948.

Black American Artists of Yesterday and Today. Black Heritage Series. Dayton, Ohio: George A. Pflaum, Publisher, 1909.

Black Art Notes. Edited and with introduction by Tom Lloyd. n.p., n.d.

Black Dimensions In Contemporary American Art. See Atkinson, J. Edward.

Black Perspectives—Teaching Guide. See: Thomas, Pearl, comp.

The Black Photographers Annual 1973. Brooklyn, NY: Black Photographers Annual, Inc.

Boning, Richard A. *Profiles of Black Americans.* Rockville Centre, N.Y.: Dexter and Westbrook, Ltd., 1969.

Boswell, Peyton, Jr. *Modern American Painting.* New York: Dodd, Mead, 1939.

Brawley, Benjamin. *Negro Builders and Heroes.* Chapel Hill: Univ. of North Carolina Press, 1937.

Brawley, Benjamin. *The Negro Genius, A New Appraisal of the Achievement of the American Negro In Literature and the Fine Arts.* New York: Biblo and Tannen, 1965.

Brawley, Benjamin. *The Negro Genius.* 2nd ed. New York: Biblo and Tannen, 1966.

Brawley, Benjamin. *The Negro In Literature and Art In the United States.* Rev. ed. New York: Dodd, Mead, 1934.

Brawley, Benjamin. *A Short History of the American Negro.* 4th ed., rev. New York: Macmillan, 1939.

325

Brown, Marion. "The Negro in the Fine Arts," in *The American Negro Reference Book*, edited by John P. Davis. Negro Heritage Library. Chicago: Educational Heritage, Inc., 1966.

Brown, Sterling. *The Negro Caravan*. New York: Dryden Press, 1942.

Bryan, Michael. *Bryan's Dictionary of Painters and Engravers*. 5 vols. New York: Macmillan, 1903-5.

Bullock, Ralph W. *In Spite of Handicaps*. New York: Association Press, 1967.

Burroughs, Margaret, et al. *National Conference of Negro Artists*. Atlanta: Atlanta Univ., 1959.

Burton, E. Milby. *South Carolina Silversmiths, 1690-1800*. Charleston, S.C.: Charleston Museum, 1942.

Butcher, Margaret J. *The Negro In American Culture*. 2nd ed. New York: Alfred A. Knopf, 1972.

Butts, Porter. *Art In Wisconsin*. Madison, Wisc.: Madison Art Assn., Wisc. Centennial Committee, and Univ. of Wisc. Division of Social Education, 1936.

Cahill, Holger, et al. *Masters of Popular Painting*. New York: Museum of Modern Art, 1938.

Cahill, Holger, and Alfred Barr, Jr., eds. *Art In America In Modern Times*. New York: Reynal and Hitchcock, 1934.

Cahill, Holger, and Alfred Barr, Jr., eds. *New Horizons In American Art*. New York: Museum of Modern Art, 1936.

Celebrating Negro History and Brotherhood: A Folio of Prints By Chicago Artists. Chicago: Seven Arts Workshop, 1956.

Chase, George Henry, and Chandler R. Post. *A History of Sculpture*. New York and London: Harper and Brothers Publishers, 1925.

Chase, Judith W. *Afro-American Art and Craft*. New York: Van Nostrand Reinhold, 1971.

Chicago Public Library Omnibus Project. *Subject Index to Literature On Negro Art Selected from the Union Catalog of Printed Materials On the Negro In the Chicago Libraries*. Chicago, 1941.

Clapp, Jane. *Art Reproductions*. New York: Scarecrow Press, Inc., 1961.

Clapp, Jane. *Sculpture Index*. Vol. 2. Metuchen, N.J.: Scarecrow Press, 1970.

Clarke, John H. *Harlem USA*. New York: Collier Books, 1971.

Clement, Clara E., and Laurence Hutton. *Artists of the 19th Century: Their Works*. Boston: Osgood, 1885.

Coen, Rena N. *The Black Man In Art*. Minneapolis, Minn.: Lerner Publications Co., 1970.

Cole, Natalie R. *Arts In the Classroom*. New York: John Day, 1940.

Craven, Thomas, ed. *A Treasury of American Prints*. New York: Simon and Schuster, 1939.

Cultural Exchange Center. *Prints By American Negro Artists*. See Roeloff-Lanner, T.V.

Cummings, Paul. *A Dictionary of Contemporary American Artists*. New York: St. Martin's Press, 1966.

Dabney, Wendell P. *Cincinnati's Colored Citizens*. Cincinnati: Dabney Publishing Co., 1926.

Daniels, John. *In Freedom's Birthplace: A Study of Boston Negroes*. Boston: Houghton Mifflin, 1941.

Dannett, Sylvia G. L. *Profiles of Negro Womanhood*. 2 vols. Negro Heritage Library. Yonkers, N.Y.: Educational Heritage, Inc., 1964 and 1966.

David, Jay. *Black Joy*. Chicago: Bill Adler Books, Inc., 1971.

Davis, John P., ed. *The American Negro Reference Book*. Negro Heritage Library. Yonkers, N.Y.: Educational Heritage, Inc., 1966.

Davis, John P., ed. *The Public Library and Reference Material On the American Negro*. New York: Phelps-Stokes Fund, 1963.

Davison, Ruth M., and April Legler, comps. *Government Publications On the Negro In America 1948-1968*. Focus: Black America Bibliography Series. Bloomington, Ind.: Indiana Univ., Summer 1969.

Desdunes, Rodolph. *Nos Hommes Et Notre Histoire; Notices Biographiques Accompagnees De Reflexion Et Des Souvenirs Personnels*. Montreal: Arbour and Dupont, 1911.

Diamond Jubilee Exposition Authority. *Cavalcade of the American Negro*. Chicago: Illinois Writer's Project, 1940.

A Dictionary of American Artists, Sculptors and Engravers. See: Young, William.

Dictionary of American Biography. Under the auspices of the American Council of Learned Societies. New York: Scribner, 1928-58.

Dixon, Vernon J., and Badi Foster. *Beyond Black or White*. Boston: Little, Brown, 1971.

Dover, Cedric. *American Negro Art*. Greenwich, Conn.: New York Graphic Society, 1966.

Dowd, Jerome. *The Negro In American Life*. New York: Negro Universities Press, 1926.

Dow, George F. *The Arts and Crafts In New England, 1704-1775*. Topsfield, Mass.: Wayside Press, 1927.

Driskell, David. *Black Dimensions In American Art*. New York: New American Library, 1970.

Drotning, Phillip T. *A Guide to Negro History In America.* New York: Doubleday, 1968.

DuBois, William Edward Burghardt. *Black Folk-Then and Now.* New York: H. Holt, 1939.

DuBois, William Edward Burghardt. *Encyclopedia of the Negro.* 2nd ed. New York: Phelps-Stokes Fund, 1946.

DuBois, William Edward Burghardt. *The Gift of Black Folk.* Boston: Stratford Co., 1924.

DuBois, William Edward Burghardt. *The Negro Artisan.* Atlanta: Atlanta Univ. press, 1902. Reprint. New York: Arno Press and *The New York Times,* 1969.

DuBois, William Edward Burghardt. *The Philadelphia Negro; A Social Study.* Philadelphia: Univ. of Pennsylvania, 1899.

DuBois, William Edward Burghardt, ed. *A Selected Bibliography of the Negro American.* Atlanta: Atlanta Univ. Press, 1905.

Dunbar, Ernest, ed. *The Black Expatriates.* New York: E.P. Dutton and Co., Inc., 1968.

Dunlap, William. *History of the Rise and Progress of the Arts of Design In the United States.* Boston: C.E. Goodspeed, 1918.

Ebony and Topaz, A Collectanea, edited by Charles S. Johnson. Black Heritage Library Collection. New York: National Urban League, 1927.

Ebony, Editors of. *The Negro Handbook.* Chicago: Johnson Publications Co., 1966.

Eliot, Alexander. *Three Hundred Years of American Painting.* New York: Time, Inc., 1957.

Encyclopedia of the Arts. See Runes, Dagobert.

English, Thomas H. *Roads to Research: Distinguished Library Collections of the Southeast.* Athens: Univ. of Georgia Press, 1968.

Fax, Elton C. *Seventeen Black Artists.* New York: Dodd, Mead, 1971.

Ferris, W. H. *The African Abroad: Or, His Evolution In Western Civilization Tracing His Development Under Caucasian Milieu.* New Haven: Tuttle, Morehouse, and Taylor Press, 1913.

Fine Arts and the Black American. See: Irvine, Betty Jo.

Ford, Alicia. *Pictorial Folk Art: New England to California.* New York: Studio Publications, 1949.

Frankhauer, Mary E. *Biographical Sketches of American Artists.* Lansing, Mich.: Michigan State Library, 1924.

Franklin, John Hope. *From Slavery to Freedom.* 3rd ed. New York: Vintage Books, 1969.

French, H. W. *Art and Artists of Connecticut.* Boston: Lee and Shephard, 1879.

Fuller, Thomas O. *Pictorial History of the American Negro.* Memphis, Tenn.: Pictorial History, Inc., 1933.

Furr, Arthur F. *History and Progress of Negroes In the United States.* Typewritten manuscript in the Boston Public Library, n.d.

Gayle, Addison. *The Black Aesthetic.* Garden City, N.Y.: Doubleday, 1971.

Geldzahler, Henry. *American Painting In the Twentieth Century.* New York: Metropolitan Museum of Art, 1965.

George Cleveland Hall Branch Library. *The Special Negro Collection At the George Cleveland Hall Branch Library.* Chicago, 1968.

Gerbrands, Adranius Alexander. *Art As An Element of Culture.* London: E.J. Bill, 1957.

Greene, Lorenzo Johnston. *The Negro In Colonial New England, 1620-1776.* New York: Columbia Univ. Press, 1942.

Groce, George C., and David H. Wallace. *The New York Historical Society's Dictionary of Artists In America, 1564-1860.* New Haven and London: Yale Univ. Press, 1957.

Gruskin, Alan D. *Painting In the U.S.A.* Garden City, N.Y.: Doubleday, 1946.

Guzman, Jessie. See *Negro Year Book.*

Hale, R. B., ed. *100 American Painters of the Twentieth Century.* New York: Metropolitan Museum of Art, 1950.

Haley, James T. *Afro-American Encyclopedia: Or, the Thoughts, Doings, and Sayings of the Race.* Nashville, Tenn.: Haley and Florida, 1896.

Harley, Ralph L., Jr. See Magazine Section.

Harvard College Library. *Afro-American Studies: A Guide to Resources of the Harvard University Library, Preliminary Edition.* Cambridge, Mass., 1969.

Harvard College. *Resources of the Harvard University Library for Afro-American and African Studies.* Cambridge, Mass., 1969.

Henderson, Harry. See Bearden, Romare, and Harry Henderson.

Howard Univ. Graduate School, Division of Social Science. *The New Negro Thirty Years Afterward: Papers Contributed To the 16th Annual Spring Conference, April 20, 21, and 22, 1955.* Washington, D.C.: Howard Univ. Press, 1955.

Huggins, Nathan Irvin. *Harlem Renaissance.* New York: Oxford Univ. Press, 1971.

Hughes, Langston. *A Pictorial History of the Negro In America.* New York: Crown, 1956.

Indiana Univ. *Fine Arts and the Black American.* See: Irvine, Betty Jo.

International Library of Negro Life and History. Under the auspices of the Assn. for the Study of Negro Life and History. New York: Publishers Co., Inc., 1967, 1968, 1969. Robinson, Wilhelmena S. *Historical Negro Biographies;* Wesley, Charles H. *In Freedom's Footsteps: from the African Background To the Civil War;* Wesley, Charles H., and Patricia W. Romero. *Negro Americans In the Civil War: from Slavery To Citizenship;* Wesley, Charles H. *The Quest for Equality: from Civil War To Civil Rights;* Romero, Patricia W., comp and ed. *I Too Am America: Documents from 1619 To the Present;* Patterson, Lindsay, comp. and ed. *The Negro In Music and Art;* Patterson, Lindsay, comp. and ed. *Anthology of the American Negro In the Theatre;* Patterson, Lindsay, comp. and ed. *An Introduction to Black Literature In America: From 1746 To the Present;* Morais, Herbert M. *The History of the Negro In Medicine;* Henderson, Edwin B. *The Black Athlete.*

Irvine, Betty Jo, and Jane A. McCabe, comps. *Fine Arts and the Black American/Music and the Black American.* Focus: Black America Bibliography Series. Bloomington, Ind.: Indiana Univ., Summer 1969.

Isham, Samuel. *The History of American Painting.* 2nd ed. New York: Macmillan, 1936.

Janis, Sidney. *They Taught Themselves, American Primitive Painters of the 20th Century.* New York: Dial Press, 1942.

Jefferson, Louise E. *Contemporary Art By Afro-Americans.* New York: Friendship Press, 196--.

Johnson, Charles S. *The Negro In American Civilization.* New York: H. Holt, 1930.

Johnson, Charles S., ed. *Ebony and Topaz, A Collectanea.* Black Heritage Library Collection. New York: National Urban League, 1927.

Johnson, James Weldon. *Black Manhattan.* New York: Alfred A. Knopf, 1930.

Keppel, Frederick P., and R. L. Duffas. *The Arts In American Life.* New York: McGraw-Hill, 1933.

Kirkland, Winifred Margaretta. *Girls Who Became Artists By Winifred & Francis Kirkland.* Freeport, N.Y.: Books for Libraries Press, 1967.

Lafollette, Susanne. *Art In America.* New York: Harper, 1929.

Larkin, Oliver. *Art and Life In America.* Rev. ed. New York: Rinehart, 1960.

Lewis, Samella S., and Ruth G. Waddy. *Black Artists On Art.* 2 vols. Los Angeles: Contemporary Crafts, Inc., 1971.

Lloyd, Tom, ed. *Black Art Notes.* n.d.

Locke, Alain. "Negro Art," in *Encyclopedia Britannica.* 14th and 15th eds.

Locke, Alain. *Negro Art: Past and Present.* Washington, D.C.: Associates in Negro Folk Education, 1936.

Locke, Alain. *The Negro In Art.* Washington, D.C.: Associates in Negro Folk Education, 1940.

Locke, Alain, ed. *The New Negro, An Interpretation.* New York: Arno Press and *The New York Times, 1968.*

Logan, Rayford, Eugene C. Holmes, and G. Franklin Edwards, eds. *The New Negro 30 Years Afterward.* Washington, D.C.: Howard Univ. Press, 1956.

McKay, George L., comp. *A Register of Artists, Engravers, Booksellers, Bookbinders, Printers and Publishers In New York City, 1633-1820.* New York: New York Public Library, 1942.

McPherson, John M., Laurence B. Holland, James M. Banner, Nancy J. Weiss, and Michael D. Bell. *Blacks In America, Bibliographical Essays.* Garden City, N.Y.: Doubleday, 1971.

Mallett, Daniel Trowbridge. *Mallett's Index of Artists: International-Biographical: Including Painters, Sculptors, Illustrators, Engravers, and Etchers of the Past and Present.* Orig. and Supplement. New York: Peter Smith, 1948.

Meglin, Nick. *On-the-Spot Drawing.* New York: Watson-Guptill Publications, 1969.

Miller, Elizabeth W. *Negro In America: A Bibliography.* Cambridge, Mass.: Harvard Univ. Press for the American Academy of Arts and Sciences, 1966.

Monro, Isabel Stevenson, and Kate M. Monro. *Index to Reproductions of American Paintings: A Guide to Pictures Occurring In More Than Eight Hundred Books.* New York: H. W. Wilson Co., 1948.

Morsbach, Mabel. *The Negro In American Life.* In conjunction with the Cincinnati Public Schools. New York: Harcourt, Brace & World, 1967.

Murray, Florence. *The Negro Handbook, 1942.* New York: Malliet and Co., 1942.

Murray, Florence. *The Negro Handbook, 1944.* New York: Current Reference Publications, 1944.

Murray, Florence. *The Negro Handbook, 1946-7.* New York: Current Books, Inc., 1947.

Murray, Florence. *The Negro Handbook, 1949.* New York: Macmillan, 1949.

Murray, Freeman Morris Henry. *Emancipation and the Freed In American Sculpture: A Study In Interpretation.* Washington, D.C.: The Author, 1916.

Myers, Carol L., ed. *Black Power In the Arts.* Flint, Mich.: Flint Board of Education, 1970.

National Conference of Artists. *A Print Portfolio By Negro Artists: A Souvenir In Observance of the Emancipation Proclamation Centennial 1863-1963.* Chicago, 1963.

The Negro Almanac, edited by Harry A. Ploski. New York: Bellwether Publishing Co., 1967.

Negro Book Club, Inc. *Negro Book Club's Guide to African American Books, Records, Visual Aids, Maps, Film Strips and Art.* New York, 1969.

The Negro Handbook, composed by Editors of Ebony. Chicago: Johnson Publications Co., 1966.

The Negro Heritage Library. Yonkers, N.Y.: Educational Heritage, Inc., 1964-6. Dannett, Sylvia G. L. *Profiles of Negro Womanhood.* 2 vols.; Davis, John P., ed. *The American Negro Reference Book.* 2 vols.; Evans, Lancelot, ed. *Emerging African Nations and Their Leaders.* 2 vols.; Cain, Alfred E., ed. *The Winding Road to Freedom; A Martin Luther King Treasury;* Christmas, Walter, ed. *Negroes In Public Affairs and Government.*

The Negro In Music and Art. See Patterson, Lindsay.

Negro Year Book, edited by Jessie Guzman. New York: Univ. Place Book Shop, 1941-6.

Nordness, Lee. *Objects: USA.* New York: Viking Press, 1970.

Ovington, Mary White. *Portraits In Color.* New York: Viking Press, 1927.

Painting In the United States. Pittsburgh: Carnegie Institute, 1944, 1947.

Patterson, Lindsay, comp. and ed. *The Negro In Music and Art.* International Library of Negro Life and History. Under the auspices of the Assn. for the Study of Negro Life and History. New York: Publishers Co., Inc., 1967.

Pearson, Ralph M. *The Modern Renaissance In American Art Presenting the Work & Philosophy of 54 Distinguished Artists.* New York: Harper, 1954.

Pinchbeck, R. B. *The Virginia Negro Artisan and Tradesman.* Richmond: William Byrd's Press, 1926.

Ploski, Harry A., ed. *The Negro Almanac.* New York: Bellwether Publishing Co., 1967.

Ploski, Harry A., and Ernest Kaiser, eds. "The Black Artist," in *Afro USA.* New York: Bellwether Publishing Co., 1971.

Ploski, Harry A., Ernest Kaiser, and Otto J. Lindenmeyer, eds. 'The Black Artist," in *Reference Library of Black America.* New York: Bellwether Publishing Co., 1971.

Porter, Dorothy B. *The Negro In the United States, A Selected Bibliography.* Washington, D.C.: Library of Congress, 1970.

Porter, Dorothy B. *A Working Bibliography On the Negro In the United States.* Reproduced by Univ. Microfilms for the National Endowment for the Humanities Summer Workshops in the Materials of Negro Culture, 1968.

Porter, James A. *Modern Negro Art.* New York: Dryden Press, 1943. Reprint. New York: Arno Press, 1969.

Porter, James A. "The Negro Artist." Master's Thesis, New York Univ., 1937.

Porter, James A. "The Transcultural Affinities of African Negro Art," in *Africa Seen By American Negroes.* Dijon: Presence Africaine, 1958.

Prime, A.C. *The Arts and Crafts In Philadelphia, Maryland and South Carolina, 1721-1785.* Baltimore: Walpole Society, 1929.

Prince George's County Memorial Library, Oxon Hill Branch. *Selective List of Government Publications About the American Negro.* Oxon Hill, Md., Feb. 1968.

Randall, Roslyn Walker. See Walker, Roslyn.

Redding, Saunders. *The Negro.* Washington, D.C.: Potomac Books, Inc., 1967.

Richardson, Ben. *Great American Negroes.* Revised by William A. Fahey. New York: Thomas Y. Crowell Co., 1956.

Ritchings, G. F. *Evidences of Progress Among Colored People.* Philadelphia: George S. Ferguson Co., 1899.

Robinson, Wilhelmena S. *Historical Negro Biographies.* International Library of Negro Life and History. Under the auspices of the Assn. for the Study of Negro Life and History. New York: Publishers Co., Inc., 1967.

Rodman, Seldon. *Conversations With Artists.* New York: Devin Adair, 1957.

Rodman, Seldon. *Renaissance In Haiti: Popular Painters In the Black Republic.* New York: Pellegrini and Cudahy, 1948.

Roelof-Lanner, T.V., ed. *Prints By American Negro Artists.* Los Angeles: Los Angeles Cultural Exchange Center, 1965.

Rogers, Joel A. *Africa's Gift to America: the Afro-American In the Making and Saving of the United States.* New York: Joel A. Rogers, 1961.

Rollins, Charlemae Hill. *The Showed the Way.* New York: Thomas Y. Crowell, 1964.

Roucek, Joseph S., and Thomas Kiernan, eds. *The Negro Impact On Western Civilization.* New York: Philosophical Library, 1970.

Runes, Dagobert D., and Harry G. Schrickel, eds. *Encyclopedia of the Arts.* New York: Philosophical Library, 1946.

St. Gaudens, Homer. *The American Artist and His Times.* New York: Dodd, Mead, 1941.

Schatz, Walter. *Directory of Afro-American Resources.* New York: R.R. Bowker, 1970.

Schoener, Allon, comp. *Harlem On My Mind: Cultural Capital of Black America, 1900-1968.* New York: Random House, 1968.

Schrickel, Harry G. See Runes, Dagobert D., and Harry G. Schrickel.

Scruggs, L.A. *Women of Distinction: Remarkable In Works & Invincible In Character.* Raleigh, N.C.: L.A. Scruggs, 1893.

Shikes, Ralph E. *The Indignant Eye.* Boston: Beacon Press, 1969.

Siegel, Jeanne. "Four American Negro Painters: 1940-1965, Their Choice and Treatment of Themes." Master's Thesis, Columbia Univ., 1966.

Simmons, Gerald L. *Exposures In Black.* Detroit: Ulozi Photographers, c. 1968.

Simmons, William J. *Men of Mark, Eminent, Progressive & Rising.* Cleveland: Revel, 1887. Reprint. New York: Arno Press and *The New York Times,* 1968.

Smith, Ralph Clifton. *A Biographical Index of American Artists.* Baltimore: William & Wilkins Co., 1930.

Spradling, Mary, ed. *In Black and White: Afro-Americans In Print.* Kalamazoo, Mich.: Kalamazoo Library System, 1971.

Stull, Edith. *Unsung Black Americans.* New York: Grosset & Dunlap, 1971.

Sutton, Denys. *American Painting.* London: Avalon Press, 1948.

Taft, Lorado. *The History of American Sculpture.* New York: Macmillan, 1903.

Thiel, Yvonne Greer. *Artists and People.* New York: Philosophical Library, 1959.

Thieme, Ulrich, and Felix Becker. *Allgemeines Lexikon Der Bildenden Kunstler.* Leipzig, Germany: Verlag Von Wilhelm Engelmann, 1908.

Thomas, Pearl, comp. *Black Perspectives—Teaching Guide.* New York: Scholastic Book Services, 1971.

Thompson, Robert Farris. "African Influence on the Art of the United States," in *Black Studies In the University,* A Symposium, edited by Armstead L. Robinson, et. al. Yale Univ., 1969.

Troup, Cornelius V. *Distinguished Negro Georgians.* Dallas: Royal Publishing Co., 1962.

Tuckerman, Henry T. *Book of Artists: American Artist Life, Comprising the Biographical and Critical Sketches of American Artists: Preceded By An Historical Account of the Rise and Progress of Art In America, With An Appendix Containing An Account of Notable Pictures and Private Collections.* New York: Putnam, 1882.

Waddy, Ruth G. See Lewis, Samella S., and Ruth G. Waddy.

Walker, Anne Kendrick. *Tuskegee and the Black Belt, A Portrait of A Race.* Richmond, Va.: Dietz Press, Inc., 1944.

Walker, Roslyn. *A Resource Guide To the Visual Arts of Afro-Americans.* South Bend, Ind.: South Bend Community School Corp., 1971.

— Welsh, Erwin K. *The Negro In the US: A Research Guide.* Bloomington, Ind.: Indiana Univ. Press, 1965.

Werlein, Mrs. Philip. *The Wrought Iron Railings of Le Vieux Carré.* New Orleans: The Author, 1925.

West, Earle H., comp. *A Bibliography of Doctoral Research On the Negro: 1933-1966.* Ann Arbor, Mich.: Univ. Microfilms, 1969.

Weyl, Nathaniel. *The Negro In American Civilization.* Washington, D.C.: Public Affairs Press, 1960.

Wheadon, Augusta Austin. *The Negro From 1863 To 1963.* New York: Vantage Press, 1964.

Whiting, Helen Adele. *Negro Art, Music & Rhyme for Young Folks.* Book 2. Washington, D.C.: Associated Publishers, Inc., 1938.

Who's Who In American Art, A Biographical Directory of Contemporary Artists, Editors, Critics, Executives, Etc., 1901-1973. New York: R.R. Bowker.

Who's Who In Colored America: A Biographical Dictionary of Notable Living Persons of African Descent In America, edited by Thomas Yenser. New York: Thomas Yenser, 1933.

Who's Who In Commercial Art and Photography: A Guide To Artists, Photographers, Agents, Studios, Representatives and Buyers of Art In the Graphics Field. New York: Director's Art Institute, Inc., 1960.

Wilson, Joseph. *Sketches of the Higher Classes of Colored Society In Philadelphia, By A Southerner.* Philadelphia: Merrihew and Thompson, 1841.

Woodruff, Hale A. *The American Negro Artist.* Ann Arbor, Mich.: Univ. of Michigan Press, 1956.

Woodson, Carter G. *A Century of Negro Migration.* Washington, D.C.: Assn. for the Study of Negro Life and History, 1918.

Woodson, Carter G., and Charles H. Wesley. *The Story of the Negro Retold.* Washington, D.C.: Associated Publishers, Inc., 1959.

Works, Monroe N. *Bibliography of the Negro In Africa and America.* New York: H.W. Wilson, 1929.

Yenser, Thomas. See *Who's Who In Colored America.*

Young, William, ed. and comp. *A Dictionary of American Artists, Sculptors and Engravers From the Beginnings Through the Turn of the Twentieth Century.* Cambridge, Mass.: Wililam Young and Co., 1968.

MAGAZINES

ABA: *A Journal of Affairs of Black Artists.* Dorchester, Mass.: National Center of Afro-American Artists.

Adams, Agatha Boyd. "Contemporary Negro Arts," *University of North Carolina Extension Bulletin.* June 1948.

"African Art—Harlem," *American Magazine of Art.* Oct. 1932, p. 244.

"Afro-American Artists 1800-1950," *Ebony.* Vol. 23, pp. 116-22.

"Afro-American Issue," *Art Gallery.* April 1968.

"Afro-American Issue," *Art Gallery.* April 1970.

"Afro-American Slide Program," *Art Journal.* Fall 1970, p. 85.

Akston, Joseph James. "Editorial: The Question of Black Art," *Arts.* May 1971, p. 5.

Allen, Cleveland G. "Our Young Artists," *Opportunity.* June 1923.

Allen, William. "In the Galleries," *Arts.* Nov. 1967.

Allison, Madeline G. "Stories in Sculpture," *Opportunity.* March 1924, pp. 81-3.

"Amateur Artists," *Ebony.* March 1950, pp. 44-6.

"American Negro Art at Downtown Gallery," *Design.* Feb. 1942, pp. 27-8.

"American Negro Art," *Design.* Feb. 1941-Feb. 1942.

"American Negro Art," *New Masses.* New York, Dec. 30, 1941, p. 27.

"Amer. Negro Art Given Full Length Review in NY Show," *Art Digest.* Dec. 15, 1941.

"And the Migrants Kept Coming," *Fortune.* Nov. 1941, pp. 102-9.

Andrews, Benny. "The Black Emergency Cultural Coalition," *Arts.* Summer 1970, pp. 18-20.

"Art at the University," *Howard University Bulletin.* March 1957.

"Art by Negroes in the McMillen Building," *Art Digest.* Oct. 15, 1941, p. 11.

"Art by Negroes," *Milwaukee Institute Bulletin.* Feb. 1942.

"Art Education for Negroes," *Design.* Dec. 1944, p. 31.

"An Art Exhibit Against Lynching," *Crisis.* April 1935, p. 107.

Art Gallery. Second Afro-American Issue. April 1970.

Art Gallery. Second Afro-American Issue. April 1968.

"Artists Aid in Negro Cultural Development," *Scrapbook of Art and Artists of Chicago.* 1956, p. 48.

"Art of the Americas: From Before Columbus to the Present Day," *Art News Annual.* Vol.

18. 1948. Reprint. New York: Simon and Schuster, 1948.

"Art of the Negroes at Grand Rapids," *Art News.* March 1, 1943, p. 6.

"The Arts and the Black Revolution Issue," *Arts In Society.* I. II. Vol. 5, No. 3, Summer-Fall 1968.

The Arts Quarterly. Vols. 1-2. New Orleans: Dillard Univ., April/June 1937-Dec. 1939.

"Art," *Time.* Special issue: Black America 1970. April 6, 1970, pp. 80-7.

Ashton, Dore. "African and Afro-American Art: The Transatlantic Tradition at the Museum of Primitive Art," *Studio.* Nov. 1968, p. 202.

"Atlanta's Annual Exhibition of Painting and Sculpture by Negroes," *Time.* April 9, 1951.

"Atlanta's Annual," *Time.* April 9, 1945.

Atlanta Univ. *Atlanta University Bulletin.* July issues carry accounts of Atlanta Univ. Art Exhibitions.

A.V. "Contemporary Art," *Arts.* Oct. 1956, p. 58.

"Awards at Atlanta University," *Art Digest.* May 1, 1944, p. 26.

Baker, James H., Jr. "Art Comes to the People of Harlem," *Crisis.* March 1939, pp. 78-80.

Balch, Jack. "Democracy at Work: The People's Art Service Center in St. Louis," *Magazine of Art.* Feb. 1943, pp. 66-8.

"Baltimore: Art by Negroes," *Art News.* Feb. 11, 1939, p. 17.

Barnes, Albert C. "Negro Art & America," *Survey.* March 1, 1925, pp. 668-9.

Barnes, Albert C. "Negro Art, Past & Present," *Opportunity.* May 1926, p. 148.

Barnes, Albert C. "Primitive Negro Sculpture and its Influence on Modern Civilization," *Opportunity.* May 1928, pp. 139-40, 147.

"The Barnes Foundation," *Opportunity.* Nov. 1927, p. 321.

Bearden, Romare. "The Negro Artist & Modern Art," *Opportunity.* Dec. 1934.

Bearden, Romare. "The Negro Artist's Dilemma," *Critique.* Nov. 1946, pp. 16-22.

Bement, Alon. "Some Notes on a Harlem Art Exhibit," *Opportunity.* Nov. 1933.

Bennett, Gwendolyn B. "The American Negro Paints," *Southern Workman.* March 1928, pp. 111-2.

Bennett, Gwendolyn B. "The Future of the Negro in Art," *Howard University Record.* Dec. 1924, pp. 65-6.

Bennett, Mary. "The Harmon Awards," *Opportunity.* Feb. 1929, pp. 47-8.

"Biggest Art Show," *Ebony.* Aug. 1946.

Binsse, Harry Lorin. " 'Modern Negro Art,' James A. Porter. New York: Dryden Press," *Liturgical Arts.* Nov. 1943.

BIBLIOGRAPHY—MAGAZINES

"Black Art Inspires White Artists," *Literary Digest*. May 1924, pp. 30-1.

"The Black Artist in America: A Symposium," *Metropolitan Museum of Art Bulletin*. Jan. 1969.

"Black Art Program in Boston," *Todays Art*. Dec. 1, 1970.

"Black Art: What Is It," *Art Gallery*. April 1970.

"Black Madonnas," *Ebony*. Dec. 1959, p. 142.

Black Shades: A Black Art Newsletter. Washington, D.C., 1970-.

Bloom, Janet. "5+1," *Arts*. Dec. 1969/Jan. 1970, p. 56.

Bontemps, Arna. "Special Collections of Negroana," *Library Quarterly*. July 1944, pp. 187-206.

"Bootstrap Operation as a Source for Exceptional Hand Screened Fabrics," *Interiors*. Sept. 1970, p. 12.

Boswell, Peyton, Jr. "Fifth Annual at Atlanta University," *Art Digest*. April 15, 1946, p. 3.

Bowling, Frank. "Critique: Discussion on Black Art," *Arts*. April, May, Sept., and Dec. 1969.

Bowling, Frank. "It's Not Enough to Say 'Black Is Beautiful'," *Art News*. April 1971, pp. 53-5.

Bowling, Frank. "The Rupture: Ancestor Worship, Revival, Confusion or Disguise; Black Artists," *Arts*. Summer 1970, pp. 31-4.

Bowling, Frank. "Silence: People Die Crying When They Should Love; The Nature of Black Art," *Arts*. Sept. 1970, pp. 31-2.

Brown, Evelyn S. "The Harmon Awards," *Opportunity*. March 1933.

Burroughs, Margaret G. "To Make a Painter Black," *Black Seventies*, edited by Floyd Barbour. Boston, 1972.

Butler, Joseph T. "The American Way with Art," *Connoisseur*. March 1971.

Caffin, Charles H. "Exhibition of the Society of American Artists," *International Studio*. 1904, pp. 261-72.

Callaway, Thomas J. "The American Negro Exhibit at the Paris Exposition," *Hampton Negro Conference*. Hampton Institute Press, 1901, pp. 74-80.

Carline, R. "Dating and the Provenance of Negro Art," *Burlington Magazine*. Oct. 1940, pp. 115-23.

Catlett, Elizabeth. "A Tribute to the Negro People," *American Contemporary Art*. Winter 1940, p. 17.

Clay, Jean. "The Implication of Negritude," *Studio*. July 1966, pp. 51-3.

"College Art News," *Art Journal*. April 1969, pp. 328-9; Spring 1972, p. 330.

"Comments: Negro Art Annual," *Art Digest*. April 15, 1946, p. 3.

Conlon, James E., and James E. Kennedy. "An Afro-American Slide Project," *Art Journal*. Winter 1970-1, pp. 164-5.

Conroy, F. "Salvation Art," *Metropolitan Museum of Art Bulletin*. Jan. 1969, pp. 243-88.

"Contemporary Negro Art at Marino Gallery," *Arts*. Oct. 1956, p. 58.

Conway, M.D. "The Negro as an Artist," *Radical*. Vol. 2. 1867, p. 39.

Cooke, Paul. "The Art of Africa for the Whole World: An Account of the First World Festival of Negro Arts (Premier Festival Mondial des Arts Nègres) in Dakar, Senegal— April 1-24, 1966," *Negro History Bulletin*. Jan. 25, 1967.

Craig, Randall J. "Focus on Black Artists: A Project for Schools and Community," *School Arts*. Nov. 1970, pp. 30-3.

"Creative Art of Negroes," *Opportunity*. Aug. 1923, pp. 240-5.

"Creative Art of the American Negro," *Baltimore Museum of Art News*. 1941-2.

Daval, Jean-Luc. "Lettre de la Suisse Romande, et de Zurich: Geneve. Huits Artists Afro-Americain," *Art International*. Oct. 20, 1971.

Dawson, Charles C. "The Negro in Art," *Southern Workman*. Jan. 1929, pp. 12-4.

"The Design Works of Bedford-Stuyvesant," *Interiors*. Sept. 1970, p. 12.

DeVore, J. "Negro Art Theme Winning; Successful Brooklynite," *Crisis*. April 1963, p. 228.

Dowd, Jerome. "Art in Negro Homes," *Southern Workman*. Feb. 1901, pp. 90-5.

Dowell, J. "Politics," *Artforum*. May 1971.

Dows, Olin. "Art for Housing Tenants," *Magazine of Art*. Nov. 1938, pp. 616-21.

Drummond, Dorothy. "Coast-to-Coast," *Art Digest*. March 1, 1952, p. 12.

Drummond, Dorothy. "Philadelphia News," *Art Digest*. March 1, 1950, p. 9.

DuBois, Guy Pene. "Art by the Way," *International Studio*. March 1924, p. 322.

DuBois, William Edward Burghardt. "Criteria of Negro Art," *Crisis*. Oct. 1926, pp. 290-7.

DuBois, William Edward Burghardt. "Social Origins of American Negro Art," *Modern Quarterly*. Oct./Dec. 1925, pp. 53-6.

d'Usseau, Arnoud. "The Negro as Artist," *American Contemporary Art*. Winter 1946, p. 7.

E.K. "Negro Artists," *Art News*. Feb. 1949, p. 47.

"Evanston Art Center," *Chicago Art Institute Scrapbook*. Jan./Dec. 1939.

"Exhibition at Fort Huachuca, Ariz.," *Art Digest*. Aug. 1943, p. 15.

"Exhibition Painting and Sculpture by Negro Artists," *Montclair Art Museum Bulletin*. Feb. 1946, pp. 3-4.

"Exhibit Negro Art," *Southern Workman*. April 1924.

"Exhibit Raises Question Whether Negro Should Paint White," *Art Digest.* Feb. 15, 1931, p. 7.

"Experience of 3 Artists Points Out Value of WPA Federal Art Project," *Norfolk Journal and Guide.* July 4, 1936.

Fax, Elton C. "Four Rebels in Art," *Freedomways.* Spring 1961.

"Federal Murals to Honor the Negro," *Art Digest.* Jan. 1, 1943.

"Fifth Annual at Atlanta University; Awards," *Art Digest.* May 1, 1946, p. 11.

"Fifty-Seven Negro Artists Presented in Fifth Harmon Foundation Exhibit," *Art Digest.* March 1, 1933, p. 18.

Fine, Elsa Honig. "The Afro-American Artist: A Search for Identity," *Art Journal.* Fall 1969, pp. 32-5.

Fine Elsa Honig. "Mainstream, Blackstream and the Black Art Movement," *Art Journal.* Spring 1971, pp. 374-5.

Fire!!, edited by Wallace Thurman. Vol. 1, No. 1. 1926. Reprint. Westport, Conn.: Negro Universities Press, 1970.

"First Negro National, Atlanta University," *Magazine of Art.* May 1942, p. 185.

"Fisk Art Center: Stieglitz Collection Makes It Finest in South," *Ebony.* May 1950, pp. 73-5.

"Fisk Universities Dedicates Alfred Stieglitz Collection," *Crisis.* March 1950, pp. 157-9.

F.L.K. "American Negroes as Artists," *Survey.* Sept. 1, 1928, pp. 648-9.

"Fourth Annual at Atlanta University," *Art News.* April 15, 1945, p. 8.

Fuller, Hoyt W. "World Festival of Negro Art," *Ebony.* July 1966, pp. 96-102.

"Full Length Review in New York Show at Downtown Gallery," *Art Digest.* Dec. 15, 1941, p. 5.

Gaither, Edmund B. "The ABA Idea," *ABA: A Journal of Affairs of Black Artists.* Vol. 1, No. 1.

Gaither, Edmund B. "The Evolution of the Afro-American Artists," *Artists Proof.* Vol. 2, pp. 24-33.

Gaither, Edmund B. "The Lender Ought to Know," *ABA: A Journal of Affairs of Black Artists.* Vol. 1, No. 1.

Gaither, Edmund B. "Visual Arts and Black Aesthetics," *ABA: A Journal of Affairs of Black Artists.* Vol. 1, No. 1.

Garver, T.H. "Dimensions of Black Exhibition at La Jolla Museum," *Artforum.* May 1970, pp. 83-4.

Ghent, Henri. "And So It Is," *School Arts.* April 1969.

Gibson, Martha Jane. "The Amistad in Play & Murals," *Arts Quarterly.* June 1939, pp. 8-14, 30.

Goffman, Kimbal. "Negro Life Is Art," *Arts Quarterly.* Sept. 1939, pp. 16-26.

"Graphic Viewpoints; Black Artist in Graphic Communication," *Industrial Design.* Jan. 1971, pp. 60-3.

Greene, Carroll, Jr. "The Afro-American Artist," *Art Gallery.* April 1968, pp. 12-25.

Greene, Carroll, Jr. "Afro-American Artists: Yesterday and Now," *The Humble Way.* Houston, Texas: Public Relations Dept. of Humble Oil and Refining Co. Vol. 8, No. 3, 1968.

Greene, Carroll, Jr. "Perspective: The Black Artist in America," *Art Gallery.* April 1970.

Hagstrom, Frieda. "The Negro in the New Art Education," *Design.* June 1943.

"Harlem Goes in for Art," *Opportunity.* April 1939.

"Harlem Library Shows Negro Art," *Art News.* May 20, 1933, p. 14.

Harley, Ralph L., Jr. "A Checklist of Afro-American Art & Artists," *The Serif.* Kent, Ohio: Kent State Univ. Libraries, Dec. 1970.

"Harmon Awards Announced for Distinguished Achievement Among Negroes in Fine Arts for 1929," *Art News.* Feb. 8, 1930, p. 17.

"Harmon Exhibit of Negro Art, Newark Museum," *Newark Museum Bulletin.* Oct. 1931, p. 178.

"Harmon Foundation Exhibition of Painting and Sculpture. Art Center," *Art News.* Feb. 21, 1931, p. 12.

"Harmon Foundation Spreads Public Appreciation of Negro Art," *Art Digest.* June 1935, p. 23.

H.B.L. "Negro's Art Lives in His Wrought Iron," *New York Times Magazine.* Aug. 8, 1926.

Henderson, Rose. "First Nation-Wide Exhibition of Negro Artists," *Southern Workman.* March 1928, pp. 121-6.

Herring, James V. "The American Negro as Craftsman and Artist," *Crisis.* April 1942, pp. 116-8.

Herring, James V. "The Negro Sculpture," *Crisis.* Aug. 1942, pp. 261-2.

Herskovitz, Melville J. "Negro Art: African & American," *Journal of Social Forces.* Dec. 1926, pp. 291-8.

Holbrook, Francis C. "A Group of Negro Artists," *Opportunity.* July 1923, pp. 211-3.

"Honoring Negro History; Exhibition at the RoKo Gallery," *Art Digest.* Feb. 15, 1949, p. 20.

Hughes, Langston. "The Negro Artist and the Racial Mountain," *The Nation.* June 23, 1926, pp. 692-3.

"In a Black Bind," *Time.* April 12, 1970.

"Introduction to the Negro in American History. Gallery of Modern Art," *Arts.* Sept. 1969, p. 58.

Jackson, Dorothy. "The Black Experience in Graphic Design," *Print.* Nov./Dec. 1968, pp. 48-51.

Jacobs, Jay. "The Cinque Gallery," *Art Gallery.* April 1970, pp. 50-1.

Jacobs, Jay. "Two Afro-American Artists," *Art Gallery.* April 1968, pp. 26-31.

Johnson, James Welden. "Race Prejudice and the Negro Artist," *Harper's.* Nov. 1928, pp. 769-76.

Jones, Lois M. "An Artist Grows Up in America," *Aframerican Woman's Journal.* Summer/Fall 1942, p. 23.

Jones, Walter. "Critique to Black Artists," *Arts.* April 1970, p. 16.

The Journal of the National Conference of Artists. Jefferson City, Mo.: Lincoln Univ.

Judd, Donald. "In the Galleries," *Arts.* Nov. 1964, p. 60.

Junier, Allen, ed. *Newsletter of the National Conference of Negro Artists.* Nov. 1959.

J.W.L. "Art and the Negro," *Art News.* May 1941, p. 6.

J.W.L. "Negro in Art," *Art News.* Dec. 19, 1941, p. 24.

Kagan, Norman. "Black American Cinema," *Cinema.* Vol. 6, No. 2. Beverly Hills, Cal.: Spectators International, Inc.

Kaufman, Arthur. "The Newly Born Lamb," *Crisis.* June/July 1965, p. 363.

Kay, Jane Holtz. "Artists as Social Reformers," *Art In America.* Jan./June 1969.

Kendrick, Ruby Moyse. "Art at Howard University: An Appreciation," *Crisis.* Nov. 1932, pp. 348-9.

Kiah, Virginia. "Black Artists," *Savannah Magazine.* Savannah, Ga.: Savannah Magazine, Inc., April 1972, p. 14.

Koethe, John. "Boston—Black Is Political," *Art News.* Oct. 1970, p. 30.

Lane, James W. "Afro-American Art on Both Continents," *Art News.* Oct. 15-31, 1941, p. 25.

Lane, James W. "Negro in Art," *Art News.* Dec. 15-31, 1941, p. 24.

"Leading Negro Artists," *Ebony.* Sept. 1963, p. 131.

"Leading Young Artists," *Ebony.* April 1958.

Lewis, T. "Frustration of Negro Art: Vitiating Influence of Color Prejudice," *Catholic World.* April 1942, pp. 51-7.

Locke, Alain. "Advance' on the Art Front," *Opportunity.* March 1939.

Locke, Alain. "The American Negro as Artist," *American Magazine of Art.* Sept. 1931.

Locke, Alain. "Chicago's New Southside Art Center," *Magazine of Art.* Aug. 1941, p. 320.

Locke, Alain. "Negro Art in America," *Design.* Dec. 1942, pp. 12-3.

Locke, Alain. "Youth Speaks: The Artistic Vanguard," *Survey.* March 1925.

Long, Fern. "A Cultural Operation Crossroads," *Crisis.* Dec. 1946, pp. 367-8.

Lowenfeld, Viktor. "New Negro Art in America," *Design.* Sept. 1944, pp. 20-1.

Lumpkin, G., and E. Shenity. "Artist in a Hostile Environment," *World Tomorrow.* April 1926, pp. 108-10.

McConnell, Roland C. "Importance of Records in the National Archives on the History of the Negro," *Journal of Negro History.* Vol. 34. 1949, pp. 135-52.

McGleughlin. "Exhibition of Negro Art," *Baltimore Museum Quarterly.* 1938-9, pp. 10-4.

Mashek, Joseph. "Black Artists at the Visual Arts Gallery," *Artforum.* Sept. 1970, pp. 79-80.

M.B. "An Introduction to the Negro in American History," *Arts.* Sept./Oct. 1969, p. 58.

Merry, Ruth C. "Art Talent and Racial Background," *Journal of Educational Research.* Sept. 1938.

" 'Modern Negro Art' by J.A. Porter, a Review," *Journal of Aesthetics and Art Criticism.* 1944-5, p. 112.

" 'Modern Negro Art' by J.A. Porter, Review," *Art Digest.* Nov. 15, 1943, p. 21.

" 'Modern Negro Art' by J.A. Porter, Review," *College Art Journal.* March 1944, pp. 122-4.

" 'Modern Negro Art' by J.A. Porter, Review," *Liturgical Arts.* Feb. 1944.

"Monuments to Two Greats," *Ebony.* Sept. 1946, pp. 35-9.

Morrison, A. "New Surge in the Arts," *Ebony.* Aug. 1967, pp. 134-6.

Motley, Willard F. "Negro Art in Chicago," *Opportunity.* Jan. 1940.

Munro, Thomas. "Art: Good and Bad Negro Art," *The Nation.* March 2, 1927.

"Mural Painting 'The Light'," *Howard University Bulletin.* July 1940, pp. 16-7.

"The Negro Annual," *Art Digest.* May 15, 1934, p. 18.

"Negro Annual at Atlanta University," *Art Digest.* April 15, 1943, p. 14.

"Negro Annual at Atlanta University," *Art News.* April 15, 1943, p. 7.

"Negro Annual Sponsored by Harmon Foundation," *Art Digest.* May 15, 1934, p. 18.

"Negro Art Annual at Atlanta University," *Art Digest.* May 1, 1942, p. 9.

"Negro Art at Lyric Theatre," *Art News.* May 6, 1933, p. 6.

"Negro Art Exhibition," *Baltimore Museum News.* June 1940, p. 45.

"Negro Art from Cleveland's Karamu House," *Art Digest.* Jan. 15, 1942, p. 19.

"Negro Artist Comes of Age: Albany Exhibition," *Art News.* Jan. 1, 1945, p. 9; Feb. 1-14, 1945, pp. 16, 29-30.

"The Negro Artist Comes of Age," *Albany Institute of History & Art Journal.* Dec. 1944.

"Negro Artist Comes of Age; Exhibition, Albany Institute," *Pictures.* Jan. 1945, p. 33.

"Negro Artist Comes of Age," *Brooklyn Museum Bulletin.* Nov. 1945.

"The Negro Artist Comes of Age," *Munson-Williams-Proctor Institute Bulletin.* Utica, Oct. 1945.

"Negro Artist Comes of Age," *Rhode Island School of Design Notes.* Jan. 1946.

"Negro Artists' Annual Sponsored by Dillard University," *Art Digest.* March 1, 1941, p. 13.

"Negro Artists at RoKo Honor National Negro History Week," *Art News.* Feb. 1949, p. 47.

"Negro Artists Reveal Genius in Trenton Show," *Art Digest.* April 15, 1935, p. 19.

"Negro Artists Show," *Art News.* Jan. 1, 1945, p. 16.

"Negro Artists: Their Works Win Top U.S. Honors," *Life.* July 22, 1946, pp. 62-5.

"Negro Artists Third Annual at Atlanta University," *Art Digest.* March 1, 1944, p. 17.

"Negro Art Prizes," *Art News.* May 1, 1944, p. 7.

"Negro Art Scores without Double Standards at the Albany Institute," *Art Digest.* Feb. 1, 1945, p. 8.

"Negro Art Show G Place Gallery, Washington," *Art News.* July 1944, p. 6.

"Negro Art Week," *Chicago Art Institute Scrapbook.* Aug. 1927/March 1928, pp. 43-4, 47, 50, 68.

"The Negro as Artist & Subject," *Magazine of Art.* April 1941, p. 216.

"Negroes Exhibit Their Art," *Pictures On Exhibit.* Feb. 1939, pp. 8-9.

"Negroes Sponsor Own Art, Dallas," *Art Digest.* June 1932, p. 7.

"The Negro in Art," *Art Digest.* June 1, 1944, p. 15.

"Negro in Art at Downtown Gallery," *Art News.* Dec. 15, 1941, p. 24.

"Negro in Art; Exhibition, G Place Gallery, Washington," *Art Digest.* June 1944, p. 15.

"The Negro in Art: How Shall He Be Portrayed, A Symposium," *Crisis.* April 1926, pp. 219-20, 278-9.

"Negro Prize Winners," *Art Digest.* Jan. 1, 1930, p. 11.

"Negro Students of Karamu House Exhibit at Associated American Artists Galleries," *Pictures.* Jan. 1942, pp. 31-2.

"Negro Winners," *Art Digest.* May 1, 1946, p. 11.

"Negro World's Fair," *Newsweek.* Sept. 9, 1940.

"Newark Exhibition," *Art Digest.* April 15, 1944, p. 20.

"News and Comment: The Negro in Art," *Magazine of Art.* April 1942, p. 147.

"New Yorkers Win Honors at the 10th Annual Painting, Sculpture and Print Exhibition for Negro Artists at Atlanta University," *Art Digest.* April 15, 1951, p. 13.

"Nineteen Young American Artists," *Life.* Articles on Art. March 20, 1950.

"Now Showing: The Black Artists," *Contact.* • Sept. 1970.

"Object Diversity," *Time.* April 6, 1970, p. 80.

"On Black Artists," *Art Journal.* Spring 1969, p. 332.

"Paintings by Negro Artists," *William Rockhill Nelson Gallery of Art Bulletin.* Kansas City, April 1942, pp. 2-3.

Parks, James D. "An Experiment in Painting the Local Scene," *Design.* Feb. 1946, pp. 10-2.

"The Passing Shows," *Art News.* Nov. 15, 1943, p. 22.

Pierce, Delilah W. "The Significance of Art Experiences in the Education of the Negro," *Negro History Bulletin.* March 1952, p. 106.

Pierre-Noel, Lois Jones. "American Negro Art in Progress," *Negro History Bulletin.* Oct. 1967, pp. 6-7.

Pincus-Witten, R. "Black Artists of the '30s at the Studio Museum in Harlem," *Artforum.* Feb. 1969, pp. 65-7.

"Politics," *Artforum.* May 1970.

Porter, James A. "Art Reaches the People," *Opportunity.* Dec. 1939, pp. 375-6.

Porter, James A. "Four Problems in the History of Negro Art," *Journal of Negro History.* Jan. 1942, pp. 9-36.

Porter, James A. "The Negro Artist and Racial Bias," *Art Front.* March 1936, p. 8.

Porter, James A. "Negro Art on Review," *American Magazine of Art.* Jan. 1934, pp. 33-8.

Porter, James A. "Versatile Interests of the Early Negro Artist," *Art In America.* Jan. 1936, pp. 16-27.

"Princeton Group Arts," *Crisis.* Jan. 1951, pp. 19-22.

"Pyramid Club, Tenth Annual Exhibition of Paintings and Sculpture," *Art Digest.* March 1, 1950, p. 9.

"Racial Strength," *Time.* April 9, 1951.

Rankin, Allen. "The Lost 10,000 Years," *Colliers.* June 22, 1946, p. 67.

"Recent Work by Negro Artists," *Montclair Art Museum Bulletin.* Feb. 1947, p. 3.

Reed, Ishmael. "The Black Artist: Calling a Spade a Spade," *Arts.* May 1967.

Richardson, Ben. "New Horizons for the Negro Artist," *American Contemporary Art.* Winter 1946, pp. 8-10.

Rich, Daniel Catton. "Fifty Years at Chicago," *Magazine of Art.* Dec. 1939, pp. 704-9, 722-4.

"RoKo and A.C.A. Will Participate in Negro History Week," *Art Digest.* Feb. 1, 1946, p. 10.

Rose, Alvin W. "Negro Art and the Great Transformation," *Negro History Bulletin.* Nov. 1959.

Rose, Barbara. "Black Art in America," *Art In America.* Sept./Oct. 1970.

"San Francisco," *Artforum.* Oct. 1970.

"Saturday Morning Art Class," *Negro History Bulletin.* April 1942, p. 158.

Schejeldahl, P. "New York Letter," *Art International.* Oct. 1969, pp. 76-7.

Schomburg, A.A. "Paintings by Negro Artists," *Milwaukee Institute Bulletin.* Jan. 1932, pp. 2-3.

Schuyler, George S. "The Negro-Art Hokum," *The Nation.* Vol. 122, No. 31, pp. 662-3.

Schuyler, George S. "Negro in the New Order," *Modern Negro Quarterly.* V.F. Calverton Memorial Issue. Fall 1940, pp. 84-7.

Schwartz, N. "The Metropolitan Museum of Art: Cultural Power in a Time of Crisis," *Metropolitan Museum of Art Bulletin.* Jan. 1969.

Schwartz, Therese. "The Political Scene," *Arts.* April 1971.

Schwarz, J. "Interview with W. Burch," *Metropolitan Museum of Art Bulletin.* Jan. 1969, pp. 243-8.

Shapiro, David. "652 Broadway," *Art News.* April 1971.

Siegel, Jeanne. "Why Spiral?," *Art News.* Sept. 1966, pp. 48-51, 67-8.

"Six Paintings of City Life," *Arts Quarterly.* Dec. 1939, pp. 13-9.

Sligh, Reed. "Amateurs," *Life.* April 16, 1951.

Smith, H.L. "Negro Artist in America Today," *Negro History Bulletin.* Feb. 1964, pp. 111-2.

"Spring Annuals," *Art News.* April 15, 1945, pp. 8-9.

Stone, Dennis. "Negro Artists from Illinois at the Oak Park Public Library," *Art Scene.* n.d.

Strickland, Edward. "Our 'Forgotten' Negro Artists," *Masses & Mainstream.* Sept. 1954, pp. 34-40.

"Studio Watts Learning Center for the Arts," *Art Journal.* Fall 1969, p. 35.

Survey Graphic. March 1925.

Sweeney, James Johnson. "African Negro Art," *New Republic.* April 10, 1935.

Tarshis, J. "BlackMan's Art Gallery, San Francisco; Exhibit," *Artforum.* Dec. 1970, p. 85.

Taylor, A.E. "The American Colony of Artists in Paris," *International Studio.* June 1912.

"Third Annual Exhibition of Paintings, Sculpture, and Prints at Atlanta University," *Art News.* May 1, 1944, p. 7.

Thompson, W.O. "Collins and DeVillis—Two Promising Painters," *Voice of the Negro.* Dec. 1905, p. 687.

Thurman, Wallace. "Negro Artists and the Negro," *New Republic.* Aug. 31, 1927.

Thurman, Wallace. See *Fire!!*

"To Encourage Negro Art," *Crisis.* Nov. 1924.

Tucker, P. "Poor People's Plan," *Metropolitan Museum of Art Bulletin.* Jan. 1969, pp. 243-88.

Turner, S. "Black Art Seminar," *Brooklyn Museum Annual.* 1969-70, pp. 208-13.

"12th Annual Invitation Exhibition at the Pyramid Club, Philadelphia," *Art Digest.* March 1, 1952.

"Two Negro Artists Win Awards in Artists for Victory Exhibit," *Opportunity.* Jan. 1943.

Usseau, Arnoud d'. See d'Usseau, Arnoud.

"Wall of Respect: Artists of Organization of Black American Culture Paint Mural in Chicago Ghetto," *Ebony.* Dec. 1967, pp. 48-50.

Ward, Francis, and Val Gray Ward. "The Black Artist—His Role in the Struggle," *Black Scholar.* Jan. 1971, p. 23.

Wechsler, Lawrence. "The Negro Sympathetically Rendered," *Art News.* Feb. 18, 1939.

Werner, A. "Black Is Not a Colour," *Art and Artists.* May 1969, pp. 14-7.

"What Is Black Art?," *Newsweek.* June 22, 1970.

Whatley, JoAnn. "Meeting The Black Emergency Cultural Coalition," *ABA: A Journal of Affairs of Black Artists.* Vol. 1, No. 1.

Wilson, Edward, and James A. Porter. "CAA and Negro Colleges," *Art Journal.* Winter 1968-69, p. 228.

Winslow, Vernon. "Negro Art and the Depression," *Opportunity.* Feb. 1941.

Wolf, Ben. "Negro Art Scores without Double Standards," *Art Digest.* Feb. 1, 1945, p. 8.

Wood, Jerry. "New Print Process," *Crisis.* Dec. 1940, p. 379.

Woodruff, Hale A. "Negro Artists Hold Fourth Annual in Atlanta," *Art Digest.* April 15, 1945, p. 10.

"WPA Art Center Opened by Chicago Negro Community," *Museum News.* April 1, 1941.

Wright, C. " 'American Negro Art' by C. Dover, a Review," *Studio.* Jan. 1961, p. 29.

"X to the 4th Power," *Arts.* Sept. 1969, p. 58.

Young, J.E. "Two Generations of Black Artists. California State College, Los Angeles," *Art International.* Oct. 1970, p. 74.

Young, Mahonri S. "Letter from USA: 'To See New Things'," *Apollo.* Feb. 1968, p. 141.

"Young Negro Art Impresses New York: Hampton Institute Exhibition at Museum of Modern Art," *Art Digest.* Oct. 15, 1943, p. 25.

"Young Negro Artists," *Design.* Nov. 1943, p. 7.

Young, Stark. "Primitive Negro Sculpture," *New Republic.* Feb. 23, 1927.

NEWSPAPERS

"About Art and Artists," *New York Times.* Nov. 3, 1955, p. 28.

"AFRICOBRA Creates for Blacks," *Bay State Banner.* Oct. 1, 1970.

"Afro-American Art a Cultural Experience for All—Fine Arts Museum to Display Work of Black Artists," *Record American.* Boston, May 19, 1970.

"Afro-American Artists, Museum of Fine Arts Announce Black Art Goal," *Minuteman.* May 28, 1970.

Afro-American. Baltimore: Afro-American Co., 1892-.

"Afro-American Paintings at Boston Museum," *Fence Viewer.* Jan. 20, 1972.

Afro-American. Washington, D.C.: Afro-American Co., 1933-.

"Afro-Art," *Jewish Advocate.* Jan. 20, 1972.

Albright, Thomas. "New Black Art Shows and Old Techniques," *San Francisco Chronicle.* Oct. 14, 1968.

Almelo, Frederik Van. See Van Almelo, Frederik.

Andrews, Benny. "On Understanding Black Art," *New York Times.* 1970.

"Anita Loos Lauds Henri Ghent, Ex-Director, Comunity Gallery," *Art Workers Newsletter.* April 1973.

"Art: Afro-American Artists: New York & Boston," *News.* Amesbury, Mass., June 17, 1970.

"Art Center, Crawford (Pittsburgh), Opens; Activities to be Devoted to Negro Culture Development," *New York Times.* Feb. 2, 1942.

"Artists Praise Lynching Exhibit," *Boston Chronicle.* March 1, 1935.

"Art Should Inspire Us Says Woman Artist of Los Angeles," *Californian News.* Feb. 22, 1935.

"At Boston Museum—Afro-American Art," *New Bedford Sunday Standard Times.* May 10, 1970.

"At New York Art Exhibit," *Washington Afro-American.* March 30, 1935.

Bentsen, Cheryl. "Life in the Back of the Gallery," *Newsday.* May 10, 1971.

Berkman, Florence. "Afro-American Exhibit Fosters Understanding of Black Artists," *Times.* Hartford, Conn., May 24, 1970.

Berkman, Florence. "Message Differs in Black Art," *Times.* Hartford, Conn., June 15, 1970.

Berkman, Florence. "Some Black Artists Irate over Whitney Exhibit," *Times.* Hartford, Conn., April 25, 1971.

Berryman, Florence S. "Colored Artists' Exhibit Attracts Wide Attention," *Sunday Star.* Washington, D.C., Feb. 22, 1942.

Berryman, Florence S. "Negro Artists of Chicago, George Neal Protegés, Exhibit Works Here," *Sunday Star.* Washington, D.C., Feb. 23, 1941.

Berryman, Florence S. "W.P.A. Exhibit at Howard," *Sunday Star.* Washington, D.C., May 18, 1941.

"Bigger Budget Asked for Museum Shows," *Dallas News.* April 15, 1939.

"Black Art Exhibit Opens Sunday," *Herald.* Belmont, Mass., May 14, 1970.

"Black Artists Exhibition May 19," *News.* Malden, Mass., March 26, 1970.

"Black Artists Work on View at Museum," *Brookline Chronicle Citizen.* Brookline, Mass., May 14, 1970.

"Black Artists' Work on View at Museum," *Citizen Item.* Allston-Brighton, Mass., May 14, 1970.

"Black Artists' Work on View at Museum," *News.* Newburyport, Mass., May 16, 1970.

"Black Artist," *Times.* Beverly, Mass., April 1, 1970.

"Black Art Program Joint Effort," *Times.* Peabody, Mass., June 12, 1970.

"Black Arts Festival Opens Next Wednesday," *Boston Globe.* May 12, 1972.

"Black Crafts," *Christian Science Monitor.* May 11, 1972.

"Black Show," *Times.* Gloucester, Mass., May 16, 1970.

Bloomfield, Arthur. "Top Black Artists," *San Francisco Examiner.* Nov. 4, 1970.

Bonosky, Phillip. "Invisible Americans: A Lesson in Black Art," *Daily World.* Nov. 23, 1968, p. 8.

Bourne, Kay. "Black Artists Shown at Museum," *Bay State Banner.* May 28, 1970.

Bourne, Kay. "Quiet, Powerful Exhibit," *Bay State Banner.* Oct. 7, 1971.

Brun, Caron Le. See Le Brun, Caron.

Burrows, Carlyle. "Harlem Artists Make Bid for Recognition," *New York Herald Tribune.* July 17, 1932.

Canaday, John. "Negroes in Art: An Exhibition Examines 250 Years of Pictorial Social History," *New York Times.* May 24, 1969.

Canaday, John. "Sculpture Is the Strength of New Black Artists' Show," *New York Times.* Oct. 8, 1969.

"Cavalcade of Negro Art at Hotel Diplomat May 9," *Daily Worker.* New York, May 5, 1948.

Chandler, Dana C., Jr. "Re: MFA From: Dana C. Chandler, Jr.," Response to Charles Giuliano's Museum of Fine Arts article in *Boston After Dark.* March 1970.

Chatfield-Taylor, Rose. "Howard U Holds Negro Exhibit," *Washington Post.* Feb. 16, 1941.

Chatfield-Taylor, Rose. "Negro Artists Prove Skill in D.C. Display," *Washington Post.* Jan. 5, 1941.

"Chicago Active in Effort to Establish Community Art Center," *Chicago Defender.* May 20, 1939.

"College Art Association Assembles Negro Art Exhibition," *New York Times.* May 1, 1934.

Collins, Florence. "Artists of Both Races Use Colored Themes in Exhibit," *Afro-American.* April 28, 1934.

"Colored Artists Show Paintings," *Washington Daily News.* Feb. 13, 1932.

"The Community Art Center," *Chicago Defender.* March 1, 1941.

Corwin, Charles. "Looking Back on the Departed Art Season," *Daily Worker.* New York, June 12, 1950.

Cross, Mariam Dungan. "Black Art Exhibit at Kaiser Center," *Oakland Tribune.* Oct. 13, 1968.

"Culture Plan Hits Snag as Clash Occurs," *New York Amsterdam News.* Feb. 6, 1937.

Danikian, Caron Le Brun. *Herald Traveler.* Boston, Oct. 10, 1971.

Derrickson, Howard. "Scholastic Art Show Best in Recent Years," *New York Times.* Feb. 17, 1952.

Driscoll, Edgar J., Jr. "Art/Afro-American, A Smashing Round-Up," *Boston Globe.* May 17, 1970.

Driscoll, Edgar J., Jr. "Art Show Reflects Black Rage, Pride," *Boston Globe.* April 28, 1971.

Driscoll, Edgar J., Jr. "50 Boston, New York Black Artists Included in BMFA Spring Exhibit," *Boston Globe.* March 21, 1970.

Driscoll, Edgar J., Jr. "Museum, Black Center Join Hands," *Boston Globe.* May 19, 1970.

Driscoll, Edgar J., Jr. "Showcase for Black Artists," *Boston Sunday Globe.* July 6, 1969. p. A73.

"Exhibition of Work by Negro Artists," *Afro-American Presbyterian.* Feb. 23, 1923.

". . . Exhibition of Works by Negro Artists . . . ," *Washington Star.* Nov. 5, 1933.

"Exhibition Sponsored by the Harmon Foundation Assembled by the College Art Association," *New York Times.* May 6, 1935.

"Expression in Black," *Chicago Sun Times.* March 25, 1970.

Faxon, Alicia. "Afro-American Exhibits Museum of Fine Arts," *Journal.* Concord, Mass., Jan. 20, 1972.

Finley, Skip. "Black Owned Newbury Street Gallery Closes," *Bay State Banner.* April 16, 1971.

"Five Local Artists Get Atlanta U. Awards," *New York Times.* April 4, 1948.

"5000 Jobless Go to School on First Day," *New York Herald Tribune.* Dec. 17, 1932.

Frankenstein, Alfred. "What Ever Happened to . . . ," *San Francisco Sunday Examiner and Chronicle.* Oct. 26, 1969.

Frank, Peter. "Black Art: Aesthetic, Cultural Success," *Columbia Daily Spectator.* Dec. 5, 1969.

Freelon, Allan. "The Negro in Art," *Philadelphia Independent.* Dec. 22, 1935.

Gaither, Edmund Barry. "From Edmund B. Gaither," Response to Charles Giuliano's Museum of Fine Arts article in *Boston After Dark* (New title: *Boston Phoenix*). March 1970.

Gerson, Sareen R. "Black Art NY-Hub Set for Museum of Fine Arts," *Citizen.* Sudbury, Mass., March 19, 1970.

Gerson, Sareen R. "Black Art NY-Hub Set for Museum of Fine Arts," *Minuteman.* March 19, 1970.

Ghent, Henri. "Art Mailbag: White Is Not Superior," *New York Times.* Dec. 8, 1968.

Giuliano, Charles. "Five Black Artists," *Boston After Dark* (New title: *Boston Phoenix*). March 4, 1970.

Giuliano, Charles. "Museum of Fine Arts: What the Museum Is Doing for Black Art," *Boston After Dark* (New title: *Boston Phoenix*). March 11, 1970.

Glueck, Grace. "America Has Black Art on Her Mind," *New York Times.* Feb. 27, 1969.

Glueck, Grace. "Black Show under Fire at the Whitney," *New York Times.* Jan. 31, 1971.

Glueck, Grace. "Minority Artists Find a Welcome in a New Showcase," *New York Times.* Dec. 23, 1969, p. 22.

Glueck, Grace. "Negro Art from 1800 to 1950 Is on Display at City College," Oct. 16, 1967.

Glueck, Grace. "Negroes' Art Is What's in Just Now," *New York Times.* Feb. 27, 1969.

Glueck, Grace. "1930's Show at Whitney Picketed by Negro Artists Who Call It Incomplete," *New York Times.* Nov. 18, 1968.

Gordon, Eugene. "Negro Arts to Keynote 2-day Talks," *Daily Worker.* New York, April 28, 1939.

Gray, Lovett S. "Central Harlem's Studio Museum: A Workshop for Black Artists," *Art Workers Newsletter.* April 1973.

Grillo, Jean B. "Art: 19th Century Black Art," *Phoenix* (New title: *Real Paper*). Boston, Jan. 26, 1972.

Grillo, Jean B. "Big Art at MIT," *Phoenix* (New title: *Real Paper*). Boston, n.d.

Grillo, Jean B. "Black Artists: Three Views," *Phoenix* (New title: *Real Paper*). Boston, n.d.

Grillo, Jean B. "Black Art-White Museum," *Phoenix* (New title: *Real Paper*). Boston, May 23, 1970.

Grillo, Jean B. "Elma Lewis: A New Show a New Showplace," *Boston After Dark* (New title: *Boston Phoenix*). Aug. 16, 1970.

Grillo, Jean B. "Where Down Home Meets Back Home," *Boston After Dark* (New title: *Boston Phoenix*). Sept. 1970.

Haas, Joseph. "A Big, Brilliant & Exciting Exhibition of Black Art," *Chicago Daily News.* Jan. 16-7, 1971.

"Harlem Sees Some Negro Art," *New York Herald Tribune.* Sept. 17, 1933.

Harris, Ruth G. "Four of the New Federal Arts Projects Murals," *New York Times.* Jan. 2, 1938.

Haskell, Ernest, Jr. "Black American Art from Joshua Johnston to Gaither," *Times Record.* Maine, Feb. 10, 1972.

Haydon, Harold. "Coming of Age of Black Art," *Chicago Sun Times.* July 26, 1970.

Hinchcliffe, Diane. "Black Art Exhibit: Future Looks a Little Brighter," *Chronicle-Citizen.* Brookline, Mass., June 4, 1970.

Hirsch, Samuel. "Two-Day Program of Black Arts to Be Held Here in June," *Boston Herald Traveler.* May 12, 1972, p. B18.

Hollingsworth, Alvin. "Wealth of Expression in Black Artists' RISD Show," *Providence Sunday Journal.* June 29, 1969, pp. 5-6.

"Home Folk: Africa," *Christian Science Monitor.* April 8, 1971.

"Howard University Gallery: Paintings by Three Artists Are Displayed," *Washington Star.* Feb. 18, 1940.

"Howard University Gallery," *Sunday Star.* Washington, D.C., Dec. 7, 1941.

"Independent Art Show Opens Tomorrow," *Washington Post.* April 21, 1935.

"In the Realm of Art: The Government's Role," *New York Times.* Jan. 3, 1937.

Jewell, Edward Alden. "In Abstract Vein," *New York Times.* March 2, 1947, p. 7.

Jewell, Edward Alden. "Stress on Modern," *New York Times.* Dec. 15, 1946, p. 9.

Jordan, Robert A. "Roxbury Students Build African Hut," *Boston Globe.* June 26, 1970, p. 9.

Kienzle, Connie. "Blacks Pour Out Soul, Pride at Their Art Show," *Pittsburgh Press.* Feb. 23, 1967.

Kramer, Hilton. "Black Art and Expedient Politics," *New York Times.* June 7, 1970, p. 19.

Kramer, Hilton. "Black Art Becomes Politics on Canvas," *New London* (Conn.) *Day.* June 6, 1970.

Kramer, Hilton. "Black Currents in the Mainstream," *Baltimore Sun.* June 7, 1970.

Kramer, Hilton. "Black Experience and Modernist Art," *New York Times.* Feb. 14, 1970, p. 23.

Kramer, Hilton. "Exhibit Attempts Answers: What's the Role of Black Art?," *State Journal.* Lansing, Mich., June 14, 1970.

Kramer, Hilton. "Is Politics Submerging Black Art?," *Courier-Journal and Times.* Louisville, Ky., June 7, 1970.

Kramer, Hilton. "So Black Is Beautiful; But Is It Art?," *Baltimore Morning Sun.* May 31, 1970.

Kramer, Hilton. "Toward a Definition of 'Black Art'," *Times Record.* Brunswick, Me., n.d.

Kramer, Hilton. "Trying to Define 'Black Art': Must We Go Back to Social Realism?," *New York Times.* May 31, 1970.

Kramer, Hilton. "What Is Black Art?," *Berkshire Eagle.* Pittsfield, Mass., June 6, 1970.

Lang, Bette Ann. "She Taught the Inmates . . . and They Taught Her," *Art Workers Newsletter.* April 1973.

Le Brun, Caron. "Black Art," *Boston Herald Traveler.* Sunday Supplement. May 24, 1970, pp. 10-4.

Le Brun, Caron. "Blacks' Art on Display," *Boston Herald Traveler.* May 26, 1970.

Loercher, Diana. "AFRICOBRA at the National Center of Afro-American Artists' Museum," *Christian Science Monitor.* Sept. 1970.

Loercher, Diana. "Afro-American Artists Abroad," *Christian Science Monitor.* Aug. 1, 1970.

Loercher, Diana. "Afro-American Center & Museum of Fine Arts Form Alliance," *Christian Science Monitor.* May 20, 1970.

Loercher, Diana. "Art: Idioms of Blackness at the Elma Lewis School," *Christian Science Monitor.* July 10, 1970.

Loercher, Diana. "Black Artists Exhibition Reveals Visual Eloquence," *Christian Science Monitor.* March 2, 1970.

Loercher, Diana. "National Center of Afro-Amer. Artists' Art & Benefit Premier," *Christian Science Monitor.* May 4, 1971.

Lowe, Romona. "New York Inter-Racial Gallery Presents Best of Flourishing New Negro Art," *Chicago Defender.* May 19, 1945.

McCausland, Elizabeth. "American Negro Art of 19th and 20th Centuries," *Springfield* (Mass.) *Union and Republican.* Dec. 21, 1941.

Mechlin, Leila. "Notes of Art and Artists," *Washington Star.* Nov. 5, 1933.

Mechlin, Leila. "75th Anniversary Exhibition at Howard," *Sunday Star.* Washington, D.C., March 29, 1942.

Miller, Donald. "Black Art Exhibition Impressive: Show Traditional Mixture of Abstract Realistic," *Pittsburgh Post Gazette.* Feb. 27, 1969.

"MIT Symposium: Art in Civic Scale," *Chronicle.* Cambridge, Mass., May 27, 1971.

"Mrs. Roosevelt Feature Guest at Art Center," *New York Amsterdam News.* Dec. 25, 1937.

"Murals Battle Continues at New York Hospital," *Afro-American*. March 21, 1936.

"Museum of Fine Arts to Hold Black Art Show," *Chronicle*. Ipswich, Mass., April 30, 1970.

"Museum of Fine Arts to Hold Black Art Show," *Herald*. Danvers, Mass., April 30, 1970.

"Museum of Fine Arts to Hold Black Art Show," *Tri-Town Transcript & Pennysaver*. April 29, 1970.

"Negro Art Center Marks Tenth Year," *New York Times*. June 19, 1938.

"Negro Art Gallery Established at CCC," *Norfolk Journal and Guide*. March 21, 1936.

"Negro Art in New York," *Washington Post*. Dec. 14, 1942.

"Negro Artists Paintings on Display at University (Howard)," *East Tennessee News*. Knoxville, Tenn., June 6, 1932.

"Negro Artists Win Prizes: 3 New Yorkers among Those Cited at Atlanta U. Display," *New York Times*. April 1, 1951.

"Negro Arts Group Gives Three Prizes," *New York Times*. Jan. 5, 1930.

"Negro College Art Show," *Chicago Sun Times*. July 2, 1970.

"Negro Has Given Much to Art, Survey Shows," *Boston Herald Traveler*. Feb. 23, 1933.

"Negro Students Hold Their Own Art Exhibition," *New York Herald Tribune*. Feb. 15, 1935.

"Negro Temple of Art," *Dayton Newsweek*. June 19, 1941.

"New Project to House Works of Negro Artist," *Los Angeles Sentinel*. Dec. 21, 1945.

"Noted Works Included in Painting Exhibit at Howard University," *Washington Evening Star*. March 11, 1942.

"128 Entries in Eighth Annual Art Exhibit," *Iowa Bystander*. Dec. 6, 1935.

"Paintings of Afro-Amer. Artists Now at Museum," *Chronicle*. Needham, Mass., Jan. 27, 1972.

Paris, Jean. "Black Art Experience in Art," *Long Island Press*. Jamaica, N.Y., June 14, 1970.

"People's Art Center Staff Show Opens: 11 Exhibitors Represented by Paintings, Sculpture and Varied Crafts," *St. Louis Post-Dispatch*. Feb. 6, 1949.

Porter, James A. "Negro Artists Gain Recognition after Long Battle," *Pittsburgh Courier*. July 29, 1950.

Porter, James A. "Progress of the Negro in Art during the Past 50 Years," *Pittsburgh Courier*. 1950. Reprint.

"Prejudice Raises Its Ugly Head, Art Fraternity 'Backs Up'," *Philadelphia Independent*. Dec. 13, 1942.

Preston, Malcolm. "Art: Black Exhibit," *Boston Herald Traveler*. April 19, 1971.

"Preview Party to Open Show by Thirteen Black Artists," *Citizen*. Belmont, Mass., May 14, 1970.

"Protests Cannot Halt Lynchings Exhibition New York: Art Gallery Closed to NAACP, But Show Will Go on Says White," *Afro-American*. Feb. 16, 1935.

Rainey, Ada. "Exhibit of Negro Art Work Begins," *Washington Post*. March 15, 1942.

"'Renaissance in Art Not Over Yet' Is Belief of Van Vechten, the Author," *Afro-American*. Sept. 22, 1934.

"Rhode Island: In Maximum Security, Prisoners' Art Negates Blankness," *Art Workers Newsletter*. April 1973.

Roosevelt, Eleanor. "Negro Paintings at Howard Were Inspiring," in "My Day" column for the *Washington Daily News*. March 3, 1941.

Rotan, Charles. "Chicago's Artists Exhibit for the Many," *Daily Worker*. New York, July 6, 1958.

"School Art League Praised for Work," *New York Times*. Dec. 6, 1936.

Setlik, Robert. "Cultural Cross Currents 19th Century Style," *Patriot Ledger*. Quincy, Mass., Jan. 20, 1972.

Sherman, Marjorie. "Afro-America Gets Biggest Show," *Boston Globe*. May 18, 1970.

Sherman, Marjorie. "Afro-American Works Score Smash Hit," *Boston Globe*. May 24, 1970.

Sherman, Marjorie. "Museum Gala Toasts Black Artists," *Boston Globe*. May 25, 1970.

"Simple Expression Is Keynote of First PWAP Exhibit Here," *Washington Herald*. April 29, 1934.

Stuttaford, Genevieve. "A Black Artist's View —Oakland Museum Art Show," *San Francisco Chronicle*. Oct. 8, 1968.

Tuttle, Worth. "Negro Artists Developing True Social Art," *New York Times*. May 14, 1933.

Van Almelo, Frederik. "In the American Grain," *Boston After Dark* (New title: *Boston Phoenix*). May 26, 1970, p. 24.

"View Prize Winners at Negro Fair," *Chicago News*. Aug. 3, 1940.

"Views Finished Product," *Chicago Defender*. Feb. 20, 1932.

"Visual Arts & Black Aesthetics," *Bay State Banner*. Feb. 18, 1970.

Wald, Martin. "Artistic Talent Blooms Behind Bars in Tombs," *Art Workers Newsletter*. April 1973.

Walsh, Rose. "Artists to Meet Public at Art Exhibit Preview," *Record American*. May 19, 1970.

Watson, Jane. "New Gallery of Art to Open Today," *Washington Post*. March 28, 1943.

"When You Think of Culture Think of Roxbury—Not Boston," *Muhamad Speaks.* Sept. 17, 1971.

"Winthrop Students Visit Arts Center," *Bay State Banner.* March 19, 1970.

"Working on Hampton Mural," *Chicago Defender.* Feb. 20, 1943.

"Works by 3 Philadelphia Artists Are Shown by Gallery at H(oward) U(niversity)," *Washington Post.* Feb. 11, 1940.

CATALOGUES

Acts of Art Gallery. New York. *Black Women Artists 1971.* New York, June 22-July 30, 1971.

Acts of Art Gallery. New York. *Rebuttal Catalogue: Catalogue of the Rebuttal Exhibition to the Whitney Exhibition.* New York, 1971.

Addison Gallery, Phillips Academy. Andover, Mass. *The Black Photographer* (1908-1970): *A Survey.* Sponsored by the James Van Der-Zee Institute. Andover, Mass.: Addison Gallery, Feb. 19-April 4, 1971.

Aesthetic Dynamics. Wilmington, Del. *Afro-American Images 1971.* Memorial exhibition to James A. Porter. Held at the State Armory, Wilmington, Del., Feb. 5-26, 1971.

Africobra. See: Studio Museum in Harlem.

Afro-American Artists: New York & Boston. See: Museum of Fine Arts. Boston.

Afro-American Artists: Since 1950. See: Brooklyn College.

Afro-American Images 1971. See: Aesthetic Dynamics.

Afro-American Slide Depository Catalog. Univ. of South Alabama, Art Dept. Mobile, Ala., 1972.

Afro-American Women in Art. See: Alpha Kappa Alpha Society.

Albany Institute of History and Art. *The Negro Artist Comes of Age; A National Survey of Contemporary American Artists.* Albany, N.Y., Jan. 3-Feb. 11, 1945.

Alpha Kappa Alpha Society. Greensboro, N.C. *Afro-American Women in Art: Their Achievements in Sculpture and Painting.* Greensboro, N.C., 1969.

American Council for American Unity. *Art for the Home.* New York, 1945.

American Greetings Gallery. *New Voices—15 Black Artists.* New York: American Greeting Gallery, Pan American Building.

American Negro Exposition. Chicago. *The Art of the American Negro 1851-1940.* Exhibition arranged by Alonzo Aden. Introduction by Alain Locke. Chicago, 1940.

Anacostia Neighborhood Museum. See: District of Columbia Art Assn.

An Art Commentary on Lynching. See: Arthur Newton Galleries.

Art Institute of Chicago. *Exhibitions by Artists of Chicago and Vicinity.* Chicago, 1923.

Art Institute of Chicago. *Exhibition by Artists of Chicago and Vicinity.* Chicago, 1931.

Art Institute of Chicago. *Negro in Art Week,* Nov. 16-23, 1927. Chicago: Guston, 1927.

The Art of Black America. See: Shorewood Reproductions, Inc.

Art of the American Negro. See: Harlem Cultural Council.

Art of the American Negro 1851-1940. See: American Negro Exposition.

Art-West Associated North, Inc. See: Oakland Museum. *New Perspectives in Black Art.*

Arthur Newton Galleries. New York. *An Art Commentary on Lynching.* Introduction by Sherwood Anderson and Erskine Caldwell. New York: Newton Galleries, Feb. 1935.

Assn. for the Study of Negro Life and History, *Exhibition of Works by Negro Artists at the National Gallery of Art.* Washington, D.C., Oct. 31-Nov. 6, 1933.

Atlanta Univ. *Exhibition.* Arranged by Hale Woodruff and the Harmon Foundation. Atlanta, Feb. 1934.

Atlanta Univ. *Exhibition of Paintings by Negro Artists of America.* Foreword by Alain Locke. Atlanta, April 19-May 10, 1942.

Atlanta Univ. *Exhibition of Paintings by Negro Artists of America.* Atlanta, April 4-May 2, 1942.

Atlanta Univ. *Third Annual Exhibition of Paintings, Sculpture and Prints by Negro Artists.* Atlanta, April 2-30, 1944.

Atlanta Univ. *Fifth Annual Exhibition of Paintings, Sculpture, and Prints by Negro Artists.* Atlanta, April, 1946.

Augusta Savage Studios, Inc. New York. *First Annual Exhibition Salon of Contemporary Negro Art.* New York, June 8-22, 1939.

Baltimore Museum of Art. *Contemporary Negro Art.* Baltimore, Feb. 3-19, 1939.

Barnet Aden Gallery. Washington, D.C. *Eighteen Washington Artists.* Introduction by James A. Porter and Agnes Delano. Washington, D.C., 1953.

Black Artist in Graphic Communication. See: Gallery 303.

Black Arts Today. See: San José State College.

Black Dimensions in Contemporary American Art. See: Books. Atkinson, J. Edward.

The Black Experience. See: Lincoln Univ.

The Black Photographer. See: Addison Gallery, Phillips Academy.

Black Reflections: Seven Black Artists. See: Flint Community Schools.

Black Women Artists. See: Acts of Art Gallery.

A Black Women's Art Exhibit. See: Normacel Gallery.

Boston Community Lecture Series. See: National Center of Afro-American Artists.

Boston Negro Artists Assn. *The Black Artist in America: A Negro History Month Exhibition.* Boston: Boston Public Library, Feb. 1973.

Boston Negro Artists Assn. *10th Anniversary Exhibition at the Boston Public Library.* Boston: Boston Public Library, Jan. 1973.

Boston Public Library. See: Boston Negro Artists Assn.

Bowdoin College. Brunswick, Me. *Portrayal of the Negro in American Painting.* Catalog of a circulating collection interpreting the Negro in art. Brunswick, Me., 1964.

Boykins School of Arts and Crafts. See: Greenwich Village Galleries.

Brandeis Univ. *12 Black Artists from Boston* (Presented by the Afro-American Organization). Rose Art Museum, Brandeis Univ. Waltham, Mass., 1969.

Brockman Gallery. Los Angeles. *Contemporary Black Imagery: 7 Artists.* Los Angeles, Oct. 10-30, 1971.

Brooklyn College. *Afro-American Artists: Since 1950, An Exhibition of Paintings, Sculpture, and Drawings.* Brooklyn, April 15-May 18, 1969.

California Arts Commission. See: Univ. of California.

California Black Artists. See: College of Marin.

California Black Craftsmen. See: Mills College Art Gallery.

California. Univ., Los Angeles. *The Negro in American Art: One Hundred and Fifty Years of Afro-American Art.* Catalog by James A. Porter. Co-sponsored by the California Arts Commission. Los Angeles, Sept. 11-Oct. 16, 1966. Also shown at Davis: Univ. of California, Nov. 1-Dec. 15, 1966; San Diego: Fine Arts Gallery, Jan. 6-Feb. 12, 1967; Oakland Art Museum, Feb. 24-March 19, 1967.

Carnegie Institute. *Pittsburgh International Exhibition of Contemporary Painting.* Pittsburgh, 1955.

Century of Progress Exhibition. *Catalog.* Chicago World's Fair, 1933-4. Chicago, 1933.

Chase, Judith W. *Catalog of Slide Lectures on Afro-American History and Art.* Charleston, S.C.: The Audio Visual Library of the Old Slave Mart Museum of Charleston, 1970.

Chicago Women's Club Committee on Race Relations. *The Negro in Art Week, Exhibition Program.* Chicago, Nov. 16-23, 1927.

Chicago World's Fair. See: Century of Progress Exhibition.

Coalition 70. See: Staten Island Museum.

College of Marin, Art Gallery. *California Black Artists.* Kentfield, Calif., March 13-April 10, 1970.

Columbia Univ., Urban Center. See: Harlem Cultural Council.

Commodore Hotel, New York. *Exhibition.* Arranged by Rev. Maurice F. Noonan and the Harmon Foundation. New York: Propagation of Faith Mission, 1934.

Community Church Art Gallery. New York. *A Tribute to the Life of Martin Luther King, Jr.* New York, April, 1969.

Contemporary Black Artists. See: Ruder & Finn Fine Arts.

Contemporary Black Imagery. See: Brockman Gallery.

Contemporary Negro Art. See: Baltimore Museum of Art, 1939.

Dartmouth College, Hopkins Center Art Galleries. *6 Black Artists.* Hanover, N.H., Jan. 10-21, 1968.

Delphic Studios. New York. See: Harmon Foundation. *An Illustrated Review of Their Achievements.*

DerZee Institute. See: James Van DerZee Institute.

The Detroit Artists Market. *Seven Black Artists.* Detroit, 1969.

Detroit Institute of Arts. *Other Ideas.* Detroit, 1969.

Dickinson Univ. See: Fairleigh Dickinson Univ.

Dillard Univ. Art Rooms. *Fourth Annual Exhibit of Paintings, First Annual Exhibit of Photographs by Negroes.* New Orleans, April 14-27, 1940.

Dimensions of Black. See: La Jolla Museum of Art.

District of Columbia Art Assn. *Exhibition '71.* Washington, D.C.: Smithsonian Institution Press: May, 1971.

District of Columbia Art Assn. *D.C. Art Assn. 2nd Annual.* Anacostia Neighborhood Museum. Washington, D.C., 1970.

District of Columbia Schools. See: Howard Univ. *Art Exhibit: Public Schools of the D of C.*

Dickson Art Center. See: California University, Los Angeles.

Dix Artistes Nègres des États Unis. See: United States Committee for the First World Festival of Negro Art.

Doty, Robert. *Contemporary Black Artists in America.* New York: Whitney Museum of American Art, April 6-May 16, 1971.

Downtown Gallery. New York. *American Negro Artists Exhibition.* New York, 1941.

Downtown Gallery. New York. *American*

Negro Art: Nineteenth and Twentieth Centuries. New York, Dec. 9-Jan. 3, 1942.

Drew Seminary. New Jersey. *Exhibition of Paintings, Sculpture and Photography.* Assembled with the assistance of the Harmon Foundation. New Jersey, 1934.

Driskell, David C. See: Fisk University.

Dunbar High School. See: Tanner Art League.

DuSable Museum of African American History. Chicago. *Contemporary Black Artists.* 1970-71 illustrated calendar. Chicago, 1970.

Dwight Art Memorial. See: Mount Holyoke College.

Edmonton Art Gallery. Edmonton, Canada. *The Washington Artists: 1950-1970.* Edmonton, 1970.

Eighteen Washington Artists. See: Barnet Aden Gallery.

Everson Museum of Art. Syracuse. *From Within: Selected Works by Artists/Inmates of New York State Correctional Facility at Auburn (Maximum Security).* Organized with the aid of a grant from Ruder & Finn Fine Arts. Shown at the National Collection of Fine Arts, Washington, D.C., Feb. 2-March 25, 1973.

The Evolution of Afro-American Artists: 1800-1950. See: New York. City College of New York.

Exhibitions by Artists of Chicago and Vicinity. See: Art Institute of Chicago.

Exhibition of Works by Negro Artists at the National Gallery of Art. See: Assn. for the Study of Negro Life & History.

Fairleigh Dickinson Univ. Art Gallery. *Some Negro Artists.* Madison, N.J., Oct. 20-Nov. 20, 1964.

Fifteen Afro-American Women. See: North Carolina A & T State Univ.

Fifteen Under Forty; Paintings by Young New York State Black Artists. Albany, N.Y.: Division of the Humanities and the Arts, 1970.

The First Baptist Church. Macon, Georgia. *Exhibition.* Macon, Ga., May, 1934.

First World Festival of Negro Arts, Dakar. See: United States Committee for the First World Festival of Negro Arts.

Fisk Univ. Ballentine Hall. *39th Arts Festival Exhibition. Sculpture by Richard Hunt; Paintings by Sam Middleton.* Assembled by David C. Driskell. Nashville, Tenn., April 21-May 17, 1968.

Fisk Univ. Art Galleries. *Three Afro-Americans: Paintings by Merton Simpson, Sculpture by Earl Hooks, Photography by Bobby Sengstacke.* Foreword by David C. Driskell. Nashville, Tenn., April 20-May 15, 1969.

Flint Community Schools. *Black Reflections: Seven Black Artists.* Flint, Mich., 1969.

Fort Huachuca, Ariz. *Exhibition of the Works of 37 Negro Artists.* Huachuca, Ariz., 1943.

Forum Gallery. New York. *The Portrayal of the Negro in American Painting.* New York, 1967.

From Within: Selected Works by Artists/Inmates of New York State Correctional Facility at Auburn. See: Everson Museum of Art.

The G Place Gallery. *New Names in American Art.* Foreword by Alain Locke. Washington, D.C., June 13-July 4, 1944.

Gallery 303. New York. *The Black Artist in Graphic Communication.* New York, Jan. 9-Feb. 1, 1970.

Georgia State Teachers and Agricultural College. *Exhibition.* Forsyth, Ga., 1934.

Ghent, Henri. See: Musée Rath.

Greene, Carroll, Jr. *Afro-American Artists: 1800-1968.* Slides and commentary. Baldwin, N.Y.: Prothmann Assoc., 1968.

Greenwich Village Galleries. *Autumn Exhibition of the Primitive African Art Center and the Boykins School of Arts and Crafts, Inc.* New York, Nov. 16-31, 1932.

Harlem Community Art Center. *Harlem Art Teachers Exhibit.* New York, Oct. 17, 1938.

Harlem Cultural Council. *The Art of the American Negro: Exhibition of Paintings.* New York, June 27-July 25, 1966.

Harlem Cultural Council. *Negro Artists of the 19th Century.* New York, 1966.

Harlem Cultural Council. *New Black Artists.* Organized in cooperation with the School of the Arts, and the Urban Center of Columbia Univ. Brooklyn Museum, Oct. 7-Nov. 9, 1969; Columbia Univ., Nov. 20-Dec. 12, 1969. New York: Printed by Clarke & Way, 1969.

Harlem On My Mind. See: Schoner, Allon, ed.

Harmon Foundation. *The Art of the Negro.* Traveling exhibition arranged in cooperation with the College Art Assn. New York, 1934.

Harmon Foundation. *Cumulative Biographical Reference Index of Contemporary Negro Artists.* New York, n.d.

Harmon Foundation. *Exhibition of Fine Art by American Negro Artists.* Arranged in cooperation with the Commission on the Church and Race Relations, Federal Council of Churches. New York: International House, 1928-1935.

Harmon Foundation. *Exhibit of Productions by Negro Artists.* New York, 1933.

Harmon Foundation. *Negro Artists: An Illustrated Review of Their Achievements.* In cooperation with Delphic Studios. New York, April 22-May 4, 1935.

Harmon Foundation. *Non-Jury Exhibit of Works of Negro Artists.* New York, 1933.

Harmon Foundation. *Select Picture List.* New York, n.d.

Herron Museum. See: John Herron Museum.

Hollis Unitarian Church. Hollis, Long Island. *Exhibition.* Arranged under the auspices of the Harmon Foundation. Hollis, N.Y., 1933.

Howard Univ. Gallery of Art. *American Paintings 1943-1948.* Foreword by Charles Seymour, Jr. Washington, D.C., Oct. 22-Nov. 15, 1948.

Howard Univ. Gallery of Art. *Art Exhibit: the Public Schools of the District of Columbia.* Washington, D.C., May 3-11, 1931.

Howard Univ. Gallery of Art. *The Art of the American Negro.* Sponsored by the Assn. for the Study of Negro Life and History. Assembled by Alonzo J. Aden. Washington, D.C., Oct. 31-Nov. 15, 1937.

Howard Univ. Gallery of Art. *Exhibition of Graphic Arts and Drawings by Negro Artists.* Washington, D.C., Jan. 5-Feb. 29, 1950.

Howard Univ. Gallery of Art. *Exhibition of Negro Artists of Chicago.* Presented in observance of National Negro History Week and the 75th anniversary of the proclamation of the 13th amendment. Washington, D.C., 1941.

Howard Univ. Gallery of Art. *Exhibition of Paintings, Museum Donor Purchase Program.* Washington, D.C., Feb. 14-March 20, 1964.

Howard Univ. Gallery of Art. *Exhibitions of Paintings by Negro Artists.* Washington, D.C., May 18-25, 1932.

Howard Univ. Gallery of Art. *An Exhibition of Paintings by Three Artists of Philadelphia: Laura Wheeler Waring, Allan Freelon and Samuel Brown.* Foreword by James A. Porter. Washington, D.C., Feb. 1-29, 1940.

Howard Univ. Gallery of Art. *Exhibition of Paintings, Prints and Drawings by the Faculty of the Department of Art.* Washington, D.C., 1957.

Howard Univ. Gallery of Art. *Genre Painting XV to XX Century.* Organized by the College Art Assn. Washington, D.C., Jan. 6-18, 1936.

Howard Univ. Gallery of Art. *The Negro in the American Scene.* Washington, D.C., March 9-April 12, 1942.

Howard Univ. Gallery of Art. *New Vistas In American Art.* Foreword by James A. Porter. Washington, D.C., 1961.

Howard Univ. Gallery of Art. *Oil Paintings, Watercolors and Prints by Negro Artists.* Exhibition lent through the courtesy of the W.P.A. Federal Art Project. Introduction by Russell C. Parr. Washington, D.C., April 15-May 31, 1939.

Howard Univ. Gallery of Art. *Ten Afro-American Artists of the Nineteenth Century.* Catalog by James A. Porter. Washington, D.C., Feb. 3-March 30, 1967.

Howard Univ. Gallery of Art. *Trends in Amer-ican Drawings.* Foreword by David A. Wilkie. Assembled by James V. Herring. Washington, D.C., Nov. 3-Dec. 31, 1952.

Hudson River Museum. *Contemporary Black Artists.* See: Studio Museum in Harlem.

8 (Huit) Artistes Afro-Américains. See: Musée Rath, Genève.

Illinois, Univ. of. *Contemporary American Painting and Sculpture.* Urbana, Ill., Feb. 27-April 3, 1955.

Institute of Modern Art. Boston. *Paintings, Sculpture by American Negro Artists.* Text by James A. Porter. Boston, Jan. 5-20, 1943.

International House. New York. See: Harmon Foundation. *Exhibition of Fine Art by American Negro Artists.*

James A. Porter Gallery of Art. See: Howard Univ.

James Van DerZee Institute. New York. *The Black Photographer 1908-1970: A Survey.* Phillips Academy. Andover, Mass.: Addison Gallery of American Art, 1971.

John Herron Art Museum. Indianapolis. *Fifth Biennial Ceramic Exhibition.* Indianapolis, 1959.

La Jolla Museum. *Dimensions of Black.* Edited by Jehanne Teilhet. San Diego, 1970.

Lee Cultural Center. Philadelphia. See: Philadelphia Department of Recreation.

Lee Nordness Galleries. New York. *Twelve Afro-American Artists—1969.* In collaboration with the N.A.A.C.P. Special Contributions Fund and the Smithsonian Institution. New York, Jan.-Feb. 1969.

Lincoln Univ. Jefferson City, Mo. *Black Arts Festival.* Jefferson City, Oct. 1969.

Lincoln Univ. Jefferson City, Mo. *The Black Experience.* Statements by Romare Bearden and Jay Jacobs. Jefferson City, 1970.

Lincoln Univ. Jefferson City, Mo. *Festival of the Arts.* Jefferson City, Dec. 14-March 7, 1970.

Los Angeles County Museum of Art. *Three Graphic Artists: Charles White, David Hammons, Timothy Washington.* Los Angeles County Museum of Art, Jan. 26-March 7, 1971; Santa Barbara Museum of Art, March 20, 1971-April 18, 1971.

Lyric Theatre. New York. *Exhibition.* Special exhibition held on the occasion of *Run Little Children.* New York, 1933.

McMillen Inc. Galleries. New York. *Contemporary Negro Art.* New York, Oct. 16-Nov. 7, 1941.

MARC. See: Metropolitan Applied Research Center.

Marino Art Galleries. New York. *American Negro Art by Living Negro Artists.* New York, Nov. 1-24, 1956.

Marino Art Galleries. New York. *Contemporary Negro Art.* New York, Sept. 8-27, 1956.

Massachusetts Artists Centennial Album. Boston: J.A. Osgood & Co., 1875.

Menil Foundation. *The Deluxe Show.* Houston, 1971.

Methodist Episcopal Church. Orange, N.J. *Exhibition.* Under the auspices of the Harmon Foundation. Orange, N.J., 1933.

Metropolitan Applied Research Center. New York. *Six Painters.* New York, Nov. 15-Dec. 20, 1971?.

Metropolitan Museum of Art. New York. *American Painting in the Twentieth Century.* Catalog by Henry Geldzahler. New York, 1965.

Michigan. Univ. of. *Eight New York Painters.* Statement by Hale Woodruff. Ann Arbor, Mich., July 1-21, 1956.

Mills College Art Gallery. *California Black Craftsmen.* Oakland, Calif., Feb. 15-Mar. 8, 1970.

Minneapolis Institute of Arts. *Contemporary Black Artists.* Touring exhibition organized by the Institute and Ruder & Finn, New York. Minneapolis Institute of Arts, 1968.

Minneapolis Institute of Arts. *Thirty Contemporary Black Artists.* Organized with the assistance of Ruder & Finn Fine Arts, New York. Minneapolis Institute of Arts, Oct. 17-Nov. 24, 1968.

Mount Holyoke College, Warbe Gallery. *A New Vitality in Art: The Black Woman.* Catalog by G. Garrison and P. Long. South Hadley, Mass., 1972.

Mount Holyoke College, Dwight Art Memorial. *Ten Afro-American Artists.* Foreword by Henri Ghent. South Hadley, Mass., Nov. 6-26, 1969.

Musée Rath. Genève, Suisse. *8 (Huit) Artistes Afro-Américains; Exposition Organisée en Collaboration avec Henri Ghent.* Genève, 1971.

Museum of Fine Arts. Boston. *Afro-American Artists: New York & Boston.* Organized in collaboration with the National Center of Afro-American Artists. Special Consultant: Edmund B. Gaither. Boston, May-June, 1970.

Museum of Modern Art. New York. *In Honor of Dr. Martin Luther King, Jr.* New York: Museum of Modern Art, Oct. 31-Nov. 3, 1968.

Museum of Modern Art. New York. *Social Comment in America.* Text by Dore Ashton. New York: Museum of Modern Art, 1968.

National Assn. for the Advancement of Colored People. New York. *Art Exhibition of Negro Expression.* Sponsored by Minars Furniture. New York, April 1964.

National Assn. for the Advancement of Colored People. Education Committee. *A Most*

Memorable Showing of Negro Creative Art. New York, n.d.

National Assn. for the Advancement of Colored People. Special Contribution Fund. *Twelve Afro-American Artists.* Preface by Roy Wilkins; essay by Carroll Greene, Jr. New York: Lee Nordness Galleries, 1969.

National Center of Afro-American Artists. *AFRICOBRA: A New Black Exhibition From Chicago.* Boston, Sept. 13-Oct. 11, 1970.

National Center of Afro-American Artists. *Afro-American Artists: New York & Boston.* See: Museum of Fine Arts. Boston.

National Center of Afro-American Artists. *Community Lecture Series Presents Local Afro-American Artists: Graphics, Paintings, Sculpture.* Boston, April 6-27, 1969.

National Center of Afro-American Artists. Five Famous Black Artists Presented By the Museum of the National Center of Afro-American Artists: Romare Bearden: Jacob Lawrence: Horace Pippin: Charles White: Hale Woodruff. Boston, Feb. 9-March 10, 1970.

National Center of Afro-American Artists. *19th Century Afro-American Artists: Duncanson & Bannister.* Boston, Jan. 13, 1972.

National Center of Afro-American Artists. *Our Elders: Crite & Dames.* Boston, Sept.-Oct. 1971.

National Center of Afro-American Artists. *Reality Expanded.* Boston, 1973.

National Center of Afro-American Artists. *Taking Care of Business.* Boston, 1972.

National Center of Afro-American Artists. *Three Boston Black Artists: Milton Johnson, Al Smith, & Richard Yarde.* Boston, Nov. 14-28, 1971.

National Center of Afro-American Artists. See: Also: Museum of Fine Arts. Boston.

National Gallery of Art. Washington, D.C. *Exhibition of Works by Negro Artists at the National Gallery of Art.* Sponsored by the Assn. for the Study of Negro Life and History. Washington, D.C., Oct. 31- Nov. 6, 1933.

The Negro Artist Comes of Age. See: Albany Institute of History and Art.

Negro Artists of the 19th Century. See: Harlem Cultural Council.

Negro Heritage Committee. See Alpha Kappa Alpha Society.

The Negro in American Art: 150 Years of Afro-American Art. See: California Univ. at Los Angeles.

The Negro in Art Week. See: Art Institute of Chicago. See Also: Chicago Women's Club Committee on Race Relations.

Negro Library Assn. *First Annual Exhibit of Books, Manuscripts, Paintings, Sculptures, etc., by the NLA at Carlton Ave. YMCA.* Chicago, Aug. 7-16, 1918.

Nelson Gallery of Art. See: William Rockhill Nelson Gallery of Art.

Newark Museum. Newark, N.J. *Black Artists: Two Generations.* Newark, N.J., May 13-Sept. 6, 1971.

New Black Artists. See Harlem Cultural Council.

New Jersey State Museum. *Arts and Crafts Exhibition.* Sponsored by the Harmon Foundation and the New Jersey State Museum Advisory Board. Trenton, N.J., March 31-April 30, 1935.

New Perspectives in Black Art. See: Oakland Museum.

New School for Social Research. New York. *Protest and Hope.* Exhibited at Wollman Hall. New York, Oct. 24-Dec. 2, 1967.

New School for Social Research. Art Center. *Landscape in Recent American Painting.* New York, Feb. 12-March 7, 1963.

Newton Galleries. See: Arthur Newton Galleries.

New Voices—15 Black Artists. See: American Greetings Gallery.

New York. City College of New York. *The Evolution of Afro-American Artists 1800-1950.* Catalog by Carroll Greene, Jr. Organized in cooperation with the Harlem Cultural Council and the New York Urban League. New York: City College, 1967.

New York Public Library. *We-Us-I 70: New Works From Weusi Artists: Sixth Annual Exhibit of Paintings & Graphics.* New York, Oct. 5-31, 1970.

New York Public Library. 135th Street Branch. *Catalog of the Negro Arts Exhibit.* New York: New York Public Library, 1921.

New York Public Library. 135th Street Branch. *Harlem Art Work Shop Exhibition.* Organized in association with the Harmon Foundation and the Harlem Adult Committee. New York, 1933.

New York State Education Department. *Fifteen Under Forty: Paintings By Young New York State Black Artists.* Saratoga, N.Y.: Gallery Museum, Hall of Springs, July 1-31, 1970.

New York. State Univ. at Stony Brook. *5 + 1 (Five Plus One).* Stony Brook, N.Y., 1969.

Nicholas Roerich Museum. New York. *Paintings & Sculpture By Four Tennessee Primitives.* New York, Jan. 12-Feb. 9, 1964.

Nitchie School of Lip Reading. New York. *Exhibition.* Under the auspices of the Harmon Foundation. New York, 1933.

Nordness Galleries. See; Lee Nordness Galleries.

Normacel Gallery. Detroit, Mich. *A Black Women's Art Exhibit.* Detroit, July 19, 1970.

North Carolina A & T State Univ. Greensboro, N.C. *15 Afro-American Women.* Sponsored by the A & T Univ. Lyceum Program. Taylor Gallery, Bludord Library. Greensboro, N.C., March 1-31, 197-.

Nyumba-Ya-Sanae. New York. *Exhibition of Art By Leading Afro-American Artists.* New York, n.d.

Oakland Museum. *Black Untitled.* Oakland, Calif., Oct. 1970.

Oakland Museum. *Black Untitled II: Dimensions of the Figure.* Oakland, Calif., Nov.-Dec. 1971.

Oakland, Museum. *The Metal Experience.* Oakland, Calif., June 5-July 4, 1971.

Oakland Museum. *New Perspectives In Black Art.* Art of Art-West Associated North. Oakland, Calif., Oct. 5-26, 1968.

Oak Park Library, Oak Park, Ill. *Exhibit of Black Artists.* Organized for the Library by Margaret Burroughs of the South Side Community Art Center. Oak Park, Ill., n.d.

Other Ideas. See: Detroit Institute of Art.

Philadelphia Department of Recreation. *Love . . . and the Black Community.* An art exhibit. Lee Cultural Center. Philadelphia, 197-.

Philadelphia Division of Art. See: Philadelphia School District.

Philadelphia School District. Board of Education. Division of Art. *Afro-American Artists 1800-1969.* Produced in cooperation with the Museum of the Philadelphia Civic Center. Philadelphia, 1969.

Phillips Academy. Andover, Mass. See: Addison Gallery.

Phillips Memorial Gallery. Washington, D.C. *Three Negro Artists: Horace Pippin, Richmond Barthé and Jacob Lawrence.* Washington, D.C., 1946.

Pittsburgh Community College. *Sixteen Black Artists at Community College.* Organized in association with the Bethesda United Presbyterian Church and the Black League for Afro-American Culture. Pittsburgh, Pa., n.d.

Porter, James A. *Ten Afro-American Artists of the 19th Century.* Washington, D.C.: Howard Univ. Gallery of Art, 1967.

Porter, James A. *The Negro In American Art: One Hundred and Fifty Years of Afro-American Art.* Los Angeles: Univ. of Calif., 1966.

Powell House. New York. *Exhibition of Contemporary American Art.* New York, April, 1945.

Propagation of Faith Mission. See: Commodore Hotel.

Pyramid Club. Philadelphia. *Second Annual Fall Review of Paintings and Sculpture: 1956.* Philadelphia, Oct. 26-Nov. 26, 1956.

Rainbow Sign Gallery. Berkeley, Calif. *Black Arts Day II.* Berkeley, Calif., Sept., 1972.

Rice Univ. Houston, Texas. *Some American History By Larry Rivers and Others.* Houston, 1971.

Riverside Museum. *Eight Plus Eight.* New York: Riverside Museum, 1969.

Rockford College. *Creativity and the Negro.* Rockford, Ill., March 3-12, 1965.

Roerich Museum. See: Nicholas Roerich Museum.

Ruder & Finn Fine Arts. New York. *Contemporary Black Artists.* Traveling exhibition—an expanded version of exhibition organized by the Minneapolis Institute of Arts, which grew out of *New Voices: 15 New York Artists,* organized by the Studio Museum in Harlem. New York: Ruder & Finn Fine Arts, 1969.

San José State College. *Black Arts Today.* San José, Calif., March 17-28, 1972.

School of Visual Arts. Visual Arts Gallery. *Black Artists 1970.* New York: United Black Artists, 1970.

Schoner, Allon, ed. *Harlem On My Mind.* New York: Metropolitan Museum of Art, 1969.

Seven Black Artists. See: The Detroit Artists Market.

Sherman Hotel. Philadelphia. *Afro-American Art Exhibition.* Organized by David C. Driskell. Philadelphia, 1968.

Shorewood Reproductions, Inc. *The Art of Black America.* New York: Shorewood Reproductions, 1969.

Six Black Artists. See: Dartmouth College.

Smith College. Museum of Art. *Paintings, Sculpture By American Negro Artists.* Introduction by James A. Porter. Also exhibited at the Boston Institute of Modern Art. Northampton, Mass., Feb. 18-March 7, 1943.

Smith-Mason Gallery of Art. Washington, D.C. *National Exhibition of Black Artists 1971.* Washington, D.C., Nov. 30, 1971.

Smithsonian Institution. *Catalogue of An Exhibition of Paintings and Sculpture By American Negro Artists At the National Gallery of Art.* Exhibition in connection with William E. Harmon Awards for Distinguished Achievement Among Negroes. Washington, D.C., May 16-29, 1929. May 30-June 8, 1930.

Smithsonian Institution. *Exhibition of Works By Negro Artists At the National Gallery of Art.* Sponsored by the Assn. for the Study of Negro Life and History. Washington, D.C., Oct. 31-Nov. 6, 1933.

South Alabama. Univ. of South Alabama. *Afro-American Slide Depository Catalog.* Mobile, Ala.: Dept. of Art, Univ. of South Alabama, 1971.

South Side Community Art Center. Chicago.

Chicago Collectors Exhibit of Negro Art. Chicago, April 8-May 3, 1945.

South Side Community Art Center. Chicago. *Exhibition of Book Illustrations By Jacob Lawrence, Charles Sebree, Vernon Winslow.* Chicago, June 9-30, 1941.

South Side Community Art Center. Chicago. *National Negro Art Exhibition.* Chicago, 1941.

South Side Community Art Center. *Opening Exhibition of Paintings By Negro Artists.* Chicago, Dec. 15, 1940-Jan. 28, 1941.

Spiral Gallery. New York. *First Group Showing.* May 15-June 5, 1965.

The Spiral Group. *The Spiral.* Long Island Univ., New York, 1964-66.

State Armory. Wilmington, Del. See: Aesthetic Dynamics.

Staten Island Museum. New York. *Coalition 70.* Text by Barry Leo Delaney. New York, March 8-April 19, 1970.

Studio Museum in Harlem. *AFRICOBRA II.* New York, 1971.

Studio Museum in Harlem. *Afro-Haitian Images & Sounds Today.* New York, Feb. 14-March 30, 1969.

Studio Museum in Harlem. *Black Artists of the 1930's.* New York, 1968.

Studio Museum in Harlem. *Contemporary American Black Artists.* Sponsored by the Smithsonian Institution and the Studio Museum. Exhibit at the Hudson River Museum, Yonkers, New York, 1970.

Studio Museum in Harlem. *Five Contemporary African American Artists; Paintings and Drawings.* New York, 1969.

Studio Museum in Harlem. *Harlem Artists 69.* New York, July 22-Sept. 7, 1969.

Studio Museum in Harlem. *Invisible Americans: Black Artists of the 30's.* New York, Nov. 19-Jan. 5, 1969.

Tanner Art Galleries. Chicago. *The Art of the American Negro (1851-1940).* Text by Alain Locke. Chicago, July 4-Sept. 2, 1940.

Tanner Art League. Washington, D.C. *Catalogue of the Third Annual Exhibition of the Tanner Art League.* Washington, Dunbar High School, May 15-June 3, 1922.

Ten Afro-American Artists of the Nineteenth Century. See: Porter, James A.

Ten American Negro Aritsts Living and Working In Europe. Copenhagen, Denmark: Den. Frie-Osho Plads, 1964.

Texas Centennial Exposition. *Exhibit: Productions of Boys and Girls Under Art Construction.* Dallas, June 19-Nov. 29, 1936.

Texas Centennial Exposition. *Exhibition of Fine Arts Productions by American Negroes.* Dallas: Hall of Negro Life, 1936.

Texas Centennial Exposition. *Thumbnail Sketches of Exhibiting Artists.* Dallas, 1936.

Texas. University. *Afro-American Artists Abroad.* Introduction by James E. Lewis. Austin, Texas, May 29-June 3, 1970.

Tuskegee Institute. George Washington Carver Museum. *Historical Dioramas. Contributions of Negro People to World Civilization.* Created as the Court of Honor for the American Negro Exposition, Chicago. Tuskegee Institute, 1940.

Twelve Afro-American Artists—1969. See: Lee Nordness Galleries.

Twelve Black Artists From Boston. See: Brandeis Univ.

Tyler School of Art. *Seven By Seven: An Exhibition of Seven Works By Each of Seven Artists.* Philadelphia: Temple Univ., Oct. 14-Nov. 1, 1970.

United Black Artists. See: School of Visual Arts.

United States Committee for the First World Festival of Negro Arts, Dakar, Senegal. *Ten Negro Artists From the United States (Dix Artistes Nègres Des États Unis).* New York: U.S. Committee for the 1st World Festival of Negro Arts, Inc.; Distributed by October House, 1966.

United States. Library of Congress. *75 Years of Freedom; Commemoration of the 75th Anniversary of the Proclamation of the 13th Amendment to the Constitution of the United States.* Washington, D.C.: United States Printing Office, 1943.

United States. Works Projects Administration. Illinois. *Subject Index to Literature On Negro Art.* Chicago: Chicago Public Library, 1941.

Van DerZee Institute. See: James Van Der Zee Institute.

The Washington Artists. See: Edmonton Art Gallery.

Washington, Intercollegiate Club. *The Negro In Chicago 1779-1929.* Chicago, 1929.

The Washington School. *Exhibition.* Terre Haute, Indiana, 1934.

Whitney Museum of American Art. See: Doty, Robert.

William Rockhill Nelson Gallery of Art. *Painting By Negro Artists.* Kansas City, Mo., 1942.

Wilmington, Del. Aesthetic Dynamics. See: Aesthetic Dynamics.

World's Fair. Chicago. See: Century of Progress Exhibition.

Xavier Univ. *Emancipation Proclamation Centennial National Art Exhibition.* 1963.

Young Women's Christian Assn., Montclair, N.J. *Exhibition of Paintings and Drawings By James A. Porter and James Lesesne Wells.* Montclair, April 16-30, 1930.